TEACHING AND LEARNING IN THE COLLEGE CLASSROOM

SECOND EDITION

EDITED BY

KENNETH A. FELDMAN
Department of Sociology
State University of New York at Stony Brook

MICHAEL B. PAULSEN
Department of Educational Leadership, Counseling, and Foundations
University of New Orleans

ASHE READER SERIES
Bruce Anthony Jones, Series Editor

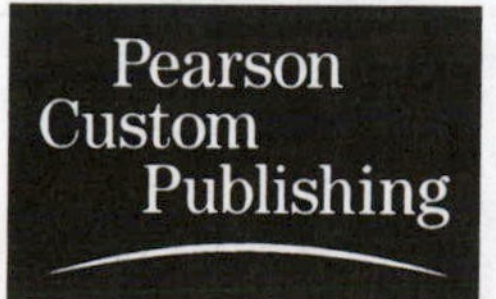

Cover art: Matisse Dream by George Herman.

Printed in the United States of America

10 9 8 7 6 5 4 3 2

Please visit our web site at www.pearsoncustom.com

ISBN 0-536-01065-X
BA 97677

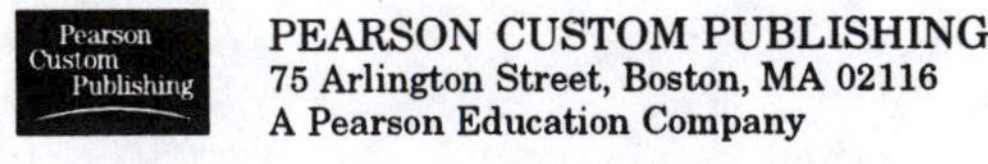

PEARSON CUSTOM PUBLISHING
75 Arlington Street, Boston, MA 02116
A Pearson Education Company

TO:
JUNE AND LAUREY

Copyright Acknowledgements

Grateful acknowledgment is made to the following sources for permission to reprint material copyrighted or controlled by them:

"The Past, Present, and Future in College Teaching: Where Does Teaching Fit?" by Barbara Schneider Fuhrmann and Anthony F. Grasha, reprinted by permission from A Practical Handbook for College Teachers, 1983.

"Research on College Teaching: The Historical Background," by Wilbert J. McKeachie, reprinted by permission from *Journal of Educational Psychology*, 82, 1990.

"Scholarship Over Time," (Chapter 1) and "Enlarging the Perspective," (Chapter 2), by Ernest L. Boyer, reprinted from *Scholarship Reconsidered: Priorities of the Professoriate*, 1990, Princeton University Press.

"Learning Theory and Research," by Cameron Fincher, reprinted by permission from *Higher Education Handbook of Theory and Research*, Vol. 1, edited by J.C. Smart, 1985, Agathon Press.

"Student Cognition," (Chapter 3) and "Student Motivation," (Chapter 4), by Wilbert J. McKeachie, Paul R. Pintrich, Yi-Guang Lin, David A.F. Smith, and Rajeev Sharma, reprinted by permission from *Teaching and Learning in the College Classroom: A Review of the Research Literature*, 1990.

"Toward Comprehensive Theories of Adult Learning," by Sharan B. Merriam and Rosemary S. Caffarella, reprinted from *Learning in Adulthood: A Comprehensive Guide*, 1991, Jossey-Bass Publishers, Inc.

"Learning Styles and Disciplinary Differences," by David A. Kolb, reprinted from *The Modern American College: Responding to the Realities of Diverse Students and a Changing Society*, edited by A.W. Chickering and Associates, 1981, Jossey-Bass Publishers, Inc.

"Intellectual, Psychosocial, and Moral Development in College: Four Major Theories," by Joanne Kurfiss, reprinted from *A Handbook on Values Development and Lutheran Church-Related College*, edited by J.P. Balas and J.R. Judy, 1988, Thiel College.

"Issues of Gender in Teaching and Learning," by Blythe McVicker Clinchy, reprinted from *Journal on Excellence in College Teaching*, Vol. 1, 1990, Office for the Advancement of Scholarship and Teaching.

"An Emerging Conceptualization of Epistemological Beliefs and Their Role in Learning," by Marlene Schommer, reprinted by permission from *Beliefs About Text and Instruction with Text*, edited by Ruth Garner and Patricia A. Alexander, 1994, Lawrence Erlbaum Associates, Inc.

"Taking Student Diversity into Account," by Nancy Chism, reprinted from *Teaching Tips: Strategies, Research, and Theory for College and University Teachers* by Wilbert J. McKeachie with chapters by Nancy Chism, Robert Menges, Marilla Svinicki and Claire Ellen Weinstein, 1994, D.C. Heath.

"Racial Identity Development: Understanding Racial Dynamics in College Classrooms and on Campus," by Rita Hardiman and Bailey W. Jackson, reprinted from *New Directions for Teaching and Learning*, No. 52, Winter 1992, Jossey-Bass Publishers, Inc.

"Effective College Teaching from the Students' and Faculty's View: Matched or Mismatched Priorities?" by Kenneth A. Feldman, reprinted by permission from *Research in Higher Education*, 28, Plenum Publishing Corporation.

"New Faculty as Teachers," by Robert Boice, reprinted by permission from *Journal of Higher Education*, 1991, Ohio State University Press.

"Visible, Vulnerable, and Viable: Emerging Perspectives of a Minority Professor," by Jacquelyn Mitchell, reprinted from *Teaching Minority Students: New Directions for Teaching and Learning*, edited by J.H. Cones, J.F. Noonan, and D. Jahna, No. 16, 1983, Jossey-Bass Publishers, Inc.

"Questioning in College Classrooms," by Carol P. Barnes, reprinted from *Studies of College Teaching: Experimental Results, Theoretical Interpretations and New Perspectives* by C.L. Ellner and C.P. Barnes, 1983, Macmillan Publishing Company.

Excerpts from "Gender and University Teaching: A Negotiated Difference," by Anne Statham, Laurel Richardson, and Judith A. Cook, 1991, State University of New York Press.

"Disciplinary Differences in Classroom Teaching Behaviors," by Harry G. Murray and Robert D. Renaud, reprinted from *New Directions for Teaching and Learning*, No. 64, Winter 1995, Jossey-Bass Publishers, Inc.

"The College Classroom: Some Observations on the Meanings of Student Participation," by David A. Karp and William C. Yoels, reprinted by permission from *Sociology and Social Research*, 60, 1976.

"The Role of Gender in College Classroom Interactions: A Social Context Approach," by Katherine Canada and Richard Pringle, reprinted by permission from *Sociology of Education*, 68, July 1995, American Sociological Association.

"Classroom Incivilities," by Bob Boice, reprinted from *Research in Higher Education*, Vol. 37, No. 4, 1996, Human Sciences Press.

"Interrupting Patriarchy: Politics, Resistance and Transformation in the Feminist Classroom," by Magda Lewis, reprinted by permission from *Harvard Educational* Review, 60, 1990.

"Identifying Exemplary Teachers and Teaching: Evidence from Student Ratings," by Kenneth A. Feldman, reprinted by permission from *Effective Teaching in Higher Education: Research and Practice*, edited by Raymond P. Perry and John C. Smart, 1997, Agathon Press.

"How College Affects Students," by Ernest T. Pascarella and Patrick T. Terenzini, 1991, Jossey-Bass Publishers, Inc.

"The Dynamic Interplay of Student Motivation and Cognition in the College Classroom," by Paul R. Pintrich, reprinted by permission from *Advances in Motivation and Achievement: Motivation Enhancing Environments*, Vol. 6, edited by M. Maehr and C. Ames, 1989, JAI Press.

"College Classroom Interactions and Critical Thinking," by Daryl G. Smith, reprinted from *Journal of Educational Psychology*, Vol. 69, 1977, American Psychiatric Association.

"The Effects of Verbal and Nonverbal Teacher Immediacy on Perceived Cognitive, Affective, and Behavioral Learning in the Multicultural Classroom," by Judith A. Sanders and Richard L. Wiseman, reprinted by permission from *Communication Education*, 39, 1990, Speech Communication Association.

"Research on Cooperative Learning" in Cooperative Learning: Increasing College Faculty Instructional Productivity, by David W. Johnson, Roger T. Johnson, and Karl A. Smith, reprinted by permission from *ASHE-ERIC Higher Education Report*, No. 4, 1991. Washington D.C.: The George Washington University, School of Education and Human Development. Please call the ERIC Clearinghouse on Higher Education at 1-800-773-3742 for a complementary Publication Catalog of other titles available in the ASHE-ERIC Higher Education Report Series. Also, more information on this and other higher education topics are available on our website at http://www.gwu.edu/~eriche.

"Teaching Styles and Effects on Learning," (Chapter 1), by Paul L. Dressel and Dora Marcus, reprinted from *On Teaching and Learning in College*, 1982, Jossey-Bass Publishers, Inc.

"What Constitutes Masterful Teaching?" (Chapter 1), by Joseph Lowman, reprinted from *Mastering the Techniques of Teaching*, 1984, Jossey-Bass Publishers, Inc.

"Inside Feminist Classrooms: An Ethnographic Approach," by Frances Maher and Mary Kay Thompson Tetreault, reprinted from *Teaching For Diversity*, No. 49, edited by L.B. Border and N. Van Note Chism, 1992, Jossey-Bass Publishers, Inc.

"What It Means to Be a Critically Reflective Teacher," (Chapter 1), by Stephen D. Brookfield, reprinted from *Becoming a Critically Reflective Teacher*, 1995, Jossey-Bass Publishers, Inc.

"Seven Principles for Good Practice in Undergraduate Education," by Arthur W. Chickering and Zelda F. Gamson, reprinted by permission from *AAHE Bulletin*, March 1987, a publication of the American Association for Higher Education.

"Practical Proposals for Motivating Students," by Donelson R. Forsyth and James H. McMillan, reprinted from *New Directions for Teaching and Learning: College Teaching from Theory and Practice*, No. 45, edited by R.J. Menges and M.D. Svinicki, 1991, Jossey-Bass Publishers, Inc.

"Effective Social Arrangements for Teaching and Learning," by Janet Mancini Billson and Richard G. Tiberius, reprinted from *New Directions for Teaching and Learning: College Teaching from Theory and Practice*, No. 45, edited by R.J. Menges and M.D. Svinicki, 1991, Jossey-Bass Publishers, Inc.

"The Kolb Model Modified for Classroom Activities," by Marilla D. Svinicki and Nancy M. Dixon, reprinted from *College Teaching*, No. 35, 1987, Heldref Publications, 1319 Eighteenth St. N.W. Washington D.C. 20036-1802. Reprinted by permission of the Helen Dwight Reid Educational Foundation. Copyright © 1987.

"What Is Collaborative Learning?" by Barbara Leigh Smith and Jean T. MacGregor, reprinted from *Collaborative Learning: A Sourcebook for Higher Education*, edited by Anne S. Goodsell, Michelle R. Maher, Vincent Tinto, Barbara Leigh Smith, and Jean MacGregor, 1992, National Center on Postsecondary Teaching, Learning, and Assessment.

"Talking About Race, Learning About Racism: The Application of Racial Identity Development Theory in the Classroom," by Beverly Daniel Tatum, reprinted by permission from *Harvard Educational Review*, Vol. 61, No. 1, Spring 1992. Copyright © 1992 by the President and Fellows of Harvard College. All rights reserved.

"Implementing the Seven Principles: Technology as Lever," by Arthur W. Chickering and Stephen C. Ehrmann, reprinted from *AAHE Bulletin*, Vol. 49, No. 2, October 1996, American Association for Higher Education.

Excerpts from "Taking Teaching Seriously: Meeting the Challenge of Instructional Improvement," by Michael B. Paulsen and Kenneth A. Feldman, reprinted by permission from *ASHE-ERIC Higher Education Report*, No. 2, 1995. Washington D.C.: The George Washington University, School of Education and Human Development. Please call the ERIC Clearinghouse on Higher Education at 1-800-773-3742 for a complementary Publication Catalog of other titles available in the ASHE-ERIC Higher Education Report Series. Also, more information on this and other higher education topics are available on our website at http://www.gwu.edu/~eriche.

"Instructional Interventions: A Review of the Literature on Efforts to Improve Instruction," by Maryellen Weimer and Lisa Firing Lenze, reprinted by permission from *Higher Education: Handbook of Theory and Research*, Vol. 7, edited by J.C. Smart, 1991, Agathon Press.

"Introduction to Classroom Research," by K. Patricia Cross and Mimi Harris Steadman, reprinted from *Classroom Research: Implementing the Scholarship of Teaching*, 1996, Jossey-Bass Publishers, Inc.

"The Teaching Portfolio: Capturing the Scholarship in Teaching," by Russell Edgerton, Patricia Hutchings, and Kathleen Quinlan, reprinted from *American Association for Higher Education*, 1991.

"Possible Items for Inclusion," by Shore, reprinted from *The Teaching Dossier*, 1986, Canadian Association of University Teachers.

Excerpt from *"Taking Teaching Seriously: Meeting the Challenge of Instructional Improvement,"* by Michael B.Paulsen and Kenneth A. Feldman, reprinted from ASHE-ERIC Higher Education Report, No. 2, 1995.

"From Teaching to Learning: A New Paradigm for Undergraduate Education," by Robert B. Barr and John Tagg, reprinted from *Change*, Vol. 27, No. 6, November/December 1995, Heldref Publications, 1319 Eighteenth St. N.W. Washington D.C. 20036-1802. Reprinted with permission of the Helen Dwight Reid Educational Foundation. Copyright © 1995.

Contents

D. Instruction and Learning Outcomes in the Classroom

PART IV UNDERSTANDING AND IMPLEMENTING EFFECTIVE TEACHING AND LEARNING

A. General Models and Teaching Styles

B. Specific Strategies and Classroom Implementation

Acknowledgments

We are delighted that the ASHE Reader Advisory Board—in conjunction with the immediate-past and current editors of the ASHE Reader Series, Barbara Townsend and Bruce Anthony Jones, respectively—asked us to put together a second edition of "Teaching and Learning in the College Classroom." The first edition was a labor of love for us, and so was the second. We did not labor alone, however, for we had a splendid panel of advisors for each edition. Some of the advisors we selected were on both panels, some only on one of the two; but all of them gave us unusually thoughtful comments about the viewpoints, topics and selections of this Reader. We are most grateful, then, to the following persons for their participation either on one of the two advisory panels or on both of them (denoted by an asterisk by their names): Robert Boice; William E. Cashin; K. Patricia Cross (*); Joanne Gainen; Anastasia S. Hagen; Samuel E. Kellams; Wilbert J. McKeachie (*); Robert J. Menges; Albert B. Smith; Joan S. Stark; Laura M. Stough; Marilla D. Svinicki (*); Barbara K. Townsend (*); and Maryellen Weimer (*). We also would like to thank Lori Bittker, editor at Simon and Schuster, for her enthusiasm about our efforts and her efficiency in seeing this second edition to its completion and publication.

Introduction to the Reader

The purpose of the present reader, like that of its predecessor published in 1994, is to increase the awareness and understanding of the most important issues, practices and research associated with the principles of effective teaching and learning in the college classroom. The analysis of teaching and learning in the college classroom is a complex matter. By considering many different aspects of students, teachers, and their interaction in the classroom, we again have tried to capture much of this complexity. Although the reader is geared to students taking graduate courses in college teaching and learning, we hope nevertheless that it will also serve as a source book for other sorts of audiences, including faculty members, faculty and instructional developers, administrators, undergraduates, and still others with a general interest in higher education.

In our selection of readings we have given much weight to empirical studies and to evidence based on carefully gathered data, yet we have tried not to slight philosophical views and informed speculations. Both quantitative and qualitative research are included; and many different research and theoretical perspectives are represented—educationist, feminist, humanistic, psychological, sociological, anthropological, and more. We have included well-known as well as little-known pieces. Some articles in the reader have a radical point of view, others a conservative one; some of the articles may provoke; others will be reinforcing. Nor are the readings of the same stylistic stripe: they vary from research reports to literature reviews to essay-like pieces to practioner-oriented articles. As in the first edition of this reader, then, we have been unabashedly eclectic in selecting readings for this book.

The variety of readings have been organized around certain clearly focused goals, purposes and themes. Graduate courses in college teaching and learning offered by higher education programs across the country continue to grow in importance in step with the shifting concerns of our academic cultures. This reader is intended to help those who design and teach such courses to better meet the needs of the increasingly diverse groups of students attracted to the study of teaching and learning. Most students who take classes on this topic fall into one of the following four rather distinct clusters with different overlapping goals: (l) future higher education scholars with special interests in college teaching and learning; (2) current or future instructors from a wide variety of disciplines who wish to improve their teaching effectiveness; (3) current M.A. level college instructors who need a doctorate with a curriculum and instructional emphasis to continue teaching; and (4) current or future academic or nonacademic administrators who wish to increase their awareness of the most important issues and practices in the field. All four of these groups of students are intended to be served by the content and organization of this reader.

Although some of the readings new to this second edition of "Teaching and Learning in the College Classroom" are concerned with issues and topics not previously considered, the general substance of the reader is essentially the same. The number and ordering of the major sections of the reader have been changed, however. The six major parts or subareas of the first edition have been recombined and reordered to make the "flow" of the presentation smoother and more effective. The reader is now divided into four major subareas. Part I ("The Evolution of College Teaching and Learning in America") examines the nature and practices of college teaching and learning from 1600 to the present, reviews the origins and evolution of research conducted in this field between 1920 and 1990, and traces the development of teaching as an act of scholarship in the history of American higher education. Part II ("Understanding Students as Learners"), in examining learning theory and related research as it applies to post secondary settings, addresses the important implications associated with student diversity. Part III ("Understanding Students and Teachers in the Classroom") first focuses on teacher and student expectations, teacher behaviors and practices, and student-teacher interactions; it then provides evidence about student cognitive and noncognitive outcomes, as these outcomes are related to the instructional activities in the classroom and to the effectiveness of the teacher. Part IV ("Understanding and Implementing Effective Teaching and Learning"), in addition to introducing some general models of teaching and specific teaching strategies for their classroom implementation, reviews the literature on models and techniques for improving teaching, presents some examples of recent innovations for instructional improvements, and considers certain important extra-classroom influences on teaching and learning.

Because each of the four parts or subareas of the reader has its own general theme, we have written a separate introduction for each of them. Each introduction embeds the readings in a framework relevant to the subarea. At the end of this volume, we have included a sampling of additional readings that represent the readings in the subareas. These additional readings help to give a fuller view of relevant topics and partially compensate for our having to be highly selective in picking readings for this collection.

PART I

The Evolution of College Teaching and Learning in America

Introduction

Wisdom, it is said, comes from experience and the time to reflect upon it. In shaping a future with more effective ideas and practices for teaching and learning, more advanced methods of research in the area, and better interpretation and application of relevant findings, we might well reflect upon the fabric of history that has shaped our present. Some historical traditions were good and their contemporary influences still are; others have been or should be changed. The three readings selected for Part I establish historical perspective for reflections about the art and science of effective teaching and learning in American higher education.

The reading by Fuhrmann and Grasha presents a broad overview of the three-hundred-year history of college teaching and learning in America. The authors review and summarize the traditional beliefs, attitudes, goals and behaviors that characterized teaching and learning processes during the colonial period (1600-1800), the nineteenth century, and the twentieth century. To this information, they add their speculations about the future. For each historical period, they ask current teachers to indicate the extent of their agreement (or disagreement) with a list of specific items that illustrate the teaching-learning traditions of the era. Such an exercise is intended to help teachers identify and clarify some of the historical influences on and antecedents of their contemporary ideas and approaches to teaching and learning.

The reading by McKeachie traces the history of research on college teaching and learning from the 1920s to the present. McKeachie highlights both substantive findings and methodological advances associated with evolving research on the following topics: class size; lecture versus discussion; student-centered discussion; independent study and peer learning; evaluation of teaching; teaching and technology; and the impact of cognitive psychology. His concluding section presents particularly illuminating speculations about the future of research on college teaching and learning.

Finally, in a reading excerpted from his book, *Scholarship Reconsidered*, Boyer examines the nature of the scholarly work of faculty and the historical influences on the meaning of scholarship. Boyer's work has influenced many faculty and administrators in higher education to conceive of teaching (and service as well) more like we have long thought of research, as an act or form of scholarship (as important and valuable as research). During the Colonial period, the emphasis that British colleges and universities placed on the moral and intellectual development of students helped establish "the image of the scholar as teacher" in American higher education. During the nineteenth century, the high value that Americans placed on service to society as an important component of faculty work was established as an important aspect of the missions of land grant colleges. Also in the nineteenth century, many of the leaders in American higher education who had completed their graduate work at German universities were successful in establishing research and the advancement of knowledge as critical aspects of the scholarly work of faculty. However, since World War II, American higher education has developed a more restricted conception of scholarship in which research and publication is viewed as a symbol of academic prestige and is rewarded more than teaching and other aspects of faculty work. Boyer expresses his concern about such a restricted view and proposes a much more inclusive, multidimensional view of scholarship. The paradigm he presents includes the scholarship of research (discovery and integration), service (application) and teaching; he argues that these dimensions of scholarly activity are highly interdependent and inseparable from one another.

This reading by Boyer is included in Part I for several reasons. First, it traces the development of teaching as an act of scholarship in the history of American higher education. Second, it has lead to a growing literature that elaborates on the meaning of the scholarship of teaching (Cross and Steadman, 1996; Menges and Weimer, 1996; Paulsen and Feldman, 1995; Schon, 1995). Third, the very contents of this ASHE Reader represent one form in which aspects of the scholarship of teaching can be documented. Thus, this collection of readings contains reports of quantitative and qualitative studies of teaching and learning in the college classroom, articles synthesizing such research in an effort to offer research-based strategies for effective teaching, and narratives or case studies documenting the wisdom of practice. We believe that this book provides examples of the scholarship of teaching as well as models to inspire and guide ongoing contributions to the expanding volume of such scholarship.

References

Cross, K.P., and Steadman, M.H., (1996). *Classroom research: Implementing the scholarship of teaching*. San Francisco: Jossey-Bass.

Menges, R.J., and Weimer, M. (1996). *Teaching on solid ground: Using scholarship to improve practice*. San Francisco: Jossey-Bass.

Paulsen, M.B., and Feldman, K.A. (1995). Toward a reconceptualization of scholarship: A human action system with functional imperatives. *Journal of Higher Education 66*, 615–640.

Schon, D.A. The new scholarship requires a new epistemology: Knowing in action. *Change, 27* (6), 26–34.

The Past, Present, and Future in College Teaching: Where Does Your Teaching Fit?

BARBARA SCHNEIDER FUHRMANN AND ANTHONY F. GRASHA

In the three hundred years of college teaching in the United States, the teacher's role has remained, until quite recently, relatively stable. Development has certainly occurred, and we will detail that development in the remainder of this chapter. However, in comparison to the upheavals experienced in the development of books and educational technology, the deeper insights into learning processes reached by a tremendous amount of research, and the vast physical and social changes taking place on campuses, the teaching role has changed remarkably, and quite regrettably, little. Undoubtedly, this cannot continue. This book and others that highlight college teaching as a vital and evolving profession are but one bit of tangible evidence that teaching must and will change to meet better the needs of students in the last decades of the twentieth century. For such changes to occur, we must begin to think actively about the changes in teaching that are possible for the future. Alvin Toffler notes that our current teaching activities could be enhanced by modifying them to meet our personal images of the future. To break with the past, each of us must bring new ideas into our current instructional practices.

What are the new ideas in teaching that we must take into account? We obviously have no crystal ball that will accurately outline the details of such things. To suggest that we know for sure would certainly be pretentious. Several of our ideas are incorporated into the content of other chapters of this book, but they are only our best guesses regarding the future. What is more important is that everyone who teaches begin to speculate about the future. Each of us must examine our current teaching-learning assumptions, goals, values, and methods to determine whether they will help our students and us meet the challenges of the future. To begin this analysis, it is important first to determine the origins of some of our current educational ideas and practices. Such insights may help us decide whether we are hopelessly buried in the past. And a careful review of why we hold various beliefs and use particular methods may help us find ways to free ourselves from whatever binds we find ourselves in. This is not to suggest that all traditional goals, values, and methods are inappropriate. As we will soon illustrate, there are many beliefs and practices in higher education that have their origins as far back as the sixteenth and seventeenth centuries, and some of these beliefs and practices are still considered useful. Rather, our goal is to identify only those traditions that are producing problems for us in meeting the emerging needs of our students and disciplines. These are typically goals, values, and methods that make our teaching less flexible than it should be. Finally, we must begin to speculate about the future to determine what new beliefs and practices help us modify our current practices. The brief overview we present of past, present, and future ideas in college and university teaching in the United States should assist you in such an analysis.[1]

"The Past, Present, and Future in College Teaching: Where Does Teaching Fit?" by Fuhrmann, Barbara Schneider, and Anthony F. Grasha, reprinted by permission from *A Practical Handbook for College Teachers,* 1983.

The Evolution of College Teaching

The Colonial Period (1600–1800)

During the seventeenth and eighteenth centuries, the role of the college instructor in colonial colleges was a paternalistic one in which hearing lessons and supervising conduct were equally important. Higher education was designed for the sons of the elite, with the express purposes of promoting the Christian religion, training young men for the ministry, infusing moral standards in otherwise temptable young minds, and disciplining the mental faculties. Indeed, as Francis Rosecrance documents, all but one of the first nine colleges founded in the United States were established primarily to train ministers, and secondarily to make higher education available to the sons of the elite. These purposes were approached through a rigidly prescribed curriculum of Greek, Latin, mathematics, and so-called moral truths. All were delivered by a single instructor, who was usually a *tutor*—a recent graduate of the institution. The tutor was not much older than his students and was filling time until he received his call to the ministry—the profession assumed by the vast majority. A hidden, unspoken agenda of the colonial colleges was to maintain a socially stratified society by separating the elite (college educated) from the masses. This tiny elite was created by the development of a strongly cohesive unit—the college class. All the men who entered in any one year became a class, a group that took all their instruction together, usually from one tutor who had the total responsibility for delivering the curriculum. Their collective struggle, day by day, year by year, against the inherent rigidity and prescription provided them with a cohesiveness not often matched by any but the most oppressed minorities.

Life in the colonial colleges was bleak—bare, unpleasant rooms and a day that began at sunrise. Following early morning chapel was a class period, then breakfast. After breakfast came alternating periods of class and study time, then lunch and perhaps a short recreational period. The afternoon pattern repeated that of the morning, with a second recreational period before supper time. After supper came more study, then evening chapel and bedtime. John Brubacher and Willis Rudy describe both the students' lot and that of the tutors: "When not attending class or engaged in recreation students were supposed to be in their rooms studying. Indeed tutors made regular rounds to guard against the devil's finding occupations for idle minds" (1958, p. 81).

Being solely responsible for all the activities of a class, including the evening study time, was an impossible burden for young, inexperienced tutors. Most were openly hated by their students, who frequently used every opportunity to retaliate against the unpleasantness of college life by abusing their tutor in all conceivable ways, including breaking his windows and laying traps for him.

The curriculum, which was impractical and expensive, continued the old English tradition of preparing "gentlemen and scholars." It created a learned and cultured group consisting of clergymen and the sons of the rich to lead and develop the fledgling country.

Teaching methods in colonial days consisted of recitation, lecture, disputations, and forensics, with the greatest amount of time and energy being given to *recitation*. Because the purpose of higher education was primarily discipline rather than meaningful learning, the heavy emphasis on recitation served well. In the recitation session, the tutor often sat at a raised desk, on which was a box containing the names of the students. The tutor drew a name from the box and named a passage or specific content for the student to recite.

> The heart of the recitation consisted of an exchange between the tutor and the student, the tutor citing and the student reciting. The citation was usually an assignment in a textbook, but might just as well be a previous lecture or scientific demonstration. In the recitation the student proved he had learned his lesson, at least the portion for which he was called on in class [Brubacher and Rudy, 1958, p. 82].

Obviously, the emphasis was on the lowest order of cognitive skill—pure memory. But the purpose of training in diligence and responsibility was fulfilled. Occasionally a particularly talented tutor raised the level of recitation to approximate a tutor-student discussion, and even more rarely a student might be challenged to interpret or even to offer an opinion. On the whole, however, recitation was mere reproduction and became the battleground between student and tutor where each tried to outwit the other.

During this period, *lecturing* emerged as a supplement to recitation. Books were not abundant, and the ancient lecture method gave students access to information they otherwise could not obtain. The instructor read his notes and students diligently copied them. In turn, the notes were used as another basis for recitation assignments. In the rather rigid atmosphere of the colonial classroom, lecturing periods provided, in addition to new information, a short break from the constant demands of recitation. Those of us who use the lecture method so frequently today may find it hard to believe that it once was a somewhat novel experience for students—and a welcomed one at that.

Colonial college students were required not only to study Latin and Greek, but to converse in Latin as well. Practice was encouraged by the use of the method of *disputations*, in which the tutor assigned a debatable thesis that concerned the nature of the soul or some other abstract concept. The student then had either to agree or disagree with the thesis through a series of syllogisms. Other students were then invited to offer differing views, using the same syllogistic reasoning process. When all students who were called on or volunteered had finished "disputing" the thesis, the tutor summarized the arguments and closed the exercise with his own opinion on the matter. About the middle of the eighteenth century, syllogistic disputations began to be replaced by public debate (*forensics*), including debate over more popular issues. Until the nineteenth century, however, the recitation method remained at the heart of the process of higher education.

Testing in the colonial colleges had each student questioned orally in public by anywhere from five to twenty examiners. The examiners were college personnel and other learned citizens from the local community. Marks were not given, but judgments were passed on both the student and his tutor. It was therefore to the tutor's advantage that his students performed well. Thus, when it was his turn to question, he was likely to give easy or leading questions to his own students and difficult ones to others. The game between tutors and students continued.

Are there ways in which your current teaching practices reflect some of the general ideas regarding educational practices present in the colonial period? Of course, we do not have the same type of tutor-student relationship. But there are a number of current educational goals, values, and practices that were popular during this period also. Table 1.1 contains several that we have identified. As you review the information in this table, consider whether your current teaching practices reflect some of the same things. Then think about whether those that do reflect the colonial period are still useful. We believe that some of them probably are valuable parts of our current educational environments. But each of us must decide which ones are still useful based on a personal analysis of their current advantages and disadvantages.

The Nineteenth Century

By the end of the eighteenth century, the impracticality and elitism of college became an issue, and a new emphasis was born. New colleges were founded, with a wider appeal, and college began to be "recognized as a means of getting ahead, not just as a means of registering that one's father had" (Rudolph, 1965, p. 36).

Francis Rosecrance also notes that early-nineteenth-century religious awakenings combined with westward expansion to influence the development of many small church-related colleges across the midwestern United States. The vast majority of these failed, but not before their democratizing effect was felt.

Concurrent with this broader appeal and purpose was the influence of scholars who attended German universities, where intellect and scholarly endeavor rather than rote memory were encouraged. Paternalism had been the hallmark of the eighteenth century; democracy became the hallmark of the nineteenth (Brubacher and Rudy, 1958).

The German influence was supported by the rise of science. Both the curriculum and its attendant teaching methodology began to broaden. Natural philosophy (science) and new methods (increased use of lectures, demonstrations, and laboratory methods) were added to the curriculum but were staunchly resisted by traditionalists. The controversy among lecture, other methods, and recitation dominated much of the century. Supporters of the recitation method pointed out that in comparison to German universities, American colleges were mere secondary schools, and the students in them required discipline and the development of their "mental faculties" rather than learned wisdom. In addition, they argued, "natural philosophy" and its methods are practical and popular and therefore do not belong in the classical curriculum. Proponents of the lecture method suggested it challenged the professor to be prepared and to present material not otherwise available. Further, the artistic possibilities of a good lecture were cited. As it already had in the German universities, lecture eventually dominated the scene in American higher education. It remains a dominant teaching procedure that is fraught with controversy and criti-

Table 1.1
General Educational Goals, Values, and Practices from the Colonial Period

Review each of the statements listed below. They represent several of the goals, values, and practices that were implicit in our description of the colonial period. Rate yourself on a scale from 1 to 5, where 1 represents total disagreement and 5 represents total agreement with the statement. *Sum the ratings for your responses to these items. We will ask you to do something with them later.* For those items you rated 3, 4, or 5, how do they appear in your current educational practices? What are their advantages and disadvantages? What implications do they have for the future if you continue to use them in your teaching?

- The instructor is an expert and should have the last word in resolving debates on content.
- Instructors should prescribe in detail the course content, assignments, and methods of evaluation.
- Colleges and universities should serve a highly selected population of students.
- Student learning is facilitated when the students are highly dependent on the instructor for information.
- Our capability to think logically and rationally is enhanced by courses in mathematics, ancient languages, and philosophy.
- Recreational activities should be a very low priority in college.
- A student's first obligation is to study what is prescribed and thus build his or her mental capacities.
- Learning is hard work and demands personal sacrifice and discipline.
- Students are basically lazy and need to be goaded into learning information.
- Repeating verbatim what they have learned, in class or on a test, is a useful activity for students.
- If a student has not learned, then the instructor has failed as a teacher.
- Students should learn what the instructor thinks is important.
- Teachers know what students need to learn.
- The classroom learning process is often a battle between the students and the instructor.

cism. The arguments over the lecture method will probably continue into the future, just as they have occurred since its introduction in our colleges and universities.

One particular form of the lecture was associated with the rise in popularity and respectability of science: a form known as the experimental lecture. Here the professor performed an experiment to demonstrate the principle that was the subject of the lecture. These demonstrations eventually led to the development of the laboratory method. Early in the century, the laboratory was viewed as the private domain of the professor. Gradually this domain was opened to students, at first only to watch, but later to participate in the professor's experiments. Involvement of students in this way eventually led to the discovery that students might learn inductively as well as deductively. Thus, the science laboratory as a teaching device was born. Finally, by the end of the nineteenth century, "at every step—definition of the problem, collection of data, formulation of a hypothesis, testing—the professor was sympathetic guide and critic" (Brubacher and Rudy, 1958, p. 88), but the student did the discovering and formulated the conclusions.

Science was responsible also for the introduction of seminars, which were supported by the new influx of German educators. From seminars and laboratories emerged a new relationship between teaching and research, a relationship that virtually changed the nature of higher education in America. Specialized courses were developed, research libraries and significant laboratory space and equipment were constructed, research papers became a popular teaching method, learned societies of earnest, like-thinking students and faculty developed, and graduate education was introduced.

Specialization began to appear in the curriculum, with the evolution of the colonial "natural philosophy" into the various scientific disciplines—geology, biology, physics, and chemistry; the colonial "moral philosophy" into the social specialties—economics, anthropology, sociology, and political science; and the colonial "classics" into language and literary specialties. With specialization, the earliest attempts at an elective rather than a prescriptive curriculum also occurred.

Also during the nineteenth century, the so-called collegiate way was born. At first, because colleges were usually located away from populous areas, residence accommodations were required. Later the idea of the ivory tower, isolated from its surroundings and providing all that its students might need, became a tradition, if not a principle, of American higher education. In the residential, often pastoral, college, the extracurriculum developed. Debating clubs and literary societies for intellectual challenge, fraternities and student activities for social needs, and athletics for physical needs became as important as (if not more important than) the curriculum itself.

By the end of the nineteenth century, colleges began seriously to question themselves. Concerns over standards and excellence were raised. There was some anxiety that learning was simply not taken particularly seriously. College education had broadened, deepened, and become popular. Student evaluation had moved from public examination to written exams with marks (0–100) and grades (A–E), but student motivation often remained low. Near the end of the century, emerging institutions experimented with manual labor as a means of teaching educational principles, encouraging interest, and providing financial support for students. This movement, however, was hardly more than a justification for using student labor to construct needed facilities, and it was short lived. The century ended with college education popular, but all too often less than meaningful.

As you did after examining the colonial period, turn to Table 1.2 and assess to what extent your current teaching practices reflect some of the educational goals and practices that were present during the nineteenth century. Think about those that do reflect the last century in terms of how well they serve your needs and those of your students. What are their advantages and disadvantages?

The Twentieth Century

If the seventeenth and eighteenth centuries in higher education are characterized as paternalistic, and the nineteenth century as democratic, the twentieth century is nothing less than revolutionary. The century began with the prospect of an ever-increasing student population, many of whose aims conflicted with the traditional scholarly ones that the colleges had relatively recently adopted. In the early 1900s, social needs outweighed academic ones. As John Brubacher and Willis Rudy note, "Many a twentieth-century father sent his son to college less to sharpen his wits than to polish his manners" (1958, p. 259). Owen Johnson, in his early-twentieth-century novel *Stover at Yale*, criticized educational habits severely, charging that students learned nothing. Colleges, he pointed out, were mere "social clearing houses" organized not only to serve social purposes, but actually to prevent learning. Student dissatisfaction with the curriculum eventually led to significant reforms, particularly those that directed more attention to practical subjects. In attempts to motivate the generally unintellectual student population, innovations of numerous kinds were tried. Preceptors were used to guide and stimulate students and to personalize the curriculum for them; honors instruction as a reward for excellence was begun; independent study became a way to encourage academic endeavor; and periods of work were alternated with periods of study in an attempt to make learning practical.

On a broader scale, three reform viewpoints or philosophies of higher education developed—the utilitarian or vocational view, which emphasizes job and career training; the scientific or intellectual view, which emphasizes research and the development of new knowledge; and the liberal or general education view, which emphasizes social development as well as intellectual and vocational development. These three viewpoints have remained prominent on university campuses, never completely comfortable in compromise, but rather living in a somewhat strained coexistence—even today.

Early Experimental Approaches

During the first half of this century, no single reform emerged as the one wave of the future, but the influence of John Dewey led to much experimentation, especially in the areas of lifelong learning needs and inductive rather than deductive methods.

Table 1.2
General Educational Goals, Values, and Practices from the Nineteenth Century

Review each of the statements listed below. They represent several of the goals, values, and practices that were implicit in our description of the nineteenth century. Rate yourself on a scale from 1 to 5, where 1 represents total disagreement and 5 represents total agreement with the statement. *Sum the ratings for your responses to these items. We will ask you to do something with them later.* For those items you rated 3, 4 or 5, how do they appear in your current educational practices? What are their advantages and disadvantages? What implications do they have for the future if you continue to use them in your teaching?

- A college education is for more than just a highly selected student population.
- Rote memory should not be emphasized in college.
- Teachers can learn from their students.
- A college education should prepare people to assume a job.
- Lecturing has positive benefits for students.
- Colleges should teach subjects that are practical and popular.
- Students need hands-on experiences in laboratories and other settings to learn.
- Teachers need to take a less directive role in prescribing what students should learn.
- Students know what they need to learn and should be encouraged to pursue such interests.
- Specialization within a field is an important goal of education.
- Colleges must help meet the social, physical, and intellectual needs of students.
- Teachers should help students develop the capacity to become independent learners.
- Students should be taught to think both inductively and deductively.
- Recreational activities should be an important part of the college environment.

One experimental approach was that of integrating disciplines for the purpose of realistically treating current issues. Thus the survey course was born, designed to interest young people in using their minds to tackle world and national problems. In this way psychology, sociology, and economics might be combined in a course entitled "Youth in Contemporary Society."

Another approach combined the development of divisions, such as physical sciences, social sciences, and humanities, with the idea of *general education.* A student who in colonial days would have followed a single prescribed curriculum, and who in the late nineteenth century might have had a free choice of electives, now had to master the basics (with a combination of prescribed electives) in each division before selecting an area of specialization. General education was seen as the basis for the widely informed and well-educated person. Through the universal adoption of the general education principle, professors began to differentiate standards for majors and nonmajors. Sometimes they even described their professional status by the number of major and nonmajor courses taught.

A third innovation was the Great Books approach to curriculum. Built on the idea that a classic book is always contemporary and relevant, the Great Books concept built anywhere from a year's study to an entire four-year curriculum on the study of specific, identified "classics."

Changes Since 1950

Now, in the second half of the twentieth century, revolutionary changes in the world have challenged all previous views. Lewis Mayhew specifies the profound revolutions occurring since World War II as "the revolt of colonial peoples, the revolution in weaponry, the explosion of knowledge, the urbanization and technocratization of the society, and undreamed-of affluence" (1969, p. ix). The veterans of World War II and later wars brought with them to American universities an attitude of sobriety and seriousness. The "rah-rah" days of Joe College, football, and fraternities spawned in the era of extracurriculum began to wane.

The Cold War and the launching of Sputnik created a panic during which all attention was given to academic excellence. Fear led to an emphasis on technology as the only way to progress and excel. The academic boom in the decade between 1958 and 1968 saw many large research grants, curriculum reforms (especially in the sciences and technology), additional faculty positions, and better salaries. New courses and curricula developed, with the emphasis on production and efficiency. Many institutions became intoxicated with growth. New courses and programs of study were added before the long-range implications of the growth were assessed. Cuts in budgets because of declining resources in the 1970s would later eliminate as frills some of the changes of the 1960s. Yet such changes continued during the 1960s without much realization that a temporary boom in money and students was feeding the growth.

It took the Vietnam War and the student protest movement on campuses during the late 1960s to force another reevaluation of the goals and methods of higher education. Students demanded (perhaps somewhat naively and destructively) a greater voice in the affairs of the university and a realignment of the purposes of academe. Now, at least partly because of student radicalism, we are seeing higher education's responsibility to the community increased. Most important, the aim of education is no longer viewed as the study of externals. The traditional views and methods will no longer suffice in an era when the demand by students is for relevance, meaning, and preparation for the work world. Instead of the "pitcher" theory of education, in which the teacher holds the pitcher full of knowledge and pours out what he or she chooses into the receptacles of student minds, a new view is evolving. In this view teacher and student are partners, though not equal partners, in the challenge of learning—learning about the world, each other, themselves, and ways of managing their lives.

The Vietnam War and the campus and societal unrest of the 1960s made higher education systems more sensitive to issues of relevance, meaning, and job preparation, and declining resources during the 1970s and 1980s forced them to focus even more on such issues. Colleges and universities found themselves having to operate with less funding and fewer students than they enjoyed during the boom years of the 1960s. Inflation, high interest rates, cuts in expenditures by foundations, state governments, and the federal government, and fewer eighteen- to twenty-one-year-old students made institutions take a hard look at what offerings and services they could reasonably provide. Some institutions folded; others searched for ways to survive. One part of surviving was opening the doors to what Pat Cross describes as the "new students." Such students were generally older, highly interested in acquiring vocational skills, and either changing careers or, in the case of many women, formulating career plans for the first time. Continuing education and lifelong learning became very important concepts that guided academic programs. At the same time, institutions took steps to eliminate the "fat" and frills from their systems, and a back-to-basics attitude began to emerge. Course offerings and programs that a decade earlier were innovative and creative suddenly were eliminated or cut to conform to new budget realities. Those that survived were the ones considered absolutely essential to preserve the discipline or to meet the immediate needs of the influx of new students. Institutions found themselves needing to extend their reach to new student populations and to develop vocationally relevant curricula while holding the line on costs.

Learning Theories

The twentieth century in higher education is also characterized by systematic attempts to develop teaching methods and practices based on theories of learning. The research literature on human learning has been used as a foundation for educational innovations. Three points of view tend to dominate this experimentation. They are the humanistic, behavioral, and cognitive views of learning. In a later chapter, we present in detail their assumptions and methods. For now, let us briefly examine a few of their principles and how they have influenced instruction in the twentieth century.

Instead of assuming that students will learn merely by passively digesting the pearls of wisdom transmitted to them by their professors, the humanistic view recognizes that learning is something that students must do for themselves. Teachers must not merely transmit, but must involve and engage students in the activities of discovery and meaning making. This emphasis on student needs and the study of oneself as part of the study of humanity is sometimes also called student-centered education, or affective education. Teachers are encouraged to guide and direct less and to facilitate or act as a catalyst for students to initiate and take responsibility for their own learning. Personal feelings and values, concerns with minority issues and sexism, and a reexamination of the content of the college curriculum are part of this approach. It is an attempt to personalize education. It represents a reaction against the excesses of the technological emphasis in education during the late 1950s, an emphasis that some people believed tended to dehumanize individuals, to bend, staple, and mutilate the spirits of students who felt left out by the increased structure, cognitive priorities, behavioral orientation and efficiency of the stress on technology.

The behaviorist point of view has also had an impact on educational practices during this century. During the early part of the twentieth century, John Watson introduced the idea that our behaviors are controlled by stimuli in our environments. He believed that anyone could be taught to become anything—doctor, lawyer, merchant, thief—by the proper manipulation of environmental stimuli. B.F. Skinner began in the 1930s to modify the earlier ideas of Watson and develop what he called a technology of operant conditioning. This technology stressed the need to shape behaviors in small steps and to reward each small success a learner had. It also emphasized that organisms learn at different rates and that some custom designing of learning environments is necessary to accommodate such variations. Skinner's work began with pigeons, rats, and other animals during the 1930s, and it was not until the late 1940s and early 1950s that educational applications began to appear. Teaching machines, token economies in the classroom, personalized systems of instruction such as the Keller Plan, learning contracts, and computer-assisted instruction have evolved based on behavioral principles.

Although behaviorism emphasized the role of environmental stimuli in controlling a learner's actions, the student's cognitive capability was not ignored. Procedures were developed to help students solve problems and make decisions more effectively, to use mental images to assist their learning of foreign languages and other subjects, and to develop cognitive procedures to monitor and control by themselves their ability to learn.

Regardless of their merits, the attempts at reforms based on principles of learning have been less than spectacular. To date, it is not a general practice for people systematically to develop their teaching based on principles of learning. In fact, some students and faculty seem to display passivity, apathy, and even overt hostility and cynicism when suggestions are made to substitute new methodologies for the old. One issue is that the nontraditional, unconventional, alternative ideas represent attitudes that (1) put the student first and the institution second; (2) concentrate more on the student's needs than the institution's convenience; (3) encourage diversity of individual opportunity rather than uniform prescription; and (4) deemphasize time, space, and course requirements in favor of competence and performance. Such beliefs run counter to many of the past experiences of students and faculty. Thus, they raise anxiety in students who want more structure or are simply afraid of deviating from the ways they learned in the past. Faculty often charge that new methods lack academic rigor or are based on ideas that are not well researched.

The reactions to nontraditional forms of teaching based on principles of learning are simply another reflection of the traditional-nontraditional controversy that has occurred throughout this and past centuries in higher education. But there need not be a quarrel between the traditional, with its emphasis on academic excellence and depth of inquiry, and the nontraditional, with its emphasis on lifelong learning and self-education. The nontraditional approaches can augment, fortify, and enhance more traditional philosophy and methods, can add new perspectives and horizons to educational opportunity and possibility, and will sometimes show that traditional forms have a necessary and perhaps irreplaceable role to play. We think, then, that the prevailing attitude today and for the future is that the traditionalist and nontraditionalist are not adversaries. One cannot supplant or supersede the other; they are inseparable partners in the single purpose of promoting learning. The traditionalist attitude of rigor and discipline is worthy of note by the nontraditionalist, and the traditionalist must take note of the nontraditionalist emphasis on independent study, flexible patterns, and lifelong enrichment. It may even be said that true creativity can come only from a dialectical synthesis of tradition and antitradition. Traditional forms that remain vital must be preserved, while those that have outlived their usefulness must be replaced by creative, relevant ones. This creativeness in the art of teaching is the wave of both the present and the future in higher education.

Earlier we asked you to assess your current practices to determine their origins in the colonial period and the nineteenth century. Whether you continue to endorse current goals and practices that originated during these periods depends on how helpful you perceive them to be. Table 1.3 contains ideas based on our discussion of the twentieth century. Try a similar analysis with the statements in this table and see if it provides additional insights into your teaching.

Table 1.3
General Educational Goals, Values, and Practices from the Twentieth Century

Review each of the statements listed below. They represent several of the goals, values, and practices that were implicit in our description of the twentieth century. Rate yourself on a scale from 1 to 5, where 1 represents total disagreement and 5 represents total agreement with the statement. *Sum the ratings for your responses to these items. We will ask you to do something with them later.* For those items you rated 3, 4, or 5, how do they appear in your current educational practices? What are their advantages and disadvantages? What implications do they have for the future if you continue to use them in your teaching?

- Students should alternate course work with job experience related to their major field of study.
- Education is a lifelong process that does not end with formal training.
- Students should learn to study and work on academic matters independently.
- It is important to stress practical subjects in a college curriculum.
- Vocational and career training is an important mission of a college or university.
- Colleges and universities must stress the development of new knowledge as one of their goals.
- Interdisciplinary course offerings should be encouraged in a college curriculum.
- The goal of education is to produce a well-educated person trained in a liberal arts tradition.
- Self-awareness is an important part of what students should learn in college.
- Teachers should be less directive and act more as facilitators of a student's learning.
- Teachers need to personalize their instruction to meet the unique needs of their students.
- Learning proceeds best if students are taught in small, discrete steps and rewarded after each step.
- Teachers should help students develop problem-solving and decision-making skills.
- Teaching methods should be developed based on theories of human learning.

The Future

> Just as all education springs from some image of the future, all education produces some image of the future [Toffler, 1974, p. 3].

Alvin Toffler, Benjamin Singer, and other futurists argue that we must integrate future possibilities into our current educational practices. To illustrate this need, Toffler describes a mythical South American Indian tribe that teaches its young the old ways. They learn how to build and ride canoes, the types of fish that live in their lakes and how to catch them, as well as other important aspects of their culture. Because they seldom venture beyond the rather immediate boundaries of their tribe, they are unaware of a hydroelectric dam that is under construction upstream from their territory. In a few years the dam will be completed and their lakes will dry up. What has the tribe done to prepare itself for this event? What can it do if it is so tradition bound?

The metaphor is important and timely, because many of us assume that the main features of our present educational, social, economic, and political systems will continue indefinitely. Yet history shows that we can expect upheavals in our current ways of living. In our experiences, we find students and colleagues who say, "That is true, but it won't happen for a while and certainly not in my lifetime." Or they assume that even if some upheavals occur, their personal lives will remain relatively unaffected. In a series of experiments, Toffler finds similar tendencies in the people with whom he has worked. Participants in his research write about future scenarios as if they will happen "out there" to other people. The future is rather impersonal. They describe their lives as continuing much as they are today. For example, people developed scenarios of a future with antigravity cars, the destruction of large parts of the earth, cures for cancer, test-tube babies, a United States–Soviet Union alliance against China, accidental nuclear explosions, and robot computers holding political office in the United States. What would happen to their lives? One participant wrote, "I'll move into my own apartment, attend interior-design school, get a driver's licence, buy a dog, get married, have children, and die at a ripe old age."

Clearly, there is a need for people to become sensitive to the possibilities of change and the probable effects on their lives. Futurists generally argue that our educational system could do a much better job of integrating the future into current curricula. They suggest that having no image or a false image of the future destroys the relevance of the educational effort. Yet our present educational systems, including higher education, are not seen as showing much concern. Today's schools and universities are perceived as past and present bound. Technological and social change is outracing the educational system, and our social reality is transforming itself more rapidly than our educational images of that reality. Students apparently are not taught to understand their investments in the future, to transfer classroom learning to future possibilities, to help change immature institutions, or to see themselves as individuals who can influence the future.

Benjamin Singer adds that the concept of the future is closely tied to the motivation of the learner. How people see their future is directly connected to their academic performance and their ability to cope with a high-change society. The future is not so much a subject as it is a perspective. Introducing it into our curriculum helps us to organize our knowledge in new ways. To these ideas we might add that such things will occur only if our current educational goals and practices are flexible and amenable to change. That is, to make use of a future perspective, our teaching methods will undoubtedly have to alter.

How to integrate ideas about the future into our teaching is an issue. The following are some possibilities for how this might occur:

- Developing personal images or scenarios about future developments in a field might help students increase their sensitivity to the future. In classroom discussions, students might sometimes be asked to forecast developments in a field and defend their answers.
- Teachers might ask students to speculate on the future images held by prominent historical figures or people in their field and what role these images might have had in their actions. For example, what images of the future guided Hitler, Nixon, Freud, Skinner, Goffman, Darwin, Sagan, or any other people who are relevant to a topic of discussion?
- Cooperative experiences and job-related courses might be developed in all fields. Thus disciplines like classics, philosophy, and history might have to change dramatically. Disciplines like psychology, education, and anthropology might have to do even more than they currently do. To accomplish such things, more long-range planning and forecasting need to be done in such disciplines than currently.
- To cope with change, students need to be able to go beyond current facts and knowledge. They will need to be able to bring themselves up to date. Thus they need to learn how to learn as part of their formal education. Classroom procedures might stress teaching people how to seek and find resources for solving problems, how to work independently, how to benefit from working with other people, and how to ask the right kinds of questions. Classrooms must stress teaching people skills for learning as well as specific content.
- New classroom materials are needed to help students understand themselves better; to recognize their investment in the future; to help them feel more in control of their lives; to understand the nature of change; and to help them mature so they can help change immature institutions. What they learn needs to be thought about in terms of its personal implications.
- Students and faculty need to be increasingly concerned with moral issues. The future is not predetermined, but is subject to our influence. People need to become more concerned with values. Students must learn to understand their values clearly enough to make consistent and effective choices. Their values must be challenged and students asked to justify them explicitly in the classroom.
- To integrate future possibilities into the classroom and to improve the teaching of subjects that are rapidly changing, new approaches to teaching are needed. The information explo-

sion in the study of human learning needs to be put to greater use in the design of instructional procedures. Institutions might demand that faculty pay more attention to the literature on learning when designing course procedures. Furthermore, the use of new teaching methodologies must be encouraged. Thus, computer-assisted instruction, simulations, role plays, classroom theater, practicum experiences, and "think tank" procedures should increase.

It is important to note that integrating a future perspective into education is not only to suggest what the world will look like next year or in the next hundred years. Such speculation is fun and often the topic of science fiction books and articles. Rather, the task is to have such images but also to suggest things that might be done today to help create desirable parts of those future images. We must remember that the future is something we help to create. It is not something that will occur without our participation.

Thus the question "What is the future of teaching in higher education?" is not answered well by simply describing scenarios of classrooms in the twenty-first century. Rather, we must suggest things that can be integrated today into our educational systems to create a future perspective and foundations for future practice. Based on the discussion in this section, several ideas for what might be done are listed in Table 1.4. As you did with the other time periods, rate the extent to which you agree or disagree with the statements.

Table 1.4
General Educational Goals, Values, and Practices for the Future

Review each of the statements listed below. They represent several of the goals, values, and practices that were implicit in our discussion of the future of higher education. Rate yourself on a scale from 1 to 5, where 1 represents total disagreement and 5 represents total agreement with the statement. *Sum the ratings for your responses to these items. We will ask you to do something with them later.* For those items you rated 3, 4, or 5, how do they appear in your current educational practices? What are their advantages and disadvantages? What implications do they have for the future if you continue to use them in your teaching?

- Speculation about the future is an important topic for discussion in the classroom.
- Students should be encouraged to develop personal images or scenarios about future developments in all disciplines.
- Having no image about the future destroys the relevance of the educational effort.
- Today's educational practices are too past and present bound.
- Technological and social change is outpacing the capacity of the educational system.
- Students should be taught to understand their investment in the future.
- Classrooms should stress teaching people skills for how to learn as well as specific content.
- Students need to learn about how to cope with the changes in the world around them.
- Students need to learn how to become effective change agents.
- Classroom practices need to become more bound to the research data on human learning.
- Teachers should use more of the advances in computers, video recorders, and other new technologies as part of their classroom methods.
- Students need to learn how to work independently to a greater extent as well as how to work better with other people.
- The values that underlie our disciplines need to be discussed as part of classroom learning.
- Education should help students develop a sense of personal control over their lives and their environment.

The History of College Teaching and You

After each section of this chapter, we suggested that you rate the extent to which you agree or disagree with the statements presented in the tables. Your total ratings should give you a good idea of which historical periods have influenced your current beliefs about education most and least. Most people find that their current beliefs are a composite of each historical period but that each period did not influence them equally. You may want to examine your ratings and the specific beliefs you agreed and disagreed with by answering the following questions:

- How satisfied am I with the beliefs that I have about education?
- What advantages and disadvantages do they have for me?
- How comfortable am I with the time period that seems to influence my beliefs most? Am I old fashioned, or do my beliefs help me to meet the needs of today's student?
- Do I need to change or modify any of the beliefs I hold?

You may want to think about your responses to these questions as you read the next chapter on examining and clarifying your values as a teacher. Your responses should give you a place to begin to examine your personal values as an instructor.

Summary

In this chapter, we have surveyed the landscape of the history of teaching in the United States from its beginning in colonial days to its as yet unheralded future. We have presented this history in terms of the goals, values, and practices that provided the guiding ideas in the colonial period (1600–1800), the nineteenth century, and the twentieth century, and those that will probably influence future developments.

In the colonial period, college instruction was guided largely by paternalistic ideas that college students should be selected, disciplined, dependent upon instructors, taught to develop rigidly prescribed mental facilities, and generally forced to subscribe to academic requirements into which they had no input and over which they felt no control.

The nineteenth century emphasized democracy, both in its attempt to provide higher education for the broad population rather than only the elite, and in its involvement of students in the process of learning. Consistent with this broadly democratic attitude was the emphasis on subjects that were practical, the concept of specialization as a goal of education, the introduction of job training and experiential learning, the mutual intellectual development of student and teacher, and the social aspect of higher education.

In the twentieth century, revolutionary ideas and behaviors sparked experimentation and innovation. The result has been that alongside traditional views now exist views of education based on humanistic concerns, learning theories, and behaviorist notions. Teaching can, [sic] and is, viewed from all three perspectives, with the result being a wide variety of approaches from which modern faculty can select.

Our presentation of the dominant ideas from each of these periods, along with our best guess as to prevailing ideas of the future, are offered as a stimulus for you to examine your own values, goals, and behaviors in both an introspective and a historical analysis. It's only with a clear idea of both the past and the present that we can thoughtfully influence the future.

Note

1. A complete history of higher education is beyond the scope of this book. Instead, we have elected to highlight several trends that have occurred during the development of higher education in the United States since the colonial period. One must keep in mind that the origins of some ideas found in this country during the colonial period and the nineteenth century lie partly in educational goals and practices found in European universities.

References

Bell, W. Social Science: The future as a missing variable. In A. Toffler, ed., *Learning for Tomorrow: The Role of the Future in Education*. New York: Vintage Books, 1974.

Brubacher, J.S., and Rudy, W. *Higher Education in Transition*. New York: Harper & Row, 1958.

Cross, P. *Accent on Learning*. San Francisco: Jossey-Bass, 1976.

Johnson, O.H., Dink Stover at Yale, about 1909. In S. Bellman, ed., *The College Experience*. San Francisco: Chandler, 1962.

Mayhew, L.B. *Colleges Today and Tomorrow*. San Francisco: Jossey-Bass, 1969.

McDanield, M. Tomorrow's curriculum today. In A. Toffler, ed., *Learning for Tomorrow: The Role of the Future in Education*. New York: Vintage Books, 1974.

Rosecrance, F.C. *The American College and Its Teachers*. New York: Macmillan, 1962.

Rudolf, F. *The American College and University: A History*. New York: Vintage Books, 1965.

Singer, B.D. The future focused role image. In A. Toffler, ed., *Learning for Tomorrow*. New York: Vintage, 1974.

Skinner. B.F. *Beyond Freedom and Dignity*. New York: Alfred Knopf, 1971.

Toffler, A. *Future Shock*. New York: Random House, 1970.

Toffler, A. *Learning for Tomorrow: The Role of the Future in Education*. New York: Vintage Books, 1974.

Watson, J.B. *Behaviorism*. Chicago: University of Chicago Press, 1924.

Wilson, L., ed. *Emerging Patterns in American Higher Education*. Washington, D.C.: American Council on Education, 1965.

Research on College Teaching: The Historical Background

WILBERT J. MCKEACHIE

Experimental research on college teaching began with single variable studies of class size and lecture vs. discussion. During the 1930s, research on student ratings of teachers began, and following World War II, studies of college teaching and learning became more common. In the decades from then to the 1980s, research moved to concern with a broader range of variables, to analyses of interaction between student and classroom variables, and to attention to processes as well as products resulting from teaching. Research on college teaching clearly meets Conant's criteria for a scientific field: progress in theory, methods, and established knowledge. Moreover, we now have demonstrated that educational research can contribute to educational practice.

Has research on college teaching made progress? Conant (1947) argued that a field could be called scientific when knowledge has accumulated, progress is evident in the development of new conceptual schemes resulting from experiments and observations, and the conceptual schemes lead, in turn, to more research. He suggested that one of the tests of whether a field qualifies would be to imagine the reaction of the pioneers in the field if they were to be brought back to life and viewed the current status of the research and theory. Would they acknowledge that there had been progress?

What would Carl E. Seashore, Edward L. Thorndike, or J. B. Edmondson say if they were to examine the research on college teaching today? In this article, I will choose a few of the significant studies in major areas of research on college teaching to subject our field to Conant's (1947) test.

World War I gave American psychologists their first opportunity to demonstrate the usefulness of psychological methods on a large scale. By the end of the war, 1,700,000 soldiers had taken Army Alpha or Beta tests of intelligence. Psychologists came out of the war with a greater sense of competence and confidence that empirical methods could solve important practical problems such as college teaching (e.g., Jones, 1923). Although educators had written scholarly works about college teaching in prior years (Klapper, 1920; Seashore, Angell, Calkins, Sanford, and Whipple, 1910), it was in the decade of the 1920s that researchers began a sustained empirical attack on the problems of college teaching.

As in other areas, the focus of research on college teaching shifted from decade to decade; therefore, this article will not follow a strictly chronological order. Rather than lose the sense of continuity in research on a particular problem, I will follow selected topics from their beginnings to the present; the topics, which will be discussed in the order in which they first appeared on the research scene, include class size, lecture versus discussion, student-centered discussion, independent study and peer learning, evaluation of teaching, teaching and technology, and the impact of cognitive psychology.

In addition to summarizing the substantive results, I shall highlight methodological lessons to be learned. My background in social, personality, and cognitive psychology undoubtedly influences both the selection and the interpretation of the studies reported. I view effective teaching and learning as a

"Research on College Teaching: The Historical Background," by Wilbert J. McKeachie, reprinted by permission from *Journal of Educational Psychology*, 82, 1990.

search has made and of its continuing promise and that this article will provide a useful perspective for the articles in this special issue. It is not, however, intended to be a comprehensive "Psych. Bulletin type" research review. For such a review, see Dunkin and Barnes (1986), McKeachie, Pintrich, Lin, and Smith (1986), and the triennial reviews of instructional psychology in the *Annual Review of Psychology*. Also useful is Menges and Mathis's (1988) *Key Resources on Teaching, Learning, Curriculum, and Faculty Development*.

Class Size

Early Research

Are small classes more effective than large classes? This was probably the first major question that research on college teaching tried to answer. Size does not seem to be a conceptually exciting variable. Yet, as we shall see, psychologists have, as in other studies, developed a conceptual understanding that makes the size variable more psychologically interesting.

Among the first investigators of class size were Edmondson and Mulder (1924), who compared the performance of students enrolled in a 109-student class with that of students enrolled in a 43-student class of the same course in education. Achievement of the two groups was approximately equal; the small class had a slight edge on an essay and the midsemester tests, and the large class had a slight edge on quizzes and the final examination. Students reported a preference for small classes.

Edmondson and Mulder's (1924) results stimulated the Committee of Research at the University of Minnesota to begin a classic series of studies of class size. In 59 experiments that involved such widely varying subjects as psychology, physics, accounting, law, and education, the results of 46 favored the large classes for achievement measured largely by classroom examinations (Hudelson, 1928).

Support for small classes, however, came from studies in the teaching of French conducted by Cheydleur (1945) at the University of Wisconsin between 1919 and 1943. With hundreds of classes ranging in size from 9 to 33, Cheydleur found consistent superior performance on objective departmental examinations for small classes.

Post-World War II experiments were also favorable to small classes. Macomber and Siegel's (1957a, 1957b, 1960) experiments at Miami University are particularly important because, in addition to conventional achievement tests, they included measures of critical thinking and problem solving, scales measuring stereotypic attitudes, and tests of student attitudes toward instruction. Statistically significant differences favored the smaller classes (particularly for high-ability students). When retention of knowledge was measured 1–2 years after completion of the courses, small differences favored the smaller classes in eight of the nine courses compared (Siegel, Adams, and Macomber, 1960).

Few instructors are satisfied with the achievement of knowledge if it is not remembered, if the students are unable to use it in solving problems in which the knowledge is relevant, or if the students fail to relate the knowledge to relevant attitudes. If one takes these more basic outcomes of retention, problem solving, and attitude differentiations as criteria of learning, the weight of the evidence favors small classes, a conclusion consistent with Glass and Smith's (1979) classic but controversial meta-analysis of class size research at all educational levels.

What Did We Learn?

The methodological lesson for both researchers and teachers is to measure higher level outcomes as well as knowledge.

What about theory? The early researchers were simply interested in answering a practical question, but there are both practical and theoretical reasons why class size should make a difference. The larger the class, the less the sense of personal responsibility and activity, and the less the likelihood that the teacher can know each student personally and adapt instruction to the individual student. Nonetheless, it seems plausible that the effect of class size on learning depends on what the teacher does. We lack descriptive studies of teacher behavior in college classes of differing sizes, but it seems likely that in larger classes, faculty members typically require less written work and spend more time lecturing and less in discussion. Thus the effect of class size also depends on the relative effectiveness of lecture and discussion, and it is not surprising that shortly after the first research on class size, experiments comparing lecture and discussion began to appear.

Lecture Versus Discussion

Early Research

Only a year after Edmondson and Mudler's (1924) and Mueller's (1924) studies on class size, Bane (1925) published a comparison of lecture and discussion[1] teaching methods. Not only was Bane's research pioneering in studying teaching methods in college; he also introduced an important methodological advance by obtaining a measure of delayed recall after the course examination as well as the conventional final examination score. There was little difference between his groups on the immediate test, but there was significant superiority for discussion on the measure of delayed recall.

In a well-designed study of teachers of adult education courses, Solomon, Rosenberg, and Bezdek (1964) found that those who stressed lectures produced higher achievement on a factual test but were not as effective as other teachers on a test of comprehension. Other studies also supported the superiority of discussion for higher level outcomes (reviewed by McKeachie, 1984).

What Did We Learn?

In general, later research supported Bane's (1925) earliest findings: Lecture tends to be at least equal to, and often more effective than, discussion for immediate recall of factual knowledge on a course examination, but discussion tends to be superior for long-term retention. Current cognitive theory would explain this finding in terms of greater likelihood of elaboration or deep processing when students are actively engaged in discussion.

The method of testing delayed recall, such as Bane used, is all too seldom used. The typical use of final course examinations, for which students have crammed, as the primary outcome measure is a major reason for the small effects often found in research on college teaching.

Student-Centered Discussion

Early Research

Interest in discussion methods seems to be a cyclical function, peaking in even-numbered decades: the 1940s, 1960s, and 1980s. Although there were a number of experiments on lecture versus discussion in the 1930s, the next peak of interest occurred after World War II when two independent movements in psychology converged to produce a spate of experiments on nondirective, group-centered, or student-centered discussion methods. Carl Roger's nondirective approach to counseling and Kurt Lewin's "group dynamics" movement both spilled over into research on "student-centered" or "group-centered" teaching.

Both the Rogerian and the Lewinian position emphasized movement away from the teacher's role as expert and authority to a role of facilitating student responsibility for learning. Thus student-centered discussion went beyond conventional discussion methods in emphasizing (a) much more interaction between students and (b) student responsibility for decisions about goals and activities of the class. Accompanying this was a shift away from thinking of subject-matter knowledge as the only goal of education. Although cognitive goals were still recognized as being important, student-centered classes accepted the expression of feelings and development of group cohesion as important mechanisms for achieving "gut" learning: learning linked to motivation, attitudes and deeper understanding (McKeachie, DeValois, Dulany, Beardslee and Winerbottom, 1954).

A pioneering study of this genre preceded World War II. Zeleny (1940) found that a group-centered method was superior to a recitation method not only in cognitive outcomes but also in changes in self-confidence, leadership, and other personality variables.

Another early comparison of student-centered and instructor-centered instruction was that made by Faw (1949). A class was divided into three discussion groups; one group was taught by a student-centered method, one was taught by an instructor-centered method, and one alternated between the two methods. In comparison with the instructor-centered class, the student-centered class was characterized by more student participation, no correction by the instructor of inaccurate statements, lack of instructor direction, and more discussion of ideas related to personal experiences.

Scores on the objective course examination based on the textbook showed small but significant differences favoring the student-centered method. In the area of major interest, emotional growth, Faw's (1949) method of evaluation was to ask students to write anonymous comments about the class. In general, comments indicated that the students felt that they received greater social and emotional value from the student-centered discussion groups.

Following the model of Lewin, Lippitt, and White's study (1939) of authoritarian, democratic, and laissez faire group climates, the staff of the University of Michigan's general psychology course set up an experiment in 1947, using three styles of teaching: recitation, discussion, and group tutorial (Guetzkow, Kelly, and McKeachie, 1954; McKeachie, 1951). In comparison with discussion and tutorial methods, the more autocratic recitation method proved to produce not only better examination scores but also greater interest in psychology, as measured by the election of advanced courses in psychology. Furthermore, students liked the recitation method better than the other methods. The greater gains in knowledge produced by the recitation method fit in with the general principle that feedback aids learning, for students in the recitation sections had weekly or semiweekly quizzes.

Despite the immediate superiority of the recitation method, two motivational outcomes favored the discussion and tutorial methods: (a) The students in discussion sections were significantly more favorable than the other groups in attitude toward psychology, and (b) a follow-up of the students 3 years later revealed that 7 men each from the tutorial and discussion groups majored in psychology, whereas none of those in the recitation group did so. Women majoring in psychology came about equally from all three groups.

Wispe (1951) carried out an interesting variation of the student-centered versus instructor-centered experiment. Instead of attempting to control the instructor personality variable by forcing instructors to teach both instructor-centered and student-centered classes, Wispe selected instructors who were rated as naturally permissive or directive. He then compared their sections of the Harvard course in "Social Relations." He found no difference in final examination scores between students taught by different methods. Students preferred the directive method, and the poorer students gained more in directive classes.

Whereas scores on objective final examinations seem to be little affected by teaching method, there are, in addition to the positive changes in adjustment reported by Asch (1951), Faw (1949), Moore and Popham (1959), Slomowitz (1955), and Zeleny (1940), other indications that student behavior outside the usual testing situation may be influenced. Bovard (1951a, 1951b) and McKeachie (1954) found that student-centered classes showed greater insight (as rated by clinical psychologists) into problems of the young women depicted in the film "The Feeling of Rejection." As in the studies of class size and lecture discussion, we find that the favorable effects of student-centered teaching methods emerge in the more subtle, "higher level" outcomes rather than in factual knowledge. These results parallel those found by Giaconia and Hedges (1982) in their meta-analysis of recitation on open education.

Although most of these studies were carried out in the late 1940s, they were not published until the 1950s and were thus still in the current literature when a new impetus to student-centered learning came to the fore—independent study. This movement in the late 1950s, followed by the sensitivity training movement in the 1960s, maintained interest in student-centered teaching despite the post-Sputnik panic about out-of-date and ill-organized scientific content.

What Did We Learn?

The studies of student-centered classes carried methodology forward by pointing to a broader range of outcomes involving attitudes, motivation, and personality variables. In addition, Wispe's (1951) method of studying natural variation rather than manipulated differences in teaching led to greater use of this method in later studies.

One methodological feature was important for the field of psychology in general. These were among the first studies to look at attribute-treatment interactions (ATIs). Even before Cronbach's (1957) classic article, "The Two Disciplines of Scientific Psychology," Remmers (1933) had reported that more intelligent students achieved more with a higher proportion of class time in recitation, whereas less intelligent students profited more from a larger proportion of time in lecture.

Independent Study and Peer Learning

The World War II veterans bulge had barely passed when leaders in higher education began warning colleges and universities that they would face even greater strains on their facilities when the postwar "baby boomers" reached college age. The projected rapid increase in enrollments would not be matched by an increase in PhDs to teach; so mechanisms to handle more students with few faculty needed to be found. Advocates of television, teaching machines, and computers predicted enormous gains in efficiency if faculty conservatism could be overcome. The research on the effectiveness of technology, disappointingly, provided little support for these proposed panaceas.

One potential solution, however, went beyond the problem of teaching greater numbers to emphasize an important goal of education—training autonomous learners (students who would presumably be better equipped for lifelong learning because they experienced less teaching in college and practiced independent study). Thus the period spawned a number of studies of learning with reduced formal classroom instruction. Some of these sent individual learners off to study by themselves; others involved small-group, peer-learning experiences.

With the support of the Ford Foundation's Fund for Advancement of Education, a number of colleges experimented with large programs of independent study. As with other comparisons of teaching methods, few large differences were found between the achievement of students working independently and that of students taught in conventional classes. Moreover, the expected gains in independence also often failed to materialize. Students taught by independent study did not always seem to develop greater ability or motivation for learning independently. Nevertheless, a number of encouraging results emerged.

Favorable results on independent study were obtained in the experiments carried out at the University of Colorado by Gruber and Weitman (1960). In a course in freshman English in which the group met in class about 90% of the regularly scheduled hours and had little formal training in grammar, the self-directed study group was significantly superior to control groups on a test of grammar. In a course in physical optics, groups of students who attended class without the instructor learned fewer facts and simple applications but were superior to students in conventional classes in performing difficult applications and learning new material. Moreover, the areas of superiority were maintained in a retest 3 months later when the difference in factual knowledge had disappeared. In educational psychology, an experimental class meeting once a week with the instructor and twice a week in groups of 5 or 6 students without the instructor was equal to a conventional three-lecture-a-week class in mastery of content, but tended to be superior on measures of curiosity. In another experiment, students in self-directed study paid more constant attention to a lecture than did students in conventional classes.

Different kinds of learning may take place out of class than in class. The experiment reported by McKeachie, Lin, Forrin, and Teevan (1960) involved a fairly high degree of student-instructor contact. In this experiment, "tutorial" students normally met with the instructor in small groups only weekly or biweekly, but students were free to consult the instructor whenever they wished. The results of the experiment suggest that the "tutorial" students did not learn as much from the textbook as students taught in conventional lecture periods and discussion sections, but they did develop stronger motivation both for course work and for continued learning after the course. This was indicated not only by responses to a questionnaire administered at the end of the course but also by the number of advanced psychology courses later elected.

Webb and Grib (1967) reported six studies in which student-led discussions were compared with instructor-led discussions or lectures. In two of the six studies, significant differences in achievement tests favored the student-led discussions. In the other four, differences were not significant. Both students and instructors reported that the student-led discussions increased student motivation. Students reported that the sense of freedom to ask questions and express their own opinions is a major advantage of the student-led discussions. It makes theoretical sense that this opportunity to expose individual conceptions and misconceptions and compare one's ideas with those of others should contribute to learning if the group contains sufficient resources of knowledge and higher level thinking.

The Pyramid Plan

The most impressive findings on the results of student-led discussion come from the research on the Pyramid Plan at Pennsylvania State University (Carpenter, 1959; Davage, 1958, 1959). The basic plan may be represented by a description of their experiments in psychology. Each "Pyramid Group" of psychology majors consisted of 6 freshmen, 6 sophomores, 2 juniors (who were assistant leaders), and a senior (who was group leader). The group leaders were trained by a faculty supervisor. A control group received comparable special attention by being given a special program of lectures, films, and demonstrations equal to the time spent in discussion by the Pyramid Groups. The results on such measures as attitude toward psychology, knowledge of the field of psychology, scientific thinking, use of library for scholarly reading, intellectual orientation, and resourcefulness in problem solving were significantly favorable to the Pyramid Plan. Moreover, a follow-up study showed that more of the Pyramid students continued as majors in psychology. Unfortunately, this program was never widely publicized and apparently was not adopted on other campuses.

The independent study movement thus extended student-centered teaching to peer teaching and learning. The sensitivity training movement of the 1960s was also based on the underpinnings of student-centered teaching—Lewinian and Rogerian theories.

T-Groups

During the 1960s, sensitivity training (T-groups, encounter groups) became the fad for high-level business executives as well as for government workers, teachers, and students. Originating in the group dynamics theories and practice of Kurt Lewin and his followers, sensitivity training groups met the 1960s generation's desire for self-analysis, confrontation of stereotypes, and overthrowing norms restricting the expression of personal needs and feelings. Many universities developed courses involving sensitivity training, and many faculty members incorporated elements of sensitivity training in conventional courses.

A number of studies of T-group effectiveness were carried out, some in academic settings. In general, the results were favorable, particularly in participants' self-reports of gains in self-understanding and sensitivity to others' feelings and behavior (see review by P. B. Smith, 1975).

The College Classroom

The decade of the 1960s was a period when federal funding of educational research resulted in substantial progress in our understanding of teaching and learning. The study to which I most often refer dates from this period. Combining quantitative and qualitative approaches, using data from observations and questionnaires, focusing on feelings underlying verbal expressions, and yet concerned with the goal of productive educational "work," *The College Classroom* (Mann et al., 1970) provides an unequaled source of insights with respect to student characteristics, teacher roles, and the development of the class as a working group over the course of a semester. The book describes the development of four introductory psychology classes over a semester; that development began with a phase in which the teachers' behaviors emphasized the roles of "formal authority" and "facilitator" while the student "heroes" and "snipers" tested the teachers' tolerance for student autonomy. During the first 2 weeks, much of the teacher's effort was to socialize the students into the methods and viewpoints of the field.

In a second phase, the teachers became dissatisfied with the students' lack of work, the dependence of the "anxious-dependent" students, and the excessive irrelevance of the participation of the "attention getters." Teachers, who had previously been trying to facilitate independent, autonomous work, were likely to become more punitive and authoritarian. Nonetheless, during this second period, the students and teachers began to gain a better understanding of the kind of work and involvement that was needed, and in the third phase, coming after 4 to 5 weeks, anxious dependence diminished, the classes became more collegial and cooperative, and effective work occurred.

As the term continued, the teacher assumed more control but now moved more toward a situation in which the teacher was leading a joint exploration of the subject matter with contributions from both students and teacher. The last phase, "Separation," was characterized by warmth, yet also by the beginnings of withdrawal.

Although the phases described in *The College Classroom* are not likely to be precisely replicated in other classes, most teachers will recognize some resonance with their own experience. *The College Classroom* thus helps both teachers and students understand and think about the unique development of their own classes and the sort of interaction that can facilitate productive development.

Peer-Learning, Cooperative-Learning

The forces of cognitive revolution in psychology and education swept over the "touchy-feely" movement of the 1960s, but student-centered, peer-group learning survived and emerged in new cognitively oriented forms in the 1970s and 1980s as the most effective method for helping students to achieve cognitive goals.

One of the best-developed systems for helping pairs of students learn more effectively is the "Learning Cell" developed by Marcel Goldschmid of the Swiss Federal Institute of Technology in Lausanne (Goldschmid, 1971). The Learning Cell, or student dyad, refers to cooperative learning in pairs in which students alternate asking and answering questions on commonly read materials:

1. To prepare for the learning cell, students read an assignment and write questions dealing with the major points raised in the reading proper or other related materials.
2. At the beginning of each class meeting, students are randomly assigned to pairs, and one partner, *A*, begins by asking the first question.
3. After having answered and perhaps having been corrected or given additional information, the second student, *B*, puts a question to *A*, and so on.
4. During this time, the instructor goes from dyad to dyad, giving feedback and asking and answering questions.

A variation of this procedure has each student read (or prepare) different materials. In this case, *A* "teaches" *B* the essentials of his or her readings and then asks *B* prepared questions, whereupon they switch roles.

The effectiveness of the learning cell method was first explored in the large (250-student) psychology course (Goldschmid, 1970) in which four learning options were compared: seminar, discussion, independent study (essay), and learning cell. Students in the learning cell option performed significantly better on an unannounced experiment and rated their ongoing learning cell's effectiveness higher regardless of the size of the class, its level, or the age of the students (Schirmerhorn, Goldschmid, and Shore, 1975).

"Pay to be a tutor, not to be tutored" is the message from these studies of peer tutoring. For example, Annis (1983) compared learning under five conditions:

1. Students read a textbook passage.
2. Students read the passage and were taught by a peer.
3. Students did not read the passage but were taught by a peer.
4. Students read the passage and prepared to teach it to other students.
5. Students read the passage and taught it to another student.

The results demonstrated that teaching resulted in better learning than did being taught. In a similar study, Bargh and Schul (1980) also found positive results: the largest part of the gain in retention was attributable to students' deeper studying of material when preparing to teach. The research in higher education is congruent with research at other levels of education demonstrating the effectiveness of peer teaching and learning (Johnson, Maruyama, Johnson, Nelson, and Skon, 1981).

What Did We Learn?

These results fit well with contemporary theories of learning and memory. Preparing to teach, teaching, questioning, and explaining involve active thought, analysis, selection of main ideas, and processing the concepts into one's own thoughts and words. The greater freedom, found by Webb and Grib (1967), of students to admit confusion and ask questions in peer learning groups also fits with current cognitive-instructional theory stressing the importance of restructuring incorrect or inadequate cognitive structures or schemata. Motivational effects of peer learning and independent study also fit well with motivation theorists' emphasis on the importance of personal control of one's environment. The results of these studies complement those of peer tutoring in elementary and high school classes. In their meta-analysis, Cohen, Kulik, and Kulik (1982) found favorable effects on learning, attitudes, and self-concept.

Methodologically, the studies in this group extended even further the list of relevant outcome measures to include, in addition to factual learning, simple versus difficult applications of concepts, retention of knowledge months later, scientific thinking, resourcefulness in problem solving, intellectual orientation, attention to lectures, ability to learn independently, student acceptance of responsibility for learning, student motivation for continued learning (assessed by both questionnaires and election of advanced courses), choosing to major in the area of the course, use of the library for scholarly reading, curiosity, attitudes, self-understanding, sensitivity to others' feelings and behavior, and effectiveness as a leader or group member.

But the most important methodological advance evidenced in these studies was the move toward more detailed analysis of the processes responsible for outcomes. Whereas in earlier studies, such as McKeachie's (1951, 1958), researchers had used observers and student ratings to describe classroom processes involved in the experimental comparisons, the detailed inferential coding of every verbal act represented in *The College Classroom* study by Mann et al. (1970) carried the analysis of interaction between teacher and students to a new level. Similarly, the processes responsible for the success of peer learning were analyzed in the studies by Webb and Grib (1967), Gruber and Weitman (1960), and Bargh and Schul (1980). Thus these studies were early representatives of the process-product paradigm (Mitzel, 1960).

Evaluation of Teaching

Early Studies

Anyone who carries out research on teaching effectiveness quickly runs into the problem of evaluating the outcomes of teaching. Obviously, one first looks at student learning, and the studies cited above typically include measures of student achievement. But if one takes increased interest and motivation for learning as important outcomes, it is hard to come up with better measures than the students' own perceptions of their interest. Not only can students' provide data about the effects that instruction has had on them, but they also have an excellent opportunity to observe what the teacher does and what the course requires. Thus student reports of instruction have commonly been used as a source of data, not only for research, but also to improve teaching and to evaluate teaching for personnel decisions.

Once again we go back to the 1920s for the beginnings of this active field of research on college teaching. In 1927, Herman Remmers published the first of an impressive series of reports on his Purdue Rating Scale for Instructors. In that series, basic questions about validity and reliability were confronted and answered with a good deal of clarity. Unfortunately, even today many faculty raise questions that were well handled by Remmers and his students and by later research that reinforced and extended his conclusions (see Marsh, 1987):

1. Do students' judgments agree with those of peers or administrators? Yes.
2. Do students change their minds after they have been out of college long enough to appreciate the sterling qualities of teachers whom they failed to appreciate while enrolled? No.
3. Can the poorer students' judgments be disregarded? No. When a teacher is particularly effective with the poorer students, these students rate the teacher higher than do other students.
4. When several teachers are teaching sections of the same course, do the teachers whose students score highest on the achievement tests get the highest ratings? Yes, a result most convincingly demonstrated by Cohen's (1981) meta-analysis of 68 validity studies.

One might surmise that the area of research on students' rating of faculty would have been exhausted by the extensive series of research studies carried out in the past 60 years and comprehensively reviewed by Costin, Greenough, and Menges (1971), by Feldman (1978), and by Marsh (1984, 1987). However, two current lines of research seem particularly worthy of special mention.

One of these is the series of well-controlled laboratory studies involving videotaped presentations of teaching carried out by Raymond P. Perry and his associates at the University of Manitoba (Perry, Abrami, and Leventhal, 1979). Originally, the methodology was devised to investigate the "Dr. Fox effect"—named after the pseudonymous "Dr. Fox," an actor whose animation and expressiveness seduced an audience of professionals into giving high ratings to a lecture devoid of content. The Manitoba research group showed that expressiveness was positively related to learning with content held constant but that student ratings of an expressive teacher were perhaps overly generous. However, the basic findings turned out, as most research does, to reveal complex interactions. More recently the method has been turned to investigations of students' "learned helplessness"—a drop in performance following failure.

A second line of research investigates the relationship between instructor personality, instructor behavior, and teaching effectiveness. Erdle, Murray, and Rushton (1985) found two personality factors, "Achievement Orientation" and "Interpersonal Orientation," that relate to classroom behavior factors "Charisma" and "Organization." Research on student rating of instructors has often yielded somewhat similar factors (e.g., Cranton and Smith, 1990 [this issue]: Smalzreid and Remmers, 1943). Personality characteristics related to effective teaching vary, depending on the type of course (Murrah, Rushton, and Paunonen, 1990 [this issue]).

What Have We Learned?

Despite faculty doubts about the ability of students to appreciate good teaching, the research evidence indicates that students are generally good judges—surprisingly so, in view of the fact that most research on student evaluation has been carried out in introductory classes, in which one would expect the students to be less able to evaluate than in more advanced classes. Moreover, ratings are robust. Potentially contaminating variables, such as time of day, class size, or required versus elective classes, make a difference, but not a large enough difference to cause researchers to misclassify a good teacher as "poor." Although one should also get evidence from other sources of a teaching evaluation is to lead to an important personnel decision, student ratings are the best validated of all the practical sources of relevant data.

But, in addition to what we have learned about evaluating teaching, the student rating research has contributed to the broader field of research on college teaching. The student rating literature led the way in the substantive identification of classroom *processes* affecting learning outcomes. This area of research also made it clear that different students reacted differently to the same teacher. This truth was at first taken to be a telling blow against the validity of student ratings, but, as early as 1949, attribute-treatment interactions had been demonstrated in student learning, and these interactions paralleled the ATIs in student ratings (Elliot, 1949). Furthermore, the research indicated not only that there were general attributes of effective teaching, such as clarity of explanations and enthusiasm, but also that there are a variety of ways in which teachers can be effective.

Finally, an important methodological contribution was the use (by Raymond R. Perry and the University of Manitoba group) of films to enable researchers to manipulate variables in well-controlled laboratory experiments.

Teaching and Technology

From Films to Computers

Instructional films came into widespread use during World War II, and research on uses of film in instruction continued after World War II. Carpenter and Greenhill (1955, 1958), working at Pennsylvania State University, had produced a series of studies of instructional films, and so they were well positioned to take advantage of the interest of the Ford Foundation's Fund for the Advancement of Education in encouraging the use of television for college-level instruction. During the mid-1950s, television seemed to offer great promise for coping with the great hordes of students expected to arrive as a result of the baby boom. Although many faculty members decried the loss of face-to-face contact with students, others embraced the chance to be among the first to appear on television. (In fact, I was one such [McKeachie, 1952].) Grants by the Fund led to a large number of well-controlled studies of the effectiveness of television, particularly as an alternative to large lectures for semester-long courses.

The results of this research may be used either to exalt or to damn television. Essentially, they indicated that although students learn nearly as much information in courses taught by television as in courses taught conventionally, live classes tend to be superior (e.g., Schramm, 1962; Sullivan, Andrews, Hollinghurst, Maddigan, and Noseworthy, 1976). Most television students learned the information needed to pass examinations, and most did not object strongly to the televised classes, although they preferred live instruction.

A course adapted for television by the addition of supplementary visual aids proved to be no more effective than televised lecture-blackboard presentations. In fact, at both Pennsylvania State University (Carpenter and Greenhill, 1955, 1958) and New York University (Adams, Carter, and Smith, 1959), the "visual" productions tended to be less effective than "bare bones" television.

The bloom of hopes for educational television had hardly begun to fade when a new technology threatened to eliminate the need for television. Teaching machines were to revolutionize education, increasing the efficiency of teaching manyfold. Skinner (1954) wrote,

> We are on the threshold of an exciting and revolutionary period, in which the scientific study of man will be put to work in man's best interests. Education must play its part. It must accept the fact that a sweeping revision of educational practices is possible and inevitable. (p. 97)

Skinner further stated, "The technical problem of providing the necessary instrumental aid is not particularly difficult" (p. 95), and "If the teacher is to take advantage of recent advances in the study of learning, she [or he] must have the help of mechanical devices" (p. 95).

So persuasive were Skinner's writings that many of the major electronic and book companies moved quickly into the teaching machine movement. Programs for teaching were written in accordance with carefully specified behavioral objectives, and, in some of the early research, human beings simulated teaching machines to test the material. It soon became apparent that programmed learning material could be presented in text like form as effectively as by machine. Programmed books and booklets were designed to permit students to learn without formal classroom instruction or, in some cases, to be used as an adjunct to other teaching materials.

The research on teaching machines and programmed learning failed to reveal the dramatic gains expected by Skinner and the corporations that invested in the field. Nonetheless, programmed learning was not as unsuccessful educationally as it was commercially. Students do learn from the programs, but learning is generally slower than with conventional printed materials (but faster than with lectures; N. H. Smith, 1962). Reviews by Kulik, Cohen, and Ebeling (1980), Lange (1972), Nash, Muczyk, and Vettori (1971), and Schramm (1964) show programmed instruction to be slightly superior to traditional instruction in about 40% of the over 100 research studies reported, equally effective in about half the studies, and seldom less effective.

Although programmed learning was not an enormous success, two related methods proved to be more effective. One of these was the Keller Plan, or Personalized System of Instruction, a self-paced, mastery oriented, modular system of instruction that produced not only superior end-of-course achievement but also superior retention (Kulik, Kulik, and Bangert-Drowns, 1988).

The other was Postlethwait's Audio-Tutorial method, which also involves a modularized self-instructional approach. Postlethwait developed slides, audiotapes, demonstration experiments, and other materials for modules of his introductory botany course (Postlethwait, Novak, and Murray, 1972). The results were so encouraging that the method was widely used in laboratory courses. A meta-analysis by Kulik, Kulik, and Cohen (1979) showed a significant positive effect on student achievement. It should be noted that there is little evidence of the value of conventional laboratory courses, although a few studies suggest that specific attention to scientific thinking does produce gains (see review by Hofstein and Lunetta, 1982).

The teaching machine revolution was quickly lost in the apparent brilliance of an even more glamorous technological competitor—the computer. By the early 1960s, the claims for teaching machines paled beside those made for the computer. Clearly, the flexibility offered by the computer could individualize learning much more than could the teaching machine. In fact, however, the first educational programs for computers differed little from the branching programs offered in many printed programmed-learning materials. Once again, manufacturers, research sponsors, and those interested in educational technology found that it is easier to envision the potential of educational technology than to develop the educational software that achieves this potential. By the early 1970s, it was apparent that the initial hopes had not been sustained. Nonetheless, some progress was made and, with the widespread use of microcomputers, the 1980s have seen a revival of optimism, with somewhat less grandiose visions of the role of the computer in education. In their meta-analysis of research on computer-based education, Kulik, Kulik, and Cohen (1980) found that computers made small but significant contributions to achievement. The greatest successes, however, were achieved with drill and practice programs—not the stuff of our dreams.

What Have We Learned?

Probably the most important thing we learned from the research on technology was to be skeptical about claims for revolutionary advances in education brought about by technology. We also learned that technology does not substitute for teachers; there is little likelihood that the classroom will be robotized. However, technological tools can facilitate student learning. How much learning takes place still depends on student activity and thought.

Technology has been methodologically useful in helping us examine the microprocesses of education, as exemplified in the research of Tobias (1988, in press).

Although "think-aloud" techniques and protocol analysis have less commonly been used in research on college student learning than in research with children, these methods, often used in connection with research with computers, provide an additional tool in our research kit, particularly as we move into cognitive approaches concerned not only with classroom processes but also with cognitive processes of students and teachers.

The Cognitive Era

Applications of Cognitive Psychology

The shift from behaviorism to cognitivism in psychology occurred gradually, even though it seemed to move with exciting speed during the decades of the 1960s and 1970s. Its impact on instructional research came in various forms, but one of the most striking effects was that deriving from research carried out at the University of Gothenburg by Ference Marton and his associates (Marton and Säljö, 1976a, 1976b; Svensson, 1976). Using a phenomenological-like approach that Marton calls *phenomenography*, the Swedish researchers described the differing ways in which students approach textbook assignments. "Surface processors" read the assignment straight through with little attempt to think about the purpose of the author or about the relationship between the assigned reading and their own previous knowledge; "deep processors," on the other hand, are more likely to look for cues to the organization and purpose of the reading and to relate it to previous chapters or other learning. Svensson (1976), in a study of student learning over the course of a semester, similarly found contrasts between those who approached study holistically and those who were characterized as atomists. Examinations in different disciplines differed in the extent to which a holistic approach was necessary, but atomistic students generally did less well. These studies represented well the move from a focus on instructional materials to a focus on the students.

The Gothenburg studies stimulated researchers in Great Britain, Australia, and the United States to devise questionnaires and develop remedial programs for students whose approaches to learning were rigid and ineffective. Thus the focus in research on instruction shifted from the teacher to the students. Diagnosis of deficiencies in study skills has shifted to a greater emphasis on deep processing (or elaboration) and on meta-cognition—the ability to think about one's own learning and thinking and to choose effective strategies for different learning situations (Biggs, 1976; Entwistle, Hanley, and Hounsell, 1979; Weinstein, Underwood, Wicker, and Cubberly, 1979). Courses designed to teach students how to be more effective learners have been devised (see McKeachie, Pintrich, and Lin, 1985; Weinstein, Goetz, and Alexander, 1985; Weinstein and Mayer, 1986). Traditional topics of research such as test anxiety have benefited from theoretical analysis based on cognitive psychology (McKeachie, 1984; Tobias, 1985). Research on college teaching has become more closely integrated with that at other levels of education (e.g., De Corte, Lodewijks, Parmentier, and Span, 1987; Goldschmid, 1971; Palincsar and Brown, 1984). Cognitive theory and research has spilled over into the areas of college classrooms so that "teaching thinking" has become a major theme of educational discussions in higher education, as well as in business and in other levels of education (McMillan, 1986).

What Have We Learned?

Cognitive theory has provided a conceptual base for understanding the results of the earlier studies and for providing guidance for instruction (e.g., Bjork, 1979). Small classes and discussion methods tend to be effective because students are actively processing material rather than passively listening and reading.

Cognitive research, both in the laboratory and in the classroom, has given us a much more detailed account of how problem solving occurs in different disciplines, and this in turn is influencing textbooks and teachers. Motivation theory, too, is beginning to help us understand why some students fail to achieve up to capacity. We are now beginning to see the relationships between active deep processing and intrinsic motivation for continued learning as these relationships are affected by teaching methods that provide guidance and yet also provide opportunities for students to feel responsible and efficacious as learners.

What of the Future?

Recently someone asked me if we had made any progress in learning about college teaching since I began doing research in 1946. The answer is obvious, I hope, in the preceding pages. Moreover, the advances continue. But, as I told my questioner, the greater the advance, the greater the complexity ahead. The circle separating what we know from the unknown becomes even larger.

We now realize that the variables influencing learning are almost numberless. Because their interactions change from day to day, we need to move from pretest-posttest measures to studies of ongoing processes, from single-variable studies to individual students interacting in groups, and from studies of outcomes of learning to studies of what goes on in the thoughts, feelings, and desires of students. The frontier of knowledge about college teaching thus becomes even more challenging. And I suspect that the progress in the next decade will be even greater than in past decades. We have more researchers, better tools, and more comprehensive cognitive, motivation, and instructional theories. We have a clearer and more comprehensive grasp of the goals of education—the intertwining of intrinsic motivation for learning with elaboration, metacognition, and "mindful" learning.

We now know that we can teach thinking skills; in the next decade, we will gain a better understanding of how to go beyond discipline-specific skills to more broadly transferable intelligence.

We now know learning skills and strategies that generally help students to learn more effectively; in the next decade, we will better understand which strategies are most effective for which students with which material and which goals.

We now know that intrinsic motivation and a sense of self-efficacy have much to do with learning strategies and the mindfulness of student learning; in the next decade, we will gain a better understanding of the kinds of instructional methods that facilitate such motivation and that integrate learning with basic values.

We now know that peer-teaching is a very effective method of learning; in the next decade, we will gain a better understanding of how to structure peer-learning groups and when and where to use them.

We now know more about the processes leading toward educational outcomes; in the next decade, we will gain a better understanding of the way in which individual differences in motives and cognition interact with teaching methods and how the interactions change as courses develop, learners learn, and learning is assessed (see Covington and Omelich, 1988; Mann et al., 1970; Tobias, 1988).

We now know that students can evaluate teaching effectively; in the next decade, we will gain a better understanding of the validity of peer review of course materials, how various aspects of teaching contribute to learning outcomes, and how to teach students to evaluate their own gains in thinking and in knowledge.

We now know that faculty teaching can be improved with consultation; we will gain a better understanding of how consultation, training, and feedback can be combined to achieve greater effectiveness.

We now know that educational research can be of practical help to faculty members and institutions; in the next decade, we will better understand how to avoid the misuse of research and how to get more effective links to practice.

Do we meet Conant's (1947) criteria for a scientific field? I believe that if Edward L. Thorndike, Carl E. Seashore, J. B. Edmondson, and Herman Remmers could see us today, there would be a ringing chorus, "Yes"!

Note

1. *Recitation, discussion,* and *seminar* are sometimes used interchangeably. I think of recitation as involving student participation in which students answer fairly specific questions assessing their knowledge of the assigned lesson; discussion, on the other hand, is more likely to involve broader questions with openness to alternative points of view; a seminar typically involves a student presentation followed by discussion and usually implies a small group with advanced students.

References

Adams, J.C., Carter, C.R., and Smith, D. R. (Eds.) (1959). *College teaching by television*. Washington, DC: American Council on Education.

Annis, L.F. (1983). The processes and effects of peer tutoring. *Human Learning, 2*, 39–47.

Asch, M.J. (1951). Non-directive teaching in psychology: An experimental study. *Psychological Monographs, 65*(4).

Bane, C.L. (1925). The lecture vs. the class-discussion method of college teaching. *School and Society, 21*, 300–302.

Bargh, H.A., and Schul, Y. (1980). On the cognitive benefits of teaching. *Journal of Educational Psychology, 72*, 593–604.

Biggs, J.B. (1976). Dimensions of study behavior: Another look at ATI. *British Journal of Educational Psychology, 46*, 68–80.

Bjork, R.A. (1979). Information-processing analysis of college teaching. *Educational Psychologist, 14*, 15–23.

Bovard, E.W., Jr. (1951a). Group structure and perception. *Journal of Abnormal and Social Psychology, 46*, 398–405.

Bovard, E.W., Jr. (1951b). The experimental production of interpersonal affect. *Journal of Abnormal and Social Psychology, 46*, 521–528.

Carpenter, C.R. (1959, March). *The Penn State pyramid plan: Interdependent student work study grouping for increasing motivation for academic development*. Paper presented at the 14th National Conference on Higher Education, Chicago.

Carpenter, C.R., and Greenhill, L.P. (1955). *An investigation of closed-circuit television for teaching university courses* (Instructional Television Research Project No. 1). University Park: Pennsylvania State University.

Carpenter, C.R., and Greenhill, L.P. (1958). *An investigation of closed-circuit television for teaching university courses* (Instructional Television Research Project No. 2). University Park: Pennsylvania State University.

Cheydleur, F.D. (1945, August). Criteria of effective teaching in basic French courses. *Bulletin of the University of Wisconsin* (Monograph 2783).

Cohen, P.A. (1981). Student ratings of instruction and student achievement: A meta-analysis of multisection validity studies. *Review of Educational Research, 51*, 281–309.

Cohen, P.A., Kulik, J.A., and Kulik, C.-L.C. (1982). Educational outcomes of tutoring: A meta-analysis of findings. *American Educational Research Journal, 19*, 237–248.

Conant, J.B. (1947). *On understanding science*. New Haven: Yale University Press.

Costin, F., Greenough, W. T., and Menges, R. J. (1971). Student ratings of college teaching: Reliability, validity, and usefulness. *Review of Educational Research, 41*, 511–535.

Covington, M.V., and Omelich C.L. (1988). Achievement dynamics: The interaction of motives, cognitions, and emotions over time. *Anxiety Research, 1*, 165–183.

Cranton, P., and Smith, R.A. (1990). Reconsidering the unit of analysis: A model of student ratings of instruction. *Journal of Educational Psychology, 82*, 207–212.

Cronbach, L.J. (1957). The two disciplines of scientific psychology. *American Psychologist, 12*, 671–684.

Davage, R.H. (1958). *The pyramid plan for the systemic involvement of university students in teaching-learning functions*. Unpublished manuscript, Division of Academic Research and Services, Pennsylvania State University.

Davage, R.H. (1959). *Recent data on the pyramid project in psychology.* Unpublished manuscript, Division of Academic Research and Services, Pennsylvania State University.

De Corte, E., Lodewijks, H., Parmenteir, R., and Span, P. (Eds.) (1987). *Learning and instruction: European research in an international context* (Vol. I). Oxford, England: Pergamon/Leuven University Press.

Dunkin, M.J., and Barnes, J. (1986). Research on teaching in higher education. In M. C. Wittrock (Ed.), *Handbook of research on teaching* (3rd ed., pp. 754–777). New York: Macmillan.

Edmondson, J.B., and Mulder, F.J. (1924). Size of class as a factor in university instruction. *Journal of Educational Research, 9,* 1–12.

Elliot, D.N. (1949). *Characteristics and relationships of various criteria of teaching.* Unpublished doctorial dissertation, Purdue University.

Entwistle, N., Hanley, M., and Hounsell, D. (1979). Identifying distinctive approaches to studying. *Higher Education, 8,* 3655–3680.

Erdle, S., Murray, H.G., and Rushton, J.P. (1985). Personality, classroom behavior, and student ratings of college teaching effectiveness: A path analysis. *Journal of Educational Psychology, 77,* 394–407.

Faw, V.A. (1949). A psychotherapeutic method of teaching psychology. *American Psychologist, 4,* 104–109.

Feldman, K.A. (1978). Course characteristics and college students' ratings of their teachers: What we know and what we don't. *Research in Higher Education, 9,* 199–242.

Giaconia, R.M., and Hedges, L.V. (1982). Identifying features of effective open education. *Review of Educational Research, 52,* 579–602.

Glass, G.V., and Smith, M.L. (1979). Meta-analysis of research on class size and achievement. *Educational Evaluation and Policy Analysis, 1,* 2–16.

Goldschmid, M.L. (1970). Instructional options: Adapting the large university course to individual differences. *Learning and Development, 1,* 1–2.

Goldschmid, M.L. (1971). The learning cell: An instructional innovation. *Learning and Development, 2,* 1–6.

Gruber, H.E., and Weitman, M. (1960, April). *Cognitive processes in higher education: Curiosity and critical thinking.* Paper presented at the meeting of the Western Psychological Association, San Jose, CA.

Guetzkow, H.S., Kelly, E.L., and McKeachie, W. J. (1954). An experimental comparison of recitation, discussion, and tutorial methods in college teaching. *Journal of Educational Psychology, 45,* 193–209.

Hofstein, A., and Lunetta, V.N. (1982). The role of the laboratory in science teaching: Neglected aspects of research. *Review of Educational Research, 52,* 201–217.

Hudelson, E. (1928). *Class size at the college level.* Minneapolis: University of Minnesota Press.

Jones, H.E. (1923). Experimental studies of college teaching. The effect of examinations on permanence of learning. *Archives of Psychology, 10*(68), 5–70.

Johnson, D.W., Maruyama, G., Johnson, R., Nelson, D., and Skon, L. (1981). Effects of cooperative, competitive, and individualistic goal structures on achievement: A meta-analysis. *Psychological Bulletin, 89,* 47–62.

Klapper, P. (Ed.) (1920). *College teaching.* Yonkers-on-Hudson, NY: World Book Co.

Kulik, J.A., Cohen, P.A., and Ebeling, B.J. (1980). Effectiveness of programmed instruction in higher education: A meta-analysis of findings. *Educational Evaluation and Policy Analysis, 2,* 51–64.

Kulik, J.A., Kulik, C.-L.C., and Bangert-Drowns, R.L. (1988, May). *Effectiveness of mastery learning programs: A meta-analysis.* Ann Arbor: University of Michigan, Center for Research on Learning and Teaching.

Kulik, J.A., Kulik, C.-L.C., and Cohen, P.A. (1979). Research on audio-tutorial instruction: A meta-analysis of comparative studies. *Research on Higher Education, 11,* 321–341.

Kulik, J.A., Kulik, C.-L.C., and Cohen, P. (1980). Effectiveness of computer-based college teaching: A meta-analysis of findings. *Review of Educational Research, 50,* 525–544.

Lange, P.C. (1972). Today's education. *National Education Association, 61,* 59.

Lewin, K., Lippitt, R., and White, R.K. (1939). Patterns of aggressive behavior in experimentally created social climates. *Journal of Social Psychology, 10,* 271–299.

Macomber, F.G., and Siegel, L. (1957a). A study of large-group teaching procedures. *Educational Research, 38,* 220–229.

Macomber, F.G., and Siegel, L. (1957b). *Experimental study in instructional procedures* (Progress Report No. 2). Oxford, OH: Miami University.

Macomber, F.G., and Siegel, L. (1960). *Experimental study in instructional procedures* (Final Report). Oxford, OH: Miami University.

Mann, R.D., Arnold, S. M., Binder, J.L., Cytrynbaum, S., Newman, B. M., Ringwald, B. E. Ringwald, J. W., and Rosenwein, R. (1970). *The college classroom.* New York: Wiley.

Marsh, H.W. (1984). Student's evaluations of teaching: Dimensionality, reliability, validity, potential biases, and utility. *Journal of Educational Psychology, 76,* 707–754.

Marsh, H.W. (1987). *Student's evaluations of university teaching: Research findings, methodological issues and directions for future research.* Elmford, NY: Pergamon.

Marton, F., and Säljö, R. (1976a). On qualitative differences in learning: I. Outcome and process. *British Journal of Educational Psychology, 46,* 4–11.

Marton, F., and Säljö, R. (1976b). On qualitative differences in learning: II. Outcome and process. *British Journal of Educational Psychology, 46,* 115–127.

McKeachie, W.J. (1951). Anxiety in the college classroom. *Journal of Educational Research, 45,* 153–160.

McKeachie, W.J. (1952). Teaching psychology on television: *American Psychologist, 7,* 503–506.

McKeachie, W.J. (1954). Student-centered instruction versus instructor-centered instruction. *Journal of Educational Psychology, 45,* 143–150.

McKeachie, W.J. (1958). Students, groups, and teaching methods. *American Psychologist, 13,* 580–584.

McKeachie, W.J. (1984). Does anxiety disrupt information processing or does poor information processing lead to anxiety? *International Review of Applied Psychology, 33,* 187–203.

McKeachie, W.J., DeValois, R. L. Dulany, D. E., Jr., Beardslee, D. C., and Winterbottom, M. (1954). Objectives of the general psychology course. *American Psychologist, 9,* 140–142.

McKeachie, W.J., Lin, Y.-G., Forrin, B., and Teevan, R. (1960). Individualized teaching in elementary psychology. *Journal of Educational Psychology, 51,* 285–291.

McKeachie, W.J., Pintrich, P. R., and Lin, Y.-G. (1985). Learning to learn. In G. d'Ydewalle (Ed.), *Cognition, information processing and motivation.* (pp. 601–618). North Holland: Elsevier Science Publishers.

McKeachie, W.J., Pintrich, P. R., Lin, Y.-G., and Smith, D. A. F. (1986). *Teaching and learning in the college classroom: A review of the research literature.* Ann Arbor: University of Michigan, National Center for Research to Improve Post-Secondary Teaching and Learning.

McMillan, L. (1986, March 5). Many professors now start at the beginning by teaching their students how to think. *The Chronicle of Higher Education,* pp. 23–55.

Menges, R.J., and Mathis, B. C. (1988). *Key resources on teaching, learning, curriculum, and faculty development.* San Francisco: Jossey-Bass.

Mitzel, H.E. (1960). Teacher effectiveness. In C. W. Harris (Ed.), *Encyclopedia of educational research* (3rd ed., pp. 1481–1486). New York: Macmillan.

Moore, M.R., and Popham, W.J. (1959, December). *The role of extraclass student interviews in promoting student achievement.* Paper presented at the joint session of the American Association for the Advancement of Science and American Educational Research Association, Chicago.

Mueller, A.D. (1924). Class size as a factor in normal school instruction. *Education, 45,* 203–277.

Murray, H.G., Rushton, J.P., and Paunonen, S.V. (1990). Teacher personality traits and student instructional ratings in six types of university courses. *Journal of Educational Psychology, 82,* 250–261.

Nash, A.N., Muczyk, J. P., and Vettori, F.L. (1971). The relative practical effectiveness of programmed instruction. *Personnel Psychology, 24,* 297–418.

Palincsar, A.S., and Brown, A.L. (1984). Reciprocal teaching of comprehension-monitoring activities. *Cognition and Instruction, 1,* 117–175.

Perry, R.P., Abrami, P.C., and Leventhal, L. (1979). Educational seduction: The effect of instructor expressiveness and lecture content on student ratings and achievement. *Journal of Educational Psychology, 71,* 107–116.

Postlethwait, S.W., Novak, J., and Murray, H.T., Jr. (1972). *The audio-tutorial approach to learning.* Minneapolis, Burgess.

Remmers, H.H. (1933). Learning, effort, and attitudes as affected by three methods of instruction in elementary psychology. *Purdue University Studies in Higher Education* (Monograph No. 21).

Schirmerhorn, S., Goldschmid, M.L., and Shore, B.S. (1975). Learning basic principles of probability in student dyads: A cross-age comparison. *Journal of Educational Psychology, 67,* 551–557.

Schramm, W.L. (1962). Learning from instructional television. *Review of Educational Research, 32,* 156–167.

Schramm, W.L. (1964). *The research on programmed instruction.* Washington, DC: U.S. Government Printing Office.

Seashore, C.E., Angell, J. R., Calkins, M.W., Sanford, E.C., and Whipple G.M. (1910). Report of the committee on the American Psychological Association on the teaching of psychology. *Psychological Monographs, 12,* 1–93.

Siegel, L., Adams, J.F., and Macomber, F.G. (1980). Retention of subject matter as a function of large-group instructional procedures. *Journal of Educational Psychology, 51,* 9–13.

Skinner, B.F. (1954). The science of learning and the art of teaching. *Harvard Educational Review, 24,* 86–97.

Slomowitz, M. (1955). A comparison of personality changes and content achievement gains occurring in two modes of instruction (Doctoral dissertation, New York University, 1955). *Dissertation Abstracts, 15,* 1790.

Smalzreid, N.T., and Remmers, H.H. (1943). A factor analysis of the Purdue Rating Scale for Instructors. *Journal of Educational Psychology, 34,* 363–367.

Smith, N.H. (1962). The teaching of elementary statistics by the conventional classroom method vs. the method of programmed instruction. *Journal of Educational Research, 55,* 417–420.

Smith, P.B. (1975). Controlled studies of sensitivity training. *Psychological Bulletin, 82,* 597–622.

Solomon, D., Rosenberg, L., and Bezdek, W.E. (1964). Teacher behavior and student learning. *Journal of Educational Psychology, 55,* 23–30.

Sullivan, A.M., Andrews, E.A., Hollinghurst, F., Maddigan, R., and Noseworthy, C.M. (1976). The relative effectiveness of instructional television. *Interchange, 7*(1), 46–51.

Svensson, L. (1976). *Study skills and learning.* Goteberg, Sweden: Acta Universitates, Gothenburgensis.

Tobias, S. (1985). Test anxiety: Interference, defective skills, and cognitive capacity. *Educational Psychologist, 20,* 135–142.

Tobias, S. (1988, August). *Adapting instruction to student charaterization.* Presidential address of Division of Educational Psychology, American Psychological Association, Atlanta, GA.

Tobias, S. (in press). Teaching strategic text review by computer and interaction with student characteristics. *Computers in Human Behavior.*

Webb, N.J., and Grib, T.F. (1967). *Teaching process as a learning experience: The experimental use of student-led groups* (Final Report, No. HE-000-882). Washington, DC: U.S. Department of Health, Education, and Welfare.

Weinstein, C.E., Goetz, E.T., and Alexander, P.A. (Eds.) (1985). *Learning and study strategies: Issues in assessment, instruction, and evaluation.* San Diego, CA: Academic Press.

Weinstein, C.W., and Mayer, R.E. (1986). The teaching of learning strategies. In M. Wittrock (Ed.), *Handbook of research on teaching* (3rd ed., pp. 315–327). New York: Macmillan.

Weinstein, C.E., Underwood, V.L., Wicker, F.W., and Cubberly, W.E. (1979). Cognitive learning strategies: Verbal and imaginal elaboration. In H. F. O'Neill, Jr., and C. D. Spielberger (Eds.), *Cognitive and affective learning strategies* (pp. 45–75). New York: Academic Press.

Wispe, L.G. (1951). Evaluative section methods in the introductory course. *Journal of Educational Research, 45,* 161–168.

Zeleny, L.D. (1940). Experiment appraisal of a group learning plan. *Journal of Educational Research, 34*(1), 37–42.

from Scholarship Reconsidered: Priorities of the Professoriate

Ernest L. Boyer

Scholarship over Time

Several years ago, while completing our study of undergraduate education, it became increasingly clear that one of the most crucial issues—the one that goes to the core of academic life—relates to the meaning of scholarship itself. In *College: The Undergraduate Experience in America*, we said, "Scholarship is not an esoteric appendage; it is at the heart of what the profession is all about . . ." and "to weaken faculty commitment for scholarship . . . is to undermine the undergraduate experience, regardless of the academic setting." The challenge, as we saw it, was to define the work of faculty in ways that enrich, rather than restrict, the quality of campus life.

Today, on campuses across the nation, there is a recognition that the faculty reward system does not match the full range of academic functions and that professors are often caught between competing obligations. In response, there is a lively and growing discussion about how faculty should, in fact, spend their time. Recently, Stanford University president Donald Kennedy called for more contact between faculty and students, especially in the junior and senior years, a time when career decisions are more likely to be made. "It is time," Kennedy said, "for us to reaffirm that education—that is, teaching in all its forms—is the primary task" of higher education.

Several years ago, the University of California completed a study of undergraduate education, recommending that more weight be placed on teaching in faculty tenure decisions. In the East, the University of Pennsylvania, in its faculty handbook, now states that "the teaching of students at all levels is to be distributed among faculty members without regard to rank or seniority as such." In the Midwest, Robert Gavin, president of Macalester College, recently reaffirmed his institution's view of the liberal arts mission as including not only academic quality, but also internationalism, diversity, and service.

It is *this* issue—what it means to be a scholar—that is the central theme of our report. The time has come, we believe, to step back and reflect on the variety of functions academics are expected to perform. It's time to ask how priorities of the professoriate relate to the faculty reward system, as well as to the missions of America's higher learning institutions. Such an inquiry into the work of faculty is essential if students are to be well served, if the creativity of all faculty is to be fully tapped, and if the goals of every college and university are to be appropriately defined.

While we speak with pride about the great diversity of American higher education, the reality is that on many campuses standards of scholarship have become increasingly restrictive, and campus priorities frequently are more imitative than distinctive. In this climate, it seems appropriate to ask: How can each of the nation's colleges and universities define, with clarity, its own special purposes? Should expectations regarding faculty performance vary from one type of institution to another? Can we, in fact, have a higher education system in this country that includes multiple models of success?

Other issues within the academy must be candidly confronted. For example, the administrative structure has grown more and more complex, the disciplines have become increasingly divided, and academic departments frequently are disconnected from one another. The curriculum is fragmented, and the edu-

"Scholarship Over Time," (Chapter 1) and "Enlarging the Perspective," (Chapter 2), by Ernest L. Boyer, reprinted from *Scholarship Reconsidered: Priorities of the Professoriate*, 1990, Princeton University Press.

cational experience of students frequently lacks coherence. Many are now asking: How can the work of the nation's colleges and universities become more intellectually coherent? Is it possible for scholarship to be defined in ways that give more recognition to interpretative and integrative work?

According to the dominant view, to be a scholar is to be a researcher—and publication is the primary yardstick by which scholarly productivity is measured. At the same time, evidence abounds that many professors feel ambivalent about their roles. This conflict of academic functions demoralizes the professoriate, erodes the vitality of the institution, and cannot help but have a negative impact on students. Given these tensions, what is the balance to be struck between teaching and research? Should some members of the professoriate be thought of primarily as researchers, and others as teachers? And how can these various dimensions of faculty work be more appropriately evaluated and rewarded?

Beyond the campus, America's social and economic crises are growing—troubled schools, budget deficits, pollution, urban decay, and neglected children, to highlight problems that are most apparent. Other concerns such as acid rain, AIDS, dwindling energy supplies, and population shifts are truly global, transcending national boundaries. Given these realities, the conviction is growing that the vision of service that once so energized the nation's campuses must be given a new legitimacy. The challenge then is this: Can America's colleges and universities, with all the richness of their resources, be of greater service to the nation and the world? Can we define scholarship in ways that respond more adequately to the urgent new realities both within the academy and beyond?

Clearly, the educational and social issues now confronting the academy have changed profoundly since the first college was planted on this continent more than 350 years ago. Challenges on the campus and in society have grown, and there is a deepening conviction that the role of higher education, as well as the priorities of the professoriate, must be redefined to reflect new realities.

Looking back, one can see that scholarship in American higher education has moved through three distinct, yet overlapping phases. The colonial college, with its strong British roots, took a view of collegiate life that focused on the student—on building character and preparing new generations for civic and religious leadership. One of the first goals the English settlers of Massachusetts pursued, said the author of a description of the founding of Harvard College in 1636, was to "advance *Learning* and perpetuate it to Posterity." Harvard College, patterned after Emmanuel College of Cambridge, England, was founded to provide a continuous supply of learned clergy for "the city on the hill" that the Massachusetts Puritans hoped would bring redemptive light to all mankind.

The colonial college was expected to educate and morally uplift the coming generation. Teaching was viewed as a vocation—a sacred calling—an act of dedication honored as fully as the ministry. Indeed, what society expected of faculty was largely dictated by the religious purposes of the colleges that employed them. Students were entrusted to tutors responsible for their intellectual, moral, and spiritual development. According to historian Theodore Benditt, "professors were hired not for their scholarly ability or achievement but for their religious commitment. Scholarly achievement was not a high priority, either for professors or students."

This tradition, one that affirmed the centrality of teaching, persisted well into the nineteenth century. Young scholars continued to be the central focus of collegiate life, and faculty were employed with the understanding that they would be educational mentors, both in the classroom and beyond. In 1869, the image of the scholar as *teacher* was evoked by Charles W. Eliot, who, upon assuming the presidency of Harvard College, declared that "the prime business of American professors . . . must be regular and assiduous class teaching."

But change was in the wind. A new country was being formed and higher education's focus began to shift from the shaping of young lives to the building of a nation. As historian Frederick Rudolf says of the new generation of educators: "All were touched by the American faith in tomorrow, in the unquestionable capacity of Americans to achieve a better world." It was in this climate that Rensselaer Polytechnic Institute in Troy, New York, one of the nation's first technical schools, was founded in 1824. RPI became, according to Rudolf, "a constant reminder that the United States needed railroad-builders, bridge-builders, builders of all kinds, and that the institute in Troy was prepared to create them even if the old institutions were not."

In 1846, Yale University authorized the creation of a professorship of "agricultural chemistry and animal and vegetable physiology." In the same decade, Harvard president Edward Everett stressed his institution's role in the service of business and economic prosperity. The college took Everett's message to heart. When historian Henry Adams asked his students why they had come to study at Cambridge, the answer he got was unambiguous: "The degree of Harvard College is worth money to me in Chicago."

The practical side of higher learning was remarkably enhanced by the Morrill Act of 1862, later called the Land Grant College Act. This historic piece of legislation gave federal land to each state, with proceeds from sale of the land to support both education in the liberal arts and training in the skills that ultimately would undergird the emerging agricultural and mechanical revolutions. The Hatch Act of 1887 added energy to the effort by providing federal funds to create university-sponsored agricultural experiment stations that brought learning to the farmer, and the idea of education as a democratic function to serve the common good was planted on the prairies.

Something of the excitement of this era was captured in Willa Cather's description of her fellow students and her teachers at the University of Nebraska in the 1890s: "[They] came straight from the cornfields with only summer's wages in their pockets, hung on through four years, shabby and underfed, and completed the course by really heroic self-sacrifice. Our instructors were oddly assorted: wandering pioneer school teachers, stranded ministers of the Gospel, a few enthusiastic young men just out of graduate school. There was an atmosphere of endeavor, of expectancy and bright hopefulness about the young college that had lifted its head from the prairie only a few years ago."

Thus, American higher education, once devoted primarily to the intellectual and moral development of students, added *service* as a mission, and both private and public universities took up the challenge. In 1903, David Starr Jordan, president of Stanford University, declared that the entire university movement in the twentieth century "is toward reality and practicality." By 1908, Harvard president Charles Eliot could claim: "At bottom most of the American institutions of higher education are filled with the modern democratic spirit of serviceableness. Teachers and students alike are profoundly moved by the desire to serve the democratic community. . . . All the colleges boast of the serviceable men they have trained, and regard the serviceable patriot as their ideal product. This is a thoroughly democratic conception of their function."

Skeptics looked with amusement, even contempt, at what they considered the excesses of utility and accommodation. They long resisted the idea of making the university itself a more democratic institution and viewed with disdain Ezra Cornell's soaring pledge in the 1860s to ". . . found an institution 'where any person can find instruction in any study.'" Some critics even viewed the agricultural experiment stations as a betrayal of higher education's mission. They ridiculed the "cow colleges," seeing in them a dilution of academic standards. Others recoiled from the idea that non-elite young people were going on to college.

Still, a host of academics flocked to land-grant colleges, confident they had both the expertise and the obligation to contribute to building a nation. They embodied the spirit of Emerson, who years before had spoken of the scholarship of "action" as "the raw material out of which the intellect moulds her splendid products." In this tradition, Governor Robert LaFollette forged, in Wisconsin, a powerful link between the campus and the state, one that became known nationally as the "Wisconsin Idea." After visiting Madison in 1909, social critic Lincoln Steffens observed: "In Wisconsin the university is as close to the intelligent farmer as his pig-pen or his tool-house; the university laboratories are part of the alert manufacturer's plant. . . ."

The idea that professors could spread knowledge that would improve agriculture and manufacturing gave momentum to what later became known as *applied* research. In the 1870s and 1880s, many agreed that education was, above all, to be considered useful. In commenting on the link between the campus and applied agricultural research, historian Margaret Rossiter presented this vivid illustration: "The chief activities of a professor of agriculture . . . were to run field tests with various fertilizers and to maintain a model farm, preferably, but rarely, without financial loss." Over the next thirty years, these agricultural sciences developed at a rapid pace, vastly increasing the knowledge that scholars could apply.

Service during this expansive period had a moral meaning, too. The goal was not only to *serve* society, but *reshape* it. Andrew White, the first president of Cornell University, saw graduates "pouring into the legislatures, staffing the newspapers, and penetrating the municipal and county boards of America. Corruption would come to an end; pure American ideals would prosper until one day they governed the entire world." Sociologist Edward Shils, in describing the spirit of the times, observed that "the concept of improvement was vague and comprehensive, signifying not only improvement of a practical sort but spiritual improvement as well."

This ideal—the conviction that higher education had a moral mission to fulfill—was especially important to those who organized the American Economic Association in 1885, under the leadership of Richard Ely. Soon after joining the newly formed faculty at Johns Hopkins University, Ely wrote to the president, Daniel Coit Gilman, that the fledgling association would help in the diffusion of "a sound Christian political economy." Most faculty were less zealous. Still, in this remarkable era marked by continued emphasis on liberal education and values, the faculty's role was energized by determined efforts to apply knowledge to practical problems.

Basic research, a third dimension of scholarly activity which can be traced to the first years of the Republic, also began to take hold. The earliest research effort was largely led by investigators *outside* the academy—people such as Thomas Jefferson; the mathematician Nathaniel Bowditch; the pioneer botanists John and William Bartram; and the intrepid astronomer Maria Mitchell, who set up an observatory on lonely Nantucket Island and, on one October night in 1847, discovered a new comet. When President Jefferson sought a scientific leader for the first of the great western explorations, he did not go to the colleges, where science was not yet well developed. Instead, he looked within government and selected his personal secretary, Meriwether Lewis, who was known to have a keen eye for the natural world. Before the expedition, Lewis was sent to Philadelphia, where he received careful training in astronomy, botany, and mineralogy from members of the American Philosophical Society.

Still, colleges themselves were not wholly devoid of scientific effort. As early as 1738, John Winthrop of Harvard, the first academic scientist, had a laboratory in which to conduct experiments. He later persuaded the lawmakers in Massachusetts to sponsor America's first astronomical expedition. These early scientists traveled to Newfoundland in 1761 to observe the transit of Venus. Moreover, George Ticknor and Edward Everett, who attended a German university in 1815, are believed to have been the first Americans to go abroad to pursue advanced scholarly studies. Upon their return, they called, even then, for the introduction at Harvard of the German approach to scholarship.

Yet, change came slowly. The new sciences were very much on the edges of academic life and expectations were modest. As Dael Wolfle wrote: "Professors were hired to teach the science that was already known—to add to that knowledge was not expected. . . . " Consider also that when Benjamin Silliman became the first chemistry professor at Yale in 1802, there were only twenty-one other full-time scientific faculty positions in the United States.

By the mid-nineteenth century, however, leading Atlantic seaboard colleges were giving more legitimacy to the authority of scientific effort and a few were beginning to transform themselves into research and graduate institutions. For example, Harvard's Lawrence Scientific School and Yale's Sheffield Scientific School were forerunners of the academy's deep commitment to the scholarship of science. Graduate courses in philosophy and the arts were established, and America's first Doctor of Philosophy was conferred at Yale in 1861. And the Massachusetts Institute of Technology, which opened its doors at the end of the Civil War, soon was recognized as a center of scientific investigation.

In the late nineteenth century, more Americans who, like Ticknor and Everett, had studied in Europe were profoundly influenced by the research orientation of the German university and wanted to develop a similar model here. G. Stanley Hall, first president of Clark University, wrote in 1891, "The German University is today the freest spot on earth. . . . Nowhere has the passion to push on to the frontier of human knowledge been so general." Some, it is true, resisted the German influences. The prominent American humanist Irving Babbitt argued that the Ph.D. degree led to a loss of balance. He complained about the "maiming and mutilation of the mind that comes from over-absorption in one subject," declaring that German doctoral dissertations gave him "a sort of intellectual nausea."

Still, research and graduate education increasingly formed the model for the modern university. Academics on both continents were moving inevitably from faith in authority to reliance on scientific rationality. And to men like Daniel Coit Gilman, this view of scholarship called for a new kind of university, one based on the conviction that knowledge was most attainable through research and experimentation. Acting on this conviction, Gilman founded Johns Hopkins University in 1876, a step described by Shils as "perhaps the single, most decisive event in the history of learning in the Western hemisphere."

In the 1870s, the universities of Pennsylvania, Harvard, Columbia, and Princeton, in that order, also began to offer programs leading to the Ph.D. degree, and the University of Chicago, founded in 1891, made the degree "the pinnacle of the academic program." By 1895 William Rainey Harper, president of this newly formed university, could require "each appointee to sign an agreement that his promotions in rank and salary would depend chiefly upon his research productivity."

By the late nineteenth century, the advancement of knowledge through *research* had taken firm root in American higher education, and colonial college values, which emphasized teaching undergraduates, began to lose ground to the new university that was emerging. Indeed, the founders of Johns Hopkins University considered restricting study on that campus to the graduate level only. In the end, some undergraduate education proved necessary, but the compromise was reluctantly made, and for many professors, class and lecture work became almost incidental. Service, too, was viewed as unimportant. Some even considered it a violation of the integrity of the university, since the prevailing Germanic model demanded that the professor view the everyday world from a distance.

It should be stressed, however, that throughout most of American higher education the emphasis on research and graduate education remained the exception rather than the rule. The principal mission at most of the nation's colleges and universities continued to be the education of undergraduates. And the land-grant colleges, especially, took pride in service.

But in the 1940s, as the Great Depression gave way to a devastating war, the stage was set for a dramatic transformation of academic life. At that historic moment, Vannevar Bush of M.I.T. and James Bryant Conant of Harvard volunteered the help of the universities in bringing victory to the nation. In 1940, Bush took the lead in establishing the National Defense Research Committee which, a year later, became the Office of Scientific Research and Development. Academics flocked to Washington to staff the new agencies and federal research grants began to flow. Universities and the nation had joined in common cause.

After the war, Vannevar Bush urged continuing federal support for research. In a 1945 report to the President entitled *Science: The Endless Frontier*, he declared: "Science, by itself, provides no panacea for individual, social, and economic ills. It can be effective in the national welfare only as a member of a team, whether the conditions be peace or war. But without scientific progress no amount of achievement in other directions can insure our health, prosperity, and security as a nation in the modern world." The case could not have been more clearly stated. Higher learning and government had, through scientific collaboration, changed the course of history—and the impact on the academy would be both consequential and enduring.

Soon, a veritable army of freshly minted Ph.D.s fanned out to campuses across the country. Inspired by their mentors, this new generation of faculty found themselves committed not only to their institutions, but also to their professions. Young scholars sought to replicate the research climate they themselves had recently experienced. Academic priorities that had for years been the inspiration of the few now became the imperative of the many. In the new climate, discipline-based departments became the foundation of faculty allegiance, and being a "scholar" was now virtually synonymous with being an academic professional. Christopher Jencks and David Riesman, capturing the spirit of that period, declared that an *academic revolution* had taken place.

In 1958, Theodore Caplow and Reece McGee defined this new reality when they observed that while young faculty were hired as *teachers*, they were evaluated primarily as *researchers*. This shift in expectations is vividly revealed in two national surveys conducted by The Carnegie Foundation for the Advancement of Teaching. Twenty-one percent of the faculty surveyed in 1969 strongly agreed that it is difficult to achieve tenure without publishing. By 1989, the number had doubled, to 42 percent (table 1). The change at comprehensive colleges—from 6 percent to 43 percent—is especially noteworthy since these institutions have virtually no doctoral programs and only limited resources for research. Even at liberal arts colleges, where teaching has always been highly prized, nearly one in four faculty strongly agreed in 1989 that it is difficult to get tenure without publishing.

Meanwhile, the nation's colleges and universities were experiencing another remarkable social transformation—the revolution of rising expectations. In 1947, Harry S Truman appointed a President's Commission on Higher Education and almost overnight the mission of higher education in the nation was dramatically redefined. In its landmark report, this panel of prominent citizens concluded that America's colleges and universities should no longer be "merely the instrument for producing an intellectual elite." Rather, the report stated, higher education must become "the means by which every citizen, youth, and adult, is enabled and encouraged to carry his education, formal and informal, as far as his native capacities permit."

In response to this expansive vision, the nation moved from an *elite* to a *mass* system of higher education, to use sociologist Martin Trow's helpful formulation. New colleges were built, new faculty hired,

Table 1
In My Department It Is Difficult for a Person to Achieve Tenure If He or She Does Not Publish
(Percentage Saying "Strongly Agree")

	1969	1989
All Respondents	21%	42%
Research	44	83
Doctorate-granting	27	71
Comprehensive	6	43
Liberal Arts	6	24
Two-Year	3	4

Please see Appendix C for a definition of institution classifications.
Source: The Carnegie Foundation for the Advancement of Teaching, 1969 and 1989 National Surveys of Faculty.

and the G.I. Bill of Rights, first authorized in 1944, changed the entire tradition of who should go to college. Almost eight million former servicemen and women benefited from the legislation. In the years to come, younger brothers and sisters, and eventually sons and daughters, followed in the footsteps of the veterans. Higher education, once viewed as a privilege, was now accepted as a right.

But even as the mission of American higher education was expanding, the standards used to measure academic prestige continued to be narrowed. Increasingly, professors were expected to conduct research and publish results. Promotion and tenure depended on such activity, and young professors seeking security and status found it more rewarding—in a quite literal sense—to deliver a paper at a national convention in New York or Chicago than teach undergraduates back home. Lip service still was being paid to maintaining a balance between *collegiate* responsibilities and *university* work, but on most campuses the latter had clearly won the day.

Research *per se* was not the problem. The problem was that the research mission, which was appropriate for *some* institutions, created a shadow over the entire higher learning enterprise—and the model of a "Berkeley" or an "Amherst" became the yardstick by which all institutions would be measured. Ernest Lynton, Commonwealth Professor at the University of Massachusetts, in commenting on the new priorities, concluded that developments after the Second World War "established too narrow a definition of scholarship and too limited a range of instruction." Ironically, at the very time America's higher education institutions were becoming more open and inclusive, the culture of the professoriate was becoming more hierarchical and restrictive.

Thus, in just a few decades, priorities in American higher education were significantly realigned. The emphasis on undergraduate education, which throughout the years had drawn its inspiration from the colonial college tradition, was being overshadowed by the European university tradition, with its emphasis on graduate education and research. Specifically, at many of the nation's four-year institutions, the focus had moved from the student to the professoriate, from general to specialized education, and from loyalty to the campus to loyalty to the profession.

We conclude that for America's colleges and universities to remain vital a new vision of scholarship is required. What we are faced with, today, is the need to clarify campus missions and relate the work of the academy more directly to the realities of contemporary life. We need especially to ask how institutional diversity can be strengthened and how the rich array of faculty talent in our colleges and universities might be more effectively used and continuously renewed. We proceed with the conviction that if the nation's higher learning institutions are to meet today's urgent academic and social mandates, their missions must be carefully redefined and the meaning of scholarship creatively reconsidered.

Enlarging the Perspective

Since colonial times, the American professoriate has responded to mandates both from within the academy and beyond. First came teaching, then service, and finally, the challenge of research. In more recent years, faculty have been asked to blend these three traditions, but despite this idealized expectation, a wide gap now exists between the myth and the reality of academic life. Almost all colleges pay lip service to the trilogy of teaching, research, and service, but when it comes to making judgments about professional performance, the three rarely are assigned equal merit.

Today, when we speak of being "scholarly," it usually means having academic rank in a college or university and being engaged in research and publication. But we should remind ourselves just how recently the word "research" actually entered the vocabulary of higher education. The term was first used in England in the 1870s by reformers who wished to make Cambridge and Oxford "not only a place of teaching, but a place of learning," and it was later introduced to American higher education in 1906 by Daniel Coit Gilman. But scholarship in earlier times referred to a variety of creative work carried on in a variety of places, and its integrity was measured by the ability to think, communicate, and learn.

What we now have is a more restricted view of scholarship, one that limits it to a hierarchy of functions. Basic research has come to be viewed as the first and most essential form of scholarly activity, with other functions flowing from it. Scholars are academics who conduct research, publish, and then perhaps convey their knowledge to students or apply what they have learned. The latter functions grow *out of* scholarship, they are not to be considered a part of it. But knowledge is not necessarily developed in such a linear manner. The arrow of causality can, and frequently does, point in *both* directions. Theory surely leads to practice. But practice also leads to theory. And teaching, at its best, shapes both research and practice. Viewed from this perspective, a more comprehensive, more dynamic understanding of scholarship can be considered, one in which the rigid categories of teaching, research, and service are broadened and more flexibly defined.

There is a readiness, we believe, to rethink what it means to be a scholar. Richard I. Miller, professor of higher education at Ohio University, recently surveyed academic vice presidents and deans at more than eight hundred colleges and universities to get their opinion about faculty functions. These administrators were asked if they thought it would be a good idea to view scholarship as more than research. The responses were overwhelmingly supportive of this proposition. The need to reconsider scholarship surely goes beyond opinion polls, but campus debates, news stories, and the themes of national conventions suggest that administrative leaders are rethinking the definitions of academic life. Moreover, faculty, themselves, appear to be increasingly dissatisfied with conflicting priorities on the campus.

How then should we proceed? Is it possible to define the work of faculty in ways that reflect more realistically the full range of academic and civic mandates? We believe the time has come to move beyond the tired old "teaching versus research" debate and give the familiar and honorable term "scholarship" a broader, more capacious meaning, one that brings legitimacy to the full scope of academic work. Surely, scholarship means engaging in original research. But the work of the scholar also means stepping back from one's investigation, looking for connections, building bridges between theory and practice, and communicating one's knowledge effectively to students. Specifically, we conclude that the work of the professoriate might be thought of as having four separate, yet overlapping, functions. These are: the scholarship of *discovery*; the scholarship of *integration*; the scholarship of *application*; and the scholarship of *teaching*.

The first and most familiar element in our model, the *scholarship of discovery*, comes closest to what is meant when academics speak of "research." No tenets in the academy are held in higher regard than the commitment to knowledge for its own sake, to freedom of inquiry and to following, in a disciplined fashion, an investigation wherever it may lead. Research is central to the work of higher learning, but our study here, which inquires into the meaning of scholarship, is rooted in the conviction that disciplined, investigative efforts within the academy should be strengthened, not diminished.

The *scholarship of discovery*, at its best, contributes not only to the stock of human knowledge but also to the intellectual climate of a college or university. Not just the outcomes, but the process, and especially the passion, give meaning to the effort. The advancement of knowledge can generate an almost palpable excitement in the life of an educational institution. As William Bowen, former president of Princeton University, said, scholarly research "reflects our pressing, irrepressible need as human beings to confront the unknown and to seek understanding for its own sake. It is tied inextricably to the freedom to think freshly, to see propositions of every kind in everchanging light. And it celebrates the special exhilaration that comes from a new idea."

The list of distinguished researchers who have added luster to the nation's intellectual life would surely include heroic figures of earlier days—Yale chemist Benjamin Silliman; Harvard naturalist Louis Agassiz; astronomer William Cranch Bond; and Columbia anthropologist Franz Boas. It would also include giants of our time—James Watson, who helped unlock the genetic code; political philosopher

Hannah Arendt; anthropologist Ruth Benedict; historian John Hope Franklin; geneticist Barbara McClintock; and Noam Chomsky, who transformed the field of linguistics; among others.

When the research records of higher learning are compared, the United States is the pacesetter. If we take as our measure of accomplishment the number of Nobel Prizes awarded since 1945, United States scientists received 56 percent of the awards in physics, 42 percent in chemistry, and 60 percent in medicine. Prior to the outbreak of the Second World War, American scientists, including those who fled Hitler's Europe, had received only 18 of the 129 prizes in these three areas. With regard to physics, for example, a recent report by the National Research Council states: "Before World War II, physics was essentially a European activity, but by the war's end, the center of physics had moved to the United States."' The Council goes on to review the advances in fields ranging from elementary particle physics to cosmology.

The research contribution of universities is particularly evident in medicine. Investigations in the late nineteenth century on bacteria and viruses paid off in the 1930s with the development of immunizations for diphtheria, tetanus, lobar pneumonia, and other bacterial infections. On the basis of painstaking research, a taxonomy of infectious diseases has emerged, making possible streptomycin and other antibiotics. In commenting on these breakthroughs, physician and medical writer Lewis Thomas observes: "It was basic science of a very high order, storing up a great mass of interesting knowledge for its own sake, creating, so to speak, a bank of information, ready for drawing on when the time for intelligent use arrived."

Thus, the probing mind of the researcher is an incalculably vital asset to the academy and the world. Scholarly investigation, in all the disciplines, is at the very heart of academic life, and the pursuit of knowledge must be assiduously cultivated and defended. The intellectual excitement fueled by this quest enlivens faculty and invigorates higher learning institutions, and in our complicated, vulnerable world, the discovery of new knowledge is absolutely crucial.

The Scholarship of Integration

In proposing the *scholarship of integration*, we underscore the need for scholars who give meaning to isolated facts, putting them in perspective. By integration, we mean making connections across the disciplines, placing the specialties in larger context, illuminating data in a revealing way, often educating nonspecialists, too. In calling for a scholarship of integration, we do not suggest returning to the "gentleman scholar" of an earlier time, nor do we have in mind the dilettante. Rather, what we mean is serious, disciplined work that seeks to interpret, draw together, and bring new insight to bear on original research.

This more integrated view of knowledge was expressed eloquently by Mark Van Doren nearly thirty years ago when he wrote: "The connectedness of things is what the educator contemplates to the limit of his capacity. No human capacity is great enough to permit a vision of the world as simple, but if the educator does not aim at the vision no one else will, and the consequences are dire when no one does." It is through "connectedness" that research ultimately is made authentic.

The scholarship of integration is, of course, closely related to discovery. It involves, first, doing research at the boundaries where fields converge, and it reveals itself in what philosopher-physicist Michael Polanyi calls "overlapping [academic] neighborhoods." Such work is, in fact, increasingly important as traditional disciplinary categories prove confining, forcing new topologies of knowledge. Many of today's professors understand this. When we asked faculty to respond to the statement, "Multidisciplinary work is soft and should not be considered scholarship," only 8 percent agreed, 17 percent were neutral, while a striking 75 percent disagreed (table 2). This pattern of opinion, with only slight variation, was true for professors in all disciplines and across all types of institutions.

The scholarship of integration also means interpretation, fitting one's own research—or the research of others—into larger intellectual patterns. Such efforts are increasingly essential since specialization, without broader perspective, risks pedantry. The distinction we are drawing here between "discovery" and "integration" can be best understood, perhaps, by the questions posed. Those engaged in discovery ask, "What is to be known, what is yet to be found?" Those engaged in integration ask, "What do the fndings *mean*? Is it possible to interpret what's been discovered in ways that provide a larger, more comprehensive understanding?" Questions such as these call for the power of critical analysis and interpretation. They have a legitimacy of their own and if carefully pursued can lead the scholar from information to knowledge and even, perhaps, to wisdom.

Table 2
Multidisciplinary Work Is Soft and Should Not Be Considered Scholarship

	Agree	Neutral	Disagree
All Respondents	8%	17%	75%
Research	7	9	84
Doctorate-granting	6	13	80
Comprehensive	8	14	78
Liberal Arts	8	16	77
Two Year	9	27	63

Source: The Carnegie Foundation for the Advancement of Teaching, 1989 National Survey of Faculty.

Today, more than at any time in recent memory, researchers feel the need to move beyond traditional disciplinary boundaries, communicate with colleagues in other fields, and discover patterns that connect. Anthropologist Clifford Geertz, of the Institute for Advanced Study in Princeton, has gone so far as to describe these shifts as a fundamental "refiguration, . . . a phenomenon general enough and distinctive enough to suggest that what we are seeing is not just another redrawing of the cultural map—the moving of a few disputed borders, the marking of some more picturesque mountain lakes—but an alteration of the principles of mapping. Something is happening," Geertz says, "to the way we think about the way we think."

This is reflected, he observes, in:

> . . . philosophical inquiries looking like literary criticism (think of Stanley Cavell on Beckett or Thoreau, Sartre on Flaubert), scientific discussions looking like belles lettres *morceaux* (Lewis Thomas, Loren Eisley), baroque fantasies presented as deadpan empirical observations (Borges, Barthelme), histories that consist of equations and tables or law court testimony (Fogel and Engerman, Le Roi Ladurie), documentaries that read like true confessions (Mailer), parables posing as ethnographies (Castañeda), theoretical treatises set out as travelogues (Lévi-Strauss), ideological arguments cast as historiographical inquiries (Edward Said), epistemological studies constructed like political tracts (Paul Feyerabend), methodological polemics got up as personal memoirs (James Watson).

These examples illustrate a variety of scholarly trends—*interdisciplinary, interpretive, integrative*. But we present them here as evidence that an intellectual sea change may be occurring, one that is perhaps as momentous as the nineteenth-century shift in the hierarchy of knowledge, when philosophy gave way more firmly to science. Today, interdisciplinary *and* integrative studies, long on the edges of academic life, are moving toward the center, responding both to new intellectual questions and to pressing human problems. As the boundaries of human knowledge are being dramatically reshaped, the academy surely must give increased attention to the *scholarship of integration.*

The Scholarship of Application

The first two kinds of scholarship—discovery and integration of knowledge—reflect the investigative and synthesizing traditions of academic life. The third element, the *application* of knowledge, moves toward engagement as the scholar asks, "How can knowledge be responsibly applied to consequential problems? How can it be helpful to individuals as well as institutions?" And further, "Can social problems *themselves* define an agenda for scholarly investigation?"

Reflecting the *Zeitgeist* of the nineteenth and early twentieth centuries, not only the land-grant colleges, but also institutions such as Rensselaer Polytechnic Institute and the University of Chicago were founded on the principle that higher education must serve the interests of the larger community. In 1906, an editor celebrating the leadership of William Rainey Harper at the new University of Chicago defined what he believed to be the essential character of the American scholar. Scholarship, he observed, was regarded by the British as "a means and measure of self-development," by the Germans as "an end in itself," but by Americans as "equipment for service." Self-serving though it may have been, this analysis had more than a grain of truth.

Given this tradition, one is struck by the gap between values in the academy and the needs of the larger world. Service is routinely praised, but accorded little attention—even in programs where it is most appropriate. Christopher Jencks and David Riesman, for example, have pointed out that when free-standing professional schools affiliated with universities, they lessened their commitment to applied work even though the original purpose of such schools was to connect theory and practice. Professional schools, they concluded, have oddly enough fostered "a more academic and less practical view of what their students need to know."

Colleges and universities have recently rejected service as serious scholarship, partly because its meaning is so vague and often disconnected from serious intellectual work. As used today, service in the academy covers an almost endless number of campus activities—sitting on committees, advising student clubs, or performing departmental chores. The definition blurs still more as activities beyond the campus are included—participation in town councils, youth clubs, and the like. It is not unusual for almost any worthy project to be dumped into the amorphous category called "service."

Clearly, a sharp distinction must be drawn between *citizenship* activities and projects that relate to scholarship itself. To be sure, there are meritorious social and civic functions to be performed, and faculty should be appropriately recognized for such work. But all too frequently, service means not doing scholarship but doing good. To be considered *scholarship*, service activities must be tied directly to one's special field of knowledge and relate to, and flow directly out of, this professional activity. Such service is serious, demanding work, requiring the rigor—and the accountability—traditionally associated with research activities.

The *scholarship of application*, as we define it here, is not a one-way street. Indeed, the term itself may be misleading if it suggests that knowledge is first "discovered" and then "applied." The process we have in mind is far more dynamic. New intellectual understandings can arise out of the very act of application—whether in medical diagnosis, serving clients in psychotherapy, shaping public policy, creating an architectural design, or working with the public schools. In activities such as these, theory and practice vitally interact, and one renews the other.

Such a view of scholarly service—one that both applies and contributes to human knowledge—is particularly needed in a world in which huge, almost intractable problems call for the skills and insights only the academy can provide. As Oscar Handlin observed, our troubled planet "can no longer afford the luxury of pursuits confined to an ivory tower. . . . [S]cholarship has to prove its worth not on its own terms but by service to the nation and the world."

The Scholarship of Teaching

Finally, we come to the *scholarship of teaching*. The work of the professor becomes consequential only as it is understood by others. Yet, today, teaching is often viewed as a routine function, tacked on, something almost anyone can do. When defined as scholarship, however, teaching both educates and entices future scholars. Indeed, as Aristotle said, "Teaching is the highest form of understanding."

As a *scholarly* enterprise, teaching begins with what the teacher knows. Those who teach must, above all, be well informed, and steeped in the knowledge of their fields. Teaching can be well regarded only as professors are widely read and intellectually engaged. One reason legislators, trustees, and the general public often fail to understand why ten or twelve hours in the classroom each week can be a heavy load is their lack of awareness of the hard work and the serious study that undergirds good teaching.

Teaching is also a dynamic endeavor involving all the analogies, metaphors, and images that build bridges between the teacher's understanding and the student's learning. Pedagogical procedures must be carefully planned, continuously examined, and relate directly to the subject taught. Educator Parker Palmer strikes precisely the right note when he says knowing and learning are communal acts. With this vision, great teachers create a common ground of intellectual commitment. They stimulate active, not passive, learning and encourage students to be critical, creative thinkers, with the capacity to go on learning after their college days are over.

Further, good teaching means that faculty, as scholars, are also learners. All too often, teachers transmit information that students are expected to memorize and then, perhaps, recall. While well-prepared lectures surely have a place, teaching, at its best, means not only transmitting knowledge, but *transforming* and *extending* it as well. Through reading, through classroom discussion, and surely through comments and questions posed by students, professors themselves will be pushed in creative new directions.

In the end, inspired teaching keeps the flame of scholarship alive. Almost all successful academics give credit to creative teachers—those mentors who defined their work so compellingly that it became, for them, a lifetime challenge. Without the teaching function, the continuity of knowledge will be broken and the store of human knowledge dangerously diminished.

Physicist Robert Oppenheimer, in a lecture at the 200th anniversary of Columbia University in 1954, spoke elegantly of the teacher as mentor and placed teaching at the very heart of the scholarly endeavor: "The specialization of science is an inevitable accompaniment of progress; yet it is full of dangers, and it is cruelly wasteful, since so much that is beautiful and enlightening is cut off from most of the world. Thus it is proper to the role of the scientist that he not merely find the truth and communicate it to his fellows, but that he teach, that he try to bring the most honest and most intelligible account of new knowledge to all who will try to learn."

Here, then, is our conclusion. What we urgently need today is a more inclusive view of what it means to be a scholar—a recognition that knowledge is acquired through research, through synthesis, through practice, and through teaching. We acknowledge that these four categories—the scholarship of discovery, of integration, of application, and of teaching—divide intellectual functions that are tied inseparably to each other. Still, there is value, we believe, in analyzing the various kinds of academic work, while also acknowledging that they dynamically interact, forming an interdependent whole. Such a vision of scholarship, one that recognizes the great diversity of talent within the professoriate, also may prove especially useful to faculty as they reflect on the meaning and direction of their professional lives.

PART II

Understanding Students as Learners

Introduction

Although learning theory, along with attendant research, has served as a basis for instructional improvement, college teachers do not commonly use formal principles of learning in planning their everyday teaching. One possible explanation for their not doing so is that very few graduate programs include coursework to develop this kind of pedagogical knowledge that informs the practice of teaching. Lee Shulman's (1987) research expands our conception of the knowledge base for teaching, while confirming that it includes a knowledge of learning, learners and their diverse characteristics. The selected readings in Part II provide an introduction to this knowledge. Three related questions are addressed. First, what have the traditional schools of thought taught us about human learning? Second, what does the latest research tell us about how college students—including those of nontraditional age—learn? And third, what are the important teaching and learning implications of the diverse characteristics of students? The first and second questions are addressed in the readings for Section A on theories of learning. The third question is addressed in the readings for Section B on the similarities and differences among learners.

A. Theories of Learning

The first reading in Section A, by Fincher, provides an overview of the evolution of traditional behavioral, cognitive, and developmental conceptions of human learning as they relate to teaching and learning in institutions of higher education. As a provisional consensus, he views behavioral processes as primarily related to skills, proficiency, and competency learning; cognitive processes as related to conceptual, symbolic, and verbal learning; and developmental processes as related to the acquisition of attitudes, beliefs, and values.

Whereas Fincher presents the historical foundation necessary for the study of the principles of learning, the second reading, by McKeachie and his associates, reviews in some detail the growing contributions from research in cognitive psychology that enhance our understanding of how college students learn. The framework of the authors' expansive review is based on a model of student cognition in which students' knowledge structures, motivational beliefs, and use of learning strategies mediate the impact of instructional activities on academic performance. Their synthesis of recent advances in this area served as the foundation for an extensive research program undertaken in association with the National Center for Research to Improve Postsecondary Teaching and Learning. In Part III (Section D) of this reader, the reading by Pintrich describes some results of this research that show significant relationships among student motivation, cognition and achievement in the college classroom.

The largest single demographic source of enrollment growth in the 1980s and 1990s has come from students of nontraditional age. Their presence sustains the efforts of researchers and teachers to enhance the academic success of the adult learner. The next reading, by Merriam and Caffarella, is from the authors' book, *Learning in Adulthood* (1991). The authors review, evaluate and synthesize a variety of notable efforts to develop comprehensive theories of adult learning. They examine three broad categories of theories of adult learning: those based on the characteristics of adult learners, including Knowles' andragogy and Cross' model of the characteristics of adults as learners (CAL); those based on the life situations—responsibilities, roles, and experiences—of adults, including the theory of margin developed by McClusky, Knox's proficiency theory, and Jarvis' comprehensive model of learning within a social context; and those with a cognitive focus based on reflection and the construction of experience and meaning, including Mezirow's theory of perspective transformation and Freire's theory of conscientization. Based on their synthesis of these theories, the authors extract several key features of adult learning.

B. Learners: Similarities and Differences

Whereas the last reading in Section A addresses the unique features of learning for adults (that is, for students of nontraditional age), the five readings in this section address the teaching and learning implications associated with student diversity in terms of learning style and major field of study, stage of moral and intellectual development, epistemological beliefs, gender, ethnicity and racial identity development. Whether students are of traditional or nontraditional age, they are diverse in terms of their preferred learning styles and their major fields of study. In the first reading of this section, Kolb presents his well-known experiential learning cycle with its four phases of concrete experience, reflective observation, abstract conceptualization, and active experimentation. The underlying dimensions of this cycle form the logical basis for his model of four distinct learning styles, each representing a preferred way to process information. He reports that variations in learning styles are strongly related to the inquiry norms of various major fields of study. Generally, the natural sciences and mathematics are associated with the abstract-reflective (assimilator) style, the science-based professions (for example, engineering) are related to the abstract-active (converger) style, the social professions (for example, education) are related to the concrete-active (accommodator) style, and the humanities and social sciences are related to the concrete-reflective (diverger) style. The reading by Svinicki and Dixon in Part IV (Section B) suggests specific teaching strategies that address each of these learning styles.

The next reading, by Kurfiss, compares the various theoretical assumptions and underlying frameworks of four perspectives on the developmental stages of college students: Piaget's theory of cognitive development; Perry's theory of epistemological development; Erikson's theory of identity and psychosocial development; and Kohlberg's theory of moral development. Each theory emphasizes a unique aspect of overall human development with specific implications for how students learn. For each theory, Kurfiss presents a critique (for example, in terms of gender or cross-cultural generalizability) and an extensive set of teaching implications.

An invaluable contribution to the literature on intellectual development—which had been previously dominated by the earlier work of Perry (1970) on the intellectual development of male college students—is presented in the next reading by Clinchy. She provides a rich, personal account of the experiences that led her and her colleagues to the discoveries about the epistemological beliefs and intellectual development of female college students (ultimately reported in their book, *Women's Ways of Knowing* [Belenky, Clinchy, Goldberger and Tarule, 1986]). The distinction made by the author (and her colleagues) between "separate knowing" as a dominant, highly-valued way of knowing, and "connected knowing" as a suppressed and undervalued but emergent and potent way of knowing, has profound implications for effective classroom instruction.

Schommer, in the fourth reading of this section, presents the conceptual framework underlying her well-known theory of epistemological beliefs, reviews the recent research supporting the validity of the theory, and explains the ways in which the theory has increased our understanding of how students learn. The theory, which views students' epistemological beliefs as multidimensional, analyzes beliefs about both the nature of knowledge and the nature of the acquisition of knowledge or learning. The dimensions of beliefs about the nature of knowledge are viewed as ranging along several continua based on the certainty of knowledge (from absolute to tentative), the structure of knowledge (from simple isolated facts to complex interwoven concepts), and the source of knowledge (from authority to reason). The dimensions of students' beliefs about the nature of the acquisition of knowledge or learning are viewed as varying along continua based on the learner's control of knowledge acquisition (from the ability to learn as fixed to the ability to learn as changeable) and the learner's speed of knowledge acquisition (from learning taking place quickly or not at all to learning taking place more gradually). Recent research has shown that epistemological beliefs of students are related to their motivational beliefs, their use of learning strategies, and their academic performance (Hofer and Pintrich 1997), and also appear to differ across their major fields of study in college (Paulsen and Wells, in press).

In most instances, today's college classrooms are multicultural settings in which learning by individuals from diverse backgrounds can be either enhanced or inhibited, depending in no small part on the attitudes and behaviors of teachers in such settings. In the next reading, Chism emphasizes the rapidly-expanding presence of previously underrepresented groups in today's college classrooms and focuses her review of the relevant literature on what she views as four broad categories of needs expressed by students from these groups. In brief, she concludes that students need to feel welcome in their classrooms, to be treated as individuals by teachers and other students, to have opportunities to participate fully in class activities, and to be treated fairly. In addition to reviewing and synthesizing the literature on the impact of selected variables on the learning experiences of women and minority students, the author offers concrete suggestions to help increase instructor self-awareness and facilitate change in attitudes and behaviors.

Hardiman and Jackson, in the last reading of this section, point out that the classroom and other campus settings frequently constitute arenas in which students and faculty interact and transition from one stage or status to another in the development of their individual racial identities. The authors define racial identity as "a sense of self in the context of one's racial group membership, which . . . changes over time to become more congruent with one's range of experiences, personal beliefs, and other dimensions of self-identity." Social diversity on college campuses—that is, the growing presence of previously under-represented groups—has been associated with expanding efforts to study and understand the diverse world views held by different individual members of the same racial or cultural groups and the ways in which different racial or cultural groups view the world in terms of their different experiences with social injustice. Inter-group and intra-group differences in experiences with social injustice form the basis for the construction of models of the stages or statuses traversed by individuals as they develop their racial identities. The authors point out that the various ways social oppression manifests itself—for example, racism, sexism and ethnocentrism—affect the self-concepts, world views and behaviors of members of both the "dominant" (e.g. White Americans) and "target" (e.g. Black Americans) groups in existing social systems. Based on their pioneering work, Hardiman and Jackson present five-stage models of both Black and White American racial identity development; they explain in some detail the ways in which various life experiences of Blacks and Whites promote their development and transitions through the naive, acceptance, resistance, redefinition and internalization stages of the formation of racial identities (see the reading by Tatum in Part IV, Section B, of this book for an examination of how specific teaching strategies can be used to assist students as they move through the various stages of racial identity development).

References

Belenky, M.F., Clinchy, B.M., Goldberger, N. R., and Tarule, J. M. (1986). *Women's ways of knowing: The development of self, body, and mind*. New York: Basic Books.

Hofer, B.K., and Pintrich, P.R. (1997). The development of epistemological theories: Beliefs about knowledge and knowing and their relation to learning. *Review of Educational Research 67*, 88-140.

Merriam, S.B., and Caffarella, R.S. (1991). *Learning in adulthood: A comprehensive guide*. San Francisco: Jossey-Bass.

Paulsen, M.B., and Wells, C.T. (in press). Domain differences in the epistemological beliefs of college students. *Research in Higher Education 39*(4).

Perry, W.G. (1970). *Forms of intellectual and ethical development in the college years*. New York: Holt, Rinehart and Winston.

Shulman, L. (1987). Knowledge and teaching: Foundation of the new reform. *Harvard Educational Review, 57*, 1-22.

A. Theories of Learning

Learning Theory and Research

CAMERON FINCHER

The relevance of learning theory and research for higher education is not a much discussed topic on college and university campuses. College instruction is not a research-based function, and much of what passes for classroom teaching cannot be derived from either learning or instructional theory. A preponderance of teaching methods and techniques, no doubt, is based on casual observation, conscious imitation, or intuitive guesswork and *not* on the uses and applications of sound learning principles. How students cope with academic tasks and demands is a subject that frequently surfaces in educational waters, but the emphasis on such matters seldom turns to learning as a psychological or educational explanation. Recent research in cognitive style, the bilaterality of the human brain, and information-processing models of intelligence arouses interest in response acquisition and modification, but a varying use is made of learning and development as explanatory constructs.

The intent of this chapter is to review the tenuous relationship of learning theory and research with education beyond high school, and to suggest that the psychology of learning is by no means irrelevant to learning and teaching in institutions of higher education. The loss of popularity on the part of psychology, in general, may be attributed to an ascendancy of economics and sociology as those two disciplines became much concerned with distributive effects in education at all levels. There is also cause for the opinion that a psychology of individual differences, once regarded as the backbone of progressive education, has been displaced by a sociology of groups, as reflected in the many resolutions of group conflict that have taken place on college campuses. The reassertion of developmental psychology as a dominant force in education, however, suggests that economic and sociological determinism may have run their course of popularity and that a reaffirmation of the importance of teaching and learning in higher education is not only in order—but in the making!

What Is Learning?

The uses and applications of learning theory and research in higher education are impeded, undoubtedly, by the difficulties of defining learning in terms that are educationally relevant. There is an element of disservice in operational definitions that may serve experimental design and analysis well but push teachers and instructors into semantic quagmires. If we thus look for an authoritative definition of learning, we would hope to find one in the fifth edition of Ernest Hilgard's classic, *Theories of Learning*. Having instructed several generations of psychology students in learning theory and research, such a classic surely supplies a well-fashioned definition that would make sense to all who are interested in the psychology of learning. Much to our disappointment, we find that Bower (1981)—now the senior author—defines learning as follows (p. 11):

> Learning refers to the change in a subject's behavior or behavior potential to a given situation brought about by the subject's repeated experiences in that situation, provided that the behavior change cannot be explained on the basis of the subject's native responses tendencies, maturation, or temporary states (such as fatigue, drunkenness, drives, and so on).

Unfortunately for those who learn and teach in college, Bower's definition is much too utilitarian. Those of us who plan and organize five-hour courses and two-hour seminars will not think of our classroom as "situations" in which "repeated experiences" are crucial. Furthermore, despite great pressure

"Learning Theory and Research," by Cameron Fincher, reprinted by permission from *Higher Education Handbook of Theory and Research,* Vol. 1, edited by J. C. Smart, 1985, Agathon Press.

from enlightened deans and department heads to cast our instructional objectives in behavioral terms, we will not observe changes in either behavior or behavior potential as often as we would prefer. We will observe, of course, that on many occasions "temporary states" of our students are more influential than our lectures or group discussions.

The most significant weakness of Bower's definition for higher education, however, is the failure to link learning directly to instruction. College and university faculty are hard pressed to accept responsibility for the learning that takes place under conditions of classroom instruction, much less the learning that may result from "native response tendencies" and "maturation." And despite a great deal of speculation about the changes in behavior that would have taken place *without* college attendance, students apparently learn best when they are well instructed. Thus the uses and applications of learning theory and research on college and university campuses are dependent upon the conditions of instruction that prevail in academic settings. One effort to define learning in educational terms is as follows:

> [Learning is] a process of acquiring and integrating through a systemized process of instruction or organized experience varying forms of knowledge, skill, and understanding that the learner may use or apply in later situations and under conditions different from those of instruction. [Fincher, 1978, p. 420]

Such a definition is obviously an optimistic one. The intent is to specify that: (1) some learning can and does result from instruction but it can also result from other forms of organized experience; (2) the process of learning can and does include cognitive, behavioral, and experimental dimensions or components; (3) learning should be seen in relation to its future uses or applications and its transfer to situations and conditions; and (4) learning and teaching are dual processes that must be treated systematically if they are to make educational sense. As a definition, it is quite compatible with Robert Gagne's (1977) more concise definition (p. 3):

> Learning is a change in human disposition or capability, which persists over time, and which is not simply ascribable to processes of growth.

Both definitions should serve, furthermore, to specify that learning is something more than a change in performance. We infer that learning has taken place when we observe and/or record a change in performance, but we should never equate, as too many have done in recent years, learning with the performance we observe. In its broadest sense, learning can be defined as a process of progressive change from ignorance to knowledge, from inability to competence, and from indifference to understanding. In much the same manner, instruction—or education—can be defined as the means by which we systematize the situations, conditions, tasks, materials, and opportunities by which learners acquire new or different ways of thinking, feeling, and doing.

Learning and Development

If learning and teaching are complementary processes of which we should be mindful, learning and development are even more so. It is obvious that learning in infancy and early childhood is dependent upon the growth and maturation of the individual. Certain skills, such as walking and talking, cannot be learned until the child reaches some particular level of neuromuscular maturation. Growth and/or maturation are thus defined as changes that are not dependent upon learning, and parents are often advised to withhold various forms of training until their child is sufficiently mature. Whereas learning may occur as the result of direct stimulation and encouragement, maturation is viewed as a natural, unfolding process that cannot be accelerated without appreciable risk.

What is obvious in children is not so obvious in adolescents and adults. Stages of development are discernible throughout life, but the influence of developmental stages on student learning in college is a relationship but recently studied. Nevitt Sanford's (1962) classic, *The American College*, was most effective in calling attention to the importance of developmental processes in college students, but student development on most campuses continues as a responsibility of deans of students and not as an academic function. The recent reemergence of developmental psychology, nonetheless, suggests a robust interest in the changes that may be attributed to development instead of formal instruction. As the expected goals and outcomes of higher education have become more diverse and as many older, more mature students have taken advantage of educational opportunities, the need for a better understanding of learning *and* development has intensified. The popularity of adult development, in particular, is indicative of the need to study more systematically the continuing behavioral changes that occur in early adult years, mid-life, and old age.

Learning Conditions

The conditions under which learning occurs on college campuses are many and varied. The major factors within the learning situation may be identified as: (a) the individual differences on the learners themselves—their academic ability, their previous preparation at the secondary level, and the various motives or incentives that bring them to the college classroom; (b) the nature of the learning materials, tasks, and equipment that will be involved in academic course work—including the structure and content of the academic programs themselves; (c) the nature and quality of instruction the learner receives—the conditions of practice, guidance, mode of presentation, etc.; and (d) situational or environmental variables that may be both subtle and complex in their influence on learning outcomes.

Although there has been widespread interest in institutional characteristics, such as campus climate or environment, research has not been highly successful in demonstrating the impact of such characteristics on student learning *per se*. Cooley and Lohnes (1976), among many educational researchers, believe that the individual differences of learners will always account for the larger proportion of variance in learning outcomes. Institutional, as opposed to program, characteristics are too far removed from classroom instruction to have immediate and direct influence on what students learn and how well they learn. The influence of course organization and content, instructional methods, and teacher expectations can be appreciable, however, and the means by which student performance is evaluated can sometimes be a major determinant of learning.

Other variables, conditions, and situations affecting learning at the college level include those as simple as class size and those as complex as the various forms of reinforcement, feedback, or knowledge of results. Although the research supporting the influence of such variables is less than rigorous, the consistency with which some findings are reported and their compatibility with human expectations give them appreciable credence.

Class size is the perfect example. As one of the simplest classroom variables that might affect learning, class size is seldom dismissed as irrelevant. Small classes are consistently preferred to large classes by teaching faculty, and research, with all its faults, appears to support their good judgment in such matters. Glass and Smith (1979) recently brought the blessings of meta-analysis to bear on the topic and they readily conclude that small classes do indeed contribute to student learning. Suggested but not yet demonstrated is a point of diminishing returns for class smallness. For most college faculty, it is distinctly possible that some classes are too small to bring out the best of professorial behavior. In other words, there is no evidence that the best teaching-learning arrangement is a one-on-one confrontation between Mark Hopkins and a student on the other end of the log.

Order of presentation is a condition of instruction that joins many curricular debates. Whether the presentation of subject matter in a course is to be logical—proceeding from the general to the specific or building from the specific to the general—or chronological is often a matter of controversy that research cannot resolve without bringing in the nature and content of the subject matter. A random order is never advocated, but the manner in which some undergraduate courses are organized could have the same effects.

The extent to which college instructors can reinforce student learning is necessarily limited. Faculty members seldom have the influence that classmates, peers, and other groups have, but they do control academic credit and grades. The constructive use of course examinations or instructor-made tests for purposes of feedback or knowledge of results is only hinted at in research literature, but the negative aspects of irresponsible examining and grading practices have been documented (Milton and Edgerly, 1977). A direct implication is that course examinations have both motivational and information properties that more college instructors would do well to exploit. In many classes, midterms and end-of-course examinations are the only opportunities students have for active participation. In virtually all classes, however, course examinations are a major determinant of final grades.

More than any other learning psychologist, Robert Gagne (1977) has tried to specify the conditions under which human learning occurs. In Gagne's view, learning takes place when external events in the form of stimuli and internal events in the form of memories affect the learner in such a way as to produce a change in performance. Instruction is defined as external events that are deliberately planned and arranged. The internal events that effect changes in performance are accounted for by information-processing models of learning and memory. The outcomes of learning are thus varied, but Gagne believes that most of them can be subsumed under five major capabilities: (1) intellectual skills, (2) cognitive strategies, (3) verbal information, (4) motor skills, and (5) attitudes. The events of learning *per se* are identified as: (a) sensory attending and selective perception, (b) storage in short-term memory, (c) encoding, (d) storage in long-term memory, (e) retrieval and response generation, and (f) feedback or reinforcement.

Much to his credit, Gagne has been directly concerned with the educational implications of his research. By defining instruction as the deliberate arrangement of the required conditions of learning, Gagne has given strong emphasis to instructional planning, design, management, and development. Many faculty members in higher education will see Gagne's views as being more relevant to industrial and/or military training and development than to college teaching, but there are many implications in his work that deserve attention. The most pertinent may be the emphasis that Gagne gives the structure or organization of instruction and the advantages of breaking down learning tasks into their less complex components. The inescapable message in all of Gagne's writing is that if instruction is to assist or enhance student learning, instruction must be designed for that specific purpose.

Methods of Instruction

Following the individual differences of learners, the most important condition of learning surely must be the methods of instruction that are employed for purposes of education, training, or development. Faith in methods of instruction is so pronounced in educational circles that Cross (1976) writes of an instructional revolution that has taken place as new or different methods of instruction have supplanted traditional or conventional methods in college classrooms. Technological change and innovation are forces that have spurred numerous efforts to instruct students in a better, easier, more efficient manner than lectures and classroom discussions. Many of these efforts have taken the form of individualized, self-paced modes of instruction in which the learner achieves a mastery of specific units and/or modules before proceeding to advanced or more specialized units (Baker, 1973; Frase, 1975).

The rubric of individualized instruction includes a host of alternative arrangements under which college students learn. Many of the assumptions built into individualized modes of instruction are variations on themes enunciated by an older generation of psychologists who took a functionalistic approach to learning and who worked within a context of human associative learning (see McGeoch and Irion, 1952). Others are the articulation of behavioral principles that were either explicit or implied in the work of experimental psychologists working in the field of learning. Keller (1968), in the most dramatic example, turned behavioral psychology to good advantage by building into an instructional system such assumptions as: (a) self-pacing, according to the time that the learner has; (b) breaking the learning task down into more manageable units; (c) using classroom lectures primarily for motivational purposes; (d) detailed assignments that actively involved learners; and (e) frequent testing and immediate feedback.

In viewing the individualization of learning as an alternative to classroom lectures and group discussions, Cross (1976) points out that self-pacing, active participation, clear and explicit goals, small lesson units, and feedback are basic principles upon which all individualized education is based. The application of these principles can be found in programmed instruction, computer-assisted instruction, and individually prescribed instruction, (IPI) as well as Keller's personalized system of instruction (PSI). The ordering of learning sequences so that students will master each step as they proceed is a principle that is crucial to mastery learning, audio-tutorial methods, and various other learning systems. Effectiveness in the application of such a principle is contingent upon knowledge of results for the learner and implies either self-grading tests and examinations or other means of immediate and direct feedback. The assessment of learner performance and direct reporting of the results are instructional chores for which the computer is particularly well adapted.

As mentioned previously, technological applications are strong features of many efforts to provide alternatives to traditional methods of instruction. The use of technology almost always imply, however, that learning tasks and materials must be analyzed in terms of the subgoals and subskills that learners may pursue and apply. Learning must be viewed as a process consisting of steps, stages, or phases that must be articulated, and the uses of technology must be seen as instrumental to particular parts of the process instead of the overall sequence of events. It is for this reason, as well as others, that technological innovations have not had the impact on teaching and learning that many of their early advocates anticipated.

Before leaving the subject of instructional methods, it is well to suggest that most of the instruction in most college classrooms continues along conventional lines. McKeachie and Kulik (1975) believe that each instructional advance has failed to meet the high expectations with which it was greeted. There is little doubt that Keller's PSI is an attractive mode of instruction for most students, that students will spend more time and effort working with the system, and that they will report learning more than they would have in lecture courses. Unfortunately, Keller's PSI and all other individualized learning require forms of self-management that many learners have not mastered. Kulik, Kulik, and Cohen (1979) report that the completion rate for PSI courses is as high as it is for conventional courses, but given the appreciable self-selection that is involved in PSI courses and the experience of high withdrawal rates on many campuses, it is best to conclude that alternative learning is not an alternative for all students.

Trends in Theory and Research

Theory and research in learning have been dominated by the schools of psychology that gained ascendance in the early years of the 20th century and by the generation of psychologists who sought during the 1930s and 1940s to establish general theories of behavior based on learning. The influence of the early behaviorists, gestaltists, and associationists is still in evidence, and despite the hegemony of cognitive psychology in the past twenty years the theoretical and empirical questions raised by Edward L. Thorndike, John B. Watson, Edwin R. Guthrie, Clark L. Hull, Edward C. Tolman, Kurt Lewin, and B. F. Skinner are seldom ignored for long. Whether answered by their many productive students or by later generations of researchers, the questions posed early in learning research continue to provide either a point of departure or a critical background for theory and research. Some of the more crucial questions may be identified as follows:

1. How many kinds of learning are necessary to account for the behavior in which psychologists are interested? Distinctions were quickly made between classical conditioning, in which the conditioned response was autonomic, and instrumental conditional, in which the learned response was muscular. Skinner's respondent and operant behavior required a somewhat similar distinction, and Mowrer's (1960) work is an explicit two-factor theory of learning, with its distinctions between "sign learning" and "solution learning." Gagne's work implies that there are at least five kinds of learning that are relevant to education.

2. Are there basic processes of learning that can account for the acquired behavior of humans, apes, rats, pigeons, and other species not obviously governed by instinct? Watson apparently believed conditioning to be such a mechanism, and Hull contended that the same principle of reinforcement was involved in all learned behavior. Association has been accepted by many as a basic process underlying ideational or verbal learning. Other psychologists, such as Gagne, see a need for several basic forms of learning, such as learning to respond to signals, trial-and-error or stimulus-response learning, and associative or sequential learning. Related to this question are the nature and extent of learning that may be species-specific and whether or not there are processes of human learning that cannot be ascribed to other species or computers.

3. What is *it* that is learned? Do we learn specific responses and/or patterns of behavior, or do we learn to connect or associate responses to differential stimuli and/or situations? In learning, do we acquire habits and skills *or* cognitive structures, in the form of expectancies, schemata, or images? In learning to run a maze, does a rat learn to follow a path or to go to a particular place where food is waiting? This may be the basic question that separates behaviorists from cognitivists.

4. What are the necessary conditions of practice in response acquisition? Can learning occur without practice or some form of trial-and-error? Is a response acquired instantly as an insight into the inner relations of a problem? Guthrie is the foremost advocate of one-trial or

all-or-none learning, while Hull best represents the view that learning proceeds in incremental stages. Thorndike believed most fervently in trial-and-error learning, while the gestalt psychologists, of course, are responsible for much of what we know about insight learning.

5. What is the nature of the reinforcement that presumably accounts for the fixation of a learned response? Is it drive reduction, as the S-R theorist so often contends, or is it confirmation of an expectancy, as Tolman so aptly proposed? Does contiguity of stimulus and response alone account for the acquisition of a response, as classical conditioning apparently implies, or is such further kind of feedback of knowledge of results necessary for a response to become part of a learner's repertoire? Reinforcement is apparently all-important to a good Skinnerian, while gestaltists make good use of their concept of closure.
6. To what extent are consciousness, memory, active attention, and other central states of human nervous system involved in learning? Working with animals as laboratory subjects, behaviorists have preferred not to involve mental or unspecified brain states as explanatory constructs in learning. Skinner knowingly treats inner states or conditions as unknown and irrelevant variables. Cognitive theorists, needless to say, regard inner events, states, or conditions as crucial.
7. And finally, how can we account for the disappearance of acquired behavior after it has been well mastered? Do skills and habits dissipate for lack of reinforcement? Because we no longer use them frequently? Or because of interference from later learning? This question has been important to psychologists because the best evidence of experimental control might be the fashioning of a learned response, its extinction, and then its restoration. Such a feat can give solid credence to the psychologist's explanation of the particular response and the research methods employed.

The Status of Theory

Theories of learning should serve, as theories in other disciplines do, to define a field of inquiry in terms of its boundaries and its significant features. To serve well, a theory should incorporate the empirical or research findings that are accepted by active researchers and it should suggest new or different lines of inquiry and analysis that should be fruitful. The extent to which a theory implies application to professional or practical problems is a lesser criterion in the eyes of theorists and front-line researchers.

Judged by the research that has been stimulated over the past fifty years, behavioral theories of learning have been enormously successful. Although not successful in accomplishing its specific objective to generate a general theory of behavior, Clark Hull's hypothetico-deductive system has been most productive in stimulating experimental inquiry into the problems and issues of learning. Although avowedly a theoretical, B. F. Skinner's work has been quite provocative. In much the same manner, Kurt Lewin's writings have influenced at least two generations of researchers and theorists. E. R. Guthrie's work did not lead to a clustering of psychologists known as "Guthrienians," but his work does continue to be discussed and his influence is still evident. Much the same can be said for E. L. Thorndike and E. C. Tolman.

The theoretical issues of the 1930s and 1940s entered a new phase in the 1950s when the lines were rather clearly drawn between neo-behaviorists and cognitive theorists, a group strongly influenced by gestalt psychology. Unfortunately for the educational uses of learning theory, researchers sought better control of their experimental variables and resorted to explanatory constructs that would enable them to predict responses and/or acquired behavior that was highly specified. Such research was guided by miniature theories and models—not by grand systems or theories. The outcome in many instances was a careful experimental verification of acquired behavior that was less and less consequential for training, development, and educational purposes.

There is appreciable irony, therefore, in the possibility that as higher education encountered a need for systematic, verified knowledge about learning processes and their implications for education beyond high school, learning theory and research were quite remote. There was little that active researchers and learning theorists could tell college faculty about the learning that took place in their classrooms. There was almost nothing that learning researchers could say about what took place in libraries, laboratories, and computer centers.

Not the least failure of learning theory was the inability of researchers to agree on an acceptable typology for learning. Neither the neo-behaviorists nor the cognitive psychologists offered a taxonomy that made sense to college instructors who were as specialized in their research and teaching interests as the psychologists were in theirs.

A taxonomy with some promise did emerge in the 1950s when Bloom et al. (1956) published a taxonomy of educational objectives in the "cognitive domain." Cognitive objectives were divided into six major categories identified as: (1) knowledge, (2) comprehension, (3) application, (4) analysis, (5) synthesis, and (6) evaluation. A later volume (Krathwohl, Bloom, and Masia, 1964) dealt with the "affective domain" of educational outcomes and identified five categories as: (1) awareness, (2) responding, (3) valuing, (4) organizing, and (5) generalizing. A third volume, dealing with psychomotor skills, appeared much later, after interest in educational taxonomies was no longer apparent. For a while Bloom's taxonomy, as the first volume became known, was discussed among college and university faculty members, but interest was not sustained except for occasional research projects and a few planning efforts. Neither the affective nor the psychomotor "domains" had great appeal for college faculty, a fact that may be attributed to the reluctance of faculty members to find out what a "domain" was and to take seriously educational objectives expressed as gerunds.

A more direct application of learning theory may be seen in the efforts of some psychologists to translate theories of learning into a workable theory of instruction. Jerome Bruner (1960, 1966) set the pace for later psychologists by emphasizing the structure of knowledge as the content of what is taught and the scholar's methods of inquiry as the means by which students should learn. Bruner saw a theory of instruction as prescriptive insofar as it set forth rules for achieving knowledge or skills. A theory of instruction is also normative, as it establishes criteria for learning and states the conditions under which those criteria are met.

Atkinson (1972), Glaser (1976), and of course Gagne (1974) contributed significantly to developing theories of instruction by advocating, respectively, a decision-theoretic analysis of the instructional process, the systematic analysis of competent performance, and the implications of educational technology. In 1969 instructional psychology was officially recognized as an established area of inquiry and analysis when Gagne and Rohwer published the first review of related research in the *Annual Review of Psychology*.

Recent Research Trends

In reviewing the psychology of learning between 1960 and 1980, James Greeno (1980) sees a radical shift from studying changes in behavior to a concern with stochastic models that specify the probability of learned responses. The statistical analysis of rote memory, paired associates learning, and problem-solving protocols gives better insight into the structure and processes of memory. Learning, if that is what such researchers are studying, is viewed as structural networks of concepts and actions that link network components in schematic form. Although Greeno suggests that the time is now right for the analysis of learning as the acquisition of knowledge, his view of learning and knowledge is better comprehended as the analysis and/or processing of language.

Bower (1981) sees research on the learning process as accelerating and speculates that several thousand psychologists and scientists in related fields are now at work on the problems of learning. Unfortunately for those who seek some unity or coherence in learning theory, behavioral research is increasingly diversified and much better suited for identifying "subproblems" or subjects for further in-depth analysis than for arriving at working organizations that might be applicable in training, development, and education. Only in the area of behavioral modification and biofeedback does there appear to be a concern for direct and immediate application.

Cognitive psychologists also appear to be overly concerned with model building and the networking of subroutines in cognition. Much of this research has resulted in better comprehension of short-term memory, the functions of organization in long-term memory, and the different kinds of memory that may be utilized in information processing, but the educational implications of many suggestive leads are often ignored. In many cases where the educational implications of research might be discussed, there is a marvelous leap from minute research details to global and sweeping instructions for classroom teachers.

Glaser (1982, 1984) provides a welcome antidote to structural networking by suggesting that: (a) knowledge may be specific to the fields of study where that knowledge was acquired; and (b) the domain-specific knowledge we have acquired may influence appreciably the way in which we acquire new knowledge, solve problems, and comprehend or process information. Glaser is even more on target when he contends that a psychology of instruction should understand and facilitate the changes in cognition and performance that occur as each of us moves from status as a novice to status as an expert. A theory of instruction cannot be based on "artificial laboratory tasks" but must be related to the analysis of educational processes and outcomes.

General Principles of Learning

The advances of learning theory tell us little about the empirical findings, warranted generalizations, or laws of learning presumably established by learning research. There are many reasons why a general theory of behavior did not emerge from the confident efforts of theorists in the 1930s and 1940s, but something of a mystery is involved in the fate of lawlike hypotheses in which learning was the primary explanatory construct. The robustness of learning theory and research in the 1950s apparently convinced many psychologists that lawlike hypotheses or general principles of learning had been experimentally verified and thus the application of those hypotheses or principles to education was sufficiently warranted.

Granting the disappointments of theory construction in the 1950s and the increasing interest in model building, there were at that time a dozen or more empirical findings that many psychologists believed to be substantiated by the research literature. These psychologists need not agree on the theoretical underpinnings or explanatory constructs involved in the establishment of empirical findings, but they could acknowledge a creditable research basis for some well-intended generalizations or working hypotheses. Among the most visible were the following:

1. Learning is dependent upon the capacities of the learner.
2. Learning is a function of the conditions of practice and/or instruction imposed upon the learner.
3. Learning materials and tasks are more easily mastered when they are meaningful, i.e., when they are suitably organized, have a logically related part or components, and specify the conditions or circumstances under which they will be used or applied.
4. Learning is facilitated by knowledge of results—especially if that knowledge is immediate and specific.
5. The transfer of learning is dependent upon the similarities of the learning tasks and/or the similarities of principles and work methods that can be applied in the transfer situation.
6. Learning is related to the degree and quality of learner motivation, i.e., learners apparently perform better when motivation is intrinsic (self-generated?) instead of extrinsic (imposed by others?) *and* reward is to be preferred over punishment.
7. Learning is also related to the learner's level of aspiration—and the learner's experiences with success or failure in striving to reach certain levels of aspiration.

The wording of these principles obviously cuts across several fields of research and a diversity of theoretical preferences. The principles are derived from the work of earlier generations and reveal the influence of Hermann Ebbinghaus and Ivan Pavlov. "Laws of association" are very much a part of these tenets and date as far back as Aristotle's laws of similarity, contrast, and contiguity. Their value as learning principles, however, may be seen in the research they stimulated. Derived from or implicit in such principles are the following corollaries and/or testable hypotheses:

1. Learning is an active process and not the passive reception of stimuli or information.
2. Motivation is a necessary condition of learning, but excessive motivation may not be conducive to learning effectiveness.

3. Intrinsic motivation may be preferable to extrinsic motivation but is seldom possible with human subjects—thus researchers must be satisfied to control incentives and not motives *per se*.
4. Some experience with success is necessary to develop a tolerance for failure.
5. Guidance in training can be effective if given early and in relatively small doses.
6. Transfer of training is facilitated by an understanding of relationships—*but* there is no substitute for repetitive practice in the acquisition and development of a skill.
7. Training methods must take into consideration not only the product of learning methods but the process as well, i.e., consideration must be given not only to "what to do" but "how to do it."

The Decline and Fall?

In his contribution to Sanford's *The American College*, Wilbert McKeachie (1962) provided a commendable review of learning research as it then related to the problems of college instruction. If general principles and/or laws of learning were not firmly established, they still gave good instruction and guidance to college instructors who would but take the time to test their implications. Twelve years later in two articles, McKeachie (1974, 1974b) found the status of such principles of learning to be much in doubt. He pointed out that previously accepted principles or laws had been derived mostly from research involving animals, which better control of experimental variables was permissible but unlikely to produce assistance in classroom instruction. In studies with human subjects, who have greater ability to conceptualize and relate, the "laws of learning" were fading.

McKeachie believed that only two principles of learning held consistently. These were: (1) active participation is still better than passive learning, and (2) meaningful learning is still more effective than rote memory. Other principles apparently do not hold because education is an interactive situation in which the conditions, materials, and tasks of learning are different—and much more complex. The learning of students in school and college thus is an interaction of numerous complex variables over an extended period of time.

In 1966 Hilgard, in the third edition of his authoritative *Theories of Learning* (and coauthored for the first time with Gordon Bower), pointed out that learning might be better understood as a form of species-specific behavior and as theory-related constructs. Research had resulted in better analyses of learning tasks and the struggle for theoretical supremacy was no longer a private affair for behaviorists; the camps were now divided into behavioral and cognitive theorists. Under the former's banner, Hilgard and Bower found such principles as (a) active learning, (b) repetitive practice, (c) reinforcement, and (d) drive constructs as motivation. New or emerging principles located under behavioral banners were: (a) stimulus generalization and discrimination as a kind of *modus operandi*, (b) the acquisition of novel responses through the imitation of models, and (c) the necessity of dealing with conflicts and frustrations.

In the cognitive camp Hilgard and Bower found: (a) new implications for the perceptual features of the task, i.e., how it appeared to learners; (b) the organization of complex wholes out of simplified wholes instead of disjointed parts; (c) the supremacy of learning with understanding; (d) feedback as correct information; (e) the relevance of goal setting; and (f) findings concerning divergent and convergent thinking. A third group of theorists, dealing with social/personal and motivational characteristics, evidently subscribed to principles related to: (a) the abilities of learners, (b) the cultural relativity of learning, (c) developmental concepts, (d) the motivational properties of internal states, (e) the organization of values and motives, and (f) group influences.

It is significant that where the second edition of Hilgard (1956) concludes with discussions of education and training—and research implications that would bridge the gap "from the laboratory to the classroom"—the concluding chapters of the 1966 edition cast the application of learning principles in a research and development mold. Hilgard saw at least six stages in a process ranging from basic research to developmental efforts leading to advocacy and adoption. The "era of great debates" was obviously over in 1966 and general theories were no longer advocated by great men—with the exception, of course, of B. F. Skinner.

Jumping the fourth edition of Hilgard and Bower (1975), we find in Bower's (1981) fifth revision a concluding chapter dealing with "Applications to Education." Principles of learning are reduced to "ideas from learning theory useful in education," and such recognition that can be given older concepts and principles is at the expense of Bower's cautious wording. The presence of behaviorists (or S-R theorists) and cognitivists, nonetheless, is much in evidence:

1. For the behaviorist, educational goals should be specified in concrete—behavioral terms. This should only be done through careful analysis of learning tasks or skills—and it should permit a "shaping procedure" in which complex skills are acquired through a sequence of less complex tasks.
2. Active responding (manipulating, relating, reciting, etc.) is still advantageous to learning.
3. For academic skills like reading, writing, and arithmetic, there is still no substitute for recitation and repeated practice.
4. Prescribed study guides may indeed have a place in college. Rehearsal-and-review techniques, such as Frank Robinson's (1946) SQ3R method of study, can help!
5. Reinforcement can be effective if directed to "task-relevant behaviors." It will be more effective, however, if students learn to direct and reinforce their own study and learning tasks.
6. Counterconditioning might be effective in coping with test anxiety.
7. The learner's motives are best translated as goals and interests—and goal setting can be effective in motivating students.
8. Learning can be facilitated through the "perpetual structuring" of learning tasks when "the essential features of the problem" are highlighted.
9. Understanding, as opposed to rote memorization, is still preferable.
10. Mnemonic devices and other memory aids can be effective when factual details must be remembered.

It is obvious from Bower's comprehensive survey of learning theory and research (577 pages, over 1,250 references) that the applications of learning theory and research to education have been directed primarily to the development of theories of instruction. One answer to questions about the status of learning theory and research thus must be that much of the interest and effect was channeled into the development of instructional theories and/or systems. The search for uniform, lawlike regularities in learning became, for many researchers, a process of developing systems and models that could account for highly specific behavioral patterns under conditions of instruction.

Of Time and Place

A more definite detouring of learning principles occurred in 1977 when Cronbach and Snow published *Aptitudes and Instructional Methods*. Summarized in that volume is a massive amount of research on aptitude/treatment interactions (ATI) and a convincing mass of evidence that generalizations from learning research are not easily warranted. Because the aptitudes, abilities, and interests of students interact in diverse ways with instructional conditions and methods, the inferences to be drawn from learning research may be confined to specific results on particular occasions. The relation of human differences to learning outcomes is thus reintroduced with detrimental impact on broad or sweeping generalities.

Unlike programmed instruction and mastery learning, the interactions of learner characteristics and instructional methods imply that time or learning rate is not the dominant variable affecting learning outcomes. Neither does the Cronbach-Snow volume suggest that systematic modes of instruction can greatly reduce individual differences in learning performance. To the contrary, there is ample evidence that individual differences influence both the amount of learning and the rate of learning under any given instructional conditions. Also implied is the possibility that instructional effectiveness may be facilitated or impeded by learner characteristics in subtle and unanticipated ways.

The direct implication of Cronbach and Snow's work is that in education, training, and development we must be satisfied with tentative conclusions, particular conjectures, or probabilistic truths instead of definitive research findings. Researchers should be reluctant to generalize their findings beyond their research subjects, their specific characteristics, the particular mode of instruction involved, and the peculiarities of the learning situation investigated. Learning principles thus become highly qualified and carry the full length of implication, they become statements about specific occurrences at a particular time and place. To wit: some students can learn some subjects better under some teachers than they can learn other subjects under other teachers.

Gagne and Dick (1983) reported six years later that interest in aptitude/treatment interactions remained high, with continuing study of learner characteristics such as anxiety, achievement via independence as opposed to achievement via conformity, and crystallized versus fluid or analytic intelligence. New learner attributes thus continue to be identified by researchers, and ATI research continues unabated.

Learning and Cognitive Psychology

The influence of cognitive psychology is quite evident in the directions taken by learning theorists and researchers since 1960. Miller, Galanter, and Pribram (1960) introduced many psychologists to the seminal work of Herbert Simon and other researchers who were making excellent use of computers in simulating human decision-making and problem-solving behavior. In his presidential address to the American Psychological Association, D. O. Hebb (1960) spoke of behaviorism as only the first stage of a revolution in psychology and urged his colleagues to get on with the second stage—the study of mental and/or mediating processes. Other psychologists began to take seriously the work of Piaget (Berlyne, 1964), and of course, 1960 was the year in which Bruner's *Process of Education* was published with modest expectations by Harvard University Press.

The significance of cognitive theory is seen most quickly in its impact on verbal learning and memory. Anderson and Bower (1973) were among many researchers who reintroduced the study of memory as a valuable contribution to research on learning, convincing their readers in the meantime that the modeling of short-term and long-term memory gave good insight into the information-processing capabilities of learners. The investigation of mnemonic devices (Bower, 1970; Higbee, 1979) is again permissible and the study of mental imagery (Paivio, 1971; Shepard, 1978) is again shown to be fascinating, as well as worthwhile. And in 1980, Donald A. Norman could entitle an article "What Goes On in the Mind of the Learner" without fear of psychologic excommunication.

As the star of cognitive psychology rose, verbal learning could be interpreted as the encoding and retrieval of information that may be organized in many ways. The ease or efficiency with which information could be retrieved became a matter of its mode of representation and whether or not it was encoded for ready access. Bruner (1966) wrote convincingly of enactive, iconic, and symbolic forms of representation. Knowledge was at last recognized by psychologists as the encoding of propositions in which the basic unit of thought was a subject-predicate coupling. Human facility in recalling meaningful materials was thus clarified because such materials have a structure that is more than just its sequence.

For education, the impact of cognitive psychology has been stated best by Wittrock and Lumsdaine (1977) in contrasting cognitive and behavioristic models (p. 418):

> By contrast, a cognitive approach emphasizes the elaborations which the learner performs on information more than the features of instruction. Cognitive approaches emphasize that one can learn from observing others, by watching a model, by viewing a demonstration, by listening to a lecture, by being told, by reading a book, by constructing images, and by elaborating words into sentences.

Never have traditional modes of learning and teaching been given a stronger or more timely reprieve!

Cognitive Styles

Nowhere is the contrast between behaviorists and cognitivists more pronounced than in the cognitivists' enthusiasm for cognitive styles. Behaviorists can appreciate, perhaps, the importance of structure or organization in cognition and perceive some degree of similarity of such constructs with those of learning capacities or learning abilities that may, on occasion, appear to be general. The notion of individualized, habitual, or preferential modes of information processing may impress the behaviorist, nonetheless, as producing too loose a rack on which to hang explanatory constructs of learning. The extent to which cognitive styles are characteristic or typical, have adaptive value, or serve as organizational or controlling mechanisms is unknown to behaviorists; cognitivists are never in doubt about the existence of cognitive styles and find their study fascinating.

Messick (1976) has identified cognitive style as an individual's preferred way of organizing what he or she sees and remembers or thinks about. The test of a cognitive style is evidently in the consistency with which individuals organize and process information in a characteristic manner. Learning and other behavior thus are seen as functions of individual differences in cognitive and creative functioning. Other personal characteristics, or personality traits, are viewed in a context of the individual's "stylistic consistencies."

Tyler (1978) has written of the different styles of conceptualization and the patterning of activities that may be the most important characteristics of individuals. Although the term "structure" has too many architectural connotations to please Tyler, she believes the meaning of individuality to be found in the organized processes and activities that serve the individual's purposes in life.

Carefully distinguishing between cognitive styles and intellectual abilities, Messick defines over a dozen cognitive styles that he believes to be substantiated by research. Among these are conceptualizing styles, such as Tyler described. Children apparently form concepts by using functional relations, while adolescents are inclined to analyze the descriptive features of what they observe. Having gone through such previous stages, adults evidently rely more heavily on the inferences they can make from categories or classes.

Other cognitive styles identified by Messick are: (1) breadth of categorization, in which individuals show a preference for inclusive or exclusive categories; (2) compartmentalization, in which ideas and objects may be isolated in discrete, rigid categories; (3) conceptual complexity versus conceptual simplicity; (4) leveling versus sharpening in the recall of memories; (5) reflection versus impulsivity in thinking; and (6) risk taking versus cautiousness in judgment.

The cognitive style that has been most carefully studied, however, is that of field independence versus field dependence (Witkin, 1976). Research on this particular style began in the 1950s and has continued since that time. The polarized ends of the continuum appear to be analytical thinking and global thinking. One end suggests a pronounced tendency to articulate the separate figures and features of what is observed and to resist domination by the global or totalistic characteristics of one's perceptions. The other end is a preferred reaction to people, places, and events as an undifferentiated complex. As Witkin and other researchers make clear, there are no social or cultural criteria by which others can decide which mode of perception is the best for everyone.

The relevance of field dependence or independence for education has been underscored by Witkin (1976), Tyler (1978), Cross (1976), and others. Witkin views the application of cognitive styles to education as being in its beginning phase but thinks that tests emerging from the research on cognitive styles might eventually replace intelligence tests. He believes field independence to be particularly relevant to the decisions and choices that college students must make in their selection of a major field and subsequent career. Tyler points out that field-dependent teachers may prefer group discussion as a mode of teaching instead of lectures and individual projects. Field-dependent learners may prefer social forms of reinforcement for the studying they do, and they may be more easily attracted to careers that involve human services. Cross finds much about field dependency that pertains to the New Students she describes in her book, *Beyond the Open Doo*r. Both groups are people-oriented, sensitive to the judgment of others, and somewhat deferential to authority. Neither group is noted for analytical problem solving, active participation in class discussions, or firm control of their individual destinies.

In their studies of aptitude/treatment interactions Cronbach and Snow (1977) gave good attention to cognitive styles. Cognitive skills, structures, and styles qualify as characteristics of learners that may forecast the probability of success and thus are included under the category of aptitude. Cronbach and Snow doubt, however, the cognitive styles and other such contrasts can be measured so as to give information that is independent of general abilities. They conclude that studies on conceptual level, cognitive complexity, and field dependence are too inconsistent to permit generalizations.

Learning Strategies

If the distinctions among cognitive structures, skills, and styles are difficult to specify, they are even more difficult for cognitive styles and cognitive strategies. Messick (1976) assures us that (p. 6):

> . . . it is important to distinguish cognitive styles, which are high level heuristics that organize and control behavior across a wide variety of situations, from cognitive strategies, which are decision-making regularities in information processing that at least in part are a function of the conditions of particular situations.

As much as some of us may think that Messick and his cited authorities have confused cognitive strategies with cognitive tactics, there is a possibility that styles are generalized and unconsciously acquired while strategies are deliberately adopted. Cronbach and Snow (1977) place "style" midway between "ability" and "strategy" and more or less suggest that strategies are the operations of organizing and processing while styles are the consistent manner in which we do so. The extent to which strategies are a function of style is, nonetheless, an open question. Cognitive styles appear much more relevant for the study of perception and personality than they do for the investigation of learning. In the latter, there is better reason to believe that consciously employed strategies are more likely to be verified as a determinant of learning.

The ingenious maneuvers of college students to obtain course credits and high grades are indicative of the great diversity of learning skills and strategies that they bring to the college classroom. Students may or may not recognize knowledge, competence, and personal development as the substantive and enduring values of higher education, but there can be no doubt that they see academic credits and grades as a means to academic credentials. The strategies and tactics that college students display in such quests are undoubtedly stylistic on many occasions, and the difference between styles and strategies, insofar as understanding learner behavior is concerned, may be meaningless. Both styles and strategies would seem closely tied to an incredible range of student sophistication concerning educational goals, learning outcomes, and instructional purposes.

Efforts to measure or assess learning styles and/or strategies have been made by Reichmann and Grasha (1974), Canfield (1976), and others. Reichmann and Grasha define six learning styles that they believe to be characteristic of students: (1) independent learning—by students who like to think for themselves and work on their own; (2) dependent learning—by students who learn only what is required; (3) collaborative learning—in which students cooperate and share ideas; (4) competitive learning—in which students seek to outperform each other; (5) participant learning—in which students may learn the most from class discussion and interaction; and (6) avoidant learning—as shown by uninterested or overwhelmed students.

Canfield views learning styles in terms of the conditions under which learning occurs, the content of what is learned, and the dominant mode by which students learn. Independence in learning, deference to authority, competitiveness, and peer relations, as conditions of learning, would appear to correspond to similar scales in Reichmann and Grasha's inventory. Learning content, however, is seen as basically numeric, qualitative, inanimate, or people-oriented. Dominant modes of learning are identified as listening, reading, iconic, and direct experience. Also germane to Canfield's view of learning are the expectations of learners, as reflected in predicted levels of student performance.

Unfortunately for those who would use inventories of learning styles or strategies in their instruction, the technical merits of such inventories are limited. The reliability of many of the scales must be suspect because of their brevity, and the construct of validation of the inventories is by no means assured. It is significant, therefore, that Reichmann and Grasha speak of their efforts as a rational approach to developing and assessing the construct validity of an inventory.

The possibilities of matching learning styles or strategies with learning conditions and opportunities and with teaching styles has intrigued many researchers (for example, Andrews, 1981; Domino, 1971; and Salomon, 1972). The matching of learner characteristics with instructional treatment is based, of course, on expectations of interactions between learning and teaching efforts that will benefit learners. Cross (1976) points out that teachers, too, have cognitive styles and will teach by methods they find comfortable unless they consciously attempt teaching strategies that accommodate learner strategies. She concludes from her discussion that both teacher and students should gain insight into teaching and learning styles. She rejects any notion of "automatic matching" as counterproductive and rightly surmises that students and teachers will be happier and more productive if they are learning and teaching by methods that are compatible with personal preferences.

Messick (1976) has given attention to the problems of matching teaching and learning methods and suggests several models for matching. These include: (a) corrective matches, (b) compensatory matches, (c) capitalization matches, and (d) various combinations thereof. In combining corrective, compensatory, and capitalization models, Messick sees no reason why instruction treatments should not compensate for learner deficiencies at the same time that learner advantages or strengths are exploited.

Elsewhere in the same volume, Seymour Wapner (1976) expresses the belief that the matching of educational treatment and learner characteristics is beneficial only for subject-matter achievement. If the intent of education is to promote flexible and creative thinking, more might be gained through the mismatching of students and teachers. Wapner would seek a synergistic effect by putting learners in learning situations where opposition, contradiction, and obstacles were necessary conditions for the learner's development.

Irrespective of the difficulties in defining, assessing, and applying cognitive styles and/or learning strategies in college and university instruction, there are many reasons to believe that higher education is the beneficiary of cognitive theory and research. The greater bulk of research calls attention to teaching and learning as dual processes affecting learning outcomes and advocates a more serious effort to match teaching and learning efforts in an educationally relevant manner. Whether matched for their compatibility or their synergistic effect, the interaction of teaching styles and/or methods and learning strategies is a major challenge to undergraduate education.

Learning and Developmental Psychology

A historical view of learning suggests that in a more optimistic era there was an affinity between education and psychology that promised scientific status to both. At the time psychology was the most rapidly developing of the behavioral and social sciences, and the behavioral sciences were perceived as the basis for educational theory and practice. In a period of rapid social change, however, the relevance of behavioral psychology has often been submerged by developmental concepts and principles that explain more satisfactorily how change occurs. The same is true of differential psychology, or the psychology of individual differences.

If previously the variations of human behavior and learning were explained by individual capacities, aptitudes, abilities, interests, and preferences, there has been since the mid-1970s an appreciable inclination to explain changes in behavior by the differential development of learners. When individual A differs from individual B, the explanation might be that while each develops at his or her own pace, both are going through stages or phases of development that all are likely to go through. Individual differences in learning are thus a matter of timing—and patience presumably solves many personal problems, in the manner that Drs. Gesell and Spock once assured parents that problems of infancy and early childhood would be solved.

Leona Tyler (1978) suggests that the individual differences of learning cannot be explained without attention to the different schedules of development that learners undergo. Psychometricians who were once content to demonstrate the wide range of capacities and dispositions evident among individuals should now be dis-enamored with variation as such and become more attentive to the developmental progress individuals make as they grow and mature. Pace and phasing have their own regularities, and where once fatalism was associated with individual differences, a more realistic viewpoint implies that if individuals will continue to develop, they will eventually get to where they want to. Such a change in viewpoints is not only optimistic, but is also constructive, with profound implications for whatever we try to learn and to teach.

Benjamin Bloom (1976) says much the same thing in quite a different manner. It is his contention that schooling need not result in accentuated learner differences but could result in a more similar or common outcome for everyone. Bloom proposes that the purpose of schooling is not to produce individual differences in learning but to reduce them. While he is obviously aware that individual differences in learners will persist, he is convinced that if instruction takes place in the right way, there will be less—not more—variation in the learning that students do. To accomplish this, the schools must offer something approaching a uniform curriculum and must agree on a finite set of learning and teaching objectives that they have not agreed upon in the past.

The arrival of pluralism and diversity in education has meant too frequently that any explanation of achievement or accomplishment in terms of individual capabilities is suspect. Differences in interests, motives, and cognitive styles are permissible, but differences in aptitudes, readiness, or predisposition are suspected of genetical or hereditarian biases that are unacceptable in an egalitarian society.

In their concern with pluralism and diversity, educators have permitted many psychological insights to slip by the wayside. Too often there has been a romanticism attached to student needs and interests with the result that curricular change sometimes has been predicated on the basis of some inexcusably faulty psychology. One need not be a psychologist or a cynic to suspect that much curricular reform has been advocated with unrealistic expectations about what students were capable of learning, willing to study and learn, and actually would learn. Open classrooms, alternative schools, and nontraditional programs have occasionally been advocated for populations of students that must surely be hypothetical. Reformers and advocates of change have indeed been able to see in students what neither the students nor their teachers could see without remarkable distortions of vision.

Personal Development

The extent to which personal development has been, can be, or should be a focal point of the undergraduate curriculum is a matter of debate. Concepts of student development have remained outside the undergraduate curriculum as such, and much that would seem to be a proper concern of a liberal or general education has been able to gain a quasi-curricular status only.

The campus function in which developmental concepts have been well received, however, is the area of student services. The concept of student development became quite relevant during the 1960s, and many professionals in student services now view student development as their primary function. Miller and Prince (1978) have provided a comprehensive student development model that fully integrates developmental thinking into all areas of student affairs. They believe a developmental view should permeate all education beyond high school, focusing directly on student goals and objectives, methods of assessing progress toward those goals, and managerial techniques for organizing a developmental environment in which academic programs and student affairs would be fully merged.

It is obvious that models and theories of student development have been influenced by the developmental stages, cycles, or phases described by Piaget, Erikson, and other developmental psychologists. Developmental stages or life cycles are progressive in the sense of representing qualitative changes with increasing age. The sequence of changes is expected to be uniform but may be accelerated or retarded by environmental or cultural events. Each stage or cycle represents a structured or organized experience for the individual and may take the form of an alternation of differentiation and integration as a basic growth process.

Developmental models for students in higher education have been influenced not only by the concepts and research findings presented in Sanford's *The American College* but also by Feldman and Newcomb's (1976) extensive survey of the developmental research on college students up to that time. Both volumes offered a positivistic view of developmental change within the college setting and suggested that higher education has a liberalizing effect on the attitudes and values of students. More noticeably, college students are believed to become more confident, less dogmatic, more oriented to intellectual values, less prejudiced, better able to handle personal impulses, and less conservative on political issues. An important conclusion of Feldman and Newcomb's work is that higher education is a means by which adolescents can become adults, and continued development should be one of the goals of a college education. Such conclusions about student development have been confirmed by the later work of Bowen (1977) and Astin (1978).

Chickering (1969) has also presented a view of education in which adolescents become adults by developing their competence, emotions, autonomy, identity, interpersonal relations, purpose, and integrity. Colleges can accelerate movements among the "vectors of change" and can set tasks and conditions that will provide a bridge from one status to the other—but they can also erect barriers and retard progress. Chickering concludes, much as Feldman and Newcomb, that the impact of education is dependent upon the developmental status of the student at entry.

Perry (1970), in another frequently cited study, has identified nine stages of intellectual and ethical development in a longitudinal study of Harvard and Radcliff students. Concepts and values apparently evolve from right-or-wrong, true-or-false distinctions through a phase of skepticism and relativism to an age of commitment where meaningful choices and decisions are made and a sense of personal style and identity achieved.

Developmental concepts are increasingly advocated by a number of specialists who see a need for both the secondary school and the college to provide education for human development. These advocates believe that cognitive skills, moral reasoning, and personal character develop by stages that have a logical and predictable sequence. Lawrence Kohlberg and his co-workers (1979) have described the phases or stages that the adolescent goes through in his or her moral development. Much like Piaget's stages of cognitive development, Kohlberg's stages of moral development proceed in something of an inexorable manner, unfolding as much from internal forces as by the stimulus of outside forces. Jane Loevinger (1979) has described similar stages for ego development. Parsons, Johnston, and Durham (1979) have offered a cognitive-developmental model for aesthetic experience, suggesting in turn that intellect, morals, aesthetic sensitivities, and emotions develop in much the same manner—i.e., stages can be delineated and a sequence for development through those stages can be expected.

The conflict between formal instruction and experiential learning, traditional and nontraditional study, conventional and alternative learning, has not lessened the difficulties of providing student services within a setting where instruction is sometimes perceived as the only legitimate function. Yet there does seem to be a trend toward either using the curriculum as a means of student development or devising curricular approaches to developmental objectives (Miller and Prince, 1978). The organization of student development laboratories, mini-courses, and other quasi-curricular approaches has introduced an instructional component that relies heavily on developmental concepts and principles. Many of these efforts have been in response to new demands by students. Course and laboratory approaches have dealt with such popular and immediately relevant topics as human sexuality, human potential, group process, collegiate lifestyles, communication skills, nonverbal communication, race relations, and female potential. Other attempts have dealt more directly with leadership, self-awareness, assertiveness training, creativity, personal decision making, and academic development. Even more recently, workshops and seminars have been offered with the themes of inquiry development, inquiry strategies, developing higher-level thinking abilities, interpersonal influence, and facilitating inquiry. Such instructional efforts are said to place an emphasis on techniques, to be competency based, and to include practice in specific competencies.

The disadvantages of such quasi-curricular solutions are thought to be their excessively narrow focus on the student as subject matter, the caliber of professional training and experience on the part of course or lab leaders, and their unintended impact as a counterforce to academic and intellectual development. A more serious reservation may be the extent to which such concepts and techniques are teachable on a college campus. A contradiction may be involved in the sense that some forms of behavior are obviously developed and must be learnable but may not be teachable with the staff, resources, and situation at hand.

Quasi-curricular solutions in higher education are seldom successful in producing a lasting effort on problems and issues that may be personal. A pattern for such curricular efforts may be seen in previous efforts to deal with critical thinking, personal adjustment, study skills, and speed reading. Each has known its moment of popularity in higher education, but each has failed to find a suitable place in the curriculum per se, and each has been subject to cycles of erosion and rediscovery. The need for direct instruction in reading and study skills was rediscovered on many campuses with the advent of disadvantaged students. Regardless of whether it was called remedial, developmental, or compensatory studies, the results often demonstrated the difficulties of short-term, quasi-curricular solutions to long-term, personal deficiencies.

Adult Development

The arrival of adult students on college campuses has left some student development specialists with their models outmoded. As Harrington (1977) has pointed out, adult students now outnumber their younger classmates, and higher education is not only expected to teach them but to help them solve their own developmental problems. The popularity of Gail Sheehy's (1976) book *Passages* suggest that adults do indeed have problems and that much of adult life is a matter of getting through its predictable crises.

Hodgkinson (1974) has discussed adult development in terms of its relevance for administrators and faculty members who must continue to cope with various crises in the college or university setting.

Faculty members continue to make career choices for much of their professional lives. They may often consider options that open with experience and additional preparation, such as administration, and they must reconcile the conflicting demands of instruction, research, and service for purposes of career advancement. The crises of the thirties and forties do not appear radically different for faculty members and college administrators. Marital difficulties, divorce, career menopause, personal fears, social inadequacies, professional disappointment, and institutional frustrations are all part of the pattern for many faculty members. The necessities of coping with change may accompany new job opportunities, moving one's family, making community adjustments, and altering interpersonal relations. Identity crises may accompany professional growth and upward mobility as well as threaten personal aspirations that are inordinate.

The relevance of adult development for students in higher education has been delineated in good style by Cross (1981), Chickering (1981), Knox (1977), and Weathersby and Tarule (1980). No doubt is left about the presence of adult learners on college campuses and about the impact their presence has had or will have. Supporting evidence is provided by Aslanian and Brickell (1980), Peterson (1979), and Solmon and Gordon (1981). Antecedents for such interest in older or nontraditional students may be found in Knowles (1973) and others working in the field of adult or continuing education prior to the 1970s.

Cross does for adult learners what she did so well for the New Student. She introduces adult learners as new participants in organized learning activities and explains why they seek participation. Adult learners are likely to come from higher rather than lower socioeconomic classes and to have a higher level of educational attainment than the general population. A majority of them are women and, as a group, they are predominantly white. The reasons for seeking further learning are varied but can be described as personal and practical. They are not interested in knowledge "for knowledge's sake alone," but they do want to become better informed and they do have curiosities that they would satisfy by continuing their education. If barriers did not exist in the form of educational expenses, institutional regulations and requirements, and personal values or dispositions, there are reasons to believe adult learners would be more numerous and thus even more prominent on college campuses.

A lack of learning ability is not a barrier for most adult learners. Cross cites an abundance of evidence to suggest that learning is a function of age but only because of eventual declines in reaction time, vision, and hearing. Since each of these declines is characteristic of later rather than middle age and since there is no inevitable decline in intellectual functioning, rates of participation for adult learners could be increased significantly. A study in the University System of Georgia disclosed that performance on academic ability tests, such as the Scholastic Aptitude Test (SAT), need not be a barrier to most adult learners. When compared to entering freshmen of traditional age, older students entering college for the first time did less well only on the mathematics section of the SAT. Lower math scores are readily explained by time since high school graduation and by the subjects studied there; they do not imply a lack of quantitative ability or analytical capacities, as traditional users of the SAT have sometimes assumed (Fincher, 1983).

In brief, the impact of adult learners on teaching and learning is not felt in the learning abilities and accomplishments that typify adult learners but in the different demands and expectations they bring with them. Research gives good support to their expectation that they will be taught and evaluated differently. Adult learners are more likely to set their own learning pace, and they have definite preferences for the teaching styles that college faculty might use (Warren, 1974).

For many researchers, however, the significance of adult learners on college campuses is to be found in life-span development or the life-cycle stages. To recast institutional missions in such a manner would be to make development the heart and soul of college and university curricula. Other observers, less sanguine about adult development, see life-span development not as the content of college curricula but as a perspective that future faculty members and administrators will need (Fincher, 1981).

A Provisional Consensus

Given the abundance of implications that learning theory and research have for higher education, does it make sense to look for signs of convergence? Granting the behaviorists and the cognitivists all their theoretical and methodological differences, what can we borrow and reconcile for purposes of improving learning and teaching in American colleges? In theoretical expositions there are surely insights and viewpoints that are useful, and in empirical research findings there must be some working generalizations that are worth applying. Field-dependent educators should concede to field-independent psychologists the limitations of time and place in theory construction and verification but listen again to Ralph Tyler (1976). It was his contention that we know a great deal about stimulating and guiding learning and need not wait for final or conclusive answers from experimental research.

If, as some cognitivists suggest, we can learn from observation, we can see much on college campuses that would signify behavioral, cognitive, and developmental dimensions in student learning. We do observe changes in student behavior and we attribute many of those changes to instruction. We do detect changes in attitudes, beliefs, and values as students move from freshman classes to senior seminars and we acknowledge that personal development is difficult to program. And on many occasions, if we are observant, we can infer that students do indeed "process" knowledge and information in interesting and idiosyncratic ways. And if we reread what behavioral, cognitive, and developmental psychologists have written about the processes of learning and teaching, we might conclude that all of them are right.

The purposes of a college education have been much debated since the 1960s but they have seldom been in doubt. Students still attend college for a mixture of benefits and advantages they hope to gain. No one has contended since Cardinal Newman that higher education should serve a single, unitary purpose, and the American university might well be the most utilitarian institution since the medieval church. Yet there is reason to believe that both the objectives and the outcomes of higher education can be distilled into three major, dominant concerns: (1) knowledge, (2) competence, and (3) values.

The permissible variations are many. Howard Bowen (1977) has found more than 1,500 educational goals in the literature of Western civilization but describes "a well-educated person" with eleven characteristics. In turn, his eleven characteristics are easily sorted as either knowledge or information; skills, proficiencies, or competencies; or attitudes, beliefs, and values. All fit into the psychologically primitive categories of knowing, doing, or feeling—as those terms were once used.

If educators could agree that the behavioral, cognitive, and developmental outcomes of education are knowledge, competence, and understanding, three kinds of learning will suffice for an explanation of how those outcomes are attained. Learning theory and research suggest a form of conceptual/symbolic/verbal learning that leads to knowledge as an organized structure of information. In much the same manner, theory and research imply a form of skills/proficiency/competency learning that leads to competent or proficient performance in such activities as arts and crafts, athletics, and professional occupations.

Neither conceptual/symbolic/verbal learning nor skills/proficiency/competency learning is strictly behavioral or cognitive in form and substance, but no serious harm is done in viewing conceptual learning as primarily cognitive and skills learning as mostly behavioral. Mastery might be a useful way of identifying the outcomes of both kinds of learning—as in mastering a body of technical or specialized knowledge, or in mastering a complex skill that requires timing and sensitive manipulation. Mastery should be easier to specify, however, for skills learning because it presumably would be more observable. Both knowledge and competence, nonetheless, must be inferred from performance because neither knowledge nor competence is overt.

The acquisition of attitudes, beliefs, and values calls for a third kind of learning that may be best identified as experiential learning. "Understanding" is the most accurate term to use in discussing the outcomes of experiential learning, and it is unfortunate that the term is used in conceptual/symbolic/verbal learning when "comprehension" would be more appropriate. As the end product of experiential learning, understanding should be used in the sense of Gordon Allport's (1961) apprehension of events and experiences in relation to a larger significance or context. Understanding thus is similar in many respects to the notion of realization, as used in "realizing" a desire or ambition. It is also similar to the concept of self-actualization as used by Maslow and other personality theorists. As the outcome of experiential learning, understanding is evidenced in the choices or decisions the learner makes and in observed lines of actions that the learner may follow. Krathwohl et al. (1964) describe similar outcomes in their taxonomy of learning objectives in the affective domain.

If educators do agree that the major outcomes of learning are knowledge, competence, and understanding, they could then agree that the psychological antecedents need not be the same. Conceptual/symbolic/verbal learning might be preceded by plans or intentions to learn particular concepts, principles, facts, details. Strategies might be effective in directing the acquisition of skills, and needs or expectations might be significant antecedents of experiential learning and the understanding that presumably follows.

The three kinds of learning identified here are not without intuitive appeal and each may be observed on college campuses, or inferred from student behavior. While learners are acquiring knowledge and competence, they may also be acquiring new or different attitudes, beliefs, and values that alter their understanding of particular events and activities. Students may be greatly influenced by personal-social experiences that may or may not affect the formal instruction they receive in class. Concurrently with instruction, students may undergo changes in tastes, preferences, viewpoints, sentiments, and other facets of personality and character. Quite often experiential change will begin with an awareness of discomfort or doubt that spurs the learner to attempt to relieve or improve the situation. Having made some effort to change his state of awareness, the learner might then step back or withdraw in an attempt to make sense of the experience. This might lead, in turn, to a second effort that will permit the learner to consolidate or internalize the experience and gain an understanding that was not possible previously.

Similar "stages of learning" can be inferred from conceptual and skills learning. Cognitive learning, in particular, begins with an initial stage of attending to or receiving information and makes some effort to order or arrange the information for further processing. Intermediate stages are inferred when the learner assimilates information, recalls and interprets it at a later date, or reorganizes and verifies the information so that it can be integrated with other information. Only when the information is integrated into a large body of information does it become knowledge.

The process of skills acquisition may be more observable, with more evidence of trial-and-error learning in its early stages. Most skills learning begins, nonetheless, with an attentive selection of movements, functions, and activities that are appropriate to the task. Suitable subskills may be encoded, stored, retained, retrieved, and applied in various stages and reinforced by their effects. Mastery of specific skills or competence will later be judged from the learner's performance and will be regarded as the competency, efficiency, or ease with which the learner does what he or she could not do in the beginning.

In brief, the behavioral, cognitive, and developmental dimensions of learning suggest three forms, channels, or levels through which knowledge, competence, and understanding are attained. Within each of the three kinds of learning, stages or phases can be described as initial, intermediate, and closing. For conceptual skills, and experiential learning, the stages of progression are both similar and different. It all suggests that learning is complex, but it need not be mysterious.

Summary and Conclusions

Learning theory and research are often reviewed in the professional literature of psychologists and educational researchers. The intent of this review, however, has been specific. The relevance of learning theory and research for higher education has not been strongly emphasized in the past two decades, and there has been, some of us believe, a noticeable absence of psychological influence on curricula planning and development, instructional improvement, and the assessment or evaluation of learning. Neglect thus provides a harsh contrast with earlier periods in which the bonds of psychology and education were quite strong.

An effort has been made to define learning as the acquisition of knowledge, skill, and understanding under conditions of instruction and for later use or transfer. To serve well the purpose of education, a definition of learning should be descriptive of what actually takes place in education as well as specifying the crucial features of learning as a complex process.

The review of learning conditions and methods of instruction, as they relate to learning in higher education, has been somewhat perfunctory because both topics have either been covered more thoroughly elsewhere or are covered in other chapters of this volume. The comprehensive review of trends in theory and research is precluded by the highly specific focus of learning models and by the voluminous outpouring of research papers that address closely defined research topics or problems.

General principles of learning have been reviewed, however, with particular attention to their applicability in college instruction. Although eroded by later research, most general principles of learning would not seem disconfirmed as much as they appear to be forgotten. Where they have survived, they can be seen as a general condition of learning and not as a productive line of experimental inquiry. There are good reasons, nonetheless, to believe that efforts on the part of college instructors to adapt and to apply general principles of learning would be in the best interests of learners. Efforts to apply general principles would at least facilitate the organization of course objectives and requirements, and they should encourage a more systematic approach to instruction *per se*.

The influence of cognitive psychology and developmental psychology on learning theory and research is seen in the widespread use of cognitive and developmental concepts. Cognitive psychology has redirected many behavioristic trends, and developmental psychology has virtually replaced differential psychology. The implications for college instruction are quite pronounced, and both cognitive and developmental concepts bring a much-needed perspective to higher education in general. Information-processing models are relevant to student learning efforts, and personal development, as opposed to acquired knowledge and competence, is still a valid reason to attend college.

The attempt to synthesize cognitive, behavioral, and experiential concepts into a three-level, multiple-stage "schema" for learning is provisional only. The effort borrows generously from various researchers and theorists with no sense of liability for the misuse of constructs and insights. The schema does provide some economy of conceptualization, however, and it should suggest a better perspective on the multiple purposes and outcomes of a college education. There are many differences in what students study and learn in college, their reasons for attending, and the outcomes that are expected, but there are also many similarities. Furthermore, there are occasions when the similarities should be underscored and the differences should be reexamined. The remaining years of the twentieth century may be such a time.

References

Allport, G.W. *Pattern and Growth in Personality*. New York: Holt, Rinehart and Winston, 1961.

Anderson, J.R., and Bower, G. H. *Human Associative Memory*. Washington, D.C.: V. H. Winston, 1973.

Andrews, J.D.W. Teaching format and student style: Their interactive effect on learning. *Research in Higher Education*, 1981, *14*, 161–178.

Aslanian, C.B., and Brickell, H.M. *Americans in Transition: Life Changes as Reasons of Adult Learning*. New York: The College Board, 1980.

Astin, A.W. *Four Critical Years*. San Francisco: Jossey-Bass, 1978.

Atkinson, R.C. Ingredients for a theory of instruction. *American Psychologist*, 1972, *27*, 921–931.

Baker, E.L. The technology of instructional development. In Robert M.W. Travers (ed.), *Second Handbook of Research on Teaching*. Chicago: Rand McNally, 1973.

Bandura, A. *Social Learning Theory*. Englewood Cliffs, N.J.: Prentice-Hall, 1976.

Bandura, A., and Walters, R.H. *Social Learning and Personality Development*. New York: Holt, Rinehart & Winston, 1963.

Berlyne, D.E. Recent developments in Piaget's work. Reprinted in R.J.C. Harper, C.C. Anderson, C.M. Christensen, and S.M. Hunka (eds.), *The Cognitive Processes: Readings*. Englewood Cliffs, N.J.: Prentice-Hall, 1964.

Bloom, B.S. *Human Characteristics and School Learning*. New York: McGraw-Hill, 1976.

Bloom, B.S., Englehart, M.C., Furst, E.J., Hill, W.H., and Krathwohl, D.R. *Taxonomy of Educational Objectives: Handbook I: Cognitive Domain*. New York: David McKay, 1956.

Bowen, H.R. *Investment in Learning: The Individual and Social Value of American Higher Education*. San Francisco: Jossey-Bass, 1977.

Bower, G.H. Analysis of a mnemonic device. *American Scientist*, 1970, *58*, 496–510.

Bower, G.H., and Hilgard, E.R. *Theories of Learning*. 5th ed. Englewood Cliffs, N.J.: Prentice-Hall, 1981.

Brown, A.L., Campione, J.C., and Day, J.D. Learning to learn: On training students to learn from texts. *Educational Researcher*, 1981, *10*, 14–21.

Bruner, J. *The Process of Education*. Cambridge, Mass.: Harvard University Press, 1960.

Bruner, J.S. *Toward a Theory of Instruction*. Cambridge, Mass.: Harvard University Press, 1966.

Canfield, A.A. Learning styles inventory manual. Ann Arbor, Mich.: Humanics Media, 1980.

Chickering, A.W. *Education and Identity.* San Francisco: Jossey-Bass, 1969.

Chickering, A.W. *Experience and Learning: An Introduction to Experiential Learning.* New Rochelle, N.Y.: Change Magazine Press, 1977.

Chickering, A.W., and Associates. *The Modern American College: Responding to the New Realities of Diverse Students and a Changing Society.* San Francisco: Jossey-Bass, 1981.

Cooley, W.W., and Lohnes, P. R. *Evaluation Research in Education: Theory, Principles, and Practice.* New York: Irvington, 1976.

Coombs, A.W. Fostering maximum development of the individual. In William Van Til (ed.), *Issues in Secondary Education.* Chicago: National Society for the Study of Education, 1976.

Cronbach, L.J., and Snow, R.E. *Aptitudes and Instructional Methods: A Handbook for Research on Interactions.* New York: Irvington, 1977.

Cross, K.P. *Beyond the Open Door: New Students to Higher Education.* San Francisco: Jossey-Bass, 1971.

Cross, K.P. *Accent on Learning: Improving Instruction and Reshaping the Curriculum.* San Francisco: Jossey-Bass, 1976.

Cross, K.P. *Adults as Learners.* San Francisco: Jossey-Bass, 1981.

Dirkes, M.A. The role of divergent production in the learning process. *American Psychologist,* 1978, *33,* 815–820.

Domino, G. Interactive effects of achievement orientation and teaching style on academic achievement. *Journal of Educational Psychology,* 1971, *62,* 427–431.

Feldman, K.A., and Newcomb, T.M. *The Impact of College on Students.* San Francisco: Jossey-Bass, 1976.

Fincher, C. What is learning? *Engineering Education,* 1978, *68,* 420–423.

Fincher, C. Higher education as a stage of transition. *Research in Higher Education,* 1981, *15,* 377–380.

Fincher, C. *Adult Learners and the SAT in the University System of Georgia.* Athens: Institute of Higher Education, University of Georgia, 1983.

Frase, L.T. Advances in research and theory in instructional technology. In Fred N. Kerlinger (ed.), *Review of Research in Education.* Vol. 3. Itasco, Ill.: Peacock, 1975.

Gagne, R.M. Educational technology and the learning process. *Educational Researcher,* 1974, *3,* 3–8.

Gagne, R.M. *The Conditions of Learning.* 3d ed. New York: Holt, Rinehart & Winston, 1977.

Gagne, R.M., and Briggs, L.J. *Principles of Instructional Design.* New York: Holt, Rinehart & Winston, 1974.

Gagne, R.M., and Dick, W. Instructional psychology. *Annual Review of Psychology,* 1983, *34,* 261–295.

Gagne, R.M., and Rohwer, W.D., Jr. Instructional psychology. *Annual Review of Psychology,* 1969, *20,* 318–418.

Glaser, R. Components of a psychology of instruction: Toward a science of design. *Review of Educational Research,* 1976, *46,* 1–24.

Glaser, R. Instructional psychology: Past, present, and future. *American Psychologist,* 1982, *37,* 307–318.

Glaser, R. Education and thinking: The role of knowledge. *American Psychologist,* 1982, *39,* 93–104.

Glass, G.V., and Smith, M.L. Meta-analysis of research on class size and achievement. *Educational Evaluation and Policy Analysis,* 1979, *1,* 2–16.

Goldstein, H., Krantz, D.L., and Rains, J.D. *Controversial Issues in Learning.* New York: Appleton-Century-Crofts, 1965.

Greeno, J.G. Psychology of learning, 1960–1980: One participant's observations. *American Psychologist,* 1980, *35,* 713–728.

Guthrie, E.R. *The Psychology of Learning.* Rev. ed. New York: Harper & Row, 1952.

Hansen, K.H. (ed.). *Learning: An Overview and Update.* Washington, D.C.: U.S. Office of Education, 1976.

Harlow, H.F. The formation of learning sets. *Psychological Review,* 1949, *56,* 51–65.

Harlow, H.F. The nature of love. *American Psychologist,* 1958, *18,* 673–685.

Harrington, F.H. *The Future of Adult Education: New Responsibilities of Colleges and Universities.* San Francisco: Jossey-Bass, 1979.

Hebb, D.O. The American revolution. *American Psychologist,* 1960, *15,* 735–745.

Higbee, K.L. Recent research on visual mnemonics: Historical roots and education fruits. *Review of Educational Research,* 1979, *49,* 611–629.

Hilgard E.R. (ed.). *Theories of Learning and Instruction. Sixty-third Yearbook of the National Society for the Study of Education.* Chicago: University of Chicago Press, 1964.

Hill, W.F. *Learning: A Survey of Psychological Interpretations.* 3d ed. New York: Harper & Row, 1977.

Hodgkinson, H.L. Adult development: Implications for faculty and administrators. *Educational Record,* 1974, *55,* 263–264.

Hull, C.L. *Principles of Behavior.* New York: Appleton-Century-Crofts, 1943.

Jenkins, J.J. Remember that old theory of memory? Well, forget it. *American Psychologist,* 1974, *29,* 785–795.

Katona, G. *Organizing and Memorizing: Studies in the Psychology of Learning.* New York: Columbia University Press, 1940.

Keller, F.S. Good-bye, teacher. . . *Journal of Applied Behavior Analysis,* 1968, *1,* 79–89.

Knowles, M.S. *The Adult Learner.* Houston: Gulf, 1973.

Knox, A.B. *Adult Development and Learning.* San Francisco: Jossey-Bass, 1977.

Kohlberg, L., and Gilligan, C. The adolescent as philosopher: The discovery of the self in a postconventional world. In R.L. Mosher (ed.), *Adolescents' Development & Education: A Janus Knot.* Berkeley, Calif.: McCutchan, 1979.

Kohlberg, L., and Mayer, R. Development as the aim of education. In R.O. Mosher (ed.), *Adolescents' Development and Education: A Janus Knot.* Berkeley, Calif.: McCutchan, 1979.

Krathwohl, D.R., Bloom, Benjamin S., and Masia, B.B. *Taxonomy of Educational Objectives: Handbook II: Affective Domain.* New York: David McKay, 1964.

Kulik, J.A., Kulik, C.C., and Cohen, P.A. A meta-analysis of outcome studies of Keller's personalized system of instruction. *American Psychologist,* 1979, *34,* 307–318.

Lewin, K. *Principles of Topological Psychology.* New York: McGraw-Hill, 1936.

Loevinger, J. Stages of ego development. In R.L. Mosher (ed.), *Adolescents' Development & Education: A Janus Knot.* Berkeley, Calif.: McCutchan, 1979.

McGeoch, J.A., and Irion, A.L. *The Psychology of Human Learning.* New York: Longmans, Green, 1952.

McKeachie, W.J. The decline and fall of the laws of learning. *Educational Researcher,* 1974(a), *3,* 7–11.

McKeachie, W.J. Instructional psychology. *Annual Review of Psychology,* 1974(b), *25,* 161–193.

McKeachie, W.J. Implications of cognitive psychology for college teaching. In W.J. McKeachie (guest editor), *Learning, Cognition, and College Teaching.* New Directions for Teaching and Learning Series. San Francisco: Jossey-Bass, 1980(a).

McKeachie, W.J. (guest editor). *Learning, Cognition, and College Teaching.* New Directions for Teaching and Learning Series. San Francisco: Jossey-Bass, 1980(b).

McKeachie, W.J. Procedures and techniques of teaching: A survey of experimental efforts. In N. Sanford (ed.), *The American College.* New York: Wiley, 1962.

McKeachie, W.J., and Kulik, J.A. Effective college teaching. In F.N. Kerlinger (ed.), *Review of Research in Education.* Ithaca, Ill.: Peacock, 1975.

Messick, S., and Associates. *Individuality in Learning: Implications of Cognitive Styles and Creativity for Human Development.* San Francisco: Jossey-Bass, 1976.

Miller, G.A., Galanter, E., and Pribram, K.H. *Plans and the Structure of Behavior.* New York: Holt, Rinehart & Winston, 1960.

Miller, T.K., and Prince, J.S. *The Future of Student Affairs: A Guide to Student Development for Tomorrow's Higher Education.* San Francisco: Jossey-Bass, 1978.

Milton, O. *Alternatives to the Traditional: How Professors Teach and How Students Learn.* San Francisco: Jossey-Bass, 1972.

Milton, O., and Associates. *On College Teaching.* San Francisco: Jossey-Bass, 1978.

Milton, O., and Edgerly, J.W. *The Testing and Grading of Students.* New Rochelle, N.Y.: Change Magazine Press, 1977.

Mowrer, O.H. *Learning Theory and Behavior.* New York: Wiley, 1960.

Norman, D.A. What goes on in the mind of the learner. In W. J. McKeachie (guest editor), *Learning, Cognition, and College Teaching.* New Directions for Teaching and Learning Series. San Francisco: Jossey-Bass, 1980.

Paivio, A. *Imagery and Verbal Processes.* New York: Holt, Rinehart and Winston, 1971.

Parsons, M.J., Johnston, M.A., and Durham, R.F. A cognitive-development approach to aesthetic experience. In R. L. Mosher (ed.), *Adolescents' Development and Education: A Janus Knot.* Berkeley, Calif.: McCutchan, 1979.

Perry, W.G. *Forms of Intellectual and Ethical Development in the College Years.* New York: Holt, Rinehart & Winston, 1970.

Peterson, R.E., and Associates. *Lifelong Learning in America.* San Francisco: Jossey-Bass, 1979.

Posner, M.I., and Keele, S.W. Skill learning. In Robert M.W. Travers (ed.), *Second Handbook of Research on Teaching.* Chicago: Rand McNally, 1973.

Reichmann, S.W., and Grasha, A.F. A rational approach to developing and assessing the construct validity of a student learning style scales instrument. *Journal of Psychology,* 1974, *87,* 231–223.

Robinson, F.P. *Effective Study.* New York: Harper and Brothers, 1946.

Salomon, G. Heuristic models for the generation of aptitude-treatment interaction hypotheses. *Review of Educational Research,* 1972, *42,* 327–343.

Sanford, N. (ed.). *The American College: A Psychological and Social Interpretation of the Higher Learning.* New York: Wiley, 1962.

Sheehy, G. *Passages: Predictable Crises of Adult Life.* New York: E.P. Dutton, 1976.

Shepard, R.N. The mental image. *American Psychologist,* 1978, *33,* 125–137.

Skinner, B.F. *The Behavior of Organisms: An Experimental Analysis.* New York: Appleton-Century-Crofts, 1938.

Skinner, B.F. *Science and Human Behavior.* New York: Macmillan, 1953.

Skinner, B.F. *The Technology of Teaching.* New York: Appleton-Century-Crofts, 1968.

Snow, R.E. Individual differences and instructional theory. *Educational Researcher,* 1977, *6* (10), 11–15.

Solmon, L.C., and Gordon, J.J. *The Characteristics and Needs of Adults in Postsecondary Education.* Lexington, Mass.: Lexington Books, 1981.

Spady, W.G. Competency based education: A bandwagon in search of a definition. *Educational Researcher,* 1977, *6,* 9–14.

Spence, K.W. *Behavior Theory and Conditioning.* New Haven, Conn.: Yale University Press, 1956.

Thorndike, E.L. *The Psychology of Learning.* New York: Teachers College, 1913.

Tolman, E.C. *Purposive Behavior in Animals and Men.* New York: Appleton-Century-Crofts, 1932.

Travers, R.M.W. (ed.). *Second Handbook of Research on Teaching: A Project of the American Educational Research Association.* Chicago: Rand McNally, 1973.

Tyler. L.E. *Individuality: Human Possibilities and Personal Choice in the Psychological Development of Men and Women.* San Francisco: Jossey-Bass, 1978.

Tyler, R.W. What we have learned about learning: Overview and update. In Kenneth H. Hansen (ed.), *Learning: An Overview and Update.* A report of the Chief State School Officers 1976 Summer Institute. Washington, D.C.: USOE, 1976.

Wapner, S. Commentary: Process and context in the conception of cognitive style. In S. Messick and Associates, *Individuality in Learning.* San Francisco: Jossey-Bass, 1976.

Warren, J.R. Adapting instruction to styles of learning. *ETS Findings,* 1974, *1,* 1–5.

Watson, J.B. *Psychology From the Standpoint of a Behaviorist.* Philadelphia: Lipincott, 1919.

Weathersby, R.P., and Tarule, J. M. *Adult Development: Implications for Higher Education.* Washington, D.C.: American Association for Higher Education, 1980.

Wilson, J.D. *Student Learning in Higher Education.* New York: Halsted Press, 1981.

Witkin, H.A. Cognitive styles in academic performance and in teacher-student relations. In S. Messick and Associates, *Individuality in Learning.* San Francisco: Jossey-Bass, 1976.

Wittrock, M.C. The cognitive movement in instruction. *Educational Researcher,* 1979, *8,* 5–11.

Wittrock, M.C., and Lumsdaine, A.A. Instructional psychology. *Annual Review of Psychology,* 1977, *28,* 417–459.

from Teaching and Learning in the College Classroom: A Review of the Research Literature

WILBERT J. MCKEACHIE, PAUL R. PINTRICH, YI-GUANG LIN, DAVID A.F. SMITH, AND RAJEEV SHARMA

III. Student Cognition

A. Knowledge Structure

In recent years, educational and instructional psychologists have emphasized the importance of meaningful learning (Ausubel, 1963, 1968; Greeno, 1978, 1980). The main focus is on the question of how students organize and represent knowledge and the role of students' cognitive structure in learning. At the same time, there is concern about subject matter structures in different disciplines (Schwab, 1962). The approach of curriculum development and curriculum evaluation based on Gagne's notion of a learning hierarchy (1970) emphasizes the importance of content structure in curriculum preparation (Shavelson, 1981). The work of these theorists suggests that, to understand student acquisition of knowledge and to improve instruction, it is necessary to investigate both the structure of subject matter and the student's internal representation of the structure of subject matter.

1. Definition of Constructs

a. Content Structure

Content structure, as a structure of subject matter, is defined as "the web of concepts (words, symbols) and their interrelationships in a body of instructional material" (Shavelson & Geeslin, 1975, p. 201). Content structure is the structure of the subject matter (Phillips, 1983). Content structure consists of *propositional structure,* including the meaning of concepts and operations, and *procedural structure,* including sets of rules or heuristics that specify the step-by-step procedures for solving a problem or attaining a goal (Shavelson, 1981). The content structure of a course may be derived from the instructional material, consisting of lectures, textbooks, syllabi, handouts, exams, etc. Shavelson and Geeslin (1975) and Geeslin and Shavelson (1975) employed the directed graph method (Harary, Norman, & Cartwright, 1965) to examine the content structure of physics and mathematics texts used in college or high school. They first identified 14 key concepts in a physics text and then identified the sentences and equations containing two or more of these key concepts. The resulting digraph, considered a representation of content structure, has points (corresponding to concepts) and lines indicating the relationships between concepts. The distance between pairs of key concepts forms a distance matrix, which may be analyzed by multidimensional scaling and clustering techniques. Shavelson and Geeslin have used such content structures as criteria to measure the progress of students' learning in physics and mathematics.

"Student Cognition," (Chapter 3) and "Student Motivation," (Chapter 4), by Wilbert J. McKeachie, Paul R. Pintrich, Yi-Guang Lin, David A. F. Smith, and Rajeev Sharma, reprinted by permission from *Teaching and Learning in the College Classroom: A Review of the Research Literature,* 1990.

Donald (1983) has studied the content structures in 16 university courses representing different disciplines. She asked professors to rate the key concepts in terms of salience, inclusiveness, and degree of abstractness. The professors then used these key concepts to construct a tree and described the relationships of each link in the tree structure. The tree structure illustrated the dominant relationships of key concepts in the course.

Donald found that the relationship most frequently found among the key concepts was the superordinate-subordinates relationship. She also found that natural science, humanities, and social sciences courses differed in the form of tree structures of key concepts. The natural science courses showed greater use of dependency or causal relationships between key concepts, whereas the social science and humanities courses showed greater use of similarity relationships.

Meyer (1975, 1977) used a method based on case grammar (Fillmore, 1968) and semantic grammar of propositions (Grimes, 1975) to identify the structure of a prose passage. The content structure was revealed as a hierarchically arranged tree structure that displayed the content of the passage. The nodes in the tree represented the content words; the lines among the nodes showed spatially how the content is organized; and the labels stated and classified the relationships among the content. She found that the ideas' positions and the pattern of specific relations in the content structure are important factors influencing learning and recall.

Stewart (1980, 1982, 1984) and Finley and Stewart (1982) have used conceptual maps and structural networks to portray the knowledge of both concepts and propositions. In constructing a network, one first lists all the important concepts, their meanings, and their important propositions. The most important proposition is selected from the list as a starting point and then additional concepts are added to the core. Labeled lines connecting the concepts describe the relationships among the concepts. In addition to this method of representing conceptual knowledge, these authors have developed a method for representing procedural knowledge. A flowchart is used to represent procedural knowledge in a series of steps of subgoals to be solved.

A science curriculum represented in this way will enable the curricular developer (1) to survey the knowledge domain in a discipline, (2) to select appropriate subsets of knowledge for students to learn, (3) to sequence the curriculum content in a meaningful way, and (4) to suggest the appropriate teaching technique to present the information. The combination of conceptual and procedural knowledge presents a meaningful problem-solving model for science students. Stewart (1982) and Finley and Stewart (1982) have applied these techniques to represent structures in genetics and ecology.

These studies on the characteristics of content structure of instructional material may help educators in designing a curriculum and in adapting teaching strategies to different instructional materials.

b. Cognitive Structure (Knowledge Structure)

It is generally agreed that cognitive structure or knowledge structure may be considered as a mental structure of organized knowledge stored in a learner's memory (Ausubel, 1963; Ausubel, Novak, & Hanesian, 1978; Shavelson, 1974). As a hypothetical construct, cognitive structure refers to the organization of different kinds of knowledge and information in long-term memory (Shavelson, 1972). We will use the terms cognitive structure and knowledge structure interchangeably.

Some theorists (e.g., Rumelhart & Ortony, 1977; Spiro, 1977) have considered cognitive structures to be schemata. "Cognitive structures (schemata) are cumulative, holistic, assimilative blends of information" (Spiro, 1977, p. 137). According to Mandler (1985), a schema is "a category of mental structures that stores and organizes past experience and guides our subsequent perception and experience" (p. 36). Cognitive structure, as prior knowledge, is viewed as one of the most important variables in determining meaningful learning and retention (Ausubel, 1968).

Different theories of memory have postulated different kinds of components and different representations for cognitive structures. *Declarative knowledge*, represented by concepts and propositional networks, and *procedural knowledge*, consisting of intellectual skills, production systems, and heuristic rules, are two closely related components of the cognitive structure (Anderson, 1980; E. Gagné, 1978; Greeno, 1978; Shavelson, 1981). Gagné and White (1978) and White (1985) also include images and episodes as components of cognitive structure. Anderson (1983) proposes spatial images as a kind of knowledge representation that preserves the configuration or pattern of elements. Episodes (recollections of events) are derived from personal experiences. Therefore, they have special meaningful connections and significance for the individual's knowledge structure.

2. Knowledge Structures in Different Subject Domains

Most studies of knowledge structure have been exploratory approaches investigating the feasibility of different techniques to assess, infer, or represent knowledge structure. These studies have involved a variety of subject matter areas.

Several studies have investigated the development and change of knowledge structure as a result of instruction and learning. For example, Shavelson (1972) and Geeslin and Shavelson (1975) have studied the correspondence between content structure and the cognitive structures of students after being taught physics and mathematics. Such research tests the construct validity of the knowledge structure concept and at the same time provides evidence for the value of the techniques used for assessing knowledge structure.

Many studies were carried out in science education and used high school students as the subjects of investigation. Some of these studies are concerned with the methodological issues, and the results and findings are of value for postsecondary education.

...

4. Developing Students' Cognitive Structures

a. Teaching Knowledge Structures

The importance of organization and structure in the acquisition of knowledge and learning is revealed in the top-down approach of teaching, which is based on the notion of concept hierarchies in the conceptual structure of subject matter. Potentially, teachers could influence the development of students' knowledge structures by (1) presenting the structure and organization of instructional materials in a meaningful way, (2) requiring students to actively organize the learning material, and (3) activating the learner's cognitive structure and linking the instructional material to students' knowledge structures. The general goal is to develop and restructure students' knowledge structures.

Organizing instructional material. There is some evidence showing that comprehension, understanding, and recall are influenced by text structure and organization (Brooks & Dansereau, 1983; Kintsch & Yarbrough, 1982; Meyer, 1975, 1977; Yekovich & Kulhavy, 1976). Kintsch, Kozminsky, Streby, McKoon & Keenan (1975) and Miller, Perry, and Cunningham (1977) found that superordinate propositions were recalled better than subordinate propositions. The encoding and retrieval of information are facilitated by organization of learning material (Glynn & Di Vesta, 1977).

Organizing learning material. Teaching students how to organize the learning material trains them to pay close attention to the relationships among concepts and to the meaning of propositional networks. The construction of a concept map (Novak & Gowin, 1984) is not only a means to assess students' existing knowledge but also is a strategy to train students how to actively organize and integrate the learning material (Novak, 1985). Geva (1983) found that requiring students to pay close attention to the hierarchical coherent aspects of text and to construct text flowcharts significantly facilitated comprehension for less skillful readers. Naveh-Benjamin and Lin (1988) showed, in real classroom settings, that providing students with a graphic representation of the instructor's hierarchical structure of the materials at the beginning of a given unit in the course results in better organization of the materials for this course unit. In addition, providing such a representation helped these students to create a better organization in a subsequent unit, when these students were compared with control students.

Spatial learning strategies, such as networking, mapping, schematizing, and concept structuring (Holley & Dansereau, 1984a) require learners to organize and structure the learning materials in some systematic ways. Hence these learning strategies should improve learning and facilitate formation and development of adequate and meaningful knowledge structures.

Linking instructional material to students' knowledge structures. According to Ausubel (1977), "the principal function of advance organizers is to bridge the gap between what the learner already knows and what he needs to know before he can successfully learn the task at hand" (p. 168). Mayer's assimilation encoding theory (1979) tries to explain the function of advance organizers in terms of activation of anchoring knowledge in long-term memory. The interaction and integration with the incoming information results in meaningful learning. Teaching by analogies, models, metaphors, and examples are also ways to bring the receiving information in line with existing knowledge to generate meaningful learning.

b. Learning and Transferring Learning

Rumelhart and Norman (1978) consider learning to be of three different forms: (a) accretion, (b) tuning, and (c) restructuring. These learnings involve the encoding, organizing, and restructuring of information in terms of existing cognitive structure to create a new cognitive structure. The result of this learning is continuous development and creation of new cognitive structure.

Ausubel (1968) has clearly stated the importance of cognitive structure in learning and transfer:

> In meaningful learning, therefore, cognitive structure is always a relevant and crucial variable, even if it is not deliberately influenced or manipulated so as to ascertain its effect on new learning. (p. 128)
>
> Thus a transfer situation exists whenever existing cognitive structure influences new cognitive functioning irrespective of whether it is in regard to reception learning or problem solving. (p. 130)

Royer (1979), using a schema theory, considers that "the transfer of learning involves the activation of a previously acquired schema when one encounters a new learning situation" (p. 65).

Royer and his associates found that acquired prior knowledge influences the storage location of prose materials (Royer, Perkins, & Konold, 1978) and the facilitative transfer in prose learning (Royer & Cable, 1976). They also showed that prose materials relating to existing knowledge structures were less prone to retroactive inhibition (Royer, Sefkow, & Kropf, 1977).

Several authors in the book *Cognitive Structure and Conceptual Change* (West & Pines, 1985) have advocated different ways of facilitating conceptual change and learning. Champagne, Gunstone, and Klopfer (1985) used confrontation strategy to produce conceptual change. Strike and Posner (1985) emphasize the relevance of the learners' current conceptions in generating new knowledge. In their view, learning is a process of transforming conceptions. All learning and teaching result in development and change of cognitive structure. Pines (1985) considers the study of development and the function of cognitive structure to be a psychological as well as an epistemological problem. These authors' approaches would undoubtedly add some additional dimensions and pose problems for the investigation of knowledge structure and its development. But at the same time, it would also broaden the investigators' horizons to enable them to study and analyze cognitive structure in a more subtle and insightful way.

B. Learning Strategies

The previous section stressed the role of prior knowledge in learning. Although the content and structure of knowledge are important, they may not be sufficient for all learning or problem solving (Pintrich et al., 1986). Educators at all levels have been increasingly concerned about generalizable cognitive skills such as those for learning, problem solving, and critical thinking. The next two sections focus on these generalizable cognitive skills.

1. Defining Learning Strategies

As Weinstein and Mayer (1986) point out, recent research on teaching and learning has focused on the active role of the learner in student achievement. Obviously, the subject matter content a student knows when taking on a new task will influence his or her performance. Accordingly, theories about prior knowledge and knowledge structure are important components of a theory of learning. Many of these knowledge-driven models, however, do not address how the student originally acquired that knowledge. Research on learning strategies deals with how students acquire and modify their knowledge and skills (Weinstein & Mayer, 1986).

Weinstein and Mayer (1986) have proposed four main components of information processing, all of which can be influenced by the use of learning strategies. The four components are: (1) selection, (2) acquisition, (3) construction, and (4) integration. The *selection* component concerns the control of attention to certain stimuli or information in the environment and transfer of that information to working memory. Corno and Mandinach (1983) label this phase "alertness and selectivity." The *acquisition* phase involves the transfer of information from working memory to long-term memory for permanent storage. In the *construction* phase the student actively builds connections between ideas in working memory. Mayer (1982, 1984) and Bransford (1979) refer to this process of construction as schema development, which results in the new information being held together by a coherent outline or organization (Weinstein & Mayer, 1986). The *integration* phase involves connecting prior knowledge with incoming information (cf. Corno & Mandinach's "connection" component). In our own discussion of the different types of learning strategies we will refer to these different phases of information processing as *attention, encoding, organization*, and *retrieval*.

There are many different definitions of learning strategies. Weinstein and Mayer (1986) define learning strategies as thoughts and behaviors that a learner engages in during learning and that are intended to influence the encoding process. This includes basic memory processes as well as general problem solving. This is a very broad definition of learning strategies and encompasses almost all cognitive processes.

In contrast, Tobias (1982) has distinguished between *macrolevel* learning strategies, such as reviewing, note taking and comprehension monitoring, that complement the more *microlevel* basic cognitive processes, such as attention and encoding. These macroprocesses concern the students' processing of instructional input, whether this input is from a teacher, a textbook, or another medium. The focus on macroprocesses is more molar than molecular, and parallels Sternberg's (1985) distinction between metacomponents and cognitive processes. As Tobias (1982) sees it, these macroprocesses are at the nexus of research on the psychology of learning performed by cognitive psychologists and research on the psychology of instruction performed by educational psychologists.

In this paper and in our research program, we will concentrate on the macrolevel cognitive strategies rather than on the basic microlevel processes. The choice of this focus is made on theoretical, methodological, and practical grounds for two reasons:

1. A number of researchers (e.g., Paris et al., 1983) have limited the definition of learning strategies to cognitive processes that are intentional and under the control of the learner. Some of the more basic memory processes and microlevel processes of intelligence (see Sternberg, 1985) are not really under the control of the student; they are part of every individual's basic information-processing equipment and are elicited automatically by various tasks.

2. Some of the basic cognitive microprocesses are difficult to measure unless the researcher uses an experimental design with highly specified experimental tasks and collects reaction times. This is neither practical nor ecologically valid in our research program.

Our research will be field-based and we will often rely on students' self-reports. Although there are problems with self-report data (e.g., Nisbett & Wilson, 1977), it can be used if treated as just one source of data on the phenomena of interest (Ericsson & Simon, 1984). Accordingly, we will also use other performance measures to triangulate on the cognitive macroprocesses of interest. In using self-report measures rather than experimental tasks there is a trade-off between decreased construct validity (Cook & Campbell, 1979) and increased external validity.

Our focus on global or macrolevel learning strategies includes both students' *use* of them as well as their *knowledge* about them. Paris et al. (1983) have discussed three types of knowledge about learning strategies that are important to informed use: declarative, procedural, and conditional knowledge. Declarative knowledge is defined as propositional knowledge about task characteristics, strategies, and personal abilities (cf. Anderson, 1985; Brown et al., 1983; Flavell, 1979). *Declarative knowledge* concerns the content or *what* about tasks, strategies, and the self. For example, students can know that reviewing notes before an exam is a good strategy. They also may know something about themselves in terms of their skill in reviewing notes. However, this declarative knowledge is not enough for good performance. *Procedural knowledge* involves students knowing how to execute various cognitive strategies. That is, it is not enough for students to know about the strategies, they must know how to use them properly and efficiently.

The final type of knowledge, *conditional knowledge*, is a term coined by Paris et al. (1983) to describe the knowledge about *when* and *why* to use strategies. It is not enough just to know about various strategies and how to use them, but students must be able to use them in a flexible and strategic manner. For example, students might know about the efficacy of skimming a chapter in a reading assignment (declarative knowledge) and even how to skim (procedural knowledge), but not know when skimming is best used or why it might be used in different situations depending on the students' goals (conditional knowledge). Given these three types of knowledge about strategies and their differential implications for performance, it is important to assess students' level of knowledge in all three areas.

There are many learning strategies and different taxonomies for classifying them (e.g., Dansereau, 1985; Pressley, 1986; Weinstein & Mayer, 1986). We have adopted a rather general framework that groups strategies into three broad categories: *cognitive, metacognitive*, and *resource management* (see Table 2). The cognitive category includes strategies related to the students' learning or encoding of material as well as strategies to facilitate retrieval of information. The metacognitive strategies involve strategies related to planning, regulating, monitoring, and modifying cognitive processes. The resource management strategies concern the students' strategies to control the resources (i.e., time, effort, outside support) that influence the quality and quantity of their involvement in the task.

a. Cognitive Strategies

The basic cognitive learning strategies are outlined by Weinstein & Mayer (1986) as rehearsal, elaboration, and organizational strategies. Each of these three types of strategies also has a basic and complex version, depending on the complexity of the task.

Basic rehearsal strategies involve reciting or naming items from a list to be learned. This strategy is related to the attention and encoding components as the learner brings information into working memory (Weinstein & Mayer, 1986). Basic rehearsal strategies are best used for simple tasks and activation of information in working memory rather than acquisition of new information in long-term memory. Rehearsal strategies for complex tasks such as learning material from a text include strategies most college students use in their day-to-day studying. For example, saying the material aloud as one reads (shadowing), coping the material over into a notebook, taking notes as one reads, and underlining or highlighting sections of the text.

As Weinstein and Mayer (1986) point out, these strategies are assumed to influence the attention and encoding processes, but they do not appear to help students construct internal connections among the information or integrate the information with prior knowledge. For example, Meyer and Cook (1980) found that students who were asked to shadow a text passage remembered more of the details and facts about the passage than a control group who did not repeat the words to themselves. However, the control group remembered more of the conceptual information and performed better on a creative problem-solving task that required use of the text material.

Weinstein and Mayer (1986) conclude that rehearsal strategies need to be supplemented with other learning strategies that help the student organize and integrate the information in long-term memory, not just bring it into working memory.

Elaboration strategies help students store information into long-term memory by building internal connections between items to be learned (Weinstein & Mayer, 1986). Basic learning tasks that can be performed more efficiently with elaboration strategies include learning foreign language vocabulary (paired-associate learning) and free recall list learning like learning to name all the parts of the brain (Weinstein & Mayer, 1986). Research has shown that the mnemonic keyword (Pressley, Levin, & Delaney, 1982) is one of the best techniques for learning vocabulary.

The **keyword method** essentially involves the building of two types of links between the foreign word and its English counterpart. First, a verbal acoustic link is formed between the words by choosing an English word that sounds similar to the foreign word. Second, this new word (the keyword) that sounds like the foreign word is paired with the English definition of the foreign word in a mental image that helps the reader remember the links between all three words. There has been a great deal of research on the keyword method (see review by Pressley et al., 1982) that suggests students are not very adept at building their own keyword links. If instructors are going to use the keyword method, better performance usually results if the links are provided by the teacher or the textbook.

Other elaboration strategies for basic tasks include **simple imagery**, which is useful for learning lists. This strategy involves the creation of an image that helps the learner remember the list. The "method of loci" is one example of this strategy. The method of loci involves the use of the image of the learner's house and its layout (e.g., hallway, living room, dining room, etc.). To learn a list of words in order (serial list learning), the learner pairs the first word with an object in the first room of the house and constructs an image of that word in the object in the first room. The second word and image of it is paired with a

Table 2
A Taxonomy of Learning Strategies

Strategy	*Basic Tasks (e.g., memory for lists)*	*Complex Tasks (e.g., test learning)*	*All Tasks*
I. Cognitive Strategies			
A. Rehearsal Strategies	Reciting list	Shadowing Copy material Verbatim note taking Underlining text	
B. Elaboration Strategies	Keyword method Imagery Method of loci	Paraphrasing Summarizing Creating analogies Generative note taking Question answering	
C. Organizational Strategies	Clustering Mnemonics	Selecting main idea Outlining Networking Diagramming	
II. Metacognitive Strategies			
A. Planning Strategies			Setting goals Skimming Generating questions
B. Monitoring Strategies			Self-testing Attention-focus Test-taking strategies
C. Regulating Strategies			Adjusting reading rate Re-reading Reviewing Test-taking strategies
III. Resource Management Strategies			
A. Time Management			Scheduling Goal setting
B. Study Environment Management			Defined area Quiet area Organized area
C. Effort Management			Attributions to effort Mood Self-talk Persistence Self-reinforcement
D. Support of Others			Seeking help from teacher Seeking help from peers Peer/group learning Tutoring

second object in the room or in the next room. When the learner wants to remember the list, he or she imagines walking through the house and recalling each image on entering a room. Of course, this method works best when the list to be remembered is made up of concrete words (i.e., a shopping list). The task is more difficult when the list includes abstract words or concepts that do not readily lend themselves to images.

Weinstein and Mayer (1986) classify learning from text or prose as complex tasks. Elaboration strategies that assist the learner on these tasks include paraphrasing, summarizing, creating analogies, generative note taking, explaining, and question asking and answering (Weinstein & Mayer, 1986). These strategies help the learner integrate and connect the new information with prior knowledge. For example, by paraphrasing what they are reading, learners actively connect the new text information with prior knowledge and organizational framework for that subject matter area. In the same fashion, generative note taking where students do not take notes verbatim but try to write notes in their own words and connect them to prior knowledge should result in better storage and retrieval of the information.

Organizational strategies help the learner select appropriate information and also construct connections among the information to be learned. For basic memory tasks, the most common organizational strategy is clustering (Weinstein & Mayer, 1986). Clustering involves the grouping of the words to be learned into taxonomic categories that reflect some shared characteristics or attributes. This grouping process results in the learner being actively involved in the task and should result in better performance (Weinstein & Mayer, 1986).

The more interesting and useful organizational strategies for college students involve the complex task of learning from texts. Weinstein and Mayer (1986) have identified selecting the main idea as an important cognitive goal. There have been a variety of techniques developed to help learners identify the main ideas in a text. Weinstein and Mayer (1986) summarize several of these techniques. One technique, networking, helps students identify the connections among the ideas in a passage by having them classify the types of links among the ideas (see Dansereau et al., 1978; Dansereau et al., 1979; Holley et al., 1979; for more details). Another type of outlining procedure was developed by Meyer (1975, 1981). It trains students to recognize five types of structures found in expository texts. A third type of outlining procedure (Cook, 1982) helps students identify prose structures. All these techniques help the students select the main ideas from a text by analysis of the text structure. It is assumed that through this analysis, students will come to understand the material better and be able to integrate it with prior knowledge.

b. Metacognitive Strategies

The term metacognition is a popular term used by a variety of researchers in cognitive, educational, and instructional psychology. As Brown et al. (1983) point out, the term has a number of definitions, making it a "fuzzy" concept. It is most often used to refer to two aspects of cognitive life: (1) the awareness of and knowledge about cognition and (2) the control and regulation of cognition (Brown et al., 1983; Flavell, 1979).

The **awareness** aspect of metacognition refers to the learners' knowledge of person, task, and strategy variables that influence performance. According to Flavell (1979), awareness of person variables refers to knowledge about the self in terms of cognitive performance (e.g., knowing that you are a fast reader, a poor writer, etc.). This aspect of metacognition is closely related to motivational constructs such as perceived competence and self-concept.

Task-variable knowledge includes information about the difficulty of various tasks and the different demands of academic tasks. Strategy-variable knowledge concerns the learner's knowledge about different strategies and how to use them (i.e., declarative and procedural knowledge; cf. Flavell, 1979; Paris et al., 1983). Although this knowledge about person, task, and strategy variables is important, metacognitive learning strategies involve the control and regulation aspect of metacognition more than the knowledge aspect. Accordingly, in this section we concentrate on the control and regulation aspect of metacognition as it relates to learning strategies.

Brown et al. (1983) note that there are three general processes that make up metacognitive activities: **planning, monitoring,** and **self-regulation**. These activities are closely related to metacognitive knowledge, although they can be distinguished theoretically. In addition, the distinction between what is cognitive and what is metacognitive is often difficult to make. We use this distinction, however, because of its theoretical and heuristic value (Brown et al., 1983). Therefore, in our description of the various metacognitive strategies, there may be some aspects that other researchers would classify as cognitive, not metacognitive, activities.

Planning activities include setting goals for studying, skimming, generating questions before reading the text, and doing a task analysis of the problem. All these activities help the learner plan the use of strategies and the processing of information. In addition, they help to activate, or to prime, relevant aspects of prior knowledge that make organizing and comprehending the material easier. Brown et al. (1983) summarize various planning models that have been suggested by cognitive psychologists. Much of the research on planning, and metacognition in general, suggests that good learners engage in more planning and more metacognitive activities than poor learners (cf., Pressley, 1986).

Students have relatively good metacognitive ability in predicting their readiness for examinations (Leal, 1987). Thus the high anxiety reported by many test-anxious students lacking effective study skills may well be the result of realistic appraisals of test performance as hypothesized by Benjamin, McKeachie, Lin, and Holinger (1981).

However, Tobias (1987) found that students' uses of learning strategies in a computer-controlled experiment of reading strategies did not correlate well with the students' reports of the strategies they normally used. While this may be a function of the difference between the laboratory situation and normal studying of text, it seems likely, as Tobias suggests, that students may neither know which strategies are most effective nor be aware of their own strategies for learning. It may well be that students have a general sense of their readiness, or lack of readiness, for an examination, but relatively less awareness of what to do to remedy deficiencies.

That this may be the case is demonstrated by Tobias's results indicating that mandatory review following an error in answering an adjunct question resulted in better performance than voluntary, student-controlled review.

Nonetheless, students are able to adjust their strategies to fit the demands of the situation. Sagerman and Mayer (1987) gave students four science passages to read. For one group each passage was followed by verbatim questions; for a second group by conceptual questions; and for a third group by no questions. The verbatim group did better in answering verbatim questions on the fourth passage than did the control group, but not on the conceptual questions. The conceptual group did better than the verbatim group on both conceptual and verbatim questions. These results fit well with evidence on the advantage of essay over objective testing for student learning. (See Chapter V, Section J.)

Monitoring activities are an essential aspect of metacognition. Weinstein and Mayer (1986) see all metacognitive activities as partly comprehension monitoring. We take a broad view of monitoring to include self-monitoring during any cognitive activity. Monitoring activities include tracking of attention as one reads, self-testing while reading a text to insure comprehension of the material, use of certain kinds of test-taking strategies (i.e., monitoring speed and adjusting to time available), and monitoring comprehension of a lecture. These various monitoring activities assist the learner in understanding the material and integrating it with prior knowledge.

What do students do when they are assigned very difficult reading? Waern and Rabenius (1987) report that students predominantly turn to memorizing. The result in the experiment conducted by Waern and Rabenius was comprehension little better than guessing on a post-test.

Self-regulation activities are related to monitoring activities. For example, as learners monitor the comprehension of a text, they can regulate their reading speed to adjust for the difficulty of the material. This continuous adjustment and fine-tuning of cognition is an important component of metacognition (Brown et al., 1983). Other forms of self-regulation behavior include re-reading portions of a text to increase comprehension, reviewing material, and using test-taking strategies (i.e., skipping questions and coming back to them later in the exam). These self-regulating activities are assumed to improve performance by assisting learners in checking and correcting their behavior as they proceed on a task.

German and Dutch research on learning and instruction is reviewed in the volume edited by Beukhof and Simons (1986). Friedrich and Mandl (1986) point out that metacognition is being related to broader concepts of motivation and action control in German research and that training in metacognitive self-regulation has been less successful than might have been expected in view of the correlations between metacognition and learning performance. Dutch results are similarly mixed (Simons & Vermunt, 1986). This may be due to the interactions between learning strategies, prior knowledge, and the specific learning task. Training in learning strategies and metacognition may not be helpful if one is so lacking in necessary content knowledge as to be completely confused. At the other end of the prior knowledge continuum, training may also be of little value either, because the learner already has effective strategies and thinking about them metacognitively may simply divert capacity from the learning task itself.

c. Resource Management Strategies

Resource management strategies include a variety of strategies that assist students in managing the environment and the resources available. These resources include the time available for studying, the actual study environment, others such as teachers and peers, as well as learners themselves (in terms of effort, mood, and persistence). These strategies could be seen as both cognitive and metacognitive in nature, but they are different enough to warrant a separate category. These strategies help students adapt to the environment as well as change the environment to fit their needs (cf., Sternberg, 1985).

Time management is a classic area included in most traditional study programs (e.g., Deese & Deese, 1979; Johnson, Springer, & Sternglanz, 1982). Thomas and Rohwer (1986) note that time management is an important self-management activity in studying. There are different levels of time management, varying from monthly and weekly scheduling to managing an evening of studying. Of course, this kind of scheduling involves planning and regulation activities that are metacognitive in nature. It is probably useful for students to have a weekly schedule for studying that helps organize their time, but this schedule also needs to be flexible enough to allow for adaptations in light of course demands (e.g., mid-terms, finals). At a more microlevel, students also need to manage time while actually studying. For example, if a student has set aside three hours one evening for studying, he or she must be able to schedule the use of those three hours efficiently. This involves setting realistic goals.

Another resource that must be managed by the student is the **study environment**. As Deese and Deese (1979) point out, students' study environments are an important aspect of their studying. It is probably useful for students to have a defined area for studying. This area can be in a variety of settings (e.g., library, study hall in dormitory, individual dorm room, or kitchen table). The nature of the setting is not as important as the fact that the student recognizes that this particular location is set aside for studying. It should be relatively free of distractions, both visual and auditory. Accordingly, it should be organized and quiet. It is probably not possible to have quality engagement in studying when there are many distractions (e.g., other students talking, loud music or television on, children in the room, etc.). The student needs to organize the study environment in such a way as to increase attention.

Another aspect of the environment that the student must learn to manage is the **support of others**. The student needs to know when and how to seek and obtain help. The source of this help can be teacher or peers. This aspect of resource management is related to Sternberg's (1985) notion of practical intelligence in that good students know when they don't know something and are able to identify someone to provide some assistance. There is a large body of research that shows that peer help or peer tutoring can facilitate student achievement (e.g., Webb, 1982). In addition, the work on reciprocal teaching (e.g., Palinscar, 1986; Palinscar & Brown, 1984) demonstrates the power of individual teacher help. However, many students do not seek help appropriately or at all. Many college instructors can probably testify to the lack of student attendance at review sessions even after the session was set up at the students' requests.

A study of Ames and Lau (1982) found that students' actual use of a review session was related to their attributional pattern and past performance. Students who did poorly on earlier exams, but attributed their poor performance to low effort and a lack of course specific knowledge rather than a general ability deficit were much more likely to seek help than students who attributed their poor performance to lack of interest, the difficulty of the exam, or the instructor. This study demonstrates that motivational patterns are related to students help-seeking behavior and need to be considered in examining students' general learning strategies. Karabenick and Knapp (1988) found that help-seeking was greater among students who had moderate need for help, and less among students with much need or little need for help. Students who expected grades above A [sic] or below C+ sought academic assistance less than those expecting B- or C+.

The last resource management strategy is directly related to students' motivational patterns. This strategy concerns students' general **self-management** in terms of effort, mood, self-talk, and self-reinforcement. Dansereau (1985) has discussed this aspect of learning strategies in terms of support strategies that help the student develop and maintain a good internal state. For Dansereau (1985), one of the most important strategies is mood-setting or mood maintenance. This is the M in Dansereau's "MURDER" scheme for learning strategies. Weinstein and Mayer (1986) term strategies for managing effort and mood, affective learning strategies. Effort management may be one of the most important learning strategies. A good student knows when to increase efforts and persist on the task as well as when maximal effort is not required for success. Corno and Rohrkemper (1985) discuss the importance of students' regulating their cognitive learning strategies in combination with their effort management. Students who are able to regulate both cognitive and motivational aspects of their behavior are termed self-regulating learners (Corno & Rohrkemper, 1985).

Another aspect of effort management concerns the students' attributions for success and failure (discussed in more detail in the motivation section of this paper). Attributing failure to lack of effort suggest that success may come by trying harder. This attribution leads to a higher expectancy for success and should help the student maintain commitment to the task. Other internal perceptions of the student are important to involvement besides attributions. Meichanbaum and Asaranow (1978) have shown that positive self-talk or self-coaching (similar to general cognitive therapy techniques) can help students succeed at difficult tasks.

Students need to have instruction, including modeling, in how to use these self-coaching techniques (Dansereau, 1985). Positive self-talk can help students halt the defeating "self-perturbing ideations" that Bandura (1982) has focused on in his work on self-efficacy.

Another aspect of this self-management category that is related to the cognitive-behavior modification model is self-reinforcement. If students are able to set-up simple plans to reward themselves for accomplishing their goals, this can help them maintain their involvement in the task. For example, a student may decide that every hour spent studying merits a "reward" of a five-minute break. This kind of self-management can help the student maintain attention and involvement, which results in better performance.

2. Teaching Learning Strategies

The preceding description of the different types of learning strategies documents the wide variety of strategies available to students. Although some students seem to be able to acquire and use these strategies on their own, most students do not acquire them or at least do not use the strategies in the most effective manner. Accordingly, there is a need to teach students how to use learning strategies. This may sound easy to do, but there are a number of problems associated with teaching learning strategies. There are issues related to training and also to the transfer and generalizability of the strategies.

Much research shows what learning strategies can be taught (e.g., Chipman, Segal & Glaser, Chipman & Glaser, 1985; Weinstein & Mayer, 1986). There are, however, disagreements about what strategies should be taught and how to teach these strategies. Levin (1986) has suggested that there are four important principles to follow in learning strategy instruction. They are:

1. The instructor should teach different learning strategies for different tasks. As Levin notes, this is just a restatement of the old cliche. "Different tools for different jobs." However, it is an important principle to remember in training learning strategies. There is no one best learning strategy. Strategies have to be adapted to the task demands as well as the learners' knowledge (Levin's third principle).

2. Strategies should have identifiable components. Here Levin (1986) suggests that strategies should be able to be decomposed into multiple components related to particular information processing variables and operations. This multiple component approach has several advantages. Students can learn the components and then adapt and combine them in different ways depending on the task. Second, research on multiple component strategies programs will help us avoid the somewhat simplistic evaluations of strategy programs that result in a "works/does not work" outcome. We need to know how and why different strategies work in different contexts, not just whether some global program works. Thus the familiar SQ3R study method (Survey, Question, Read, Recite, Review) should be taught not as a recipe to be used routinely without thought but rather as consisting of five components, each related to a cognitive theory of learning.

3. Learning strategies must be considered in relation to students' knowledge and skills. This third principle of Levin's is simply that there must be a "match" between the student and the strategy. Students must have the prerequisite skills to master certain strategies. Levin (1986) notes that processing capacity differences between children of different ages and adults may result in some strategies being useful for older children and adults but not for younger children. In our own work (e.g., McKeachie Pintrich, & Lin, 1985a, 1985b), we have found that the efficacy of a general learning strategy course for college students was related to the students' basic skill and aptitude levels. Students who had very poor reading skills and low general aptitude levels did not benefit from the program as much as other students. Some minimum level of competency seemed to be required to be able to use the strategies effectively. For example, if students cannot decode words, then it is useless to teach them sophisticated reading comprehension strategies.

4. Learning strategies that are assumed to be effective must be empirically validated. This principle of Levin is similar to comments made by Sternberg (1983). There must be empirical data on the effectiveness of various strategies and general strategy programs if we are to learn more about how to teach learning strategies. This includes evaluating techniques that are very effective in laboratory settings but may not be effective when moved into the ecologically valid setting of the classroom. As many researchers and program developers know, the leap between research and practice is a large one. If empirical data is not collected on the effectiveness of these programs, we will not progress in our understanding of learning strategies and how to teach them.

These principles are general issues to consider in learning-strategy instruction. At a more practical level, there are several other principles that should be considered. First, a variety of researchers have noted that direct instruction in strategies is not only useful for students, but almost required (McKeachie et al., 1985a, 1985b; Pressley, 1986). Students need to be taught both task specific strategies as well as general cognitive and metacognitive strategies (e.g., Paris et al., 1983; Pressley, 1986). Another important aspect of teaching strategies is modeling the strategies for students and providing guided practice in the use of strategies (Corno & Snow, 1986; Paris et al., 1983; Pressley, 1986). This suggestion on direct instruction of strategies follows the general model of direct instruction in any content domain (e.g., Rosenshine & Stevens, 1986).

However, Thornton et al. (1990) have suggested that: (a) Training for learning strategies may be more effective if it identifies students' existing strategies and strengthens them. (b) Short-term training strategies may not be very effective for college students as they may prefer and continue to use their own strategies. They also reported that spontaneous learning strategies employed by mature learners may be as effective as strategies imposed on them, even when explicit training is given in the use of the imposed strategies.

This content-domain issue brings us to the issue of transfer and generalizability. There is a long and continuing controversy on the domain-specificity of problem-solving skills (Campione & Armbruster, 1985; Glaser, 1984). As Campione and Armbruster (1985) point out, the issue revolves around the training of general cognitive strategies versus specific knowledge-based strategies. Most of the learning-strategy training programs would be placed on the general cognitive strategy side of this dichotomy.

There is evidence that learning strategies can be taught and generalized beyond the original instructional context. For example, courses designed to enhance study skills have long been successful (e.g., Kulik, Kulik, & Schwalb, 1983). Dansereau (1985) and Weinstein and Underwood (1985) provide description of two successful programs to improve learning strategies. Weinstein and Mayer (1986) review the research on learning strategies performance and the success of different programs in teaching strategies. Learning strategy training programs should show transfer not only of the original strategies taught, but also that achievement in other areas is influenced (cf. Sternberg, 1983).

One aspect of the transfer problem in teaching learning strategies is learning with awareness (Campione & Armbruster, 1985). Most learning strategies programs attempt to make students aware of the various strategies available to them. However, as we have noted, there are two aspects of awareness or metacognition that need to be considered in the teaching of learning strategies: knowledge about cognition and regulation of cognition (Brown et al., 1983).

Most learning strategy training programs teach both of these aspects of metacognition. Knowledge about cognition includes knowledge about the person, task, and strategy variables that influence performance (Flavell, 1979). These person, task, and strategy variables parallel the factors of the tetrahedral model: criterial task, materials, learner, and activities (Brown et al., 1983). Students need to know how task characteristics (i.e., recall vs. recognition) and the nature of materials (i.e., visual vs. linguistic) influence their learning. In the same manner, knowledge about their own abilities and characteristics (e.g., knowing they are better at recognition tasks such as multiple choice tests) will help students adapt their learning to the task. Finally, knowledge about various cognitive strategies or activities should improve learning. Most strategy training programs focus on the latter aspect of the tetrahedral model (Brown et al., 1983) by teaching students about the various memory strategies (i.e., rehearsal, imagery, elaboration) and other strategies for attention, problem solving, and comprehension.

Knowledge about cognition, however, does not necessarily lead to improved cognition. Students need to learn how to regulate their cognition through executive control of their resources (e.g., attention, memory, effort, and time). Teaching about self-regulation of cognition is easier than fostering actual regulation of cognition. Most learning strategy programs teach students about the importance of planning their study activities, regulating their attention, and monitoring their comprehension of readings and lectures. There is no guarantee, however, that students will internalize these strategies and become self-regulating. The problem of getting students to actually use the strategies and become self-regulating in other situations besides the training program is one all learning strategy programs must confront.

Motivational factors play a role in the transfer of learning strategies to other situations. Parts et al. (1983) have proposed three types of knowledge important for strategic learning: declarative, procedural, and conditional knowledge. They define *declarative knowledge* as propositional knowledge of task characteristics and personal abilities (cf. Brown et al., 1983; Flavell, 1979). *Procedural knowledge* is defined as knowing about how to execute various cognitive processes and skills (i.e., how to use elaboration, how to skim). The new term, *conditional knowledge,* introduced by Paris et al. (1983), is defined as knowing when and why to use strategies. Paris et al. argue that it is not enough just to know how to use strategies, but that students must be motivated to use them in a flexible and strategic manner. If they have both the motivation and conditional knowledge of why a particular strategy works, they will be more likely to use it in an appropriate situation.

The transfer issue is not an easy one to resolve. Strategy training programs can attempt to increase transfer by directly teaching students how to apply the strategies to different tasks. In addition, it is important to combine cognitive, metacognitive, resource management, and motivational strategies in a program in such a way that the student can use them to become a self-regulating learner. In the end analysis, our goal, is to have students become active learners and take control of their own learning.

Various programs and models have been used to teach learning strategies. Chipman, Segal, and Glaser (1985) and Segal, Chipman, and Glaser (1985) describe a variety of programs to teach thinking and learning skills. Chance (1986) and Nickerson, Perkins, and Smith (1985) also summarize a variety of programs. These programs range from general training programs (e.g., Sternberg, 1986) to rather specific learning strategy programs (e.g., training in the key word method (Pressley, Levin, & Delaney, 1982). In between are several programs to teach general learning strategies and study skills (e.g., Dansereau, 1985; McKeachie et al., 1985a, 1985b; Pintrich, McKeachie, & Lin 1987; Shenkman & Cukras, 1986; Weinstein & Underwood, 1985). These college students (or high school students) general learning strategies and demonstrate positive effects on academic achievement.

Although our review is intended to focus on research, we would be serving our readers badly if we did not include a book review in the winter 1984 issue (published in August 1987) of *Contemporary Education Review*. The review, "Are there programs that can really teach thinking and learning skills?" by Pressley, Cariglia-Bull, and Snyder (1984), not only provides an incisive critique and analysis of the programs for improving thinking and learning skills described in the book reviewed—*Thinking and Learning Skills, Volume I: Relating Instruction to Research* (Segal, Chipman, & Glaser, 1985)—but also gives the reader a brief introduction to Pressley's own good Strategy User model. The reviewers point out the need for better experimental data both on the overall effectiveness of the programs and on the interactions between particular skills and the student's knowledge base in different content areas.

. . .

C. Thinking and Problem Solving

While we treat "thinking and problem solving" as a separate topic, let us make it clear that there is a continuum running from what is usually termed "learning" to "problem solving" and "creativity." We usually say that someone has *learned* when they display the effects of training or experience in a context similar to that in which the learning occurred. We talk about "transfer of learning" when the learning is displayed in a situation somewhat different from that in which the original learning occurred. If the transfer situation is so different that the use of the learning encounters some barrier or difficulty, we speak of "problem solving." When the situation is greatly different and the distance of transfer needed is greater still, we speak of "creativity." But even a simple learning task, such as reading a textbook assignment, requires thinking. Selecting an approach to maximize one's learning is a problem-solving activity quite comparable to that involved in designing an experiment or solving a puzzle.

1. Defining the Construct

Current cognitive and instructional research stresses the role of prior knowledge in learning (Glaser, 1984; Pintrich et al., 1986). For example, it is obvious that college students' previous knowledge in chemistry or mathematics will have an important influence on their performance in these courses in college. However, even though content knowledge is critical, it may not be sufficient for effective problem solving. Docky (1988) suggests that "prior knowledge" involves not only knowledge of facts and principles, but also knowledge of categories of problems and of approaches to problems. Thus, as contrasted with novices, the experts' "prior knowledge" enables the expert to apply knowledge effectively in solving new problems. The problem of teaching generalizable cognitive skills is particularly crucial for higher education, since for most college students, life after college will not draw so much on specific content knowledge of chemistry, mathematics, history, psychology, etc., as on their abilities to learn effectively, solve problems, reason, evaluate, and make decisions.

When faculty members talk about teaching critical thinking, problem solving, or reasoning, they typically are referring to teaching students to use their learning in new situations to solve problems, reach decisions, or make evaluations with respect to standards of excellence.

The faculty at Alverno College (Mentkowski & Strait, 1983), who have spent over a decade developing a curriculum to teach critical thinking, describe their educational goal of achieving cognitive skills and integrative abilities in terms of "complex systems of intellectual development rather than quantifiable sets of skills" (Loacker, Cromwell, Fey, & Rutherford, 1984, p. i). This definition temporarily bypasses some of the difficult problems of analysis and measurement by pointing to holistic, global, qualitative methods of assessing the outcomes of education. Nonetheless, one would like to be somewhat more specific about the outcomes of a specific course or curriculum. While the systems of intellectual development are undoubtedly intertwined in complex ways, we should be able to tease out the components of thinking taught in different subject matter domains as well as differentiable cognitive skills generalizable across two or more domains.

Much highly skilled intellectual performance does not require thinking. One may learn to apply standard methods of solution so automatically that no thinking is necessary. In mathematics or science, for example, the student may solve many problems by automatically applying a standard algorithm. Elshout (1985) describes a "zone of problematicity" as that area lying between the area where problems are so difficult and complex that the problem solver cannot solve them and the area where the problem solver can automatically apply the correct procedure to arrive at a solution. The zone of problematicity thus is different for problem solvers of differing degrees of expertness. From this perspective, the task of higher education becomes that of increasing the area in which thinking is not required as well as of developing strategies and skills for dealing with problems in the zone of problematicity.

In a review of studies on inductive reasoning Ropo (1987) highlighted the importance of inductive reasoning in academic achievement. According to Pellegrino and Glaser (1982) inductive reasoning consists of the following processes:

1. *Encoding or representing the problem*. In this, the individual forms a mental model of the problem.

2. *Inference processes*. The individual identifies or generates relational features shared by two or more encoded elements.

3. *Rule assembly or monitoring*. The individual organizes individual relational features into simple or complex structures.
4. *Comparison or match processes*. In this, the individual evaluates similarities among relational structures.
5. *Discrimination processes*. The individual chooses between competing relational structures.
6. *Decision and output processes*. In this final stage, the individual determines and produces the output of the problems.

Research on problem-solving and general thinking skills has a long history in psychology. Recent volumes edited by Chipman, Segal, and Glaser (1985) and Segal, Chipman, and Glaser (1985) highlight both the theoretical and practical work being conducted in this area. The entire winter 1984 issue of *Review of Educational Research* deals with problems in the teaching and learning of reasoning skills. Fredericksen (1984) demonstrates the applicability of cognitive theories to instruction in problem solving. Glaser (1984) provides an excellent overview of the critical issues involved in attempting to teach generalizable cognitive skills. Essentially, the research suggests that there are five critical issues that must be addressed in future research:

1. Can general cognitive skills be taught?
2. How can current knowledge-based structural cognitive theories be applied to the teaching of general problem-solving skills?
3. How can instruction best be designed to foster these skills?
4. How can cognitive skills learned in one domain of knowledge be transferred to another domain?
5. How can we assess the effectiveness of teaching critical thinking?

2. Teaching Critical Thinking

Support for a positive answer to the first question above—that of the teachability of general intellectual skills—comes from studies of the impact of education on intelligence. Balke-Aurell (1982) has shown that general, or "fluid," intelligence increases with increased education. Verbal, or "crystallized," intelligence is also enhanced by education in general, while spatial/technical ability is particularly enhanced by education in such fields as engineering and science. Individuals involved in work demanding verbal functioning continue to develop increased verbal ability.

A number of scholars have applied current theories of cognitive psychology to programs for teaching thinking. Four book-length programs have been developed by major figures in cognitive psychology—Hayes (1981), Bransford and Stein (1984), Sternberg (1986), and Nickerson, Perkins, and Smith (1985).

Problem Solving and Discussion. Studies such as Balke-Aurell's encourage hope about the potential value of education for educational development, but we now need to determine what kinds of education are most facilitative. Most of the programs to teach intelligence have been targeted at children. Evidence of their success is less than one would desire but still somewhat encouraging. All of these programs involve a component of active discussion or dialogue.

Similarly, at the level of higher education, Smith (1977) observed twelve college classrooms in different disciplines and found that student participation, teacher encouragement, and student-to-student interaction were positively related to critical thinking outcomes. This fits well with both the pre-college research and with the results of other research on college teaching methods, which found discussion to be superior to lecture in experiments using measures of thinking or problem solving (McKeachie, 1986).

Supporting the conclusion that discussion is likely to increase opportunities for students to practice critical thinking is the finding by Fischer and Grant (1983) that in small classes student responses showed greater use of analysis, synthesis, and evaluation than in large classes.

Mayer (1989) described three programs for training thinking. One was structure training in which students learned how to outline sections of their science textbooks. Second was representation training, in which students learned how to translate sentences from mathematical word problems into concrete diagrams. Third was conceptual model training in which students learned how to describe what goes on inside the computer for several BASIC computer programming statements. All the training programs had the following elements:

1. They considered thinking as a collection of skills instead of as a unitary activity.
2. Training was focused on the methods and strategies for problem solving rather than on getting the right answers in the problem; that is, the *process* was emphasized in comparison to the product.
3. Thinking-skill instruction was integrated within existing subject material domain instead of being taught in a domain-independent, general problem-solving course.

Problem Solving in Content Courses. Turning to research on teaching problem solving in particular courses, we get some additional hints of possible answers to the "how to teach" question. The typical teacher—teaching problem solving in a discipline such as mathematics—assumes that the way to do it is to have students solve lots of problems. This is not a bad assumption, but teachers can probably do better by being more explicit about the specific methods and strategies to be used and by noting differences in the approaches useful for novices as compared with those used by experts. Working in thermodynamics, Konst, Wielenga, Elshout, and Jansweijer, (1983) have found that beginners need to go through an orientation phase involving: (1) bringing order out of chaos; (2) discovering uncovered ideas; (3) developing strategies; (4) and avoiding jumping to conclusions. In studies of medical problem solving Elstein, Shulman & Sprafka, (1978) found that, in areas of no prior knowledge, a strategy focusing on one approach should be preferred; with more knowledge, simultaneous multiple-hypothesis testing is efficient. Thus problem solving instruction for beginners needs to differ from that for students with more experience. Problem representation is a key task for all problem solving but particularly so for beginners dealing with ill-defined problems.

Standard courses in logic apparently are not very successful in teaching practical skills in reasoning beyond the formal settings of problems used in logic courses. In a study of student development during logic courses, Cheng, Holyoak, Nisbett, and Oliver (1986) found that abstract teaching needed to be coupled with examples of concrete instances to be effective. In contrast to the difficulty in teaching thinking using formal logic training, instruction using a pragmatic reasoning schema did generalize to reasoning on other problems for which the schema was relevant. These results support these researchers' claim, that neither of the two dominant views of reasoning is sufficient. One is the view that people use syntactic rules of logic that transcend subject matter; the other is that reasoning depends upon domain-specific knowledge. Cheng et al. propose that people often use "pragmatic reasoning schemas"—general rules defined with respect to classes of goals and types of relationships.

In contrast to the lack of generalizability of courses in logic, training in statistics does generalize to everyday problems involving inferences about events perceived to be subject to random variability. Nisbett, Fong, Lehman, and Cheng (1987) reviewed research demonstrating that even brief formal training in inferential rules can enhance their use in reasoning in non-classroom situations.

Nisbett et al. (1987) show that transfer occurs when individuals have an intuitive grasp of an abstract rule, such as the law of large numbers, and are given this abstract rule or are given training on examples. The law of large numbers involves the principle that one needs larger samples when generalizing about populations that vary more in the relevant attribute than when generalizing about populations that vary less. Thus people are more willing to assume that all tribesmen on a remote island are brown based on a small sample of brown, fat, tribesmen, than that all are fat.

Studies of the effect of graduate training in psychology, chemistry, medicine, and law showed little difference among students at the beginning of training but significant differences after two years both for scientific and everyday problems in the use of statistical, methodological, and conditioning reasoning. Chemistry training had no effect, law produced improvement in the logic of conditional but not in statistical or confounded variable problems, while students in psychology and medicine gained on all three types of problems. These studies open up a new area of research on pragmatic reasoning rules as well as hope for dramatic improvements in teaching reasoning.

Mettes, Pilot, and Roossink (1981) describe a successful attempt to integrate subject matter and problem-solving in a thermodynamics course. Heuristics and problem-solving methods were presented with content in a step-by-step "Programme of Actions and Methods." General problem-solving strategies, such as working backwards, making sketches, and taking extensive notes to reduce the load on working memory, were tied directly to solving problems in the subject matter.

As we shall see in a later section of this monograph, peer learning is very effective. Schoenfeld (1980) uses peer learning extensively in teaching heuristics for mathematical problem solving. He challenges students to bring him hard problems. He then demonstrates and makes explicit such strategies as thinking of alternative approaches, evaluating the alternatives in terms of one's ability to carry them out in the time available, and monitoring progress. His own struggles teach students that one often comes to dead ends and must start over. Small group discussions and problem solving lead to student self-regulation with the teacher gradually fading out. At the end of each session, students and teacher take turns summarizing a solution episode, analyzing what they did and why.

Guided Design. "Guided Design" is a method of course organization and teaching developed by Wales (Wales & Stager, 1977) to teach engineering students problem solving and decision making. Guided design courses involve textbook and problem-solving assignments out of class and small-group decision making in class. The class time is spent on a sequence of open-ended problem-solving projects (perhaps three to five projects in a term). In one of Wales' classes, they were:

1. Developing Better Housing in a Rain Forest
2. Making University Campus Buildings Accessible
3. Providing Water and Power to a Mountain Cabin

Each guided design project involves use of subject matter from the text and is guided by printed material prepared by the teacher. The first printed instruction describes the situation and specifies the students' roles (e.g., Peace Corps workers). Student groups then identify the problem and set a goal for their work. After completing this step they are given a printed sheet showing how other groups have responded. Students are not asked to agree with other groups but to consider the other viewpoints. Similar feedback and directions are given at each step of the problem-solving process; for example:

1. Identify situation.
2. Set goal.
3. Gather information. (What information is needed? Where can it be obtained? Who will get what?)
4. Consider possible solutions. (List three or more ways to attain the goal.)
5. Consider constraints. (List limiting factors.)
6. Choose a solution. (Test solutions for positive and negative consequences before choosing.)
7. Analyze solution. (Identify important factors to be considered in working out the details of the solution.)
8. Synthesize analysis. (Produce a detailed solution.)
9. Evaluate solution. (How can the solution be evaluated?)

Students who took the guided design course showed better achievement in advanced courses and were less likely to drop out of engineering than comparable previous students.

Laboratory Teaching. Laboratories are believed to be important in teaching problem solving in the sciences but there is some evidence that they only achieve problem-solving goals if taught with a special emphasis on problem solving. While reviews of research on laboratory teaching find that laboratory courses are effective in improving skills in handling apparatus of visual-motor skills, laboratories generally are not very effective in teaching scientific method or problem solving (Shulman & Tamir, 1973; Bligh, Jacques, & Piper, 1980).

Lawrenz (1985), however, taught an inquiry oriented physical science lab using a three-phase learning cycle of (1) exploration, (2) invention, and (3) application. In all three phases students interacted in small groups. Significant gains were found on a pre-test/post-test measure of formal reasoning.

Bainter (1955) found that a problem-solving method was superior to traditional laboratory manual methods in teaching students to apply principles of physics in interpreting phenomena. Lahti (1956) also found a problem-solving method to be superior to more conventional procedures in developing students' abilities to design an experiment.

All of these studies point to the importance of developing understanding, rather than teaching problem solutions by going through a routine series of steps. Whether the laboratory is superior to the lecture-demonstration in developing understanding and problem-solving skills probably depends on the extent to which understanding of concepts and general problem-solving procedures are emphasized as opposed to "cookbook" methods.

Verbalization. One of the critical elements in learning, retention, and transfer of problem-solving skills is verbalization. Ahlum-Heath and di Vesta (1987) showed in a controlled experiment that practice with verbalizing the reason for taking a step before the step was taken resulted in improved performance. Verbalization was most helpful during the initial stages of learning.

The Alverno College Experience. Explicit verbalization is an important element of the Alverno College program. In teaching critical thinking throughout the college, the Alverno College faculty (Loacker et al., 1984) stress *explicitness, multiple opportunities to practice in different contexts*, and *emphasis on developing student self-awareness and self-assessment*. Growth in critical thinking abilities occurred over four years of college as demonstrated both on locally developed measures and on Stewart's Analysis of Argument, the *Watson-Glaser Critical Thinking Appraisal*, and the Kolb *Learning Styles Inventory*.

Summary. In summary, problem solving can be taught, but most success in teaching has come when the problem-solving skills have been explicitly developed in the context of existing subject matter, courses, or modules. Evidence for transfer to other subject matter domains is generally lacking.

Overall, the research on teaching problem solving, or other skills in thinking, is less conclusive than one would like. McMillan (1986) summarizes his review of critical thinking research as follows. "The results failed to support the use of specific instructional or course conditions to enhance critical thinking but did support the conclusion that college in general appears to improve critical thinking."

. . .

IV. Student Motivation

Although there are many models of motivation that may be relevant to college student learning (see Weiner, 1980b, for a review of general motivational models), we have chosen to use a general expectancy-value model to organize our review. Expectancy-value models are essentially cognitive models of motivation, in contrast to psychodynamic models (e.g., models based on Freudian or psychoanalytic theory), ego-psychology models (e.g., models based on Erikson's theory), learning theory or drive models (models based on Spence's or Hull's theories), or humanistic models (models based on Maslow's or Rogers' theories). Since we are primarily concerned with student cognitive development in our research program, rather than personality or social development, a cognitive model of motivation fits nicely with this focus.

Attribution theory (Weiner, 1979, 1985a, 1986), which has dominated research on motivation during the past two decades, relates nicely to expectancy-value theory. When one succeeds or fails at a task, the degree to which one attributes success or failure to effort, ability, or external factors determines one's expectancy of success on the task in the future. Although the sections of this literature review may treat cognition and motivation separately, one of the hallmarks of our research program is the examination of cognitive and motivational constructs taken together in the context of the college classroom.

Expectancy-value models are derived from Atkinson's (1964) model of achievement motivation. Recent cognitive reformulations of Atkinson's model have made the role of students' perceptions or cognitions central to achievement dynamics (e.g., Dweck & Elliott, 1983; Eccles, 1983; Nicholls, 1984; Weiner, 1985a, 1986). In Atkinson's model, the students' probability of success was defined objectively in terms of task difficulty. Several researchers, (e.g., Eccles, 1983; Weiner, 1985a, 1986) have pointed out that it is not the actual task difficulty that determines the students' expectancy for success but the students' perceived probability of success, given their perceptions of the task difficulty and their perceived ability. Accordingly, in these newer cognitive models of motivation, students' perceptions about themselves and the task are the most important components of motivation.

Figure 2 displays the general relationships between the expectancy and task value components and their relationship to achievement. Figure 2 is based on Eccles' (1983) expectancy-value model with additions and refinements added to integrate the various motivational constructs of other researchers. The six general constructs in the middle of the figure (i.e., student goal orientation, task value, student efficacy, control and outcome beliefs, perceptions of task difficulty, perceived competence, test anxiety and affect, and expectancy for success are all student perception constructs assumed to mediate the relationship between the college classroom environment and student involvement and achievement.

This is not to say that environmental characteristics may not have direct effects on student involvement or achievement, but that our predictive model will be stronger and more complete if student perceptions of the environment are included. Little research in higher education has addressed motivational issues using an expectancy-value model. Accordingly, our review focuses on the relevant higher education research when available, but it also includes research from developmental and educational psychology. Our goal is to provide a framework for organizing motivational constructs that will be useful both for theory and for guiding research on motivation for higher education.

A. The Expectancy Path

The expectancy path in Figure 2 is at the bottom of the figure and flows from students' efficacy, control, and outcome beliefs to their perceptions of the task, and from their perceived self-competence to expectancy. Expectancy, in combination with task value, is assumed to lead to task involvement and subsequent achievement. The relationship among the expectancy components are described below.

1. Expectancy

The expectancy component is defined as the student's belief about his or her probability of success (or failure) on a particular task. As Eccles (1983) has pointed out, there is a long history in motivational research documenting the importance of expectancies for academic performance, task persistence, and task choice (e.g., Atkinson, 1964; Covington & Omelich, 1979a, 1979b; Crandall, 1969; Dweck & Elliott, 1983; Feather, 1969; Lewin, 1938; Veroff, 1969). Expectancies can be specific or general. For example, students can believe they will fail a midterm exam in chemistry because they did not study (a specific short-term expectancy). A more generalized expectancy would be students' beliefs about their potential for receiving a good grade in chemistry, while an even more generalized expectancy would be the perception that they will do well or poorly in all future science courses or in college in general.

Figure 2
Components of Motivation

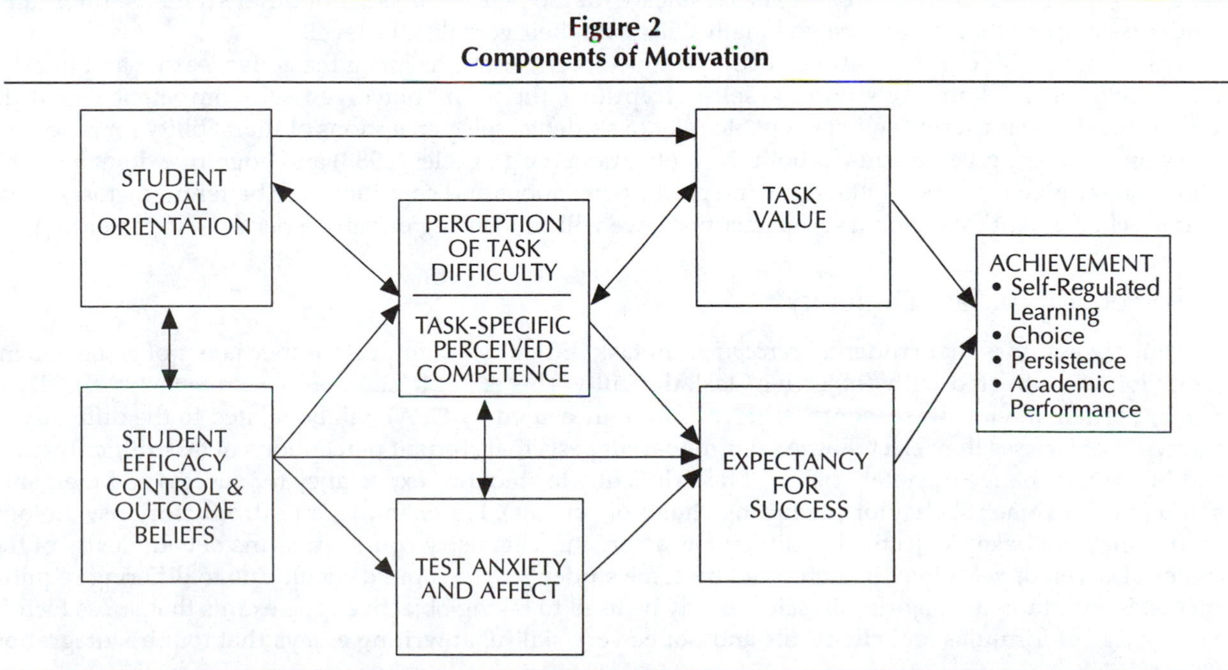

2. Perceived Self-Competence, Self-Concept

As Figure 2 demonstrates, there are two other types of student perceptions that play a direct role in expectancy formation: perceived self-competence and perceptions of task difficulty. Perceived self-competence is not the same as expectancy for success or actual ability. Self-competence is defined as students' *perceptions* of their ability to accomplish a particular task. As such, it should be isomorphic to actual ability, but it is not necessarily identical to actual ability. It differs from expectancy for success in that a student can have a high perceived competence for a task, but, under certain conditions (i.e., stress, an extremely difficult or boring task, a biased teacher), not have a high expectancy for success. It is the interaction of the student's perception of task difficulty and perceived competence that is assumed to produce the student's expectancy (Dweck & Elliot, 1983; Eccles, 1983). In addition, perceived competence can vary along the specific to global dimension as does expectancy, however, it is generally assumed to be more stable than expectancy (Harter, 1983).

The construct of perceived self-competence is related to the self-concept literature (e.g., Harter, 1983; Shavelson & Bolus, 1982; Marsh et al., 1984) as well as the self-efficacy literature (e.g., Bandura, 1982). A long history of research demonstrates that self-concept is correlated with achievement, with positive self-concepts related to higher achievement (see reviews by Harter, 1983; Purkey, 1970; Rosenberg, 1979; Wylie, 1974, 1979). Although there is a continuing controversy on the causal predominance of self-concept over achievement (cf., Caslyn & Kenny, 1977; Dweck, 1975; Eccles, 1983; Scheirer & Kraut, 1979; Shavelson & Bolus, 1982), we do not plan to enter into this debate. Rather, we believe that self-concept and achievement are inextricably linked in a synergistic fashion. Our goal is to examine how students' perceived competence is related to their use of cognitive strategies, task involvement, and subsequent achievement, not whether past achievement or self-concept is causally predominant in predicting future achievement.

Recent research on self-concept (e.g., Marsh & Shavelson, 1985; Shavelson & Bolus, 1982) suggests that self-concept is best characterized as being both task specific and global in nature. That is, students have both fairly domain-specific self-concepts (e.g., a self-concept for mathematics, science, English, sports or physical activity, social skills, etc.) and more global self-concepts that are made up of the domain-specific self-concepts. This distinction parallels the discussion between domain-specific cognitive skills and more global, generalizable cognitive skills (Pintrich et al., 1986).

Marsh, Byrne, & Shavelson (1988) found that verbal and math self-concepts were nearly uncorrelated. Verbal achievement positively affected verbal self-concept but negatively affected math self-concept, while math achievement positively affected math self-concept but negatively affected verbal self-concept. Self-concepts are a function of external and internal comparison processes. Externally, students compare their own math and verbal skills with the perceived skills of other students. Internally, students compare their self-perceived math skills with their verbal skills level.

In keeping with our general social-cognitive perspective, emphasizing the active learner and our dynamic relationships among students' self-perceptions, the term "perceived self-competence" is used rather than the static term "self-concept" to refer to students' self-perceptions of their ability for academic tasks. In addition, given results in both the motivational (e.g., Eccles, 1983) and cognitive domains (e.g., Stevenson & Newman, 1986) that domain-specific perceptions and cognitions are better predictors of academic achievement than global self-perceptions, we will be focusing on fairly specific self-perceptions.

3. Perceptions of Task Difficulty

Our model assumes that students' *perceptions* of task difficulty are important mediators of achievement behavior as contrasted with "objective" task difficulty. This is not to say that objective task difficulty is not important; obviously, students' achievement (if measured by GPA) will be related to the difficulty of the types of courses they elect. Rather, our model suggests that student perceptions of task difficulty may modulate and change the relationship of task difficulty to students' expectancy for success and their subsequent achievement behavior (including choice of courses). For example, an introductory psychology course may not be as "objectively" difficult as an organic chemistry course in terms of complexity of the material covered, yet it may be perceived by some students to be more difficult due to differing requirements. Some students majoring in science may be used to taking objective type exams that stress factual knowledge of formulas and chemicals and not be very skillful at writing essays that require integration of different abstract psychological theories. Consequently, these students may perceive the writing of a psychology paper to be more "difficult" than taking an exam in chemistry. In contrast, other students may perceive the chemistry course as much more difficult. These differing perceptions of task difficulty should lead to different expectancies for success.

The exact relationship of perceived task difficulty to expectancy is not clear. As Eccles (1983) points out, perceptions of task difficulty should be inversely related to expectancy. However, in her review of this construct, Eccles suggests that the literature on the relationship between perceived task difficulty and expectancy is not straightforward. First, Eccles notes that many experimental studies (e.g., Atkinson & Birch, 1970; Kukla, 1978; Meyer, Folkes, & Weiner, 1976; Weiner, 1972, 1974) show that students' persistence and choice of tasks is a curvilinear function of perceived task difficulty; tasks of moderate difficulty seem to elicit the most choice and persistence, while easy and very difficult tasks result in lower levels of choice or persistence. However, since many of these laboratory studies use tasks with low ecological validity (e.g., anagrams, ring toss games), it is not clear that the curvilinear function generalizes to actual college student achievement behavior (Eccles, 1983).

While Eccles suggests that there might be a simple negative relationship between task difficulty and choice of courses (courses perceived to be harder should be chosen less), task difficulty also interacts with task value to produce choice. For example, pre-med courses might be perceived as being very difficult, but because these courses have high task-value for some students (e.g., they have a high utility value for students who have a goal of becoming a doctor), these courses may be selected by pre-med students, even if their expectancy for success in these courses is low. Accordingly, there is not a simple relationship between task difficulty, expectancy for success and achievement behavior. Research needs to be done to clarify these relationships in ecologically valid settings with ecologically valid tasks. Our research represents one attempt to address this gap in the literature.

4. Test Anxiety and Affect

In our model, test anxiety is placed near the perceived-competence construct. We are not proposing that it is the same construct as perceived competence, as others have (e.g., see Nicholls, 1976), but that it is closely tied to perceived competence. Generally, test anxiety is assumed to have two components, a worry (or cognitive) component and an emotionality component. Given previous research demonstrating that the cognitive component is most closely associated with performance decrements (Tobias, 1985), we will focus on the cognitive component in our research, although we will include emotionality. Our model also assumes that student beliefs influence test anxiety and that test anxiety is negatively related to expectancy for success (see Figure 2). As will become clear in the following discussion, we also link test anxiety to students' cognitions as well as to task characteristics.

On the basis of a meta-analysis review of 562 studies relating test anxiety and academic achievement, Hembree (1988) found that test anxiety causes poor performance and relates inversely to students' self-esteem and directly to their fear of negative evaluation and defensiveness.

There are many different theoretical explanations for the well-documented finding that test anxiety interferes with performance. Two general theoretical models have been suggested: a cognitive skills deficit model and an attentional-interference model (Tobias, 1985).

Cognitive skills deficit model. The cognitive skills deficit model generally includes two components: a learning strategies or skills deficit and a test-taking skills deficit (Tobias, 1985). The research, as reviewed by Tobias, shows that the learning skills deficit component is consistently related to anxiety and performance, while the research is somewhat contradictory on the test-taking skills deficit component. The learning skills deficit component of the cognitive deficit model (e.g., Benjamin, McKeachie, Lin, & Holinger, 1981; Culler & Holahan, 1980) includes study skills such as active reading, reviewing material, comprehension monitoring, and metacognition that can be called macrolevel cognitive processes (e.g., Tobias, 1982) as well as microlevel cognitive processes that make up basic information processing activities (e.g., elaboration, rehearsal, and imagery techniques for memory, see Weinstein & Mayer, 1986). As Tobias (1985) has pointed out, a variety of researchers have shown that students high in test anxiety often have less effective study skills, which leads to less effective processing of information in the encoding and acquisition phase of learning (in other words, poor preparation) and a subsequent decrement in performance. In line with this research, the cognitive learning skills deficit component of our general model is proposed as a mediator of anxiety's influence on performance (see Figure 2).

In contrast to the learning skills deficit, which is assumed to operate before the student takes the exam, the test-taking skills deficit is assumed to operate at the time of the exam. Students who do not have good test-taking strategies might do poorly on the exam even if they are well-prepared (i.e., have good learning strategies). Tobias (1985) suggests that students with low test-taking strategies (e.g., lack of knowledge about differences in how to answer multiple choice vs. essay questions) become aware that they are doing poorly in the exam. This awareness results in students' becoming anxious and the onset of attentional-interference problems. Test-taking skills are not synonymous with the attentional-interference effects of anxiety, however. Paulman and Kenney (1984) have shown that test anxiety and test-taking skills have separate effects on performance.

Attentional-interference model. The attentional-interference model suggests that anxious students' drop in performance (Wine, 1971) is due to the occurrence of interfering and distracting thoughts (e.g., "I'm really failing this exam; I don't know what to do.") that divide the students' attention between these "self-perturbing ideations" (see Bandura, 1982) or task-irrelevant thoughts and the task relevant thoughts about the actual exam. With worry occupying much of the processing capacity of the students' minds, it is no surprise that the highly anxious student does poorly on the exam, even if well prepared.

Deffenbacher (1988) compared the effect of four different types of test anxiety on performance decrement and found that worry (cognitive concern and preoccupation about performance) was the greatest source of performance decrement.

Darke (1988), on the basis of three separate but interrelated experiments, concluded that anxiety affects various inferential reasoning tasks differently. There was no performance deficit for anxious students when inferring anaphoric relations. (Anaphoric relations are those essential to the understanding of the text and can be made in an automatic manner.)

Cognitive capacity synthesis of deficit and interference models. A recent cognitive capacity formulation by Tobias (1985) has suggested that the deficit and interference models should not be seen as mutually exclusive but rather as inversely complementary. The model assumes that students have a limited cognitive capacity to process information at any one time. The model also proposes that the cognitive components of learning strategies and test-taking skills tend to increase the amount of cognitive capacity available to the student for any one task, while, in a complementary but inverse fashion, the interference components decrease the cognitive capacity available. If this is so, then good learning strategies and test-taking skills should reduce the cognitive demands on the student when the student is taking the exam while interfering thoughts increase cognitive demands. For example, if the student is well prepared (because of good study skills) and has good test-taking strategies (allowing him or her to activate the appropriate schema for the type of test questions), then his or her cognitive capacity is free to deal with any interfering anxious thoughts that may arise in the testing situation. Accordingly, the model predicts a disordinal interaction between cognitive skills and the interference aspect of test anxiety. Students high in cognitive skills and low in the interference aspect of test anxiety should perform at the highest level, while students low in cognitive skills but high in interfering thoughts should suffer the largest performance decrement. Students with low skills and low amounts of interference and high skills and high interference should be at intermediate levels of performance in Tobias' (1985) model.

This model represents an important integration of the cognitive and interference models of anxiety based on a general information-processing model. However, it does not include a cognitive-motivational component. Recent reviews (e.g., Pintrich et al., 1986) have suggested the need to integrate cognitive-motivational constructs with cognitive constructs. It is becoming clear to various researcheres that cognitive strategies (e.g., learning strategies and test-taking strategies) are not recruited and employed in isolation from motivational components. Accordingly, there is a need for the addition of motivational components, such as ability and effort attributions and expectancies for success, to the cognitive capacity model. Covington (1985) has begun to explore the interactions between anxiety and students' attributional patterns. He has found that students' attributions of success or failure to their own lack or adequacy of ability mediate some of the effects of anxiety. He also found that effort attributions did not mediate anxiety effects, mainly because high-anxious students reported that they tried as hard as other students. Pintrich (1986) also found that high and low-anxious students did not differ in their effort, but that high-anxious students had lower levels of cognitive skills than low-anxious students. However, Pintrich did find that the relationship of these cognitive skills to student performance was mediated through effort. That is, having high levels of cognitive skills did not lead directly to improved performance, it was only the motivated and effortful use of these strategies that led to improved performance.

Types of test-anxious students. A different way to synthesize study skills and interference models has recently been suggested by Naveh-Benjamin, McKeachie, and Lin (1987). Instead of claiming that both skill deficiency and interference from worry occur in all highly test-anxious students, these authors suggest that different types of such students possess different types of deficits. A first type includes highly test-anxious students with good study skills who do not have problems in encoding and organizing (learning) the information, but rather have a major problem in retrieval for tests, probably due to interfering thoughts. A second type includes highly test-anxious students with poor study habits who have problems in all stages of processing, both in learning the information and in retrieving it. Such a distinction was supported by results comparing performance of these types of highly test-anxious students in evaluative and non-evaluative situations. Results showed that those highly test-anxious students with good study skills did well on a task requiring organizational skills in a non-evaluative situation. In such a situation they were able to use their knowledge without interfering thoughts. However, in an evaluative situation they did as poorly as the other highly test-anxious students who lack study skills. In contrast, highly test-anxious students with poor study skills performed poorly in a non-evaluative situation as well as on tests.

Further support for the above distinction between two types of highly test-anxious students was obtained in a study by Naveh-Benjamin (1985) which showed that each of the above types of highly test-anxious students benefited from different training programs. Desensitization and study-skills training show that highly test-anxious students with good study habits benefit more from a desensitization training program that reduced their interfering thoughts. These students showed a greater decrease in anxiety and an improvement in course performance over the semester in comparison with a group of the same type of students who received study skills training. In contrast, those highly test-anxious students with poor study habits benefited more from a training program intended to improve their study skills. These students showed a greater decrease in anxiety and an increase in course grades over the semester in comparison with a group of the same type of students who received desensitization training.

Covington & Omelich (1988) suggested that test anxiety is a cluster of interrelated factors whose relationships to cognitions, motivation, and ultimately to test performance, change as an individual progresses through the achievement cycle. They also reported that the detrimental effect of test anxiety of performance is more of a result of poor study strategies than of anxiety. Similarly Covington and Omelich (1987) examined the hypothesis that anxiety inhibits college students' test performance by "temporarily blocking" previously learned responses. Following a midterm examination, college students were administered the same test items under non-evaluative conditions. They found that subjects reacted differently to difficult and easy test items. Performance on difficult test items was not affected by the evaluative or non-evaluative conditions. However, the interference phenomena was found to be true for easy items. The "blocking hypothesis" was not confirmed totally but it provided some evidence to the fact that interference at the time of test may be related to the previous preparation of the subject matter. In short, anxiety won't affect you if you don't know the answer, but it might block performance on items you otherwise would be able to answer.

5. Student Efficacy, Control, and Outcome Beliefs

The fifth component of the expectancy path in our model is the individual's beliefs about efficacy, control and outcome. There have been a number of constructs and theories proposed about the role of these beliefs in student achievement. For example, early work on locus of control (e.g., Rotter, 1966) found that students who believed that they were in control of their behavior and could influence the environment tended to achieve at higher levels. Although this general idea of internality is still represented in current motivational theories, newer models stress that these perceptions of control may be more situationally specific in contrast to stable personality traits and that locus of causality is a separate construct from controllability (Weiner, 1985a, 1986). Accordingly, our approach is to conceptualize these beliefs about efficacy, control and outcome in a more dynamic, social cognitive perspective. We have incorporated the ideas from several different theories in this section, but a good starting point is attributional theory.

Attributional theory proposes that students' causal attributions for success and failure, not actual success or failure, mediate future expectancies. A large number of studies (see reviews by Weiner, 1985a, 1986) have shown that students who tend to attribute success to ability (e.g., "I did well on that exam because I'm smart") will expect to do well on future exams because ability is assumed to be stable over time. In contrast, students who tend to attribute their success to other causes (e.g., task difficulty, an easy exam, or extra effort) will not have as high expectancies because the task or effort can change over time. In failure situations, stable attributions to ability have detrimental effects on expectancy. That is, students who attribute their poor performance to ability (e.g., "I did poorly because I'm not very smart") will tend to have lower expectancies for future exams. Just the opposite is true of unstable attributions for failure. Students who attribute failure to effort tend to have higher expectancies because they can change their level of effort for the next exam or in the case of attributing failure to a difficult exam, expect that the next exam will be less difficult.

Many attributions can be provided for most achievement situations (e.g., ability, skill, sustained effort, unstable effort, luck, task difficulty, mood, illness, fatigue, other people, interest, knowledge, and attention; see Weiner, 1980b, 1985a, 1986 for reviews). However, it is not the actual attributions per se that seem to determine consequences but their common causal dimensions (Weiner, 1985a, 1986). The three main dimensions on which attributions can be placed include *locus, stability*, and *controllability*, although intentionality and globality are other dimensions that have appeared in some analyses (Weiner, 1985b, 1986). It is the causal properties of the dimensions that relate to future expectancy and behavior.

The *locus* dimension refers to the internal or external nature of the cause in relation to the individual. For example, ability and effort are internal causes, while task difficulty and luck are external causes. It was assumed that having an internal locus-of-causality is good (Rotter, 1966). However, this one-dimensional locus-of-control formulation has proven too simplistic and inadequate to account for the data (Weiner, 1986). The other dimensions of stability and controllability also need to be included in the model since believing that the cause of failure is one's own inherent lack of ability is not likely to lead to greater success.

The *stability* of an attribution refers to the manner in which the cause may fluctuate over time. For example, ability (or, more appropriately, aptitude) is an internal cause that is assumed to be stable over time, while effort (also an internal cause) is assumed to be changeable over time. Luck and task difficulty are both external causes that are assumed to be unstable. Weiner (1986) has suggested that the stability dimension is most closely related to changes in expectancy for success in the achievement context. According to Weiner's expectancy principle, attributions to stable causes (e.g., ability) should result in more positive expectancies for the outcome in future situations, while attributions to unstable causes may result in a different expectancy or an unchanged expectancy for the outcome.

The *controllability* dimension refers to the individual's ability to control the cause. For example, mood, fatigue, and effort are all internal and unstable causes, yet effort is generally under the individual's volitional control while mood and fatigue are not (Weiner, 1986). In the same manner, aptitude (an internal and stable cause) is not considered to be under the individual's control, while skill (an internal and unstable cause) can be brought under the individual's control. While stability is assumed to relate to expectancy change, controllability and locus are assumed to relate to students' affective reactions in Weiner's (1986) model.

Attributional theory is a theory of how people reason about causes of events. Researchers have shown that individuals tend to show consistent patterns in their attributional reasoning over time and across different achievement tasks. These patterns have been shown to be related to achievement behavior. These different patterns can be grouped according to three dimensions of causality: stability, internality, and controllability.

Students' beliefs about the stability of achievement. A few attributions seem to predominate in most achievement contexts. Weiner (1986) suggests that the two most important attributions in the achievement domain are effort and ability. Although these two attributions are understood intuitively by most people, recent theory and research by Nicholls (1984) and Dweck and Elliott (1983) suggest that individuals can differ in their conceptions of ability. Young children believe abilities are learnable skills. As they grow older they develop the misconception that ability is an unchangeable aptitude.

In the skill-based model, students assume they can improve with effort and that skill rises with increased mastery of the task. Dweck and Elliot (1983) term this an "incremental" approach to ability. In contrast, in the aptitude model, ability is seen as capacity (Nicholls, 1984), setting a limit on improvement of performance as well as on the efficacy of effort for improvement. Dweck and Elliott (1983) term this an "entity" approach to ability.

These conceptions of ability should be related to students' expectancy and perceived competence. Students who have a skill-based or incremental model of ability will assume that effortful behavior will help them improve, resulting in a higher expectancy for success. In addition, they will tend to judge their competence in terms of their own self-mastery of a task, rather than in relation to others' performance. In contrast, students with an entity or aptitude theory will tend to see their past performance as limiting their future performance, which is not debilitating if one perceives oneself as having high aptitude and has had success in the past, but it can be debilitating if one does not have a pattern of past success and high perceived competence. These constructs are relatively new and have been investigated with younger children but have not been explored in great detail with college students. In our work we will examine these constructs and their relationships to perceived competence, expectancy, and performance.

Students' beliefs about the internal or external locus of achievement. The locus of causality dimension has generated a variety of models concerning the individuals' pattern of intrinsic or extrinsic control (e.g., Lefcourt, 1976; Rotter, 1966). The general message of all these models is that a general pattern of perception of internal control results in positive outcomes (i.e., higher achievement, high self-esteem), while sustained perceptions of external control result in negative outcomes. For example, Deci (1975) and de Charms (1968) have discussed perceptions of control in terms of the students' belief in self-determination. De Charms (1968) coined the terms "origins" and "pawns" to describe students who believed they were able to control their actions and students who believed others controlled their behavior.

More recently, Connell (1985) has suggested that there are three aspects of control beliefs: an internal source, an external source or powerful others, and an unknown source. Students who believe in internal sources of control are assumed to perform better than students who believe powerful others (e.g., teachers, parents) are responsible for their success or failure and better than those students who don't know who or what is responsible for the outcomes.

These models generally assume that perception of internal control is a positive condition and external or unknown control is negative. Reviews of research in this area are somewhat conflicting, however. For example, Stipek and Weisz (1981) in a review of research on perceived control and academic achievement conclude that there is little relationship between perceptions of control and elementary students' academic achievement. In contrast, Findley and Cooper (1983), in a larger review that included studies of college students and adults, found a small but significant positive relationship between perception of internal control and academic achievement. Findley and Cooper also found evidence for a curvilinear relationship between perceptions of internal control and achievement. They found that the relationship was strongest for young adolescents (e.g., junior high school students) and weakest for elementary students (first through third grade) and college students. This curvilinear relationship by age may be responsible for the conflicting findings of previous reviews if the review did not sample or analyze by age of subject. In addition, Findley and Cooper found that the positive relationship was stronger for males than females. These findings suggest that for college students, the relationship between perceptions of internal control and achievement may not be straightforward.

Almost all the models concerned with internal orientation automatically assume that higher levels of internal control result in positive outcomes. However, this may not necessarily be the case. There may be times when perceptions of internal control may be debilitating (e.g., Covington & Beery, 1976). Harter (1985) has proposed a refinement of the general internal-external orientation with her construct of beneffectance. The neologism, beneffectance, is formed by combining effectance motivation (White, 1959) and beneficence, meaning good outcomes (see Greenwald, 1980). Harter proposes that beneffectance involves the individual's tendency to attribute successful outcomes to internal causes and attribute failure outcomes to external causes. This hedonic bias should result in more positive outcomes. As expected, students who tend to have a high level of beneffectance, tend to perform better on academic tasks and have higher expectancies for future success (Harter, 1985).

Students' beliefs about the controllability of achievement. As Weiner (1986) points out, the controllability dimension is related to the internal dimension as well as the intentionality dimension, but they can be separated on conceptual grounds. In fact, most of the early social learning research on locus of control confounded the internality and controllability dimensions (Weiner, 1986). The controllability dimension concerns the individual's perception that events are controllable. The most common attributional pattern related to this dimension is one that has been labeled "learned helplessness" (e.g., Seligman, 1975). The negative aspect of this pattern has been the focus of much of the research, hence the negative label. The basic pattern is that individuals perceive no association or contingency between their own behavior and the environment in terms of outcomes, other's behavior (i.e., the teacher's), rewards, and punishments. This lack of perceived contingency can lead to passivity, anxiety, lack of effort, and lower achievement levels (Weiner, 1980b). This attributional pattern is related to students' efficacy beliefs.

Students' self-efficacy has been defined as individuals' beliefs that their performance capabilities in a particular domain (Bandura, 1982; Schunk, 1985). The construct of self-efficacy includes students' judgments about their ability to accomplish certain goals or tasks by their actions in specific situations (Schunk, 1985). This approach implies a relatively situational or domain specific construct rather than a global personality trait. In an achievement context, it includes students' confidence in their cognitive skills to perform the academic task. In terms of our model these beliefs about self-efficacy should be related to task difficulty perceptions as well as expectancy for success. In addition, it is important to distinguish these perceptions of efficacy from students' beliefs about outcome. As Schunk (1985) has pointed out, outcome expectations refer to persons' beliefs concerning their ability to influence outcomes, that is, their belief that the environment is responsive to their actions. This belief that outcomes are contingent on their behavior leads individuals to have higher expectations for success and should lead to more persistence. These beliefs are distinct from students' self-appraisals of their ability to master task (Schunk, 1985). Accordingly, beliefs about self-efficacy and outcome can vary. For example, a student may believe that she has the capability to perform well on exams, but at the same time, expect a poor grade because of a tight grading curve in the class or a belief that the instructor's criteria for evaluating the exam are arbitrary. These beliefs about the grading system would lead the student to expect a lower outcome than her self-efficacy beliefs would predict. It is important, therefore, to assess not only students' self-perceptions of efficacy but also their beliefs about the responsiveness of the environment to their actions.

Deboer (1986) found that students' decisions to continue to science depended on self-perceived ability; self-ability depended on students' belief that they had succeeded in the past.

Wood and Locke (1987) examined the relationship between academic self-efficacy, grade goals, ability and performance in college course. They found that self-efficacy was significantly related to academic performance and to self-set academic grade goals. Grade goals and ability were in turn related to course performance.

Smith, Pintrich, and Doljanac (1988) also reported a strong direct relationship between self-efficacy and academic performance, but suggested that this relationship was moderated by personal and situational factors. For example, intrinsic motivation enhanced the relationship between self-efficacy and academic performance, while learning strategies, particularly those involving deep processing of information, weakened the link. Females were found to be more sensitive than males to situational norms and expectations that enhanced their self-efficacy. Therefore, to be effective, interventions aimed at enhancing self-efficacy should take into account students' cognitive coping style, intrinsic motivation, and personal and situational factors.

In addition to the notion of controllability, a number of researchers have suggested that intentionality is an important dimension of achievement beliefs. For example, an effort attribution for success or failure can be seen as intentional. A student must purposively exert effort in an intentional manner. In contrast, a study-strategy attribution for success or failure generally would not be considered intentional. Students do not intentionally use a poor study strategy that leads to failure (Weiner, 1985a). They usually don't use a particular strategy because they don't have the knowledge of the strategy (declarative knowledge), how to use it (procedural knowledge) or don't recognize the situation as appropriate for the strategy (conditional knowledge). Of course, intentionality is not orthogonal to control. It seems likely that any attribution that can be considered intentional would also be controllable. In addition, as Weiner (1986) points out, logically, intention is not a characteristic of an attribution, it is a characteristic of an action or individual and best described as motivational orientation. As such, Weiner (1985a) leaves intentionality out of his general attributional model and classification of attributions along causal dimensions. The concept of intentionality as a motivational orientation, however, has important implications for our research on student learning. Recent work by Kuhl (1983, 1985), Corno (1986) and Skinner (1985) has addressed the relationship between intentionality and the individual's control of their actions and their cognition and learning. Basically, this research shows that students who believe they have control over their behavior and act accordingly (with volition) perform better than students who do not have this type of motivational orientation. Since much college learning takes place outside the classroom and is under the control of the student, these concepts of control, volition, and intention are important aspects of students' motivational orientations. Accordingly, we have included these beliefs in our model of motivation.

Beginning freshmen who explain failure as the result of fixed ability often receive lower grades than comparable students who explain failure in terms of external, unstable, or specific causes. Students with a negative explanatory style are less likely to have specific academic goals and make less use of academic advising than those with a more positive style of explaining failure (Peterson & Barrett, 1987). Thus one method of improving student performance may be to help students recognize the possibility of developing needed skills as well as clarifying academic goals.

McCombs (1987a) provides support for this view in a review of research and theory indicating that, for students to develop the motivation necessary for self-directed learning, they must believe that they have the ability to achieve the level of competence necessary for reaching personally meaningful goals. McCombs suggests that if we are to provide useful suggestions for teachers, we need better methods of assessing students' goals, their evaluations of their competencies, and their assessment of the personal significance of particular learning tasks as well as their belief in the ability to assume self direction and take responsibility for their own learning. This is the direction of NCRIPTAL research, as exemplified by our Motivated Strategies for Learning Questionnaire.

McCombs (1986) lists six principles:

1. Human behavior is basically motivated by needs for self-development and self-determination.
2. The self-system operates as the base set of "filters" through which all information is processed, transformed, and encoded.
3. The self-referent nature of this filtering process maintains the illusions of control or self-determination that lie at the base of self-esteem maintenance.
4. Self-reference can become an effective strategy for generating motivation to learn and for producing more effective learning.
5. Affect plays a major role in self-system development, motivation, and the engagement of self-regulated learning processes and strategies.
6. Autonomous learning is an inherently natural process driven by the need to fulfill self-development and self-determination goals.

In McCombs' model, needs for self-development and self-determination lead to self-system structures—goals, values, beliefs. Self-system structures interact with self-evaluative processes to determine outcome expectancies, which, in turn, generate affect, which influences motivation leading to performance. Performance outcomes cycle back to affect self-system structures, and self-regulation processes interact with metacognitive and cognitive structures to produce a dynamic system.

McCombs (1987b) has developed a test battery to assess self-evaluations of competence and personal control.

B. The Task-Value Path

The task-value path in the model has been less developed than the expectancy path (Eccles, 1983; Parsons & Goff, 1980). In our formulation, we have followed Eccles' conceptualization of task value and student goals. The general flow of the model is from students' goal orientation to task values. A simple example of the flow follows. A young woman decides that she would like to become a doctor. She may then adopt this career goal as one of her life goals. This goal adoption then influences her value for certain kinds of tasks in college (e.g., choosing pre-med courses over other types of courses). The causal flow and definitions of the constructs are explored in more detail below.

1. Task-Value Component

The task-value component was originally conceived as the value an individual attached to success or failure on a task. This value, like probability for success, was defined in objective task terms by Atkinson (1964) in his achievement motivation theory. However, as Eccles (1983) points out, task value can be conceived of in more subjective, broader, and individualistic terms (cf. Parsons & Goff, 1978, 1980; Raynor, 1974; Spenner & Featherman, 1978). This more subjective focus includes the characteristics of the task as well as the needs and goals of the student. Three components of task value have been proposed by Eccles (1983) as important in achievement dynamics: the attainment value of the task, the intrinsic value or the intrinsic interest value of the task, and the utility value of the task for future goals. There has been very little research on these components of task value.

a. Attainment Value

This component of task value refers to the students' perception of the task's ability to provide a challenge, fulfill certain achievement needs, and to confirm a salient aspect of the self (e.g., competence). For example, students who think of themselves as "smart" and perceive a certain course as both a challenge and a confirmation of "smartness" (e.g., organic chemistry), would have a high attainment value for this course (Eccles, 1983). High attainment value should lead to more involvement in the task.

b. Intrinsic, or Interest, Value

The intrinsic, or interest, value of a task refers to the individual's inherent enjoyment of the task. Intrinsic interest is assumed to influence students' involvement in the task and their future achievement. Interest in the task is partially a function of the individual's preferences as well as aspects of the task (e.g., Malone, 1981). Interest is not always related to successful goal achievement. A student may be so interested in a given subject that they spend their time on reading accessory sources and fail to complete requirements.

c. Utility Value

In contrast to the "means" or "process" motivational dynamic of intrinsic task value, utility value refers to the "ends" or instrumental motivation of the student (Eccles, 1983). Utility value is determined by the importance of the task in facilitating the student's goals. For example, organic chemistry may not be an inherently interesting task or have high attainment value for a student, but because the student has a goal of becoming a doctor, the course has a high utility value for the student. This instrumental aspect of college students' motivational dynamics may play an important role in their choice of classes and their ultimate involvement in the course.

2. Motivational Views of Student Goal Orientation

Student goals influence the degree to which they value certain tasks, as the last example of the pre-med student demonstrates. Student goals can be conceptualized along a continuum from the global level (in terms of career goals and life goals) to the more specific level, referring to the students' approach to a particular task, exam, or course. We take a fairly task-specific approach to student goals, in keeping with our general model of examining cognition and motivation in relationship to the instructional and task environment that students confront in college. Although a number of researchers have discussed student goals, there are three general perspectives, an intrinsic motivation model, a self-worth model, and a cognitive goal formation model. They range, in order, from more to less general views of student goal structure. However, these models are not intended to subsume one another. Rather, they represent relatively distinct ways of thinking about a student's motivation to learn.

a. Intrinsic Motivation Model

Intrinsic motivation is the expectation that engaging in, or completing, a task will be enjoyable. Thus it includes both attainment value and interest. Human beings, like other animals, are inherently curious about things that differ from their previous experience. (If the difference is too great, however, we become anxious.) We are born problem solvers, enjoying solving challenging problems. What is seen as an enjoyable challenge obviously depends on each individual's previous experience. Intrinsic motivation for learning contrasts with extrinsic motivation—in which the motivation is determined by values not inherent in the task such as grades, vocational utility, or praise.

Research and theory in intrinsic motivation have a long and varied history. This perspective on human motivation began as an effort to make sense of our propensity to actively seek engagement with the surrounding environment and was only recently reconceptualized as an inherent part of a student's motivation to learn in the classroom. Examples of this early perspective are provided by the work of Woodworth, McDougal, Allport, White, and others. Woodworth (1958) argued that only when an activity is energized through some inherent aspect of its process or substance will it be performed freely and effectively. McDougal (1908) viewed intrinsic motivation as an innate human propensity. This early work received support from research on the reinforcing qualities of exploratory behavior among nonhumans (Nissen, 1930; Montgomery & Segall, 1955), which demonstrated that the exploration of novel environmental stimuli is both an intrinsically rewarding activity (Harlow, 1950; Harlow, Harlow, & Meyer, 1950; Premack, 1959, 1963), and a secondary reinforcer of other responses (Butler & Harlow, 1957).

Research focusing on the functional properties and goals of intrinsic motivation, including the reduction of psychological incongruity (cf. Hunt, 1971; McClelland et al., 1953; Berlyne, 1971), cognitive dissonance (Festinger, 1957), and the reduction of uncertainty (Kagan, 1972), suggests that intrinsic motivation may be most fruitfully conceptualized as serving the needs of humans to deal effectively with their environments (White, 1959). In this way, intrinsic motivation is related to control beliefs and perceived competence from the expectancy side of the model. This concept encompasses the motivation to engage in activities including exploration, manipulation, attention, thought, and communication (Deci, 1975).

The intrinsic motivation to effectively interact with the environment may be quite undifferentiated in children (White, 1959; Deci & Ryan, 1985), while becoming progressively differentiated into more specific motives like mastery, cognizance, and achievement among adolescents and adults. Particular motives become more salient to a person's make-up through experiences as different aspects of environments call for different types of effective functioning (de Charms, 1968).

While we question, with White (1959), the correctness of conceptualizing this propensity among humans in terms of simple drive states, two points seem well established. Humans, as well as other animals, appear to readily engage in the exploration and manipulation of stimulus objects within their environments, and the intrinsic incentives inherent in these activities appear to be important motivators of behavior (cf., Deci, 1975).

Intrinsic motivation to learn has been conceptualized in a somewhat different way. In large part, this differentiation is due to the need of educational researchers to capture important aspects of the classroom environment and characteristics of the student that are relevant to classroom learning. Consequently, we find that the basic propensity to pursue a sense of personal causality and competence is often joined with learning that enables the student to sustain the desire to learn (Corno & Rohrkemper, 1985). This reflects the development of cognitive and other academically related skills that include abilities to pursue achievement through one's own efforts, the ability to delay immediate gratification for less proximal but highly valued rewards, and a gradual reduction in fear of failure (Weiner, 1979; Corno & Rohrkemper, 1985). Harter and her colleagues (1985) have developed an instrument designed to assess a student's present capacity for intrinsically motivated learning.

She has proposed five student-centered dimensions of the intrinsic motivation to learn in the classroom. They are: challenge, curiosity, mastery, independent judgment, and internal evaluative criteria. These dimensions parallel some of the aspects of the models of Dweck and Elliott's (1983) and Nicholls' (1984). Each dimension can be conceptualized as a continuum along which individuals can vary. The challenge dimension refers to the individual's preference for challenging tasks or easy tasks. The curiosity dimension is anchored at one end by the student's tendency to work to satisfy his own interests and curiosity rather than working to please others (parents, instructors) or to obtain good grades. The students' preference for working out problems alone in contrast to relying on the instructor for assistance makes up the mastery dimension. A related dimension is the student's belief that she or he is capable of making judgments about what to do versus being dependent on the instructor for guidance. The last dimension concerns the student's reliance on internal criteria for judging success and failure versus reliance on external criteria (e.g., grades, social comparison) for judging performance.

A study by Koestner, Zuckerman, and Koestner (1987) suggests that the problem is even more complex. These researchers examined the relationships between praise, type of involvement, and intrinsic motivation. They found that intrinsic motivation was enhanced when a puzzle was presented as a game rather than as a measure of intelligence. Praise was not necessary, but praise for ability rather than effort resulted in a greater increment in intrinsic motivation. Higher levels of intrinsic motivation were associated with better performance.

This description of intrinsic motivation joins together, then, descriptors of person and social environment. It suggests that humans have a need to seek optimal levels of stimulation and sense of competence. By implication, it also suggests that the environment must provide students with appropriate opportunities and resources for such activities. Finally, our conceptualization of an intrinsic motivation to learn indicates that the individual comes to possess what Weiner (1979) has termed "personal responsibility factors." These factors or capacities enable the individual effectively to pursue involvement with intrinsically interesting education tasks.

b. Self-Worth Model

Covington and Beery (1976) have proposed a self-worth model of motivation that assumes that one of the driving forces of students' motivational dynamics is the maintenance of self-worth. In this model, students are not necessarily intrinsically motivated for challenge or mastery, but rather are motivated to increase their feelings of self-worth and self-esteem or at least protect their self-worth. In this model, the classroom context is seen as a competitive system with an inordinate emphasis on student ability (Covington & Beery, 1976). This classroom context encourages students to prefer to be seen by others as succeeding through ability rather than effort (Covington & Omelich, 1979a; 1979b). In addition, the model assumes that the nature of the classroom system produces more failure experiences than success experiences for most students. This system also distributes grades (or other rewards) on a fixed basis in an unequal distribution (e.g., grading on a curve). Under this system, with a scarcity of rewards and an emphasis on ability, students will tend to have a motivational orientation or goal to avoid failure rather than strive for success (Covington, 1985).

This failure-avoidance goal will result in a variety of strategies to avoid failure. The key attributional mechanism for failure-avoiding strategies concerns the nature of effort and ability. If students try hard at an academic task (a paper, an exam) and fail or do poorly, they often have no other attribution to make for poor performance except lack of ability. This lack-of-ability attribution is very damaging to the individual's sense of self-worth and individuals will try to avoid this event. In contrast, if they do not try hard and then do poorly, they can avoid the lack-of-ability attribution by noting that they did not try hard enough. Hence, effort is a double-edged sword. Effort increases the probability of success, but it also increases the potential for lack-of-ability attributions if failure occurs (Covington & Omelich, 1979a; 1979b). There are many different strategies to avoid effort. For example, students may avoid effort by choosing not to participate in a variety of educational activities, by skipping classes, sleeping in class, etc. (cf., Astin, 1985). A more sophisticated strategy involves setting extremely difficult goals, such as electing an overload of difficult courses for a semester. This strategy (if it results in failure) allows the student to make a task-difficulty attribution for poor performance and avoid the lack-of-ability attribution.

Another popular effort-avoiding strategy involves procrastination, such as cramming for an exam and writing papers the night before the due date. These strategies allow the individual to avoid lack-of-ability attributions because, if poor performance results from these activities, students always can say that they would have done better if they had studied more or started the paper earlier. In addition, the procrastination strategy presents students with a "bonus" if they do well on the exam or paper. In this case, they can conclude that they must be smart (an ability attribution) because they did so well with so little studying or preparation. Of course, another strategy to avoid failure is to structure the situation so that the probability of achieving success is quite high. In experimental studies this results in students choosing easy tasks (Covington & Beery, 1976). The college analog of this behavior is the election of extremely easy courses, solely on the basis of ease of obtaining a high grade without consideration of the students' overall curriculum plans or career goals.

c. Cognitive Goal Formation Model

Dweck and Elliott (1983) and Nicholls (1984) have proposed two basic types of goals students can adopt as they engage in a task: performance goals (or an ego-involved orientation) and learning goals (or a mastery orientation). Essentially, students who adopt a performance goal will focus on their own ability to do the task, their performance in relation to some normative, rigid, or immediate standard, and on their obtained outcome, and they will tend to see errors as examples of failure. This is similar to the self-worth goal orientation model. In contrast, students who approach a task with a learning goal will focus on the process of how to do the task, their performance in relationship to their past performance or a personal standard that is flexible, and their involvement in the task in contrast to the outcome, and they will tend to see errors as useful (Dweck & Elliott, 1983). This is similar to the intrinsic goal orientation model.

This cognitive goal formation model encompasses aspects of the intrinsic motivation model as well as the self-worth model. It is a fairly recent formulation and has not been researched as much as the other two models. The cognitive goal model synthesizes the other models but is more process-oriented and predicts that students will have different orientations for different tasks. For some tasks, students may be driven by a performance goal; for example, they may just want to get a good grade; in other cases, they may adopt a learning goal to strive to master the task.

d. Motivational Models: Conclusions

It is obvious from these examples that students' motivational orientations are an important component of any motivational model of student behavior. Motivational orientation influences students' level of involvement in a task, their value for the task, and their expectancy and perceived competence for the task. The question for researchers remains whether students are intrinsically motivated for mastery, challenge, and learning, or are motivated to enhance their self-worth and ability perceptions, or some combination of both, depending on the situation and their past experience and history. Our research will attempt to address this question by examining students' motivational orientation in relation to other motivational variables, cognition, and instruction.

C. Antecedents of Motivational Constructs

Students' motivation is influenced by a variety of environmental antecedents. There is very little ecologically valid research on the general expectancy-value model we have proposed here in the college setting. Consequently, we not only summarize existing literature but also point out potential research areas that need to be investigated. Many of the possible environmental antecedents are aspects of other research programs in NCRIPTAL and will not be discussed here. These include school-wide variables, such as institutional climate (Peterson, Cameron, Mets, Jones, & Ettington, 1986), or curriculum variables (Stark & Lowther, 1986). Of most concern to our research program are environmental variables at the course level, such as instructor characteristics, format and structure of the class, grading practices, and types of exams.

1. Instructor Characteristics

While another program in the Center is doing research on faculty members (Blackburn et al., 1986), our interest is in instructors' instructional styles and teaching strategies. Chapter V discusses the cognitive outcomes of different teaching methods; here we are concerned with how different teaching strategies affect motivational constructs.

Dunkin's (1986) review of teaching in higher education mainly focuses on cognitive outcomes, but he notes several findings related to motivation. First, in his summary of the Michigan meta-analysis (e.g., Kulik, Kulik, & Cohen, 1979), Dunkin (1986) notes that the Keller Plan does result in more student satisfaction than conventional instruction. The general mechanism assumed to be operative here is that students' choice and control over the pace of their learning results in more satisfaction. This notion of student choice and control has been promulgated by intrinsic motivation researchers for all grade levels (e.g., Deci, 1975).

Other faculty characteristics that Dunkin reviewed included socio-emotional qualities and lecturing characteristics. Again, Dunkin focused mainly on the cognitive outcomes of these characteristics. The motivational outcomes have seldom been evaluated, except for general student attitudes. It would seem likely that positive faculty characteristics, such as praise and encouragement, would be related to student's motivation, but Dunkin notes that the results are equivocal in the few studies that have addressed this issue. Clearly, there is a need for more research in this area.

In terms of lecturer characteristics, Baumgart (1976) found six types of faculty roles (i.e., reflexive judge, data input, stage setter, elaborator, probe, and cognitive engineer). Baumgart found that students engaged in more higher level thought and expressed more positive evaluations when the instructor performed the role of reflexive judge. Dunkin notes that this type of research is valuable by demonstrating the differential effects of different aspects of teaching behavior. Again, there is a need for more research that examines students' cognition and motivation as conceptualized in our review.

2. Other Course Variables

Many other course variables can influence motivational variables. These include the format of the class (e.g., lecture, discussion, lab section, etc.), grading practices, and types of tasks assigned for the course. In Chapter V, there is a review of many of these aspects of the class environment. However, one aspect that has been investigated from a motivational perspective is the nature of the reward system in the classroom. In particular, researchers who have investigated intrinsic motivation have focused on this aspect of the classroom environment.

As students of this area well know, controversy over the value of intrinsic motivation to learn is not new. Over four decades ago Dewey (1938) wrote of the continuing debate over whether education is best oriented toward fostering development of the students from within or whether it is better oriented toward formation from without. A microcosm of this debate presently focuses on whether intrinsic incentives versus extrinsic rewards are the more effective motivators of learning and whether intrinsic motivation is undermined by extrinsic rewards. We now turn to a brief review of some of the major points in this ongoing debate.

An instructive way of addressing the relationship between intrinsic motivation to learn and extrinsic rewards is to disaggregate the process into components, including initial engagement with the activity, the actual process of working the activity through to its conclusion, disengagement from the task, and subsequent reengagement (Condry & Chambers, 1981). This procedure focuses our attention on the learning process rather than simply on intrinsic interest, enabling us to avoid intellectually interesting, but pedagogically inconsequential distinctions between intrinsic and extrinsic rewards.

a. Engagement

The impetus for much of the research on the "hidden costs" to learning of extrinsic rewards is based on a single, important set of observations. In sum, the observations are: there is an inverse relationship between an individual's attitude toward an activity and the salience of extrinsic justification for engaging in it (Lepper & Greene, 1975). In situations where salient external incentives are expected at the outset, the findings from over-justification research suggest that students tend to engage in that activity for the reward rather than for any inherent challenge or the possibility of learning it may provide (Deci, 1971; Lepper, Greene, & Nisbett, 1973).

Further, some evidence indicates that subjects who anticipated being judged by an external source (Maehr & Stallings, 1972) or who were persuaded that they would be paid for undertaking learning problems (Condry & Chambers, 1981) took on significantly easier tasks than those working under intrinsically oriented conditions. This finding is especially salient because the potential for students to be "distracted" from seeking out optimal challenge appears to be most pronounced when an activity is first being learned (Condry & Chambers, 1981; Harter, 1981).

Finally, it is argued that extrinsic rewards tend to curtail free choice in the engagement phase of any activity (Corno & Rorhkemper, 1985; Condry & Chambers, 1981; Harter, 1981). One implication of this finding is that the level of active self-involvement will also tend to be less under conditions of extrinsic incentives. The finding that the motivators of initial engagement are crucial to what is eventually learned will not come as a surprise to most astute practitioners. The result of such work is that the nature of the motivators of initial engagement with any learning activity will almost certainly have direct implications for how a student defines optimal levels of personal investment and challenge for that activity and, in turn, on whether a student is oriented toward learning new material or simple performance.

This is not to say that it is always a mistake to use grades or other extrinsic motivators to get students engaged. If intrinsic interest is low, extrinsic motivators may be necessary to get students involved in a task. Once the student gets involved and makes progress, it may be possible to reduce the extrinsic rewards until the student is weaned and interested enough to proceed without the threat of a bad grade (Bandura & Schunk, 1981; Lepper & Green, 1978; Lepper, 1988).

b. Process

The problematic relationship between extrinsic rewards and learning continues during the learning stage, with the possibility that the foregoing effects may be generalized to actual performance. Lepper and his colleagues (1973) have noted that, as compared with children expecting no reward, children expecting a reward for pictures drawn during an experimental session tended to draw more pictures, but of lower quality. In a study of concept-attainment, Condry and Chambers (1981) introduced subjects to a learning task and then asked them to work through one on their own. They found that participants who were paid to do the problems proceeded in a way that was more "answer oriented." This is similar to the ego-involved motivational orientation. Members of this group sought less information, made more premature guesses, made more redundant choices, and in the end, needed as much or more information before achieving the correct solution. Their conclusion is instructive:

> Learning requires that one develop some skills and habits such as attention to specific aspects of the informational array, formation of meaningful questions, perception of relationships, and integration of information. Our research suggests that these skills, what we prefer to call strategies of learning, are different under the two motivational contexts we have described. Intrinsically motivated subjects attend to and utilize a wider array of information; they are focused on the way to solve the problem rather than the solution. They are, in general, more careful, logical, and coherent in their problem-solving strategies than comparable subjects offered a reward to solve the same problems. (p. 69)

Such findings strongly advise against uncritically using grades as a primary motivator of learning. However, we agree with Deci's distinction between informational versus controlling feedback (Deci, 1975). Information that is intended or experienced as pressure to perform, think, and feel in a particular way will tend to facilitate an extrinsic orientation toward learning. Information experienced as providing effective feedback in the context of relative choice or autonomy will tend to enhance intrinsic engagement in an activity (Deci, 1975; Ryan, Connell, & Deci, 1985). Consequently, we suggest restraint in using incentives simply to control student learning behaviors.

c. Disengagement and Reengagement

Disengagement refers to the point at which a student terminates his or her involvement with a task, while reengagement refers to a willingness to persist or return to a task later (Condry & Chambers, 1981). Disengagement may occur under conditions of choice, wherein a student decides that he or she is willing to leave a task. In intrinsically motivated situations we would expect termination to occur when the questions leading to initial engagement with the activity have been resolved, a sense of mastery has been developed, one's curiosity has been satisfied, or other tasks or interests draw one away from the activity (Condry & Chambers, 1981). Disengagement may also occur when the teacher decides that the demands associated with an activity have been met or when its incentive value has been exhausted.

While the requirements of mass education may seem to call for employing extrinsically determined termination of involvement with particular learning activities (e.g., term paper deadlines, time limits on work in laboratory courses, exam dates), this is largely inconsistent with requirements of intrinsically oriented learning. For example, in studies of motivation among children (Condry & Chambers, 1981), Condry notes that when asked to work out problems without offering answers until they were certain of their soundness, significantly more of those in the extrinsic context guessed before they "logically had sufficient information."

The largely behavioral literature on token economies argues convincingly that in the presence of valued forms of extrinsic reward, students can be induced to engage in an activity to secure such rewards. However, research demonstrates that in the presence of such rewards subjects are much less likely to seek reengagement in a given activity relative to those working under intrinsic reward conditions (Lepper, Greene, & Nisbett, 1973). Replication of these findings involving substantial variations in the nature of the contingency imposed, the target activity, and the rewards employed have substantiated these initial findings (Greene & Lepper, 1974; Lepper & Greene, 1975). We conclude that extrinsically based learning situations suffer in attractiveness to students because they tend to emphasize the fact that the activity is simply a means to an extrinsic end (Lepper & Greene, 1978; McKeachie, 1986), and that the locus of causality for involvement with the task lies outside oneself (Deci, 1975; Ryan, Connell, & Deci, 1985).

In an earlier section we indicated that the intrinsic motivation to learn was based on the propensity of humans to seek optimal levels of stimulation and to move toward both the mastery of challenging situations and the reduction of uncertainty. Further, we suggested that sustaining an intrinsic motivation to learn also depends on a student's ability to actively and successfully engage in the learning process.

Interacting with the properties of the individual are characteristics of the instructional environment that together influence achievement. In the following section we will review some of the attributes of classroom environments supportive of intrinsic motivation.

d. Structural and Evaluative Components of the Classroom

While we caution against generalizing too quickly from the results of research examining developmentally dissimilar groups, Corno and Rohrkemper's (1985) analysis of primary school classrooms does identify several influential environmental characteristics. They identify four general dimensions of settings in which academic training usually occurs. These dimensions will both foster and impede the intrinsic motivation to learn.

Task *flexibility* is linked to learning options and academic goals that are explicitly stated or implicitly expressed in a particular lesson or task. Higher levels of flexibility tend to be more supportive of intrinsic motivation in such cases. As was discussed earlier, the *reward structure* of a course is an important classroom attribute, with more informational forms of incentives tending to support intrinsic motivation and intrinsically motivated performance. The form of *evaluation* employed is also important, with privately rendered, relatively specific forms of feedback especially effective (Corno & Rohrkemper, 1985). McKeachie (1986) also notes that the calculus used to evaluate students has implications for their interpersonal relationships, with "grading on the curve" often disrupting the development of cooperative and mutually supportive orientations to learning among students.

Finally, the *timing and emphasis* of feedback on performance should be (1) informative in terms of pinpointing the probable source of student errors, (2) encouraging, and (3) provided in a natural context that displays performance recognition by a source student respects (Corno & Rorhkemper, 1985, p. 81; McKeachie, 1986, Chaps. 8 & 9). Under such conditions argue these researchers, a sense of growing competence and self-worth tend to support intrinsic engagement with learning.

In our view, a universally optimal configuration of assignments, exercises, lectures, and discussions for all subject areas does not exist. Whether an instructor is employing term papers, programmed learning, computers as instructional tools, audiovisual techniques, laboratory teaching, or instructional games and simulations (McKeachie, 1986, Chaps. 10–17); the motivational principles for intrinsic motivation are the same. They continue to involve enhancing a student's sense of self-determination as a result of engaging in activities (Ryan, Connell, & Deci, 1985) and supporting a student's pursuit of optimal levels of academic stimulation. Teachers must weigh the familiarity of their students with these techniques, the set of aptitudes associated with a particular group of students, and the resources they have at their disposal, in conjunction with these principles, while developing appropriate vehicles for teaching certain subjects (McKeachie, 1986; Corno & Rohrkemper, 1985).

e. The Teacher as Focal Point and Model

One of the most important forms of influence on a student's intrinsic motivation to learn in the classroom may simply be the instructor. Beyond determining the substantive content and organizational structure of the course, the instructor may embody those characteristics that help his or her students develop intrinsic appreciation for course material.

In continuing study of the development of self-regulation skills among grade and high school students, Corno and her colleagues (1983, 1985) indicate that the teacher who is able to promote intrinsically motivated engagement in learning does not simply display mastery of correct procedure. The instructor must also develop and display the capacity to discuss difficult aspects of task performance and indicate how they might be managed or overcome. In effect, a coping model of activity should be periodically presented along with suggestions of how students can learn from the task. McKeachie and his associates' (1985a, 1985b) research on the development of a course intended to teach undergraduates at the University of Michigan how to learn more effectively, points up the motivational importance of an instructor's efforts to go beyond simple presentation of information. He or she must also learn to foster the development of general cognitive learning strategies that may be flexibly brought to bear on questions of importance in their discipline.

Moreover, the lecturer's own attitudes and enthusiasm may have an important effect on students' intrinsic motivation to learn. McKeachie (1986) indicates that:

Research on student ratings of teaching as well as on student learning indicates that the enthusiasm of the lecturer is an important factor in affecting student learning and motivation. Not only is the lecturer a model in terms of motivation and curiosity, the lecturer also models ways of approaching problems, portraying a scholar in action in ways that are difficult for other media or methods of instruction to achieve. In fact there is some evidence suggesting that one of the advantages of live professors is the tendency of people to model themselves after individuals whom they perceive as living, breathing, human beings with characteristics that can be admired and emulated. (p. 71)

Toward Comprehensive Theories of Adult Learning

SHARAN B. MERRIAM AND ROSEMARY S. CAFFARELLA

How easy it would be to explain adult education to legislators, public school personnel, educators, and the general public if we had but a single theory of adult learning—a theory that differentiated adults from children, that included all types of learning, and that was at once elegant and simple. But just as there is no single theory that explains human learning in general (see Chapter Seven), there is no single theory of *adult* learning. Nor is there likely to be one. Nearly twenty years ago Kidd observed that "no such magical or scientific theory is likely to arise or be formulated" (1973, p. 188). Brookfield (1986) compares the search to the quest for the Holy Grail, and Cross states flatly that there will be not one but "many theories useful in improving our understanding of adults as learners" (1981, p. 112).

What we do have at this point are suggestions, constructs, tentative formulations, and models, rather than fully developed theory. Houle (1972), for example, has developed a model or "system" as he calls it, for analyzing activities that take place in various learning situations. Kidd (1973) proposes adopting the concept of "mathetics" in an effort to focus our research efforts on learning rather than teaching. This chapter examines the theory-building efforts that we do have. Each theory reviewed here focuses on adult learning and adheres to a broad definition of theory as a set of interrelated concepts or principles that attempt to explain a phenomenon. If a theory helps us to understand how adults learn, we should be able to predict when and how learning will take place and, as educators, arrange for its occurrence. Adult learning theory can be divided into three categories: those anchored in adult learners' characteristics, those based on an adult's life situation, and those that focus on changes in consciousness.

Theories Based on Adult Characteristics

The best-known theory of adult learning is andragogy, defined by Knowles (1980) as "the art and science of helping adults learn" (p. 43). It is based upon five assumptions, all of which are characteristics of adult learners:

1. As a person matures, his or her self-concept moves from that of a dependent personality toward one of a self-directing human being.
2. An adult accumulates a growing reservoir of experience, which is a rich resource for learning.
3. The readiness of an adult to learn is closely related to the developmental tasks of his or her social role.
4. There is a change in time perspective as people mature—from future application of knowledge to immediacy of application. Thus an adult is more problem-centered than subject-centered in learning (Knowles, 1980, pp. 44–45).
5. Adults are motivated to learn by internal factors rather than external ones (Knowles, 1984, p. 12).

"Toward Comprehensive Theories of Adult Learning," by Sharan Mirriam and Rosemary S. Caffarella, reprinted from *Learning in Adulthood: A Comprehensive Guide*, 1991, Jossey-Bass Publishers, Inc.

From each of these assumptions (the fifth was added after the original four), Knowles draws numerous implications for the design, implementation, and evaluation of learning activities with adults. This theory, or "model of assumptions" as Knowles also calls it (1980, p. 43), has given adult educators "a badge of identity" that distinguishes the field from other areas of education, especially childhood schooling (Brookfield, 1986, p. 90). Many would agree with Bard (1984) that andragogy "probably more than any other force has changed the role of the learner in adult education and in human resource development" (p. xi).

It has also caused more controversy, philosophical debate, and critical analysis than any other concept proposed thus far. One of the early points of criticism was Knowles's original inference that andragogy, with all its technological implications for instruction, characterizes adult learning and that pedagogy, with another set of implications, characterizes childhood learning. He later clarified his position by stating in essence that andragogy-pedagogy represents a continuum and that the use of both techniques is appropriate at different times in different situations regardless of the learner's age (Knowles, 1980, 1984). Since andragogy now appears to be situation-specific and not unique to adults, technically it does not qualify as a theory of adult learning.

As a theory to explain how adults learn, andragogy has been critiqued on other grounds. Hartree (1984) observes that it is not clear whether Knowles has presented a theory of learning or a theory of teaching, whether adult learning is different from child learning, and whether there is a theory at all—perhaps these are just principles of good practice. The assumptions, she notes, "can be read as descriptions of the adult learner . . . or as prescriptive statements about what the adult learner *should* be like" (p. 205). Because the assumptions are "unclear and shaky" on several counts, Hartree (1984) concludes that while "many adult educators might accept that the principles of adult teaching and conditions of learning which he evolves have much to offer, and are in a sense descriptive of what is already recognized as good practice by those in the field, conceptually Knowles has not presented a good case for the validity of such practice. . . . Although he appears to approach his model of teaching from the point of view of a theory of adult learning, he does not establish a unified theory of learning in a systematic way" (pp. 206–207).

Brookfield (1986), who also raises the question of whether andragogy is a "proven theory," assesses to what extent a "set of well-grounded principles of good practice" can be derived from andragogy (p. 98). He argues that three of the assumptions are problematic when drawing inferences for practice: Self-direction is more a desired outcome than a given condition, and being problem-centered and desiring immediate application can lead to a narrow reductionist view of learning. Brookfield finds only the experience assumption to be well grounded (p. 98).

Davenport and Davenport (1985) review the use of the term *andragogy* and chronicle the history of the debate as to whether it is in fact a theory. They note that andragogy has been classified "as a theory of adult education, theory of adult learning, theory of technology of adult learning, method of adult education, technique of adult education, and a set of assumptions" (p. 157). They are a bit more optimistic than other critics for andragogy's chances of possessing "the explanatory and predictive functions generally associated with a fully developed theory" (p. 158). For them the issue can be resolved through empirical studies that test the underlying assumptions.

A few studies have attempted to do just that. At least three studies have focused on the relationship between andragogical assumptions and instruction. Beder and Darkenwald (1982) asked teachers who taught both adults and preadults if their teaching behavior differed according to the age of the students. Teachers reported viewing adult students differently and using more andragogical techniques. Gorham (1985), however, actually observed teachers of adults and preadults. She found no differences in how a particular teacher instructed adults or preadults, although teachers claimed that they did treat the two age groups differently. Beder and Carrea (1988) found that training teachers in andragogical methods had a positive and significant effect on attendance but no effect on how teachers were evaluated by the students. Yet another study draws from Knowles's assumption that adults are self-directing and thus like to plan their own learning experiences. Rosenblum and Darkenwald (1983) compared achievement and satisfaction measures between groups who had planned their course and those who had it planned for them. No differences were found in either achievement or satisfaction.

A second attempt at theory building that rests on characteristics of adults is Cross's characteristics of adults as learners (CAL) model. Cross (1981) offers it as "a tentative framework to accommodate current knowledge about what we know about adults as learners" (p. 234). Based on differences between children and adults, it consists of two classes of variables: personal characteristics and situational characteristics. As can be seen in Figure 13.1, personal characteristics include physical, psychological, and sociocultural dimensions. These are continua and reflect growth and development from childhood into adult life. Situational characteristics focus on variables unique to adult participants—for example, part-time versus full-time learning and voluntary versus compulsory participation.

Cross believes that her model incorporates completed research on aging, stage and phase developmental studies, participation, learning projects, motivation, and so on. The model can also be used to stimulate research by thinking across and between categories. It might be asked, for example, whether there is a "relationship between stage of ego development and voluntary participation in learning" or whether transition points in development "generate extra amounts of volunteer learning" (p. 248). Rather than suggesting implications for practice, as Knowles's andragogy does, Cross's model offers a "framework for thinking about *what* and *how* adults learn" (p. 248).

Although the CAL model is intended to be a comprehensive explanation of *adult* learning, the variables may be too broadly defined: What situational characteristics when combined with which personal characteristics lead to explaining different types of learning, for example? Probably a more serious problem with the model is its focus on the *characteristics* of adults, which tells us little about how adults actually learn or if they learn differently than children. Furthermore, the personal characteristics can apply to children as well as adults since they are on continua reflective of growth from childhood into adulthood. Nor do the situational characteristics neatly divide between children and adults. Some adult learners are full time and some participate because of mandatory continuing education requirements; some preadults are part-time learners and some learning is done on a voluntary basis. The CAL model has yet to be empirically tested.

Theories Based on an Adult's Life Situation

Andragogy and the CAL model are explanations of adult learning emanating from the characteristics of adult learners. The three theories reviewed in this section—McClusky's theory of margin, Knox's proficiency theory, and Jarvis's model of the learning process—are anchored in an adult's life situation with its attendant experiences, roles, and responsibilities.

McClusky presented his theory of margin in a 1963 publication followed by discussions of application in 1970 and 1971. Adulthood is a time of growth, change, and integration in which one constantly seeks balance between the amount of energy needed and the amount available. This balance is conceptualized as a ratio between the "load" of life, which dissipates energy, and the "power" of life which allows one to deal with the load. The energy left over when one subtracts load from power McClusky called "margin in life." He describes how the theory works: "Margin may be increased by reducing Load or increasing Power, or it may be decreased by increasing Load and/or reducing Power. We can control both by modifying either Power or Load. When Load continually matches or exceeds Power and if both are fixed and/or out of control, or irreversible, the situation becomes highly vulnerable and susceptible to

Figure 13.1
Characteristics of Adults as Learners: A Conceptual Framework

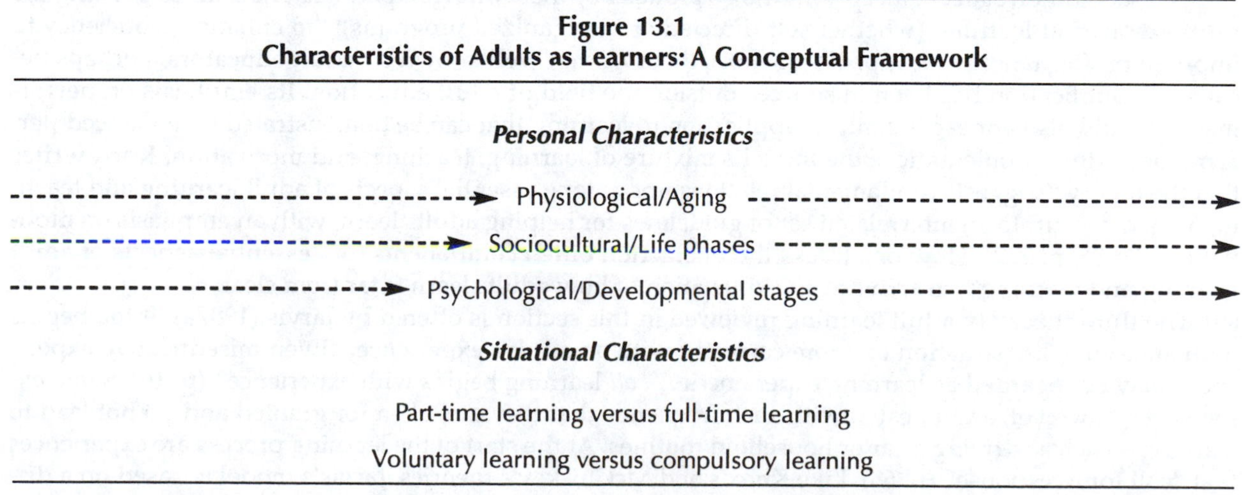

Source: Cross, 1981, p. 235.

breakdown. If, however, Load and Power can be controlled, and, better yet, if a person is able to lay hold of a reserve (Margin) of Power, he is better equipped to meet unforeseen emergencies, is better positioned to take risks, can engage in exploratory, creative activities, is more likely to learn, etc., i.e. do those things that enable him to live above a plateau of mere self subsistence" (1970, p. 83).

This theory, he argues, helps to explain the dynamics of adult learning. A learning situation requires the expenditure of resources—that is, "a necessary condition for learning is access to and/or the activation of a Margin of Power that may be available for application to the processes which the learning situation requires" (1970, p. 84). The situational focus of this theory is reflected in his recognition that "adjustments of Load to Power become matters of overarching concern as a person accumulates and later relinquishes adult responsibilities and modifies the varying roles which the successive stages of the life cycle require" (1970, p. 84). Using the theory of margin as a conceptual framework, Main (1979) studied adult learning and teaching. Its greatest application, however, has been with middle-aged and older adults. Using an instrument developed to measure margin in life, Stevenson (1980) compared the load, power, and margin patterns of independent older adults, nursing home residents, and young and middle-aged adults. Baum (1980) tested the theory using a randomized sample of 100 widows.

McClusky's theory has appeal in that it speaks to the everyday events and life transitions that all adults encounter (see Chapter Six). It is perhaps a better counseling tool than it is an explanation of adult learning. In fact, there is a striking similarity between McClusky's power, load, and margin concepts and the components of Schlossberg's model for counseling adults in transition. In her model, one assesses the ability to work through a transition by assessing the relative strength of four factors: the situation, the self (internal strengths), external supports, and strategies one has developed to handle stress (Schlossberg, 1984, 1987).While certainly life events and transitions precipitate many (and some would say the most potent) learning experiences, McClusky's model does not directly address learning itself but rather *when* it is most likely to occur. One might also question whether "a necessary condition for learning" (McClusky, 1970, p. 84) is a reserve of energy or margin of power. This may seem to apply more readily to formal learning situations; informal learning can occur under conditions of stress or, in McClusky's terms, when load is greater than power.

Knox's (1980) proficiency theory also speaks to an adult's life situation. Adult learning, he writes, is distinctive on at least two counts: "the centrality of concurrent adult role performance" (p. 383) and the "close correspondence between learning and action beyond the educational program" (p. 384). Proficiency, as defined by Knox, is "the capability to perform satisfactorily if given the opportunity," and this performance involves some combination of attitude, knowledge, and skill (1980, p. 378). At the core of his theory is the notion of a discrepancy between the current and the desired level of proficiency. This concept of proficiency helps explain "adult motivation and achievement in both learning activities and life roles. Adults and society expect that individual adults will be proficient in major life roles and as persons generally" (1985, p. 252). A model representative of the theory contains the following interactive components: the general environment, past and current characteristics, performance, aspiration, self, discrepancies, special environments, learning activity, and the teacher's role.

The set of interrelated concepts in Knox's proficiency theory hinge upon what he defines as being the purpose of adult learning (whether self-directed or in organized programs): "to enhance proficiency to improve performance" (1980, p. 399). Knox's theory is not well known by adult educators, perhaps because its publication has been in sources outside the field of adult education. Its emphasis on performance would also appear to limit its application to learning that can be demonstrated by enhanced performance. More problematic is the model's mixture of learning, teaching, and motivation. Knox writes that the theory "suggests fundamental relationships among essential aspects of adult learning and teaching which constitute an interrelated set of guidelines for helping adults learn, with an emphasis on motivation" (1985, p. 252). How one tracks the interaction of ten components (or "essential aspects of adult learning and teaching") to arrive at an explanation of how adults learn is far from clear.

The third theory of adult learning reviewed in this section is offered by Jarvis (1987a). It too begins with an adult's life situation or, more correctly, with an adult's experience: "Even miseducative experiences may be regarded as learning experiences . . . *all* learning begins with experience" (p. 16). Some experiences, however, are repeated with such frequency that they are taken for granted and do not lead to learning—such as driving a car or household routines. At the start of the learning process are experiences that "call for a response" (p. 63). Like Knox's and McCluskey's theories, Jarvis's model is based on a discrepancy between biography (all that a person is at a particular point in time) and experience—an incident that a person is unprepared to handle. This "inability to cope with the situation unthinkingly, instinctively, is at the heart of all learning" (p. 35)

For Jarvis, all experience occurs within a social situation, a kind of objective context within which one experiences life: "Life may be conceptualized as an ongoing phenomenon located within a sociocultural milieu which is bounded by the temporality of birth and death. Throughout life, people are moving from social situation to social situation; sometimes in conscious awareness but on other occasions in a taken-for-granted manner" (p. 64). Jarvis's model of the learning process begins with the person moving into a social situation in which a potential learning experience occurs. From an experience there are nine different routes that a person might take, some of which result in learning, and some of which do not. Presumption, nonconsideration, and rejection do not result in learning. The six other responses (preconscious, practice, memorization, contemplation, reflective practice, and experimental learning) represent six different types of learning. The nine responses form a hierarchy: The first three are nonlearning responses, the second three are nonreflective learning, and the final three are reflective learning. These latter three, Jarvis says, are the "higher forms of learning" (1987a, p. 27). Of the nonlearning responses, one can respond in a mechanical way (that is, presume that what has worked before will work again); one can be too preoccupied to consider a response; or one can reject the opportunity to learn. The nonreflective learning responses can be preconscious (that is, a person unconsciously internalizes something); one can practice a new skill until it is learned; or learners can acquire information "with which they have been presented and learn it, so that they can reproduce it at a later stage" (p. 33). The three higher forms of learning call for more involvement. Contemplation is thinking about what is being learned and does not require a behavioral outcome; reflective practice is akin to problem solving; experimental learning is the result of a person experimenting upon the environment.

In his book on the model Jarvis explains how each of the nine responses coincides with the visual representation of the learning process. As in Figure 13.2, a person enters a social situation, has an experience, and can exit (box 4) unchanged by ignoring the event or taking it for granted. One might also go from the experience (box 3) to memorization (box 6) and exit either unchanged (box 4) or changed (box 9). For a higher type of learning, a person might go from the experience to reasoning and reflecting (box 7) to practice experimentation (box 5) to evaluation (box 8) to memorization (box 6) and to being changed (box 9).

Figure 13.2
A Model of the Learning Process

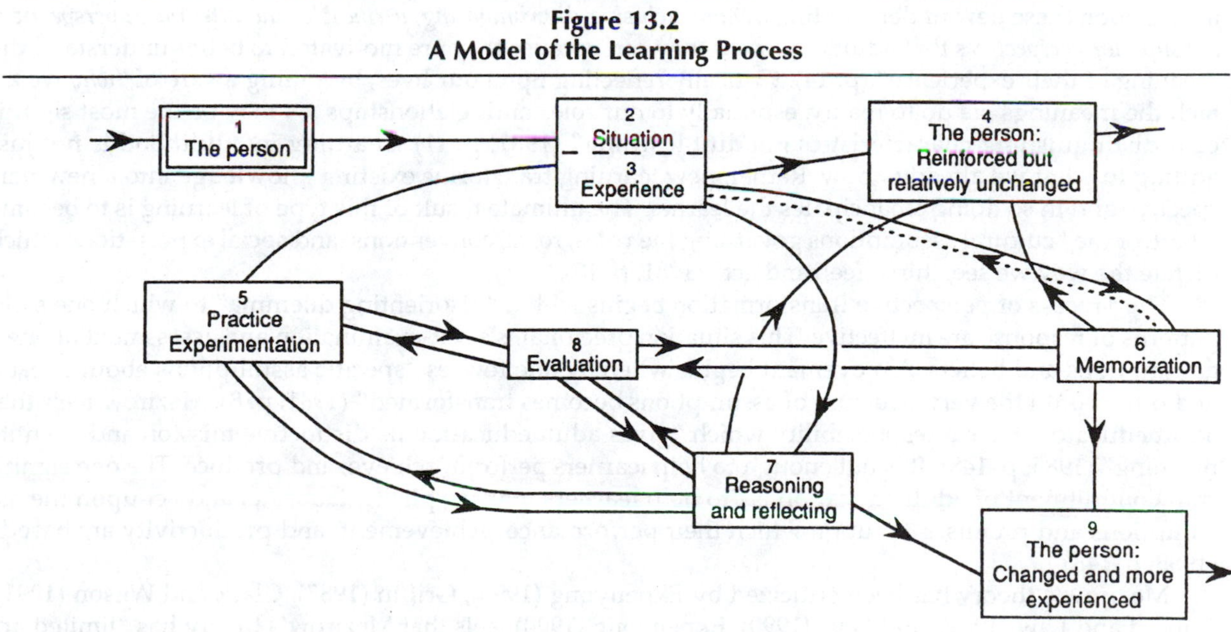

Source: Jarvis, 1987a, p. 25. Reprinted by permission.

More than the theories based on adult characteristics or the other two theories discussed in this section, Jarvis's model does deal with learning per se. The thoroughness of his discussion, which concentrates on explaining the responses one can have to an experience, is a strength of the model. These responses encompass multiple types of learning and their different outcomes—a refreshingly comprehensive view of learning. Furthermore, his model situates learning within a social context; learning is an interactive phenomenon, not an isolated internal process. There is some question, however, as to whether his model is unique to adults. Although it was constructed from research with adult learners and has been used by Jarvis with adults in various settings, he himself suspects that "it is as valid for children as it is with adults. . . . There may be a relationship between the frequency of use of these different types of learning and the age of the learner, [but] no evidence exists at present that might verify this" (Jarvis, 1987a, pp. 35–36).

Theories Based on Changes in Consciousness

The theories so far discussed attempt to explain the phenomenon of adult learning from the perspective of adult characteristics and adult social roles, responsibilities, and experiences. The theoretical formulations discussed in this section have a stronger cognitive focus in that they deal with the mental construction of experience and inner meaning. Reflection upon the content of one's environment and one's experiences is a common component of the theories reviewed here. Reflective thought, some propose, may even be *the* thought structure to emerge in adulthood and "a necessary prerequisite to asking questions, and discovering problems" (Allman, 1983, p. 114).

The most developed "theory" in this group is Mezirow's notion of perspective transformation. Drawing from the writings of the German philosopher Jurgen Habermas, Mezirow defines three areas of cognitive interest: technical or instrumental, which is task-related; practical or dialogic, which involves social interaction; and emancipatory, which is characterized by interest in self-knowledge and insights gained through self-reflection. Recently Mezirow has reduced these three domains to two: Emancipatory learning is now operative in the technical and practical domains (1989). It is this emancipatory learning that Mezirow (1990) equates with perspective transformation: "Perspective transformation is the process of becoming critically aware of how and why our presuppositions have come to constrain the way we perceive, understand, and feel about our world; of reformulating these assumptions to permit a more inclusive, discriminating, permeable, and integrative perspective; and of making decisions or otherwise acting upon these new understandings. *More inclusive, discriminating, permeable, and integrative perspectives are superior perspectives* that adults choose if they can because they are motivated to better understand the meaning of their experience" (p. 14). Critically reflecting upon our lives, becoming aware of "*why* we attach the meanings we do to reality, especially to our roles and relationships . . . may be the most significant distinguishing characteristics of adult learning" (1981, p. 11). Learning in adulthood is not just adding to what we already know. Rather, new learning transforms existing knowledge into a new perspective and in so doing emancipates the learner. The ultimate result of this type of learning is to become aware of the "cultural assumptions governing the rules, roles, conventions, and social expectations which dictate the way we see, think, feel, and act" (1981, p. 13).

The process of perspective transformation begins with a "disorienting dilemma" to which one's old patterns of response are ineffective. This situation precipitates a self-examination and assessment of one's assumptions and beliefs. A movement begins whereby one revises "specific assumptions about oneself and others until the very structure of assumptions becomes transformed" (1981, p. 8). Mezirow feels that adult educators have a responsibility which "gives adult education its distinctive mission and even its meaning" (1985, p. 148). It is not enough to help learners perform, achieve, and produce. The one significant commitment of adult education is "to help learners make explicit, elaborate, and act upon the assumptions and premises . . . upon which their performance, achievement, and productivity are based" (1985, p. 148).

Mezirow's theory has been criticized by Ekpenyong (1990), Griffin (1987), Clark and Wilson (1991), Collard and Law (1989), and Hart (1990). Ekpenyong (1990) feels that Mezirow's theory has "limited application" (p. 165). A more comprehensive understanding of adult learning, according to Ekpenyong, is to be found in philosopher Thomas Kuhn's notion of paradigm-transition. Griffin argues that Mezirow has presented not so much a theory as a "set of prescriptions for good practice on the part of professional adult educators who are committed to facilitating self-directed adult learning" (1987, p. 183). Indeed,

Mezirow (1981) outlines a "charter for andragogy" stressing the adult educator's role as one of "enhancing the learner's ability for self-direction" (p. 21). Clark and Wilson (1991) point out that Mezirow's orientation toward autonomy uncritically reflects the values of the dominant culture in our society—masculine, white, and middle class. In Griffin's (1987) opinion, Mezirow fails to provide an ideological basis for adult education as social policy. Collard and Law (1989) fault Mezirow for his lack of attention to the social context and to social change as the natural outcome of perspective transformation. For Mezirow, however, change need not be just social change; it can also be epistemic (knowledge-related) or psychic (relating, for example, to unresolved childhood dilemmas that influence adult behavior). Mezirow (1989) writes: "Social action may develop, and it is desirable and appropriate that it do so. But this is the learner's decision, not the educator's. . . . Educators do not set out to effect specific political action; this is indoctrination" (p. 173). Hart (1990) contends that Mezirow is too "rationalist" in that "he tries to systematize the areas of 'distortions' requiring . . . fundamental changes or transformations . . . without directly criticizing current economic, social, and political arrangements which are inherently tied to these 'distortions'" (p. 127).

More than the other theories discussed here, Mezirow's perspective transformation deals directly with the process of learning. Furthermore, although some would contest the notion, Mezirow claims that this type of learning is unique to adulthood (1981). The combination of these factors—that is, a theory about learning itself which is perhaps unique to adults—makes Mezirow's theory particularly promising for understanding adult learning. A recent publication by Mezirow and Associates (1990) cites programs that have stimulated critical reflection and offers practical methods for helping adults engage in critical reflection that can result in transformative learning. Only a few research studies have focused on perspective transformation. Hunter (1980), Cochrane (1981), and Williams (1985) studied perspective transformation related to health practices, withdrawal experiences, and spouse abuse, respectively. Young (1986) was able to change the perspectives of workshop participants (toward a global, future-oriented worldview) with a contextual learning intervention. Boyd and Fales (1983) studied the relationship of reflection to meaning transformation and delineated a process with stages much like the stages of perspective transformation.

One educator who does espouse social change as a necessary corollary to critical reflection is Freire. His "theory" is more precisely a theory of education (of which learning is an important component) in contrast to Mezirow's focus on the learning process itself. Freire is a Brazilian educator whose theory of adult education is set within a larger framework of radical social change. Education for Freire is never neutral; it either oppresses or liberates. Conscientization—"the process in which men, not as recipients, but as knowing subjects, achieve a deepening awareness both of the sociocultural reality which shapes their lives and of their capacity to transform that reality"—is what takes place in an authentic educational encounter (1970a, p. 27). Increasing awareness of one's situation involves moving from the lowest level of consciousness, where there is no comprehension of how forces shape one's life, to the highest level of critical consciousness. Similar to Mezirow's "critical reflectivity" (1981), critical consciousness is marked by a thorough analysis of problems, self-awareness, and self-reflection.

Within Freire's theory of education for social change are components relevant to adult learning situations. He distinguishes between "banking" and "problem-posing" education. In traditional banking education, deposits of knowledge are made into student receptacles; in problem posing, teachers and students cooperate in a dialogue that seeks to humanize and liberate. Central to the learning is a changed relationship between teacher and student. They are coinvestigators into their common reality: the sociocultural situation in which they live. Dialogue is the method by which this sharing takes place and by which consciousness is raised. Generative themes, concerns that are posed by the learners themselves, become the content of a learning situation. The ultimate goal is liberation, or praxis, "the action and reflection of men upon their world in order to transform it" (1970b, p. 66).

Freire has operationalized his theory of education into techniques that have demonstrated success in combating illiteracy, especially in the Third World. Its application in North America has been limited, owing perhaps to the necessary corollary of social change. Some have suggested that conscientization is not comprehensive enough to explain various types of learning that an adult might experience; others contend that the emphasis on active involvement, experiential learning, and dialogue is not new. If taken out of its political context, conscientization shares with perspective transformation the idea that *adult* learning is the process of becoming aware of one's assumptions, beliefs, and values and then transforming those assumptions into a new perspective or level of consciousness. This "awakening . . . proceeds to action, which in turn provides the basis for new perception, new reflection" (Lloyd, 1972, p. 5).

In summary, Mezirow's and Freire's approach to adult learning emphasizes the importance of inner meaning and mental constructs in defining the nature of learning in adult life. More so than the theories based on learner characteristics or adult life position, the formulations described in this section give rise to philosophical and ethical issues: What right do adult educators have to tamper with the worldview (mental set, perspective, paradigm, or state of consciousness) of the learner? How is the goal of educational intervention to be determined? What is the educator's responsibility for the action component of praxis? These questions are addressed in Chapter Fifteen.

Summary

This chapter has reviewed seven different theory-building efforts in adult learning. Knowles's andragogy and Cross's CAL model were discussed together in that they both stress adult learners' characteristics. Three theories—McClusky's theory of margin, Knox's proficiency theory, and Jarvis's model of the learning process—are solidly anchored in the adult's life situation. Finally, Mezirow's perspective transformation and Freire's conscientization were treated together as theories that focus on changes in consciousness.

In assessing the theory-building efforts in adult learning, one can ask how well the seven theories reviewed in this chapter explain learning—in particular, adult learning. One can ask if the theory is comprehensive, that is, includes all types of learning. Rachal suggests that one can also ask how practical the theory is and how universal its application might be (1986).

No single theory fares well when all of these criteria are brought to bear. Each has strengths and weaknesses, most of which have been discussed in this chapter. Four of the theories reviewed here (those of Knowles, Cross, Knox, and McClusky) reveal more about the learner's characteristics, his or her life situation, and the desired outcomes of learning than they do about learning. While these theories help us understand the learner and to some extent the motives for participation, they do little to advance our understanding of the learning process. Three focus on the process of learning itself—Jarvis's, Mezirow's, and Freire's—but only one, Mezirow's perspective transformation, claims to explain learning that is unique to adults. This claim has yet to be supported by research. Indeed, none of the theories is supported by a substantial body of research. Until there is more empirical support, the criterion of universality, or how well predictions derived from theory hold up, is a moot point. Finally, while most of these theories address implications for practice (see especially Mezirow and Associates, 1990), only Knowles' andragogy has been widely applied in practice (Knowles and Associates, 1984).

A phenomenon as complex as adult learning will probably never be adequately explained by a single theory. Each of the seven attempts reviewed in this chapter contributes something to understanding how adults learn and, by extension, how educators can enhance the process. At least four components of adult learning can be extracted from these theories: (1) self-direction or autonomy as a characteristic or goal of adult learning; (2) breadth and depth of life experiences as content or triggers to learning; (3) reflection or self-conscious monitoring of changes taking place; and (4) action or some other expression of the learning that has occurred. While one theory to explain all adult learning may never emerge, the process does stimulate inquiry, reflection, and research, all of which will eventually provide us with some of the answers to our questions about adult learning.

Note

Much of the material in this chapter is based on an earlier article by Sharan B. Merriam titled "Adult Learning and Theory Building: A Review" in *Adult Education Quarterly*, 1987, 37 (4), 187–198.

B. Learners: Similarities and Differences

Learning Styles and Disciplinary Differences

DAVID A. KOLB

Along the Cleveland heights there is a vantage point where I can view the university spreading beneath me toward the horizon—in the foreground is the new medical complex of concrete and glass towers placed among older yellow brick hospitals and laboratories. To the left, stretched along the road that separates it from the medical buildings is the long, low, steel, glass and brick home of the natural science laboratories.

Nested against this brick and steel spine, lie vestiges of science past. One side, the old physics building, large and austere with a red tile roof slowly turning black, and tall, narrow windows that belie the high-ceilinged dark rooms within. On the other side, two black stone fortress-like buildings, one capped by an observatory telescope. Paralleling these buildings around a mall punctuated at one end by a towering smokestack and at the other by a computer center office tower, lie the squat, functional ceramic brick and concrete buildings of the engineering and management schools, almost defiantly ugly, as though to emphasize that appearances are secondary to reality.

In the distance across Euclid Avenue, still another world—strong gothic stone buildings beside awkward Victorian red brick constructions, the old Western Reserve campus now home for the humanities and social sciences. Beyond is the flashy, contemporary law school building, its black one-way windows revealing as little inside as a state trooper's sunglasses. And finally, the serene, classic beauty of Severance Hall and the Museum of Art.

I have stopped here several times as I framed this essay. The diversity that lies below is staggering—not one university but many, each with its own language, norms, and values, its own ideas about the nature of truth and how it is to be sought. By crossing the street, or in some cases even the hallway, I can visit cultures that differ on nearly every dimension associated with the term. There are different languages (or at least dialects). There are strong boundaries defining membership and corresponding initiation rites. There are different norms and values about the nature of truth and how it is to be sought. There are different patterns of power and authority and differing criteria for attaining status. There are differing standards for intimacy and modes for its expression. Cultural variation is expressed in style of dress, furnishings, architecture, and use of space and time. Most important, these patterns of variation are not random but have a meaning and integrity for the members. There is in each department or profession a sense of historical continuity and in most cases historical mission.

While there are obviously points of interpretation among these "cultures" and in some cases, true integration, I want here to emphasize the themes of differentiation and diversity.

In considering the student careers that are spawned and shaped in the university community and the university's responsibility for the intellectual, moral, and personal development of its members, we have often emphasized the unitary linear trend of human growth and development at the expense of acknowledging and managing the diverse developmental pathways that exist within different disciplines and professions. These paths foster some developmental achievements and, as we shall see, inhibit others. The channels of academic specializations are swift and deep, the way between them tortuous and winding. For example, these days the major career transitions in college are from science to the humanities (Davis, 1965). When I taught at M.I.T., I served for a while as a freshman adviser. Two or three of my stu-

"Learning Styles and Disciplinary Differences," by David A. Kolb, reprinted from *The Modern American College: Responding to the Realities of Diverse Students and a Changing Society,* edited by A. W. Chickering and Associates, 1981, Jossey-Bass Publishers, Inc.

dents in each group faced the awkward realization near the end of their freshman year that a career in engineering was not quite what they had imagined it to be. What to do? Transfer to a liberal arts school and possibly lose the prestige of an M.I.T. education? Endure the institute's technological requirements and "bootleg" a humanities major? Switch to management? Most decided to wait and see but, in so doing, experienced a distinct loss of energy and increase in confusion. I felt powerless about what to advise or even how to advise.

It was only later that I was to discover that these shifts represented something more fundamental than changing interests—that they stemmed in many cases from fundamental mismatches between personal learning styles and the learning demands of different disciplines. That disciplines incline to different styles of learning is evident from the variations among their primary tasks, technologies and products, criteria for academic excellence and productivity, teaching methods, research methods, and methods for recording and portraying knowledge. Disciplines even show sociocultural variation—differences in faculty and student demographics, personality and aptitudes, as well as differences in values and group norms. For students, education in an academic field is a continuing process of selection and socialization to the pivotal norms of the field governing criteria for truth and how it is to be achieved, communicated, and used, and secondarily, to peripheral norms governing personal styles, attitudes, and social relationships. Over time these selection and socialization pressures combine to produce an increasingly impermeable and homogeneous disciplinary culture and correspondingly specialized student orientations to learning. This, briefly, is the thesis I will attempt to articulate in this chapter.

In reviewing the research on differences among academic disciplines, I have been struck by the fact that relatively little comparative research has been done on academic disciplines and departments. In fact, Biglan (1973a) has stated:

> One of the most easily overlooked facts about university organization is that academic departments are organized according to subject matter . . . While the organization of university departments has received increasing attention from social scientists . . . the way in which subject matter characteristics may require particular forms of department organization has not been examined [p. 195].

The reason for this lies in the same difficulties that characterize all cross-cultural research—the problem of access and the problem of perspective. The relatively closed nature of academic subcultures makes access to data difficult, and it is equally difficult to choose a perspective for interpreting data that is unbiased. To analyze one system of inquiry according to the ground rules of another is to invite misunderstanding and conflict and further restrict access to data.

Studying disciplines from the perspective of learning and the learner offers some promise for overcoming these difficulties, particularly if learning is defined not in the narrow psychological sense of modification of behavior but in the broader sense of acquisition of knowledge. The access problem is eased because every discipline has a prime commitment to learning and inquiry and has developed a learning style that is at least moderately effective. Viewing the acquisition of knowledge in academic disciplines from the perspective of the learning process promises a dual reward—a more refined, epistemology that defines the varieties of truth and their interrelationships and a greater psychological understanding of how individuals acquire knowledge in its different forms. Over fifteen years ago, in the distinguished predecessor to this volume, *The American College*, Carl Bereiter and Mervin Freedman envisioned these rewards:

> There is every reason to suppose that studies applying tests of these sorts to students in different fields could rapidly get beyond the point of demonstrating the obvious. We should, for instance, be able to find out empirically whether the biological taxonomist has special aptitudes similar to his logical counterpart in the field of linguistics. And there are many comparisons whose outcomes it would be hard to foresee. In what fields do the various memory abilities flourish? Is adaptive flexibility more common in some fields than in others? Because, on the psychological end, these ability measures are tied to theories of the structure or functioning of higher mental processes, and because, on the philosophical end, the academic disciplines are tied to theories of logic and cognition, empirical data linking the two should be in little danger of remaining for long in the limbo where so many correlational data stay [1962, pp. 567-568].

It is surprising that, with the significant exception of Piaget's pioneering work on genetic epistemology, few have sought to reap these rewards.

The research that has been done has focused primarily on what from the above perspective are the peripheral norms of academic disciplines rather than the pivotal norms governing learning and inquiry. Thus, studies have examined political and social attitudes and values (Bereiter and Freedman, 1962; Kirtz, 1966), personality patterns (Ral, 1956), aspirations and goals (Davis, 1964), sex distribution and other demographic variables (Feldman, 1974), and social interactions (Biglan, 1973b; Hall, 1969). The bias of these studies is no doubt a reflection of the fact that psychological research has until quite recently been predominantly concerned with the social and emotional aspects of human behavior and development. Concern with cognitive or intellectual factors has been neatly wrapped into concepts of general intelligence. Thus, most early studies of intellectual differences among disciplines were only interested in which discipline had the smarter students (for example, Wolfle, 1954; Terman and Oden, 1947).

In the fifteen years since *The American College* was written, there has been a great burgeoning of research and theory focused on intellectual development and cognitive style—on how one comes to know his world and cope with it. The preceding chapters in this volume reflect this new focus of concern. As a result, we now have new tools and concepts available for the study of the learning process. My own research work during this time has focused on an approach to learning that seeks to integrate cognitive and socioemotional factors into an "experiential learning theory."

Experiential Learning Theory

The experiential learning model represents an integration of many of the intensive lines of research on cognitive development and cognitive style. The result is a model of the learning process that is consistent with the structure of human cognition and the stages of human growth and development. It conceptualizes the learning process in such a way that differences in individual learning styles and corresponding learning environments can be identified. The learning model is a dialectical one, similar to Jung's (1923) concept of personality types, according to which development is attained by higher-level integration and expression of nondominant modes of dealing with the world.

The theory is called *experiential learning* for two reasons. First, this term ties the theory historically to its intellectual origins in the social psychology of Kurt Lewin in the forties and the sensitivity training of the fifties and sixties. Second, it emphasizes the important role that experience plays in the learning process, an emphasis that differentiates this approach from other cognitive theories of the learning process. The core of the model is a simple description of the learning cycle—of how experience is translated into concepts, which, in turn, are used as guides in the choice of new experiences.

Learning is conceived as a four-stage cycle (see Figure 1). Immediate concrete experience is the basis for observation and reflection. An individual uses these observations to build an idea, generalization, or "theory" from which new implications for action can be deduced. These implications or hypotheses then serve as guides in acting to create new experiences. The learners, if they are to be effective, need four different kinds of abilities: *Concrete Experience* abilities (CE), *Reflective Observation* abilities (RO), *Abstract Conceptualization* abilities (AC), and *Active Experimentation* (AE) abilities. That is, they must be able to involve themselves fully, openly, and without bias in new experiences (CE); they must be able to observe and reflect on these experiences from many perspectives (RO); they must be able to create concepts that integrate their observations into logically sound theories (AC); and they must be able to use these theories to make decisions and solve problems (AE). Yet this ideal is difficult to achieve. Can anyone become highly skilled in all these abilities, or are they necessarily in conflict? How can one be concrete and immediate and still be theoretical?

A closer examination of the four-stage model indicates that learning requires abilities that are polar opposites, and that the learner, as a result, must continually choose which set of learning abilities to bring to bear on various learning tasks. More specifically, there are two primary dimensions to the learning process. The first dimension represents the concrete experiencing of events, at one end, and abstract conceptualization at the other. The other dimension has active experimentation at one extreme and reflective observation at the other. Thus, in the process of learning, one moves in varying degrees from actor to observer, from specific involvement to general analytic detachment.

These two dimensions represent the major directions of cognitive development identified by Piaget. In his view, the course of individual cognitive development from birth to adolescence moves from a phe-

Figure 1
The Experimental Learning Model

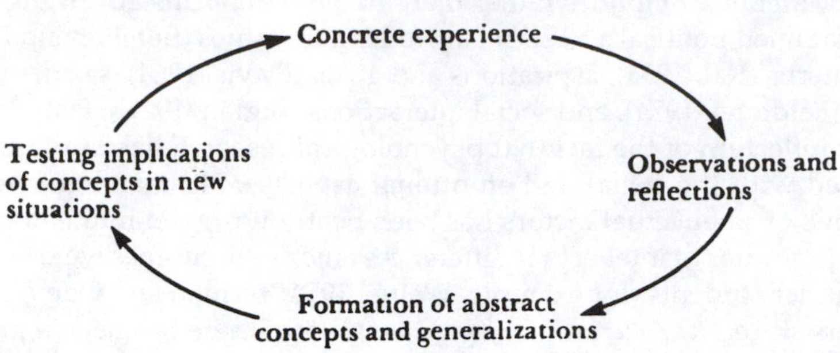

nomenolistic (concrete) view of the world to a constructivist (abstract) view from an egocentric (active) view to a reflective internalized mode of knowing. Piaget also maintains that these have also been the major directions of development in scientific knowledge (Piaget, 1970). Much other research has focused on one or the other of these two basic dimensions.

Many other cognitive psychologists (for example, Flavell, 1963; Bruner, 1960, 1966; Harvey, Hunt, and Schroeder, 1961) have identified the concrete-abstract dimension as a primary dimension on which cognitive growth and learning occur. Goldstein and Scheerer (1941, p. 4) suggest that greater abstractness results in the development of the following abilities:

1. To detach our ego from the outer world or from inner experience.
2. To assume a mental set.
3. To account for acts to oneself; to verbalize the account.
4. To shift reflectively from one aspect of the situation to another.
5. To hold in mind simultaneously various aspects.
6. To grasp the essential of a given whole; to break up a given into parts to isolate and to synthesize them.
7. To abstract common properties reflectively; to form hierarchic concepts.
8. To plan ahead ideationally, to assume an attitude toward the more possible, and to think or perform symbolically.

By contrast, concreteness, according to these theorists, represents the absence of these abilities, the immersion in and domination by one's immediate experiences. Yet the circular, dialectical model of the learning process would imply that abstractness is not exclusively good and concreteness exclusively bad. Witkin's (1962, 1976) extensive research on the related cognitive styles of global versus analytic functioning has shown that both extremes of functioning have their costs and benefits; the analytic style includes competence in analytical functioning combined with an impersonal orientation, while the global style reflects less competence in analytical functioning combined with greater social orientation and social skill. Similarly, when we consider the highest form of learning—through creativity insights—we note a requirement that one be able to experience anew, freed somewhat from the constraints of previous abstract concepts. In psychoanalytic theory, this need for a concrete childlike perspective in the creative process is referred to as "regression in service of the ego" (Kris, 1952). Bruner (1966), in his essay on the conditions for creativity, emphasizes the dialectical tension between abstract and concrete involvement. For him, the creative act is a product of detachment and commitment, of passion and decorum, and of a freedom to be dominated by the object of one's inquiry.

The active-reflective dimension is the other major dimension of cognitive growth and learning that has received a great deal of attention from researchers. In the course of cognitive growth, thought becomes more reflective and internalized, based more on the manipulation of symbols and images than overt actions. The modes of active experimentation and reflection, like abstractness and concreteness, stand in opposition to one another. Kagan and Kogan's (1970) research on the cognitive-style dimension of reflection-imulsivity suggests that extremes of functioning on this continuum represent opposing definitions of competence and strategies for achieving. The impulsive strategy is based on seeking reward for active accomplishment, while the reflective strategy is based on seeking reward through the avoidance of error. Reflection tends to inhibit action and *vice versa*. For example, Singer (1968) has found that children who have active internal fantasy lives are more capable of inhibiting action for long periods of time than are children with little internal fantasy life. Kagan and others (1964) have found, however, that very active orientations toward learning situations inhibit reflection and thereby preclude the development of analytic concepts. Herein lies the second major dialectic in the learning process—the tension between actively testing the implications of one's hypotheses and reflectively interpreting data already collected.

Individual Learning Styles

As a result of our hereditary equipment, our particular past life experience, and the demands of our present environment, most of us develop learning styles that emphasize some learning abilities over others. Through socialization experiences in family, school, and work, we come to resolve the conflicts between action and reflection and between immediate experience and detached analysis in characteristic ways. Some people develop minds that excel at assimilating disparate facts into coherent theories, yet these same people may be incapable of, or uninterested in, deducing hypotheses from those theories. Others are logical geniuses but find it impossible to involve themselves in active experience. And so on. A mathematician may emphasize abstract concepts, while a poet may value concrete experience more highly. A manager may be primarily concerned with the active application of ideas, while a naturalist may concentrate on developing observational skills. Each of us develops a unique learning style, which has both strong and weak points. Evidence for the existence of consistent unique learning styles can be found in the research of both Kagan and Witkin, cited earlier (Kagan and Kogan, 1970). Their research, while supporting Piaget's view that there is a general tendency to become more analytic and reflective with age, indicates that individual rankings within the population tested remain highly stable from early years to adulthood. That is, individuals seem to develop consistent and distinctive cognitive styles.

We have developed a brief self-descriptive inventory called the Learning Style Inventory (LSI) to measure differences in learning styles along the two basic dimensions of abstract-concrete and active-reflective (Kolb, 1976a). Although the individuals tested on the LSI show many different patterns of scores, we have identified four statistically prevalent types of learning styles. We have called these four styles the Converger, the Diverger, the Assimilator, and the Accommodator. The characteristics of these types are based both on research and clinical observation of these patterns of LSI scores.

Convergers' dominant learning abilities are Abstract Conceptualization and Active Experimentation. Their greatest strength lies in the practical application of ideas. We have called this learning style the *Converger* because persons with this style seem to do best in those situations, like conventional intelligence tests, where there is a single correct answer or solution to a question or problem (Torrealba, 1972). These persons organize knowledge in such a way that, through hypothetical-deductive reasoning, they can focus it on specific problems. Liam Hudson's (1966) research in this style of learning (using different measures than the LSI) shows that convergers are relatively unemotional, preferring to deal with things rather than people. They tend to have narrow interests and often choose to specialize in the physical sciences. Our research shows that this learning style is characteristic of many engineers (Kolb, 1976a).

Divergers have the opposite learning strengths from those of the Convergers. They are best at Concrete Experience and Reflective Observation. Their greatest strength lies in imaginative ability. They excel in the ability to view concrete situations from many perspectives and to organize many relationships into a meaningful "gestalt." We have labeled this style *Diverger* because persons of this type perform better in situations that call for generation of ideas, such as "brainstorming" sessions. Divergers are interested in people and tend to be imaginative and emotional. They have broad cultural interests and tend to specialize in the arts. Our research shows that this style is characteristic of persons with humanities and liberal arts backgrounds. Counselors, organization development consultants, and personnel managers often have this learning style.

Assimilators' dominant learning abilities are Abstract Conceptualization and Reflective Observation. Their greatest strength lies in the ability to create theoretical models. They excel in inductive reasoning, in assimilating disparate observations into an integrated explanation (Grochow, 1973). They, like the convergers, are less interested in people and more concerned with abstract concepts, but less concerned with the practical use of theories. It is important that the theory be logically sound and precise. As a result, this learning style is more characteristic of the basic sciences and mathematics than of the applied sciences. In organizations, this learning style is found most often in the research and planning departments (Kolb, 1976; Strasmore, 1973).

Accommodators have the opposite strengths from those of the Assimilators. They are best at Concrete Experience and Active Experimentation. Their greatest strength lies in doing things, in carrying out plans and experiments and becoming involved in new experiences. They tend to be risk-takers more than persons with the other three learning styles. We have labeled this style *Accommodator* because persons with this style tend to excel in situations that call for adaptation to specific immediate circumstances. In situations where the theory or plan does not fit the facts they will most likely discard the plan or theory. (The opposite type, the Assimilator, would be more likely to disregard or reexamine the facts.) They tend to solve problems in an intuitive trial-and-error manner (Grochow, 1973), relying heavily on other people for information rather than their own analytical ability (Stabel, 1973). Accommodators are at ease with people but are sometimes seen as impatient and "pushy." Their educational backgrounds are often in technical or practical fields such as business. In organizations, people with this learning style are found in "action-oriented" jobs, often in marketing or sales.

It is important to stress that these types should not become stereotypes. Perhaps the greatest contribution of research on cognitive style has been the documentation of the diversity and complexity of cognitive processes and their manifestation in behavior. Three important dimensions of diversity have been identified:

1. Within any single theoretical dimension of cognitive functioning it is possible to identify consistent subtypes. For example, it appears that the dimension of cognitive complexity-simplicity can be further divided into at least three distinct subtypes: (1) the tendency to judge events with few variables versus many, (2) the tendency to make fine versus gross distinctions on a given dimension, and (3) the tendency to prefer order and structure versus tolerance of ambiguity (Vannoy, 1965).

2. Cognitive functioning in individuals will vary as a function of the area or content it is focused on—the so-called *cognitive domain.* Thus, an individual may be concrete in interactions with people and abstract in work (Stabel, 1973), and children will analyze and classify persons differently than nations (Signell, 1966).

3. Cultural experience plays a major role in the development and expression of cognitive functioning. Lessor (1976) has shown consistent differences in thinking style across different American ethnic groups; Witkin (1967) has shown differences in global and abstract functioning in different cultures; and Bruner and others (1966) have shown differences in the rate and direction of cognitive development across cultures. Though the evidence is not conclusive, it would appear that these cultural differences in cognition, in Michael Cole's words, "reside more in the situations to which cognitive processes are applied than in the existence of a process in one cultural group and its absence in another" (1971, p. 233). Thus, Cole found that African Kpelle tribesmen were skillful at measuring rice but not at measuring distance. Similarly, Wober (1967) found that Nigerians functioned more analytically than Americans when measured by a test that emphasized proprioceptive cues, whereas they were less skilled at visual analysis.

Inquiry Norms of Academic Disciplines

My first hint that experiential learning theory might provide a useful framework for describing variations in the inquiry norms of academic disciplines came when we examined the undergraduate majors of a large sample of 800 practicing managers and graduate students in management. We found that, although these individuals shared a common occupation, they showed variations in learning style that were strongly associated with their undergraduate educational experience (Kolb, 1976b). Figure 2 shows the average Learning Style Inventory scores for various undergraduate majors reported by the managers. (Only majors with more than ten respondents are included.) Undergraduate business majors tended to

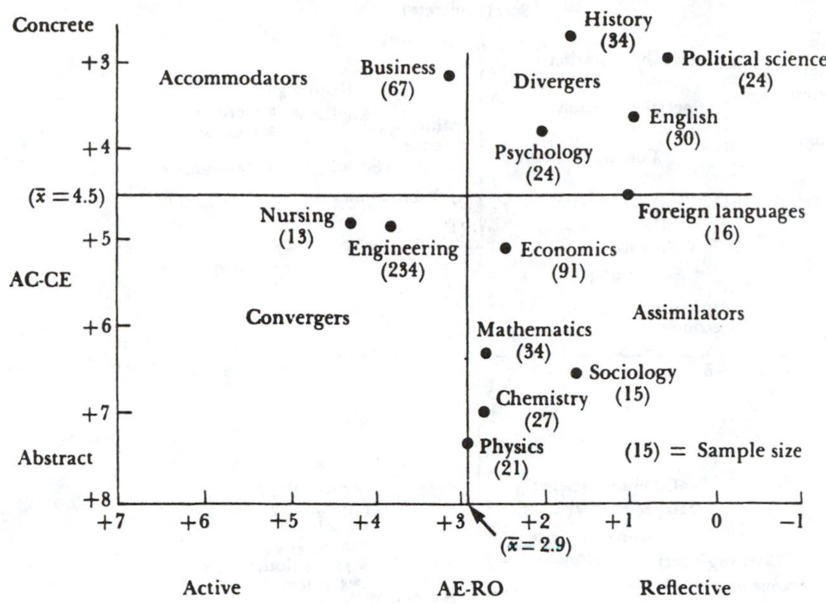

Figure 2
Learning Style Inventory Scores on Active-Reflective (AE-RO) and Abstract-Concrete (AO-CE) Dimensions by College Major

have accommodative learning styles, while engineers, on the average, fell into the convergent quadrant. History, English, political science, and psychology majors all had divergent learning styles. Mathematics and chemistry majors had assimilative learning styles, as did economics and sociology majors. Physics majors were very abstract, falling between the convergent and assimilative quadrants. These data suggested that undergraduate education was a major factor in shaping individual learning style, whether by the process of selection into a discipline, or by socialization in the course of learning in that discipline, or both.

Results from other studies are consistent with these findings. Anthony Biglan (1973a) used a method well suited to answering these questions in his studies of faculty members at the University of Illinois and at a small western college. Using the technique of multidimensional scaling, he analyzed the underlying structures of scholars' judgments about the similarities of subject matter in different academic disciplines. The procedure required faculty members to group subject areas on the basis of similarity, without any labeling of the groupings. Through a kind of factor analysis, the similarity groupings were then mapped onto an *n*-dimensional space, *n* being determined by closeness of fit and interpretability of the dimensions. The two dimensions accounting for the most variance in the University of Illinois data were identified by Biglan as *hard-soft* and *pure-applied*. The mapping of the academic disciplines on this two-dimensional space (Figure 3), reveals a great similarity between Biglan's data and the clustering of data on the learning style dimensions of abstract-concrete and reflective-active. Of the twelve disciplines common to the two studies, nine are in identical quadrants. Business (assumed equivalent to accounting and finance) is accommodative in learning style terms. Engineering is convergent, whereas physics, mathematics, and chemistry are assimilative. The humanistic fields of history, political science, English, and psychology fall into the divergent quadrant. Foreign languages, economics, and sociology were divergent in Biglan's study rather than assimilative. Biglan reported that the pattern of relationships between disciplines shown by the small college data was very similar to that shown by the Illinois data.

These two studies suggest that the abstract-concrete and active-reflective dimensions identified by experiential learning theory differentiate sharply among academic disciplines. A more extensive data base is needed, however. The learning style data came from a single occupation, and in the case of some academic areas sample sizes were small. Biglan's study was limited to two universities, and differences here could be attributed to the specific characteristics of these academic departments.

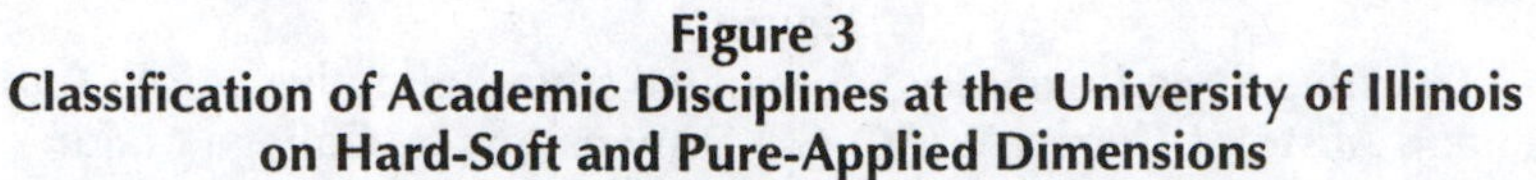

Figure 3
Classification of Academic Disciplines at the University of Illinois on Hard-Soft and Pure-Applied Dimensions

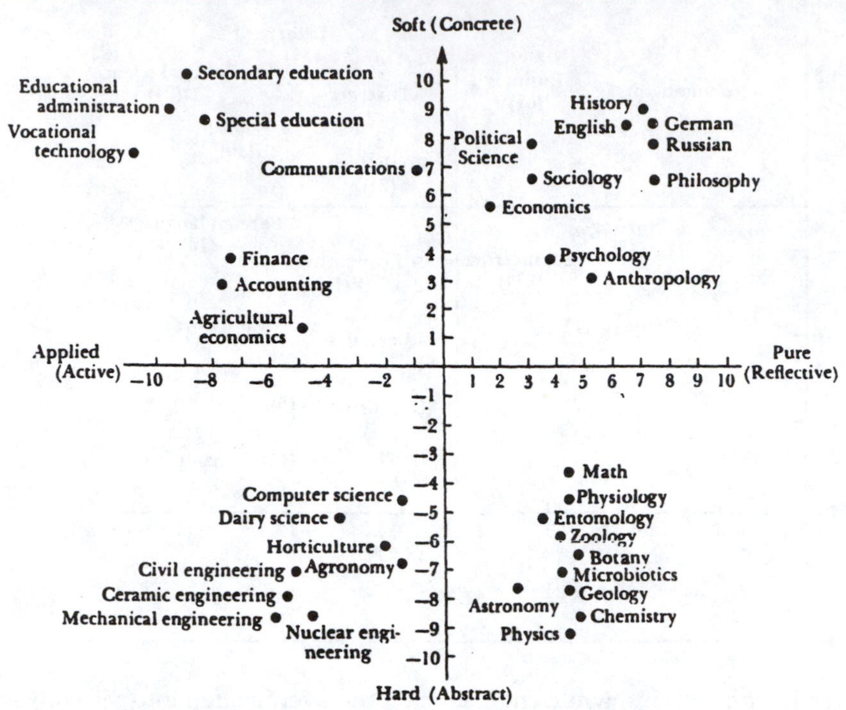

In search of a more extensive and representative sample, I examined data collected in the Carnegie Commission on Higher Education 1969 study of representative American colleges and universities. These data consisted of 32,963 questionnaires from graduate students in 158 institutions and 60,028 questionnaires from faculty in 303 institutions. Using tabulations of this data reported in Feldman (1974), I created ad hoc indexes of the abstract-concrete and active-reflective dimensions for the forty-five academic fields identified in the study. The abstract-concrete index was based on graduate students' responses to two questions asking how important undergraduate backgrounds in mathematics and humanities were for their fields. Mathematics is an abstract field, relying heavily on models, theories, and symbolic manipulation, whereas the humanities are concrete, involving human feelings, intuition, and metaphorical representation of knowledge. There was, as predicted, a strong negative correlation (-.78) between the answers to the mathematics and humanities questions. The index was computed using the percentage of graduate student respondents who strongly agreed that either humanities or mathematics was very important:

$$\frac{\%\ \text{Math important} + (100\text{-}\%\ \text{Humanities important})}{2}$$

Thus, high index scores indicated an abstract field in which a mathematics background was important and humanities not important.

The active-reflective index used faculty data on the percentage of faculty in a given field who were engaged in paid consultation to business, government, or other organizations. This seemed to be the best indicator on the questionnaire of the active, applied orientation of the field. As Feldman (1974) observed, "Consulting may be looked upon not only as a source of added income but also as an indirect measure of the 'power' of a discipline, that is, as a chance to exert the influence and knowledge of a discipline outside the academic setting" (p. 52). The groupings of academic fields based on these indexes are shown in Figure 4.

The indexes reveal a pattern of relationships among academic fields that is highly consistent with Biglan's study and the managerial learning style data. The results suggest that the commonly accepted division of academic fields into two camps, the scientific and the artistic, or abstract and concrete (for example, Snow, 1963; Hudson, 1966), might be usefully enriched by the addition of a second dimension,

Figure 4
Concrete-Abstract and Active-Reflective Orientations of Academic Fields Derived from the Carnegie Commission Study

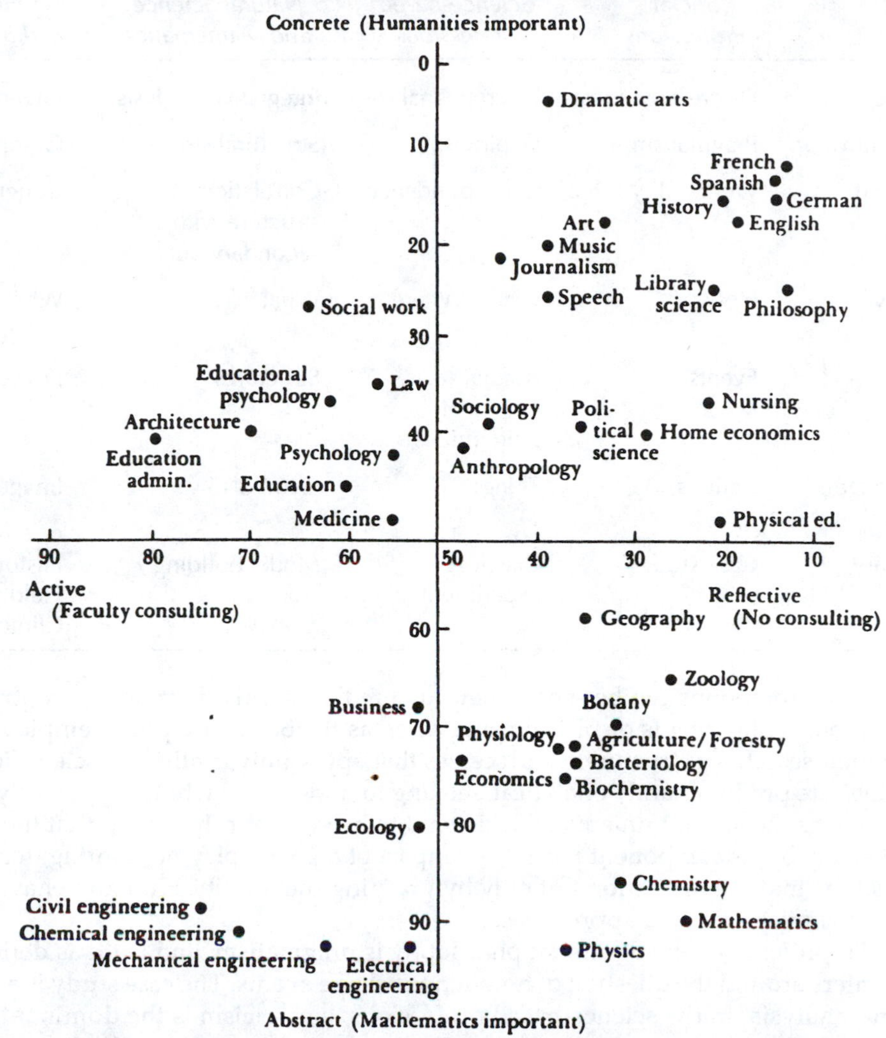

namely, active-reflective or applied-basic. When academic fields are mapped on this two-dimensional space, a fourfold typology of disciplines emerges. In the abstract-reflective quadrant are clustered the *natural sciences and mathematics,* while the abstract-active quadrant includes the *science-based professions,* most notably the engineering fields. The concrete-active quadrant encompasses what might be called the *social professions,* such as education, social work, and law. The concrete-reflective quadrant includes the *humanities and social sciences.* Further evidence for the validity of this typology can be seen in the different ways that knowledge is structured and created in these fields.

Knowledge Structures and Inquiry Processes

When one examines the four major groupings of disciplines just cited—the natural sciences and mathematics, the science-based professions, the social professions, and the humanities and social sciences—it becomes apparent that what constitutes valid knowledge differs widely from one to another. This is easily observed in differences in how knowledge is reported (for example, numerical or logical symbols, words or images), in inquiry methods (for example, case studies, experiments, logical analysis), and in criteria for evaluation (for example, practical versus statistical significance). Currently we are developing a typology that describes the basic structural dimensions of different knowledge systems (see Table 1). In

Table 1
A Typology of Knowledge Structures and Inquiry Processes in Four Types of Academic Disciplines

Discipline Type	*Social Professions*	*Science-based Professions*	*Natural Science and Mathematics*	*Humanities and Social Science*
Inquiry strategy	Discrete synthesis	Discrete analysis	Integrative analysis	Integrative synthesis
Dominant philosophy	Pragmatism	Empiricism	Structuralism	Organicism
Theory of truth	Workability	Correspondence	Correlation of structure with secondary qualities	Coherence
Basic inquiry question	How	When, Where	What	Why
Basic units of knowledge	Events	Natural laws, empirical uniformities	Structures	Processes
How knowledge is portrayed	Actions	Things	Symbols	Images
Typical inquiry method	Case study	Classical experiment	Model building	Historical analysis Field study Clinical observation

this typology, the professions can be seen to employ predominantly discrete injury strategies, aimed at understanding particular events or phenomena, whereas the basic disciplines employ more integrated strategies, in their search for structures or processes that apply universally. The scientific professions and basic disciplines are predominantly analytical, seeking to understand wholes by identifying their component parts, whereas the social-humanistic fields tend to be synthetic, believing that the whole can never be explained solely by its component parts. The impact of a poem, play or painting, for example, cannot be understood by analytic dissection but only by grasping the totality. Human behavior and economic systems require similar synthetic approaches.

In the social professions the dominant philosophy is pragmatism, and truth as defined by workability. Inquiry centers around the question of how actions shape events. The case study is a common method of inquiry and analysis. In the science-based professions, empiricism is the dominant philosophy, and correspondence is the main criterion for truth. Thus, knowledge is created by locating phenomena in time (when) and space (where). Here the emphasis is on the analysis, measurement, and categorization of observable experience and the establishment of empirical uniformities defining relationships between observed categories (natural laws), with a minimum of reliance on inferred structures or processes that are not directly accessible to public experience. The classical experimental method is the typical inquiry method.

Mathematics and natural science are dominated by a structuralist philosophy, which seeks to distinguish the primary, essential elements and relationships in a phenomenon from the secondary, accidental relationships. Piaget (1968) defines these structures as follows:

> As a first approximation we may say that a structure is a system of transformations. Inasmuch as it is a system and not a mere collection of elements and their properties, these transformations involve laws: the structure is preserved or enriched by the interplay of its transformation laws, which never yield results external to the system nor employ elements that are external to it. In short, the notion of structure is comprised of three key ideas: the idea of wholeness, the idea of transformation, and the idea of self-regulation [p. 5].

Thus, quantitative model building is a typical inquiry method. The humanities and the social sciences share an organicist philosophy concerned with basic processes. The primary criterion for truth is coherence, a meaningful "gestalt" that integrates phenomena. Here there is a concern with ultimate values, with why things are as they are. The anthropological field study, historical analysis, and clinical observation are typical inquiry methods.

Some fields seem to include within their boundaries considerable variation in inquiry norms and knowledge structures. Several of the professions (particularly management, medicine, and architecture) are themselves multidisciplinary, including specialties that emphasize different learning styles. Medicine requires both a concern for human service and scientific knowledge. Architecture has requirements for artistic and engineering excellence. Management involves skills at both quantitative and qualitative analysis. Several of the social sciences, particularly psychology, sociology, and economics, can vary greatly in their basic inquiry paradigms. Clinical psychology emphasizes divergent learning skills, while experimental psychology emphasizes convergent skills; industrial and educational psychology emphasize practical, accommodative skills. Sociology can be highly abstract and theoretical (as in Parsonian structural functionalism) or concrete and active (as in phenomenology or ethnomethodology). Some economics departments may employ very convergent models of inquiry, emphasizing the use of econometric models in public policy; others may employ divergent modes, emphasizing economic history and philosophy.

This brief description cannot do justice to the complexity and variation of inquiry processes and knowledge structures in various disciplines. Nevertheless, it may suggest how the forms of knowledge in different fields can be differentially attractive and meaningful to individuals with different learning styles. Indeed, every field will show variation on these dimensions within a given department, between departments, from undergraduate to graduate levels, and so on. The purpose of this analysis is not to pigeonhole fields but to identify useful dimensions for describing variations in individual learning styles and in the inquiry processes of different disciplines, in order to better understand and manage the educational process.

. . .

Note

I am indebted to David Brown, Arthur Chickering, and Suresh Srivastva for their comments and suggestions on this chapter.

Intellectual, Psychosocial, and Moral Development in College: Four Major Theories

JOANNE KURFISS

Introduction

Most faculty in liberal educational environments would like to believe that they are successfully achieving the lofty goals carried in their institutional catalogs. Yet lacking a common language for discussing such goals, lacking clarity as to the nature of the goals, lacking a sense of what the ideal student is really like, and lacking in empirical means of determining how successful they are in achieving any kind of positive outcome, faculty are susceptible to challenges of all kinds, not the least of which is that they should be "training" students for "useful" careers and vocations in a very direct and pragmatic (and measurable) way.

How can these challenges be addressed without injustice to the values and goals which independent colleges represent? In this paper, we present four models, four "languages," if you will, four "lenses" for viewing students, educational goals, and learning environments. Each offers a different perspective; taken together they provide a beginning for our continuing efforts to improve the educational experience. They are neither exclusive nor exhaustive; numerous other models exist. Our hope is that the reader will be enticed to learn more about these models, and to share the new perspectives gained with colleagues, encouraging them to join together in an ongoing enterprise which can mean the difference between business as usual and a new and engaging interaction with students, parents, alumni, and the social context in which we teach.

In general, theories of cognitive and psychological development trace paths from simplicity and absolutism to complexity and relativism, from concreteness to abstractness, and from external to internal regulation of behavior. This is not surprising in view of our culture's idealization of such values as individual responsibility (internal or self-regulation), critical analysis (abstractness and complexity; differentiation of ideas), and tolerance (relativity of values). What may be surprising to some is the diversity of current theories of development which specify intervening steps or stages and suggest conditions and processes that encourage movement through those stages. These theories have powerful implications for educators who desire to engage students fully in the learning process while encouraging their evolution as thinking and caring human beings.

Each of the four theories presented in this paper emphasizes a unique aspect of the total developmental process. Piaget's model describes the development of structures and processes which characterize mature logical thinking. Perry provides a closer look at students' beliefs about the nature of knowledge and authority, identifying and chronicling epistemological assumptions that profoundly affect students' reactions to and ability to learn from various instructional strategies. Relationships between Perry's "positions" and Erikson's model of identity development are described, and their implications for curriculum design explored. Finally, Kohlberg's stage theory and Gilligan's critique provide two important perspectives on the development of systems for analyzing moral and value issues, and suggest instructional

"Intellectual, Psychosocial, and Moral Development in College: Four Major Theories," by Joanne Kurfiss, reprinted from *A Handbook on Values Development in Lutheran Church-Related College,* edited by J. P. Balas and J. R. Judy, 1988, Thiel College.

processes most likely to enhance this development. by keeping in mind the major dimensions noted above, the reader will be able to discern the commonalties which unite these theories and make them so relevant to teaching and learning in today's liberal arts college.

All the models presented share a basic methodological foundation. They were developed on the basis of extensive listening to and observation of individuals at various points in their growth. Piaget's "clinical method" involved observing and interacting with children as they attempted to solve specific concrete or formal operational tasks. Perry and his associates interviewed dozens of students at Harvard, meeting their study participants once a year for lengthy, open-ended conversations about "What stood out" about the past year. Kohlberg used moral dilemmas, and Erikson drew from clinical experiences and biographies. Each listened with the "third ear," attempting to discern patterns, to hear a world-view, and to give credence and respect to the intellectual work that created whatever world-view emerged.

Thus a major contribution of these theorists is the example of empathic listening each provides. A primary purpose in reviewing these theories is to provide a framework for more sensitive listening—not to categorize or label students, but to establish a series of potential contexts for understanding each learner's present way of construing the work, for appreciating the progress it represents over past constructions, and for respecting the learner's need to proceed to the next most likely construction at his or her own pace.

For each of these theorists we will briefly summarize and critique their major ideas. Each section will conclude with an analysis of the specific implications of the theory for teaching and learning in Project QUE colleges. These stage theories are not without their limitations, so we preface our remarks with some qualifying observations.

First, to some degree all four theories describe linear, progressive movement through age-related stages. Regressions, defined as use of an earlier stage, seem contradictory to the notion of orderly forward progress. Yet when approaching a new task, searching for a creative solution to some problem, producing a work of art, or coping with occasional levels of high stress many learners behave in ways characteristic of earlier stages of development (Kris, 1952). The challenges of college, which include entering new environments, assuming new roles and responsibilities, or encountering increased or differing challenges to their self-image or sense of self-esteem, may inhibit use of skills and structures evident in other situations (Barber, 1981; Knefelkamp, 1982). For example, adults returning to school after a long absence may fail to use problem-solving strategies or social skills they use at home or at work on a daily basis. Such regression may be adaptive and is not often temporary and limited to the situation presenting the challenge; hence, Kohlberg's term "functional regression."

Three of the four theories are based on research with adolescents and/or young adults. Only Erikson attempts to describe experiences and images common to adults. Furthermore, most of the observations about developmental stages have been made about males, and all have been made about people living in European-American cultures. Recent research on women's development challenges basic assumptions of Kohlberg's model, and research on Erikson's identity periods reveal a variety of sex differences, as we shall see. Sex differences are also emerging in research on Perry's stages as well. Although Piaget's work has held up fairly well in cross-cultural research, and Kohlberg's stages are based on cross-cultural data, critics have attacked all of these models for one form or another of ethnocentrism or methodological flaws.

Thus we make no claim for the universality or total generalizability of these theories; we offer them as entry points for common thinking about students, learning, and academic environments. They provide perspectives on the teaching/learning process that are invaluable for those who choose to approach the educational process reflectively. They can help us ask better questions about what we are doing, why we are doing it, and how we can do it more effectively. At the same time, their inadequacies have already stimulated new questions and can be expected to generate increased understanding of learning in all its many forms.

Piaget: Cognitive Development

The Theory

Piaget's ideas provide a foundation for understanding cognition, which is central to the tasks of educators. Once Piaget's ideas are understood, subsequent ideas should be relatively easy to grasp.

Three essential axioms of Piaget's theory are that:

1. Knowing is ultimately based on activity, both physical and mental, an interaction between self and environment.

2. Development is a gradual and progressive reorganization of mental structures used to "make sense" of the world.

3. Learning (other than rote learning) occurs when the learner acts to resolve discrepancies between beliefs and new information which does not fit those beliefs.

Piaget's theory is founded on a "constructionist" or "interactionist" epistemology. That is, he emphasizes the active participation of the knower in the process of understanding the world. "The world" as we know it is the product of inherent properties of mind interacting with inherent properties of the environment. We do not arrive with a "blank slate"—either at birth or at college. We do not learn solely because we are rewarded for learning, but because our primary mission, cognitively at least, is to make sense of the world. Even as infants we are like little scientists, testing hypotheses, using our theories to understand our experiences, trying to fit new experiences into old theories, and modifying our theories only when the evidence of their inadequacy overwhelms us.

Piaget documented this view by studying closely the behavior of his infant children (Piaget, 1954), as well as numerous children and adolescents in his native Switzerland. Observing infants, he noted their continual use of bodily action as a means of understanding their world. For instance, as soon as the infant is capable of doing so, it applies its habit of sucking things to a new problem: learning about nonnutritive objects (the familiar "everything into the mouth" period). Later, the infant studies the paths of moving objects by dropping them repeatedly from the crib. Piaget labeled the first two years the "sensory-motor" period because of the infant's use of its senses combined with bodily or "motor" activity to make sense of the world.

In Piaget's view, the child's interactions stimulate progressive reorganization of mental structures (the child's equivalent to models, theories, and paradigms about what to expect from the environment). A primary characteristic of reorganized stages is that they become more general and abstract. We come to rely less and less on direct experience and physical activity, simplifying by integrating common experiences and using increasingly sophisticated representational systems (including but not limited to language) to store what we know. Thus the infant "knows" that when she drops her toy it will fall because she has observed a simple cause-effect relation between her action and the behavior of the object. As a formal operational thinker, she will be able to use an algebraic formula or write a paragraph to describe symbolically what was known through action in her infancy.

Cognitive abilities in childhood are, of course, intermediate between those of toddlers and adolescents. Simple relationships between events and objects come to be understood and taken for granted. The child understands that she and her brother can have the same amount of milk shake even if the glasses are different sizes. But the child's emerging logic is only effective in dealing with tangible objects and **observable** events (even if not **directly** observed). Problems requiring proportional relations, reasoning about improbable situations, or isolation of factors which combine to determine the outcomes of events are not yet solvable by the child in this "concrete operational" period. The mental structures necessary to solve such problems, termed "formal operations," generally appear during adolescence, under favorable conditions. Most traditional college-level instruction is conducted under the assumption that students reason formally. This assumption has recently been challenged, as we shall see.

Table 1 summarizes various mental processes which Piaget has identified as "formal" in nature (Inhelder and Piaget, 1958), and indicates responses to such tasks expected of a student who is still a concrete learner. As an example, a formal thinker will devise a series of tests to determine the factors influencing flexibility of rods (Figure 1): when testing each hypothesized factor, this person will hold all other factors constant and vary **only** the factor being checked, but a concrete learner will confound the factors (question, Figure 1) without realizing the implications for his conclusions.

As another example, a concrete learner can observe and make simple generalizations about which of a group of objects will float, but will be at a loss to explain unexpected events such as a large object floating (a block of wood) or a small object sinking (a needle once it breaks the surface tension of the water). Only a formal learner can provide a logical explanation when a prediction is disconfirmed, and go on to make a general statement about the behavior of floating objects. This is formal operations; thought is gen-

Table 1
Formal Task/Concrete Learner

Formal Operation Required	Concrete Operational Response
Hypothetical Reasoning (reasoning about possible outcomes; e.g., projections, forecasting, speculating)	Rejection of hypothetical premises that contradict "reality"; stopping when an "actual" solution is found; inability to consider further alternatives.
Deductive Reasoning (reasoning from a general rule or principle to a specific instance; ("If . . . then" reasoning)	Drawing of invalid conclusions; failure to consider logical relationships inherent in the problem; failure to recognize relevance of a previously "learned" principle to a specific situation.
Proportional Reasoning (reasoning about relationships that can be expressed in the form x/y = a/b)	Attempts to use algorithms or rote formulas—not necessarily correctly. Use of additive relationships where ratios should be constructed.
Systematic Combination of Elements (generating a list of all possible combinations of three or more variables)	Failure to use an orderly, organized, planned approach. Failure to identify all combinations and/or duplications of responses. May require reminders to use a previously learned system.
Holding Variables Constant (establishing a trial procedure to isolate the effects of a single factor, exclude irrelevant factors, or separate out the combined effects of related variables)	Failure to separate effects of individual variables; failure to establish critical diagnostic tests of a hypothesis; ignoring of dis-confirming or contradictory evidence; inability to relate multiple variables; reasoning limited to one or two variables at a time.
Correlational Analysis (determining whether two events co-vary or act independently)	Focus on positive associations without recognition of possible disconforming cases.
Probabilistic Reasoning (estimating or calculating the change that a given event will occur; includes proportional reasoning)	Failure to grasp sampling concepts; insistence on actual "counts" as only way to determine outcomes; use of addition and subtraction to calculate relationships.
Propositional, Verbal, or Symbolic Reasoning (reasoning about relationship between statements, observations, or symbols)	Efforts to "capture" all information for later rote memorization; literal interpretation of symbols.
Complex Problem Solving (requires transformation of familiar procedures or generalization to a new context)	Tendency to treat each problem as if it were a new one; difficulty establishing a context of related problems; "forgetting" of previously learned procedures or failure to recognize their relevance for present problem (lack of transfer of knowledge); preference for step-by-step, "cookbook" instruction in how to solve each new type of problem that arises.

**Based on Inhelder & Piaget (1958)*

eral, abstract, and complex. It is also internally regulated, since it is independent of the concrete reality of rods (they could be variables in a psychological experiment) or the particular floating objects used.

As a corollary, we note that a major cognitive achievement of the formal period is the ability to reason about possibilities or hypothetical situations. Thus, given a new object such as a golf practice ball or jar top, the formal thinker can study it and make a reasonable prediction as to whether it will float, drawing on the general rule he or she has "constructed" about flotation.

Figure 1
Flexible Rods Problem*

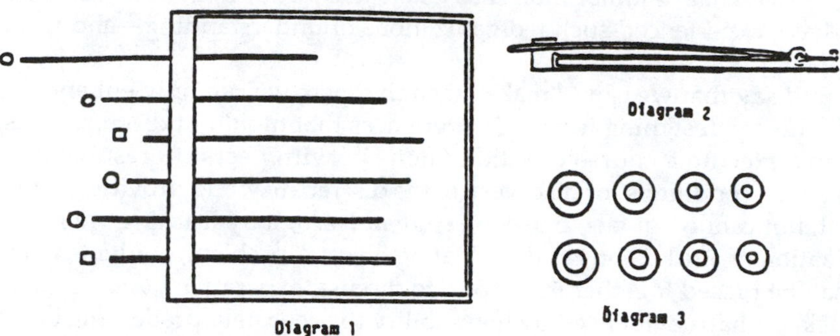

Diagram I illustrates a top view of an apparatus which can be used to test the flexibility of rods which vary in cross-sectional shape (square or round), thickness (10mm² or 16mm²), and material (brass, steel, or wood). The user can adjust the lengths of the rods as shown in Diagram 2. The apparatus includes a set of weights (Diagram 3) which can be placed on the ends of the rods. Flexibility can be judged by the closeness of the weighted rod top to the water in the apparatus (Diagram 2).

1. Using this apparatus, how would you determine which variable(s) affect the flexibility of the rods? Describe your suggested procedure in detail below.

2. What would you do to find out if square rods bend more than round rods?

3. What would you do to find out if brass rods bend more than wooden ones?

4. If you had a 40 cm. square, steel rod with 10mm cross-section and a 50 cm. square, steel rod with 16mm cross-section, could you compare them to determine whether thickness affects flexibility? Why or why not?

**Tomlinson-Keassey, and Campbell, n.d.: based on Inhelder and Piaget (1958).*

What are the conditions for development of this type of reasoning? Throughout the early years, the child is acquiring a backlog of concrete, action-based experiences in the world. Without these experiences, the mind has nothing to act upon, and would have difficulty developing. But experience alone is not sufficient. Some experiences are clearly more likely than others to stimulate the mind to act. What characterizes those more "stimulating" experiences? This questions is addressed by Piaget's third "axiom":

> Learning (other than rote learning) occurs when the learner acts to resolve discrepancies between beliefs and new information which does not fit those beliefs.

Piaget terms the reaction to discrepancies "disequilibration." With this language, he suggests a process whereby the cybernetic system of the mind seeks to rectify an imbalance between two normal, everyday processes: assimilation (the incorporation of information into a pre-existing understanding of "the way the world is") and accommodation (adjusting one's understanding to encompass variations in the external world).

As adults, our understanding is normally sufficient to avoid the need for making major accommodations; we assimilate most events or information and make minor, unnoticed adjustments as necessary. In fact, we **prefer** to assimilate; accommodation requires effort. Only when we experience major discrepancies are we aware of accommodation (and perhaps our resistance to it!), often expressed in the emotional reaction of surprise. We **accommodate** our thinking in order to **assimilate** as much available, relevant information as possible.

But the cognitions of the growing young person are only partially developed, so that they are more often susceptible to surprises. In education, a once-popular term for such times of surprise was "teachable moments." When the learner responds to unexpected information by adjusting a particular structure of understanding, we say that "equilibration" has taken place. The "light bulb" comes on. As teacher and learners, all of us have experienced such reorganizations of understanding—and wished we knew how to make them happen.

Piagetians would say that we can't "make" them happen; we can only enhance their probability of occurrence. We do this by designing learning experiences that highlight discrepancies, and then letting the learner plan and execute a course of action (alone or with peers) to resolve the discrepancy. The teacher can establish the conditions for discovery of the discrepancy, and provide support for the learner's efforts to resolve it, but cannot, in fact, make the student learn, if by learning we mean something other than rote memorization of a rule. Thus in the "floating objects" problem, students who have not grasped the general rule can be placed together in a group to discuss, experiment, and arrive at a deeper understanding of the task, perhaps evidenced by their ability to accurately predict the behavior of five or six new objects, and to write out a rule which predicts floating behavior in general. In the process, they work out "secrets" of organizing and recording observations, planning experiments eliminating irrelevant information—many of which, with encouragement, they will apply to new problems and eventually use spontaneously. Contrast this with the usual didactic methods of teaching (telling students about) concepts of density and specific gravity. Fuller (1980) has documented the ineffectiveness of these methods, even with college level students in physics.

What does this have to do with higher education? Don't college-age students have well-developed structures, and are they not, therefore, relatively immune to surprises of this sort? And since they are generally far into adolescence, are they not formal thinkers, capable of using purely verbal, symbolic, abstract processes to understand what is presented to them?

The answer is not, in all three cases. First, while college students generally have experience with and knowledge of the physical world, they have rarely been educated to confront and work out discrepancies between casual observations (e.g., wood blocks and battleships, though large, **do** float), assumptions (large things sink), and what they memorize in school. They often bring with them to college strongly held misconceptions about how things are in the world. We all know it is still possible to surprise college students, no matter how worldly or blasé they may appear to be. For instance, even students with younger siblings are surprised to learn about the capabilities and limitations of infants and young children. They often react by subjecting their siblings (or their own offspring) to extensive developmental testing to verify their new learning, demonstrating Piaget's idea that learning requires activity in the service of equilibration. Second, use of formal operations by entering freshmen, at least as measured by traditional Piagetian tasks, may be the exception rather than the rule (McKinnon, 1976). Many freshmen are "transitional"; they may reason formally in limited areas, in areas which interest them and where they have experience, or they may use a mix of concrete and formal strategies. At one state university, 50 percent of a sample of entering freshmen scored at the concrete operational level on a Piagetian test battery (McKinnon and Renner, 1971). This is reflected in students' difficulty with seemingly basic concepts such as density in physics, multiple causality in history, or graphs and proportionality in science and math. We also find students unskilled in using processes such as interpretation in literature, separating observation from inference in writing or psychology, and planning experiments in science or social science classes. All of these require formal thought. If instruction does not provide opportunities to explore formal concepts actively the concrete thinker must rely on rote recall to get by.

Many developmentalists attribute the rarity of formal thought to students' lack of opportunity, during earlier school years, **to act upon** questions, problems, or discrepancies which they themselves have discovered. Action is both the most natural and the most effective way for young people to learn. Without it there is little or no opportunity to exercise, challenge, and extend the structures and capabilities of thought. The fact that Piagetian programs in high school and colleges (such as DOORS, ADAPT, SOAR, STAR, and others; see Fuller, 1978, 1980) have succeeded to some extent in reversing the damage done in earlier schooling is the basis for our optimism about the developmental approach to instruction. With careful attention to planning and use of developmentally based methods in designing educational programs, we may be able to overcome many of the serious learning deficits we see in students today.

Critique

A major source of criticism directed to Piagetian theory by educators concerns its focus on skills and tasks associated with the natural sciences and mathematics. With some analytical effort, one can see how formal operations are used in writing a coherent essay, analyzing a short story, or understanding themes and patterns in history. However, it is less clear how formal operations relate to creativity and the capacity to visualize or describe a specific concrete experience—skills that are central to the arts of many of the humanities. Recent research on left and right hemisphere specialization (the so-called "split brain" research) is highly speculative and controversial; however, it does suggest that much of what Piaget describes as the movement from concrete to formal operations involves left hemisphere functions. Most of the functions generally attributed to the right hemisphere (intuitive, emotional, spatial, musical) seem to be neglected by Inhelder and Piaget's model.

Does the movement from concrete to formal operations mean the emerging dominance of left hemisphere functions at the expense of right hemisphere functions, or is there a parallel development in the right hemisphere? Are there stages of development in the capacity of learners to be creative, synthesizing information in novel ways, to portray an idea, setting, or feeling in a particularly sensitive manner via paint, sounds, or words? Is there a developmental step beyond formal operations that incorporates both left and right hemisphere functions, or are we seeing differences in individual styles of expression such as those described in Holland's typology (1966)? Certainly capacities of the formal operational thinker such as the ability to generate multiple combinations and to think about hypothetical situations are relevant to creative thought and productions, but creativity seems to demand more than logic.

A final criticism is that Piaget has not, in fact, defined the most advanced cognitive stages. For instance, Arlin (1974) has claimed that problem **finding** is a developmentally more advanced task than problem **solving**, emphasized by Piaget. Riegel (1973) has argued that the search for equilibration is not a realistic model of thought, but that mature reasoning requires a kind of creative acceptance of conflict. He suggests that a dialectic between formal and sensory-motor or concrete processes (perhaps analogous to left- and right-brain processes in hemispheric lateralization terminology) energizes thought, making it adaptable to situations; this view offers potential for understanding the interplay of cognition and intuitive/affective/creative processes.

In part, perhaps, because their work focused on the logical thought processes of young people, Inhelder and Piaget clearly did not exhaust the possibilities of this vast and challenging domain of inquiry. However, Piaget was certainly not unaware of these questions. He explored relationships between cognition and affect at each stage of development in at least one essay (Piaget, 1968). And a colleague notes that Piaget's seeming inattention to the affective domain was more a result of his deep humility in the face of such processes than a consequence of a belief that they were unimportant (Papert, 1980)

Teaching Implications

Given what we do know about the movement from concrete to formal operations, several specific suggestions can be made concerning the design of educational settings. First, the Piagetian model of learning implies—perhaps even necessitates—heavy reliance on "hands-on," problem-oriented modes of instruction that provide numerous points of contact with experiences or knowledge familiar to the learner, particularly when learners have not achieved formal operations. Second, research on contemporary college students suggests that a faculty member working with students at introductory levels can assume that the majority are at best transitional. For these students, Piaget's model suggests that a) their future careers will benefit from instruction designed to stimulate formal reasoning, and b) they will learn "content" better if it is firmly grounded in concrete experiences, with formal concepts developed or "constructed" in a joint venture between student, professor, and subject, emphasizing understanding rather than simply "coverage." This in turn means that expectations concerning what can be accomplished in the classroom may need to be revised.

A professor approaching this situation might begin by identifying the central, critical concepts or principles of a course—probably no more than a dozen in all. These principles should then be taught using hands-on experiences, multiple examples, laboratory problems, and applications in numerous contexts to provide the necessary concrete foundation for understanding. Terminology, theoretical models, or symbolic representations of relations can be introduced more effectively once the concrete foundation is established. Later concepts may need less emphasis on the concrete if earlier ones are firmly grasped. In some cases, formal concepts are actually learned more quickly with this approach, as in the case of a philosophy professor teaching logic in an ADAPT course (in Fuller, 1978). Less central concepts may be covered through readings or modules using various forms of instructional technology (slide/tapes, computer-assisted instruction, videotape or videodisc, etc.).

To the extent that a faculty member dwells on the presentation of specific facts and tests for the acquisition of details (dates, statistics, events, outcomes) where there is no clear reason for memorizing these, students will not be encouraged to move toward formal operations, but will instead be rewarded for using learning strategies that enable them to remain at the concrete stage. They will have covered more but will learn less, in the sense of retaining and integrating knowledge in a meaningful way.

Some of the students in a college classroom will be using formal operations: they will learn from the initial presentation of abstract concepts and will not need the extensive background required by concrete or transitional learners. These students can check or consolidate their learning by helping other students, so long as they are willing to do so , and are able to refrain from "giving the answers" to their less fortunate peers. Of course, whether or not this will succeed depends greatly on the social environment of the classroom and the norms of the institution. Traditionally, students devalue the potential for learning from peers; while desirable, these arrangements require special sensitivity if they are to work well. The professor also may consider meeting the needs the needs of more advanced students by increasing individual options within the course structure. Some students might attend special sessions where principles are expanded upon, or might be given additional and more challenging problems to work out, perhaps with access to a tutor.

For both concrete and formal learners, laboratory experiences provide flexibility needed to meet the needs of a heterogeneous group. Faculty in the sciences often combine lectures with laboratory experiences in the humanities and social sciences to complement lectures. Studio work in the arts, participation in theater performances, translation of a short story into a newspaper article or television screenplay (or vice versa), writing musical compositions within certain parameters or using kitchen utensils or microcomputers for instruments can provide lab-like experiences in humanities and fine arts disciplines. Lab experiences can also be designed in history (compare original documents with later writings about them; do research on local history using primary documents) or philosophy (make an ethical choice and defend it). In any discipline, laboratory experiences must avoid "cookbook," here-is-how-to-do-it approaches. Emphasis should be on exploration, experimentation, and identifying and solving problems at least partially selected by students. Group work is valuable to stimulate exchange and critique of ideas in a peer-centered (as opposed to authority-centered) situation.

A model which has proven useful in a variety of programs is the Learning Cycle, developed by Karplus (1974) for public school science teaching and adapted by Fuller and others (1978, 1980) for use in a variety of disciplines at the college level. The ADAPT program at the University of Nebraska-Lincoln provided a model followed in recent years by several other institutions. Fuller and associates (1978, 1980) provide descriptions of learning cycles in disciplines ranging from algebra to economics, literature, and philosophy—essential reading for anyone who intends to pursue this approach. The Learning Cycle model is briefly summarized in Table 2. Kurfiss (1982) provides suggestions for effective use of the model.

Perry: Epistemological Development

The Theory

While Piaget chronicles development of ability to use logical thinking, William G. Perry, Jr., has chronicled the evolution of beliefs about what constitutes knowledge, truth, and fact, and the role of authorities in defining and conveying knowledge. The later positions shift to issues arising from the problems of making commitments in a relativistic context as epistemological reflection generalizes to personal choice and action (Perry, 1970). His "positions" share some characteristics with Piaget's stages; for example, they are orderly in their sequence, both logically and psychologically (Kurfiss, 1975, 1977). The more advanced the position, the more likely it is to require formal reasoning. The processes which are presumed to stimulate development include disequilibration; more will be said of this shortly.

Although Perry's original work identified nine positions, grouping these into four major periods makes the scheme more manageable and accessible on first exposure. These periods are somewhat arbi-

Table 2
The Three Phases of the Learning Cycles Model*

1. **Exploration**
   In this phase, students are provided with structured opportunities to explore the "raw data" relevant to the concept to be learned. "Hands-on" experiences, opportunities to sort or categorize examples, experimentation with materials illustrating variations on a theme, recall of related experiences—all can be used to focus the student's attention on the concept. The key is to provide a base of experience which will allow the student to relate the concept to something "real" in his/her world, and which may also lead the student to question previously acquired knowledge.
2. **Intervention**
   If the exploration phase has been properly structured, students will make discoveries or will have questions about the concept. When the instructor sees that they are ready to crystallize these discoveries, the process shifts from exploration to identification of the observations, principles, rules, or other regularities which the students have found. The teacher will want to guide but not dominate this phase; often it will be best to provide terminology only when students have clarified the ideas to which labels are to be applied. The invention phase stresses induction of general ideas from a variety of particular experiences, past and present.
3. **Application**
   In this phase, students are encouraged to search out or work with other examples of the newly discovered/invented concept. These may be teacher or student generated, or both. The application phase may involve a new, concrete experience using the concept in a novel way. The idea is to help the student generalize from the particular instance just learned to broaden his/her understanding of other circumstances or situations in which the concept applies.

**Based on the work of Robert Karplus (1974); adapted from Fuller (1978, 1980)*

trarily defined, since the positions, grouping these into four major periods makes these scheme more manageable and accessible on first exposure. These periods are somewhat arbitrarily defined, since the positions shade gradually into one another; for those who intend to pursue the topic further I have indicated specifically which of Perry's positions I am including in the four periods below.

I. **Dualism** (Perry's positions 1 and 2): For the Dualist, knowledge is absolute; there is Truth and Falsity, Right and Wrong, Good and Bad. "For every question there is a simple answer" would be a characteristic Dualist statement. Authorities are those who have the Answers. Disagreement among them is unthinkable—facts are facts! Belief systems are not chosen, they are given—unquestioned, unanalyzed backdrops to the student's experience.

II. **Multiplicity** (Perry's positions 3 and 4 Multiplicity Correlative): Most knowledge is still viewed as absolute, as in Dualism. But in some fields or on some questions, we don't have its grey areas, and authorities may **not** be infallible. But the reaction to this realization may be rather anti-establishment. Values? Ideology? Why have any? Just do what seems right at the time; "Go with the flow." In response to a low grade on an essay exam, a student may contend that since there is no one right answer, all we have is opinion, and one opinion is just as good as another. This form of epistemological nihilism is particularly common among sophomores.

Liberal educators may realize their greatest potential influence by developing strategies to overcome the tendency for this belief structure to persist through graduation. A common path out of this position is to attempt to discover and use the "rules of the game" to the students' best advantage. Thus, presentation of a balanced, documented "opinion" in a paper may become a strategy for managing the grey areas, but one adopted only to satisfy the instructor and get the grade. The irony is that the tools of independent thinking are acquired as the student discovers and seeks to conform to "what the professor wants," as Perry (1970) wryly notes.

Regardless of motives, however, the student who can articulate principles for the use of critical thinking processes has already slipped into the next position.

III. **Relativism** (Perry's 4 Relativism Subordinate, 5, and 6): As noted above, and given the right conditions, students will begin to discern patterns or regularities in the way their professors (and others) approach grey areas of knowledge. They may recognize such strategies as analysis of evidence, comparison of interpretations, or designing experiments. At first this recognition may come in a limited area of study, but at some point a flip-flop occurs and the student comes to view the grey areas as the rule rather than the exception. Procedures for negotiating within uncertainty begin to be articulated by the student (e.g., "I try to present a balanced view, look at the evidence on both [or all] sides, and then come to a conclusion that seems most reasonable.") The context within which facts are viewed is recognized as having a bearing on how those facts will be interpreted. Authorities are now recognized as fellow seekers of understanding, different primarily in that they are experienced at making sense of the profusion of knowledge in their fields. During this period, students may feel that belief systems are difficult to think about because so many good arguments exist for any one approach, "no matter how you look at it." Toward the end of this period (Position 6), they begin to experience the necessity of choosing despite the difficulties involved. They also realize at some point during this period that this state of affairs is relevant to their own life choices, a disconcerting discovery for many.

IV. **Commitment in Relativism** (Positions 7, 8, and 9): Skilled in rational (formal operational) processes and drawing upon the accumulated learning and experience of the college years, the student can commit herself to the opinions, ideologies, values, and interests with which she will identify. Recognition of the fallibility of her choices, acceptance of responsibility for their consequences, and willingness to accept others; right to their own choices characterize the commitments of the Relativist. There is full recognition that choices restrict one from some choices and open the way to others; there may be sadness accompanying specific decisions as well as positive feelings and apprehension about the future. Commitments may not be made all of a sudden, though a gradual realization that a particular direction is being taken may occur. A student may reaffirm or reject old beliefs; either way, the decision is based on a **conscious** consideration of alternatives as opposed to the blind acceptance of the Dualist.

Throughout these four periods we again see the trends which recur in developmental models: from concrete and simplistic to abstract and complex thought processes; from absolute to relativistic belief systems, and from external to internal control, as the student increasingly reflects upon and takes responsibility for actions, choices, and the selection/formulation of a world view. What characteristics of college environments contribute to the changes documented by Perry and others? Perry (1970) suggests that students' growth is enhanced when we create the sense of being participants in a "community of scholars." In such a community, students observe and engage with faculty in a variety of contests, all of which encourage critical analysis, empathetic discussion, and reflection of ideas, information, and choices. Many independent colleges provide ideal environments in this respect, and there is considerable evidence that students who participate in this type of community do progress more rapidly, on a variety of measures of maturity, than do students who do not become thus engaged (Chickering, 1974; Chickering and McCormick, 1970; Winter, Stewart, and McClelland, 1981). Characteristics of college settings which appear to encourage epistemological development include the following:

1. Faculty openly expressing doubt rather than adopting an authoritative stance; willing to consider the ideas of others but able to provide a rational defense of their own position(s).
2. De-emphasis on rote learning, lecture teaching, and "objective" testing; students expected to defend ideas through critical analysis.
3. Faculty available for and open to interactions with students.
4. Disagreement and lively debate about ideas among students and between students and faculty encouraged. For instance, argument over personal values might be expected to take precedence over gossip, television, or fashion as topics of conversation (Kurfiss, 1975, p. 97).

Disequilibration is also relevant to the question of transition mechanisms in Perry's model, particularly for students in Dualistic or Multiplicity positions (1 through 4 M.C.). An optimum amount of disequilibrium is generally considered to be induced by stretching the student to consider ideas approximately one position beyond his own. This is termed the "+I principle" by developmental psychologists. Applying this concept we hypothesize that for development to occur, Dualists must be helped to discover that authorities disagree and that often there is no single right answer, while students in Multiplicity must discover that although there are not always right answers, authorities do have methods useful in studying and comparing ideas. Relativists can benefit from observing that although commitments are difficult, people do make them; and authority figures persist in making judgments and defending them even while tolerating—even welcoming discussion of—the views of those who disagree. They can even remain friends through their disagreements—sometimes! And they can give you an "A" on a well-reasoned paper even if it presents a view completely contradictory of their own.

Creating disequilibrium about such fundamental assumptions requires the counterbalancing influence of supports appropriate to the concerns likely to be salient at each position. This may be especially true for some Dualists, who may reject or deny the possibility that truths long held are not absolute, or whose concrete way of thinking may be too limited to handle the complex differentiation of ideas demanded by many college courses. In the later periods. Relativism and beyond, disequilibrium may be less important than guidance, encouragement, objectivity, and support for those facing major life decisions such as choice of a major, or whether to get married, move away from home, or even transfer to another college.

Although Perry's initial study and validating sample drew from a rather restricted population (Harvard males, traditional-aged, during the late 50s and the 60s), subsequent research has provided evidence of the relevance of the sequence in other settings. For instance, the sequence and cohesiveness of the positions were experimentally validated using a sample of sophomores and seniors at a large state university (Kurfiss, 1975, 1977). Clinchy and Zimmerman (1981) have found the scheme provides a useful framework for studies of women's development in a women's college, although they note some differences from men's experiences. Goldberger (Goldberger, Marwine, and Paskus, 1978) has used it with young students, and Daloz (Daloz, Noel, and Miller, 1980) has studied its relevance for reentry students in a nontraditional setting; he and his colleagues have found the scheme useful as a guide in counseling, guidance, and program planning for both men and women. Progress in other settings may not be as rapid as it was in the Harvard sample, but the assumptions and behavior of students have changed little over the intervening years. Many researchers find modal positions of freshmen at around Position 3, the pivot-point from Dualism to Multiplicity; seniors may be Relativists yet not have a strong sense of Commitment (as found, for instance, among Clinchy and Zimmerman's students, 1975).

Critique

The use of Perry's scheme in both research and teaching has been hampered by the lack of consistency within individuals that would enable practitioners to make global judgments or ratings of an individual's level of functioning in this domain. To be useful as well as accurate, an assessment must consider the differential development that is likely to occur in specific contexts encountered by the student. Students are likely to be more advanced in areas of interest and expertise (for instance, their major academic area or a favored avocation) than in areas of relative ignorance, disinterest, or inexperience (Kurfiss, 1977). Even among professional adults we find dualistic attitudes with respect to disciplines other than their own. For instance, Cronbach and Meehl (1952) note that psychologists tend to believe physicians can always confirm or disconfirm their diagnoses simply by opening up the patient. This is, of course, not possible for clinical psychologists, so they are far more relativistic about their own diagnoses than the physicians'. Perry interviewers often find that students who accept a relativistic world view in literature or political science firmly believe that in biology, history, or mathematics, "They have all the answers."

The lack of consistency in rates of progress is often compounded by another phenomenon, the fact that when entering any new and challenging situation, people tend to use earlier positions, at least temporarily ("functional regression," noted earlier). Entering college or starting a new job can easily stimulate such backpedaling. Thus any cross-sectional slice of an individual's development will show a complex, mixed, and highly differentiated picture of intellectual and ethical development. Perry uses the image of a spiral to capture the sense of non-linear expansion as the individual matures. Nonetheless, many professional educators have found that with practice, they can detect stage implications in students' words and emotional reactions, and have developed skill in responding appropriately.

Teaching Implications

Nothing so complex as the maturing human intellect is likely to be captured in a single theoretical model. Yet the framework provided by Perry has proven to be a rich source of stimulation for practitioners both in student services and faculty development (Parker, 1978). Perry's theory has precipitated a wealth of research on the teaching/learning process in college settings, and on relationships between intellectual development and other descriptors such as ego development using Loevinger's scale (Goldberger et al., 1978) and learning style as measured by Holland's typology (Cornfeld and Knefelkamp, 1977). The intellectual progress charted by Perry also can be shown to parallel Erikson's description of the four periods of identity development (Kurfiss, 1981), as will be discussed later.

Next we turn to the curricular and instructional implications of Perry's analysis. While assessment of progress along the Perry continuum has posed significant methodological problems, researchers have been able to demonstrate that educational experiences taking "Perry level" into account do enhance developmental processes (Widick and Simpson, 1976). Further, the Perry scheme has been used effectively for several years as a faculty development tool at the University of Minnesota (Parker, 1979). Related assessment procedures involving analysis of students' use of relativistic thinking skills have recently enabled researchers to identify differential outcomes for three types of colleges: a two-year community college, a four-year state teachers college, and a liberal arts institution (Winter, Stewart, and McClelland, 1981). Although entry characteristics of students in each setting differed, statistical analysis suggested that changes in critical thinking and flexibility in the use of argumentation skills, as well as independence of thought, could not be due to entry differences alone. This research supports the proposal that college settings can be enhanced by deliberate design to favor developmental outcomes, and that progress toward developmental goals can be assessed.

The most detailed translation of Perry's framework into a working model for instructional design is provided by Knefelkamp (1981). The model takes seriously the students' task of making sense of the world, a large part of which is the classroom. The ego-threatening nature of classroom learning experiences is squarely acknowledged; the instructor is challenged to create a learning environment that provides sufficient stimulation to explore new areas of knowledge and of self, with sufficient support to keep the students' anxiety about the process at a manageable level. Assessment of students on a variety of measures, both cognitive and affective, is recommended, although not always possible. The data are analyzed in light of students' perceptions of such classroom issues as roles of student, faculty, and peers; evaluation processes and the nature of knowledge; abilities; and probable areas of challenge and support. The learning environment is then analyzed in terms of four continua of challenge and support, described by Knefelkamp (1981, 1982):

1. Degree of structure, defined by Knefelkamp (1981) as the "amount of framework and direction provided to students," in the form of instructions, guidelines, practice sessions, and use of relevant examples.
2. Degree of diversity, construed as amount and complexity of tasks, information, perspectives, or methods offered or required of students.
3. Degree of experiential (as opposed to "vicarious") learning provided.
4. Degree of personalism provided; that is, how successfully has the spirit of the "community of scholars" been recreated in the classroom.

Subject matter and course goals are assessed as well, and both teaching and evaluation methods are self-consciously planned to create a balance between student needs for content learning and desired development goals defined by faculty and/or students. The model has been applied in a variety of disciplines with considerable success. Cornfeld and Knefelkamp have also balanced stage information with styles as described by Holland (1966) to address diversity within levels.

One serious problem that arises is that of student heterogeneity: How do you teach a class for students at two or more different developmental levels? Knefelkamp (1982) recommends, based on numerous studies of contemporary undergraduates, that the instructor assume students are either late Dualists, entering Multiplicity, or in transition between the two. The course can then be designed to encourage both recognition of multiple perspectives and ways of thinking about and comparing perspectives.

Students should have opportunities to express their views both in writing and in groups, but should always be expected to explain **why** they think as they do. Supports can be provided by explaining **why** this type of analysis is necessary, which incidentally provides a consistent role model on the part of the faculty member, and by explaining the purposes of assignments and activities in such a way that students at various levels can tune in on the rationale that addresses their concerns. For instance, when using small groups with Dualistic students, it is wise to instruct them to take notes and to listen for knowledge contributed by their peers (Knefelkamp, 1982). To reinforce this instructional set, the professor should visit the groups to lend her authority to the enterprise, but must refrain from correcting or pontificating in answer to students' questions. She should, however, emphasize points made by students ("That's interesting; I hadn't thought of it that way before.") or, redirect discussion to bring in quiet members. Supports such as these give students the opportunity to learn what it means to "think with" others and encourages their recognition of themselves as participants in the process of making sense, rather than recipients of the predigested learning of others.

Erikson: Identity and Psychosocial Development

The Theory

Erik Erikson, a psychoanalyst concerned with the tension between psychological needs and social constraints, has proposed a developmental sequence based on age-related issues and extending across the entire life span. In each of Erikson's eight "ages," a particular conflict or tension must be addressed. The ages, beginning in infancy and evolving through the life span, address the following issues: trust vs. mistrust; autonomy vs. shame and doubt; initiative vs. guilt; industry vs. inferiority; identity vs. role confusion; intimacy vs. isolation; generativity vs. stagnation; and integrity vs. despair. Figure 2 shows how Erikson construes the relationships between these eight issues and the individual's overall development. In any given period, one issue is usually predominant; that is, the individual experiences heightened vulnerability and potential in that area (Erikson, 1968). A resolution on the negative side is not necessarily permanent, but can slow progress on later issues since, as the diagram shows, each builds on those preceding it as well as influencing those to follow.

While not a cognitive theory, Erikson's developmental blueprint is helpful in designing a supportive context in which learning can take place. It also suggests issues which are likely to be salient for learners in various life stages, though not in as much detail or with the empirical support of more recent adult development models. However, his views on identity development, which peaks during late adolescence, are especially well developed, and have received considerable empirical support in recent years (Constantinople, 1969; Marcia, 1966; Adams, Shea and Fitch, 1979). Since identity is a crucial issue for many college students, both traditional and non-traditional, acquaintance with the characteristics of this period can be helpful in educational planning. Finally, as mentioned earlier, Erikson's model bears a close relationship to Perry's; clarification of the parallels may provide insight on the intellectual (and hence academically "treatable") level about what may appear at first glance to be purely psychological issues normally considered outside the realm of appropriate (and comfortable) areas of interaction with students.

Since all the eight issues remain at least somewhat salient throughout life, we can consider their implications for the identity-level student in various learning situations. For example, Table 3 suggests ways in which tasks or courses requiring problem-solving can be structured to minimize "psychological interference" in the students' attempts to address an intellectual problem. Erikson's framework can also be used to guide selection of specific issues or topics to emphasize. For instance, themes of love and identity are likely to be salient for young people; older, returning students may be more concerned with issues of caring for others (generativity) or integrating the various strands of life (integrity). Chickering (1981) offers numerous suggestions on this topic drawing from a variety of models of adult development.

Because of his keen interest in identity development, Erikson examined that period in depth in several of his writings. He formulated the concept of a "psychosocial moratorium," a period of exploring personal alternatives and of deliberate avoidance of enduring commitments while the young adult seeks "a niche which is firmly defined and yet seems to be uniquely made for him" (Erikson, 1968, p. 156). This relatively sensible approach to the emerging challenges of adult life contrasts with a response Erikson terms "identity role confusion." Here the pulls and demands become overwhelming and can, in extreme

Figure 2
Erikson's Eight Ages*

	1	2	3	4	5	6	7	8
VIII								INTEGRITY vs DESPAIR
VII							GENERATIVITY vs STAGNATION	
VI							INTIMACY vs ISOLATION	
V	Temporal Perspective vs Time Confusion	Self-Certainty vs Self-Consciousness	Role Experi-mentation vs Role Fixation	Apprentice-ship vs Work Paralysis	IDENTITY vs IDENTITY CONFUSION	Sexual Polarization vs Bisexual Confusion	Leader- and Followership vs Authority Confusion	Ideological Commitment vs Confusion of Values
IV				INDUSTRY vs INFERIORITY	Task Identi-fication vs Sense of Futility			
III				INITIATIVE vs GUILT	Anticipation of Roles vs Role Inhibition			
II		AUTONOMY vs SHAME DOUBT			Will to Be Oneself vs Self-Doubt			
I	Mutual TRUST vs MISTRUST				Recognition vs Autistic Isolation			

cases, lead to various forms of psychological paralysis. Some young adults, of course, never seem to recognize the predicament they are in. They coast in a world not entirely of their own making, but one defined largely by powerful, usually adult, authority figures. some voluntarily adopt **in toto** the ideologies of cult leaders or other surrogate authorities, apparently in retreat from newly perceived social demands. These individuals experience a kind of psycho-social "foreclosure." These three within the identity period, as well as successful ego achievement, have been observed among normal college student populations (Marcia, 1966; Podd, 1972; Adams, Shea and Fitch, 1979). Table 4 relates these four periods to the four major periods outlined above with respect to Perry's theory of development in college.

Critique

The themes of Erik Erikson have been widely accepted and used by child development practitioners, as well as by faculty in the humanities, for many years. The film "Wild Strawberries" created by Ingmar Bergman, lends itself well to analysis in terms of Erikson's model (Erikson, 1976). However, behaviorally-oriented psychologists take exception with the psychoanalytic bent of his theories and the inferential rather than observational basis of his conclusions. How do you "operationalize" an "identity"?

Although the concept of Identity (like the concept of Commitment) is very global, efforts to clarify and assess it have been successful. As we have noted, students tend to be working on a variety of issues simultaneously in their lives, progressing at different rates in different areas. Therefore, researchers using both the Perry model and the Eriksonian perspective have found it useful to design assessment instru-

Table 3
Supportive Structures for Problem Solving Activity
An Eriksonian Checklist

Basic Trust
Can the student trust the environment to support and to yield to efforts to influence it? Is the environment controllable in known and significant ways?

Autonomy
Is the student given some opportunity to exercise his/her will? Is the student given some real choice about either: a) whether, when, or how to approach a problem? b) which of several problems to approach?

Initiative
Is the problem such that the student's curiosity can be aroused by it? Can a starting point be discovered that will lead the student into further exploration? Does the problem present a significant yet approachable challenge, as opposed to an overwhelming complexity?

Industry
Is the problem structured so that sustained effort will be rewarding, so that working through obstacles and frustrations will be satisfyingly productive? Does working the problem enhance the student's understanding of and/or facility with the technology of his/her society?

Identity
Is the problem structured to involve sufficient risk that solving it confirms the student's sense of self in meaningful ways? does solving the problem have the potential to clarify or enhance the student's perception of himself or herself as capable of meeting challenges effectively? Does it provide a developmentally appropriate opportunity to experience the rewards of investing the self in interaction with the artifacts of the society?

Intimacy
Does the problem-solving context provide opportunities to learn with and from peers?

Generativity
Are there opportunities for those who have special skills or understanding to share those with others and to help others grow in their own abilities?

Integrity
Does the process build the student's experience of continuity with an earlier self and enable the student to feel "wholesome" or "oneness" with rather than alienation from that self? Where wholeness is necessarily challenged by the nature of the task, are supports provided to balance this stress?

ments that examine specific aspects of the overall process. Marcia's system (1966) and Adams' Objective Measure of Ego Identity Status (OM-EIS; Adams, Shea and Fitch, 1979) probe specific issues such as occupational identity, religion, or marriage.

Like any other model of development based on the experiences of a particular culture, Erikson's metaphor of the life cycle can be challenged as potentially ethnocentric. For instance, there is evidence that the Identity "crisis" takes a different form, or may not occur at all, even in other Western cultures (McNassor, 1967). In fact, it is likely that the crisis is not experienced by many youth even in our own society. We lack sufficient cross-cultural longitudinal data to respond one way or another to this criticism, although data exists to show that college and non-college youth are not comparable on developmentally relevant dimensions (Trent and Medsker, 1968).

On the other hand, compared to other developmental models, Erikson's theory is far more sensitive to ethnic and sex differences, and to the impact of major social and cultural forces on the developing individual. He explicitly addresses the developmental experience of blacks (Erikson, 1968). And a growing body of evidence supports his observation (1968) that women's identity development progresses differently from men (Fitch, 1981; Grotevent, 1981). Erikson's writing on the lives of G. B. Shaw (1968), Luther (1958), and Gandhi (1969) reveal his attention to the interplay of internal and external forces.

Table 4
Relationships Between "Psychosocial" (Eriksonian) and "Epistemological" (Perry) Models of Adolescent/Early Adult Development*

I. Foreclosure Dualists

Students in Dualism and Foreclosure share a restricted view of the world, a tendency to accept parental and other authority views without question, and a desire for easy answers to complex questions. Political beliefs, values, career choice, and many other aspects of identity may be foreclosed, that is, accepted as "real" without any questioning ("crisis," in Eriksonian language) of their validity for the individual.

II. Diffusion Pre-relativist

These two share an inability to sort out the "chaos" which is just beginning to be perceived. For one, chaos is in terms of the plurality of truths; for the other, the terms are life choices, value options, heroes to identify with, and other psychological issues.

III. Moratorium Relativist

Both are actively exploring alternatives, using rational processes, and consciously delaying commitments until they "feel ready." The term "Identity Crisis" refers to the final throes of this process.

IV. Ego Identity Achiever Committed Relativist

Both have made conscious choices about who and what they are/will be, although certainly not necessarily in all areas of life.

**From Kurfiss, 1981.*

Teaching Implications

What kinds of experiences can college environment provide to encourage healthy identity development? Erikson describes the role of developing "Fidelity" (1965) in making mature identity possible. Fidelity is the ability to invest oneself in a task, person, issue, etc.: it is a precursor to the full-blown commitment which marks Identity Achievement. Opportunities for such trial commitments are developmentally appropriate for Moratorium students, and they will create them if they are not provided (witness the massive student movement in the 60s). Internship programs lasting a term or longer enable them to test their ability to stick with a challenge. On the other hand, Foreclosure students may benefit from less intensive experiences, which encourage them to try out or observe roles or occupations they had not considered for themselves. To insure their attention to and involvement in these experiences, supports should be built in. These might include allowing the person to select experiences freely, to attend with friends, and to work with adults he or she can identify with.

Diffusion students are likely to drop out of (and into) classes, programs, and college itself and hence may be difficult to engage or motivate. Perhaps these students are most likely to find something of value in course material that focuses directly on Identity as an object of study. Of course, the prevalence of Identity and Intimacy issues in the traditional-aged student population suggests these would be themes of interest for the majority of those students, though their incorporation into the curriculum would of course need to take different forms at different points in any particular program.

One of the practical implications of Erikson's stage theory concerns distinctions between the psychological—and educational—needs of 18–20 year old learners and older adult learners. For instance, while the younger adult learner may be most interested in an issue of identity, the older student might find such a program to be of little value, instead being attracted to a program in which generativity is evoked. The mature student may benefit from serving as a tutor or career counselor to younger students, or offering an internship rather than taking one himself. In the process the older student learns more about his own job by being encouraged to reflect on and discuss the job with young interns. The intern brings a "theory rich/experience poor" background, while the older student who is offering the internship brings a "theory poor/experience rich" perspective. The two have much to gain from one another. Their developmental stages, in terms of Erikson's theory, are compatible, allowing for the "mutual regulation" that he sees as an important process in psychosocial development (Erikson, 1968).

Several other suggestions emerge from Erikson's theory that are directly applicable to the college classroom and the traditional-aged student. First, the college classroom should reflect Erikson's observations that all past and future stages of development are reflected in the present stage. Thus, an educational experience should be diversified and reflect a variety of development themes, while focusing on the primary developmental tasks of the predominant age group in the classroom. A college curriculum should anticipate future stages of the student's development, while providing a basis for reflection on and distillation of the learnings from the student's previous stages of development. From classroom exercises, questioning techniques and assignments stressing connections and relationships to curricular designs that stress integration of psychological concerns with social realities and potentials, a vast continuum of possibilities for developmentally stimulating instruction can be envisioned.

Eriksonian theory emphasizes the role of constructive tension between inner and outer forces; the working out of these conflicts is never an emotionally sterile process. Thus faculty would be wise to be sensitive to the interrelationships between academic and personal development. Erikson reminds us that we cannot separate the head from the heart. He encourages us to pay attention to the ways in which emotional and interpersonal needs provide a substructure for learning of a more cognitive nature. Thus, a faculty member should be just as concerned about her role as an advisor as about her role as an instructor and should teach principles and processes in her discipline through themes and experiences that relate directly to the student's developmental concerns.

Finally, and perhaps most importantly, Eriksonian theory would encourage us to look carefully at the "moratorium" that 18 to 22 year old students seem to need in their lives. Do we provide safe places in which students can test out alternative identities, alternative life styles, and alternative value systems? How do we encourage this exploration without condoning unethical or irresponsible behavior? Clearly, this safe place must include sensitivity to Sanford's (1966) concept of providing support as well as challenge.

The factor of **trust** seems to be crucial. Students must trust the intentions as well as the competencies of faculty if they are to explore alternative structures and styles during this moratorium. They may never have another opportunity in their lives to explore alternatives with both relative freedom and relative maturity of vision. A college teacher misses a tremendous opportunity for both personal and professional satisfaction if he or she does not strive to be available as a sensitive resource to students at this point in their development.

Implications for Faculty Development

The theme of generativity emerges for faculty as well as for students, and is relevant in planning for professional development programs. Whereas most people in our society move into the role of teacher or mentor to younger people when they reach the stage of generativity, the college faculty member (as well as elementary and secondary school teachers) is placed in the teaching role much earlier in his career. At this developmental stage, according to Erikson, there is little dominant concern about such generative issues as conveying something of one's self, one's experiences, and one's heritage to the next generation. Baldwin's research (1981) suggests that professional contributions may be a more pressing concern at this time, and workload pressures are as great during this period as any other. Can a teacher be an effective mentor, when she is still working out a professional identity, perhaps still being guided by her mentor?

Unfortunately, pleasure from teaching declines gradually over the course of the professorial career (Baldwin, 1981) during which—according to Erikson—generativity should be increasing. Almost paradoxically, teaching, in liberal arts colleges at least, maintains a high degree of importance throughout this time. How can this information be used in designing professional development programs for faculty? The decline in pleasure from teaching may reflect a lack of freshness or direction, which could be counteracted by varying the tasks involved, stimulating the faculty member's sense of generativity.

Generativity may be provided when experienced faculty are given opportunities to teach in a new area or new environment, thereby breaking out of old habits and roles. Serious career questioning seems to be most common late in the assistant professor phase and also during the pre-retirement years. Faculty who are especially susceptible at these points might be encouraged to try new approaches to teaching, particularly if they can see that these approaches are based on empirically sound theories of how human beings move toward their potential. Interdisciplinary teaching may, in part, be the answer. Alternatively, faculty might be given an opportunity to teach at another college or outside a college classroom (corporate training, high school teaching, consultation/training with city or state officials and staff, etc.) (Furniss, 1981). Faculty may also welcome opportunities to serve as mentors to younger faculty. For younger faculty, Baldwin suggests allowing them to teach specialized upper-division courses to capitalize on their professional currency and desire to share this crucial aspect of their identity. For all faculty, increased knowledge of students and their development may help make teaching and advising more satisfying, challenging experiences.

Kohlberg: Moral Development

The Theory

As students address issues of identity, they invariably come up against moral and ethical issues which they must learn to resolve. We will examine one of several stage theories in this area, recognizing that others exist and have merit. However, Kohlberg's theory of moral development has demonstrated considerable explanatory power. It also lends itself well to application, as the stages are relatively distinct, although students may use reasoning from more than one of the stages in discussing various issues.

Lawrence Kohlberg (1958) created a novel research paradigm to study the development of moral thinking. He presented subjects with short, anecdotal dilemmas and then analyzed the patterns which emerged in the reasons they gave for their choices on a particular issue. The classic case is that of Heinz and the druggist. Heinz must decide whether to steal a drug which can save the life of his ailing wife. The druggist, of course, has refused to extend credit and is making a large profit on the medication. Other dilemmas involve euthanasia, faithfulness to a paralyzed spouse, and reporting of a reformed criminal who has escaped detection by authorities.

By now the reader can probably anticipate the general outlines of the Kohlberg state progression. Initially concrete and egocentric, the young moral philosopher uses increasingly general and relativistic reasoning. Kohlberg divides the sequence into three major periods each with two substages, as follows:

I. Pre-conventional

1. Punishment/obedience orientation. Right and wrong are defined in terms of whether or not an act is punished. Goodness is obedience (without question) of authority. An early childhood orientation.

2. Marketplace orientation. Right is what helps me get what I want from you. God is that which provides hedonistic pleasure. Later childhood (often seen in juvenile delinquents).

II. Conventional

3. Good boy/girl orientation. Conform to the expectations of those who care for you in order to earn their approval.

4. Law and order orientation. Obey the laws, maintain—even defend—the social system, and abide by majority rule.

III. Post Conventional

5. Social contract orientation. Laws are made by members of a society and can be changed by them, particularly where injustices are or have been perpetuated by old laws. Citizens implicitly agree to abide by a social contract as participants in their society. The U.S. Constitution expresses this type of morality.

6. Orientation to universal ethical principles. There are some principles and rights that are overriding, e.g., justice, honesty, equality, life. It is on this basis that social relativists (Stage 5) argue that a law is "unjust"—it violates their sense of what is universally "right"—although they might claim that there are no absolutes. Civil disobedience is justified when the "system" fails to respond to claims of injustice.

Rest (1973) has demonstrated that while we can understand all stages up to and including our own, and in some cases on above that, comprehension of reasoning two or more stages beyond our own level is rare. Furthermore, when confronted with more advanced reasoning that we cannot understand, we translate or assimilate it to something we *can* understand, in other words, to a lower-stage reasoning. Rest found that we tend to reject or disapprove of reasoning below our own level. The net effect of all this is neatly illustrated in the case of the Berkeley "Free Speech" demonstrations of the 1960s. Among the demonstrators were students using both Stage 2 ("I have a right to say what I want; the administration can't tell me what I can and can't do!") and Stage 6 ("Freedom of speech is a basic human right.") reasoning. Stage 4 observers could not hear the Stage 6 arguments as such, but they could understand the Stage 2 reasoning—and quite naturally condemned all those protesting. Interestingly, a higher proportion of Stage 6 demonstrators were arrested than any other group (Haan, Smith, and Block, 1968), illustrating Kohlberg's claim that the higher the stage, the more congruence between belief and action. Furthermore, Stage 5 individuals tended to function as mediators, attempting to translate the Stage 6 arguments of protestors into language which would be appreciated by Stage 4 observers.

Critique

During the past decade, several major criticisms have been voiced by theorists and practitioners who have studied Kohlberg's model. One of Kohlberg's colleagues, Carol Gilligan, has questioned the applicability of this model to many student populations. Gilligan (1981) finds that Perry's model, which explicitly recognizes the dilemmas of context, provides a missing link in understanding the full range of moral development. "Context" in most moral dilemmas means the consequences for and feelings of those human beings touched by the situation. In Kohlberg's model, use of such information in moral reasoning is viewed as "concrete," not universal in nature, and hence not indicative of the "highest," i.e., most abstract, stages of moral judgment. Thus women, who tended to use such reasoning more often than men, were scored at Stage 3 or 4 more frequently than men. Yet in her work with women contemplating abortions, Gilligan found that while they *could* use abstract and universal principles when discussing moral issues, when they dealt with very real and complex situations, they necessarily considered concrete circumstances and feelings as part of their analysis (Gilligan, 1977). She reasoned that to call this "lower-level" reasoning or a sign of "regression" was to do violence to what is, in fact, a very highly developed, empathetic approach to moral questions. Gilligan concludes that Kohlberg's theory is in need of significant revision in order to take these criticisms into account.

Kohlberg is often criticized because he focuses on moral reasoning without attempting to relate this reasoning to actual behavior. Some research has supported his claim, noted above, that at the higher stages, congruence between belief and action is greater than at lower stages. While moral reasoning and moral behavior are no doubt intertwined, the latter requires empathy, personal integrity, self-sacrifice, and courage as well as reasoning ability. These "nonrational" characteristics are also developmental in nature (Loevinger, 1976; Weathersby and Tarule, 1980); the precise quality of the interaction between these characteristics remains to be clarified.

Kohlberg also proposes that the highest level of moral reasoning may prescribe behavior that violates specific laws and/or societal norms (as in the case of civil disobedience). While this perspective is compatible with a western conception of justice and personal responsibility, it may limit cross-cultural applicability of Kohlberg's model, for in many cultures, individualistic decision-making is considered inappropriate and destructive, the group being the ultimate arbiter of morality. Furthermore, while Western culture claims to value human life above all else, other cultures feel that life is not worth living when one is deprived of one's land. Educators must be sensitive to these and other differences if they are to use a Kohlbergian framework to prepare students—both domestic and international—to live in an increasingly international community.

Teaching Implications

While Kohlberg's model is not without its flaws, when its weaknesses are counterbalanced by attention to criticisms such as those described, it offers a rich resource for design of instruction to enhance moral thinking. Numerous educational applications have sprung from the model, ranging from democratic classrooms in racially mixed areas (Wasserman, 1976), to a district-level intervention in a group of public schools (Sullivan and Dockstader, 1978). Whitely (1978) reports on a program at the college level. A detailed analysis of theory and review of applications appears in Munsey (1980); included in that collection is a Kohlbergian analysis of the development of religious faith (Folwer, 1980).

The original instructional model used dilemmas as a starting point for classroom discussion. Dilemmas may be real (such as a classroom discipline problem) or imaginary (whether to identify a friend who was seen shoplifting). The discussion begins with a clarification of the students' thoughts in response to the situation; once this is accomplished, dis-equilibration is induced by raising questions about the adequacy of the students' logic. For instance, is the prescribed response one that could safely be generalized to all other people in a similar situation? What would be the consequences? Students can be encouraged to view the situation from the point of view of each of the actors to determine whether their proposed resolution would be fair to all concerned. While these approaches are effective with young people, college students may benefit from use of dilemmas drawn from history, literature, drama, philosophy, sociology, or other fields. Chickering (1976, pp. 100–106) has provided numerous suggestions for doing just that.

Kohlberg has introduced the concept of the "justice structure" of an environment—its governing moral and ethical dynamics, which can be expressed in terms of the six moral stages. Faculty should be aware that many students are highly sensitive to morality and injustice, and highly responsive to the justice structure provided by the college environment. They frequently enter in a Stage 4 or possibly Stage 5 frame of mind. If the justice structure they encounter in college emphasizes maintenance of rules and regulations and following of established, unchallengeable procedures, they will find little to challenge their Stage 4 reasoning or consolidate Stage 5. In contrast, if the environment encourages open discussion of ethical and moral questions, and if the system is responsive to claims of unfairness or injustice, they will come to understand the evolutionary process of law which is embodied in our Constitution. As always, clear rationales, tolerance of disagreement, and empathetic role models are positive conditions for growth and development.

Kohlberg's successful use of moral dilemmas, which are in effect simple case studies, reinforces the claims of other theorists and practitioners for the value of interactive methods of instruction in the college classroom. Case studies with a value orientation can be useful for encouraging moral reasoning in many courses, as noted above. Keeping in mind Gilligan's criticisms, case studies should be written, discussed, and evaluated within a specific content rather than as abstract, universal dilemmas. If one is concerned about the cognitive bias of the model, case studies could be drawn from real life or from field experiences designed to require courage as well as rationality. Of course, they may be difficult to set up, but whether by design or by coincidence, students who are put in a position to make difficult moral decisions should be given ample opportunity for debriefing (in case or in private, as appropriate) and for reflection on the process and its consequences. Journals, poetry, and other written materials can serve as an excellent medium for "working out" of conflicts which may be engendered by such experiences.

Kohlberg's work should encourage college educators to recognize the need for and appropriateness of moral deliberations in all areas of inquiry. Even in science courses, students should be confronted with moral and ethical decisions and implications of what they are learning. Perhaps in today's world we should say **especially** in science courses. The point is that no subject is value-free, no fact is context-free, and no observation is purely objective. Until students recognize this, they cannot be said to be fully and properly "educated." Whatever model of moral reasoning or development is used, the following guidelines suggest the kind of climate we must attempt to create if we are to achieve this goal. Students should:

Be active in developing and defending their own positions

Be challenged to probe deeply the justifications for human choices, especially their own

Confront standards and points of view that counter their personal perspectives

Be encouraged and enabled to assume the role of someone with a contrasting point of view

Wrestle with problems that have no simple solutions (Morrill, 1980, p. 101)

All of these guidelines suggest a far more interactive, discussion-centered student-dominated classroom setting than most faculty are accustomed to using. Faculty whose natural style does not favor these approaches will need support from their colleagues if they are to succeed. The importance and central nature of the challenge are such that we must work to create these opportunities for our students, and grow to be comfortable with them ourselves. In the long run, the learning from such discussions well may be as great for the professor as for the students, and the process will be a stimulating one.

Conclusion

"The success of education," Carol Gilligan notes, "depends on its leading students to question that which formerly was taken for granted." Chickering (1969) has pointed out that environments consistent in their outlook, theme, and tone are most influential in students' development. In a similar vein, programs such as DOORS and ADAPT have demonstrated the power of concerted faculty effort to assist students in acquiring skills needed for the new tasks they face in college and adult life. And Winter, et al., (1981) have confirmed that student outcomes do reflect goals emphasized in college catalogs. The theories presented enable us to be more intentional about achieving the goals we identify as desirable for our students. They provide a common language with which faculty can engage in campus-wide dialog about the purposes and methods of education. But most important of all, they remind us that if we want to be effective and if we hope to provide students with the makings of a "better world," we must first arouse their involvement in learning. And to do this we must do no less than what one historian and veteran teacher describes as "speaking to the deepest concerns of students" (Ward, 1981, p. 381). We must be convinced of the importance and central nature of the concerns to which we devote precious classroom time. And we must include in our concerns the courage to make thinking, feeling, and social responsibility explicit aims of the educational venture.

> It was the absence of such questioning in the testimony of [Adolph] Eichmann [during his trial for exterminating millions of Jews] that has led [Hannah] Arendt [*The Life of the Mind*, 1978] to see, in his thoughtless obedience, the evil of our time and to wonder if the activity of thought might stand as an impediment to its recurrence. (Gilligan, 1981, p. 156)

For colleges willing to make the commitment, developmentally designed program planning and course design have the potential for greatly enhancing the learning and growth which takes place under their guidance and, as a consequence, vastly increasing the satisfaction and the contributions of faculty and students alike.

References

Adams, G., Shea, J., and Fitch, S. Toward the Development of a Measure of Ego-Identity Status. *Journal of Youth and Adolescence*, 1979, *8*(2), 223–237.

Arlin, P.F. Problem Finding: The Relation Between Selected Cognitive Process Variables and Problem-Finding Performance. Unpublished doctoral dissertation, University of Chicago, 1974.

Barber, Nancy. Authoritarian Regression in an Educational Setting: a Study of Development in Graduate Students. Unpublished candidacy paper, The Wright Institute, Berkeley, CA, 1981.

Baldwin, R.G. and Blackburn, R.T. The academic career as a developmental process: Implications for high education. *Journal of Higher Education*, 1981 *52*(6), 598–614.

Chickering, A.W. *Commuting vs. Resident Students: Overcoming the Inequities of Living Off Campus.* San Francisco: Jossey-Bass, 1974.

Chickering, A.W. *Education and Identity*. San Francisco: Jossey-Bass, 1969.

Chickering, A.W. Developmental Change as a Major Outcome. M. Keeton (ed.) *Experiential Learning: Rationale, Characteristics, and Assessment.* San Francisco: Jossey-Bass, 1976, 62–106.

Chickering, A.W. The Life Cycle. In A.W. Chickering (ed.) *Modern American College.* San Francisco: Jossey-Bass, 1981, 16–50.

Clinchy, B. and Zimmerman, C. Epistemology and Agency in Undergraduate Women. In P. Perun (ed.) *The Undergraduate Women: Issues in Educational Equity.* Boston: D.C. Heath & Co., 1981.

Constantinople, A. An Eriksonian Measure of Personality Development College Students. *Developmental Psychology*, 1969, *I*, 357–372.

Cornfeld, J.L. and Knefelkamp, L.L. Combining Student Stage and in the Design of Learning Environments: Using Holland Typologies and Perry Stages. Presented at the American College Personnel Association, Denver, 1977.

Cronback and Meehl. Construct Validity in Psychological Tests. *Psychological Bulletin*, 1955, *52*, 281–302.

Daloz, L., Noel, J., and Miller, M. Mentoring Strategies. Working Conference on Adult Education and Program Design, Denver, Colorado, June, 1980.

Erikson, E.H. *Gandhi's Truth: On the Origins of Militant Non-violence.* New York: Norton, 1969.

Erikson, E.H. *Identity: Youth and Crisis.* New York: Norton, 1968.

Erikson, E.H. Reflections on Dr. Borg's Life Cycle. *Daedalus*, 1976, *105*(2), 1–23.

Erikson, E.G. *Young Man Luther*. New York: Norton, 1958.

Erikson, E.H. Youth: Fidelity and Diversity. In E.H. Erikson (ed.) *The Challenge of Youth*. Garden City, NY: Anchor Books, 1965.

Fitch, S. Identity and Intimacy: Erikson's Psychosocial Developments in Adolescence and Young Adulthood. *Symposium on Current Issues in the Study of Identity Formation*. Denver, CO: Rocky Mountain Psychological Association, 1981.

Fowler, J. Moral Stages and the Development of Faith. In B. Munsey (ed.) *Moral Development, Moral Education and Kohlberg*. Birmingham, AL: Religious Education Press, 1980.

Fuller, R.G. and Associates. *Multidisciplinary Piaget-Based Programs for College Freshmen.* Lincoln, NE: University of Nebraska-Lincoln, 1978.

Fuller, R.G. (ed.) *Piagetian Programs in Higher Education.* Lincoln, NE: University of Nebraska-Lincoln, 1980.

Gilligan, C. In a Different Voice: Women's Conceptions of Self and Morality. *Harvard Educational Review*, 1977, *47*(4), 481–517.

Goldberger, N., Marwine, A., and Paskus, J. The Relationship Between Intellectual Stage and the Behavior of College Freshmen in the Classroom. Presented at the annual meeting of the Eastern Psychological Association, 1978.

Grotevent, H. Sex Differences in Styles of Occupational and Inter-Personal Identity Formation. *Symposium on Current Issues in the Study of Identity Formation.* Denver, CO: Rocky Mountain Psychological Association, April, 1981.

Haan, N., Smith, M.B., and Block, J. Moral Reasoning of Young Adults: Political-Social Behavior, Family Background, and Personality Correlates. *Journal of Personality and Social Psychology*, 1968, *10*, 133–201.

Holland, J.L. *The Psychology of Vocational Choice: A Theory of Personality Types and Model Environments.* Wathmore, MA: Blaisdell, 1966.

Inhelder, B. and Piaget, J. *The Growth of Logical Thinking from Childhood to Adolescence.* New York: Basic Books, 1958.

Karplus, R. *Science Curriculum Improvement Study: Teachers Handbook.* Berkeley, CA: Lawrence Hall of Science, 1974.

Knefelkamp, L. "Developmental Instruction." Unpublished summary, University of Maryland, 1981.

Knefelkamp, L. AAHE Workshop on Developmental Instruction. Washington, DC, March 6, 1982.

Kohlberg, L. The Development Modes of Moral Thinking and Choice in the Years Ten to Sixteen. Unpublished doctoral dissertation, University of Chicago, 1958.

Kris, Ernst. *Psychoanalytic Explorations in Art.* New York: International University Press, 1952.

Kurfiss, J. Cognitive Development: *Sine Qua Non* of Identity Achievement? Symposium on Current Issues in the Study of Identity Formation. Denver, CO: Rocky Mountain Psychological Association, 1981.

Kurfiss, J. Late Adolescent Development: A Structural-Epistemological Perspective. Unpublished doctoral dissertation, University of Washington, 1975.

Kurfiss, J. Notes on the Design of Effective Learning Cycles. Paper presented at the Third Annual Conference on Reasoning, Piaget, and Higher Education. Denver, Colorado, April, 1982.

Kurfiss J. Sequentiality and Structure in a Cognitive Model of College Student Development. *Developmental Psychology,* 1977, *13*(6), 565–571.

Marcia, J.D. Development and Validation of Ego Identity Status. *Journal of Personality and Social Psychology,* 1966, *3*, 551–558.

McKinnon, J.W. The College Student and Formal Operations. In J.W. Renner (ed.) *Teaching and Learning with the Piaget Model,* Norman, Oklahoma: University of Oklahoma Press, 1976.

McKinnon, J. and Renner, J. Are Colleges Concerned with Intellectual Development? *American Journal of Physics,* 1971, 39, 1047–1052.

McNassor, D. Social Structure for Identity in Adolescence: Western Europe and America. *Adolescence,* 1967, 2, 311–334.

Munsey, B. (ed.) *Moral Development, Moral Education, and Kohlberg: Basic Issues in Philosophy, Psychology, Religion and Education.* Birmingham, AL: Religious Education Press, 1980.

Papert, Seymour *Mindstorms: Children, Computers, and Powerful Ideas.* New York: Basic Books, 1980.

Parker, C.A. *Encouraging the Development of College Students.* Minneapolis: University of Minnesota Press, 1978.

Perry, William G., Jr. *Forms of Intellectual and Ethical Development in the College Years.* New York: Holt, Rinehard, & Winston, 1970.

Piaget, J. *The Construction of Reality in the Child.* New York: Basic Books, 1954.

Podd, M.H. Ego Identity Status and Morality: The Relationship Between Two Developmental Constructs. *Developmental Psychology,* 1972, *6*, 497–507.

Rest, J.R. Developmental Psychology as a Guide to Value Education: a Review of "Kohlbergian" Programs. *Review of Educational Research,* 1974, *44*, 241–259.

Rest, J.R. Hierarchical Nature of Moral Judgment: a Study of Patterns of Comprehension and Preference. *Journal of Personality,* 1973, *41*, 86–109.

Riegel, K.F. Dialectical Operations: The Final Period of Cognitive Development. *Human Development,* 1973, *16*, 356–370.

Sanford, N. *Self and Society: Social Change and Individual Development.* New York: Atherton Press, 1966.

Sullivan, P.J. and Dockstader, M.F. Values Education and American Schools: Worlds in Collision? In Sprinthall and Mosher (eds.) *Value Development as an Aim of Education.* Schenectady, NY: Character Research Press, 1978, 69–113.

Tomlinson-Keasey, C. and Campbell, T. Cognitive Pretest and Postest Material.

Ward, P. History. In A. Chickering (ed.) *The Modern American College.* San Francisco: Jossey-Bass, 1981, 376–382.

Wasserman, E.R. Implementing Kohlberg's "Just Community" Concept in an Alternative High School. *Social Education,* 1976 (April), 203–207.

Whitely, J.A. Developmental Intervention in Higher Education. *Moral Education Forum,* 1978, 3(4) 1–13.

Widick, C. and Simpson. The Use of Developmental Concepts in College Instruction. Conference on Student Development, University of Minnesota, May, 1976.

Winter, D., Stewart, A., and McClelland, D. *A New Case for the Liberal Arts.* San Francisco: Jossey-Bass, 1981.

Issues of Gender in Teaching and Learning

BLYTHE MCVICKER CLINCHY

When I ask myself—Does gender matter in college teaching and learning?—I come up with two mutually contradictory answers. One is, I don't know. The other is yes. Because it's hard to frame an argument around two contradictory propositions, I shall tell you a story instead of presenting an argument. In stories, conflicts and contradictions are allowable and even desirable. The story I'd like to tell is about the ways in which my thinking about gender and teaching and learning has evolved over the years.

The Wellesley Study

I first chose to study women not because I was especially interested in them, but because they were there. I *was* concerned about learning—more precisely, my students' failure to learn—and, because I was and am teaching at a women's college, my students happened to be women.

At the time, I was team teaching an introductory psychology course with my friend and colleague, Claire Zimmerman. Because the class was large, usually between 150 to 200 students, we were forced to do most of our teaching in lectures, a style uncomfortably close to what the revolutionary educator Freire called "the banking model" (1974, p. 63). In the banking model, the teacher deposits information in the students' heads, and the students' task is to store the deposits.

The banking image may be too mechanical to capture this process. The women students we've talked with tend to use biological metaphors. They speak of teachers "spoon feeding" information into them, which they "regurgitate" on exams or convert into "bullshit" papers. Perhaps the biological model captures the reality more accurately than does the mechanical model, because it involves transformation; what comes out is not exactly what went in.

It became obvious to Claire and me that this was the case in Psychology 101. What came out of the students in papers and exams was distressingly discrepant from what we thought we had deposited. Because we were both cognitive psychologists, we proceeded to intellectualize our frustration by studying the transformations the students made. We began to collect examples of these transformations. We called them "common errors." Notice that the term "error" implies that we said it right and they got it wrong. As teachers so often do, we blamed the victim.

As time went on, we began to see that these errors were systematic transformations that were not idiosyncratic but common to many students. For example, we learned that when the lecturer mentioned a possibility or made a qualified statement (e.g., "Freud may have come to this conception of anxiety because. . ." or "Freud based his concept of anxiety partly on. . ."), many students, in their exams, converted the statement into an absolute ("Freud came to this view because. . ." or "Freud based his concept of anxiety. . ."). Another example most teachers will recognize is that when we asked students, on an exam, to compare and contrast two perspectives, they gave us two discrete lists. If we asked them to compare and contrast Freud's and Piaget's conceptions of children's play, they gave us Freud's view, then Piaget's view. Period.

Claire and I noticed that students in our upper-level courses rarely made these errors. Because we were both interested in cognitive development, we wondered whether we might be looking at a develop-

"Issues of Gender in Teaching and Learning," by Blythe McVicker Clinchy, reprinted from *Journal on Excellence in College Teaching,* Vol. 1, 1990, Office for the Advancement of Scholarship and Teaching.

mental phenomenon. Perhaps the younger students were filtering the lecturer's words through cognitive structures different from ours and from those of the older students. That is, perhaps in the course of the college years, students changed not only in the amount they knew (the content of their knowledge), but also in their ways of knowing (their cognitive structures). This possibility seemed remote, because we had been taught in graduate school that qualitative changes in ways of knowing (as opposed to quantitative increments in amount of knowledge) ended in early adolescence.

The Work of Perry

It was at this point that Claire came upon Perry's book, *Forms of Intellectual and Ethical Development in the College Years* (1968/1970). Perry was not trained in cognitive-developmental theory. Although he was and is a gifted counselor and teacher of counselors, his only advanced degree was a master's in English literature, so he didn't realize that no qualitative changes in thinking could occur in the college years. It seemed to him, just listening to students as they came in for counseling year after year, that they did change. So the poor fellow, relying on his own experience rather than cognitive-developmental dogma, just blundered his way into a developmental study.

He and his associates interviewed samples of Harvard undergraduates (140 in all) repeatedly each year across their four years at the college. Since Perry was not trained in psychological research methodology, his interview technique was elegantly simple. After explaining that he was interested in the students' experiences at Harvard, he asked just one standard question, "Why don't you start with whatever stands out for you about the year?" (Some of my more ardently feminist colleagues regard this question as phallic and prefer to ask, in their interviews, "What stays with you about the year?") The interviewer then simply listened carefully, inviting the students to clarify their comments and elaborate upon them.

On the basis of the students' responses, Perry constructed a scheme tracing the development of what psychologists would now call "naive" or "natural" or "vernacular" epistemology. Perry's scheme defines a sequence of moves through a series of positions from which students view the world of knowledge, truth, and value. The scheme begins with a position he calls "dualism." Dualists are absolutists; they assume that there is one right answer to every question, and they see the world in terms of black and white, right and wrong, true and false. At the next position, "multiplicity," gray areas appear, and there are no absolute right answers. Truth is personal and private, there are as many truths as there are persons, all opinions are equally valid, and everyone is his or her own authority and has a right to his or her own opinion. Ultimately, one comes to the next position and sees that some opinions are better than others and that truth is "contextual," that is, the meaning of a phenomenon depends upon the context in which it is embedded and upon the perspective from which it is viewed.

Perry's scheme seemed to offer a way of conceptualizing our informal observations, so we decided to launch our own longitudinal study at Wellesley. Our main goal at the start of this work was to fill in Perry's scheme. He had given us a schematic, sketchy outline of development; we wanted to flesh it out, to elaborate and articulate it in richer detail. We saw ourselves as Perry's helpers. He had generated the really important ideas; we were just sort of tidying up after him. Gender was not a central concern. In a request for funding the project, we did propose to test the applicability of the scheme to a female sample. But our hearts really weren't in this proposal; we were confident that it *was* applicable.

Perry himself had already dismissed the issue of gender. Included in his sample of 140 were 28 women, or 20% of the sample. However, in a passage early in his book, a passage I hardly noticed at the time, but which now seems to me remarkable, Perry wrote, "With the few exceptions which will be noted, the illustrations and validations in this study will draw on the reports of the men" (1968/1970, p. 16). With few exceptions, then, the voices of the women students were excluded from Perry's account of forms of intellectual and ethical development in the college years. This is just one of many instances in which, as Gilligan (1982) pointed out, women have been systematically excluded from the stage of theory building in developmental psychology. Nearly always the investigator has been male, and all or nearly all of his informants have been male, yet the theories that emerge from these studies are assumed to apply to all human beings, regardless of gender (or class or race, or even national origin). Perry's book is not called "Forms of Intellectual and Ethical Development in College *Men*"; it is called "Forms of Intellectual and Ethical Development in the College *Years*."

Perry could reply, however, that he was justified in dismissing the issue of gender. In an attempt to establish the reliability of rating the students' interviews for position, Perry assembled a group of judges and asked them to rate 20 cases of four-year sequences, using the scheme. Included among the 20 were 2 women. (Note that the percentage of women has now dropped from 20% to 10%.) Perry reports that although "the judges engaged in a lively discussion of the differences between men and women" (1968/1970, p. 16), they concluded that these were differences in content rather than structure. It is not clear what Perry means by this distinction. Minimally, he seems to mean that while the women's interviews (note, only two sets of interviews) may have sounded different, they could be coded for position as easily as the men's. The scheme, then, could be seen as gender-fair or gender-blind.

At first, Claire and I reached much the same conclusions in coding our own data. We were able to place nearly all of the women in terms of the scheme, and we observed in most of the women a regular progression, in small steps, across the four years. I say "nearly all" and "most of" the women. In one corner of my office there accumulated an ugly pile of transcripts—we called them "anomalies"—that refused to be wedged into the scheme. What they had to say just didn't seem relevant. So we left them out.

On the whole, however, most of the Wellesley women seemed to move smoothly through dualism and multiplicity into a position Perry called "relativism subordinate." At this position, the student learns that her professors want her neither to accept as truth anything an authority says *nor* to treat all opinions as equally valid, but to adopt an analytical, critical approach, using the tools of the discipline to interpret and evaluate the material she is studying. Most of the Wellesley women caught on to this approach. They learned to construct complex, contextual arguments and interpretations, marshalling evidence to support their views. They learned to compare and contrast interpretations. They learned that this was the kind of thinking the professors wanted, and they learned how to deliver it.

So far, the women looked to us like Perry's men. But then things seemed to go wrong. According to Perry, the student sees critical thinking at first as merely an academic exercise and practices these skills only to survive the system, to get good grades. But gradually, through some mysterious, unarticulated process, the student comes to realize that this kind of complex, critical thinking is not just a procedure that professors make you use to solve academic problems. And it is not just the way They—uppercase T, denoting Authority—want you to think; it's the way they—dethroned to lowercase t—think too. The students and their teachers now become colleagues. The President of Harvard welcomes you to the community of scholars, and you become one of *them*. "The irony," Perry says, "is that in merely trying to conform, the student becomes an independent thinker."

This happy ending occurred for too few of our students, only about half of the seniors we interviewed. The others learned to conform, all right, but they did not become independent thinkers. They remained frozen in a schoolgirl mode, performing the cognitive tasks they were ordered to perform, often with considerable skill, but without joy or conviction and sometimes, ultimately, with despair.[1]

In *Women's Ways of Knowing* (Belenky, Clinchy, Goldberger, & Tarule, 1986), we tell the stories of some of these women. For example, Simone[2], nominated by the science faculty at her college as the best student of her year, told us that she could write "good papers" when she tried. By good papers, she meant papers that teachers liked. Simone, herself, didn't like them much. She says:

> I can write a good paper, and someday I may learn to write one that I like, that is not just bullshit, but I still feel that it's somewhat pointless. I do it, and I get my grade, but it hasn't proved anything to me. The problem is that I don't feel terribly strongly about one point of view, but that point of view seems to make more sense. It's easier to write the paper supporting that point of view than the other one, because there's more to support it. And it's not one of my deep-founded beliefs, but it writes the paper. (p. 110)

Simone doesn't write the paper. "It" writes the paper. The voice that speaks in these good papers is not Simone's. Whose voice is it?

A sophomore we call Katie refers to this voice as the "should-voice." In a paper written for a women's studies class, Katie tells of her struggles with writing.

> For years I have been taught in school that writing academic papers I must strive to be objective, I must avoid the personal, . . . I must not deal with feelings and responses and reactions so much, but rather with ideas and evidence and arguments...I must push away the personal voice (and) construct some separate, objective, analytical voice. Yet, if writing is the setting down of ideas, where are my ideas to come from if I cannot allow myself to listen to the personal response?

Katie understands now that her teachers have been trying not to silence her personal voice but only to shape it, so that it communicates more clearly. But writing remains difficult for her.

> Writing is still a stage of conflict, a struggle to communicate, with two voices competing for my one mouth . . . The me-voice is loud because it is what I am truly thinking. Yet, the should-voice is strong because it has come from many other people, people in positions of power and apparent superiority, many times, over many years.

For Perry's students, the should-voice seems to evolve easily into a me-voice. But Katie and Simone remain stuck in subordinate schoolgirl positions, and the me-voice and the should-voice remain at odds. For Katie, the two voices compete, and for Simone, the should-voice silences the me-voice. Both are very able women students, and they are not alone. Another able student, the philosopher Ruddick, writes, "In college I learned to avoid work done out of love. My intellectual life became increasingly critical, detached, and dispensable" (1977, p. 135). Simone appears to have dispensed with hers. During her senior year she aborted her honors thesis, withdrew her applications to the most prestigious graduate schools in the country, and returned to her hometown to marry her high school boyfriend and take a low-level job.

I wanted to understand better this phenomenon of arrested development. What caused it, and how general was it? Did women in other institutions experience the same collision between their own voices and the official institutional voice?

The Project on Education for Women's Development

With questions like this in mind, I joined three developmental psychologists from other institutions, Mary Belenky, Nancy Goldberger, and Jill Tarule, in a three-year project called "Education for Women's Development," supported by the U.S. Department of Education's Fund for the Improvement of Post-Secondary Education (FIPSE). That study led ultimately to our book, *Women's Ways of Knowing* (Belenky, Clinchy, Goldberger & Tarule, 1986). We interviewed in depth 135 women varying widely in age, social class, race, and ethnic background, and coming from a wide range of institutions, including elite, traditional colleges; a progressive college concentrating on the arts; an "early college" with entering students two years younger than the norm; low-residency programs for older students; and an inner city community college. We also interviewed women with little formal education who were clients from social agencies concerned with maternal and child health. This time, the decision to interview women and only women was deliberate. It is a decision we have been challenged incessantly to defend from the very inception of the project to the present day. In our book, we try to explain the decision.

> In our study we chose to listen only to women. The male experience has been so powerfully articulated that we believed we would hear the patterns in women's voices more clearly if we held at bay the powerful templates men have etched in the literature and in our minds. (p. 9)

We believed that if we allowed those powerful male voices to intrude, they would deafen us to the words of the women. When the male voice intrudes, it becomes the standard, and the women's voices are heard, if they are heard at all, as deviations from the male voice. We wanted to listen to the women in their own terms.

In attempting to understand the women's ways of knowing, we began by trying to classify them in terms of Perry's positions. These positions are defined in terms of the *nature* of truth: truth as single and absolute, as multiple, and as relative to context. The positions we finally defined owe much to and are built upon Perry's work. Yet, as we read and reread the interview transcripts, we also tried to stay close to the women's own images. We combed the interviews for what we came to call "growth metaphors," and one metaphor occurred repeatedly. Over and over the women spoke of their growth in terms of gaining a voice. As in Katie's paper, these women saw the themes of voice and self and mind as closely intertwined. (Katie's paper is not just about her problems as a writer. It is about her problems as a person and a knower.) These observations led us to revise our definitions of the epistemological positions to emphasize the *source* of knowledge and truth, rather than the *nature* of knowledge and truth. In reading an interview, we asked ourselves, How does the woman conceive of herself as a knower? Is knowledge seen as originating outside or inside the self? Can it be passed down intact from one person to another, or does it well up from within? Does knowledge appear effortlessly in the form of intuition or revelation, or is it attained only through an arduous procedure of construction?

Epistemological Positions

Some of the women we interviewed took a position we call *received knowledge*. These women, like Perry's dualists, rely on authorities, although the authorities do not always occupy authoritative roles; some are friends and lovers. The women count on these authorities to supply them with the right answers, to tell them who they are and what they should believe. Truth, for the received knower, is external. She can ingest it, but she cannot evaluate it or create it for herself. The received knowers are the students who sit there, pencils poised, ready to write down every word the teacher says.

A second mode of knowing that we identified we call *subjectivism*. Subjective knowledge is, in a sense, the opposite of received knowledge. While received knowers see knowledge as "out there," lodged in the minds of authorities, subjective knowers look inside themselves for knowledge. For them, truth is internal, in the heart or the gut. Truth is personal: You have your truths, and I have mine. The subjectivist relies on the knowledge she has gleaned from her own, firsthand, personal experience. She carries the residue of that experience in her gut in the form of intuition.

The subjectivist makes judgments in terms of feelings: An idea is right if it feels right. For example, in the Wellesley study we asked the students what they did when competing interpretations of a poem were being discussed in English class. How would they choose which one was right? One student said, "I usually find that when ideas are being tossed around, I'm usually more akin to one than another. I don't know—my opinions are just sort of *there*." Another said, "With me it's almost a matter of liking one more than another. I mean, I happen to agree with one or identify with it more."

Now, it is possible that if we studied men we would find these positions, but we think they might often take a somewhat different tone. For instance, there is in the subjectivist statements I've just quoted a humble, self-deprecatory tone that does not appear in the statements of Perry's multiplists. The male multiplist says he has a right to his own opinion, and no teacher has the right to call him wrong. Some of the subjectivists we interviewed say the same thing. But more often—and *very* often in the more traditional and self-consciously rigorous colleges—the subjectivists said things like, "This is *just* (or *only*) my opinion," and they felt strongly that it would be wrong to "inflict" their opinions on anyone else. I am suggesting that there may be a gender difference at the subjectivist and received knowledge positions. But this is one of those questions I can't answer, because researchers (I and others) are only beginning to use the positions we defined to study men.

I want to concentrate in this article on the position that for many subjectivists, at least at Wellesley, is the next developmental step after subjectivism. We call it *procedural knowledge*. I want to dwell on this position, because it is here that the issues of gender, teaching, and learning intersect most meaningfully for me. There are several reasons for this. First, I think that much of my own teaching is devoted to helping students reach this position. I want my students to pay close attention to whatever it is we're studying, to examine it seriously and carefully. I don't want them just to swallow my interpretations of an experiment, for instance, but I also don't want them to wallow in their own gut reactions to the experiment.

The women we've interviewed have taught me to respect received knowledge and subjectivism in ways that I never did before, to see the virtues of these positions, and to see them as real achievements, rather than just something to be "gotten over" like measles or chicken pox or adolescence. Nevertheless, as a teacher, I want my students to move beyond these positions. Students who rely exclusively on received or subjective knowledge are not, in some sense, *really thinking*. The received knower's ideas come ready-made from the professor; the subjectivist's opinions are, as one student said, "just there." Neither the received knower nor the subjectivist has any systematic, deliberate procedures for developing new ideas or for testing the validity of ideas. What college seems to do for many students is to help them develop procedures for understanding and evaluating ideas. Most of the more advanced college students we interviewed had reached the position of procedural knowledge.

Separate Knowing

I want now to describe the two types of procedures we identify in *Women's Ways of Knowing*. Even after several years of research, when we began writing the book, we saw only one procedure. Now we call that procedure *separate knowing*. I won't spend much time describing separate knowing, because you know what it is, whether you've heard the term before or not. It's the "it" that writes Simone's papers. It's the "should-voice" in Katie's head—an objective, analytical voice, one that exercises care and precision.

Separate knowing is emphasized in activities like critical thinking, scientific method, and textual analysis. Some people just call it "thinking." We used to, too, but now we claim it's only one kind of thinking.

The heart of separate knowing is detachment. The separate knower holds herself aloof from the object she is trying to analyze. She takes an impersonal stance. She follows certain rules or procedures to insure that her judgments are unbiased. All of our various disciplines and vocations have these impersonal procedures for analyzing things. All of the various fields have impersonal standards for evaluating things, criteria that allow you to decide whether a novel is well constructed or an experiment has been properly conducted or a person should be diagnosed as epileptic.

We academicians tend to place a high value on impersonality. For example, some of us pride ourselves on blind grading. We read and grade a student's paper without knowing who wrote it, so as not to let our feelings about the person affect our evaluation of the product. In separate knowing, you separate the knower from the known. The less you know about the author, the better you can evaluate (and, some would say, even understand) the work.

A couple of years ago, a group of us were planning a series of lectures in a team-taught interdisciplinary course, and some of us tried to entice the man who was going to lecture on Marx to tell the students a bit about Marx as a person. The lecturer argued strongly that Marx's biography was irrelevant to his theory and would only lead students astray, deflecting their attention from the ideas to the man. He finally grudgingly agreed to, as he put it, "locate Marx" within an intellectual tradition. That was as personal as he was willing to get.

Separate knowing often takes the form of an adversarial proceeding—not hostile, of course, but adversarial. The separate knower's primary mode of discourse is the argument. For example, one of the young women we interviewed who was a proficient separate knower said, "As soon as someone tells me his point of view, I immediately start arguing in my head the opposite point of view. When someone is saying something, I can't help turning it upside down." Another said, "I never take anything someone says for granted. I just tend to see the contrary. I like playing devil's advocate, arguing the opposite of what somebody's saying, thinking of exceptions to what the person has said or thinking of a different train of logic." These young women are playing what the writer Elbow (1973) calls "the doubting game." They think up opposing positions. They look for what is wrong with whatever it is they are examining. It could be a text or a painting or a person or anything at all.

Teachers report that they often have trouble inducing their women students to play the doubting game. In *Women's Ways of Knowing*, we retell a story told to us by a sophomore, about a time when, as she put it, the professor "gave" the class his interpretation of James' novel, which she referred to as *The Turning* (sic) *of the Screw*. Everyone silently, dutifully wrote it down. The professor, exasperated, tossed his notes into the air and said, "Listen. This is just my interpretation. You should be ripping it apart. You're just sitting there. Come on, start ripping at it." But the student was unable to rip into it. "Basically," she said, "I agreed with it."

Michael Gorra, an assistant professor of English at Smith College, a women's college, tells a similar story in an article in *The New York Times* called, "Learning to Hear the Small, Soft Voices" (1988). Gorra complains that he has trouble getting a class discussion off the ground, because the students refuse to argue, either with him or with one another. He tells about a recent incident in which two students, one speaking right after the other, offered diametrically opposed readings of an Auden poem.

> The second student didn't define her interpretation against her predecessor's, as I think a man would have. She didn't begin by saying, "I don't agree with that." She betrayed no awareness that she had disagreed with her classmate, and seemed surprised when I pointed it out. (p. 32)

Gorra has found the feminist poet Rich helpful in trying to understand this phenomenon. In an essay called, "Taking Women Students Seriously" (1979), Rich says that women have been taught since early childhood to speak in "small, soft voices" (p. 243). Gorra adds:

These women could recognize disagreement, all right, but they didn't deal with disagreement by arguing. For instance, a woman we call Grace said that when she disagreed with someone, she didn't start arguing in her head; she started trying to imagine herself into the person's situation. She said, "I sort of fit myself into it in my mind, and then I say, 'I see what you mean.'" She added, "There's this initial point where I kind of go into the story, you know? And become like Alice in Wonderland falling down the well."

It took Claire and me a long time to hear what Grace was saying. We thought at the time she was just revealing her inability to engage in critical thinking. To us, her comment indicated not the presence of a different way of thinking but the absence of any kind of thinking, not a difference but a deficiency. Now we see it as an instance of a genuine procedure. We call it *connected knowing*, and, as we go back over the interviews we have done with women over the years, we find it everywhere. We find it, for example, in that ugly pile of interviews in the corner of my office that we were unable to code. Further, we understand why many women have a proclivity toward connected knowing.

Here is an especially clear illustration of connected knowing, from a college student we call Priscilla:

> When I have an idea about something, and it differs from the way another person's thinking about it, I'll usually try to look at it from that person's point of view, see how they could say that, why they think they're right, why it makes sense.

Now, contrast this quotation with those illustrating separate knowing. When you play devil's advocate, you take a position contrary to the other person's, even when you agree with it, even when it seems intuitively right. Priscilla turns this upside down. She allies herself with the other person's position even when she disagrees with it. Another student illustrates the same point. This woman said she seldom played devil's advocate. She said, "I'm usually a little bit of a chameleon. I really try to look for pieces of truth in what the person says, instead of going contrary to him. Sort of collaborate with him."

These women are playing what Elbow (1973) calls "the believing game." Instead of looking for what's wrong with the other person's idea, they try to see why it makes sense, how it might be right. Connected knowers are not dispassionate, unbiased observers; they deliberately bias themselves in favor of the thing they are examining. They try to get right inside it, to form an intimate attachment to it. This imaginative attachment is at the heart of connected knowing. Priscilla tries to get behind the other person's eyes, "to look at it from that person's point of view." This is what Elbow means by "believe." You must suspend your disbelief, put your own views aside, and try to see the logic in the idea. You need not ultimately agree with it. But while you are entertaining it, you must, as Elbow says, "say yes to it." You must empathize with it, feel and think with the person who created it. Emotion is not outlawed, as in separate knowing. But reason is also present. The self is not obliterated. You use your own experience as a means of understanding what produced the idea you are attempting to understand.

The connected knower believes that in order to understand what a person is saying, one must adopt the person's own terms. One must refrain from judgment. In this sense, connected knowing is uncritical. But it is not unthinking; it is a personal way of thinking, and it involves feeling. The connected knower takes a personal approach even to an impersonal thing like a philosophical treatise. She treats the text, as one Wellesley student put it, "as if it were a friend." In Buber's terms (1970), the text is a "thou," a subject, rather than an "it," an object of analysis.

So, while the separate knower takes nothing at face value, the connected knower, in a sense, takes everything at face value. She doesn't try to evaluate the perspective she is examining; she tries to understand it. She does not ask whether it is right; she asks what it means. When she says, Why do you think that? She doesn't mean, What evidence do you have to back that up? She means, What in your experience led you to that position? She is looking for the story behind the idea. The voice of separate knowing is argument; the voice of connected knowing is a narrative voice.

Women spend a lot of time sharing stories of their experience. It sometimes seemed to us that first-year college students spent most of their time this way. This may help to account for the fact that many students of intellectual development among college students show that the major growth occurs during the first year.

We call these conversations *connected conversations*. These conversations may begin rather like clinical interviews. In this sort of interviewing, a still, soft voice is an asset. The skilled interviewer says little; mainly, she listens. But the listening is active, although it may appear passive. The skilled interviewer offers support and invites elaboration at the proper moment. If we cultivate and nourish our students' skills in connected knowing, students can begin to engage in fully mutual connected knowing, in which each person serves as midwife to each other person's thoughts, and each builds on the other's ideas. Some of the women we interviewed cherished memories of class discussions that took this form, with students and teachers drawing out and entering into one another's ideas, elaborating upon them, and building together a truth none could have constructed alone.

Gender in the Academy

Let me make some points of clarification. First, I want to make it very clear that when I say that women have a proclivity toward connected knowing, I am not saying that women will not or cannot think. I *am* saying that many women would rather think *with* someone than think *against* someone. I am arguing against an unnecessarily constricted view of thinking as analytic, detached, and divorced from feeling.

Similarly, I do not object to the cultivation of separate knowing in the academy. I believe it is important to teach the skills of separate knowing. But I do object to an educational system that places nearly exclusive emphasis on separate knowing and fails to acknowledge with respect, let alone to nourish, the skills of connected knowing.

When a woman (or anybody) with a proclivity toward connected knowing enters an environment that fails to recognize connected knowing as a legitimate way of knowing, she feels disconfirmed as a thinker. Such women may become highly adept in separate knowing, but, as they say, "it doesn't feel right." It feels lonely, ungenerous, fraudulent, and futile. Thus it never becomes a "me-voice." It remains a separate voice, separate from the self. The me-voice, being ignored, may fail to develop further or may even wither away.

This, to me, is the really insidious effect of an education that emphasizes separate knowing to the virtual exclusion of connected knowing. Like Ruddick (1977), many of the students we interviewed had removed themselves from their work and dissociated thinking and feeling. They had learned, to paraphrase Ruddick, to think only about things they didn't care about and to care only about things they didn't think about.

What is it like for the male undergraduate? In research that Annick Mansfield and I and other colleagues are doing now, exploring separate and connected knowing in men and women, we are finding, so far, that men usually describe themselves as more comfortable and adept in argument than women do. Most of the men interviewed have said that they like to argue and have found argument useful in sharpening their thinking. In a sense, then, educational practices based on an adversarial model may be more appropriate—or at least less stressful—for men than for women.

Typically, the men's responses to our questions about connected knowing reflect an ambivalence similar to the women's attitudes toward argument. These men said they knew they ought to try harder to enter the other person's perspective, but it made them uneasy, and they found it difficult to do, so they didn't do it much. It is possible that men like this might feel as constricted in the kind of connected class discussion I envisage as the women seem to feel in Professor Gorra's classroom. In a connected class, these men might grow silent, and the teacher would worry about what it was in the men's upbringing that had inhibited their intellectual development.

But not all the men would grow silent. Although the preliminary results of our research confirm our hunch that the two modes are probably gender-related, it is clear that they are not gender-exclusive. We are not talking about genetic incapacity here. Many men have said to us, in person or in writing, "Why do you call it '*women's* ways of knowing?' I'm a connected knower too."

Many of these men are college professors, and they are feeling as constricted by the exclusively adversarial style of their institutions as the women professors and students are. One man wrote to me:

> I took up the study of English literature because I fell in love with the metaphysical poets. But now I find that to get promoted at my institution I must write macho criticism in which I tear my loved ones apart.

Some of the men are considering leaving academic life, divorcing themselves both from their colleges and their disciplines in order, as one expressed it, "to put my heart and mind together again."

That is what Ruddick had to do. Years after earning a Ph.D. and becoming a mother, Ruddick's intellect came alive. In rearing her two children, Ruddick developed a way of knowing that was simultaneously separate and connected. She watched the children closely, attentively, in detail, her attention sharpened rather than clouded by her love for them. As a sort of hobby, she began to study Virginia Woolf, and she found that the way of thinking she developed in reading Woolf was closer to the way of thinking she used in rearing children than to the way she had been taught in college and graduate school. She writes:

> I seemed to learn new ways of attending...This kind of attending was intimately connected with caring; because I cared I reread slowly, then found myself watching more carefully, listening with patience...The more I attended, the more deeply I cared. The domination of feeling by thought, which I had worked so hard to achieve, was breaking down. Instead of developing arguments that could bring my feelings to heel, I allowed feelings to inform my most abstract thinking...I now care about my thinking and think about what I care about. (1984, p. 151)

Ruddick has returned to philosophy, but not to mainstream philosophy[3], and she has returned to college teaching, but not to traditional college teaching. Reconstructing her professional life around her new ways of knowing, she has invented new forms of philosophy and new styles of teaching. It is this sort of reconstruction that I would like to see all teachers achieve, as men and women, learners and thinkers, and critics and lovers of ideas, so that we can do the work we care about and care about the work we do, and help our students to achieve earlier and with less suffering, the integration of separate and connected knowing.

Notes

1. For a fuller description of these findings, see Clinchy, B., & Zimmerman, C. Epistemology and agency in the development of undergraduate women. In P. Perun (Ed.), *The undergraduate woman: Issues in educational equity*. Lexington, MA: D.C. Heath.
2. All informants' names are pseudonyms.
3. See, for example, her recent book, *Maternal Thinking: Toward a Politics of Peace*, Beacon Press, 1989.

References

Belenky, M.B., Clinchy, B.M., Goldberger, N.R., and Tarule, J.M. (1986). *Women's ways of knowing*. New York: Basic Books.

Buber, M. (1970). *I and thou*. New York: Scribner.

Elbow, P. (1973). *Writing without teachers*. London: Oxford University Press.

Freire, P. (1971). *Pedagogy of the oppressed*. New York: Seabury.

Gilligan, C. (1982). *In a different voice: Psychological theory and women's development*. Cambridge, MA: Harvard University Press.

Gorra, M. (1988, May 1). Learning to hear the small, soft voices. *The New York Times Sunday Magazine*, pp. 32, 34.

Perry, W.G. (1968/1970). *Forms of intellectual and ethical development in the college years*. New York: Holt, Rinehart & Winston.

Rich, A. (1979). *On lies, secrets, and silence: Selected prose—1966–1978*. New York: Norton.

Ruddick, S. (1977). A work of one's own. In S. Ruddick & P. Daniels (Eds.), *Working it out* (pp. 128–143). New York: Pantheon.

Ruddick, S. (1984). New combinations: Learning from Virginia Woolf. In C. Asher, L. DeSalvo, and S. Ruddick (Eds.), *Between women* (pp. 137–159). Boston: Beacon Press.

An Emerging Conceptualization of Epistemological Beliefs and Their Role in Learning

Marlene Schommer

All around us there are clues to suggest that individuals' beliefs about the nature of knowledge and learning may be influencing how they approach learning. For example, a college undergraduate declares, "When I went to my first lecture, what the man said was just like God's word, you know. I believed everything he said, because he was a professor . . ." (Perry, 1968, p. 18).

Beliefs, such as this, may contribute to the numerous problems of poor learners. For example, some students fail to think critically. Some fail to integrate information. Some fail to see the complexity and uncertainty of information. Some fail to persist in their studying at the first sign of making an error. And lest you think that these problems will go away in time, I invite you to imagine these students as adults. These problems can be re-framed in day-to-day adult life. For example, some adults follow cultist leaders without question. Some fail to see the big picture in world events. Some give up on themselves at the first sign of difficulty. It would seem addressing these problems at the student level may decrease the problems at the adult level.

Recently, researchers started investigating students' beliefs about the nature of knowledge and learning, or epistemological beliefs (e.g., Feltovich, Spiro, & Coulson, 1989; Schoenfeld, 1983, 1985; Steinbach, Scardamalia, Burtis, & Bereiter, 1987) in an attempt to determine some of the contributing factors to problems like these. For example, if students believe that knowledge is characteristically isolated bits, then they may assume that being able to list and define terms in a chapter qualifies as understanding. In other words, this belief in simple knowledge serves as a standard for understanding. In turn, if "to understand" means being able to define terms, then the student would select a study strategy consistent with achieving this standard, namely memorizing. The ultimate consequence of this chain of events would be an oversimplified knowledge representation of the chapter content.

One possible objection to this line of research is that beliefs are far too messy to study in an objective, scientific, and scholarly manner. Pajares (1992) has suggested that in order to cope with the fuzziness of beliefs, we need to clearly conceptualize them, articulate precise meanings, and test key assumptions. With this advice in mind I have written this chapter for several purposes: (a) to introduce an emerging theory of individuals' beliefs about the nature of knowledge and learning, or epistemological beliefs, (b) to review research that tests aspects of this theory, and (c) to highlight the critical role of epistemological beliefs in learning. My ultimate goal is to entice researchers, practitioners, and philosophers to question, test, and revise the theory that I present.

Underlying assumptions of this line of work are that individuals have an unconscious system of beliefs about what knowledge is and how it is acquired. These epistemological beliefs have subtle, yet important effects on how individuals comprehend, monitor their comprehension, problem solve, and persist in the face of difficult tasks. Epistemological beliefs are likely to have direct effects on individuals' intellectual performance, as well as indirect effects that are mediated through other aspects of cognition. In this chapter I do acknowledge limitations of this theory. Each limitation serves as an invitation to the reader, to revise the theory after thoughtful questioning and careful investigation. In the first section of

"An Emerging Conceptualization of Epistemelogical Beliefs and Their Role in Learning," by Marlene Schommer, reprinted by permission from *Beliefs About Text and Instruction with Text*, edited by Ruth Garner and Patricia A. Alexander, 1994, Lawrence Erlbaum Associates, Inc.

this chapter I present a brief history of the study of epistemological beliefs. This is followed by the introduction of a theory of epistemological beliefs, research that tests aspects of the theory, limitations of the theory, and final comments.

A Brief History

Although there have been several attempts to describe personal epistemology as a component of human development (Broughton, 1978; Chandler, 1987; Gilligan & Murphy, 1979) and personality (Pepper, 1942; Royce & Powell, 1983; Toulmin, 1972), it has been William Perry, Jr.'s (1968) theory of college students' beliefs about the nature of knowledge that has received substantial attention among researchers interested in education (e.g., Knefelkamp & Slepitza, 1976; Touchton, Wertheimer, Cornfeld, & Harrison, 1977). Based on interviews and survey responses of college undergraduates, Perry theorized that students progress through a series of nine intellectual stages. In the early stages students see knowledge as either right or wrong with authority figures knowing the answers (dualism). As students progress through college they encounter conflicting opinion among experts. In time, they come to recognize different points of view, yet persist in searching for the right answer. Eventually students conclude that one point of view is as good as another (multiplicity). As students enter new stages of development they begin to perceive knowledge as correct relative to various contexts (relativism). The right/wrong belief is now subordinate to relativistic thinking. According to Perry, when students reach the final stage of development, they realize that there are multiple possibilities for knowledge and that there are times when one must make a strong, yet tentative commitment to some ideas (commitment).

Early attempts to link epistemological beliefs to metacomprehension based on Perry's work have produced mixed results. Ryan (1984), using several items from Perry's questionnaire, classified students as either highly dualistic (knowledge is right or wrong) or highly relativistic (validity of knowledge is context dependent). When students were asked what their criteria were for determining if they had comprehended a textbook chapter, dualists reported using fact-oriented standards, such as free recall, whereas relativists reported using context-oriented standards, such as paraphrasing and application. In contrast, Glenberg and Epstein (1987), using Ryan's scale to predict students' accuracy in monitoring their comprehension, found that the scale "accounted for little variance and, thus tended to waste degrees of freedom" (p. 87).

An Emerging Theory of Epistemological Beliefs

In order to resolve these conflicting results, I have reconceptualized epistemological beliefs and initiated a series of experiments to test aspects of this reconceptualization. This reconceptualization is presented as an initial effort to generate a loose-knit theory of epistemological beliefs.

Like Perry, I approach epistemological beliefs with a psychologist's background rather than with a philosopher's background. Unlike Perry, I have chosen to label my theory with the umbrella term epistemology. I borrow this philosophical term because the focus of this theory is on individuals' beliefs about what knowledge is and how knowledge is acquired.

Personal Epistemology Is a System of More or Less Independent Beliefs

Ryan's interpretation of Perry's work assumes that personal epistemology is unidimensional and develops in a fixed progression of stages. A more plausible conception is that personal epistemology is a system of more or less independent dimensions. That is, epistemological beliefs may be far too complex to be captured in a single dimension. Consequently, I propose that epistemological beliefs be conceived as a system of relatively independent beliefs.

By *system* of beliefs, I mean that there is more than one epistemological dimension to consider. I have proposed five epistemological dimensions, each dimension having a range of possible values: *CERTAINTY* of knowledge, ranging from knowledge is absolute to knowledge is tentative; the *STRUCTURE* of knowledge, ranging from knowledge is organized as isolated bits and pieces to knowledge is organized as highly interwoven concepts; the *SOURCE* of knowledge, ranging from knowledge is handed down by authority to knowledge is derived through reason; the *CONTROL* of knowledge acquisition, ranging from the ability to learn is fixed at birth to the ability to learn can be changed; and the *SPEED* of the knowledge acquisition, ranging from knowledge is acquired quickly or not-at-all to knowledge is acquired gradually. Although these five epistemological dimensions do not encompass all possible aspects of epistemological beliefs, they do serve as a starting point into this line of investigation.

Several studies support the notion of a system of epistemological beliefs. In order to test the multidimensionality of an epistemological belief system, a questionnaire (Schommer, 1990) was developed that tapped individuals' preferences to statements about knowledge and learning. For example, "Successful students learn quickly," "Scientists can ultimately get to the truth," and "Most words have one clear meaning." The questionnaire was administered to 260 college undergraduates. Factor analysis yielded four factors suggesting four epistemological dimensions. Factor titles stated from the naive perspective are as follows: (a) *fixed ability*, (b) *simple knowledge*, (c) *certain knowledge*, and (d) *quick learning*. This factor structure has been replicated with another college group of over 400 students (Schommer, Crouse, & Rhodes, 1992), with over 1,000 high school students (Schommer, 1993), and by different investigators (Dunkle, Schraw, & Bendixen, 1993).

Other researchers have found evidence for all five epistemological dimensions. Jehng, Johnson, and Anderson (1993) developed a questionnaire by revising the Schommer (1990) questionnaire and adding aspects of Spiro's (1989) questionnaire. Using confirmatory factor analysis, Jehng et al. indicate that there is evidence of five epistemological dimensions that reflect the five beliefs hypothesized.[1] Although additional means of measuring epistemological beliefs needs to be developed, these studies support the multidimensionality of personal epistemology.

I have also hypothesized that these epistemological beliefs are relatively independent. By that I mean that individuals are not *necessarily* sophisticated (or naive) in all beliefs concurrently. For example, individuals may believe that the solution to poverty is highly complex, yet once the solution is found, it will be an absolute solution.

Some supporting evidence for the independence of epistemological dimensions within epistemological belief systems is found in Schommer and Dunnell's study (1994). The development of gifted and non-gifted high school students' epistemological beliefs was compared. In the early years of high school, no differences were found in epistemological beliefs between groups. By the end of high school, the gifted students were less likely to believe in simple knowledge and quick learning, yet they maintained less sophisticated beliefs in fixed ability and certain knowledge. At least in this sample of students, there was no evidence to suggest that gifted students' beliefs were developing in synchrony.

Epistemological Beliefs Are Characterized as Frequency Distributions

I propose that individuals' epistemological beliefs are best characterized as frequency distributions, rather than a single point along each dimension. With this characterization of epistemological beliefs, the distinction between the naive learner and the sophisticated learner becomes a matter of the shape of the distribution. Figure 2.1 shows two hypothetical epistemological distributions. Individuals with a sophisticated epistemological belief in the certainty of knowledge would believe that there are a few things in this world that are certain, some things that are temporarily uncertain, and many things that are either unknown or constantly evolving. With this particular distribution a sophisticated learner by default would be a critical reader, that is, always questioning what is read since many facts may be tentative or unknown. Yet, with enough accumulated evidence, the sophisticated individual would hold a small set of facts as basic concepts that hold true through time.

I also show the hypothetical epistemological distribution of naive learners. They would have a restricted epistemological belief distribution. Naive individuals would believe much knowledge is absolute and the remainder of knowledge is temporarily unknown. In time, experts may find the answers. Their epistemological distribution either does not include any notion that some knowledge is constantly evolving or the likelihood of uncertainty is so slim, that it would take an extraordinary event for them to acknowledge uncertainty. With this epistemological distribution, naive individuals will, by default, fail to read critically. When information is explicitly or implicitly stated as tentative, they may distort information.

For example, naive individuals may be more susceptible to advertisements for the cure of baldness or the best diet yet. They may also be more susceptible to phone market scams that promise great prizes or cheap luxurious property in a retirement village. Alternatively, sophisticated individuals will be more skeptical of these solicitations. Furthermore, when sophisticated individuals read newspapers and maga-

Figure 2.1
The upper pie chart shows the hypothesized belief in certainty distribution of a naive learner. The lower pie chart shows the hypothesized belief in certainty distribution for a sophisticated learner.

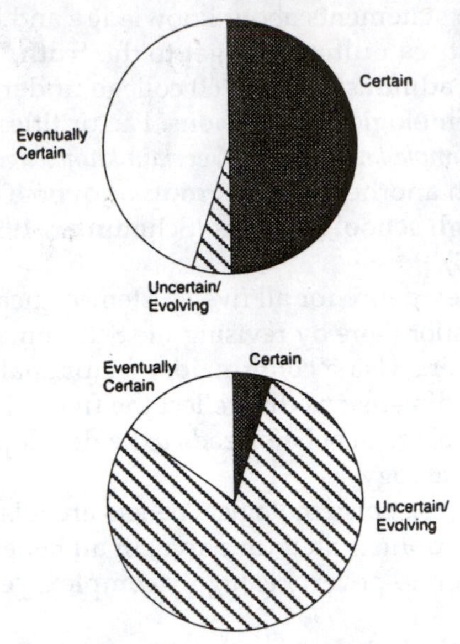

zine articles, they may be more likely to question factual, as well as editorial articles. Yet, when enough evidence is accumulated, sophisticated readers can be influenced to believe what they read.

Support for the distribution hypothesis is found in Perry's descriptions of students' educational views, as well as research examining the effects of epistemological beliefs on learning. Although Perry (1968) has not characterized personal epistemology as a distribution, his description of incoming college freshmen is consistent with it. He reported that the freshmen did not entertain any possibility of uncertain knowledge. And he theorized that when students began to believe in relativistic knowledge, then dualistic beliefs took on a subordinate function. The right/wrong belief was an exception to the rule. In agreement with Perry, I am suggesting that sophisticated individuals do entertain the possibility of absolutes.[2] They believe there are few absolutes and many uncertainties.

Although there is no empirical evidence to support the "distribution" hypothesis, per se, there is research evidence that supports the notion that a strong belief in certainty hinders text comprehension. In two separate studies (Schommer, 1988, 1990) college students were presented text information that was explicitly tentative. After reading the passages, students rated their confidence in their comprehension. The final paragraph at the end of each passage had been omitted. Students were asked to imagine that they were the authors of the passage. They were to write a concluding paragraph based on what they had just read. Students' concluding paragraphs were coded for the reflection of certainty or uncertainty. Analyses revealed that the more students believed in certain knowledge, the more likely they were to write inappropriately absolute conclusions. There is also research evidence that suggests strong beliefs in quick learning, simple knowledge, and fixed ability hinder learning, as well.

A strong belief in quick all-or-none learning has been found to predict the comprehension of mathematical, social, and physical science texts. Based on extensive analysis of mathematical problem solving protocols of experts and novices, Schoenfeld (1983, 1985) suggests that many high school students (novices) believe mathematics problems should be solved in less than 10 minutes. Students considered more mental investment as a waste of time. In the Schommer (1990) study, students read either a physical science passage or social science passage. In addition to writing a concluding paragraph, students rated their confidence in understanding the passage and completed a mastery test. To measure depth of students' understanding, conclusions were categorized according to the degree to which students elaborated on the passage information. To test their comprehension, tests were scored for accuracy. And to test for comprehension monitoring, the degree of agreement between students' confidence in their comprehension and their actual test performance was compared. After controlling for verbal ability, regression analyses indicated that the more students believed in quick learning, the more likely they were to write impoverished conclusions, perform poorly on the mastery test, and be over confident in their understanding of the text material.

In a more recent study (Schommer, 1993), the epistemological beliefs of over 1,000 high school students were assessed. After controlling for general intelligence, regression analyses revealed that the more students believed in quick learning, the more likely they were to have a low overall grade point average.

Strong belief in simple knowledge (i.e., knowledge is fragmented and isolated) has been found to predict medical science, physical science, and mathematical text comprehension. In a provocative study of medical students' understanding of biomedicine, Feltovich et al. (1989) indicate that epistemological beliefs influence students' understanding of complex medical concepts. The major roadblock to conceptual understanding was a "reductive bias" or tendency to oversimplify and reduce new information into a single framework. Students tended to oversimplify complex and irregular structures, rely on single mental representations, and compartmentalize knowledge components. Songer and Linn (1991) examined students' views of science and their effect on an integrated understanding of thermodynamics. Students were asked questions about the work of scientists; about the nature of scientific knowledge; and about the relevance of science outside the classroom. Students who held a rich, integrated view of science, for example, related science in the classroom with science outside the classroom and who recognized the interrelationship among scientific concepts, outperformed students with the opposite views in understanding thermodynamics. Schommer, Crouse, and Rhodes (1992) found that the more students believed in complex, interrelated knowledge, the more likely they were to successfully comprehend statistical text.

There is evidence to suggest a strong belief in fixed ability predicts children's persistence in learning. Work done by Dweck (see Dweck & Leggett, 1988) in the last 10 years provides evidence for the influence of children's beliefs about the nature of intelligence and persistence. She has found that some children have a predominant belief that intelligence is a fixed entity, whereas others believe it is incremental, that is, it can be improved. When engaging in an easy task, these two groups of children will perform similarly. When confronted with a difficult task, children with an entity theory will interpret the situation as reflecting a lack of intelligence. They will display "helpless" behavior. That is, they will engage in negative self-talk, such as "I'm failing," perseverate on the same study strategy, and finally cease to try. Incremental theorists, on the other hand, will perceive the difficulty of the task as a challenge. They will engage in positive self-talk, such as "I must try harder and longer." They will also try alternative study strategies. Ultimately, although both groups have similar ability, the incremental theorists will outperform the fixed theorists.

Epistemological Beliefs Have Both Direct and Indirect Effects

I propose that epistemological beliefs have indirect, as well as direct effects on other aspects of cognition. The indirect effects of epistemological beliefs make their manifestation subtle. Nonetheless, the effects are important. For example, if individuals believe knowledge is organized as isolated bits and pieces, this belief in turn may effect the standards by which they judge accurate comprehension (Baker, 1984, 1985) and the study strategies they select when studying. In this example, they might be convinced that reciting definitions constitutes comprehension, and rehearsing definitions would he a means to meet this standard of comprehension.

Research from text comprehension studies provides some support for the direct and indirect effects of epistemological beliefs. The finding that students with strong beliefs in certain knowledge tend to write absolute conclusions for tentative text information (Schommer, 1990) provides some evidence of the direct effect of epistemological beliefs. Evidence for indirect effects comes from the investigation of statistical text comprehension (Schommer et al., 1992). College students completed the epistemological questionnaire, a study strategy inventory (Weinstein, Palmer, & Schulte, 1987), read a statistical passage, rated their confidence in their comprehension, and completed a mastery test. Regression analyses revealed that the less students believed in simple knowledge, the better they performed on the mastery test and the more accurately they assessed their own understanding. Path analyses indicated both direct and indirect effects of belief in simple knowledge. The less students believed in simple knowledge, the more sophisticated study strategies they reported using. The more sophisticated study strategies they used, the better they performed on the mastery test.

This conclusion must be considered tentative however, since students were asked to rate how they *typically* studied (rather than how they studied for the task they had just completed) and the assessment was based on self report, rather than with on-line measures. Nevertheless, this study does provide enough evidence to suggest future research on the interaction of epistemological beliefs with other aspects of cognition is likely to reveal the subtle, yet important influence of these beliefs.

Epistemological Beliefs are Influenced by Experience

An important issue to address is the development and modification of epistemological beliefs. Whether children are born with an "epistemological scheme" is unclear. What does seem evident is the influence of environmental factors that instill and modify children's beliefs about knowledge. In 1984 at the presidential address for the annual meeting of the American Educational Research Association, Richard C. Anderson stated that:

> It stands to reason that beliefs about knowledge that a child develops will be influenced by those of his parents. Parents' beliefs about knowledge will be conditioned by educational and occupational status. . . . Later, teachers become mediators of experience. (1984, p. 8)

I propose that individuals' beliefs are influenced by experience. Although empirical evidence is limited as to the sources of epistemological beliefs, there is some research that points to the contribution of both teaching and upbringing to personal epistemology. Beers (1988) in interviewing teachers regarding their classroom goals, found their objectives to be less content-oriented and more philosophically oriented.

> Few were interested in transmitting their content per se. . . . It seemed that these teachers were primarily concerned with helping them [students] develop particular attitudes and thinking styles. A biologist, for example, said that she "hated facts," and spoke of "getting students excited about the way the world works." . . . When these teachers were discussing their educational goals, they were referring to a set of epistemological assumptions. . . . Teachers . . . may be unaware of the role that epistemological assumptions play in their interactions with students, but this role may be profound. (p. 87)

Indeed, Schoenfeld (1983) has suggested that students' beliefs about quick and easy mathematical solutions and failure to integrate mathematical concepts may be a product of how they are taught. For example, teachers may emphasize memorizing formulas and ignore conceptual understanding in their teaching and/or testing of mathematics.

I am presently conducting research to investigate the development of epistemological beliefs. In the first year of a 4-year longitudinal study (Schommer, 1993), the epistemological beliefs of students in a high school were assessed. Differences in epistemological beliefs between students across high school years and between genders were examined. Belief in simple knowledge, certain knowledge, and quick learning decreased from freshman to senior years. Girls were less likely to believe in quick learning and fixed ability. Results from the longitudinal study will be needed to determine if the difference in epistemological beliefs across the school years is due to sophisticated students remaining in school through their senior year and less sophisticated students dropping out, or students' beliefs actually changing. As intriguing as this longitudinal study is, we will not be able to tease apart the influence of education versus life's experiences on students' epistemological beliefs.

To control for the confound between personal experiences and formal education, I carried out a study examining the epistemological beliefs of adults (Schommer, 1992). To decrease the confound between age (a measure of experience) and education, adults from all walks of life were studied. One third of the sample of adults had no more than a high school degree. Another third of the sample had no more than a college undergraduate degree. The remaining portion of the adults had been exposed to postgraduate work. These adults completed the epistemological questionnaire and a demographic/upbringing survey. Epistemological factor scores were regressed, first, on age and demographic/upbringing variables, then, on educational level.

Demographic characteristics and upbringing factors predicted the adults' epistemological beliefs. The older adults were, the less likely they were to believe in fixed ability. The more they had been allowed to question their parents, the less likely they were to believe in fixed ability and quick learning.

The less they had been pushed to get good grades, the less likely they were to believe in simple knowledge. The less strict they had perceived their parents to be, the less likely they were to believe in quick learning. The more they had been allowed to make their own decisions, the less likely they were to believe in certain knowledge. And the more education their father had, the less likely they were to believe in simple knowledge and certain knowledge. Women were less likely to believe in quick learning and certain knowledge.[3] In short, the more their parents encouraged them to think deeply and to think for themselves, the more likely they were to hold sophisticated epistemological beliefs as adults.

When background knowledge was controlled, education also predicted epistemological beliefs.[4] The higher educational level achieved, the less likely adults believed in simple and certain knowledge. It is interesting to note aspects of epistemological beliefs that deal with knowledge, per se, are predicted by education. Beliefs about self, the speed and control of learning, are predicted by personal experience. In other words, beliefs about knowledge, which the perceivers can *think* is distant from them, may be modified by education. On the other hand, beliefs about the learning which intimately involves the self, may be firmly established early in the individual's home life and resistant to change from factors outside the family.

Although these results reveal that education predicts personal epistemology above and beyond, age, parents' education, and upbringing, interpretation of the data must be made with caution. As in the high school study (Schommer, 1993), we cannot determine if adults' beliefs change because they experienced formal education or if adults who decided to pursue higher education have more sophisticated epistemological beliefs. Future longitudinal studies may help resolve this issue.

Domain Independence of Epistemological Beliefs Varies With Experience

Throughout all the research I have reported an underlying assumption is that epistemological beliefs are domain independent. There is one recent study that suggests college students in different majors have different epistemological beliefs (Jehng et al., 1993). But we cannot tell from this information if students in a particular domain believe consistently across domains. For example, business majors may believe *all knowledge* is cut and dried. Whereas, social science majors may believe *all knowledge* is tentative. Jehng et al. do not address the domain specificity issue, per se. I am presently conducting a series of studies to address this issue. For now I would like to theorize just how complex this investigation is likely to be.

I propose that the issue of domain specificity is far more complex than simply saying epistemological beliefs either are, or are not, domain independent. Essentially, I suggest that the issue of domain specificity may be intimately related with individuals' experiences.

A hypothesis to be tested is that the degree of domain specificity will vary with either age or education. Setting aside for the moment the issue of whether age or education (or both) affects individuals' epistemological views, let us assume that experience is the influence. Now let me present to you a testable hypothesis. Young children will most likely have domain-independent beliefs. The level of sophistication of these beliefs is directly dependent on the home environment of the child. When the child enters school, the teacher and the child's peers now begin to influence his or her epistemological beliefs. It may be at this time in children's lives that they begin to acquire stereotypes of domains resulting in different epistemological beliefs for different domains. The domain specificity tendency may continue until sometime in adulthood. When an individual acquires a substantial amount of experience, they will develop a sophisticated epistemological point of view in the domain of their expertise. The real mystery is whether their epistemological bent for their area of expertise will generalize to other domains. It is such a tentative point, that I prefer to wait for empirical evidence before I draw any conclusions. The main point is that the question of domain specificity is not easily resolved. There may be times in an individuals' life when their beliefs are consistent across domains and other times, when their beliefs will vary across domains.

Reflections on the Epistemological Theory

It is important to consider the LIMITATIONS of this loose-knit epistemological theory and the supporting research.

1. I write this theory with a psychologist's background, rather than a philosophers' background. This adds strength to the theory in that aspects of the theory are based on empirical findings and psychological explanations of human learning. On the other hand, the

conceptualization of epistemological beliefs, that is, the description of individual dimensions and the completeness of the *system* of beliefs would be enhanced by a philosopher's contribution to the theory.

2. This theory is influenced by my own personal background and from the background of the psychologists who have influenced me with their research and thinking. Hence, the theory is written from a limited cultural perspective. Contributions from individuals with different cultural perspectives and different areas of expertise are likely enrich the conceptualization of epistemological beliefs.
3. The assertion as to what constitutes naive and sophisticated epistemological beliefs is somewhat vague and perhaps presumptuous. Essentially, I entertain the notion that as long as individuals are willing to consider all possibilities, for example, both certain knowledge and uncertain knowledge, and their default is uncertain knowledge, then they are sophisticated. This is controversial. And although never explicitly asserted, I have come to believe that great scholars share similar epistemological beliefs across all domains. Perhaps this is not so. It may be that great engineers need to have a different epistemological beliefs compared to great sociologists.[5] These issues remain to be tested.
4. Varied measures of epistemological beliefs are needed to confirm the notion of a *system* of beliefs and to be sensitive to the *distribution* of beliefs. No single measure could possibly capture all aspects of individuals' epistemological belief systems. Belief systems in general, will almost always need to be inferred (Rokeach, 1960). By using multiple measures such as questionnaires (e.g., Jehng et al., 1993; Perry, 1968; Schommer, 1990; Spiro, 1989), dilemma resolutions (e.g., Kitchener, 1986), and interviews (e.g., Perry, 1968), a more complete picture of individuals' epistemological beliefs may be derived.
5. The suggestion that epistemological beliefs have both direct and indirect effects only begins to address the complexity of their effects. It is likely that within individuals' system of beliefs, certain patterns of beliefs may have unique effects on learning. For example, does an individual who has strong beliefs in certain and complex knowledge approach a learning task differently compared to an individual who has strong beliefs in uncertain and simple knowledge?
6. Finally, I have not addressed the issue of affect. The study of epistemological beliefs is clearly dealing with "hot cognition." Beliefs, by definition, are emotion-laden. That is why beliefs can drive behavior. That is why they are resistant to change. Presently, I am in the process of analyzing epistemological interviews in search of affective information.

Final Comment

To summarize the epistemological theory to date, I have proposed an epistemological belief system that is multidimensional. These epistemological dimensions are more or less independent. At least five beliefs have been considered including the Source, Structure, and Certainty of Knowledge, and the Speed and Control of the Acquisition of Knowledge. Individuals' beliefs are better described in terms of distributions rather than a single point along each continuum. Epistemological beliefs affect learning both directly and indirectly. Their effects are often mediated by other aspects of cognition. The development of these beliefs may be due to cultural, familial, and educational influences. Whether epistemological beliefs are domain-specific or not depends on the developmental level of the individual.

To summarize the research to date, there is evidence that suggests epistemological beliefs affect comprehension, metacomprehension, interpretation, and persistence. These effects have been found among individuals of all ages and with varied educational backgrounds. These effects may be mediated by other aspects of cognition. There is evidence to suggest that both upbringing and education influence individual's epistemological beliefs. There appear to be age and gender differences, as well.

I hope I have achieved my goals for writing this chapter. If you have finished reading this chapter and are now convinced that epistemological beliefs, as difficult as they may be to conceive and measure, are too important to ignore, then I have achieved my most important goal. If you find yourself in doubt about the conception, the measure, and the findings of epistemological beliefs, to date, then I have achieved another goal, to entice you to reflect, research, and revise the conceptualization of epistemological beliefs. I do not believe that a single conceptualization of epistemological beliefs, a single measure of epistemological beliefs, or a single researcher of epistemological beliefs, will successfully capture this complex phenomenon. By explicitly writing this theory, I hope to encourage teachers to consider the epistemological beliefs of their students, as well as themselves during instruction and testing, and to entice researchers to embrace this conceptually challenging phenomenon in their thoughts and in their investigations.

Notes

1. Jehng et al. (1993) chose to reconceptualize the epistemological dimension I refer to as the structure of knowledge. In their questionnaire this factor, stated from the naive perspective, reflects a belief in orderly process. This bears a strong resemblance to my conception that knowledge is simple. Jehng et al.'s emphasis is that the *process* of learning is simple, whereas my conceptualization emphasizes that *knowledge*, itself, is simple.
2. I suspect that an individual who has the opposite belief, that is, never entertains the notion of certainty, may have problems as well. This may lead to depression and despair. Chandler (1987) has theorized that adolescents are incredible skeptics and this can account for certain aspects of identity crises during development.
3. In an earlier study (Schommer & Dunnell, 1994), high school girls were less likely to believe in fixed ability and quick learning
4. The statistical confound between age and education was decreased substantially. The zero order correlation between age and education was –.11.
5. Although I report that Jehng et al. (1993) found students in different majors have different epistemological beliefs, I do not consider these students as "great experts." They were in the early stages of developing their expertise. For example, based on conversations with professors in physics, psychology, and education, I come to suspect that naive beliefs in certainty last into the early years of graduate school.

References

Anderson, R. C. (1984). Some reflections on the acquisition of knowledge. *Educational Researcher, 13*(9), 5–10.

Baker, L. (1984). Children's effective use of multiple standards for evaluating their comprehension. *Journal of Educational Psychology, 76*, 588–597.

Baker, L. (1985). Differences in the standards used by college students to evaluate their comprehension of expository prose. *Reading Research Quarterly, 20*, 297–313.

Beers, S. E. (1988). Epistemological assumptions and college teaching: Interactions in the college classroom. *Journal of Research and Development in Education, 21*, 87–93.

Broughton, J. (1978). Development of concepts of self, mind, reality, and knowledge. *New Directions for Child Development, 1*, 75–100.

Chandler, M. (1987). The Othello effect. *Human Development, 30*, 137–159.

Dweck, C. S., & Leggett, E. L. (1988). A social-cognitive approach to motivation and personality. *Psychological Review, 95*, 256–273.

Dunkle, M. F., Schraw, G. J., & Bendixen, L. (1993, April). *The relationship between epistemological beliefs, causal attributions, and reflective judgment*. Paper presented at the annual meeting of the American Educational Research Association, Atlanta, GA.

Feltovich, P. J., Spiro, R. J., & Coulson, R. L. (1989). The nature of conceptual understanding in Biomedicine: The deep structure of complex ideas and the development of misconceptions. In D. Evans & V. Patel (Eds.), *The cognitive science in medicine* (pp. 113–172). Cambridge, MA: MIT Press.

Gilligan, C., & Murphy, J. M. (1979). Development from adolescence to adulthood: The philosopher and the dilemma of the fact. *New Directions for Child Development, 5*, 85–99.

Glenberg, A. M., & Epstein, W. (1987). Inexpert calibration of comprehension. *Memory & Cognition, 10*, 597–602.

Jehng, J. J., Johnson, S. D., & Anderson, R. C. (1993). Schooling and students' epistemological beliefs. *Contemporary Educational Psychology 18*, 23–35.

Kitchener, K. S. (1986). The reflective judgment model: Characteristics, evidence, and measurement. In R. A. Mines & K. S. Kitchener (Eds.), *Adult cognitive development* (pp. 76–91). New York: Praeger.

Knefelkamp, L. L., & Slepitza, R. (197G). A cognitive-developmental model of career development: An adaptation of the Perry Scheme. *The Counseling Psychologist, 6*, 53–58.

Pajares, M. F. (1992). Teacher's beliefs and educational research: Cleaning up a messy construct. *Review of Educational Research, 62*, 307–332.

Pepper, S. C. (1942). *World hypotheses*. Berkeley: University of California Press.

Perry, W. G., Jr. (1968). *Patterns of development in thought and values of students in a liberal arts college: A validation of a scheme*. Cambridge, MA: Bureau of Study Counsel, Harvard University. (ERIC Document Reproduction Service No. ED 024315)

Rokeach, M. (1960). *Open and closed mind*. New York: Basic Books.

Royce, J. R., & Powell, A. (1983). *Theory of personality and individual differences: Factors, systems, and processes*. Englewood Cliffs, NJ: Prentice-Hall.

Ryan, M. P. (1984). Monitoring text comprehension: Individual differences in epistemological standards. *Journal of Educational Psychology, 76*, 248–258.

Schoenfeld, A. H. (1983). Beyond the purely cognitive: Beliefs systems, social cognitions, and metacognitions as driving forces in intellectual performance. *Cognitive Science, 7*, 329–363.

Schoenfeld, A. H. (198S). *Mathematical problem solving*. New York: Academic Press.

Schommer, M. (1988, April). *Dimensions of tacit epistemology and comprehension*. Paper presented at the annual conference of the American Educational Research Association, New Orleans.

Schommer, M. (1990). Effects of beliefs about the nature of knowledge on comprehension. *Journal of Educational Psychology, 82*, 498–504.

Schommer, M. (1992, October). *Predictors of epistemological beliefs: Comparing adults with only a secondary education to adults with post-secondary education*. Paper presented at the Mid-western Educational Research Association, Chicago.

Schommer, M. (1993). Epistemological development and academic performance among secondary students. *Journal of Educational Psychology, 85*, 1–6.

Schommer, M., Crouse, A., & Rhodes, N. (1992). Epistemological beliefs and mathematical text comprehension: Believing it's simple doesn't make it so. *Journal of Educational Psychology, 84*, 435–443.

Schommer, M., & Dunnell, P. A. (1994). A comparison of epistemological beliefs between gifted and non-gifted high school students. *Roeper Review, 16*, 207–210.

Songer, N. B., & Linn, M. C. (1991). How do students' views of science influence knowledge integration? *Journal of Research in Science Teaching, 28*, 761–764.

Spiro, R. J. (1989). *Epistemological beliefs questionnaire*. University of Illinois, Center for the Study of Reading, Champaign, IL. [Unpublished raw data]

Steinbach, R., Scardamalia, M., Bunis, P. J., & Bereiter, C. (1987). Children's implicit theories of knowledge and learning. Presented at *The American Educational Research Association*, Washington, D.C.

Touchton, J. G., Wertheimer, L. G., Cornfeld, J. L., & Harrison, K. H. (19771. Career planning and decision-making: A developmental approach to the classroom. *The Counseling Psychologist, 6*, 42–47.

Toulmin, S. (1972). *Human understanding: Volume I: General introduction and part I.* Princeton, NJ: Princeton University Press.

Weinstein, C., Palmer, D. R., & Schulte, A. C. (1987). *Learning and study strategies inventory*. Clearwater, FL: H & H Publishing Co.

Taking Student Diversity into Account

NANCY CHISM

Traditional discussions of student differences have focused on variations in cognitive style, cognitive development, motivation, speed, and preferred physiological modality. Recently, discussion of difference has centered on social diversity as well. As the demographic makeup of the traditional college-going population has changed, students who have previously been underrepresented, given the total population, are attending college (Levine et al., 1989). More students who are older than the traditional 17–22-year-old range are now reentering the education system; women now constitute half or more of the total population at many institutions; students of diverse racial and ethnic backgrounds are a greater presence on campus (following a decline in participation during the 1980s); students with physical or learning disabilities are attending and self-identifying in higher numbers; and gay, lesbian, and bisexual students (who have heretofore been a largely "invisible" population) are becoming increasingly articulate about their participation.

Although these groups are different from one another and even different within each group (for example, as Nieves-Squires [1991] notes, the label "Hispanic" is used to refer to people from more than five major social groups, each of which is further differentiated internally by gender, socioeconomic, and other differences), the groups are united by a past and current experience of both blatant and subtle forms of exclusion in higher education and in society more generally. Within each group, there is a sense of patterns of values, ways of thinking and acting, and a spirit of community that are distinct enough to be considered "cultural" characteristics.

A persistent theme connected with social diversity in higher education has been disappointing retention rates and discouragement on the part of many traditionally underrepresented students. Although research on the issue is in its infancy, it is clear that students from diverse groups identify the quality of relationships they have with faculty as a critical factor influencing their learning and comfort level with the institution. Although financial aid, residential life, and a host of other factors are important, students have reported in several studies that positive in- and out-of-class relationships with their teachers can enable them to overcome constraints and achieve academic success (Sedlacek, 1983; Ferguson, 1989; Astin, 1975).

Some faculty members are unconvinced that there are any teaching issues surrounding social diversity. Others, who are in the process of evaluating their role in responding to student social diversity, often wonder whether attention to difference will fragment and irritate social relations and prevent, rather than encourage, student success. Many worry about "canon" issues, fearing a watering down of the curriculum. They may fear that the purposes of social diversity will call upon them to treat students preferentially—a practice that they have always been careful to avoid. They may also feel that they are walking on eggshells or that whatever action they take will be misinterpreted. But it is clear that the problems need to be addressed openly. The payoff is not only for the students themselves but for the colleges and universities who profit from truly embracing the opportunity to let previously unheard or unheeded voices enrich and broaden ways of thinking and knowing.

The main teaching issues connected with social diversity fall into two broad categories: curriculum and instructional strategies issues. The first, curriculum issues, is the most frequently debated. Socially diverse groups have claimed that the content of most courses is very narrowly focused on the Western intellectual tradition, specifically the experience of the mainstream European-descended male. The effect is

"Taking Student Diversity into Account," by Nancy Chism, reprinted from *Teaching Tips: Strategies, Research, and Theory for College and University Teachers* by Wilbert J. McKeachie with chapters by Nancy Chism, Robert Menges, Marilla Svinicki and Claire Ellen Weinstein, 1994, D. C. Heath.

that they feel marginal to the academic experience. They see no role models and feel that their experience is not valued. Secondly, students from diverse groups often feel that the way in which instruction takes place inhibits their academic success. They argue that classroom interactions, academic discourse, cognitive style, and other aspects of teaching and learning are also based on a male European cultural style that does not permit their full participation and excludes insights from other cultures. Majority as well as minority students, then, experience an education that is far too narrow given the possibilities.

The literature on the needs expressed by students from previously underrepresented groups (Green, 1988; Pemberton, 1988; Hall and Sandler, 1982; Steele, 1992) bears several messages for faculty to consider: 1) These students need to feel welcome; 2) they need to feel that they are being treated as individuals; 3) they need to feel that they can participate fully; and 4) they need to be treated fairly.

Feeling Welcome

Students from socially diverse groups frequently report experiencing alienation on college campuses. They recount instances of overt hostility, ignorance, and insensitivity, as well as more subtle messages they receive that their cultural heritage is not valued. In student-teacher interactions, overt problems can result from comments that are openly racist, such as "Black people never contributed anything of worth to society," or homophobic, such as "Gay men are immoral and don't belong on campus," or sexist, such as "The women in this class will probably have trouble with this concept." Although students report that most faculty do not voice such overt hostility, they pick up on more subtle cues, often entangled in instructors' attempts to be humorous, such as jokes about sexual orientation, physical disabilities, or women. The message received is that there is an underlying resentment about the presence of students who "don't fit." Many times, well-meaning but ignorant statements are the cause for discomfort. A faculty member who was in the habit of following his slips into profanity with "My apologies to the ladies" was seen as patronizing by his women students; one teacher who addressed a student with a learning disability with exaggerated enunciation made the student feel that it was assumed he was dull-witted.

Language is a cue to the instructor's stance for many students. When instructors refer to groups in terms that the groups do not prefer, such as "homosexual" for gay and lesbian students, or "Oriental" for Asian-American students, or "gals" for women, they give off a signal that they are not in tune with new developments in language preference, which is often interpreted by students as an uncaring or insensitive attitude. Students expect instructors to be aware of the dialogue around them and to demonstrate appropriate social skills. The emphasis is not so much on policing language or "political correctness" as it is on being considerate in addressing people as they wish to be addressed.

Welcoming not only involves being personally sensitive as the instructor but also helping all students to display welcoming behavior in the classroom. Most students from diverse groups say they more frequently hear insensitive comments from fellow classmates than from faculty. They emphasize that faculty must monitor classroom behavior and address problems when they occur as part of the learning experience. Rather than hurriedly passing over the comment of a student who refers to "niggers on welfare," it is important for instructors to openly discuss issues surrounding the negative image and language choice of the response, even if embarrassment is a possibility. Teaching for diversity not only involves being more welcoming to diverse groups but also means increasing the sensitivity of majority students to cultural differences.

For students from diverse groups to feel valued, instructors must go beyond neutrality. Frequently, the students experience alienation because their presence is not acknowledged at all. They are upset that instructors do not call them by name. Students expecting, according to their cultural background, to engage in formal greetings or "small talk" before an interpersonal exchange begins often interpret the impersonal, businesslike behavior of many instructors as instances of personal rejection. They frequently use the term "invisible" to describe how they feel. Although majority students sometimes describe the same feeling, it is experienced more deeply by students who are from a group that has traditionally experienced exclusion, since they are more likely to take it personally. Teachers who acknowledge diversity at the beginning of a course by indicating that they welcome different perspectives and want to accommodate different needs set the tone for students to feel respected and free to communicate with the teacher.

One of the biggest problems with helping underrepresented students feel welcome is large class size. They can feel lost and may also feel that the peer environment is more likely to get out-of-hand since classroom management is more of a challenge to the teacher. Students from non-dominant racial and ethnic groups, for example, often say that they are very hesitant to speak out on issues about people from their groups in large group settings because they fear physical violence and slurs that the instructor will not witness. Attempts by instructors to manage large class environments well and to increase personal contact with students by engaging in informal conversation before class, scheduling out-of-class visits with students, or working closely with small groups of students on a rotating basis are especially important gestures that can be made to students experiencing the "outsider" syndrome.

Messages in the Curriculum

Similarly, students from non-mainstream groups fail to find their culture or perspective acknowledged in the curriculum. For example, works by or about people of color or gay, lesbian, or bisexual people are noticeable by their absence. References are often minimized or negative. One gay student reported looking forward to the day when his American history instructor would lecture on a section of the text that dealt with the gay pride movement, only to hear the instructor say that he would not deal with the "so- called Stonewall Riots." Another reported that a human sexuality instructor said that the class would skip the chapter on homosexuality because the course was only about "normal" sexuality. In an ethics class, another student reported, the treatment of homosexuality was one of three sections in the text that the instructor chose to omit because of time constraints. The students report that examples used in classes and assignments consistently presume a heterosexual orientation. When these things happen, students report feeling that their point of view, their culture, their heritage is not welcome. They look for role models of scholars, practitioners, and artists in their field of study and find few examples that would encourage them to persist in school. Simple attempts at inclusion can be of enormous importance to students seeking validation. They can also increase the breadth of exposure of majority students.

As many scholars have noted (Banks, 1988; Butler, 1989; Sleeter, 1991; Toombs and Tierney, 1992), rethinking the curriculum often begins with including references to or about scholars or issues connected with socially diverse groups, but ultimately involves a transformative approach whereby the entire assumptions and content of a given field are reconsidered from the perspectives of diverse people. Transformation in sociology, for example, could begin with attention to eliminating stereotyped references that occur or including mention of the work of some current sociologists of color, but would move on to rethink some basic ways of doing or thinking about sociology in light of feminist epistemology or other paradigms. Often the scholarship necessary to revise courses is underdeveloped or hard to access. It takes both personal and institutional commitment and much original scholarship to do this work.

Being Treated as an Individual

Stereotyping

While students from diverse groups are very eager that their social group be welcomed on campus, they also want to be treated as individuals. One barrier that prevents this is stereotyping. Images of the African-American student as a "dumb jock" or "special admissions", student, of the female sorority student as a "fluffhead," or of the lesbian student as an "argumentative dyke" influence teacher expectations, often in unconscious ways. Stereotypes that are ostensibly positive, such as the "math whiz" Asian American or the "wise" older student, are also problematic since they may place unrealistically high expectations on some students. Teachers do not have to voice these stereotypes for students—they often get the message indirectly. For example, a faculty member may lavish excessive praise on a Native-American student, causing the student to feel that the expectations for him are low because of his ethnicity. An instructor might consistently ask female students, rather than males, to take notes for students who are ill, or ask males, rather than females, to lead lab groups.

Tokenism

Students from diverse cultural groups also feel that their individuality is not acknowledged when they are called upon as representatives of their group. When teachers say, "John, how do disabled people feel about this issue?" they potentially put the student in an uncomfortable position. John may not have an opinion; he may feel that there is likely to be a range of opinions on the topic among students with disabilities; and he might feel put on the spot. While it is understandable that faculty might want to include the student in the treatment of a topic and hear the voice of the "local expert," most students want to be respected as individuals and to contribute on their own volition when these issues are addressed. Likewise, many underrepresented students who are invited to serve on committees or panels are very wary of being the "token" member and want to participate based on their personal qualities rather than social group membership.

Mentoring

Individual nurturing through mentoring relationships is also important, yet women and students of color report much lower instances of being mentored than male European Americans (Hall and Sandler, 1982; Blackwell, 1990). In commenting on the reasons for the lack of mentoring and graduate associateships reported by minority graduate students, Blackwell concludes that faculty do not choose students who are different from themselves, since there is a "tendency for faculty members to consciously or subconsciously attempt to reproduce themselves through persons chosen as their protegees" (p. 8). Keeping an open mind about having work go in a new direction or appreciating stylistic differences as potentially complementary or liberating are often involved in mentoring previously underrepresented students.

Full Participation

The Dominant Classroom

Valuing people who think and act in ways that are consistent with the traditional culture of the institution often leads to inadvertent or deliberate exclusion of those who are different. Usually faculty are unaware that they are operating within a cultural perspective, since the dominant culture is taken for granted. As Adams (1992) describes, this culture is uncomfortable for many students from socially diverse groups because in its most extreme form it is "narrow in that it rules out nonverbal, empathic, visual, symbolic, or nuanced communication; it neglects the social processes by which interpersonal communication, influence, consensus, and commitment are included in problem solving; it overlooks the social environment as a source of information . . .; it ignores the values and emotions that nonacademics attach to reasons and facts" (p. 6).

The disjuncture between the dominant classroom culture and the culture of many students can be extreme. Collett and Serrano (1992) point out that for students who have not had a great deal of mainstream culture experience and whose native language is not English, the differences are enormous. Many scholars have pointed out differences between particular cultures and academic culture. Hofstede (1986), for example, talks about differences in whether the individual or group is valued, whether there are large or small power distances between people, whether the culture seeks certainty or tolerates ambiguity, and whether the culture stresses the "masculine" characteristics of material success and assertiveness or the "feminine" characteristics of quality of life and interpersonal relationships. She describes the classroom culture as very different from the cultural expectations of many groups. Much has been written about the differences between an Afro-centric versus Eurocentric worldview (Asante, 1987 and 1988; Branch-Simpson, 1988), the Afro-centric stressing harmony, egalitarian social relations, a fluid notion of time and space, the social world, nonverbal communication, holistic thinking, intuitive reasoning, and approximation; and the Eurocentric stressing competition, power, numerical precision, abstract thinking, verbal communication, analytical thinking, logic, and quantitative accuracy. This literature portrays American classrooms as valuing the Eurocentric worldview.

Cognitive Styles

There is not a clear consensus on whether one can draw implications on learning styles from cultural styles or whether particular learning styles are associated with particular groups. In the case of some of the populations being discussed, such as gay, lesbian, and bisexual students, there is no present evidence to indicate that there are clear patterns. For some other groups, such as students with learning disabilities, there are clear differences (by definition) connected with the disability. The literature on nontraditional- age students (from the adult education literature), women, and students of color does discuss patterns. These descriptions must be viewed with caution, however, since talking about broad patterns across groups of people who have many intragroup differences can lead to stereotyping and overgeneralization. On the other hand, if descriptions of styles are considered as tools to illustrate differences rather than as applicable to every individual in the categories described, they can be helpful.

When scholars talk about major differences in cognitive and social-interactional styles across various cultures, they often use the work of learning style theorists and apply their constructs, which are usually polar opposites, such as abstract vs. concrete thinking, to a particular cultural group. Anderson and Adams (1992), for example, use Anderson's categories of relational and analytical and Witkin and Moore's (1975) categories of field independence and field dependence (also termed "Held sensitivity") to illustrate differences in style. They argue that women from the European-American culture and men and women from Native-American, Hispanic, and African-American cultures often exhibit a style that is relational and field dependent. They suggest that many people from these groups are more improvisational and intuitive than sequential and structured; more interested in material with social or concrete content than abstract material; more holistic than analytic; and more cooperative than competitive. Most European-American males (most faculty members) and Asian-American males would tend to fall into the opposite categories. They have been socialized through their culture and the academic tradition to value analytic, structured, abstract approaches. The danger that this research warns against is that faculty might view differences from the traditional norm as deficits, devaluing the work of some students and preventing them from learning well.

Gender Differences

Similarly, there is a body of literature on cognitive development in women that discusses patterns in the way women take in and process information. Belenky et al. (1986) and Baxter Magolda (1992) have looked closely at epistemological development. Their findings are often compared with a model posed by Perry (1970), whose research was conducted with a sample of students that was mostly male. (See page 248 of the 8th edition of *Teaching Tips* for a description of his work.) Although the recent studies resist the strict association of one pattern with male students and one with females, they do discuss contrasting styles that are gender-related. Both Belenky et al. and Baxter Magolda find that development in the women they studied culminates in levels of thinking that are as complex as those described by Perry but are qualitatively different at each stage in gender-related ways. Baxter Magolda, for example, describes four levels of epistemological reflection: absolute, transitional, independent, and contextual knowing. There are rough parallels to these within the schemes of both Perry and Belenky et al. Within each of the first three levels described by Baxter Magolda, however, students demonstrate contrasting approaches, generally termed "relational" and "abstract." For example, transitional knowers, the most prevalent type of knowers among traditional-age college students, demonstrate two patterns: the interpersonal pattern, found more frequently in women, and the impersonal, found more frequently in men. Although both genders are transitional knowers in that they view knowledge as uncertain (at least in some areas) and understanding as more important than acquiring and remembering information, they demonstrate different gender-related patterns (see Table 22-1). The patterns described by Belenky et al. are compatible with these findings.

One area of research that documents how different ways of knowing affect classroom learning is the literature on classroom participation. Several researchers, such as Sadkar and Sadkar (1992), Allen and Niss (1990), and Trujillo (1986), have found in empirical studies that in classroom discussion white males speak more frequently and for longer periods than white females and males and females of color and that the latter are treated deferentially by teachers. Clearly, the style associated with European-American males is dominant in many American college classrooms, making it difficult for others to participate.

Table 22-1
Gender-Related Patterns of Thinking in Traditional-Age College Students

Interpersonal	*Impersonal*
Want to exchange ideas with others	Want to debate ideas
Seek rapport with the instructor	Want to be challenged by the instructor
Want evaluation to take individual differences into account	Want fair and practical evaluation
Resolve uncertainty by personal judgment	Resolve uncertainty by logic and research

Working with Different Styles

What can faculty do about styles? First, teachers can be aware that different styles exist. They can reflect on their own style and on the extent to which their preference for a style leads to teaching practices that exclude others. They can be alert to stylistic differences among their students, drawing upon the literature on gender and cultural differences, being careful to note individual characteristics of a particular student before assuming that he or she will demonstrate characteristics associated with her or his group.

Secondly, teachers can use varied instructional approaches. Moving between lecture, discussion, small group work, experiential learning, simulations, and other strategies allows more possibilities for students to find learning opportunities and for all to expand their own stylistic repertoires. Similarly, using redundancy in teaching modalities, such as visual aids accompanying verbal descriptions, helps students with different stylistic preferences or physical abilities to learn. Providing for options in assignments, such as a choice of an individual term paper or a collaborative project, or options in assessment, such as the choice of an essay or oral exam, is another helpful approach.

Third, teachers can evaluate work from multiple perspectives. For example, rather than viewing a personal narrative by a nontraditional-age student as "subjective, emotional, and unscholarly" it can be seen as an alternative kind of contribution to the traditional footnoted and impersonal paper, each valuable in a different way. Welcoming comments that seek synthesis and understanding rather than argumentation and analysis can promote more balanced discussion. Rewarding collaboration as well as individual effort can affirm those students whose strengths and values are in social interaction.

Being Treated Fairly

Egalitarian treatment of students is a very valued norm in American higher education. Grading anonymously, giving all students the same amount of time to complete a test or assignment, and requiring the same number and type of assignments by each student are common practices. Teachers often say, "I treat all students the same." Yet a closer look reveals that they do not treat all students the same, nor should they. Students with disabilities are often allowed more time for exams, the help of a reader, or a special setting for taking the test. Non-native speakers may be allowed to use dictionaries during test- taking and their work may be graded more for content than expression of ideas. Equal treatment involves not necessarily *same* treatment, then, but treatment that respects the individual needs of particular learners.

While teachers may readily accept different treatment for students who are disabled, non-native speakers, or even those older students who have hearing impairments or work slowly, they find it much more difficult to justify different treatment based on gender or cultural characteristics. Once again, however, beginning with the individual student is important. It is important to have expectations that are appropriate to the student. Some disjuncture between the student's point of entry and the dominant culture may occur and balance should be sought. For example, students coming from cultures where time is viewed fluidly may have difficulty understanding that due dates will be interpreted literally or that class begins promptly on the hour. Most students have learned to be bicultural and to operate under different sets of assumptions based on the cultural context. Others, however, may need help. It may be necessary to have individual conversations with such students emphasizing the expectations or giving reminders about due dates. It may be important to tolerate a few mistakes before penalizing students or to rethink the cultural-embedment of the rule. A conversation at the start of the course on expectations and standards, coupled with a clear syllabus, can help communications immeasurably.

Teachers can also consider cultural or gender-related issues that may impact class discussion. Many female students or male and female students from Native-American or Asian-American backgrounds have been socialized to value listening more than speaking. For them, a class participation grading scheme based on number of contributions in class may be problematic. Fair treatment might be based on quality of comment rather than quantity or on performance in dyad or small group, rather than whole class, conversation. Students who are from more reflective than spontaneous cultures can be helped by giving the class time for silent thought before responses are solicited. They may need to learn the culture. Conversely, students from the dominant culture may learn from them, incorporating the strengths of silent reflection into class routines. Myra and David Sadkar (1992) recommend that teachers ask an observer to record participation levels in their classes to give them a sense of the patterns that are occurring so that they may avoid the pitfall of unequal discussion.

Inherent in all discussion about fairness is mutuality. The need for order and routine must be balanced by appreciation for variation and richness of perspective. Strongly forcing students from nontraditional backgrounds to acculturate to the institution in order to succeed prevents the institution from learning and expanding its potential. Pervading considerations of social diversity are issues involved in the ongoing revitalization of colleges as places of learning.

Supplementary Readings

L. Border and N. Chism (eds.), *Teaching for Diversity, New Directions in Teaching and Learning, 49* (San Francisco: JosseyBass, 1992). This collection of essays treats the following topics: the culture of the classroom, learning styles of diverse learners, gender equity in the classroom, feminist pedagogy, and developing programs to promote inclusive teaching. Descriptions of successful programs and a resource guide are included.

J. H. Cones, J. F. Noonan, and J. Jahna (eds.), *Teaching Minority Students, New Directions in Teaching and Learning, 16* (San Francisco: Jossey-Bass, 1983). This sourcebook contains many insightful chapters on how majority faculty and others can explore their own racial assumptions in order to work more effectively with underrepresented students.

M. F. Green (ed.), *Minorities on Campus: A Handbook for Enhancing Diversity* (Washington, D.C.: American Council on Education, 1988). Chapter 8 of this overview volume deals directly with teaching, learning, and curriculum issues. Many program examples are given.

G. Pemberton, *On Teaching the Minority Student: Problems and Strategies* (Brunswick, ME: Bowdoin College, 1988). This guide discusses problems and specific strategies for interactions both in and outside the classroom.

Racial Identity Development: Understanding Racial Dynamics in College Classrooms and on Campus

RITA HARDIMAN AND BAILEY W. JACKSON

In recent years, educators in higher education have paid increased attention to the ways that interactions among students from diverse social groups are manifested everywhere on campus. Of particular concern are the effects of these interactions on both the social and academic life of the campus community. It is apparent that these interactions are not what they could or should be. As the academy first tried to increase the numbers of students from underrepresented social groups and then established academic and social support programs, its efforts were divided between integration of socially diverse populations into the existing campus community and creation of shared multicultural communities that maintained the integrity of diverse social groups. Instead of expecting students from underrepresented social groups to conform to preexisting college norms, college faculty and administrators now seem to be open to the new perspectives and expectations these students bring with them to the campus and classroom (Levine, 1991). This shift in the understanding and definition of diversity could have significant implications for campus climate, student interactions, student personnel programming, and the curriculum.

It is useful to note that the most significant shift in the evolution of approaches to social diversity on campus can be described as a shift from asking *who* is on campus to understanding *how* each group views the world as a function of its experiences with social injustice and the influence of cultural orientation (Border and Chism, 1992; Jones, 1990; Jackson and Hardiman, 1988; Ho, 1987). It is clear to us that these two issues, which we differentiate for emphasis, are not only related but indeed inseparable and must be factored in if we are to have any understanding of student identity. In other words, it is difficult if not impossible to understand group differences merely as differences in cultural expression. We must also recognize that the various manifestations of social oppression, such as racism, ethnocentrism, or sexism, have a significant impact on the worldview, self-concept, self-esteem, and behavior of both those who benefit from the system of social oppression (dominants) and those who are victims of this system (targets).

In this chapter we focus on the intersection of social diversity and social justice at the individual level of personal belief, attitude, and behavior, by presenting a model of racial identity development that makes several assumptions: the identity development of both dominant and targeted group members is influenced by White racism in the United States; this identity development can be described as shifts in worldview or consciousness in sequential stages; individual interactions within groups as well as between groups are influenced by the developmental stage of one's racial identity (Jackson, 1976a, 1976b; Hardiman, 1982). We understand *racial identity* to mean a sense of self in the context of one's racial group membership, which includes all aspects of that group's culture. Racial identity development theory "concerns the psychological implications of racial group membership; that is, belief systems that evolve in reaction to perceived differential racial group membership" (Helms, 1990, p. 4; see also Cross, Parham, and Helms, in press; Abrams and Hogg, 1990; Smith, 1991). We understand this perceived racial group membership as developmental, in that, as with other developmental processes, one's racial identity changes over time to become more congruent with one's range of experiences, personal beliefs, and other dimen-

"Racial Identity Development: Understanding Racial Dynamics in College Classrooms and on Campus," by Rita Hardiman and Bailey W. Jackson, reprinted from *New Directions for Teaching and Learning,* No. 52, Winter 1992, Jossey-Bass Publishers, Inc.

sions of self-identity.

In the early 1970s, one of the authors pioneered in what has since emerged as the field of racial identity development and, writing independently of Cross, developed the model of Black identity development that closely resembles the model reported here (Jackson, 1976a, 1976b; Cross, 1971, 1978). Jackson's work was germinating during the latter years of the contemporary civil rights movement and focused on how Black Americans develop individual identities around their understanding of their Blackness—that is, their social group identification and affiliation within the social context of racism. Both Jackson and Cross argued not only that Black Americans constitute a distinct cultural group, but also that their cultural group has experienced a history of systemic oppression as a racial minority. Therefore, their individual identities as Blacks and as Americans are affected both by Black culture and by American racism.

The work of Hardiman (1979), a colleague with Jackson at the University of Massachusetts, became the first model of White identity development, that is, the first model to describe how members of a dominant racial identity group (Whites) develop a consciousness of racial identity.

This chapter will present a synthesis of both authors' evolving work on the development of racial identity in Black and White Americans. (We use the racial/color designators in this chapter, rather than the ethnic terms African American or European American, to highlight the "discrimination" rather than the "diversity" aspect of the interaction.) The racial identity development model will help teachers and administrators alike understand the developmental processes that Black and White students are undergoing (see Tatum, 1992; Mann and Moser, 1991) and, in fact, may assist faculty and staff in understanding their own racial identity processes. It describes how racism affects the development of a sense of group identity for Blacks and Whites by examining the increasingly conscious attention both dominant group members (Whites) and target group members (Blacks) experience as they struggle with racism and strive to attain liberated racial identities in a persistently racist environment. The authors are White and Black, respectively, and have each focused their research and writing on those two racial groups. However, the reader should not assume that we view racism as uniquely a Black-White issue. Racism in the United States affects all targeted racial groups as well as persons of mixed heritage. Other racial identity models are also available; see Kim (1981) for Asian Americans, Hayes-Bautista (1974) for Chicanos, and Wijeyesinghe (1992) for Black/White biracial identity factors. These racial identity development models can be viewed as road maps of the journey from an identity in which racism and domination are internalized to an identity that is affirming and liberated from racism. This road map highlights five major points of reference, each point descriptive of a stage or predominant mode of consciousness. *Stage* is a convenient metaphor for states of consciousness or worldviews that are developmental in nature and that change over time in response to experience and knowledge to become more complex and more adequate internal reference points for examining and understanding one's own beliefs, values, and behaviors.

We have named the five stages (1) *naive*, without consciousness of social identity; (2) *acceptance* of the prevailing social definitions of Blackness and Whiteness; (3) *resistance*, the rejection of the racist definition of Blackness and Whiteness; (4) *redefinition*, suggesting the renaming of one's racial identity; and (5) *internalization*, the integration of the redefined racial identity into all aspects of the self (see Figure 2.1). The acceptance and resistance stages are described in relation to two possible manifestations, passive (unconscious) or active (conscious). The stages of redefinition and internalization involve by their very nature, conscious, active choices and therefore have no passive-stage manifestations, whereas the naive stage is by definition not conscious.

The transition from one stage to another usually occurs when an individual recognizes that his or her current worldview is either illogical or contradicted by new experience and information, detrimental to a healthy self-concept or no longer serving some important self-interest. During the transition periods, a person may appear to him or herself and to others to be in two stages simultaneously, for indeed they are exiting from one stage and entering the next stage at the same time.

The racial identity development model will be presented as follows in this section. There will be a general overview of the stage of development presented, to be followed by separate descriptions of the nature of each stage for a White person and a Black person.

Stage One—Naive

The naive stage of consciousness describes the consciousness of race in childhood, when there is little or

Figure 2.1
Stages of Racial Identity Development

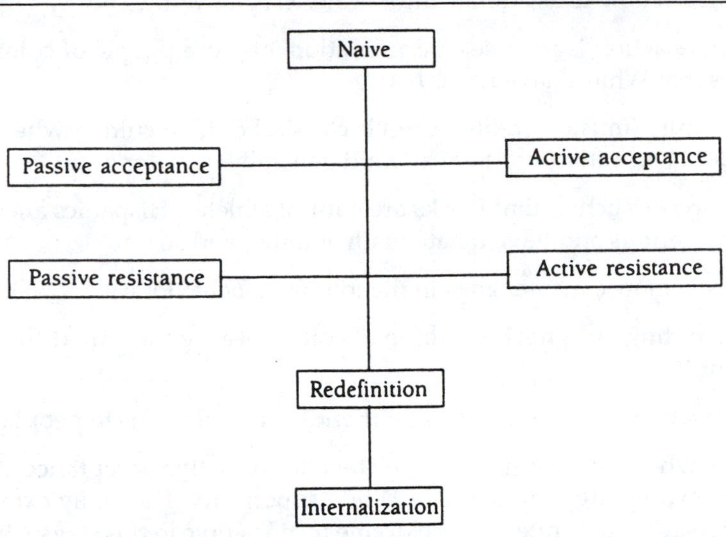

no social awareness of race per se (Derman-Sparks, Higa, and Sparks, 1980). During this period members of both dominant groups and target groups are vulnerable to the logic system and worldview of their socializing agents (for example, parents, teachers, the media, and significant others). Children at this stage become aware of the physical differences and some obvious cultural differences between themselves and others, and while they may not feel completely comfortable with people who are different, they generally do not feel fearful, hostile, or either inferior or superior. They may display a curiosity about or an interest in understanding the differences between people, but they have not yet learned to see some differences as more normal, or correct, or valued than others in the social world. This stage generally covers the developmental period between birth and about four years of age.

In the transition from naive to acceptance, two related changes take place in the racial worldviews of both Blacks and Whites. One is that children begin to learn and adopt an ideology about their own racial group and as well as other racial groups. They internalize many covert and some overt messages, that being Black means being less than, that Whiteness equals superiority or normality, beauty, importance, and power. The second change is that members of both racial groups begin to learn that there are formal and informal rules, institutions, and authority figures that permit some behaviors and prohibit others, and that people encounter negative consequences for stepping out of these rules regarding how the races relate to each other.

Stage Two—Acceptance

The naive stage of consciousness is followed by a stage of acceptance. In one sense, the stage of acceptance represents the absorption, whether conscious or unconscious, of an ideology of racial dominance and subordination which touches upon all facets of personal and public life. A person at this stage has accepted the messages about racial group membership, the superiority of the dominant group members and the dominant culture, and the inferiority of target group people and cultures.

Acceptance Stage for Whites

For Whites in passive acceptance, there may not be any conscious identification with being White. Whiteness is taken for granted and seen as normal. Whites in passive acceptance are thus more subtly racist in perpetuating dominant beliefs and actions, because they are unable to see themselves as racists or as actively prejudiced people, whom they describe as being actively or vocally against targeted racial groups (such as the Ku Klux Klan). In this stage White people may hold the following attitudes and beliefs:

> That Blacks, Asians, Native Americans, and some Hispanics are "culturally deprived" and need help to learn how to assimilate into "American" or White society
>
> That affirmative action is reverse discrimination, because people of color are being given opportunities that Whites have never had
>
> That White culture (music, art, literature) is classical or high culture whereas the culture of people of color is primitive, craft not art, and generally of lower class
>
> Various stereotypes such as that Blacks are natural athletes, Hispanics are naturally violent, Asians are mysterious and have innate math abilities, and so on.

Whites in passive acceptance may engage in the following behaviors:

> Excluding, avoiding, or ignoring people of color, because they are different or strange or not quite right
>
> Patronizing behavior, such as being extra friendly and solicitous to people of color.

In contrast, Whites who move from the naive stage to the active acceptance stage tend to be more vocal and forthright in expressing their sense of White superiority. They may express consciousness of White identity and pride in being White. In the extreme form, people in this stage may actually join White supremacist organizations. The recent emergence of "White student unions" may be one contemporary example of this tendency. Various forms of racial harassment and acting out are also indicative of the active acceptance stage, made easier on college campuses by the influence of alcohol and peer pressure.

Acceptance Stage for Blacks

The Black person in the acceptance stage of consciousness follows the prevailing notion that "White is right." This person attempts to gain resources—approval, sense of worth, goods, power, money—by accepting and conforming to White social, cultural, and institutional standards, more as an unexamined response to the dominant social mode than an examined explicit pattern of behavior consciously adopted for personal survival. The internal acceptance of these standards as a worldview requires the rejection and devaluation of all that is Black. A Black person who consciously (active acceptance) or unconsciously (passive acceptance) adopts the prevailing White view of the world weakens his or her positive self-concept or positive view of Black people. This consciousness typically causes a Black person to avoid interactions with other Blacks and to desire interactions with Whites, a behavioral pattern that may at first seem to conform to the dominant mode of traditional college campuses or the expectations of some White peers or teachers. Black people in this stage may exhibit these beliefs and behaviors:

Beliefs:

> People are people, and if Blacks just work hard they will be judged by their merits.
>
> There is no race problem. The problem is with those Blacks who don't want to work and better themselves. They are messing it up for the rest of us.
>
> White people are generally smarter than Black people, and White people get ahead because they work harder at succeeding than Blacks do.

Behaviors:

> Seeks interaction with and validation from Whites and White social groups and avoids organizations, committees, social groups that focus on race or racism
>
> Goes along with or excuses racist behavior on the part of Whites.

The transition from acceptance to resistance marks a period that can be confusing and often painful for both targets (Blacks) and dominants (Whites). The transition generally evolves over time and usually results from a number of events that have a cumulative effect. People in an acceptance consciousness begin to be aware of experiences that contradict the acceptance worldview experiences they had earlier ignored or passed off as isolated, exceptional events. Gradually, as a person begins to encounter more dissonant issues, the isolated incidents form a discernible pattern. The contradictions that initiate the transition period can arise from interactions with people, social events, information presented in classes, stories in the media, or responses to so-called racial incidents on campus. Many students of color as well as White students were shaken by overt acts of harassment and hostility toward students of color in the late 1980s. Many who had seen racism as a 1960s issue began to reevaluate their thinking in the light of the numerous acts of disrespect and violence on campus.

Dominant group members experience difficult emotions as they exit the acceptance stage and enter into the resistance consciousness. These range from guilt and embarrassment at having been naive or foolish enough to believe the racist messages they received, to anger and disgust at the people and institutions that taught them. Emotions seem to be especially intense for those who were enthusiastic supporters of the acceptance worldview. As their way of viewing the world crumbles, they are often afraid and uncertain what the implications of this new awareness will be. Target group members who begin to exit from the stage of acceptance typically share a reluctant acknowledgment of their collusion with their own victimization and an emerging understanding of the harmful effects of holding on to the acceptance consciousness. In Freireian terms, the members of these target groups begin to become aware of the many ways they have played host to their oppressor.

Stage Three—Resistance

The initial questioning that begins during the exit phase of acceptance continues with greater intensity during the third stage, resistance. The worldview that people adopt at resistance is dramatically different from that of acceptance. At this stage members of both target and dominant groups begin to understand and recognize racism in many of its complex and multiple manifestations—at the individual and institutional, conscious and unconscious, intentional and unintentional attitudinal, behavioral, and policy levels. Individuals become painfully aware of the numerous ways in which covert as well as overt racism affect them daily as members of racial identity groups.

Resistance Stage for Whites

There are two manifestations of the resistance stage, as there are for the acceptance stage. For Whites in passive resistance there are the beginnings of a critical consciousness of the existence of racism and White people's relationship to it, but it is generally an awareness accompanied by little action or behavioral change. Whites in passive resistance may see the problem but feel personally impotent to affect it. There is a prevailing feeling that the issue is too big and nothing can be done about it, especially by only one concerned person. The active resistance stage is quite different, however. White persons who acquire the active resistance consciousness have a more deeply developed critical consciousness about racism, and also have a sense of personal ownership of the problem. That is, they are aware that they too are racist, and that whatever they do or fail to do is either part of the problem or part of the solution. At this stage, Whites understand that they have internalized racial prejudice, misinformation, and lies about themselves as Whites and about people of color. They also realize that their behavior has been racist in at least a passive sense and perhaps at times in active, conscious ways.

The resistance stage engenders powerful emotions in White persons, ranging from embarrassment and anger to disbelief, shame, guilt, and occasionally despair. Some Whites in active resistance become so distressed at being part of an oppressive dominant group that they distance themselves from other Whites and White culture by gravitating to communities of color and trying to adopt a new identity. This response is particularly common among college-age students who live in a campus environment where exploring new identities, political orientations, and different roles is commonplace. This behavior also reflects the confusion of White students at this stage, who are in a process of rejecting the racism and oppressiveness of White individuals, institutions, and culture and as such do not want to see themselves as part of that group. Another indicator of the learning process is the realization that confronting and changing the White community is the special responsibility of Whites who are antiracist. The focus of energy shifts, from being a good "liberal" to people of color, to being a real agent of change with one's

White peers.

At the active resistance stage, White people may hold the following types of attitudes and beliefs:

Racism in the United States is White racism and I have been infected with it.

The cultures of Black, Latino, Asian, and Native people have been misrepresented by racism.

Racism is systemic and is not simply prejudice or discrimination in one facet of life.

Whites in active resistance may show the following behavioral indicators:

Indiscriminately challenging racism in many spheres, by letter writing, picketing, and verbal confrontations

Expressing solidarity with people of color through wearing buttons, participating in marches, donating money, and so on

Distancing themselves from White culture and people, and simultaneously "adopting" or borrowing the traditions and cultural expressions of communities of color.

Whites in passive resistance may have attitudes and beliefs similar to those of Whites in active resistance, but the behavioral indicators may be absent. For many Whites in passive resistance, a key indicator of the stage may be attempts to "drop out."

Resistance Stage for Blacks

The acknowledgment of the existence of racism and its negative effects is typical of one who is exiting the acceptance stage. This stage is usually followed by the first manifestation of the resistance stage—active, often vehement questioning. Once a Black person has acknowledged the existence of racism, he or she usually desires to find out more about it. These values, moral codes, and codes of personal and professional development, handed down by the dominant White culture and those who collude with their victimization, are the first things to be scrutinized through the lens of this new consciousness. Gradually the target group member becomes more skilled at identifying the existence of racist premises that have been woven into the fabric of social experience. This person finds that his or her hostility toward White people, as well as toward fellow Blacks (or other targeted people of color) who collude with White people, is intensifying.

The often overt expression of hostile reactions to the existence and effects of racism marks the transition from the entry to the adoption phase of the resistance stage. It is at this point in the resistance stage that the Black individual has fully internalized the antithesis of the acceptance stage of development. It is here that the person fully experiences anger, pain, and rage. The combination of these emotions with a more intellectual understanding of the manifestations and effects of racism may appear to be all consuming. Some Black students who enter this stage during their college years may find it difficult to remain focused on course work, especially if that work seems irrelevant to their emerging concern for Blackness and for racial issues. We have seen some students at this stage become heavily involved with student groups and with campus efforts that have an activist focus. Many of these students are motivated, capable, and gifted academically. Their turning away from their course work is not due to inability. Rather they are drawn in a compelling and often consuming way to engage in social action, through seminars, teach-ins, demonstrations, and other efforts to confront racism and effect change on their campus regarding racial issues. In other instances, the Black person may find that to experience the resistance stage fully results in the loss of the "benefits" that were acquired when the acceptance consciousness was adopted. Blacks may choose the path of passive resistance, in the hope that they will be able to stay in favor with White society while rejecting racism. Typically, this strategy proves too frustrating and contradictory to sustain. For most Blacks at this stage the primary task is to discontinue the pattern of collusion with their own victimization. It is time to cleanse their consciousness of those internalized racist notions that have served to stifle or retard their personal development and to stop passively accepting the racism of their environment.

During the course of the resistance stage, the Black person discovers a greater scope for action and a sense of personal power. At this stage, students who rail against the "system" discover that they can make that system respond. While the power that is gained at this stage is not of the same type and quantity available to the dominant group, it is power nonetheless. The student recognizes that to varying degrees and in a variety of situations, he or she can stop things from happening. For many this is the first lesson in personal and social power. Also during the course of the resistance stage, the person begins to recognize that a considerable amount of energy has been put into unlearning as well as undoing considerable earlier programming about his or her identity as a Black person. The primary focus at this stage is the exact reverse of acceptance: it is directed toward being clear about "who I am not." This person is now ready to put energy into the questions "Who am I? Who are we?" Some indicators of the resistance stage for Blacks may include the following attitudes and behaviors:

Challenging and confronting Whites, especially those in positions of authority; and challenging or writing off Black faculty and administrators who are seen as not Black enough or as colluding with the White system

Testing the credentials of Black staff and faculty to determine whether they are truly revolutionary

Denigrating all that is White, and simultaneously glorifying all that is Black, in an unrelenting manner.

Stage 4—Redefinition

The transition from resistance to redefinition occurs when members of both racial groups realize that they do not really know who they are, racially speaking, or what their racial group membership means to them. At resistance, they recognized that their sense of themselves as Whites or as Blacks has been defined for them in a White racist environment, and they actively sought to question it and reject aspects of it. Now they are no longer actively consumed by rejection, but the loss of prior self-definition of Blackness or Whiteness leaves them with a void. Attempts to grapple with the question what it means to be White and antiracist, or what it means to be Black, lead to the redefinition stage.

Redefinition Stage for Whites

Having experienced a period of conflict at the resistance stage, Whites are now beginning to move beyond this conflict toward a resolution and a new racial identity. They begin to refocus or redirect their energy in order to define Whiteness in a way that is not dependent on racism or on the existence of perceived deficiencies in other groups.

Before this stage, Whites are not terribly concerned with their racial identity. Up to this point they have been focusing on people of color as "different from" or deficient or developing a consciousness of racism and reacting to it. The consequences of experiencing the resistance stage has left Whites feeling negative about their Whiteness, confused about their role in dealing with racism, and isolated from much of their racial group. Therefore, developing a deeper understanding of the meaning of Whiteness and its connection to racism, together with those aspects of White European American culture that affirm their own needs as individual members of that social group, is a necessary part of the redefinition stage for Whites. In contrast to the negative feelings about being White at the earlier Resistance stage, Whites at redefinition can begin to develop a new sense of comfort and identification with their cultural heritage. This recognition of the strengths of White culture and people results in a feeling of pride in the group membership, without a personal feeling of superiority, and without disclaiming the larger system of societal dominance focused on at the earlier resistance stage. There is a recognition that all cultures and racial groups have unique and different traits that enrich the human experience, and that no race or culture is superior to another. They are all unique, different, and adaptive.

Redefinition Stage for Blacks

The redefinition stage is the point in the developmental process at which the Black person is concerned with defining himself or herself in terms that are independent of the perceived strengths or weaknesses of Whites and the dominant White culture. The redefinition stage is particularly significant because it is here that Black people shift their attention and energy away from a concern for the nature of their interaction with dominants toward a concern for primary contact and interaction with other Blacks at the same stage of consciousness. Unlike the Black person at the acceptance and resistance stages, the Black person with a redefinition consciousness is not concerned either with emulating or rejecting dominants and dominant culture. The redefining person does not see interaction with dominants as necessary and useful in the quest for a positive or nurturing sense of self and racial identity. Because renaming is the primary concern in this person's life, he or she begins a search for paradigms that will facilitate the accomplishment of this task.

This search can begin in a number of places, but for most Black people it seems to begin with the conscious or unconscious formation of a new reference group. As mentioned above, it is critical that this new reference group consist of other Blacks with a redefinition perspective. Black people at this stage are particularly concerned with the perspective of other Black people and as a consequence tend to limit their interactions to Blacks, where this is an option. But this type of behavior is often viewed negatively by members of both dominant and target groups at earlier stages of consciousness. Whereas students in the resistance stage who are members of targeted groups are generally labeled troublemakers, students in redefinition may be labeled separatist or self-segregating. Black students at this stage have a particular need to participate in, or create where none exist, programs, centers, or housing units where they can interact closely and maintain dialogue with other Black students in the same stage. While some Black students in redefinition may begin to see connections between the racism that Blacks experience and the racism experienced by other people of color (Native Americans, Hispanics, and Asian Americans), they may not be invested in forming alliances or coalitions with members of those groups. The psychological tasks at this stage are very in-group (that is Black) centered, and adopting a multicultural worldview, rather than a Black worldview, may be premature at this point.

It may be difficult for non-Blacks to interact with Blacks who are occupied with redefinition issues. Non- Blacks may fail to understand that the redefinition stage is chiefly concerned with engaging in relationships and activities that will further the search for new and different ways of redefining one's self and one's social group membership. Old allegiances are being reevaluated. Thus many relationships that appeared essential in the past seem not to be as important at this stage.

The search for a new understanding of Blackness often begins by reclaiming the group heritage. Revisiting or uncovering their heritage or culture, Blacks often find values, traditions, customs, philosophical assumptions, and concepts of time, work, and family that are appealing and nurturing. They find that many elements of Black culture that have been handed down through the generations still affect their lives, and the uniqueness of their group becomes clearer. They come to understand that they are more than the victims of racism, more than just people who are not the same as the dominant group. These targets come to experience their Blackness in a way that engenders pride.

Indicators of the redefinition stage for Blacks include:

- Literally changing their names, taking on African or Muslim names
- Demonstrating a concern for presenting a Black perspective or an African or Afrocentric perspective in a variety of settings
- Changing friendships, academic major, career directions, or choice of living situation and redirecting energy and focus from White-oriented choices to Black people and Black-oriented concerns.

The redefinition stage is seen less often in the traditional college-age White student than in the Black college student. In fact, although more students of color may enter this stage during college, their numbers are not large. It is more likely that both White students and Black students will enter college at the (passive) acceptance stage and experience primarily the (active or passive) resistance stages only during their college years. For this reason we have chosen to provide more detail about these earlier two stages and have restricted our description of redefinition and internalization to the basics.

Stage 5—Internalization

The transition from the redefinition stage to the internalization stage occurs when an individual begins to integrate some of the newly defined values, beliefs, and behaviors into all aspects of life. As with any other developmental task, it takes time and a variety of opportunities for the new aspects of a person's identity to begin the process of integration with the rest of that person's identity. When the redefined sense of racial identity is fully integrated, the new values or beliefs occur naturally and are internalized as a part of the person.

Indicators of internalization for Blacks include:

Recognition that their Black identity is a critical part of them, but not the only significant aspect of their identity

Ability to consider other identity issues, and other issues of oppression, since some resolution of the struggle for a redefined Black identity has occurred

Ability to work effectively with Blacks at all stages of identity development in assisting them to deal with whatever issues their stage of development presents, and not judge or act punitively toward Blacks who are at earlier stages, but help them achieve a positive Black identity.

Indicators of internalization for Whites include:

A clear sense of their own self-interests as members of the White group in ending racism; acting on that self- interest to confront racial oppression proactively

An understanding of the uniqueness of their cultural backgrounds; not seeing others as "culturally different" and Whites as "normal," but rather understanding how White European American culture is different as well.

Applications and Conclusions

It perhaps is self-evident at this point in our discussion that college campuses are frequently the arena in which the processes of developing the racial identity of students, faculty, and staff are visibly played out. One has to look no further than White student unions and acts of racial harassment to see Whites in active acceptance. One can also see the stage of active resistance and occasionally redefinition appearing in the "Third World Affairs" pages of student newspapers and in race-specific cultural and social centers, such as Malcolm X centers, Latino student caucuses, and American Indian student centers. It should also be clear that our campuses are places where students and others interact with each other from their respective, frequently clashing stages of racial identity development. How should faculty and administrators respond?

1. *It should be our goal as educators to facilitate development in students, not stifle it or hide from it.* As difficult as it is to do, we believe that it is necessary first to acknowledge and accept wherever a student is in his or her developmental journey, not to condemn or try to hasten it. Only if we understand and respond to each student's developmental stage can we expect that student to grow at his or her own pace.

   It is not easy for faculty and administrators to absorb students' anger as expressed at the resistance stage. Well-intentioned administrators are particularly vulnerable to onslaughts from students who are (rightfully) angered by acts of racism or harassment on campus. We have seen administrators disregard students' anger or call for an investigation or a policy change, dismissing the behavior as mere adolescent "acting out" or, more cynically, as the "annual Spring protest." As difficult as it may be, administrators, especially those who are White, do represent a power structure that students must confront: first, because most institutions frankly deserve to be challenged, since no campus is free of racism; second, because students need to exercise their emerging sense of empowerment, as full citizens; third, because their often newly established perspective, within resistance, focuses their attention on resistance as a total and absorbing worldview. We have also seen errors in misinterpreting White students' assaults against students of color as "pranks" or late adolescent acting out rather than expressions of a worldview of active acceptance of White supremacy. We describe active acceptance as a "stage," but our experience is that not all students will move beyond it, and students should not be allowed to violate other students' rights because "it is just a stage they are going through."

2. *As faculty and staff, we should look at these stages in the light of our own life experiences.* Where are we in our own racial identity development process? None of us are neutral players in this world; we bring all our "baggage" to our profession. Our racial identity development stage influences the curriculum we develop, our choice of bibliography, and even how we organize our classroom environments. For example, we know of a recent situation where a White professor, acting out of "liberal" beliefs, refused to begin a class until the Black students dispersed themselves around the classroom, and stopped "segregating" themselves.

3. *We should not be surprised by the ways in which our students interact.* "Vertical" social group relationships (dominant and targeted) and "horizontal" relationships (within or across targeted groups) (Jackson and Hardiman, 1988) can express themselves in sharp differences of ideology or belief, which can seem confusing if one looks for monolithic ethnic and cultural expressions without considering the role of individual racial identity filters as well.

4. *We should understand broad differences in social identity perspective.* Recognizing that social identity is the generic of which racial identity is a particular instance (Jackson and Hardiman, 1988; Jones, 1990) will enable college teachers and administrators to prepare for differences of understanding and belief by students across their range of social group differences as filtered through their individual developmental lenses. For example, Black male students may be at one perspective in their racial identity (active resistance, perhaps, or redefinition), but at another concerning sexism or anti-Semitism (passive or active acceptance possibly); similarly, Jewish female students may be in active resistance or redefinition with regard to their Jewish identity and at another place on racism or heterosexism. The same unevenness among racial, ethnic, and other social identity profiles is just as likely to characterize faculty and administrators as students.

In this chapter we have presented a model of racial identity development for Black and White Americans and discussed the application of racial identity development stages as filters for understanding the divergent and often conflicting behavior of students on campus as they grapple with racial issues. We also argued at the beginning of this chapter for the consideration of issues of dominance and oppression in our discussions of diversity issues in higher education, because we see social group differences and their accompanying forms of group bias and discrimination as inseparable.

We have suggested in this chapter that faculty and administrators' failure to understand and respect the development of racial identity in their students can lead to inappropriate and ineffective responses to volatile racial situations on campus. We present this model to inform behavior and the selection of strategies and responses, but we caution against anyone's using this model simplistically to label or stereotype or pigeonhole students or others. We present the stages for purposes of initial understanding, as if a person were to move neatly in totality from one stage to the next, whereas the reality is that most people are in several stages simultaneously, holding simultaneously different perspectives on the complex range of issues and questions that enter into their equally complicated racial identity. Rather than misusing it as a set of labels or new stereotypes, our hope is that readers will use this model to understand better the racial identity component of their own developmental processes, identify the individual characteristics or cues that constitute the broad brush strokes called "developmental stages," and thereby understand and respect the racial identity developmental processes that are likely to be stimulated by rapid changes in our social world and refracted back even more intensely onto our college campuses.

References

Abrams, D, and Hogg, M. A. (eds). *Social Identity Theory: Constructive and Critical Advances*. New York Springer-Verlag, 1990.

Border, L. L. B., and Chism, N. V. N. (eds.). *Teaching for Diversity*. New Directions for Teaching and Learning, no. 49. San Francisco: Jossey-Bass, 1992.

Cross, W. E., Jr. "The Negro-to-Black Conversion Experience: Toward a Psychology of Black Liberation." *Black World*, 1971, *20* (9), 13–27.

Cross, W. E., Jr. "Models of Psychological Nigrescence: A Literature Review." *Journal of Black Psychology*, 1978, *5* (1), 13–31.

Cross, W. E., Jr. *Shades of Black: Diversity in African-American Identity*. Philadelphia: Temple University Press, 1991.

Cross, W. E., Jr., Parham, T. A., and Helms, J. E. "Nigrescence Revisited: Theory and Research." In R. L. Jones (ed.), *Advances in Black Psychology*. Vol. 1. Berkeley, Calif.: Cobb & Henry, in press.

Dalton, J. C. (ed.). *Racism on Campus: Confronting Racial Bias Through Peer Interventions*. New Directions for Student Services, no. 56. San Francisco: Jossey-Bass, 1991.

Derman-Sparks, L, Higa, C. T., and Sparks, B. "Children, Race and Racism: How Race Awareness Develops." *Interracial Books for Children Bulletin*, 1980, *11* (3, 4), 3–9.

Hardiman, R. "White Identity Development Theory." Unpublished manuscript, University of Massachusetts, Amherst, 1979.

Hardiman, R. "While Identity Development: A Process-Oriented Model for Describing the Racial Consciousness of White Americans." Unpublished doctoral dissertation, University of Massachusetts, Amherst, 1982.

Hayes-Bautista, D. E. "Becoming Chicano: A 'Dis-Assimilation' Theory of Transformation of Ethnic Identity " Unpublished doctoral dissertation, University of California, San Francisco, 1974.

Helms, J. E. *Black and White Racial Identity: Theory, Research and Practice*. Westport, Conn.: Greenwood Press, 1990

Ho, M. K. *Family Therapy with Ethnic Minorities*. Newbury Park, Calif: Sage, 1987

Jackson, B. W. "Black Identity Development." In L. Golubschick and B. Persky (eds.), *Urban Social and Educational Issues*. Dubuque, Iowa: Kendall/Hunt 1976a.

Jackson, B. W. "The Function of a Theory of Black Identity Development in Achieving Relevance in Education for Black Students." Unpublished doctoral dissertation, University of Massachusetts, Amherst, 1976b.

Jackson, B. W., and Hardiman, R. "Oppression: Conceptual and Developmental Analysis." In M. Adams and L. S. Marchesani (eds.), *Racial and Cultural Diversity, Curricular Content and Classroom, Dynamics: A Manual for College Teachers*. Amherst: University of Massachusetts, 1988.

Jones, W. T. "Perspectives on Ethnicity." In L. V. Moore (ed.), *Evolving Theoretical Perspectives on Students*. New Directions for Student Services, no. 51. San Francisco: Jossey-Bass, 1990

Kim, J. "Processes of Asian American Identity Development: A Study of Japanese American Women's Perceptions of Their Struggle to Achieve Positive Identities as Americans of Asian Ancestry." Unpublished doctoral dissertation, University of Massachusetts, Amherst, 1981.

Levine, A. "Editorial: The Meaning of Diversity " *Change*, 1991, *23* (5), 4–5.

Mann, B. A., and Moser, R. M. "Model for Designing Peer-Initiated Activities to Promote Racial Awareness and an Appreciation of Differences " In J. Dalton (ed.), *Racism on Campus: Confronting Racial Bias Through Peer Interventions* New Directions for Student Services, no 56. San Francisco: Jossey- Bass, 1991.

Smith, E. J. "Ethnic Identity Development: Toward the Development of a Theory Within the Context of Majority/Minority Status." *Journal of Counseling & Development*, 1991, *70* (1), 181–188.

Tatum, B. D. "Talking About Race, Learning About Racism: The Application of Racial Identity Development Theory in the Classroom." *Harvard Educational Review*, 1992, *62* (1), 1–24.

Wijeyesinghe, C. "Towards An Understanding of the Racial Identity of Bi-Racial People: The Experience of Racial Self-Identification of African-American Euro-American Adults and the Factors Affecting Their Choices of Racial Identity." Unpublished doctoral dissertation, University of Massachusetts, Amherst, 1992.

PART III

Understanding Students and Teachers in the Classroom

Introduction

The college classroom is an interactional setting, a social system in miniature. Like any such social setting, the classroom can be analyzed in terms of the psychological characteristics of its participants, the interpersonal relationships and dynamics found in it, the normative forces that emerge within it, the wide social and cultural forces that impinge on it, and both the short-range and long-range consequences for the participants themselves. Each reading in Part III touches on one or another of the psychological, interpersonal, social and cultural aspects of the classroom. The readings have been divided into four sections: teacher and student expectations; teacher behaviors and practices; student-teacher interactions; and instruction and learning outcomes in the classroom.

A. Teacher and Student Expectations

Neither teachers nor students enter the classroom empty-handed; they bring with them a wide range of values, attitudes, goals, dispositions, and personal characteristics. Thus, the terms of the interaction between students and teachers are partially set before they even enter the classroom. Especially important in this regard are the expectations about teaching and learning held by the two groups. The three readings in this section are about such expectations and, in the last two readings, the way in which these expectations are (or are not) realized in the classroom.

The first reading, by Feldman, presents a synthesis of 31 studies in which students and faculty (at the same colleges) specified the instructional characteristics they considered important to good teaching and effective instruction. It was found that students and faculty were generally similar, though not identical in their views. The differences that did exist between the two groups across the various studies showed a pattern of students placing more importance than faculty on teachers being interesting, having good elocutionary skills, and being available and helpful. Students also emphasized the outcomes of instruction more than faculty did. Faculty placed more importance than did students on teachers being intellectually challenging, motivating students and setting high standards for them, and encouraging self-initiated learning.

The second and third readings, by Boice and by Mitchell, are directly about teachers' expectations and only indirectly about students' expectations. Boice presents results from a study of four cohorts of new faculty at two college campuses. He documents how the teaching styles and performance of these faculty members are determined, in part, by their actual experiences in conjunction with the expectations they have about themselves as teachers, about what students expect and want from them, about balancing the demands of teaching with those of researching, publishing and other activities, and about relationships with their more established colleagues. Mitchell describes and examines her personal expectations and perspectives as a minority professor in relation to the expectations and perceptions of students, colleagues and community residents. She does so in terms of what she sees as the visibility, vulnerability and viability of minority professors in the white academic community. She concludes that, although minority professors in predominantly white universities are immersed in systems of dual expectations, rules, and judgments created by institution and ethnicity, they can be viable members of both systems.

B. Teacher Behaviors and Practices

Many of the activities and much of the interaction in the classroom are initiated by the teacher. Important in understanding the dynamics of the college classroom, then, is the knowledge gained by systematic and reliable description or measurement of what teachers actually do when they teach. In the first of the three articles in this section, Barnes describes and analyzes instructor questioning as a potentially important facet of the instructional process. Her research is based on 40 classes at two public and two private undergraduate institutions. Each instructor gave permission to audiotape four class sessions. Among the findings of this study are that the majority of the teachers' questions were at low cognitive levels, that the most common questioning pattern was teacher lecture followed by a low-level cognitive question followed by more lecture, that there were no differences in questioning levels between beginning and advanced classes within each discipline group studied, and that there appeared to be a significant difference in the cognitive levels of teachers' questions between small and large schools but not between public and private institutions.

Statham, Richardson, and Cook also studied the questioning behavior of teachers in the classroom, but in this case as only one of the many behaviors and practices of teachers. As a source of data in this research, 167 teachers were observed in their classroom by trained observers who used a time-unit method to code, at five-second intervals, various dimensions of teaching behavior. Another source of data came from semi-structured, open-ended interviews with a purposive sample of 30 teachers (equally divided between women and men) almost all of whom were selected from the observation sample. From Statham, Richardson and Cook's book, all of Chapter 3 ("Basic Instructional Activities in Academia"), and the summaries of Chapter 4 ("Authority Management in the Classroom") and Chapter 5 ("Personalizations: Look into My Life") have been excerpted to form the second reading of this section. Because the focus of the authors' book is the possible gendered aspects of teaching, a major consideration of these chapters is the similarities and differences in teaching behaviors and practices of female and male teachers.

Gender of the teacher is not the only potential source of differences in teaching practices, as shown by the research of Murrray and Renaud (whose study is reprinted as the last reading of this section). Observing 401 faculty members in the classroom who were teaching undergraduate lecture or lecture-discussion courses at the University of Western Ontario, these researchers found differences in faculty's teaching behaviors by academic disciplines. Natural and social science teachers more frequently showed behaviors that facilitated structuring or organizing of the subject matter, whereas arts and humanities teachers behaved more frequently in ways that fostered student participation.

C. Student-Teacher Interactions

In the preface to their now classic and still valuable study of the college classroom, Richard Mann and his associates (1970) wrote the following about what they referred to as the "other part of teaching and learning":

> "This book presents a study of some of . . . the interpersonal and emotional events that occur in the classroom. It is by no means an assault on the importance of the content of education. It merely expands the focus to include aspects of the teacher-student interchange that are often ignored. The fact that as teachers we so often ignore the noncontent issues of the classroom can be traced partly to our ignorance and partly to our pessimism. Our ignorance is revealed when we find out how little we understand about what caused a particularly sluggish class or a confusing, violent interchange over a minor issue. Our ignorance is revealed when we find that for unknown reasons things which 'worked' one term flop terribly the next" (p. v).

In their consideration of the "world of emotional and interpersonal realities" in the classroom, they introduce the idea of the "internal workings" of the college classroom. It is these internal workings of the classroom—the emotional and interpersonal realities of the classroom, and the social and cultural ones as well—to which the readings of this section are directed.

In the first reading, Karp and Yoels study the meaning of student participation in the college classroom. They bring observational and questionnaire data to bear on both the organizational features of the college classroom and the situational definitions of the classrooms held by teachers and students. They maintain that these features and definitions promote an orientation of noninvolvement on the part of students. As one aspect of their argument, they suggest that college instructors appear to define the classroom as an instance of "focused" interaction whereas students appear to define it as an instance of an "unfocused" gathering.

One of Karp and Yoels's several specific findings is that in the ten classrooms they studied, male students played a more active role in the classes than did female students regardless of the teacher's gender although with female instructors the percentage of female participation sharply increased. The next selection, by Canada and Pringle, also contains data on the importance of gender to interaction in the college classroom. These researchers studied classroom interactions during the first five years of a former women's college's transition to mixed-sex education. They found that this interaction was altered by the transition and by the gender composition of the classes. Although male and female professors initiated comparable numbers of interactions in all-female classrooms, female professors initiated many more interactions and male professors initiated much fewer interactions in the mixed-sex classrooms. Moreover, the increasing presence of male students in the mixed-sex classrooms was associated with an overall decrease in professor-initiated interactions, student-initiated interactions, and female student-initiated follow-up interactions; at the same time, male student-initiated follow-up interactions increased.

Not all activities and behaviors in the classroom—by either teachers or students—are desirable or wanted ones. The third reading in this section, by Boice, analyzes class disturbances or, as he refers to them, "classroom incivilities." Based on this researcher's systematic observations of large survey courses, he found the most problematic classroom incivilities to be teachers displaying aloof, distancing mannerisms, teachers discouraging student involvement with fast-paced lectures, students' noisiness and indifference, students coming late and leaving early, and students' sarcastic remarks or gestures. As part of his analysis, Boice suggests some procedures that might work to lower the level of these classroom incivilities.

The last reading of this section, written by a teacher about her classroom experiences, is rich in ethnographic detail about classroom dynamics and the way in which larger social and cultural forces play a part in shaping these dynamics. Lewis focuses on the psychological, social and gender dynamics of a feminist classroom. She relates the strategies she uses in specific instances to subvert the status quo of classroom interaction between men and women, and suggests a specific framework that articulates the terms of feminist teaching.

D. Instruction and Learning Outcomes in the Classroom

By the end of a course, students are expected (and assumed) to be different in some way from the way they were when they began the course. For example, they are assumed to know more about the subject matter of the course than they did. The may also think differently about certain matters; or, perhaps, they have been reinforced in their previous beliefs. They may appreciate certain aspects of their world more (or less) than they did before. These changes, it is further assumed, have something to do with the educational processes encountered in the classroom—instruction by the teacher, class discussions, assignments to be mastered by the student, and the like. The selections in this section of the reader provide evidence about student outcomes, as these outcomes are linked to the teacher and the variety of instructional activities found in the classroom.

Some teachers and some classes, of course, are more satisfactory to students and have more impacts on them than others. One way of gauging the effectiveness of teachers and classes is through the use of student ratings. Much research has been done on these ratings. Indeed, Cashin (1995) has pointed out that there are probably more studies of student ratings than all the other ways used to evaluate teaching combined. In the first selection, Feldman explores various interpretations that can be made of information gathered from students about their teachers, and considers the possible half-truths and myths that continue to circulate about teacher and course evaluations. He concludes that "current research evidence does show that when teacher evaluation forms are properly constructed and administered . . ., the global and specific ratings contained in them, as interpreted with appropriate caution, are undeniably helpful in identifying exemplary teachers and teaching." Even so, student ratings are only one source of data about teaching and should be used in combination with other sources of data if one wishes to make a judgment of all the components of teaching. These other sources include evidence of student learning, alumni ratings, peer (colleague) evaluations, instructor self-evaluations, observations by external observers, and experimental manipulations (Marsh and Dunkin, 1992).

Teaching comprises many different elements—a multidimensionality that instruments of teacher evaluation usually attempt to capture. In his article on student ratings, Feldman reviews the results of two different sets of studies that are useful for establishing the differential importance (to effective teaching) of various dimensions. The first set provides evidence of the magnitude of the correlations of various aspects of instruction with students' achievement in the class. The second set gives the magnitude of correlations between student ratings of specific attitudinal or behavioral characteristics of teachers and students' overall evaluation of the teachers. Both methods of determining the importance of instructional dimensions indicate that the teacher's preparation and course organization, the teacher's clarity and understandableness, the teacher's stimulation of students' interest, and the student-perceived outcome or impact are the dimensions most strongly correlated with student achievement and with the overall evaluation of the teacher. Correlation does not prove causation, of course; thus it is of more than routine interest that Murray (1991) concluded from his review of experimental studies (either field experiments or laboratory experiments) that classroom teaching behaviors in what he calls "the clarity domain" and "the enthusiasm domain" (which would include stimulation of students' interest) do appear to be causal antecedents rather than mere correlates of various instructional outcome measures.

In the second selection of this section, Pascarella and Terenzini offer a broad review of influences on students' subject matter knowledge and academic (usually verbal and quantitative) skills as well as on their general intellectual and cognitive competencies (reasoning skills, critical thinking, intellectual flexibility, etc.). They, too, consider teacher behaviors and practices along various instructional dimensions, again finding teacher clarity to be one of the important factors in student learning. These analysts go past a consideration of teacher behaviors and practices to review the research on such influences as the curriculum, patterns of course work, class size, types of instructional approaches (lecture vs. discussion, team teaching, individualized instruction, etc.), and student involvement.

Pintrich's study, excerpted in this section as the third selection, reminds us that the individual students in a college classroom are not alike and thus may be differentially affected by instruction. The underlying premise of this study is that because students are active processors of information, the effects of instruction are mediated by their cognitive and motivational characteristics (see the reading by McKeachie and his associates in Part II [Section A] of this book for a fuller discussion of these characteristics). The findings suggest that the motivational and cognitive components of student learning do not operate in isolation from one another, but rather support and complement one another synergistically. The research further suggests that different types of students may benefit from different types of interventions to help them become more active learners and better critical thinkers.

The last three readings of this section present additional data on outcomes as related to classroom processes and teacher behaviors. In her research, Smith investigates how various classroom processes—teacher's encouragement, praise, and use of student ideas; the amount and kind of questioning by the teacher, the amount and kind of student participation; and peer-to-peer interaction—influence the cognitive outcome of critical thinking. Sanders and Wiseman find in their research that teacher immediacy behaviors enhance the students' perceived cognitive, affective and behavioral learning in the multicultural classroom. Moreover, similarities and difference can be found in the effect of teacher immediacy cues across cultural groups. While immediacy appears to be positively associated with various outcomes for all groups, the levels of the association vary. Further, some immediacy cues appear to have pancultural effects while others hold particular salience only for certain ethnicities. Johnson, Johnson and Smith review the research on the likely outcomes of classrooms that implement cooperative efforts of students (contrasted with classrooms based on competitive or individualistic efforts of students). They find that "promotive interaction" in the classroom results in a number of important outcomes, which they divide into three broad categories (effort exerted to achieve, quality of relationships among participants, and participants' psychological adjustment and social competence). They conclude that the more students work in cooperative learning groups, the more they learn, the better they understand what they are learning, the easier it is for them to remember what they learn, and the better they feel about themselves, about each other, and about the class as a whole.

References

Cashin, W. E. (1995). *Student ratings of teaching: The research revisited* (IDEA paper No. 32). Manhattan, KS: Center for Faculty Evaluation and Development, Kansas State University.

Mann, R. D., Arnold, S. M., Bender, J., Cytrynbaum, S., Newman, B. M., Ringwald, B., Ringwald, J., and Rosenwein, R. (1970). *The college classroom: Conflict, change and learning*. New York: Wiley.

Marsh, H. W., and Dunkin, M. J. (1992). Students' evaluations of university teaching: A multidimensional perspective. In J. C. Smart (Ed.), *Higher education: Handbook of theory and research* (Vol. 8, pp. 143-233). New York: Agathon Press.

Murray, H. G. (1991). Effective teaching behaviors in the college classroom. In J. C. Smart (Ed.), *Higher education: Handbook of theory and research* (Vol. 7, pp. 135-172). New York: Agathon Press.

A. Teacher and Student Expectations

Effective College Teaching From the Students' and Faculty's View: Matched or Mismatched Priorities?

KENNETH A. FELDMAN

Thirty-one studies were located in each of which students and faculty specified the instructional characteristics they considered particularly important to good teaching and effective instruction. Students and faculty were generally similar, though not identical, in their views, as indicated by an average correlation of +.71 between them in their valuation of various aspects of teaching. In those studies with relevant data, the differences that did exist between the two groups showed a pattern of students placing more importance than faculty on teachers being interesting, having good elocutionary skills, and being available and helpful. Students also emphasized the outcomes of instruction more than faculty did. Faculty placed more importance than did students on teachers being intellectually challenging, motivating students and setting high standards for them, and encouraging self-initiated learning. The results of the present analysis were compared with those of an earlier analysis of the importance of various specific aspects of instruction in terms of their correlations with students' overall evaluations of teachers in actual rating situations.

An earlier synthesis (Feldman, 1976b) analyzed college students' views on teachers and their judgments of the instructional effectiveness of various attitudes, behaviors, and pedagogical practices of instructors. Students' conceptions about good teaching, of course, may or may not match the conceptions of the instructors themselves. To give only one example of a presumed mismatch in preferences, it is sometimes said that students place greater importance on lectures being entertaining or interesting than do faculty. Any such differences in student and faculty views might well contribute to the tensions found in some college classrooms (see, for example, Mann et al., 1970). Moreover, if the faculty and students of a college do not agree as to what constitutes effective teaching, then faculty members may well be leery of students' overall ratings of them, believing their students may use different priorities than they themselves would in arriving at overall evaluations. Baum and Brown (1980) explicitly make this point, putting the matter strongly, as follows:

> From the very beginning of their use, faculty have expressed reservations about the meaning (validity) of student responses regarding teaching effectiveness. Put simply, faculty have argued that they and students use different criteria in evaluating teaching. Naturally, faculty view their own standards as being more relevant for, or consistent with, the long-run mission of higher education. (p 234)

The present analysis explores the extent to which students and faculty, in fact, do differ in the criteria each group uses in evaluating teaching. To this end, studies were located in which both students and faculty at the same school or schools were asked to indicate the instructional characteristics they considered important to good teaching. As with the other analyses in the present series on college teaching and students' assessments of it,[1] the research reviewed has been restricted to studies of students and teachers at colleges and universities in the United States and Canada.

"Effective Teaching from the Students' and Faculty's View: Matched or Mismatched Priorities?" by Kenneth A. Feldman, reprinted by permission from *Research in Higher Education*, 28, Plenum Publishing Corporation.

Degree of Similarity Between Faculty and Students

Thirty-one studies were found in which students and faculty at the same school(s) were asked about the importance of various components of teaching. The most common way in these studies of determining each group's criteria for evaluating teaching was to ask both students and faculty to specify the attitudes, behaviors, and pedagogical practices of teachers that they felt were the most important to "good" teaching or "effective" instruction. (Occasionally, "effective" teaching was more closely specified in terms of student learning.) Sometimes, students and faculty were asked to characterize "best" or "ideal" teachers. Another procedure used was to ask students and faculty to rate various instructional characteristics in terms of their importance in judging a teacher or their importance for inclusion on an evaluation form.

In each study, the differential importance of the various attitudes, behaviors, and practices to effective teaching was determined for both students and faculty. Correlating the results for the two groups indicates the degree of "agreement"—that is, similarity—between students and faculty across the various components of good teaching. In some cases, the relevant correlation is actually given in the study, whereas, in other cases, it had to be calculated from the data that were given. A summary of each study, including the pertinent correlation(s), is given in Table 1.

As can be seen in this table, many of the studies showed relatively high correlations between students and faculty with respect to the differential importance each group attached to various components of teaching. Indeed, some 12 of the 31 studies had correlations of at least +.85 (and 9 of these had correlations of +.90 or higher). Across all 31 studies, the average correlation was + .71 (combined Z = + 21.858; $p < .001$),[2] which indicates a substantial, though clearly not total, similarity between the criteria students and faculty use in judging effective teaching.

With certain exceptions, to be noted, the results of studies varied little when divided by major type of sample used. Sixteen of the studies[3] each sampled student and faculty across departments or academic fields at a university or four-year college. For these studies, the average correlation between students and faculty across the instructional characteristics considered important to good teaching was + .84 (combined Z = + 19.421; $p <.001$), not much different from the average correlation of + .76 (combined Z = + 11.406; $p < .001$) for the six studies[4] using (presumably) schoolwide samples of students and faculty at junior or community colleges.

The remaining studies were done with students (and sometimes faculty also) in particular classes or within academic divisions. Again, results for a study (Blazek, 1974) of students in sections of a secondary education course and teachers of these sections ($r = +.77$) and for the two studies (Crawford and Bradshaw, 1968; Wittmaier, 1975) of students in psychology classes and of teachers more widely selected from the school as a whole (average $r = +.88$) were fairly similar to each other as well as to the studies already noted that used a wider sampling of students at the schools under study. Likewise, in the research by Freilich (1983), whose student data came from freshman engineering students and from students in a general chemistry course but whose faculty data came from instructors "in a wide variety of disciplines," the correlation in question was also high (rho = +.75).

There are some exception to these high correlations. Using data from Table 1 in Marques, Lane, and Dorfman (1979), it can be shown that whereas the student-faculty correlations are high (and statistically significant) for the academic divisions of the social sciences ($r = +.88$), the humanities ($r = +.85$), and engineering ($r = +.80$) at the school under study, the pertinent correlation for the natural sciences is only +.16 (and is statistically insignificant). Moreover, for the four different studies of faculty members in business schools and students in their classes (Baum and Brown, 1980; Stevens, 1978; Stevens and Marquette, 1979; Wotruba and Wright, 1975), none of the correlations was statistically significant, although each was positive. The average correlation across these studies is + .26, whose combined Z of + 1.684 also is not statistically significant ($p = .092$). Finally, the research by Norr and Crittenden (1975), based on data from 25 faculty members in a sociology department and 1,114 students in 52 classes, produced a statistically insignificant inverse correlation (rho) of –.35. It is not clear from the report of the investigators whether the classes involved were only sociology classes or were more widely spread across the particular college.[5]

The Nature of Student-Faculty Dissimilarity

The average correlation between students and teachers, while high, is not so large as to preclude some dissimilarity between them in the exact importance each group places on any particular instructional

Table 1
Summary of Studies with Data on the Differential Importance of Various Components of Teaching (from Which the Extent of Similarity Between the Two Groups Can Be Determined)

Baril and Skaggs (1976): 1,369 sophomores, juniors, and seniors compared with 418 faculty members at the University of Maine, Orono (year not given) when indicating for each of 156 items "the importance . . . for inclusion on an evaluation form."

$r = +.89^*$ (as given on p. 185); $Z = +11.116^*$ ($p < .001$)

Baum and Brown (1980): 179 students compared with 50 faculty members in the School of Business and Economics at California State University, Northridge (year not given) when weighting each of 10 "common aspects of the teaching process" as to its "relative importance in determining teaching effectiveness."

$r = +.001^*$ (as calculated from data given in Table 1, p. 236); $Z = +0.003^*$ ($p = .998$)

Blai (1974): 411 students compared with 23 faculty members at Harcum Junior College in Bryn Mawr, Pennsylvania (Fall 1973) when responding to 14 forced–choice questions pertaining to the "characteristics of the 'better' junior college teacher."

$r = +.35^*$ (as calculated from data given on pp. 1–3); $Z = +1.310^*$ ($p = .190$)

Blazek (1974): 196 undergraduate students enrolled in the first required secondary course at Northern Illinois University compared with 10 faculty members teaching sections of this course (Spring 1974) when rating each of 37 items as to how important it is "for the measurement of teaching effectiveness in the general instructional situation." [Note: Excluded from consideration for the present analysis is an item for overall evaluation of the course.]

$r = +.77^*$ (as calculated from data given in Table 23, p. 81); $Z = +4.684^*$ ($p < .001$)

Breed (1927): 100 students compared with 56 faculty members at the University of Chicago (year not given) when ranking 34 "qualities desirable in instructors in college courses conducted by the lecture–discussion method."

For 5 items dealing with "knowledge and organization of subject matter", $r = +.96$ (as calculated from data in Table 1, p. 248) and $Z = +2.147$). For 11 items dealing with "skill in instruction," $r = +.95$ (as calculated from data in Table 1, p. 248) and $Z = +3.151$. For 10 items dealing with "personal qualities," $r = +.97$ (as calculated from data in Table 1, p. 248) and $Z = +3.067$.

Average $r = +.96^*$; average $Z = +2.788^*$ ($p = .005$)

Brewer and Brewer (1970): 280 freshmen and 92 upperclassmen compared with 54 members of the faculty and administration at De Paul University (year not given) when picking one trait from each of 10 pairs of traits according to "which was more important for good college teaching."

When comparing the group of freshmen with the group of faculty/administrators, $r = +.94$ (as calculated from data given in Tables 1 and 3 on pp. 244 and 245) and $Z = +2.973$. When comparing the group of upperclassmen with the group of faculty/administrators, $r = +.93$ (as calculated from data given in Tables 1 and 3 on pp. 244 and 245) and $Z = +2.941$.

Average $r = +.94^*$; average $Z = +2.957^*$ ($p = .003$)

Bridges et al. (1971): 741 students compared with 201 faculty members at "a large university" (year not given) when describing the "six outstanding characteristics of the *best* college teacher" they have known, results of which were classifiable into 24 categories with frequency distributions given.

$r = +.76^*$ (as calculated from data given in Table 2, p. 55); $Z = +3.723^*$ ($p < .001$)

Crawford and Bradshaw (1968): 36 faculty members compared with 158 undergraduate students in four university classes in psychology (school and year not given) when choosing from each of 13 pairs of descriptive statement the one considered "more essential or critical to effective University teaching."

Two groups of professors (associate and full professors; instructors and assistant professors) and six groups of students (high, average and low ranking females; high, average, and low ranking males) produced 12 separate *r*'s ranging from +.72 to +.92 (as given in Table 4, p. 1084).

Average $r = +.83^*$; average $Z = +2.990^*$ ($p = .003$)

Table 1 *continued*

Delaney and Coons (1976): 1,405 undergraduates compared with 369 faculty members at "a large metropolitan university" (year not given) when judging the importance of 4 "criteria of teaching effectiveness."

r (rho) = + 1.00* (as calculated from data given in Figure 1, p. 5); Z = + 2.000* (p = .045)

Evaluation and Examination Service (1974): 1,127 undergraduate and graduate students compared with 1,344 faculty members at the University of Iowa (Spring 1974) when indicating whether each of 111 items was an "important factor" in determining how much students learn in courses.

r = + .85* (as calculated from data given in Tables 1–3, pp. 7–16; Z = + 8.955* (p < .001)

Freilich (1983): 107 students in a general chemistry courses for freshman engineering students at Purdue University and 106 students in a general chemistry course for liberal arts/science students at California State University Hayward compared with 23 teachers ("several faculty members and a few experienced graduate teaching assistants in a wide variety of disciplines") (year not given) when evaluating 28 questionnaire items in terms of the five most important and the five least important in helping students learn.

r (rho) = + .75* (as calculated from data given in Table 2, p. 219; Z = + 3.969* (p < .001)

Hartung (1972): students compared with teachers in the junior colleges in North Carolina (year not given) when evaluating each of 67 characteristics in terms of its "importance. "

r (rho) = + .90* (as given on p. 147); Z = +7.367* (p < .001)

Hussain and Leestamper (1968): 283 students compared with 186 teaching and administrative faculty at New Mexico State University (Fall 1967) when rating 60 "criteria of teaching effectiveness."

r = +.94* (as given on p. 12); Z = +7.281* (p < .001)

Jenkins et al. (n.d.): 90 students compared with 27 faculty members at Highland Community College in Freeport, Illinois (year not given) when rating each of 60 teacher behaviors as to its "importance to good instruction."

r (rho) = +.86* (as given on p. 19); Z = +6.662* (p < .001)

Krupka (1970): 60 students compared with a group of faculty members at Northampton Area Community College (year not given) when ranking 10 items on the Instructor Rating Questionnaire as to their "importance in judging a teacher." [Note: Excluded from consideration for the present analysis is an item for overall evaluation of the teacher and an item for overall evaluation of the course.]

r = + .94* (as calculated from data given in the table on p. 2); Z = + 2.973* (p = .003)

Lovell and Haner (1955): junior and senior students compared with faculty members at Grinnell College (Spring 1954) when indicating whether each of 107 items applied as a descriptive item about best, average, or worst professors.

r = +.75* (as given on p. 299); Z = +7.758* (p < .001)

Marques et al. (1979): 35 male undergraduates compared with 37 male faculty members (distributed among the academic divisions of engineering, humanities, natural sciences, and social sciences) at Rice University (year not given) when assigning an overall rating of teaching effectiveness to hypothetical instructors whose profiles varied in the values assigned to 7 "quantified cues reflecting instructor performance on dimensions thought to be related to teaching effectiveness."

r = +.88* (as calculated from data in Table 1 on p. 844, averaging across data for the four academic divisions); Z = + 2.328* (p = .020)

Murray et al. (1982): 602 undergraduates (February 1981) compared with 666 full-time faculty members (December 1980) at the University of Western Ontario when rating 13 factors in terms of their "relative importance as components of university teaching. "

r = + .74* (as calculated from data given in Table 4, p. 57); Z = + 2.668* (p = .008)

Table 1 *continued*

Norr and Crittenden (1975): 1,114 students in 52 classes compared with 25 sociology faculty members at the University of Illinois, Chicago Circle (year not given) when rating 5 dimensions of teaching (multi–item scales) in terms of their "importance for good teaching."

r (rho) = –.35* (as calculated from data given in Table 1, p. 341); Z = –0.990* (*p* = .322)

Odom (1943): 121 undergraduate students compared with 26 faculty members at a "southern liberal arts college" (year not given) when listing "traits that they believed a good college teacher should possess," results of which were classified into 36 categories and then rank ordered.

r (rho) = + .76* (as calculated from data given in Table 1 on p. 111); Z = +4.560* (*p* < .001)

Perry (1969): a group of students compared with a group of faculty members at the University of Toledo (year not given) when judging each of 60 behaviors as to how warranted it was "for evaluation of effective teaching behavior."

r = +.91* (as calculated from data given in the table on p. 18 and continued on p. 22); Z = + 7.049* (*p* < .001)

Romine (1974): 1,237 undergraduate and graduate students compared with 268 faculty members at the University of Colorado (year not given) when rating the significance of 40 items as to their contribution "to an effective instructional climate" (that is, "one in which students are well satisfied with courses and in which they are strongly motivated to study and learn").

r = + .65* (as calculated from data given in Table 1 on p. 141); Z = +4.111* (*p* < .001)

Romine and Newport (1973): 2,058 students compared with 325 faculty members "located in 29 community junior college in 15 states of the North Central Region" (year not given) when rating the significance of 70 attributes in terms of their contribution to an "effective instructional climate in which satisfying and successful teaching and learning occur."

r (rho) = +.84* (as calculated from data given in Table 1 on pp. 18–27); Z = + 7.028*(*p* < .001)

Rotem (1975): students in 36 undergraduate courses compared with the instructors of these courses at the University of California, Santa Barbara (Winter 1975) when rating 8 types of behaviors in terms of how often an "ideal" teacher would engage in them. (Note: This information was gotten *before* 18 of the instructors participated in an experiment to find out the effects of their receiving feedback from their students, early in the semester, on their performance in the classroom.)

r = +.99* (as calculated from data in the tables on pp. 112 and 114, with means on each item being averaged across the experimental and control groups); Z = + 2.800* (*p* = .005)

Shatz and Best (1986): 106 students compared with 45 faculty members at "a four-year midwestern university" (year not given) when identifying which of the 35 items of the Students' Evaluations of Educational Quality (SEEQ) were "important enough to be included in a course evaluation questionnaire" and which of these important items were the "most important."

r (rho) for "important" items = + .71 (as given on p. 241) and Z = +4.200; *r* (rho) for the "most important" items = + .75 (as given on p. 241) and Z = 4.437.

Average *r* (rho) = +.73*; average Z = +4.319* (*p* < .001)

Stevens (1978): 572 students compared with 226 faculty members "at a College of Business in a southwestern university (year not given) when rating the importance (in terms of student learning) of 10 "teaching traits and behaviors that are commonly exhibited in a classroom situation."

r = + .50* (as calculated from data given in Table 1, p. 20); Z = + 1.581* (*p* = .114)

Stevens and Marquette (1979): 135 students enrolled in business courses compared with 55 faculty members in the College of Business at Kent State University (year not given) when judging each of 10 traits as to its "relative importance in determining teaching effectiveness."

r = + .43* (as calculated from data given in Table 1, p. 211); Z = + 1.360* (*p* = .174)

Table 1 *continued*

Whitley (1982): 112 students compared with 61 full–time instructors at Meridian College (year not given) when ranking 16 "characteristics of good instruction" as to their "perceived importance."

r (rho) = + .67* (as calculated from data given in Table 4, p. 12); Z = + 2.600* (p = .007)

Wittmaier (1975): 60 students in an introductory psychology course compared with 23 faculty members at a "small liberal arts college" (year not given) when rating 5 different teaching styles (multi–item scales) in terms of their "importance to good teaching."

r = + .92* (as calculated from data given in Table 1 on p. 25); Z = + 2.057* (p = .040)

Wotruba and Wright (1975): 350 students compared with a representative sample of 60% of the faculty members in the School of Business Administration at San Diego State University when rating each of 18 items as to its "importance . . . in evaluating faculty." (Note: The exact rank of the last 8 ranked items is not given in the article, so each of these items was considered tied at rank 14.)

r (rho) = + .10* (as calculated from data given in Table 2 on p. 660); Z = +0.424* (p = .672)

Yourglich (1955): 101 undergraduate students compared with 35 faculty members at a "university in the Pacific Northwest" (year not given) when listing traits thought to comprise the "ideal teacher" (as subsequently classified by the researcher into 19 categories for which frequency of mention was determined).
r = +.75* (as calculated from data given in Table 2, p. 60); Z = +3.269* (p < .001)

Note: If a product-moment correlation (r) between the students' view and the faculty's view of the importance of various components of teaching was not given explicitly in a study, it was calculated when possible from data that were given. A rank–order correlation (rho)—either as presented in a study or as calculated from data in it—is given only when r was not given or could not be calculated. Following the suggestion of Glass, McGaw, and Smith (1981, Table 5.8), rho's are treated as r's. Multiplying r by $\sqrt{N}$ (where N, in this case, is the number of items in a study that were considered by both students and faculty in terms of importance to good teaching) yields a generally conservative estimate approximation to Z, the standard normal deviate (see Rosenthal 1984, p. 107). The r's that have been used to calculate the average r's given in the text are marked by asterisks in the table, as are the Z's that have been used to produce combined Z's. The probability levels (p's) associated with the Z's are two-tailed.

characteristic. To see whether any patterns could be found with respect to whether students were more likely to emphasize certain components of teaching and faculty other components, the exact rank order of various instructional characteristics were compared across studies. The intent was to find out whether there were any *consistencies* across these studies in terms of specific instructional characteristics students felt to be more important than did teachers, and vice versa. Because the procedures used to accomplish this objective involved the systematic comparison of the differential importance of various instructional characteristics to students and faculty, only those studies could be used that gave sufficient information to allow the instructional characteristics in the study to be coded into the categories of the present analysis and to be rank-ordered in terms of their importance to students and to faculty. Consequently, nine studies were eliminated at this point,[6] leaving 22 studies for further consideration. These 22 studies included the four studies that sampled teachers in business schools and the students enrolled in business courses. Because the relative importance placed by these students on various instructional characteristics was essentially unrelated to that of these faculty members, as noted earlier, the results of these four studies, for the most part, are considered separately throughout the present analysis. This leaves 18 studies as the *core* set of studies for consideration.

The instructional characteristics in these studies have been coded into a set of categories whose names and contents can be found in the Appendix. Nineteen of these coding categories are those that have been used previously in this series (in Feldman, 1976b, 1983, 1984, 1987) and are given as Instructional Dimensions Nos. 1–19 in the Appendix. Three additional categories were added for the present analysis so that more of the instructional characteristics investigated in the studies could be coded and used (see Instructional Dimensions Nos. 20–22 in the Appendix). As a consequence, most of the pedagogical attitudes, behaviors, and practices found in the studies under consideration could be coded into one of these 22 instructional dimensions.

In each of the studies under consideration, either the instructional characteristics in them were originally rank-ordered in importance (for students and for faculty separately) or data are presented in them from which such rankings can be derived. In order to establish comparability among these studies, the rank of each instructional characteristic in a study has been standardized by dividing that rank by the number of characteristics in the study. For an instructional characteristic, say teacher enthusiasm, to rank fourth in importance out of 60 characteristics is hardly the same as ranking fourth out of 10 such characteristics, as the standardized ranks would show: .07 vs. .40 (i.e., 4/60 vs. 4/10). Note that the smaller the fraction, the greater the rank-ordered importance of the characteristic.

The Appendix gives the standardized ranks in the form of fractions for students and for faculty of each instructional characteristic (in each study) that was codable into one of the 22 general instructional dimensions under consideration. Table 2 is based on (and, in part, is a condensation of) the fuller array of data presented in the Appendix. This table shows the standardized rank in decimal form (for students and faculty) for each general instructional dimension for each study that had at least one instructional characteristic codable into that dimension. If more than one of the instructional characteristics in a particular study was coded into the same general instructional dimension, the individual standardized ranks were averaged to produce the standardized rank for that study for that particular instructional dimension. For each study with data relevant to a particular instructional dimension, the *difference* between the standardized rank for students and that for faculty is also given. (A positive difference between standardized ranks indicates that students place more importance on the instructional dimension than does the faculty, whereas a negative difference indicates that the faculty places more importance on the dimension than do students.) Finally, for each of the general instructional dimensions, the table gives the *average* standardized rank (across the relevant studies) for students and for faculty as well as the average differences between these two average standardized ranks (henceforth called the average standardized difference).

To give some idea of the scale or "meaning" of the standardized differences (either as individual cases or as averages), it should be noted that a standardized difference of –.10 or +.10 is equivalent to a difference of one rank if 10 characteristics are being ranked, or a difference of two ranks if 20 characteristics are being ranked, and so forth. Likewise, an average standardized difference of –.15 or +.15 is equivalent to a difference of three ranks were 30 characteristics being ranked, or a difference of six ranks were 40 characteristics being ranked, and so on.

The average standardized differences shown in Table 2 for the core set of studies under consideration are not very large, as would be expected since the importance placed by students and teachers on various instructional characteristics is fairly similar (indicated by the sizable correlation across studies discussed previously). The largest average standardized differences are +.22 for Instructional Dimension No. 1 (students place more importance than do faculty on teachers stimulating students' interest), –.24 for Instructional Dimension No. 21 (students place less importance than do faculty on teachers encouraging self-initiated learning on the part of students), and –.18 for Instructional Dimension No. 17 (students place less importance than do faculty on teachers challenging students intellectually and encouraging their independent thought.

Also shown in Table 2 are smaller differences of –.13 for Instructional Dimension No. 20 (students place less importance than do faculty on teachers motivating students to do their best and setting high standards of performance for them), +.10 for Dimension No. 7 (students place more importance than do faculty on teachers' elocutionary skills), and +.10 for Dimension No. 19 (students place more importance than do faculty on teachers' availability and helpfulness to students) as well as the even smaller differences of +.08 for Dimension No. 12 (students place more importance than do faculty on the perceived outcome or impact of instruction), +.08 for Dimension No. 18 (students place more importance than do faculty on teachers being concerned about students, showing respect for them, and being friendly), and –.08 for Dimension No. 2 (students place less importance than do faculty on teachers' enthusiasm for the subject or for teaching). On the remaining dimensions, students and faculty differ less, if at all, in their preferences.

To consider the four studies of business school instructors and students adds a certain amount of information to the analysis, but not as much as might be expected because they present no information for several of the pertinent instructional dimensions. Moreover, for others of the dimensions, only one of the studies has relevant data, and for none of the dimensions is there information from two of the studies. However, as seen in the Appendix, six of the dimensions do have data from either three or all four of the

Table 2
Importance (Standardized Ranks) of Various Instructional Dimensions for Students and Faculty (Individual Studies and Averages)

Instructional Dimension	Importance Stated by Students	Importance Stated by Faculty	Difference
No. 1. Teacher's Stimulation of Interest in the Course and Its Subject Matter			
Blazek (1974)	.54	.70	+.16
Brewer and Brewer (1970)	.10	.20	+.10
Bridges et al. (1971)	.08	.21	+.13
Evaluation and Examination Services (1974)	.14	.26	+.12
Krupka (1970)	.20	.20	.00
Marques et al. (1979)	.29	.29	.00
Odom (1943)	.58	.92	+.34
Romine (1974)	.33	.75	+.32
Romine and Newport (1973)	.27	.46	+.19
Youglich (1955)	.26	.97	+.71
Average	.28	.50	+.22
No. 2. Teacher's Enthusiasm (for Subject or for Teaching)			
Blazek (1974)	.27	.26	–.01
Brewer and Brewer (1970)	.40	.40	.00
Bridges et al. (1971)	.21	.17	–.04
Evaluation and Examination Services (1974)	.16	.13	–.03
Murray et al. (1982)	.62	.46	–.16
Odom (1943)	.78	.44	–.34
Romine (1974)	.09	.10	+ .01
Romine and Newport (1973)	.13	.05	–.08
Whitley (1982)	.25	.13	–.12
Average	.32	.24	–.08
No. 3. Teacher's Knowledge of the Subject			
Blazek (1974)	.43	.53	+.10
Brewer and Brewer (1970)	.20	.30	+.10
Bridges et al. (1971)	.44	.25	–.19
Delaney and Coons (1976)	.25	.25	.00
Evaluation and Examination Service (1974)	.49	.43	–.06
Freilich (1983)	.14	.05	–.09
Hussain and Leestamper (1968)	.23	.32	+.09
Jenkins et al. (n.d.)	.48	.10	–.38
Krupka (1970)	.10	.10	.00
Marques et al. (1979)	.57	.43	–.14
Murray et al. (1982)	.15	.19	+.04
Odom (1943)	.03	.03	.00

Table 2 *continued*

Perry (1969)	.33	.18	–.15
Romine (1974)	.13	.08	–.05
Romine and Newport (1973)	.34	.32	–.02
Whitley (1982)	.06	.06	.00
Yourglich (1955)	.32	.26	–.06
Average	.28	.23	–.05
No. 4. Teacher's Intellectual Expansiveness (and Intelligence)			
Bridges et al. (1971)	.50	.29	–.21
Evaluation and Examination Service (1974)	.32	.43	+.11
Hussain and Leestamper (1968)	.69	.60	–.09
Jenkins et al. (n.d.)	.74	.67	–.07
Odom (1943)	.58	.48	–.10
Perry (1969)	.68	.49	–.19
Romine (1974)	.48	.64	+.16
Romine and Newport (1973)	.54	.54	.00
Yourglich (1955)	.54	.32	–.22
Average	.56	.50	–.06
No. 5. Teacher's Preparation; Organization of the Course			
Blazek (1974)	.30	.57	+.27
Bridges et al. (1971)	.56	.59	+.03
Evaluation and Examination Service (1970)	.01	.05	+.04
Freilich (1983)	.28	.26	–.02
Hussain and Leestamper (1968)	.05	.10	+.05
Jenkins et al. (n.d.)	.15	.14	–.01
Krupka (1970)	.30	.40	+.10
Perry (1969)	.08	.10	+.02
Romine (1974)	.03	.03	.00
Romine and Newport (1973)	.07	.03	–.04
Whitley (1982)	.50	.31	–.19
Yourglich (1955)	.87	.74	–.13
Average	.27	.28	+.01
No. 6. Clarity and Understandableness			
Blazek (1974)	.26	.31	+.05
Bridges et al. (1971)	1.00	1.00	.00
Evaluation and Examination Service (1974)	.21	.19	–.02
Freilich (1983)	.07	.36	+.29
Murray et al. (1982)	.08	.19	+.11
Romine (1974)	.50	.54	+.04
Romine and Newport (1973)	.38	.31	–.07
Yourglich (1955)	.11	.18	+.07
Average	.33	.39	+.06

Table 2 *continued*

No. 7. Teacher's Elocutionary Skills			
Bridges et al. (1971)	.63	.50	–.13
Evaluation and Examination Service (1974)	.60	.69	+.09
Hussain and Leestamper (1968)	.38	.43	+.05
Jenkins et al. (n.d.)	.27	.70	+.43
Krupka (1970)	.80	.90	+.10
Murray et al. (1982)	.69	.92	+.23
Perry (1969)	.45	.43	–.02
Romine (1974)	.23	.33	+.10
Romine and Newport (1973)	.16	.26	+.10
Average	.47	.57	+.10
No. 8. Teacher's Sensitivity to, and Concern with, Class Level and Progress			
Bridges et al. (1971)	.33	.54	+.21
Evaluation and Examination Service (1974)	.37	.50	+.13
Hussain and Leestamper (1968)	.12	.08	–.04
Jenkins et al. (n.d.)	.03	.13	+.10
Perry (1969)	.10	.13	+.03
Romine (1974)	.25	.28	+.03
Romine and Newport (1973)	.36	.20	–.16
Average	.22	.27	+.05
No. 9. Clarity of Course Objectives and Requirements			
Blazek (1974)	.27	.26	–.01
Delaney and Coons (1976)	.75	.75	.00
Evaluation and Examination Service (1974)	.42	.38	–.04
Freilich (1983)	.46	.38	–.08
Krupka (1970)	.70	.50	–.20
Marques et al. (1979)	1.00	1.00	.00
Romine (1974)	.80	.43	–.37
Romine and Newport (1973)	.34	.16	–.18
Whitley (1982)	.56	.69	+.13
Wittmaier (1975)	1.00	1.00	.00
Average	.63	.56	–.07
No. 10. Nature and Value of the Course Material (Including Its Usefulness and Relevance)			
Blazek (1974)	.91	.88	–.03
Evaluation and Examination Service (1974)	.40	.52	+.12
Freilich (1983)	.59	.52	–.07
Hussain and Leestamper (1968)	.16	.35	+.19
Jenkins et al. (n.d.)	.24	.20	–.04
Murray et al. (1982)	.38	.31	–.07
Perry (1969)	.22	.28	+.06

Table 2 *continued*

Romine (1974)	.32	.44	+.12
Romine and Newport (1973)	.28	.29	.01
Whitley (1982)	.94	.75	−.19
Wittmaier (1975)	.67	.67	.00
Average	.46	.47	+.01
No. 11. Nature and Usefulness of Supplementary Materials and Teaching Aids			
Blazek (1974)	.54	.47	−.07
Bridges et al. (1971)	.77	.60	−.17
Evaluation and Examination Service (1974)	.18	.40	+.22
Freilich (1983)	.44	.59	+.15
Hussain and Leestamper (1968)	.78	.74	−.04
Jenkins et al. (n.d.)	.62	.65	+.03
Murray et al. (1982)	.38	.31	−.07
Perry (1969)	.77	.81	+.04
Romine (1974)	.68	.90	+.22
Romine and Newport (1973)	.21	.29	+.08
Average	.54	.58	+.04
No. 12. Perceived Outcome or Impact of Instruction			
Blazek (1974)	.70	.57	−.13
Evaluation and Examination Service (1974)	.65	.51	−.14
Romine (1974)	.18	.60	+.42
Romine and Newport (1973)	.19	.37	+.18
Average	.43	.51	+.08
No. 13. Instructor's Fairness; Impartiality of Evaluation of Students; Quality of Examinations			
Blazek (1974)	.03	.39	+.36
Brewer and Brewer (1970)	.30	.10	−.20
Bridges et al. (1971)	.13	.38	+.25
Evaluation and Examination Service (1974)	.46	.47	+.01
Freilich (1983)	.93	.89	−.04
Hussain and Leestamper (1968)	.37	.44	+.07
Jenkins et al. (n.d.)	.41	.39	−.02
Krupka (1970)	.60	.70	+.10
Murray et al. (1982)	.38	.23	−.15
Odom (1943)	.08	.33	+.25
Perry (1969)	.38	.49	+.11
Romine (1974)	.95	.51	−.44
Romine and Newport (1973)	.55	.39	−.16
Whitley (1982)	.69	.63	−.06
Average	.45	.45	.00

Table 2 *continued*

No. 14. Personality Characteristics ("Personality") of the Instructor			
Brewer and Brewer (1970)	.90	.80	–.10
Bridges et al. (1971)	.59	.55	–.04
Freilich (1983)	1.00	1.00	.00
Hussain and Leestamper (1968)	.63	.58	–.05
Jenkins et al. (n.d.)	.57	.65	+.08
Krupka (1970)	.60	1.00	+.40
Odom (1943)	.48	.50	+.02
Perry (1969)	.62	.66	+.04
Romine (1974)	.60	.80	+.20
Romine and Newport (1973)	.26	.41	+.15
Whitley (1982)	.88	1.00	+.12
Yourglich (1955)	.50	.42	–.08
Average	.64	.70	+.06
No. 15. Nature, Quality, and Frequency of Feedback from the Teacher to Students			
Blazek (1974)	.46	.49	+.03
Evaluation and Examination Service (1974)	.55	.58	+.03
Freilich (1983)	.14	.11	–.03
Hussain and Leestamper (1968)	.42	.51	+.09
Jenkins et al. (n.d.)	.43	.57	+.14
Perry (1969)	.43	.61	+.18
Romine (1974)	.65	.68	+.03
Romine and Newport (1973)	.34	.25	–.09
Whitley (1982)	1.00	.94	–.06
Average	.49	.53	+.04
No. 16. Teacher's Encouragement of Questions and Discussion, and Openness to Opinions of Others			
Blazek (1974)	.26	.12	–.14
Brewer and Brewer (1970)	.55	.55	.00
Bridges et al. (1971)	.31	.56	+.25
Delaney and Coons (1976)	.50	.50	.00
Evaluation and Examination Service (1974)	.61	.46	–.15
Freilich (1983)	.67	.77	+.10
Hussain and Leestamper (1968)	.34	.29	–.05
Jenkins et al. (n.d.)	.24	.27	+.03
Murray et al. (1982)	.85	.77	–.08
Odom (1943)	.19	.26	+.07
Perry (1969)	.30	.28	–.02
Romine (1974)	.93	.50	–.43
Romine and Newport (1973)	.57	.50	–.07

Table 2 *continued*

Whitley (1982)	.59	.66	+.07
Wittmaier (1975)	.67	.67	.00
Average	.51	.48	–.03
No. 17. Intellectual Challenge and Encouragement of Independent Thought (by the Teacher and the Course)			
Bridges et al. (1971)	.54	.60	+.06
Evaluation and Examination Service (1974)	.82	.76	–.06
Hussain and Leestamper (1968)	.46	.38	–.08
Jenkins et al. (n.d.)	.49	.35	–.14
Marques et al. (1979)	.86	.71	–.15
Murray et al. (1982)	.31	.08	–.23
Perry (1969)	.47	.28	–.19
Romine (1974)	.48	.13	–.35
Romine and Newport (1973)	.57	.30	–.27
Whitley (1982)	.81	.38	–.43
Average	.58	.40	–.18
No. 18. Teacher's Concern and Respect for Students; Friendliness of the Teacher			
Blazek (1974)	.20	.36	+.16
Brewer and Brewer (1970)	.70	.70	.00
Bridges et al. (1971)	.04	.04	.00
Evaluation and Examination Service (1974)	.69	.61	–.08
Freilich (1983)	.46	.20	–.26
Hussain and Leestamper (1968)	.39	.31	–.08
Jenkins et al. (n.d.)	.23	.25	+.02
Marques et al. (1979)	.71	.86	+.15
Murray et al. (1982)	.46	.62	+.16
Odom (1943)	.50	.78	+.28
Perry (1969)	.38	.31	–.07
Romine (1974)	.45	.51	+.06
Romine and Newport (1973)	.17	.34	+.17
Whitley (1982)	.28	.53	+.25
Wittmaier (1975)	.17	.50	+.33
Yourglich (1955)	.37	.58	+.21
Average	.39	.47	+.08
No. 19. Teacher's Availability and Helpfulness			
Evaluation and Examination Service (1974)	.17	.07	–.10
Hussain and Leestamper (1968)	.26	.29	+.03
Jenkins et al.(n.d.)	.12	.24	+.12
Krupka (1970)	.50	.60	+.10
Murray et al. (1982)	.46	.62	+.16
Perry (1969)	.25	.36	+.11

Table 2 *continued*

Romine (1974)	.50	.78	+.28
Romine and Newport (1973)	.55	.46	–.09
Whitley (1982)	.31	.56	+.25
Yourglich (1955)	.53	.68	+.15
Average	.37	.47	+.10
No. 20. Teacher Motivates Students to Do Their Best; High Standards of Performance Required			
Blazek (1974)	.59	.58	–.01
Bridges et al. (1971)	.83	.67	–.16
Hussain and Leestamper (1968)	.34	.17	–.17
Jenkins et al. (n.d.)	.44	.32	–.15
Perry (1969)	.31	.18	–.15
Romine and Newport (1973)	.93	.76	–.17
Whitley (1982)	.63	.44	–.19
Average	.58	.45	–.13
No. 21. Teacher's Encouragement of Self–initiated Learning			
Evaluation and Examination Service (1974)	.72	.34	–.38
Freilich (1983)	.71	.60	–.11
Romine (1974)	.84	.38	–.46
Romine and Newport (1973)	.72	.70	–.02
Average	.75	.51	– .24
No. 22. Teacher's Productivity in Research and Related Activities			
Brewer and Brewer (1970)	.90	.80	–.10
Hussain and Leestamper (1968)	.95	.91	–.04
Jenkins et al. (n.d.)	.98	.98	.00
Perry (1969)	.97	.88	–.09
Romine and Newport (1973)	.76	.85	+.09
Average	.91	.88	–.03

Note: This table shows the individual and average standardized ranks (as explained in the text) for students and faculty (and the differences between them) for each of the instructional dimensions under consideration, and it is based on data in the Appendix for the 18 "core" studies. Had the four studies of business school instructors and students in business courses been included, results for some of the instructional dimensions (namely No.'s 7, 8, 10, 11, 12, 14, 21, and 22) would not be affected because none of the instructional characteristics considered in these four studies were coded into these dimensions. For the remaining dimensions, the average standardized ranks for students and for faculty, and the corresponding average standardized differences between them, would be the following: No. 1 (.35, .61, +.26); No. 2 (.33, .28, –.05); No. 3 (.26, .23, –.03); No. 4 (.59, 52, –.07); No 5 (.29, .41, +.12); No. 6 (.38, .38, .00); No. 9 (.60, .58, –.02); No. 13 (.40, .51, + .11); No 15 (.52, .55, +.03); No. 16 (.53,.47, –.06); No. 17(.65,.38, –.27); No. 18 (.39, .46, +.07); No. 19 (.38, .46, +.08); No. 20 (.67, .50, –.17). The average standardized difference for each dimension (either including the four studies done at business schools or excluding them) has been gotten by subtracting the average standardized ranks for students from the average standardized rank for faculty. Averaging the individual differences between the standardized ranks for students and for faculty should produce exactly the same result, although occasionally the average standardized difference figured this way (not shown in the table) is off by .01 due to rounding error.

studies, and most of these show large differences between students and faculty. Reviewing the average standardized ranks involved, as calculated from the data presented in the Appendix, it is clear that these studies show that students in business courses place much less emphasis than do faculty members of business schools on instructors intellectually challenging students and encouraging independent thought (Dimension No. 17: .83 vs. .33) and (to a smaller extent) on teachers setting high standards of performance and motivating students to do their best (No. 20: .83 vs. .60). At the same time, these students place much more importance than faculty on an instructor's fairness and impartiality of evaluation (No. 13: .24 vs. .69), preparation and organization (No. 5: .37 vs. .80), and stimulation of students' interest (No. 1: .53 vs. .90). No difference exists on average between the two regarding the importance of the teacher's friendliness as well as concern and respect for students (No. 18: .43 vs. .43).[7]

Student and faculty judgments of importance can also be compared by examining the rank order of the average standardized ranks of the instructional dimensions for students and for faculty in the core group of studies, as shown in Table 3. This table is based on Table 2 and repeats the average standardized ranks of that table. In this case, however, these average standardized ranks are themselves ranked from 1 (high) to 22 (low) for students and faculty separately. The instructional dimensions in Table 3 have been reordered so that they are listed from highest to lowest in importance to students. The rank-order correlation (rho) between the rank ordering of the dimensions of students and that for faculty is + .69 ($p < .001$), and the correlation coefficient (r) between the average standardized ranks for the students and the faculty is +.80 ($p < .001$).

Some of the differences between students and faculty in the importance they attach to various instructional dimensions appear more striking when using this second method of comparison. It can be seen from Table 3 that the largest differences between students and faculty in the rank order of their preferences are for Instructional Dimensions No. 17, intellectual challenge (rank 17.5 for students vs. rank 6 for faculty); No. 1, stimulation of interest (rank 3.5 for students vs. rank 13.5 for faculty); and No. 20, motivating students and setting high standards (rank 17.5 for students vs. rank 7.5 for faculty). More modest differences are found for Dimension No. 7, elocutionary skills (rank 12 for students vs. rank 19 for faculty); No. 12, perceived outcome of instruction (rank 9 for students vs. rank 15.5 for faculty); No. 21, encouragement of self-initiated learning (rank 21 for students vs. rank 15.5 for faculty); and No. 11, usefulness of supplementary materials (rank 15 for students vs. rank 20 for faculty). Still smaller, or "borderline," differences are found for Dimension No. 15, feedback to students (rank 13 for students vs. rank 17 for faculty); No. 19, availability and helpfulness (rank 7 for students vs. rank 10 for faculty); and No. 2, enthusiasm (rank 5 for students vs. rank 2 for faculty). Students and faculty preferences show little if any differences in the rank placement of the remaining dimensions.[8]

Thus, for the group of studies, the two methods of comparison give similar though not identical results. Both methods produce relatively large differences for Instructional Dimensions No. 1 and No. 17 (students placing greater emphasis than faculty on teachers being interesting or stimulating and lesser emphasis on their being intellectually challenging). Instructional Dimensions No. 20 and No. 21 show relatively large differences using one of the two methods, but more modest differences using the other (students placing less emphasis than faculty on teachers motivating students, setting high standards for them, and encouraging self-initiated learning). Both methods found moderate or small differences for Instructional Dimensions No. 7 (students placing greater emphasis than faculty on the teacher's elocutionary skills), No. 12 (students placing greater emphasis than faculty on perceived outcome or impact of instruction), No. 19 (students placing greater emphasis than faculty on teachers being available and helpful), and No. 2 (students placing less emphasis than faculty on teachers being enthusiastic). Instructional Dimensions No.'s 11, 15, and 18 show differences for only one of the two methods and not for the other (and for the last of these three dimensions, even the differences that are found are relatively small).[9]

Considering results for *both* methods of comparison as well as for *both* sets of studies (i.e., the set excluding the four studies of faculty and students at business schools and the set including them), the most consistent and largest student-faculty differences are those showing that students place more importance than do faculty on teachers being interesting and having good elocutionary skills and that faculty place more importance than do students on teachers being intellectually challenging, motivating and setting high standards for students, and encouraging self-initiated learning (Dimensions Nos. 1, 7, 17, 20, and 21). To a lesser extent students give greater emphasis than faculty to the outcomes of instruction (No. 12), and to a still smaller extent (and somewhat inconsistently across methods and sets of studies), they view the availability and helpfulness of teachers (No. 19) as more important to good teaching than faculty do.

Table 3
Importance (Average Standardized Ranks and Their Rank Ordering) of Various Instructional Dimensions for Students and Faculty

Instructional Dimension	Importance Stated by Students	Importance Stated by Faculty
No. 8. Teacher's Sensitivity to, and Concern with, Class Level and Progress	.22 (1)	.27 (3)
No. 5. Teacher's Preparation; Organization of the Course	.27 (2)	.28 (4)
No. 3. Teacher's Knowledge of the Subject	.28 (3.5)	.23 (1)
No. 1. Teacher's Stimulation of Interest in the Course and Its Subject Matter	.28 (3.5)	.50 (13.5)
No. 2. Teacher's Enthusiasm (for Subject or for Teaching)	.32 (5)	.24 (2)
No. 6. Clarity and Understandableness	.33 (6)	.39 (5)
No. 19. Teacher's Availability and Helpfulness	.37 (7)	.47 (10)
No. 18. Teacher's Concern and Respect for Students; Friendliness of the Teacher	.39 (8)	.47 (10)
No. 12. Perceived Outcome or Impact of Instruction	.43 (9)	.51 (15.5)
No. 13. Instructor's Fairness; Impartiality of Evaluation of Students; Quality of Examinations	.45 (10)	.45 (7 5)
No. 10. Nature and Value of the Course Material (Including Its Usefulness and Relevance)	.46 (11)	.47 (10)
No. 7. Teacher's Elocutionary Skills	.47 (12)	.57 (19)
No. 15. Nature, Quality, and Frequency of Feedback from the Teacher to Students	.49 (13)	.53 (17)
No. 16. Teacher's Encouragement of Questions and Discussion, and Openness to Opinions of Others	.51 (14)	.48 (12)
No. 11. Nature and Usefulness of Supplementary Materials and Teaching Aids	.54 (15)	.58 (20)
No. 4. Teacher's Intellectual Expansiveness (and Intelligence)	.56 (16)	.50 (13.5)
No. 17. Intellectual Challenge and Encouragement of Independent Thought (by the Teacher and the Course)	.58 (17.5)	.40 (6)
No. 20. Teacher Motivates Students to Do Their Best; High Standards of Performance Required	.58 (17.5)	.45 (7.5)
No. 9. Clarity of Course Objectives and Requirements	.63 (19)	.56 (18)
No. 14. Personality Characteristics ("Personality") of the Instructor	.64 (20)	.70 (21)
No. 21. Teacher's Encouragement of Self–Initiated Learning	.75 (21)	.51 (15.5)
No. 22. Teacher's Productivity in Research and Related Activities	.91 (22)	.88 (22)

Note: The average standardized ranks given in this table are taken directly from Table 2 and have themselves been ranked from 1 (high) to 22 (low) for students and faculty. These ranks are given in parentheses. In addition, the instructional dimensions have been reordered so that they are listed from highest to lowest in importance to students. As in Table 2, the data presented are based on 18 "core studies." When the four studies of faculty and students in business schools are included, the ranks of the average standardized ranks (see note to Table 2) for the 22 instructional dimensions are the following: Instructional Dimension No. 8 (rank 1 for students. rank 2 for faculty); No. 3 (2, 1); No. 5 (3, 6); No. 2 (4, 3); No. 1 (5, 20); No. 6 (6.5, 4.5); No. 19 (6.5, 7.5); No. 18 (8, 7.5); No. 13 (9, 13); No. 12 (10, 13); No 10 (11, 19.5); No. 7 (12, 17); No. 15 (13, 16); No. 16 (14, 9.5); No. 11 (15, 18.5); No. 4 (16, 15); No. 9 (17, 18.5); No. 14 (18, 21); No. 17 (19, 4.5); No. 20 (20, 11); No. 21 (21, 13); No. 22 (22, 22).

Certain differences, all small, were dependent on the method or set of studies used. For both sets of studies, students felt it slightly more important than did faculty for teachers to be friendly, concerned, and respectful of students (No. 18) when the comparison was in terms of average standardized differences but not when these average standardized differences themselves were ranked and compared. Moreover, for both sets of studies, students placed somewhat more importance than did faculty on the nature and usefulness of supplementary materials and teaching aids (No. 11) and on the nature, quality, and frequency of feedback (No. 15) when this latter, but not the former, method of comparison was used. For both methods of comparison, students placing slightly less emphasis than faculty on teachers' enthusiasm (No. 2) showed up only when the four studies of business teachers and students in business courses were excluded, whereas students placing slightly greater emphasis than faculty on teachers' organization and preparation (No. 5) and on their impartiality and fairness (No. 13) showed up only when business teachers and students were included.

Focusing on differences overlooks the many dimensions on which students and faculty are more or less similar in their views. Thus it is important to note that across sets of studies and methods, students and faculty alike place high importance[10] on teachers being knowledgeable about the subject matter of the course, clear and understandable, and sensitive to (and concerned with) class level and progress (Instructional Dimensions Nos. 3, 6, and 8). Compared to these instructional dimensions, both groups feel it of either moderate or moderate-to-low importance for teachers to be intellectually expansive and intelligent, and open to student questions, class discussion, and the opinions of others (Dimension Nos. 4 and 16) and for the course material to be valuable, useful, and relevant (No. 10). Of clearly low importance to students and faculty, relative to the other dimensions, is the clarity of course objectives and requirements, the overall "personality" of the instructor, and the extent of the teacher's research activities (Nos. 9, 14, and 22). Moreover, some of the differences discussed earlier that varied by the set of studies or the method of comparison used not only were inconsistent but also were so small that students and faculty were in fact more similar than different across the sets of studies and methods. Thus both students and faculty essentially placed high importance on enthusiasm (No. 2) and preparation and organization (No. 5) of instructors, and moderate importance on the instructor's impartiality and fairness (No. 13) as well as on the friendliness of the instructor and the concern or respect he or she shows for students (No. 18).

Instructional Characteristics Important to Overall Evaluation of Actual Teachers

Asking students for their opinions on the characteristics important to effective teaching is not the same as asking them to evaluate specific teachers (or their courses) in actuality, although their general views on good teaching presumably are a critical influence on such evaluations. If it is assumed that each students' overall evaluation of an instructor is an additive combination of the student's evaluation of specific aspects of the teacher and his or her instruction, weighted by the student's estimation of the relative importance of these aspects to good teaching, then it would be expected that students' overall assessment of instructors would be more highly associated with instructional characteristics that students generally consider to be more important to good teaching than with those they consider to be less important (cf. Crittenden and Norr, 1973). If so, then a rank ordering of various specific instructional characteristics that is based on how strongly students' evaluation of actual teachers on these characteristics correlate with the students' overall assessment of these same teachers should be highly similar, if not identical, to the rank ordering of these characteristics when students "merely" indicate the degree of importance of these characteristics to good teaching.

There are factors that might come into play that would reduce the similarity of these two rank orderings, however. For one, the differential weights of various specific instructional characteristics that students imply they use (or will use) in evaluating their teachers—determined by asking them about their ideal or best teachers or about the importance of various instructional characteristics to good teaching—are not necessarily the weights they actually use, in practice, when they form and report an overall impression of each of their current teachers (see, especially, Permut, 1973). For another, it is altogether possible that a characteristic considered by students to be highly important to good teaching does not particularly differentiate the better from the poorer teachers in actual teacher-rating situations. For example, excellent knowledge of the subject matter, already shown to be seen by students as important to good teaching, may indeed be a characteristic of teachers who receive high global ratings from students. But this does not automatically or necessarily mean that less globally effective teachers are any less knowledgeable. These lower-rated teachers, too, may be highly expert in their subject. If so, this would be a case where the instructional dimension of subject-matter knowledge simply does not discriminate (or, perhaps, discriminates only weakly) among teachers with respect to their overall ratings on teacher evaluation forms.

Correlational analysis between specific and overall student evaluations of teachers, then, offers prima facie evidence of the importance of various specific instructional characteristics in discriminating among students' global assessment of teachers. Presumably it also supplies information about the "weights" students attach to these characteristics in terms of their importance to effective teaching, although the extent to which this is the case has not yet been determined by research. At any rate, it is of some worth to compare the importance of various instructional characteristics to good teaching as determined by the views students have directly expressed on the matter (as well as by faculty views) with their "importance" as determined by the strength of their correlation with actual overall ratings of teachers. Ideally, actual ratings of teachers would be available from exactly the same students whose views about good teaching were sought. Barring this, ratings from students at the same schools made at about the same time would be a reasonable substitute. Unfortunately, as far as can be determined, neither set of data is currently available. None of the studies asking students about the components of good teaching (on which Tables 2 and 3 are based) also obtained specific and overall ratings of the teachers at the schools under consideration.

An alternative procedure is available, but it is less satisfactory, and any analysis based on it is exploratory. The earlier article (Feldman, 1976b), mentioned at the outset of the present report, located some 23 studies containing correlations between students' overall evaluations of their instructors and their ratings of various specific attitudinal and behavioral characteristics of these instructors. In this earlier investigation, average standardized ranks were calculated for various instructional dimensions, including 18 of the dimensions used in the present analysis (Nos. 1–13, 15–19, as given in Table 2 and footnote 5 of the earlier article). It is these average standardized ranks that can be compared to those of the present study. Note that this alternative procedure introduces yet another source of variation, and thereby an additional complexity, into the analysis. To an unknown extent, any differences found in the importance of specific instructional characteristics may be due to the use of different students and schools rather than to the fact that importance is being determined by analyzing actual student ratings of teachers.

Shown in Table 4 are the average standardized ranks for the 18 instructional dimensions (and their rank ordering) based on the correlations between students' specific evaluations of teachers on these instructional dimensions and their overall evaluations of these same teachers. Repeated in this table (from Table 3), for purposes of comparison, are the average standardized ranks for these particular 18 dimensions, based on the extent to which students and faculty saw them as being of importance to effective teaching. The ranks of these average standardized rankings are again given (this time running from 1 to 18).

The association between the importance of these eighteen dimensions to effective teaching as viewed by students and by faculty is still high (rho = +.66, $p < .01$; $r = +.71$, $p < .01$), although a little lower than when all 22 dimensions were used. However, neither the student nor the faculty indications of the importance of the instructional dimensions are significantly related to importance of these dimensions in terms of discriminating among students' overall evaluation of teachers in actual rating situations. For the student-student comparison, rho is +.34 ($p > .05$) and r is +.36 ($p > .05$); for the faculty-student comparison, rho is + .28 ($p > .05$) and r is + .31 ($p > .05$). It thus becomes of particular interest to see where, and exactly how, the three indicators of importance differ as well as where they might be similar. In order not to put too fine a point on the comparisons, given the several methodological and interpretive difficulties discussed, comparisons are made in terms of high (1–6), medium (7–12), and low 13–18) ranks.

The teacher's preparation and organization, clarity and understandableness, and sensitivity to, and concern with, class level and progress (Instructional Dimension Nos. 5, 6, and 8) are of especial importance in all three ways. That is, students and faculty view them as highly important when asked about the components of good teaching, and they are of high importance in discriminating among the global ratings received by teachers from their students. The teacher's enthusiasm and his or her knowledge of the subject (Dimensions No. 2 and No. 3) are also of high importance in the views of students and faculty, but they are of only moderate importance in differentiating among students' actual overall assessment of teachers. Being able to stimulate their interest (No. 1) is highly important to students, both when they ex-

Table 4
Importance (Average Standardized Ranks and Their Rank Ordering) of Various Instructional Dimensions for Students (Two Indicators) and Faculty (One Indicator)

Instructional Dimension	Importance Stated by Students	Importance Stated by Faculty	Importance Shown by Correlation with Overall Evaluations
No. 8. Teacher's Sensitivity to, and Concern with, Class Level and Progress	.22 (1)	.27 (3)	.40 (5)
No. 5. Teacher's Preparation; Organization of the Course	.27 (2)	.28 (4)	.41 (6)
No. 3. Teacher's Knowledge of the Subject	.28 (3.5)	.23 (1)	.48 (9)
No. 1. Teacher's Stimulation of Interest in the Course and Its Subject Matter	.28 (3.5)	.50 (12.5)	.20 (1)
No. 2. Teacher's Enthusiasm (for Subject or for Teaching)	.32 (5)	.24 (2)	.46 (80)
No. 6. Clarity and Understandableness	.33 (6)	.39 (5)	.25 (2)
No. 19. Teacher's Availability and Helpfulness	.37 (7)	.47 (9)	.74 (17)
No. 18. Teacher's Concern and Respect for Students; Friendliness of the Teacher	.39 (8)	.47 (9)	.65 (13)
No. 12. Perceived Outcome or Impact of Instruction	.43 (9)	.51 (14)	.28 (3)
No. 13. Instructor's Fairness; Impartiality of Evaluation of Students; Quality of Examinations	.45 (10)	.45 (7)	.72 (15.5)
No. 10. Nature and Value of the Course Material (Including Its Usefulness and Relevance)	.46 (11)	.47 (9)	.70 (14)
No. 7. Teacher's Elocutionary Skills	.47 (12)	.57 (17)	.49 (10)
No. 15. Nature, Quality, and Frequency of Feedback from the Teacher to Students	.49 (13)	.53 (15)	.87 (18)
No. 16. Teacher's Encouragement of Questions and Discussion, and Openness to Opinions of Others	.51 (14)	.48 (11)	.60 (12)
No. 11. Nature and Usefulness of Supplementary Materials and Teaching Aids	.54 (15)	.58 (18)	.72 (15.5)
No. 4. Teacher's Intellectual Expansiveness (and Intelligence)	.56 (16)	.50 (12.5)	.54 (11)
No. 17. Intellectual Challenge and Encouragement of Independent Thought (by the Teacher and the Course)	.58 (17)	.40 (6)	.39 (4)
No. 9. Clarity of Course Objectives and Requirements	.63 (18)	.56 (16)	.45 (7)

Note: The average standardized ranks given in the first two columns for the 18 dimensions under consideration are taken from Table 3 and have been (re)ranked from 1 to 18 (with the ranks shown in parentheses). The average standardized ranks given to Column 3 come from Feldman (1976b, see Table 2 and footnote 5); they, too, have been ranked from 1 to 18 (with the ranks given in parentheses).

press their views about good teaching and when they actually rate teachers; however, faculty regard this dimension as moderate to low in importance.

No one dimension is of moderate importance in all three ways, although Dimension No. 16 (the teacher's openness to question, discussion, and the opinion of others) is of moderate-to-low importance for all three. In the eyes of both students and faculty, the nature and value of the course material and the instructor's fairness, concern and respect for students, friendliness, availability, and helpfulness (Dimension Nos. 10, 13, 18, and 19) are of moderate importance as components of good teaching, although they are only of low importance in discriminating among teachers' overall ratings. Students place moderate emphasis on the teacher's elocutionary skills (No. 7), both in their expressed views and when actually rating teachers, but the faculty themselves do not see this instructional characteristic as particularly important to good teaching. No matter the indicator used, the nature and usefulness of supplementary material and teaching aids, as well as the nature, quality, and frequency of feedback from the teacher to students (Nos. 11 and 15) register low in importance relative to the other dimensions.

The four remaining dimensions show particularly interesting discrepancies. The clarity of course objectives and requirements (No. 9) are said by both students and faculty to be of low importance to effective teaching, yet this dimension ranks in seventh place (just short of being in the top third) in correlating with overall ratings of teachers. Based on the views they express, the outcome of instruction (No. 12) is moderately important to students and of less importance than to faculty, but this dimension is highly correlated with the overall student assessment of teachers in actual rating situations. The teacher's intelligence and intellectual expansiveness (No. 4) are moderately important to faculty and also to students when they actually discriminate among the overall performances of teachers, but this aspect of instruction is of less importance to students when they express their views on good teaching. Finally, intellectual challenge and encouragement of independent thought (No. 17) are highly important to good teaching say the faculty, although students see them of low importance; yet when students actually assess their teachers, this dimension turns out to be highly important in discriminating among teachers.

Summary, Comments, and Suggestions for Additional Research

College teachers have been known to voice concern that students and faculty have different ideas about what is important to good teaching and effective instruction. One of the arguments brought up against the use of students' evaluations of teachers, in fact, is that students do not always use appropriate criteria in evaluating their teachers. Indeed, the chief premise behind the so-called Dr. Fox effect, accounting in part for the great interest in the presumed phenomenon, is that students value authoritative style, showmanship, wit, and other forms of teachers' expressiveness at the expense of substance, meaning, and course content (see, *inter alia*, Abrami, Leventhal, and Perry, 1982; Marsh, 1984; Naftulin, Ware, and Donnelly, 1973). The purpose of the present analysis was to draw together what is known about the similarities and dissimilarities between faculty and students in their views on effective college teaching, so that a consideration of these various concerns and issues would be better grounded empirically.

As it happens, extant evidence shows faculty members not to be much different from students in their views on good teaching—at least in terms of the expressed importance the two groups place on various components of teaching. Across the 31 relevant studies reviewed here, the average correlation between students and faculty in their valuation of these components is +.71. From the studies at hand, the strength of this association is about the same, on average, for universities and four-year colleges as it is for community colleges. It is possible, of course, that future multischool studies, using more finely grained categories of schools, might show that there are certain specific types of universities or colleges where these associations are likely to be particularly strong and others where they are likely to be weak or nonexistent.

The strength of the association in question may vary within colleges, of course. Thus it was found that, for each of the four studies of teachers and students at business schools within colleges, the association between faculty and students was not sufficiently large to be statistically significant. Because each of these studies was done at a different college, results would seem to have some generalizability, although further replication at still other colleges would be desirable. Assuming that the lack of association between students and faculty at business schools is not an ungeneralizable fluke, it would be worth pursuing what there is about such settings, or about the teachers and students in them, that creates this lack of similarity in their views. There may also be other divisions, programs, or academic fields within colleges where associations between faculty and student views on good teaching are low, and perhaps some where they are particularly high, but what they are cannot be told from the few existing pieces of research that have focused on faculty and students within particular subdivisions or subfields in colleges.

Research is also needed on whether there are certain types of students who are either much more or much less likely to have views similar to those of faculty in general. For example, are students who are academically successful more similar to faculty in their views as to what contributes to effective instruction than are students who are not particularly successful academically? Do male and female students, or students at different class levels in college, differ in the extent to which their views are similar to those of faculty? Crawford and Bradshaw (1968) and Yourglich (1955) have done some research in this area, but their work offers only the beginnings of what might be done. College teachers are not an undifferentiated lot, of course, so they, too, could be divided into subtypes before comparing them with students. Here, one would want to explore the extent of similarity between the opinions of certain types of teachers with those of students in general as well with certain types of students in particular.

If the average correlation of +.71 indicates a general similarity between students and faculty in their views of good teaching, its size nevertheless leaves room for some particular differences between them. One interest of the present investigation was whether there were any consistencies across studies in the ways that students and faculty in fact were dissimilar (as well as similar). The responses gathered from students and faculty about the components of good teaching were coded into 22 instructional dimensions. The average standardized ranks for students and for faculty on these dimensions were compared, as were the ranks of these average standardized ranks, for a "core" set of 18 studies that excluded the four studies done at business schools as well as for an expanded set of studies that included them. In addition, these results were compared with those given in an earlier analysis of studies showing the correlations between students' actual ratings of teachers on 18 of these 22 dimensions and the students' overall ratings of these teachers.

Across the various sets of studies and methods of comparison, it is clear that students and faculty were similar in placing high importance on teachers being prepared and organized, clear and understandable, and sensitive to class level and progress; and both groups generally placed moderate importance on teachers being open to class discussion and the opinions of others. Moreover, each of these pedagogical aspects was of a corresponding level of importance in students' actual overall assessment of their teachers in rating situations (as shown by the relative sizes of the correlations between specific and overall evaluations).

Students and faculty were also generally similar in their views about the importance of certain other instructional components, but in each of these instances, the components were not of a corresponding level of importance with respect to discriminating among students' overall ratings of instructors. Thus, faculty and students were similar in attributing high importance to the instructor's enthusiasm and his or her knowledge of the subject matter, but in actual rating situations, these two aspects of instruction were only moderately important in their "contribution" to the overall rating of teachers. Likewise, faculty and students were similar in placing moderate importance on the instructor's fairness and impartiality of evaluation, his or her friendliness as well as concern and respect for students, and the nature and value of the course material, but in actual ratings situations these instructional dimensions were low in importance. Faculty and students both felt that teachers being intellectually expansive was of moderate to low importance, but this aspect of instruction was unequivocally moderate in importance in discriminating among teachers' overall evaluations by students. Finally, faculty and students alike said that the clarity of course objectives and requirements was of low importance to good teaching or effective instruction, although in actuality this pedagogical aspect turned out to be of moderate, if not high, significance in discriminating among the overall quality or effectiveness of teachers when they were evaluated by students.

It might also be noted that faculty and students were similar in believing the "personality" of the instructor and his or her productivity in research and related activities to be relatively unimportant to good teaching, but it is unknown from the sources used for the present analysis whether these two dimensions were also of low importance in rating situations. For the dimension of the nature, quality, and frequency of feedback from teachers to students and that of the nature and usefulness of supplementary material and teaching aids, results varied enough across different methods and sets of studies to create some ambiguity about the similarity (or lack of it) between students and faculty. It is not clear whether students placed moderate or low emphasis on these two aspects of instruction, although it is clear in both cases that faculty thought them to be of low importance (and both were of low importance in discriminating among the overall instructional performance of teachers as perceived by students) .

All told then, students and faculty were clearly similar in their views about the importance of 13 of the 22 instructional dimensions under study (although the importance of the dimensions in actual rating situations did not always match), and for two other dimensions results were somewhat inconsistent across sets of studies and methods of comparison. For the remaining seven instructional dimensions, students and faculty showed consistent differences in terms of the views they expressed about the importance of each. Students strongly emphasized the importance of the teacher stimulating their interest in the course and in its subject matter (and this dimension was highly important in its contribution to the overall assessment of actual teachers), but faculty considered this dimension to be of moderate or even low importance (depending on the particular set of studies reviewed). The dimension of instructor availability and helpfulness showed a smaller difference between students and faculty. Students felt this dimension to be of moderate-to-high importance, whereas faculty thought it to be more unequivocally moderate in importance (and, in practice, the dimension was only of low importance in discriminating among the overall ratings of teachers). Students clearly felt the outcome or impact of instruction to be of moderate importance (and this dimension was highly associated with students' overall ratings of teachers); faculty, however, viewed this particular aspect as having lesser (moderate-to-low) importance. Although students placed moderate importance on teachers' elocutionary skills (and this dimension was also a moderate contributor to the overall assessment of teachers), faculty felt this instructional aspect to be of low importance. Students placed low importance, but faculty high importance, on teachers intellectually challenging students and encouraging their independent thought; yet this dimension was a strong correlate of students' overall ratings of teachers, suggesting it was of high importance to students when they actually discriminated among teachers as to their overall performances. Students also placed low importance on teachers setting high standards of performance and motivating students to do their best as well as on encouraging self-initiated learning, whereas faculty saw these aspects of teaching as moderate in importance; no information was available in the sources used for the present analysis regarding the significance of these two dimensions in discriminating among teachers' overall ratings.

The fact that certain similarities and differences in the criteria students and faculty use in determining good teaching can be found across studies creates some confidence in their existence. Nevertheless, it would be of interest to see if the similarities and differences that have been found hold up as more studies are done. It would be of even greater interest if future studies could discover how these similarities and differences are affected by type of school, type of academic division and field within schools, and type of student and teacher.

It should be emphasized that comparing the importance of various components of teaching (from either the student or faculty view) with the importance of these components in actual rating situation was done exploratory in this analysis. Any generalizations based on these particular comparisons are tentative, at best. This is mainly so because data for actual ratings involved a different set of studies—with different students and faculty at different schools—from the set of studies used to obtain students and faculty views. An obvious need thus exists for future research in which the data on the views of students and faculty and the data on the actual specific and overall student ratings of faculty are collected from matching samples.

Even with such data, there are at least two different explanations for any differences that are found between the importance of pedagogical components when measured by students' stated views and the importance of these components when determined by the size of their associations with the overall evaluations of teachers. The differential weights for the various pedagogical characteristics that students, in effect, say they use (or will use) in evaluating their teachers—determined by asking them about the importance of various characteristics to good teaching (or about their "ideal" or "best" teachers)—may not necessarily be the weights they actually use, in practice, when forming an overall impression of each of their teachers and globally evaluating them. Quite apart from the question of the correspondence of these weights, moreover, traits that students consider to be important to good teaching may not of necessity be exactly the same traits that actually discriminate among teachers in terms of the overall evaluations they receive. Teachers receiving high overall ratings from students may be higher than other teachers on some, but not all, of the specific components considered by students to be highly important to good teaching. Conversely, teachers receiving low overall ratings are not necessarily lower than other teachers on every trait seen as highly important to good teaching.

Another consideration needs mentioning at this point. The present analysis has avoided couching its argument in terms of the "agreement" or "disagreement" between students and faculty about the components of effective teaching. At least by one sense of these words, to say that faculty agree (or disagree) with students and that students agree (or disagree) with faculty implies that the similarity (or dissimilarity) is explicit and known to both groups. The implication is that the groups are mutually aware of their similarities and differences. This may or may not be true, which suggests another area of research. Students could be asked whether they thought faculty would agree or disagree with the importance they place on various components of teaching. Similarly, faculty members, having expressed their own preferences, could be asked whether they thought students would agree or disagree. Each group could even be instructed to rate the importance of various components as they thought the other groups would rate them. The degree of mutual awareness of similarity and dissimilarity in views between the two groups could thus be established.

Finally, it is important to recognize that discovering the similarities and dissimilarities between faculty and students in the importance they place on various components of teaching (including the extent of their mutual awareness of these similarities and dissimilarities) is merely the beginning of a research agenda. What really needs to be known is how such similarities or dissimilarities come into play in the actual interaction between students and teachers in the classroom. Moreover, do these similarities and dissimilarities affect how well instructors actually teach or how much students learn, and what are the exact mechanisms at work? Empirical answers to questions such as these should prove especially beneficial to the study and practice of higher education.

Notes

1. See Feldman (1976a,b, 1977, 1978, 1979, 1983, 1984, 1986, 1987).
2. Rosenthal (1978, 1984) discusses several methods of combining independent probabilities (from different studies) to get an overall estimate of the probability that the separate *p* levels would have been obtained were the null hypothesis true in each of the cases. Adding up the separate Z's dividing the resultant sum by the square root of the number of studies perhaps is the simplest and most routinely applicable of the methods, and it is the one used in the present analysis.
3. Baril and Skaggs (1976); Breed (1927); Brewer and Brewer (1970); Bridges et al. (1971); Delaney and Coons (1976); Evaluation and Examination Service (1974); Hussain and Leestamper (1968); Lovell and Haner (1955); Marques et al. (1979); Murray et al. (1982); Odom (1943); Perry (1969); Romine (1974); Rotem (1975); Shatz and Best (1986); and Yourglich (1955).
4. Blai (1974); Hartung (1972); Jenkins et al. (n.d.); Krupka (1970); Romine and Newport (1973); and Whitley (1982).
5. The degree of student-faculty similarity may also vary for different subgroups of students and faculty. Crawford and Bradshaw (1968) calculated correlations between subgroups of students (male, female; high, average, and low ranking students, as based on grade-point averages) and subgroups of faculty members (associate and full professors; instructors and assistant professors). Student-faculty correlations varied across the various combination of subgroups from a high of .92 to a low of .72 (all of which are statistically significant), as follows: high ranking male students x instructors/assistant professors (r = +.92); high ranking female students x instructors/assistant professors (r = +.90); high ranking male students x associate and full professors (r = + .89); average ranking female students x instructors/assistant professors (r = + .88); average ranking male students x instructors/assistant professors (r = + .85); average ranking male students x associate and full professors (r = + .85); low ranking female students x associate and full professors (r = + .83); average ranking female students x associate and full professors (r = + .81); high ranking female students x associate and full professors (r = +.80); low ranking male students x associate and full professors (r = +.76); low ranking female students x instructors and assistant professors (r = + .74); low ranking male students x instructors and assistant professors (r = +.72). Data given in Tables 2 and 4 in Yourglich (1955) can be used to calculate the rank-order correlation between the preferences of faculty as a whole and those of each of the four class levels of students. The lowest rank-order correlation is for the comparison between faculty and freshmen (rho = +.41) and is not statistically significant. The rank-order correlations for the comparisons involving sophomores (+.65), juniors (+.60), and seniors (+.57) not only are higher but also are statistically significant.
6. Each of the following studies gave the general correlation between students' and faculty's judgments of the importance of various instructional characteristics, as reported in Table 1 of the present analysis, but none of these studies gave specific information about the importance of *each* characteristic: Crawford and Bradshaw (1968); Hartung (1972); Lovell and Haner (1955); and Rotem (1975). Breed (1927) did present the ranks of various instructional characteristics, but separately within certain subdivisions of these

characteristics rather than across them; thus a single overall rank ordering for students and one for faculty cannot be obtained from the data presented. From data in Norr and Crittendon (1975) and Shatz and Best (1986), the ranking of multi-item scales measuring various instructional components can be obtained, but the rank of separate items within the scales cannot. The kind of questionnaire items about instruction found in Blai (1974) and the format of the questionnaire itself do not lend themselves to the coding scheme and data analysis of the present investigation; and thus this study, too, has been excluded from further consideration.

7. The note to Table 2 shows the results when data from the four studies of faculty and students in business schools *are added to* the results from the core set of studies (including those cases where only one of the four studies had data relevant for a particular dimension). Considering the nine instructional dimensions that showed the largest average standardized differences (even if small) between faculty and students for the core set of studies, five show the same or highly similar differences when the fuller set of studies is used (Dimension Nos. 7, 13, 18, 19, and 21), whereas three dimensions now show larger differences (Dimension Nos. 1, 17, and 20). The previously small average standardized difference for Dimension No. 2 becomes even smaller, to the point where it is insignificant as a difference between students and faculty. In addition, the expanded group of studies now show "new (albeit relatively small) average standardized differences for Dimensions No. 5 (+.12) and No. 13 (+.11).

8. When the results from the four studies done at business schools are added to the results from the core set of studies (see the note to Table 3), Instructional Dimensions No. 1, No. 17, and No. 21 show larger differences between the student and faculty rankings. The differences in ranks for the other seven dimensions originally showing such differences (Nos. 2, 7, 11, 12, 15, 19, and 20) become somewhat smaller. Because the differences for two of these particular dimensions (Nos. 2 and 19) were very small to begin with, the decrease means that faculty and students no longer show meaningful differences in the importance they place on them. Finally, for four instructional dimensions, the fuller set of studies show small differences not found using only the core set of studies: Dimension No. 16 (rank 14 for students vs. rank 9.5 for faculty), No. 13 (rank 9 for students vs. rank 13 for faculty), No. 5 (rank 3 for students vs. rank 6 for faculty), and No. 14 (rank 18 for students vs. rank 21 for faculty). Incidentally, adding the four studies lowers rho and r somewhat (to + .60 and + .72, respectively).

9. Comparing methods produces somewhat different results when the four studies of faculty and students at business schools are added to the core set of studies. The following four dimensions show large or fairly large differences between students and faculty for both methods: Nos. 1, 17, 20, and 21. Moderate or small differences are found for Dimension Nos. 5, 7, 12, and 13 for both methods. Dimension Nos. 11. 14, 15, 16, and 19 show differences (relatively small ones) for only one of the two methods and not the other.

10. For purposes of general comparison, a rank between 1 and 7 is considered as placing high importance on the particular instructional dimension, whereas ranks 8–15 and ranks 1–22 are considered to indicate moderate and low importance, respectively.

References

Abrami, P. C., Leventhal, L., and Perry, R. P. (1982). Educational seduction. *Review of Educational Research* 52(3): 446–464.

Baril, G. L., and Skaggs, C. T. (1976). Selecting items for a college course evaluation form. *College Student Journal* 10(2): 183–187.

Baum, P., and Brown, W. W. (1980). Student and faculty perceptions of teaching effectiveness. *Research in Higher Education* 13(3): 233–242.

Blai, B., Jr. (1974). Viewpoints—to each his own! A parallel-perceptions inquiry. Bryn Mawr, Pa.: Office of Research, Harcum Junior College.

Blazek, H. D. (1974). Student perceptions of college teaching effectiveness. Unpublished doctoral dissertation, Northern Illinois University.

Breed, F. S. (1927). Factors contributing to success in college teaching. *Journal of Educational Research* 16(4): 247–253.

Brewer, R. E., and Brewer, M. B. (1970). Relative importance of ten qualities for college teaching determined by pair comparisons. *Journal of Educational Research* 63(6): 243–246.

Bridges, C. M., Ware, W. B., Brown, B. B., and Greenwood, G. (1971). Characteristics of best and worst college teachers. *Science Education* 55(4): 545–553.

Crawford, P. L., and Bradshaw, H. L. (1968). Perception of characteristics of effective university teachers: a scaling analysis. *Educational and Psychological Measurement* 28(4): 1079–1085.

Crittenden, K. S., and Norr, J. L. (1973). Student values and teacher evaluation: a problem in person perception. *Sociometry* 36(2): 143–151.

Delaney, E. L., Jr., and Coons, E. E., Jr. (1976). Differing views on the criteria and purposes of student ratings of instruction. Paper read at the annual meeting of the Association for Institutional Research.

Evaluation and Examination Service (1974). Student Perceptions of Teaching (SPOT): 2. Asking the right questions. Research Report No. 76. Iowa City: Evaluation and Examination Service, University of Iowa.

Feldman, K. A. (1976a). Grades and college students' evaluations of their courses and teachers. *Research in Higher Education* 4(1): 69–111.

Feldman, K. A. (1976b). The superior college teacher from the students' view. *Research in Higher Education* 5(3): 243–288.

Feldman, K. A. (1977). Consistency and variability among college students in rating their teachers and courses: A review and analysis. *Research in Higher Education* 6(3): 223–274.

Feldman, K. A. (1978). Course characteristics and college students' ratings of their teachers: what we know and what we don't. *Research in Higher Education* 9(3): 199–242.

Feldman, K. A. (1979). The significance of circumstances for college students' ratings of their teachers and courses. *Research in Higher Education* 10(2): 149–172.

Feldman, K. A. (1983). Seniority and experience of college teachers as related to evaluations they receive from students. *Research in Higher Education* 18(1): 3–124.

Feldman, K. A. (1984). Class size and college students' evaluations of teachers and courses: a closer look. *Research in Higher Education* 21(1): 45–116.

Feldman, K. A. (1986). The perceived instructional effectiveness of college teachers as related to their personality and attitudinal characteristics: a review and synthesis. *Research in Higher Education* 24(2): 139–213.

Feldman, K. A. (1987). Research productivity and scholarly accomplishment of college teachers as related to their instructional effectiveness: a review and exploration. *Research in Higher Education* 26(3): 227–298.

Freilich, M. B. (1983). A student evaluation of teaching techniques. *Journal of Chemical Education* 60(3): 218–221.

Glass, G. V., McGaw, B., and Smith, M. L. (1981). *Meta-Analysis in Social Research.* Beverly Hills, Calif.: Sage.

Hartung, A. B. (1972). Teaching excellence. *Improving College and University* 20(3): 146–147.

Hussain, K. M., and Leestamper, R. (1968). Survey on criteria of teaching effectiveness at New Mexico State University. Las Cruces: New Mexico State University. (ERIC Document Reproduction Service No. ED 023 365)

Jenkins, C., Baker, R. Emerson, D., Hagerty, D., and Tune, D. (n.d.). Evaluation of community college instruction: a background study. Freeport, Ill.: Highland Community College.

Krupka, J. G. (1970). Report on faculty and student evaluation of Instructor Rating Questionnaire. Northampton, Pa.: Northampton County Area Community College.

Lovell, G. D., and Haner, C. F. (1955). Forced-choice applied to college faculty rating. *Educational and Psychological Measurement* 15(3): 291–304.

Mann, R. D., Arnold, S. M., Binder, J. L., Cytrynbaum, S., Newman, B., Ringwald, B. E., Ringwald, J. W., and Rosenwein, R. (1970). *The College Classroom: Conflict, Change, and Learning.* New York: Wiley.

Marques, T. E., Lane, D. M. and Dorfman, P. W. (1979). Toward the development of a system for instructional evaluation: Is there consensus regarding what constitutes effective teaching? *Journal of Educational Psychology* 71(6): 840–849.

Marsh, H. W. (1984). Students' evaluation of university teaching: dimensionality, reliability, validity, potential biases, and utility. *Journal of Educational Psychology* 76(5):707–754.

Murray, H. G., Newby, W. G., Crealock, C., Bowden, B., Gailey, T. D., Oswin, J., and Smith, P. (1982). Evaluation of teaching at the University of Western Ontario: Report submitted by Provost's Advisory Committee on Teaching and Learning (July).

Naftulin, D. H., Ware, J. E., Jr., and Donnelly, G. A. (1973). The Doctor Fox lecture: a paradigm of educational seduction. *Journal of Medical Education* 48(7): 630–635.

Norr, J. L., and Crittenden, K. S. (1975). Evaluating college teaching as leadership. *Higher Education* 4(3): 335–350.

Odom, C. L. (1943). An objective determination of the qualities of a good college teacher. *Peabody Journal of Education* 21(3): 109–116.

Permut, S. E. (1973). Cure utilization patterns in student-faculty evaluation. *Journal of Psychology* 83: 41–48.

Perry, R. R. (1969). Evaluation of teaching behavior seeks to measure effectiveness. *College and University Business* 47(4): 18, 22.

Romine, S. (1974). Student and faculty perception of an effective university instructional climate. *Journal of Educational Research* 68(4): 139–143.

Romine S., and Newport. D. L. (1973). Defining, assessing, and improving community junior college instructional climate. Boulder, Colo.: Higher Education Center, School of Education, University of Colorado.

Rosenthal, R. (1978). Combining results of independent studies. *Psychological Bulletin* 85(1): 185–193.

Rosenthal, R. (1984). *Meta-Analytic Procedures for Social Research.* Beverly Hills, Calif.: Sage.

Rotem, A. (1975). The effects of feedback from students to university professors: an experimental study. Unpublished doctoral dissertation, University of California, Santa Barbara.

Shatz, M. A., and Best, J. B. (1986). Selection of items for course evaluation by faculty and students. *Psychological Reports* 58: 239–242.

Stevens, G. E. (1978). Teaching by whose objectives? The view of students and teachers. Unpublished manuscript. (ERIC Document Reproduction Service No. ED 193 580).

Stevens, G. E., and Marquette, R. P. (1979). Differing student and faculty perceptions of teaching effectiveness and the value of student evaluations. *POD Quarterly* 1(4): 207–219.

Whitley, I. (1982). Students' and teachers' perceptions of good instruction. Unpublished manuscript, Meridian Junior College.

Wittmaier, B. C. (1975). Teaching styles: a comparison of faculty and student preferences. *Improving College and University Teaching Yearbook 1975,* pp. 249–251. Corvallis: Oregon State University Press.

Wotruba, T. R., and Wright, P. L. (1975). How to develop a teacher–rating instrument: a research approach. *Journal of Higher Education* 46(6): 653–663.

Yourglich, A. (1955). Study on correlations between college teachers' and students' concepts of "ideal-student" and "ideal-teacher." *Journal of Educational Research* 49(1): 59–64.

New Faculty as Teachers

ROBERT BOICE

In the midst of growing concerns for college teaching [1] we produce more and more useful advice about ways to improve instruction [8]. Yet, we know almost nothing about how (and how quickly) professors establish their teaching styles. And, it follows, we too rarely consider strategies for dealing with their teaching in its formative stages.

This article depicts the experience of new faculty as teachers over periods of one and two years and across two large campuses. It shows a surprisingly slow pattern of establishing comfort and student approval, of moving beyond defensive strategies including overpreparation of lecture content, and of looking for supports in improving teaching. The few prior efforts at observing new faculty have been enlightening but limited to smaller groups, to fewer observations, or to nonteaching activities [3, 5, 6].

The aim of this study, though, is not simply to document the teaching experiences of new faculty but to answer four related questions. First, do initial teaching patterns, adaptive and maladaptive, tend to persist? Second, what can we learn from the experiences of new faculty who master teaching quickly and enjoyably? Third, how does success in teaching correspond to prowess in areas including the establishment of collegial supports and of outputs in scholarly writing? And, fourth, how do initial teaching experiences compare at a "teaching" (comprehensive) and at a "research" (doctoral) campus?

Methods

The four cohorts of new faculty described here came from two campuses, (1) a comprehensive university with some thirty-five thousand students and about one thousand faculty and (2) a doctoral campus with some fifteen thousand students and some one thousand faculty. Both campuses hired similar numbers of new tenure-track faculty during the study years of 1985 to 1990, from fifty to seventy per year.

Cohorts

Table 1 shows the composition of the four cohorts, two of them from the former campus and two of them from the latter campus. Cohorts 2 and 3 overlapped as the author transferred his faculty development programs from the first campus to the second during 1988–89.

At Campus 1, all but one to three new faculty per cohort volunteered for interviews conducted in their offices over successive semesters. The few individuals who did not participate were inaccessible because of their commitments off campus. At Campus 2, all but twelve to fifteen new faculty per cohort volunteered to participate in the same format of interviews. Campus 2, much less publicly committed to teaching than Campus 1, differed most obviously in the influence of department chairpeople; at Campus 2 (but never at Campus 1), five of some forty chairs advised their new faculty not to participate in a program that might interfere with research productivity.

In most other ways the two groups of new faculty were alike. They came to campus with similar levels of scholarly productivity, of teaching experience, and of doctoral credentials from prestigious univer-

"New Faculty as Teachers," by Robert Boice, reprinted by permission from *Journal of Higher Education*, 1991, Ohio State University.

Table 1
Distribution of Background Types of Interviewees across Cohorts for Both Campuses (number of participants during second years are shown parenthetically)

	Background Category		
Year cohort began, Campus 1	Inexperienced	Returning	Experienced
1987	14 (10)	5 (3)	29 (28)
1988	19 (14)	2 (2)	47 (46)
Year cohort began, Campus 2			
1988	19 (17)	6 (5)	16 (15)
1989	25	4	11

At both study campuses, a critical distinction emerged between types of new faculty. They differentiated themselves as (a) inexperienced (with less than two years beyond the doctorate), (b) returning (from careers outside academe and/or teaching), and (c) experienced (including full-time teaching at another campus).

The most obvious difference between the two campuses was teaching load. Campus 1 had an official load of twelve classroom hours a week (that is, four separate courses per semester). Most of its new hires received three hours of release time in year 1 on campus; thereafter, only a minority of successful applicants who demonstrated productive beginnings continued to receive reduced teaching loads. Campus 2 had a two-course (or six hours a week) load except for some humanities faculty who carried three courses. The majority of new faculty at Campus 2 in the science areas had teaching loads of one course or less for their first year or two on campus.

The key faculty under study here are the inexperienced newcomers and returning newcomers; experienced new faculty serve as comparisons. Most inexperienced and returning new faculty in this sample had minimal experience as classroom teachers during graduate school ($N = 17$ at Campus 1 and $N = 12$ at Campus 2 taught their own classes as graduate students). Fewer still reported any systematic training including teaching practice ($N = 8$ at Campus l; $N = 5$ at Campus 2).

Interview Formats

The interview format resembles that used in prior research with new faculty by a variety of researchers [7]; copies can be obtained from the author. Each participant in this study was interviewed during successive semesters. Essentially, I asked new faculty about their experiences and plans as teachers, colleagues, and scholarly writers. These visits to new faculty, however, consisted of much more than preplanned interviewing. Interactions usually lasted one hour, often longer, always in informal fashion with prods for open-ended answers beyond responses to structured questions. Thus, except for replies to set questions, individuals chose what to emphasize and develop.

Participants were recruited by means of phone calls in which they were asked to give an hour of their time for a confidential interview about their experience as a new faculty member on campus. Where new faculty expressed ambivalence about participating, the author visited them during their posted office hours to repeat the request. This modicum of social pressure was sufficient to enlist almost all faculty who would otherwise not have participated; the result was a representative sample of individuals who volunteered and who, invariably, indicated satisfaction in having done so. As indicated above, this strategy worked except in some cases at Campus 2 where chairs (distributed across campus) had cautioned their new faculty not to participate.

A critical condition for all new faculty was the assurance that I would not relate information about the participation or answers of individuals to anyone. Administrators, who routinely asked about the involvement or responses of individual faculty, were given the kinds of generalized and/or anonymous results reported here.

My own role in this study was multifaceted and reflects my training, first as an ethologist and then as a psychotherapist; that is, I interacted with new faculty as an observer, researcher, helper, and colleague. I began initial interviews by explaining this complexity of interactive stances as part of explaining the project's purpose. No one expressed discomfort with my multifaceted role or with the prospect of waiting to learn the results of repeated interviews in manuscripts like this one.

Results

Interview formats produced both qualitative and quantitative results. Interviewees responded to requests to rate experiences on 10-point Likert scales (for example, rate your recent comfort in the classroom), to specify experiences including teaching practices (for example, number of colleagues with whom they discussed teaching), and to elaborate on quantitative answers (for example, "how do you suppose students would describe you as a teacher?").

Analysis of these interviews is presented in terms of successive semesters on campus. Within each semester (for example, the first semester on campus), data are presented as a conglomerate of all cohorts studied; then, contrasts are drawn between backgrounds (as inexperienced, returning, and experienced), and between campuses. Where appropriate, individualistic patterns of new faculty are described to give a sense of how new faculty (1) experienced problems and supports as teachers, (2) showed ready promise as successes or as failures at teaching, and (3) responded to opportunities for help as teachers.

First Semester

Initial contacts with new faculty at orientation workshops (before the onset of formal interviews) revealed various common concerns. Because both campuses required publication for tenure, newcomers supposed that they would feel more pressured to write than to do anything else during coming semesters; they worried that teaching would suffer in the process. No one at orientation expressed concerns about social supports; in the exuberance of meeting other new faculty, campuses seemed easy places to make friends. Moreover, new faculty just arriving on campus often reaffirmed their attraction to academe as a place where autonomy is highly valued (as in this typical comment during orientation by an inexperienced new faculty member at Campus 1):

> I'm not sure that I need this sort of thing [that is the orientation day]. I have people I can rely on back at _______ if I need them, but I think I know what I need to do. [In response to my question about whether she would be interested in having a mentor on campus?] No, I think I am too busy for that . . . and I'm not sure what such a person could tell me. That's why I decided to become a professor; I like to have good people around me but I prefer to manage on my own.

By the midpoint of the first semester, when interviews were well underway, two surprising realities had set in. First, a lack of collegial support and of intellectual stimulation dominated complaints. Second, investments in lecture preparation dominated workweeks. Writing and other things that "could wait" were put aside until new faculty had time and energy left over from teaching.

Collegial support. One specification of new faculty's experience can be seen in analyses of reported collegial help in terms of advice about teaching (see table 2). Three results stand out. First, general levels of collegial support evidenced as advice were anything but universal; senior faculty were unlikely to say much beyond initial small talk. Second, most of what they did say that could have been credited as informative and supportive tended to be far more gossipy than new faculty would have preferred. And third, of all the kinds of advice and support, counsel about teaching was least often reported (table 2). This comment from an inexperienced newcomer at Campus 1 was normative:

> No, no one has said much about teaching. Mostly, I've been warned about colleagues to avoid. A lot of it is gossip and complaining. I can only think of two specific things that have been said about teaching here. One is how bad the students are . . . about how unprepared and unmotivated they are. The other one, that maybe two people mentioned, was a warning about the need to set clear rules and punishments on the first day of class. All in all, I'm pretty disappointed with the help I've gotten.

This inattention to teaching surprised new faculty at both campuses. Inexperienced and returning faculty were not confident that they knew how to teach (although their senior colleagues seemed to assume that they did). Almost all new faculty felt that they should have gotten more concrete help such as syllabi from courses that preceded theirs. And, the majority of new faculty at both campuses reported

Table 2
Percentage of New Faculty Reporting High Overall Levels and Specific Kinds of Collegial Support in Terms of Advice Offered by Senior Colleagues

Category		Campus 1	Campus 2
High overall support:	1987	48% (*N* = 23)	
	1988	48% (*N* =33)	42% (*N* = 17)
	1989		40% (*N* = 16)
Type of advice:			
None:	1987	10% (*N* =5)	
	1988	19% (*N* = 13)	18% (*N* = 7)
	1989		20% (*N* = 8)
Gossip and politics:	1987	54% (*N* = 26)	
	1988	50% (*N* = 34)	59% (*N* = 24)
	1989		47% (*N* = 16)
Teaching-related:	1987	4% (*N* = 2)	
	1988	3% (*N* = 2)	4% (*N* = 2)
	1989		6% (N = 3)

that they had not been given appropriate strategies for coping with difficult students, especially those who disrupted classes or who might complain to departmental chairs. (At each campus, rumors spread quickly about new faculty who suffered embarrassment and other punishments as a result of such complaints).

Another way of documenting inattention to teaching can be seen in a single datum: Less than 5 percent of new faculty in their first semesters at either campus could identify any sort of social network for discussing teaching. Moreover, no new faculty were in departments where colleagues met occasionally to discuss teaching (in ways akin to departmental discussions about, say, the scholarly literature).

These questions about support produced another surprise. At both campuses, nurturance was no greater for inexperienced and returning faculty than for experienced newcomers, despite the seemingly greater need of the former. At Campus 2, curiously, experienced new faculty reported receiving by far the most useful advice and encouragement; this was part of a general pattern where already accomplished professors were welcomed by their new colleagues.

When I asked new faculty about what sort of help they needed most as teachers, the answer was nearly universal: they imagined that the hardest tasks would be learning the appropriate level of lecture difficulty for students. The follow-up question, about how senior faculty could provide such help, produced a hint about why new faculty were passive in soliciting assistance. That is, new faculty could not imagine how anything short of direct classroom experience could provide the answer they needed.

Another question asked for specific plans to coteach. New faculty's plans (12 percent and 20 percent intentions to coteach for the two cohorts at Campus 1; 8 percent and 4 percent at Campus 2) and the results of those plans (less than 3 percent at both campuses for new faculty who were actually in class simultaneously with another instructor) evidenced little use of this collegial device for helping new faculty acculturate to teaching a new population of students.

Finally, new faculty in inexperienced and returning categories commonly reported some distress over their senior colleagues' attitudes about teaching. At Campus 1, interviews with new faculty produced this rank-ordered list of what they disliked about their seniors: (1) burnout, (2) overconcern with campus politics, (3) complaints about campus resources, and (4) negativism toward students. Campus 2 produced the same list except for the omission of the first complaint.

Taken together, senior faculty at both campuses seemed unable, unasked, or unwilling to provide the kinds of modeling as teachers that new faculty found themselves wanting as semester 1 progressed. At Campus 1, only five new faculty specified senior colleagues who acted as models of a sort (three instances were department chairs). At Campus 2, only 6 such specifications were made (three of them for chairs).

Casual comments from chairs suggested a reason why they were more likely than other senior colleagues to offer help; they felt obligated to give advice where other faculty might have felt they were overstepping their bounds. The majority of chairs, however, expressed the same Social Darwinistic logic that I heard from their senior colleagues; that is, the best faculty seem to figure these things out on their own.

Work and plans. Close behind concerns for a lack of collegial supports came distress over workloads. Table 3 shows that new faculty, in their predictions of typical workweeks during semester 2 anticipated a balance of time spent on lecture preparation and on scholarly writing. A curious quality of these estimates was that they only remotely reflected ongoing patterns at the midpoint of semester 1. New faculty including the two experienced associate professors quoted here, the first at Campus 1 and the second at Campus 2, invariably described their beginning patterns as temporary aberrations:

> As soon as I have my classes under control, I'm going to spend a lot more time on my writing. I need to get at least two papers finished (actually one just needs revision) this semester. [In response to my question about how ready he was to teach his classes?] I have taught these courses before. And, I spent some time this summer going over my notes. I thought that I would be spending very little time preparing for classes. But now I find that I'm doing a lot of modification. I'm trying to simplify some things. And, much as I always have done . . . now that I think about it . . . I find myself always trying to improve the content of my notes. I want to be sure that I'm up-to-date.
>
> I'm not settled down yet. I'm still trying to figure out what will work with students here. So, my typical workweeks, as you call them, are not typical yet. I find myself spending much more time than I planned on my classes. I want to find a way to make the students a little less obviously bored and disinterested. Once I do that I will get back to writing and the other things I have to do.

Self-descriptions as teachers. Here again, the result was remarkably uniform across groupings when new faculty were asked to list their strengths as teachers. My rank-orderings of the most common answers sorted themselves into categories of kindred responses:

1. I am well-prepared and knowledgeable (Campuses 1 and 2)
2. I am interested in students (Campus 1)
   I am good at explaining/conceptualizing (Campus 2)
3. I am good at explaining/conceptualizing (Campus 1)
   I am a motivator (Campus 2)

In this context, new faculty implied what they considered the basis for good teaching in terms of this uniform estimate: good teaching equals clear, knowledgeable, and, possibly, inspiring lectures.

Self-generated lists of weaknesses as teachers produced this rank-ordering:

1. I ask too much of students (Campus 1)
   None (Campus 2)
2. None (Campus 1)
   I ask too much of students (Campus 2)
3. I am disorganized (Campuses 1 and 2)

Table 3
New Faculty's Median Estimates of Typical Workweeks, in Hours per Week, during the Coming Semester (Semester 1, Year 1)

Academic Activity	Year Cohort Began 1987 (Campus 1)	1988 (Campus 1)	1988 (Campus 2)	1989 (Campus 2)
Teaching	9.0	8.0	4.5	5.0
Lecture Prep	13.0	13.0	8.0	7.5
Scholarly Writing	13.3	14.0	7.0	9.0

Fewer than four new faculty in any of the four cohorts studied here indicated an awareness that their teaching prowess could depend on more than issues of content and of clear, enthusiastic presentation. Given that the majority of new faculty already saw themselves as doing adequately or better in these regards, three other outcomes may have been foregone.

For one thing, a near majority of new faculty had no plans for improving their teaching (and all but a few who did specified improvements to content, organization, and motivation). For another thing, fewer than four faculty per cohort described their classroom styles as anything more than what Fink [5] and others have labeled "facts-and-principles lecturing." And, finally, only two newcomers at each campus had firm plans to visit the classrooms of colleagues for tips on teaching. When asked to explain this disinterest, the remaining respondents answered much like this inexperienced new hire at Campus 2:

> Frankly, I never thought of it. I'm not sure what I would learn. I really think it's a matter of simply learning what the students here can handle and of lowering my standards in general. Besides, I'm not sure I would be welcome in my colleagues' classes.

Second Semester

In general, second semesters proved disappointing for new faculty. They felt no more settled-in, successful at teaching, or productive at writing than they had in semester 1. For most of these new faculty, semester 2 was the nadir of reported experience at their new campuses and in their recall of overall careers.

Collegial support. Estimates of collegial support declined for all groupings in semester 2. Table 4 shows this result in terms of new faculty who rated collegial contacts as generally poor. Ratings in this category during semester 1 had been at least 10 percent higher for all groups except the inexperienced members of cohort 2.

The drop in perceived collegiality by semester 2 seemed to have a reliable concomitant. New faculty talked openly about a growing sense of disillusionment—usually as in this excerpt from the comments of an inexperienced new hire at Campus 1 (cohort 1):

> I'm beginning to see how hopeless things really are here. I don't think I was told how bad things are here and I hold the older people—the same people who painted such a rosy picture during my interview—responsible. It makes me feel all the more alienated here . . . all the more determined to just do my work quietly and to leave as soon as I can.

Table 4 mirrors another related dimension of disappointment for new faculty; feelings of intellectual understimulation continued into semester 2, more so for new faculty at Campus 1. Consistent with that difference, newcomers to Campus 1 held generally lower estimates of the professional competence of their senior colleagues. As before, one grouping contradicted the experience of loneliness and understimulation—the experienced faculty hired at Campus 2.

Reports of understimulation went beyond collegial prods to reflect and write; by semester 2 it grew to strong salience as a factor that might undermine newcomers' commitment to teaching. This concern was equally prominent at both campuses and it often took the form of these comments from returning faculty at Campuses 1 and 2:

Table 4
Semester 2 Ratings of Collegiality as Poor

	Background of New Faculty		
Year Cohort Began	Inexperienced	Returning	Experienced
1987 (Campus 1)	30% ($N = 3$)	50% ($N = 1$)	64% ($N = 18$)
1988 (Campus 1)	15% ($N = 2$)	50% ($N = 1$)	57% ($N = 27$)
1988 (Campus 2)	33% ($N = 6$)	83% ($N = 5$)	25% ($N = 4$)
1989 (Campus 2)	40% ($N = 10$)	50% ($N = 2$)	27% ($N = 3$)

> One thing I worried about in returning to a campus job was whether I could handle the teaching. I guess I didn't presuppose that I would get lots of help but I certainly didn't expect to be surrounded by colleagues who don't seem to care about teaching. When I talk about it in the department I feel like I am violating a rule of silence.
>
> One big reason why I left my job at ________ was because I thought I would enjoy teaching. Now I wonder how I can avoid becoming just as negative about teaching as this campus is. It isn't just that people don't care; teaching is seen as a negative and as something that we rarely discuss except to complain about.

Self-descriptions as teachers. Changes in self-descriptions were almost nonexistent, except in the few new faculty who had become participants in the author's faculty development programs by semester 2 ($N = 14$, 18, 8, and 17 over the four cohorts who participated in programs that coached them through changes in teaching assumptions and practices). Whereas participants persisted in the short run as facts-and-principles lecturers, during semester 2 they began to list plans for changes in teaching, such as setting learning goals and effecting critical thinking. Even so, the transition to trying new tactics came slowly; most new faculty who planned to improve their teaching wanted to wait until year 2, when they would presumably be less busy and more confident.

Work patterns. In semester 1, new faculty of all groupings predicted changed work patterns that would allot equal time to teaching and to scholarly writing (table 3). Table 5 shows that the reality of demands for time had changed little since the initial interviews. By semester 2, averages for lecture preparation remained far higher than deemed desirable by new faculty; Campuses 1 and 2 reported a mean exceeding twenty-one hours and sixteen hours, respectively, across all experience types. Even the small subgroup of newcomers to science departments at Campus 2 (with teaching loads of one course or less) routinely expressed surprise that they had spent three to four hours a week preparing for each hour of classroom presentation. Another surprise for new faculty who paused to calculate their work loads was the realization that core workweeks were only about thirty hours long.

Thus, anticipations of spending far more time at writing by semester 2 went unfulfilled. Original estimates of workweeks with a balance of hours per week spent on teaching and writing persisted at a ratio of at least 15:1. Most surprising, these imbalances were as characteristic of experienced faculty as of other new hires at both campuses.

New faculty's immediate concern with this pattern related to a near absence of scholarly and grant writing. The result was an increasing frustration with teaching as a task whose demands overshadowed its rewards. But, with prods during these interviews to reflect about the reasons for spending so much time preparing lectures, new faculty realized their own contributions to the problem. That is, the majority of them spontaneously admitted to overpreparing in the sense of having too much material to present without hurrying their lectures and in terms of trying to be too perfectionistic beyond the level that could be rewarded in most classes.

A final pattern characterized new faculty in regard to habits. Despite having no immediate plans to effectively change their workweeks, new hires invariably predicted more productive and effective schedules in the near future. Moreover, nearly all new faculty saw upcoming summers as times when they would, at last, catch up on writing.

Table 5
Actual Core Work Weeks during Semester 2 (cf. table 3) in Mean Hours

Academic Activity	Year Cohort Began: 1987 (Campus 1)	1988 (Campus 1)	1988 (Campus 2)	1989 (Campus 2)
Teaching	8.5	8.2	4.0	4.1
Lecture Prep	23.7	21.0	17.2	16.1
Scholarly Writing	0.8	0.6	1.1	1.3
Committees	3.3	2.8	4.0	3.8

Teaching evaluations. During semester 1, all but a few new faculty (eleven at Campus 1 and eight at Campus 2) declined offers made during the first interview to help them conduct early, informal student evaluations of their teaching. The stated reasons at both campuses are typified in this comment noted from an inexperienced new hire at Campus 2:

> I already do that in my own way. I ask students to tell me how I am doing . . . and if they have any questions. I think I'm doing fine in that regard. So I don't really see the need to go through this.

By semester 2, at both campuses and across all groupings, poor teaching ratings became a reality for the majority of new faculty. Table 6 shows that most new faculty were rated as mediocre according to campus-generated, compulsory teaching evaluations administered at the end of semester 1. In terms of this measure, new faculty reported that they generally fared far worse as teachers than they had anticipated.

Although this result held across campuses, two limitations merit mention. First, faculty at Campus 2 were less surprised at their generally poor ratings; their students, especially undergraduates, were seemingly more open in expressing their dissatisfaction during classes in terms of bored expressions, audible conversations among themselves, and exiting classes early. In retrospect, new faculty at Campus 2 reported realizing that they should have paid more attention to obvious signs that students would rate them unfavorably. Second, nearly half of new faculty at Campus 2 did not receive the printouts of the analyses of their student evaluations during semester 2. Even though this campus had made special efforts to devise and institutionalize a student evaluation device in the few years prior, it had not followed up to see that faculty were getting the results.

Although Campus 1, which prided itself for caring about teaching, did a far better job of getting feedback from its teaching evaluations to faculty, it did little better in supplementing printouts with consultation from chairs or colleagues. That is, only a handful of new faculty at either campus ($N = 5$ and 4, respectively) were counseled by departmental colleagues about what their numerical ratings meant or how they translated into alternative ways of teaching.

Third Semester

New faculty in semester 2 expected that their return to campus after summer vacation would mark the end of campus experience as one of busily catching up. They hoped to be rested and ready to assume a less harried schedule. Once again, realities differed from plans.

Even before contacts were reestablished in the third interview, casual meetings left the impression of disappointing progress during first summers. As a rule, new faculty did not settle down to productive writing as planned; instead, they spent most of the summer resting up from what they generally described as the busiest, most stressful year of their lives. Then, when and if they felt compelled to do something productive with the last parts of their first summers, they most often spent them in preparing and revising course plans and lectures. The stated reason (typified in this note from an inexperienced newcomer at Campus 1) was this:

Table 6
New Faculty Who Received Student Evaluation Scores (Global) below Departmental Means (Semester 1)

	Background of New Faculty		
Year Cohort Began	Inexperienced	Returning	Experienced
1987 (Campus 1)	57% ($N = 8$)	75% ($N = 4$)	57% ($N = 16$)
1988 (Campus 1)	57% ($N = 8$)	50% ($N = 1$)	43% ($N = 20$)
1988 (Campus 2)	67% ($N = 12$)	83% ($N = 5$)	56% ($N = 9$)
1989 (Campus 2)	68% ($N = 17$)	67% ($N = 2$)	64% ($N = 7$)

> What I realized when I finally felt like getting back to work was that I needed to be better prepared for my classes than I was last year. I realize that as long as I'm struggling to have good enough notes and problems, I will never get around to writing.

Almost without exception, newcomers reported feeling another disillusionment upon returning for year 2: They still did not feel that they were a real part of campus.

Collegiality. By around the midpoint of semester 3, reports of collegial support had reached new (albeit still modest) heights. New faculty continued to complain about loneliness and understimulation, but they were often better able to identify colleagues with whom they had regular and substantial interactions. Nonetheless, this phenomenon was not universal. Two groups evidenced no gains in collegial support for activities including teaching: returning faculty at both campuses, and experienced faculty at Campus 1. Their comments about this continuing predicament are echoed in this remark by a returning full professor at Campus 2:

> No point kidding myself; I'm a bit hurt by it all. I thought that by now I would have some friends . . . or at least some colleagues who feigned an interest in what I'm doing. But evidently, this is how things are going to be. I'm just going to have to make the best of a bad situation. It's hard to want to spend time at things like teaching when no one here seems to care.

And where collegiality had improved, changes came from sources other than those expected by new faculty (beyond the senior faculty who invited a minority of new hires for one-time, welcoming dinners in their homes). As a rule, inexperienced newcomers found the collegiality they valued most from other new faculty. An oft-heard comment in this context: "It's like the blind leading the blind."

Self-descriptions as teachers. In the main, self-descriptions continued unchanged. The great majority of new faculty in their second year on campus still saw good teaching (including their own aspirations for excellence) in terms of little more than content and enthusiasm. The hoped-for trend toward more involvement in faculty development programs (and in goals for more active student learning) had grown only slightly (to nineteen and eleven in cohorts 1 and 3, the two groups studied into year 2). By semester 3, six more individuals identified themselves as having brought more enlightened concepts of teaching to campus than they had displayed or even discussed during year 1. This was usually evidenced as an inclination to have parts of classes devoted to student participation. The single reason stated for this delay was waiting to feel settled as teachers before taking risks.

The great majority of new faculty in year 2 persisted in describing their classroom styles as strict facts-and-principles lecturing. My visits (with prior permission of new faculty and with my appearances at unpredictable times) to the classrooms of samples of ten of these faculty at each campus confirmed these self-descriptions. A similar sampling of new faculty who claimed to be using student-oriented approaches (see Weimer [8] for a definition of this concept), in contrast, confirmed self-descriptions in only slightly more than half my visits. These self-described innovators who were lecturing in "content only" fashion during my visits usually offered an explanation like this one made by an experienced newcomer to Campus 2:

> You have to realize that I don't always do this. When I have a better class, one that is better prepared and better prepared to participate, then I can focus around break-out groups and that sort of thing. Besides, to be honest with you, I don't feel all that confident here yet. These students are not shy about letting professors know when they don't like something.

In fact, by semester 3 little had changed for most new faculty as teachers. When asked, as in semester 1, what plans they had for improving as teachers, the answers at both campuses reflected the rank-ordering listed earlier in this article: (1) none, (2) teaching at lower levels of difficulty, and (3) preparing lectures with better and more organized content.

Student evaluations. Given the formalized student rating systems for teaching used at both campuses, new faculty got no printouts about semester 2 until semester 3. Two things stood out in my discussions of these ratings with new faculty: first, student ratings (except for some of the teachers with student-oriented styles mentioned earlier and for a near majority of experienced new faculty) had not improved. Second, new hires reported feeling ambivalent about these generally discouraging results. On one hand, the ratings seemed so remote in time that they could be dismissed as irrelevant to teaching in what had since become more comfortable surrounds. On the other hand, the ratings seemed finally to force many new faculty to admit that this was an unanticipated, unhappy state of affairs that had to be addressed. Resulting plans, seen just above, suggested little immediate promise for improved teaching.

Work patterns. Disappointments about teaching were matched, for most new faculty, by frustrations with continuing imbalances in workweeks. The result of assessing the self-reported workweeks of new faculty in semester 3 produced a result closely similar to that already seen for semester 2 (table 5). Despite firm expectations to the contrary, new faculty generally persisted in patterns where teaching preparation dominated other activities.

Plans. By the third semester, new faculty uniformly set more modest goals for productivity and for balance of teaching preparation with other activities. Still, they continued to hope that the time would come soon when they could put the priority of teaching behind them (as in this comment from an inexperienced new hire at Campus 1):

> I just need to get to the point where I feel that I am in control of my classes. I mean that my notes and overheads have to be better organized. I mean that the materials have to be at a level appropriate for students. [In response to my question about when he would know that his notes were well-enough prepared?] Good question. Maybe never; I might always be repreparing my notes. [In response to my question about when he would feel comfortable about balancing teaching preparation with other activities such as social life and writing?] I think, really, that will come when students seem to like what I'm doing . . . and when I like what I'm doing.

Again, new faculty were asked to specify their plans for improving their teaching. Rank-orderings of their most common responses produced responses nearly identical to those listed for prior semesters. In brief, beliefs about the best ways of finding improved teaching, classroom comfort, and student acceptance revolved around notions of better lecture preparation and lowered standards. Increasingly, though, new faculty in their third semester were attributing their negativism about improving teaching to students, specifically to their lack of preparation and motivation.

Fourth Semester

Although new faculty continued to predict that each new semester would bring the sense of feeling accepted and "on track" for career goals, semester 4 rarely brought those desired results. Instead, semester 4 brought another self-rated low for new faculty. Exceptions to this rule were inexperienced new faculty who found strong bonds with other junior faculty that promised scholarly productivity, inexperienced new faculty at Campus 1 who participated in campus faculty development programs, and experienced newcomers at Campus 2 who had reestablished research productivity. In contrast, the new faculty who showed the most obvious signs of maladjustment were returning new faculty. As a rule, then, the socialization periods at these two campuses lasted well beyond the fourth semester.

Collegiality. Overall, new faculty at both campuses rated collegial support as lowest in semester 4. Returning new faculty, as just indicated, were most vocal in making this complaint. As indicated in the following comment from Campus 1, they had usually come from settings where they experienced more friendly and appreciative colleagues:

> Sometimes I feel like a failure here. No one cares what I'm doing . . . except in the critical comments I got in my annual review. They make a big deal of my one poor teaching rating but not one of them has offered to help. This system would be considered madness in industry. They wouldn't go to the trouble to recruit a doctoral-level specialist and then watch him or her fail.

In a preliminary sense, semester 4 may have been a critical period of sorting out people who would establish happy bonds with their campus and those who would remain estranged. Overall, about half the new faculty studied into semester 4 showed signs of establishing social networks and of finding comfort with job demands such as teaching. While they as a rule, had not yet found the kind of balance mentioned several times in this manuscript, they were anticipating it in seemingly more realistic ways.

Student ratings. Semester 4 brought feedback on student ratings of new faculty's teaching in semester 3, the juncture at which some new faculty reported expecting a turnaround in student appreciation. But this did not happen on the average; increases over semesters 1 and 2 were slight except for participants in faculty development programs, for a group of self-starters to be described later, and for most experienced new faculty.

Three things about new faculty's reactions to these ratings stood out in interviews in semester 4. First, new faculty now tended to attribute disappointing ratings to their students' inabilities to handle challenging material. Second, new faculty almost never (except for the minority who participated in faculty development programs) sought out advice for ways of translating ratings into alternative styles of teaching. Third, even in the face of two disillusioning ratings, new faculty generally supposed that their usual plans for improvement (that is, better organization, lowered standards) offered the best likelihood for improved ratings.

Self-descriptions as teachers. Consistent with what we have just seen, new faculty showed few changes from earlier answers about their self-images as teachers. One slight change at both campuses was the valence associated with teaching: increasingly, teaching was depicted as even less fun than it had been in semester 1. A related change: some interviewees, especially returning new faculty, volunteered the possibility that they would never be considered good teachers. These preliminary admissions were not, however, accompanied by a sense of relief; these were people who apparently wanted to teach well and who did not find comfort in the prospect of chronically mediocre ratings.

Work patterns. By this fourth interview, new faculty generally expressed dismay with how they were allotting their time. With the exceptions of small groups who were making regular time for scholarly productivity, new faculty showed work weeks similar to those seen earlier (table 5). On the average, new faculty at both campuses were producing manuscripts at rates well below the mean of one-plus per year necessary to meet usual expectations for tenure decisions. For the first time, new faculty in this unbalanced pattern openly expressed resentment toward the demands of teaching as they saw them. That is, teaching, despite its signal lack of rewards, seemed to demand preparation to the exclusion of other important things.

Plans. At the end of their second year on campus, new faculty placed heavy expectations on the coming summer session. Here again they hoped to catch up on neglected activities, especially regarding social life and writing. But this time new elements crept into interview comments. New faculty no longer reported being as busy and stressed as they had been in semesters 1–3; they supposed that they would not have to spend the coming summer resting. Moreover, plans for writing seemed more realistic; suddenly, plans were accompanied by realizations that, for most interviewees, *any* writing of substance would be progress. Thus, plans now specified, say, mornings at writing and afternoons at family outings (and not the entire days imagined in plans made a year earlier). This excerpt from my notes on an inexperienced newcomer to Campus 2 reflects the tone of trying to be realistic amidst a disillusioning semester:

> Things are overdue, that's for sure. Maybe this summer will be the turning point. I have to make something work; I have to take better care of myself and of my career. Students may have to accept me for what I am. . . . I am not perfect, but I try hard to bring good material to class. And, when I think of it, I may have to accept myself for what I am. I certainly have to accept the fact that I'm not producing great scholarship at a great rate. But I think that I will produce some good stuff, slowly but surely. [In response to my question about what, assuming that progress, would remain as important goals for year three on campus?] That's easy. I need to work harder to find friends, maybe even collaborators. I need to feel like I belong here.

Comparisons of Novice and Veteran Teachers

As I analyzed the results of interviews over semesters, I integrated them with other observations. For example, my repeated sampling of the classroom performances of inexperienced new faculty ($N = 8$), of returning new faculty ($N = 3$), and experienced new faculty ($N = 6$) suggested surprisingly few differences in superficial teaching styles during semesters 1 and 2. That is, most faculty new to campus, regardless of level of experience as teachers, were lecturing in facts-and-principles style. All but a few newcomers obviously focused on presenting lots of content organized in terms of concepts and lists. All but a few lectured in rapid-fire fashion. The obvious difference between veteran and novice teachers emerged in other dimensions including more classroom comfort and confidence for the former.

By semesters 3 and 4 nearly half of the teachers veteran to teaching had further relaxed their styles to include somewhat more student participation. During comments to me after class, these experienced professors described the change as feeling settled and comfortable with the students. Curiously, experienced new faculty who evidenced no apparent changes in classrooms from year 1 reported having experienced similar improvements in comfort, not necessarily in regard to students but in terms of worrying about their teaching. For them, the transition evidenced itself as a reduction in feeling pressured about lecture preparation.

Inexperienced and returning new faculty generally reported no such transitions in comfort or in time saved during years 1 and 2 at either campus. They were, according to my observations and their interview comments, still teaching in facts-and-principles style during semester 4. And by their own admissions, they were still primarily concerned about avoiding punishment (for example, widely known complaints made by students to campus administrators). They were continuing, in their own description, to teach defensively.

How persistent is this general pattern? In a pilot study with two cohorts at Campus 1 immediately preceding the cohorts studied here, I found that inexperienced (*N*= 18 and 13) and returning (*N* = 3 and 6) new faculty persisted in this same pattern during their first three and four years on campus. Even where they had, on occasion, ceased overpreparing lectures (usually by semesters 5 or 6), they stuck to the same facts-and-principles style that had characterized their performances in semester 1.

Another bit of evidence already mentioned corroborates the notion that faculty tend to stick to initial styles: the majority of experienced new faculty sampled here were lecturing, by their own reckoning, in the same facts-and-principles manner they had used as novices. Curiously, only a few of them were able to specify any significant changes as teachers beyond (a) increases in the confidence that results from experience and (b) decreases in the demands that they made on students in terms of assignments and tests.

These data stimulated two related inquiries: what characterizes novice professors who seem to start as excellent teachers and what causes other colleagues to move in similar directions by their second year on campus?

Inexperienced Newcomers Who Found Quick Comfort

I selected three inexperienced new faculty in each cohort who began as exemplary teachers. Criteria for inclusion were: clearly superior students ratings as teachers; my own classroom ratings (of comfort, enthusiasm, organization, student rapport and involvement, clarity of presentation, and active student learning); and new faculty's own self-descriptions as comfortable, as innovative, and as interested in active student learning.

Analysis of my notes about these twelve individuals produced the following list of characteristics that, in combination, distinguished them from their peers:

1. Positive attitudes about students at these state universities
2. Lectures paced in relaxed style so as to provide opportunities for student comprehension and involvement
3. Low levels of complaining about their campuses including collegial supports
4. Evidence of actively seeking advice about teaching (especially the mechanics of specific courses), often from a colleague in the role of a guide or mentor
5. A quicker transition to moderate levels of lecture preparation (that is, less than 1.5 hours per classroom hour), usually by semester 3
6. A generally (*N* = 4 at Campus l; *N* = 3 at Campus 2) superior investment in time spent on scholarly and grant writing (mean = 3.3 hours per workweek)
7. A greater readiness to become involved in campus faculty development programs (*N* = 2, 3, 2, and 3, respectively, over the four cohorts).

Ten other new faculty who were not fast starters made transitions that brought them to obvious comfort and well above average student ratings during year 2. All but four of the individuals who met this description were experienced new faculty. The four inexperienced newcomers in this category evidenced gradual movement toward items 1–3 of the list above; by semester 3 and 4, for example, they were complaining less about colleagues and students. These new hires, however, did not seem to seek out the collegial support characteristic of the sample just described. Instead they showed a determination to adjust on their own.

New Faculty Active in Campus Faculty Development Programs

Although new faculty were routinely contacted in the repeated interviews that formed the basis of this manuscript, only a minority of them followed up on admonitions to participate in campus faculty development programs. As a rule, new hires told me that they felt too busy to participate; most said that they would participate once they felt settled in, particularly after acquiring a sense of control over their teaching. Indeed, junior faculty at both campuses who counted as regular participants in campus faculty development programs most often came from cohorts in their fourth through sixth years on campus. The reason for this general delay in participation seemed clear: junior faculty admitted waiting until the pressures of meeting standards for tenure were near.

Nonetheless, the apparent benefits for new faculty who participated in faculty development programs (for example, workshops on teaching and writing, feedback on classroom performance and student evaluations including early and informal ratings, and prearranged interactions with exemplary senior faculty for advice on activities including teaching) were substantial. Earlier we saw that participants were highly represented in the group that found immediate comfort and success at teaching. Although these new faculty were vocal in attributing their successes and comfort to participation in development programs, they might well have achieved similar progress by virtue of their seemingly more optimistic styles.

Participation in campus faculty development programs did not obviously affect tendencies to lecture in facts and principles style, at least during the first two years on campus. Only two of the new faculty picked as exemplary made significant inroads into involving students in class discussion that exceeded 15 percent of class time or in teaching higher-order skills in ways that included writing-intensive courses.

What short-term participation in faculty development did seem to affect was classroom comfort and time management. That is, these participants evidenced less overpreparation for lectures, more relaxed pacing during lectures, more comfort with lecturing and with students, fewer complaints about busyness, and more time on scholarly writing. Consistent with these differences, participants displayed more confidence about their careers, more satisfaction with teaching, and quicker assimilation to their new campuses.

Discussion

The main premise of this article, namely, that we need to know more about how new faculty establish teaching styles, was generally confirmed. The study of new faculty from two large campuses suggested the following generalities about how new faculty begin as teachers:

1. They teach cautiously, equating good teaching with good content [8]. Thus, most faculty observed here stuck to what Axelrod [2] designated a facts-and principles style of lecturing.
2. They teach defensively, so as to avoid public failures at teaching [4]. New faculty routinely worried aloud about criticisms of their teaching, especially the sort that would earn repeated listings in reports of tenure committees. This meant that new faculty tried to get their facts straight; whatever else, they did not want to be accused of not knowing their material. Other factors, such as students who seemed to complain capriciously and maliciously, seemed beyond the control of new faculty.
3. They often blame external factors for teaching failures as indicated in student ratings. Three of the most common of these attributions were to poor students, heavy teaching loads, and invalid rating systems.
4. They are passive about change and improvement [5]. They assume that casual comments from students (and perhaps from colleagues) are sufficient to gauge prowess at teaching.

They reluctantly seek outside help from resources including faculty development programs. And when asked to specify plans for improvement, even in the wake of poor ratings and admitted dissatisfaction, they are unable to specify alternatives beyond improving lecture content and making assignments and tests easier.

5. New faculty's primary goals as teachers revolve around time management and punishment; they do not expect to enjoy teaching until they no longer have to spend large amounts of time preparing for it and until it no longer offers prospects of public criticism. Only then, they suppose, can they attend to subtle aspects of teaching, such as moving beyond a facts-and-principles format (perhaps by teaching critical thinking).
6. Experienced new faculty claim that their defensive and factual styles of teaching are regressions from how they had taught recently at other campuses. They too complained of worrying about public complaints and about heavy investments in new lecture notes.
7. New faculty establish comfort, efficiency, and student acceptance only slowly if at all. In preliminary studies at Campus 1, large groups of new faculty were systematically interviewed and observed for periods as long as four years. Only a minority made verifiable progress in any of these areas except for lessened preparation time. Broader progress in the samples studied here were limited to the handfuls of new faculty who persisted as participants in campus faculty development programs.

Although this evidence for the effectiveness of faculty development programs must be considered preliminary, it offers bright promise in an otherwise dreary picture of how new faculty develop as teachers. It suggests, as we just saw, that new faculty can be aided in finding balance; the study samples did less overpreparing, they got students more involved in classes, and managed more productivity on scholarly projects. Moreover, participating new faculty received significantly higher student ratings, the measure used for administrative assessments of teaching at both campuses.

A related conclusion of this article concerns the generality of the findings just reviewed across two campuses with different priorities for teaching. That is, new faculty at the campus with little public emphasis on teaching showed the same tendencies as their counterparts at the "teaching campus." Specifically, the two groups were closely similar in terms of:

1. An initial concern for teaching well and for earning the respect and gratitude of students.
2. Worries about eliciting public complaints about their teaching and strategies of teaching more for correctness than for innovation and student learning.
3. A tendency to prepare more lecture material than could be presented and assimilated in comfortable fashion, usually in a facts-and-principles format.
4. A tendency to plan few changes in teaching beyond easing standards for students who were seen as the main problem in teaching well.
5. Putting off scholarly writing until feeling settled as teachers.

Curiously, the two campuses had similar demands for publication rates (that is, about 1.0 to 1.5 manuscripts accepted in referred outlets per year, depending on department).

Another point expands this preliminary picture. There was no observable difference in teaching performance between new faculty at the two campuses. This observation extended beyond classroom performance and students ratings in approximately similar rating forms; it included stated interests in teaching, time spent with students outside class, and attempts to seek help in improving teaching. No doubt, this finding would surprise faculty at the teaching campus who commonly asserted the teaching superiority of their campus in comparison with research campuses.

What this kind of direct and sustained examination of new faculty as teachers can tell us, then, is that professors often begin in styles that persist in disappointingly narrow fashion. One suggestion in this study is that we might do better to safeguard new faculty from all but private and formative evaluations of their classroom performance for a year or two. Such precautions might reduce the reliance of new faculty on facts-and-principles formats of lecturing as defenses against possible criticisms.

A second suggestion concerns faculty development. Involving new faculty in programs that helped them refrain from overpreparing facts and that assisted them in finding comfort with increased student participation produced two measurable improvements here. One was improved comfort and ratings as teachers; the other was improved comfort and productivity as productive scholars.

The final suggestion is that we can learn something of value about how new faculty could develop as teachers from observing individuals who excel quickly. These colleagues assumed unusually positive and proactive stances, especially in terms of seeking help.

What remains to be seen is if university campuses will provide the kinds of safety, supports, and formative feedback that appear essential to early comfort and success at teaching. In my experience as a faculty developer and consultant at a variety of campuses, management favors conditions that produce poor morale and tolerates the resulting low productivity. Why? Part of the reason, I suspect, owes to the autonomy so highly valued in academe; we tend to let new faculty "sink or swim" on their own, perhaps so that they can take full credit for their work. But the rest of this neglect has roots in our externalized world view. We have yet to learn much about ways of making our own work more effective and satisfying.

References

1. Association of American Colleges. *Integrity in the College Curriculum: A Report to the Academic Community.* Washington, D.C.: Association of American Colleges, 1985.

2. Axelrod, J. *The University Teacher as Artist: Toward an Aesthetics of Teaching with Emphasis on the Humanities.* San Francisco: Jossey-Bass, 1973.

3. Boice, R. "New Faculty as Colleagues." *International Journal of Qualitative Studies in Education,* in press.

4. Eble, K. E. "Preparing College Teachers of English." *College English,* 33 (Winter 1972), 385–406.

5. Fink, L. D. *The First Year of College Teaching.* San Francisco: Jossey-Bass, 1984.

6. Sorcinelli, M. D. "Faculty Careers: Satisfactions and Discontents." *To Improve the Academy,* 4 (1985), 44–62.

7. Turner, J. L. and R. Boice. "Starting at the Beginning: Concerns and Needs of New Faculty." *To Improve the Academy,* 6 (1987), 41–55.

8. Weimer, M. *Improving College Teaching.* Jossey-Bass, 1990.

Visible, Vulnerable, and Viable: Emerging Perspectives of a Minority Professor

JACQUELYN MITCHELL

The presence today of many minority faculty members on college and university campuses represents the most recent stage of a historic movement to eliminate the legal barriers to full citizenship erected by race, creed, or prior state of servitude. This movement was animated by a sense of the injustice perpetuated by legislation and social sentiment that systematically excluded members of certain racial and ethnic groups from access to educational facilities that could enable them to realize their potential and to enjoy their rights as American citizens. Largely through the efforts of the National Association for the Advancement of Colored People (NAACP), de jure segregation of graduate and professional education was formally ended in the early 1950s. Following this success, the NAACP, armed with sociological and psychological research findings, successfully challenged the doctrine of separate but equal educational facilities in elementary schools. The Supreme Court ruled in the classic 1954 *Brown* vs. *Board of Education of Topeka* case that separate but equal was inherently unequal and therefore unconstitutional. Schools were mandated to integrate with all deliberate speed. As a result of this decree, many minority children found themselves thrust into experimental integrated educational settings that espoused culturally incongruent philosophical and social ideologies.

The tactics devised to accomplish the legal mandate placed many students in integrated settings. Formal inclusion in the majority school culture was intended to counteract the exclusionary legacy of past practices. However, student differences—racial, ethnic, linguistic, and economic—became salient markers that kept the newcomers apart from the culture that they had integrated. While busing became symbolic of the intrusion of government into the private realm of neighborhoods and schools, the children who rode the buses and attended the schools experienced a new form of visibility that made them vulnerable in ways that previous generations had not experienced. Media treatment of the civil rights movement caused even children who did not participate directly in busing programs to experience this new visibility.

Thrust into a variety of programs promising new opportunities, minority students became the pawns in the battle of an egalitarian society with its heritage of discriminating practices and prejudicial attitudes. Schools became the major battlefront as the rhetoric of equality advocated educational correctives for the traditions of inequality embedded in social structure. Compensatory education became the means, but its consequences served only to highlight for students the social ambiguities implicit in the notion of compensation.

Frequently, economic boundaries were crossed in order to integrate schools, and minority students paid a penalty for not having the same economic benefits as their white peers. Many discovered that the cultural norms of their respective communities were evaluated negatively in schools, and their dialects and behaviors were often the source of derision. At the same time, they learned that their mere presence was potent enough to create a new phenomenon of rejection—white flight. But, the most subtle form of socialization of this new environment emerged with the school's use of so-called objective tests that created new forms of internal segregation.

"Visible, Vulnerable, and Viable: Emerging Perspectives of a Minority Professor," by Jacquelyn Mitchell, reprinted from *Teaching Minority Students: New Directions for Teaching and Learning,* edited by J. H. Cones, J. F. Noonan, and D. Jahna, No. 16, 1983, Jossey-Bass Publishers, Inc.

Minority students viewed what the schools saw as grouping by ability somewhat differently, since those in the special education and language remediation programs are primarily black, Native American, and Hispanic peers. The explanation proffered by experts for the poor performance of minority students on standardized tests intensified the discrepancy between the rhetoric and the reality of integration. Families that invested heavily in their children's future only to see them geographically and culturally transferred to a different world found themselves called the cause of their children's failure.

To students whose academic ability was confirmed by the objective criteria of schools, the rhetoric of equality through education held out special promise and a different form of contradiction. Their ability to conform to the norms associated with the dominant culture suggested that they departed from the norms associated with their ethnicity. Although education enlightens, it cannot whiten technicolor reality. As these students came to see their success as rooted in their unique individuality, they frequently became estranged from their family and community. Yet, the knowledge that they gained made them aware that a large number of their peers who did not make it had been victims of societal conditions, not of lack of individual ability. They became frustrated by the inequities that turned many of their friends into combat soldiers in Vietnam, inmates in prison, or workers in low-status occupations. For many, these contradictory experiences fostered a new consciousness in which individualism became the exception and collective experiences became the norm of their understanding of workings of society.

It is not surprising that many of those who entered college rebelled against the institutional labeling that denied their ethnic identity. Some substituted ethnic for egalitarian concerns and sought to devise new means of expressing their collective identity. Others fought for their right to participate in a variety of traditional areas of study that had excluded minorities. Individuals from both groups succeeded in qualifying as the new generation of Ph.D.s available for academic positions. Precisely because students in the second group succeeded in traditional fields, far less is known about their struggles, dilemmas, and despair than those who followed different routes. As former students holding the newly elevated status of professor, these exceptions—some might call them the fortunate ones—became at once minorities within the majority culture and minorities within their minority culture. Socialized to individualistic identities, these minority scholars also became accustomed, especially in the elite colleges and universities, to serving as conspicuous symbols in a setting that also contained all the problems associated with the professional role.

In moving from the role of student to that of professor, these scholars continued to function as pioneers but in a drastically different environment. Their environments were structured to some extent by their discipline, and by the professors with whom they worked. However, the professional role required them to assume new authority and unfamiliar responsibilities.

While the experiences involved in mastering this new role can be described in terms of marginality, discontinuity, or dissonance, this chapter will examine the living experiences of scholars in the process of actively constructing their social reality as members of their academic and of their ethnic community. To communicate this experience, I will characterize the process in terms of the tensions and challenges that one must confront in one's self and the contradictions and limitations in communities and institutions that one must recognize and articulate.

This chapter will describe and examine my personal perspectives as a minority professor in three related domains: being visible, being vulnerable, and being viable in the white academic community—distinct phases that capture the complexity and contradictory nature of the roles in which we have been cast. Of course, the opinions and interpretations expressed in this chapter are mine and do not necessarily reflect those of other minority professors.

Visibility: Reflections

"I am invisible," says Ellison's (1972, p. 3) Invisible Man, "because people refuse to see me. . . . as though I have been surrounded by mirrors of hard distorted glass. . . . You ache with the need to convince yourself that you do exist in the real world. . . . You curse and swear to make them recognize you. And, alas, it's seldom successful." For the aspiring nontraditional scholar, Ellison's masterful treatment of the paradoxical plight of the invisibility of the most visible is particularly poignant. While coming to see one's self as others do, the minority scholar often discovers that the hallowed halls of ivy are lined with strange reflections. From the initial interview for the position to the four-to-eight-year struggle for tenure, minority scholars confront dual systems of expectations, rules, and judgments from within their institution and from within their ethnic community.

Our physical appearance invariably evokes unconscious attitudes and unfounded presumptions regarding our competence as scholars and our viability as faculty members. It begins in university search committee meetings when faculty members view minority candidates with fixed, biased convictions and are unable to separate issues of ethnicity from issues of qualification. Thus, minority applicants are penalized during recruitment procedures, and those who are hired remain minority members for the duration of their tenure in the minds of most other faculty.

To the minority applicant, competition for an academic position on the fair and open job market seems neither fair nor open, and university affirmative action hiring policies often seem perfunctory at best. Furthermore, "the most limited opportunities for status mobility among [minorities] call for stiffer competition than occurs among whites" (Ogbu, 1982, p. 427). In fact, minority scholars realize that their chances for securing a university appointment are significantly reduced unless ethnicity is clearly a prerequisite for the position. For example, a psychology department may be searching for a black psychologist, not for a psychologist who is black—a denotation considerably more meaningful than the semantic differences imply.

Even minority scholars selected for the final applicant pool regard their inclusion with caution, knowing that an invitation to come for an interview or to present a colloquium frequently means something other than it seems. While such an invitation may truly indicate genuine interest in and serious consideration of the applicant's candidacy, the minority applicant also recognizes that his or her presence on a campus as a viable candidate can be exploited to demonstrate the university's stated commitment to affirmative action goals. Invitations in such cases are a sham—nothing more than diversionary tactics to obscure actual intent. Ironically, the minority candidate who gets hired may also experience doubt, being unable to discern whether qualification or ethnicity was the decisive factor in his or her selection or whether it was both.

Inside the university, pressures associated with visibility reflect conflicting demands. Senior faculty and members of the administration warn minority scholars to place more emphasis on research and less on committee work and service obligations. Yet, many of the same people then ask, even urge, the minority scholar to get involved in recruiting a new faculty member, presenting a minority perspective in class or on a committee, counseling a minority student who has academic difficulties, or speaking to an outside group. The same people who evaluate the faculty member for advancement and for tenure ask these things seemingly unaware of the number of invitations that we must consider. Although "many of us resent this yoke . . . , [at] the same time [we] recognize our social responsibility to pursue and explain ethnic issues. Strangely enough, we often demand from ourselves what whites expect from us, while realizing the futility of accomplishing this goal to anyone's satisfaction" (Mitchell, 1982, p. 36).

Implicit in our visibility are the representative roles that we are forced to take. We are assumed to be less competent, yet we are also expected to replicate our white colleagues' output in both quantity and quality. We are chastised for spending excessive time with our students, but we are also relied on to reduce their isolation and cultural shock. We are criticized for participating in ethnically related community and university events, and we are given little recognition for our service contributions, but at the same time we are viewed as a critical link with the ethnic community.

Pressures regarding visibility and representation come also from the minority community. Poor communities have many needs and few people with clout. While such communities are often suspicious that minority faculty have lost interest in their affairs, they also request highly tangible services, such as membership on boards, assistance preparing applications for funding and grants, and advocacy for the children. Their needs are so immediate and their regard for the research process is so low that they often view refusal as an indication of snobbery or as a rejection of ethnic identity.

Typically, with few other minority faculty nearby as friends, relationships with minority students and with community people can both take on great importance and create conflicting demands. Our visibility affects both our professional and our personal life. Colleagues, community residents, and students react to it and develop perceptions about us because of it. Such perceptions, combined with the conflicts, demands of the role, and personal needs, create pressures that can jeopardize our health, happiness, and productivity. We become vulnerable to inner and outer demands by trying to create and maintain a feasible balance and meaningful synthesis of self, ethnicity, and profession—no small task.

Vulnerability: The Pitfalls of Reflections

DuBois (1961 [1903], pp. 16–17) evokes "a peculiar sensation, this double consciousness, this sense of always looking at one's self through the eyes of others, of measuring one's soul by the tape of a world that looks on in amused contempt and pity. One ever feels his twoness—an American, a Negro; two souls, two thoughts, the unreconciled strivings; two warring ideals in one dark body whose dogged strength alone keeps it from being torn asunder." The double consciousness that DuBois describes aptly conveys the discrepancies between achieved and ascribed status conflicts that many minority social scientists experience. The crux of the problem lies in the differential rankings given to research, teaching, and services by the university, community, and individual. While the university emphasizes publishing, teaching, and service—in that order—in evaluating its faculty, the community places service first and publishing last. However, many minority professors find that teaching consumes their time and interest and believe that it should weigh most heavily.

Of course, all new faculty members experience anxiety about publication because the university gives such primacy to this area of their performance. Minority faculty members whose area of specialization involves ethnic communities are particularly vulnerable to conflicts between the criteria of the university and the community. Their consciousness of the differences between the two perspectives not only intensifies their vulnerability but frequently overshadows their need to establish in their own mind the personal standards and criteria for constructing a viable professional identity.

Expedience convinces some to adhere to the criteria articulated by the university. The issue then becomes one of the kinds of articles and the journals in which they will appear. Journals that have high status in the academic community tend to emphasize studies that further the development of methodological practices and theoretical models. From this perspective, the aspects of an ethnic community in which the researcher focuses become the means to methodological or theoretical ends. At the same time, when the researcher identifies with the group studied, the resulting work implies a self-referential level that the work of nonminority faculty members seems not to possess. Moreover, member status can also encourage the appropriation of such studies for ends other than those normally associated with publications. They are quoted out of context by policy makers and attacked both by members of the ethnic community and by other academicians for sacrificing the community's needs or interests to their own self-interest.

Minority scholars who attempt to use community criteria as the basis for publications encounter different problems. Within ethnic communities, rigorous but esoteric research is often viewed as damaging, if not worthless. The research that counts in these communities is the research that advocates change, that helps to get money, and that speaks in plain language. While such work can be judged for its inherent quality, its real value lies in the role that it plays in achieving community goals. The university tends to be unsympathetic to publications that are answerable to a particular set of cultural beliefs. It views them as too particularistic or subjective. However, this response tends to reaffirm the community's view of the university as a racist institution concerned only with perpetuating the image of ethnic communities as disorganized, deviant, or pathological. These experiences heighten the minority scholar's sense of distance from nonminority colleagues and increases his or her alienation from the university.

The vicious cycle that traps minority faculty members transforms the dictum Publish or Perish into Publish and Perish. The image of the dedicated and prolific scholar that prevails in academia rules out entangling alliances with interests and concerns outside the ivory tower. The impact of pressures exerted by alternative cultural or ethnic perspectives is not recognized, and it will not be recognized until sufficient numbers of minority faculty members create a literature that can form such a view. In the meantime, the university's culture is the sole standard in evaluation for tenure.

While problems created by publications are frequently aired, the complications that arise from teaching receive relatively little attention. The issue surfaces during disputes about tenure, because minority faculty members feel that the university does not appreciate the extent of their contributions in this area. Again, the difficulty involves a discrepancy between the established traditions of academia and the modifications that ethnic diversity necessitates in that tradition.

Faculty members of color are unwittingly cast into positions of role model. When a traditional faculty member functions in that role, status is accorded in terms of discipline, not of ethnicity. In contrast, the minority role model's position is more often derived from ethnic than from academic identity. We are compelled by our disproportionately small number to accept this responsibility, and we are thrust into these positions virtually without choice. The stress in balancing visibility and role model status makes us vulnerable to pressures from both minority faculty and students. By virtue of our color, we symbolize each other, and we represent, both in the eyes of the other and in our own, each other's competencies and weaknesses. As a result, we often use criteria far harsher than traditional university standards to judge each others' behavior. In all cases, "a negative sanction [received] from one's own ethnic group [is] far more devastating than one received from whites" (Mitchell, 1982, p. 37). The situation for the female ethnic professor is even more complicated. In addition to serving as a role model for profession and race, ethnic women must also assume the role for gender. The accountability and time demands that the female ethnic professor encounters are especially pressing, given the fact that minority women occupy even fewer positions than minority men.

The difficulty of negotiating between the university's assumptions and the students' ethnically conditioned expectations is increased by our vulnerability to student-initiated evaluations of performance. Past treatment gives students their own understanding of the institution's perspectives on minorities as members of the university. In general, such treatment has reinforced an association between minority status and low competence that activates ethnically acquired defense reactions in minority students. This reaction encourages group strategies for protecting individual members from the corrosive effects of a hostile environment. The identity shared by minority students and faculty members and the protective strategies can interfere with the critical and evaluative functions that professors must fulfill if their students are to learn. Thus, while students see university treatment of minority faculty and students as an expression of institutional racism, minority faculty members who accept this definition of the situation are hindered by students' limited understanding of the role of the professor. The efforts that minority faculty members make to fulfill that role are often misconstrued by students as attempts to deny shared ethnic identity, and students are led to interpret the professor's definition of the situation as a denial of ethnicity. In any case, whether the faculty member is seen as loyal to the ethnic group or as loyal to the university, he or she is not seen as an individual. Consequently, this dilemma becomes the primary element of our visibility and the source of great stress; the self is obscured by the social category.

Stereotypes also exist for those among us who struggle to assert our individuality and independence. Under such circumstances, we may be accused of wanting to deny racial or ethnic heritage, and we may be criticized for seeking assimilation to the "idealized" white world. The conformist directives from our reference groups and from the university lock us into symbols and images. It is not just the white academic structure that boxes us in and that sanctions our behavior according to prescribed norms and values but the ethnic community as well. Ironically, the same kind of boxing in exists within the ethnic academic community, and the demands placed on us to reflect ethnically established standards and beliefs are just as intense, if not more so; we become locked in to our ethnicity.

Students' needs, students' estrangement from home and community, and students' feelings of cultural isolation subject minority faculty to demands that encroach on scarce research time. Minority students often expect minority faculty to make themselves available beyond regularly scheduled office hours believing that they "owe" them the time because of their shared ethnic membership. Minority faculty are also expected to give more time and help, to be understanding when papers are turned in late, and to bend university standards because such standards do not reflect the minority belief system. Resentment can flair if we attempt to maintain professional standards and establish professional distance. Under such circumstances, it becomes difficult to discourage students of color from dropping by our office to chat and considerably more difficult to persuade them to seek the academic and personal counseling they need from the appropriate centers on campus. Many minority students are distrustful of and reluctant to use these resources and reject them outright. They come to us because they believe that we are better able than white professors to empathize with their circumstances academically and personally. As role models by design, we represent for them what they can become. We are the minorities who have made it. We have mastered the tricks of the trade, and we have learned how to negotiate the system successfully. They want to learn those skills from us. It is difficult for them to understand that developing such skills requires time for research, cognition, and privacy. If we attempt to discourage them from visiting during hours set aside for preparation or research, we face resentment. Indeed, we can be scorned as "white ethnics."

Caught between pressing academic and ethnic needs, minority faculty may be forced to resort to the strategy of playing one demand against the other in order to service. For example, in an attempt to deter students from visiting after office hours, we may plead faculty commitments; that is, we may use an institutional excuse to counter students' demands. We do, in fact, spend many hours with students. As a result, our research time is substantially curtailed. This can place us in academic jeopardy. By the same token, however, university demands consume a great deal of our time, although the administration seems to have little if any understanding of the time and emotional constraints under which we are forced to produce. The enormous amount of time that we spend with students is not taken into consideration when our level of productivity is compared with that of white colleagues. As a result, the minority scholar must plead ethnic demands to the university with regard to his or her academic productivity in the same way that he or she is forced to use institutional demands to explain and offset ethnic ones. In interacting both with students and with administrators, we deny ourselves, and we are unable to admit to personal preference, to demand social space, or to pursue individual interests and needs. In these situations, we are vulnerable to dual constraints, trapped as we are in the dilemma created by trying to treat the double bind as if it were rational.

Viability: Beyond the Reflections

The trick that minority faculty members, burdened with ethnic and professional demands that often are philosophically and culturally disparate in their orientation, must master requires disentangling and objectifying the realities of both worlds. The tension and stress experienced by minority faculty members stem largely from the absence of established images that prescribe their behavior as members of the ethnic and academic community. In this regard, we retain an either-or perspective from our history of legal segregation and social separation. Individuals who attempt to choose between the two groups remain hopelessly trapped in illusions and unavoidably perpetuate that legacy. Only those who realize that the dilemma can be resolved only by disentangling past group norms and statuses from the options available to individuals today are likely to appreciate that the way in which they as individuals perform with new professional roles will eventually shape the norms and statuses of the group in the future. In other words, to escape the binds of visibility we need to rephrase the problems in terms that increase the bicultural awareness that enables individuals to establish the personal and professional criteria needed for building new levels of understanding in students. The process is neither simple nor easy. Bicultural awareness demands recognizing both the differences between two realities and the similarities that they share. Bicultural awareness is the view from the other side of the mirror.

I have discussed some of the ways in which ethnic communities and universities differ. For minority members to become viable, they must situate themselves in the overlap between the two environments. Ironically, the attention given to ethnic communities in the formal literature reflects the fragmented images of separate disciplinary perspectives. This makes it difficult to locate the areas of similarity between ethnic communities and academia. We also know, however, that human forms of collective organization are grounded in the need for survival. We can work to create a more coherent image of our ethnic communities in terms of the standards that they use for selecting and inculcating patterns of behavior that increase the groups' capacity to survive. Since these standards are used to evaluate members' performance, they include criteria for excellence. The personal criteria that we come to use for structuring our personal and professional life are derived from our experiences of the standards of excellence in our social environment. The fact that members of various ethnic groups have aspired to and achieved the status of academician indicates that ethnic and university criteria for excellence are compatible. Our task is to eliminate the distorting effects of our former exclusion from participation by using our knowledge of the symbolic orders or meaning with our own community to inform and expand the theoretical perspectives and methodologies of our academic discipline. The excellence that we incorporate into our teaching, research, and community service becomes the standards and values informing the future.

It is this criterion for excellence that gives individual minority professors a basis for constructing a personally satisfying balance between their ethnic and their professional identity. Such a balance lessens their vulnerability and increases their viability both in the ethnic and in the university community. As minority faculty members devise teaching techniques that enable students from diverse backgrounds to move back and forth between their ethnic community and the university, we give content to new categories of understanding. In contributing to the literature of our discipline on ethnic communities, we shape the form of this understanding. By participating in formulation of policy within the university, we demonstrate the efficacy of this new level of understanding for pragmatic action. Through our innovations in teaching and our additions to the literature, we broaden the university's capacity to respond productively to an increasingly complex world.

The differences that make us so visible in academic settings lose their social reverberations of past inequity as increasing numbers of minority faculty members confront their vulnerability and strive to link their visibility with the viability common to the university and the ethnic community. We cannot operate competently from within the set of expectations of either. Instead, we need consciously to pursue membership in both reference groups as we seek to become viable members of academia. We become viable only when we operate effectively in our ethnic and university roles and contribute significantly to the development of both and to the advancement of self.

References

DuBois, W. F. B. *The Souls of Black Folk.* Greenwich, Conn.: Fawcett, 1961 [1903].

Ellison, R. *The Invisible Man.* New York: Vintage, 1972.

Mitchell, J. "Reflections of a Black Social Scientist: Some Struggles, Some Doubts, Some Hopes." *Harvard Educational Review,* 1982, *52*(1), 27–44.

Ogbu, J. "Minority Education and Caste." In N. R. Yetman and C. H. Steele (Eds.), *Majority and Minority: The Dynamics of Race and Ethnicity in American Life.* (3rd ed.) Boston: Allyn & Bacon, 1982.

B. Teacher Behaviors and Practices

Questioning in College Classrooms

CAROL P. BARNES

Most people who have been to college believe they can describe what goes on in college classrooms. However, thorough descriptive studies of what actually takes place in these classes are rather scarce. As we have noted, without an accurate picture of teaching, further research will lack the necessary theoretical support. In chapter 4, the cognitive levels of both professors' and students' discourse were described. This study attempts to describe another aspect of the college-teaching process—questioning. It focuses on the cognitive levels and patterns of professors' questions and tries to answer the following:

1. What cognitive levels are elicited by the questions of college instructors?
2. What questioning patterns are present in college instruction? Do these cognitive levels and patterns differ across
   Institution types—private and public?
   Institution size—small and large?
   Beginning and advanced courses?
   Subject areas—humanities/arts/social sciences, and math/science/engineering?
3. In examining the data developed in the study
   Is there a relationship between the cognitive level of the professor's questions and the general cognitive level of the professor's talk?
   Is there a relationship between the cognitive level of the professor's questions and the general cognitive level of the students' talk?

Because there was so little descriptive research on collegiate instruction, the variables selected for this study were carefully chosen. Research on student rating of instructors tends to show the potential value of instructor-student classroom interaction,[1] and the research on class structure suggests the value of discussions and student-centered instruction.[2] Consequently, instructor questioning seemed to be a variable that might reveal an accurate picture of an important facet of the collegiate instructional process.

This decision to study questioning behavior is further supported in studies of questioning in high-school classes. Frequently the researchers found that the majority of all teacher questions were on the lowest cognitive level,[3] yet questions eliciting abstract thinking seemed to be the most effective for moving students toward high levels of understanding.[4]

In general, the great bulk of research over the century has suggested that, in fostering the important cognitive and affective outcomes to which colleges are committed, the instructor's questions may be a crucial factor. On both elementary and secondary levels, questions have been shown in certain studies to relate to critical thinking, to achievement, and to attitude toward the subject. On the college level, however, their role in the teaching process has been only superficially evaluated.

Given the importance of analyzing a professor's questions, then, one must certainly ask how this behavior differs across a multiplicity of variables. Does instructors' questioning behavior change over the course level? among subject areas? across institution size? among institution types? This study attempted to shed light on these questions.

"Questioning in College Classrooms," by Carol P. Barnes, reprinted from *Studies in College Teaching: Experimental Results, Theoretical Interpretations, and New Perspectives* by C. L. Ellner and C. P. Barnes, 1983, Macmillan Publishing Company.

Procedures

The sample of professors in this study is identical to that in chapter 4. The same audio tapes were used for analysis in both studies.

As was noted in chapter 4, the researchers wished to be as unobtrusive as possible, and considerable discussion was given to the question of whether or not to inform the professors of the taping schedule. Lamb studied the effects of the presence of three different observers on the questioning pattern of second-year probationary teachers.[5] He concluded that different observation conditions do not affect the questioning pattern of teachers, except in one instance: teachers observed for an expressed administrative purpose of contract renewal asked a significantly higher number of opinion questions than did teachers being observed for an inservice purpose. Since this study carried no overt threat, and since the professor had no knowledge of what was being studied other than college teaching, it was assumed that knowing when the session would be taped would not appreciably affect teaching. Thus the study involved a sample of forty professors drawn from a population of full-time undergraduate faculty at four institutions. Thirty were from large schools, ten from small schools.

Each tape was coded first, using the Amidon Multiple Category system (MCS—see figure 5–1). These data were then placed in a 24 x 24 matrix and percentages computed for each category. While coding the MCS for each question asked by a professor, the researcher coded a further breakdown according to the Aschner-Gallagher System for Classifying Thought Processes in the Context of Classroom Verbal Interaction (A-G) in figure 5–2. These observations were then recorded on the Aschner-Gallagher tally sheet. A second researcher coded a random sample of at least two tapes per professor using the Florida Taxonomy of Cognitive Behavior (FTCB—figure 4–1). Since each major category of the FTCB contains several items, and the developers of the system do not report that these are accurately sequential within the major categories, only the total number of teacher and pupil tallies for each major category was computed. Thus for each professor, four MCS matrices, four A–G tally sheets, and at least two FTCB displays were available for analysis.

Figure 5–1
Amidon Modified Category System (MCS)

Teacher Talk	1. Accepts Feeling
	2a. Praises
	2b. Praises Using Public Criteria
	2c. Praises Using Private Criteria
	3. Accepts Idea Through: a) Description
	b) Inference
	c) Generalization
	4. Asks: a) Cognitive Memory Question
	b) Convergent Question
	c) Divergent Question
	d) Evaluative Question
	5. Lectures
	6. Gives Direction
	7a. Criticizes
	7b. Criticizes Using Public Criteria
	7c. Criticizes Using Private Criteria
	8. Pupil Response: a) Description
	b) Inference
	c) Generalization
	9. Pupil Initiation: a) Description
	b) Inference
	c) Generalization
	10. Silence
	11. Confusion

Figure 5–2
Aschner-Gallagher System

- I. Cognitive Memory (C-M)
  - Scribe (Scr)
  - Recapitulation (Re)
    - Quoting (Req)
    - Repetition (Rep)
    - Recounting (Rec)
    - Review (Rev)
  - Clarification (Cl)
    - Clarif. Meaning (Clm)
    - Clarif. Qualification (Clq)
  - Factual (F)
    - Fact stating (Fs)
    - Fact detailing (Fd)
    - Factual monologue (Fm)
- II. *Convergent Thinking (C-T)*
  - Translation (Tr)
  - Association (As)
  - Explanation (Ex)
    - Rational Expl. (Exr)
    - Value Expl. (Exv)
    - Narrative Expl. (Exn)
  - Conclusion (Con)
    - Generalization (Gen)
    - Summary Concl. (Cons)
    - Logical Concl. (Conl)
- III. *Divergent Thinking (D-T)*
  - Elaboration (El s/f)
  - Divergent Association (Ad s/f)
  - Implication (Imp s/f)
  - Synthesis (Syn)
- IV. *Evaluative Thinking (E-T)*
  - Unstructured (U)
    - Rating (URa)
    - Judgment (UJu)
  - Structured (S)
    - Structured Probability (Svp)
    - Structured Choice (Svc)
  - Qualification (Q)
    - Qualified Judgment (Qj)
    - Counter Judgment (Qc)

Figure 5–2 *continued*

V. Routine (R)			______
Management (M)		______	
Question (Mq)	______		
Procedure (Mp)	______		
Aside (Ma)	______		
Nose Counting (Mnc)	______		
Feedback (Mfb)	______		
Structuring (St)		______	
Self Structuring (Sts)	______		
Structuring Others (Sto)	______		
Future Structuring (Stf)	______		
Class Structuring (Stc)	______		
Verdict (V) + or –		______	
Agreement (Agr) + or –		______	
Self-Reference (S)		______	
Dunno (Du)		______	
Muddled (Mu)		______	
Humor (Hu)		______	

The MCS matrices and coding sheets were then examined to ascertain the professor's questioning pattern. It was possible to group these patterns into seventeen distinct groups, plus one group of "other"—patterns used very infrequently, and one group of "no questions asked."[6]

Several different statistical procedures were employed in examining the cognitive levels and questioning patterns. In dealing with the cognitive levels elicited by the questions of college instructors, frequency count, mean, and simple T test were used. To describe the questioning patterns present in college instruction, a cross-tabulated frequency count was made. A chi square was used to describe the differences in these patterns across the variables of institution size and type, course level, and discipline. To determine the relationship between the cognitive level of professor questions and the general cognitive level of teacher and student talk, a Pearson Correlation Coefficient was computed.

Results and Discussion

The portion of total class time spent in professor questioning was determined by summing the percentage in all subcategories of the questioning category (cognitive memory, convergent, divergent and evaluative) on the Amidon Multiple Category System (MCS). Table 5–1 illustrates both means and standard deviations for each institution in the sample, for beginning and advanced courses and for the two discipline groups (humanities/social sciences/arts and math/science/engineering).

The range of the percentages of total class time spent questioning was 0.03 to 20.80. The values of 0.03 and 20.80 were single cases. If these two cases are omitted, the range was 0.20 to 9.20.

There was no significant difference in the mean percentage of the total class time occupied by professors' questions across any of the variables examined.

Cognitive Levels Elicited by the Questions of College Professors

The Amidon MCS was used to determine the cognitive levels elicited by the questions of college professors. In this system, questions are ranked according to the type of thinking elicited: cognitive memory, convergent, divergent, and evaluative. The remaining tables describe the percentage of questions present in each of these cognitive levels and how they vary across institution type, size, course level, and discipline.

Table 5-1
Percentage of Total Class Time Spent in Professor Questioning

	$\overline{X}$	S.D.	N
By School			
Large Public	3.68	2.97	15
Small Public	4.99	3.32	5
Large Private	2.44	2.23	15
Small Private	5.81	8.49	5
By Discipline			
Math/Science	2.48	2.28	14
Humanities/Social Sciences	4.27	4.40	26
By Level			
Beginning	3.99	4.50	20
Advanced	3.30	3.16	26
Total	3.65	3.86	40

The overwhelming percentage of all questions asked by college professors, regardless of institution were on the lowest cognitive level (cognitive memory). The grand mean for this level was 82.33 percent. With the exception of the small public institution, the means for the cognitive memory level were between 80 and 82 percent. The small public college had a cognitive-memory level mean of 91.51 percent.

This same distribution was also seen across the level of convergent thinking, divergent thinking, and evaluative thinking. The large public, large private, and small private colleges appear fairly close in percentages; whereas the small public school has consistently fewer of the higher-level questions.

When using a t-test to determine the differences in cognitive level of questions between private and public institutions, no significant differences were found. Questioning level was thus independent of institution type.

When the institutions were grouped as small and large and a t-test was performed to determine the difference in cognitive level of questions, it was found that the convergent-thinking questioning level did differ across the variable of institution size, with large schools having a significantly higher percentage of questioning time spent at this level.

Since there was little difference in the individual cognitive levels of questions across the variables of institution size and type, a chi-square analysis was computed to determine whether discrete institutions were independent of questioning level.

When all four institutions were compared over the four questioning levels, it was found that institution was, in fact, *not* independent of questioning level. Whereas a t-test did not indicate a significant difference for each one of the cognitive questioning levels individually, taken together a lack of independence was shown: $\chi^2 = 27.09$, df = 9, $P \geq .01$.

The large private institution had a high incidence of divergent-thinking questions and the small public institution had a low incidence of divergent-thinking and evaluative-thinking questions.

Differences in Percentage in Each Professor Cognitive-Questioning Level between Beginning and Advanced Courses

In a t-test for difference between means in the questioning levels between beginning and advanced courses, no significant difference was found. It should be noted that the cognitive-memory level was almost identical in beginning and advanced course and that the evaluative-thinking level was also almost identical. Divergent thinking was somewhat higher in the beginning courses but not significantly higher.

T-tests of the differences in percentage in each cognitive-questioning level between beginning and advanced courses within each discipline group (science/math/engineering and humanities/social sciences/arts) were also calculated. No significant differences were found on any questioning level.

Table 5-2
Percentage of Total Questions in Each Cognitive Level, by Institutions

	Cognitive-Questioning Level			
	Cognitive Memory	Convergent Thinking	Divergent Thinking	Evaluative Thinking
Large Public	80.13	15.42	1.99	2.45
Small Public	91.51	7.95	0.28	0.26
Large Private	81.95	12.89	3.60	1.56
Small Private	80.33	14.39	2.80	2.48
Column X	82.33	13.40	2.43	1.85

Differences in Percentage in Each Professor Cognitive-Questioning Level between Disciplines

The cognitive memory questioning level was significantly different (at the 0.03 level) between the two major discipline groups—humanities and math/science. In the math/science/engineering group, professors asked significantly more cognitive-memory questions than did the humanities/social sciences/arts professors (table 5–4). It must be noted, however, that both groups essentially asked a large number of cognitive-memory questions. On the other questioning levels, however, no significant differences were found.

Aschner-Gallagher System Data on Professor Questioning

In order to examine the questioning behavior of professors in a somewhat more detailed manner than was possible with MCS, the Aschner-Gallagher system was employed to analyze only the professors' questions, not the entire class session.

This system, in general, yields a more detailed breakdown of each subscript of the questioning categories in the Amidon MCS. Additionally, it adds a fifth category, "routine." As noted in the description of the instrumentation, the MCS groups most routine questions into the cognitive-memory category. It treats rhetorical questions as lecture and humorous questions as praise with no criteria. The A–G system brings both of these (rhetorical and humor) under the major heading of Routine; each has its own coding category. Although these differences account for only a small portion of the questioning, they do give a slightly different picture of professor questioning from that which the MCS gives. If a future researcher is particularly interested in routine questions as separate from cognitive memory questions, he may wish to add this fifth category to the MCS.

It must also be noted that with the MCS a single question may be tallied three times if it is of nine-seconds duration, whereas with the A-G system questions are not tallied by duration but by a shift from

Table 5-3
Percentage of Questions in Each Professor Cognitive Level, by Beginning and Advanced Courses

	Questioning Level			
	Cognitive Memory	Convergent Thinking	Divergent Thinking	Evaluative Thinking
Beginning	82.43	12.71	3.05	1.81
Advanced	82.22	14.08	1.81	1.88
Total	82.33	13.40	2.42	1.85

Table 5-4
Percentage of Questions in Each Cognitive Level, by Discipline

	Questioning Level			
	Cognitive Memory	Convergent Thinking	Divergent Thinking	Evaluative Thinking
Humanities	79.74	14.40	3.35	2.51
Math/Sciences	87.08	11.57	0.73	0.63

one category or subcategory to another. Thus a nine-second question calling for fact stating would receive only one cognitive-memory-fact stating code, whereas in the MCS it would be coded as three cognitive-memory tallies. This accounts for the slight differences in percentages in the major categories.

Regardless of the classification system used, the majority of all professors' questions were on the lowest cognitive level. With the A–G system, it is further noted, of those questions on the lowest level, 56.10 percent were designed to elicit a statement of facts from the students. No other particularly unusual findings are seen.

No correlations were made between the data obtained from the A–G system and the MCS or FTCB systems: A–G was used simply to provide a more descriptive analysis of the overall sample.

Discussion of Questioning Levels

Since there appears to be a relation between professors' higher level questions and student outcomes such as achievement, positive attitudes toward the subject, and critical thinking (see note 2) there are a number of implications for instructional development. Because it is apparent that professors asked mostly very low-level questions, it appears that they did not generally utilize questioning to its fullest extent. The current level may be effective for knowledge acquisition, but if critical thinking, for instance, is valued as an outcome, then different levels of questioning need to be considered. It may be of interest to future researchers to study whether or not such outcomes as critical thinking and positive attitude are, in fact, stated goals, and to study whether or not professors' questioning differs in relation to the variability of these goals.

Added to the problem of goals is that of institutional type. In examining these data, it was found that, although there appeared to be no significant difference in the cognitive levels of professors' questions between public and private institutions, there did appear to be a difference in professor questioning levels between small and large schools. A chi-square analysis performed over the entire data sample showed that questioning levels were not independent of institution; that is, they did in fact differ across each separate institution. Professors at large schools asked more convergent thinking questions such as "What is there about the position of New York City that accounts for its importance?" than did professors at small schools. When discrete institutions were examined, professors at the large private schools tended to ask more divergent thinking questions such as "How might the lives of the people of New York City be different if the city were located in the torrid zone?" and professors in small public schools tended to have a low incidence of both divergent- and evaluative-thinking questions.

Table 5-5
Percentage of Professor-Questioning Episodes in Major Categories of Aschner-Gallagher System

	Percentage of Total Questioning Episodes
Cognitive Memory (I)	62.67
Convergent Thinking (II)	13.72
Divergent Thinking (III)	2.34
Evaluative Thinking (IV)	2.50
Routine (V)	18.71

The finding that large-school professors gave more attention to questions above the cognitive-memory level than did professors at small schools may indicate, as suggested earlier, a difference in institutional goals, or it may indicate that professors adapted their teaching to different types of students. Future researchers might be interested in how much impact the academic or social characteristics of the students have on teaching.

Although differences in professors' cognitive-questioning levels were discovered between institutions, these were not present between beginning and advanced courses. Not only was there no significant difference between course levels, but there was in fact, a very close relationship. One might expect beginning courses to deal with more factual information than advanced courses and for advanced courses to synthesize and relate these concepts and to draw hypotheses and conclusions from them; but this did not happen. The study then tested the possibility that there was a difference in questioning levels between beginning and advanced classes within each discipline group, the assumption being that in linear and sequential disciplines such as mathematics, science, and engineering, one might find more low-level questions in the beginning courses and more high-level questions in advanced courses. No questioning differences were found, however, between the course levels within the two discipline groups. Apparently professors' general questioning strategies do not change from beginning to advanced courses, regardless of the subject being taught.

When the differences in questioning level between disciplines were examined, the only variability was found at the cognitive-memory level, with science/math/engineering professors asking a significantly larger proportion of low-level questions than did the humanities/social sciences/arts professors.

There are several possible explanations for this heavy reliance on low-level questions: (1) low-level questions are by far the easiest to ask; (2) professors may often use low-level questions simply to "wake up" the class (such questions as "Are you with me?" and "Did you all get that?" sometime serve this function); (3) low-level questions generally bring predictable responses from the students and thus may create a more comfortable situation for the professor; (4) professors may not recognize higher-order questions. Thus, if the professor is actually attempting to facilitate critical thinking, for example, but is uncomfortable with higher-order questions or cannot easily formulate them, faculty developers may wish to include the topic of questioning in their programs.

Researchers may also find curvilinear relationship between critical thinking, for example, and higher level questions. There may well be an optimum proportion of high- and low-level questions and either extreme is less than optimally productive.

Questioning Patterns

Another potentially important aspect is the questioning pattern. Questioning patterns are an important aspect of an instructor's questioning skills. What does a professor say immediately before he asks a question? What kind of question does he ask? To begin to answer these questions, the primary (most frequent) and secondary (next most frequent) questioning patterns were isolated from the MCS tally sheets. These were combined into nineteen groups. Table 5–6 describes these nineteen most common questioning patterns.

A brief description of the five most frequent patterns appears below.

1. 4A-5 (4B-5) Professor lecture followed by cognitive-memory or convergent thinking question followed by more lecture.
2. 4A-10-5 Professor lecture followed by cognitive-memory question followed by silence followed by lecture.
3. 4A-8-3-5 Professor lecture followed by cognitive-memory question followed by a restricted (statement or answer to a question directed specifically to a particular student) student response followed by an acceptance or use of the student's idea followed by lecture.
4. 4A-9-5 Professor lecture followed by cognitive-memory question followed by unrestricted (statement or answer to a question which was asked of the total class and which any student was free to answer) student response followed by lecture.
5. 4A-8-5 Professor lecture followed by cognitive-memory question followed by restricted student response followed by lecture.

Table 5-6
Order of Frequency of Summed Primary- and Secondary-Questioning Patterns of College Professors

1.	5-4A-5 (5-4B-5)	11.	5-4B-9-9-5
2.	5-4A-10-5	12.	5-4A-9-3-4A(B) (5-4A-8-3-4A(B))
3.	5-4A-8-3-5	13.	5-4B-10-5
4.	5-4A-9-5	14.	5-4A-8-2A (3A)-8 (9)-5
5.	5-4A-8-5	15.	5-4B-8-2A-4 (5-4B-8-2A-4)
6.	5-4A-8-4 (5-4A-9-4)	16.	5-4B-9-9-2A-3-9-5
7.	5-4A-9-2A-5 (5-4A-9-3-5)	17.	5-4A-10-10-9
8.	5-4B-8-2A-5 (5-4B-8-3-5)	18.	No questions asked
9.	5-4A-8-2A-5	19.	Unusual patterns used only once
10.	5-4A-10-4A		

Legend (Category numbers and letter subscripts are those used in the Amidon MCS.)

2A Professor praises.
3 Professor uses or accepts student ideas.
4A Professor asks cognitive memory question.
4B Professor asks convergent-thinking question.
5 Professor lectures.
8 Student gives answer to a question directed specifically to him.
9 Student gives answer to a question that was asked of the total class (a question that any student was free to answer).
10 Silence.

The most frequent questioning pattern of college professors involves lecturing, asking a low-level question, and then lecturing some more. Often this return to lecturing after a question was to give additional information to aid the students in answering the question. At other times the professors simply answered their own questions. It must be noted that these are not rhetorical questions, since rhetorical questions are coded as lecture with the MCS.

Consistent with both primary- and secondary-questioning patterns, the professor's question followed a section of lecture. On occasion professor questions would follow student responses, but these were not of primary or secondary frequency.

These five most frequent summed primary and secondary professor questioning patterns accounted for 61.54 percent of all patterns. In the sum of patterns 1 and 2, neither of which involve any student response, 31.93 percent of all questioning patterns of professors elicited no student participation.

Table 5-7
Five Most Frequent Primary and Secondary Professor-Questioning Patterns

Pattern number	Percentage of Total Primary and Secondary Patterns
1	18.08
2	13.85
3	10.77
4	10.38
5	8.46
Total 1–5	61.54

Due to the small expected frequencies in patterns 6–19, further analyses were performed using only patterns 1–5.

Table 5–8 shows evidence indicates that, with summed primary and secondary questioning patterns 1–5, questioning patterns were not independent of institutions (p 0.001). The large private institution had a high frequency of patterns 2 and 3 and a moderate frequency of pattern 1. The large public institution had a high frequency of patterns 3 and 4. The small public institution had a high frequency of pattern 1, and the small private had a high frequency of pattern 4.

Primary and secondary questioning patterns 1–5 were summed for beginning and advanced courses. Table 5–9 suggests that the summed patterns 1–5 were not independent of course level (p 0.01). Beginning courses had more patterns 2 and 3; advanced courses had more patterns 1 and 5.

Primary and Secondary questioning patterns 1–5 were summed for the two discipline groups. From table 5–10 it is clear that, even when comparing the five most frequent patterns, questioning patterns were independent of discipline.

Discussion of Questioning Patterns

The general finding that professors seem to rely on fairly restrictive questioning patterns—those eliciting no student response or those that are a simple lecture-question-answer-lecture sequence—might imply that professors are not aware of the potential of their own questioning patterns. In conference, several of the professors in the study indicated they had never given any particular thought to this aspect of the questioning process and consequently relied on a few patterns that seemed comfortable to them.

Although the potential impact of questioning pattern has not yet been determined, it seems possible that what precedes and follows a professor's question may well determine how that question affects students. That is, the pattern lecture-low level question-student response-lecture may give the impression that the professor is checking up on the students' preparation for the class; whereas if the professor followed the response by an elaboration of the student's idea, it might suggest that he was attempting to involve students in the actual content of class session—two totally different strategies. The sequence of questions over a class period may also be an important area for investigation.

Relationship between the Cognitive Level of Professors' Questions and the General Cognitive Level of Professor and Student Verbal Behavior

To test the relationship between the cognitive level of professors' questions and the professors' and students' overall cognitive levels, a Pearson Correlation Coefficient was calculated between each cognitive-questioning level of each professor (4A,B,C,D) on the MCS and each professor's specific verbal cognitive levels (1.0 - 7.0) as identified by the FTCB.[7] No significant correlations were found between the cognitive memory or divergent questioning levels and any specific verbal-cognitive level of professors.

Two possible relationships were found at each of the convergent-thinking and evaluative-thinking levels. Convergent thinking showed a positive correlation with professor cognitive level 3.0 (interpretation) ($r = 0.3354$, $p = 0.003$); it also showed a positive relationship with level 4.0 (application) ($r = 0.9009$, $p = 0.018$). Evaluative thinking was positively related to cognitive level 2.0 (translation) ($r = 0.4475$, $p =$ 0.–27[sic]); it was also positively related to cognitive level 3.0 (interpretation).

Table 5-8
Differences in Professors' Questioning Patterns across Institutions

	Pattern Number				
	1	2	3	4	5
Large Public	17	6	11	17	8
Small Public	12	9	4	1	4
Large Private	14	20	13	3	7
Small Private	4	1	0	6	3

$^2 = 43.6329$ $df = 12$ p .001

Table 5-9
Differences in Professors' Questioning Patterns across Course Levels

	Pattern Number				
	1	2	3	4	5
Beginning	9	17	15	7	7
Advanced	22	6	8	9	13

^{2} = 14.8234 *df* = 4 *p* .01

It must be noted, however, that since a 4 x 20 table was computed, by chance one would expect to obtain four correlations significant at the .05 level—the exact number obtained. Thus one must regard these significant correlations with caution.

The same calculations were performed between professor's cognitive questioning level and student cognitive level. No significant relationships were found.

Correlations were computed between the modal cognitive level for each professor and the questioning level of that professor. No significant relationships were found (table 5–11). When the median professor cognitive level with the level of professors' questions were compared, however, some relationships were found. In table 5–12 it is seen that, as the median professor cognitive level went up, the frequency of questions in the cognitive-memory category went down; and as the median professor cognitive level went up, the frequency of professor questioning at the convergent-thinking level went up. Thus it seems that professors' questioning was related in some respects to their overall cognitive level.

In a comparison of the modal student-cognitive level with professor questioning levels, several possible relationships were revealed (table 5–13). It was seen that as the percentage of professor questioning at the cognitive-memory level increased, the cognitive level of the student tended to decrease ($r = 0.2362$, $p = 0.002$). As the percentage of professor questioning at the convergent-thinking level increased, the student cognitive level tended to increase ($r = 0.19$, $p = 0.028$). As the percentage of professor questioning at the divergent-thinking level increased, the student cognitive level tended to increase ($r = 0.3394$, $p = 0.027$). Thus the modal student-cognitive level appeared to be positively correlated to the level of the professor's questions.

The median student-cognitive level, when compared with the cognitive level of professor's questions showed a significant relationship only in the cognitive-memory category. As the professor asked fewer cognitive-memory questions, student cognitive levels went up.

The association of the level of a professor's questions to both his and the students' overall cognitive levels produced a positive correlation between the cognitive level of the professor's questions and both his and the student's overall cognitive levels. An inverse relationship was found between the professor's frequency of low-level questions and both his and the students' overall cognitive levels.

These relationships were more clear at some cognitive levels than at others, however, and were not found across all variables. For example when each single professor and student cognitive level was compared with each single professor questioning level, relationships were found only between (1) a professor's convergent questions and the cognitive levels of interpretation and application, and (2) his evaluative questions and the cognitive level of translation. However even these may be suspect because of the

Table 5-10
Differences in Professors' Questioning Patterns across Disciplines

	Pattern Number				
	1	2	3	4	5
Humanities	17	13	14	7	15
Math/Sciences	14	10	9	9	5

^{2} = 3.93515 *df* = 4 *p* 0.4

Table 5-11
Correlation Between Level of Professor's Questions and Modal and Median Professor Cognitive Level

	Questioning Level			
	Cognitive Memory	Convergent Thinking	Divergent Thinking	Evaluative Thinking
r	0.0541	0.0785	0.0083	0.0224
N	147	102	33	28
P	0.258	0.216	0.482	0.455

Pearson correlation coefficient between cognitive level of professor's questions (based on MCS) and modal professor cognitive level (based on FTCB).

Table 5-12
Pearson Correlation Coefficient between Cognitive Level of Professor's Questions and Median Professor-Cognitive Level

	Questioning Level			
	Cognitive Memory	Convergent Thinking	Divergent Thinking	Evaluative Thinking
Professor *Median* *r*	–0.1436	0.1876	0.1072	–0.0989
N	147	102	33	28
P	0.041	0.029	0.276	0.308

Table 5-13
Pearson Correlation Coefficient between Cognitive Level of Professors' Questions and Modal Student-Cognitive Level

	Questioning Level			
	Cognitive Memory	Convergent Thinking	Divergent Thinking	Evaluative Thinking
r	–0.2362	0.19	0.3394	0.1952
N	147	102	33	28
P	.002	0.028	0.027	0.16

Table 5-14
Pearson Correlation Coefficient between Cognitive Level of Professor's Questions and Median Student-Cognitive Level

	Questioning Level			
	Cognitive Memory	Convergent Thinking	Divergent Thinking	Evaluative Thinking
Median *Student* *r*	–0.1894	0.01133	0.2415	–0.1417
N	147	102	33	28
P	0.011	0.128	0.088	0.236

number of comparisons made. With this single comparison model no relationships were found between any one cognitive level of students and any one level of the professor's questions.

On the other hand, when both modal and median scores of the overall professor and student cognitive levels were computed and compared to the cognitive levels of the professor's questions, there were several significant relationships. These measures of central tendency yielded an overall picture of the cognitive level of each class, depicting more accurately the differences between classes. Thus they revealed relationships not found when each single cognitive level and each questioning level were compared. One might conclude that there appear to be some relationships between the cognitive level of professors' questions and the overall cognitive level of the class, but the exact nature of this relationship is not totally clear.

In this study the specific relationships that were found between the professor's overall cognitive level and the levels of his questions were (1) as the percentage of a professor's low-level questions went down, his median cognitive level went up; (2) as the percentage of the professor's convergent-thinking questions went up, his median cognitive level went up. No relationship was found between professor modal-cognitive level and professor questioning level.

The specific relationships between the overall student cognitive level and the professor's questioning levels were generally consistent with the findings concerning overall professor cognitive levels. It was found that (1) as the percentage of professors' low-level (cognitive-memory) questions increased, the students' median and modal cognitive levels decreased; (2) as the percentage of professors' convergent-thinking questions increased, modal student levels increased; and (3) as the percentage of professors' divergent questions increased, modal student cognitive levels increased.

Summary and Implications

While a variety of descriptive information was obtained from this study, the following seem to be the most important findings:

1. A very small portion of most college classes was spent in professor questioning. This percentage of time spent questioning did not vary significantly across institution type, size, course level, or academic field.
2. The great majority of the questions asked by college professors were at the lowest cognitive level ($X = 82.33$ percent).
3. There appeared to be no significant difference in the cognitive level of professors' questions between public and private institutions.
4. When questioning levels of professors were compared according to the size of the institution, only convergent thinking appeared to differ; large-school professors asked significantly more convergent-thinking questions than did small-school professors.
5. In an overall chi-square analysis of questioning levels, questioning level was not independent of the individual institutions in the sample.
6. Questioning level was not only *not* significantly different between beginning and advanced courses, but was surprisingly similar across the course levels.
7. Questioning level varied between disciplines only at the cognitive-memory level, with science/math/engineering professors asking significantly more low-level questions than did humanities/social sciences/arts professors.
8. Primary questioning patterns did not vary significantly across institution size, type, course level, or discipline.
9. The most common questioning pattern was professor lecture followed by a low-level (cognitive-memory) question, followed by more lecture.
10. Five questioning patterns accounted for 61.54 percent of all primary and secondary questioning patterns of college professors.

11. 31.93 percent of all questioning patterns of college professors in this sample elicited no student participation.
12. Summed primary and secondary patterns 1–5 were not independent of institution or course level, but they were independent of discipline.
13. In a comparison of each professor and student cognitive level with each professor-questioning level, few relationships were found.
14. In a comparison of the modal professor-cognitive level with the professor-questioning level, no significant relationships were found; but a comparison of the median cognitive level of the professors with questioning levels revealed that professors' median cognitive levels decreased as their low-level questions increased, and their median cognitive levels increased as the frequency of their convergent-thinking questions increased.
15. As the frequency of professors' questions in the cognitive-memory level increased, the modal student-cognitive level decreased. As the frequency in the professor's convergent-thinking questioning level increased, the modal student cognitive level increased.
16. As the frequency of professors' questioning in cognitive memory increased, the median student level decreased.

The results of the study raise several questions. Probably most fundamental is why are the majority of the professors' questions at such low cognitive levels? Second, why are significant differences found among institutions? Is it simply a matter of institutional goals or are different types of students responsible? Do small public institutions ignore the goal of critical thinking or do they simply take less able students?

Another aspect of the data that merits attention is the great similarity of questioning between beginning and advanced courses. One would expect beginning courses to deal with more factual information than advanced ones, and for advanced courses to attempt, then, to synthesize and relate concepts, to draw hypotheses and conclusions; but this did not happen. Furthermore, there was no difference in questioning and advanced classes within each discipline group. Apparently professors' general questioning strategies do not change from beginning to advanced courses regardless of the subject being taught. Needed, though, are studies examining courses taught by the same professor at both beginning and advanced levels. Perhaps each individual professor does change questioning strategies, but these differences are buried by computing group means.

Also of potential interest is the possibility of a curvilinear relationship between outcomes such as critical thinking, and higher-level questions. It may well be that there is an optimum proportion of high- and low-level questions to reach this goal, and that either extreme is less than optimally productive.

Two additional questions arise from the data on the relationship of the cognitive levels of student and professor; foremost is why is there an apparent lack of relationship between the highest levels of professors' questions (divergent and evaluative) with any general cognitive levels? It may well be that due to the low frequency of professors' questions at these levels, significant relationships will be difficult to uncover, and that controlled experiments will be necessary to investigate this relationship further. Second, because of its methodology, this study could not reveal which is the dependent variable: do higher student and professor general-cognitive levels cause the professor's cognitive-questioning levels to rise, or do higher level professor questions cause the overall cognitive levels to rise? This certainly needs to be determined.

In general, then, when viewing the questioning process in the college classroom, one sees that professor questioning occupies a very small portion of the total class time, the cognitive level of the professors' questions is usually very low, but appears to be related to overall cognitive level of both professor and students; and often professors' questioning patterns elicit no student response. Overall there are very few major differences in questioning across any of the variables examined. Additional studies of questioning patterns in which causal relationships between levels of questioning and student achievement may be established are warranted.

Our sense of mythology suggests that in colleges one would expect to find inquiring young minds being challenged by the intellectual and perceptive questions of learned professors—extensive Socratic dialogues and an active interchange of ideas. In this respect, the findings of this study were disappointing. Not only were many of the classes void of intellectual interchange between professor and students, but they also lacked excitement and vigor. One of the primary tools at the professor's disposal to infuse this atmosphere into his classroom is questioning, an age-old technique, but one which has not yet been tapped for its full potential.

For institutions and professors who wish to improve teaching, it seems reasonable that some attention be directed toward an analysis of questioning patterns in college classrooms. This analysis, although not exhaustive, does suggest topics for study in this area. It may be that questioning levels and patterns are not what is important, that instead we should look harder at cognitive levels, as is suggested in chapter 4. The main point however, is that today little of the actual teaching *process* is being examined at all. The results of this study clearly indicate that what we achieve with our efforts to improve college teaching could not be any worse than what we are doing by habit. We may be in a situation where it is better to be ineffective and trying than to be ineffective and not trying.

Notes

1. A.B. Hartung, "Teaching Excellence," *Improving College Teaching* 20(1972): 146–147; M. Hildebrand, "The Character and Skills of the Effective Professor," *Journal of Higher Education* 44 (1973):41–50; M. Hildebrand, R.C. Wilson, and E.R. Dienst, *Evaluating University Teaching* (Berkeley, Calif.: Center for Research and Development in Higher Education, University of California, 1971); G.V. Walsh, "One in Five Made Us Think," *Improving College and University Teaching* 20 (1972):153–155.

2. W.J. McKeachie, *Research on College Teaching: A Review* (Washington, D.C.: ERIC Clearinghouse on Higher Education, 1970) ERIC Document Reproduction Service No. ED043 789.

3. T.H. Adams, "The Development of a Method for Analyses of Questions Asked by Teachers in Classroom Discussion." Doctoral diss., Rutgers University, 1964. University Microfilms No. 64-11, 475; A. Bellack, *The Language of the Classroom* (New York: Teachers College Press, Columbia University, 1966); O.L. Davis, Jr., and D.C. Tinsley, "Cognitive Objectives Revealed by Classroom Questions Asked by Social Studies Student Teachers," *Peabody Journal of Education* 45 (July 1967):21–26; V.M. Rogers, "Modifying Questioning Strategies of Teachers, Questioneze," *Journal of Teacher Education* 23 (1972):58–62.

4. N.F. Furst, "The Multiple Languages of the Classroom," Paper presented at the meeting of the American Educational Research Association, New York, February 1967; M.D. Gall, "Use of Questions in Teaching," *Review of Educational Research* 40 (Dec. 1970): 707–721.

5. M.L. Lamb, "The Effects of Different Classroom Observation Conditions on Questioning Patterns of Teachers." Doctoral diss., University of Oklahoma, 1970. University Microfilms No. 71-12584.

6. A complete discussion of the instrumentation is included in C.P. Barnes, "A Descriptive Study of the Questioning Behavior of College Instructors." Doctoral diss., Claremont Graduate School, 1975.

7. Note that S. Labovtiz, "The Assignment of Numbers to Rank Order Categories," *American Sociological Review* 35 (1970):515–524, indicates that even if assumptions concerning equal interval data are violated, as they are in this study, the Pearson r may still be used. It is a more powerful statistic than the Spearman Rank Order or the Kendall and the results are nearly identical. This was tested and found to be true in this study.

from Gender and University Teaching: A Negotiated Difference

ANNE STATHAM, LAUREL RICHARDSON, AND JUDITH A. COOK

Basic Instructional Activities in Academia

The faculty members we interviewed and observed used a diversity of strategies and techniques in the classroom. In general, university professors have a great deal of flexibility in performing the teaching aspect of their role. In most cases norms of academic freedom and personal autonomy preclude all but minimal interference. Certain activities, however, occur in most classrooms. These include carefully organizing lectures and other presentations so that they are easy to follow, soliciting students' feedback and checking the adequacy of explanations, and correcting any misinformation the students may have acquired. In the interest of promoting understanding and motivation among students, professors also encourage students' participation. This participation, sometimes taken for granted at the elementary and secondary levels, might be more difficult to achieve at the college level. Hence, the concerns and skills of women professors in facilitating interpersonal communication might be particularly valuable in helping them to manage the requirements of the professorial role.

We focus on two aspects of these activities: structured presentations and participatory learning. Both are common activities for university teachers (Centra 1987; McKeachie 1986). They are emphasized in teacher education as most effective (Rosenshine and Furst 1973) and are referred to as most appropriate (Duncan and Biddle 1974). Although there is no reason to assume that males and females will differ on the dimension of structured classroom presentations, women might be more likely than men to use participatory learning in their classrooms if they are more concerned with establishing interpersonal relationships and enhancing their students' sense of agency. Some recent evidence shows that women secondary teachers do, in fact, generate more student participation (Good et al. 1973; Brophy and Good 1974); Thorne suggests that this difference may carry over to the college level, in view of women's generally cooperative and symmetrical style of interaction (1979).

If women professors do make greater use of the participatory model, this difference would increase the amount of classroom time in which students are discussing the material, as we expected. We reasoned that learning in women's classrooms might focus primarily on the students as active participants rather than on the professor as the purveyor of knowledge.

Information Exchange as Good Teaching

Information exchange was the major goal in the classrooms we observed. Much of the classroom time was spent on lectures and presentations by the professor. A significant, though smaller, portion of time was given to interaction with the students. Although professors are not required to generate student involvement, some use of the participatory model is suggested for teachers in general (Duncan and Biddle 1974; Rosenshine and Furst 1973) and is counted among good teaching behaviors by university professors (Wotruba and Wright 1974). This approach presumably will increase the student's investment in the learning process. Because such investment is likely to facilitate the learning process, we expected some type of active participation by students to occur in most of the classrooms we observed.

Excerpts from "Gender and University Teaching: A Negotiated Difference," by Ann Statham, Laurel Richardson, and Judith A. Cook, 1991, State University of New York Press.

We constructed specific measures to examine these behaviors. The two major dimensions of instruction specified above—structured presentations by the professor and participatory learning by the students—underlie the types of measures constructed. Structured presentations by the professor include two different sets of behaviors. The first set consists of managerial classroom behaviors such as giving assignments, making announcements, and going over the syllabus. These behaviors facilitate the learning process but are neither substantive (i.e., students will not be tested on them) nor evaluative. Second are the ordered substantive behaviors such as giving lectures, reviewing material covered, and emphasizing particular points. These behaviors are manifestly intended to convey knowledge; the students will be tested on this material.

Accordingly, we created two variables to measure the structured presentation dimension. We combined all managerial behaviors into a single variable called managerial behaviors. Such management of the classroom might affect how students learn the substantive material, as well as influence their judgments of a professor's competence and likability and the tenor of the class as a whole. Second, all behaviors that were subscripted as representing ordering, reviewing, or explicitly emphasizing certain substantive points were combined into a variable called ordered substantive presentations. In addition to these two variables, we constructed a combination measure of miscellaneous behaviors that occurred only infrequently: teacher's manipulation of artifacts (which makes presentation much clearer), unspoken behaviors (such as writing on the board, which also should clarify presentation), and professor's self-judgments of incorrectness (an indicator of the extent to which clarity of presentation is a valued goal). This latter measure summed all judgments of incorrectness subscripted as referring to self (see table 3.1).

The second dimension involves the quantity and the quality of professor/student interaction or the use of students' participatory learning. Generating students' involvement is a complex task, and doing so may overlap with the professor's structured presentations. For example, a professor could organize the classroom presentation in such a way as to facilitate feedback from students. The feedback might be used to check whether the professor is communicating with the class, but it also might be used as a way of involving students in their education. Recognizing the potential overlap, we decided to consider any input from the students as an indication that students' involvement was encouraged. Yet, because we also recognized the complexity involved, we distinguished among the levels of effort a professor expended to generate students' involvement. We divided behaviors into those which indicated minimal or mild use of participatory learning and those which indicated extensive use.

Mild efforts to involve students involve exchanges that require minimal feedback, such as the recitation of the "right" answer or a "yes" answer to a question such as "Do you understand?" Such behaviors in themselves suggest that professors are acquiescing in form to the principle of involving students but are not necessarily endorsing the spirit of this approach. The spirit is found in classrooms managed by professors who exert a stronger effort to involve students. In such classrooms, professors engage their students in exploring ideas about the material, in asking questions, and in sharing opinions. Through the use of humor, for example, they create classroom climates that are pleasant and warm. Their pedagogy may be experiential, such that students examine the artifacts being described, flip coins to "see" probability theory, or engage in sociodramas and mock debates. These behaviors—the encouragement of students' ideas and opinions and the use of humor and experiential teaching methods—we view as examples of strong efforts to involve students.

Table 3.1
Proportion of Classroom Time Spent in Structuring Activities
(Observation Material)

Structured Presentations	Female Professors	Male Professors
Managerial behaviors	.039	.033
Presentation of material	.632	.704
Other/miscellaneous	.001	.001
	(correcting self, manipulating artifacts)	

Note: No significant sex differences are found in any of these behaviors when sex ratio of department faculty, professor's rank, class size, and course level are controlled in regression format.

We constructed several measures to tap mild efforts to involve students. First, we considered the proportion of initiations by professors (presenting material) to be a negative indicator of use of the participatory model. Other measures seemed to be indirect indicators of limited use. They included proportion of time spent in professor's responses to students' questions, teacher's solicitations of clarifications ("What do you mean by that?"), and managerial solicitations ("Are there any questions?"). All three of these indicators involve the students only minimally in classroom interaction. They may serve simply to inform the professor of the students' comprehension rather than eliciting their active participation in initiating classroom discussion (see table 3.2).

Another subset of behaviors indicated extensive use of participatory learning. These behaviors, involving fuller student participation in the classroom, are a combination of all instances where students manipulated artifacts or engaged in other forms of experiential learning. We also created measures of teachers' general solicitations of students' input and of all student solicitations (questions or invitations to respond further). All of these behaviors indicated fuller student participation, in which students did more than take notes from lectures, ask for clarification, or respond to limited queries by the teacher (See table 3.2).

Several other measures served as indicators of the extent to which the classroom climate lent itself to a give-and-take between professor and students. We calculated total input by students as well as the proportion of time in which students presented material. We also measured the proportion of time given to professor's and students' laughter. These may be general indicators of the extent to which students' participation was encouraged; they certainly represent interaction patterns that may make the atmosphere more receptive to involvement by students (see table 3.2).

From several sets of data we gain multiple perspectives on these activities. The interview material allows us to explore the levels of commitment to good teaching held by male and female professors and to examine its meaning to them, including the salience of the teaching role, the professors' claimed commitment to structured presentations and to encouraging students' participation, their use of humor, and an additional concept related to the involvement of students, namely whether the classroom focus is on the professor or on the students.

Table 3.2
Proportion of Classroom Time Spent Encouraging and Permitting Students' Participation (Observation Material)

	Women Professors	*Men Professors*
Mild Efforts to Involve Students		
Responding to questions	.083	.090
Soliciting clarification	.013	.012
Checking students' understanding	.024	.017[a]
Strong Efforts to Involve Students		
Soliciting students' input	.047	.029[a]
Soliciting responses from students	.051	.037[a]
Experiential presentations and activities	.023	.007[a]
Professors' and students' thought	.021	.007[a]
Professors' and students' laughter	.016	.013[a]
Participation by Students		
Total student input	.152	.096[a]
Students presenting material	.035	.013[a]
Students' solicitations of information	.017	.013[a]

[a] Significant sex differences occur at .05 level, controlling for sex ratio of department faculty, professor's rank, class size, and course level in regression format.

The observational data permit us to examine sex differences in actual behaviors, including structured presentations, mild and strong efforts to involve students as participatory learners, and the actual amount of input by students.

Although our indicators of perceptions and attitudes regarding good teaching are not identical with the indicators of actual teaching behaviors, they emerge from the same theoretical perspectives. Hence, we will explore whether or not sex differences are consistent across the two sets of data.

Neither the status inconsistency/role conflict perspective nor the contextual/woman-centered perspective would lead us to propose that sex differences in overall basic instructional techniques would be great. Both males and females are socialized into an academic culture that values certain teaching activities; both males and females are in a situational context that demands at least an adherence to the goal of communicating knowledge in as clear a way as possible. If women are less secure in that context, as proposed by the status inconsistency/role conflict perspective, they are likely to compensate by thorough preparation and careful ordering of material, thus making their performance of this teaching behavior similar to that of their male colleagues. If they are not insecure in this context because they have already mastered the prerequisite skills (as attested by the attainment of the Ph.D.), as the contextual/woman-centered perspective would argue, they would still be similar to the male professors in the care given to organization of materials.

Although we do not expect the sex differences to be great, we propose that women professors will emphasize the importance of teaching more than men, will invest more effort in involving students, and will achieve higher levels of interaction with their students. Whether viewed from the status inconsistency/role conflict perspective or the contextual/woman-centered perspective, women are expected to be concerned more often with the well-being of others and to invest more in the establishment of relationships; these concerns are likely to carry over into the academic context and the teaching role. Thus, both perspectives predict similar outcomes concerning these behaviors.

The Salience of Teaching

The salience of teaching for university professors can vary a great deal. For some, teaching may be a highly salient role; for others it may be perfunctory and virtually ritualistic. For this reason we considered it necessary to examine the importance of teaching to the faculty; we did so through the interviews.

Being highly committed to teaching does not mean that one is an excellent teacher, nor is the reverse necessarily true. Even so, differences in the salience of the teaching role by sex may affect the amounts and kinds of satisfaction that males and females derive from teaching; in turn this satisfaction might affect their behavior.

Our interviews covered four issues that we used as indicators of the salience of the teaching role: (1) attitude toward teaching, (2) importance of being an excellent teacher, (3) amount of time spent discussing teaching, and (4) amount of time spent preparing for class. We assigned each respondent a score from 4 (high) to 0 (low) on each of the indicators; we summed these indicators into a single scale with a range of 16 (dedicated to teaching) to 0 (not invested in teaching). In addition, respondents volunteered information concerning the amount of life involvement they had in teaching, i.e., the relevance of teaching to their general state of well-being and to the management of their other role responsibilities. Each of the researchers responsible for the interviews independently rated from 0 (low) to 4 (high) each respondent's life involvement in teaching. The coders agreed on all but two judgments; those were negotiated. Life-involvement judgment scores stand as secondary or confirmatory data for the salience-of-teaching scores because there was considerable agreement between the two.

The mean salience-of-teaching scores and the mean life-involvement scores by rank and by sex reveal no overall gender differences (table 3.3). (To preserve confidentiality we do not present the specific scores of individual faculty members.) There are, however, interactions between gender and rank. Specifically, commitment decreases as rank increases: male and female professors seem to be equally dedicated; assistants are most dedicated and full professors least. The main gender difference occurs at the associate level, where the women are more dedicated than the men; women associates are closer to the assistant professors in their degree of dedication, whereas male associates show midrange salience in teaching scores.

Table 3.3
Mean Scores for Salience of Teaching, Life Involvement, and Involvement of Students, by Rank (Interview Material)

	Salience of Teaching[a]		Life Involvement[b]		Involvement of Students[a]	
	Females	Males	Females	Males	Females	Males
Rank						
Assistant	12.0	12.2	3.2	3.0	13.2	12.4
Associate	10.6	7.6	3.2	2.4	12.0	8.0
Full	5.4	4.4	1.4	.8	7.8	7.6
Overall mean	9.4	8.0	2.6	2.0	11.0	9.3

[a] Range possible: 0–16.
[b] Range possible: 0–4.

The Life Course of the Teaching Role: Composites

Although we found no sex differences in overall salience of teaching, we conjectured that teaching nevertheless might be salient for men and for women for different reasons. To explore this possibility, we constructed separate composites of male and female dedicated teachers based on the interview materials. These composites—the male ideal-typic dedicated teacher and the female ideal-typic dedicated teacher—do not represent any particular professor but depict a blending of characteristics found among the dedicated teachers.

The male ideal-typic dedicated professor sees teaching as "the most exciting, stimulating, varied profession that exists." He "loves it." He wants to do well at it. He spends nearly all of his time preparing, seeing students, and talking about teaching to his colleagues. A major portion of his preparation time and much of his conversation are devoted to "the mechanics of teaching," "designing teaching techniques," and sending memos to his colleagues about his ideas. Transferring content is not enough; "you must *find a way* to get the material into their heads." Teaching is a calling, a "mission much broader than the subject matter." Part of that mission is to find ways to teach his colleagues to teach better, to recognize students as human beings, and to devise techniques that work. When the techniques are successful, the professor feels good. When they flop, he designs new ones. He orders the remainder of his life around his teaching. This may mean that his wife "chooses" not to be employed or helps him with his curriculum planning and course presentation, that he "sacrifices" being an "ideal husband/father," or that in order to have any time to himself he "has to get out of town."

The female dedicated professor, as an ideal type, sees teaching as extremely valuable and important, perhaps "her most important professional contribution," "the thing [she does] which has the greatest value." She is "highly devoted" and "ego-involved." She "loves it." She spends a considerable amount of time preparing, thinking about it, counseling students; and talking about her teaching, especially with colleagues who are friends. For her, teaching means "communicating the subject matter *and* working with the students." Both are equally important. ("I get to read books I'm interested in and talk about them with others (students).") Students' responses are extremely important to her; she sees them as valid judges of her teaching excellence. She wants feedback, including negative feedback, so she can improve. If her class goes well, she shares her elation with colleague-friends; if it goes badly, "if the students become disenchanted—for whatever reason—everything else in (her) life feels out of whack"; doing a poor job makes her feel "depressed for hours—even into the evening." She knows she is a role model for her students, especially her female students, and strives to find ways to encourage them to succeed and at the same time to differentiate themselves from her—to find their own paths toward success.

The ideal-typic dedicated male professor and the ideal-typic dedicated female professor are similar in some ways. They both love teaching, want to be excellent at it, and expend a considerable amount of time preparing for it and talking about it. Both have high life involvement with teaching. Males, however, tend to be oriented more technically toward their teaching, and females more interpersonally. This difference can be seen in several ways. First, males discuss their dedication in terms of strategies and methods of teaching, whereas females focus on the content and on the students. Second, males talk to colleagues about those methods, whereas females tend to talk to colleague-friends about their feelings concerning a particular class or student. Third, male professors feel bad when a technique flops and rectify the situation by devising a different method. A bad teaching experience can be "turned around" by a new technique. On the other hand, female professors report feeling very bad and depressed when their classes go poorly. For them, rectification comes from obtaining students' input and evaluations. Fourth, dedicated males view teaching as a calling, a "mission." Their job is not only to teach students to enjoy learning—an abstract mission—but to teach other teachers—an external goal. Female professors do not report the same messianic zeal, but rather view themselves as individual role models who have a responsibility to create a more personal and more individualized relationship with their students.

Thus dedicated teaching seems to have different meanings for men and for women; the impact of dedicated teaching on their lives is different, both emotionally and structurally. Males tend to view the role as a "career" or a "cause" and to structure their private lives accordingly; wives and children accommodate to the demands of dedicated teaching. Female dedicated teachers apparently do not expect their families' lives to accommodate to the time demands resulting from their dedication. Unlike the males, however, they frequently mention the emotional consequences of dedicated teaching in terms of their feeling of well-being or depression. Dedicated males either do not experience these emotional consequences or erase them quickly by refocusing on teaching as a technical problem. Females focus on the relationship they develop with the students; males are more concerned with interactions with students, a precursor to involving the students in their learning. Thus, although teaching itself might not be much more important for women, the practice of participative teaching might have greater significance.

Almost directly opposite to those dedicated teachers are male and female professors—mostly at the full rank—who can be described as disinterested in teaching, not as devoted, dedicated, or involved. To what extent do male and female professors experience this noninvolvement in similar or dissimilar ways? To address this question, we constructed ideal-typic portraits of the male disinterested professor and the female disinterested professor.

The male disinterested professor sees teaching as "at best ancillary to the role of scholar/researcher," and at worst "the temptation of the devil," a waste of his talent and energy. Excellence in teaching is not a "priority" or a "primary motivation." He devotes little time to preparing for class, but he brings to teaching his "years of reading." Only occasionally does he discuss his teaching, and then with friends or spouse. He believes that students must motivate themselves; "spending time with such unformed and uninformed minds" is deadly to one's own development and growth.

The ideal-typic female disinterested professor views teaching at best as "what I do for a living," and at worst as "a chore, an interruption." Excellence in teaching is not important; in any case, "teaching takes up too much time." She rarely talks about it, and then primarily to a friend or spouse. Preparation time is minimal, but her "whole intellectual life is preparation." Students' feelings are not very interesting; their ideas, not very stimulating; and their evaluations, not very important. They are not her "constituency"; they are not the persons whose approval she seeks. She feels role-model pressures but believes that her life is her own and that she can act in ways judged appropriate by herself, not by her students. As these two ideal-typic constructions make clear, these men and women sound very similar; occasionally their language is nearly identical.

Disinterested professors spend a minimal amount of time preparing for and talking about teaching, have low ego involvement in being excellent teachers, and do not hold teaching as a priority. They have other interests. In the male professors' accounts, these other interests are specified as research and scholarship. That specification is not found in the women's accounts. We might view this finding as a continuation of the male *career* investment mode that was noted among the male dedicated teachers. That is, the male noninvested professors, although not concerned with teaching, make it clear that they are invested in the scholarship/research/writing aspects of the professorial role. The female professors do not specify the nature of their other commitments and interests. Further, although it is clear that teaching has lost its emotional salience for the noninvested women, the interviews give no sense that other aspects of their role have captured their emotional investment. Consequently we might hypothesize that as females move through the ranks, they become more like the males in the sense of abandoning the expressive dimension but are less likely to adopt the "career" and "mission" alternatives.

In summary, then, dedication to teaching is associated with gender and with rank. Dedication decreases as rank increases; the decrease is more rapid for men than for women. By looking at the ideal-typic male and female dedicated teachers, however, we find that the meanings of that dedication differ greatly by gender. Dedicated male professors are more technical or technique-focused in their orientation, whereas dedicated female professors are more relational or concerned with interpersonal relationships. Finally, the meaning of the teaching role for the disinterested professors is quite similar for both sexes; both men and women lack a personalized, affective orientation toward teaching.

Teaching as Structuring and Presenting

Behavior

Overall, men and women professors did not differ significantly in the importance they attached to the teaching role. Hence, we did not expect them to differ in their efforts to communicate the material clearly. In fact, both men and women spent a great proportion of their classroom time presenting material to their students. Even so, we noted great variety in how these presentations were handled. Some professors walked expansively around the classroom, making eye contact with virtually every student. Others stood quietly behind podiums, talking through a microphone to huge rooms full of students. Some were very dramatic; others were dry, crisp, and to the point. Some gender differences in style might have existed, but there were no gender differences in time spent presenting classroom material. Both sexes spent considerable time presenting material (see table 3.1); other related structuring activities took considerably less time. Men spent slightly more time presenting material, and women engaged somewhat more often in managerial (noncontent-related) activities, but these differences were not statistically significant when possibly confounding factors were controlled.[1]

Preferences for Structuring

The interviews contain more detailed information about professors' preferences for structuring classroom sessions. Although the structure and clarity of the material presented to the students are important features of teaching, our interviewees expressed preferences for different types of classroom structure. They differed in opinions regarding whether teachers should have a set agenda in mind for each classroom session. Here we discuss three types of structure: tight, loose, and "deceptive." As with the observation material, the use of these structures was not associated with gender or with rank.

Some of the professors described a style that involved careful preparation and tight organization. One male associate professor in the humanities explained, "You lecture as clearly and in as organized a fashion as you can." A woman full professor in home economics noted, "I outline, usually, or go with transparencies, but I get them organized, I don't like to be in a class myself where the teacher is fumbling around."

Other professors described a looser style that involved less preparation and granted more organizational responsibility to students. A male professor in the humanities said:

> I make a practice of not reading [students' papers] that are going to be discussed in class ahead of time so I don't have preconceptions about them. Somebody in the class is going to be a critiquer so they read it aloud and start talking about it.

Similarly, a woman associate professor in home economics gave the following example:

> I have a plan in mind but if students bring up some relevant subject matter we'll go with it because that's where they are. That's the teachable moment. That's the time to make use of that.

Other professors reported a style that was essentially a mixture of the tight and the loose. This style was described as one in which professors maintained an organized presentation of ideas while making it appear as if students controlled the classroom. That is, professors were able to orchestrate students' "spontaneous" presentation of ideas and insights to conform to their own plan for presenting information effectively; the class appeared deceptively loose. Two examples, one from a male and one from a female professor, are illustrative:

> It's an easy, free-going class, though all the time I'm pulling the strings underneath. Someone describing me would say: "He's apparently very easy-going, deceptively loose," but underneath there's a very tight structure (male assistant, humanities).

> There really is structure. I have in mind things that ought to be covered in a session but I let the students move in agendas of their own but try to get us back to what the agenda really is (female full, social sciences).

Although there were no gender differences in faculty members' reported use of any one of the three styles, we found an interesting difference in students' reactions, according to the professors' accounts. Women who described their style as loose and unstructured were more likely to report hostile reactions from students. As a woman assistant professor in home economics noted, "Some [students] get very upset if there is not a lot of structure." Several women felt that students saw a looser teaching style, when used by a woman, as indicative of incompetency. As one female associate professor in the humanities explained:

> They think that I am too disorganized. I give the impression of not having things laid out in rigid structures. A lot of our students want coverage . . . I'm not a coverage person.

In summary, then, although all of the professors observed spent most of their classroom time presenting and structuring material, those whom we interviewed reported teaching styles that varied widely in degree of structure. The following orientations toward planning and organizing were evident in these descriptions: men were as likely as women to choose each of the styles, but women were more likely than men to report students' resentment of looser, less structured approaches. The data suggest that women's attempts to soften their presentations by loosening the class structure may incur resentment among students.

Students' Involvement

Structuring material is one aspect of teaching; generating students' involvement is another. Basically it is difficult to know whether students are absorbing material unless they provide a minimal amount of feedback. Waiting until examination time is both too late and too punitive a way to correct misunderstandings. Some instructors see their role as "teaching how to learn"; desiring more expanded involvement by students, they include them in a more complex array of activities.

Efforts to involve students can be seen in the observational data along two dimensions: mild and strong efforts. Mild efforts are activities designed to check students' understanding; strong efforts attempt to incorporate students more fully into the learning enterprise. Because we found no gender differences in the salience of teaching or in the structuring of material, we expected little difference in the mild efforts to involve students. Overall, these activities are simply an expansion of efforts to convey the material; the instructors are checking to make certain the material has been understood. We expected, however, to find gender differences in the strong efforts to involve students, given (nonfull professor) women's greater emphasis on the relationships they develop with their students, particularly on helping them to develop as learners.

Behavior and Perceptions

In observing these professors in their classrooms, we found few gender differences in what we call their "mild" efforts to involve students. These differences (table 3.2) are not statistically significant for the most part. Both sexes spent similar proportions of time answering and clarifying students' questions. These behaviors include asking, "By that do you mean. . . ?" "Where are you confused?" "I'm not sure I understand your question." Some students raised their hands to ask questions; others spoke out spontaneously. Some questions were posed as jokes that relieved the tension in a lengthy and technical explanation, others were asked seriously in quiet classrooms.

We noted gender differences, however, in one of these mild efforts, namely checking students' understanding. Women spent more time trying to determine whether students grasped the material. Women professors might ask directly whether the students understood or might devise quick methods for testing their understanding. They seemed to play a more active role in ensuring students' understanding, whereas men were more inclined to respond to students' questions once they had been asked.

More striking gender differences emerged when we looked at the professors' "strong" efforts to involve students. These activities include asking directly for students' input ("Does anyone know the answer to that question?" "Any thoughts about this?") and waiting to receive it, providing the opportunity for performing certain activities rather than simply talking about them (including the manipulation of artifacts), pausing for reflection or thought (by both student and professor), and laughing (usually together). All of these occurrences in the classroom suggest that more is going on than presentation of material; they indicate more interaction between student and professor. In the interviews, female professors echoed this concern with checking students' comprehension. Some professors felt that they were particularly sensitive to students who were confused but afraid to speak up, as in the following:

> I think I am extremely conscious of nonverbal cues and I don't think men are. Just out of all my experiences I can tell when a student is in distress and doesn't understand. I can tell when he or she wants to say something but isn't quite ready to raise the hand (associate, humanities).

In fact, women described more teaching techniques designed to determine when students were confused or misunderstood the material, and tended to let the correction of this situation guide their teaching. One woman, an associate professor in the natural sciences, explained:

> If the [student's] question indicates a lack of understanding of something that we have done previously or that has been in the [homework] problems—that the student has missed, generally then you do more than just interrupt [your lecture]. You may digress and rebuild because you don't want a stone out of place in mathematics.

As in the mild efforts, women might ask directly whether the students understood, or might devise quick methods for testing their understanding, as with applications ("Usually at the beginning of the class hour I will go over previous content and students will do the summary parts, which gives me an opportunity to see where they are."). These strategies were largely absent from the men professors' descriptions. Women seemed to be more active in ensuring that students understood, whereas men tended to respond to students' questions after they had been asked. Some of the activities were attempts to create a warm, pleasant atmosphere.

Other indicators show the outcomes of women professors' efforts to encourage students' participation: students had a significantly greater amount of total input in women's classes, presented significantly more material, and made a significantly greater number of solicitations than in male professors' classes. (See Table 3.2)

The interview material confirmed these findings. Many of the women professors described teaching styles that involved seeking students' input, using techniques such as asking questions, calling on students to define difficult terms, fostering group discussions, and requiring presentations by students as in the following:

> I find students' questions stimulating. The interrelation with students stimulates me. They make observations on points that I've missed or they ask me pertinent questions that I hadn't thought to ask (female, associate, humanities).

> I feel like I'm asking them to be not just rational and reasoning but also to feel things, be emotional. I expect them to not only think about the characters in the book but to feel about them, tell me who they hate and who they like. It's very important to me to respond that way to novels (female, assistant, humanities).

> In undergraduate courses I would say I carry the course on questions, ask a lot of questions. That I frequently stop and have the students work for me. The class is generally broken up between a much smaller segment of lecture—of my talking—(and) my response to difficulties that students are having with problems and some time generally for students to verbalize their own work—present it in some way (female, associate, natural sciences).

Not only did women professors describe a variety of methods to solicit students' input; they spoke more often about making genuine use of these contributions rather than merely giving students "time to talk." That is, they mentioned listening to what the students had to say and then incorporating this input into the classroom material. As one woman associate professor in English explained:

> The thing that students have always said about me in my evaluations is that I listen. And that very few professors do. They have a sense that I am really listening to what they say. I am conscious of that because I've worked at it.

In addition, women often said that they used experiential teaching methods in which they encouraged students to learn by doing and by experiencing the subject matter. They were more likely than men to list a number of such strategies when asked to do so (e.g., videotapes, case studies, interviewing a professional in the field, bringing in guest speakers for participatory small groups, creating performance art). Thus, in the women's but not the men's descriptions of their classes, time frequently was devoted to students' solicitations and students' presentations of material as an intentional pedagogical technique, as the following two women noted:

> I allow the discussion to take the direction the students essentially create, and go from there; at least when I'm at my best I do (female, associate, humanities).
>
> For an upper-division graduate course there would be a lot more lecture. I think I'm more inclined to interrupt my lecture with questions [for the students] than my colleagues are, and that my students are more inclined to interrupt me with questions. So that there would be, within the lecture, quite a bit of exchange between teacher and class (female, associate, natural sciences).

It is highly relevant to our argument that all but one of the strong attempts to involve students in the classroom occurred in women's classrooms significantly more often than in men's. Women strive more than men to create situations in which students are involved participants. The only classroom behavior that did not differ significantly was laughter, although even this occurred slightly more often in women's classrooms.

Humor. Our interviews provide additional insight with regard to laughter. Although we found no significant gender differences in the amount of laughter that occurred in classrooms, there were differences in the reasons men and women gave for the use of humor. As before, these gender differences seemed to interact with rank.

Male professors, especially assistants, used humor to "relax the class" and to encourage students' participation. Humor, by their accounts, helped informalize the class, as exemplified in the following statement by an assistant professor in the natural sciences:

> I'm lewd. I use semi-lewd humor because some of the things in the course relate to touchy sorts of things that need just a little humor to break the ice.

Men also used humor as "entertainment" to enliven their classes. They reported feeling good when their "jokes" were well received.

Female assistant professors rarely reported using humor purposefully in their classrooms, but tenured women frequently reported using it. Sometimes they used humor to deflect situations that were potentially a challenge to their authority, as the following two quotes illustrate:

> [When students are rude], I just outsnide them in class (full, social science).
>
> If they make a snide comment I try to keep it on a joking basis (associate, humanities).

The tenured women used humor for entertainment, as did the men. As one woman stated, "I use a lot of humor and funny illustrations . . . I put on a show." Some said it was an essential ingredient of teaching, as expressed in the following excerpt: "I don't think I've done a good job of teaching if we haven't laughed during a class period."

Thus, untenured males and tenured females are likely to claim humor as a strategy for good teaching. "Entertainment" is used by male assistants and by tenured women to create a friendlier and more pleasant atmosphere. Male assistants, however, are also likely to use it to "take the edge off" and to enhance students' participation, whereas tenured women use it to control inappropriate participation by students. In view of the options potentially available to women in situations where a student is "obnoxious" and "out of line" (such as directly confronting him or her, removing him or her from the classroom), women's use of humor suggests that they are trying to handle the situation in a way which disrupts only minimally the "open," "nonthreatening," "warm and personal" classroom environments they try to create.

Preferences for Involving Students

To assess the faculty members' preference for involving students, we used four kinds of information from the interviews: (1) stated use of an interactive class format, (2) desire for students' input in class, (3) desire for students' input in the form of evaluations by students, and (4) the professor's attitude toward students' opinions. We formed a single measure, commitment to involving students, by assigning each interviewed professor a score of 0 (low) to 4 (high) on each indicator and summing the scores for all four indicators. Hence, this measure, ranging from 0 to 16, reflects a professor's claimed commitment to involving students.

Nearly all faculty members claimed that they used an interactive classroom format such as lecture-discussion or question periods. Even the faculty in the natural sciences, where it is claimed sometimes that the interactive format is inappropriate, stated their preference for this approach.

Our respondents prefer the participatory model almost universally (table 3.3). In addition, there are no overall gender differences, although sex and rank interact. The lower the rank, the greater the claimed preference for involving students. As with the salience-of-teaching scores, female associates are closer in claimed preferences to assistants (both male and female), whereas male associates are closer in claimed preferences to full professors (both male and female).

Although male and female assistants score similarly, as do male and female full professors, we wanted to know whether the meaning of participatory education is the same for both sexes: do they have the same reasons for preferring it? To answer this question we drew upon the interview material both of faculty members who claimed strong preferences for involving students and of those who claimed little preference, and constructed ideal-typic portraits.

The male professors who are strongly committed to involving students discuss students' input as necessary and valuable because "we need to find what the students want to learn and what they expect" so we can "then do it." "Students won't learn unless motivated and interested." Further, because it is difficult to get students to discuss, sometimes it is necessary to "throw away a period just to induce them talking . . . and chattering about the material." Most of the interaction, however, takes place between student and professor.

The female professors who are committed to involving students, on the other hand, discuss students' input as desirable and valuable primarily because "through the interchange they (the students) develop a commitment to ideas"; "the process of learning is the learning." Eliciting discussion is not difficult because the professor creates a classroom atmosphere that is warm, relaxed, open, and nonthreatening. Best of all is the interaction that occurs between student and student, in which they "relate to each other, listen to each other."

Male professors who are strongly committed to involving students, then, see the interactive process as potentially a "time waste," difficult to sustain, primarily a relationship between professor and student, and valuable only to the extent that it enables them to find out what the students want to learn so they can teach it. On the other hand, female professors view the interaction as valuable in and of itself, and see themselves as creating non-threatening classroom atmospheres in which students can exchange ideas with each other, all for the purpose of increasing their learning capacity. Obviously these are very different attitudes toward the value of participatory education.

In contrast, males who are not strongly committed to involving students view students' input "as not a very useful thing" because "not everybody's opinion is equally good." They do "not even try to talk to the students" about their preferences and opinions regarding their education. Students are not able to evaluate because they lack basic competence.

Females who are not committed to involving students view students' evaluations primarily as judgments about the professor's personality rather than her competence. Students are "not particularly thoughtful" in those evaluations: "I know whether I'm prompt, prepared, or organized." These professors may not "even bother to read" the evaluations. They encourage classroom interaction, however, and will "*let* students move in agendas of their own (emphasis ours)" or will encourage questions to the professor, and they will "try not to talk down."

These less committed professors are fairly similar in their lack of respect for students' opinions of their teaching styles, but they differ in their classroom interaction patterns. Males tend to downplay such interaction almost entirely, whereas females adopt the model of students' interacting with the professor (rather than with other students) that prevailed among the younger men who strongly preferred student involvement.

Locus of Learning: Professor or Student?

Our analyses of the meanings of students' involvement and dedicated teaching for males and for females led us to an interesting conclusion; men and women professors seem to have very different attitudes towards students. Women professors, especially those who are dedicated to teaching and involving students, value students' contribution as an end in itself; for these women, stimulating students' interest and motivation is not simply a pedagogical technique. Dedicated female teachers see students as valuable sources of learning. Students' participation is a source of stimulation and learning for these women as well as for other students; affective relationships formed with students also are an important part of teaching. Even the women professors who do not prefer involvement by students encourage classroom interaction, albeit between student and professor.

Male professors do not mention the value of students as contributors, as collaborators, or as sources of knowledge or stimulation. Nor do they mention the importance of relationships that they form with students. Rather they see themselves as the *center* of the classroom, as the source of knowledge. Male dedicated teachers discuss the methods they might devise to convey the material more effectively; males who prefer students' involvement talk about the necessity of "permitting" students' participation in order to motivate the students or to find out what they know and what they want to learn. They do not regard students as having a genuinely active part in the learning process.

We term this stance toward students "locus of learning." Male professors tend to see the locus as almost entirely in themselves; female professors tend to see it as in the students. The gender difference is most visible in faculty members' assessments of "good" and "bad" classroom experiences, to which we now turn.

Professors' Best and Worst Classroom Experiences

In the interviews, we asked professors to describe a particular classroom experience that they felt was especially positive or rewarding and a classroom experience that they found especially negative or disappointing. Almost without exception, professors' descriptions of the best classes emphasized a high degree of involvement by students in the learning process (related to the blanket endorsement of students' involvement, as discussed above). This involvement was generated in a variety of situations, including interaction between students, interaction between a student and the professor with the rest of the class as audience, and periods during the professor's lecture when students listened attentively. Some professors described students' involvement in the context of a class discussion in which students became excited and "caught up" in relating their ideas and opinions: "Everybody was sort of leaping in saying things and getting involved and enthusiastic" (female, assistant). In other cases involvement occurred when some or all of the students were able to relate what they were learning to their personal lives: "We talked about heart attacks, and one student was crying because her father died of a heart attack, so it was a very emotional experience and the class all liked it" (male, assistant). In still other descriptions, involvement was fostered through simultaneous but independent intellectual discoveries in which students seemed suddenly to gain insight during a lecture: "It was one of those moments where the whole lecture section suddenly wakes up and you see that there is some comprehension" (male, associate).

In this sense the two sexes were highly similar, but the men and the women differed in one important way. Women were more likely to describe situations as most rewarding when students increased their independence from the professor, took charge of the progression of ideas, pursued topics outside the course requirements, or anticipated professors' major points. The following quotes provide examples:

> [It happens] when a class starts to take over and I find that they're generating their own ideas and getting to the questions that I wanted to ask before I have to ask them, so that they move the discussion along (female, associate, humanities).

> I'd gotten to the statement of the theory near the end of the class but I didn't have enough time to put the argument together. The next time we got back together they had constructed the argument. They were able to see exactly how this all fits together. That was exciting (female, assistant, natural sciences).

> I could see them talking to each other, sharing ideas, relating to each other. They were not talking to me, they talked to me as if I were anyone else, a member of the class (female, assistant, social sciences).

On the other hand, men were more likely to describe their best classes as those in which they, as professors, had played a crucial part in generating students' involvement. In these descriptions, what made the class "best" was not only that students became highly involved in learning but also that the men felt satisfaction from being able to foster this kind of atmosphere. The following quotes are illustrative:

> It was occasions when everyone would be talking, every one would be well read. It's like I motivated them to some extent. There was a good exchange of ideas based on the material presented so that when I walked in that room it was like I turned them on in some way or another (male, assistant, social sciences).

> I had, in fact, covered the material well, conveyed the important facts and yet, in a sense, I entertained them and kept them interested in it. I had a little story to tell and it went over well and contributed to the atmosphere in the classroom (male, associate, social sciences).

> There was a lecture I gave on the counter culture of the sixties that really struck home since I was a graduate student then and I used a lot of my own experiences. It really seemed to get things across to students . . . to the extent that they got up and applauded at the end of the lecture (male, assistant, humanities).

The professors' descriptions of their worst classes showed the same gender difference in perceptions of locus of learning. For the women, the worst classes were those in which the students' contribution to the classroom was lacking in some way ("They were completely disinterested"; "They had all been assigned to read a book and nobody had read it"; "I think the students were just all bad."). Among the men, however, descriptions of worst class experiences tended to focus on the teacher's deficiencies ("I skipped some material and had to go back and got confused"; "The most embarrassing ones are where you go in and actually get lost in your own explanation"; "When I use teaching techniques that just flop terribly.").

In sum, these findings constitute fairly strong evidence for gender differences in locus of learning. Males and females take different stances toward the students and have different perceptions of the student's role and competence in the classroom. Women professors tend to see students as more valuable contributors and as playing a more integral part in the learning process. Given this difference, we might predict more accurately the gender differences in students' involvement as observed in the classroom.

Students' Behaviors

Our observations permit us to say how much students actually participated in these classrooms. Although the total amount of student input is important in this regard, specific types of input might be more exact indicators of the "locus of learning" concept discussed above. In this situation students become a source of learning, along with the professor. Thus we give special attention to students' attempts to solicit information on their own from the instructor and to students' presentations of their own material or information. We expect all of these activities to occur more frequently in women's classrooms, particularly those in which the locus of learning is said to be with the student.

These gender differences do exist (see bottom panel of table 3.2). Students have significantly more input into women's classes. About one-sixth of the time in these classes, students are presenting material themselves (e.g., giving information from other sources or from class sources, short reports). They spend a smaller portion of that time soliciting information from the instructor.

Women, according to the interviews, are more likely to view their students as active, important contributors to the class. Our observational material confirms this point. Women are more likely to use techniques that increase the total amount of students' input into the classroom and to use teaching strategies that are student-centered rather than professor-centered. Although both males and females use similar teaching strategies, women's classes typically are different from men's classes in that students participate more and do so more independently.

Effect of Rank

As in the interview material, we found that the professor's rank affected these gender differences. We tested for this gender difference by estimating regression equations for all of the behaviors considered here that included a sex/rank interaction term. We found two significant interactions: those for presentation of information and for soliciting students' input. In both instances, gender differences were greater (and significant) for professors at ranks above assistant. Both assistant men and assistant women were quite likely to have involved students; tenured men were less likely to have done so. On the basis of the results from the interview data, this gender difference among tenured professors might be due largely to differences among associate professors (the majority of our tenured women). Women full professors might become more similar to men full professors in their divestiture of the teaching role; we cannot test this possibility with this sophisticated statistical technique, however, because there are not enough women full professors in the sample (or university) and because of the cross-sectional nature of our research design. Even so, tabular analysis shows that in keeping with the interviews, the women full professors we observed reduced their investment in teaching, particularly in participatory teaching.

Summary

These results show a marked gender difference in teaching styles. Although both sexes give the bulk of their time to structuring and presenting material, women professors are more likely than men to encourage students' input, particularly in ways that allow for a more independent student role. This difference is reflected in the behaviors we observed, as well as in the interview material dealing with attitudes toward students. Women professors view students as active collaborators in the learning process; hence, they give them more latitude in the classroom. These gender differences are especially true of associate professors; men assistants adopt the more female-typed participatory model, and female full professors divest themselves of this involvement.

Although these gender differences appeared, others did not. Women were not more committed to the teaching role nor to involving students. Both genders adopted normative stances typical of those in the teacher role, emphasizing the importance of teaching to approximately the same degree. Both were equally concerned with the clarity and structure of their presentations. Both believed that students' involvement was essential for successful teaching. The major difference was in their attitudes toward students, which conditioned the amount and the quality of student involvement that they encouraged and received. Women professors' tendency to make fuller use of students' input gives students greater latitude in the classroom, allowing them to contribute more substantively to the class. This possibility is related to the way in which authority is managed in the classroom, the topic of the following chapter.

. . .

Authority Management in the Classroom

Summary

These results show important gender differences in the management of classroom authority. Although both sets of data suggest few gender differences in the challenges that professors actually receive in the classroom, marked differences exist in *perceptions* of challenges to authority and in strategies for managing them. The differences are interesting, especially when related to differences in basic instructional behaviors. The men themselves make the connection between their authority position and their ability to involve students in the classroom. They may not realize, however, that their authority management strategies may deter students' involvement. Whatever their awareness, this lack of involvement clearly troubles them. The men, then, use their authority at the cost of involvement by students.

The women's position is the opposite. They share authority and receive students' input, but not without cost. The women (especially untenured professors) struggle to assert their authority position. To handle this situation, the women in our interview sample, especially assistant professors, acted to establish the legitimacy of their authority position; they felt that students had more doubts about their competence than about that of male professors. Even so, their strategies for establishing legitimacy seemed designed to avoid students' resentment. The women used less direct, less harsh, less punitive means of dealing with students than male professors, and granted considerably more subject-matter authority to their students. Women were, however, quite firm in their stands on authority; they made full use of their evaluative authority, and as their rank increased, they reported themselves to be quite adept at confronting direct challenges by students. As they approached the end of their careers, they seemed to derive more satisfaction from their teaching than did the men.

Although the double binds hypothesized by the role conflict/status inconsistency literature do seem to exist for women, particularly in their perceptions, they were not nearly as pronounced as one might expect. In fact, women seemed to establish and maintain their authority in the classroom with relative ease, being careful not to disrupt their relationships with students in the process. This finding provides support for the contextual/woman-centered approach, which predicts that women's greater repertoire of interpersonal techniques and skills allow them to manage conflict situations effectively. This possibility will become clearer in chapter 6 when we consider students' reactions to the professors we studied. Meanwhile, we turn to personalizations, the final category of teaching behaviors that we considered.

. . .

Personalizations: Look Into My Life

Summary

These findings demonstrate that men and women professors are quite different in their attempts to personalize their classroom atmospheres. Neither sex showed a greater tendency toward self-revelation in the classroom, though our interview data suggest that the content of women's revelations might have been more personal. The greatest gender difference concerned women's attempts to relate to their students' personal situations. In our interview data, female professors reported more of these attempts; our observational data *show* women making more of these attempts. Female professors more often used examples relevant to the students' personal lives and encouraged students to relate their own experiences to the class. In essence, they seemed to focus more on the student as a total person, incorporating students' experiences into classroom presentations, listening to students' problems in their offices, and chatting with students outside the classroom.

Although these behaviors simply might make the situation more comfortable for women because of prior sex-role conditioning, they could serve another pragmatic function. The women believed that they enhanced the students' learning potential by making the students the focus of learning. From the woman-centered/contextual perspective, such a strategy shows the strengths of women's responses to a particular situation. From a role conflict/status inconsistency perspective, we could argue that personalizations enable women to establish their authority in the classroom without violating sex-appropriate behavioral norms. Along these lines, the women professors adopted a more formalized, less interactive position only when grades were at issue, while the men engaged in direct interaction and authority with students who came to their offices. For whatever reason, personalizing behaviors appear to be especially important to women professors; men, on the other hand, are less likely to use these methods and might in the end, be less satisfied with the relationships they form with students as a result. In the previous chapter, we showed that the men were unhappy with this outcome because they wished to reduce the distance between themselves and students.

Professors' concern with their students' feelings about them may influence their perception of role conflict in the professorial role. Accordingly we turn now to the question of how students react to the differences we have discussed in basic instructional techniques, authority management, and personalizations, as measured by students' evaluations.

Notes

1. We performed significance tests with regression equations predicting the proportion of time spent in each activity with variables measuring sex of professor (1 = female), sex ratio of the professor's department (1 = male-dominated; 0 = nonmale-dominated), professor's rank, class size, and course level. Thus, all reported gender differences held true while we controlled simultaneously for the professor's departmental sex ratio, rank, class size, and course level. . . .

Disciplinary Differences in Classroom Teaching Behaviors

Harry G. Murray and Robert D. Renaud

Student ratings of teachers and courses have been shown to provide reliable and valid information on instructional quality in higher education. Results vary somewhat from study to study, but the weight of evidence indicates that student ratings (1) are stable across items, raters, and time periods; (2) are affected to only a minor extent by extraneous variables such as class size and severity of grading; (3) are consistent with ratings of the same teachers made by colleagues, alumni, and trained classroom observers; and, most important of all, (4) are significantly correlated with more objective indicators of teaching effectiveness, such as student performance on common final examinations in multiple-section courses (Centra, 1993; Marsh and Dunkin, 1992).

Academic discipline appears to be one area in which student ratings of teaching do differ systematically. Feldman (1978) reviewed research in this area and concluded that, on average, student ratings are highest for arts and humanities teachers, lowest for science, mathematics, and engineering teachers, and intermediate for social science teachers. Cashin (1990) reached essentially the same conclusion in an analysis of standardized student rating data for approximately one hundred thousand classes across North America.

Although there is clear and consistent evidence that student instructional ratings are higher for some academic fields (for example, humanities) than for others (for example, sciences), the reasons for these differences remain to be determined. Franklin and Theall (1992) compared teachers in humanities, business, and science and engineering in terms of instructional goals, teaching methods, and grading practices. They found that humanities teachers tended to emphasize "thought" goals more so than "fact" goals and to use discussion and independent projects rather than lecturing alone. Given that both of these teaching practices were independently shown to correlate with student ratings, the use of these practices provides a possible explanation for higher student ratings in arts and humanities courses. Cashin (1990) suggested several other possible explanations for differences in student ratings, including student attitudes, course difficulty, and actual differences in teaching effectiveness among disciplines.

The goal of research reported in this chapter was to determine whether teachers in different academic fields differ in the frequency with which they exhibit specific classroom teaching behaviors and, if so, whether these differences could be responsible for differences in student ratings of overall teaching effectiveness. Teachers in three academic fields—namely, arts and humanities, social sciences, and natural sciences and mathematics—were systematically observed in the classroom to assess the frequency of occurrence of specific "low inference" teaching behaviors. These behaviors include asking questions of students, writing key terms on the blackboard, and addressing individual students by name. Correlations were then derived, separately for each academic field, between behavioral frequency estimates and end-of-term student ratings of teaching.

Previous research (Murray, 1983, 1985) has demonstrated strong correlations between low-inference classroom teaching behaviors and student ratings of instructional quality. Furthermore, at least one previous study (Erdle and Murray, 1986) has reported differences among academic disciplines in the frequency of low-inference teaching behaviors. The present study sought to confirm these results in a larger and more diverse sample of teachers, and to articulate more explicitly the hypothesis that classroom

"Disciplinary Differences in Classroom Teaching Behaviors," by Harry G. Murray and Robert D. Renaud, reprinted from *New Directions for Teaching and Learning,* No. 64, Winter 1995, Jossey-Bass Publishers, Inc.

teaching behaviors are responsible for disciplinary differences in perceived teaching effectiveness. (For a different interpretation, see the Cashin and Downey chapter in this volume.)

Observing 401 Teachers

The sample investigated in this study consisted of 401 faculty members teaching undergraduate lecture or lecture-discussion courses with enrollment of thirty or higher at the University of Western Ontario. Each of these individuals had participated previously in one of a series of classroom observation studies carried out by the first author, the results of which were aggregated into one archival data file for purposes of the present study. The 401 teachers could be divided into three general academic fields: arts and humanities ($n = 117$); social sciences ($n = 149$); and natural sciences and mathematics ($n = 135$).

The academic departments included in each disciplinary group are listed in Table 3.1. In terms of Biglan's (1973) taxonomy (see the Editors' Notes), the academic fields compared in this study appear to vary mostly in terms of the "hard" versus "soft" dimension.

Classroom Observations

Classroom teaching behaviors were assessed by trained observers who visited regular classes taught by participating instructors. Each instructor was observed by three to twelve different observers ($M = 7.45$).

Each observer attended three individually selected one-hour class segments taught by an instructor over a three-month period. Classroom observers were paid for their work, and before visiting classes they were given approximately four hours of training in recording low-inference teaching behaviors from videotaped samples. Instructors gave written permission for classroom observation to occur but did not know exactly when the observations would take place.

Observers summarized their three hours of observation of a given instructor on a standardized behavioral rating form called the Teacher Behaviors Inventory (TBI) (Murray, 1983). Each of the one hundred items of the TBI describes a specific low-inference teaching behavior (for example, "signals the transition from one topic to the next"; "maintains eye contact with students"), which the observer rates on a 5-point frequency-of-occurrence scale: 1 = almost never; 2 = rarely; 3 = sometimes; 4 = often; 5 = almost always. Ratings were averaged across observers to obtain mean frequency ratings of each of one hundred teaching behaviors for each of 401 instructors. The reliability of observer mean ratings of individual TBI items has averaged .75 in previous studies, indicating that classroom observers show substantial interrater agreement in their assessment of specific teaching behaviors.

Student Ratings

Overall teaching effectiveness of participating instructors was measured by formal end-of-term student ratings for the course in which classroom observation took place. Student evaluation of teaching is required in all courses at the University of Western Ontario, and most of the instructors included in the present study were evaluated by means of the same 10-item evaluation form with a 5-point agree-disagree

Table 3.1
Composition of Disciplinary Groups

Arts and Humanities	*Social Sciences*	*Natural Sciences and Mathematics*
English	Psychology	Chemistry
Philosophy	Sociology	Physiology
French	Political science	Physics
Classics	Economics	Biochemistry
Visual arts	Geography	Geology
Modern languages	Anthropology	Mathematics
History		Biology
Music		Applied mathematics
		Computer science
		Anatomy

rating scale. To obtain a single, comparable measure of overall teaching effectiveness for each instructor, ratings were averaged across all items of the evaluation form.

Comparing the Disciplines

A preliminary analysis was undertaken to determine whether there were differences among arts, social science, and natural science disciplines in mean student ratings of overall teaching effectiveness. Consistent with previous studies (for example, Cashin, 1990; see also Cashin and Downey and Franklin and Theall in this volume), mean student ratings were significantly higher for arts and humanities teachers (3.96) than for social science teachers (3.82), which in turn were significantly higher than for natural science and mathematics teachers (3.69).

Teaching Behaviors by Discipline

In order to obtain a manageable set of teaching behavior variables for use in statistical analyses, the one hundred items from the Teacher Behaviors Inventory were grouped into factors or dimensions on the basis of factor loading in previously reported factor analyses (Murray, 1983, 1985; Erdle and Murray, 1986). Any of the one hundred TBI items that failed to show a strong and consistent relation to a single factor was deleted. This resulted in the retention of a total of sixty-four TBI items loading on a total of ten factors. Table 3.2 shows the individual teaching behaviors defining each of the ten factors. Alpha reliability coefficients for the ten factors ranged from 63 to .88 and averaged .82, indicating a high level of internal consistency among the items constituting a particular factor. Instructors were assigned scores on each of the ten teaching behavior factors by averaging frequency-of-occurrence ratings across the individual teaching behaviors defining a particular factor.

Table 3.3 shows group mean frequency ratings of each of the ten teaching behavior factors for instructors in the three disciplinary groups, arts and humanities, social sciences, and natural sciences and mathematics. A multivariate analysis of variance showed that the disciplinary groups differed significantly with respect to the frequency of occurrence of all teaching behavior factors taken collectively. Univariate analyses of variance indicated that six of the ten factors, namely Interaction, Organization, Pacing, Disclosure, Rapport, and Mannerisms, differed significantly across academic fields. Inspection of Table 3.3 reveals that teachers of arts and humanities subjects were more likely than social science or natural science teachers to use behaviors in the Interaction, Rapport, and Mannerisms categories (for example, addressing individual students by name, encouraging student participation, maintaining eye contact with students), whereas teachers in the social and natural sciences were more likely than arts teachers to

Table 3.2
Definition of Teaching Behavior Dimensions

Clarity	Uses concrete examples
	Stresses most important points
	Fails to define new terms*
	Gives multiple examples
	Suggests memory aids
	Repeats difficult ideas
	Writes key terms on blackboard
	Answers student questions thoroughly
Expressiveness	Moves about room while teaching
	Gestures with hands and arms
	Speaks expressively or "dramatically"
	Exhibits facial gestures
	Uses humor
	Reads lecture verbatim from notes*
	Gestures with head or body
	Smiles or laughs

Table 3.2 *continued*

Interaction	Encourages students to ask questions Addresses individual students by name Asks questions of class as a whole Asks questions of individual students Praises students for good ideas Incorporates student ideas into lecture Talks with students before or after class Uses a variety of teaching methods
Organization	Reviews topics from previous lectures Puts outline of lecture on blackboard Gives preliminary overview of lecture Uses headings and subheadings to organize lecture Signals transition from one topic to the next Summarizes periodically Explains how each topic fits into the course
Pacing	Dwells excessively on obvious points* Covers very little material in class sessions* Sticks to the point in answering questions Digresses from major theme of lecture Fails to take the initiative in class*
Disclosure	States teaching objectives Advises students how to prepare for exams Provides sample exam questions Tells students what is expected on assignments Reminds students of test assignment dates
Interest	Describes personal experiences related to subject Points out practical applications of concepts Presents thought-provoking ideas Relates subject matter to student interests States own point of view on controversial issues Relates subject matter to current events
Rapport	Offers to help students with problems Shows interest in student ideas Announces availability for consultation Shows tolerance for other points of view Is flexible regarding deadlines and requirements Is fair and impartial in interactions with students Shows concern for student progress
Mannerisms	Avoids eye contact with students* Shows distracting behaviors* Rocks or sways on heels* Plays with chalk or pointer* Says "um" or "ah" *
Speech quality	Voice fades in midsentence* Does not speak clearly* Speaks in a monotone* Stutters, mumbles, or slurs words* Speaks too softly*

*Negatively worded items were reverse coded in complying factor scores, such that a rating of 5 represented low-frequency occurrence of the teaching behavior in question.

Table 3.3
Mean Rated Frequency of Occurrence of Teaching Behaviors in Different Disciplinary Groups

Teaching Behavior Dimension	*Disciplinary Group*		
	Arts and Humanities	*Social Sciences*	*Natural Sciences and Mathematics*
Clarity	3.44	3.57	3.52
Expressiveness	3.33	3.27	3.19
Interaction	3.53	3.08	2.99
Organization	2.86	3.21	3.20
Pacing	3.71	3.90	3.74
Disclosure	3.41	3.19	3.42
Interest	3.12	3.09	2.95
Rapport	4.00	3.76	3.68
Mannerisms	4.15	4.03	3.94
Speech quality	4.10	4.01	3.99

show behaviors loading on the Organization and Pacing factors (for example, putting outline of lecture on blackboard, sticking to the point in answering questions); and arts and natural science teachers were more likely than social science teachers to exhibit Disclosure behaviors (for example, stating teaching objectives).

In summary, the results shown in Table 3.3 support the view that teachers in different academic disciplines do in fact differ in the frequency with which they exhibit certain specific classroom teaching behaviors, with arts and humanities teachers behaving more frequently in ways that foster student participation, and natural science and social science teachers more frequently showing behaviors that facilitate structuring or organization of the subject matter.

Teaching Behaviors and Student Ratings

To determine whether there were differences among academic fields in the correlation of teaching behavior factors with overall teaching effectiveness, teacher mean scores on the ten teaching behavior factors were correlated separately in each disciplinary group with mean student ratings of teaching. Consistent with previous research (Murray, 1983, 1985), Table 3.4 shows strong correlations between teaching behaviors and perceived teaching effectiveness. Correlation of individual teaching behavior dimensions with overall effectiveness ranged as high as .65, and twenty-nine of the thirty correlation coefficients listed in Table 3.4 were statistically significant. However, comparison of correlation coefficients across

Table 3.4
Correlation of Teaching Behaviors with Overall Teacher Effectiveness Rating in Different Disciplinary Groups

Teaching Behavior Dimension	*Disciplinary Group*		
	Arts and Humanities	*Social Sciences*	*Natural Sciences and Mathematics*
Clarity	.498	.562	.647
Expressiveness	.308	.402	.446
Interaction	.417	.441	.502
Organization	.359	.361	.439
Pacing	.511	.464	.609
Disclosure	.254	.405	.220
Interest	.352	.557	.435
Rapport	.316	.591	.579
Mannerisms	.513	.455	.255
Speech quality	.496	.625	.650

disciplinary groups within each dimension of teaching, using Fisher's r-to-z transformation, revealed that only two of thirty pairwise differences were statistically significant. The correlation of Rapport with student instructional rating was significantly lower in arts and humanities (.316) than in either social sciences (.591) or natural sciences (.579). Given that approximately 1.5 significant results would be expected by chance alone among 30 correlations, the data in Table 3.4 are best interpreted as reflecting purely random, nonsignificant group differences.

In summary, despite differences among academic fields in the frequency of occurrence of specific teaching behaviors, the contribution of these same behaviors to overall teaching effectiveness seems to be very similar in different academic fields. Although natural science teachers may be more likely to exhibit organizational behaviors than are humanities teachers, the extent to which organizational behaviors "pay off" in higher student ratings seems to be essentially the same in humanities as in natural sciences.

Conclusions

The present research suggests that *teachers of different academic disciplines differ in the frequency with which they exhibit specific classroom teaching behaviors, but they do not differ in the correlation of these teaching behaviors with student evaluations of overall teaching effectiveness.* These findings are generally consistent with what has been reported in previous research by Solomon (1966), Pohlmann (1976), and Erdle and Murray (1986). These investigators all found behavioral differences among academic fields similar to those reported here (for example, humanities teachers encouraged student participation more than science instructors); and all found nonsignificant differences among academic fields in the correlation of specific teaching behaviors with overall teaching effectiveness.

Thus, contrary to the currently popular view (for example, Shulman, 1989) that what constitutes effective teaching is embedded in context and varies systematically from one discipline to another, research to date on specific low-inference teaching behaviors indicates that what makes an effective teacher, at least in the eyes of students, is pretty much the same regardless of academic discipline. With specific reference to Shulman (1989), the present findings might be interpreted to mean that *although a teacher must have "pedagogical content knowledge" within a certain academic discipline in order to develop effective teaching activities in that discipline, it is nonetheless true that effective teachers in all disciplines tend to use the same generic teaching activities or teaching behaviors.* As a case in point, effective teachers in all academic disciplines may use concrete examples to explain concepts, but the content of these examples will vary with the discipline and will be effective only to the extent that the teacher knows how to translate the discipline into terms that students can understand. Whether these generic teaching behaviors generalize across other relevant dimensions (for example, class size, teacher and student gender) remains to be determined by further research.

Do the findings of this research provide an answer to the original question of why student ratings of teaching differ across academic disciplines? The fact that natural science and social science teachers were less likely than arts teachers to exhibit Interaction and Rapport teaching behaviors that are known to be positively correlated with student instructional ratings would seem to provide an obvious explanation of why natural science and social science teachers tend to receive lower student ratings, on average, than arts and humanities teachers. On the other hand, natural science and social science teachers were more likely than arts teachers to show teaching behaviors in the Organization and Pacing categories that are similarly known to be positively correlated with student ratings.

Perhaps the best summary statement of the present findings is that arts and humanities teachers scored higher than social science and natural science teachers on six of the ten teaching behavior dimensions listed in Table 3.3. In other words, it appears that arts and humanities teachers tend to exhibit a wider range of teaching behaviors that contribute positively to student instructional ratings than social science or natural science teachers do, and this finding provides one possible explanation as to why student ratings differ across academic disciplines.

Implications for Faculty Evaluation and Faculty Development

The fact that correlations between classroom teaching behaviors and student instructional ratings were generally similar across academic disciplines has implications both for faculty evaluation and for faculty development.

The implication for faculty evaluation is that, at least with respect to courses taught by the lecture method, the factors contributing to student ratings of teaching are similar in different academic fields, and thus it is reasonable for student rating forms to be similar or perhaps even identical in content in different fields or departments.

The implication for faculty development is that it is not really necessary to focus on different teaching behaviors in working with instructors from different disciplines, but only to encourage instructors in each discipline to increase the frequency of teaching behaviors that are positively correlated with student ratings but tend, for whatever reason, to occur relatively infrequently in that discipline.

References

Biglan, A. "The Characteristics of Subject Matter in Different Academic Areas." *Journal of Applied Psychology*, 1973, *57* (3), 195–203.

Cashin, W. E. "Students Do Rate Different Academic Fields Differently." In M. Theall and J. Franklin (eds.), *Student Ratings of Instruction: Issues for Improving Practice*. San Francisco: Jossey-Bass, 1990.

Centra, J. A. *Reflective Faculty Evaluation*. San Francisco: Jossey-Bass, 1993.

Erdle, S. and Murray, H. G. "Interfaculty Differences in Classroom Teaching Behaviors and Their Relationship to Student Instructional Ratings." *Research in Higher Education*, 1986, *24*, 115–127.

Feldman, K. A. "Course Characteristics and College Students' Ratings of their Teachers: What We Know and What We Don't." *Research in Higher Education*, 1978, *9*, 199–242.

Franklin, J., and Theall, M. "Disciplinary Differences: Instructional Goals and Activities, Measures of Student Performance, and Student Ratings of Instruction." Paper presented at the annual meeting of the American Educational Research Association, San Francisco, April 1992.

Marsh, H. W., and Dunkin, M. J. "Students' Evaluation of University Teaching: A Multidimensional Perspective." In J. C. Smart (ed.), *Higher Education: Handbook of Theory and Research*. Vol. 8. New York: Agathon Press, 1992.

Murray, H. G. "Low-Inference Classroom Teaching Behaviors and Student Ratings of College Teaching Effectiveness." *Journal of Educational Psychology*, 1983, *75*, 138–149.

Murray, H. G. "Classroom Teaching Behaviors Related to College Teaching Effectiveness." In J. G. Donald and A. M. Sullivan (eds.), *Using Research to Improve Teaching*. San Francisco: Jossey-Bass, 1985.

Pohlmann, J. T. "A Description of Effective College Teaching in Five Disciplines as Measured by Student Ratings." *Research in Higher Education*, 1976, *4*, 335–346.

Shulman, L. S. "Toward a Pedagogy of Substance." *American Association for Higher Education Bulletin*, 1989, *41* (10), 8–13.

Solomon, D. "Teacher Behavior Dimensions, Course Characteristics, and Student Evaluations of Teachers." *American Educational Research Journal*, 1966, *3*, 35–47.

C. Student - Teacher Interactions

The College Classroom: Some Observations on the Meanings of Student Participation

David A. Karp and William C. Yoels

This study utilizes a symbolic interactionist approach to the investigation of student behavior in the college classroom. Ten classes were selected for observation in a Northeastern university. Data were gathered throughout the semester on the interactions occurring in these selected classes. At the end of the semester students and teachers in the classes which had been observed were given questionnaires dealing with the factors deemed important in influencing students' decisions on whether or not to talk in class.

Our observational data indicate that the number of students participating in a given class is not affected by the size of the class. In addition a small percentage of students account for the majority of interactions in both small and large classes. Less than 10% of the observed interactions involved cases in which students responded to the comments or questions of other students. Less than 10% of the interactions involved instances in which instructors directly called on specific students.

Student responses to questionnaire items asking about factors preventing them from participating in class indicated a high degree of concern with issues such as "not having done the assigned reading;" "not knowing enough about the subject matter," etc. In contrast, instructors placed a great deal of emphasis on items such as "students appearing unintelligent in the eyes of other students" "the possibility that student comments might negatively affect their grades."

Our explanation of these findings involves a treatment of the organizational features of the college classroom and the situational definitions arising from such features. We have specified three of these "organizational features": (1) the "consolidation of responsibility"—students know that a small percentage of the class can be relied upon to do most of the talking; (2) instructors are very unlikely to call on specific students; (3) students are tested infrequently and the tests that are given are usually announced in advance. These "organizational features" of the college classroom, then, promote an orientation of non-involvement on the part of students.

We conclude our study by speculating on the dilemma faced by college instructors who wish to have extensive classroom dialogues with students. Borrowing from Goffman, we suggest that college instructors define the classroom as an instance of "focused" interaction while students define it as an instance of an "unfocused" gathering.

A recent report on the employment of sociologists and anthropologists indicated that 97% of the sociologists in the United States were teaching either full-time or part-time in an institution of higher education (NIHM: 1969). While sociologists earn their "daily bread" by teaching, they earn their scholarly reputations by engaging in research studies of almost every conceivable kind of social setting except, it seems, that of the college classroom. The failure to explore the "routine grounds" of our everyday lives as teachers is testimony to the existence of the college classroom as part of what Alfred Schutz (1962) referred to as "the world as taken-for-granted."

"The College Classroom: Some Observations on the Meanings of Student Participation," by David A. Karp and William C. Yoels, reprinted by permission from *Sociology and Social Research*, 60, 1976.

There has been considerable research on the classroom, but typically investigators have centered their inquiries on primary and secondary school settings. Several works have portrayed the social structure and operation of the classroom as it is influenced by broader institutional arrangements (Boocock, 1972; Jackson, 1968; Waller, 1932; Hollingshead, 1949; Holt, 1964, 1967). Other investigators have concerned themselves with more specific features of the primary and secondary school classrooms. Among other issues, researchers have been concerned with *teacher effectiveness* (Medley and Mitzel, 1963; Cogan, 1958; Ojemann and Wilkinson, 1939), *leadership style* (Lewin *et al.*, 1939; White and Lippitt, 1962), *teacher expectation effects* (Rosenthal and Jacobson, 1968; Brophy and Good, 1974), the nature of *classroom interaction* (Flanders, 1960; Bales, 1952), *communication structures* in the classroom (Bavelas, 1962; Leavitt, 1958; Adams, 1969), and the like.

While there has been, alternatively, a good deal written about higher education in general, there has been comparatively little research specifically on the *college classroom*. That which has been done reflects largely the work of educational psychologists and focuses on student/teacher personality characteristics as they relate to various aspects of classroom interaction (McKeachie and Lin, 1971; Mason, 1970; Bowers, 1962; Rees, 1969; Feenberg, 1972). With the exception of Robert Sommer's (1967, 1969) work on "classroom ecology," which employed observational techniques, the research on college classrooms relies heavily on questionnaires administered to students and teachers. The intent of these questionnaires has been to measure various personality dimensions of students and teachers and to relate these to a number of classroom behaviors. The form of explanation in these studies is best described as "variable analysis" (Blumer, 1956). The present study is based on the premise that the types of studies briefly characterized above do not uncover certain salient elements of the college classroom as a special social context.

Rarely have researchers attempted to consider the processes through which students and teachers formulate definitions of the classroom as a social setting. The problem of how students and teachers assign "meaning" to the classroom situation has been largely neglected in the various studies mentioned. Although writing about primary and secondary school classrooms, we would suggest that the following statement from Jackson's (1968:vii) *Life in Classrooms* holds true for college classrooms as well. He writes that:

> Classroom life . . . is too complex an affair to be viewed or talked about from any single perspective. Accordingly, as we try to grasp the meaning of what school is like for students and teachers, we must not hesitate to use all the ways of knowing at our disposal. This means we must read and look and listen and count things, and talk to people, and even muse introspectively. . .

The present study focuses on the meanings of student participation in the college classroom. Our examination of this problem will center on the way in which definitions of classrooms held by students and teachers relate to their actual behavior in the classroom.

Methods of Study

In an attempt to investigate the issues mentioned above we initiated an exploratory study of classroom behavior in several classes of a private university located in a large city in the northeastern United States. Our familiarity with the literature on the "words-deeds" problem (Deutscher, 1973; Phillips, 1971) led us to employ a two-fold process of data collection—namely, systematic observation of classroom behavior in selected classes, accompanied by questionnaires administered at the end of the semester in the classes under observation. None of the previously reviewed studies employed this type of research strategy, and it was hoped that such an approach would yield insights not attainable from reliance on a single data gathering procedure. In addition to the foregoing procedures we also drew upon our numerous years of experience as both students and teachers in college classrooms.

Ten classes were selected for observation. The observers were undergraduate and graduate sociology students who were doing the research as part of a Readings and Research arrangement. The classes were not randomly selected but were chosen in terms of the observers' time schedules and the possibility of their observing behavior in the classrooms on a regular basis throughout the semester. The observed classes were located in the following departments: sociology, philosophy, English, psychology, economics, theology. While the classes are certainly not a representative sample of all classes taught in this university, questionnaire responses from an additional sample of students in classes selected at random at the end of the semester indicate a remarkable similarity to the questionnaire responses of the students in the ten classes under observation.[1]

At the end of the semester a questionnaire was distributed in class to the students in the ten classes which had been under prior observation. A shortened version of this questionnaire was also given to the teachers of these classes. Questionnaire items centered on factors deemed important in influencing students' decisions on whether to talk or not in class.[2]

Findings

Table 1 presents a summary of selected observational items by class size. Classes with less than 40 students have a higher average number of interactions per session than those with more than 40 students. More important, however, is the fact that in both categories of class size the *average number* of students participating is almost identical. Moreover, a handful of students account for more than 50 percent of the total interactions in both under 40 and over 40 classes. In classes with less than 40 students, between 4 and 5 students account for 75 percent of the total interactions per session; in classes of more than 40 students between 2 and 3 students account for 51 percent of the total interactions per session. From the limited data presented here it would appear that class size has relatively little effect on the average number of students participating in class. Such a finding is particularly interesting in view of the fact, as indicated in table 5, that more than 65 percent of both male and female students indicated that the large size of the class was an important factor in why students would choose not to talk in class.

Data also indicate that students have a conception of classroom participation as being concentrated in the hands of a few students. Ninety-three percent of the males and 94 percent of the females strongly agreed or agreed with the item "In most of my classes there are a small number of students who do most of the talking." Such a conception is in congruence with the observations of actual classroom behavior noted in table 1.

The students' conception that a handful of students do most of the talking is also coupled with annoyance on the part of many students at those who "talk too much." Responses to a questionnaire item indicated that 62% of the males and 61% of the females strongly agreed or agreed with the item "I sometimes find myself getting annoyed with students who talk too much in class."

Students also believe it possible to make a decision very early in the semester as to whether professors really want class discussion. Ninety-four percent of the males and 96% of the females strongly agreed or agreed with the item "students can tell pretty quickly whether a professor really wants discussion in his/her class."

Students were also asked whether the teacher's sex is likely to influence their participation in class. The overwhelming response of both male and female students to this question is that the professor's sex makes *no difference* in their likelihood of participating in class. Over 93% of the males and 91 percent of the female students answered "No Difference" to this question. In effect, then, both male and female students tend to define the classroom as a situation in which the sexual component of the professor's identity is completely irrelevant.

The contrast between what students say about the previous item and what they actually do in classroom is highlighted in table 2. The data indicate a very clear-cut relationship between the sex of the teacher and the likelihood of male or female participation in class. In male taught classes men account for

Table 1
Summary Table by Class Size of Selected Observational Items

Average number of interactions per class	Average number of students participating	Average % of students present participating	Average number of students making two or more comments	% of those present making two or more comments	% of total interactions accounted for by those making two or more comments
25.96	9.83	47.84	4.64	25.06	75.61
19.40	9.88	23.98	2.70	5.74	51.0

[a] The smallest class contained 12 students; the largest class contained 65 students.

Table 2
Observed Classroom Interaction by Sex of Student and Sex of Teacher

Sex of	% of observed interactions				% of students in classes[a]			
	Male	Female	Total	N	Male	Female	Total	N
Male	75.4	24.6	100.0	565	52.0	48.0	100.0	152
Female	57.8	42.2	100.0	774	51.5	48.5	100.0	163
Total	65.3	34.7	100.0	1139	51.7	48.3	100.0	315

Note: $\chi 2 = 44.05$, df = 1, $p < .001$

[a] Refers to the number of students answering the questionnaires in class

75.4 percent of the interactions, three times the percentage for women—24.6 percent. In female taught classes, men still account for more of the interactions than women—57.8 percent to 42.2 percent—but the percentage of female participation increases almost 75 percent from 24.7 percent in male taught classes to 42.2 percent in female taught classes. Female student participation is maximized under the influence of female professors.

Since the participation of men and women may be a function of their proportion in class, the right-hand side of table 2 presents data on the composition of the male and female taught classes. In both male and female taught classes the percentage of male and female students is almost equal, therefore eliminating the possibility that the rate of male-female participation is a function of male student over-representation in these classes.

Table 3 presents observational data regarding what the students were responding to when they participated in classroom interactions. There was very little student-to-student interaction occurring in the ten classes under observation. Ten percent of the total number of classroom interactions involved cases in which students responded to the questions or comments of other students. Table 3 indicates quite dramatically that the actions of the teacher are indeed most crucial in promoting classroom interaction. Questions posed by the teacher and teacher comments accounted for 88 percent of the classroom interactions. Especially significant is the fact that very few cases occur in which the teacher directly calls on a particular student to answer a question (category labeled "Direct" under TQ). The percentage for the Direct Question category is 9.9 percent, compared to 46.3 percent for the Indirect Question in which the teacher poses a question to the class in general. Indeed, it might be argued that the current norm in college classrooms is for both students and teachers to avoid any type of direct *personal confrontation* with one another. It might be that "amicability" in the classroom is part of the larger process, described by Riesman (1950) in *The Lonely Crowd*, in which the desire to "get ahead" is subordinated to the desire to "get along." In the college classroom "getting along" means students and teachers avoiding any situation that might be potentially embarrassing to one or the other.

Table 4 indicates that in male taught classes male students are more likely than female students to be directly questioned by the instructor (7.1 percent to 3.1 percent). In addition, men are twice as likely as female students (30.3 percent to 15.0 percent) to respond to a comment made by a male teacher. In female

Table 3
Source of Interaction by Sex of Student

	Source of "Stimulus"							
	Teacher Question		Teacher	Student	Student	Source not		
	Direct	Indirect	Comment	Question	Comment	specified	Total	N
Sex of Student								
Male	10.0%	46.5%	31.9%	3.6%	3.3%	1.5%	99.8%	840
Female	9.8%	45.9%	31.3%	1.6%	8.9%	2.2%	99.7%	437
Total	9.9%	46.3%	31.7%	2.9%	7.2%	1.8%	99.8%	1277[a]

[a]62 cases were excluded because of insufficient information.

Table 4
Source of Interaction by Sex of Student, Controlling for Sex of Teacher

	Source of "Stimulus"							
	Teacher Question		Teacher	Student	Student	Source not		
	Direct	Indirect	Comment	Question	Comment	specified	Total	N
Sex of Student								
				Male Taught Classes				
Male	7.1%	55.3%	30.3%	1.9%	2.6%	2.6%	99.8%	419
Female	3.1%	67.4%	15.0%	3.9%	3.9%	6.3%	99.6%	126
Total	6.2%	58.1%	26.7%	2.3%	2.9%	3.4%	99.6%	545
				Female Taught Classes				
Male	12.8%	37.7%	33.4%	5.4%	9.9%	.4%	99.6%	421
Female	12.5%	37.2%	37.9%	.6%	10.9%	.6%	99.7%	311
Total	12.7%	37.5%	15.3%	3.4%	10.3%	.5%	99.7%	732

taught classes the percentage of male and female responses are almost identical in each category under observation. Of interest here is the fact that female teachers are equally likely to directly question male and female students (12.8 percent versus 12.5 percent).

Table 5 presents the student responses to a series of items concerning why students would choose not to talk in class. The items are ranked in terms of the percentage of students who indicated that the particular item was important in keeping them from talking. As the rankings indicate, male and female stu-

Table 5
Percentage of Students Who Indicated That an Item Was an Important Factor in Why Students Would Choose Not to Talk in Class, by Sex of Student (in Rank Order)

Male			Female		
Rank	Item	%	Rank	Item	%
1.	I had not done the assigned reading	80.9	1.	The feeling that I don't know enough about the subject matter	84.8
2.	The feeling that I don't know enough about the subject matter	79.6	2.	I had not done the assigned reading	76.3
3.	The large size of the class	70.4	3.	The feeling that my ideas are not well enough formulated	71.1
4.	The feeling that my ideas are not well enough formulated	69.8	4.	The large size of the class	68.9
5.	The course simply isn't meaningful to me	67.3	5.	The course simply isn't meaningful to me	65.1
6.	The chance that I would appear unintelligent in the eyes of the teacher	43.2	6.	The chance that I would appear unintelligent in the eyes of other students	45.4
7.	The chance that I would appear unintelligent in the eyes of other students	42.9	7.	The chance that I would appear unintelligent in the eyes of the teacher	41.4
8.	The small size of the class	31.0	8.	The small size of the class	33.6
9.	The possibility that my comments might negatively effect my grade	29.6	9.	The possibility that my comments might negatively effect my grade	24.3
10.	The possibility that other students in the class would not respect my point of view	29.6	10.	The possibility that the teacher would not respect my point of view	21.1
11.	The possibility that the teacher would not respect my point of view	12.3	11.	The possibility that other students in the class would not respect my point of view	12.5

dents are virtually identical in their conceptions of what factors inhibit or promote their classroom participation. The items accorded the most importance—not doing the assigned reading, ignorance of the subject matter, etc.—are in the highest ranks. The lowest ranking items are those dealing with students and teachers not respecting the student's point of view, the grade being negatively affected by classroom participation, etc.

In comparing the teachers' rankings of these same items with that of the students, it appears that, with one important exception, the rankings are very similar. About 42 percent of both male and female students ranked as important the item concerning the possibility that other students would find them unintelligent. Eighty percent of the teachers, on the other hand, indicated that this was likely an important factor in keeping students from talking.

Discussion

Although we did not begin this study with any explicit hypotheses to be tested, we did begin with some general guiding questions. Most comprehensive among these, and of necessary importance from a symbolic interactionist perspective, was the question, "What is a college classroom?" We wanted to know how both students and teachers were defining the social setting, and how these definitions manifested themselves in the activity that goes on in the college classrooms. More specifically, we wanted to understand what it was about the definition of the situation held by students and teachers that led to in most instances, rather little classroom interaction.

What knowledge, we might now ask, do students have of college classrooms that makes the decision not to talk a "realistic" decision? There would seem to be two factors of considerable importance as indicated by our data.

First, students believe, that they can tell very early in the semester whether or not a professor really wants class discussion. Students are also well aware that there exists in college classrooms a rather distinctive "consolidation of responsibility." In any classroom there seems almost inevitably to be a small group of students who can be counted on to respond to questions asked by the professor or to generally have comments on virtually any issue raised in class. Our observational data (table 1) indicated that on the average a very small number of students are responsible for the majority of all talk that occurs in class on any given day. The fact this "consolidation of responsibility" looms large in students" consciousness is indicated by the fact, reported, earlier, that more than 90 percent of the students strongly agreed or agreed with the statement "In most of my classes there are a small number of students who do most of the talking."

Once the group of "talkers" gets established and identified in a college classroom the remaining students develop a strong expectation that these "takers" can be relied upon to answer questions and make comments. In fact, we have often noticed in our own classes that when a question is asked or an issue raised the "silent" students will even begin to orient their bodies towards and look at this coterie of talkers with the expectation, presumably, that they will shortly be speaking.

Our concept of the "consolidation of responsibility" is a modification of the ideas put forth by Latane and Darley (1970) in *The Unresponsive Bystander*. In this volume Latane and Darley developed the concept of "the diffusion of responsibility" to explain why strangers are often reluctant to "get involved" in activities where they assist other strangers who may need help. They argue that the delegation of responsibility in such situations is quite unclear and, as a result, responsibility tends to get assigned to no one in particular—the end result being that no assistance at all is forthcoming. In the case of the classroom interaction, however, we are dealing with a situation in which the responsibility for talking gets assigned to a few who can be relied upon to carry the "verbal load"—thus the *consolidation of responsibility*. As a result, the majority of students play a relatively passive role in the classroom and see themselves as recorders of the teacher's information. This expectation is mutually supported by the professor's reluctance to directly call on *specific* students, as indicated in table 3.

While students expect that only a few students will do most of the talking, and while these talkers are relied upon to respond in class, the situation is a bit more complicated than we have indicated to this point. It would appear that while these talkers are "doing their job" by carrying the discussion for the class as a whole, there is still a strong feeling on the part of many students that they ought not to talk *too much*. As noted earlier, more than 60 percent of the students responding to our questionnaire expressed annoyance with students who "talk too much in class." This is interesting to the extent that even those who talk very regularly in class still account for a very small percentage of total class time. While we have no systematic data on time spent talking in class, the comments of the observers indicate that generally a total of less than five minutes of class time (in a fifty-minute period) is accounted for by student talk in class.

A fine balance must be maintained in college classes. Some students are expected to do most of the talking, thus relieving the remainder of the students from the burdens of having to talk in class. At the same time, these talkers must not be "rate-busters." We are suggesting here that students see "intellectual work" in much the same way that factory workers define "piece-work." Talking too much in class, or what might be called "linguistic rate-busting," upsets the normative arrangement of the classroom and, in the students' eyes, increases the probability of raising the professor's expectations vis-a-vis the participation of other students. It may be said, then, that a type of "restriction of verbal output" norm operates in college classrooms, in which those who engage in linguistic rate-busting or exhibit "over-involvement" in the classroom get defined by other students as "brown-noses" and "apostates" from the student "team." Other students often indicate their annoyance with these "rate-busters" by smiling wryly at their efforts, audibly sighing, rattling their notebooks and, on occasion, openly snickering.

A second factor that insures in students' minds that it will be safe to refrain from talking is their knowledge that only in rare instances will they be directly called upon by teachers in a college classroom. Our data (table 3) indicate that of all the interaction occurring in the classes under observation only about 10 percent were due to teachers calling directly upon a specific student. The unwillingness of teachers to call upon students would seem to stem from teachers' beliefs that the classroom situation is fraught with anxiety for students. It is important to note that teachers, unlike students themselves, viewed the possibility that "students might appear unintelligent in the eyes of other students" as a very important factor in keeping students from talking (table 6). Unwilling to exacerbate the sense of risk which teachers believe is a part of student consciousness, they refrain from directly calling upon specific students.

The direct result of these two factors is that students feel no obligation or particular necessity for keeping up with reading assignments so as to be able to participate in class. Such a choice is made easier still by the fact that college students are generally tested infrequently. Unlike high school, where homework is the teacher's "daily insurance" that students are prepared for classroom participation, college is a situation in which the student feels quite safe in coming to class without having done the assigned reading and, not having done it, safe in the secure knowledge that one won't be called upon.[3] It is understandable, then, why such items as "not having done the assigned reading" and "the feeling that one does not know enough about the subject matter" would rank so high (table 5) in students' minds as factors keeping them from talking in class.

In sum, we have isolated two factors relative to the way that classrooms actually operate that make it "practically" possible for students not to talk in class. These factors make it possible for the student to pragmatically abide by an early decision to be silent in class. We must now broach the somewhat more complicated question: what are the elements of students' definitions of the college classroom situation that prompt them to be silent in class? To answer this question we must examine how students perceive the teacher as well as their conceptions of what constitutes "intellectual work."

Table 6
Percentage of Teachers Who Indicated That an Item Was an Important Factor in Why Students Would Choose Not to Talk in Class (in Rank Order)

Rank	Item	%
1.5	The large size of the class	80
1.5	The chance that I would appear unintelligent in the eyes of other students	80
4	The feeling that I don't know enough about the subject matter	70
4	The feeling that my ideas are not well enough formulated	70
4	The possibility that my comments might negatively effect my grade	70
6	The course simply isn't meaningful to me	50
7.5	I had not done the assigned reading	40
7.5	The chance that I would appear unintelligent in the eyes of the teacher	40
9.5	The possibility that the teacher would not respect my point of view	30
9.5	The possibility that other students in the class would not respect my point of view	30
11	The small size of the class	10

By the time that students have finished high school they have been imbued with the enormously strong belief that teachers are "experts" who possess the "truth." They have adopted, as Freire (1970) has noted, a "banking" model of education. The teacher represents the bank, the huge "fund" of "true" knowledge. As a student it is one's job to make weekly "withdrawals" from the fund, never any "deposits." His teachers, one is led to believe, and often led to believe it by the teachers themselves, are possessors of the truth. Teachers are in the classroom to *teach*, not to *learn*.

If the above contains anything like a reasonable description of the way that students are socialized in secondary school, we should not find it strange or shocking that our students find our requests for criticism of ideas a bit alien. College students still cling to the idea that they are knowledge seekers and that faculty members are knowledge dispensers. Their view of intellectual work leaves little room for the notion that ideas themselves are open to negotiation. It is simply not part of their view of the classroom that ideas are generated out of dialogue, out of persons questioning and taking issue with one another, out of persons being *critical* of each other.

It comes as something of a shock to many of our students when we are willing to give them, at best, a "B" on a paper or exam that is "technically" proficient. When they inquire about their grade (and they do this rarely, believing strongly that our judgment is unquestionable), they want to know what they did "wrong." Intellectual work is for them dichotomous. It is either good or bad, correct or incorrect. They are genuinely surprised when we tell them that nothing is wrong, that they simply have not been critical enough and have not shown enough reflection on the ideas. Some even see such an evaluation as unfair. They claim a kind of incompetence at criticism. They often claim that it would be illegitimate for them to disagree with an author.

Students in class respond as uncritically to the thoughts of their professors as they do to the thoughts of those whom they read. Given this general attitude toward intellectual work, based in large part on students' socialization, and hence their definition of what should go on in classrooms, the notion of using the classroom as a place for generating ideas is a foreign one.

Part of students' conceptions of what they can and ought to do in classrooms is, then, a function of their understanding of how ideas are to be communicated. Students have expressed the idea that if they are to speak in class they ought to be able to articulate their point logically, systematically, and above all completely. The importance of this factor in keeping students from talking is borne out by the very high ranking given to the item (table 5) "the feeling that my ideas are not well enough formulated."

In their view, if their ideas have not been fully formulated in advance, then the idea is not worth relating. They are simply unwilling to talk "off the top of their heads." They feel, particularly in an academic setting such as the college classroom, that there is a high premium placed on being articulate. This feeling is to a large degree prompted by the relative articulateness of the teacher. Students do not, it seems, take into account the fact that the teacher's coherent presentation is typically a function of the time spent preparing his/her ideas. The relative preparedness of the teacher leads to something of a paradox vis-a-vis classroom discussion.

We have had students tell us that one of the reasons they find it difficult to respond in class involves the professor's preparedness; that is, students have told us that because the professor's ideas as presented in lectures are (in their view) so well formulated they could not add anything to those ideas. Herein lies something of a paradox. One might suggest that, to some degree at least, the better prepared a professor is for his/her class, the less likely are students to respond to the elements of his lecture.

We have both found that some of our liveliest classes have centered around those occasions when we have talked about research presently in progress. When it is clear to the student that we are ourselves struggling with a particular problem, that we cannot fully make sense of a phenomenon, the greater is the class participation. In most classroom instances, students read the teacher as the "expert,"[4] and once having cast the professor into that role it becomes extremely difficult for students to take issue with or amend his/her ideas.

It must also be noted that students' perceptions about their incapacity to be critical of their own and others' ideas leads to an important source of misunderstanding between college students and their teachers. In an open-ended question we asked students what characteristics they thought made for an "ideal" teacher. An impressionistic reading of these responses indicated that students were overwhelmingly uniform in their answers. They consensually found it important that a teacher "not put them down" and that a teacher "not flaunt his/her superior knowledge." In this regard the college classroom is a setting pregnant with possibilities for mutual misunderstanding. Teachers are working under one set of assumptions about "intellectual work" while students proceed under another. Our experiences as college teachers lead us to believe that teachers tend to value *critical* responses by students and tend to respond critically themselves to the comments and questions of college students. Students tend to perceive these critical comments as in some way an assault on their "selves" and find it difficult to separate a critique of their thoughts from a critique of themselves. Teachers are for the most part unaware of the way in which students interpret their comments.

The result is that when college teachers begin to critically question a student's statement, trying to get the student to be more critical and analytical about his/her assertions, this gets interpreted by students as a "put-down." The overall result is the beginning of a "vicious circle" of sorts. The more that teachers try to instill in students a critical attitude toward one's own ideas, the more students come to see faculty members as condescending, and the greater still becomes their reluctance to make known their "ill formulated" ideas in class. Like any other social situation where persons are defining the situation differently, there is bound to develop a host of interactional misunderstandings.

Before concluding this section, let us turn to a discussion of the differences in classroom participation rates of male versus female students. Given the fact that men and women students responded quite similarly to the questionnaire items reported here, much of our previous discussion holds for both male and female students. There are some important differences, however, in their *actual behavior* in the college classroom (as revealed by our observation data) that ought to be considered. Foremost among these differences is the fact that the sex of the teacher affects the likelihood of whether male or female students will participate in class (table 2). Clearly, male and female teachers in these classes are "giving off expressions" that are being interpreted very differently by male and female students. Male students play a more active role in all observed classes regardless of the teacher's sex, but with female instructors the percentage of female participation sharply increases. Also of interest, as indicated in table 4, is the fact that the male instructors are more likely to directly call on male students than on female students (7.1 percent to 3.1 percent), whereas female instructors are just as likely to call on female students as on male students (12.5 percent to 12.8 percent). Possibly female students in female taught classes interpret the instructor's responses as being more egalitarian than those of male professors and thus more sympathetic to the views of female students. With the growing involvement of women faculty and students in feminist "consciousness" groups it may not be unreasonable to assume that female instructors are more sensitive to the problem of female students both inside and outside the college classroom.

With the small percentage of women faculty currently teaching in American universities it may well be that the college classroom is still defined by both male and female students as a setting "naturally" dominated by men. The presence of female professors, however, as our limited data suggest, may bring about some changes in these definitions of "natural" classroom behavior.

Implications

For the reasons suggested in the last few pages, it may be argued that most students opt for non-involvement in their college classroom. This being the case, and because organizational features of the college classroom allow for non-involvement (the consolidation of responsibility, the unwillingness of professors to directly call on specific students, the infrequency of testing), the situation allows for a low commitment on the part of students. The college classroom, then, rather than being a situation where persons must be deeply involved, more closely approximates a situation of "anonymity" where persons' obligations are few.

We can now perceive more clearly the source of the dilemma for college instructors who wish to have extensive classroom dialogues with students. To use the terminology generated by Goffman (1963) in *Behavior In Public Places*, we can suggest that instructors are treating the classroom as an instance of "focused" interaction while students define the classroom more as an "unfocused" gathering. Focused gatherings are those where persons come into one another's audial and visual presence and see it as their obligation to interact. These are to be distinguished from unfocused gatherings where persons are also in a face-to-face situation but either feel that they are not privileged to interact or have no obligation to do so.[5]

It may very well be that students more correctly "read" how professors interpret the situation than vice versa.[6] Knowing that the teacher expects involvement, and having made the decision not to be deeply involved, students reach a compromise. Aware that it would be an impropriety to be on a total "away" from the social situation, students engage in what might be called "civil attention." They must *appear* committed enough to not alienate the teacher without at the same time showing so much involvement that the situation becomes risky for them. Students must carefully create a show of interest while maintaining non-involvement. A show of too great interest might find them more deeply committed to the encounter that they wish to be.

So, students are willing to attend class regularly and they do not hold private conversations while the teacher is talking; they nod their heads intermittently, and maintain enough attention to laugh at the appropriate junctures during a lecture, and so on. Students have become very adept at maintaining the social situation without becoming too involved in it. Teachers interpret these "shows" of attention as indicative of a real involvement (the students' performances have proved highly successful) and are, therefore, at a loss to explain why their involvement is not greater—why they don't talk very much in class.

Footnotes

1. Some relevant demographic characteristics of the students in the ten classes under observation are as follows: sex: males—52 percent, females—48 percent; year in college: freshmen and sophomores—60 percent, juniors and seniors—40 percent; father's occupation: proprietor—7 percent, management or executive—21 percent, professional—34 percent, clerical and sales—15 percent, skilled worker—16 percent, unskilled worker—7 percent; religious affiliation: Catholic—79 percent, Protestant—7 percent, other—14 percent. In comparing the students in the observed classes to those students in unobserved classes which were selected at random at the end of the semester, the following differences should be noted: the observed classes contain more women (48 percent) than the unobserved classes (33 percent); there were twice as many freshmen in the observed classes (31 percent) than in the unobserved classes (14 percent); there were twice as many students whose fathers were in clerical and sales occupations in the observed classes (15 percent) than in the unobserved classes (8 percent).
   The questionnaire responses of the students in the unobserved classes are not reported here since these were selected only to check on the representativeness of the students in the original ten classes under observation.
2. Spatial limitations preclude a full treatment of the methodology and findings. More complete details are available from the authors.
3. We have no "hard" data concerning student failure to do the assigned reading other than our own observations of countless instances where we posed questions that went unanswered, when the slightest familiarity with the material would have been sufficient to answer them. We have also employed "pop" quizzes and the student performance on these tests indicated a woefully inadequate acquaintance with the readings assigned for that session. The reader may evaluate our claim by reflecting upon his/her own experience in the college classroom.
4. This attribution of power and authority to the teacher may be particularly exaggerated in the present study due to its setting in a Catholic university with a large number of students entering from Catholic high schools. Whether college students with different religious and socio-economic characteristics attribute similar degrees of power and authority to professors is a subject worthy of future comparative empirical investigation.
5. If we think of communication patterns in college classrooms as ranging along a continuum from open-discussion formats to lecture arrangements, the classes studied here all fall toward the traditional lecture end of the continuum. Thus, generalizations to other formats, such as the open discussion ones, may not be warranted by the present data.
6. Of interest here is the recent study by Thomas *et al.* (1972) in which support was found for the "theoretical proposition that role-taking ability varies inversely with the degree of power ascribed to social positions" (1972:612).

References

Adams, R. S., 1969. "Location as a Feature of Instructional Interaction." *Merrill-Palmer Quarterly of Behavior and Development* 15:309–321.

Bales, R. F., 1952. "Some Uniformities of Behavior in Small Social Systems." Pp. 146–159 in G. E. Swanson *et al.*, (eds.), *Readings in Social Psychology*, revised edition. New York: Holt.

Bavelas, A., 1962. "Communication Patterns in Task-Oriented Groups." Pp. 669–682 in D. Cartwright and A. Zander (eds.), *Group Dynamics*, Evanston, Ill.: Row, Peterson and Company.

Blumer, H., 1956. "Sociological Analysis and the Variable." *American Sociological Review* 21: 683–690.

_____, 1969. *Symbolic Interactionism*. Englewood Cliffs, N.J.: Prentice-Hall.

Boocock, S., 1972. *An Introduction to the Sociology of Learning*. Boston: Houghton Mifflin.

Bowers, N. D. and R. S. Soar, 1962. "The Influence of Teaching Personality on Classroom Interaction." *Journal of Experimental Education* 30: 309–311.

Brophy, J. and T. Good, 1974. *Teacher-Student Relationships: Causes and Consequences*. New York: Holt, Rinehart and Winston.

Cogan, M. L., 1958. "The Behavior of Teachers and the Productive Behavior of Their Pupils." *Journal of Experimental Education* 27: 89–124.

Deutscher, I., 1973. *What We Say/What We Do*. Glenview, Ill.: Scott, Foresman and Company.

Feenberg, L., 1972. "Faculty-Student Interaction: How Students Differ." *Journal of College Student Personnel* 13: 24–27.

Flanders, N., 1960. Teacher Influence, Pupil Attitudes and Achievements. U.S. Department of Health, Education and Welfare, Office of Education, Cooperative Research Monograph No. 12.

Frere, P., 1970. *Pedagogy of the Oppressed*. New York: Seabury Press. Glaser, B. and A. L. Strauss.

_____, 1967. "Awareness Contexts and Social Interaction." *American Sociological Review* 29: 669–679.

Goffman, E., 1963. *Behavior in Public Places*. New York: Free Press.

_____, 1969. *Strategic Interaction*. Philadelphia: University of Pennsylvania Press.

Hollingshead, A. B., 1949. *Elmtown's Youth*. New York: Wiley.

Holt, J., 1964. *How Children Fail*. New York: Delta.

_____, 1967. *How Children Learn*. New York: Pitman.

Jackson, P., 1968. *Life in Classrooms*. New York: Holt, Rinehart and Winston.

Latane, B. and J. Darley, 1970. *The Unresponsive Bystander: Why Doesn't He Help?* New York: Appleton-Century-Crofts.

Leavitt, H. J., 1958. "Some Effects of Certain Communication Patterns on Group Performance." Pp. 546–563 in E. E. Maccoby *et al.* (eds.), *Readings in Social Psychology*, third edition, New York: Holt.

Lewin, K., R. Lippitt, and R. K. White, 1939. "Patterns of Aggressive Behavior in Experimentally Created 'Social Climates.'" *Journal of Social Psychology* 10:271–300.

Mason, J. L., 1970. "Study of the Relationship Between the Behavioral Styles of Classroom Teachers and the Quality of Teacher-Student Interpersonal Relations." *Educational Leader* 28:49–56.

McKeachie, W. L. and Y. Lin, 1971. "Sex Differences in Student Response to College Teachers: Teacher Warmth and Teacher Sex." *American Educational Research Journal* 8: 221–226.

Medley, D. M., and H. E. Mitzel, 1963. "Measuring Classroom Behavior by Systematic Observation." Pp. 247–328 in N. L. Gage (ed.), *Handbook of Research on Teaching*. Chicago: Rand McNally.

Milgram, S., 1963. "Behavior Study of Obedience." *Journal of Abnormal and Social Psychology* 67:371–378.

National Institute of Mental Health, 1969. Sociologists and Anthropologists: Supply and Demand in Educational Institutions and Other Settings. Chevy Chase, Maryland: U.S. Government Printing Office.

Ojemann, R. H. and F. R. Wilkinson, 1939. "The Effects on Pupil Growth of an Increase in Teacher's Understanding of Pupil Behavior." *Journal of Experimental Education* 8: 143–147.

Phillips, D., 1971. *Knowledge From What*? Chicago: Rand McNally and Co.

Rees, R. D., 1969. "Dimensions of Students' Points of View in Rating College Teachers." *Journal of Educational Psychology* 60: 476–482.

Riesman, D., 1950. *The Lonely Crowd*. New Haven: Yale University Press.

Rosenthal, R. and L. Jacobson, 1966. "Teachers' Expectancies: Determents of Pupils' IQ Gains." *Psychological Reports* 19: 115–118.

Schutz, A., 1962. *Collected Papers*: I. The Problem of Social Reality. Edited by Maurice Natanson. The Hague: Martinus Nijhoff.

Sommer, R., 1967. "Classroom Ecology." *Journal of Applied Behavior Science* 3: 489–503.

_____, 1969. *Personal Space*. Englewood Cliffs, N.J.: Prentice-Hall.

Thomas, D. L., D. D. Franks, and J. M. Calonico, 1972. "Role-Taking and Power in Social Psychology." *American Sociological Review* 37: 605–614.

Waller, W., 1932. *The Sociology of Teaching*. New York: Wiley.

White, R. and R. Lippitt, 1962. "Leadership Behavior and Member Reaction in Three 'Social Climates.'" Pp. 527–553 in D. Cartwright and A. Zander (eds.), *Group Dynamics*. Evanston, Ill.: Row, Peterson.

The Role of Gender in College Classroom Interactions: A Social Context Approach

Katherine Canada and Richard Pringle

This study examined the social construction of gender differences in classroom interactions during the first five years of a former women's college's transition to mixed-sex education. The classroom interaction patterns of male and female professors and students were considerably altered by the transition and by the gender composition of the classes. For example, male and female professors initiated comparable numbers of interactions in the all-female classrooms, but female professors initiated many more interactions and male professors initiated much fewer interactions in the mixed-sex classrooms. Also, in the mixed-sex classrooms, the increasing presence of male students was associated with an overall decrease in professor-initiated interactions, student-initiated interactions, and female student-initiated follow-up interactions and with an overall increase in male student-initiated follow-up interactions. The authors interpret these gender differences as arising out of an emerging gender politic that was largely absent in the all-female student environment, but to which the mixed-sex community, during the period of observation, fundamentally acquiesced.

Increasingly, it seems, the promise of coeducation is regarded suspiciously. Whether comparing the educational outcomes of all-female and mixed-gender schools and colleges (Lee 1992; Lee and Bryk 1986; Riordan 1990, 1992; Smith 1990; Tidball 1989, 1992), assessing gender equity within mixed-sex educational settings (Hall and Sandler 1982; Krupnick 1985; Sadker and Sadker 1994), investigating the social construction of gender differences (Eagly 1987; Eccles 1989; Maccoby 1988, 1990; Thorne 1993), or unveiling the social consignment of male privilege and dominance (Holland and Eisenhardt 1990; Hughes and Sandler 1988; Koss, Gidycz, and Wisniewski 1987; Sanday 1990), researchers have found that mixed-sex education, at least as it is typically configured, may pose notable disadvantages for girls and women (see American Association of University Women 1992; Moore, Piper, and Schaefer 1993 for recent reviews).

Review of Research

Single-Sex versus Mixed-Sex Education

It has been reported that in comparison to women who attend mixed-sex colleges, women who attend women's colleges have greater self-esteem at graduation (Astin 1977; Miller-Bernal 1993; Riordan 1990; Smith 1990), have less gender-stereotypic career aspirations (Bressler and Wendell 1980; Carnegie Commission 1973), are more engaged in college activities (Miller-Bernal 1993; Smith 1990), are more likely to enter certain traditionally male professions (Tidball 1985, 1986; Tidball and Kistiakowsky 1976), are more likely to earn higher salaries (Conaty, Alsalam, James, and To 1989; Riordan 1994), and are more likely to reach high levels of achievement in their careers (Oates and Williamson 1978; Rice and Hemmings 1988; Tidball 1973; 1980). Also, the career advantage bestowed by an all-female institution may increase with the time one spends in it (Riordan 1994). Unfortunately, as others have noted, it is impossible to determine, on the basis of the nonequivalent groups design used in these studies, the degree

"The Role of Gender in College Classroom Interactions: A Social Context Approach," by Katherine Canada and Richard Pringle, reprinted by permission from *Sociology of Education,* 68, July 1995, American Sociological Association.

to which the unusual success of women's college graduates is attributable to single-sex education per se; to environmental factors favored by, but not necessarily exclusive to, single-sex education; or to self-selection factors, such as the socio-economic level, intelligence, and motivation of entering students (cf. Oates and Williamson 1978, 1981; Rice and Hemmings 1988; Smith 1990; Stoecker and Pascarella 1991; see also, Tidball 1989).

In addition to studies at the postsecondary level, a number of studies have examined the relative outcome advantages of single-sex and mixed-sex schooling at the secondary level (see Moore et al. 1993 for a comprehensive review). Like its postsecondary counterpart, this research has been plagued by problems inherent in nonequivalent groups design. Although most studies have favored the all-female model on many of the same dimensions just mentioned in the context of postsecondary schools, some studies that have attempted to control statistically for preexisting differences have reported mixed results (see, for example, Lee and Bryk 1986, 1989; Marsh 1989a, 1989b).

Some may argue that sufficient countervailing evidence exists (see, for example, Marsh 1989b; Marsh, Owens, Myers, and Smith 1989), and others would almost certainly remain skeptical about particular aspects of the alleged advantage (see Giele 1987; Marsh, Smith, Marsh, and Owens 1989; Oates and Williamson 1981; Stoecker and Pascarella 1991). However, we interpret the evidence, especially at the postsecondary level, as leaning strongly to the advantage of single-sex education for women. In their careful review of this research, Moore et al. (1993:35) stated:

> Considering the general direction of the research and giving more weight to those studies with carefully drawn samples, a reasoned choice of background controls, adequate efforts to compare similar entities, and overall statistical rigor, we conclude that there is empirical support for the view that single-sex schools may accrue positive outcomes, particularly for young women.

Nevertheless, we are skeptical of efforts to assess, once and for all, which is better: single-sex or mixed-sex education. Such comparisons invariably rely on central tendencies and are therefore inclined to disregard each category's potential for change, which may be better represented by variability or even theory. Instead, we regard the evidence that all-female education holds advantages for girls and women as an indication that so-called coeducation, *as it is typically configured*, is "failing at equity" (Sadker and Sadker 1994), that sound educational production[1] aimed at what Lee, Marks, and Byrd (1994:98) referred to as "positive engenderment," or the "conscious effort to provide equitable education for both sexes, including attempts to counter sexism and its residual effect," lags far behind where it should be.

One reason for this delay, beyond widespread indifference, is that in spite of many educational programs designed to promote positive engenderment, such as the National Women's History Project, the National SEED Project, and Project Kaleidoscope, there is a lack of practical knowledge of how all-female educational environments confer advantages, so, in turn, little is known about the transferability of these advantages to mixed-gender settings. Certainly, some of the outcome studies have attempted to isolate the operative factors. For example, Tidball (1989; see also Miller-Bernal 1993; Smith 1990) argued that women's colleges bestow their advantages indirectly through the critical mass of female role models, the special valuation of women, and the unparalleled opportunities for leadership and engagement with academics that such environments afford. In addition to these advantages, Riordan (1994:491) proposed others: mitigation of the values of the youth culture, fewer gender-based disparities in curricular opportunities, less gender bias in interactions between teacher and student, less gender stereotyping in peer interactions, a "proacademic parent/student choice," special programs for women, and receptivity to women's learning styles. But, for the most part, emphases on outcome do not lend themselves easily to investigations of the mechanisms whereby advantages accrue. In principle, studies of gender equity in the classroom do.

Gender Equity in the Classroom

The role of gender in the dynamic of the mixed-sex college classroom is a potential source of insight into the success of the all-female educational model. Consistent with several of the factors listed earlier, gender inequity in mixed-sex classrooms, compared to its relative absence in all-female classrooms, could be a major, but potentially correctable, weakness in the mixed-gender approach. It was in this spirit, or so it seems to us, that in the title of their provocative article, Hall and Sandler (1982) raised the pivotal question: "The classroom climate: a chilly one for women?" and then went on to suggest, on the basis of their review of a wealth of both quantitative and qualitative evidence, that gender influences interactions in educational environments and that the effects are particularly detrimental to the education of women. The report challenged educators to consider the consequences of prior socialization and gender expectations on students' experiences in coeducational environments and called for heightened awareness that teachers' behaviors can communicate differential expectations for male and female students.

Although Hall and Sandler addressed a wide range of possible negative gender influences on female students in academe, their claim that faculty members are responsible for, or at least inadvertently contribute to, the educational disadvantages for women stimulated the most research (see Bennett 1988; Constantinople, Cornelius, and Gray 1988; Cornelius, Gray, and Constantinople 1990; Crawford and MacLeod 1990; Krupnick 1985; Long, Sadker, and Sadker 1986). Although these studies generally found little, if any, evidence that faculty themselves impose the chilly climate, they and related studies (such as Boersma, Gay, Jones, Morrison, and Remick 1981; Brooks 1982; Irvine 1985; Karp and Yoels 1976; Sternglanz and Lyberger-Ficek 1977) have consistently shown that male and female students *do* behave differently in mixed-sex classrooms. For example, most reported disproportional numbers of classroom interactions involving male students.

However, rather than explore the educational implications of the observed differences and call for educational programs and environments that would minimize the differences or their negative consequences for women, many of the authors downplayed the gender differences for a variety of reasons. Some of the reasons they gave were that the differences were smaller than the observed differences associated with factors other than gender (Constantinople et al. 1988; Cornelius et al. 1990); were not "pervasive or robust" (Constantinople et al. 1988:547; see also Gray, Cornelius, and Constantinople 1989); were not due to discrimination by the faculty (Brooks 1982; Constantinople et al. 1988; Cornelius et al. 1990; Crawford and MacLeod 1990; Sternglanz and Lyberger-Ficek, 1977); were stylistic (Boersma et al. 1981); and, by implication, were immutable and therefore natural.

Similar differences between boys and girls have been observed in primary and secondary classrooms, and like the research on postsecondary classrooms, the focus of these studies was on exonerating teachers at the expense of probing the differences observed (see Brophy 1985 for a review). It is the differences between the behaviors of male and female students and, for that matter, between the male and female professors, and the circumstances in which those differences occur, not "who is to blame," that interests us, for there is reason to believe that such differences are socially constructed—and are constructed most readily in mixed-sex groups—and that the differences are symptomatic of a gender politic that pervades the educational and societal landscape (cf. Maccoby 1990). The relative success, on average, of women's colleges may be due to the relative ease with which gender politics can be held at bay in those settings while the educational process is allowed to proceed.

If, as this review suggests, all-female and mixed-sex schools differ, on average, along certain dimensions that are key to positive engenderment, Lee et al. (1994) suggested that mixed-sex institutions themselves vary along some of the same continua. These researchers examined the relative incidence of six kinds of sexism in the classrooms of 21 independent secondary schools of three different gender compositions: all boys, all girls, or mixed. Although each type of school had its share of sexist or negatively engendering events in the classrooms, considerable variations in the volume and kinds of sexism were evinced between and within the types of schools. So, although "the major form of classroom sexism treated in the literature—gender domination (either boys dominating discussions or teachers recognizing boys more often than girls)—was by far the most prevalent form of sexism in the coeducational schools" (p. 104), "explicitly sexual incidents" were observed only in the boys' schools, whereas "gender reinforcement" and "embedded discrimination" were more common in single-sex than in mixed-sex schools.

It is interesting that events that Lee et al. (1994) categorized as "equitable" or as promoting positive engenderment occurred with the greatest frequency in the girls' schools. But what was notable was that the degree of sexism observed in each type of school, including the mixed-gender schools, varied considerable. Two of the mixed sex schools were essentially nonsexist and, indeed, could be classified as promoting positive engenderment. Lee et al. concluded that circumstances, including an institution's gender mix, but more important, an institution's policy stance with regard to engenderment, have notable effects on the incidence and kinds of sexism that students experience.

Social Construction of Gender Differences

Studies on sex differences and gender roles in group interactions, if generalizable to the classroom, lead us to expect differences between the dynamics in classes with only female students and those in mixed-gender classes (Deaux and Major 1987; Eagly 1987; Eccles 1989; Maccoby 1988, 1990; Ragins and Sundstrom 1989). Regarding this expansive research literature, we make the following two general comments.

First, in many contexts, most boys and girls, left to themselves, associate and play with children of the same sex (see Maccoby 1988; Maccoby and Jacklin 1987). One important consequence is that within their same-sex groups, boys and girls learn and develop interaction styles that tend to be "restrictive" and "enabling," respectively. In mixed-gender groups, these styles clash in ways that usually favor boys' dominance of group interactions. These patterns continue through adulthood. Within their same-sex groups, however, both males and females are often highly interactive, and dominance and leadership are commonplace (see, for example, Aries 1982; Carli 1989; Lockheed and Hall 1976). In mixed-gender groups, however, the enabling interactive strategy adopted more often by females, in the face of the restrictive strategy adopted more often by males, favors male leadership of the group; males generally dominate interactions and monopolize desirable items shared by the group, including toys, computers, information, or access to an instructor (see, for example, Canada and Brusca 1991; Carli 1989; Lockheed and Hall 1976; Maccoby 1990; Powlishta 1987; Sadker and Sadker 1994).[2]

Second, the social roles, or the gender-stereotypic beliefs of the dominant culture, hold that males are more *agentic*, meaning that they tend to be more assertive and controlling, and females are more *communal*, meaning that they tend to be more concerned with the welfare of others (Eagly 1987). Attributes in common with being agentic include "aggressive, ambitious, dominant, forceful, acts as leader." Attributes in common with being communal include "affectionate, able to devote self completely to others, eager to smooth hurt feelings, helpful, kind, sympathetic, loves children, . . . awareness of feelings of others . . . gentle, soft-spoken" (Eagly 1987:16).

To the extent that people incorporate these gender beliefs into internalized rules that govern their own behavior and into expectations concerning the behavior of others, males and females ought to act differently, especially in situations that, based on norms, carry clear gender prescriptions. An important corollary is that, especially in mixed-gender groups, for a female to be highly interactive or dominant or otherwise to show leadership traits requires her to cross her gender-prescribed role, an act that, at the least, would be more difficult than behaving in accordance with her prescribed role, but at worst would be expected to invoke social penalties.[3]

These findings, like those of Lee et al. (1994), demonstrate the power of the social context, particularly gender composition, in the governance of gender differences. Without alternative mechanisms or policies to hold gender politics at bay, we would expect gender differences within mixed-sex classrooms to parallel those found in other mixed-gender settings. That is, in mixed-sex classrooms, female students, educated and expected to enable, would be inclined to relegate themselves to the role of audience to the more restrictive interaction style of male students. And male students, educated to restrict, would be inclined to assume positions of leadership and dominance.

The results from the research on interaction patterns in mixed-sex college classrooms and on single-sex and mixed-sex educational outcomes largely support this conclusion. However, the fact that the studies revealed varying degrees of adherence to the pattern raises the intriguing hypothesis that the inconsistency across studies reflects classroom and institutional attributes that either contribute to or mitigate students' and professors' tendencies to behave in gender-stereotypic ways. Although whether the classroom does or does not include men is certainly a powerful social context variable insofar as the social construction of gender differences is concerned, many additional factors can be expected to operate, so that some mixed-gender classrooms and schools would be more gender stereotypic than would others (Maccoby 1990). Giele (1987), for example, demonstrated that, on many outcome variables, female graduates of Oberlin College, the nation's first coeducational college, compare favorably with those of two of the seven sister colleges. Oberlin's long-standing commitment to the education of women may be a significant factor. Furthermore, Eccles (1989) showed that mixed-sex, seventh-grade mathematics classrooms vary in their "girl-friendliness," which has a direct impact on girls' interest in and commitment to the subject matter. She characterized girl-friendly classes as having relatively low levels of competition and public drill and high levels of contact between individual students and the teacher.

Understanding how institutional and classroom cultures may enhance positive engenderment is a priority. It is not enough to determine which educational model, all female or mixed sex, serves women better. That approach presumes that the central tendencies capture the essential feature of the categories. Rather, the goal is to understand better the conditions and processes that bring about the differences.

Consignment of Male Privilege

When we think of the social context within which classroom interactions occur, we think of an ever-widening series of concentric circles that define the ever-broadening historical , geographic, social-cultural, and circumstantial perspectives one can bring to bear on the particular classrooms that are observed. It is sheer folly to think that single-sex and mixed-sex educational practices can exist apart from these factors, that in comparing one with the other, one can somehow capture and evaluate their essences. Classrooms exist in context. Many are on campuses in which academic considerations play second fiddle to a youth culture predominated by athletics, parties, and romance (see, for example, Coleman et al. 1966). Holland and Eisenhardt (1990) described a campus "culture of romance" in which, unlike men who have a variety of pathways to status, women have one primary pathway to status: attractiveness to men. Sanday (1990) described a campus culture that colludes to privilege men and to allow rapes, even gang rapes, to occur.

That women are treated as second-class citizens of many college and university communities is a central theme in the vast and growing feminist scholarship on education and is the background of Title IX and other efforts to enlighten educators to the perils of sexual harassment (cf. DuBois, Kelly, Kennedy, Korsmeyer, and Robinson 1985; Hughes and Sandler 1988; Paludi 1990) and the chilly climate (DuBois et al. 1985; Hall and Sandler 1982; Lockheed and Klein 1985; Sadker and Sadker 1994). The consequences for women of attending "unfriendly" schools and classrooms certainly include the sobering ones that their confidence that they will be taken seriously will be repeatedly undercut and that their career aspirations and achievements will be systematically derailed. However, schools and classrooms choose, implicitly at least, either to resist or to conform to these patterns. After examining the relationship of institutional policies and characteristics, on the one hand, and the incidence and severity of sexism within independent secondary schools, on the other hand, Lee et al. (1994:115) concluded:

> Our results suggest that strong policies on the equitable treatment of male and female students make a difference. Such policies, if carefully enforced and periodically monitored by observations in classrooms, are translated into gender-equitable behaviors of teachers and students in classrooms and can profoundly affect students' experiences.

A College in Transition to Coeducation

When a small liberal arts, women's college announced its intention to become coeducational in 1987, we began a longitudinal study of its transition. This report focuses on our quantitative analyses of the changing classroom dynamic accompanying the first five years following the announcement. Our approach was to compare female students' behaviors in single- and mixed-sex classrooms and to compare both with the classroom behaviors of the entering male students. Our principle goal was to describe female students' interaction patterns in different settings, thereby highlighting and clarifying the relationship between gender and social context in college classroom environments.

Although we kept an eye on the broader concentric rings that define this college's culture, the particular social context variables we investigated were institutional- and classroom-level variables, which included the type of institution, the gender mix of students, the gender of the professors, the class size, and the class level. Our question was, What roles do gender and these social context variables play in the initiation, establishment, and continuation of classroom interactions between students and professors? In contrast to past research (see, for example, Cornelius et al. 1990), in which the emphasis was on describing social context variables as overriding the role of gender in influencing classroom dynamics, we focused on investigating gendered classroom behaviors as socially constructed variables that are influenced by social contexts. This approach is congruent with theoretical perspectives (such as those of Deaux and Major 1987; Maccoby 1990; Statham, Richardson, and Cook 1991) and research traditions (see, for example, the introduction in Thorne, Kramarae, and Henley 1983) that conceptualize gender as a variable variable, rather than as an immutable, inevitable trait that defines and directs behaviors.

Method

The Sample

The school

The college began admitting men in the fall of 1987, and we collected classroom data during the spring semesters of 1987, 1988, 1990, and 1991. As was true throughout its history, students at the college during this period were overwhelmingly white and middle and upper-middle class. Approximately 5 percent were African American; 10–15 percent were students of color.

The classrooms

During the spring semesters of 1987 and 1988, we collected data in 46 all-female student classrooms: 24 introductory-level classes in 1987 and 22 upper-level classes in 1988. During the spring semesters of 1990 and 1991, we collected data in 57 mixed-sex classrooms: 33 introductory-level classes in 1990 and 24 upper-level classes in 1991. In all, we made requests to visit 130 classrooms and were denied permission in only 5 instances—a participation rate of 96 percent.

Excluded from the sample because their classroom interactions were less public or too difficult to code were foreign language, speech, dance, and studio classes. Although we initially tried to observe laboratory sessions, we eventually excluded them for similar reasons. Classes taught by either of the authors and classes with fewer than five students enrolled were also excluded. Classes that met these constraints and were subsequently observed were nevertheless excluded from the analyses if during our classroom visit, an appreciable portion of the period was "team taught" or was devoted to students delivering formal, oral presentations or the professor divided the students into small-group discussions for most of the period. Five of the 115 classes that we actually observed were excluded for these reasons, and an additional seven were excluded because they were laboratory sessions, leaving a total of 103. For the analyses reported here, that is, for analyses that focused on the impact of the transition to mixed-sex education, we excluded an additional 10 classes because there was one male student or male visitor in a classroom that otherwise belonged to the single-sex classroom cohort (4 cases, 1988-89) or because there were no male students in a classroom that otherwise belonged to the mixed-sex classroom cohort (6 cases, 1990–91).

In 1987 and 1988, the observational sample was selected randomly from the pool of all eligible classes. The only stipulation on the random process was that each discipline (such as history, biology, or sociology) should be included in the sample at least once. In 1990 and 1991, our aim was to repeat observations in as many as possible of the classrooms that had been observed during the 1987 and 1988 codings. Our attempts were hindered by the fact that some courses were not offered every year or were replaced by new ones; these issues were particularly evident at the 200 and 300 levels. Nevertheless, in 1990, 20 observations were conducted in classes that had been included in the 1987 sample; in 1991, 10 observations were in classes that had been included in 1988. The remaining classrooms observed in 1990 and 1991 were randomly selected from the pool of eligible courses. No attempt was made to balance artificially the gender of professors and the size of classes across class levels (introductory versus upper level) and/or the type of school (single sex versus mixed sex). Similarly, no attempt was made to balance the proportion of male students across the various types of mixed-sex classes.

Table 1 presents basic descriptive information for the classrooms included in this report, broken down by year, type of school, class level, and gender of professors. As indicated, the observed class sizes were small, ranging from 3 to 42 students present (median = 13) and varied with the gender of the professors, class level, and type of school. Also, the proportion of male students present within the mixed-sex classrooms was small, ranging from 5 to 64 percent (median = 22 percent).

The students

In all, 1,282 students were observed and included in this analysis. Although classes were visited only once, some students and faculty were observed more than once in different courses; therefore, the number of students and professors observed represents totals, rather than the number of unique participants.

Table 1
Class Size and Proportion of Males, by Type of School and Professor's Sex[a]

	Single-Sex School		Mixed-Sex School			
	Female Professor	Male Professor	Female Professor		Male Professor	
	Class Size	Class Size	Class Size	P(male)	Class Size	P(Male)
Mean	9.1	13.5	16.3	.22	15.2	.28
Median	9.0	11.0	14.0	.20	16.6	.26
Range	3–17	3–28	3–42	.05–.64	4–29	.10–.60
SD	4.1	8.6	9.6	.14	7.4	.14
N	21	21	27	—	24	—
$N_{I/U}$	7/14	13/8	15/12	—	17/7	—

[a]N, $N_{I/U}$ and P(male) are the number of classes, the number of introductory- and upper-level classes, and the proportion of male students, respectively.

Procedure

We used a modified version of INTERSECT (Sadker, Sadker, Bauchner, and Hardekopf 1984) to observe classroom interactions. To provide ample opportunity for the establishment of a classroom interaction pattern, classrooms were observed during a three-to-five-week span in the middle of the semester of observation. Each classroom was observed once. We conducted the observations in 83 (89 percent) of the classrooms included in the following analyses; the remaining 10 (11 percent) were conducted by two research assistants.

On a day prearranged with the professor, the observer arrived early to choose a peripheral seat with a clear view of both the professor and the students. Although the duration of the classes varied, observations were conducted for 30 minutes of the scheduled class time. During the first 10 minutes of a class, the observer diagrammed the classroom, specifying the locations of the professor and each student. Each student was identified by a seating-chart number and by gender. Systematic observations of the classroom interactions began 10 minutes into the class and continued for 30 minutes, or until the class was otherwise over.[4]

Results

Preliminary Considerations

Some of the apparent inconsistencies in the classroom interaction literature may actually reflect the lack of explicitness about what constitutes a classroom interaction and which aspects of classroom interactions are being investigated. We took a more formal and deliberate approach by developing a model of classroom interactions, fundamental aspects of which were borrowed directly from our interpretation of INTERSECT (Sadker et al. 1984), the classroom observation system we used to collect data. We will detail the development and evaluation of the model in separate reports and present only an overview here. The model, summarized in Figure 1, has four key assumptions:

1. In traditional college classrooms the entire classroom dynamic occurs within an asymmetrical power structure in which the professor has higher status and exerts greater control than the students.
2. The asymmetrical power structure shapes the local classroom context, which, along with other contextual factors, affects the incidence and types of classroom interactions.
3. Each interaction link or exchange is composed of three parts or levels: dialing, responding, and evaluating.

Figure 1
A Model of Classroom Interactions as Configured in Traditional College Classrooms

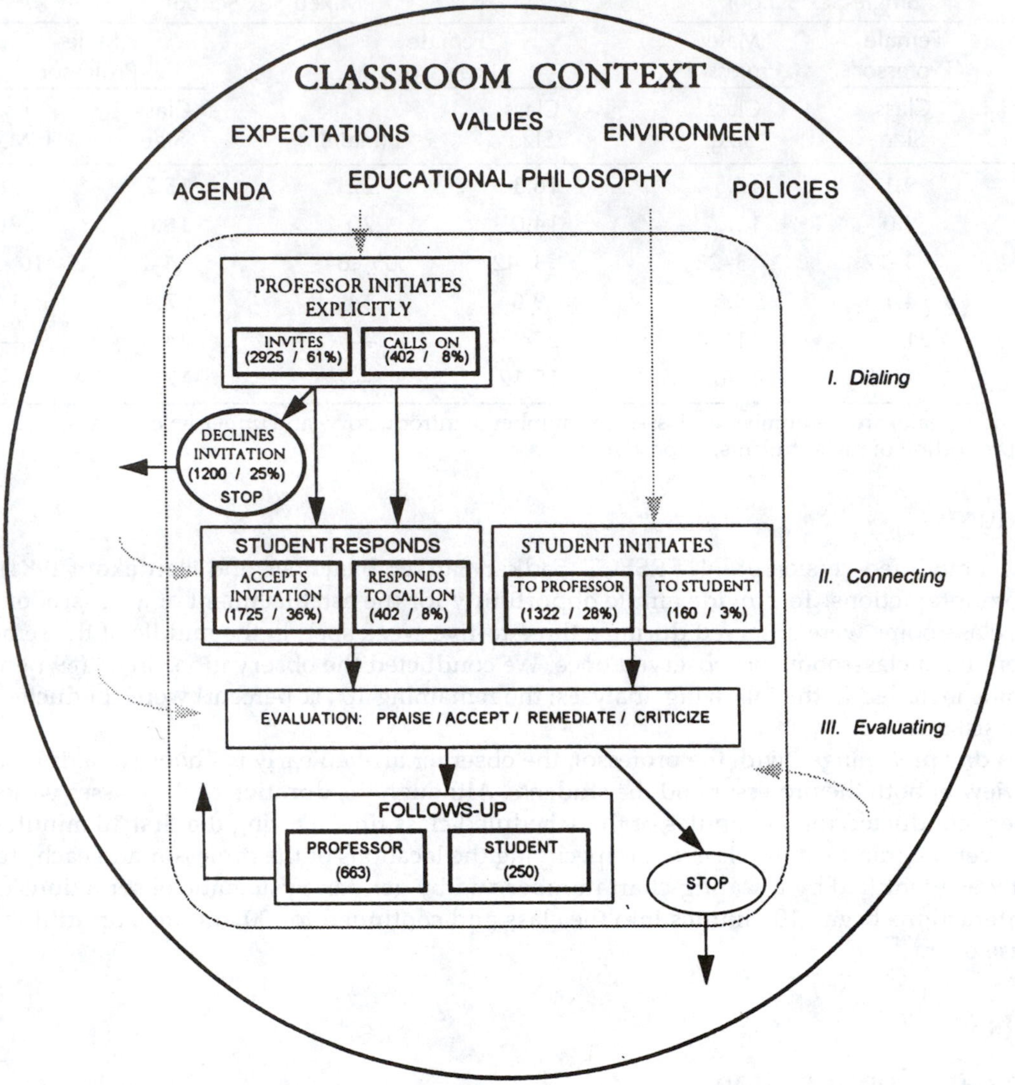

Note: Lighter arrows represent contextual influences that are assumed to operate at every level, darker boxes or ellipses = the dependent variables, and the total observed frequencies and unconditional probabilities are in parentheses.

4. Exchanges have the potential of being linked together, chainlike, forming classroom interactions of various lengths and complexity that can sometimes take on the appearance of a conversation between a student and professor or, in principle, between students.[5]

An exchange begins when the professor attempts, within the first level, to engage verbally, or "dial," his or her students, either implicitly, by simply helping to create conditions that favor student-initiated interactions, or explicitly, by raising a question or otherwise requiring some sort of response from the students. A student's response establishes a connection, which defines the second level. In the third level the professor implicitly or explicitly evaluates the student's message. An interaction can terminate at this point, a one-link interaction (one exchange), or it can continue through the cycle any number of times. An extended interaction is represented in the model by a series of successive and connected loops through the interaction sequence by the professor and a single student.

We used this model to create a taxonomy of classroom interactions. The portions of the taxonomy that are most concerned with establishing or failing to establish interactions are detailed in Figure 1. The taxonomy distinguishes between interactions initiated explicitly by the professor and those that are not (referred to as student-initiated interactions). Initiations by professors are of two types: an invitation to interact, usually in the form of a question directed to the class as a whole, and a requirement to interact, whereby the professor calls on a student directly. A professor's invitations can be accepted by one or more students, but often are not. Students' initiations can be directed either to the professor or to other students. Once an interaction is established and then cycles through the student's comment and the professor's evaluation, either the student or the professor can choose to keep it going by initiating a follow-up exchange.

Design and Analytic Strategy

Our aim was to assess the role of the gender composition of the group and other contextual factors in constructing gender differences within the classroom. We focused on aspects of the classroom dynamic that the literature on classroom and group interactions indicates are often highly gendered, namely, those that deal directly with the initiation, establishment, and continuation (or the failure therein) of classroom interactions. Our independent or predictor variables (the "social context" variables), included type of school (single sex versus mixed sex), sex of the professor, sex of the student, class size (number of students), class level (introductory versus upper level), and the proportion of males in the class. We selected five dependent or criterion variables that represent behaviors occurring within Levels 1 and 2 of the model (dialing and connecting). These variables were classroom totals for professors' invitations to interact (including separately those invitations that were accepted and those that were not), professors' call-ons, professors' follow-ups, students' initiations with the professor, and students' follow-ups. Students sometimes initiated interactions with other students, but because such interactions were so uncommon, they were not included in these analyses.

Because we used an unbalanced design and because of intercorrelations among independent variables, we used a hierarchical, general linear model approach to analyzing the effects of the independent variables and their interactions. The professor's sex, type of school, class level, and student's sex were all "effect" coded, with female, single-sex, and introductory courses coded as -1 and male, mixed-sex, and upper-level courses coded as +1. For each dependent variable, we examined three classes of models: (I) the overall school-type effects, that is, the "effects" of professor's sex, class level, class size, and school type on the class totals, ignoring the student's sex; (II) the school-type effects for female students only, that is, the effects of professor's sex, class level, class size, and school type on the adjusted female student totals; and (III) student's gender effects, that is, the effects of professor's sex, class level, class size, student's sex, and proportion of male students on the adjusted cohort totals for the mixed-sex classes.

Data were transformed as follows: For each classroom or classroom cohort the observed frequency of each type of interaction was tallied. Because some classrooms were not observed for exactly 30 minutes, either because of the brevity of the class (8 cases) or because of the observer's error of coding too long (4 cases), each class total was normalized to a 30-minute observation period.[6] Also, to avoid spurious effects involving class size, we chose not to base our analyses of cohort activity levels on the activity level per cohort member. Instead, we normalized the 30-minute cohort totals to reflect the interaction volume expected had the cohort in question been as large as the class itself (see the appendix). These adjusted totals provided a common response metric across analyses. Finally, because the dependent variables and class size were positively skewed, we applied square root or logarithmic transformations, depending solely on which resulted in minimal skew, to class size and to each of the dependent variables (J. Cohen and P. Cohen 1975).[7]

Separate hierarchical analyses were performed for each of the dependent variables for each of the analytic conditions (I-III). The resulting statistical models summarized in Tables 2–4, respectively, were based on data transformed to correct for skew.

Single-Sex versus Mixed-Sex Effects

Invitations

The total number of invitations to interact extended by professors during an observation period is equal to the number of invitations accepted by students plus the number of invitations declined. As indicated in Table 2, there were significant negative effects of class size and class level on the number of invitations. Also, as is illustrated in Figure 2, there was a significant interaction involving the sex of the professor and the type of school in that the number of invitations extended by female professors increased with the transition to mixed-sex education, whereas the number of invitations extended by male professors decreased. Male- and female-led all-female classes had statistically equivalent and intermediate numbers of invitations. This pattern of results was almost exactly replicated for invitations accepted and for invitations declined. To see if students were more inclined or less inclined to accept invitations in the mixed-sex classrooms, we performed additional analyses on the ratio of invitations accepted to invitations extended. In general, accepted invitations were more common than declined invitations (a ratio of 1.5 to 1), and this ratio was unaffected by type of school. Apparently, the observed changes in the totals of accepted and unaccepted invitations represent changes in the total number of invitations extended by the professors, rather than fundamental shifts in the willingness of students to respond.

Professor call-ons

Professors seldom began an interaction by calling on students directly. Only 8 percent of all interactions were of this type, or about 2.5 per 30 minutes of class. There were no significant effects for the call-on interactions, so those results are not included in Table 2.

Table 2
Determinants of Overall Patterns of Classroom Interaction, Irrespective of Students' Sex[a]

	Professor Invitation			Student	
Predictor	(Total)	Decline	Accepted	Initiation	Follow-up
School type (S)				.10* (6.6)	
Class size (N)	–.35* (4.2)	–.22 (2.7)	–.30* (3.9)	–.16** (18.5)	–.08** (5.3)
Class level (L)	–.78** (18.3)	–.67** (20.7)	–4.2** (7.2)		
Professor's sex (P)		–.97 (3.8)	–.23 (2.5)		
P × S	–.36* (4.3)	–.33** (5.5)	–.26 (3.2)	–.29* (4.8)	
P × N		.26 (3.8)			
S × L					–.07* (4.1)
P × S × N				–.10** (7.5)	
Constant	6.2** (97.0)	3.8** (56.1)	4.9** (77.8)	1.6** (133.3)	.70** (27.9)
R	.46	.51	.39	.46	.40

$^*p \leq .05$, $^{**}p \leq .01$.

[a] Table entries are unstandardized coefficients (*F*-ratios in parentheses). Models are based on a hierarchical, GLM approach. Model parameters reflect skew-correction transformations: square root for N, invitations extended, invitations declined, and invitations accepted; logarithmic for student initiations with the professor and student-initiated follow-ups. School type (S), class level (L), and professor's sex (P) were "effect" coded, so that single-sex schools, introductory classes, and females = –1, and mixed-sex schools, upper-level classes, and males = +1. Only significant factors and those approaching significance are shown here.

Figure 2
The Relationship of School Type to the Predicted Mean Number of Invitations to Interact Delivered by Male and Female Professors over a 30-Minute Class Period

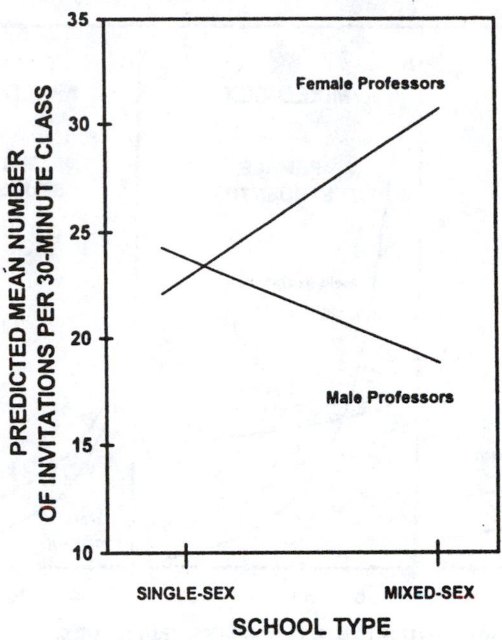

Student initiations

The analyses revealed a negative effect of class size and a positive effect of school type on the student-initiation totals. Also, school type interacted with professor's sex and together, they interacted with class size (see Table 2). These various effects were due primarily to a much higher number of student-initiated interactions in small and middle-size, male-led, mixed-sex classes than in others. Although this particular interaction is not shown here, it is nearly identical to the one illustrated in Figure 3A-B, which presents comparable information for the Type II analytic condition or, in other words, for the female students considered separately.

Although they are complex and interact with one another and with class size, two aspects of these findings are of special interest here. First, the number of student-initiated interactions was greater in the mixed-sex than in the all-female student classrooms. Second, for single-sex classes, the student-initiated interaction patterns in male- versus female-led classrooms were nearly equivalent (see Figure 3A), but for the mixed-sex classes, the patterns within male- versus female-led classrooms were different (see Figure 3B). So here, as with professors' invitations, the mixed-sex classroom made the professor's sex an important determinant of the interactive dynamics.

Professor follow-ups

Analyses of the numbers of professor-initiated follow-up exchanges revealed no main effects and no interactions. Hence, that model is not reported in Table 2. Taking into consideration a weak and non-significant effect of class size, the mean number of professor follow-ups per class was estimated at 4.2 for the median class size of 13 students.

Student follow-ups

There was a negative effect of class size. In addition, school type interacted with class level, so that the introductory, single-sex classrooms had approximately half as many student follow-ups as there were in each of the other three types of classrooms. The transition to mixed-sex education was therefore

Figure 3
The Relationship of Class Size to the Predicted Mean Adjusted Total Number of Student Initiations to the Professor per 30-Minute Class Period, per Each Student Cohort

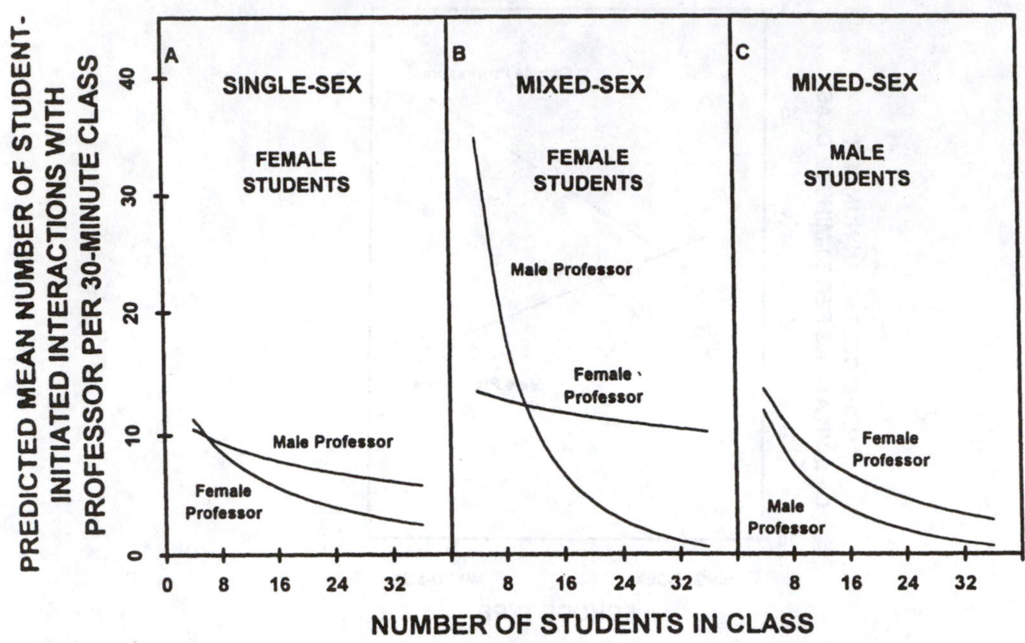

accompanied by an increased willingness by introductory-level students to follow up an initial exchange with another and/or by an increased tolerance or encouragement by the professors for such exchanges. When the college was all female, that relatively higher rate of student follow-ups was not evident until students entered upper-level classes.

Gender Cohort Totals

The foregoing analyses ignored students' gender and focused on how mixed-sex education and other factors (professor's sex, class size, and class level) affected the prominent features of the classroom dynamic. The results reported next consider the additional issue of students' gender. First, we consider how the transition and the other contextual factors influenced interactions involving the female students. Then we consider how students' gender and the other contextual factors influenced the adjusted cohort totals in the mixed-sex classrooms.

Female students

When only the female students' interactions were considered, so that the hierarchical analyses were performed on the adjusted total frequencies for the female student cohorts, the results, summarized in Table 3, closely duplicated those described earlier and will not be restated here. That these results for the female student cohorts so closely duplicated those obtained for the classroom totals indicates that the shifts in the overall pattern of classroom interactions that accompanied the transition from single-sex to mixed-sex education also held for the classroom interaction patterns of the female students themselves. This finding is not surprising, given that female students still far outnumbered male students during the period of observation. Even so, it is important to emphasize that the overall changes wrought by mixed-sex education were not simply due to the inclusion of male students who behaved differently from female students; rather, female students and both male and female professors behaved differently than they did in the single-sex classrooms. We turn now to the mixed-sex classrooms themselves.

Table 3
Determinants of Patterns of Classroom Interaction, Female Students Only[a]

	Professor		Student	
Predictor	Invitation Accepted	Follow-up	Initiation	Follow-up
School type (S)			.09* (5.5)	
Class size (N)	−.31* (4.6)*		−.16** (16.3)	
Class level (L)	−.46** (9.6)			−.07* (4.0)
Professor's sex (P)	−.23 (2.7)	.37** (7.1)		
P × S	−.26 (3.4)		.35* (6.3)	
P × N		−.08* (5.1)		
S × L				.09* (6.4)
P × S × N			−.11** (9.2)	
Constant	4.7** (78.6)	.73** (353.7)	1.6** (116.5)	.36** (98.2)
R	.40	.29	.45	.31

*$p \leq .05$, ** $p \leq .01$.

[a]Table entries are unstandardized coefficients (*F*-ratios in parentheses). Models are based on a hierarchical, GLM approach. Model parameters reflect skew-correction transformations: square root for N, and invitations accepted: logarithmic for student initiations with the professor and for professor- and student-initiated follow-ups. School type (S), class level (L), and professor's sex (P) were "effect" coded, so that single-sex schools, introductory classes, and females = −1, and mixed-sex schools, upper-level classes, and males = +1. Only significant factors and those approaching significance are shown here.

Students in Mixed-Sex Classrooms

The analyses of the mixed-sex classrooms included a somewhat different set of variables. In addition to examining again, now in the mixed-sex context, effects of professor's sex, class size, and class level, we also examined how the behavior of the male student cohort compared with that of the female student cohort and whether or not participation patterns were related to the proportion of male students in the class. The results are summarized in Table 4.

Professor invitations accepted

Consistent with the earlier findings, there was a positive effect of professor's sex in that the adjusted total number of invitations accepted was greater for mixed-sex classes led by female professors than for mixed-sex classes led by male professors. This effect of professor's sex was not related to student's sex. In the results reported in the previous sections, we stated that the female professors extended a greater number of invitations in mixed-sex classrooms than did the male professors. In the analyses we report here, we learned that the male and female students were equally likely to accept those invitations. What was interesting, however, was that there was an overall effect of the proportion of male students—classes with higher proportions of male students were associated with fewer adjusted total numbers of invitations accepted, irrespective of class size and the sex of students or professors.

On the basis of the regression in Table 4, the magnitude of the effect was such that the mean number of predicted invitations accepted dropped from 27 when the proportion of males in the class was set at zero to 3 when the proportion of males was set at 1.0.

Table 4
Gender Differences in Classroom Interaction Patterns in Mixed-Sex Classrooms[a]

	Professor		Student	
Predictor	Invitation Accepted	Follow-up[b]	Initiation	Follow-up
Student's sex (S)		–.13** (7.4)	–.11* (4.6)	–.19* (5.3)
Class size (N)		–.11* (5.9)	–.19** (10.8)	–.06 (2.7)
Class level (L)			.32** (7.8)	
Professor's sex (P)	–1.6* (5.1)			
Proportion males (M)	–3.6* (4.2)		–.98* (3.8)	
P × S				–.37* (6.5)
P × N	.42* (5.1)			
P × L	.49* (5.5)			
M × S				.69* (5.7)
M × L	–.26 (2.5)		–1.16* (6.3)	
P × S × N				.09* (6.2)
Constant	5.2** (26.4)	1.00** (33.0)	1.86** (40.7)	.56** (14.9)
R	.43	.34	.45	.38

*$p \leq .05$, ** $p \leq .01$.

[a] Table entries are unstandardized coefficients (F-ratios in parentheses). Models are based on a hierarchical, GLM approach. Model parameters reflect skew-correction transformations: square root for N, and invitations accepted; logarithmic for student initiations with the professor and for professor- and student-initiated follow-ups. Class level (L), professor's sex (P), and student's sex (S) were "effect" coded, so that introductory classes and females = –1 and upper-level classes and males = +1. Only significant factors and those approaching significance are shown here.

[b] The PLNM interaction was marginally significant; however, when included in the model, the overall model was not significant. Here the four-way interaction was folded back into error variance. These effects should be interpreted cautiously, (see text, note 8).

In addition to these first-order effects, there were two interactions. First, the effect of professor's sex interacted with class level. In these mixed-sex classes, female professors extended more interactions and therefore had more of them accepted than the male professors did. However, the higher number for female professors was greater for introductory- than for upper-level classes. Second, the effect of professor's sex also depended on class size; the greater number of invitations extended by the female professors (and accepted) diminished with the larger classes because for the female-led classes, but not for the male-led classes, there was a negative effect of class size.

Professor call-ons

As in the previous analyses of professor call-ons, none of the predictor variables nor their interactions was significant and, consequently, no model is reported in Table 4. In mixed-sex classes, male and female students were apparently equally, albeit rarely, called on.

Student initiations to professor

The joint effects of class size and professor's sex are shown separately for male and female students in mixed-sex classes in Figure 3B-C. Within mixed-sex classes, the adjusted total number of student initiations was greater for female than for male students (see Table 4). Indeed, the totals for initiations by male students were comparable to those for female students in the single-sex classrooms. In other words, the earlier finding that the number of student initiations per class increased with mixed-sex education was apparently exclusive to female students. In addition, there was a positive effect of class level and negative effects of class size and the proportion of male students. The latter finding was especially interesting: as the proportion of males in a class increased, both the male and the female students initiated fewer and fewer interactions.

Professor follow-ups

The hierarchical analysis of the professor follow-ups in mixed-sex classes revealed a four-way interaction involving professor's sex, class level, class size, and proportion of male students (see Table 4, footnote b). Four-way interactions are extremely difficult to interpret under the best circumstances, and the complexities surrounding unbalanced designs and hierarchical analyses only compound the problem. So, we can offer no coherent description, let alone an interpretation, of this particular finding.[8]

Student follow-ups

For mixed-sex classes, the adjusted total number of student follow-ups was greater for female than for male students, but that effect was, in turn, dependent on the proportion of male students in the class (see Table 4). Indeed, the greater number of follow-ups by female students is a *y*-intercept difference and therefore assumes that the proportion of male students is zero. As shown in Figure 4, as the proportion of male students increased, the adjusted total number of female student follow-ups decreased and the adjusted total number of male student follow-ups increased. Recall that the totals are "adjusted" to reflect the male and female student follow-up *rates* (see the appendix). In other words, the differences reflect "per student" differences.

Figure 4
The Relationships of the Proportion of Males in the Class to the Predicted Mean Adjusted Total Number of Male and Female Student-initiated Follow-ups over a 30-Minute Class Period

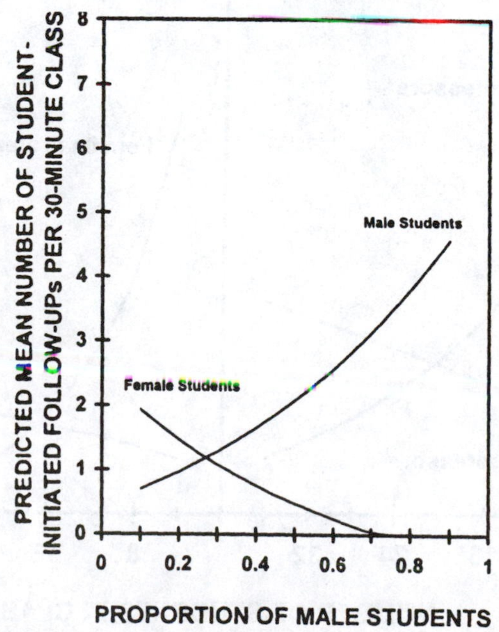

In addition, the effect of student's sex interacted with professor's sex, which in turn, depended on class size. This interaction, illustrated in Figure 5, is an interesting cross-sex effect: The total number of student follow-ups in which the student's gender matched the professor's gender was unaffected by class size and was relatively low. In contrast, the total number of student follow-ups by students of the opposite sex from the professor was relatively high in the smaller classes, but decreased with class size.

In sum, the data show that the males' and females' behaviors differed in many ways. However, in every instance, the nature of the differences, even their very existence, depended on circumstance.

Male versus Female Professors

Within the mixed-sex classes, female professors initiated 63 percent more interactions than did male professors (see Figure 2). The opposite was true for the student-initiated interactions: Mixed-sex classes led by male professors, when they were small to intermediate in size, were associated with many more student-initiated interactions than were comparable-size classes led by female professors (see Figure 3). In effect, female-led, mixed-sex classes were more professor driven and were less student driven than were male-led, mixed-sex classes. These findings would lead one to believe, on the basis of the mixed-sex classes considered in isolation, that male and female professors differ stylistically in how they govern their classrooms. But contrary to what this narrow view would indicate, male and female professors initiated intermediate and statistically equivalent numbers of interactions within the all-female student classes (see Figure 2). Similarly, these male- and female-led classes did not differ in their numbers of student-initiated interactions. Clearly, the "stylistic" difference that seems to have existed between male and female professors when they led mixed-sex classes was not at all evident when they led all-female classes. The difference in style was socially constructed.

Figure 5
The Relationship of Class Size to the Predicted Mean Adjusted Total Number of Male and Female Student-initiated Follow-ups to Male and Female Professors over a 30-Minute Class Period

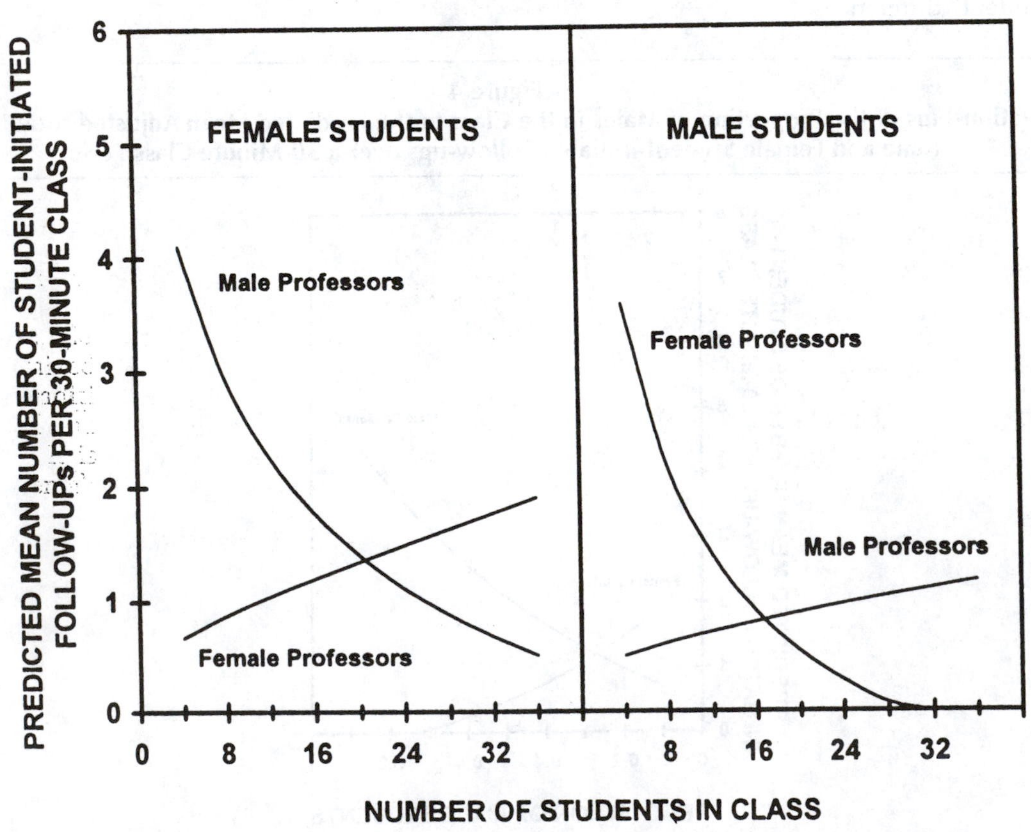

These various professor-sex findings both corroborate and extend Statham et al.'s (1991) finding that female and male professors negotiate their authority in different ways. Statham et al. conducted their research at a mixed-sex institution, and the classrooms they studied were mixed sex. Like Statham et al., we found that female and male professors tend to behave differently in mixed-sex classrooms. We also found, however, that in single-sex classrooms, female and male professors tend to behave in similar ways.

For faculty, this finding indicates that with regard to the specific classroom behaviors we observed and analyzed, the single-sex classrooms provided an environment within which female and male professors behaved similarly, which suggests that within that circumscribed domain, gender did not matter. For female students, this finding of gender differences in professors' styles and behaviors in mixed-sex classrooms is particularly interesting and potentially disturbing when it is considered in light of Tidball's (1989) assertion that the high number of female faculty who serve as role models for women students is one of the main reasons women from single-sex colleges outpace women from mixed-sex institutions in their entry into traditional male fields and career accomplishments.

It is not the case that the number of female faculty at the college under study declined since the move to mixed-sex education; the percentage of female professors remained high (over 50 percent) during the course of the research. However, our findings suggest a qualifier to Tidball's assertion: Not only are female students at women's colleges exposed to *more* female faculty members than are their counterparts at mixed-sex colleges, but they are also privy to a different type of female role modeling in the classroom. Specifically, female students at women's colleges reap the benefits of classrooms in which female and male professors model similar behaviors; in relation to their mixed-sex counterparts, the female professors behave more malelike, and the male professors behave more femalelike. Our findings suggest that male students in mixed-sex classes are similarly deprived of the opportunity to interact with female and male professors who are behaving in similar ways; therefore, their opportunities to observe and interact with females in environments in which gender does not matter are reduced.

Male versus Female Students

There were several differences in the manner in which male and female students interacted in the mixed-sex classrooms, and in every case, the difference depended on the social context. First, although the effect depended somewhat on class size and professor's sex, female students in the mixed-sex classes initiated more interactions than did male students (see Figure 3). One might suppose, on the basis of this finding, considered in isolation, that female students are more inclined than are male students to participate in the classroom dynamic. However, female students in the single-sex classroom initiated interactions in a manner and level almost exactly equivalent to that of the male students in mixed-sex classrooms.

Second, male and female students in mixed-sex classrooms differed in their numbers (rates) of student follow-ups: Female students started with a higher rate than did male students, but as the proportion of male students in a class increased, the female student follow-up rate decreased and the male student follow-up rate increased. The functions crossed, and hence the student follow-up rates were equal when the proportion of male students was .27 (see Figure 4). Had one examined the difference between male and female students' rates of engagement in conversation-style interactions and examined classrooms that had roughly equal proportions of male and female students, as did Boersma et al. (1981), then one would likely conclude, as they did, that male and female students have a different interaction style, with males being more likely than females to engage in conversationlike interactions with the professor. Here, too, the gender difference depends on the social context, in this case, on the proportion of male students in the class.

Third, in the mixed-sex classes, female students were more likely to engage in student follow-ups when the professor was male than when the professor was female (see Figure 5), suggesting a cross-gender affiliation between female students and male professors (cf. Boersma et al. 1981). However, there was no such effect among the single-sex classes: The student follow-up rates were unrelated to the professor's sex, which suggests that this so-called cross-gender affiliation was socially constructed in the mixed-sex classrooms.

Discussion

There are countless ways in which gender differences could arise within mixed-sex college classrooms. Our observational techniques, combined with the particular sampling and statistical procedures we used, like casting a net into a single region of the sea, permitted us to examine some small subset of these possibilities. We did not, for example, even attempt to collect data on the content of interactions. We focused instead on classroom and cohort tallies of certain well-defined behaviors that served to initiate, establish, and maintain verbal exchanges or interactions between students and professors. Nor were we able to follow individual students in detail, an approach that would have undoubtedly revealed many individual exceptions to the general trends emphasized here (see for example, Thorne 1993).

But with regard to those trends, within this domain alone we documented a variety of ways in which gender matters. The behaviors of female students and of both male and female professors were strongly related to whether or not male students were present in the classroom, and the behaviors of both female and male students in mixed-sex classes were related to the proportion of male students. The gender of the professor was also important, and these variables sometimes interacted in complex ways. Simply, the shift from all-female to mixed-sex classrooms was accompanied by profound changes in the nature of the dynamic of classroom interaction. That these data indicate that gender mattered in the mixed-sex classrooms in ways that it did not in the all-female classrooms is not surprising. They are consistent with several independent literatures that have documented ways in which gender matters in a variety of educational and group-interaction contexts.

These student-centered gender differences arising with mixed-sex education are consistent with Maccoby's (1990; see also, Greeno 1989) claims that the verbal and interactive behaviors of females are often strongly affected by the presence of males. The behaviors of women and girls, particularly those of European descent, are greatly affected by the gender composition of the group such that gender differences seem most pronounced in mixed-gender settings. The gender differences observed in our study of classroom interactions can be viewed similarly. We propose that they are a product of a kind of mixed-sex education that takes a laissez-faire approach to engenderment, which is to say, one that largely acquiesces to the broader culture's construction of gender.

Theorizing Gender in Classrooms

From the perspectives of the gender dynamics that ordinarily pervade mixed-sex classrooms and mixed-sex community youth culture, reviewed earlier, it is not hard to imagine events in the mixed-sex classroom that would trigger the kinds of changes we observed during the early phases of the college's transition. For example, one would expect the restrictive interaction styles of the entering male students to have been off-putting to the upperclasswomen who had gotten used to and learned to appreciate its absence. Similarly, some professors might have recognized in the restrictive style of the male students the kind of locution and verbal aggressiveness that they themselves had been taught to value. Others, more sensitive to gender issues or perhaps more vulnerable to the aggressive style because they were women or otherwise favored a more egalitarian and noncompetitive pedagogy, might have felt disconcerted and challenged for leadership within their own classrooms. Mix into this classroom cauldron a tendency by male students to evaluate female students and professors in terms of their attractiveness, as opposed to their intellectual capabilities and contributions, and related tendencies by male students to expect and to exert male privilege, and you have a gender politics in the classroom that was nearly absent in the single-sex environment.

The nature and volatility of the mixture just mentioned may be sufficient to induce the noted bifurcation between the ways in which male and female professors negotiate their classroom interactions. If a female professor believes that her classroom agenda is being challenged in some way, perhaps by body language (we frequently observed males sitting together in the back row, with their feet propped up, seemingly indifferent to the classroom dynamic), perhaps by silence (often the same male students did not participate in class), perhaps by the content of an interaction (we occasionally observed male students making agenda-challenging comments, such as "I resent your bringing that up!"), what recourse does she have? She can openly challenge the student or students, but that may be difficult to do and may, particularly if she does not have tenure, be professionally risky, especially at an institution that measures the success of its transition to coeducation by the number of its full-time male students. She may, instead, try to keep the agenda alive by asking more questions of the class.

Why did the female students initiate more interactions than the male students? We simply do not know. This behavior may have reflected their reaction to implicit and/or explicit comments by the male students. Or it may have been an attempt to "enable" the professor's agenda. Another possibility is that during these first five years of the transition to mixed-sex education, female students were inclined to contest male privilege and domination in the classroom, perhaps because of the residual effects of the all-female environment, such as pedagogical habits and expectations and the high proportion of female role models. Knowing the content of these interactions may help clarify their role in the classroom dynamic. Therefore, this issue awaits further study.

Interpreting the findings on the male and female students' follow-ups seems more clear cut. For whatever reason, when the proportion of male students was high, women in the new mixed-sex classrooms were not as likely as they were in the single-sex classrooms to enter deliberately into a sustained conversation with the professor. Male students, on the other hand, became increasingly willing to enter into such conversations as the proportion of male students increased. The issue can be understood in terms of intimidation. Note that the neutral point in Figure 4, the point where the two functions cross or, in other words, the female-to-male split that resulted in equal rates of student follow-ups for the two cohorts, is at .7/.3, *not* .5/5. That is, female students were more intimidated by male students than vice versa.

What, on the surface, appears to be an alternative explanation is that by ranking classes in accordance with the proportion of males in them, we may, in fact, have ranked them in accordance with the greater interest they evoked in males than females. For example, the classes with the higher proportions of males may have been those that are supposedly, or so the stereotype would have it, of greater interest to males, such as mathematics, computer science, and the natural sciences. By this alternative account, the relative lack of participation of the females in the student-initiated follow-ups would have been due to their lack of interest or skill in the subject—an intimidation by the subject matter, rather than an intimidation by the presence of male students. From our point of view, however, silencing is silencing. Also, we place little stock in this "essentialist" approach because the point is that these very classes were, when the college was single sex, populated by conversant female students. Now they are not.

The Challenge of Coeducation

We interpret our findings as evidence of the need for increased attention to issues of gender and gender equity in higher education. Though we acknowledge a need for educational reforms to address these issues, we are not ready to conclude, at this time, that the gendered outcomes reported in this article are themselves the things that need to be "corrected." Instead, we believe that these outcomes are the footprints of a gender politic or dynamic that now exists both in the college's classrooms and throughout the college campus that did not exist when the institution was single sex. What we measured, the changing volume of various types of interactions, signaled the entry of some changed circumstances, like a cloud chamber registers the passing of some otherwise invisible and unnoticed subatomic intruder. Given the total circumstance, the differences we observed may be more a reflection of the professors' and female students' survival tactics in response to the altered environment than a direct view of the altered environment itself. Given the reality of the gender politic, raising the number of invitations, for example, may be the best possible negotiation available to the female professors as they search for alternative pedagogies to achieve their educational goals in mixed-sex classes.

The wholesale entry of the gender politic itself occurred within a context. This study is a partial case history of an institution trying to find its way through difficult economic and demographic circumstances. As an all-female institution facing a less-than-critical mass of students for the foreseeable future, it looked to mixed-sex education as a means of increasing its recruitment pool. During the internal discussions of what it would mean to become coeducational, members of the community, and indeed the official proclamations of the institution itself, repeatedly stated the claim that mixing men with women would make little or no educational difference.

That gender does not matter in the domain of education is an institutional stance that Laird (1989) referred to as the "negative claim." That the institution under study maintained its negative claim throughout the period of study is clear: During its first five years, the success of the transition to coeducation was measured internally by the number of male students who were recruited. Furthermore, by the time our project ended, the institution had not established a single communitywide workshop, venue of discussion, database, or policy pertaining to the new role of gender in the business and mission of the college. Toward the end of our project, when we met with the person who was, at that time, president of the college to summarize our findings and concerns, she, too, expressed concern but informed us that "gender equity is not the guiding principle of this college." We would take her statement one step further and say that at least during the period of our research, the college's concern for survival overrode other concerns and values it might otherwise have held, including gender equity.[9]

Naturally, a college that makes the negative claim would not be easily alarmed. The tolerance for the gender politic, the tolerance for quiet students and dominant students in the classroom, and the tolerance for letting things sort themselves out as they will seem to us to guarantee the status quo as our society as a whole defines it, and that, as the literature amply documents, is far too frequently at the expense of female students. We end with this challenge: Making the negative claim is itself a social context. No one yet knows what is possible of a mixed-sex educational environment that soundly rejects the negative claim and aims instead for gender equity.

Appendix

Preliminary analyses indicated nearly ubiquitous and precipitously negative effect of class size on interaction "rate," defined as the number of interactions by a specific cohort (such a classroom or the female students within a classroom) divided by the number of students in the cohort. Also, these class-size effects were nonlinear, leveling off at nearly zero for the larger classes. Because classroom-interaction totals were not greatly affected by class size, converting from totals to rates by dividing by class size or cohort size produces asymptotically decreasing functions. The complexity of the situation is compounded by the fact that single-sex classes led by female professors ended to be smaller than other classes (see Table 1). A function describing the class-size effect for those classes would be expected to show a steeper decline (a steeper regression function) than would the others by virtue of the function never having the opportunity to reach asymptote. Consequently, in the regression analyses, class size would *appear* to have a more profound effect on the single-sex, female-led classes than on others, and that would tend to produce spurious main effects involving school type and professor's sex. We approached the problem by analyzing, in model types II and III, "adjusted totals," rather than response rates, per se. When partitioning classrooms into student cohorts, we used the interaction rates of the cohorts (for example, female students in mixed-sex classes) to compute the interaction volume expected had the cohort been as large as the class itself, or

$$T_a = (T_c/N_c)N$$

where T_a is the adjusted total frequency, T_c is the cohort total frequency, N_c is the number of students in the cohort, and N is the number of students in the class. In this way, we used a common metric across all analyses, and, even though the adjusted total is computed on the basis of cohort response rates, the transformation avoids the strongly asymptotic and nonlinear aspects of the nonadjusted rates.

Notes

1. In the sense of the social production theory of education that posits practitioners and students as active agents of resistance and change (Arnot 1982, 1984; Kessler, Ashenden, Connell, and Dowsett 1985; Weiler 1988). Regarding social production theory's application to gender, see related positions of Chafetz (1990); Epstein (1988); Hansot and Tyack (1988); Holland and Eisenhardt (1990); Laird (1989); and Lee, Marks, and Byrd (1994).

2. These patterns may vary considerably by race, ethnicity, and other circumstances (see for example, Orenstein 1994; Thorne 1993). That they are situational—not essential, not universal, but socially constructed and reproduced, and therefore potentially modifiable—is one of the central themes of this article.

3. For example, the penalty may be direct, as in lower evaluations of a female's leadership performance (see S. L. Cohen, Bunker, Burton, and McManus 1978), or indirect, as in the group's overall negative appraisal of competence that seems to arise from members' attempts to interpret their negative and largely unconscious and automatic affective responses (such as facial expressions) to female leadership (see Butler and Geis 1990). Also, see Ragins and Sundstrom (1989) for a review.

4. During the last 10 minutes of class, the students and the professor completed the Classroom Environment Survey (CES; Fraser, Treagust, and Dennis 1986). The observer briefly explained the purpose of the study and asked the students for permission to link the data collected with other data held by the registrar. Results pertaining to these various data sets, including the CES, will be reported elsewhere.
5. We do not claim that this model represents either an ideal or a universal pedagogy. Our own conceptions of the ideal are changing and depart markedly from this model. Also, the fact that we had such difficulty applying INTERSECT to the dynamics observed in laboratories and studios and to other classes characterized by small-group discussions and formal student presentations suggests that the model cannot be universal. Nevertheless, our data and firsthand experiences speak well for the model's wide applicability. Still, the classrooms depicted by this model are rather traditional and probably are most likely to be found in traditional educational settings. When the circumstances differ, say, for example, when the professor, the department, the institution, and/or the students are inclined to challenge asymmetrical power structures or to support democratic classrooms and other critical pedagogies, radically different configurations may result (see Freire 1970/1990; Maher and Tetreault 1994).
6. We used the following transformation:

   $$T_{30} = (T/t)30$$

   where T_{30} is the normalized total, T is the observed total, and t is the actual observation period. Of the 12 (13 percent) classes affected by these adjustments, all but 3 were observed for at least 25 minutes. The shortest observation periods were 16 and 20 minutes.
7. Skew is of little practical consequence when designs are balanced, but it can have serious statistical implications when they are not (Pedhazur 1982). We chose to be cautious with this issue and to perform our analyses on scores transformed to correct for skew. In every case a transformation was found that eliminated a significant departure from normality as determined by both a skew/(standard error of skew) criterion (<2.0) and by a Kolmogorov-Smirnov test of normality. In effect, these transformations helped to minimize the chance that statistically significant effects might be artifacts of the nature of our sampling and measuring procedures.
8. If we ignore the interaction and fold the variance associated with the interaction back into error variance, we are left with two simple overall effects: the adjusted total numbers of the professor follow-ups in mixed-sex classes decreased with class size and were greater for female than for male students. This strategy has some justification in that the overall statistical model that includes the four-way interaction and its lower-order factors did not reach or approach statistical significance. Also, when the four-way interaction is loaded first, adding the class size and student gender effects, both resulted in significant (and independent) increases in R^2. Thus it seems that whatever is happening in the four-way interaction itself does not contradict that, overall, there was a negative effect of class size and a negative effect of student's sex on professor follow-ups. Clearly, these two effects do not tell the whole story, however, and we prefer to interpret them cautiously. But it is noteworthy that there may have been a tendency for professors to initiate more follow-up interactions with female students than with male students.
9. Our comments here pertain, of course, to the institution considered as a whole, not to individuals.

References

American Association of University Women. 1992. *How Schools Shortchange Girls.* Washington, DC: AAUW Educational Foundation.

Aries, Elizabeth J. 1982. "Verbal and Nonverbal Behavior in Single-Sex and Mixed-Sex Groups: Are Traditional Sex Roles Changing?" *Psychological Reports* 51:127–34.

Arnot, Madeleine. 1982. "Male Hegemony, Social Class, and Women's Education." *Journal of Education* 164:64–89.

____________. 1984. "A Feminist Perspective on the Relationship Between Family Life and School." *Journal of Education* 166:5–24.

Astin, Alexander. 1977. *Four Critical Years.* San Francisco: Jossey-Bass.

Bennett, Sheila Kishler. 1988. "The Effect of Gender of Instructor and Gender of Student on Classroom Interaction: An Observational Study of Mixed-Gender Classrooms in a Women's College." Unpublished manuscript, Emory University, Atlanta.

Boersma, P. Dee., Debora Gay, Ruth A. Jones, Lynn Morrison, and Helen Remick. 1981. "Sex Differences in College Student-Teacher Interactions: Fact or Fantasy?" *Sex Roles* 7:775–84.

Bressler, Marvin and Peter Wendell. 1980. "The Sex Composition of Selective Colleges and Gender Differences in Career Aspirations." *Journal of Higher Education* 51:650–63.

Brooks, Virginia R. 1982. "Sex Differences in Student Dominance Behavior in Female and Male Professors' Classrooms." *Sex Roles* 8:683–90.

Brophy, Jere. 1985. "Interactions of Male and Female Students with Male and Female Teachers." Pp. 115–42 in *Gender Influence in Classroom Interaction*, edited by L. C. Wilkinson and C. B. Marrett. New York: Academic Press.

Butler, Dorè, and Florence L. Geis. 1990. "Nonverbal Affect Responses to Male and Female Leaders: Implications for Leadership Evaluation." *Journal of Personality and Social Psychology* 58:48–59.

Canada, Katherine and Frank Brusca. (1991). "The Technological Gender Gap: Evidence and Recommendations for Educators." *Educational Technology Research and Development* 39:43–51.

Carli, Linda L. 1989. "Gender Differences in Interaction Style and Influence." *Journal of Personality and Social Psychology* 56:565–76.

Carnegie Commission on Higher Education. 1973. *Opportunities for Women in Higher Education*. New York: McGraw-Hill.

Chafetz, Janet Saltzman. 1990. *Gender Equity: An Integrated Theory of Stability and Change*. Newbury Park, CA: Sage Publications.

Cohen, Jacob and Patricia Cohen. 1975. *Applied Multiple Regression/Correlation Analysis for the Behavioral Sciences* (2nd ed.). Hillsdale, NJ: Lawrence Erlbaum Associates.

Cohen, Stephen L., Kerry A. Bunker, Amy L. Burton, and Phillip D. McManus. 1978. "Reactions of Male Subordinates to the Sex-Role Congruency of Immediate Supervision." *Sex Roles* 4:297–311.

Cleman, James S., Ernest Q. Campbell, Carol J. Hobson, James McPartland, Alexander M. Mood, Frederic D. Weinfeld, and Robert L. York. 1966. *Equality of Educational Opportunity*. Washington, DC: U.S. Government Printing Office.

Conaty, Joseph C., Nabeel Alsalam, Estelle James, and Duc-Le To. 1989, August. "College Quality and Future Earnings: Where Should You Send Your Sons and Daughters to College?" Paper presented at the 48th meeting of the American Sociological Association, San Francisco.

Constantinople, Anne, Randolph Cornelius, and Janet Gray. 1988. "The Chilly Climate: Fact or Artifact?" *Journal of Higher Education* 50:527–50.

Cornelius, Randolph R., Janet Gray, and Anne P. Constantinople. 1990. "Student-Faculty Interaction in the College Classroom." *Journal of Research and Development in Education* 23:189–97.

Crawford, Mary and Margo MacLeod. 1990. "Gender in the College Classroom: An Assessment of the 'Chilly Climate' for Women." *Sex Roles* 23:101–22.

Deaux, Kay and Brenda Major. 1987. "Putting Gender into Context: An Interactive Model of Gender-Related Behavior." *Psychological Review* 94:369–89.

DuBois, Ellen Carol, Gail Paradise Kelly, Elizabeth Lapovsky Kennedy, Carolyn W. Korsmeyer, and Lillian S. Robinson. 1985. *Feminist Scholarship: Kindling in the Groves of Academe*. Urbana: University of Illinois Press.

Eagly, Alice H. 1987. *Sex Differences in Social Behavior: A Social-Role Interpretation*. Hillsdale, NJ: Lawrence Erlbaum Associates.

Eccles, Jacquelynne S. 1989. "Bringing Young Women to Math and Science." Pp. 36–58 in *Gender and Thought: Psychological Perspectives*, edited by Mary Crawford and Margaret Gentry. New York: Springer-Verlag.

Epstein, Cynthia Fuchs. 1988. *Deceptive Distinctions: Sex, Gender, and the Social Order*. New Haven, CT: Yale University Press.

Fraser, Barry J., David F. Treagust, and Norman C. Dennis. 1986. "Development of an Instrument for Assessing Classroom Psychosocial Environment at Universities and Colleges." *Studies in Higher Education* 11:43–54.

Freire, Paulo. 1990. *Pedagogy of the Oppressed*, Myra Bergman Ramos, trans. New York: Continuum. (Original work published 1970).

Giele, Janet Zollinger. 1987. "Coeducation or Women's Education? A Comparison of Alumnae from Two Colleges: 1934–79." Pp. 91–109 in *Educating Men and Women Together*, edited by Carol Lasser. Urbana: University of Illinois Press.

Gray, Janet, Randolph Cornelius, and Anne Constantinople. 1989, March. "The Effects of Student Gender on Participation in the College Classroom." Paper presented at the annual meeting of the American Educational Association, San Francisco.

Greeno, Catherine G. 1989. "Gender Differences in Children's Proximity to Adults." Unpublished doctoral dissertation. Stanford University, Stanford, CA.

Hall, Roberta M. and Bernice R. Sandler. 1982. *The Classroom Climate: A Chilly One for Women?* Washington, DC: Project on the Status and Education of Women, Association of American Colleges.

Hansot, Elizabeth and David Tyack. 1988. "Gender in American Public Schools: Thinking Institutionally." *Signs: Journal of Women in Culture and Society* 13:741–60.

Holland, Dorothy C. and Margaret A. Eisenhardt. 1990. *Educated in Romance: Women, Achievement, and College Culture.* Chicago: University of Chicago Press.

Hughes, Jean O'Gorman and Bernice R. Sandler. 1988. *Peer Harassment: Hassles for Women on Campus.* Washington, DC: Project on the Status and Education of Women, Association of American Colleges.

Irvine, Jacqueline Jordan. 1985. "Teacher Communication Patterns as Related to the Race and Sex of the Student." *Journal of Educational Research* 78:338–45.

Karp, David A. and William C. Yoels. 1976. "The College Classroom: Some Observations on the Meanings of Student Participation." *Sociology and Social Research* 60: 421–39.

Kessler, S., D. J. Ashenden, R. W. Connell, and G. W. Dowsett. 1985. "Gender Relations in Secondary Schooling." *Sociology of Education* 58:34–48.

Koss, Mary P., Christine A. Gidycz, and Nadine Wisniewski. 1987. "The Scope of Rape: Incidence and Prevalence of Sexual Aggression and Victimization in a National Sample of Higher Education Students." *Journal of Consulting and Clinical Psychology* 55:162–70.

Krupnick, Catherine G. 1985. "Women and Men in the Classroom: Inequity and Its Remedies." *On Teaching and Learning: Journal of the Harvard-Danforth Center* 1:18–25.

Laird, Susan. 1989, March. "Co-education: A Philosophical Anomaly?" In Susan Laird (Chair), *Needed: Research on Co-Education.* Symposium conducted at the annual meeting of the American Educational Research Association, San Francisco.

Lee, Valerie E. 1992. "Single-Sex Schooling: What Is the Issue?" Pp. 39–46 in *Single Sex Schooling: Proponents Speak Out* (special report from the Office of Educational Research and Improvement, U.S. Department of Education, Vol. 2), edited by Debra K. Hollinger and Rebecca Adamson. Washington, DC: U.S. Department of Education.

Lee, Valerie E. and Anthony S. Bryk. 1986. "Effects of Single-Sex Secondary Schools on Student Achievement and Attitudes." *Journal of Educational Psychology* 78:381–95.

__________________. 1989. "Effects of Single-Sex Schools: Response to Marsh." *Journal of Educational Psychology* 81:647–50.

Lee, Valerie E., Helen M. Marks, and Tina Byrd. 1994. "Sexism in Single-Sex and Coeducational Independent Secondary School Classrooms." *Sociology of Education* 67:92–120.

Lockheed, Marlaine E. and Katherine Patterson Hall. 1976. "Conceptualizing Sex as a Status Characteristic: Applications to Leadership Training Strategies." *Journal of Social Issues* 32:111–24.

Lockheed, Marlaine and Susan S. Klein. 1985. "Sex Equity in Classroom Organization and Climate." Pp. 189–217 in *Handbook for Achieving Sex Equity through Education*, edited by Susan Klein. Baltimore, MD: Johns Hopkins University Press.

Long, Joan E., David Sadker, and Myra Sadker. 1986, April. "The Effects of Teacher Sex Equity and Effectiveness Training on Classroom Interaction at the University Level." Paper presented at the annual meeting of the American Educational Research Association, San Francisco.

Maccoby, Eleanor E. 1988. "Gender as a Social Category." *Developmental Psychology* 26:755–65.

__________________. 1990. "Gender Relationships: A Developmental Account." *American Psychologist* 45:513–20.

Maccoby, Eleanor E. and Carol Nagy Jacklin. 1987. "Gender Segregation in Childhood." Pp. 239–87. In *Advances in Childhood Development and Behavior* (Vol. 20), edited by E. H. Reese. New York: Academic Press.

Maher, Frances A. and Mary Kay Thompson Tetreault. (1994). *The Feminist Classroom: An Inside Look at How Professors and Students Are Transforming Higher Education for a Diverse Society.* New York: Basic Books.

Marsh, Herbert W. 1989a. "Effects of Attending Single-Sex and Coeducational High Schools on Achievement, Attitudes, Behaviors, and Sex Differences." *Journal of Educational Psychology* 81:70–85.

__________________. 1989b. "Effects of Single-Sex and Coeducational Schools: A Response to Lee and Bryk." *Journal of Educational Psychology* 81:651–53.

Marsh, Herbert W., Lee Owens, Margaret R. Myers, and Ian D. Smith. 1989. "The Transition from Single-Sex to Co-Educational High Schools: Teacher Perceptions, Academic Achievement, and Self-Concept." *British Journal of Educational Psychology* 59:155–73.

Marsh, Herbert W., Ian D. Smith, Margaret Marsh, and Lee Owens. 1989. "The Transition from Single-Sex to Co-educational High Schools: Effects on Multiple Dimensions of Self-Concept and on Academic Achievement." *American Educational Research Journal* 25:237–69.

Miller-Bernal, Leslie. 1993. "Single-Sex versus Coeducational Environments: A Comparison of Women Students' Experiences at Four Colleges." *American Journal of Education* 102:23–54.

Moore, Mary, Valerie Piper, and Elizabeth Schaefer. 1993, December. "Single Sex Schooling and Educational Effectiveness: A Research Overview." Pp. 7–68 in *Single-Sex Schooling: Perspectives from Practice and Research* (special report from the Office of Educational Research and Improvement, U.S. Department of Education, Vol. 1), edited by Debra K. Hollinger and Rebecca Adamson. Washington, DC: U.S. Department of Education.

Oates, Mary J., and Susan Williamson. 1978. "Women's Colleges and Women Achievers." *Signs: Journal of Women in Culture and Society* 3:795–806.

__________________. 1981. "Comments on Tidball's 'Women's Colleges and Women Achievers Revisited.'" *Signs: Journal of Women in Culture and Society* 6:342–45.

Orenstein, Peggy. 1994. *Schoolgirls: Young Women, Self-Esteem, and the Confidence Gap*. New York: Doubleday.

Paludi, Michele A. (Ed.). 1990. *Ivory Power: Sexual Harassment on Campus*. Albany: State University of New York Press.

Pedhazur, Elazar J. 1982. *Multiple Regression in Behavioral Research: Explanation and Prediction* (2nd ed.). New York: Holt, Rinehart, & Winston.

Powlishta, K. K. 1987, April. "The Social Context of Cross-Sex Interactions." Paper presented at the biennial meeting of the Society for Research in Child Development, Baltimore, MD.

Ragins, Belle Rose and Eric Sundstrom. 1989. "Gender and Power in Organizations: A Longitudinal Perspective." *Psychological Bulletin*, 105:51–88.

Rice, Joy K. and Annette Hemmings. 1988. "Women's Colleges and Women Achievers: An Update." *Signs: Journal of Women in Culture and Society* 13:546–59.

Riordan, Cornelius. 1990. *Girls and Boys in School: Together or Separate?* New York: Teachers College Press.

______________. 1992. "The Case for Single-Sex Schools." Pp. 47–54 in *Single-Sex Schooling: Proponents Speak Out* (special report from the Office of Educational Research and Improvement, U.S. Department of Education, Vol. 2), edited by Debra K. Hollinger and Rebecca Adamson. Washington, DC: U.S. Department of Education.

______________. 1994. "The Value of Attending a Women's College: Education, Occupation, and Income Benefits." *Journal of Higher Education* 65:486–510.

Sadker, Myra and David Sadker. 1994. *Failing at Fairness: How America's Schools Cheat Girls*. New York: Maxwell Macmillan.

Sadker, Myra, David Sadker, Joyce Bauchner, and Celia Hardekopf. 1984. "Observer's Manual for Intersect: Post-Secondary Form—Interactions for Sex Equity in Classroom Teaching." Unpublished manuscript, American University, Washington, DC.

Sanday, Peggy Reeves. 1990. *Fraternity Gang Rape: Sex, Brotherhood, and Privilege on Campus*. New York: New York University Press.

Smith, Daryl G. 1990. "Women's Colleges and Coed Colleges: Is There a Difference for Women?" *Journal of Higher Education* 61:181–95.

Statham, Anne, Laurel Richardson, and Judith A. Cook. 1991. *Gender and University Teaching: A Negotiated Difference*. Albany: State University of New York Press.

Sternglanz, Sarah Hall and Shirley Lyberger-Ficek. 1977. "Sex Differences in Student-Teacher Interactions in the College Classroom." *Sex Roles* 3:345–52.

Stoecker, Judith L. and Ernest T. Pascarella. 1991. "Women's Colleges and Women's Career Attainments Revisited." *Journal of Higher Education* 62:394–409.

Thorne, Barrie. 1993. *Gender Play: Girls and Boys in School*. New Brunswick, NJ: Rutgers University Press.

Thorne, Barrie, Cheris Kramarae, and Nancy Henley. 1983. *Language, Gender and Society*. Rowley, MA: Newbury House.

Tidball, M. Elizabeth. 1973. "Perspective on Academic Women and Affirmative Action." *Educational Record* 54:130–35.

______________. 1980. "Women's Colleges and Women Achievers Revisited." *Signs: Journal of Women in Culture and Society* 5:504–17.

______________. 1985. "Baccalaureate Origins of Entrants into American Medical Schools." *Journal of Higher Education* 56:385–402.

______________. 1986. "Baccalaureate Origins of Recent Natural Science Doctorates." *Journal of Higher Education* 57:606–20.

______________. 1989. "Women's Colleges: Exceptional Conditions, Not Exceptional Talent, Produce High Achievers." Pp. 157–72. In *Educating the Majority: Women Challenge Tradition in Higher Education*, edited by Carol S. Pearson, Donna L. Shavlik, and Judith G. Touchton. New York: Macmillan.

______________. 1992. "Educational Environments and the Development of Talent." Pp. 55–61 in *Single-Sex Schooling: Proponents Speak Out* (special report from the Office of Educational Research and Improvement, U.S. Department of Education, Vol. 2), edited by Debra K. Hollinger and Rebecca Adamson. Washington, DC: U.S. Department of Education.

Tidball, M. Elizabeth and Vera Kistiakowsky. 1976. "Baccalaureate Origins of American Scientists and Scholars." *Science* 193:646–52.

Weiler, Kathleen. 1988. *Women Teaching for Change: Gender, Class, and Power*. South Hadley, MA: Bergin & Garvey.

Classroom Incivilities

ROBERT BOICE

The scattered, little-known literature on classroom disturbances depicts their aversive nature and growing costs, but rarely in higher education. Here I summarize a five-year study of classroom incivilities (CI) at a large research university. In systematic observations of large survey courses, I ranked the most problematic CI as (1) teachers displaying aloof, distancing mannerisms; (2) teachers discouraging student involvement with fast-paced lectures; (3) students' noisiness and indifference; (4) students coming late and leaving early; (5) students' sarcastic remarks/gestures; and so on. High levels of CI corresponded to low levels of student attentiveness and note-taking—and to low levels of teacher enthusiasm, clarity/organization, and immediacies (i.e., expressions of warmth and approachability). High CI meant fast-paced lectures, student confusion/annoyance, and perceptions of teachers as uncaring and incompetent. The key indicator of CI may be teachers' deficits in immediacies, particularly during the first few days of classes. Immediacy was coached here with demonstrable reductions in CI.

We may know classroom incivilities best from news accounts about intimidation and violence directed at high-school teachers. The topic has become a chief concern of educational leaders:

> What people really want are their own schools and they want the schools to be safe and orderly. It is insane to set up a system where we move 98 percent of our kids away from the 2 percent who are dangerous instead of moving the 2 percent who are okay. . . . Independent surveys and our own polls show that the overwhelming majority of Americans put school safety at the top of their concerns. (Shanker, 1995, p. 48)

We say comparatively little about classroom incivilities in higher education. Still, there are at last signs of a growing concern even within our ivy towers:

> Caught in this web of laxity, indiscrimination, and materialism, the young, by the time they are ready to enter college, have established within themselves a mental fixity born of fear and disorientation that is strikingly narcissistic in its monadic self-encapsulation, in its fear and resentment of authority, and in its conformist rigidity and intellectual lassitude. The result is the high-tech barbarian: rude, without sympathy for culture, crude in his tastes, raucous in his behavior, enthralled by the loud pulse of his music and devoted to the accumulation of megabucks and the amassment of the shining baubles of tawdry affluence. (Bartlett, 1993, p. 308)

I too had paid little attention to classroom incivilities (CI), even to occasional incidents in my own classes, until I undertook a decade of observing new faculty cope as teachers. Then CI emerged as a major factor, frequently dominating classes, often making or breaking novice teachers. I remember wondering: Why isn't this problem the subject of more study? Why don't we recognize its commonness and cost in higher education? In my search for answers, I found that more information is available than I had realized, most of it, though, from different, more indirect vantages than I had hoped for. Still, they establish a useful background. These are four extant views as I understand them.

"Classroom Incivilities," by Bob Boice, reprinted from *Research in Higher Education,* Vol. 37, No. 4, 1996, Human Sciences Press.

1. CI as Taboo, as Embarrassing

Social psychologists study the reason why we do not persistently question people's failings or seriously examine their excuses, or why we resist admitting our own struggles with problems that presumably reveal our intelligence, including teaching. Doing so can be an embarrassment, a social impropriety (Snyder and Higgins, 1988). Nonetheless, some of our colleagues do better than we at facing up to the taboo. Psychotherapists acknowledge why they dislike admitting annoyance with difficult patients. Such a disclosure might be interpreted by colleagues as a sign of poor therapeutic skills (Fremont and Anderson, 1988).

The point of digging into such a dark corner of professional activity is to show why we typically neglect or distance ourselves from CI. It helps explain why what we know about CI is so amicably remote.

2. CI as More Studied/Publicized Among Teachers with Less Status and Privacy

Elsewhere in the profession of teaching, in the lower grades, accounts of student disruptiveness proliferate. News reports routinely depict urban schools, even some rural settings, in terms of insolent, indifferent students (Coles, 1993). Elementary schools now obviously require programs of violence prevention (Goleman, 1993); students at surprisingly young ages find school a nightmarish experience of sexual and other aggressive taunts (Baringer, 1993). By early adolescence they commonly talk about the pain of enduring mean, boring teachers—and they act in classes accordingly (Manegold, 1993). Soon after, they often demand the good grades requisite for college but without interest in learning (Lee, 1993). This atmosphere, of course, demoralizes and exhausts teachers (Toby, 1993). It even turns immigrant students away from the good study habits they had imported (Associated Press, 1994).

But when we look past the dramatic, we can learn practical things about the nature and prevention of CI. Examples: Disorder (inside and outside the classroom) may engender a loss of community spirit and with it a lessening of the informal social controls that maintain interest and order. Teachers accustomed to working amid disorder suppose that little can be done to change it and do less to discourage the rudeness, violence, and demoralization that follow (Toby, 1993). In settings where teachers establish truces with classes, by demanding little and getting it, a few intimidating students can discourage open displays of interest in other class members. Even there, solutions for CI are possible. Briefly angry but caring confrontations with students can enable the teacher and most of the students to break the hold of fear and foreignness on both sides (Coles, 1993). And when classes discuss what provokes anger, students share ways of resolving conflicts more peaceably (Goleman, 1993).

3. CI as More Readily Acknowledged Among Other Doctoral-Level Practitioners

We can also profit by looking at the experiences and reactions of other practitioners who must deal with difficult patients and clients. Physicians place most of the responsibility for misbehavior on patients; there is little onus for doctors whose patients resist and noncomply. Still, physicians (far more than professors) are coached in ways of reducing the stress and burnout that come with manipulative, controlling, uncooperative patients. These are common admonitions: (a) understand the causes of resistance (e.g., fear and misinformation) and respond impersonally; (b) balance caring with objectivity; (c) have confidence you are doing the right thing; and (d) find more peer support and hobbies (Smith and Stendler, 1983).

Therapists model another bold move not typically considered by teachers facing resistance. They publicly acknowledge which of patients' behaviors annoy them most (e.g., impositions such as late-night, nonemergency calls) and which should be tolerated (e.g., "dynamic" struggles that patients display in working through difficult problems—Fremont and Anderson, 1988). More important, they constantly and firmly remind patients of what behaviors help or hinder therapy (Tryon, 1986).

Because of this openness and inquisitiveness, I think, therapists are far more likely than teachers to suppose that their successes rely on practicing the right skills, not on inheriting the right genes. Hill and Corbett (1993) show why the skills approach has found widespread acceptance with therapists. Early research by Carl Rogers established the value of skills like a "focused voice" that has an irregular pace, moderate to high energy levels, and variable accents. Robert Carkhuff added more credibility to this skills assumption by demonstrating that early training of therapists is best aimed at teaching basic ways of working: problem-solving and decision-making skills (cf. usual emphases on teaching graduate students about diagnosing pathologies). Process researchers, as they call themselves, even show the teachability of more advanced skills. Norman Kagan pioneered research that identified two skills essential to expertise: learning to share patients' perceptions of how therapy sessions progress and knowing how to get beyond performance anxieties that inhibit already learned skills. The upshots of this tradition may be worth noticing in higher education. Therapists boast a sharing of ideas between humanists and behaviorists, because the same skills prove to be essential to either approach. Said another way, empathic, warm, skilled therapists require no theoretical orientation (only skills like interpretation and nonverbal immediacy—e.g., smiling, facing, moving, and moderate distancing). Where these practices are missing, Hill and Corbett note, so is adequate awareness and anticipation of client reactions, especially of the negative kind.

4. CI as Higher Education Approaches It

We are, clearly, decades behind therapists in empirically evaluating what affects success among college teachers in domains including CI (Weimer and Lenze, 1991). And when we do approach the awkward topic of trouble in the classroom, we do so with monumental indirectness. We talk abstractly about the breakdown of traditional student-faculty relationships but not specifically about how it demoralizes faculty (Wilson, 1990). We blame deteriorating conditions of teaching on democratic tendencies to admit underqualified students into college, without addressing the immediate problems of ever more crowded classrooms (Henry, 1994). And on the few occasions when faculty development practitioners examine CI on their own campuses, the information is often held back from public distribution. I know of two large campuses where such studies/programs were kept from publication by administrators concerned about institutional image. Another, particularly sound program produced a report that was effectively limited to a campus newspaper (BQ, 1990). Its facilitator identified common disruptive classroom behaviors on her campus (e.g., students conversing with neighbors; students coming to class late and leaving early; students expressing direct anger about course content or tests). She also listed seemingly effective interventions for CI: (a) defining acceptable behaviors at the outsets of semesters; (b) decreasing students' anonymity by knowing and using their names; (c) encouraging active learning that involves students in classroom endeavors. Unfortunately, this model program remains nearly invisible.

This same tradition, the one that perpetuates obscurity for CI, encourages another oversight: We rarely ask whether some kinds or degrees of CI might be adaptive in our classrooms. Still, there are hints of alternative ways of conceptualizing CI. One clue lies in representations of traditionally acceptable students. They can be seen as so eager to please authority figures, so oversensitive to negative evaluations as to approach what psychotherapists label as a dependent personality disorder (Bornstein and Kennedy, 1994). So it is, possibly, that school impresses many independent students, including the bulk of people who find greatness, as uncongenial and irrelevant (Simonton, 1994). Another irreverent hint is that traditional teachers may err in adhering too closely to academic norms of rationality, impersonality, and formality—so much so that even positive emotions are discouraged in students (Bowen, Seltzer, and Wilson, 1987). What does it matter? For one thing, emotions help learners to focus attention on important topics, to persevere, and to find inspiration. For another, emotional expression makes teachers seem more human to students. And third, consider that cultures different from our own (usually white) orientation see a value for, say, emotional trash-talking as a leveler and motivator (DeJonge, 1993). There is a point to this alternative literature: It reminds us that in looking for ways to moderate CI, we can go too far. After all, the ultimate of psychological health and functioning, self-efficacy, depends not only on success but also on learning to reinterpret stressful events in more tolerant, optimistic ways (Bandura, 1986; Perry et al., 1993).

Even higher education's few empirically based accounts of CI are generally abstract and indirect. In an extensively documented program, Amada (1992) treats CI largely as a mental health problem; more students with schizophrenia, manic-depression, and personality disorders are coming to our campuses. Their incivilities are best treated in campus mental health centers (or, in extreme cases, with legal action). What makes Amada's approach indirect and limited? The bulk of CI needs to be dealt with in and near the classroom by teachers themselves; only extremely disruptive or disturbed students require formal treatment.

Another drawback to our own little-known research on CI is that it tends to prove the obvious. Wyatt (1992), for example, found students more likely to cut classes they did not like. Even so, some of these confirming studies help clarify things. Examples: Not just absences but cheating (another form of CI) relate to disliking a class, particularly when students see it as irrelevant to their careers (Didner, 1992). And, more interesting, CI can be conceptualized, at least in survey responses, to fall into three general reciprocities between students and teachers. Both especially dislike people in the other role who come to class late. Students dislike teachers who run overtime; teachers loathe class members who pack up early. Both complain about counterparts who cut or cancel classes (Appleby, 1990).

Other more surprising research may prove even more useful. Tracking studies suggest that most newcomers to teaching rely on personal experiences as students, not on direct observations of their own students, to determine when difficulties are likely to arise in classes (Lenze and Dinham, 1994). Similarly, novices often make erroneous assumptions about their students' prior knowledge. With the right kinds of experience, though, teachers develop enhanced sensitivity to problems such as inattention (Fogarty, Wang, and Creek, 1983). Most uncommon in this genre are assumptions that teachers commit CI. In fact, some of our colleagues are guilty of lapses in dealing fairly and empathically with diverse students (Williams, 1994). In samplings of core courses at large public universities, as many as a third of faculty treated students with unmistakable rudeness and condescension. In a few cases they physically assaulted students who pressed them for answers or help (Boice, 1986, 1993b), perhaps about as often as students assaulted professors. In many more instances (we do not know the exact figures) professors take advantage of teaching dynamics to sexually and otherwise compromise students.

The most experienced researchers on CI assume that students and teachers are partners in generating and exacerbating it. They even report its commonness and its varieties: In a typical class of 30, 5 or 6 students resist doing what the teacher wants (and just one troublesome student can ruin an entire class for everyone). CI typically means missing classes, cheating, refusing to participate, coming unprepared, and distracting teachers and other students. Kearney and Plax (1992) remind us that some kinds of student (and teacher) resistance can be labeled constructive (as when substantive questions are pressed), even though most teachers react to any kind of confrontation as problematic.

What other roles do teachers play? How they present themselves may be the most telling factor, at least in initiating CI. In laboratory simulations, Kearney and Plax find that students decide to resist and misbehave depending largely on how they interpret two interrelated kinds of teacher behaviors. One is a matter of whether the teacher employs mostly prosocial motivators (e.g., "Do you understand?" and "You can do better") or antisocial motivators (e.g., threats and guilt induction). The second is about immediacy—the extent to which the teacher gives off verbal and nonverbal signals of warmth, friendliness, and liking (e.g., forward leans, smiles, purposeful gestures, eye contact). With positive motivators and, particularly, immediacy, student inclinations to CI drop off dramatically. But without these skills, teachers are seen as cold, uncaring, and incompetent by their students—as deserving targets of incivilities. So, according to Kearney and Plax, power in classrooms is relational. Teachers have the power (if they have the skills) to use motivators and immediacies to moderate CI. And students have the power and the skills (far more than most teachers appreciate) to effectively undermine teachers who seem not to care about them.

Something else is worth knowing about skills of immediacy. They can be taught. Resulting improvements bring skills to levels already exhibited by experienced, successful teachers who, for instance, exhibit a large array of positive motivators (Plax and Kearney, 1992). This research on communication in teaching may be a significant breakthrough in understanding the origins, preventives, and correctives for CT. (Many of us, incidentally, already know parallels to immediacy in older research on expressiveness and enthusiasm.) Given that leap forward, do we know enough to begin setting up programs to moderate CI?

Why These Varied Perspectives Leave Us Short

Consider what we have learned from the four perspectives on CI: It seems to be increasingly problematic, at least in K-12 classes. It is usually left undiscussed, most so (probably) in higher education. It involves common complaints such as teachers running overtime and students clamoring to leave early. Its costs include discomfort, danger, and derailed learning. It has attracted informal study and faculty workshops at some campuses, but in generally unpublicized ways. And, while tradition holds students mostly responsible for CI, emerging research suggests that teachers' underuse of positive motivators and immediacies may be more powerful. Teachers themselves can be uncivil.

Then consider that we still do not know much about (a) the frequency and kinds of CI in any broad sampling of college classes; (b) its costs (and benefits) for students and teachers in live college classrooms; (c) why some of our colleagues encounter more CI than others of us (although we have one hint from Kearney and Plax's research); (d) how CI relates to turning points—within classes or within teaching careers; and (e) how to teach the skills for moderating CI. In this paper I describe my own systematic but modest attempts to illuminate these unknowns. First I outline the methods for observing and analyzing CI and some usual kinds and costs of CI. Next I report how types of teachers (new vs. senior faculty) compare in CI experiences. And finally, I portray intervention programs that coach the skills of tempering CI. By the end, I conclude that those of us interested in teaching improvement owe CI more attention.

Direct Studies of CI

With so few clear precedents, I began by observing inductively and theoretically, much as I once did as an ethologist learning the social dynamics of pack rats or grasshopper mice. I had little idea what to expect and I took notes on almost everything until normative behavior patterns and individual differences grew familiar. Here, though, the classes I tracked offered an advantage over the communities of desert rodents I once haunted. Students and faculty proved to be eager reporters and interpreters of CI. After two years of patient observation and discussion, I had derived a working taxonomy of CI and I felt prepared to undertake the more formal study I report here. Still, my work needs corroboration and extension to other campuses and investigators. These reports about intemperance may even need some tempering; the locale for these observations is near enough to New York City so that the incivilities could be near maximum.

Assessment Scheme

Classroom Ratings

These were difficult for me to refine to the point where its components were few enough for reliable rating and rich enough to capture much of the complexity of CI. During the pilot stage, I winnowed the rating system from a larger list by opting for 10 items that proved reliable (with at least 80% agreement between a graduate assistant and me) and valid (by correlating items with the impressions of teachers, students, and independent observers). Table 1 shows the final rating scheme. In after-class interviews with students, I had them rate the day's meeting, using similar rating schemes to those in Table 1 (see Table 4).

Pilot work revealed that upper-level undergraduate courses were too diverse in size, content, and teaching styles to permit the broad, basic generalities I wanted to draw here. So, this study was limited to large (enrollment over 100) survey courses (nominally at freshman and sophomore levels) in easily accessible, centrally located lecture halls. And here, despite my collections of pilot data about CI at several universities, I report on one large, public research campus with about 10,000 undergraduates and 1,500 faculty. I balanced courses for study between sciences, social sciences, and humanities.

I asked permission of teachers to visit their courses. I showed them anonymous examples of what kinds of information I record. I assured them that I would report as much of what I observed about their classes to them as they wanted to hear (but always with a balance, as in my notes, of what they did well and what they might have done differently). And I got their permission to interview a small sample of students from their classes immediately after each observed period ended, in a balanced fashion that would encourage evaluations of what was satisfying and what was bothersome. Over a three-year period, I asked 16 colleagues to let me monitor and assess their classes. All agreed and all persisted in brief weekly conversations with me about my ratings and their experiences with CI for at least one full semester. (And most did all this despite initial feelings that they would have too little interest or time to persist. Some of these stayers are individuals whom colleagues assured me would not cooperate. Said another way, my subject faculty were not exceptionally compliant.)

Table 1
Classroom Rating Form (S = Student, T = Teacher, 10 = optimal level)

A. Notes About Class Prior to and Including Formal Start:

B. Category Rated (1–10)	First Segment	Middle Segment	Final Segment
1. background noise			
2. S attentiveness			
3. S note-taking			
4. T immediacy			
5. T pace			
6. T enthusiasm			
7. room comfort			

C. Counts of:
1. T neg. motivators
2. T CI
3. S CI

D. Notes on Things Done Well:

E. Notes on CI (with parenthetic ratings of inappropriateness):

F. Notes on Things That Could Have Been Done Differently:

Participants and Interviews/Ratings

Eight of the faculty I observed were senior; eight were junior (i.e., in their first three years of teaching). Of each of those groups, I adjudged half (in preliminary scans of potential participants) to be clearly excellent or deficient as teachers compared to their age/experience cohorts. I used student ratings, collegial nominations, and campus awards to help make these distinctions. I ended up selecting only those teachers whose ratings were uniformly high or low in all these dimensions; the decisions were easy. With rare exceptions I visited their courses at least once per week in 12 weeks of the study semesters. Usually, to make my schedule manageable, I attended only the first and last 20 minutes (including the 5-minute periods before sessions formally began and after they ended) of what were typically 80-minute classes. Occasionally, I sampled middle segments of classes or even entire sessions.

I sat near the rear of classes so that I could come and go without disturbing them. And I located myself so that I could see most students while closely observing four of them at note-taking. As I made my own notes and periodic ratings, I identified 2–4 students to interview after class. Here too I tried for balance; roughly half my interviews were with students I judged to be diligent listeners and notetakers and question askers, half with students I saw as casual, indifferent participants. (I cued no one about memberships in subgroups.) I also stopped and interviewed students and teachers who exhibited salient forms of CI that day. Surprisingly few students and faculty denied me these 3–5 minute interactions (only, I believed, because they were rushing elsewhere). I was often told, somewhat jokingly, that my great height and unmistakably professorial mien induced compliance, but I sensed that students and teachers liked to talk about their classroom experiences, at least to someone who would not use the information against them. Those who admitted to CI usually seemed relieved to talk about it and to explain what had happened (often, to ponder ways of avoiding repetitions).

In routine interviews with students after classes, I took notes on their comments and I asked them to rate (on 10-point scales) (a) the worth of the teaching for the day; (b) the interest/immediacy of the teacher; (c) the clarity and organization of the material presented (most concretely, how easily and memorably it could have been put into useful notes); (d and e) the degree to which all students seemed involved in the class session and the extent of their own; and (f and g) the extent/severity of CI and the degree that it hindered or helped their involvement and learning. I prodded for incidents that were perceived as CI and, one by one, asked for the 405 interviewees' reactions to them.

After classes I asked students (half of them diligent and half not) to show me their notes of the day. From these 230 sharings I noted length, content, and apparent thoroughness/understanding. And then I asked students why they had taken notes in the way they had (and how well they understood a central concept from the day's class). Here too students were remarkably cooperative (although surprised; for many, this was the first time anyone other than a peer had looked at their notes); they liked the attention and its implicit caring. On some occasions I photocopied students' notes and then shared them (after ensuring their anonymity) with faculty. (Professors looking at notes taken by their students, particularly poor teachers, were amazed at how different students' perceptions were from what they thought they had presented in class.)

Weekly interviews with faculty usually took place in their offices or by phone (because immediately after classes they were typically occupied with students asking questions). In their 192 regular meetings with me, teachers answered questions and made ratings, much as I depicted above for students. I specifically asked them to recall awkward moments and incivilities in classes that had met a day or two earlier. I also asked and reasked them about their longer-term experiences with CI, particularly about especially salient, difficult incidents. Only with repeated recollections did these teachers/reporters move beyond superficial evaluations of what had happened to more process-oriented accounts (see Boice, 1993a, for a description of this method).

Analysis

I report only descriptive statistics; sample sizes and variabilities made more demanding analyses questionable. I focus on representative frequencies and experiences connected with CI.

General Patterns

Common Perceptions of CI

Much of what I noted as instances of CI confirms the existence of the kinds suggested in the literature. Both students and teachers were annoyed by lateness, early or late stopping, and each other's cutting or canceling. And students were clearly responsive to the kinds of motivators and levels of immediacy that their teachers typically displayed. But on the study campus, these were only part of the picture and evidently not the most crucial—at least at a first glance. The picture grows clearer as I move from general norms to patterns of individual differences and of their correlates.

After listing each category (below), I present three kinds of data parenthetically: (a) the percentage of courses in which the particular kind of CI was noted in at least three class meetings per semester; (b) the mean percentage, in those designated courses, of daily sessions where the CI was noted; and (c) the percentages of those classes overall that produced ratings of intensity/disruptiveness of at least 5 out of 10 in interviewees. That is, the indices depict the commonness (in two ways) and then the intensity of CIs. (Why did I pick the number 3 to indicate a minimal level of CI? The truly exemplary, immediate teachers in the sample had even fewer.) Teachers and students agreed only in ranking only these three kinds of CI as strongly disturbing:

1. Students conversing so loudly that lecturers and student discussants could not be heard throughout a third or more of class meetings (68% of all courses—71% of classes in those courses—88% of incidents rated as significant).
2. Students confronting teachers with sarcastic comments or disapproving groans. A typical example, one that came after teachers finished giving assignments, was the student remark "You're kidding!" . . . accompanied by sneers and the noises of notebooks slamming shut (62%—37%—50%).

3. The presence of one or perhaps two "classroom terrorists" whose unpredictable and highly emotional outbursts (usually as insulting complaints or as intimidating disagreements) made the entire class tense (25%—75%—68%).

After these three common perceptions of CI, students and teachers diverged on the rank ordering and content of other bothersome kinds. For *students*, who perceived half-again as many incidents of CI as did their teachers, the following categories ranked as next most common:

4. Teachers seen as distant, cold, and uncaring, i.e., lacking in immediacy (81% of all courses—60% of classes in those courses—80% of incidents rated highly disturbing).
5. Teachers who surprised them with test items and grades that they had not prepared for or anticipated (43%—19%—88%).
6. Teachers who came 5 min.+ late to class and/or who canceled classes without advance warning (75%—51%—37%).
7. Students who taunted/belittled fellow class members (37%—34%—56%).

Teachers, in contrast, produced these fourth through seventh rankings of CI in their classes:

4. Students who seemed reluctant to participate by answering or asking questions, or reluctant to display interest (87% of all courses—60% of classes in those courses—64% of CI rated high).
5. Students who came to class unprepared (56%—53%—71%).
6. Students who imposed by demanding make-up exams or extended deadlines for projects (68%—21%—72%).
7. Students who arrived late and left early, disruptively (62%—45%—51%).

A preliminary glance at these second-level (but still intrusive) experiences of CI reveals interesting differences and similarities between students and faculty. Examples: Students seemed far less likely than faculty to notice when other students were not participating or being civil in class; both sides particularly disliked classroom terrorists for the pallor they cast over whole semesters. My own class observations using the format in Table 1 produced similarities and differences to the rank orderings just seen:

1. Teachers alienating themselves from students via negative comments and nonimmediate nonverbals (75% of courses—59% of classes in those courses—61% of CI rated high).
2. Teachers distancing themselves from students via fast-paced, noninvolving lectures (81%—55%—58%).
3. Students conversing so loudly that lecturers and discussants could not be clearly heard (62%—80%—69%).
4. Students coming late and leaving early, without apparent attempts to be unobtrusive (62%—50%—71%).
5. Students making sarcastic remarks/gestures (68%—43%—69%).
6. Teachers eliciting student mistrust via surprises on tests and grading (43%—15%—89%).
7. Teachers and students being intimidated, distracted, and demoralized by a classroom terrorist (25%—88%—93%).

Why were my own conclusions different from those of the teachers and students whose classes I analyzed (even though students and I were closely similar in attributing the highest levels of CI to classes of teachers whom I had preselected as deficient in prior semesters)? It was a matter of timing. If I had included my earliest pilot observations, my rank orderings would more closely have resembled those of teachers and students (who at this stage were also inexperienced observers of CI). What became clear with systematic practice at noticing CI is the importance of its patterning over a semester. CI usually gets set in its course on the first few days of classes. Not until teachers' negativities confirm students' skepticism (and exacerbate the playful or exploratory CI of settling in and of testing how teachers will respond) do incivilities become salient and problematic.

Exceptions of sorts occurred in two circumstances. In one, teachers evidently gave off such strong cues of nonimmediacy and low self-esteem that classes quickly, almost imperceptibly, escalated to chronically high and aversive levels of CI. (I observed this pattern in four cases, two of them amongst novice teachers prerated as deficient, two with senior teachers prejudged as deficient.) In another exception, something traumatic happened during the semester that changed the course of student-faculty relationships from what had been established: Students revolted after particularly demanding, surprising exams—and their teacher (senior, deficient) responded in kind. In the third exception, two classes were dominated by student terrorists and the other students blamed the teachers for not handling the problem (one novice-deficient; one novice-exemplar).

Which source of information about CI is most important? All three perspectives on CI seem vital. Not until I presented all three vantages in a follow-up semester, where teachers were looking again at CI as they taught a new round of classes, was there evidence of understanding that translated into reliably changed practices in classrooms. Anon, I mention more about what happens in such interventions, but here I turn to something that faculty apparently needed to appreciate beforehand: knowing what CI is, its generality among other teachers, what prices it exacts, and how students experience it.

Representative Comments About CI from Students

The following excerpts typify what I entered in my general notes after classes:

1. About how teachers seem to alienate and distance themselves from students on the first days of class: (a) "He seemed very smart, very businesslike. I was impressed that he talked so far over our heads. But I got the feeling that he didn't really like students, not ones like me . . . that was pretty much when I gave up on him and decided to lag it." (b) "Who is he kidding? He doesn't want to teach us. He starts by telling us that he won't be talking to us outside class, only his TAs will. He tells us that his lectures won't count on tests. In other words, don't bother me, don't bother to come to class. It pisses me off to think I'm paying for this. . . . If he doesn't care, why should I?" (c) "We just wasted time today. Okay, so it's nice that we had a short class, but I wanted to know what it's going to be about, what the requirements are. Not a good start!" (d) "It's not good when the class begins so confused. I don't think she is going to be able to handle this class; it's going to be too much for her. She lets people insult her. That's dumb." (e) "I'll tell you what turned me off. He's a snob. So he went to school at Harvard. So? If he's so much better than us, what's he doing wasting his time here with us?"
2. About fast-paced lectures: (a) "'Whoa' is what somebody should have said. Impossible to keep up. I just quit trying to take notes." (b) "What a jerk. He doesn't look to see if we can stay with him . . . with his blackboards full of stuff, off in space far, far away." (c) "It's hard to understand what is going on in here. If you catch on to one thing, you're already way behind on the next one."
3. On students conversing during class: (a) "Now this really makes me mad. You couldn't hear a thing that was going on. Almost nothing. I finally lost interest and tried to read something for my next class." (b) "I put the responsibility on him. He's not a good teacher if he doesn't take the effort to be heard." (c) "I don't understand this. Why doesn't she just tell some of those guys to shut up? Who's in charge?" (d) "Why was I talking through most of the class? Because the class is boring and I don't like the professor. Because the lectures don't matter; everything is in the book. I'm only here because they take roll."
4. On students arriving late and leaving early: (a) "All this coming and going, like a train station, makes it hard to concentrate. A stop should be put to it." (b) "Well I am usually late. I guess when I have a prof who doesn't make a big deal about it, I probably do it for sure. He doesn't seem to know who we are."
5. About sarcasm and catcalls in class: (a) "Don't like it. It shows disrespect. It makes the atmosphere unpleasant. . . . It just fits in with the general hubbub here, where everyone

seems to be doing their own thing." (b) "Sure. I jeered at him and I'll probably do it again. I don't like the man. He's a nerd. He doesn't explain things. He disses students who don't catch on right away. Not a nice man." (c) "Somebody has to complain. The assignments are unreal. This course takes more of my time than all the others put together. . . . If I liked him, if I thought all this hard work was worthwhile, I would probably be quiet. But I get agitated, nervous in this class, and I sit there feeling that something has to be done. All I did, you know, was a bit of a groan. Well?"

6. About students being surprised on tests and grades: (a) "No way, man, were we prepared for this test. It was hard, tricky. Some of it wasn't what we talked about in class. Not even [in] the review session [that] her TA did. It is totally unfair." (b) "I studied like mad for this test and I thought I knew it pretty well. I came to every class and worked like mad to get all the notes, even by borrowing other people's notes. I'm used to getting As and Bs. I got a C-. I can't believe it."

7. On the presence of classroom terrorists: (a) "Whew, is it unreal? She, all by herself, is screwing up everything. Everything. She talks all the time. She gets out of control, I think. She attacks anyone else who argues with her. I feel sort of, how can I say it?, frightened by her." (b) "Why isn't something being done about him? I think he's dangerous. He's drunk, I guess; you can smell it. Maybe crazy. And he gets so loud and aggressive. I hate it." (c) "As it is, [the teacher] tries to act like nothing bad is happening. Ridiculous." (d) "Yeah, today, once more I made a fool of myself. I talked way too much; I got too excited. You know, I always hope I won't do these things again. Then the class gets boring because no one asks questions. So before I know it, I'm talking and then arguing. [In response to my question, *What might help you have better self-control in class?*] Well, some teachers tell me, in a nice way, in private, to shut up, or wait my turn, and then I do."

Common kinds of CI as perceived by teachers (again, I categorize these interview data using my own taxonomy, one based on my rank orderings of the most common, bothersome CIs):

1. About how they are perceived by students during the first few classes: (a) "[shrugs] I couldn't really tell you that much. I was nervous and I just wanted to get through it." (b) "Who knows? I mean, there are definitely some in there who don't like me, or the class or whatever. That's probably par with such poor students." (c) "Really, who cares? This isn't what matters. My chairman told me not to pay too much attention to this, just to get through it." (d) "There's an easy thing I learned to make a better impression. Took a while to figure it out. I spend time finding out who they are and why they are in class. I talk about myself and why I like the course. I show them I care and it makes a world of difference."

2. On presenting material at a fast, noninvolving pace: (a) "Was I? Yeah I was, wasn't I? Darn. I know I tend to do it. I try not to. But I guess I do it without being much aware of it." (b) "Suppose so; I didn't really notice. Well, there's a lot to get covered and they've got accept that. We're not in there for a picnic. This is a science course and I have covered all the basics so they will be prepared to take the next courses." (c) "I know I was rushing. I was exhausted at the end . . . couldn't sleep later that day. And the worst thing, I didn't really connect with them. It wasn't at all what I hoped for, what I had imagined in my mind's eye." (d) "You know what I'm noticing, maybe because I'm talking with you about this, is that when I rush, they get more unruly, noisier. Right?"

3. On student noise in class: (a) "Yes, there was lots of noise and disorder, I guess, in the class. It was upsetting, but what can you do? These are not very good students." (b) "I can't say I noticed it much; you may be overreacting." (c) "Let's hope it quiets down soon. I'd just as soon they didn't come to class if they aren't going to listen." (d) "Well there was some of it at first but you notice it isn't always so bad now. I'll tell you why, in my opinion: When the material is stuff I really like, it must be I show more enthusiasm. Then they settle down and take notes."

4. On students coming late and leaving early: (a) "I try not to pay attention to them; I really can't make them do anything they don't want to, including being in college." (b) "I notice it, yes. I don't like it, no. I spoke about it on the first day but without much apparent success. That's how they are here." (c) "There wasn't so much of it, not for this school. The good students are okay." (d) "I know this class is bad and I have had classes with very little of this problem. There are some trouble-makers in this class, you know, and they make the difference." (e) "I started the semester, you saw it, by telling them why it is important to be there on time and what not. I'm nice but firm about it and I don't have much trouble with it."
5. On sarcastic, catcalling students: (a) "Oh that. That's the way kids get raised on Long Island. Disrespect at home, disrespect at school." (b) "To tell you the truth, I haven't mentioned it to anyone before, but it bothers me. [Long pause.] A lot. It hurts me and it makes me feel unfit to be a teacher. Like quitting." (c) "I grew up in the city and so I'm not so shocked. I can live with it and I can give as good as I get." (d) "That can be dealt with, you know. I'm going to win over some of those tough guys with their hats on backwards by getting to know them, just by giving them attention and help."
6. On students being surprised by tests and grades: (a) "Of course—for most of them. I give hard tests but I also provide everything they need to do well. Reviews, homework, you name it. Those who do the work get the good grades." (b) "I was surprised too. They should have done much better, I think. I don't know why they didn't." (c) "Well, yes, I am a hard grader. I'm no panderer and never will be." (d) "I guess I should have given them some practice questions but I got behind and had too much to do."
7. On classroom terrorists: (a) "This is a disaster. I wasn't ready for someone like ____________ and I don't know what to do except to write off the whole semester. I think, I hope, that the rest of the students understand it is out of my control." (b) "What a bad dream! This has now happened several times to me; I had one in my first class too. This is what makes me want to get out of teaching." (c) "What can be done about someone like this, an insane person? I could use some help with this." (d) "Well I shudder at this sort of thing but I'm trying to put out the fire. He and I are meeting, here in my office, to talk things over and I think, based on past experience, that it will help. [*How did you learn this approach?*] That's a good question. I imagine I just learned it on my own. I've never heard these things discussed. They should be."

Interim Summary

In these general patterns, then, differences in student and faculty perceptions of CI were predictable. Students usually saw teachers as the main culprits, and vice versa. But that conceptualization oversimplifies CI and makes it seem inevitable and hopeless. It casts teachers and students as natural adversaries. Throughout the study, I couldn't miss noticing that some teachers (almost always those picked for having been good teachers beforehand) were less affected by and less often involved in CI (even with many of the students present whom I had seen exhibiting CI with other professors). When I finally analyzed the data by subtypes and patterns, I felt reassured about prospects of depicting only some teachers in a negative way, as unskilled individuals who need help in managing CI.

Specific Patterns

Here, then, I sort out those individuals who suffered most and least from CI. I look more carefully at the roles of timing and experience in CI. I highlight some uncommon experiences (and common but generally unnoticed incidents) tied to incivility that devastate teachers. And here, at last, I get to mention how my other observations of classroom teaching relate to CI.

New Faculty Versus Senior Faculty as Teachers

Curiously, novice teachers were no more likely to have classes with markedly high levels of C (i.e., in the top quartile of all classes so rated). Still, they (particularly amongst those pregrouped as deficients) more often encountered it, typically for entire semesters at chronic but moderate, disheartening levels. Senior faculty evidenced a more bimodal pattern; as a rule, they either had very little CI or lots of it in their classes (overall, in accord with their predesignations as good or poor teachers). It seemed to me that senior teachers had settled into habits of liking teaching, of treating students with general enthusiasm, fondness, and immediacy—or not.

Some new faculty, though, fell into similar patterns with surprising swiftness; those who treated their undergraduates with disdain and distance approached the worst levels seen in their poorest counterparts with extensive experience. But what kept disdainful, defensive newcomers from exposure to as much CI? Students themselves suggested an answer. They could usually spot novice teachers and they felt inclined to go easier on them (e.g., "He's new. He doesn't know better. Maybe he needs some time").

There is also a telling variation in these data that casts experience into a stronger role than I first had. Senior teachers displayed more kinds of positive motivators (e.g., ways of coaching students to make better answers in class) and more depth of skill at expressing immediacies (e.g., ease at walking about the classroom and making eye contact with a variety of students). Evidently, complex skills such as composing, writing, and teaching require some 10 years of regular, deliberate practice before true expertise is achieved (Ericsson and Charness, 1994). Only a lucky few of us ordinarily get the supports, coaching, and rewards that sustain such extensive practice (Simonton, 1994).

While the dimension of inexperience-experience mattered, it was overshadowed by the two factors predicted by Plax and Kearney (1992). What influenced CI more, evidently, were kinds of motivators used and degrees of immediacy displayed. Table 2 helps make the point by arraying my two indices of motivator valences and of immediacy against teachers partitioned by CI levels.

These data help buttress the other indications that teachers' incivilities weighed heavily in CI. Moreover, Table 2 reaffirms the observation that experience alone does not suffice to lessen CI. Indeed, some teachers may grow more adversarial and uncivil to their students (who respond in kind).

There is an important exception to this pattern, one that occurred in survey classes whose students were mostly nonmajors enrolled to meet graduation requirements. Where the teachers of these captive audiences tailored their teaching to cover problem solving and listing in lock-step ways that clearly prepared students for tests, classes were only moderately inclined to CI. Where one teacher tried to infuse these classes with more conceptual material and attempts to teach critical thinking, students became generally uncivil (even with moderately high degrees of teaching immediacy present). What we usually consider the best approaches to teaching are not always the best moderators of CI. But, and this is important, most are in my experience.

The data in Table 2 leave a neighboring question unanswered. What role do students play in these results? The best answer may rely on analyses of how CI develops over the course of semesters.

Table 2
Relationship Between Ratings of Motivation/Immediacy and CI

Group (and Level of CI)	My Ratings of: % of Motivators Used Positively	$\bar{X}$ Level of Immediacy
New Faculty (best quartile)	81	6.2
New faculty (worst quartile)	56	3.7
Senior Faculty (best quartile)	93	7.6
Senior Faculty (worst quartile)	42	3.2

How Timing Affects CI

Consider how classes in the study began. To an impressive extent, students started semesters with reserve, respect, and optimism; they were sometimes unruly (often because they were greeting friends and testing limits in playful ways). On first days of class, they showed generally moderate to low levels of CI. Even in the required, nonmajor classes I mentioned above (and in one especially threatening statistics course), students waited for teachers to make the first move. Where the first days of class were marked by conspicuously positive motivators and strong immediacies, CI dropped off to at least moderately low levels and generally stayed there. Early periods in courses may have been the crucial turning point for CI. Table 3 shows how clearly good starts related to CI.

There were also, in most courses I observed, other potential turning points in semesters. Students seemed primed to exhibit CI before and after first and second exams (especially big tests such as midterms), and near deadlines for major projects. When teachers helped prepare students for tests and projects with approximations (e.g., practice tests; preliminary deadlines for preliminary versions of projects), reactions were subdued or more optimistic. One other series of events proved pivotal: Where students got to talk with faculty outside class in friendly, egalitarian fashion, CI levels were lower. Students were candid in explaining why: "When you get to know him, he's a pretty nice guy. Not so intimidating after all. . . . That was when I realized that he cares about students, that he wants me to do well in the course. No, now I wouldn't dream of giving him a hard time."

A Single-Case History of a Class Over the Semester

Another way of appreciating the patterning of CI may be seen in synopses of courses. I depict the following case because its teacher was a veteran member of the faculty, a renowned scientist, but a novice at teaching large, core courses. (Prior he had been considered an excellent teacher for advanced majors; he was pregrouped here among exemplars.) What follows are a few excerpts from that semester [I denote incidents I rated as CI in brackets (and rating levels in parentheses); higher ratings indicate *more* favorable conditions]:

> Class 1: First 10 min. after formal start (with friendly greeting), room is full, Ss quiet. T makes efforts to answer S questions but misses many hands [CI]; his pacing and patience are good (ratings = 6,7) but he isn't cueing Ss when to take notes. When he presents problems (that he claims are easy) on the board, Ss near me are clearly confused and get the wrong answers. . . . T doesn't notice, assumes everyone gets it [CI]. Class ends with moderate background noise (5), much of it due to students' confusion.
>
> Class 2: T is more hurried (pace = 4), less immediate (4) today; writes more on board . . . and

Table 3
Patterns of CI During Semesters for Subgroups of Courses with Good or Subpar Starts ($N = 4$ per Subgroup)*

	Time of Rating (and $\bar{X}$ Counts of Salient CI per Class)					
Course	(My Focus)	Day 1	Day 2	Day 3	Fifteenth Mtg	Last Mtg
New Fac.	T	3.0	3.5	3.8	4.3	3.3
(Good start)	S	4.3	2.0	3.3	1.8	2.3
New Fac.	T	5.8	5.5	8.3	4.0	8.3
(Subpar)	S	3.9	9.5	10.5	10.3	11.3
Senior Fac.	T	1.5	1.3	0.8	0.5	1.3
(Good start)	S	3.5	2.0	2.0	0.5	2.5
Senior Fac.	T	5.2	6.8	9.0	6.3	8.8
(Subpar)	S	8.0	17.0	17.8	12.3	16.0

*My ratings of teachers (T) and of students (S) appear in alternate rows.

twice misses clusters of raised hands [2CI]. Background noise goes from 7 to 3 [i.e., it gets worse] within 15 min.; note-taking from 4 to 2.

Class 3: Begins with exam information and Ss listen quietly (noise rating = 9); next, T stresses need to proceed quickly, without being able to cover everything completely. He then rushes (pace = 3) with mannerisms that clearly discourage questions ("Can you hold off on that question?" [CI]. His immediacy ratings drop (7 to 4) despite his continuing enthusiasm; noise goes from 8 to 3; the room is now so noisy that students in back cannot hear T [CI].

Class 5: S attendance down markedly for first time, from a start of about 120 (Day 1) to about 50 today. Students are generally attentive only to demonstrations (6), but take few notes on them (3).

Class 10: Attendance down to 22; most Ss noisy (4) but otherwise passive (involvement rating = 3). Pacing of T increases as noise level goes up (or is it the other way round?).

Class 15: *N* = 30; 5 leave, noisily, after writing down assignments [CI]. I interview all early leavers; all claim they are busy and have things to do (e.g., renew driver's license), that they work better on their own. In class, no takers when T poses question and waits for answer [CI]; when he then writes on the board material that he says is critical, about half of Ss take notes on it (5). After class, Ss angry about confusion they experience; in later interview with T, he attributes the anger to the cumulative nature of the course ("They didn't learn the early material, so they are lost now").

Class 18: Attendance = 15; Ss start fairly quiet (6), but inattentive (3). Four Ss leave and return, loudly, with lunches [CI]. Even when he tells Ss that one of the three problems he is solving on the board will be on the test, only about half of Ss take notes on them. Non-note-takers sit slumped, with feet up on top of chairs in front of them, talking loudly [CI].

Class 22: T asks Ss to stay after and ask questions; no one does.

Class 25: T describes new, interactive format for getting Ss to answer his questions (while he does so, not one S smiles or nods); only one question elicited, a rude and cynical remark [CI].

Class 27: Nine Ss eating lunch loudly [CI]; T now seems not to notice when noise grows past point where he cannot be heard by Ss in back half of class (rating = 3) [CI].

Class 29: *N* = 25 attendance. Ss who come 10 to 15 minutes late (N = 6 today) now take extended time getting settled in (e.g., noisily rifling through packs/purses) [CI]; some chatting at full volume with friends as they walk in [CI]. T now using several negative motivators per class (e.g., Calmly: "Haven't you read the syllabus?"). Four Ss sit through class with Walkmans on [CI]; one S shouts complaint while leaving at 20-minute mark ("You've lost us!") [CI].

Final Class: *N* = 28; many students here today I haven't seen since first few classes. They are insolent (e.g., shoes off, feet way up, bodies slumped way down, negative facial cues) [CI]. Despite maintaining a generally high level of enthusiasm through class (8 down to S), T shows first signs of being ruffled (head down, no eye contact; immediacy = 3 by end of class), of anger toward some especially unruly Ss [CI for T; CI for Ss]. His attempts to lecture today constantly interrupted by demands for clarification about the final exam, one of them rude [CI]. Almost all Ss leave class abruptly at end, in midst of T's final attempt to wish them success [CI].

Uncommonly Traumatic Kinds of CI

Some of the most upsetting incidents were the least visible, the least likely to be admitted by teachers in ordinary circumstances. Usually these CIs were embarrassing and indelibly hurtful. Faculty were disconcerted by students' personal comments on formal evaluations at ends of semesters (e.g., "she dresses badly"), even when the great majority of their students' comments were positive. They often found it hard not to key in on students who displayed especial disdain and disapproval in class ("Did you notice him? He just sits there, arms folded, glaring at me, shaking his head in disapproval"). But most devastating were incidents where students went to departmental chairpeople to complain about a teacher—and where faculty perceived that chairs assumed them guilty until proven otherwise. In my experience, all three of these problems can be moderated by more humane practices. Student evaluations can be screened by a neutral third party to exclude or edit personally hurtful, nonconstructive comments. Newcomers can be coached to realize that even the best teachers do not please everyone (or want to). Chairs can handle students' complaints by asking students to first discuss concerns with professors, then by approaching colleagues in ways that do not put them on the defensive (e.g., "Can you help me think what we could do to make this student happier in our classes, less likely to complain to me?").

Another incident that demoralized teachers in two cases here was student cheating; in both cases apparent culprits acted defensively and angrily. The tension produced in such confrontations seemed to distract these professors from their work and exacerbate their health problems. One teacher who handled a similar problem in a way that apparently limited incivility bears mentioning: He put some of the responsibility on his students to solve the dilemma (his report to me of a private conversation: "Look, I need your help with this uncomfortable situation. The two of you turned in papers that seem very much alike. How can we figure out what happened and what to do?").

How CI Relates to Other Behaviors of Teachers

Tables 4 and 5 suggest that the general indices of teaching prowess used here over semesters were negatively related to levels of CI. Students' ratings of classroom experiences (Table 4) show all the expected relationships: How students related the worth of the teaching just experienced, its clarity and organization, its pacing, the overall involvement of the class members in what was going on, and their own involvement—all these estimates were generally lower as noted incidents of CI increased. And, in classes with the highest, most chronic levels of student-noted CI, students' ratings of the effects of incivilities were also highest. So, in these constantly disrupted and distracting classrooms where students often appeared to be more detached and indifferent than in other courses, CI continued to be noticed and disliked. If habituation occurred, it was largely limited to external reactions. In courses with high levels of CI, even where attendance was required, students most often cut classes or left early.

Table 5, based on my own classroom ratings, adds to this picture of how CI relates to teaching styles and environmental conditions. Background noise levels were, not surprisingly, highest in classes with high course ratings of CI. In the worst examples, teachers were upstaged by a constant buzz of conversations, paper shufflings, openings of food and drink containers, fidgets, and coughs. (Francis Galton, the pioneer of psychology, would have been pleased at corroboration of his results of measuring boredom in lecture and concert halls over a century ago.)

Student attentiveness followed much the same pattern (Table 5). While a minority (usually about 10–20%) of students remained obviously involved in the courses with high CI, their peers typically did not attend to the teacher or to classroom discussions with the teacher. Instead, about a third of the remainder usually sat passively, sometimes listening, sometimes closing their eyes and drowsing, sometimes looking around the room. Another third usually read or wrote for other classes, put on makeup, or ate. The final, most salient third spent most class periods conversing, greeting latecomers, even moving

Table 4
Students' Ratings (10 = maximum) of Classes Juxtaposed Against CI Counts

CI Level for Class (My Rating)	Rating Item					
	Worth of T	Pace	Clarity/Org.	Class Involv.	Personal Involv.	CI Effect
Worst quartile	3.3	2.5	3.8	4.3	4.3	7.5
2nd quartile	3.0	3.3	4.5	4.0	4.8	5.8
3rd quartile	5.5	6.2	5.0	6.2	5.3	3.9
Best quartile	7.0	6.0	8.3	7.8	8.0	2.3

Table 5
My Own Overall Ratings of Courses in Terms of CI Level Compared to My $\bar{X}$ In-Class Ratings of Classroom Conditions (where 10 = optimal and where 1 = unacceptable)

Level of CI for Class	Rating Item					
	Noise	S Attentiveness	Note-Taking	T Enthus.	T Pace	Room Comfort
Worst quartile	2.2	3.8	1.8	3.0	2.6	5.2
2nd quartile	4.5	3.2	1.5	3.1	3.0	4.8
3rd quartile	5.6	6.0	3.1	6.4	7.2	4.8
Best quartile	9.1	7.3	4.5	7.1	7.6	5.6

around the room to engage new conversations.

Note-taking was not a regular activity of most of the students in these classes, even where CI was low and involvement high (Table 5). These undergraduates, if they took notes at all, typically entered only a few lines at the beginning of classes (e.g., announcements, assignments) and some of the salient points or diagrams or equations put on the board. That is, notes for the day usually comprised about a half-page in the notebooks of 50% of the students, regardless of classroom climate. (Still I only twice saw students with nothing on which to take notes.) Better note-takers (overall about a quarter of the students I observed) usually entered two or three pages of writing and diagrams, but often with little explication beyond lists, definitions, and graphics that were proffered with emphasis in class. The best note-takers typically produced 3–5 pages in their notebooks per class. They were unique in several ways: in noting explanations and examples; in adding their own questions and reminders about what they were processing; in politely trying to interrupt professors for explanations.

How did other, more normal students in these large survey courses explain their general lassitude? Their answers often amazed me (and too, the teachers with whom I shared them; such occasions reminded us that we had never before gotten to know introductory students well, except perhaps for outstanding performers). In high CI courses, normal students usually explained their uninvolvement in terms of retribution (e.g., "I'm not going to do anything for him" [speaking of his teacher]). When pressed for more explanation, these same students generally made excuses about not needing to pay attention in class (e.g., "Everything is in the book" [a belief that often proved demonstrably untrue in tests]; "I'll figure it out later" [also unverified, as a rule, in my informal checks]). To a lesser extent students offered the same attributions for noninvolvement in low CI classes. What made their answers different was their additional claim that by listening instead of taking notes, they comprehended more of what was presented in class [this assumption proved untrue in all but a few students when I then asked them for explanations of key concepts from the day's class, particularly after a few days' delay]. In high CI classes, again, students made even fewer notes and offered even fewer excuses for not doing so.

Teachers' levels of enthusiasm (Table 5)—that traditional index of good practice—also accorded with the pattern of what I deemed successful behaviors. But in everyday occurrence, it seemed more a by-product of immediacy, where students repaid warmth with enthusiasm, than of a traitlike quality of teachers that showed itself regardless.

The same can be said for pacing (Table 5). Fast pacing was clearly incompatible with the signs of involvement I have been calling immediacy; teachers who took the trouble to establish eye contact, to listen and encourage, to move about while looking for comprehension, necessarily proceeded more slowly than did counterparts talking and/or writing nonstop on the board. What was more interesting was what had presumably happened to the pacing of some teachers with experience. The best senior teachers were nearly unique at displaying rhythms in their gaits, usually sauntering but sometimes galloping with excitement. In may ways their styles resembled those of successful therapists mentioned earlier, whose strengths included a "focused voice."

Room conditions (Table 5) proved an enigma to me. I went into these observations that CI would vary in obvious ways with poor classroom conditions such as overheated, stuffy rooms and dim lighting. It did not, except in one short-lived condition: Where classes began as overcrowded, with more students enrolled than seats, with many students clamoring to "add" an already filled class, chaos marked the day. And with it (at least until the problem was resolved) came CI. But this kind of CI was different from most that I saw; it was usually not personally directed at the teacher. Still, it was disconcerting and it seemed to contribute to bad starts that endured in three junior faculty I observed.

Uncommonly Considered Origins

Here I refer to origins of CI outside classrooms, CI factors about which we still have much to learn. These are possibilities: One was a sense communicated by central administrators that they cared little about classroom conditions ("You know those people in administration just tell them [students] to just go ahead and burst into my class, even though they know it's overenrolled. The students they send over are already agitated and angry. They [administrators] care about maximizing enrollments but not about us. . . . The classes get unruly because of them, and I find myself caring less and less about teaching"). The second was the behavior of faculty toward students elsewhere. Because I found the most reliable access to faculty during their posted office hours, I noticed which individuals treated student visitors with immediacy. My distinct impression was that low levels of immediacy in offices was associated with high CI in classrooms. And, third, only some of the teachers, those who fared best on most ratings, had taken immediacy/involvement to the next level, of enlisting students from classes as actual collaborators (in presenting classroom materials; in helping with research outside class). Teachers who scored lowest on immediacy and highest on CI, in contrast, supposed that such collaborations were impositions on students.

Situations Where CI Is Tolerable, Perhaps Even Helpful

Earlier I suggested that CI might serve useful functions under the right conditions. In my own observations, the reality proved somewhat at odds with what I had expected. The better-rated, more immediate teachers simply perceived occasional, moderate incidents (of what could have been CI) differently than did other teachers. If exemplary teachers noticed these disruptions as incivilities, they did not let on. Instead, they usually treated them respectfully, by listening carefully, as though they had been offered up as well-intentioned comments or cues. These are typical excerpts from my notes of such interactions:

> S in row 5 emits loud "uugh" and sinks in his chair. T: "Oh no [laughs gently], I've worn you down, worn you out with all this. I do that sometimes. So thanks for alerting me. What do you think? Would it help if I stop and go through it again with you?"
>
> S____________ abruptly interrupts: challenges point T just made: "I *know* that's wrong . . . " T listens cheerfully. Says: "Well, you might be right about that. I can always stand to be corrected; I can survive that. Can you come by my office and we'll share resources?"
>
> T: "I'm seeing some big yawns and abandoned note-taking. I'm sorry. I'm losing you. Let's all stand and stretch for a minute and then we'll backtrack a bit."

So these excerpts show how teachers maintain immediacy (and its kin, optimism) through what could have been CI (but were not generally rated so by teachers or students). And they hint at how CI, in moderation, can help improve classes. Socially skilled, positive responses by teachers to student frustration help calm classrooms. They reengage students who had been distancing themselves from the class. And, according to teachers who tolerate and use them best, such distractions can, if treated imaginatively and optimistically, provide breaks in the action, even helpful cues for redirection or changed pacing.

How Early Experiences with CI Affected Teachers' Styles and Attitudes

This study provides glimpses of what probably were turning points in some new faculty's teaching careers. Each of the four new faculty here who taught amid CI described the experience as traumatic and disillusioning. Consider this representative comment [after an unruly first day of a class]: "This is what I'll be doing for a living? I hope I prove better at publishing. . . . Can I imagine solutions? Sure. I'll concentrate on my graduate teaching. I'll write grants to get time off from teaching."

Other observations incline me to think that these initial reactions are lasting. Senior teachers faring badly here recalled early experiences and decisions similar to the one just excerpted. (And the most successful did not.) In related studies, where I tracked new faculty longer, these traumatic events and resulting impressions of undergraduates as adversaries were among the few early turning points that derailed careers (Boice, 1993a). The faculty at midcareer who display the most depression and oppositionalism seem to suffer most from long-standing patterns of student disapproval (even in departments where only research, not teaching, is overtly rewarded—Boice, 1986, 1993b).

In my notes from two decades of offering workshops on teaching for junior faculty, the same basic problem has seemed dominant. The most urgent, common questions from novices are about classroom management, especially about maintaining classroom control, dignity, and student involvement. New teachers first want help with unruly students who disrupt, demand extra effort, cheat, and make teaching miserable. Curiously, this is not the focus of most published advice for newcomers.

A Trial Program to Ameliorate Teachers' Contributions to CI

Merely observing and eliciting comments about teachers' exposure to CI is an intervention. When these participants asked me, inevitably, about how often CI happened to their colleagues, my answers relieved them. Many had imagined their own experiences as unique ("You never hear such things mentioned"). When I brought up incidents that they had not noticed, they tried harder to notice and understand CI. And when, eventually, they inquired about what colleagues did to cope with CI, they typically tried emulating the strategies I summarized. This did not produce generally impressive outcomes during these same semesters; entrenched patterns of CI in such large classes are not easily turned around. Most teachers experiencing high CI wanted to bring it under control almost immediately, and when attempts went badly, they resumed old styles. Still, all of these teachers expressed an interest in trying new strategies in future semesters.

In the formal intervention phase, I again observed, noted, and interviewed weekly. But this time I actively coached faculty with repeated reminders, before and after classes, about the general patterns of actions/attitudes that distinguished low CI teachers. And, to make this difficult transition more realistic, I concentrated my measurements and feedback on what I assumed was the most crucial and practical category: immediacy. Its specifics included (a) arriving at classes early, for informal chats with students coming in the door and after they had taken seats around the room; (b) deliberate practice at presenting parts of classes with active focus/moderate pacing, forward leans and open body postures, smiling and direct eye contact, walking about while lecturing/listening; (c) salient reminders in class notes of times to pause, slow, and check student note-taking for involvement/comprehension; and (d) taking care, in meetings with students after class and in office hours, to listen patiently and reflectively while avoiding signs of impatience (e.g., reading materials on one's desk while students talked).

Six of the ten teachers I invited as participants stayed throughout the intervention program (the other four concluded that immediacy was a dishonest expression of their personalities). All six showed reliably observable gains of about 30-50% in my measures of immediacy (with no apparent differences between four novices and two seniors who had fared badly in the prior semester). And all six evidenced far lower levels of CI than before (three in nearly identical courses; three in less demanding survey courses). So my data about the modifiability of CI in teachers and their classes are only suggestive but promising.

Conclusions

Overall, CI was more common than uncommon; it occurred in significant ways (i.e., disruptively in at least three class meetings during a semester) in over two-thirds of the courses I tracked. Of those large survey courses, about half showed chronic, disheartening patterns of CI. In the high CI courses, both students and faculty usually reported annoyance and demoralization. But whatever the setting, faculty (even novices who had little time to habituate to CI) noticed far less of it than did their students. And faculty took less personal responsibility for CI.

Faculty Awareness of CI

The faculty with the keenest appreciation of CI's nature and liabilities were, ironically, least likely to experience it. They were the teachers of the four classes I observed where CI was virtually absent (and where other indices of teaching such as enthusiasm, pacing, and organization rated highest). Why did other faculty often overlook CI? As a rule, their attitude was reminiscent of physicians' putative reaction to resistant patients: What the teacher offers is undoubtedly valuable, and when students frustrate the teacher the loss is only theirs. Indeed, high CI professors often acted like specialized kinds of doctors, psychoanalysts who imagined that student resistance proved the meaningful difficulty of the material under discussion. In their defense, though, these professors typically knew no better. No one talks or writes much about the nature of CI or its preventives; most novice teachers I have tracked through first days of classes were simply puzzled by the ruckus in their classes. (A typical comment: "These students are certainly not the kind of student I was.") The solution that occurs to most faculty in this situation seems unacceptable. They imagine that students can be won over only with pandering—easy assignments/tests and entertainment in place of serious classroom material. In the usual vicious cycle that follows, faculty often find ways to confirm this misbelief. When they alternate distant, demanding styles with periodic bouts of lowered standards (e.g., "Okay, I'll drop your lowest test score"), students quiet, but only temporarily.

Costs of CI

Another finding here is that CI matters deeply. The differences between classrooms with a lot and those without it were dramatic. With persistent CI, students grew more and more uninvolved, oppositional, combative. Their teachers found their own seemingly innocent remarks and gestures (often emitted without their conscious awareness) escalating into adversarial interactions with students. Even when the CI was largely limited to a single, disruptive individual (what faculty and students often call a classroom terrorist), teachers were surprised to discover the increased difficulty of teaching . . . and that the other students held them responsible for not squelching the terror. Among new faculty I have tracked closely, experiences of unmanaged and unsettling CI constitute a turning point that can ruin professorial careers (Boice, 1993a). Why? New faculty tend to spend most of their time preparing for teaching (even in research universities), and when they fail at teaching, they lose the self-efficacy they need to meet challenges of research/scholarship and collegiality/professional networking. Promising newcomers overwhelmed by CI, especially women, too often decide to abandon professorial careers (or worse yet, resign themselves to lifetimes of marginal performance and rewards for the sake of job security). The irony is that observers from a distance imagine that pressures to publish are the only villains.

Faculty Role in CI

The most important point in this study is the one usually overlooked. Clearly, teachers were the most crucial initiators of CI. And, as a rule, their most telling provocations occurred during the first few days of courses. Conversely, professors who most consistently displayed immediacies and positive motivators were least involved in incidents of CI, their own or their students'. In the intervention project I report here, teachers practicing a simple regimen of immediacies showed clear improvements in the CI levels of their classes. These data are not yet conclusive but they suggest the worth of pursuing the usually taboo topic of CI more openly and caringly.

How General Are These Findings?

When I made similar observations at large, public universities more distant from large cities like New York, I generally saw somewhat less CI (but still at levels that were often problematic). The exception came at comprehensive campuses where classes were small ($N = 30$ or less) and teachers were openly interested in teaching (e.g., Appalachian State University). Unfortunately, it is this type of institution that seems to have little generality in terms of CI. At another campus with only moderate CI (California State University at Long Beach), I was able to ferret out the suggestion of another crucial factor. Where new faculty resembled students in terms of SES and educational background (particularly when faculty were graduates of the same campus), they established easier rapport and acceptance with classes. Long Beach's strength in teaching seemed to lie in the commonness of this match. The study campus of this article may be the polar opposite; many of its faculty are from private school, Ivy League backgrounds. Still, few of these faculty, except for some senior-level types, expressed openly negative attitudes toward teaching and students. Instead, they seemed to work as hard and long as their counterparts at other campuses I have studied. Their notes were as well crafted, their lectures were as well organized (in my view, at least), and they seemed to care as much about student approval. What they seemed to lack was mostly the immediacy that could have made their classrooms more rewarding, less uncivil. The same diagnosis we usually make for students who act barbarically could be applied to teachers: "Mediocrity is an intellectual impairment" (Bartlett, 1993, p. 308).

What Will Make CI Difficult to Change?

We know some of the answers. First, CI is rarely mentioned in higher education. Second, CI has enormous momentum, growing from the roots upward, that is already out of control in many K-12 settings. At every campus I observe, senior faculty spontaneously talk about the rise of student incivility over the past two decades. Third, attempts to study CI may be seen as threats to the autonomy of faculty who have always been expected to figure their own styles as teachers, in jealously guarded privacy. At the least, investigations about CI will bring discomforts.

What about CI could be easily changed (given the right timing and supports)? In a way, as we have seen, solutions for CI are easy. Preventives and correctives evidently rely on little more than simple training in social skills such as eye contact and other signals of warmth and approachability. The problem, though, is that we, those of us concerned with teaching improvement, would have to work much harder. Usual palliatives such as books of advice and visits to the office of faculty developers will not suffice, so far as I can see. The reason is that much of CI, especially its initiating incidents, goes unnoticed and unsuspected. Someone accustomed to seeing it (and to noting its occurrence diplomatically and supportively) must be present in the classroom for a while.

How Much CI Is Desirable?

If we agree that CI merits more study (and even that intervention is acceptable), the question remains about how much CI is optimal and tolerable. We might better ask the question this way, in two parts: When and how should we choose to turn CI into positive communicators and motivators (as did the exemplars we saw earlier)? And when should we set clear limits on its expression? The second question is no small matter. When students act in racist, sexist, and other exploitive and aggressive ways, teachers must know how to stop the disruption in its tracks. What helps? On most of our campuses, we are already doing some of the right things: seminars for faculty and students about the nature and costs of harassment; growing pressures for teachers to begin courses with clear explanations of what behaviors are unacceptable (sometimes even referring to teacher behaviors); and setting up easier ways to report these forms of CI. One other thing may help limit intolerable CI: Classrooms with generally low levels of CI overall had no terrorists. In this study, the student members of such courses not only scored low on dimensions like indifference and inattention, but gave high ratings of teachers' use of positive motivators and immediacies. Courses with high immediacy and low CI, so far as I can tell, somehow discourage serious incidents of incivility and terrorism. One student I had seen terrorize another course suggested reasons why he did not in a course with low levels of CI: "Everyone likes her and she cares about the students; you don't get so antsy in here."

Relating CI to Research and Theory in Higher Education

Consider this brief sampling of ready connections between the seemingly distant problem of CI and our own customary inquiries in the literature. Higher educators already know that students learn by becoming involved, especially in scholarly conversations with professors (e.g., Pascarella and Terenzini, 1991). Tinto (1975) makes a similar point: Students become integrated into campuses (and, so, thrive until graduation) to the extent that they can share normative attitudes and values of peers. Negative interactions reduce student integration, perhaps even with teachers. In my own studies, new faculty who failed to integrate with students (i.e., by not holding some similar attitudes and values) evidenced poor expectations and outcome as teachers.

Higher educators also know what helps contribute to immediacy: Cohen's (1981) taxonomy of crucial teaching dimensions includes rapport (e.g., accessibility, empathy, and friendliness). Wilson, Gaff, Dienst, Wood, and Bavry (1975) are among the many researchers to demonstrate that effective teachers not only use effective examples and analogies but communicate clear accessibility to students in and out of class. Overall, this literature makes involvement sound much like immediacy: The more students are involved in "learning activities" including note-taking, discussions, and questioning, the greater the content acquisition (Johnson and Butts, 1983).

There is, then, a shared theme in the immediacy that moderates CI and in involvement theory. Pace's (1984) and Astin's (1984) pioneering notions of involvement in higher education help explain the general patterns of CI seen in this study. The involvement that predicts student success requires high-quality student efforts including a great amount of physical and psychological energy devoted to the academic experience. Student involvement, by definition, seems to be incompatible with CI and its fundamental quality of sullen passivity. There are many other suggestions of similarity between involvement and immediacy. Willis (1993), for instance, analyzed Astin's forms of student involvement and concluded they are a mixture of affective experience, learning outcomes, and classroom interaction. Higher education researchers even specify roles that teachers can play in maximizing student involvement. Perry, Hechter, Menec, and Weinberg (1993), for instance, propose attributional retraining as a way of enhancing students' motivation and achievement by changing how students think about their successes and failures. Good teachers already use forms of attributional retraining, however inadvertently, when they earn the trust and optimism of students who would otherwise experience distancing and helplessness in classes.

What, then, can an awareness of immediacy's role in CI add to already well-established conceptualizations of involvement? Teacher behaviors of warmth and approachability, because they are central to immediacy, must also be crucial to student involvement. In usual studies of involvement, as in traditional looks at CI, we may attribute too large a role to students, too small a part to teachers. (Without classroom immediacies of teachers, how can most students manage involvement in learning?) If, finally, we can see CI as a mere problem of uninvolvement, perhaps we can more easily move past our longstanding reservations about facing up to this embarrassing but important topic.

References

Amada, G. (1992). Coping with the disruptive college student. A practical model. *Journal of American College Health* 40: 203–215.

Appleby, D. C. (1990). Faculty and student perceptions of irritating behaviors in the college classroom. *Journal of Staff, Program, & Organization Development*, Spring: 41–46.

Associated Press (1994). Becoming American, bad habits and all. *New York Times*, February 23: B7.

Astin, A. W. (1984). Student involvement: A development theory for higher education. *Journal of College Student Personnel* 40: 288–305.

Bandura, A. (1986). *Social Foundations of Thought and Action.* Englewood Cliffs, NJ: Prentice-Hall.

Baringer, F. (1993). School hallways as gantlets of sexual taunts. *New York Times*, June 2: B7.

Bartlett, S. J. (1993). Barbarians at the door. *Modern Age*, Summer: 296–311.

Boice, R. (1986). Faculty development via field programs for middle-aged, disillusioned faculty. *Research in Higher Education* 25: 115–135.

Boice, R. (1993a). New faculty involvement for women and minorities. *Research in Higher Education* 34: 291–341.

Boice, R. (1993b). Primal origins and later correctives for midcareer disillusionment. *New Directions in Teaching and Learning* 55:33–41.

Bornstein, R. W., and Kennedy, T. D. (1994). Interpersonal dependency and academic performance. *Journal of Personality Disorder* 8: 240–248.

Bowen, D. D., Seltzer, J., and Wilson, J. A. (1987). Dealing with emotions in the classroom. *The Organizational Behavior Teaching Review* 7(20): 1–14.

BQ (1990). Suggestions for responding to disruptive classroom behavior. *The Campus Chronicle*, April 27: 3–4.

Cohen, P. (1981). Student ratings of instruction and student achievement: A meta-analysis of multisection validity studies. *Review of Educational Research* 51: 281–309.

Coles, R. (1993). When volunteers are sorely tested. *Chronicle of Higher Education* 39(35):A52.

DeJonge, P. (1993). Talking trash. *New York Times Magazine*, June 6: 30–38.

Didner, J. (1992). Survey reveals high level of academic fraud. *Stony Brook Statesman*, February 10: 3.

Ericsson, K. A., and Charness, N. (1994). Expert performance: Its structure and acquisition. *American Psychologist* 49: 725–747.

Fogarty, J. L., Wang, M. C., and Creek, R. (1983). A descriptive study of experienced and novice teachers' interactive thoughts and actions. *Journal of Educational Research* 77: 22–32.

Fremont, S. K., and Anderson, W. (1988). Investigation of factors involved in therapists' annoyance with clients. *Professional Psychology: Research and Practice* 19: 330–335.

Goleman, D. (1993). Schools try to tame violent pupils one punch and taunt at a time. *New York Times*, August 19: B11.

Henry, W. A. (1994). *In Defense of Elitism*. New York: Doubleday.

Hill, C. E., and Corbett, M. M. (1993). A perspective on the history of process and outcome research in counseling psychology. *Journal of Counseling Psychology* 40: 3–24.

Johnson, R., and Butts, D. (1983). The relationships among college science student achievement, engaged time, and personal characteristics. *Journal of Research in Science Teaching* 20: 357–366.

Kearney, P., and Plax, T. G. (1992). Student resistance to control. In V. P. Richmond, and J. C. McCroskey (eds.), *Power in the Classroom* (pp. 85–99). Hillsdale, NJ: Erlbaum.

Lee, F. R. (1993). Disrespect rules. *New York Times*, Education Supplement (Section 4A): 16.

Lenze, L. F., and Dinham, S. M. (1994). Examining pedagogical knowledge of college faculty new to teaching. Paper presented at the American Educational Research Association, New Orleans, April.

Manegold, C. S. (1993). To Crystal, 12, school serves no purpose. *New York Times*, April 8: A1 & B7.

Pace, R. C. (1984). *Measuring the Quality of College Student Experiences. An Account of the Development and Use of the College Student Experiences Questionnaire.* Los Angeles: Higher Education Research Institute. UCLA.

Pascarella, E. T., and Terenzini, P. T. (1991). *How College Affects Students*. San Francisco: Jossey-Bass.

Perry, R. P., Hechter, F. J., Menec, V. H. and Weinberg, L. E. (1993). Enhancing achievement motivation and performance in college students: An attributional retraining perspective. *Research in Higher Education* 34: 687–723.

Plax, T. G., and Kearney, P. K. (1992). Teacher power in the classroom. In V. P. Richmond, and J. C. McCroskey (eds.), *Power in the Classroom* (pp. 67–84). Hillsdale, NJ: Erlbaum.

Shanker, A. (1995). Classrooms held hostage. *American Educator* 19(1): 8–13, 47–48.

Simonton, D. K. (1994). *Greatness*. New York: Guilford.

Smith, R. J., and Stendler, E. M. (1983). The impact of difficult patients upon treaters. *Bulletin of the Menninger Clinic* 47: 107–116.

Snyder, C. K., and Higgins, R. L. (1988). Excuses: Their effective role in the negotiation of reality. *Psychological Bulletin* 104:23–35.

Tinto, V. (1975). Dropout from higher education: A theoretical synthesis of recent research. *Review of Educational Research* 45:89–125.

Toby, J. (1993). Everyday school violence: How disorder fuels it. *American Educator* 17(4): 4–9 & 44–47.

Tryon, G. S. (1986). Abuse of therapists by patients: A national survey. *Professional Psychology: Research and Practice* 17: 357–363.

Weimer, M., and Lenze, L. F. (1991). Instructional interventions: A review of the literature on efforts to improve instruction. In J. C. Smart (ed.), *Higher Education: Handbook of Theory and Research* (pp. 294–333). New York: Agathon.

Williams, J. A. (1994). *Classroom in Conflict: Teaching Controversial Subjects in a Diverse Society*. Albany: SUNY Press.

Willis, D. (1993). Academic involvement at university. *Higher Education* 25; 133–150.

Wilson, R. (1990). Quality of life said to have diminished on U.S. campuses. *Chronicle of Higher Education* 36(33): A1 &A 32.

Wilson, R., Gaff, J., Dienst, R., Wood, L., and Bavry, J. (1975). *College Professors and Their Impact on Students*. New York: Wiley-Interscience.

Wyatt, G. (1992). Skipping class: An analysis of absenteeism among first-year students. *Teaching Students* 20: 201–207.

Interrupting Patriarchy: Politics, Resistance, and Transformation in the Feminist Classroom

MAGDA LEWIS

In this article Magda Lewis investigates the psychological, social, and sexual dynamics of the feminist classroom as the women and men in her course struggle with the realities of violence against women and the negotiation strategies women use to succeed and survive in a patriarchal society. Lewis presents a feminist critique of patriarchy through her own feminist teaching practice within a context of both blatant and subtle forms of physical, social, emotional, and psychological violence against women. She analyzes students' resistance to such a critique, and self-consciously examines and questions the conditions under which her students make meaning of these events. Lewis shares some of the teaching strategies she has used to subvert the gendered status quo of classroom interaction between women and men by including her thoughts and reactions to her students' accounts of their experiences, perceptions, frustrations, and anger as they grapple with these issues. These stories illustrate the use of such instances as pedagogical moments of transformative power to lead students toward a more critical political perspective. Lewis concludes by suggesting a specific framework that articulates the terms of feminist teaching.

In Canada, the fall of 1989 marked a particularly hostile environment for women on university campuses. On my own campus the events surrounding our "NO MEANS NO" campaign drew national attention. "NO MEANS NO" was an educational campaign organized by the Gender Issues Committee of the undergraduate student government (Alma Mater Society) aimed at alerting young women, particularly first year women, to the forms and expressions of date rape. The reaction of a faction of the male students was to respond with a "sign campaign" that made explicit their belief that women's refusal of male sexual demands could appropriately be countered with violence ("No means tie me up") or with their own definitions of women's sexual deviance ("No means dyke"). To the extent that the signs were accompanied by active verbal threats and physical intimidation, many women experienced the threatening atmosphere as misogyny.

My campus was not the only one experiencing what appeared to be an increasing backlash to a feminist presence inside the academy. As women academics across and between campuses shared stories of violation, more and more examples of misogyny surfaced. Our isolation and small numbers (women still comprise a very small fraction of academic faculty) precluded any possibility of collective action (Brodribb, 1987; McCormack, 1987). In the face of an academic community complicit in its complacency and unwilling to acknowledge its own oppressive practices born of the sexual subordination of women, we were atomized and held inside the private spaces of our own violations. And yet, despite the isolation of our struggles, we worked with our students to create an intellectually and emotionally supportive environment for them (Lewis, 1990a).

"Interrupting Patriarchy: Politics, Resistance and Transformation in the Feminist Classroom," by Magda Lewis, reprinted by permission from *Harvard Educational Review,* 60, 1990.

massacred by a gun-wielding young man who had convinced himself that women, transposed in his own sad head into the phrase "you bunch of feminists," were the cause of his own personal misery.[1]

This incident focused, on several levels, my concerns about teaching and learning as a feminist in the academy. The historical context of our individual and collective experiences as intellectual women enabled me to see that what the media identified as the "idiosyncratic" madness of this young man actually reflected infinitely receding images of male power transformed into violence—a polished surface facing the mirror of masculine privilege. Because of our identification with a politic that makes explicit our critique of women's subordination as a function of masculine privilege, my students' and my own safety were in question. This was not the single act of a deranged mind, nor the outcome of peculiar conditions on that specific campus. That the events at the Université de Montréal could have happened on any campus in this country—indeed, any campus on this continent—became a tangible reality (Malette, 1990).

I am haunted by the image of young women—not unlike the women I teach—lined up against the wall, while their perplexed, perhaps helpless, male colleagues and male instructor vacated the classroom. I am haunted, too, by the words (reported in the media) of that young woman whose vain efforts to save herself and her women classmates were captured when she screamed at the gunman: "You have the wrong women; we are not feminists!"

The words "you have the wrong women; we are not feminists!" provides a backdrop for the question I raise: How might we bring about the social changes we desire without negating women's perspective on our reality, or turning it, yet one more time, into a self-perpetuated liability? More specifically, how might I create a feminist pedagogy that supports women's desire to wish well for ourselves when for many women the "good news" of the transformative powers of feminist consciousness turns into the "bad news" of social inequality and, therefore, a perspective and politics they want to resist. More than resistance, which, drawing on Willis (1977), I characterize as the struggles against social forms that are experienced as oppressive, transformation is the fusion of political perspective and practice. Transformation is the development of a critical perspective through which individuals can begin to see how social practices are organized to support certain interests, and the process whereby this understanding is then used as the basis for active political intervention directed toward social change with the intent to disempower relations of inequality.

In short, my agenda in this paper is to understand the basis from which I might fashion a viable feminist pedagogy of transformation out of student resistance, not to patriarchic meaning-making but to feminist politics.

Using my experiences in Foundations 490, in this article I continue to raise the dilemmas I face as a feminist teacher. I explore the possibilities and limits of feminist teaching and learning in the academy under conditions that directly contradict its intent (Lewis & Simon, 1986; Lewis, 1988a, 1989, 1990a). Foundations 490 is a sociology of education course I teach in the faculty of education at Queen's University. While it is not one of the core Women's Studies courses, it is cross-listed in the Women's Studies Programme Calendar. For this reason the course often draws students from a wide range of disciplines. The specific title of the course, "Seminar in Social Class, Gender and Race in Education," is explicitly descriptive of the course focus. In the course outline I tell students that the theoretical framework we are using draws on critical and feminist theory and method. More specifically, the course proposes to "examine and develop a critical understanding of the implications for children's educational experiences of the effects of social class background, sex/gender differences and racial background." It also proposes to "locate school practices as part of the larger social context within which schools exist."

The course format is a seminar which incorporates class discussion around assigned readings and student presentations. The class presentation component requires students to articulate the social meaning of a cultural artifact or practice of their choice. Students examine how the artifact or practice reflects the social/cultural context out of which it has risen. The purpose of the assignment is to help students develop their skills in raising questions about our culture, which they had previously taken as a given. My intention is also that, through the exercise, they might see differently how sexism, racism, class differentiation, homophobia, and so on, are embedded in concrete cultural products and social practices.

I begin the course with an introductory lecture that outlines to the students what I intend that we take up during the coming term and the perspective from which my analysis proceeds. By doing this I attempt to incorporate many aspects of women's lives articulated within feminist politics.

The course is attended by both female and male students, although women tend to outnumber the men four to one. This, in part, is accounted for by the fact that student enrollment in faculties of education is still largely skewed in favor of women, who comprise approximately 70 to 75 percent of the undergraduate teacher education complement. Because the majority of students in Foundations 490 are women, in this paper I use the general designation "student" to refer to women or to the students in general. When I refer to the men in the classroom I shall use the qualifier "male."

While in this paper I explore the context of my teaching practice and the politics of the classroom, it is not my intention to offer prescriptive and generic feminist teaching strategies abstracted from the particular situations of feminist classrooms. Although it might be possible to employ suggestive approaches, we cannot artificially construct pedagogical moments in the classroom to serve as moments of transformation toward a critical political perspective. Nor can we predict how such moments will be responded to when they arise in particular situations, given the personal histories of the students and instructors involved.

Rather, I believe questions about the politics of feminist teaching have most specifically to do with how we identify those pedagogical moments whose transformative power lies precisely in the understandings we bring to the gendered context of the classroom. Ruth Pierson (1987) provides a clear and comprehensive definition of feminism, which frames the intent of my own teaching from a feminist perspective:

> One identifiable characteristic of feminism across an entire spectrum of varieties has been the pursuit of autonomy for women. Integral to this feminist pursuit of independent personhood is the critical awareness of a sex/gender system that relegates power and autonomy to men and dependence and subordination to women. Feminists start from an insistence on the importance of women and women's experience, but a woman-centered perspective alone does not constitute feminism. Before a woman-centered perspective becomes a feminist perspective, it has to have been politicized by the experience of women in pursuit of self-determination coming into conflict with a sex/gender system of male dominance. From a feminist perspective the sex/gender system appears to be a fundamental organizing principle of society and for that reason it becomes a primary object of analysis. (p. 203)

From this perspective I raise the psychological, social, and sexual dynamics of the feminist classroom as a site where, I believe, the political struggle over meaning must be seen as the focus of our pedagogical project. It is a context in which a serious intrusion of *feminist pedagogy* must concern itself, as Rachel Blau DuPlessis (1985) suggests, not with urging our women students to "resent the treatment of [their] sex and plead for its rights" (p. 33)—a project that acts to reaffirm women's subordination and encourage our exploitation—but to examine and question self-consciously the conditions of our own meaning-making and to use it as the place from which to begin to work toward change.

In taking up the psychological, social, and sexual dynamics of the feminist classroom, in this paper I propose to examine the violence/negotiation dichotomy environment as a feature of women's educational experience. In this context, I share the strategies I employ in specific instances as a feminist teacher to subvert the status quo of classroom interaction between women and men. Finally, in the conclusion I suggest a specific framework that articulates the terms of feminist teaching.

Theoretical Framework

In the largely unchallenged practices of the school setting marked by patriarchic privilege (Corregan, 1987), for women the dynamics of contestation born of knowledge are more complex than is often implied in the resistance literature. By paying close attention to practices in the classroom, forms of discourse, directions taken in discussion, the subtleties of body language, and so on, it is clear that, for women, a dichotomy between desire and threat is reproduced and experienced inside the classroom itself.

The salience of this dichotomy for women is suggested by Kathleen Rockhill (1987) in her powerful and moving article, "Literacy as Threat/Desire: Longing to be SOMEBODY," in which she articulates women's contradictory reality as an educational dilemma. For the women in Rockhill's study, the knowledge and power made potentially available through becoming literate contradictorily also repositioned them in such a way that it threatened familial, conjugal, and ultimately economic relations. Rockhill explains:

> It is common today for education to be ideologically dressed as the pathway to a new kind of romance for women, the romance of a "career," a profession, a middle-class way of life; the image is one of a well-dressed woman doing "clean" work, important work. As such, it feeds her yearning, her desire, for a way out of the "working class" life she has known (Steedman, 1986). It is precisely because education holds out this promise for women that it also poses a threat to them in their everyday lives. This is especially true for women in heterosexual relationships when their men feel threatened by the images of power (independence and success) attached to education. (p. 315)

In the feminist classroom, the contradiction that women experience is compounded by the way in which feminist politics challenges the everyday lives they have learned to negotiate.

The complexities of student resistance to the intentions of schooling have been documented before, and indeed such accounts provide much of the data for the theoretical framework of critical pedagogy. Paul Willis's classic work, *Learning to Labour* (1977), influenced by the theoretical work of Bowles and Gintis, Althusser, Bourdieu and Passeron, and Gramsci, was one of the first. Willis's study dealt exclusively with the experiences of male students. He included women only in their relations as girl friends and mothers. In this context, it is interesting to note the irony of the title of the more recent book by Dale Spender and Elizabeth Sarah, *Learning to Lose* (1980), a study of the experiences of girls in school.

In its classic form, critical pedagogy emphasizes that student resistance to the experiences of institutionalized education is forged from the contradictions they perceive between the dominant discourse of school knowledge on the one hand and their own lived experiences of subordination and violation on the other. According to resistance theory, students struggle to mark themselves off against the dominant discourse of the school through the enactment of practices that reaffirm and validate their subjectivities as specifically classed, raced, and gendered social actors.

It is my explicit intent in the classroom to raise with students issues of social relations from a critical perspective. But I am also a feminist who has worked for many years in feminist politics across a variety of sites. My family life, my involvement with grassroots community organizations, and my intellectual work are informed in concrete ways by the politics of feminist analysis. By extension, the politics that informs my everyday life infuses my relations with students, generates the readings for the course, and suggests my classroom teaching style and practice. Yet my frustrations as a feminist teacher arise significantly from the extent to which critical thinking on transformative pedagogical practices fails to address the specifics of women's education as simultaneously a site of desire and threat.

Based on my own experiences, I know that a feminist perspective could offer understandings the students might develop and bring to bear on their own experiences (Lather, 1989). Yet I also realize that attending to feminist politics and cultural critique in the classroom requires difficult emotional work from them and from me. I know that new understandings are often experienced painfully, and that lives are transformed.

All of this has happened in Foundations 490. Yet, the forms through which such transformations have taken place are not those that I anticipated—or perhaps hoped for. As a teacher and a feminist I share the hope for the promise of education as a political project: That through the offer of a theoretical framework—analysis and critique—students would eagerly join in my enthusiasm to work for social change in their personal and public lives. Clearly there are times when women immediately embrace the intentions of feminist teaching because it helps them make a different sense of their experiences. But just as often students struggle with these new understandings as they explore the space between the public and theoretical agenda of the course and the privacy of their everyday lives, where complex negotiations across gender often take their most salient form.

In the academy, women find themselves inside institutions whose practices and intentions are historically designed to keep them outside its concrete and theoretical frames. For women students, negotiating masculine content and practices often means that they have to absorb as well as struggle to survive the violations of their subordination. My students often find more simple and, therefore, more powerful words through which to express my meaning. The legacy of the violations women experience in the academy are apparent in the following conversations:

> I don't speak in class anymore. All this professor ever talked about was men, what they do, what they say, always just what's important to men. He, he, he is all I ever heard in class. He wasn't speaking my language. And whenever I tried to speak about what was impor-

> tant to me, whenever I tried to ask questions about how women fit into his scheme all I got was a negative response. I always felt I was speaking from inside brackets, like walls I couldn't be heard past. I got tired of not being heard so I stopped speaking altogether.
>
> I often tried to bring up examples of famous women in class because I thought it was important that people should acknowledge that women had done some things too. But no one ever knew who I was talking about. There was this assumption that if someone was a woman she couldn't possibly have done anything famous. The most important thing that happened to me in high school was that one of my history teachers had a picture of Agnes Mcphail pinned above the blackboard in the classroom. We never talked about it directly but for me that became a symbol of a woman. Sometimes I got really disgusted in some of my classes but I would think of that picture in that history class and that helped me to feel less alienated.
>
> In history we never talked about what women did; in geography it was always what was important to men. The same in our English class, we hardly ever studied women authors. I won't even talk about math and science ... I always felt that I didn't belong ... sometimes the boys would make jokes about girls doing science experiments. They always thought they were going to do it better and it made me really nervous. Sometimes I didn't even try to do an experiment because I knew they would laugh if I got it wrong. Now I just *deaden* myself against it, so I don't hear it any more. But I feel really alienated. My experience now is one of total silence. Sometimes I even wish I didn't know what I know.

For me, as a feminist teacher, such statements are not only painful but revealing. The remarks suggest that the politics of my teaching should focus not on teaching women what we already know but on finding ways of helping all of us articulate the knowledge we gain from our experience.

As a begining point I agree with claim of Giroux and Simon (1988):

> We are not concerned with simply motivating students to learn, but rather *establishing the conditions of learning* that enable them to locate themselves in history and to interrogate the adequacy of that location as both a pedagogical and political question. (p. 3, emphasis added)

Yet a feminist pedagogy cannot stop here. For women, the cultural, political, and ultimately historical discourse of the everyday, the present, and the immediate are conditions of learning marked by the varied forms of patriarchic violence (Brookes, 1988; Belenkey, Clinchy, Goldberger, & Tarule, 1986; McMahon, 1986). Pedagogy, even radical pedagogy, does not easily translate into an education that includes women if we do not address the threat to women's survival and livelihood that a critique of patriarchy in its varied manifestations confronts.

The dynamics of the classroom context when the students engage a feminist analysis presents the most challenging aspects of feminist teaching (Lewis, 1988a). In what follows I explore the psychological, social, and sexual aspects of this context.

Psychological Dynamics in the Feminist Classroom

For women, tension in the feminist classroom is often organized around our historically produced nurturing capacity as a feature of our psychologically internalized role as caretakers (Lewis, 1988b). The following example is a case in point. Recently, in reference to a set of class readings dealing with peace education, my introductory presentation spoke to the connections between patriarchy, violence, and political economy. As I finished, one of the first students to speak was a young woman. She said, "As you were speaking I was wondering and worrying about how the men in the room were feeling. What you said made sense to me, but I felt uncomfortable about how the men took it." A couple of other women nodded their agreement. Such a protective posture on the part of women on behalf of men is a common drama played out in many classrooms.

Similar responses to feminist critique are not specific to mixed-gender classrooms. The absence of men in the classroom does not significantly diminish the psychological investment women are required to make in the emotional well-being of men—an investment that goes well beyond the classroom into the private spaces of women's lives, which cannot easily be left at the classroom door. The response women bring to feminist politics/analyses arises from women's social/political location within patriarchic forms, which requires that men be the focus of women's attentions. Examples range from general claims that men are also isolated and contained by patriarchy in what is required of them within the terms of masculinity, to more specific references to personal family relations aimed at exempting intimate male relations from the general population of men. The sharing of household duties is often used as an example, although the articulation of details of this shared housework is often vague. Young women growing up in physically violent and sexually violating homes know a more brutal side of the caretaking imperative.[2]

Whether or not men are bodily present in the classroom, women carry the parameters of patriarchic meaning-making as a frame from within which we struggle to articulate our own interests. How women live this experience is not specific to mixed-gender classrooms. While it is my observation that the practice of a woman-as-caretaker ideology is more obvious in the presence of men, this ideology holds sway whether or not men are present as long as women believe their interests to be served by maintaining existing relations.

This formulation is not intended to subsume the experiences of all women and men under seamless, hegemonic constructs articulated through dominant expressions of femininity/masculinity. I use Alison Jaggar's (1983) formulation of Gramsci's notion of hegemony: A concept "designed to explain how a dominant class maintains control by projecting its own particular way of seeing social reality so successfully that its view is accepted as common sense and as part of the natural order by those who in fact are subordinated to it" (p. 151). In this respect, hegemony is accomplished through an ongoing struggle over meaning not only against, but for the maintenance of, power. Lesbians and gay men experience the social constructs of femininity/masculinity differently than women and men whose emotional and psychic investment is in heterosexual relationships. However, especially in professional schools, where students' aspirations for future employment often govern their willingness to challenge the status quo, pressures to conform to the dominant social text are shared by lesbians and heterosexual women alike (Khayatt, 1987). Because lesbians and gay men often remain voiceless within such classroom dynamics, the relations between the women and men in the classroom remains a site that supports only practices that construct women's social acceptability as caretakers of men.

In the mixed-gender classroom, much of the caretaking takes the form of hard-to-describe body language displayed as a barely perceptible "moving toward"; a not-quite-visible extending of the hand; a protective stance accomplished through eye contact. However, as the young woman's question of concern has shown, just as often it is explicitly articulated. In the feminist classroom, such caretaking responses on the part of women toward men are ones that, as feminist teachers, we easily recognize and anticipate. We must choose words carefully and negotiate our analyses with the women students in ways that will not turn them away from the knowledge they carry in their experiences.

Following the young woman's comments, many of the men seemed to feel that what she said vindicated their feelings of discomfort with the way in which I was formulating the issues. Some of the men expressed this through verbal support of the woman's concern over their emotional well-being. They showed a strong inclination to redirect the discussion toward notions of world violence as a *human* and not a gendered problem. By doing so, the men attempted to reappropriate a speaking space for themselves, which they saw to be threatened by my analysis. Even more troublesome for me was the pleasure some of the men seemed to take in encouraging women to take up the caretaking on their behalf and in how the women seemed to be brought up against one another in the debate that followed. The question of whether or not feminist critique constituted a confrontational stance by women against men was the substance of the debate between the women and the men and among the women. Some of the men offered verbal support for women who agreed with them and a rebuttal of those who did not. However, the more subtle forms of pleasure-taking are difficult to describe. We do not have language that can adequately express the social meaning of the practice of relaxing back into one's chair, with a barely there smile on one's face while eyes are fixed on the object of negation. One of the reasons feminist films are a source of exceptionally powerful critique is because they can display how violation works at the level of the non-verbal (Lewis, 1990b). Yet such practices are unmistakable in their intent. The non-verbal is a social language that women—and all culturally marginal groups—have learned to read well and that does its sad work on women's emotions.

That such a dynamic should develop among the students was not a surprise. I know that, within the terms of patriarchy, women have had no choice but to care about the feelings of men. Women know that, historically, not caring has cost us our lives: intellectually, emotionally, socially, psychologically, and physically. I see this played out over and over again in my classes, and in every case it makes women recoil from saying what they really want to say and simultaneously leaves men reassured about their right to speak on behalf of us all.

For me, this dynamic presented a pedagogical dilemma. How could I question particularities of our present social organization, which requires women to work as caretakers of men not only in economic/material relations but in emotional/psychological ones as well? Furthermore, how was I to do this in ways that did not reproduce the women's strong inclination to protect the men from what was *felt* to be an indictment of men in general and the men in the classroom in particular? Specifically, how could I help them focus on social organizational practices rather than on the man sitting next to them in the classroom?

I asked them to think of instances when we might expect men to reciprocate for women the kind of caretaking practices and ego support that women are expected to extend on behalf of men. Most specifically, I asked the women if they had ever been in the company of a male friend/partner/family member/stranger who, upon seeing our discomfort at the common public display of misogyny in such examples as billboards, had ever offered support for how uncomfortable and violated such displays must make us feel. By asking students to focus on the personal, I felt that it might be possible to reposition the women and men in a social configuration that did not take a gendered hierarchy and its attendant practices for granted. Not only the women, but the men as well, admitted that they had never had such an experience. More to the point, there was general agreement that the possibility had never even occurred to them.

Through our discussion, it became clear that as a collective social practice, for men, attentiveness to other than one's self is largely a matter of choice, whereas for women, it has been a socially and historically mandated condition of our acceptability as women. This provided, for some of the students in the class, a moment of critical reflection and transformation. It also offered a framework from which to envision a set of social relations not based fundamentally on inequality. For men such transformation often appears as a willingness to listen. Less eager to talk, they sometimes acknowledge that they can see themselves on the privileged side of the gender divide and admit that they had not previously given it a lot of thought. These acknowledgments are often fairly brief and to the point: "I had never thought of it that way" is a common response. Whether or not men carry their new understanding into their public and private lives outside the classroom is unclear. If they do, they have not shared it with me. For women, transformation often means a more active process. At times, younger women have asked to bring male friends to the class with them. More frequently, students have reported that they have asked their male friends or partners to read some of the course material. And some women have reported major changes in their family life, either in terms of renegotiated practices—mostly pertaining to household responsibilities—or in a decision to end a relationship. I do not want to suggest that every student in every class experiences these transformations. Progress is slow and often tentative as students struggle with the implications of their new understanding.

By shifting our focus from the topic of discussion (the political economy and masculine forms of world violence) and refocusing on the dynamics in the classroom at that moment, we made it possible to ask what cultural/political forms might articulate caretaking as a reciprocal process between women and men. This teaching strategy is central to my pedagogical agenda: identifying the moment when students might be most receptive to uncovering how they are invested in their own meaning-making practices.

Social Dynamics in the Feminist Classroom

For many students, the social context of the feminist classroom is another sphere of tension. For the women students, the content and processes of feminist curricula and teaching can result in the classic version of consciousness raising. "Feminist method," says Catherine MacKinnon (1983), "is consciousness raising:"

> the collective critical reconstitution of the meaning of women's social experience, as women live through it.... Consciousness raising ... inquiries into an intrinsically social situation, into that mixture of thought and materiality which is women's sexuality in the most generic sense. It approaches its world through a process that shares its determination: women's consciousness, not as individual or subjective ideas, but as a collective social

> being.... The process is transformative as well as perceptive, since thought and thing are inextricable and reciprocally constituting of women's oppression, just as the state as coercion and the state as legitimizing ideology are indistinguishable, and for the same reason. The pursuit of consciousness becomes a form of political practice. (p. 255)

Reading Catharine MacKinnon has convinced me that the politic of consciousness raising has earned a bad name precisely because it is a profoundly effective practice. There is a long history to the fear of women coming together and, in that space, sharing the personal stories that become metaphorical bases for generating a theory of women's subordination (Daly, 1978). The dominant forms of discourse are aimed hegemonically at preventing women from engaging in discussions that lead toward consciousness raising; the threat of social sanctions defuse the vitality of storytelling. Telling our stories of violation and subordination in the presence of those whose advantages are highlighted and challenged by such sharing, or doing so in the presence of those who hold the discursive power to subvert the act of consciousness raising as a feminist method is, for many women, a contradictory outcome of their experiences in the feminist classroom.

I believe the following exchange demonstrates this point well. Recently, a student was making a class presentation on the topic of violence against women. A few minutes after the beginning of her presentation, a frustrated young man demanded to know why he had to talk about women and men all the time, and why the presenter did not offer "the other side of the story." This example confirms other experiences indicating that students, particularly those who benefit from the present social arrangements, often find it difficult to engage in the self-reflection required to question the unequal and violent social relations in which we ourselves are social actors.

As a feature of classroom dynamics, the unpacking and uncovering of deeply submerged social practices of domination/entitlement experienced by the "other" as subordination/oppression, which we carry in and on our gendered bodies, in our verbal expressions, in the privilege (or lack of it) of having choice, can itself become another source for experiences of oppression. For women, as for other subordinate groups, it is the fact of "knowing" that is seen to be an act of insubordination; exposing that knowledge, speaking it in public space, claiming language through which to articulate our knowledge, refusing to believe that the dominant discourse speaks for all, as it speaks on behalf of patriarchic interests, is used as the justification for continued violation.

In part, patriarchy disempowers women by marginalizing their experiences of violation in an ongoing discourse that legitimates only those ways of making sense or the telling of only those kinds of stories that do not make men "look bad" (MacKinnon, 1987, p. 154). The use of language, for example, which exchanges "wife battering" with "family violence," as a way to redirect our focus away from masculine practices is a case in point.

One way male students sometimes wish to displace the sense women make of our experience is to refocus the discussion in directions that are less disquieting for them. In the instance mentioned above, I understood the young man's demand—the tone of his voice left no doubt that it was a demand—to be an attempt to redirect the discussion away from his own social identity as a male who, whether he acknowledges it or not, benefits from the culturally, legally, and politically encoded social relations of patriarchy (MacKinnon, 1987). Yet men can no more deny the embodiment of their masculine privilege than any of us can deny the embodiment of our entitlement if we are White, economically advantaged, heterosexual, able bodied, and carrying the valued assets of the privilege of Euro-American culture. As is suggested by Biddy Martin and Chandra Mohanty (1986), "the claim to a lack of identity or positionality is itself based on privilege, on a refusal to accept responsibility for one's implication in actual historical or social relations, on a denial that positionalities exist or that they matter, the denial of one's own personal history and the claim to a total separation from it" (p. 208). Furthermore, to the extent that sexism, racism, and social class inequalities represent social systems within which we either appropriate or struggle against particular personal relations, those who embody positions of privilege are often not attracted to an articulation of their interests in the terms required by self-reflexivity.

On this occasion, I judged that, by providing for the possibility of self-reflexive critique, I might avert the tendency of such debates to degenerate into expressions of guilt and victimization that would destroy the creative potential of a feminist political discourse that speaks not only to women but to men as well. I also felt that how I presented my response was crucial. Whatever my response was, it had to be possible for women to see it as a model for how they might also take up similar challenges to their own meaning-making in ways other than to demand their right to do so—precisely the point of debate. My challenge was to create the possibility for students to be self-reflexive.

The young man's demand for the "other side" of the story about men's violence against women created the space I was looking for. In classrooms, as in other social/political spaces, women and men come together unequally (Lewis & Simon, 1986). In such a context, a pedagogical approach that fails to acknowledge how such inequality silences serves to reinforce the powerlessness of the powerless. I knew from my own experience that under such circumstances; asking women to "speak up" and intervene on their own behalf would have reproduced exactly that marginalization that the young man's demand was intended to create. Clearly, I needed to employ another strategy.

The power of teaching as dramatic performance cannot be discounted on this particular occasion. Following the question, I allowed a few moments of silence. In these few moments, as the question and the dynamics of the situation settled into our consciousness, the social history of the world was relived in the bodies of the women and men around the table. What is the "other side of the story" about violence against women! What could the women say? Faced with the demand to articulate their *reality in terms not of their own making*, the women visibly shrank into their chairs; their breathing became invisible (Rockhill, 1987a). In contrast, whether I imagined it or not, it seemed to me that the men sat more upright and "leaned into" the response that began to formulate in my head. It seemed clear to me that the young man's objections to the woman's presentation constructed women as objects of practices which were experienced by him as unproblematic; the threat of physical violence is not one which most men experience on a daily basis. By objectifying women through his question, he reinforced male privilege. I needed to find a way of repositioning us—women and men—in such a way that the young man had no options but to face his own social location as problematic.

The stage was set for dramatic performance. Reassuring the young man that indeed he was right, that "other sides" of issues need to be considered whenever possible, I wondered if *he* would perhaps be the one who could tell us about the "other side" of violence against women. My memory of this moment again focuses on the breath: the men's as it escaped their bodies and the women's as it replenished them.

Turning the question away from the women in the class created the self-reflexive space that I believed could truly challenge the men in the class to take up not women's subordination but their own positions of privilege. Given the social realities of violence against women, he was no more able to answer his own question than it might have been possible for the women to do so. At the same time, it remained for him to tell us why he couldn't answer his own question. He found himself speechless. This time the silence that followed reversed the order of privilege to name the social realities we live. The young man's failure to find a salient way of taking up the issue he had raised made it possible for the young woman to continue with her presentation without challenge to her fundamental right to do so.

The incident ended at this point and the class presentation proceeded. Reflecting on my own practice in this instance, I cannot deny that my politics embraced and supported the struggle for women's autonomy and self-determination. Working with women to create the space for our voice is fundamental to this politic. Whether the young man experienced transformation or was simply intimidated into silence was something that required sorting out. I was willing to let him undertake the hard work of doing so for himself. If I had silenced him I could only hope that perhaps the experience would provide him with a deeper understanding of an experience women encounter every day. That the incident was experienced by the women in ways that signaled a moment of possibility for them is captured by a young woman who came over to where I was distractedly picking up my papers after the long three-hour class. She lightened the load of my exhaustion with the announcement that she wanted to be a sociologist and a feminist and would I tell her "how to become it." Both her naiveté and mine embarrassed us into shared laughter; but then such fleeting moments of embrace are sometimes all we have, it seems to me, to collect ourselves and move on. Such experiences reveal the feminist classroom as profoundly relevant to women's lives.

Sexual Dynamics in the Feminist Classroom

Finally, the sexual dynamics of mixed-gender classrooms are complex and often contradictory. Particularly for younger women, at times still caught in the glare of sexual exploration and identification, the feminist classroom can feel threatening. The following example is a case in point.

Recently, during the introductory lecture I use as a way of framing the seminar session, I was addressing the educational concerns over the low number of women in mathematics and science programs. On this occasion, trying to concretize the issues for the students, I asked them to indicate, by a show of hands, which of them were preparing to be math and science teachers. A number of students raised their hands. As might be expected, many of those who raised their hands were men. However, a number of women also raised their hands. A "guffawed" and embarrassed laughter rose from the back of the room after a young man whispered a comment to a young woman who had raised her hand.

I do not generally make use of or support embarrassment as a pedagogical strategy. In this instance, however, I felt certain that I knew what the laughter was about and wanted to capture the moment as a concrete example of exactly the issues I was raising. I requested that the young man tell us what he had said. He resisted; I insisted. The use of institutional power, I believe, should not always be viewed as counterproductive to our politics. Feminism is a politic that is both historical and contingent on existing social relations. I had no problem justifying the use of my institutional power to create the possibility for privilege to face itself and own its violation publicly. Using power to subjugate is quite different from using power to liberate. The young man complied. He told us that he had whispered to the young woman that perhaps she had had a sex change.

The assumed prerogative to pass such commentary on women's choices of career and life possibilities is not, of course, new to any of us. However, in the feminist classroom such commentary and attendant laughter become overtly political issues that can be taken up as instances of gender politics. I used the incident as an example of the kind of academic environment created for women when such interactions are not treated as problematic. In doing so, I was aware that both the women and the men experienced various degrees of discomfort. Many of the men and some of the women insisted that I was making too much of an innocent joke, while many of the women and none of the men, as far as I could tell, sat quietly with faces flushed. In thinking about how I approach my teaching, I can recall the salient details of this example to understand how gender politics can be transformed into sexual dynamics in the classroom. Not only gender, but sexuality is a deeply present organizing principle in the classroom and one which enters into the dynamics of how we come together as women and men in pursuit of shared meaning.

The production of shared meaning is one of the ways we experience deeply felt moments of psychosexual pleasure, whether across or within gender. Yet, in a patriarchic culture, women and men can find the articulation of shared meaning profoundly elusive, and the desire for pleasure in conflict with mutual understanding.

While women have always found support in separate women's communities, education cells, political movements, work, and so on, these sites of solidarity have usually existed outside of the dominant male culture—a culture of which, we cannot forget, women are also an integral part. Social, political, and economic relations are articulated through the personal/collective experience we have of the world. Feminist politics insist on using these experiences as the lens through which to look at the barely perceptible yet tenacious threads that hold the social forms and forces in place. For women who refuse subordination, who refuse to pretend that we don't know, standing against these social forces has not only economic and political consequences but psycho/sexual ones as well. bell hooks (1989) comments:

> Sexism is unique. It is unlike other forms of domination—racism or classism—where the exploited and oppressed do not live in large numbers intimately with their oppressors or develop their primary love relationships (familial and/or romantic) with the individuals who oppress and dominate or share in the privileges attained by domination.... [For women] the context of these intimate relationships is also the site of domination and oppression. (p. 130)

This dynamic is seldom, if ever, talked about in the feminist classroom, and yet, it explains the conflicting emotional and analytic responses women have to the content of the course.

Exploring the sexual parameters of the conditions under which women are required to undertake their intellectual work is crucial. Finding examples is not hard; relating them is. It is with difficulty that I cite specific examples, and then only briefly, because of my own complex emotions associated with writing these words and having them stand starkly, darkly on the page to be read and reread; knowing that stories of violation violate at each retelling. These stories are not lightly told nor lightly received; they are often related in the privacy of my office. One woman's books disappeared (an event reminiscent of the one related in Janice Radway's *Reading the Romance*, 1984); another, alerted by the words, "maybe you should be reading this instead," had a copy of a pornographic magazine flung at her as she sat reading her course material; and yet another was told, as a "joke" at a social gathering, that to "celebrate" the completion of the course she would be "rewarded" by being "raped" so she could "get it out of her system" and return to her "old self." The monitoring and banning of what women read is shown in these examples to be closely associated with demands for women to conform to a particular version of male-defined sexuality. While the above may represent especially harsh examples, the antagonistic relationship drawn between women's desire for knowledge and our embodiment as sexually desirable human beings is an issue that lies always just below the surface in the classroom.

For many women, a feminist world view is deeply incorporated at the level of everyday practice. Yet, we need to be aware that by requiring women to challenge masculine constructs—as I had done in the classroom example cited above—we also require them to break with the dominant phallocentric culture. While as feminist teachers we might believe that such a break may offer the only possibilities for the resolution of this conflict, we must be aware that for many women the concrete possibility of doing so is difficult to contemplate. As Claire Duchen, quoted in Rowbotham (1989), suggests, "the tailoring of desire to the logic of politics is not always possible or acceptable" (p. 85).

Feminist critique of phallocentric culture is at once fundamentally necessary for and profoundly disruptive of the possibilities for shared meaning across gender, leaving women vulnerable to what Sheila Radford-Hill (1986) has analyzed as the potential "betrayal" and "psychosexual rejection" of women by men (pp. 168–169), attended by more or less severe economic and political consequences. None of this dynamic escapes women's awareness. "The personal is political" is not just a useful organizing concept, it is also a set of material enactments that display and reflect back how the political is personal.

As Susan Griffin (1981) suggests, a woman knows that "over and over again culture tells her that men abandon women who speak too loudly, or who are too *present*" (p. 211). Coupled with the strong cultural message that "her survival in the world depends on her being able to find a man to marry" (p. 211), many young women in the feminist classroom find themselves caught in the double bind of needing to speak and to remain silent at the same time in order to guarantee some measure of survival. While the salience of this politic is more immediately obvious in the case of heterosexual women, woman-identified (Rich, 1986, p. 57) women who do not comply, at least minimally, with acceptable forms of sexual self-presentation do not escape the consequences of marginalization and exclusion. For all women in professional schools specifically, compliance with particular displays of femininity can mean the difference between having or not having a job.

As women and men struggle over establishing and articulating shared meanings, we need to notice the reality that, for many women, such struggles often take place in the context of deeply felt commitments reverberating with emotional psycho/sexual chords and attended by the material conditions of unequal power. While perhaps these relations are lived most deeply not in the classroom itself but in those private spaces lived out between women and men beyond the classroom, for women, course content can be instrumental in raising these relations as questions.

The following is an example of how one woman took up these struggles in her private life. After a particular encounter in the classroom regarding the issue of voice/discourse discussed in the context of who has the right to name whether or not a joke is funny, she wrote me the following note:

> The articles at this point in the course ... have plunged me into the next phase of my feminist awareness, which is characterized by anger and a pervading sense of injustice.... The "feminist" anger that I feel is self-perpetuating. I get angry at the discrimination and stereotyping I run up against so I blame the patriarchal society I live in in particular, and men in general. Then I think about women who feel that feminism is unnecessary or obsolete and I get angry at that subset of women. Then I think about the good guys like Mike and Cam and I get angry because the patriarchal society biases the way I think about these men, simply because they're members of a particular gender (sex class?). Then I think about men who stereotype and discriminate against women and criticize us for being "overly sensitive" when we get uptight or even just point out or suggest humanistic egalitarian changes that are good and smart and I get REALLY angry because I realize that they're all a bunch of (expletives deleted) [sic].... One of the most difficult aspects of this anger is that I become frustrated and impatient with people who can't see the problems or don't see the urgent need for solutions. (I am writing) a lot during this time because I often can't communicate orally with people who don't at least respect my feminist views.

hooks states that feminist works that focus on strategies women who can use to speak to males about male domination and change are not readily available, if they exist at all. Yet women have a deep longing to share feminist consciousness with the men in their lives (the 'good guys'), and together work at transforming their relationships." hooks goes on to say that "concern for this basic struggle should motivate feminist thinkers to talk and write more about how we relate to men and how we change and transform relationships with men characterized by domination" (p. 130).

Yet despite their desire genuinely to share the meanings they have drawn from their experiences, for young women in the feminist classrooms, phallocentric myth-making often collides with the theoretical agenda of the course. Phallocentric myths are those beliefs that continue to marginalize women through the process of naturalizing politically created gender inequalities: "Women are not in positions of decision and policymaking because they don't want to be"; "Everybody has equal opportunity to become school principal. Women choose not to be because they like teaching better"; "If abused and battered women don't leave their partners it is because they have deviant personalities"; "Women who are raped did something wrong"; "Boys are better at math, girls are better at reading"; "Women who do math are not really women"; "Jokes, sexually offensive to women, are funny"; "There are no women in history because they didn't do anything"; "Women like staying home with children"; "Men share equally in housework"; and so on. I have heard some version of all of these statements in the classroom. While the men might express a comfortable indignation at such beliefs, they don't often understand what practices are required of them to change how they live their lives. For example, one man recently told the class that he supports his wife's career by "baby-sitting" the children while she goes to work. It is precisely this imbalance of power that constructs the women's silence, suppressed behind embarrassed laughter.

The pedagogical implications of such gender relations in the feminist classroom must be taken seriously if we are to understand how and why women students might wish both to appropriate and yet resist feminist theoretical and political positions that aim to uncover the roots of our deeply misogynist culture and give legitimacy to women's desires and dreams of possibility. As feminist teachers we need to look closely at the psycho/sexual context within which we propose the feminist alternative and consider the substance of why women may genuinely wish to turn away from the possibilities it offers.

Women know through experience that the threat to our sexuality is a way of controlling our political activities. In her review of Spender (1982), Pierson (1983) points out that there is a long history to the process of displacing women's legitimate political and intellectual critique and struggles into distorted evaluations of women's sexuality as a form of social control hammered into place by the material conditions of women's lives. The meaning that patriarchy has assigned to the term "lesbian" has resulted in its use as a pejorative term to undermine the serious political work in which women as women have been negated in resistance to a set of social relations marked by patriarchic domination. The misogyny of such a designation violates all women at all points of the heterosexual/lesbian continuum (Rich, 1986). Clearly "the regulation of speaking and silence" (Walkerdine, 1985) is not just achieved through concrete regulatory practices, but also through the emotional, psychic, and sexual sphere—articulated through the practices of patriarchic myth-making—that combine in our hearts and heads to silence us from within. Given the terms of such social conditions it would be a surprise, indeed, if women did not feel the constraints of contradictory choices and conflicting interests.

The power of patriarchic social controls on women's sexuality does not escape even (or perhaps especially) very young women. For example, within a recent three-week period, two separate groups of elementary and high school students were invited to participate in different events sponsored by the faculty where I teach. The first was a forum on women and education, attended by 150 students, at which the guest speaker, Dale Spender, presented an address entitled "Young Women in Education: What Happens to Girls in Classrooms." Three weeks later, a dramatic presentation by a feminist acting troupe, The Company of Sirens[3], presented an upbeat production called *The Working People's Picture Show*, dealing with such issues as women in the work force, day care, unionism, and sexual harassment. The question period that followed each event was telling. In each case the young women's concerns were well demonstrated by the almost identically phrased question aimed at the presenters, who were seen as the embodiment of feminist critique: "Are you married and do you have children?" I don't believe this was a theoretical question. For many young women the concern about the compatibility of feminist politics with marriage and family is the concrete realization that making public what our feminist consciousness reveals about women's experiences of patriarchy can result in potential limits on desire. To the extent that any woman who displays autonomy and independent personhood is seen as a threat to male power and therefore subjected to male violence was reaffirmed by the massacre at the Université de Montréal. Such events are not lost on young women.

My response to the sexual dynamics in the classroom is to create a context that offers "space" and "safety" particularly to women students. Men in the feminist classroom often state that the course readings and class discussions feel threatening and that they experience various degrees of discomfort. I would like to understand more about these feelings of threat and discomfort—where do they come from, what do they fear? I am concerned that all students—women and men—have access to the analyses we take up in the class. I am also concerned that all students feel equally validated in doing the hard work toward a transformed consciousness. However, this work is different for women than it is for men. Women need space and safety so that they are free to speak in order to better understand and act against the violations they have experienced in a social/cultural setting that subordinates them in hurtful and violent ways. The consciousness around which men need to do hard work is the pain of their complicity in benefiting from the rewards of this same culture. I support men in doing this hard work. Personally, I have not seen many of them try. Those who have are strong and welcome allies.

The language of "space" and "safety" is not new to discussions of feminist teaching. However, I believe that it is not always clear what practices attend these abstractions. I believe, first, that women don't need to be taught what we already know: fundamentally, that women are exempted from a culture to which our productive and reproductive labor is essential. The power of phallocentrism may undermine our initiative, it may shake the foundations of our self-respect and self-worth, it may even force us into complicity with its violence. But it cannot prevent us from knowing. Nor do women need to be taught the language through which to speak what we know.

Rather, the challenge of feminist teaching is in finding ways to make speakable and legitimate the personal/political *investments* we all make in the meanings we ascribe to our historically contingent experiences. In this context, I raise with students the contradictory reality of women's lives, wherein one's interests, at the level of practice, lie both with the dominant group and against it. Through such discussion emerges the deeply paradoxical nature of the conditions of the subordinate in a hierarchical culture marked by gender, class, and race inequalities. Approaching women's lives from this perspective means that practices previously understood by students, to be a function of choice can be seen as the result of a need to secure some measure of emotional, intellectual, and quite often physical survival (Wolfe, 1986, p. 58).

Pedagogy that is grounded in simple notions of false consciousness that articulates teaching as a mediation or, worse, as a charitable act, does not support knowledge invested with the meanings students ascribe to their own experiences. This not only buries the complexity of human choices in an unproblematized notion of self-interest but, further, can only offer validating or supplementary educational options without transforming the conditions under which we learn (Lewis, 1989). By fusing women's emotional and concrete lives through feminist critique, it is possible to make problematic the conditions under which women learn, and perhaps to make a feminist political agenda viable in women's own lives wherein they can transcend the split between personal experience and social form.

Conclusion

What are the possibilities of doing feminist politics/pedagogy in the classroom? In answering this question I want to examine the potential for feminist teaching that does more than address the concerns of the already initiated. For me, the urgency of this issue arises from my own teaching. On one hand, the often chilling stories women students share with me and each other in the context of classroom relations point to their clear understanding of the politics of gender subordination. Within the confines of traditional academic practices, the politics of personal experience are often seen to be irrelevant. In contrast, the feminist classroom can be a deeply emotional experience for many women, offering the opportunity to claim relevance for the lives they live as the source of legitimate knowledge.

On the other hand, I also hear the young woman who speaks to me in anger, who derides me for being the bearer of "bad news," and who wants to believe that our oppression/subordination is something we create in our own heads. Given the context of violence within which students are being asked to embrace a feminist politic, their concerns about their emotional, intellectual, and, quite obviously, physical safety have to be recognized as crucial. For women, overt acts of violence, like the one that occurred at the Université de Montréal, are merely an extension of their daily experiences in the psychological/

social/sexual spaces of the academy. Resistance to the emancipatory potential of a liberating politic indicates the extent of women's subordination. Thus, we cannot expect that students will readily appropriate a political stance that is truly counter-hegemonic, unless we also acknowledge the ways in which our feminist practice/politics *creates*, rather than ameliorates, feelings of threat: the threat of abandonment; the threat of having to struggle within unequal power relations; the threat of psychological/social/sexual, as well as economic and political marginality; the threat of retributive violence—threats lived in concrete embodied ways. It is any wonder that many women desire to disassociate from "those" women whose critique of our social/cultural world seems to focus and condense male violence?

The challenge of feminist teaching lies for me in the specifics of how I approach the classroom. By reflecting on my own teaching, I fuse content and practice, politicizing them both through feminist theory and living them both concretely rather than treating them abstractly. To elaborate: as I reflect on my teaching, it is clear from the detailing of the examples I provide above that feminist teaching practices cannot be separated from the content of the curriculum. Specific political moments arise exactly because of the content of the course. As is suggested by Gayle MacDonald (1989), "the process by which teaching occurs in a feminist classroom is one which is very different from technique/pedagogy used in other settings" (p. 147). I want to extend this idea by suggesting that the "difference" MacDonald identifies in the feminist classroom is that, as students articulate their interests and investments through particular social practices, a dialectic develops between students and the curriculum in such a way that the classroom dynamics created by the topic of discussion reflect the social organization of gender inequality. Indeed, the irony is that feminist critique of social relations reproduces exactly the practices we are critiquing. When these practices are reproduced, so are the attendant violations, marginalizations, struggles, and transformation which again lend themselves to be revisited by the critique of feminist politics.

An interesting case in point is the experience I have had on various occasions when I have presented some version of this argument at academic conferences. On each occasion, in responding to my presentation, some members of the audience tended to reproduce to some extent the practices that I take such great pains to critique in the text. The caretaking practices, the concern that men not feel unfairly marginalized or attacked, the willingness of men in the audience to speak unproblematically on behalf of women, and the dynamics of sexual marginalization have all played a part in the reception of my article-in-progress. My purpose here is not to suggest that every instance of critique of feminist social/cultural analysis is a display of phallocentric power or male privilege. Indeed, as feminist scholars we put our work forward in good faith and both invite and welcome articulate and substantive engagement of it (Ellsworth, 1989). My point is, rather, that responses to feminist critique often take forms that reproduce the gendered practices that I have described in this paper.

The strategies I have employed in the classroom have been directed toward politicizing not only what we take up in the class as course content but also the classroom dynamics that are generated by our topic and subsequent discussion. These practices included: shifting our focus from larger social issues to the dynamics in the classroom so that we might explore the relationship between the two; legitimating the meanings women bring to their experiences by turning challenges to these articulated meanings back on the questioner, thereby requiring the questioner to make different meanings sensible; disrupting the order of hierarchy regarding who can speak on whose behalf; requiring that men in the class own their social location by exploring the parameters of their own privilege rather than the limits on women of their oppression; providing opportunities for self-reflexive critique of unequal power relations; staying attentive to the political context of women's lives—those seemingly unconnected experiences made to seem livable by the tumble of daily life—in order to offer a vision of a future that women might embrace; attending to the ways in which women have been required historically to invest in particular and often contradictory practices in order to secure their own survival; and, finally, treating women's resistance to feminism as an active discourse of struggle derived from a complex set of meanings in which women's practices are invested.

The above suggestions are intended to be neither exhaustive nor prescriptive. Pedagogical moments arise in specific contexts: the social location of the teacher and students; the geographic and historical location of the institution in which they come together; the political climate within which they work; the personalities and personal profiles of the individuals in the classroom; the readings selected for the course; and the academic background of the students all come together in ways that create the specifics of the moment. It is not appropriate to think of what I have presented here as a "model" for feminist teaching. "Models" can only be restrictive and reductive because they cannot predict and thus cannot take into account the complexity of contingent and material realities. My intent, rather, has been to articulate how, at particular moments in my teaching, I made sense of those classroom dynamics that seemed to divide women and men across their inequalities in ways that reaffirmed women's subordination, and how making sense of those moments as politically rich allowed me to develop an interpretive framework for creating a counter-hegemony from my teaching practice. My hope is that through such shared struggles in the classroom women might embrace for themselves the politics of autonomy and self determination rather than reject it as a liability.

Notes

I wish to thank Gayle MacDonald, Barbara McDonald, Elizabeth Ellsworth, and Roberta Lamb for making helpful comments on earlier drafts of this paper.

1. This article is dedicated to the fourteen women massacred at the Université de Montréal on December 6, 1989: Genevieve Bergeron, Helene Colgan, Nathalie Croteau, Barbara Diagneault, Anne-Marie Edward, Maud Havcirnick, Barbara Marie Klueznick, Maryse Laganiere, Maryse Leclair, Anne-Marie Lemay, Sonia Pelletier, Michele Richard, Annie St-Arneault, and Annie Turcotte.

2. I thank Barbara McDonald for providing me with a deeper understanding of this reality through the work we share.

3. The Company of Sirens, 176 Robert Street, Toronto, Ontario, Canada, M55 2K3.

References

Belenky, M. F., Clinchy, B. M., Goldberger, N. R., & Tarule, J. M. (1986). *Women's ways of knowing: The development of self, voice and mind.* New York: Basic Books.

Brodribb, S. (1987). Women's studies in Canada [Special issue]. *Resources for Feminist Research.*

Brookes, A. L. (1988). *Feminist pedagogy: A subject in/formation.* Unpublished doctoral dissertation, University of Toronto.

Childers, M. (1984). Women's studies: Sinking and swimming in the mainstream. *Women's Studies International Forum,* 7(3), 161–166.

Corrigan, P. (1987). In/forming schooling. In D. Livingston & contributors, *Critical pedagogy and cultural power* (pp. 17–40). Toronto: Garamond Press.

Daly, M. (1978). *Gyn/ecology: The metaethics of radical feminism.* Boston: Beacon Press.

DuPlessis, R. B. (1985). *Writing beyond the ending: Narrative strategies of twentieth-century women writers.* Bloomington: Indiana University Press.

Ellsworth, E. (1989). Why doesn't this feel empowering? Working through the repressive myths of critical pedagogy. *Harvard Educational Review, 59,* 297–324.

Giroux, H., & Simon, R. (1988). *Critical pedagogy and the politics of popular culture.* Unpublished manuscript.

Griffin, S. (1981). *Pornography and silence: Culture's revenge against nature.* New York: Harper and Row.

hooks, b. (1989). *Talking back: Thinking feminist, thinking Black.* Boston: South End Press.

Jaggar, A. (1983). *Feminist politics and human nature.* Sussex, Eng.: The Harvest Press.

Khayatt, D. M. (1987). *Gender role conformity in women teachers.* Unpublished doctoral dissertation, University of Toronto.

Lather, P. (1988). Feminist perspectives on emancipatory research methodologies. *Women's Studies International Forum, 11,* 569–581.

Lewis, M. (1988a). *Without a word: Sources and themes for a feminist pedagogy.* Unpublished doctoral dissertation, University of Toronto.

Lewis, M. (1988b). The construction of femininity embraced in the work of caring for children: Caught between aspirations and reality. *Journal of Educational Thought, 22*(2A), 259–268.

Lewis, M. (1989). The challenge of feminist pedagogy. *Queen's Quarterly, 96*(1), 117–130.

Lewis, M. (1990a). *Solidarity work and feminist practice.* Paper presented at the annual meeting of the American Educational Research Association, Boston, MA.

Lewis, M. (1990b). *Framing: Women and silence disrupting the hierarchy of discursive practices.* Paper presented at the annual meeting of the American Educational Research Association, Boston, MA.

Lewis, M., & Simon, R. I. (1986). A discourse not intended for her: Learning and teaching within patriarchy. *Harvard Educational Review, 56*, 457–472.

MacDonald, G. (1989). Feminist teaching techniques for the committed but exhausted. *Atlantis, 15*(1), 145–152.

MacKinnon, C. A. (1983). Feminism, Marxism, method and the state: An agenda for theory. In E. Abel & E. Abel (Eds.), *The signs reader: Women, gender and scholarship* (pp. 227–256). Chicago: University of Chicago Press.

MacKinnon, C. (1987). *Feminism unmodified: Discourses of life and law.* Cambridge: Harvard University Press.

Malette, L., & Chalouh, M. (Eds.). (1990). *Polytechnique, 6 Décembre.* Montréal: Les Éditions du remue-ménage.

Martin, B., & Mohanty, C. T. (1986). Feminist politics: What's home got to do with it? In T. de Lauretis (Ed.), *Feminist studies/critical studies* (pp. 191–212). Bloomington: Indiana University Press.

McCormack, T. (1987). Feminism, women's studies and the new academic freedom. In J. Gaskell & A. McLaren (Eds.), *Women and education: A Canadian perspective* (pp. 289–303). Calgary: Detselig Enterprises.

McMahon, M. (1986). *A circuitous quest: Things that haunt me when I write.* Unpublished manuscript.

Pierson, R. R. (1983). Review of women of ideas and what men have done to them. *Resources for Feminist Research, 12*(2), 17–18.

Pierson, R. R. (1987). Two Marys and a Virginia: Historical moments in the development of a feminist perspective on education. In J. Gaskell & A. McLaren (Eds.), *Women and education: A Canadian perspective* (pp. 203–222). Calgary: Detselig Enterprises.

Radford-Hill, S. (1986). Considering feminism as a model for social change. In T. de Lauretis (Ed.), *Feminist studies/critical studies* (pp. 157–172). Bloomington: Indiana University Press.

Radway, J. (1984). *Reading the romance: Women, patriarchy and popular literature.* Chapel Hill: University of North Carolina Press.

Rich, A. (1986). *Blood, bread and poetry.* New York: W. W. Norton.

Rockhill, K. (1987a). The chaos of subjectivity in the ordered halls of academe. *Canadian Women Studies, 8*(4).

Rockhill, K. (1987b). Literacy as threat/desire: Longing to be SOMEBODY. In J. Gaskell & A. McLaren (Eds.), *Women and education: A Canadian perspective* (pp. 315–331). Calgary: Detselig Enterprises.

Rowbotham, S. (1989). To be or not to be: The dilemmas of mothering. *Feminist Review, 31*, 82–93.

Spender, D. (1982). *Women of ideas and what men have done to them.* London: Routledge and Kegan Paul.

Spender, D., & Sarah, E. (Eds.). (1980). *Learning to lose: Sexism and education.* London: The Women's Press.

Walkerdine, V. (1985). On the regulation of speaking and silence: Subjectivity, class and gender in contemporary schooling. In C. Steedman, C. Urwin, & V. Walkerdine (Eds.), *Language, gender and childhood* (pp. 203–241). London: Routledge and Kegan Paul.

Williamson, J. (1981/1982). How does girl number twenty understand ideology? *Screen Education, 40,* 80–87.

Willis, P. (1977). *Learning to labour: How working class kids get working class jobs.* New York: Columbia University Press.

Wolfe, A. (1986). Inauthentic democracy: A critique of public life in modern liberal society. *Studies in Political Economy, 21,* 57–81.

D. Instruction and Learning Outcomes in the Classroom

Identifying Exemplary Teachers and Teaching: Evidence from Student Ratings[1]

Kenneth A. Feldman

Formal or systematic evaluation by college students of their teachers has long been used to help students in their selection of courses, to provide feedback to faculty about their teaching, and to supply information for administrators and personnel committees in their deliberations on the promotion and tenure of individual faculty members. Moreover, with the increasing emphasis that many colleges and universities are currently putting on good teaching and on designating, honoring, and rewarding good teachers, the use of student ratings is, if anything, likely to increase. Yet, for all their use, student ratings of instructors and instruction are hardly universally accepted. It is no secret, for example, that some college teachers have little regard for them. For these faculty, student evaluations of teachers (or courses)—whether sponsored by the university administration, faculty-development institutes, individual academic departments, or student-run organizations—are not reliable, valid, or useful, and may even be harmful. Others, of course, believe more or less the opposite; and still others fall somewhere in between these two poles of opinion.

If the credibility of teacher evaluations is to be based on more than mere opinion, one asks what the research on their use shows. This question turns out to be more difficult to answer than might be thought because, even apart from the substance of the pertinent research, the number of relevant studies is voluminous. A few years ago, in a letter to the editor in *The Chronicle of Higher Education* (Sept. 5, 1990), William Cashin pointed out that 1,300 citations could be found in the Educational Resources Information Center on "student evaluation of teacher performance" at the postsecondary level. This same year, my own collection of books and articles on instructional evaluation numbered about 2,000 items (Feldman, 1990b). This collection has grown still larger since then, of course. It is true that, at a guess, well over one-half of the items in this collection are opinion pieces (filled with insightful observations at best and uninformed polemics at worst). Even so, this still leaves a large number of research pieces.

Luckily, this research—either as a whole or subportions of it—has been reviewed relatively often (see, among others Aubrect, 1981; Braskamp, Brandenburg and Ory, 1984; Braskamp and Ory, 1994; Centra, 1979, 1989, 1993; Costin, Greenough and Menges, 1971; Doyle, 1975, 1983; Kulik and McKeachie, 1975; Marsh, 1984, 1987; Marsh and Dunkin, 1992; McKeachie, 1979, Miller, 1972, 1974; and Murray, 1980). Cashin (1988, 1995) has even supplied particularly useful reviews of the major reviews. My own series of reviews started in the mid-1970s and has continued to the present. (See Feldman, 1976a, 1976b, 1977, 1978, 1979, 1983, 1984, 1986, 1987, 1989a, 1989b, 1990a, 1993; two other analyses—Feldman, 1988, 1992—are indirectly relevant.)

One of the best overviews in the area is that by Marsh (1987), which is an update and elaboration of an earlier review of his (Marsh, 1984). In this review, after 100 pages or so of careful, critical, and reflective analysis of the existing research and major reviews of student ratings of instruction, Marsh (1987) sums up his findings and observations, as follows:

> Research described in this article demonstrates that student ratings are clearly multidimensional, quite reliable, reasonably valid, relatively uncontaminated by many variables often seen as sources of potential bias, and are seen to be useful by students, faculty, and

"Identifying Exemplary Teachers and Teaching: Evidence from Student Ratings," by Kenneth A. Feldman, reprinted by permission from *Effective Teaching in Higher Education: Research and Practice*, edited by Raymond P. Perry and John C. Smart, 1997, Agathon Press.

> administrators. However, the same findings also demonstrate that student ratings may have some halo effect, have at least some unreliability, have only modest agreement with some criteria of effective teaching, are probably affected by some potential sources of bias and are viewed with some skepticism by faculty as a basis for personnel decisions. It should be noted that this level of uncertainty probably also exists in every area of applied psychology and for all personnel evaluation systems. Nevertheless, the reported results clearly demonstrate that a considerable amount of useful information can be obtained from student ratings; useful for feedback to faculty, useful for personnel decision, useful to students in the selection of courses, and useful for the study of teaching. Probably, students' evaluations of teaching effectiveness are the most thoroughly studied of all forms of personnel evaluation, and one of the best in terms of being supported by empirical research (p. 369).

Marsh's tempered conclusions set the stage for the present comments. This discussion first explores various interpretations that can be made of information gathered from students about their teachers (which includes a consideration of the possible half-truths and myths that continue to circulate about teacher and course evaluations). It then analyzes the differential importance of the individual items that constitute the rating forms used to evaluate teachers. The primary aim of this discussion is to see how student evaluations can be used to help identify exemplary teachers and instruction.

Truths, Half-truths, and Myths: Interpreting Student Ratings

The unease felt by some faculty, and perhaps by some administrators and students as well, in using teacher and course evaluations to help identify exemplary teachers and instruction may in part be due to the half-truths if not outright myths that have cropped up about these evaluations. Some of the myths can be laid to rest; and the half-truths can be more fully analyzed to separate the real from the imagined. To do so requires a consideration of certain factors or influences that have been said to "bias" ratings. At the moment there is no clear consensus on the definition of bias in the area of student ratings (see Marsh, 1984, 1987; and Marsh and Dunkin, 1992). I take bias to mean something other than (or more than) the fact that student ratings may be influenced by conditions not under the teacher's control or that conditions may somehow be "unfair" to the instructor (making it harder for him or her to teach well and thus to get high ratings compared to teachers in "easier" situations). Rather, bias here refers to one or more factors directly and somehow inappropriately influencing students' judgments about and evaluation of teachers or courses. In essence, the question is whether a condition or influence actually affects teachers and their instruction, which is then accurately reflected in students' evaluations (a case of *non*bias), or whether in some way this condition or influence only affects students' attitudes toward the course and students' perceptions of instructors (and their teaching) such that evaluations do not accurately reflect the instruction that students receive (a case of bias). (For a more extensive discussion of the meaning of bias as it pertains to student ratings, see Feldman, 1984, 1993; Marsh, 1987, and Marsh and Dunkin, 1992.) Implications and examples of this conceptualization of bias will be given as the discussion proceeds.

Myths

Aleamoni (1987) has listed a number of speculations, propositions, and generalizations about students' ratings of instructors and instruction that he declares "are (on the whole) myths." Although I would not go so far as to call each of the generalizations on his list a myth, some of them indeed are—at least as far as current research shows—as follow: students cannot make consistent judgments about the instructor and instruction because of their immaturity, lack of experience, and capriciousness (untrue); only colleagues with excellent publication records and expertise are qualified to teach and to evaluate their peers' instruction—good instruction and good research being so closely allied that it is unnecessary to evaluate them separately (untrue); most student rating schemes are nothing more than a popularity contest, with the warm, friendly, humorous instructor emerging as the winner every time (untrue); students are not able to make accurate judgments until they have been away from the course, and possibly away from the university for several years (untrue); student ratings are both unreliable and invalid (untrue); the time and day the course is offered affect student ratings (untrue); students cannot meaningfully be used to improve instruction (untrue). I call these statements untrue because supporting evidence was not found for them in one or another of the following research reviews: Abrami, Leventhal and Perry (1982); Cohen (1980b); Feldman (1977, 1978, 1987, 1989a, 1989b); Levinson-Rose and Menges (1981); L'Hommedieu, Menges and Brinko (1988, 1990); Marsh (1984, 1987); and Marsh and Dunkin (1992).

For the most part, Aleamoni (1987) also seems correct in calling the following statement a myth: "Gender of the student and the instructor affects student ratings." Consistent evidence cannot be found that either male or female college students routinely give higher ratings to teachers (Feldman, 1977). As for the gender of the teacher, a recent review (Feldman, 1993) of three dozen or so studies showed that a majority of these studies found male and female college teachers not to differ in the global ratings they receive from their students. In those studies in which statistically significant differences were found, more of them favored women than men. However, across all studies, the average association between gender and overall evaluation of the teacher, while favoring women, is so small (average $r = +.02$) as to be insignificant in practical terms. This would seem to show that the gender of the teacher does not bias students' ratings (unless, of course, it can be shown by *other* indicators of teachers' effectiveness that the ratings of one gender "should" be higher than the other to indicate the reality of this group's better teaching).

This said, it should also be noted that there is some indication of an interaction effect between the gender of the student and the gender of the teacher: across studies, there is some evidence to suggest that students may rate same-gendered teachers a little more highly than they do opposite-gendered teachers. What is unknown from the existing studies, however, is what part of this tendency is due to male and female students taking different classes (and thus having different teachers) and what part is due to differences in preferences of male and female students within classes (thus possibly indicating a bias in their ratings).

Half-truths and the Question of Bias in Ratings

Aleamoni (1987) also presents the following statements as candidates for the status of myth: the size of the class affects student ratings; the level of the course affects student ratings; the rank of the instructor affects student ratings; whether students take the course as a requirement or as an elective affects their ratings; whether students are majors or nonmajors affects their ratings. That these are myths is not clear-cut. Each of these course, instructor or student factors is, in fact, related to student evaluation. The real question is: "Why?"

Although the results of pertinent studies are somewhat mixed, some weak trends can be discerned: *slightly* higher ratings are given (a) to teachers of smaller rather than larger courses (Feldman, 1984; Marsh, 1987); (b) to teachers of upper-level rather than lower-level courses (Feldman, 1978); (c) to teachers of higher rather than lower academic ranks (Feldman, 1983; Marsh, 1987); (d) by students taking a course as an elective rather than as a requirement (Feldman, 1978; Marsh, 1987); and (e) by students taking a course that is in their major rather than one that is not (Feldman, 1978; Marsh, 1987). These associations do not prove causation, of course; each of these factors may not actually and directly "affect" ratings, but may simply be associated with the ratings due to their association with other factors affecting ratings.

Even if it can be shown that one or more of these factors actually and directly "affect" students' ratings, the ratings are not necessarily biased by these factors, as is often inferred when such associations are found (probably an important underlying worry of those prone to discount teacher or course evaluations). To give an example, at certain colleges and universities teachers of higher rank may in fact typically be somewhat better teachers, and thus "deserve" the slightly higher ratings they receive. To give another example, teachers in large classes may receive slightly lower ratings because they indeed are somewhat less effective in larger classes than they are in smaller classes, not because students take out their dislike of large classes by rating them a little lower than they otherwise would. So, while it may be somewhat "unfair" to compare teachers in classes of widely different sizes, the unfairness lies in the difference in teaching conditions, not in a rating bias as defined here.[2]

To put the matter in general terms, certain course characteristics and situational contexts—conditions that may not necessarily be under full control of the teachers—may indeed affect teaching effectiveness; and student ratings may then accurately reflect differences in teaching effectiveness. Although rating bias may not necessarily be involved, those interested in using teaching evaluations to help in decisions about promotions and teaching awards may well want to take into account the fact that it may be somewhat harder to be effective in some courses than in others. Along these lines, note that student ratings gathered from the Instructional Development and Effectiveness Assessment (IDEA) system are reported *separately* for four categories of class size—small (1–14 students), medium (15–34), large (35–99) and very large (100 or more)—as well as for five levels of student motivation for the class as a whole (determined by the average of the students' responses to the background question, "I have a strong desire to take this course"). The reason for this procedure is made clear to users of the evaluation instrument, as follows:

> In addition to using flexible criteria, the IDEA system also controls for *level of student motivation* of the students' desire to take the course . . . and the *size of the class*—two variables which the research has shown are correlated with student rating. . . . The IDEA system assumes that it is harder to teach large groups of students who do not want to take a course than it is to teach small groups of students who do want to take a course. IDEA controls for this by comparing an instructor's ratings, not all with "All" courses in the comparative data pool, but with "Similar" courses [same level of student motivation and same class size] as well (Cashin and Sixbury, 1993, pp. 1–2, emphasis in original).

Another candidate for the status of myth concerns students' grades. As Aleamoni (1987) words it, "the grades or marks students receive in the course are highly correlated with their ratings of the course and instructor." On the one hand, the word "highly" indeed makes the statement mythical; grades are not *highly* correlated with students' ratings. On the other hand, almost all of the available research does show a small or even modest positive association between grades and evaluation (usually a correlation somewhere between +.10 and +.30), whether the unit of analysis is the individual student or the class itself (see Feldman, 1976a, 1977; Stumpf and Freedman, 1979).

Research has shown that some part of the positive correlation between students' grades (usually expected grades) and students' evaluation of teachers is due to "legitimate" reasons and therefore is unbiased: students who learn more earn higher grades and thus legitimately give higher evaluations. This has been called the "validity hypothesis" or "validity effect" (see Marsh, 1987, and Marsh and Dunkin, 1992). Moreover, some part of the association may be spurious, attributable to some third factor—for example, students' interest in the subject matter of the course—which has been referred to as the "student characteristics hypothesis" or "student characteristics effect" (see Marsh, 1989, and Marsh and Dunkin, 1992). Yet another part of the positive correlation may indeed be due to a rater bias in the ratings, although the bias might not be large. Researchers currently are trying to determine the degree to which an attributional bias (students' tendency to take credit for successes and avoid blame for failure) and a retributional bias (students "rewarding" teachers who give them higher grades by giving them higher evaluations, and "punishing" teachers who give them lower grades by giving them lower evaluations) are at work (see Gigliotti and Buchtel, 1990; Theall, Franklin, and Ludlow, 1990a, 1990b). The second of these two biases has been called a "grading leniency hypothesis" or "grading leniency effect" (Marsh, 1987, Marsh and Dunkin, 1992). In their view of research relating grades and teacher evaluations, Marsh and Dunkin (1992) conclude as follows:

> Evidence from a variety of different types of research clearly supports the validity hypothesis and the student characteristics hypothesis, but does not rule out the possibility that a grading leniency effect operates simultaneously. Support for the grading leniency effect was found with some experimental studies, but these effects were typically weak and inconsistent, may not generalize to nonexperimental settings where SETs [students' evaluations of teaching effectiveness] are actually used, and in some instances may be due to the violation of grade expectations that students had falsely been led to expect or that were applied to other students in the same course. Consequently, while it is possible that a grading leniency effect may produce some bias in SETs, support for this suggestion is weak and the size of such an effect is likely to be insubstantial in the actual use of SETs (p. 202).

Yet another correlate of—and, therefore, a possible influence on—teacher evaluations is not mentioned by Aleamoni (1987): academic discipline of the course. Reviewing eleven studies available at the time (Feldman, 1978), I found that teachers in different academic fields tend to be rated somewhat differently. Teachers in English, humanities, arts, and language courses tend to receive somewhat higher student ratings than those in social science courses (especially political sciences, sociology, psychology and economic courses); this latter group of teachers in turn receive somewhat higher ratings than teachers in the sciences (excepting certain subareas of biological sciences), mathematics and engineering courses.

Recently, based on data from tens of thousands of classes either from the IDEA system only (Cashin and Clegg, 1987; Cashin and Sixbury, 1993) or from this system and the Student Instructional Report (SIR) of the Educational Testing Service combined (Cashin, 1990), differences among major fields similar to those in my review have been reported.

Cashin and his associates have suggested several possible causes that could be operating to produce these differences in ratings of teachers in different academic disciplines including the following: some courses are harder to teach than others; some fields have better teachers than others; and students in different major fields rate differently because of possible differences in their attitudes, academic skills, goals, motivation, learning styles, and perceptions of the constituents of good teaching. The following practical advice given by Cashin and Sixbury (1993) is informative:

> There is increasing evidence that different academic fields are rated differently. What is not clear is why. Each institution should examine its own data to determine to what extent the differences found in the general research hold true at that particular institution. If an institution concludes that the differences found at that institution are *due to something other than the teaching effectiveness of the instructors*, e.g., because low rated courses are more difficult to teach, or reflect a stricter rating response set on the part of the students taking those courses, then some control for those differences should be instituted. Using the comparative data in this technical report is one possibility. If however, it is decided that the *differences in ratings primarily reflect differences in teaching effectiveness*, that is, that the low rated courses are so rated because they are *not* as well taught, then of course no adjustments should be made (pp. 2–3, emphasis in original).

Identifying Instructional Dimensions Important to Effective Teaching

Thus far, I have explored how student ratings can be used to identify those persons who are seen by students as exemplary teachers (as well as those who are not), noting certain precautions in doing so. Now, I turn to the related topic of how exemplary teaching itself can be identified through the use of student ratings of specific pedagogical dispositions, behaviors and practices of teachers.[3] Teaching comprises many different elements—a multidimensionality that instruments of teacher evaluation usually attempt to capture. The construction of most of these instruments, as Marsh and Dunkin (1992) point out, is based on "a logical analysis of the content of effective teaching and the purposes the ratings are intended to serve, supplemented by reviews of previous research and feedback" (p. 146). Less often used is an empirical approach that emphasizes statistical techniques such as factor analysis or multitrait-multimethod analysis.

Marsh and Dunkin (1992) also note that "for feedback to teachers, for use in student course selection, and for use in research in teaching . . . there appears to be general agreement that a profile of distinct components of SETs [students' evaluations of teaching effectiveness] based on an appropriately constructed multidimensional instrument is more useful than a single summary score" (p. 146). However, whether a multidimensional profile score is more useful than a single summary score for personnel decisions has turned out to be more controversial (see Abrami, 1985, 1988, 1989a, 1989b; Abrami and d'Apollonia, 1991; Abrami, d'Apollonia and Rosenfield, 1993, 1996; Cashin and Downey, 1992; Cashin, Downey and Sixbury, 1994; Hativa and Raviv, 1993; and Marsh, 1987, 1991a, 1991b, 1994).

In earlier reviews (Feldman, 1976b, 1983, 1984, 1987, 1989a), I used a set of roughly 20 instructional dimensions into which the teaching components of relevant studies could be categorized. In recent years, I extended this set in one way or another to include more dimensions (see Feldman, 1988, 1989b, 1993). The fullest set—28 dimensions—is given in the Appendix, along with specific examples of evaluation items that would be categorized in each dimension. Unlike studies using factor analyses or similar techniques to arrive at instructional dimensions, the categories are based on a logical analysis of the single items and multiple-item scales found in the research literature on students' views of effective teaching and on their evaluations of actual teachers. Over the years, I have found the system of categorization to be useful in classifying the characteristics of instruction analyzed in various empirical studies even though it may differ from the definitions and categories found in any one of these studies.[4]

Teaching That Is Associated with Student Learning

Although all 28 dimensions of instruction found in the Appendix would seem to be important to effective teaching, one would assume that some of them are more important than others. One way of establishing this differential importance is to see how various teaching dimensions relate to student learning, which Cohen (1980a, 1981, 1987) did in his well-known meta-analytic study of relationships of student achievement with eight different instructional dimensions.[5] Based in large part on work by d'Apollonia and Abrami (1987, 1988) and Abrami, Cohen and d'Apollonia (1988), I extended Cohen's meta-analysis a few years ago by using less heterogeneous categories for coding the evaluation items and scales in the studies under review, widening the range of instructional dimensions under consideration, and preserving more of the information in the studies Cohen used in his meta-analysis (see Feldman, 1989b, 1990a). To be included in Cohen's meta-analysis or my own, a study had to provide data from actual college classes rather than from experimental analogues of teaching. The unit of analysis on the study had to be the class or instructor and not the individual student. Its data had to be based in a multisection course with a common achievement measure used for all sections of the course (usually an end-of the course examination as it turned out). Finally, the study had to provide data from which a rating/achievement correlation could be calculated (if one was not given).

The correlations between specific evaluations and student achievement from the studies under review were distributed among 28 instructional dimensions (given in the present Appendix), with weighting procedures used to take into account evaluational items or scales that were coded in more than one dimension. Average correlations were calculated for each of the instructional dimensions having information from at least three studies. These average correlations are given in Table 1, along with the percent of variance explained (r^2).[6]

Note that average r's for the instructional dimensions range from +.57 to –.11. All but one (Dimension No. 11) are positive, and all but three (Dimensions No. 11, No. 23, No. 24) are statistically significant. The two highest correlations of .57 and .56—explained variance of over 30%—are for Dimensions No. 5 (teacher's preparation and course organization) and No. 6 (teacher's clarity and understandableness). The teacher's pursuit and/or meeting of course objectives and the student-perceived outcome or impact of the course (Dimensions No. 28 and No. 12) are the next most highly related dimensions with achievement (r = +.49 and +.46). Somewhat more moderately-sized correlations—including between roughly 10% and 15% of explained variance—were found for several instructional dimensions: teacher's stimulation of students' interest in the course and its subject (Instructional Dimension No. 1, average r = +.38); teacher's motivation of students to do their best (No. 20, +.38); teacher's encouragement of questions and discussion, and openness to the opinions of others (No. 16, +.36); teacher's availability and helpfulness (No. 19, +.36); teacher's elocutionary skills; teacher's knowledge of subject (No. 3, +.34) (No. 7, +.35); clarity of course objectives and requirements (No. 9, +.35); and teacher's knowledge of subject (No. 3, +.34).

Less strongly associated with student achievement are: the teacher's sensitivity to, and concern with, class level and progress (No. 8); teacher's enthusiasm (No. 2); teacher's fairness and impartiality of evaluation (No. 13); classroom management (No. 25); intellectual challenge and encouragement of students' independent thought (No. 17); teacher's "personality" (No. 14); teacher's friendliness and respect or concern for students (No. 18); the quality and frequency of teacher's feedback to students (No. 15); the pleasantness of the classroom atmosphere (No. 26); and the nature and value of the course material (No. 10). The nature and usefulness of supplementary materials and teaching aids as well as the difficulty and workload of the course (either as a description or as an evaluation by students) are not related to student achievement. Because of insufficient data in the set of studies under consideration, the relationship of the following dimensions to student achievement is not clear from these studies: No. 4 (teacher's intellectual expansiveness); No. 21 (teacher's encouragement of self-initiated learning); No. 22 (teacher's productivity in research); and No. 27 (individualization of teaching).

Do Certain Kinds of Teaching Actually Produce Student Achievement?

It is important to recognize that the associations between specific evaluations of teachers and student achievement by themselves do not establish the causal connections between the instructional characteristics under investigation and student achievement. For example, it is possible that the correlations that have been found in some proportion of the studies (whose results were used to create Table 1) do not necessarily indicate that the instructional characteristics were causal in producing the students' achievement. Rather, as Leventhal (1975) was one of the first to point out, some third variable such as student motivation, ability or aptitude of the class might independently affect both teacher performance and

Table 1
Average Correlations of Specific Evaluations of Teachers with Student Achievement

Percent Variance Explained	Instructional Dimension	Average r
30.0%–34.9%	No. 5 Teacher's Preparation; Organization of the Course	.57
	No. 6 Clarity and Understandableness	.56
25.0%–29.9%		
20.0%–24.9%	No. 28 Teacher Pursued and/or Met Course Objectives	.49
	No. 12 Perceived Outcome or Impact of Instruction	.46
15.0%–19.9%		
10.0%–14.9%	No. 1 Teacher's Stimulation of Interest in the Course and Its Subject Matter	.38
	No. 20 Teacher Motivates Students to Do Their Best; High Standard of Performance Required	.38
	No. 16 Teacher's Encouragement of Questions, and Openness to Opinions of Others	.36
	No. 19 Teacher's Availability and Helpfulness	.36
	No. 7 Teacher's Elocutionary Skills	.35
	No. 9 Clarity of Course Objectives and Requirements	.35
	No. 3 Teacher's Knowledge of the Subject	.34
5.0%–9.9%	No. 8 Teacher's Sensitivity to, and Concern with, Class Level and Progress	.30
	No. 2 Teacher's Enthusiasm (for Subject or for Teaching)	.27
	No. 13 Teacher's Fairness: Impartiality of Evaluation of Students; Quality of Examinations	.26
	No. 25 Classroom Management	.26
	No. 17 Intellectual Challenge and Encouragement of Independent Thought (by the Teacher and the Course)	.25
	No. 14 Personality Characteristics ("Personality") of the Teacher	.24
	No. 18 Teacher's Concern and Respect for Students; Friendliness of the Teacher	.23
	No. 15 Nature, Quality, and Frequency of Feedback from the Teacher to the Students	.23
	No. 26 Pleasantness of Classroom Atmosphere	.23
0.0%–4.9%	No. 10 Nature and Value of the Course (Including Its Usefulness and Relevance)	.17
	No. 23 Difficulty of the Course (and Workload)—Description	.09
	No. 24 Difficulty of the Course (and Workload)—Evaluation	.07
	No. 11 Nature and Usefulness of Supplementary Materials and Teaching Aids	–.11

Note: This table has been constructed from data given in Table 1 in Feldman (1989b), which itself was based on information in the following studies: Benton and Scott (1976); Bolton, Bonge and Marr (1979); Braskamp, Caulley and Costin (1979); Bryson (1974); Centra (1977); Chase and Keene (1979); Cohen and Berger (1970); Costin (1978); Doyle and Crichton (1978); Doyle and Whitely (1974); Elliott (1950); Ellis and Rickard (1977); Endo and Della-Piana (1976); Frey (1973); Frey (1976); Frey, Leonard and Beatty (1975); Greenwood Hazelton, Smith, and Ware (1976); Grush and Costin (1975); Hoffman (1978); Marsh, Fleiner, and Thomas (1975); Marsh and Overall (1980); McKeachie, Lin, and Mann (1971); Mintzes (1976–77); Morgan and Vasché (1978); Morsh, Burgess, and Smith (1956); Murray (1983); Orpen (1980); Rankin, Greenmun, and Tracy (1965); Remmers, Martin, and Elliott (1949); Rubinstein and Mitchell (1970); Solomon, Rosenberg, and Bezdek (1964); and Turner and Thompson (1974). Each r given in (or derived from information in individual studies was converted to a Fisher's Z transformation (z_r) and weighted by the inverse of the number of instructional dimensions in which it was coded. For each instructional dimension, the weighted z_r's were averaged and then backtransformed to produce the weighted average r's given in this table. These r's are shown only for those instructional dimensions having information from at least three studies; thus there are no entries for Dimensions 4, 21, 22 and 27. All correlations in this table are statistically significant except those for Dimensions 11, 23, and 24.

student learning, which would account for the correlations between instructional characteristics and student achievement even if there were no direct causal connection.

Leventhal (1975) has suggested that causality can be more clearly established in studies in which students are randomly assigned to sections of a multisection course rather than self-selected into them, for the "random assignment of students . . . promotes equivalence of the groups of students by disrupting the causal processes which ordinarily control student assignment" (p. 272). It is not always possible, however, to assign students randomly to class sections. In some of the studies reviewed by Cohen (and by Feldman, 1989b), students were randomly assigned to class sections, whereas in other studies they were not. Interestingly, in his meta-analysis, Cohen (1980a) found that, for each of the four instructional dimensions that he checked, studies in which students were randomly assigned to sections gave about the same results as did studies where students picked their own class sections. Cohen (1980a) also compared studies where the ability of students in class sections was statistically controlled with studies where it was not. Again, for each of the four instructional dimensions that he checked, the correlations for the two sets of studies did not differ. Results such as these increase the likelihood that the instructional characteristics and student achievement are causally connected, although the possibility of spurious elements has not been altogether ruled out. Even with random assignment, the results of multisection validation studies may still permit certain elements of ambiguity in interpretation and generalization (Marsh, 1987; and Marsh and Dunkin, 1992; but see Abrami, d'Apollonia, and Rosenfeld, 1993, 1996).

The results of experimental studies—whether field experiments or laboratory experiments—are obviously useful here, for they can help clarify cause-effect relationships in ways that the correlational studies just reviewed cannot. Relevant research has been reviewed (selectively) by Murray (1991), who notes in his analysis of pertinent studies that either teacher's enthusiasm/expressiveness or teacher clarity (or both) has been a concern in nearly all relevant experimental research, and that these studies usually include measures of amount learned by students. In his overview of this research, Murray (1991) reports that "classroom teaching behaviors, at least in the enthusiasm and clarity domains, appear to be causal antecedents (rather than mere correlates) of various instructional outcome measures" (p. 161, emphasis added).

Although Murray's (1991) definitions of these domains are not completely identical with the definitions of pertinent dimensions of the present analysis, it is still of interest to compare his conclusions and the findings given here. Thus, in the present discussion, teacher clarity has also been shown to be of high importance to teaching, whether indicated by the correlation of teacher clarity with student achievement in the multisection correlational studies or, as will be seen in a later section of this paper, by the association of teacher clarity with the global evaluation of the teacher. As for the enthusiastic/expressive attitudes and behaviors of teachers, highlighted in Murray's (1991) analysis, the instructional dimensions of "teacher's enthusiasm (for subject or for teaching)" referred to in the present discussion is, in fact, associated with achievement in the multisection correlational studies, but only moderately so compared to some of the other instructional dimensions. However, the instructional dimension of "teacher's elocutionary skills," which assumedly is an aspect of enthusiasm/expressiveness is more strongly associated with achievement in the multisectional-correlational studies. Furthermore, note that Murray writes that "behaviors loading on the Enthusiasm [Expressive] factor share elements of spontaneity and stimulus variation, and thus are perhaps best interpreted as serving to elicit and maintain student attention to material presented in class" (p. 146). Given this interpretation, it is of relevance that the instructional dimension of "teacher's stimulation of interest in the course and its subject matter" has been found to be rather highly correlated (albeit less so than the top four dimensions) with students' achievement in multisectional correlational studies; moreover, this particular dimension is highly associated, as well, with global evaluation of instruction relative to the other instructional dimensions (to be discussed in a later section of this paper).

Underlying Mechanisms and Other Considerations

Whether the associations between student learning and teacher's attitudes, behaviors, and practices are established by correlational studies or by experimental studies, the exact psychological and social psychological mechanisms by which these instructional characteristics influence student learning need to be more fully and systematically detailed than they have been. When a large association between an instructional characteristic and student achievement is found, the tendency is to see the finding as obvious—

that is, as being a self-explanatory result. For example, given the size of the correlation involved, it would seem obvious that a teacher who is clear and understandable naturally facilitates students' achievement; little more needs to be said or explained, it might be thought. But, in a very real sense, the "obviousness" or "naturalness" of the connection appears only after the fact (of a substantial association). Were the correlation between dimension of "feedback" and student achievement a great deal larger than was found, then this instructional characteristic, too, would be seen by some as obviously facilitative of student achievement: naturally, teachers who give frequent and good feedback effect high cognitive achievement in their students. But, as previously noted, frequency and quality of feedback has not been found to correlate particularly highly with student achievement, and there is nothing natural or obvious about either a high or low association between feedback and students' achievement; and, in fact, to see either as natural or obvious ignores the specific psychological and social psychological mechanisms that may be involved in either a high or low correlation.

In short, although a case can be made that many of the different instructional characteristics could be expected to facilitate student learning (see, for example, Marsh and Dunkin, 1992, pp. 154–156 [pp. 251–253 herein]), what is needed are specific articulations about which particular dimensions of instruction theoretically and empirically are more likely and which less likely to produce achievement. A crucial aspect of this interest is specifying exactly how those dimensions that affect achievement do so—even when, at first glance, the mechanisms involved would seem to be obvious. Indeed, conceptually and empirically specifying such mechanisms in perhaps the most "obvious" connection of them all in this area—that between student achievement and the clarity and understandableness of instructors—has turned out to be particularly complex, not at all simple or obvious (see, for example, Land, 1979, 1981; Land and Combs, 1981, 1982, Land and Smith, 1979, 1981; and Smith and Land, 1980). Likewise, the mechanisms underlying the correlation between teacher's organization and student achievement have yet to be specifically and fully determined, although Perry (1991) has recently started the attempt by offering the following hypothetical linkages:

> Instructor organization . . . involves teaching activities intended to structure course material into units more readily accessible from students' long-term memory. An outline for the lecture provides encoding schemata and advanced organizers which enable students to incorporate new, incoming material into existing structures. Presenting linkages between content topics serves to increase the cognitive integration of the new material and to make it more meaningful, both of which should facilitate retrieval (p. 26).

One other consideration may be mentioned at his point. McKeachie (1987) has recently reminded educational researchers and practitioners that the achievement tests assessing student learning in the sorts of studies being considered here typically measure lower-level educational objectives such as memory of facts and definitions rather than the higher-level outcomes such as critical thinking and problem solving that are usually taken as important in higher education. He points out that "today cognitive and instructional psychologists are placing more and more emphasis upon the importance of the way in which knowledge is structured as well as upon skills and strategies for learning and problem solving" (p. 345). Moreover, although not a consideration of this paper, there are still other cognitive skills and intellectual dispositions as well as a variety of affective and behavioral outcomes of students that may be influenced in the college classroom (see for example, discussions in Baxter Magolda, 1992; Bowen, 1977; Chickering and Reisser, 1993; Doyle, 1972; Ellner and Barnes, 1983; Feldman and Newcomb, 1969; Feldman and Paulsen, 1994; Hoyt, 1973; King and Kitchener, 1994; Marsh, 1987; Pascarella and Terenzini, 1991; Sanders and Wiseman, 1990; Sockloff, 1973; and Turner, 1970).

Specific Aspects of Teaching as Related to Overall Evaluation of the Teacher

There is another way of determining the differential importance of various instructional dimensions, one that uses information internal to the evaluation form itself. If it is assumed that each student's overall evaluation of an instructor is an additive combination of the student's evaluation of specific aspects of the teacher and his or her instruction, weighted by the student's estimation of the relative importance of these aspects to good teaching, then it would be expected that students' overall assessment of teachers would be more highly associated with instructional characteristics that students generally consider to be more important to good teaching than with those they consider to be less important (cf. Crittenden and Norr, 1973). Thus, one way to establish the differential importance of various instructional characteristics is to compare the magnitudes of the correlations between the actual overall evaluations by students of their teachers and their ratings of each of the specific attitudinal and behavioral characteristics of these teachers. Otherwise put, the importance of an instructional dimension is indicated by its ability to discriminate among students' global assessment of teachers.[7]

In an analysis (Feldman, 1976b) done a while ago now, though one still of full relevance here, I located some 23 studies containing correlations (or comparable information showing the extent of the associations) between students' overall evaluations of their teachers and their ratings of specific attitudinal and behavioral characteristics of these teachers.

This information in each study was used to rank order the importance of these characteristics (in terms of size of its association with overall evaluation) and then to calculate for each study standardized ranks (rank of each item divided by the number of items ranked) for the specific evaluations in the study. Finally, for each of the instructional dimensions under consideration (see Feldman, 1976, Table 1 and note 5), standardized ranks were averaged across the pertinent studies.

These average standardized ranks are given in Column 2 of Table 2. Column 1 of this same table repeats those data previously given in Table 1 on the associations between instructional dimensions and student achievement for just those instructional dimensions considered in both analyses. The two analyses, each determining the importance of instructional dimensions in its own way, have eighteen instructional dimensions in common, although data for only seventeen of them are given in the table. Instructional Dimension No. 4 (teacher's intellectual expansiveness) has been left out, as it was in Table 1, because of insufficient data about the correlation between it and student achievement. Table 2 also shows (in parentheses) the rank in importance of each of the instructional dimensions that is produced by each of the two different methods of gauging importance of the dimensions.

There is no overlap in the studies on which the data in Columns 1 and 2 of Table 2 are based. Furthermore, because the studies considered in the student achievement analyses (Col. 1) are mostly of students in multisection courses of an introductory nature, these students and courses are less representative of college students and courses in general than are the students and courses in the second set of studies (Col. 2). Despite these circumstances, the rank-order correlation (rho) between the ranks shown in the two columns is +.61. Those specific instructional dimensions that are the most highly associated with student achievement tend to be the same ones that best discriminate among teachers with respect to the overall evaluation they receive from students. The correlation is not a perfect one, however. The largest discrepancies are for teacher's availability and helpfulness (relatively high importance in terms of its association with achievement and relatively low importance in terms of its association student's global evaluations) and for intellectual challenge and encouragement of students' independent thought (relatively low importance by the first indicator and relatively high importance by the second indicator). The other large "shifts" between the two indicators of importance are less dramatic: teacher's preparation and course organization (from Rank 1 to Rank 6, the latter still relatively high in importance), and teacher's encouragement of questions and openness to others' opinions (from rank 5.5 to rank 11).

If ranks 1 through 6 are thought of as indicating high importance (relative to the other dimensions), ranks 7–12 as indicating moderate importance, and ranks 13–17 as indicating low importance (low, that is, relative to the other dimensions, not necessarily unimportant), then the two methods determining the importance of instructional dimensions show the following pattern. Both methods indicate that the teacher's preparation and course organization, the teacher's clarity and understandableness, the teacher's stimulation of students' interest and the students' perceived outcome or impact of the course are of high importance (relative to the other dimensions). Although the teacher's encouragement of questions and openness to others' opinions as well as his or her availability and helpfulness are also of high importance in terms of the association of each with achievement, the first is only of moderate importance and the second of low importance in terms of its association with global evaluation of teachers.

Both methods of determining the importance of the instructional dimensions show the following to be of moderate importance relative to other dimensions: teacher's elocutionary skill, clarity of course objective and requirements, teacher's knowledge of subject, and teacher's enthusiasm. The importance of the teacher's sensitivity to class level and progress is also moderate by the first indicator (association with student learning) but high by the second (association with overall evaluation of the teacher), whereas the teacher's fairness and impartiality of evaluation is moderate by the first and low by the second. Each of the following five dimensions is of low relative importance in terms of its association with student achievement, although only the first three are also relatively low in importance in terms of their association with global evaluation: nature, quality and frequency of feedback to students; nature and value of

Table 2
Comparison of Instructional Dimensions on Two Different Indicators of Importance

	Instructional Dimension	Importance Shown by Correlation with Student Achievement (1)	Importance Shown by Correlation with Overall Evaluations (2)
No. 5	Teacher's Preparation; Organization of the Course	.57 (1)	.41 (6)
No. 6	Clarity and Understandableness	.56 (2)	.25 (2)
No. 12	Perceived Outcome or Impact of Instruction	.46 (3)	.28 (3)
No. 1	Teacher's Stimulation of Interest in the Course and Its Subject Matter	.38 (4)	.20 (1)
No. 16	Teacher's Encouragement of Questions and Discussion, and Openness to Opinions of Others	.36 (5.5)	.60 (11)
No. 19	Teacher's Availability and Helpfulness	.36 (5.5)	.74 (16)
No. 7	Teacher's Elocutionary Skills	.35 (7.5)	.49 (10)
No. 9	Clarity of Course Objectives and Requirements	.35 (7.5)	.45 (7)
No. 3	Teacher's Knowledge of the Subject	.34 (9)	.48 (9)
No. 8	Teacher's Sensitivity to, and Concern with, Class Level and Progress	.30 (10)	.40 (5)
No. 2	Teacher's Enthusiasm (for Subject or for Teaching)	.27 (11)	.46 (8)
No. 13	Teacher's Fairness; Impartiality of Evaluation of Students; Quality of Examinations	.26 (12)	.72 (14.5)
No. 17	Intellectual Challenge and Encouragement of Independent Thought (by the Teacher and the Course)	.25 (13)	.33 (4)
No. 18	Teacher's Concern and Respect for Students; Friendliness of the Teacher	.23 (14.5)	.65 (12)
No. 15	Nature, Quality, and Frequency of Feedback from the Teacher to Students	.23 (14.5)	.87 (17)
No. 10	Nature and Value of the Course Material (Including Its Usefulness and Relevance)	.17 (16)	.70 (13)
No. 11	Nature and Usefulness of Supplementary Materials and Teaching Aids	–.11 (17)	.72 (14.5)

Note: This table is adapted from Table 3 in Feldman (1989b). The correlations shown in Column 1 are the same as those in Table 1 of the present analysis. The higher the correlation, the more important the instructional dimension. The correlations have been ranked from 1 to 17 (with the ranks shown in parentheses). The average standardized ranks given in Column 2 originally were given in Feldman (1976b, see Table 2 and footnote 5), and are based on information in the following studies; Brooks, Tarver, Kelley, Liberty and Dickerson (1971); Centra (1975); Cobb (1956); French-Lazovik (1974, two studies); Garber (1964); Good (1971); Harry and Goldner (1972); Harvey and Barker (1970); Jioubu and Pollis (1974); Leftwich and Remmers (1962); Maas and Owen (1973); Owen (1967); Plant and Sawrey (1970); Remmers (1929); Remmers and Weisbrodt (1964); Rosenshine, Cohen and Furst (1973); Sagen (1974); Spencer (1967); Van Horn (1968); Walker (1968); Widlak, McDaniel and Feldhusen (1973); and Williams (1965). The lower the average standardized rank (that is, the smaller the fraction), the more important the dimension. The average standardized ranks in Column 2 have been ranked from 1 to 17 (with the ranks shown in parentheses). This table includes only those dimensions considered in both Feldman (1976b) and Feldman (1989b), and thus there are fewer dimensions in this table than there are in Table 1.

course material; nature and usefulness of supplementary materials and teaching aids; intellectual challenge and encouragement of independent thought (which is of relatively high importance in the strength of its association with the global evaluation of teachers); and teacher's friendliness and concern/respect for student (of moderate importance in its association with global evaluation).

Table 3 offers a summary of the results of using the two different ways considered here of determining the importance of various instructional dimensions from student ratings of teachers. By averaging (when possible) the rank order of the dimensions produced by the two methods, information in Table 2 (and, in some cases, Table 1 as well) has been used to clarify roughly the instructional dimensions into

Table 3
Summary of the Importance of Various Instructional Dimensions Based on Student Ratings

		High Importance
(Two Sources)	No. 6	Clarity and Understandableness
(Two Sources)	No. 1	Teacher's Stimulation of Interest in the Course and Its Perceived Subject Matter
(Two Sources)	No. 12	Perceived Outcome or Impact of Instruction
(Two Sources)	No. 5	Teacher's Preparation; Organization of the Course
(One Source)	No. 28	Teacher Pursued and/or Met Course Objectives
(One Source)	No. 20	Teacher Motivates Students to Do Their Best; High Standard of Performance Required
		Moderate Importance
(Two Sources)	No. 9	Clarity of Course Objectives and Requirements
(Two Sources)	No. 8	Teacher's Sensitivity to, and Concern with, Class Level and Progress
(Two Sources)	No. 16	Teacher's Encouragement of Questions and Discussion, and Openness of Opinions of Others
(Two Sources)	No. 17	Intellectual Challenge and Encouragement of Independent Thought
(Two Sources)	No. 7	Teacher's Elocutionary Skills
(Two Sources)	No. 3	Teacher's Knowledge of the Subject
(Two Sources)	No. 2	Teacher's Enthusiasm for the Subject
(Two Sources)	No. 19	Teacher's Availability and Helpfulness
		Moderate-to-Low Importance
(Two Sources)	No. 13	Teacher's Fairness; Impartiality of Evaluation of Students: Quality of Examinations
(Two Sources)	No. 18	Teacher's Concern and Respect for Students; Friendliness of the Teacher
(One Source)	No. 25	Classroom Management
(One Source)	No. 14	Personality Characteristics ("Personality") of the Teacher
(One Source)	No. 26	Pleasantness of Classroom Atmosphere
		Low Importance or No Importance
(Two Sources)	No. 10	Nature and Value of the Course (Including its Usefulness and Relevance)
(Two Sources)	No. 15	Nature, Quality, and Frequency of Feedback from the Teacher to the Student
(Two Sources)	No. 11	Nature and Usefulness of Supplementary Materials and Teaching Aids
(One Source)	No. 23	Difficulty of the Course (and Workload)—Description
(One Source)	No. 24	Difficulty of the Course (and Workload)—Evaluation

Note: By averaging (when possible) the rank ordering of dimensions produced by two different methods of determining importance of various instructional dimensions, information in Table 2 (and, in some cases, Table 1) has been used to classify instructional dimensions into one of the four categories shown in this table. As indicated in the table, for some instructional dimensions two sources of information were available (association of the instructional dimension with achievement and with global evaluations, as given in Table 2); for other instructional dimensions, only one source of information was available (association of the instruction dimension with achievement, as given in Table 1).

four categories of importance: high importance; moderate importance; moderate-to-low importance; and low (or no) importance. For most of the instructional dimensions, placement into the categories depended on information from both indicators of importance (association with achievement and association with global rating); in the other cases, classification was based on information from only one indicator (association with achievement).

Although the present paper has concentrated on data derived from student ratings of actual teachers, I want to note briefly another way of determining the importance of various instructional dimensions using different information: Those most involved with teaching and learning can be asked directly about the importance of various components of instruction. In one analysis (Feldman, 1988), I collected thirty-one studies in which both students and faculty (separately) specified the instructional characteristics they considered particularly important to good teaching and effective instruction. Students and faculty were generally similar, though not identical, in their views, as indicated by an average correlation of +.71 between them in their valuation of various aspects of teaching. However, the ordering of the instructional dimensions by either of these groups shows differences (as well as some similarities) with that based on the two indicators of importance using student ratings of actual teachers.

A few examples may be given. Similar to the results shown in Table 3, Instructional Dimensions No. 5 (teacher's preparation and organization of the course) and No. 6 (clarity and understandableness) are of high importance to students and to faculty when these groups are asked directly about what is important to good teaching and effective instruction. Further, when asked directly, students again place high importance on Dimension No. 1 (teacher's stimulation of interest), but in this case faculty (when asked directly) see this aspect of teaching as less important than do the students (when asked directly) or by the two indicators of importance derived from student evaluations (summarized in Table 3). Moreover, compared to the importance determined by the analysis of data from student evaluations, students and faculty, when asked directly, place less importance on Instructional Dimension No. 12 (perceived outcome or impact of instruction) but more importance on Dimensions No. 8 (teacher's sensitivity to, and concern with, class level and progress), No. 3 (teacher's knowledge of subject matter), and No. 2 (teacher's enthusiasm).[8]

Concluding Comments

This paper was not intended as a comprehensive review of the research literature on evaluation of college students of their teachers or on the correlates of effective teaching in college. Indeed, several topics or areas usually explored in such reviews have not been considered in this paper. To take two instances, I have ignored an analysis of whether there is a connection between research productivity and teaching effectiveness as well as a discussion of the usefulness of student ratings as feedback to faculty to improve their teaching (other than to label as myths the statements that good instruction and good research are so closely allied as to make it unnecessary to evaluate them separately and that student ratings cannot meaningfully be used to improve teaching). Rather, I have somewhat single-mindedly focused on the use of student ratings to identify exemplary teachers and teaching. In doing so, I have drawn together relevant parts of my own work over the years in addition to incorporating findings and conclusions from selected others.

Nothing I have written in this paper is meant to imply that the use of teacher evaluations is the only means of identifying exemplary teachers and teaching at the college level. The recent discussion of the multitude of items that would be appropriate for "teaching portfolios" by itself suggests otherwise (see, among others, Centra, 1993, Edgerton, Hutchings and Quinlan, 1991, and Seldin, 1991). For instance, in a project sponsored by the Canadian Association of University Teachers to identify the kinds of information a faculty member might use as evidence of teaching effectiveness, some forty-nine specific items were suggested as possible items for inclusion in a dossier (Shore and associates, 1986); only one of these items referred to student ratings (listed as "student course and teaching evaluation data . . ."). Given the diverse ways noted in these dossiers of "capturing the scholarship of teaching," as Edgerton, Hutchings and Quinlan (1991) put it, gathering teacher evaluations may or may not be the one best way to identify excellence in teaching. But it is an important way; and current research evidence does show that when teacher evaluation forms are properly constructed and administered (Feldman, 1979), the global and specific ratings contained in them, as interpreted with appropriate caution, are undeniably helpful in identifying exemplary teachers and teaching.

Notes

1. This paper is based on an earlier one (Feldman, 1994) commissioned by the National Center on Postsecondary Teaching, Learning, and Assessment for presentation at the Second AAHE Conference on Faculty Roles & Rewards held in New Orleans (January 28–30, 1994). The earlier paper benefited by the thoughtful suggestions of Robert Menges and Maryellen Weimer. As for the present paper, I am grateful to Herbert Marsh, Harry Murray, and Raymond Perry for their helpful comments. A brief version of this paper is to appear in an issue of *New Directions for Teaching and Learning*, edited by Marill Svinicki and Robert Menges (Feldman, forthcoming).
2. Using a different definition of bias, Cashin (1988) would consider the size of a class a source of bias if its correlation with student ratings of teachers were sufficiently large (but see Cashin, 1995).
3. As with overall evaluation of teachers, the characteristics of courses, of teachers themselves, and of situational context have all been found to correlate with specific evaluations. Those characteristics most frequently studied have been class size, teacher rank/experience and the gender of the teacher. Class size and the rank/experience of the teacher each correlate more highly with some specific evaluations than with others (for details, see Feldman, 1983, 1984). (The degree to which these factors actually affect teaching rather than "biasing" students in their ratings has yet to be determined.) With the possible exception of their sensitivity to and concern with class level and progress, male and female teachers do not consistently differ in the specific evaluations they receive across studies (Feldman, 1993).
4. Abrami and d'Apollonia (1990) adapted these categories for use in their own work (also see d'Apollonia and Abrami, 1988). More recently, they have made more extensive refinements and modifications to the dimensions and concomitant coding scheme (Abrami, d'Apollonia and Rosenfield, 1993, 1996).
5. These dimensions are labeled: Skill; Rapport; Structure; Difficulty; Interaction; Feedback; Evaluation; and Interest/Motivation.
6. The results given in Table 1 are similar to those shown in an analysis in d'Apollonia and Abrami (1988), although there are some differences (see Abrami, d'Apollonia and Rosenfield, 1996).
7. Limitations of this approach to determining the importance of instructional dimensions are discussed in Feldman (1976b, 1988; also see Abrami, d'Apollonia and Rosenfield, 1993, 1996).
8. Other similarities and differences can be found in Feldman, 1989b (Table 3), where data for all four indicators of the importance of various instructional dimensions—association with achievement, association with global ratings, direct report of students, and direct report of faculty—are given.

References

Abrami, P. C. (1985). Dimensions of effective college instruction. *Review of Higher Education* 8: 211–228.

Abrami, P. C. (1988). SEEQ and ye shall find: A review of Marsh's "Students' evaluation of university teaching." *Instructional Evaluation* 9: 19–27.

Abrami, P. C. (1989a). How should we use student ratings to evaluate teaching? *Research in Higher Education* 30:221–227.

Abrami, P, C. (1989b). SEEQing the truth about student ratings of instruction. *Educational Researcher* 43: 43–45.

Abrami, P. C., Cohen, P. A., and d'Apollonia, S. (1988). Implementation problems in meta-analysis. *Review of Educational Research* 58: 151–179.

Abrami, P. C., and d'Apollonia, S. (1990). The dimensionality of ratings and their use in personnel decisions. In M. Theall and J. Franklin (eds.), *Student Ratings of Instruction: Issues for Improving Practice* (New Directions for Teaching and Learning No. 43). San Francisco: Jossey-Bass.

Abrami, P. C., and d'Apollonia, S. (1991). Multidimensional students' evaluations of teaching effectiveness—generalizability of "N=1" research: Comments on Marsh, 1991). *Journal of Educational Psychology* 83: 411–415.

Abrami, P. C., d'Apollonia, S., and Rosenfield, S. (1993). The dimensionality of student ratings of instruction: Introductory remarks. Paper presented at the annual meeting of the American Educational Research Association.

Abrami, P. C., d'Apollonia, S., and Rosenfield, S. (1996). The dimensionality of student ratings of instruction: What we know and what we do not. In J. C. Smart (ed.) *Higher Education: Handbook of Theory and Research* (Vol. 11). New York: Agathon Press. *(Reprinted in this volume.)*

Abrami, P. C., Leventhal, L., and Perry R. P. (1982). Educational seduction. *Review of Educational Research* 52: 446–464.

Aleamoni, L. (1987). Student rating myths versus research facts. *Journal of Personnel Evaluation in Education* 1: 111–119.

Aubrecht, J. D. (1981). Reliability, validity and generalizability of student ratings of instruction. (IDEA Paper No. 6). Manhattan, KS: Kansas State University, Center for Faculty Evaluation and Development (ERIC Document Reproduction Service No. ED 213 296).

Baxter, Magolda, M. B. (1992). *Knowing and Reasoning in College: Gender-Related Patterns in Students' Intellectual Development.* San Francisco: Jossey-Bass.

Benton, S. E., and Scott, O. (1976). A comparison of the criterion validity of two types of student response inventories for appraising instruction. Paper presented at the annual meeting of the National Council on Measurement in Education.

Bolton, B., Bonge, D., and Marr, J. (1979). Ratings on instruction, examination performance, and subsequent enrollment in psychology courses. *Teaching of Psychology* 6: 82–85.

Bowen, H. R. (1977). *Investment in Learning: The Individual and Social Value of American Higher Education*. San Francisco: Jossey-Bass.

Braskamp, L. A., Brandenburg, D. C., and Ory, J. C. (1984). *Evaluating Teaching Effectiveness: A Practical Guide*. Beverly Hills, Calif.: Sage.

Braskamp, A., Caulley, D., and Costin, F. (1979). Student ratings and instructor self-ratings and their relationship to student achievement. *American Educational Research Journal* 16: 295–306.

Braskamp, L. A., and Ory, J. C. (1994). *Assessing Faculty Work: Enhancing Individual and Institutional Performance*. San Francisco: Jossey-Bass.

Brooks, T. E., Tarver, D. A., Kelley, H. P., Liberty, P. G., Jr., and Dickerson, A. D. (1971). Dimensions underlying student ratings of courses and instructors at the University of Texas at Austin: Instructor Evaluation Form 2. (Research Bulletin RB-71-4). Austin, Texas: University of Texas at Austin, Measurement and Evaluation Center.

Bryson, R. (1974). Teacher evaluations and student learning: A reexamination. *Journal of Educational Research* 68: 11–14.

Cashin, W. E. (1988). Student ratings of teaching: A summary of the research. (IDEA Paper No. 20). Manhattan, KS: Kansas State University, Center for Faculty Evaluation and Development.

Cashin, W. E. (1990). Students do rate different academic fields differently. In M. Theall and J. Franklin (eds.), *Student Ratings of Instruction: Issues for Improving Practice* (New Directions for Teaching and Learning No. 43). San Francisco: Jossey-Bass.

Cashin, W. E. (1995). Student ratings of teaching: The research revisited. (IDEA Paper No. 32). Manhattan, KS: Kansas State University, Center for Faculty Evaluation and Development.

Cashin, W. E., and Clegg, V. L. (1987). Are student ratings of different academic fields different? Paper presented at the annual meeting of the American Educational Research Association. (ERIC Document Reproduction Service No. ED 286 935).

Cashin, W. E., and Downey, R. G. (1992). Using global student rating items for summative evaluation. *Journal of Educational Psychology* 84: 563–572.

Cashin, W. E., Downey, R. G., and Sixbury, G. R. (1994). Global and specific ratings of teaching effectiveness and their relation to course objectives: Reply to Marsh (1994). *Journal of Educational Psychology* 86: 649–9657.

Cashin, W. E., and Sixbury, G. R. (1993). Comparative data by academic field. (IDEA Technical Report No. 8). Manhattan, KS: Kansas State University, Center for Faculty Evaluation and Development.

Centra, J. A. (1975). Colleagues as raters of classroom instruction. *Journal of Higher Education* 46: 327–337.

Centra, J. A. (1977). Student ratings of instruction and their relationship to student learning. *American Educational Research Journal* 14: 17–24.

Centra, J. A. (1979). *Determining Faculty Effectiveness: Assessing Teaching, Research, and Service for Personnel Decisions and Improvement.* San Francisco: Jossey-Bass.

Centra, J. A. (1989). Faculty evaluation and faculty development in higher education. In J. C. Smart (ed.), *Higher Education: Handbook of Theory and Research* (Vol. 5). New York: Agathon Press.

Centra, J. A. (1993). *Reflective Faculty Evaluation: Enhancing Teaching and Determining Faculty Effectiveness.* San Francisco: Jossey-Bass.

Chase, C. I., and Keene, J. M., Jr. (1979). Validity of student ratings of faculty. (Indiana Studies in Higher Education No. 40). Bloomington, Ind.: Indiana University, Bureau of Evaluation Studies and Testing, Division of Research and Development. (ERIC Document Reproduction Service No. ED 169 870).

Chickering, A. W., and Reisser, L. (1993). *Education and Identity* (2nd Ed.). San Francisco: Jossey-Bass.

Cobb, E. B. (1956). Construction of a forced-choice university instructor rating scale. Unpublished doctoral dissertation, University of Tennessee, Knoxville.

Cohen, P. A. (1980a). A meta-analysis of the relationship between student ratings of instruction and student achievement. Unpublished doctoral dissertation, University of Michigan, Ann Arbor.

Cohen, P. A. (1980b). Effectiveness of student-rating feedback for improving college instruction: A meta-analysis of findings. *Research in Higher Education* 13: 321–341.

Cohen, P. A. (1981). Student ratings of instruction and student achievement. *Review of Educational Research* 51: 281–309.

Cohen, P. A. (1987). A critical analysis and reanalysis of the multisection validity meta-analysis. Paper presented at the annual meeting of the American Educational Research Association. (ERIC Document Reproduction Service No. ED 283 876).

Cohen, S. H., and Berger, W. G. (1970). Dimensions of students' ratings of college instructors underlying subsequent achievement on course examinations. Proceedings of the 78th Annual Convention of the American Psychological Association 5: 605–606.

Costin, F. (1978). Do student ratings of college teachers predict student achievement? *Teaching of Psychology* 5: 86–88.

Costin, F., Greenough, W. T., and Menges, R. J. (1971). Student ratings of college teaching: Reliability, validity and usefulness. *Review of Educational Research* 41: 511–535.

Crittenden, K. S., and Norr, J. L. (1973). Student values and teacher evaluation: A problem in person perception. *Sociometry* 36: 143–151.

d'Apollonia, S., and Abrami, P. C. (1987). An empirical critique of meta-analysis: The literature on student ratings of instruction. Paper presented at the annual meeting of the American Educational Research Association.

d'Apollonia, S., and Abrami, P. C. (1988). The literature on student ratings of instruction: Yet another meta-analysis. Paper presented at the annual meeting of the American Educational Research Association.

d'Apollonia, S., Abrami, P. C., and Rosenfield, S. (1993). The dimensionality of student ratings of instruction: A meta-analysis of the factor studies. Paper presented at the annual meeting of the American Educational Research Association.

Doyle, K. O., Jr. (1972). Construction and evaluation of scale for rating college instructors. Unpublished doctoral dissertation, University of Minnesota, Minneapolis.

Doyle, K. O., Jr. (1975). *Student Evaluation of Instruction*. Lexington, Mass.: D. C. Heath.

Doyle, K. O., Jr. (1983). *Evaluating Teaching*. Lexington, Mass.: D. C. Heath.

Doyle, K. O., Jr., and Crichton, L. I. (1978). Student, peer, and self evaluation of college instruction. *Journal of Educational Psychology* 70: 815–826.

Doyle, K. O., Jr., and Whitely, S. E. (1974). Student ratings as criteria for effective teaching. *American Educational Research Journal* 11: 259–274.

Edgerton, R., Hutchings, P., and Quinlan, K. (1991). *The Teaching Portfolio: Capturing the Scholarship in Teaching*. Washington, D. C.: American Association for Higher Education.

Elliott, D. N. (1950). Characteristics and relationship of various criteria of college and university teaching. *Purdue University Studies in Higher Education* 70: 5–61.

Ellis, N. R., and Rickard, H. C. (1977). Evaluating the teaching of introductory psychology. *Teaching of Psychology* 4: 128–132.

Ellner, C. L., and Barnes, C. P. (1983). *Studies of College Teaching: Experimental Results, Theoretical Interpretations, and New Perspectives.* Lexington, Mass.: D. C. Heath.

Endo, G. T., and Della-Piana, G. (1976). A validation study of course evaluation ratings. *Improving College and University Teaching* 24: 84–86.

Feldman, K. A. (1976a). Grades and college students' evaluation of their courses and teachers. *Research in Higher Education* 4: 69–111.

Feldman, K. A. (1976b). The superior college teacher from the students' view. *Research in Higher Education* 5: 243–288.

Feldman, K. A. (1977). Consistency and variability among college students in rating their teachers and courses: A review and analysis. *Research in Higher Education* 6: 223–274.

Feldman, K. A. (1978). Course characteristics and college students' ratings of their teachers: What we know and what we don't. *Research in Higher Education* 9: 199–242.

Feldman, K. A. (1979). The significance of circumstances for college students' ratings of their teachers and courses. *Research in Higher Education* 10: 149–172.

Feldman, K. A. (1983). Seniority and experience of college teachers as related to evaluation they receive from students. *Research in Higher Education* 18: 3–124.

Feldman, K. A. (1984). Class size and college students' evaluations of teachers and courses: A closer look. *Research in Higher Education* 21: 45–116.

Feldman, K. A. (1986). The perceived instructional effectiveness of college teachers as related to their personality and attitudinal characteristics: A review and synthesis. *Research in Higher Education* 24: 139–213.

Feldman, K. A. (1987). Research productivity and scholarly accomplishment of college teachers as related to their instructional effectiveness: A review and exploration. *Research in Higher Education* 26: 227–298.

Feldman, K. A. (1988). Effective college teaching from the students' and faculty's view: Matched or mismatched priorities? *Research in Higher Education* 28: 291–344.

Feldman, K. A. (1989a). Instructional effectiveness of college teachers as judged by teachers themselves, current and former students, colleagues, administrators, and external (neutral) observers. *Research in Higher Education* 30: 137–194.

Feldman, K. A. (1989b). The association between student ratings of specific instructional dimensions and student achievement: Refining and extending the synthesis of data from multisection validity studies. *Research in Higher Education* 30: 583–645.

Feldman, K. A. (1990a). An afterword for "The association between student ratings of specific instructional dimensions and student achievement: Refining and extending the synthesis of data from multisection validity studies." *Research in Higher Education* 31: 315–318.

Feldman, K. A. (1990b). Instructional evaluation. *The Teaching Professor* 4: 5–7.

Feldman, K. A. (1992). College students' views of male and female college teachers: Part I—evidence from the social laboratory and experiments. *Research in Higher Education* 33: 317–375.

Feldman, K. A. (1993). College students' views of male and female college teachers: Part II—evidence from students' evaluations of their classroom teachers. *Research in Higher Education* 34: 151–211.

Feldman, K. A. (1994). Identifying exemplary teaching: Evidence from course and teacher evaluations. Paper commissioned by the National Center on Postsecondary Teaching, Learning, and Assessment for presentation at the Second AAHE Conference on Faculty Roles and Rewards.

Feldman, K. A. (forthcoming). Identifying exemplary teaching: Using data from course and teacher evaluations. In M. D. Svinicki and R. J. Menges (eds.) *Honoring Exemplary Teaching* (New Directions for Teaching and Learning). San Francisco: Jossey-Bass.

Feldman, K. A., and Newcomb, T. M. (1969). *The Impact of College on Students.* San Francisco: Jossey-Bass.

Feldman, K. A., and Paulsen, M. B. (eds.) (1994). *Teaching and Learning in the College Classroom.* Needham Heights, Mass.: Ginn Press.

French-Lazovik, G. (1974). Predictability of students' evaluation of college teachers from component ratings. *Journal of Educational Psychology* 66: 373–385.

Frey, P. W. (1973). Student ratings of teaching: Validity of several rating factors. *Science* 182: 83–85.

Frey, P. W. (1976). Validity of student instructional ratings as a function of their timing. *Journal of Higher Education* 47: 327–336.

Frey, P. W., Leonard, D. W., and Beatty, W. W. (1975). Student ratings of instruction: Validation research. *American Educational Research Journal* 12: 435–444.

Garber, H., 1964. Certain factors underlying the relationship between course grades and student judgments of college teachers. Unpublished doctoral dissertation, University of Connecticut, Storrs.

Gigliotti, R. J., and Buchtel, F. S. (1990). Attributional bias and course evaluation. *Journal of Educational Psychology* 82: 341–351.

Good, K. C. (1971). Similarity of student and instructor attitudes and student's attitudes toward instructors. Unpublished doctoral dissertation, Purdue University, West Lafayette.

Greenwood, G. E., Hazelton, A., Smith, A. B., and Ware, W. B. (1976). A study of the validity of four types of student ratings of college teaching assessed on a criterion of student achievement gains. *Research in Higher Education* 5: 171–178.

Grush, J. E., and Costin, F. (1975). The student as consumer of the teaching process. *American Educational Research Journal* 12: 55–66.

Harry, J., and Goldner, N. S. (1972). The null relationship between teaching and research. *Sociology of Education* 45: 47–60.

Harvey, J. N., and Barker, D. G. (1970). Student evaluation of teaching effectiveness. *Improving College and University Teaching* 18: 275–278.

Hativa, N., and Raviv, A. (1993). Using a single score for summative teacher evaluation by students. *Research in Higher Education* 34: 625–646.

Hoffman, R. G. (1978). Variables affecting university student ratings of instructor behavior. *American Educational Research Journal* 15: 287–299.

Hoyt, D. P. (1973). Measurement of instructional effectiveness. *Research in Higher Education* 1:367–378.

Jiobu, R. M., and Pollis, C. A. (1971). Student evaluations of courses and instructors. *American Sociologist* 6: 317–321.

King, P. M., and Kitchener, K. S. (1994). *Developing Reflective Judgment: Understanding and Promoting Intellectual Growth and Critical Thinking in Adolescents and Adults.* San Francisco: Jossey-Bass.

Kulik, M. A., and McKeachie, W. J. (1975). The evaluation of teachers in higher education. In F. N. Kerlinger (ed.), *Review of Research in Education* (Vol. 3). Itasca, Ill.: F. E. Peacock.

Land, M. L. (1979). Low-inference variables of teacher clarity: Effects on student concept learning. *Journal of Educational Psychology* 71: 795–799.

Land, M. L. (1981). Actual and perceived teacher clarity: Relations to student achievement in science. *Journal of Research in Science Teaching* 18: 139–143.

Land, M. L., and Combs, A. (1981). Teacher clarity, student instructional ratings, and student performance. Paper read at the annual meeting of the American Educational Research Association.

Land, M. L., and Combs, N. (1982). Teacher behavior and student ratings. *Educational and Psychological Research* 2: 63–68.

Land, M. L., and Smith, L. R. (1979). The effect of low inference teacher clarity inhibitors and student achievement. *Journal of Teacher Education* 30: 55–57.

Land, M. L., and Smith, L. R. (1981). College student ratings and teacher behavior: An Experimental Study. *Journal of Social Studies Research* 5: 19–22.

Leftwich, W. H., and Remmers, H. H. (1992). A comparison of graphic and forced-choice ratings of teaching performance at the college and university level. *Purdue Universities Studies in Higher Education* 92: 3–31.

Leventhal, L. (1975). Teacher rating forms: Critique and reformulation of previous validation designs. *Canadian Psychological Review* 16: 269–276.

Levinson-Rose, J., and Menges, R. L. (1981). Improving college teaching: A critical review of research. *Review of Educational Research* 51: 403–434.

L'Hommedieu, R., Menges, R. J., and Brinko, K. T. (1988). The effects of student ratings feedback to college teachers: A meta-analysis and review of research. Unpublished manuscript, Northwestern University, Center for the Teaching Professions, Evanston.

L'Hommedieu, R., Menges, R. J., and Brinko, K. T. (1990). Methodological explanations for the modest effects of feedback. *Journal of Educational Psychology* 92: 232–241.

Maas, J. B., and Owen, T. R. (1973). *Cornell Inventory for Student Appraisal of Teaching and Courses: Manual of Instructions.* Ithaca, NY: Cornell University, Center for Improvement of Undergraduate Education.

Marsh, H. W. (1984). Students' evaluations of university teaching: Dimensionality, reliability, validity, potential biases, and utility. *Journal of Educational Psychology* 76: 707–754.

Marsh, H. W. (1987). Students' evaluations of university teaching: Research findings, methodological issues, and directions for future research. *International Journal of Educational Research* 11: 253–388.

Marsh, H. W. (1991a). Multidimensional students' evaluation of teaching effectiveness: A test of alternative higher-order structures. *Journal of Educational Psychology* 83: 285–296.

Marsh, H. W. (1991b). A multidimensional perspective on students' evaluations of teaching effectiveness: A reply to Abrami and d'Apollonia (1991). *Journal of Educational Psychology* 83: 416–421.

Marsh, H. W. (in press). Weighting for the right criterion in the IDEA system: Global and specific ratings of teaching effectiveness and their relation to course objectives. *Journal of Educational Psychology.*

Marsh, H. W., and Dunkin, M. J. (1992). Students' evaluations of university teaching: A multidimensional approach. In J. C. Smart (ed.), *Higher Education: Handbook of Theory and Research* (Vol. 8). New York: Agathon Press. *(Reprinted in this volume.)*

Marsh, H. W., Fleiner, H., and Thomas, C. S. (1975). Validity and usefulness of student evaluations of instructional quality. *Journal of Educational Psychology* 67: 833–839.

Marsh, H. W., and Overall, J. U. (1980). Validity of students' evaluations of teaching effectiveness: Cognitive and affective criteria. *Journal of Educational Psychology* 72: 468–475.

McKeachie, W. J. (1979). Student ratings of faculty: A reprise. *Academe* 65: 384–397.

McKeachie, W. J. (1987). Instructional evaluation: Current issues and possible improvements. *Journal of Higher Education* 58: 344–350.

McKeachie, W. J., Lin, Y-G, and Mann, W. (1971). Student ratings of teacher effectiveness: Validity Studies. *American Educational Research Association* 8: 435–445.

Miller, R. I. (1972). *Evaluating Faculty Performance.* San Francisco: Jossey-Bass.

Miller, R. I. (1974). *Developing Programs for Faculty Evaluation.* San Francisco: Jossey-Bass.

Mintzes, J. J., (1976–77). Field test and validation of a teaching evaluation instrument: The Student Opinion Survey of Teaching (A report submitted to the Senate Committee for Teaching and Learning, Faculty Senate, University of Windsor), Windsor, Ontario: University of Windsor.

Morgan, W. D., and Vache, J. D. (1978). An Educational Production Function Approach to Teaching Effectiveness and Evaluation. *Journal of Economic Education* 9: 123–126.

Morsh, J. E., Burgess, G. G., and Smith, P. N. (1956). Student achievement as a measure of instructor effectiveness. *Journal of Educational Psychology* 47: 79–88.

Murray, H. G. (1980). *Evaluating University Teaching: A Review of Research.* Toronto: Ontario Confederation of University Faculty Associations.

Murray, H. G. (1983). Low-inference classroom teaching behaviors in relation to six measures of college teaching effectiveness. Proceedings of the Conference on the Evaluation and Improvement of University Teaching: The Canadian Experience (pp. 43–73). Montreal: McGill University, Centre for Teaching and Learning Service.

Murray, H. G. (1991). Effective teaching behaviors in the college classroom. In J. C. Smart (ed.) *Higher Education: Handbook of Theory and Research* (Vol. 7). New York: Agathon Press. *(Reprinted in this volume.)*

Orpen, C. (1980). Student evaluations of lecturers as an indicator of instructional quality: A validity study. *Journal of Educational Research* 74: 5–7.

Owen, P. H. (1967). Some dimensions of college teaching: An exploratory study using critical incidents and factor analyses of student ratings. Unpublished doctoral dissertation, University of Houston, Houston.

Pascarella, E. T., and Terenzini, P. T. (1991). *How College Affects Students: Findings and Insights from Twenty Years of Research.* San Francisco: Jossey-Bass.

Perry, R. P. (1991). Perceived control in college students: Implications for instruction in higher education. In J. C. Smart (ed.), *Higher Education: Handbook of Theory and Research* (Vol. 7). New York: Agathon Press. *(Reprinted in this volume.)*

Plant, W. T., and Sawrey, J. M. (1970). Student ratings of psychology professors as teachers and the research involvement of the professors rated. *The Clinical Psychologist* 23: 15–16, 19.

Rankin, E. F., Jr., Greenmun, R., and Tracy, R. J. (1965). Factors related to student evaluations of a college reading course. *Journal of Reading* 9: 10–15.

Remmers, H. H. (1929). The college professor as the student sees him. *Purdue University Studies in Higher Education* 11: 1–63.

Remmers, H. H., Martin, F. D., and Elliott, D. N. (1949). Are students' ratings of instructors related to their grades? *Purdue University Studies in Higher Education* 66: 17–26.

Remmers, H. H., and Weisbrodt, J. A. (1964). *Manual of Instructions for Purdue Rating Scale of Instruction.* West Lafayette, IN: Purdue Research Foundation.

Rosenshine, B., Cohen, A., and Furst, N. (1973). Correlates of student preference ratings. *Journal of College Student Personnel* 14: 269–272.

Rubinstein, J., and Mitchell, H. (1970). Feeling free, student involvement, and appreciation. *Proceedings of the 78th Annual Convention of the American Psychological Association* 5: 623–624.

Sagen, H. B. (1974). Student, faculty, and department chairmen ratings of instructors: Who agrees with whom? *Research in Higher Education* 2: 265272.

Sanders, J. A., and Wiseman, R. L. (1990). The effects of verbal and nonverbal teacher immediacy on perceived cognitive, affective, and behavioral learning in the multicultural classroom. *Communication Education* 39: 341–353.

Seldin, P. (1991). *The Teaching Portfolio.* Boston: Anker Publishing.

Shore, B. M., and associates (1986). The Teaching Dossier: A Guide to Its Preparation and Use (Rev. Ed.). Montreal: Canadian Association of University Teachers.

Smith, L. R., and Land, M. L. (1980). Student perception of teacher clarity in mathematics. *Journal for Research in Mathematics Education* 11: 137–146.

Sockloff, A. L. (1973). Instruments for student evaluation of faculty: Ideal and actual. In A. L. Sockloff (ed.). *Proceedings of the First Invitational Conference on Faculty Effectiveness as Evaluated by Students.* Philadelphia, PA.: Temple University, Measurement and Research Center.

Solomon, D., Rosenberg, L., and Bezdek, W. E. (1964). Teacher behavior and student learning. *Journal of Educational Psychology* 55: 23–30.

Spencer, R. E. (1967). Analysis of the Instructor Rating Form—General Engineering Department. (Research Report No. 253). Urbana, Ill.: University of Illinois, Measurement and Research Division, Office of Instructional Resources.

Stumpf, S. A., and Freedman, R. D. (1979). Expected grade covariation with student ratings of instruction: Individual versus class effects. *Journal of Educational Psychology* 71: 293–302.

Theall, M., Franklin, J., and Ludlow, L. (1990a). Attributions and retributions: Student ratings and the perceived causes of performance. *Instructional Evaluation* 11: 12–17.

Theall, M., Franklin, J., and Ludlow, L. (1990b). Attributions or retributions: student ratings and the perceived causes of performance. Paper presented at the annual meeting of the American Educational Research Association.

Turner, R. L. (1970). Good teaching and its contexts. *Phi Delta Kappa* 52: 155–158.

Turner, R. L., and Thompson, R. P. (1974). Relationships between college student ratings of instructors and residual learning. Paper presented at the annual meeting of the American Educational Research Association.

Van Horn, C. *An Analysis of the 1968 Course and Instructor Evaluation.* (Institutional Research Bulletin No. 2–68). West Lafayette, Ind.: Purdue University, Measurement and Research Center.

Walker, B. D. (1968). An investigation of selected variables relative to the manner in which a population of junior college students evaluate their teachers. Unpublished doctoral dissertation, University of Houston.

Widlak, F. W., McDaniel, E. D., and Feldhusen, J. F. (1973). Factor analysis of an instructor rating scale. Paper presented at the annual meeting of the American Educational Research Association.

Williams, H. Y., Jr. (1965). College students' perceptions of the personal traits and instructional procedures of good and poor teachers. Unpublished doctoral dissertation, University of Minnesota, Minneapolis.

Appendix

This appendix, with its listing of 28 instructional dimensions, first appeared in Feldman (1989b) in a slightly different version. For each of the instructional dimensions, examples of evaluation items that would be classified into it are given. For refinements and modifications to this list of dimensions and attendant coding scheme, see d'Apollonia, Abrami and Rosenfield (1993) and Abrami, d'Apollonia and Rosenfield (1996).

No. 1 *Teacher's Stimulation of Interest in the Course and Its Subject Matter:* "the instructor puts material across in an interesting way"; "the instructor gets students interested in the subject"; "it was easy to remain attentive"; "the teacher stimulated intellectual curiosity"; etc.

No. 2 *Teacher's Enthusiasm (for Subject or for Teaching):* "the instructor shows interest and enthusiasm in the subject"; "the instructor seems to enjoy teaching"; "the teacher communicates a genuine desire to teach students"; "the instructor never showed boredom for teaching this class"; "the instructor shows energy and excitement"; etc.

No. 3 *Teacher's Knowledge of Subject Matter:* "the instructor has a good command of the subject material"; "the teacher has a thorough knowledge, basic and current, of the subject"; "the instructor has good knowledge about or beyond the textbook"; "the instructor knows the answers to questions students ask"; "the teacher keeps lecture material updated"; etc.

No. 4 *Teacher's Intellectual Expansiveness (and Intelligence):* "the teacher is well informed in all related fields"; "the teacher has respect for other subject areas and indicates their relationship to his or her own subject of presentation"; "the teacher exhibited a high degree of cultural attainment"; etc.

No. 5 *Teacher's Preparation; Organization of the Course:* "the teacher was well prepared for each day's lecture"; "the presentation of the material is well organized"; "the overall development of the course had good continuity"; "the instructor planned the activities of each class period in detail"; etc.

No. 6 *Clarity and Understandableness:* "the instructor made clear explanations"; "the instructor interprets abstract ideas and theories clearly"; "the instructor makes good use of examples and illustrations to get across difficult points"; "the teacher effectively synthesizes and summarizes the material"; "the teacher answers students' questions in a way that helps students to understand"; etc.

No. 7 *Teacher's Elocutionary Skills:* "the instructor has a good vocal delivery"; "the teacher speaks distinctly, fluently and without hesitation"; "the teacher varied the speech and tone of his or her voice"; "the teacher has the ability to speak distinctly and be clearly heard"; "the instructor changed pitch, volume, or quality of speech"; etc.

No. 8 *Teacher's Sensitivity to, and Concern with, Class Level and Progress:* "the teacher was skilled in observing student reactions"; "the teacher was aware when students failed to keep up in class"; "the instructor teaches near the class level"; "the teacher takes an active personal interest in the progress of the class and shows a desire for students to learn"; etc.

No. 9 *Clarity of Course Objectives and Requirements:* "the purposes and policies of the course were made clear to the student"; "the instructor gave a clear idea of the student requirements"; "the teacher clearly defined student responsibilities in the course"; "the teacher tells students which topics are most important and what they can expect on tests"; "the instructor gave clear assignments"; etc.

No. 10 *Nature and Value of the Course Material (Including Its Usefulness and Relevance):* "the teacher has the ability to apply material to real life"; "the instructor makes the course practical"; "there is worthwhile and informative material in lectures that doesn't duplicate the text"; "the course has excellent content"; "the class considers what we are learning worth learning"; etc.

No. 11 *Nature and Usefulness of Supplementary Materials and Teaching Aids:* "the homework assignments and supplementary readings were helpful in understanding the course"; "the teacher made good use of teaching aids such as films and other audio-visual materials"; "the instructor provided a variety of activities in class and used a variety of media (slides, films, projections, drawings) and outside resource persons"; etc.

No. 12 *Perceived Outcome or Impact of Instruction:* "gaining of new knowledge was facilitated by the instructor"; "I developed significant skills in the field"; "I developed increased sensitivity and evaluative judgment"; "the instructor has given me tools for attacking problems"; "the course has increased my general knowledge"; "apart from your personal feelings about the teacher, has he/she been instrumental in increasing knowledge of the course's subject matter" etc.

No. 13 *Teacher's Fairness: Impartiality of Evaluation of Students: Quality of Examinations:* "grading in the course was fair"; "the instructor has definite standards and is impartial in grading"; "the exams reflect material emphasized in the course"; "test questions were clear"; "coverage of subject matter on exams was comprehensive"; etc.

No. 14 *Personality Characteristics ("Personality") of the Teacher:* "the teacher has a good sense of humor"; "the teacher was sincere and honest"; "the teacher is highly personable at all times in dress, voice, social grace, and manners"; "the instructor was free of personal peculiarities"; "the instructor is not autocratic and does not try to force us to accept his ideas and interpretations"; "the teacher exhibits a causal, informal attitude"; "the instructor laughed at his own mistakes"; etc.

No. 15 *Nature Quality, and Frequency of Feedback from the Teacher to Students:* The teacher gave satisfactory feedback on graded material"; "criticism of papers was helpful to students"; "the teacher told students when they had done a good job"; "the teacher is prompt in returning tests and assignments"; etc.

No. 16 *Teacher's Encouragement of Questions and Discussion, and Openness in Opinions of Others:* "students felt free to ask questions or express opinions"; the instructor stimulated class discussions"; "the teacher encouraged students to express differences of opinions and to evaluate each other's ideas"; "instructor invited criticism of his or her own ideas"; "the teacher appeared receptive to new ideas and the viewpoints of others"; etc.

No. 17 *Intellectual Challenge and Encouragement of Independent Thought (by the Teacher and the Course):* "this course challenged students intellectually"; "the teacher encouraged students to think out answers and follow up ideas"; "the teacher attempts to stimulate creativity"; "the instructor raised challenging questions and problems"; etc.

No. 18 *Teacher's Concerns and Respect for Students; Friendliness of the Teacher:* "the instructor seems to have a genuine interest in and concern for students"; "the teacher took students seriously"; "the instructor established good rapport with students"; "the teacher was friendly toward all students"; etc.

No. 19 *Teacher's Availability and Helpfulness:* "the instructor was willing to help students having difficulty"; "the instructor is willing to give individual attention"; "the teacher was available for consultation"; "the teacher was accessible to students outside of class"; etc.

No. 20 *Teacher Motivates Students to Do Their Best; High Standard of Performance Required:* "Instructor motivates students to do their best work"; "the instructor sets high standards of achievement for students"; "the teacher raises the aspirational level of students"; etc.

No. 21 *Teacher's Encouragement of Self-Initiated Learning:* "Students are encouraged to work independently"; "students assume much responsibility for their own learning"; "the general approach used in the course gives emphasis to learning on the students' own"; "the teacher does not suppress individual initiative"; etc.

No. 22 *Teacher's Productivity in Research Related Activities:* "The teacher talks about his own research"; "instructor displays high research accomplishments"; "the instructor publishes material related to his subject field"; etc.

No. 23 *Difficulty of the Course (and Workload)—Description:* "the workload and pace of the course was difficult"; "I spent a great many hours studying for this course"; "the amount of work required for this course was very heavy"; "this course required a lot of time"; "the instructor assigned very difficult reading"; etc.

No. 24 *Difficulty of the Course (and Workload)—Evaluation:* "the content of this course is too hard"; "the teacher's lectures and oral presentations are 'over my head'"; "the instructor often asked for more than students could get done"; "the instructor attempted to cover too much material and presented it too rapidly"; etc.

No. 25 *Classroom Management:* "the instructor controls class discussion to prevent rambling and confusion"; "the instructor maintained a classroom atmosphere conducive to learning"; "students are allowed to participate in deciding the course content"; "the teacher did not 'rule with an iron hand'"; etc.

No. 26 *Pleasantness of Classroom Atmosphere:* "the class does not make me nervous"; "I felt comfortable in this class"; "the instructor created an atmosphere in which students in the class seemed friendly"; "this was not one of those classes where students failed to laugh, joke, smile or show other signs of humor"; "the teacher is always criticizing and arguing with students"; etc.

No. 27 *Individualization of Teaching:* "instead of expecting every student to do the same thing, the instructor provides different activities for different students"; "my grade depends primarily upon my improvement over my past performance"; "in this class each student is accepted on his or her own merits"; "my grade is influenced by what is best for me as a person as well as by how much I have learned"; "the instructor evaluated each student as an individual"; etc.

No. 28 *Teacher Pursued and/or Met Course Objectives:* "the instructor accomplished what he or she set out to do"; "there was close agreement between the announced objectives of the course and what was actually taught"; "course objectives stated agreed with those actually pursued"; etc.

from How College Affects Students

Ernest T. Pascarella and Patrick T. Terenzini

Within-College Effects

In commenting on the body of research on the college environment conducted in the early and mid-1960s, Berdie (1967) made a particularly cogent point in a paper entitled "A University Is a Many Faceted Thing." He argued that most institutions are not monolithic organizations with a single uniform set of environmental stimuli impinging equally on all members. Rather, individuals are members of different subenvironments within the same institution that may have substantially different influences on growth and development. In terms of the acquisition of subject matter knowledge and skills, the academic program is perhaps the most salient of these subenvironments. Obviously, not all learning occurs as a result of the academic program or in classroom settings. Students clearly learn a range of valuable skills from peers, work, and extracurricular and athletic involvements, to name only a few. Yet it is undeniably the college's academic program, with its courses, classroom, laboratory, library, and related experiences, that is the major vehicle through which subject matter knowledge and skills are transmitted (for example, Bisconti, 1987; Bisconti & Kessler, 1980). This section will focus primarily on ways in which differences in the individual student's academic experience influence learning in college. Emphasis will be placed on the influence of differences in patterns of course work, the teaching/learning context, instructional approaches, teaching behavior, and the extent of student involvement or engagement in academic and related experiences. Although there are other conceptual schemes for organizing the effects of college experiences on learning (for example, Bergquist, Gould, & Greenberg, 1981), we think these categories most accurately reflect both where the preponderance of evidence exists and how it is clustered.

Patterns of Course Work

It seems reasonable to expect that what a student learns during college will depend largely on the nature of the courses he or she takes. Different patterns of courses taken should lead to the development of different kinds of knowledge and skills. The hypothesis that differential course work accounts for much of the differences in learned abilities has had considerable attention in research on the impact of secondary education (for example, Fennema & Sherman, 1977; Pallas & Alexander, 1983; Steel & Wise, 1979). While there has been a growing interest in course work patterns in postsecondary education, the bulk of inquiry has been descriptive (for example, Beeken, 1982; Blackburn, Armstrong, Conrad, Didham, & McKune, 1976; Dressel & DeLisle, 1969; Prather, Williams, & Wadley, 1976; Warren, 1975). Comparatively little attention has been devoted to determining whether differential course work leads to differential learning.

One notable exception to this is the work of Ratcliff and Associates (1988) on a single-institution sample. These researchers first residualized the nine item types of the Graduate Record Examination on student Scholastic Aptitude Test scores to produce measures of senior-year learning statistically independent of precollege academic ability. They then cluster analyzed courses on student transcripts by the residual scores on the nine item types of the GRE: quantitative comparison, antonyms, regular mathematics, analytical reasoning, sentence completion, analogies, data interpretation, reading comprehension, and logical reasoning.

"How College Affects Students," by Ernest T. Pascarella and Patrick T. Terenzini, 1991, Jossey-Bass Publishers, Inc.

The results yielded two major findings. First, high residual GRE achievement generally did not appear to be associated with course work taken in any one year. Rather, a spread of course work taken from the freshman to the senior year was most consistently associated with high GRE residuals on seven of the nine item types. This further supports the notion that significant academic learning is not concentrated in any one period during college but instead occurs over the entire span of the college years.

The second major finding of the Ratcliff and Associates (1988) study was that high residual scores on specific GRE item types were associated with specific sets of course work differing by discipline, level (that is, freshman, sophomore, junior, senior), and sequence. One course work cluster consisted primarily of lower-division courses in the arts and sciences and was associated with high residual achievement on antonyms and low achievement in analytical reasoning. A second cluster consisted primarily of business courses evenly distributed between lower and upper divisions. This group was associated with high performance in analytical reasoning and quantitative comparisons and low performance on antonym items. A third cluster consisted primarily of upper-division business and social science courses and was associated with high achievement on analytical reasoning and regular mathematics items. The fourth cluster was defined primarily by lower-division course work in mathematics and the natural sciences and was linked to high residual performance in regular mathematics. A final cluster was largely made up of lower- and upper-division courses in journalism, English, and mathematics and was associated with strong performance in regular mathematics and weak performance in analytical reasoning.

Ratcliff and Associates' (1988) findings are preliminary, and although there is some evidence of their generalizability across institutions (Ratcliff, 1988), they await more definite replication before any but the most tentative conclusion can be made. They nevertheless provide support for differential course work hypothesis at the postsecondary level. While a consistent pattern may not necessarily emerge, the results clearly suggest that the pattern of course work taken during college may have important implications for the types of learning that occur, independent of student academic ability.

The Teaching/Learning Context

Perhaps the most obvious contextual difference in the academic experience of students within the same institution is one's major field of study. The vast majority of colleges and universities require students to select a primary field of study, and this represents a significant portion of the student's total formal course work. Although the extent of requirements for majors varies, it is generally quite substantial: 30 to 40 percent of the total undergraduate course load for the typical B.A. degree and from 40 to 50 percent of the total load for the B.S. degree (Levine, 1978; Jacobs, 1986). As such, the academic major represents an important social and intellectual subenvironment for the student. For example, the major facilitates frequent contact between peers with similar academic and career interests, thus shaping acquaintance networks and reinforcing initial interests (Jacobs, 1986; Feldman & Newcomb, 1969). Moreover, it would appear that majors form somewhat distinctive instructional environments in terms of classroom environments (Astin, 1965a), the nature of the interaction between students and faculty (Gamson, 1966; Hearn & Olzak, 1981; Vreeland & Bidwell, 1966), the effort devoted to instruction (Stark & Morstain, 1978; Trow, 1977), and students' cognitive preferences and strategies for meeting course demands (Barrall & Hill, 1977; Goldman & Hudson, 1973; Goldman & Warren, 1973; Tamir & Kempa, 1977).

Given this evidence, it would seem reasonable to anticipate that one's major would provide distinctive learning outcomes during college. However, beyond the rather obvious and unsurprising finding (cited earlier) that students demonstrate the highest levels of proficiency on subject matter tests most congruent with their academic major, there is little to suggest that students become *generally* more knowledgeable during college *because* of what they major in. Again, the problem is one of separating the socialization effect of different major fields of study from the recruitment effect of students with different characteristics entering different majors to begin with. Unfortunately, in terms of estimating effects on knowledge acquisition, the few existing studies have generally not addressed this issue. In a single-institution study, for example, Dumont and Troelstrup (1981) found no statistically significant differences in average freshman-to-senior gains on the ACT achievement test composite score across five broad academic fields of study. Since amount of change is a function of a group's initial score, however, it is somewhat difficult to interpret these findings, particularly in the absence of some control for initial score.

Perhaps the most extensive evidence concerning major field of study and academic learning is provided by Adelman (1984). Adelman conducted a secondary analysis of student performance between

1964 and 1982 on the Graduate Record Examination, the Graduate Management Admission Test, the Medical College Admission Test, the Law School Admission Test, and fifteen tests of advanced achievement in specific subject areas. With the exception of engineering, students majoring in professional or occupational fields consistently had lower scores on these tests than did those majoring in traditional arts and science fields. Students majoring in engineering, science, and mathematics consistently scored the highest of all major fields. Since Adelman was unable to adjust for initial academic aptitude, however, it is difficult to causally attribute these differences to the effect of one's academic major. If not totally, then at least to a great extent, they probably reflect initial differences in academic aptitude or proficiency among students entering different major fields of study.

If there is little solid evidence one way or the other to suggest that one's academic major has a significant impact on what is generally learned in college outside of one's major field, this should not be construed as indicating that major is unimportant. As we shall see throughout the remainder of this book, one's academic major has a set of influences that extends beyond the college experience to such salient outcomes as one's career choice and income.

Class Size

A somewhat narrower context for teaching and learning than academic major is class size. Here there has been a substantial amount of research over the last sixty years concerning the influence of class size on learning in college (for example, Edmonson & Mulder, 1924; Mueller, 1924; Hudelson, 1928; Cheydleur, 1945; Nachman & Opochinsky, 1958; Simmons, 1959; Siegel, Adams, & Macomber, 1960; Hoover, Baumann, & Schafer, 1970; Attiyeh & Lumsden, 1972; Karp & Yoels, 1976; Williams, Cook, Quinn, & Jensen, 1985). In addition to the body of empirical evidence, there have been a number of reviews of the research on class size and learning (Dubin & Taveggia, 1968; Laughlin, 1976; McKeachie, 1978, 1980; Milton, 1972; Witmer & Wallhaus, 1975). The consensus of these reviews—and of our own synthesis of the existing evidence—is that class size is not a particularly important factor when the goal of instruction is the acquisition of subject matter knowledge and academic skills. Moreover, this finding appears to hold across class type (for example, lecture, discussion) and when measures of learning were standardized across content areas (Williams, Cook, & Jensen, 1984). It is probably the case, however, that smaller classes are somewhat more effective than larger ones when the goals of instruction are motivational, attitudinal, or higher-level cognitive processes (McKeachie, 1980).

Instructional Approaches

Not surprisingly, the question of the effects of different instructional approaches on academic learning and skill acquisition has been the focus of much research. This large body of research is as diverse as it is extensive. Indeed, it may well merit a book-length synthesis in and of itself. Fortunately, however, a number of scholars have undertaken syntheses of different segments of this evidence, upon which our own analysis substantially relies.

Lecture Versus Discussion

One of the initial areas of inquiry into the effects of different instructional approaches on learning is that of lecturing versus discussion. It is reasonably clear that lecturing is the overwhelming method of choice for undergraduate teaching in most institutions. Pollio (1984), for example, estimates that teachers in the typical classroom spend about 80 percent of their time lecturing to students, who in turn are attentive to what is being said about 50 percent of the time. Even so, there is little consistent evidence to suggest that lecturing is any less efficient in imparting subject matter knowledge to students than is instruction that emphasizes class discussion (Dunkin & Barnes, 1985; Kulik & Kulik, 1979; McKeachie, 1962; Ryan, 1969). The weight of evidence, as well as the findings of most literature reviews, tends to converge on this conclusion. The evidence also appears to be consistent in indicating that lecturing is a somewhat less effective instructional approach than classroom discussion when the goal of instruction is higher-order cognitive skills (critical thinking, problem solving, and the like) rather than the transmission of factual information.

Here we see a conclusion quite similar to that of the cognitive benefits of large versus small classes. Since instructional approach is not independent of class size (that is, small classes are more conducive to discussion than large classes), it is likely that these two conclusions are mutually confounding. Nevertheless, the weight of evidence makes it reasonably clear that in postsecondary education neither large or small classes nor lecture or discussion formats are more effective than the other in fostering the mastery of factual subject matter material.

Team Teaching

Another instructional approach that has received some attention in postsecondary education has been that of team teaching. By team teaching we mean the use of two or more people assigned to the same class *at the same time* for instructional purposes. Schustereit (1980) conducted a synthesis of studies pertaining to the influence of team teaching on subject matter achievement. He divided the studies reviewed into two types, those comparing classes taught by a team and those taught by one teacher and studies comparing different teaching techniques, including team teaching. Using the box score method of synthesizing research, he found inconsistent results from the studies reviewed. There were generally as many studies favoring team teaching as favoring solitary teaching. Thus, any generalization about team teaching being a consistently superior or inferior instructional technique for enhancing subject matter learning appears unwarranted.

Individualized Instruction

One characteristic of most traditional lecture or discussion instructional approaches (whether individually or team taught) has been that the pace at which instruction is provided tends to be a constant for all students, while level of achievement or subject matter proficiency tends to vary among students (Cross, 1976, 1981). In the early 1960s, however, Carroll (1963) developed a learning model that essentially reversed the relationship between what is constant and what varies in instruction. In brief, he argued that learners will succeed in learning a given task to the extent that they receive proper instruction and that they spend the amount of time they individually need to learn it. Therefore, according to Carroll, virtually all students can achieve mastery of any learning task if each is given enough time and receives competent instruction.

Although Carroll's (1963) model was developed primarily to address elementary and secondary school learning, it and the closely related mastery concepts of Bloom (1968) have significantly influenced collegiate instruction during the last two decades. Indeed, it is probably safe to say that one important strand of the intellectual heritage of Carroll and Bloom has been the development of various approaches to individualized instruction in postsecondary education. These approaches have taken various forms and are exemplified, though not necessarily exhausted, by the following:

1. *Audio-tutorial instruction (AT):* This instructional method, as developed by Postlethwaite (Postlethwaite, Novak, & Murray, 1972), involves three main components. The independent study session is the primary activity in audio-tutorial instruction. Students work independently on learning tasks in a learning center equipped with laboratory materials, audio tapes, and visual aids. The small assembly session is a weekly meeting of six to ten students and an instructor for the purpose of discussion and quizzing. A weekly meeting, the general assembly session, is used for motivational lectures, films, and major examinations.

2. *Computer-based instruction (CBI):* This approach involves the interactive use of a computer. Programmed instruction, drill and practice, and/or tutorial exercises are frequently implemented in CBI.

3. *Personalized system of instruction (PSI):* This approach was first described by Keller (1968) and has frequently been termed the Keller Plan. PSI involves the following components: (1) small modularized units of instruction, (2) study guides, (3) mastery orientation and immediate feedback on unit tests, (4) self-pacing through the material, (5) student proctors to help with individual problems, and (6) occasional lectures for motivation.

4. *Programmed instruction (PI):* This approach involves the presentation of material in a step-by-step sequential manner. It is a procedure employed in many types of individualized instructional methods.

5. *Visual-based instruction (VI):* This approach relies heavily on visually based materials (for example, slide tapes, films, and other visual instructional technology) as the main instructional vehicle for a course.

While these instructional methods or approaches differ from each other in some specific respects, they have many similarities. Perhaps the primary one is the acknowledgment of individual differences among students coupled with a concern for adapting instruction to the individual learner (Goldschmid & Goldschmid, 1974). Second, the different methods tend to modularize the course content into reasonably small, self-contained units (Dunkin & Barnes, 1985). Third, most of the methods tend to require mastery of material presented in the small units and typically provide immediate (or at least timely) feedback to students concerning their performance on mastery tests (Aiello & Wolfle, 1980; Rowe & Deture, 1975). Finally, the different methods all appear to emphasize active individual student involvement in the learning process, a feature consistent with what is known about effective learning environments (for example, McKeachie, Pintrich, Lin, & Smith, 1986; Rosenshine, 1982). Consequently, there is often less emphasis on employing the teacher in formal or traditional teaching situations such as lectures (Dunkin & Barnes, 1985).

It is our view that these and related attempts to individualize instruction constitute the single most dramatic shift in college teaching over the last two decades. Moreover, the weight of evidence from experimental studies would suggest that such approaches are reasonably effective in improving the acquisition of subject matter content (at least as measured by course-specific tests) over more traditional instructional approaches such as lecture, discussion, and combinations of lecture and discussion. The magnitude of the improvement, however, is not uniform across the different implementations of individualized instruction.

Kulik, Kulik, and Cohen (1979b) and Kulik (1983) summarized the results of forty-two studies employing the audio-tutorial (AT) method in college courses. The major criterion for a study's inclusion in this synthesis was that it had a control group taught by more traditional methods (for example, lecture, discussion) and reported the results of a common course examination. Although there was considerable variation across studies in the magnitude of the effect size (that is, the average of the AT group minus the average of the conventional group divided by the pooled standard deviation of both groups), the average effect size was .20 of a standard deviation favoring the AT group. This effect size was statistically significant (that is, non-zero) and represented an achievement advantage attributable to the AT approach of 8 percentile points. In other words, if the conventionally taught group was achieving at the 50th percentile, the AT group was, on the average, at the 58th percentile. Quite similar results have been reported in Mintzes (1975) in a narrative review of research on the audio-tutorial method and by Aiello and Wolfle (1980) in another meta-analysis based on twenty-seven studies. Aiello and Wolfle report an effect size favoring the AT group of .21, almost exactly the same as that found by Kulik and colleagues. It is also important to note that Kulik, Kulik, and Cohen (1979b) found no statistically significant differences between AT and conventional methods in the attitudes of students toward instruction or their rates of withdrawal from the course. Thus, the modest learning advantages associated with the audio-tutorial approach do not appear to come at the cost of increased course withdrawal rates or negative student attitudes toward the instruction received.

Aiello and Wolfle (1980) and Kulik, Kulik, and Cohen (1980) conducted independent meta-analyses of the effects of computer-based instruction (CBI). The former synthesis was based on eleven studies, while the latter was based on fifty-nine studies. This may account for the substantial difference in effect sizes reported: .42 for Aiello and Wolfle and .25 for Kulik, Kulik, and Cohen. Because the Kulik, Kulik, and Cohen synthesis is based on nearly five times as many studies as the Aiello and Wolfle synthesis, we are inclined to have greater faith in the representativeness of its findings. The statistically significant effect size of .25, favoring CBI over conventional instruction, represents an advantage of 10 percentile points in course achievement. Furthermore, across those studies that address the questions, computer-based instruction showed a positive and significant effect on student attitudes toward instruction and a significant reduction in the hours per week needed for instruction.

Meta-analyses of research on programmed instruction (PI) have been conducted by Aiello and Wolfle (1980) on the basis of twenty-eight studies and by Kulik, Cohen, and Ebeling (1980) on the basis of fifty-seven studies. The results of these two independent syntheses are remarkably similar. The effect size favoring PI over conventional instruction reported by Aiello and Wolfle is .27 of a standard deviation, while that reported by Kulik, Cohen, and Ebeling is .26. Again, this represents an achievement advantage attributable to the PI approach of 10 percentile points. Kulik, Cohen, and Ebeling also report the same achievement advantage for both immediate and delayed measures of achievement and no statistically significant differences between PI and conventional approaches in attitudes toward instruction, course withdrawal rates, and hours per week required for instruction.

Evidence from sixty-five studies that focused on the effects of visual-based instruction (VI) on subject matter learning has been synthesized by Cohen, Ebeling, and Kulik (1981). They report a statistically significant effect size of .15, favoring VI over conventional instructional approaches. While the typical student in the conventional approach functioned at the 50th percentile in learning, the typical student exposed to visual-based instruction was functioning at the 56th percentile (an advantage of 6 percentile points in learning). Cohen, Ebeling, and Kulik also report no significant differences between VI and conventional methods across studies in course withdrawal rate or attitudes toward the instruction received.

Finally, a substantial amount of interest has focused on synthesizing evidence that addresses the effectiveness of the Keller Plan, or personalized system of instruction (PSI), on subject matter learning (for example, Aiello & Wolfle, 1980, Block & Burns, 1976; Johnson & Ruskin, 1977; Kulik, 1982; Kulik, Kulik, & Carmichael, 1974: Kulik, Kulik, & Cohen, 1979a; Robin, 1976). This is probably due to the fact that with the possible exception of the audio-tutorial approach, PSI tends to be the most fully developed and elaborated system of instruction. Thus, it is perhaps the easiest to implement and has the added advantage of not being overly dependent on instructional hardware. Whatever the reason, there is striking consensus in each individual synthesis we reviewed to suggest that PSI is effective in fostering improved subject matter mastery over more conventional instructional approaches. This is true regardless of whether the analysis is quantitative or narrative.

The meta-analytical syntheses of PSI and learning have been conducted by Aiello and Wolfle (1980) on the basis of nineteen studies and by Kulik, Kulik, and Cohen (1979a) on the basis of sixty-one studies. The former report an effect size of .42, favoring PSI over conventional instruction, while the latter report an effect size of .49. Because of Kulik, Kulik, and Cohen's more extensive sampling of the evidence, we are inclined to have somewhat more faith in the effect that they report (although the difference in effect size between the two syntheses is probably trivial). Kulik, Kulik, and Cohen's statistically significant effect size translates into an achievement advantage of 19 percentile points attributable to the personalized system of instruction. They also found that across relevant studies, PSI was associated with a statistically significant advantage of 18 percentile points over conventional methods in students' attitudes toward the instruction received. No statistically significant differences were found between PSI and conventional methods in terms of course withdrawal rates or time required for instruction. (It is noted a recent synthesis by Kulik, Kulik, and Bangert-Drowns (1990) suggests a reconsideration of this conclusion.)

In addition to analyses of the overall effects of the personalized system of instruction on subject matter learning, there has been at least some interest in discovering which particular components of PSI contribute most to its effectiveness (Kulik, 1982; Kulik, Jaska, & Kulik, 1978; Robin, 1976). The studies cited tend to agree that the most salient aspects of PSI in terms of enhancing learning are the mastery requirement and immediate feedback on tests and quizzes. Thus, students in PSI approaches may perform better on common final examinations than students in conventional instruction, in part, at least, because they are forced to study more and have more opportunities to practice the criterion behavior (for example, Cline & Michael, 1978). There is less support for the idea that PSI features such as self-pacing and optional lectures are essential for improving learning, although they may have indirect effects by fostering greater motivation or satisfaction with instruction.

One can conclude from the extensive syntheses of research on the various forms of individualized instruction that each appears to enhance subject matter learning over traditional approaches such as lectures and/or discussion sections. Moreover, this learning advantage appears to occur without giving rise to undesirable side effects in terms of negative student attitudes toward instruction, increased course withdrawal rates, or increased time required to meet course demands. It is also clear, however, that the relative magnitude of the learning advantages attributable to individualized instruction varies quite markedly across its different implementations. Four of the five approaches reviewed (audio-tutorial, computer-based, programmed instruction, and visual-based) provide learning advantages over conventional instruction that are consistent but modest, ranging from 6 to 10 percentile points. In comparison, the learning advantage attributable to the personalized system of instruction (19 percentile points) is twice as great as any of the other approaches.[2]

A second conclusion is that the magnitude of the estimated advantage for each of the different implementations of individualized instruction is essentially independent of study characteristics. Typically, this is determined by regressing effect size on certain design characteristics of the studies included (for example, subject self-selection, randomized assignment to conditions, pretreatment equivalence of experimental and control groups). When this was done, the study design characteristics contributed little to explaining differences in study outcomes (Aiello & Wolfle, 1980; Kulik, Kulik, & Cohen, 1979a, 1979b, 1980). Consequently, one can reasonably conclude that the effects of the different forms of individualized instruction on subject matter learning are not generally biased in their direction by the methodological rigor of the research.

There is one possibly important exception to this conclusion in the research on computer-based instruction, visual-based instruction, and the personalized system of instruction. In these areas student achievement results somewhat more favorable to individualized approaches were found if different instructors implemented individualized and conventional approaches than if the same instructor implemented both. Dunkin and Barnes (1985) argue that this suggests the possibility of an instructor self-selection effect, with individualized approaches tending to attract the most motivated or effective instructors.

A final conclusion about the effects of individualized instructional approaches on student learning is that they tend to be essentially independent of the teaching/learning context. There is little evidence from any of the syntheses that individualized approaches tend to be more effective in some content areas than in others. The one exception to this is that the personalized system of instruction appeared to have stronger positive effects on learning in mathematics, engineering, and psychology than in other social sciences or the natural sciences (Dunkin & Barnes, 1985; Kulik, Kulik, & Cohen, 1979a). Of course, there is a caveat to this conclusion: Individualized instructional approaches are, by their very nature, more likely to be implemented in some content areas and/or course levels than in others. It is probably much more likely, for example, that PSI would be implemented in an introductory calculus course than in a literature course on modern European writers. Indeed, the evidence from most reviews suggests this. Consequently, although it is safe to conclude that individualized instructional approaches are equally effective across nearly all content areas *where they have been implemented*, it is also important to acknowledge that they have not been implemented equally across all possible content areas in the curriculum.

Teacher Behavior

Do differences in teaching behavior systematically influence the acquisition of subject matter knowledge by students? The answer to this question appears to be yes; and it is based on a substantial body of evidence. By and large, this evidence has focused on answering two related questions. First, what are the dimensions of more effective (versus less effective) teaching behavior? Second, how are these various dimensions of teaching behavior related to subject matter learning?

Given the concerns of this book, the first question is perhaps less important than the second. Suffice it to say that reviews of the factor-analytical studies of the dimensions of student evaluations of teaching yield about six general dimensions (Cohen, 1981; Doyle, 1975; Feldman, 1976; Kulik & McKeachie, 1975; Marsh, 1984, 1986a). While different studies employ different names for what may be the same construct, the taxonomy offered by Cohen (1981) is useful and parsimonious. His labels for the dimensions are as follows:

1. *Skill:* This dimension represents the instructor's overall pedagogical adroitness. Typical terms are the "instructor has good command of subject matter"; "the instructor gives clear explanations."

2. *Rapport:* This dimension assesses the instructor's empathy, accessibility, and friendliness; for example, "the instructor is available to talk with students outside of class."

3. *Structure:* This dimension measures how well the instructor planned and organized the course; for example, "the instructor uses class time well."

4. *Difficulty:* This dimension assesses the amount and difficulty of work expected in the course; for example, "the instructor assigns difficult reading."

5. *Interaction:* This dimension measures the extent to which students are encouraged to become actively involved in class sessions; for example, "the instructor facilitates classroom discussion."
6. *Feedback:* This dimension measures the extent to which the instructor provides feedback on the quality of a student's work; for example, "the instructor keeps students informed of their progress."

In terms of the second question, the evidence suggests that while these dimensions of students' perceptions of teaching behavior are largely independent of class size (Feldman, 1984), they have statistically significant positive correlations with course achievement (for example, Benton, 1982; Centra, 1977, 1979; Cohen, 1972; Costin, Greenough, & Menges, 1971; Follman, 1974; Frey, Leonard, & Beatty, 1975; Gage, 1974; Marsh, 1984; Marsh, Fleiner, & Thomas, 1975; McKeachie & Lin, 1978; Mintzes, 1982; Murray, 1985; Sullivan, 1985; Sullivan & Skanes, 1974). Cohen (1981) conducted a meta-analytical synthesis of much of the research on the relationship between student perceptions of teaching behavior and subject matter achievement. His overall synthesis was based on forty-one independent validity studies reporting data from sixty-eight separate multisectional courses. Of the six dimensions of teaching behavior named above, only instructor skill and course structure or organization had statistically significant mean correlations with course achievement, .50 and .47, respectively. More modest correlations were found for such dimensions of teacher behavior as rapport (average correlation = .31), feedback (r = .31), and interaction (r = .22). Cohen also reports statistically significant mean correlations between course achievement and overall student ratings of the course instructor (r = .43) and the course (r = .43).

Additional analysis by Cohen (1981) suggests that the magnitude of the association between student perceptions of instructor proficiency and course achievement is influenced by a number of study characteristics. (In this analysis only overall rating of instructor was employed as a measure of instructor proficiency.) Most notably, correlations between instructor rating and achievement were larger for full-time (versus part-time) faculty,[3] when an external evaluator (not an instructor) graded students' course achievement, and when students knew their final grades before rating the instructor. The last finding, in particular, suggests that knowledge of one's grade may bias perceptions of the quality of instruction received. Additional study characteristics such as statistical control for ability, course level, institutional setting, and a measure of the overall quality of the study had only trivial influences on the magnitude of the correlation between rating of instructor proficiency and subject matter achievement.[4]

Despite the suggestion in Cohen's (1981) synthesis that knowledge of one's grade may bias perceptions of the quality of instruction received, the body of evidence clearly suggests that subject matter learning has a nontrivial relationship with the quality of instruction received. Two dimensions of teacher behavior stand out as being particularly salient in terms of potential influence on learning. These are skill, the general classroom adroitness and pedagogical clarity of the teacher, and structure, the degree of clear organization in the course. Other factors such as instructor rapport, interpersonal accessibility, and feedback to students also appear to be positively associated with achievement but less strongly than instructor skill and course structure.

A recent synthesis of an expanded data base of studies by Feldman (1989, in press) provides an important refinement to the above conclusion regarding instructor skill and course structure. Feldman's analyses suggest that the positive association found between instructor skill and student learning depends more on instructor clarity and understandability than on other constituent factors such as instructor subject matter knowledge or sensitivity to class level and progress. Likewise, the positive association between course structure and learning is more dependent on instructor preparation and organization than on clarity of course objectives and requirements.

Teacher Clarity

Research on student evaluations of teaching is only one source of evidence on the relationship between variations in teaching behavior and variations in achievement. Other researchers have come at the issue from a somewhat different perspective. Interestingly, however, the findings from this research are in rather close agreement with the evidence just reviewed.

One perspective is to take a very micro view of teaching and focus on the effects of specific, observable behaviors on subject matter learning. One of the most developed lines of research in this area is that concerned with teacher clarity. Most of the original work on the influence of teacher clarity and achievement was conducted by Land and Smith and their colleagues (Denham & Land, 1981; Land, 1979, 1980, 1981a, 1981b; Land & Smith, 1979a, 1979b, 1981; L. Smith, 1977, 1982; Smith & Edmonds, 1978; Smith & Land, 1980). They have attempted to identify specific teacher behaviors that present clear and unambiguous learning stimuli to students versus behaviors that lead to ambiguity and confusion. Examples of the former are using examples to illustrate concepts, identifying key points, and clearly signaling topic transitions. Examples of the latter are using "vagueness terms" and "mazes." Vagueness terms are imprecise terms that confuse the learner, such as *basically, you know, so to speak, usually, kind of, I'm not sure*, and so on (Hiller, Fisher, & Kaess, 1969). Mazes are units of discourse that do not make sense, such as starts or halts in speech, redundantly spoken words, and complex tangles of words (L. Smith, 1977).

Land and Smith have attempted to estimate the effects of teacher clarity (versus vagueness or lack of clarity) on subject matter achievement through the series of experimental studies just cited. In the typical study the same instructional content was purposefully taught under different levels of teacher clarity. The basic results of this body of research suggest that independent of other influences, degree of teacher clarity has a statistically significant positive effect on subject matter achievement. Conversely, high frequencies of teacher vagueness terms and mazes, in particular, appear to inhibit learning by college students.

More recent research on teacher clarity by Hines, Cruickshank, and Kennedy (1982, 1985) has broadened the operational definition of the term to include twenty-nine different low-inference (observable) variables thought to comprise clarity in instruction. To determine the independent effect of these variables on subject matter learning, the researchers conducted a complex experiment in which thirty-two student teachers were randomly assigned to classes to teach a twenty-five-minute lesson in matrix multiplication to peers. The teachers were free to select any instructional strategy they believed effective, and all instructional sessions were videotaped so that the teacher clarity behaviors could be recorded by independent observers. Net of student perceptions of teacher clarity and student satisfaction with the instruction, observer ratings of teacher clarity accounted for a statistically significant 52 percent of the variance in mean class achievement on a common posttest. Individual teacher behaviors most strongly and positively related to achievement were using relevant examples during explanation, reviewing material, asking questions to find out if students understood, teaching in a step-by-step manner, explaining things and then stopping so that students could think about the explanation, presenting the lesson in a logical manner, and informing students of lesson objectives or what they were expected to be able to do on completion of instruction. Such behaviors, as well as those uncovered by Land and Smith, are quite consistent with student perceptions of faculty behaviors (for example, skill, structure) that are also positively associated with student learning.[5] Moreover, given the fact that many of the teaching behaviors found to be associated with enhanced subject matter learning are themselves learnable, the research on teacher clarity may have potentially important implications for the pedagogical training of college faculty. Dalgaard (1982), for example, has experimentally demonstrated that teaching-training interventions can significantly improve the classroom effectiveness of graduate teaching assistants.

Student-Faculty Informal Interaction and Effective Teaching

Another perspective on the relationship between teacher behavior and student learning takes a somewhat more macro view. Typical of this approach is the research on the relationship between student-faculty informal interaction and effective teaching conducted by Wilson, Wood, and Gaff (1974) and Wilson, Gaff, Dienst, Wood, and Bavry (1975). In a comprehensive multi-institutional study the researchers had faculty and students identify faculty members whom they (faculty and students) regarded as having a particularly significant impact on students. These "effective teachers" were then compared with other faculty not so identified on a number of teaching dimensions.[6] Aside from factors such as using examples and analogies in teaching and efforts to make courses interesting, effective teachers were also characterized by accessibility to students outside of class. Thus, not only were the effective teachers the most skillful and interesting in the classroom; they also tended to extend their contact with students to nonclassroom situations. Moreover, faculty who interacted frequently with students outside of class tended to give cues as to their "social-psychological accessibility" for such interaction through their in-class teaching behaviors.

Such teaching behaviors and personal traits are not restricted to effective teachers in four-year institutions. Guskey and Easton (1983) report markedly similar behaviors and traits as also characterizing effective teaching in urban community colleges.

Student Involvement

Several recent models of learning and student development have suggested the importance of student involvement or engagement as a key determinant of the outcomes of education (for example, Astin, 1984; Friedlander, 1980; Pace, 1976, 1984; Parker & Schmidt, 1982; Rosenshine, 1982). Not surprisingly, perhaps, a substantial body of evidence exists to suggest that the greater the student's involvement in academic work or in the academic experience of college, the greater his or her level of knowledge acquisition. This evidence is consistent whether extent of involvement is measured at the class level or in terms of broader-based types of involvement.

At the class level, for example, substantial experimental evidence suggests that students are more attentive and involved in what transpires in class when they are required to take notes, and in turn note taking has positive effects on course subject matter achievement (for example, Hult, Cohn, & Potter, 1984; Kiewra, 1983; King, Biggs, & Lipsky, 1984; Locke, 1977; Weiland & Kingsbury, 1979). Similarly, evidence reported by Johnson (1981) and Johnson and Butts (1983) suggests that the greater the proportion of time in which the student is actually engaged in learning activities (taking notes, engaging in discussion, answering questions, and the like), the greater the level of content acquisition.

Peer Teaching or Tutoring

One method by which faculty have sought to increase students' active involvement or engagement in learning is through peer teaching or tutoring (Goldschmid and Goldschmid, 1976). Most of the recent research has suggested that peer teaching and peer tutorial programs have a positive impact on learning. Bargh and Schul (1980) conducted an experiment in which one group of undergraduates studied verbal material to learn it themselves while another group studied the material for the purpose of teaching it to another person. When pretest scores were controlled statistically, students who were preparing to teach scored significantly higher on a subsequent test of content retention than their counterparts who studied only to learn it for themselves. Similar results have been reported by Annis (1983), who compared comprehension knowledge in history among randomly assigned groups of sophomore women who differed in whether they read a passage for the purpose of teaching it to another student or not. With initial reading comprehension scores controlled statistically, students who read the passage with the purpose of teaching it or who actually taught it to another student scored significantly higher on a test of comprehension than students who merely read the passage or who read it and were taught.

Perhaps the most comprehensive study in this area of research was conducted by Benware and Deci (1984). They hypothesized that learning in order to teach facilitates greater intrinsic motivational processes than simply learning to be tested and that intrinsically motivated learning is more active and results in greater conceptual learning. In order to create an intrinsic or active orientation, randomly assigned students in an introductory psychology course were asked to learn material with the purpose of teaching it to another student, while the passive orientation asked students merely to learn material in order to be tested. The results indicated significantly higher conceptual learning of the material read for the group learning to teach but no statistically significant differences in rote learning between the group learning to teach and the group learning to be tested. The group learning to teach also perceived themselves to be more actively engaged in the course than the group learning to be tested, even though they spent equal time with the material.

The experimental research on peer teaching provides reasonably strong evidence that learning material in order to teach it not only increases student involvement in the process of learning but also enhances mastery of the material itself, particularly at the conceptual level. A possible explanation suggested by Bargh and Schul (1980) is that the cognitive benefits of learning to teach result from the use of a different and more comprehensive method of study than that employed when one is merely learning material in order to be tested. This may, in part, account for the finding that tutors in PSI courses benefit even more in terms of content mastery from these courses than do students who take them (Johnson, Sulzer-Azaroff, & Mass, 1977; McKeachie, Pintrich, Lin, & Smith, 1986).

Extent and Quality of Student Effort

A somewhat more broadly based perspective on student involvement and learning has been taken by Pace (1980, 1984). A basic assumption of Pace's work is that what a student gets out of college is dependent not only upon what the college does or does not do but also on the extent and quality of effort that the student puts into college. Thus, extent of subject matter learning, as well as other outcomes of college, is a function of what the institution offers and what the student does with those offerings. To assess involvement Pace has developed fourteen "quality of effort" scales that estimate a student's use of an institution's facilities and opportunities. The scales consist of items that vary according to complexity or "quality of effort" involved in a specific activity; and the respondent indicates level of involvement on a "never" to "very often" continuum. For example, items on the classroom involvement scale range from relatively simple activities such as taking notes or underlining to more complex or higher-level cognitive activities such as efforts to explain, organize, and go beyond assignments. The fourteen scales cluster into three factors: (1) academic and intellectual experiences (for example, library, faculty, classroom), (2) personal and interpersonal experiences (for example, student acquaintances, conversation topics), and (3) group facilities and opportunities (for example, student union, clubs).

Pace (1980) administered the quality of effort scales to a sample of more than 4,000 students at all class levels at thirteen institutions. He also attempted to assess student knowledge acquisition by means of self-reported gains on two scales: general education (gaining broad general knowledge and cultural awareness) and academic and intellectual outcomes (acquiring field-specific knowledge and intellectual skills). (While there are assessment problems with such self-reports, most evidence suggests that they have moderately positive correlations, $r = .25$ to $r = .65$, with objective measures of knowledge [for example, Baird, 1976a; Berdie, 1971; Dumont & Troelstrup, 1980; McMorris & Ambrosino, 1973; Pohlmann & Beggs, 1974].) Pace found that the quality of effort students put into the academic or intellectual aspects of the college experience had statistically significant correlations of .39 with both the general education and the academic (intellectual) outcome scales. It was also the case, however, that the student's quality of effort in personal and interpersonal experiences and group facilities and opportunities had statistically significant positive correlations with the same two outcomes (ranging from $r = .19$ to $r =.40$).

To Pace, such findings suggest a basic wholeness about the college experience. In addition to academic and intellectual effort, involvement in personal and social experiences in college may contribute to learning and the development of intellectual skills. An alternative hypothesis, of course, is that involvement in personal and social experiences is associated with learning and intellectual skill development only because students who are highly involved in the academic and intellectual experience of college tend also to be involved in the personal and social experience of college (for example, Pace, 1987; Pascarella, 1985c; Pascarella & Terenzini, 1980a; Stage, 1987). Thus, if academic and intellectual efforts directly influence learning, personal and social involvements are also likely to correlate with learning but not necessarily in a causal sense.

Despite this alternate hypothesis, Pace's findings on quality of effort and learning are important, particularly since they have been supported by other studies. For example, a series of single-institution, longitudinal analyses by Terenzini and colleagues (Terenzini, Pascarella, & Lorang, 1982; Terenzini, Theophilides, & Lorang, 1984a; Terenzini & Wright, 1987a; Volkwein, King, & Terenzini, 1986) sought to determine the kinds of college experiences that were related to student self-reports of progress in academic and intellectual skill development. Using regression analysis to control statistically for salient background characteristics (for example, race, gender, secondary school achievement) and personal goals, the investigators found that a measure of classroom involvement had generally consistent, positive associations with the academic and intellectual progress measure. The classroom involvement scale measures such factors as how frequently students express their ideas in class and are intellectually stimulated by material covered in class.

Student Interactions with Faculty

Related to the concept of classroom involvement and effort is that of students' interactions and relationships with faculty. If one is willing to assume that faculty generally attach substantial value to student behaviors and attitudes that increase effort and learning (for example, Wallace, 1963, 1967a, 1967b; Pascarella, 1980) and that faculty influence on student values, behaviors, and attitudes is enhanced through informal contact beyond the classroom, it would seem to follow that student interaction with faculty is a potentially important influence on learning. A number of studies tend to confirm this notion, although the evidence is not totally consistent. Endo and Harpel (1982, 1983) conducted two longitudinal studies that looked at the influence of different measures of student-faculty interaction on self-report measures of knowledge acquisition in the senior and freshman years, respectively. Controlling for student precollege characteristics and expectations of college, Endo and Harpel (1982) found that frequency of informal contact with faculty had statistically significant positive associations with seniors' self-reports of adequacy of general knowledge and adequacy of mathematics skills. With similar statistical controls, Endo and Harpel (1983) found that frequency of informal contact with faculty also had a statistically significant positive association with freshmen's reports of their knowledge of basic facts. The researchers also found that perceived quality of relationships with faculty was significantly associated with this outcome.

In terms of the influence of *frequency* of student-faculty informal contact on self-reports of progress in academic and intellectual skill development, similar results have been reported in the longitudinal investigations of Terenzini, Theophilides, and Lorang (1984a) and Terenzini and Wright (1987a). Less supportive evidence, however, has been reported by Terenzini, Pascarella, and Lorang (1982) and Volkwein, King, and Terenzini (1986). In terms of the *quality* of students' relationships with faculty, the findings of Terenzini and colleagues are quite consistent with those of Endo and Harpel (1982, 1983). Controlling for student precollege characteristics, Terenzini and colleagues found that a measure of the extent to which a student had developed a friendly, informal, influential relationship with at least one faculty member was a statistically significant positive predictor of perceived gains in academic skill development.

In addition to the possible problems of reliability and validity of student self-reports (discussed previously), much of the research on student involvement or quality of effort and learning is plagued by potential ambiguity in causal direction. This is particularly evident in those studies that find statistically significant associations between frequency of student-faculty informal interaction and various measures of gains in academic knowledge and skills. Do frequency and quality of informal interaction with faculty enhance students' academic competence, or do initial perceptions of gains in academic knowledge and skills eventually lead students to seek informal contact with faculty beyond the classroom? Unfortunately, the designs of existing studies make it difficult, if not impossible, to answer this question.

Despite this and related methodological problems, the research that links broad-based student involvement or quality of effort during college and increases in academic knowledge and skills opens a potentially significant new area of inquiry. This is particularly true if we can gain a better understanding of those institutional policies, practices, and organizational structures that facilitate involvement or quality of effort. Some evidence does exist to suggest two important influences: living on campus (versus commuting to college) and both institutional and major department size. The former tends to facilitate involvement (for example, Astin, 1973b; Chickering, 1974a; Chickering & Kuper, 1971; Pace, 1980; Pascarella, 1984b), while the latter factors tend to inhibit it (for example, Hearn, 1987; Pascarella, 1985c; Stoecker, Pascarella, & Wolfle, 1988). Moreover, evidence from Pascarella (1985d) suggests that the effect of place of residence on student involvement during college persists irrespective of institutional size, while the inhibiting effect of attending a large institution holds even when place of residence is held constant. Chapman and Pascarella (1983) have suggested that the factors that influence different types of student involvement during college depend on a complex pattern of interactions (conditional effects) between student precollege characteristics and the type of institution attended (four-year residential, four-year commuter, two-year commuter). It is difficult, however, to draw any clear generalizations from their findings.

...

Instructional Approaches

Though not as extensive as the research on subject matter learning, a considerable body of evidence focuses on the effects of different instructional or curricular approaches on the development of general cognitive skills. Consistent with previous sections of this chapter, our synthesis of this evidence is organized according to category of cognitive skill.

Communication Skills

Trank and Steele (1983) sought to determine whether a one-semester course in rhetoric would influence the development of students' speaking and writing skills. Students were given pre- and posttests with alternate forms of the ACT COMP speech and writing tests. There was a statistically significant improvement in total score, but the effect was somewhat stronger in speaking than in writing. Trank and Steele also noted that the students who initially scored lowest showed the greatest gain. In the absence of a control group, however, it is difficult to determine whether this is a differential course effect or simply the result of regression artifacts.

Piagetian Formal Reasoning

A considerable body of inquiry has focused on the effectiveness of instructional interventions designed to increase students' formal reasoning. In our synthesis of this evidence we found one particular approach, termed *inquiry* or *learning cycle* (Karplus, 1974), to have the most consistently positive effects. The purpose of the learning cycle–inquiry approach is to move students from concrete to formal reasoning. It does this essentially by making the learning process highly inductive, or concrete, in nature. Concepts are taught in three stages: (1) exploration—students participate in an activity or laboratory with concrete materials (for example, collect data or conduct an experiment); (2) invention—students draw together ideas and/or concepts out of the concrete activities; and (3) discovery—students generalize or apply the concept (Lawson & Snitgen, 1982). For example, one might introduce the general concept of protective coloration in biology by first throwing equal numbers of red, yellow, blue, white, and green toothpicks on the grass and then seeing which color is least likely to be found.

A number of experimental and quasi-experimental studies (based largely on science content) have compared the effects of the learning cycle-inquiry approach on formal reasoning with that of the more traditional lecture/discussion approach. With the exception of Blake and Nordland (1978) and McMeen (1983), the weight of evidence indicates that the learning cycle-inquiry approach is the more effective in enhancing students' transition from concrete to formal reasoning (Baker, 1978; Campbell, 1978; Killian & Warrick, 1980; Lawson & Snitgen, 1982; McKinnon & Renner, 1971; Mele, 1978; Renner & Lawson, 1975; Renner & Paske, 1977). Although lack of complete data (for example, standard deviations) in some studies makes it difficult to determine the size of the advantage in formal reasoning due to the learning cycle-inquiry approach, our best estimate from available data is that it is about .25 of a standard deviation. This translates to an advantage of about 10 percentile points. We also found little to suggest differences in the quality of the research design between those studies that found the learning cycle-inquiry approach the more effective and those studies that did not.[3]

The learning cycle-inquiry approach was expanded into an entire freshman-year curriculum at a large state university. The purpose of this experimental curriculum (Accent on Developing Abstract Processes of Thought, or ADAPT) was to assist students in moving from concrete to formal (abstract) reasoning (Tomlinson-Keasey & Eisert, 1978a). The ADAPT program combined six disciplines (anthropology, economics, English, history, mathematics, and physics). In each discipline area, courses were taught in an inductive manner consistent with the learning cycle-inquiry approach. An additional aspect of the ADAPT program was that all freshmen enrolled in it formed a social cluster that took classes together and had close contact with peers and professors.

In order to estimate the net impact of the ADAPT curriculum on general cognitive skills, Tomlinson-Keasey and Eisert (1978a) and Tomlinson-Keasey, Williams, and Eisert (1978) conducted a quasi-experiment. The control group included freshman students who had applied to the ADAPT program but were not in the final group of participants. The two groups did not differ significantly in ACT scores or secondary school class percentile rank. Both the ADAPT and control students made statistically significant freshman-year gains on a measure of Piagetian formal reasoning, but the gains of the former were significantly greater. These results were generally replicated in a second-year evaluation of the program (Tomlinson-Keasey & Eisert, 1978b). However, in this instance the ADAPT students were initially much lower in formal reasoning than the control students. Thus, the significantly greater gains for the ADAPT group may have been the result of regression to the mean.

Critical Thinking

A substantial amount of research has been concerned with the influence of specific instructional or curricular interventions on critical thinking.[4] Much of this research has been reviewed in a synthesis by McMillan (1987). Of the twenty-seven studies McMillan reviewed, thirteen focused on the influence of specific instructional variables, and seven focused on the effect of courses. Only two of the studies used true experimental designs (random assignment of subjects to treatments); the rest were either pretest-posttest nonequivalent control group quasi-experiments or simple pre-post designs without a control group. The primary (though not exclusive) criterion measure used was the Watson-Glaser Critical Thinking Appraisal, a very broad-based, general measure of critical thinking that is not tied to academic content. In terms of specific instructional variables, six studies found no statistically significant differences, three reported mixed findings, and four found statistically significant differences favoring a particular instructional variable. However, no single instructional variable was found consistently to enhance critical thinking. Similarly, in terms of course interventions, three studies found no significant effects, three found mixed effects, and only one found significant effects.

One conclusion that can be drawn from the McMillan (1987) review is that specific instructional and course interventions have little consistent impact on the development of critical thinking. The major reason for this may be that a one-quarter or one-semester instructional experience is simply too brief and isolated to have a discernible impact on a general cognitive skill such as critical thinking. This may be particularly true as the instrument of choice for assessing critical thinking in these studies is the Watson-Glaser CTA, a measure that is oriented toward critical thinking in everyday matters rather than in academic matters.

The McMillan (1987) synthesis takes a box score approach (that is, number of studies showing significant results, number showing mixed results, and number showing no significant differences). It therefore tends to be conservative in that studies with statistically nonsignificant findings are considered to indicate a zero effect for the experimental intervention. A meta-analysis, on the other hand, would take a more liberal (Bayesian) approach and consider the size of an intervention's effect even if it were not significantly different from zero. McKeachie, Pintrich, Lin, and Smith (1986) reconsidered an unpublished version of McMillan's review from this perspective and concluded that instruction that stresses student discussion and/or places explicit emphasis on problem-solving procedures and methods may enhance critical thinking. Additional studies not included in McMillan's synthesis would lend at least some support for this position (for example, Holloway, 1976; Moll & Allen, 1982).

There has been less research on the influence of purposeful curricular interventions on critical thinking. In their second-year evaluation of the ADAPT curriculum, Tomlinson-Keasey and Eisert (1978b) compared freshman-year change scores on the Watson-Glaser CTA between students in the ADAPT program and control groups of regular university freshmen. The ADAPT students showed a statistically significant gain of more than one standard deviation, while the gains for the control groups were essentially trivial and statistically nonsignificant, averaging only about .05 of a standard deviation. Unfortunately, the pretest of the ADAPT group was more than a full standard deviation lower than that of the control groups. Consequently, the greater improvement in critical thinking for the ADAPT students may have been, in large part, the result of regression artifacts.

Somewhat more impressive evidence concerning the effects of curricular interventions on critical thinking is presented by Winter, McClelland, and Stewart (1981). They hypothesized that a curriculum experience that requires the integration of ideas, courses, and disciplines would enhance critical thinking over the more typical curriculum, which merely provides a checklist of requirements without any integrative rationale. To test this hypothesis, they compared students in two different curricula within the same institution on gains on the Test of Thematic Analysis. (Recall that the TTA is an essay measure of critical thinking.) The experimental curriculum was a joint humanities program in which students took a group of two or more courses from different but complementary subject areas. The courses focused on an integrative theme relevant to the different disciplines. The control group was made up of students in the regular courses in the same general area, covering the same material, over the same period of time. While students in the integrative program started out on the TTA higher than the controls (1.66 versus 1.22), they also showed significantly greater gains (average increase of .50 versus .08 for the controls). This is the opposite of what one would expect from regression artifacts and represents reasonably impressive evidence of a real effect, despite the absence of an equivalent control group. Winter, McClelland, and

Stewart conclude from this evidence that the experience of having to integrate two or more disciplines at the same time elicits greater cognitive growth than does simply studying the same material in separate courses without a consciously integrative structure. This is consistent with the evidence reported by Dressel and Mayhew (1954) and Forrest (1982) concerning the marked effects on critical thinking and reasoning skills of colleges that stress integrative general education in their curricula.

Postformal Reasoning

A small body of evidence suggests that college instruction can be designed to facilitate development along Perry's (1970) scheme of intellectual development. (Recall that this scheme views intellectual development as advancing through three basic stages: a dualistic right-versus-wrong stage, a relativistic stage in which facts are seen in terms of their context, and a stage in which the individual can make intellectual commitments within a context of relative knowledge). Stephenson and Hunt (1977) report the results of a course-based intervention founded on a theory of cognitive developmental instruction. This type of instruction assumes that intellectual development occurs as a result of "cognitive conflict or dissonance which forces individuals to alter the constructs they have used to reason about certain situations" (Widick, Knefelkamp, and Parker, 1975, p. 291). The experimental intervention was a freshman social science course that focused on human identity within the context of literature and psychology (readings were from such authors as Edward Albee, James Baldwin, Arthur Miller, and Sylvia Plath). The method of instruction was specifically intended to advance dualistic students toward the relativistic stage of the Perry continuum. As such, the instruction emphasized challenges to the students' values and cognitive constructs within a supportive teaching paradigm. The control groups were made up of students in a humanities class and an English class that focused on similar course content but did not include cognitive developmental instruction.

Students in both instructional conditions were pre- and posttested with an instrument developed specifically to measure position on the Perry continuum. Even though the groups were generally equal to begin with, the experimental group exhibited substantially greater stage movement (mean change of +.85 stage) than the control groups (mean change of +.25 stage). Since students self-selected themselves into both the experimental and control conditions, however, there is still the possibility that the findings may be confounded by the interaction of selection and change (that is, the reason why an individual chooses a particular mode of instruction may be a determinant of the degree of change).

Findings generally consistent with those of Stephenson and Hunt (1977) have been reported in two additional course interventions described by Knefelkamp (1974); Widick, Knefelkamp, and Parker (1975); and Widick and Simpson (1978). As with the Stephenson and Hunt study, the two course interventions sought to determine whether cognitive developmental instruction matched to the student's initial stage on the Perry scheme could facilitate progress along the continuum. Once again the instruction emphasized challenges to the students' cognitive and value structure within an overall supportive learning environment. In one intervention, without a control group, there was a pre- to postcourse gain of slightly more than .75 of a stage in the Perry continuum.[5] In the second intervention study, a greater percentage of those exposed to cognitive developmental instruction exhibited progress on the Perry continuum (63 percent) than those in the control sections (51.5 percent). The second study, however, was unclear as to how students were placed in the experimental and control sections. More recent findings similar to those of Knefelkamp (1974); Widick, Knefelkamp, and Parker (1975); and Widick and Simpson (1978) have been reported for an application of cognitive developmental instruction in an introductory course on educational foundations (Mortensen & Moreland, 1985, as reviewed in Kurfiss, 1988).

Conceptual Complexity

We uncovered only one study that dealt with the effects of instructional interventions on conceptual complexity, and that involved the ADAPT curriculum described earlier in the chapter. Tomlinson-Keasey and Eisert (1978a) compared changes in freshman-year scores on the Test of Conceptual Complexity for students in the ADAPT curriculum and regular freshmen. The Test of Conceptual Complexity appears to be a version of the Paragraph Completion Method. (Recall that conceptual complexity assessed in this manner measures the extent to which a person is capable of conceptualizing complex issues on increasingly abstract levels.) Although the ADAPT and control groups were not significantly different on the pretest, the ADAPT students increased approximately .50 of a standard deviation during the freshman year, while the control group actually decreased. The difference in the change in scores was statistically significant. Again, however, these results may be confounded by the fact that students selected the ADAPT or control curriculum. Although students in both groups were similar in conceptual complexity at the beginning of the freshman year, the reasons for their selection of one curriculum rather than the other could have been a determinant of differential change.

Teacher Behavior

As indicated in Chapter Three, there is a considerable body of research on teacher behavior and its relationship to students' learning of subject matter content. In contrast, there has been surprisingly little inquiry concerning the influence of teacher behavior on general cognitive skills. Perhaps the most useful research in this area has been conducted by D. Smith (1977, 1981), who employed a correlational design to assess the relationship between college classroom interactions and critical thinking. Critical thinking was measured by the Watson-Glaser CTA and Chickering's (1972) self-report index of critical thinking behavior. The Flanders (1970) Interaction Analysis System was used to assess four dimensions of classroom interactions. These interactions were related to changes between precourse and postcourse scores on the critical thinking appraisal and to postcourse scores on the six dimensions of the self-report index of critical thinking by means of canonical correlation (akin to multiple regression analysis with more than one dependent variable). The sample included twelve classes (138 students) distributed across disciplines, with analyses conducted at both individual and classroom levels of aggregation. The results suggest that at both levels three types of instructor-influenced classroom interactions were consistently and positively related to gains in critical thinking and to the analysis and synthesis dimensions of critical thinking behavior: the degree to which faculty encouraged, praised, or used student ideas; the degree to which students participated in class and the cognitive level of that participation; and the extent of peer-to-peer interaction in the class.

Clearly, the D. Smith (1977, 1981) research has an important methodological limitation, namely, the absence of controls for possible confounding differences in student precourse levels of critical thinking. (Indeed, research with samples of medical students suggests that student classroom participation is significantly and positively associated with precourse levels of critical thinking [Foster, 1981, 1983].) Nevertheless, the results do suggest that student critical thinking may be enhanced by teacher classroom behaviors that foster active student involvement in the learning process at a rather high level of interchange between student and teacher and between student and student. In this sense Smith's findings are quite consistent with earlier research suggesting that student-initiated discussions or verbal interactions in the classroom enhance the development of higher-order problem-solving skills over more traditional lecture approaches (for example, Beach, 1968; Romig, 1972; C. Smith, 1970). In fact, it may well be that increased student participation is an important causal mechanism underlying the positive association found between small classes and the development of higher-order cognitive processes (Dunkin & Barnes, 1985; McKeachie, 1978, 1980). Other factors being equal, student discussion is probably more likely in a class of 15 to 20 than in one of 250. The D. Smith findings, however, further suggest that amount of student-faculty and student-student interchange may not be particularly influential unless that interchange is at a reasonably high cognitive level.

The Dynamic Interplay of Student Motivation and Cognition in the College Classroom

PAUL R. PINTRICH

Introduction

The problem of how to teach students to become active, motivated, and self-regulating learners is an old but continuing issue in education. Plato struggled with this problem in his efforts to tutor the slave boy Meno. William James, in his *Talks to Teachers*, stressed the importance of not just teaching content and skills but also inculcating habit and will in students. More recently, there has been a plethora of national reports on the necessity of improving our efforts to teach students at the elementary, secondary, and post-secondary levels not only content but also "process" or "critical thinking" skills. This concern for "higher order" thinking skills reflects the assumption that knowledge in different disciplines may change rapidly in our society today. Consequently, students need to acquire not only factual knowledge and basic skills but also "critical thinking" skills which will enable them to evaluate new ideas and concepts. In terms of a psychology of learning and instruction, this issue concerns the problems of the role of domain-specific knowledge vis-a-vis general learning skills and the transfer of learning across domains (cf., Glaser, 1984; Pintrich, 1988,a,b; Pintrich, Cross, Kozma, & McKeachie, 1986).

Most of the research and theory that has addressed the problem of teaching "higher order" skills has stressed cognitive and instructional variables as important components for fostering student learning (cf., Chance, 1986; Chipman, Segal, & Glaser, 1985; Nickerson, Perkins, & Smith, 1985; Segal, Chipman, & Glaser, 1985; Sternberg, 1985). Motivational constructs are usually not discussed in these models of student cognition and thinking, or at best, given only passing and superficial attention. It seems likely, however, that cognitive skills are not learned or employed in isolation from motivation. Motivation seems to be implicated when students are taught cognitive skills, seem to learn them, but then don't employ them in all situations. Motivational constructs such as goals and values are assumed to guide students' approach to a task and, therefore, may influence their cognition (Dweck & Elliott, 1983). For example, a student who sees a difficult task as a challenge may be more willing to try different cognitive strategies to accomplish the task. Other motivational constructs such as self-efficacy may be implicated because students who are not confident of their cognitive skills may not be willing to persist in their use of them in all situations (e.g., Schunk, 1985).

At the same time, most motivational models of student achievement do not incorporate cognitive skills or strategies in their models. Almost all motivational models assume that students who have a "positive" motivational orientation (e.g., high self-efficacy, high task value, adoption of a learning goal, low anxiety, etc.) will try harder and persist longer at a task with a concommitant increase in performance. In some situations effort alone may result in satisfactory performance, but in many school situations effort alone may not be sufficient. For example, a college student may study for many hours a week, but if he is using ineffective or inefficient strategies, he will not do as well as a student who uses effective learning strategies. A motivated student without the appropriate cognitive skills will not perform well,

"The Dynamic Interplay of Student Motivation and Cognition in the College Classroom," by Paul R. Pintrich, reprinted by permission from *Advances in Motivation and Achievement: Motivation Enhancing Environments*, Vol. 6, edited by M. Maehr and C. Ames, 1989, JAI Press.

nor will a skilled student who is not motivated (cf., Paris, Lipson, & Wixson, 1983). In addition, these cognitive and motivational components need to be coordinated by the student in an effortful, yet flexible manner, so that the student is cognitively engaged in the task in a self-regulating fashion (Corno & Mandinach, 1983; Corno & Rohrkemper, 1985).

Given that much of the previous research has examined cognitive or motivational components of students learning separately, the goal of this paper is to focus on the interactive relationships between students' motivation and cognition in the college classroom. Specifically, the paper examines the relationships between students' motivational orientation and their use of cognitive learning strategies as well as their metacognitive and effort management strategies. These motivational and cognitive components are discussed in the context of the college classroom. Although there are many different ways to characterize the college classroom environment (e.g., Dunkin, 1986), the organizing construct in this paper is the academic task (cf., Doyle, 1983). A focus on the academic tasks students must accomplish in the college classroom serves to link the research in cognitive psychology on the influence of tasks on student cognition (e.g., Brown, Bransford, Ferrara, & Campione, 1983) to the motivational research on how different task and reward structures may influence students' motivational beliefs (e.g., Ames, 1981; Cogington & Omelich, 1984). In addition, a focus on academic tasks grounds the discussion of person-environment interaction at a level of analysis that allows for both nomothetic and idiographic analysis of contexts and individuals (Cantor & Kihlstrom, 1987). The remainder of this chapter outlines the theoretical framework for integrating motivational and cognitive components of college student performance, followed by a discussion of classroom tasks. The paper concludes with a presentation of some preliminary empirical results from an on-going research project on college students' motivation, cognition, and achievement in different college classrooms.

...

Empirical Findings

The following empirical results represent an initial attempt to examine the interactive relationships between student motivation and cognition and student performance on different college tasks.

Subjects

College students (n = 224) enrolled at three institutions in the state of Michigan were participants. The institutions included a four-year comprehensive state university, a small liberal arts college, and a community college. The students were enrolled in three types of courses, English composition, Introductory Biology, and Introductory Psychology reflecting the three general disciplines of humanities, natural sciences, and social sciences. There were seven classes involved in the study (2 English, 3 Biology and 2 Psychology) and six instructors (1 English, 3 Biology, 2 Psychology).

Instruments

Students were given the Motivated Strategies for Learning Questionnaire (MSLQ) at the beginning of the term. The MSLQ is a self-report questionnaire that asks students to rate themselves on a variety of motivational and cognitive items. The rating scale is 7-point Likert scale. Different versions of the MSLQ have been used since 1982 in a series of studies on college student learning (e.g., McKeachie, Pintrich, & Lin, 1985; Pintrich, 1986a,b) and the results from these studies demonstrate reasonable internal reliability of the scales and moderate correlations of the scales with academic performance. Table 1 displays the items that make up the scales that were used in the present study along with the alphas for the scales. All components of the model were not measured on this version of the MSLQ (e.g., self-esteem) and, consequently were not included in the results.

The academic achievement measures were taken from the student's actual performance in the course. These measures varied by class but generally consisted of three types of assignments or tasks: exams, essays or papers, and labs. All the courses had exams and most had essay assignments. However, only the biology courses had lab assignments. Accordingly, in the analysis of the performance data the actual number of students varies by the type of task. A fourth performance measure used in analysis of student performance was final grade in the class. Since tasks and grade distribution differed across classes, all

Table 1
Summary of Scales and Sample Items

I. *MOTIVATIONAL COMPONENTS*

A. Intrinsic Orientation (4 items, alpha = .65)
I prefer course work that is interesting and challenging so I can learn new things.
I often choose course assignments that are interesting to me even if they don't guarantee a good grade.

B. Task Value (9 items, alpha = .92)
1. Interest (3 items)
I think that the course material in this class is interesting.
I like the subject matter of this course.
2. Importance (3 items)
It is important for me to learn the course material in this class.
Understanding the subject matter in this class is important to me.
3. Utility value (3 items)
I think that what I learn in this course will be useful to me after college.
I think that the subject matter of this course is useful for me to know.

C. Control Beliefs (5 items, alpha = .68)
I think my grades in this class depend on the amount of effort I exert.
I think my grades in this class depend on the instructor's teaching and grading style (reversed).

D. Expectancy for Success (3 items, alpha = .80)
I expect to do well in this class.
I expect to receive a good grade in this class.

II. *COGNITIVE STRATEGIES*

A. Rehearsal Strategies (4 items, alpha = .65)
When I study I practice saying the material to myself over and over.
When I study for a test I copy my notes over.

B. Elaboration Strategies (11 items, alpha = .80)
When I study I translate difficult material into my own words.
I write short summaries of what I am studying.

C. Organizational Strategies (5 items, alpha = .67)
I have difficulty identifying the important points in my reading.
When I study for an exam I integrate information from different sources (e.g., lectures, readings, discussions).

III. *METACOGNITION* (13 items, alpha = .81)

A. Planning (4 items)
When I study I often skim the material to see how it is organized.
When I study I set goals for myself in order to direct my activities in each study period.

B. Monitoring (5 items)
When studying I try to determine which concepts I don't understand well.
I often find that I have been reading for class but don't know what it was all about (reversed).

C. Regulating (4 items)
I stop periodically while reading and mentally go over or review what was written.
I adjust my reading speed based on how well I understand the material.

IV. *RESOURCE MANAGEMENT STRATEGIES*

A. Time Management (3 items, alpha = .69)
I make good use of my study time.
I find it hard to stick to a study schedule.

B. Study Environment (3 items, alpha = .65)
My primary place for studying is relatively quiet and has few distractions.
I have a regular place set aside for studying.

Table 1 *continued*

C. Effort Management (3 items, alpha = .68)
When work is difficult I either give up or study only the easy parts.
Even when study materials are dull and uninteresting, I manage to keep working until I finish.

D. Help-seeking (5 items, alpha = .76)
When I can't understand the material in a course, I ask another student for help.
I ask my instructor to clarify concepts that I don't understand well.

performance data was converted to z-scores within each class before any analyses were conducted. Current analysis of the tasks focus on the product dimension. Other dimensions such as reward structure did not differ across classrooms or could not be analyzed (e.g., content) because they were confounded with class.

Results

The results section is organized into three general sections that describe: (1) the relationships between the motivational and cognitive components and student course performance, (2) the relationships between the cognitive and motivational components, and (3) the interactive or combined relationships of the motivational and cognitive components to student performance.

Table 2 displays the simple zero-correlations between the motivational and cognitive components of the model and student performance. The use of rehearsal strategies and organizational strategies was positively related to performance on exams and the final grade in the classes. Use of these strategies was not significantly related to performance on the lab or essay assignments. This pattern of results is consistent with the general finding that certain types of learning strategies may be more appropriate for certain types of tasks (cf., Levin, 1986; Weinstein & Mayer, 1986). In addition, the results also suggest that the

Table 2
Zero Order Correlations between Student Performance and Cognitive and Motivation Scales

	Student Performance			
	Exams (n = 224)	Labs (n = 75)	Papers (n = 110)	Grade (n = 224)
Cognitive Components				
Rehearsal	.21**	.12	.12	.23**
Elaboration	.08	.05	.07	.02
Organization	.23**	.13	.11	.23**
Metacognition	.31**	.29*	.19*	.31**
Resource Management				
Time	.23**	.23*	.13	.26**
Study Environment	.10	.11	.00	.12
Effort Management	.28**	.30**	.22*	.32**
Help-seeking	–.02	.32**	.12	.01
Motivational Components				
Intrinsic Orientation	.22**	.02	.19*	.22**
Task Value	.17**	.03	.13	.20**
Control Beliefs	.43**	.39**	.26**	.45**
Expectancy for Success	.45**	.27*	.26**	.45**

* p < .05, ** p < .01

MSLQ does capture two important aspects of learning strategies. The results for elaboration, however, were somewhat surprising. The elaboration scale did not correlate significantly with any of the performance measures. Given that the elaboration scale was made up of a variety of elaboration strategies (e.g., paraphrasing, creating analogies, summarizing) and these strategies may relate differentially to outcomes on different tasks, it may be that an omnibus scale like the current one may not be appropriate. Future analyses of the elaboration items will explore this possibility.

As expected, students who reported using a variety of metacognitive strategies did better on all the performance measures (see Table 2). Students who reported more planning , monitoring, and self-regulating performed better on our performance measures. Two of the resource management strategies showed consistent positive relationships with performance as expected. Good use of study time resulted in better grades in the class as well as on the exams and labs. Most importantly, students' high in effort management did well on all four performance measures. Students who were able to regulate their effort and attention did better in class than those students who were not as effortful. Study environment did not correlate significantly with any performance measures, while help-seeking only showed a positive relationship with lab performance. Given previous suggestions that help-seeking might be related to performance in a non-linear fashion (e.g., Rosen, 1983), quadratic and cubic relationships for help-seeking were examined and found to be non-significant.

The motivational components generally displayed the expected positive relationships with performance, albeit the value components of task value and intrinsic orientation did not show as consistent or as strong relationships as the expectancy components of control beliefs and expectancy for success (see Table 2). Students who stated that they were highly motivated for challenge and mastery performed at higher levels on exams, essays, and final grade than students who were not as intrinsic in their orientation. Students who were interested in the course material and thought the material was important and useful also performed better than students low in task value on exams and the final grade. Students who expected to succeed and believed that their grades were contingent on aspects of their own behavior rather than others' behavior performed at higher levels on all four outcome measures. These findings are consistent with other results on the link between motivational components and performance and suggest that the MSLQ provides valid measures of students' motivational orientation.

Table 3 displays the zero order correlations for the relationships between the motivational and cognitive components. In general, as expected, the motivational components were positively correlated with the cognitive components. Students who were more challenge and mastery oriented used more cognitive strategies and engaged in more metacognitive activities as well as managed their effort in a more positive fashion than students who were less intrinsically oriented. Students high in task value basically showed the same pattern (see Table 3). The expectancy components also were correlated in a positive fashion with the cognitive and metacognitive components, but in a somewhat stronger pattern. Students high in control beliefs were higher than students with low control beliefs in all the cognitive, metacognitive, and re-

Table 3
Zero Order Correlations between Cognitive and Motivational Components

	Motivational Components			
Cognitive Components	*Intrinsic Orient.*	*Task Value*	*Control Beliefs*	*Expectancy for Success*
Rehearsal	.27**	.20**	.31**	.27**
Elaboration	.11	.23**	.18**	.09
Organizational	.33*	.23**	.37**	.36**
Metacognition	.35**	.21**	.48**	.34**
Time Management	.18**	.05	.51**	.16*
Study Environment	.12	.03	.28**	.16*
Effort Management	.20**	.15*	.57**	.35**
Help-seeking	–.02	.08	.08	.09

* $p < .05$, ** $p < .01$

source management strategies except for help-seeking. The same pattern held for students high in expectancy for success except for elaboration and help-seeking strategies.

These results are correlational and no causal statements can be made about the directionality of the relationship between the motivational and cognitive components. However, these results suggest that both the expectancy and value components of motivation are related to students' cognitive and metacognitive strategies. Students who are generally active and self-regulating learners (e.g., high in cognitive and metacognitive activity including effort regulation) tend to be students who value and are interested in the course work. In addition, these active and self-regulating learners are even more likely to be students who have fairly high control beliefs and high expectations for success. The remaining question is how do these motivational and cognitive components work together to produce academic performance?

There are a number of potential ways to analyze the data to examine the interactive relationships between the motivational and the cognitive components and student performance. Previous research (e.g., Pintrich, 1986a,b), using some of the same motivational and cognitive measures with two different samples of college students, showed that there were few, if any bivariate or threeway interactions between the motivational and cognitive measures and student performance. For example, there were no simple bivariate interactions between students high and low in metacognition and students high and low in expectancy for success (Pintrich, 1986a,b). The same pattern held in this data set. There were no bivariate interactions between the four motivational variables and students' metacognitive activities or effort management.

Another possible way of analyzing the data is to examine the independent contributions of the motivational and cognitive components in a series of regression and path analyses. Previous studies have used this approach (Pintrich, 1986a,b) and, in general, have shown that two or three variables emerge as good predictors of performance, usually metacognition, expectancy for success, and effort management. In addition, path analyses have revealed that the direct effects of strategy use on performance are mediated by effort management and that effort management is a function of both the motivational and cognitive components (Pintrich, 1986b). These results are helpful in teasing apart the relative influences of the motivational and cognitive components on student performance, but the current data are cross-sectional and correlational making it difficult to specify the relative primacy of the motivational or cognitive components. In addition, it is not clear that these cognitive and motivational variables should work independently from one another as suggested by a simple regression analysis. Rather, if they work together in a synergistic fashion, an analysis strategy that takes into consideration the interdependence may be more illuminating. Consequently, a cluster analysis strategy which involved treating the motivational and cognitive components as interdependent was adopted for analysis of the current data.

The cluster analysis was used to create a typology of students based on the different patterns of relationships among the motivational and cognitive components between students. A casewise or P-type cluster analysis was performed using seven variables: the four motivational variables (intrinsic orientation, task value, control beliefs, and expectancy for success), the cognitive rehearsal scale, the metacognitive scale, and the effort management scale. These seven variables were selected because they showed the strongest and most consistent relationships to performance. The cluster analysis used correlations as the distance measure and a complete linkage algorithm to form clusters (Everitt, 1980). The selection of the appropriate cluster solution was based on two general criteria, parsimony and significant differences between the cluster group vectors on the scales included in the original cluster analysis and other variables (e.g., performance measures) not included in the cluster analysis (Aldenderfer & Blashfield, 1984).

As Aldenderfer and Blashfield (1984) suggest, MANOVA can be used to examine how the different groups of students generated by the cluster analysis differ on the vectors of the scales included in the original cluster analysis. Cluster solutions of four, three, or two groups of students did not generate significant differences in vectors in the MANOVA. This suggests that the cognitive and motivational patterns of the students when clustered in four or fewer groups were not that different. The five cluster solution did result in a significant difference in the MANOVA test for the vectors of the seven scales included in the original cluster analysis [$F(20,714) = 38.59$, $p < .0001$)]. This suggests that the five groups of students do differ in motivational and cognitive patterns. As Aldenderfer and Blashfield (1984) point out, this result suggests that the five group cluster solution is viable, but it also is an expected result. A better test of the validity of the cluster solution is to compare the five groups of students on variables not included in the original cluster analysis. Accordingly, the five groups of students generated by the cluster analysis were compared on the four performance measures using MANOVA and the overall F was significant [$F(16,205) = 1.95, p < .02$)]. This suggests that the five groups differ not only in their motivational and cognitive patterns, but also in their performance patterns. Given these results, the five group cluster solution was adopted as the most viable solution.

Of course, the overall MANOVA F-tests only suggest that there are differences among the five groups, they do not specify exactly how the groups differ from one another, post hoc tests are necessary. A series of univariate ANOVA post hoc tests were run to compare the five groups on the seven motivational and cognitive scales and the four performance measures. Table 4 summarizes the results from the five group cluster solution. The simple univariate ANOVAs revealed that the five clusters differed on use of rehearsal strategies [$F(4,219) = 8.39, p < .0001$] and metacognition [$F(4,219) = 3.40, p < .01$]. Cluster 1 had the lowest use of rehearsal strategies, while cluster 2 had the highest use. Clusters 3, 4, and 5 were in the intermediate range on the use of rehearsal strategies. In terms of metacognition, clusters 2 and 3 were the least likely to engage in metacognitive activity in comparison to clusters 1, 4 and 5. There were no differences between the five groups on elaboration or organizational strategies. Resource management strategies only showed two differences also. Cluster 3 was significantly lower in terms of time management in comparison to the four other groups [$F(4,219) = 3.25, p < .01$]. The groups also differed on effort management [$F(4,219) = 20.46 , p < .0001$]. Clusters 1 and 5 were much more persistent than clusters 2 and 3. In addition, clusters 2 and 4 were better at managing their effort than cluster 3, the lowest group in terms of effort management.

The motivational scales showed three differences between the clusters. Task value [$F(4,219) = 68.90, p < .0001$] was very different depending on cluster membership. Clusters 1, 3 and 5 were quite high in

Table 4
Mean Differences between Cluster Groups on Cognitive, Motivational, and Performance Measures[1]

	Cluster 1 (N = 67)	*Cluster 2* (N = 12)	*Cluster 3* (N = 65)	*Cluster 4* (N = 33)	*Cluster 5* (N = 45)
Cognition					
Rehearsal	3.93[a]	5.12[b]	4.44[c]	4.33[c]	4.42[c]
Elaboration	4.02	3.83	3.83	3.95	4.24
Organization	4.98	5.02	4.82	4.85	4.92
Metacognition	4.84[a]	4.45[b]	4.46[b]	4.86[a]	4.80[a]
Resource Management					
Time	3.82[a]	3.67[a]	3.05[b]	3.68[a]	3.85[a]
Study Environment	5.19	4.67	4.61	4.98	4.93
Effort Management	5.15[a]	4.33[b]	3.73[c]	4.77[a,b]	5.11[a]
Help-seeking	3.84	3.96	3.78	3.71	4.13
Motivation					
Intrinsic Orientation	4.31	4.07	4.32	4.06	4.05
Task Value	6.03[a]	5.00[b]	6.11[a]	3.42[c]	5.89[a]
Control Beliefs	4.69[a]	4.19[b]	4.15[b]	4.41[b]	4.21[b]
Expectancy for Success	5.78[a]	3.89[b]	5.30[c]	4.56[d]	4.13[b]
Performance					
Exams	.47[a]	–.18[b,c]	.08[b]	–.04[b,c]	–.25[c]
Essays	.15	–.61	–.01	–.23	.08
Labs	.17	–.01	–.15	.84	.29
Grade	.43[a]	–.28[b]	.09[b]	–.06[b]	–.06[b]

[1] Means with different superscripts are significantly different at the .05 level.

their perceptions of the value of the course in comparison to clusters 2 or 4. Cluster 4 was significantly lower than all four other clusters on task value. The clusters also differed on control beliefs [$F(4,219) = 5.62$, $p < .0003$], with cluster 1 individuals being much more confident of their ability to influence their grade in the class. The groups differed on expectancy for success [$F(4,219) = 27.07$, $p < .0001$] with cluster 1 having quite high expectations, followed by cluster 3 and cluster 4. Clusters 2 and 5 had the lowest expectations for success of the five groups. It should be noted that intrinsic orientation was included in the original cluster analysis, but the post hoc tests from the univariate ANOVAs did not show any significant differences between any of the five groups on this scale. This result suggests that intrinsic orientation may not be that crucial to college students' performance in comparison to other cognitive and motivational variables.

The four groups only differed significantly in terms of performance on exams [$F(4,219) = 4.58$, $p < .001$] and final grade [$F(4,219) = 3.11$, $p < .02$]. Cluster 1 students were students who received the best grades on exams and in the class with an average grade about .50 standard deviations above the sample mean. Cluster 2 students scored consistently below the mean except on labs and clusters 3, 4, and 5 showed intermediate levels of performance. Some of the mean differences between clusters were not significant on the performance measures of essays and labs because of small numbers in the clusters, making the estimates unreliable. However, it is interesting to note how the means fluctuate by task depending on cluster membership. For example, Cluster 4 had the highest lab performance mean grade but the second lowest mean for essay grades. Cluster 5 did poorly on the exam but very well on the lab. These different patterns suggest that student performance can vary by the type of task and type of student.

The five groups formed from the cluster analysis represent five relatively distinct groups of students that differ in their pattern of academic performance, motivation, cognition, metacognition, and effort management. As in factor analysis, one aspect of the interpretation of cluster analysis results involves the labeling of the clusters. Clusters 1 and 2 were the traditionally good and poor students. Cluster 1 students did well on all performance measures, used rehearsal strategies infrequently, but engaged in metacognitive activities often. In addition, they were able to regulate their effort and attention effectively. They also believed that the course material was interesting and important. They had high expectancies for success in the course and believed that their effort and ability would help them achieve a good grade.

In contrast, the cluster 2 students were the poor students in the class. They performed at low levels on the achievement measures, used very few metacognitive strategies, and did not regulate their effort effectively and did not expect to do well in the class. They were the highest in the use of more rote, rehearsal strategies and it was probably through the use of these relatively simple cognitive strategies that they were able to achieve at all in their courses.

The other three groups did not differ from one another in terms of overall performance in the class. They were all basically average students, just above or below the average for the sample. However, the pattern of their performance, motivation, and cognition did differ in interesting ways. The third cluster consisted of students who were motivated but not self-regulating. They were interested in the course, thought it was important and useful and expected to do well in the course. They did not, however, engage in much metacognitive activity and reported that their effort and attention could be easily distracted. They did best in an exam situation that was relatively structured, but did poorly in a more open lab situation that probably required sustained effort and attention as well as more planning, monitoring, and self-regulation.

In contrast, cluster 4 students were self-regulating, but not motivated for the course in terms of task value. In fact, they were extremely low in task value for the course. They did not think the course material was very interesting, useful, or important, nor did they expect to do well. They were, however, high in their use of metacognitive strategies and relatively high in effort management. These students did best in a lab situation, probably due not only to their self-regulating skills, but also because the lab situation may have engaged their interest more than other aspects of the course.

Cluster 5 students showed the same basic pattern as cluster 4 students in terms of cognitive and metacognitive strategies, but differed in their motivational patterns. These students were very motivated for the course in terms of their beliefs about interest, importance, and utility of the course material. However, these students still did not expect to succeed in the class. These students were self-regulating in terms of metacognition and effort management, they just seemed to lack confidence in their ability to do well in the course. These students did poorly in exam situations, but well on the lab and paper assignments.

Conclusions

The findings provide support for a multivariate contextual model of student learning that highlights the functional and adaptive roles of cognition and motivation for different academic tasks. In particular, the results suggest the importance of exploring the pattern of relationships among the various cognitive, metacognitive, and motivational components. Consideration of the pattern of relationships among these variables is a start on the specification of the dynamic interplay between motivation and cognition that seems to be more useful than simple linear models of student learning. For example, the cluster analysis results shed some light on the motivational dynamics of self-regulated learning, suggesting that task value and expectancy components can combine with cognitive, metacognitive, and effort management components to influence student performance. In simple regression models, task value usually drops out of the equation, resulting in an unwarranted conclusion about its lack of importance for student learning. In contrast, the cluster results suggest that task value plays an important role for some students, helping them compensate for lower levels of self-regulation (in terms of metacognition and effort management). These results parallel the findings from earlier studies (i.e., Pintrich, 1986a,b) and suggest that the motivational and cognitive components of student learning do not operate in isolation from one another, but rather support and complement one another in a synergistic manner. Students can be skilled in cognitive and self-regulating strategies, but motivational beliefs can influence how these strategies are used for different tasks.

Student performance did differ by exam, and, although the differences were not statistically different due to small samples, the pattern of results for the essays and lab assignments are suggestive of the importance of the task construct in relation to patterns of student motivation and cognition. In contrast to models of the task that stress cognitive features (e.g., Brown et al., 1983; Doyle, 1983), the present results suggest that motivational characteristics of tasks may be important also (cf., Blumenfeld et al. 1987). For example, students who have very low value for a course in general may be engaged by a laboratory assignment and consequently do very well (e.g., cluster 4 students, see Table 4). The results also suggest the importance of developing a taxonomy of tasks and examining how the different dimensions of tasks may interact to influence student motivation and cognition. The current focus on just the product dimension may be too global a focus to uncover the complexity of the relationships.

Finally, in line with a general ATI model (e.g., Corno & Snow, 1986; McKeachie et al., 1986), the cluster results suggest that different types of students may benefit more from different types of interventions to improve students' active learning and critical thinking. For example, the cluster 3 students, who are motivated but do not seem to have the cognitive and metacognitive skills, might benefit most from self-efficacy or attribution retraining programs (e.g., Forsterling, 1985). The cluster 4 students, who also have the self-regulation skills and confidence but lack the interest or value, might benefit most from interventions that attempt to change the nature of classroom tasks to increase the interest and value of the assignments (e.g., Lepper, 1985). Of course, this level of adaptive teaching may be difficult to implement on a practical basis. Nevertheless, the results do support the general ATI rationale that the effects of instruction will differ depending on the characteristics of students (Corno & Snow, 1986). Moreover, the findings point to the importance of considering motivational and cognitive characteristics of students jointly, so that we have, to paraphrase the American philosopher and psychologist William James, a psychology of student learning that encompasses the mathematician and poet, fervor with measure, and passion with correctness.

Acknowledgments

Preparation of this chapter was facilitated by a Spencer Fellowship from the National Academy of Education. Data collection was performed pursuant to a grant (#OERI-86-0010) awarded to the National Center for Research to Improve Postsecondary Teaching and Learning (NCRIPTAL) from the Office of Educational Research and Improvement/Department of Education (OERI/ED). The opinions expressed in this chapter do not reflect the positions or policies of the National Academy of Education, NCRIPTAL, or OERI/ED. An earlier version of this paper was presented at the 1987 American Educational Research Association convention in Washington, D.C.

College Classroom Interactions and Critical Thinking

DARYL G. SMITH

This exploratory study was designed to investigate the relationship between specific classroom behaviors and critical thinking. Four indicants of student involvement were measured using a modified version of Flanders's Interaction Analysis system: student participation, peer-to-peer interaction, faculty questions, and faculty encouragement and use of student ideas. Critical thinking was assessed by use of the Watson-Glaser Critical Thinking Appraisal and the Chickering behavioral self-report index. Twelve college classrooms, equally divided among disciplines, were studied using canonical correlations, analysis of variance, and univariate analyses. Student participation, encouragement, and peer-to-peer interaction consistently emerged as being significantly and positively related to critical thinking. The results, though more suggestive than definitive, have significant implications for future research methodology and for faculty development efforts.

Educational researchers and theorists alike have been concerned about effective teaching and instructional techniques for decades, for the education of students exists as one of the primary functions of all colleges and universities. The current fiscal crisis in higher education lends an urgency to these concerns. With declining enrollments, one obvious alternative for dealing with the financial problems of an institution is to improve its quality and thereby increase its attractiveness (Freedman, 1973; Group for Human Development in Higher Education, 1974; Leslie and Miller, 1974; Shulman, 1974). One means to improving the attractiveness of an institution is the continued improvement of the quality of teaching.

Unfortunately, research results have been so limited that what we can report to faculties and their institutions is of little use in efforts to improve teaching. Now, when the need for empirically based information is even more crucial to the effectiveness and survival of institutions, it is important to study the process of instruction more carefully.

Limitations of Past Research

In much of the past research dedicated to assessing the differential impact of different instructional techniques, researchers typically assessed whether the use of different methods such as lecture or discussion resulted in different student performances as measured by test results or grades. The lack of many significant findings has led some researchers to conclude that teaching method makes no difference (Bloom, 1963; Coladarci, 1958; Dressel and Mayhew, 1954; Macomber and Siegel, 1960; McKeachie, 1963). However, others have concluded that limitations in traditional research approaches may be responsible for the failure to find meaningful differences among teaching methods (Centra, 1972; Gage, 1967; McKeachie, 1974; Rosenshine and Furst, 1973). Indeed, when individual student characteristics have been considered and when more varied and sensitive sets of performance criteria have been used, some differences have been found in teaching method (McKeachie, 1970), but the results of such research have not been overwhelmingly powerful or consistent.

Another promising approach to understand the teaching-learning process better may involve the development of more accurate assessments of the processes and outcomes of instruction. In looking at past

"College Classroom Interactions and Critical Thinking," by Daryl G. Smith, reprinted from *Journal of Educatrional Psychology,* Vol. 69, 1977, American Psychiatric Association.

research, it appears that the concept of method has rarely been questioned. As one reviews the instructional literature of the past two decades, one sees the continued and prominent use of lecture and discussion methods as the primary independent variables of many instructional research programs (Lyle, 1958; Maddox, 1970; McKeachie, 1974). The risk of depending upon such molar concepts to study instruction is highlighted by Bellack's (1967) finding that in comparing classes described as either lecture or discussion, the ratio of time the teacher talks to the time students talk was nearly the same. Perhaps these terms have described the structure of the classroom rather than the behaviors which occurred. An alternative strategy to describe the process of instruction is to consider more molecular behaviors which occur in the classroom (Gage, 1967; Rosenshine and Furst, 1973). Such behaviors as questioning patterns, types of student interaction, or even overall time students talk can be considered.

Such an approach has rarely been tried in research in higher education. However, advantages of studying processes are evident both in the general field of group psychology as well as in research at lower levels of education. If we consider the classroom as an instance of a small group, the following comment by McGrath and Altman (1966), two group psychologists, seems quite pertinent. In discussing the causal relationship between inputs and outputs in the group, they noted the following:

> Too little attention has been given to systematically establishing the links in this complex chain. What has been done is to explain the relationship of inputs and outputs with insufficient attention to the ways in which input characteristics enhance or hamper final output via *intermediate processes.* (p. 65; emphasis added)

When research at lower levels of education has considered specific behaviors and the interrelationship between process and a variety of outcomes, significant relationships have been found. For example, Flanders (1970), Bellack (1967), and Gallagher and Aschner (1963) have consistently demonstrated that when specific pupil-teacher interactions vary, outcomes of instruction vary as well.

The Current Study

This study was part of a larger exploratory research project investigating the relationship between processes which occur in the classroom and learning outcomes, taking into account a range of student and faculty characteristics. This research assesses the relationship between processes which occur in the classroom and a generally accepted goal of instruction—critical thinking.

Processes

The focus of this process analysis is on active involvement, because many theorists, researchers, and writers agree that active involvement of the student in the learning process is critical (e.g., Bigge, 1964; Hilgard and Bower, 1966; McKeachie, 1974). More specifically, faculty behaviors which attempt to elicit active involvement (including encouragement and questions) and student behaviors which are indicants of that involvement (overall student participation and peer-to-peer interaction) are considered. While research on the college peer culture demonstrates that the impact of peers on values, developing independence of judgment, and in working for or against institutional goals is important (Feldman and Newcomb, 1969), the impact of peer interaction in the instructional setting has been largely unexplored.

In particular, four activities were identified as being related to involvement and were the focus of the analysis:

1. The first activity was the degree to which the faculty member encouraged, praised, or used student ideas.
2. The second activity was the degree to which the faculty member asked questions, and also the nature of the questions. Questioning, in general, not only encourages participation but also enables students to test what they have learned and to receive feedback. However, it can be seen that questions which ask for a rote memory response differ considerably from ones which ask for imaginative or evaluative responses (Sanders, 1966). As a result, questioning behavior was investigated in terms of the different levels of cognitive thinking implied.

3. The third activity was the degree to which students participated in class and the cognitive level of the participation. Again, it was believed that sheer quantity of participation might not be as important as the kind of participation.
4. The fourth activity was the degree to which there was peer-to-peer interaction in the class. Thus, it can be seen that the concern in investigating these particular behaviors is not simply based on an interest in the impact of the *quantity* of involvement but also on the *nature* of the behaviors which take place. It was expected that active involvement of students would tend to relate positively with change in or level of critical thinking (Flanders, 1970; McKeachie, 1974).

Method

Procedure

A group of 15 faculty members, teaching in a small liberal arts college and known for a variety of teaching styles, were approached to participate in the study during the fall semester. At the time, they each indicated one class which would be the focus of the study. Three faculty members were eliminated because they taught no classes with less than 40 students or did not teach in English.

During the first two weeks of the fall semester, the researcher attended each of the 12 classes to explain the nature of the study and to encourage student participation. At that time, students and faculty received a letter of explanation and a packet of test materials. The student packet included the Fundamental Interpersonal Relations Orientation-Behavior Questionnaire, one of two forms of the Watson-Glaser Test of Critical Thinking, a questionnaire soliciting demographic and attitudinal information, and permission to obtain the students' Scholastic Aptitude Test scores from the college. The faculty packet included the Fundamental Interpersonal Relations Orientation-Behavior Questionnaire and a brief questionnaire asking for basic demographic information. Packets were to be returned within two weeks.

To insure some representatives in class sessions sampled, each of the 12 classes was tape-recorded at equal intervals four times during the semester. The first taping occurred during the 2nd and 3rd weeks of the semester and the last during the 15th and 16th weeks. Coding of the tapes using a modified version of the Flanders Interaction Analysis system took place after all the taping was completed.

During the last two weeks of the semester, the researcher again attended each class to hand out final packets to those students who were participating and had filled out the first packet of information. This packet included the Watson-Glaser Critical Thinking Appraisal and a questionnaire asking for behavioral and attitudinal information. At this time, the faculty members were given a single-item questionnaire asking if they perceived that the presence of the researcher or the tape recordings affected their classroom interaction in any way.

Subjects

The subjects in the study were the 12 faculty members originally approached and the students in each of the classes designated for the study who completed both the initial and final packets of information. The total enrollment in the 12 classes was 210. Of this number, 148 (70%) completed the first packet; 138 students (65.7%) completed the second packet as well.

Of the 138 student subjects, 92% were students at the college and 8% attended other colleges in the vicinity; 75 subjects (54%) were women and 63 (46%) were men.

The 12 faculty members included 2 women and 10 men (approximately the proportion of women represented on the faculty) and were evenly divided between the humanities, social sciences, and natural sciences.

Instrumentation—Process and Outcome

Teacher-student interaction (process)

The examination of classroom processes in terms of teacher and student behavior gives a more precise description of what occurs in the classroom than the molar description of lecture and discussion. The reliance on verbal behaviors, which is true of most research, is based on the greater reliability with which verbal behavior can be observed, the fact that it is less obtrusive, and the somewhat tenuous assumption that verbal behavior is an adequate sample of total behavior (Amidon and Hough, 1967; Aschner, 1960).

One of the most frequently used and well-established instruments for recording verbal interaction in the classroom is Flanders's (1970) Interaction Analysis system. Because of the interest of many researchers in cognitive levels of behaviors as well as an interest in making refinements for specific theoretical purposes, Flanders's system has been modified many times. For the purposes of this study, a variation of Flanders's system based on work by Amidon and Hough (1967), Gallagher and Aschner (1963), and Guilford (1956) was utilized.

The modified version used in this study extended Flanders's system from 10 to 11 categories by separating "silence" from "confusion or laughter." Also, the "questioning" and student talk sections were subdivided to include four divisions for cognitive memory, convergent, divergent, and evaluative responses.

The primary processes used in the analysis to follow were (a) a combined use of the encouragement, praise, and faculty use of student ideas categories, (b) the questioning category, and (c) a combination of both student talk sections.

Data collection

From the tape recordings, I categorized the verbal behavior of every 3 sec in sequential order. If the behavior changed within the 3-sec interval, each behavior was indicated. Frequencies and percentages in each category were tallied for each class session. Peer-to-peer interaction was obtained through one additional step. Any student talk in Category 8 or 9 (though usually Category 9) which was in direct response to another student was checked as peer-to-peer interaction. The final measure was the percentage of peer-to-peer interaction in relation to total student talk. For purposes of the final analysis, the average percentages in each category for each class were calculated. In this way, each class was weighted equally, despite varying lengths of the individual class sessions.

Reliability

There are numerous ways to conceptualize reliability or to calculate an index of reliability (cf. Weick, 1968). In this study, both interrater and intrarater measures of reliability were taken. In addition, as recommended by Johnson and Bolstad (1973), a variation of odd-even reliability was used to assess consistency among the four class sessions. To limit the possibility that high interobserver or intraobserver agreement might easily be found simply due to chance, a stringent statistical measure of reliability, Cohen's K (Cohen, 1960), which uses a unit-by-unit measure of agreement rather than the more common agreement between category frequencies, was used. Interrater and intrarater reliability's were computed from 5-minute samples from six different tapes. Cohen's K was .91 for interrater reliability and .87 for intrarater reliability. The interrater agreement on units (not indicated by Cohen's K) was 95% and for the intrarater test it was 94%, indicating no substantial problem in this area.

In calculating odd-even reliability for the categories used in the study, the scores for Sessions 1 and 3 were correlated with Sessions 2 and 4 for the 12 classes. An overall average of all reliabilities was then taken and the Spearman Brown correction formula then applied. The average reliability for the six major categories (student talk, faculty talk, praise, questioning, peer-to-peer interaction, and the ID ratio) was .70. The corrected reliability was .82.

Critical Thinking (Outcome)

Operationalizing a concept such as critical thinking is not easy. Not many measures of critical thinking are available, and many simply ask for a subject's perception of a change in critical thinking (cf. Pace, 1974). Consequently, it was decided to use two instruments to try to assess the impact of different classroom processes on critical thinking: the Watson-Glaser Critical Thinking Appraisal (Watson and Glaser, 1964) and a behavioral report of activities associated with critical thinking developed by Chickering (1972).

Watson-Glaser Critical Thinking Appraisal

This test is based on Dressel and Mayhew's (1954) definition of critical thinking and includes five subtests designed to measure different aspects of critical thinking: (a) inference, (b) recognition of assumptions, (c) deduction, (d) interpretation, and (e) evaluation of arguments. Because of the limited testing time available, only three of the subtests were used in this study:

1. Inference test samples ability to discriminate among degrees of truth or falsity of inferences drawn from given data.
2. Interpretation subtest samples the ability to weigh evidence and to distinguish between (a) generalizations from given data that are not warranted beyond a reasonable doubt and (b) generalizations which, although not absolutely certain or necessary, do seem to be warranted.
3. Evaluation-of-arguments subtest samples the ability to distinguish between strong, relevant arguments and weak, irrelevant ones to a particular question (Watson and Glaser, 1964, p. 5).

Because the Watson-Glaser test was to be used for pretesting and posttesting of the subjects, each of the two forms of the test was randomly distributed to half of the subjects at the beginning of the semester. Subjects then received the alternate form for the posttest.

Chickering Critical Thinking Behaviors

Because of the known difficulty in measuring such concepts as critical thinking directly, many experimenters tend to rely on global self-report to assess development of critical thinking abilities (cf. Pace, 1974). The validity of such an approach is not clear. However, Wicker (1971) has shown that self-report measures which focus on behaviors do tend to approximate reality more closely. Based on a similar assumption, McDowell and Chickering (Note 1) developed a measure of behaviors associated with critical thinking based on the assumption that "if a program does not foster the behaviors and experiences pertinent to desired objectives it is sufficient to assume that such development is not taking place" (Chickering, 1972, p. 143).

Using Bloom's taxonomy, the inventory asks students to report the percentage of time spent in each of six activities while studying for the particular course in question. The six items are defined according to Bloom's (1963) approach:

1. Memorizing: learning specific things, words, ideas, methods, so that you can remember them pretty much in the same form in which you encountered them.
2. Interpreting: mentally putting things in different terms, translating, reorganizing, making inferences or extensions of thinking based on principles given.
3. Applying: drawing upon a variety of concepts and applying them to new problems or situations.
4. Analyzing: analyzing material (data, literary works, argumentative or discursive material, etc.) into parts and detecting relationships among parts and ways they are organized.
5. Synthesizing: organizing ideas, or parts, into new plans, relationships, or structures, as in developing plans for an experiment, writing a poem or essay, deriving principles from data, integrating information from diverse sources.
6. Evaluating: making judgments about the value of materials (concepts, evidence, theories, arguments, communications) and methods.

Analysis

Change scores

Because of the problem of self-selection in the current study, pretest and posttest measures were obtained on the Watson-Glaser test. The self-report measures of behaviors could only be obtained at the end of the course. The precise way in which change scores should be treated, however, is the subject of much controversy and at least four methods have been suggested (cf. Cronbach and Furby, 1970; Harris, 1963).

Kenny (1975) reviews each of the alternatives and suggests that the appropriate approach depends, to a large degree, on the mode of selection into groups. Because students select classes on the basis of their interest or other such factors, it is felt that the present study fits into the category described as "selection based on group differences." Because of this, standardized change scores were used in the current research.

In the case of the Watson-Glaser test, in which random-half methods were used for the pretest and posttest, standardization occurred for each form of the test as well, resulting in the standardization of four groups (Thorndike, 1971).

Unit of analysis

One of the difficulties in statistical analysis in a study such as this one, in which both individual and classroom characteristics are being studied, is that the appropriate unit of analysis is not always clear. Past research has been frequently criticized for using class means as outcome measures, thereby ignoring individual differences (Berliner and Cohen, 1973). Yet to consider the individual subject as the unit of analysis poses a problem, since we cannot assume that the error is distributed randomly. All students in a given class may be affected by the climate or behaviors occurring in the class. Because there is no easy way to avoid the problem, data using both methods of analysis are frequently reported. Thus, some boundaries were established with regard to efforts introduced by using the subject or the classroom alone as the unit of analysis.

Table 1
Means and Medians on the Process Variables for the 12 Classes

Process	Mean % class time	*Mdn*	Minimum obtained %	Maximum obtained %
% encouragement, praise, use of ideas	3.7	3.3	.8	7.3
% questioning	2.6	2.8	0	4.2
% cognitive memory	49	44	28	89
% convergent	34	34	9	65
% divergent	13	14	0	30
% evaluative	4	2	0	26
% student participation	14.2	14.2	.6	38.1
% cognitive memory	27	21	9	55
% convergent	36	33	20	58
% divergent	30	36	0	56
% evaluative	7	7	0	17
% peer-to-peer interaction	7.5	2.3	0	33.7

Multivariance procedures

Researchers in both psychology and education have recently been advocating the use of multiple measures in conducting field research (Glaser, 1973; Helmreich, Bakeman, and Scherwitz, 1973). Such an approach tends to acknowledge, statistically as well as conceptually, that the situation under study is a complex one.

The need to use multivariance procedures is essential, since the number of univariate analyses otherwise required tends to result in more frequent ad hoc and chance occurrences of significance. However, in order to facilitate interpretation, both multivariate and univariate analyses have been employed. In particular, canonical correlations have been employed to test the overall relationship between two sets of variables. In this way, the pattern employed in traditional analysis of variance procedures is followed. Only upon finding a significant overall R is one permitted to perform additional, more specific analyses.

Results

Processes

Mean and median scores for each of the process variables are shown in Table 1. Minimum and maximum scores are noted to indicate the range between the highest and lowest classes in the sample. The range is very important here, since the effects of differential behaviors can be studied only if an adequate range of behaviors is observed. The median scores when compared to the mean tend to indicate the skewness of the distribution. In all but peer-to-peer interaction, the distributions appear to be relatively symmetrical.

The average level of participation or behaviors which solicit participation was rather low. Questioning, encouragement, and student participation, together, involved an average of 20% of the class time.

Cognitive memory questions were the most frequently asked, and higher order questions occurred much less frequently. Student participation was relatively equally divided among memory, convergent, and divergent responses, though evaluative responses occurred much less frequently.

One process in which a very narrow range was observed was questioning behavior. With a range of only 4.2 percentage points, it was not possible to observe large differences between classes.

Outcomes

Table 2 gives a summary of the mean score on each of the critical thinking measures for the subject pool. The table indicates the mean raw pretest and posttest scores by form for the Watson-Glaser test, although

Table 2
Mean Scores on Critical Thinking

Critical thinking	Pretest	Posttest
Watson-Glaser (N = 138)		
Form Y/Z	45.7	43.6
Form Z/Y	42.4	44.5
Study time spent		
Memorizing (n = 137)	—	2.4
Interpreting	—	3.0
Applying	—	2.6
Analyzing	—	2.7
Synthesizing	—	2.5
Evaluating		2.3

Note: No pretest was given for the study-time categories. For the posttest study-time scores, 1 = 0%–5%; 2 = 6%–20%; 3 = 21%–50%; 4 = 51%–80%; 5 = 81%–100%.

the actual scores used for statistical tests were standardized change scores. The manual indicates that Form Z is more difficult than Form Y; the results of the present study supported this.

Because the two forms of the Watson-Glaser test were not equally difficult, an adjustment must be made to assess the overall change in critical thinking scores. On the pretest, performance on Form Y was 3.3 points higher than on Form Z. On the posttest this differential was .9. If we take an average of these two, we can estimate that Form Y tends to be 2.1 points easier than Form Z. Correcting the mean scores on Form Z to take this into consideration, we see that the posttest and pretest scores are the same. No overall change in critical thinking scores occurred over the semester. Students reported spending the least amount of time in evaluating, synthesizing, and memorizing, the highest and lowest levels of critical thinking behaviors.

Relationship of Involvement to Critical Thinking

The hypothesis to be tested was that the greater the degree of active student involvement and the higher the levels of questioning and student participation, the greater the change in or level of critical thinking.

Findings

The canonical *R* for the relationship between the process variables (student participation, peer-to-peer interaction, questioning, divergent and evaluative questions, divergent and evaluative student responses, encouragement) and the cognitive outcomes (changes in critical thinking and the three highest critical thinking behaviors) was .464, $\chi^2(20) = 44.26$, $p < .005$. Using class means, the canonical *R* was .96, $\chi^2(20) = 28.7$, $p < .10$. A separate canonical correlation between the same process variables and the set of six critical thinking behaviors for class means yielded a perfect correlation of 1.00, $\chi^2(30) = 108.68$, $p < .001$, and thus demonstrates a strong relationship between these variable sets as well.

In order to see the specific relationships involved, individual bivariate correlations were tabulated. Table 3 reveals that the three process measures most directly related to changes in critical thinking were

Table 3
Univariate Correlations Between Processes and Cognitive Outcomes for Individual (N = 138) and Class Means (N = 12)

Process	Critical thinking	Memory	Interpretation	Application	Analysis	Synthesis	Evaluation
Student participation							
Individual *M*	.2028**	–.1466*	.2866****	.0566	.3281****	.2607****	.2460**
Class *M*	.6295*	–.1923	.4225	.2902	.5478*	.5586*	.4690
Divergent and evaluative student responses							
Individual *M*	.0903	–.0083	.1333	–.1693*	.2619****	.0623	.1707*
Class *M*	.1790	–.2010	.2515	–.2810	.4741	.0917	.5740*
Divergent and evaluative questions							
Individual *M*	.0662	.0013	.2100**	–.1171	.2865****	.1801*	.1968*
Class *M*	.1445	–.0416	.3377	–.1679	.4493		.6145*
Encouragement							
Individual *M*	.2324***	–.2243***	.2576***	.1245	.3194****	.2857****	.2271***
Class *M*	.6213*	–.4295	.4306	.5022*	.5639*	.5511*	.4417
Peer-to-peer interaction							
Individual *M*	.1870*	–.2064**	.3037****	.1602*	.2443*	.2039**	.2372***
Class *M*	.5706*	–.3020	.5164*	.5322*	.4282	.4648	.4076

Note: Boxes indicate significant correlations for both units of analysis.
*$p < .05$. **$p < .01$. ***$p < .005$. ****$p < .001$.

student participation, encouragement, and peer-to-peer interaction. These three processes were also related to several of the critical thinking behaviors as well, especially analysis and synthesis. Higher level questions and participation appeared to be most consistently associated with evaluative behaviors, however. In addition, using the student as the unit of analysis, each of the processes was significantly related to evaluation and analytic behavior and all but high-level participation related to synthesizing behaviors. Using this unit of analysis, the table also reveals a negative relationship among student participation, praise, peer-to-peer interaction, and time spent memorizing.

To amplify some of the more significant findings in Table 3 and to examine further the relationships among change in critical thinking scores, reported critical thinking behaviors, and the various processes that occurred in classes, the classes were then divided into low, medium, and high levels for the process measures and an analysis of variance was conducted. (For divergent and evaluative student participation, the classes were only divided into low and high levels.) The divisions were made on the basis of natural breaks in the distributions. Figure 1 illustrates the relationship between the change in critical thinking scores and student participation, encouragement, and peer-to-peer interaction. Figure 2 is illustrative of the relationship between the six critical thinking behaviors and the process under study—in this case, student participation.

A consistent pattern between the low and high levels of the behavior under consideration is apparent. Such patterns were also found in the relationship among encouragement and peer-to-peer interaction and the six critical thinking behaviors. High-critical-thinking behaviors are more frequent with higher quantities of praise, peer-to-peer interaction, and student participation. In addition, with an increase in these processes, memorizing behaviors decrease. The middle-level behaviors do not show a consistent pattern, possibly reflecting the somewhat arbitrary separation points between low, medium, and high levels of each process. In Figure 1 we see significant differences in the mean standardized change in critical thinking scores on the Watson-Glaser test for different levels of student participation and encouragement.

Discussion

This study of collegiate instruction was designed as an exploratory investigation of some specific processes of instruction and their relationship to outcomes of instruction. The results outlined above give support to the belief that improved research strategies do indeed add to our knowledge of instruction. Although a number of relationships were found, our understanding of instruction will not be complete with one study. Rather, our knowledge will accrue as we begin to observe trends established from many research studies which serve to replicate one another using a variety of research designs and measurement techniques. The current study, employing a research design quite different from many earlier ones, adds support to the general notion of the importance of active involvement of the student in the learning process and to the need for a more molecular research strategy that provides information on actual classroom behaviors.

We must avoid simplistic conclusions that might be suggested by the positive relationships which were found. A cautious approach would contribute more to a scholarly understanding of instruction and needed research improvements than would a conclusion which implies that a simple formula to good teaching has been found. Problems of curvilinear relationships (Coats, 1966; Soar, 1968), confounding, self-selection, and observer interference, though not major here, must be kept in mind when generalizing.

Though an adequate range of behaviors was observed across the 12 classes, the overall level of student involvement was quite low. Questioning occurred only 2.6% of the time and student participation only 14.2%. In total, less than 20% of class time was spent in student participation or in encouraging involvement. There is little indication of how this figure compares to other college classrooms; however, Flanders (cited in Amidon and Hough, 1967) has indicted that for high school classes, student participation alone often accounts for 17% to 26% of class time. The active intellectual interchange, which one often imagines when envisioning a college classroom, does not take place *on the average.* This varied quite considerably among the classes, however, with student participation occupying over one third of class time in one class. The narrow range observed for the questioning behavior might account for the lack of any consistent relationships between questioning and the critical thinking variables in contrast to the striking patterns observed with the other process variables.

Figure 1
Levels of three classroom processes and changes in critical thinking scores

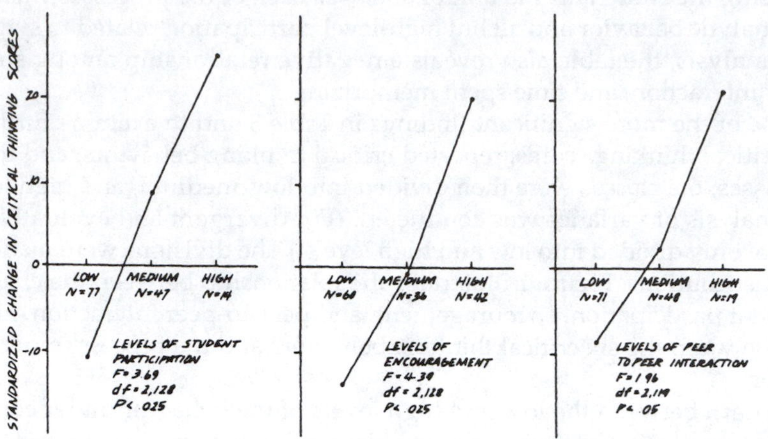

Interestingly, the mean critical thinking scores for the sample did not seem to change, though this might not be surprising given the short time span in which the study took place. Because significant differences in amount of change in critical thinking scores were found across the individual classes, it must be presumed that some students' scores declined over the semester, while other students' scores increased. In particular, as seen earlier in Figure 1, classes with low participation tended to show a decline in critical thinking. One might suggest that a decline in critical thinking could result from an emphasis on memorization and a lack of practice. Two alternative but speculative explanations might also be offered. A decline in critical thinking might have been a result of the greater emphasis in such classes on knowledge acquisition and memorization. With the end of the semester pressure of finals, students might have been under greater pressure in these classes and thus have less time to devote to the test. A decline might also be indicative of lower morale in classes with low involvement and less willingness to contribute to the study.

Figure 2
Levels of student participation and critical thinking behaviors

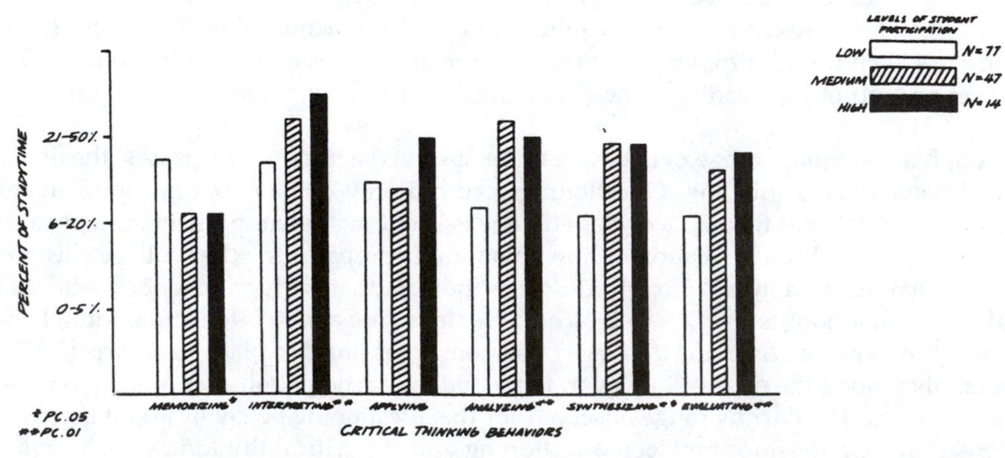

A consistent pattern was found between three main process variables and the critical thinking variable. Student participation, faculty encouragement and use of student ideas, and peer-to-peer interaction emerged as positively related to change in critical thinking and critical thinking behaviors. Efforts at student involvement, then, might be encouraged not only for the sake of student contentment, but for cognitive benefits as well. The differences in critical thinking scores and in critical thinking behaviors between classes with low- and high-level participation were dramatic, as revealed in Figures 1 and 2. The current research suggests (a) that a more molecular process-analysis strategy can reveal significant additive effects and (b) that speculation on the need for complex interaction models might be premature.

The results of the present study have major implications both for research and for faculty development and teaching. The molecular measures and complex analyses used in this study clearly proved useful. The experience gained here should be useful in designing studies which control for some of the confounding and other limitations discussed earlier. We can also conduct research which manipulates variables rather than research which just assesses associational patterns. The merger and coordination of field and laboratory work, as Glaser (1973) has suggested, are clearly required, and the present study suggests some of the more specific hypotheses to investigate.

Two additional aspects of instruction which could be incorporated into further research are the consideration of the individual faculty member's goals and a study of variations among disciplines. In the current study, some general goals of instruction were outlined and utilized as the outcomes of instruction. Whether faculty were purposely teaching for these outcomes was not investigated. Future studies might well look at the specific goals of the instructor as well as generalized goals of instruction. Variation among disciplines in goals, processes, and outcomes also needs to be investigated. The overall benefits of research such as this will lie, first, in its contribution to the accumulation of more and more refined studies of instructions within instructional and educational psychology and, second, in its stimulation of reflectiveness about teaching and learning among the faculty and student participants. The knowledge that instruction can be studied and that such studies can provide useful information may generate greater awareness than either experience or intuition.

Note

1. McDowell, J., and Chickering, A.W. *Experience of college questionnaires.* Plainfield, Vt.: Project on Student Development, 1967.

References

Amidon, E.J., and Hough, J.B. (Eds.). *Interaction analysis: Theory, research and application.* Reading, Mass.: Addison-Wesley, 1967.

Aschner, M.J. The language of teaching. *Teachers College Record,* 1960, *61,* 242–252.

Bellack, A.A. *The language of the classroom.* New York: Teachers College Press, 1967.

Berliner, D.C., and Cohen, L.S. Trait-treatment interaction and learning. In F.N. Kerlinger (Ed.), *Review of research in education.* Itasca, Ill.: Peacock, 1973.

Bigge, M. *Learning theory for teachers.* New York: Harper, 1964.

Bloom, B. Testing "cognitive ability and achievement," In N.L. Gage (Ed.), *Handbook of research on teaching.* Chicago: Rand McNally, 1963.

Centra, J.A. *Strategies for improving college teaching.* Washington, D.C.: American Association for Higher Education, 1972. (ERIC/Higher Education Research Report No. 8)

Chickering, A. Undergraduate academic experience. *Journal of Educational Psychology,* 1972, *63,* 134–143.

Coats, W.D. Investigation and simulation of the relationships among selected classroom variables (Doctoral dissertation, University of Michigan, 1966). *Dissertation Abstracts International,* 1966, *28,* 1A (University Microfilms No. 67-8228)

Cohen, J. A coefficient of agreement for nominal scales. *Educational and Psychological Measurement*, 1960, *20*, 37–46.

Coladarci, A.P. Educational psychology. *Annual Review of Psychology*, 1958, *8*, 189–212.

Cronbach, L.J., and Furby, L. How should we measure change or should we? *Psychological Bulletin*, 1970, *74*, 68–80.

Dressel, P., and Mayhew, L.B. *General education: Explorations in evaluation.* Washington, D.C.: American Council on Education, 1954.

Feldman, K., and Newcomb, T. *Impact of college on students.* San Francisco: Jossey-Bass, 1969.

Flanders, N.A. *Analyzing teaching behavior.* Reading, Mass.: Addison-Wesley, 1970.

Freedman, M. (Ed.). *Facilitating faculty development.* San Francisco: Jossey-Bass, 1973.

Gage, N.L. The need for process oriented research. In C. Lee (Ed.), *Improving college teaching.* Washington, D.C.: American Council on Education, 1967.

Gallagher, J., and Aschner, M.J. A preliminary report: Analysis of classroom interaction. *Merrill Palmer Quarterly of Behavior and Development*, 1963, *9*, 183–194.

Glaser, R. Educational psychology and education. *American Psychologist*, 1973, *28*, 557–567.

Group for Human Development in Higher Education. Faculty development in a time of retrenchment. *Change Magazine*, 1974.

Guilford, J.P. The structure of intellect. *Psychological Bulletin*, 1956, *53*, 267–293.

Harris, C.W. (Ed.). *Problems in measuring change.* Madison: University of Wisconsin Press, 1963.

Helmreich, R., Bakeman, R., and Scherwitz, L. The study of small groups. *Annual Review of Psychology*, 1973, *24*, 337–354.

Hilgard, E.R., and Bower, G.H. *Theories of learning.* New York: Appleton-Century-Crofts, 1966.

Johnson, S.M., and Bolstad, O.D. Methodological issues in naturalistic observation: Some problems and solutions for field research. In L. Hamerlynch, L. Handy, and J. Mash (Eds.), *Behavior change methodology: Concepts and practice.* Champaign, Ill.: Research Press, 1973.

Kenny, D.A. A quasi-experimental approach to assessing treatment effects in the nonequivalent control group design. *Psychological Bulletin*, 1975, *82*, 345–362.

Leslie, L.L., and Miller, H.F. *Higher education and the steady state.* Washington, D.C.: American Association for Higher Education, 1974. (ERIC/Higher Education Research Report No. 4)

Lyle, E. An exploration in the teaching of critical thinking in general psychology. *Journal of Educational Research*, 1958, *52*, 129–133.

Macomber, B.G., and Siegel, L. *Final report of the experimental study in instructional procedures.* Oxford, Ohio: Miami University Press, 1960.

Maddox, H. University teaching methods: A review. *University Quarterly*, 1970, *24*, 157–165.

McGrath, J., and Altman, I. *Small group research.* New York: Holt, Rinehart and Winston, 1966.

McKeachie, W.J. Research in teaching at the college and university level. In N.L. Gage (Ed.), *Handbook of research on teaching.* Chicago: Rand McNally, 1963.

McKeachie, W.J. *Research on college teaching: A review.* Washington, D.C.: ERIC Clearinghouse on Higher Education, 1970.

McKeachie, W.J. The decline and fall of the laws of learning. *Educational Research*, 1974, *3*, 7–11.

Pace, C.R. *The demise of diversity.* Berkeley, Calif.: Carnegie Commission, 1974.

Rosenshine, B., and Furst, N. The use of direct observation to study teaching. In R.M. Travers (Ed.), *Second handbook of research on teaching*. Chicago: Rand McNally, 1973.

Sanders, N.M. *Classroom questions: What kinds?* New York: Harper and Row, 1966.

Shulman, C.H. *Private colleges: Present conditions and future prospects.* Washington, D.C.: American Association for Higher education, 1974. (ERIC/Higher Education Research Report No. 9)

Soar, R.S. Optimum teacher-pupil interaction for pupil growth. *Educational Leadership,* 1968, *26,* 275–280.

Thorndike, R.L. *Educational measurement.* Washington, D.C.: American Council on Education, 1971.

Watson, G., and Glaser, E.M. *Watson-Glaser critical thinking appraisal manual.* New York: Harcourt, Brace and World, 1964.

Weick, K.E. Systematic observational methods. In G. Lindsey and E. Aronson (Eds.), *Handbook of social psychology.* Reading, Mass.: Addison-Wesley, 1968.

Wicker, A.W. An examination of the "other variables" explanation of attitude-behavior inconsistency. *Journal of Personality and Social Psychology,* 1971, *19,* 18–30.

The Effects of Verbal and Nonverbal Teacher Immediacy on Perceived Cognitive, Affective, and Behavioral Learning in the Multicultural Classroom

JUDITH A. SANDERS AND RICHARD L. WISEMAN

Past research has indicated that verbal and nonverbal teacher immediacy have a positive effect on perceived cognitive learning, student affect, and behavioral intent. The present study extends that research by examining the effects of immediacy in the multicultural classroom. A total of 952 college students participated in a survey regarding teacher immediacy and perceived cognitive, affective, and behavioral learning. Comparisons of the results among White, Asian, Hispanic, and Black students yielded both similarities and differences. The summed immediacy scale was positively related to all learning scales for all ethnicities. However, differences emerged in the extent of that relationship. Examination of the effects of individual immediacy behaviors on learning yielded both cross-cultural similarities and differences. Results are discussed in terms of the kinds of communication emphasized by each culture group and the need for teacher sensitivity to student differences.

Effective teacher communication is the *sine qua non* of student learning in the classroom. There is, as Hurt, Scott and McCroskey (1978) noted, "a difference between knowing and teaching, and that difference is communication in the classroom" (p. 3). Despite the fact that the search for optimal teacher communication behaviors has generated a substantial amount of research, determining the most effective communication strategies for teachers has proven an elusive task. Nonetheless, research has lead to some heuristic conclusions about enhancing teacher communication.

One factor which seems clearly linked to teaching effectiveness is immediacy. Mehrabian defines immediacy as that communication which enhances closeness to another. Immediacy behaviors reflect a positive attitude on the part of the sender toward the receiver (Mehrabian, 1969). Andersen (1985) notes that immediacy behaviors indicate approachability, signal availability for communication, increase sensory stimulation, and communicate interpersonal warmth and closeness. Support for this position was provided by Burgoon, Buller, Hale and deTurck (1984). Examining interpersonal encounters, they found that high eye contact, close proximity, forward body lean, and smiling all conveyed greater intimacy, attraction, and trust. Conversely, low eye contact, a distal position, backward body lean, and the absence of smiling and touch communicated greater detachment.

If immediacy behaviors signal approach, openness for communication, and warmth, it seems logical that such communication would enhance student-teacher relationships and potentially student learning. Indeed the research so indicates.

Nonverbal teacher immediacy

Much of the research on teacher immediacy has focused on nonverbal cues and seems to indicate that immediacy does increase teaching effectiveness. Nonverbal cues which have been identified as immediate include: eye contact, gestures, relaxed body position, directing body position toward students, smiling,

"The Effects of Verbal and Nonverbal Teacher Immediacy on Perceived Cognitive, Affective, and Behavioral Learning in the Multicultural Classroom," by Judith A. Sanders and Richard L. Wiseman, reprinted by permission from *Communication Education*, 39, 1990, Speech Communication Association.

vocal expressiveness, movement, and proximity (Andersen, 1979).

Substantial evidence indicates nonverbal immediacy increases affective learning. In her seminal research on nonverbal immediacy, Andersen (1979) found that immediacy positively influenced student affect toward teacher communication, course content, the course in general, and the course instructor. Immediacy was also positively related to student likelihood of engaging in similar communication and the likelihood of enrolling in another related course. Further, Chaiken, Gillen, Derlega, Heinen, and Wilson (1978) found that a teacher exhibiting close proxemic behavior was perceived in a more favorable light than a teacher exhibiting distant behavior. More recently, Plax, Kearney, McCroskey and Richmond (1986) found that students' perceptions of teachers' immediacy were positively related to students' affective learning.

While studies have consistently demonstrated a positive relationship between nonverbal immediacy and affective learning, the link to cognitive learning has not been as clear. Andersen (1979) found that immediacy did not predict student grades. Likewise, Chaiken et al. (1978) found no difference for student performance with immediate teachers. However, Richmond, Gorham and McCroskey (1987) argue that past measures of cognitive learning are unreliable and that a more appropriate measure is students' perceptions of cognitive learning. On that basis they found a variety of nonverbal immediacy behaviors had positive associations with both affective and perceived cognitive learning. They conclude that immediacy behaviors are significantly related to cognitive learning but suggest that the relationship between immediacy and cognitive learning may be nonlinear. Moderate immediacy may be necessary for cognitive learning and low immediacy may suppress such learning. However, high immediacy may not increase cognitive learning over that generated by moderate immediacy.

If immediacy is seen as a positive evaluative approach behavior, why would it influence cognitive learning? Andersen (1985) argues that in most instances immediacy increases arousal, setting the stage for cognitive learning. Kelley and Gorham (1988) provided support for this position when they found a positive relationship between immediacy, as defined by eye contact and physical proximity, and short-term cognitive recall. Greatest recall occurred with eye contact and high physical proximity. Eye contact with low proximity or high proximity with no eye contact produced moderate recall results. No eye contact and low proximity produced the worst recall results.

Verbal teacher immediacy

Immediacy may be verbal as well as nonverbal; that is, the words a person uses may signal approach or openness for communication as well as avoidance. Words that include the sender and the receiver in the same category, such as "we," or that increase communicator solidarity rather than distancing the sender from the receiver are seen as more immediate. Likewise, the use of humor and self-disclosure are immediacy cues (Gorham, 1988).

Research indicates that verbal cues demonstrate immediacy or nonimmediacy resulting in perceptions of approach or avoidance. Anthony (1978) found that when an individual uses immediate expressions in conversation about another, s/he conveys greater liking for and a greater desire for continued interaction with that person than one who uses nonimmediate expressions. Conville (1975) found that communicators with low verbal nonimmediacy were perceived as more authoritative and as having a more positive character than were communicators with medium and high verbal nonimmediacy. Conversely, a communicator's negative attitude toward another is reflected in low levels of verbal immediacy (Feinberg, 1971; Mehrabian, 1967). Bradac, Bowers, and Courtright (1979), reviewing the research on verbal immediacy, concluded that positive affect on the part of the source increases verbal immediacy, cognitive stress on the part of the source was negatively related to immediacy, people see high immediacy as a sign of positive affect, and verbal immediacy is related to judgments of source competence and character.

While there is little extant research on teachers' verbal immediacy, a variety of related concepts suggest that verbal immediacy should have a positive effect on teaching effectiveness. Andersen, Norton, and Nussbaum (1981) found that perceived teacher immediacy and perceived teacher communicator style were significantly related and that style was positively related to affective learning and behavioral intent but not cognitive learning. Teachers who were perceived as better were perceived as demonstrating style; specifically, they were thought to be more dramatic, open, relaxed, impression leaving, and friendly. Wheeless (1976) found that self-disclosure and solidarity were positively related and that meaningfully higher levels of self-disclosure were associated with high solidarity relations (see also, Wheeless,

1978).

The one study which has specifically examined the effects of verbal teacher immediacy, Gorham (1988), found that verbal as well as nonverbal behaviors contributed to learning. The teachers' use of humor; praise of student work, actions, or comments; and frequency of initiating and/or willingness to become engaged in conversations before, after, or outside of class were particularly significant verbal immediacy cues. Student cognitive and affective learning were also related to the following behaviors: (a) self-disclosure; (b) asking questions or encouraging students to talk, (c) asking questions that solicit viewpoints or opinions, (d) following up on student-initiated topics, (e) reference to class as "our" class, (f) asking how students feel about assignments, due dates or discussion topics, and (g) invitations for students to telephone or meet with him/her outside of class. In terms of nonverbal cues, vocal expressiveness, smiling, and relaxed body position, as well as gestures, eye contact, movement around the classroom, and to some degree touch were nonverbal immediacy behaviors significantly associated with students' perceptions of learning.

This review of the literature indicates that both verbal and nonverbal teacher immediacy are positively associated with affective learning. Moreover, there is also substantial evidence that both constructs are positively associated with cognitive learning. Unfortunately, prior research has not examined plausible ethnic differences in teacher-student interaction, especially as this interaction affects student learning and affect toward the teacher and school.

Student ethnicity

Our classrooms are becoming increasingly ethnically diverse. For example, in California it is projected there will be no majority ethnic group by the year 2010 (*The Register*, 1989). As student populations become more multicultural, how will such changes affect the teacher-student relationship? Will teacher communication behaviors effective in the traditional classroom be effective in the multicultural classroom?

Andersen's (1985) "arousal-valence theory" of the effects of immediacy helps to explain why culture could influence the results of teacher immediacy. The theory suggests that for immediacy to have effects it must be perceived by a receiver. Once perceived, immediacy generates an arousal change in the receiver. Extremely high levels of arousal result in aversion, while extremely low levels of arousal result in no behavioral change. However, moderate levels of arousal are valenced either positively or negatively resulting in behavioral responses. Andersen suggests that culture is a primary influence on valence. In other words, if the arousal change is as a result of a culturally inappropriate behavior for the receiver, negative valence will occur.

If the effects of teacher immediacy are generalizable to the multicultural classroom, communication patterns among domestic cultures must be similar. However, much research has demonstrated that there are cultural differences in communication patterns. For example, Hecht and Ribeau (1984) found that Black, Hispanic, and White respondents differed significantly in the type of communication they found satisfying. Hispanics viewed communication as a bonded relationship with internal rewards while Whites viewed communication as more self-oriented with external rewards. Satisfying communication for Hispanics seemed to revolve around nonverbal communication and acceptance of self. Whites and Blacks stressed the future of the relationship and confirmation that the message and possible relationship is accepted. Black respondents seemed to require deeper more intimate topical involvement than White subjects. Satisfaction for Blacks revolved around having their own goals fulfilled by the actions of the other. On the other hand, Whites placed more stress on emotional aspects as well as being more future oriented. Collier (1988), in her comparison of intra- vs. intercultural conversations among Whites, Mexican Americans, and Black Americans, noted:

> although some similarities in broad competencies such as politeness emerged, important differences also were evident. Mexican Americans emphasized relational climate more frequently than the other groups, Black Americans emphasized individuality in politeness and expression frequently, and White Americans showed a marked emphasis on verbal content. Intercultural conversations appear to require more unique competencies that do not involve simply applying one's own group standards nor adopting the other's rules. (p. 143)

Research has also identified differences in nonverbal behaviors and disclosure between Asian-Americans and Caucasion-Americans (Gudykunst, Sodetani and Sonada, 1987) and differences in disclosure between White and Black Americans (Gudykunst, 1986).

If people of different ethnicities evaluate communication behaviors differently, the effects of teacher immediacy behaviors may likewise have diverse results. Research by Collier and Powell (1986) lends support to this conclusion. Examining student perceptions, they did not find significant differences in the way Anglos, Hispanics, Blacks, and Asians evaluated teacher immediacy or teacher effectiveness. All four groups perceived a positive relationship between immediacy and teaching effectiveness. However, immediacy cues functioned differently for different ethnic groups. For Anglos, the degree to which the teacher oriented his/her body position toward the students contributed significantly to teaching effectiveness. For Blacks, teacher relaxedness and smiling contributed significantly to teaching effectiveness. For Asians, vocal expressiveness, smiling, and teacher relaxedness contributed significantly to teaching effectiveness.

Since there appear to be ethnic differences in appropriate communication behaviors, the valencing of arousal generated by immediacy behaviors may also vary causing divergent effects for teacher immediacy. Additional research is needed to explore the effects of immediacy in the multicultural classroom.

Research questions

To examine the effects of teacher immediacy in the multicultural classroom, we decided to compare effects for four domestic culture groups: Whites, Asians, Hispanics, and Blacks. These groups were selected because they represent the majority of ethnic groups within American colleges. Our concerns about the effects of immediacy in the ethnically diverse classroom led us to identify the following research questions:

1. Does teacher immediacy positively contribute to affective, cognitive and behavioral learning for White, Asian, Hispanic, and Black students?
2. Do immediacy cues function differently for White, Asian, Hispanic, and Black students?

Methods

Sample

A total of 952 college students from two western universities volunteered to participate in the study. The demographic characteristics of the sample included: the average age was 23.6 (sd = 5.6), 58% were female and 40.3% were seniors. The participants represented 74 academic majors. In terms of the sample's ethnicity, 65.6% were White, 14.1% were Asian, 14.2% were Hispanic, and 3.7% were Black.

Questionnaire

The first step in construction of the questionnaire was to determine the teacher the students would be evaluating. In order to allay students' fears of teacher reactions and to attain a wide variety of classes, students were asked not to rate the teacher in the class in which they received the questionnaire; rather, they were requested to rate the behavior of the teacher in the class they had had just prior to the one in which they received the questionnaire. They were asked to identify the class they were taking from the selected teacher, the teacher's gender, and the teacher's ethnicity. The rated teachers were from 68 different disciplines, 68.9% were male, 93.4% were White.

The next stages in questionnaire construction were the operationalization of the verbal and nonverbal immediacy behaviors. Andersen (1979) found that student reports of the teachers' immediacy behaviors were highly reliable when compared with trained observers. Consequently, we decided to use student reports. Modified versions of Richmond, Gorham, and McCroskey's (1987) nonverbal behavior index and Gorham's (1988) verbal immediacy behavior scale were used for this purpose. Deleting duplicative items, 13 behaviors were selected for verbal immediacy and nine were selected for nonverbal immediacy, completing a 22-item scale. Two examples of the verbal items are: "Ask questions or encourages students to talk" and "Refers to class as `our' class or what `we' are doing." Two examples of nonverbal items are: "Gestures while talking to the class" and "Stands close to students while teaching." The 22 items were rated as to the frequency of the target teacher's use of these behaviors on a five-point scale: 0 = never, 1 = rarely, 2 = sometimes, 3 = often, and 4 = very often. Gorham (1988) presents evidence that all of these behaviors load on a single factor. Our interitem reliability for these 22 items was quite high (Cronbach's alpha = .91; Cronback, 1951).

The measure for perceived cognitive learning was drawn from Richmond et al. (1987). Recognizing that the scale is subjective, they nonetheless argue that it is appropriate because:

> College students are adults with considerable experience in a school environment. We believe it is reasonable to expect them to estimate with considerable accuracy the amount they learn in a given class. In fact, it is likely that their estimate is at least as good as subjective grades provided by teachers in many classes or by tests administered in classes not based on clear behavioral objectives. (p. 581)

While their scale initially contained two items, the interitem correlation between the items was .94. Thus, we selected one item for the measure of perceived cognitive learning: "On a scale of 0-9, how much have you learned in this class (0 means you have learned nothing and 9 means you have learned more than in any other class you've had)?"

The scales measuring affective learning were drawn from Andersen (1979). Affective learning was measured in three ways: affect toward the course in general, affect toward the content of the course, and affect toward the behaviors/practices/theories recommended in this course. Four seven-point evaluative semantic differential scales were used to assess each of the three affect dimensions: good/bad, worthless/valuable, fair/unfair, and negative/positive. Interitem reliability for the 12 items comprising the affective learning scale was quite high for each of the four ethnic groups (White: Cronbach's alpha = .95; Asian: Cronbach's alpha = .96; Hispanic: Cronbach's alpha = .96; Black: Cronbach's alpha = .97).

The scale operationalizing a student's behavioral commitment was also drawn from Andersen (1979). The scale measured the likelihood of actually attempting to use the behaviors/practices/theories recommended in the course and the likelihood of enrolling in a course of related content, schedule permitting. These two behavioral dimensions of the scale were evaluated on four semantic-differential items: likely/unlikely, possible/impossible, probable/improbable and would/would not. Reliability for the behavioral learning scale was very high for each ethnic group (White: Cronbach's alpha = .94; Asian: Cronbach's alpha = .97; Hispanic: Cronbach's alpha = .91; Black: Cronbach's alpha = .97).

Data analysis

The intent of this research was to assess the relationships between teacher immediacy behaviors and various dimensions of student learning. Unfortunately, the measures for these variables tend to be very intercorrelated, leading to problems of multicollinearity in multivariate statistical designs (e.g., regression analysis). Thus, it was decided that a bivariate statistical approach would be more appropriate, viz., Pearson correlations. Since a number of correlations would need to be computed, it was further decided to use rather conservative criteria in determining statistical significance in order to minimize attributing significance to spurious relationships. The specific criteria used to assess statistical significance were: (a) that the amount of shared variance (r^2) should reach 10% and (b) that a difference between two measures of association should contribute an additional 10% of variance accounted for in the learning outcome.

Results

Correlations between summed immediacy scale and learning scales

In order to assess the relationships between the summed immediacy scale and learning scales, correlations were computed for the summed immediacy scale and learning scales for each ethnic group. Scores for items from the questionnaire that were presumed to be nonimmediate were reversed for purposes of analysis (e.g., uses monotone/dull voice when talking to the class, has a very tense body position while talking to the class). The results are summarized in Table 1 and indicate that while the levels of correlation varied, the relations between immediacy behavior and all of the learning scales were significant and positive for all ethnic groups.

Table 1
Correlations Between Summed Immediacy and Learning Scales

Learning Scale	Ethnicity			
	White	Asian	Hispanic	Black
Cognitive learning	.55(.30)*	.57(.33)	.55(.30)	.50(.25)
Affective learning	.61(.37)	.57(.33)	.66(.43)	.54(.28)
Behavioral learning	.46(.21)	.46(.21)	.44(.19)	.52(.27)

*For all correlations, $p < .002$; r^2 presented in parentheses.

While significant and positive correlations were found between the immediacy scale and all of the outcome measures—cognitive learning, affective learning, and behavioral learning—three significant differences should be noted. First, for the White, Asian, and Hispanic ethnic groups, teacher immediacy was more predictive of affective learning than behavioral learning. Second, teacher immediacy was more predictive of affective learning for Hispanic students than for Asian and Black students. Finally, for Hispanic students, teacher immediacy was more associated with affective learning than with cognitive learning. In general, it appears that teacher immediacy is an important correlate of affective learning for Hispanic students.

Table 2 presents the correlations between the teacher immediacy items and the cognitive learning measure. For all four ethnic groups, seven teacher behaviors were significantly related to perceived cog-

Table 2
Correlations Between Immediacy Behaviors and Perceived Cognitive Learning

	White	Asian	Hispanic	Black
Uses personal examples	.28(.08)*	.18(.03)	.12(.01)	.23(.05)
Encourages students to talk	.38(.14)	.37(.14)	.32(.10)	.50(.25)
Discusses student topics	.26(.07)	.36(.13)	.37(.14)	.01(.00)
Uses humor	.39(.15)	.35(.12)	.31(.10)	.52(.27)
Uses student names	.32(.10)	.31(.10)	.26(.07)	.29(.08)
Has outside discussions	.40(.16)	.51(.26)	.32(.10)	.33(.11)
Refers to "our" class	.31(.10)	.23(.05)	.40(.16)	.32(.10)
Asks about assignments	.37(.14)	.42(.18)	.28(.08)	.40(.16)
Suggests telephoning	.36(.13)	.46(.21)	.32(.10)	.25(.06)
Solicits viewpoints	.33(.11)	.50(.25)	.36(.13)	.48(.23)
Praises student work	.50(.25)	.44(.19)	.39(.15)	.39(.15)
Discusses issues unrelated to class	.25(.06)	.29(.08)	.27(.07)	.25(.06)
Addresses by first name	.24(.06)	.24(.06)	.18(.03)	.07(.00)
Gestures while lecturing	.34(.12)	.22(.05)	.25(.06)	.11(.01)
Uses dull voice (R)**	.51(.26)	.46(.21)	.54(.29)	.38(.14)
Stands close to students	.26(.07)	.19(.04)	.25(.06)	–.25(.06)
Maintains eye contact	.39(.15)	.45(.20)	.54(.29)	.19(.04)
Has tense body (R)	.33(.11)	.19(.04)	.28(.08)	.30(.09)
Moves around classroom	.26(.07)	.22(.05)	.26(.07)	.13(.01)
Looks at board/notes (R)	.20(.04)	.13(.02)	.35(.12)	.05(.00)
Stands behind podium (R)	.29(.08)	.15(.02)	.32(.10)	–.06(.00)
Smiles at students	.39(.15)	.38(.14)	.32(.10)	.32(.10)

*r^2 presented in parentheses.
**(R) indicates reverse coding.

nitive learning: (a) encourages students to talk, (b) uses humor, (c) has discussions with students outside class, (d) solicits alternative viewpoints, (e) praises student work, (e) does not use a dull voice, and (f) smiles at students. Two ethnic group differences were discovered among the correlations between cognitive learning and teacher immediacy. First, in contrast to the other ethnic groups, three immediacy behaviors were unrelated to cognitive learning for Black students, namely, maintaining eye contact, discussing student topics, and suggesting students telephone the teacher. Second, Hispanic students, more than other ethnic groups, tended to indicate a greater relationship between cognitive learning and visually-oriented immediacy behaviors, namely, maintaining eye contact, not looking at one's notes/board, and not standing behind the podium.

The correlations between the teacher immediacy items and the affective learning scale are presented in Table 3. For all four ethnic groups, affective learning was significantly related to six immediacy behaviors: (a) using humor, (b) asking students about assignments, (c) soliciting viewpoints from students, (d) praising student work, (e) maintaining eye contact, and (f) smiling at students. Two ethnic group differences in the patterns of correlations between teacher immediacy and affective learning could be discerned in Table 3. First, there was a tendency for Black students to perceive affective learning to be unrelated to three teacher immediacy behaviors that attempt to individualize instruction, namely, discussing student topics, using student names, and having discussions with students outside class. Second, Asian students tended to perceive affective learning as unrelated to the teacher encouraging students to talk and using inclusive referents such as "our class" or "we."

The correlations between the behavioral learning scale and the teacher immediacy behaviors are presented in Table 4. Only two immediacy behaviors were significantly related to behavioral learning for all four ethnic groups: using student names and maintaining eye contact with students. Six of the 22 teacher

Table 3
Correlations Between Immediacy Behaviors and Affective Learning

	White	Asian	Hispanic	Black
Uses personal examples	.30(.09)*	.26(.07)	.40(.16)	.37(.14)
Encourages students to talk	.43(.18)	.29(.08)	.44(.19)	.47(.22)
Discusses student topics	.29(.08)	.35(.12)	.41(.17)	.09(.01)
Uses humor	.43(.18)	.40(.16)	.41(.17)	.57(.32)
Uses student names	.37(.14)	.33(.11)	.28(.08)	.12(.01)
Has outside discussions	.44(.19)	.48(.23)	.44(.19)	.27(.07)
Refers to "our" class	.41(.17)	.22(.05)	.47(.22)	.34(.12)
Asks about assignments	.40(.16)	.43(.18)	.37(.14)	.41(.17)
Suggests telephoning	.39(.15)	.42(.18)	.40(.16)	.21(.04)
Solicits viewpoints	.38(.14)	.52(.27)	.44(.19)	.46(.21)
Praises student work	.55(.30)	.45(.20)	.44(.19)	.48(.23)
Discusses issues unrelated to class	.27(.07)	.31(.10)	.39(.15)	.23(.05)
Addresses by first name	.30(.09)	.22(.05)	.27(.07)	–.03(.01)
Gestures while lecturing	.34(.12)	.35(.12)	.17(.03)	.15(.02)
Uses dull voice (R)**	.50(.25)	.45(.20)	.52(.27)	.30(.09)
Stands close to students	.32(.10)	.20(.04)	.26(.07)	–.14(.02)
Maintains eye contact	.41(.17)	.46(.21)	.58(.34)	.37(.14)
Has tense body (R)	.38(.14)	.19(.04)	.37(.14)	.11(.01)
Moves around classroom	.28(.08)	.22(.05)	.31(.10)	.16(.02)
Looks at board/notes (R)	.23(.05)	.03(.00)	.29(.08)	.03(.00)
Stands behind podium (R)	.32(.10)	.04(.00)	.31(.10)	.12(.01)
Smiles at students	.41(.17)	.45(.20)	.48(.23)	.39(.15)

*r2 presented in parentheses.
**(R) indicates reverse coding.

Table 4
Correlations Between Immediacy Behaviors and Behavioral Learning

	White	Asian	Hispanic	Black
Uses personal examples	.22(.05)*	.19(.04)	.33(.11)	.48(.23)
Encourages students to talk	.31(.10)	.25(.06)	.34(.12)	.27(.07)
Discusses student topics	.25(.06)	.27(.08)	.41(.17)	.07(.00)
Uses humor	.31(.10)	.25(.06)	.25(.06)	.48(.23)
Uses student names	.35(.12)	.35(.12)	.33(.11)	.44(.19)
Has outside discussions	.35(.12)	.34(.12)	.30(.09)	.20(.04)
Refers to "our" class	.29(.08)	.26(.07)	.25(.06)	.33(.11)
Asks about assignments	.29(.08)	.38(.14)	.17(.03)	.19(.04)
Suggests telephoning	.28(.08)	.29(.08)	.19(.04)	.06(.00)
Solicits viewpoints	.27(.07)	.47(.22)	.35(.12)	.33(.11)
Praises student work	.42(.18)	.26(.07)	.40(.16)	.53(.28)
Discusses issues unrelated to class	.22(.05)	.30(.09)	.31(.10)	.24(.06)
Addressed by first name	.24(.06)	.26(.07)	.29(.08)	.10(.01)
Gestures while lecturing	.25(.06)	.32(.10)	.02(.00)	.22(.05)
Uses dull voice (R)**	.32(.10)	.26(.07)	.35(.12)	.33(.11)
Stands close to students	.26(.07)	.21(.04)	.19(.04)	–.09(.01)
Maintains eye contact	.33(.11)	.31(.10)	.33(.11)	.32(.10)
Has tense body (R)	.25(.06)	.09(.01)	.21(.04)	.62(.38)
Moves around classroom	.20(.04)	.20(.04)	.02(.00)	.05(.00)
Looks at board/notes (R)	.17(.03)	.02(.00)	.20(.04)	–.09(.01)
Stands behind podium (R)	.23(.05)	.12(.01)	.15(.02)	–.03(.00)
Smiles at students	.30(.09)	.29(.08)	.29(.08)	.40(.16)

*r^2 presented in parentheses.
**(R) indicates reverse coding.

immediacy behaviors proved unrelated to behavioral learning for all ethnic groups (suggesting students telephone, addressing teachers by first name, standing close to students, moving around the classroom, not looking at the board/notes, and not standing behind the podium). Three significant ethnic differences could be ascertained in the correlations between the behavioral learning scale and the teacher immediacy behaviors. First, the Asian students, as opposed to the other ethnic groups, perceived a greater relationship between the behavioral learning and the teacher soliciting student viewpoints, and a lesser relationship between behavioral learning and praising student work. Second, Hispanic students felt a stronger relationship between behavioral learning and the teacher discussing student topics than other ethnic students. Finally, Black students perceived a stronger relationship between behavioral learning and the teacher using humor and having a relaxed body position than did other ethnic groups.

Discussion

The present study found that teacher immediacy behaviors enhance the students' perceived cognitive, affective and behavioral learning in the multicultural classroom. However, the results suggest that there are both similarities and differences in the effects of teacher immediacy cues across U.S. cultural groups. While immediacy appears to be positively associated with learning for all groups, the levels of association vary. Further, some immediacy cues appear to have pancultural effects while others hold particular salience only for certain ethnicities.

For all ethnic groups, positive correlations were obtained between immediacy and perceived cognitive, affective, and behavioral learning. This suggests that there may be pancultural effects for teacher immediacy in terms of student learning. These results are consistent with Collier and Powell's (1986) study which found that teacher immediacy was positively related to teaching effectiveness, regardless of ethnicity.

Some differences in the relationships between immediacy and the learning variables were also observed. First, for White, Asian, and Hispanic students, immediacy was more highly related to affective learning than to behavioral learning. It may be that the behavioral implementation of the course's recommendations may entail other contingencies than teacher immediacy. Thus, behavioral learning may be more difficult for a teacher to influence than the student's affect toward the course. This is consistent with prior research which has found a lower relationship between behavioral learning and immediacy than affective learning and immediacy (Andersen, 1979; Plax et al., 1986).

Two other differences were noted in the relationship between immediacy and learning: (a) immediacy was more highly related to affective learning for Hispanic students than for Asian or Black students, and (b) immediacy was more associated with affective learning than cognitive learning for Hispanic students. Past research indicates that Hispanic students emphasize the "relational" element of communication (Collier and Powell, 1986; Hecht and Ribeau, 1984). Immediacy carries a positive relational message and so is very important in developing positive affect in the classroom for the Hispanic student. The lesser role of immediacy in affect for Black students is consistent with Hecht and Ribeau's (1984) finding that Black students emphasize topical involvement and goal fulfillment in communication, thus relegating interpersonal warmth to a lesser role. For Asian students this finding may simply reflect the cultural difference that it is normal for them to engage in less immediate communication behaviors (Gudykunst et al., 1987).

Examination of the relationships between specific immediacy behaviors and the learning outcomes also yielded cultural similarities and differences. For all ethnic groups seven immediacy behaviors were positively associated with cognitive learning: (a) encourages students to talk, (b) uses humor, (c) has discussions with students outside class, (d) solicits alternative viewpoints, (e) praises student work, (e) does not use a dull voice, (f) smiles at students. Other studies have found similar cues to be significantly related to cognitive learning (Gorham, 1988; Richmond et al., 1987).

Some ethnic differences were also noted in the relationships between immediacy behaviors and cognitive learning. First, some cues were uniquely not related to cognitive learning for certain ethnic groups. For Black students these included: maintaining eye contact, discussing student topics, and suggesting student telephone the teacher. Consistent with Hecht and Ribeau (1984) this suggests a high level of goal orientation for Black students. For Asian students, "refers to class as 'our' class" was not a significant predictor of cognitive learning. This may be indicative both of the collective nature of Asian culture and the ethnicity of the teacher; that is, Asian students may not perceive themselves as belonging to the same group as White teachers (see Gudykunst et al., in press). "Asks about assignments" was not strongly related to cognitive learning for Hispanic students. This is consistent with a feeling by Hispanic students that it is the job of the teacher to determine course methodologies (Hofstede, 1986).

Second, some cues were significant predictors of cognitive learning only for certain ethnic groups or were particularly strong predictors only for certain ethnic groups. Gestures and tense body position were significant predictors only for White students suggesting that these are important arousal factors. For Hispanic students visual immediacy cues seemed particularly important in relation to cognitive learning. Maintaining eye contact, avoiding looking at the board or notes, and avoiding standing behind the podium were significantly related to cognitive learning for these students. While maintaining eye contact was also significantly related for White and Asian students, avoiding looking at the board or notes and avoiding standing behind the podium were not significantly related to cognitive learning for other ethnic groups. These cues seem to focus on personal attention to the student and thus probably enhance the student's arousal level through positive relationship development, affirming the significance of relational communication to the Hispanic student. While encouraging students to talk and using humor were significant predictors for all ethnic groups, they were especially important to Black students suggesting they are particularly salient in enhancing the learning environment for Black students. Likewise, willingness to have discussions outside of class was particularly salient to Asian students. This last finding probably reflects a cultural reticence to speak out in front of others (Collier and Powell, 1986); Asian students prefer to interact with their teachers in a less public environment.

Pancultural relationships were also observed between immediacy behaviors and affective learning. Six immediacy behaviors were significant predictors of affective learning for all ethnic groups: (a) using humor, (b) asking students about assignments, (c) soliciting viewpoints from students, (d) praising student work, (e) maintaining eye contact, and (f) smiling at students. In contrast, two immediacy behaviors were not significant predictors for any ethnic group: (a) addressing the teacher by first name, and (b) avoiding looking at board or notes.

Several cultural differences were also isolated in the relationships between immediacy behaviors and affective learning. Consistent with Colier and Powell's (1986) finding that body orientation is particularly important to White and Hispanic students, standing close to students was significant only for White students while moving around the classroom was important only to Hispanic students. Avoiding standing behind the podium and having a relaxed body position were significant both for White and Hispanic students. Gesturing and calling students by name were significant only for White and Asian students. Using personal examples was important only to Hispanic and Black students. Discussing student topics and issues unrelated to class were important only to Asian and Hispanic students. Thus, while all of these cues contribute to overall perceptions of immediacy, some cues are more salient for particular ethnic groups.

Fewer immediacy behaviors were related to behavioral learning than cognitive or affective learning and only two were significant across cultural groups: using student names and maintaining eye contact. Conversely, six cues were not related to behavioral learning across all ethnic groups: (a) suggesting student telephone, (b) addressing teachers by first name, (c) standing close to students, (d) moving around the classroom, (e) not looking at board/notes, and (f) not standing behind the podium. Apparently these cues do not substantially affect students' intents to use the recommended behaviors or enroll in similar classes.

Several ethnic differences were also observed between the immediacy cues and behavioral learning. First, for Asian students, soliciting student viewpoints was more important and praising student work was less important in influencing behavioral learning. This suggests that use of the recommended behaviors as well as future enrollment is strongly related to allowing students to express their opinions by direct request but providing public recognition for individual student accomplishment is not. Hispanic students saw a stronger relationship between discussing student topics and behavioral intentions, and the teacher's use of humor and relaxed body position were more salient to Black students.

A review of those factors significant across learning scales for each ethnic group does provide some guidance as to the most important immediacy cues. Vocal expressiveness, smiling and eye contact appear to be the nonverbal cues with the widest pancultural effects on student learning. Using humor, soliciting student views, and praising student work appear to be the verbal cues with the greatest pancultural effects on student learning. Encouraging students to talk and referring to class as "our" class appear to be less important to Asian students. Having outside discussions and suggesting that students telephone the teacher appear less important to Black students. Asking how students feel about assignments appears to be less important to Hispanic students. Using personal examples are particularly important to Hispanic and Black students, while discussing student topics, having unrelated discussions, and avoiding standing behind the podium are particularly important to Hispanic students. Using student names and gesturing are especially significant to White and Asian students while White students feel teacher relaxation is also important. Standing close to students, calling the teacher by first name, moving around the classroom, and looking at the board or notes appear to be the less important immediacy cues across cultures. Both the similarities and differences isolated here suggest that the more effective classroom teacher will be sensitive to the cultural background of his/her students and will adjust to student expectations generated by that background.

In conclusion, this study confirmed past research which suggests that teacher immediacy is an important influence on student learning and affect toward the class. Teacher immediacy creates a supportive learning environment for the class. The present study extends upon extant research by suggesting that specific immediacy behaviors may vary in their efficacy for different ethnic groups. As the demography of our classroom becomes increasingly multicultural, a greater sensitivity to the needs and learning styles of various ethnic groups becomes more critical. Future research should continue to address how instructors can adapt their teaching styles to optimize the learning of all students.

References

Andersen, J.F. (1979). Teacher immediacy as a predictor of teaching effectiveness. In D. Nimmo (Ed.), *Communication Yearbook 3* (pp. 543–559). New Brunswick, N.J.: Transaction Books.

Andersen, J.F., Norton, R. W., and Nussbaum, J. F. (1981). Three investigations exploring relationships between perceived teacher communication behaviors and student learning. *Communication Education, 30*, 377–392.

Andersen, P.A. (1985). Nonverbal immediacy in interpersonal communication. In A. W. Siegman and S. Feldstein (Eds.), *Multichannel integrations of nonverbal behavior* (pp. 1–36). Hillsdale, N.J.: Lawrence Erlbaum.

Anthony, S. (1978). Immediacy and nonimmediacy factors in communicating interpersonal attraction. *Journal of Social Psychology, 93*, 141–142.

Bradac, J.J., Bowers, J.W., and Courtright, J.A. (1979). Three language variables in communication research: Intensity, immediacy, and diversity. *Human Communication Research, 5*, 257–269.

Burgoon, J.K., Buller, D.B., Hale, J.L., and deTurck, M.A. (1984). Relational messages associated with nonverbal behaviors. *Human Communication Research, 10*, 351–378.

Chaiken, A.L., Gillen, B., Derlega, V.J., Heinen, J.R.K., and Wilson, M. (1978). Students' reactions to teachers' physical attractiveness and nonverbal behavior: Two exploratory studies. *Psychology in the Schools, 15*, 588–595.

Collier, M.J. (1988). A comparison of conversations among and between domestic culture groups: How intra– and intercultural competencies vary. *Communication Quarterly, 36*, 122–144.

Collier, M.J. and Powell, R.G. (1986, May). *The effect of student culture/ethnicity on judgments of instructional communication*. Paper presented at the annual convention of the International Communications Association, Chicago, Illinois.

Conville, R. (1975). Linguistic nonimmediacy and self–presentation. *Journal of Psychology, 90*, 219–227.

Cronbach, L. (1951). Coefficient alpha and the internal structure of tests. *Psychometrika, 16*, 297–334.

Feinberg, L.B. (1971). Nonimmediacy in verbal communication as in indicator of attitudes toward the disabled. *Journal of Social Psychology, 84*, 135–140.

Gorham, J. (1988). The relationship between verbal teacher immediacy behaviors and student learning. *Communication Education, 37*, 40–53.

Gudykunst, W.B. (1986). Ethnicity, types of relationship, and intraethnic and interethnic uncertainty reduction. In Y. Kim (Ed.), *Interethnic Communication* (pp. 201–224). Newbury Park, CA: Sage.

Gudykunst, W.B., Schmidt, K.L., Bond, M.H., Wang, G., Gao, G., Nishida, T., Leung, K., and Barraclough, R. (in press). The influence of individualism-collectivism, self-monitoring, and predicted outcome values on communication in ingroup and outgroup relationships. *Journal of Cross-Cultural Psychology.*

Gudykunst, W.B., Sodetani, L.L., and Sonada, K.T. (1987). Uncertainty reduction in Japanese-American/Caucasian relationships in Hawaii. *Western Speech Communication Journal, 51*, 256–278.

Hecht, M.L., and Ribeau, S. (1984). Ethnic communications: A comparative analysis of satisfying communication. *International Journal of Intercultural Relations, 8*, 135–151.

Hofstede, G. (1986). Cultural differences in teaching and learning. *International Journal of Intercultural Relations, 10*, 301–322.

Hurt, H.T., Scott, M.D., and McCroskey, J.C. (1978). *Communication in the Classroom.* Reading: MA: Addison-Wesley.

Kelley, D.H., and Gorham, J. (1988). Effects of immediacy on recall of information. *Communication Education, 37*, 198–207.

McClatchy News Service (1989, February 11). State's ethnic diversity expected to increase. *The Register,* p. B10.

Mehrabian, A. (1967). Attitudes inferred from nonimmediacy of verbal communication. *Journal of Verbal Learning and Verbal Behavior, 6,* 294–295.

Mehrabian, A. (1969). Some referents and measures of nonverbal behavior. *Behavioral Research Methods and Instruments, 1,* 213–217.

Plax, T.G., Kearney, P., McCroskey, J.C., and Richmond, V.P. (1986). Power in the classroom VI: Verbal control strategies, nonverbal immediacy and affective learning. *Communication Education, 35,* 43–55.

Richmond, V.P., Gorham, J.S., and McCroskey, J.C. (1987). The relationship between selected immediacy behaviors and cognitive learning. In McLaughlin, M. L. (Ed.), *Communication Yearbook 10* (pp. 574–590). Beverly Hills, CA: Sage.

Wheeless, L.R. (1976). Self-disclosure and interpersonal solidarity: Measurement, validation, and relationships. *Human Communication Research, 3,* 47–61.

Wheeless, L.R. (1978). A follow-up study of the relationships among trust, disclosure, and interpersonal solidarity. *Human Communication Research, 4,* 143–157.

Research on Cooperative Learning

DAVID W. JOHNSON, ROGER T. JOHNSON AND KARL A. SMITH

The best answer to the question "What is the most effective method of teaching?" is that it depends on the goal, the students, the content, and the teacher. But the next best answer is, "Students teaching other students." A wealth of evidence suggests that peer teaching is extremely effective for a wide range of goals, content, and students (McKeachie et al. 1986, p. 63).

A professor at the University of Minnesota in his introductory astronomy classes of 300 to 500 students randomly assigns students to groups of four. He provides explicit directions about students' group work and maintains an extensive file system to pass information between the students and the instructor. After students become accustomed to working in groups, he often differentiates assigned roles and assigns each group member one of the roles. The recorder records the group's work by writing out the steps for solving each astronomy problem assigned. The checker makes sure that all members can explain how to solve each problem correctly (or can give an appropriate rationale for the group's answer). The encourager in a friendly way encourages all members of the group to participate in the discussion, sharing their ideas and feelings. The elaborator relates present to past learning.

Within the lesson, positive interdependence is structured by the group's agreeing on the answer and the process for solving each problem. Because the group certifies that each member has the correct answer written on the answer sheet and can correctly explain how to solve each problem, individual accountability is structured by having the professor randomly ask one group member to explain how to solve one of the problems. The cooperative skills emphasized in the lesson are checking, encouraging, and elaborating. Finally, at the end of the period, the groups process how well they are functioning by answering two questions: (1) What is something each member did that was helpful for the group, and (2) What is something each member could do to make the group even better tomorrow?

As a result of structuring this introductory astronomy lesson cooperatively, what instructional outcomes can the professor expect?

Research on Social Interdependence

Learning together to complete assignments can profoundly affect students, teaching assistants, and professors. A great deal of research has compared the relative effects of cooperative, competitive, and individualistic efforts on instructional outcomes (Johnson and Johnson 1974, 1978, 1983, 1989a; Johnson, Johnson, and Maruyama 1983; Johnson et al. 1981; Pepitone 1980; Sharan 1980; Slavin 1983). Such research began in the late 1800s with a series of studies on the factors associated with competitive performance. The amount of research that has been conducted since is staggering. During the past 90 years, over 575 experimental and 100 correlational studies have been conducted by a wide variety of researchers in different decades with different age subjects, in different subject areas, and in different settings (see Johnson and Johnson 1989a for a complete list of these studies). The research program at the Cooperative Learning Center at the University of Minnesota over the past 25 years has conducted over 85 studies to refine the understanding of how cooperation works. Far more is known about the efficacy of cooperative learning than about lecturing, departmentalization, the use of technology, or almost any other facet of education (see Johnson and Johnson 1989a for a comprehensive review of all studies and meta-analyses of the results).[1]

"Research on Cooperative Learning," in *Cooperative Learning: Increasing College Faculty Instructional Productivity,* by David W. Johnson, Roger T. Johnson, and Karl A. Smith, reprinted by permission from *ASHE/ERIC Higher Education Report,* No. 4, 1991. Washington, D.C.: The George Washington University School of Education and Human Development.

Building on the theorizing of Kurt Lewin and Morton Deutsch, one can make the premise that the type of interdependence structured among students determines how they interact with each other, which in turn largely determines instructional outcomes. This section is organized around this progression from goal structures to patterns of interaction to outcomes. Structuring situations cooperatively results in promotive interaction, structuring situations competitively results in oppositional interaction, and structuring situations individualistically results in no interaction among students. The characteristics of these three types of social interdependence are summarized in table 2. These patterns of interaction affect numerous variables, which can be subsumed within three broad and interrelated outcomes: effort exerted to achieve, quality of relationships among participants, and participants' psychological adjustment and social competence (see figure 1) (Johnson and Johnson 1989a).

Patterns of Interaction

Two Heads Are Better than One

Simply placing students near each other and allowing them to interact does not mean that learning will be maximized, high-quality peer relationships will result, or students' psychological adjustment, self-esteem, and social competencies will be enhanced. Students can obstruct as well as facilitate each other's learning. Or they can ignore each other. The way students interact depends on how faculty members structure interdependence in learning.

Positive interdependence results in students' promoting each other's learning and achievement. Promotive interaction is defined as individuals encouraging and facilitating each other's efforts to achieve, complete tasks, and produce to reach the group's goals. While positive interdependence in and of itself might have some effect on outcomes, it is the face-to-face promotive interaction among individuals, fostered by the positive interdependence, that most powerfully influences efforts to achieve, caring and committed relationships, and psychological adjustment and social competence. Students focus on increasing their own achievement and on increasing the achievement of the other members of the group. Promotive interaction is characterized by individuals':

1. Providing each other with efficient and effective assistance;
2. Exchanging needed resources, such as information and materials, and processing information more efficiently and effectively;
3. Providing each other with feedback to improve their subsequent performance of their assigned tasks and responsibilities;
4. Challenging each other's conclusions and reasoning to promote higher-quality decision making and greater insight into the problems being considered;
5. Advocating the exertion of effort to achieve mutual goals;
6. Influencing each other's efforts to achieve the group's goals;

Table 2
Characteristics of Social Interdependence

	Interdependence		
Characteristic	Positive	Negative	None
Fate	Mutual	Negatively Linked	Individual
Benefit	Mutual	Differential	Self
Time Perspective	Long-Term	Short-Term	Short-Term
Identity	Shared	Relative	Individual
Causation	Mutual	Relative	Self
Affiliation Motives	Enhance	Oppose	Oppose

Figure 1
Outcome of Cooperation

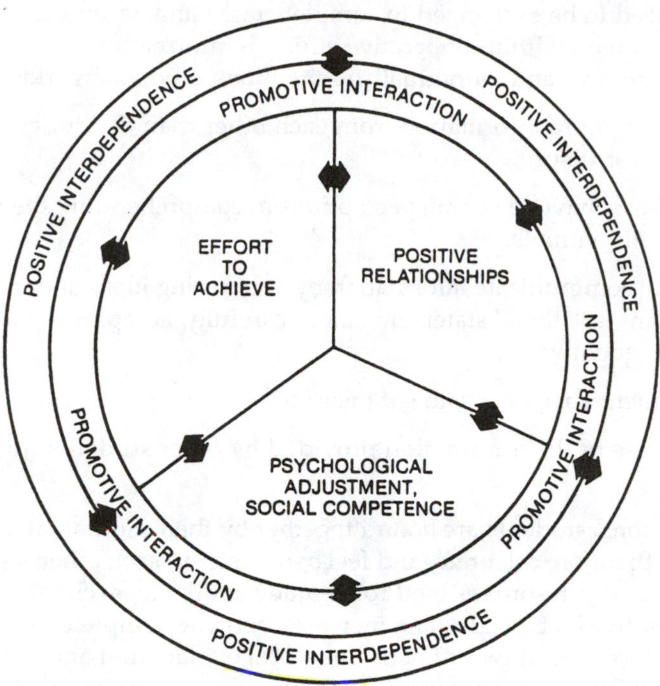

Source: Johnson and Johnson 1989a.

7. Being motivated to strive for mutual benefit;
8. Acting in trusting and trustworthy ways;
9. Exhibiting a moderate level of arousal characterized by low anxiety and stress (Johnson and Johnson 1989a).

Negative interdependence typically results in students' opposing and obstructing each other's learning. Oppositional interaction occurs as students discourage and obstruct each other's efforts to achieve. Students focus on increasing their own achievement and on preventing any classmate from achieving higher than they do. No interaction exists when students work independently without any interaction or interchange with each other. Students focus only on increasing their own achievement and ignore as irrelevant the efforts of others.

Giving and Receiving Assistance

Within most tasks, productivity is enhanced when individuals give each other relevant task-related help and assistance (Johnson and Johnson 1989a). Cooperative situations contain more consistent perceptions of more frequent helping and tutoring (including cross-ethnic and cross-handicap helping) than competitive or individualistic situations. In research on both social-psychological and applied behavior, cooperative structures have enhanced helping among group members, while competitive structures have resulted in individuals' obstructing each other's efforts to achieve, refusing to help and share and engaging in antisocial behaviors. These effects of competition are exacerbated by losing. Observational studies of actual learning groups consistently find students giving and receiving more help in cooperative than in competitive or individualistic situations.

Information Exchange and Cognitive Processes

More efficient and effective exchange and processing of information take place in cooperative than in competitive or individualistic situations (Johnson 1974; Johnson and Johnson 1989a). While a wide variety of resources might need to be exchanged to complete tasks and accomplish goals, the most common resource shared and exchanged within cooperative efforts is information.

Compared with competitive and individualistic situations, students working cooperatively:

1. Seek significantly more information from each other than do students working within a competitive goal structure;
2. Are less biased and have fewer misperceptions in comprehending the viewpoints and positions of other individuals;
3. More accurately communicate information by verbalizing ideas and information more frequently, attending to others' statements more carefully, accepting others' ideas and information more frequently;
4. Are more confident about the value of their ideas;
5. Make optimal use of the information provided by other students (Johnson and Johnson 1989a).

In cooperative situations, students are bound together by their mutual fate, shared identity, and mutual causation, and they therefore celebrate (and feel benefited by) each other's successes. Relevant ideas, information, conclusions, and resources tend to be made available, exchanged, and used in ways that promote collective and individual insights and increase energy to complete the task. Such oral discussion of relevant information has at least two dimensions—oral explanation and listening—and both benefit the giver and the receiver. The giver benefits from the cognitive organizing and processing, higher-level reasoning, insights, and personal commitment to achieving the group's goals derived from orally explaining, elaborating, and summarizing information and teaching one's knowledge to others. The receiver benefits from the opportunity to use others' resources in accomplishing his or her goals.

Exchanging information and stimulating cognitive processes might not occur in competitive or individualistic situations. In competitive situations, the exchange of communication and information tends to be nonexistent or misleading, and competition biases a person's perceptions and comprehension of others' viewpoints and positions. Individualistic situations are usually deliberately structured to ensure that individuals do not communicate or exchange information at all.

Survey research indicates that fear of public speaking is quite common among the general populations of adolescents and adults (Motley 1988). College students in particular are frequently apprehensive about speaking in the classroom (Bowers 1986). Such anxiety, however, can be significantly reduced if students are given the opportunity to first express themselves in the more comfortable social context of a small group of peers (Neer 1987). Students whose primary language is not English could especially find anxiety reduced by working in small groups in college classes.

Peer Feedback

An important aspect of promotive interaction is the opportunity for group members to provide each other with feedback about how they are fulfilling their responsibilities and completing their work. Feedback is information made available to individuals that makes possible the comparison of actual performance with some standard of performance. Knowledge of results is information provided to the person about his or her performance on a given effort. It could be in the form of qualitative information in which the person is informed that a performance is either correct or incorrect. Or it could be quantitative information about how much discrepancy exists between the person's response and the correct response. Usually, quantitative information (that is, process feedback) about the size of the discrepancy existing between actual performance and some standard of performance or how to improve one's reasoning or performance promotes achievement more effectively than qualitative information (that is, terminal feedback) about being right or wrong or what the correct answer is. Receiving personalized feedback from another person increases performance to a greater extent than does receiving impersonal feedback; peer feedback from collaborators could be especially vivid and personalized. Frequent and immediate feedback increases a student's motivation to learn (Mackworth 1970).

Challenge and Controversy

An important aspect of promotive interaction is controversy, the conflict that arises when involved group members have different information, perceptions, opinions, reasoning processes, theories, and conclusions and must reach agreement. When controversies arise, they can be dealt with constructively or destructively, depending on how they are managed and the level of interpersonal and small-group skills of the participants. When managed constructively, controversy promotes uncertainty about the correctness of one's views, an active search for more information, a reconceptualization of one's knowledge and conclusions, and, consequently, greater mastery and retention of the material being discussed. Individuals working alone in competitive and individualistic situations do not have the opportunity for such a process, and their productivity, quality of decision making, and achievement therefore suffer.

Public Advocacy and Commitment

Promotive interaction includes advocating that cooperators increase their efforts to accomplish the group's goals and publicly committing oneself to do the same. Commitment can be defined as the binding or pledging of the individual to an act or decision. To the extent that people act in the absence of coercion, commit themselves in front of others to act, or invest time, money, or personal prestige in an activity, they come to see themselves as believers in that sort of activity and develop a personal interest in it. Individuals become more committed to attitudes that are made public than to attitudes that remain private. People are particularly prone to increase their commitment to actions that they have attempted to persuade another to adopt.

Mutual Influence

During the exchange of information, individuals share ideas and information and use each other's resources to maximize their productivity and achievement. This process entails mutual influence in which cooperators consider each other's ideas and conclusions and coordinate their efforts. Participants must be open to influence attempts aimed at facilitating the accomplishment of shared goals, must trust each other *not* to use the resources being shared in detrimental ways, and must form emotional bonds that result in commitment to each other's welfare and success. Influence can be exerted in three ways within social situations: direct influence, social modeling, and situational norms. Students will be receptive to others' attempts to influence them directly to the extent that they perceive a cooperative relationship among goals attained. In cooperative situations, students benefit from the group's modeling effective and committed behaviors, skills, and attitudes. Visible and credible models who demonstrate the recommended attitudes and behaviors and who directly discuss their importance are powerful influences. Finally, achievement is influenced by whether or not the group's norms favor high performance. In cooperative situations, everyone benefits from the efforts of cooperators. Because it is in each student's best interests to encourage the productivity of collaborators, the group's norms support efforts to achieve. Furthermore, evidence suggests that in the generally competitive climate of most schools, success at academic tasks has little value for many individuals and could even be a deterrent to popularity with peers (Johnson and Johnson 1989a).

Motivation to Achieve

Achievement is a we *thing, not a* me *thing, always the product of many heads and hands*

—J. W. Atkinson

Motivation to achieve is reflected in the effort individuals commit to strive to acquire increased understanding and skills they perceive as meaningful and worthwhile. While humans might be born with a motivation to increase their competencies, motivation to achieve is basically induced through interpersonal processes, either internalized relationships or current interaction patterns within a learning situation. Depending on whether students interact within a context of positive, negative, or no interdependence, different patterns of interaction result, causing different motivational systems, which in turn affect achievement differently, determining expectations for future achievement. The motivational system promoted in cooperative situations includes intrinsic motivation, high expectations for success, high incentive to achieve based on mutual benefit, high epistemic curiosity and continuing interest in achievement, high commitment to achieve, and high persistence. The motivational system promoted in competitive situations includes extrinsic motivation to win, low expectations for success by all but those with the highest ability, low incentive to learn based on differential benefit, low epistemic curiosity, a lack of continuing interest to achieve, a lack of commitment to achieving, and low task persistence by most individuals. The motivational system promoted in individualistic situations includes extrinsic motivation to meet preset criteria of excellence, low expectations for success by all but those with the highest ability, an incentive to achieve based on self-benefit, low epistemic curiosity and continuing interest to achieve, low commitment to achieving, and low task persistence by most individuals.

Motivation is most commonly viewed as a combination of the perceived likelihood of success and the perceived incentive for success. The greater the likelihood of success and the more important it is to succeed, the higher the motivation. Success that is intrinsically rewarding is usually seen as more desirable for learning than is having students believe that only extrinsic rewards are worthwhile. The likelihood of success is perceived as greater, and success is viewed as more important in cooperative than in competitive or individualistic learning situations (Johnson and Johnson 1989a). Striving for mutual benefit results in an emotional bonding, with collaborators liking each other, wanting to help each other succeed, and being committed to each other's well-being. These positive feelings toward the group and the other members could have a number of important influences on intrinsic motivation to achieve and actual productivity. In many cases, the relationships among group members can become more important than the actual rewards given for the work being done. Consequences provided by group members (for example, respect, liking, blame, rejection) can supplement or replace those produced by task performance (for example, salary or grades). Such consequences might be important in sustaining behavior during periods when no task-based reinforcement is received.

Interpersonal Trust

To disclose one's reasoning and information, one must trust the other individuals involved in the situation to listen with respect. Trust is a central dynamic of promotive interaction. It tends to be developed and maintained in cooperative situations and tends to be absent and destroyed in competitive and individualistic situations (Deutsch 1958, 1960, 1963; Johnson 1971, 1973, 1974; Johnson and Noonan 1972). Trust includes several elements:

1. Anticipation of beneficial or harmful consequences (risk);
2. Realization that others have the power to determine the consequences of one's actions;
3. Expectation that the harmful consequences are more serious than the beneficial consequences;
4. Confidence that the others will behave in ways that ensure beneficial consequences for oneself (Deutsch 1962).

Interpersonal trust is built by placing one's consequences in the control of others and having one's confidence in the others confirmed. It is destroyed by placing one's consequences in the hands of others and having one's confidence in the others disconfirmed through their behaving in ways that ensure harmful consequences for oneself. Thus, trust includes two sets of behaviors. *Trusting* behavior is the willingness to risk beneficial or harmful consequences by making oneself vulnerable to another person. *Trustworthy* behavior is the willingness to respond to another person's taking risks in a way that ensures that the other person will experience beneficial consequences. To establish trust, two or more people must be trustworthy and trusting. In cooperative situations, individuals tend to be both trusting and trustworthy; in competitive situations, they tend to be distrusting and untrustworthy, using information to promote their own success and the other's failure.

Anxiety and Performance

Cooperation typically produces less anxiety and stress and more effective coping strategies to deal with anxiety than does competition. Anxiety is one of the most pervasive barriers to productivity and positive interpersonal relationships, generally leading to an egocentric preoccupation with oneself, disruption of cognitive reasoning, and avoidance of the situation one fears. They in turn can mean skipping school or work, cutting classes or taking long breaks, or avoiding challenging situations at school or work. Furthermore, continued experience involving even moderate levels of anxiety over a number of years can produce psychological and physiological harm. Especially for individuals with a chronic high state of anxiety, cooperation promotes a better climate for learning and work.

Summary of Promotive Interaction

Positive interdependence results in promotive interaction, which in turn promotes efforts to achieve, positive interpersonal relationships, and psychological health. Promotive interaction can be defined as individuals encouraging and facilitating each other's efforts to achieve, complete tasks, and produce to reach the group's goals. It is characterized by individuals providing each other with efficient and effective assistance, exchanging needed resources, such as information and materials, and processing information more efficiently and effectively, providing each other with feedback to improve their subsequent performance of their assigned tasks and responsibilities, challenging each other's conclusions and reasoning to promote higher-quality decision making and greater insight into the problems being considered, advocating the exertion of effort to achieve mutual goals, influencing each other's efforts to achieve the group's goals, being motivated to strive for mutual benefit, acting in trusting and trustworthy ways, and exhibiting a moderate level of arousal characterized by low anxiety and stress. Oppositional interaction results in the opposite pattern of interaction. Promotive interaction results in a number of important outcomes that can be subsumed under three broad categories: effort exerted to achieve, quality of relationships among participants, and participants' psychological adjustment and social competence.

Learning Outcomes

Different learning outcomes result from the interaction between students promoted by the use of cooperative, competitive, and individualistic goal structure (Johnson and Johnson 1989a). The numerous outcomes of cooperative efforts can be subsumed under the three broad categories cited in the previous paragraph. Because research participants have varied as to economic class, age, sex, and cultural background, because a wide variety of research tasks and measures of the dependent variables have been used, and because the research has been conducted by many different researchers with markedly different orientations working in different settings and in different decades, the overall body of research on social interdependence has considerable generalizability.

Effort to Achieve

Achievement

Over 375 studies have been conducted over the past 90 years to answer the question of how successful competitive, individualistic, and cooperative efforts are in promoting productivity and achievement (see table 3) (Johnson and Johnson 1989a). When all of the studies were included in the analysis, the average student cooperating performed at about two-thirds a standard deviation above the average student learning within a competitive (effect size = 0.67) or individualistic (effect size = 0.64) situation. When only high-quality studies were included in the analysis, the effect sizes were 0.88 and 0.61, respectively. When only the college and adult studies were included in the analysis, the results were similar. Cooperative learning promoted higher achievement than did competitive or individualistic learning (effect sizes = 0.59 and 0.62, respectively). Interestingly, competition promoted higher achievement than did individualistic learning (effect size = 0.67). Cooperative learning, furthermore, resulted in more higher-level reasoning, more frequent generation of new ideas and solutions (i.e., process gain), and greater transfer of what is learned within one situation to another (i.e., group to individual transfer) than did competitive or individualistic learning.

Table 3
Social Interdependence: Weighted Findings

	Achievement		
	Mean	Standard Deviation	Number
Total Studies			
Cooperative versus competitive	0.67	0.93	129
Cooperative versus individualistic	0.64	0.79	184
Competitive versus individualistic	0.30	0.77	38
High-Quality Studies			
Cooperative versus competitive	0.88	1.13	51
Cooperative versus individualistic	0.61	0.63	104
Competitive versus individualistic	0.07	0.61	24
Mixed Operationalization			
Cooperative versus competitive	0.40	0.62	23
Cooperative versus individualistic	0.42	0.65	12
Pure Operationalization			
Cooperative versus competitive	0.71	1.01	96
Cooperative versus individualistic	0.65	0.81	164
College and Adult			
Cooperative versus competitive	0.59	0.86	52
Cooperative versus individualistic	0.62	0.90	96
Competitive versus individualistic	0.67	0.90	17

Some cooperative learning procedures contained a mixture of cooperative, competitive, and individualistic efforts; others were "pure." The original jigsaw procedure (Aronson et al. 1978), for example, is a combination of resource interdependence (cooperative) and individual reward structure (individualistic). Teams-games-tournaments (DeVries and Edwards 1974) and student-teams-achievement-divisions (Slavin 1980) are mixtures of cooperation and intergroup competition. Team-Assisted Instruction (Slavin, Leavey, and Madden 1982) is a mixture of individualistic and cooperative learning. When the results of "pure" and "mixed" cooperative learning were compared, "pure" produced higher achievement (cooperative versus competitive, pure = 0.71 and mixed = 0.40, cooperative versus individualistic, pure = 0.65 and mixed = 0.42).

The potential value of cooperative learning in large college classes is highlighted by a recent study designed to identify what specific factors contributed to students' learning in large classes (Wulff, Nyquist, and Abbott 1987). The survey of 800 college students found that the second most frequently cited factor contributing to their learning in large classes was "other students," leading the researchers to conclude that faculty might wish to use cooperative learning in large classes (p. 29). A comparison of the cost-effectiveness of four academic strategies concluded that working with classmates is the most cost-effective support system for increasing college students' achievement (Levin, Glass, and Meister 1984).

That working together to achieve a common goal results in higher achievement and greater productivity than does working alone is so well confirmed by so much research that it stands as one of the strongest principles of social and organizational psychology. Cooperative learning is indicated whenever the goals of learning are highly important, mastery and retention are important, the task is complex or conceptual, problem solving is desired, divergent thinking or creativity is desired, quality of performance is expected, and higher-level reasoning strategies and critical thinking are needed.

Why does cooperation result in higher achievement? The critical issue in understanding the relationship between cooperation and achievement is specifying the variables that mediate the relationship.

Simply placing students in groups and telling them to work together does not of itself promote higher achievement. It is only under certain conditions that the group's efforts can be expected to be more productive than individual efforts. Those conditions are clearly perceived positive interdependence, considerable promotive (face-to-face) interaction, felt personal responsibility (individual accountability) to achieve the group's goals, frequent use of relevant interpersonal and small-group skills, and periodic and regular group processing (Johnson and Johnson 1989a).

Critical Thinking Competencies

In many subject areas, teaching facts and theories is considered secondary to the development of students' critical thinking and use of higher-level reasoning. The aim of science education, for example, has been to develop individuals who can sort sense from nonsense or who have the abilities involved in critical thinking of grasping information, examining it, evaluating it for soundness, and applying it appropriately. The application, evaluation, and synthesis of knowledge and other higher-level reasoning skills, however, are often neglected in college classes. Cooperative learning promotes a greater use of higher-level reasoning strategies and critical thinking than competitive or individualistic learning strategies (Gabbert, Johnson, and Johnson 1986; Johnson and Johnson 1981; Johnson, Skon, and Johnson 1980; Skon, Johnson, and Johnson 1981). Cooperative learning experiences, for example, promote frequent insight into and use of higher-level cognitive and moral reasoning strategies than do competitive or individualistic learning experiences (effect sizes = 0.93 and 0.97, respectively).

In addition to the research directly relating cooperative learning with critical thinking, certain lines of research link critical thinking and cooperative learning. At least three elements of teaching make a difference in college students' gains in thinking skills: (1) discussion among students, (2) explicit emphasis on problem-solving procedures and methods using varied examples, and (3) verbalization of methods and strategies to encourage development of metacognition (McKeachie 1988).

> Student participation, teacher encouragement, and student-to-student interaction positively relate to improved critical thinking. These three activities confirm other research and theory stressing the importance of active practice, motivation, and feedback in thinking skills as well as other skills. This confirms that discussions, especially in small classes, are superior to lecture in improving thinking and problem solving (p. 1).

The explicit teaching of higher-level reasoning and critical thinking does not depend on what is taught, but rather on *how* it is taught (Ruggiero 1988). "The only significant change that is required is a change in teaching methodology" (p. 12). Cooperative learning is such a change.

Research indicates that cooperative learning is an important procedure for involving students in meaningful activities in the classroom and engaging in situated cognition (Brown, Collins, and Duguid 1989; Lave 1988; Schoenfeld 1985, 1989). Higher-level writing assignments can also best be done by cooperative peer response groups (DiPardo and Freedman 1988).

Attitudes Toward Subject Area

Cooperative learning experiences, compared with competitive and individualistic ones, promote more positive attitudes toward the subject area, more positive attitudes toward the instructional experience, and more continuing motivation to learn more about the subject area being studied (Johnson and Johnson 1989a). A study comparing group discussion and lecturing found that students in discussion sections had significantly more favorable attitudes toward psychology than the other groups; a follow-up of the students three years later revealed that seven students each from the tutorial and discussion groups majored in psychology, whereas none of those in the recitation group did so (Guetzkow, Kelly, and McKeachie 1954; McKeachie 1951). Students who had opportunities in class to interact with classmates and the instructor were more satisfied with their learning experience than students who were taught exclusively by lecture (Bligh 1972). Students who participated in discussion groups in class were more likely to develop positive attitudes toward the course's subject matter (Kulik and Kulik 1979). And one of the major conclusions of the Harvard Assessment Seminars was that the use of cooperative learning groups resulted in a large increase in satisfaction with the class (Light 1990). These findings have important implications for influencing female and minority students to enter careers oriented toward science and mathematics.

Interpersonal Relationships

Interpersonal Attraction and Cohesion

Cooperative learning experiences, compared with competitive and individualistic ones and "tradition instruction," promote considerably more liking among students (effect sizes = 0.67 and 0.60, respectively) (Johnson and Johnson 1989a; Johnson, Johnson, and Maruyama 1983), regardless of individual differences in ability, sex, handicapping conditions, ethnic membership, social class, or task orientation (see table 4). Students who studied cooperatively, compared with those who studied competitively or individualistically, developed considerably more commitment and caring for each other, no matter what their initial impressions of and attitudes toward each other. When only the high-quality studies were included in the analysis, the effect sizes were 0.82 (cooperative versus competitive) and 0.62 (cooperative versus individualistic), respectively. The effect sizes were higher for the studies using pure operationalizations of cooperative learning than for studies using mixed operationalizations (cooperative versus competitive, pure = 0.79 and mixed = 0.46; cooperative versus individualistic, pure = 0.66 and mixed = 0.36). Students learning cooperatively also liked the instructor better and perceived the instructor as being more supportive and accepting academically and personally. For the college and adult studies, cooperative experiences resulted in greater interpersonal attraction than did competitive or individualistic experiences (effect sizes = 0.83 and 0.40, respectively). Competition promoted greater interpersonal attraction than did individualistic efforts (effect size = 0.84).

To be productive, a class of students must cohere and share a positive emotional climate. As relationships within the class or college become more positive, absenteeism decreases and students' commitment to learning, feeling of personal responsibility to complete the assigned work, willingness to take on difficult tasks, motivation and persistence in working on tasks, satisfaction and morale, willingness to endure pain and frustration to succeed, willingness to defend the college against external criticism or attack, willingness to listen to and be influenced by peers, commitment to peers' success and growth, and pro-

Table 4
Social Interdependence: Weighted Findings

	Interpersonal Attraction		
	Mean	Standard Deviation	Number
Total Studies			
Cooperative versus competitive	0.67	0.49	93
Cooperative versus individualistic	0.60	0.58	60
Competitive versus individualistic	0.08	0.70	15
High-Quality Studies			
Cooperative versus competitive	0.82	0.40	37
Cooperative versus individualistic	0.62	0.53	44
Competitive versus individualistic	0.27	0.60	11
Mixed Operationalization			
Cooperative versus competitive	0.46	0.29	37
Cooperative versus individualistic	0.36	0.45	10
Pure Operationalization			
Cooperative versus competitive	0.79	0.56	54
Cooperative versus individualistic	0.66	0.60	49
College and Adult			
Cooperative versus competitive	0.83	0.47	34
Cooperative versus individualistic	0.40	0.73	15
Competitive versus individualistic	0.84	0.21	2

ductivity and achievement can be expected to increase (Johnson and F. Johnson 1991; Johnson and Johnson 1989a; Watson and Johnson 1972).

In addition, when a class includes students who are different with regard to ethnicity, social class, language, and ability, cooperative learning experiences are a necessity for building positive peer relationships—especially for contemporary colleges, which are now witnessing an increasing number of international students on campus (Scully 1981) and an increasing number of African-American students attending predominantly white colleges (National Center for Educational Statistics 1984). Studies on desegregation indicate that cooperation promoted more positive cross-ethnic relationships than competitive (effect size = 0.54) or individualistic (effect size = 0.44) learning experiences (Johnson and Johnson 1989a). Cross-handicapped relationships were also more positive in cooperative than in competitive (effect size = 0.70) or individualistic (effect size = 0.64) learning experiences.

Social Support

Table 5 indicates that cooperation resulted in greater social support than did competitive or individualistic efforts (effect sizes = 0.62 and 0.70, respectively). For the high-quality studies, the results were comparable (effect sizes = 0.83 and 0.62, respectively). The pure operationalizations of cooperation promoted greater social support (compared with competition) than did the mixed operationalizations (effect sizes = 0.73 and 0.45, respectively). When cooperative and individualistic learning experiences were compared, the results were even more extreme (effect sizes = 0.77 and 0.02, respectively). When only the college and adult samples were included, the effect sizes were 0.70 and 0.36. Competitive experiences promoted less social support than did individualistic experiences (effect size = –0.45).

Social support tends to be related to several factors:

1. Achievement, successful problem solving, persistence on challenging tasks under frustrating conditions, lack of cognitive interference during problem solving, lack of absenteeism,

Table 5
Social Interdependence: Weighted Findings

	Social Support Mean	Standard Deviation	Number
Total Studies			
Cooperative versus competitive	0.62	0.44	84
Cooperative versus individualistic	0.70	0.45	72
Competitive versus individualistic	–0.13	0.36	19
High-Quality Studies			
Cooperative versus competitive	0.83	0.46	41
Cooperative versus individualistic	0.72	0.47	62
Competitive versus individualistic	–0.13	0.36	19
Mixed Operationalization			
Cooperative versus competitive	0.45	0.23	16
Cooperative versus individualistic	0.02	0.35	6
Pure Operationalization			
Cooperative versus competitive	0.73	0.46	58
Cooperative versus individualistic	0.77	0.40	65
College and Adult			
Cooperative versus competitive	0.70	0.58	29
Cooperative versus individualistic	0.36	0.37	16
Competitive versus individualistic	–0.45	0.25	5

academic and career aspirations, more appropriate seeking of assistance, retention, job satisfaction, high morale, and greater compliance with regimens and behavioral patterns that increase health and productivity;

2. A longer life, recovering from illness and injury faster and more completely, and experiencing less severe illnesses;
3. Psychological health and adjustment, lack of neuroticism and psychopathology, reduction of psychological distress, the ability to cope effectively with stressful situations, self-reliance and autonomy, a coherent and integrated self-identity, greater psychological safety, higher self-esteem, increased general happiness, and increased interpersonal skills;
4. Effective management of stress by providing the caring, information, resources, and feedback individuals need to cope with stress, reducing the number and severity of stressful events in an individual's life, reducing anxiety, and helping to appraise the nature of the stress and one's ability to deal with it constructively;
5. The emotional support and encouragement individuals need to cope with the risk that is inherently involved in challenging one's competence in striving to grow and develop (Johnson and Johnson 1989a).

The importance of social support has been ignored in education over the past 30 years. The pressure to achieve should always be matched with an equal level of social support; that is, challenge and security must be kept in balance (Pelz and Andrews 1976). Whenever increased demands and pressure to be productive are placed on students (and faculty), social support should be increased correspondingly.

Student Retention

According to the Study Group on the Conditions of Excellence in Higher Education:

> Traditional classroom teaching practices in higher education favor the assertive student. But our analysis indicates that instructors should give greater attention to the passive or reticent student. . . . Passivity is an important warning sign that may reflect a lack of involvement that impedes the learning process and leads to unnecessary attrition (National Institute of Education 1984, p. 23).

Appropriately one-half of all students who leave college do so during their freshman year (Terezini 1986), and many of the departures take place during the first semester (Blanc, Debuhr, and Martin 1983). The major reasons for dropping out of college could be failure to establish a social network of friends and classmates and to become academically involved in classes.

The greater the degree of students' involvement in their college learning experience, the more likely they are to persist to graduation (Tinto 1975, 1987). The processes of social involvement, integration, and bonding with classmates are strongly related to higher rates of retention. On the basis of research conducted over 10 years, students' involvement academically and socially in college is the cornerstone of persistence and achievement (Astin 1985), and active involvement in learning is especially critical for "withdrawal-prone" students, such as disadvantaged minorities, who have been found to be particularly passive in academic settings (Astin et al. 1972).

Cooperative learning experiences tend to lower attrition rates in college. In one study, students working on open-ended problems in small groups of four to seven were more likely to display lower rates of attrition and higher rates of academic achievement than those not involved in group learning (Wales and Stager 1978). The five-year retention rate for African-American students majoring in math or science at Berkeley who were involved in cooperative learning, for example, was 65 percent, compared to 41 percent for African-American students not involved (Treisman 1985). The percentage of African-American students involved in cooperative learning who graduated in mathematics-based majors was 44 percent, compared to only 10 percent for a control group of African-American students not participating in cooperative learning groups.

College students report greater satisfaction with courses that allow them to engage in group discussion (Bligh 1972; Kulik and Kulik 1979), and students are more likely to stay in college if they are satisfied with the learning experience (Noel 1985). Cooperative learning allows for significant amounts of meaningful discussion, enhancing students' satisfaction with the learning experience and promoting retention.

Faculty Relationships with Students

Many college faculty report that they get to know their students better when they use cooperative learning groups. The process of observing students work in small groups and then intervening seems to create more personal and informal interactions between the instructor and the students than do lectures and discussions involving the whole class. Interacting with students in small groups, for example, gives instructors a chance to learn and address students by name. "Addressing students by name" correlates significantly with students' overall satisfaction with the course and the instructor (Murray 1985). Such informal interactions also positively affect student retention (Astin 1977), for when faculty get to know students better in class, they could be more likely to interact with students informally outside the classroom. And the quantity and quality of out-of-class contact with faculty are strongly associated with students' retention (Pascarella 1980).

The Importance of Peer Relationships

Peer relationships contribute to social and cognitive development and to socialization in numerous ways:

1. *In their interaction with peers, individuals directly learn attitudes, values, skills, and information unobtainable from adults.* In their interaction with each other, individuals imitate each other's behavior and identify with friends possessing admired competencies. Through providing models, reinforcement, and direct learning, peers shape a wide variety of social behaviors, attitudes, and perspectives.

2. *Interaction with peers provides support, opportunities, and models for prosocial behavior.* In one's interactions with peers, one helps, comforts, shares with, takes care of, assists, and gives to others. Without peers with whom to engage in such behaviors, many forms of prosocial values and commitments could not be developed. Conversely, whether or not individuals engage in problem or transitional behavior, such as the use of illegal drugs and delinquency, is related to the perceptions of their friends' attitudes toward such behaviors. Being rejected by one's peers tends to result in antisocial behavioral patters characterized by aggressiveness, disruptiveness, and other negatively perceived behaviors.

3. *Peers provide models of, expectations of, directions for, and reinforcements of learning to control impulses.* Individuals frequently lack the perspective of time needed to tolerate delays in gratification. As they develop and are socialized, the focus on their own immediate impulses and needs is replaced with the ability to take longer perspectives of time. Peer interaction involving aggressive impulses like, for example, rough-and-tumble play promotes the acquisition of a repertoire of effective aggressive behaviors and helps establish the necessary regulatory mechanisms for modulating aggressive actions.

4. *Students learn to view situations and problems from perspectives other than their own.* Taking such perspectives is one of the most critical competencies for cognitive and social development. All psychological development can be described as a progressive loss of egocentrism and an increase in ability to take wider and more complex perspectives. It is primarily in interaction with peers that egocentrism is lost and the ability to take a wider perspective is gained.

5. *Relationships with peers are powerful influences on the development of the values and the social sensitivity required for autonomy.* Autonomy is the ability to understand what others expect in any given situation and to be free to choose whether to meet their expectations. Autonomous people are independent of both extreme inner- or outer-directedness. When making decisions about appropriate social behavior, autonomous people tend to consider both their internal values and the situation and then respond in flexible and appropriate ways. Autonomy is the result of the internalization of values (including appropriate self-

approval) derived from caring and supportive relationships, and the acquisition of social skills and sensitivity. Individuals with a history of isolation from or rejection by peers often are inappropriately other-directed. They conform to group pressures even when they believe the recommended actions are wrong or inappropriate.

6. *Close and intimate relationships with peers provide others with whom young people can share their thoughts and feelings, aspirations and hopes, dreams and fantasies, joys and pains.* Young people need constructive peer relationships to avoid the pain of loneliness.

7. *Peer relationships help develop a frame of reference for perceiving oneself.* Throughout infancy, childhood, adolescence, and early adulthood, a person moves though several successive and overlapping identities. The physical changes involved in growth, increasing number of experiences with other people, increasing responsibilities, and general cognitive and social development all cause changes in self-definition. The final result should be a coherent and integrated identity. In peer relationships, children and adolescents become aware of the similarities and differences between themselves and others. They experiment with a variety of social roles that help them integrate their own sense of self. In peer relationships, values and attitudes are clarified and integrated into an individual's self-definition, gender typing and its impact on one's identity, for example.

8. *Coalitions formed during childhood and adolescence provide help and assistance throughout adulthood.*

9. *Friendships during childhood and adolescence seem to decrease the risk of mental disorder.* The ability to maintain independent, cooperative relationships is a prime manifestation of psychological health. Poor peer relationships in elementary school predict psychological disturbance and delinquency in high school, and poor peer relationships in high school predict adult pathology.

10. *In both educational and work settings, peers have a strong influence on productivity.* Greater achievement is typical in collaborative situations where peers work together than in situations where individuals work alone.

11. *Students' educational aspirations could be more influenced by peers than by any other social influence.* Similarly, ambition in career settings is greatly influenced by peers. In instructional settings, peer relationships can be structured to create meaningful interdependence through learning cooperatively with peers. In cooperative learning situations, students experience feelings of belonging, acceptance, support, and caring, and the social skills and social roles required for maintaining interdependent relationships can be taught and practiced (Johnson 19890; Johnson and Johnson 1989a).

Through repeated cooperative experiences, students can develop the social sensitivity to learn what is expected from others and the active skills and autonomy to meet such expectations if they so desire. Through holding each other accountable for appropriate social behavior, students can greatly influence the values they internalize and the self-control they develop. Through belonging to a series of interdependent relationships, students learn and internalize values. Through prolonged cooperative interaction with other people, healthy social development and general trust rather than distrust of other people, the ability to view situations and problems from a variety of perspectives, a meaningful sense of direction and purpose in life, an awareness of mutual interdependence with others, and an integrated coherent sense of personal identity take place (Johnson 1979; Johnson and Matross 1977).

For peer relationships to be constructive influences, they must promote feelings of belonging, acceptance, support, and caring rather than feelings of hostility and rejection (Johnson 1980). Being accepted by peers is related to willingness to engage in social interaction, using abilities to achieve goals, and providing positive social rewards for peers. Isolation from peers is associated with high anxiety, low self-esteem, poor interpersonal skills, emotional handicaps, and psychological pathology. Rejection by peers is related to disruptive classroom behavior, hostile behavior and negative affect, and negative attitudes toward other students and school. To promote constructive influences from peers, teachers must therefore first ensure that students interact with each other and then that the interaction takes place within a cooperative context.

Psychological Health

Psychological Adjustment

When students leave college, they need the psychological health and stability required to build and maintain relationships in a career, family, and community, to establish a basic and meaningful interdependence with other people, and to participate effectively in society. Studies on the relationship between cooperation and psychological health indicate that cooperativeness is positively related to a number of indices of psychological health: emotional maturity, well-adjusted social relationships, strong personal identity, and basic trust in optimism about people (Johnson and Johnson 1989a). Competitiveness seems also to be related to a number of indices of psychological health, while individualistic attitudes tend to be related to a number of indices of psychological pathology: emotional immaturity, social maladjustment, delinquency, self-alienation, and self-rejection. Colleges and college classes should be organized cooperatively to reinforce those traits and tendencies that promote students' psychological well-being.

Accuracy of Perspective

Taking a social perspective is the ability to understand how a situation appears to another person and how that person is reacting cognitively and emotionally to the situation. The opposite of taking a perspective is egocentrism, that is, being embedded in one's own viewpoint to the extent that one is unaware of other points of view and of the limitation of one's perspective. Cooperative learning tends to promote greater cognitive and affective perspective taking than do competitive or individualistic learning experiences (Johnson and Johnson 1989a). In one study, students participating in class discussions (as opposed to listening to lectures) showed greater insight (as rated by clinical psychologists) into problems of the young women depicted in the film, *The Feeling of Rejection* (Bovard 1951a, 1951b; McKeachie 1954).

Self-Esteem

Table 6 indicates that cooperation tended to promote higher levels of self-esteem than did competitive and individualistic efforts (effect sizes = 0.58 and 0.44, respectively). When only the college and adult samples were included in the analyses, the results were similar for the comparison of cooperation and competition (effect size = 0.67) but lower for the comparison of cooperative and individualistic efforts (effect size = 0.19). Only one study compared the effects of competitive and individualistic efforts on self-esteem at the college level. High self-esteem seems desirable, because individuals with low self-esteem tend to:

1. Have low productivity because they set low goals for themselves, lack confidence in their ability, and assume that they will fail no matter how hard they try;
2. Be critical of others as well as themselves by looking for flaws in others and trying to tear them down;
3. Withdraw socially because they feel awkward, self-conscious, and vulnerable to rejection;
4. Be conforming, agreeable, highly persuadable, and highly influenced by criticism;
5. Develop more psychological problems, such as anxiety, nervousness, insomnia, depression, and psychosomatic symptoms (Johnson and Johnson 1989a).

In competitive situations, self-esteem tends to be based on the contingent view of one's competence that "If I win, then I am worthwhile as a person, but if I lose, then I am not." Winners attribute their success to superior ability and attribute the failure of others to lack of ability, both of which contribute to self-aggrandizement. Losers, who are the vast majority, defensively tend to be self-disparaging and apprehensive about evaluation, and tend to withdraw psychologically and physically. In individualistic situations, students are isolated from one another, receive little direct comparison with or feedback from peers, and perceive evaluations as inaccurate and unrealistic. The result is a defensive avoidance, and apprehension of evaluation, and a distrust of peers. In cooperative situations, however, individuals tend to interact, promote each other' success, form multidimensional and realistic impressions of each other's competencies, and provide accurate feedback. Such interaction tends to promote a basic self-acceptance of oneself as a competent person.

Table 6
Social Interdependence: Weighted Findings

	Self-Esteem		
	Mean	Standard Deviation	Number
Total Studies			
Cooperative versus competitive	0.58	0.56	56
Cooperative versus individualistic	0.44	0.40	38
Competitive versus individualistic	−0.23	0.42	19
High-Quality Studies			
Cooperative versus competitive	0.67	0.31	24
Cooperative versus individualistic	0.45	0.44	29
Competitive versus individualistic	−0.25	0.46	13
Mixed Operationalization			
Cooperative versus competitive	0.33	0.39	17
Cooperative versus individualistic	0.22	0.38	9
Pure Operationalization			
Cooperative versus competitive	0.74	0.59	36
Cooperative versus individualistic	0.51	0.40	27
College and Adult			
Cooperative versus competitive	0.67	0.93	18
Cooperative versus individualistic	0.19	0.47	5
Competitive versus individualistic	−0.46	0.00	1

Relationships Among Outcomes

Bi-directional relationships exist among achievement, quality of interpersonal relationships, and psychological health (Johnson and Johnson 1989a), and each influences the others. The more students work cooperatively, the more they care about each other. Caring and committed friendships come from a sense of mutual accomplishment, from mutual pride in joint work, and from the bonding that results from joint efforts. And the more students care about each other, the harder they will work to achieve mutual goals for learning. Long-term and persistent efforts to achieve tend to come not from the head but from the heart (Johnson and Johnson 1989c). Individuals seek out opportunities to work with those they care about. As caring increases, so do feelings of personal responsibility to do one's share of the work, willingness to take on difficult tasks, motivation and persistence in working toward the goal and willingness to endure pain and frustration on behalf of the group. All contribute to a group's productivity.

In addition, the joint success experienced in working together to get the job done enhances social competencies, self-esteem, and general psychological health. The healthier psychologically individuals are, the better able they are to work with others to achieve mutual goals. Joint efforts require coordination, effective communication, leadership, and management of conflicts. States of depression, anxiety, guilt, shame, and anger decrease the energy available to contribute to a cooperative effort.

Finally, the more positive interpersonal relationships are, the greater the psychological health of the individuals involved. Through the internalization of positive relationships, direct social support, shared intimacy, and expressions of caring, psychological health and the ability to cope with stress are built. The absence of caring and committed relationships and the presence of destructive relationships tend to increase psychological pathology. States of depression, anxiety, guilt, shame, and anger decrease individuals' ability to build and maintain caring and committed relationships. The healthier psychologically individuals are, the more meaningful and caring the relationships they can build and maintain.

Reducing the Discrepancy

With the amount of evidence available, it is surprising that the practice in college classrooms is so oriented toward competitive and individualistic learning and that colleges are so dominated by competitive and individualistic organizational structures. It is time for the discrepancy to be reduced between what research indicates is effective in teaching and what college faculty actually do. To do so, faculty must understand the role of the instructor in implementing cooperative learning. The next three sections focus on the instructor's role in using formal cooperative learning groups, informal cooperative learning groups, and cooperative base groups.

Note

1. This section summarizes the basic results from the meta-analyses on all the studies conducted up to 1989. In addition, separate meta-analyses have been conducted on the results of the 137 experimental studies that compare cooperative, competitive, and individualistic efforts at the college and adult levels. In most cases, references to individual studies are not included in this section. Rather, the reader is referred to the reviews that contain the references to specific studies that corroborate the point being made.

PART IV

Understanding and Implementing Effective Teaching and Learning

Introduction

There is no one best way to teach, although some ways may be better than others. Teachers develop enduring sets of assumptions, attitudes, values and behavioral patterns that constitute their own teaching styles. These styles are often based on implicit, personal theories of teaching rather than formal educational theories. As Rando and Menges (1991) explain, teachers tend to be unaware of theories that they tacitly create to give some structure and stability to their experiences—theories that are often shaped by the norms of academic culture regarding what is appropriate. Implicit personal theories can be made explicit through *reflection* upon experience. Personal theories can then be *analyzed* and combined with formal educational theories to *develop* and *improve* effective individual teaching styles, as well as specific teaching strategies, for classroom *implementation*. The selected readings in Part IV are intended to facilitate these processes of reflection, analysis, development, implementation and improvement of teaching and learning in higher education. The readings have been divided into three sections: general models and teaching styles; specific strategies and classroom implementation; and instructional improvement.

A. General Models and Teaching Styles

The readings in this section introduce a variety of general models of teaching. These models illustrate broad themes and perspectives on teaching as contexts within which instructors can reflect upon, analyze, and possibly modify the assumptions, attitudes, values and behaviors that constitute their own teaching styles. The first reading, by Dressel and Marcus, presents a general model that compares four distinct, alternative teaching styles or orientations across thirteen specific dimensions. Each style represents a composite of typical views and practices that are readily recognizable characteristics of some teachers on every campus. While the four styles in their model are prototypical, the authors point out that real teaching styles are usually eclectic combinations of these. The expressed purpose of their model is to provide an opportunity for teachers to compare their own views and practices, along the thirteen dimensions, with those of the four prototypes to arrive at a profile of their own eclectic style.

The second reading, by Lowman, presents an empirically-based, two-dimensional model of effective college teaching. Lowman combines research on group leadership with research on student ratings of teaching behavior to identify two independent dimensions of teaching effectiveness: intellectual excitement (clear and enthusiastic presentation) and interpersonal rapport (positive student-teacher interaction). Combining high, moderate, and low performance on each of these two dimensions yields nine distinct teaching styles. Indicators of high, moderate and low levels of performance on each dimension are articulated in some detail. This articulation permits teachers to identify styles most like their own, to reflect upon their associated teaching attitudes and behaviors, and to analyze, reinforce, or modify them as desired.

Whereas the Dressel and Marcus model and the Lowman model tend to emphasize the dominant styles and discourse of traditional pedagogy, the third and fourth selections, by Maher and Tetreault and Brookfield, respectively, present postmodernist models of feminist pedagogy and critically reflective pedagogy. Maher and Tetreault report results from their ethnographic study of eighteen feminist classrooms in six different colleges. In this article, they examine the practices of two feminist teachers and illustrate how each teacher works through the issues of defining what actually constitutes knowledge, eliciting student voice and identity, negotiating authority between teacher and students, and addressing the impact on learning of the classroom and societal position of individual students. Both teachers clearly value and encourage connected knowing as a basis for collaborative efforts to meaningfully construct knowledge. Excerpts from student journals and classroom dialogues richly illustrate feminist epistemological and interpersonal teaching practices.

In the last reading in this section, Brookfield explains his model of the "critically reflective teacher." This model is a productive blend of some features of Schon's (1983) theory of "the reflective practitioner," Argyris, Putman and Smith's (1985) "double-loop learning," Mezirow's (1991) "transformative learning" and the perspectives and transformative power associated with "critical pedagogy" (Leistyna, Woodrum, and Sherblom 1996). According to Brookfield, being an effective and critically reflective teacher requires the kind of reflection that makes possible an enhanced awareness of one's embedded paradigmatic, prescriptive and causal assumptions. For example, a paradigmatic assumption held by the author is that "adults are self-directed learners." It follows then, that a related prescriptive assumption would be that since adults are self-regulated learners, an effective teacher should provide activities that permit students to assume control over the planning, implementation and assessment of their own learning. Brookfield offers a variety of examples of such assumptions, illustrating how they could be quite effective in some situations, but clearly invalid in others. Developing the habit of reflection is, therefore, necessary to unearth one's implicit assumptions and challenge their appropriateness or validity in various situations. However, reflection in and of itself is not enough. One must also reflect using the lenses of critical theory. Since the forces of power and oppression and the inequities associated with race, class and gender in society are persistent intruders in the college classroom, it is important for teachers to "understand how considerations of power undergird, frame, and distort educational processes and interactions."

B. Specific Strategies and Classroom Implementation

The readings in this section shift the perspective on the processes of reflection, analysis and development from the global nature of teaching style to the specific nature of particular teaching strategies for classroom implementation. The specific strategies presented in this section's readings are based on formal educational theory and research in the areas of motivation, cognition, and group interaction. The first reading, by Chickering and Gamson, presents the well-known seven principles for good practice in undergraduate education. These principles, based on decades of research on effective teaching and learning, were developed by a task force of scholars who had contributed much of the related research. Each principle is carefully articulated and accompanied by a set of specific strategies for implementation. The principles and their associated specific strategies have been widely applied. Within eighteen months of initial publication, 150,000 reprints of the article were ordered. A self-assessment inventory measuring the use of specific strategies based on each principle was also published, and within a similar period of time, over 500,000 copies were ordered (Gamson, 1991).

Each of the remaining readings in this section presents a set of specific teaching strategies that addresses most, if not all, of the seven principles. Each set of strategies addresses one or more of the following instructional challenges: (1) increasing students' desire to learn (motivational strategies); (2) enhancing students' "how to learn" skills (cognitive strategies); (3) creating a classroom climate that facilitates positive group interaction (social strategies); and (4) increasing the efficiency of student learning (technological strategies). Thus, the second reading, by Forsyth and McMillan, presents a number of practical suggestions for enhancing students' desire to learn. These motivational strategies are based on the authors' thoughtful review and analysis of the need and expectancy-value theories of motivation. They conclude that effective strategies focus on promoting intrinsic motivation, providing meaningful feedback, helping students discover realistic and personally valuable learning outcomes or goals, and promoting high student expectations for successful achievement.

In addition to possessing a strong desire to learn, students need to develop learning skills to effectively process information for meaningful learning. In an article reprinted in our first edition (but not reprinted here), Svinicki (1991) presents six principles from recent research in cognitive psychology that have clear implications for effective teaching. Each principle refers to a particular aspect or phase of an effective information processing sequence. For each principle, Svinicki presents specific strategies teachers can use to help students become more efficient and effective processors of information at a particular stage or phase in the sequence. The last of the six principles emphasizes the importance of teaching students to develop and use effective learning strategies independent of the teacher's prompting. Sivinicki concludes that, in particular, students need to be made aware of what strategies are available, how to use them, when to use them, how to monitor their effectiveness, and how to adapt them to different learning situations.

A detailed account of the nature and use of these important strategies is presented in the reading by McKeachie, et al., in Part II, Section A of this second edition. The authors present numerous examples of cognitive, metacognitive, and resource-management strategies in their section on "Learning Strategies." They explain how learners use rehearsal strategies to retain new information in short-term memory, organizational strategies to select and construct connections among various aspects of the new information to be learned, and elaboration strategies to integrate and connect the new information with prior knowledge. The authors also explain how learners can effectively use metacognitive strategies to plan, monitor, and regulate their learning and use of learning strategies; and the resource-management strategies to increase their effectiveness regarding the use of time and effort, their study environment, peer interactions and other help-seeking behaviors.

Sustaining student motivation and the persistent use of effective learning strategies requires the creation of a positive classroom environment. In the third reading, by Billson and Tiberius, the authors describe such an environment in terms of an alliance between teachers and students. Based on the authors' analysis of recent research on the social context of teaching and learning, they derive five basic principles of group interaction that guide the formation of a constructive teacher-student alliance: mutual respect; shared responsibility and mutual commitment to goals; effective communication and feedback; cooperation; and security and trust. Numerous strategies are presented to assist teachers in developing a productive classroom alliance that is consistent with all five principles of effective group interaction.

The fourth reading, by Svinicki and Dixon, addresses the motivation, cognition, and interaction perspectives by presenting a range of classroom activities corresponding to each stage of Kolb's experiential learning model (see the Kolb reading in Part II of this book). The authors provide detailed strategies for every stage of the learning cycle, including content-specific illustrations for six different disciplines. They also arrange these strategies along a continuum ranging from active to passive activities that would be useful at each stage of the cycle.

The fifth reading, by Smith and MacGregor, presents various instructional formats that encourage collaborative learning among students and also address the motivational, cognitive, and social foundations for learning. The authors assert that collaborative learning structures are based on the assumption that learning, which takes place among students with diverse backgrounds and experiences, is social, active, constructive, and richly contextual. Based on their review of the literature, they clarify the educational goals and rationale for collaborative learning and explain the challenges that instructors typically face due to the culturally-embedded predilection for the lecture method in the academy. The authors present the prominent features of six broad approaches to collaborative learning—cooperative learning, problem-centered instruction, writing groups, peer teaching, discussion groups, and learning communities—and provide specific examples of each approach. Of these approaches, cooperative learning is the most highly structured and has received the most attention and support from extensive research on its effectiveness (see the selection by Johnson, Johnson, and Smith in Part III, Section D, of this book).

Increasingly, college courses across a variety of subject areas are examining the effects on human experience of such factors as race, class, and gender. While these important changes in course content have been widely addressed in the literature, the problematic aspects of the "process" of addressing issues related to race, class and gender has received less attention. If the emotional responses that emerge from learning activities that focus on such issues are not appropriately addressed, students may resist cognitive engagement in the study of such content. In the reading by Tatum, these issues are examined within the context of the author's extensive experiences in teaching a course on the Psychology of Racism, which (at the time she wrote her article) she had taught over 18 times at several different universities. Using written examples of students' thoughts, feelings and other reactions to class-related readings and discussions—drawn from students' journals and essays—Tatum identifies the primary sources of students' resistance to talking and learning about racism and elaborates on several effective strategies for facilitating positive student experiences with interracial dialogue. She not only establishes a set of clear guidelines that create a safe and conducive environment for classroom discussion but also creates assignments that provide opportunities for students to acquire self-generated knowledge about racism through performing interviews and conducting observations of settings and interactions in those settings. To assist students in understanding their own developmental processes, she establishes racial identity development theory as an important substantive component of the course (see the Hardiman and Jackson reading in Part II, Section B, of this book for more research on Black and White students' development of racial identity).

In a sense, the final reading, by Chickering and Ehrmann, brings this section full circle to a reconsideration of the seven principles of good practice in teaching and learning. The authors examine new ways to teach more effectively and efficiently by explaining "cost-effective and appropriate ways to use computers, video, and telecommunications technologies to advance the Seven Principles." While many instructional strategies may be enhanced by a variety of different technologies, just as one specific technological approach may enhance a variety of different instructional practices, the authors point out that "for any given instructional strategy, some technologies are better than others." The authors explain how each of the seven principles can be advanced through technological applications, providing illustrations of how specific technologies could be integrated with specific instructional strategies to advance each principle of good practice. They also provide guidelines and caveats regarding the important roles that students, faculty, and developers of institutional policy play in the responsible use of technology in efforts to promote more effective and efficient teaching and learning.

C. Instructional Improvement

The 1980s produced a number of national reports pointing a critical finger at the quality of college teaching (Association of American Colleges, 1985; Bowen and Schuster, 1986; Boyer, 1987; National Institute of Education, 1984). These reports made it perfectly clear that the status quo in teaching was unacceptable. This clarion call for instructional improvement, to which many responded in the 1980s, still resounds today. In order to respond meaningfully to this call, we need to confront some important challenges in improving teaching. The readings selected for Section C of Part IV address several prominent challenges, including motivating instructors to improve their teaching, clearly articulating the steps in improving teaching, and identifying, understanding and applying specific strategies that would help.

The first reading in this section, by Paulsen and Feldman, reviews the literature on models of instructional change and presents a general model of instructional improvement (consisting of the three stages of unfreezing, changing and refreezing) that is grounded in the early work on change in human systems pioneered by Lewin (1952) and elaborated by Schein (1992). This model explicitly acknowledges that the process of instructional improvement is embedded in—and influenced by—the campus teaching culture. The teaching culture provides informative feedback about an instructor's teaching effectiveness from a variety of sources including (but not necessarily limited to) the self, students, colleagues, consultants, and department chairs. Since most faculty are intrinsically motivated, disconfirming cues from these various sources of informative feedback interact with an instructor's needs for perceived competence and self-determination as a teacher, thereby stimulating the instructor's desire to explore changes in attitudes and behaviors about teaching and learning. Such changes will be sustained if one or more sources of informative feedback is sufficient to reconfirm the instructor's perceived competence and self-determination as an effective teacher. The authors use this model as an "underlying analytic framework" to summarize the literature on effective strategies for improving instruction. Each strategy is classified in terms of the source of informative feedback that is primarily responsible for initiating, directing and sustaining a particular strategy of instructional improvement.

In the second reading, Weimer and Lenze present a comprehensive review of the available empirical research on the effectiveness of strategies for improving teaching. They report on the use of workshops, consultation, instructional grants, instructional reading material, and colleagues helping colleagues. For each of these strategies, the authors provide a history, an assessment of its prevalence, a description of its use, and an assessment of its effectiveness. They conclude that most assessments of effectiveness are either based on the judgments of instructional developers who are experienced in the use of these strategies, or drawn from the opinions of teachers who have applied these strategies to improve their teaching. Such judgments are useful, but the authors acknowledge the great need for assessments of effectiveness based on measurable changes in teacher behaviors and in student achievement.

In the third reading, Cross and Steadman propose that improving teaching and learning (as well as active engagement in and implementation of the scholarship of teaching) can be achieved through classroom research. They define such research as "ongoing and cumulative intellectual inquiry by classroom teachers into the nature of teaching and learning in their own classrooms." This approach is based on the notion that instructors should collect data from students about teacher behavior and student learning at the very moment they occur in the classroom. By collecting such information regularly, teachers come to see more clearly the relationship between their teaching and their students' learning. Cross and Steadman explain that the most important characteristics of classroom research are that it is learner-centered, teacher-directed, collaborative, context-specific, scholarly, practical and relevant, and continual. They point out how classroom research has roots in educational research, faculty development, and assessment but is different from each of them. They also explain how the seven principles of good practice in undergraduate education provide a further rationale for classroom research. Finally, the authors demonstrate how teachers engaged in classroom research can be viewed as also engaged in all four dimensions of scholarship identified by Boyer (1990) (and presented in Part I of this reader): discovery; integration; application; and teaching.

The fourth reading, by Edgerton, Hutchings, and Quinlan, specifies the many uses of a teaching portfolio, including its use to improve instructional effectiveness. The teaching portfolio is essentially a documented and illustrated presentation of a teacher's best work. The authors conclude that it is particularly conducive to the improvement of teaching effectiveness for a number of reasons: (1) it engages instructors at a new level of responsibility for monitoring the quality of their teaching; (2) it requires instructors to engage in intensive reflection on their teaching to explain the underlying rationale of their approach to teaching; (3) it requires instructors to select and structure thoughtfully examples of their teaching performance; (4) it connects knowledge of subject matter with knowledge of how to teach it; and (5) it fosters the development of a campus teaching culture supportive of norms that encourage open discourse about a valued scholarship of teaching.

In an article reprinted earlier in this reader (Part III, Section C), Canada and Pringle emphasized the importance of seeing college classrooms as existing in social contexts. They pointed out that classroom interactions occur in an "ever-widening series of concentric circles" that define the circumstantial, social-cultural, geographic and historical perspectives "one can bring to bear on the particular classrooms that are observed." Such wider contexts and circumstances are also important to the analysis of improving teaching and learning in college. Thus we end this section of the reader (and the reader itself) with two different articles that bring in considerations of out-of-classroom circumstances and contexts. In the first of these last two readings, Paulsen and Feldman explicitly note that "college instructors do not teach in a vacuum." For example, teachers are part of an organization whose dominant and subordinate cultures can either positively or negatively affect their teaching and their efforts to improve their teaching. The authors focus particularly on the teaching culture that exists at a college or university. Regardless of whether a particular teaching culture is the college's dominant culture or, as may happen, a subordinate subculture, the characteristics of that culture are of great importance to teaching and its improvement. The effectiveness of most, if not all, strategies to improve instruction is enhanced by the presence of a culture supportive of teaching. From their consideration of relevant research (primarily qualitative studies, case studies, and surveys), the authors identify the characteristics of university cultures that most support teaching and its improvement.

The consideration of circumstances and contexts is of a different sort in the reading by Barr and Tagg. These authors argue that "a paradigm shift is taking hold in American higher education" because of two newly developing circumstances in higher education. The first circumstance is that colleges find it "virtually impossible . . . to respond effectively to the challenges of stable or declining budgets while meeting the increasing demand for postsecondary education." Colleges, they believe, suffer from a serious design flaw in that any attempt to increase outputs without a corresponding increase in costs and resources is a threat to quality. The second circumstance is that current "conceptions of teaching . . . are increasingly [being] recognized as ineffective." This set of circumstances, the authors maintain, is already beginning to produce a subtle but profound shift in the paradigm that governs higher education—a shift from colleges as institutions existing to provide instruction to colleges as institutions existing to produce learning. As advocates of this change, the authors of this provocative essay discuss how the shift in paradigm might be facilitated or strengthened. They also outline the many ways in which colleges based on the "Learning Paradigm" will be radically different from those now based on the "Instruction Paradigm." As part of their analysis, they explain how changes in the roles of virtually all college employees (including teachers) and the nature and use of classrooms (along with many other changes) will create vastly improved institutions of higher learning. In essence, Barr and Tagg leave us with this thought: the real challenge to colleges and universities is not to improve instruction but to improve learning.

References

Argyris, C., Putnam, R., and Smith, D. M. (1985). *Action science*. San Francisco: Jossey-Bass.

Association of American Colleges. (1985). *Integrity in the college curriculum: A report to the academic community*. Washington, D. C.: Association of American Colleges.

Bowen, H. R., and Schuster, J. H. (1986). *American professors: A national resource imperiled*. New York: Oxford University Press.

Boyer, E. L. (1987). *College*. New York: Harper and Row.

Boyer, E. L. (1990). *Scholarship reconsidered*. Princeton, NJ: Carnegie Foundation for the Advancement of Teaching.

Gamson, Z. F. (1991). A brief history of the seven principles for good practice in undergraduate education. In A. W. Chickering and Z. F. Gamson (Eds.), *Applying the seven principles for good practice in undergraduate education* (New Directions for Teaching and Learning, No. 47, pp. 5–12). San Francisco: Jossey-Bass.

Leistyna, P., Woodrum, A., and Sherblom, S. A. (1996). *Breaking free: The transformative power of critical pedagogy*. Cambridge, MA: The President and Fellows of Harvard College.

Lewin, K. (1952). Group decision and social change. In Guy E. Swanson, T. M. Newcomb and E. L. Hartley (Eds.), *Readings in social psychology* (Rev. ed., pp. 459–473). New York: Holt.

Mezirow, J. (1991). *Transformative dimensions of adult learning*. San Francisco: Jossey-Bass.

National Institute of Education. (1984). *Involvement in learning: Realizing the potential of American higher education*. Washington, D. C.: U. S. Government Printing Office.

Rando, W. C., and Menges, R. J. (1991). How practice is shaped by personal theories. In R. J. Menges and M. D. Svinicki (Eds.), *College teaching: From theory to practice* (New Directions for Teaching and Learning, No. 45, pp. 7–14). San Francisco: Jossey-Bass.

Schein, E. H. (1992). *Organizational culture and leadership*. San Francisco: Jossey-Bass.

Schon, D. A. (1983). *The reflective practitioner*. New York: Harper Collins.

Svinicki, M. D. (1991). Practical implementations of cognitive theories. In R. J. Menges and M. D. Svinicki (Eds.), *College teaching: From theory to practice* (New Directions for Teaching and Learning No. 45, pp. 27–38). San Francisco: Jossey-Bass.

A. General Models and Teaching Styles

Teaching Styles and Effects on Learning

PAUL L. DRESSEL AND DORA MARCUS

The heart of a college or university, with the exception of a few primarily graduate and research-oriented institutions, is the undergraduate program. Undergraduates and the programs in which they enroll justify much of the operational budget, the facilities, and consequently, the curriculum and faculty. In turn, the character and quality of an undergraduate program depend upon the professors and the teaching that they provide. Hence whether one discusses administration, finance, curriculum, or evaluation, some attention to teaching is essential.

In the process of writing an earlier volume, *Improving Degree Programs* (Dressel, 1980), which dealt with program and curriculum development and evaluation, the senior author found it necessary to consider the nature of the teaching process. This chapter, which draws freely on that earlier work, will further elaborate the conception of college teaching and learning expounded there, but with changes in order and emphasis to accommodate to the central themes of this volume. In particular, the discussion of teacher prototypes or orientations of classroom behavior should prove useful to teachers as a way of clarifying their own teaching performances and as profiles of possible alternative teaching styles.

Teacher Prototypes

After extensive discussion with teachers and educators, Hardy and Dressel identified and defined the following four teacher orientations (Hardy, 1976):

1. In discipline-centered teaching, the content and structure of the discipline are rigidly determined and in no way modified to meet the requirements, needs, or special concerns of either the teacher or learner.

2. In instructor-centered teaching, the teacher is the expert and the main source of knowledge in both the particular subject matter and the discipline. The instructor, around whom all class activity revolves, is the focal point in the teaching-learning process. The student is a passive recipient rather than an active participant.

3. In student-centered cognitive teaching, intellectual development is held to be the most important outcome of the teaching-learning process. Both content and teaching practices are selected and adjusted to accommodate the cognitive growth of the student toward teacher-specified objectives.

4. In student-centered affective teaching, the personal and social development of the student is the focus of the teaching-learning process. Both the content and the teaching practices are adjusted to foster the total development of each individual. The individual is expected to develop idiosyncratically rather than to adapt to content or to the demands of the teacher.

These prototypes are not empirically based. Rather, they represent a conceptually derived resolution of a complex of teachers' characteristics and a composite of teachers' thoughtful but highly subjective reactions. Teacher responses to the orientations were useful in producing a large number of statements indicative of the views and behavior that individuals related to the various orientations. These responses

"Teaching Styles and Effects on Learning," (Chapter 1) by Paul L. Dressel and Dora Marcus, reprinted from *On Teaching and Learning in College,* 1982, Jossey-Bass Publishers, Inc.

were added to the already extensive collection acquired from other studies and from teacher rating scales. Drawing upon all these materials, Hardy and Dressel then further developed the four orientations into a form to be used by teachers wishing to review and organize their views about teaching.

Additionally, an attempt was made to accommodate to recurring faculty reservations about the use of orientations or prototypes, such as the following:

- The use of prototypes is demeaning and ignores the uniqueness of individual professionals.
- Widely used typologies are likely to have values attached to them by administrators or others that lead to inequities in the appraisal of individual teachers.
- There will never be unanimity in definition of teaching types; hence typologies confuse and mislead rather than help.
- Any set of categories is a set of abstractions, whereas individuals are not merely composites but adapt their views and practices to changing circumstances.

There is some validity to these objections but accepting them entirely would not only rule out any characterizations of teaching but would also discourage evaluation of individual teachers. Furthermore, the approach actually used here effectively answers some of the objections, as later discussion will demonstrate.

We do not regard these proposed teacher types as ones to which every teacher could be readily assigned. Rather, the intent has been to define each orientation by typical views and practices which teachers might identify or contrast with their own practices and thus arrive at a profile across the orientations The individual teacher might then reflect upon this profile, evaluate, and possibly undertake to reinforce or to alter it. We do not value either consistency or rigidity in adherence to a typology. In fact, we prefer the term *orientation* rather than typology, suggesting a tendency toward the use of certain teaching behaviors rather than a rigid commitment to them. Although each of the orientations could be so defined as to be internally consistent and thereby imply a philosophy of teaching or education, most teaching styles are eclectic—not by formal choice, but by unconscious or conscious imitation of former teachers and colleagues and influenced by fortuitous circumstances and various institutional pressures.

Following is an elaboration of each of the four teaching prototypes or orientations. An exhibit of the composite results in Table 1 points up the differences among the orientations.

Discipline-Centered Teaching

In discipline-centered teaching, the course content and the structure of the discipline are rigidly defined and are not modified or rearranged to meet the requirements, needs, or special concerns of either the teacher or learner. The professorial obligation is to assure that each segment of the discipline covered by the course is presented in a sound scholarly manner. Learning is the obligation of the student. The *course content* includes those concepts, methods, theories, and materials that seem to present best that segment of the discipline as defined by scholars in the discipline. The specification of content is facilitated and reinforced by the selection of a text and of supplementary references. The preferred *method* of instruction is a series of lectures (perhaps supplemented by a text and references) planned to cover the specified content systematically and according to a fixed schedule.

The *classroom setting* tends to be formal, with emphasis on scholarly authority and objectivity. *Interactions of students and of students with the professor* deal almost exclusively with issues arising out of the classification of course content. Students are given the same or very similar assignments to be pursued through use of the text and standard reference materials. Students are *evaluated and graded* on specific skills and items of knowledge and on traditional or standard ways of presenting them. The professor's *self-image* is that of an authority in the discipline or certain of its subphases. The professor is responsible for presenting a defined segment of that discipline to students, each of whom is assumed to be motivated to acquire an understanding of it. Students are regarded as prospective majors in the discipline or in a field to which the discipline has direct relevance. Course coverage and teaching methodology are the same for all classes, regardless of heterogeneity or size. Neither *individuality* nor *creativity* is sought because *objectivity* is prized, and standards of mastery imposed by expert judgment do not accommodate student idiosyncrasies.

Teaching in the disciplinary mode may be very effective with students who are vitally interested in the course and the discipline, and especially so with graduate students. Teachers so oriented may be vital, warm human beings interested in those students who share an interest in the discipline and demonstrate potential for success in it. Such professors are frequently found in mathematics and sciences, but not solely there.

Instructor-Centered Teaching

In instructor-centered teaching, the teacher selects and develops the ideas presented to students. Students are expected to adjust to the professors and to learn more from them than from reading, discussion, or critical thought. *Students* are regarded as an admiring audience and as a source of acolytes. *Course content* is based upon personal preferences and may include practical applications or interrelations with other disciplines that the professor finds interesting and complementary (also complimentary) to his or her personal insights and scholarship. The instructional procedures are chosen to highlight the teacher's personality and eccentricities. *Classroom discussions,* which may exhibit the instructor's humor, critical facilities, and versatility, focus upon and clarify the instructor's views. *Assignments* likewise reflect the instructor's interests and points of view. The instructor (perhaps without consciously so doing) evaluates and grades students on their ability to imitate, reflect, and elaborate on professorial perspectives, conceptions, and formulations.

The professor's *self-image* is that of scholar and teacher of stature—a recognized authority. The professor may make conscious or unconscious adaptations to an audience, but the adaptations are based on affective rather than cognitive concerns. The professor radiates self-confidence and expects applause—and may deserve it. The instructor-centered teacher may not give much thought to adaptation to individual students or student groups and may even, without fully realizing it, ignore or resent student *originality* or *creativity* as competition. The *standards* of instructor-centered teachers tend to be highly personal and idiosyncratic. *Subjectivity* and *objectivity* are not always distinguishable, and they are roles of the moment rather than consistent stances. Within this instructor-centered category, there are identifiable subtypes. Some teachers consciously entertain and titillate rather than educate. Some simply and uninhibitedly express their natural personality. And some have had such a range of experiences and are so talented in communicating them that, without conscious intent, they become the course. These talented types are those whose names recur in the advice (sometimes good) given to students by other students, graduates, and professors: "Be sure to take a course from Professor X." This instructor-centered orientation is found in some of the best and most inspiring teachers and also in some of the worst. An overweening ego may make the reputation of a professor, but it may not result in good teaching.

Student-Centered Cognitive Teaching

In student-centered, cognitive teaching, the intellectual maturation of the student is regarded as the goal of the teaching-learning process. Both content and teaching techniques are chosen to foster the cognitive development of the student. Emotions (affect) are not ignored but are expected to be controlled and directed by intellect. The cognitively oriented teacher regards students as individuals who are becoming self-reliant and capable of self-direction. The knowledge that they will acquire and the ways they will use it are not predictable by the teacher. This cognitive emphasis is conjoined with an awareness that affect often directs and controls cognition. Affect, then, is to be recognized and brought under control to achieve more rational behavior. It may also be acknowledged that, in the nature of the human being, there are moments in which affect reigns supreme. There is joy in scholarship and intellectual performance.

Course content is chosen to be interesting, stimulating, and productive of student intellectual growth. *Teaching methods* or learning experiences, chosen primarily to encourage or even force students to think, may include student discussions, Socratic dialogue, experiments, lectures, demonstrations, exhibits—any experience that stimulates curiosity, thought, and understanding. The *classroom atmosphere* may be exciting and yet relaxed, encouraging participation of students and stimulating them to become creative, analytical, and logical in their thinking. *Student discussions and interactions* are used as processes to encourage understanding and application of concepts and principles. However, the teacher, always focusing on cognitive development, may intervene and redirect discussion whenever it strays from the point. *Assignments* are designed to require and develop cognitive abilities and to motivate the student toward self-reliance and intellectual maturity. Students are *evaluated and graded* on their ability to define and solve problems that require new resources and strategies.

The teacher's *self-image* is that of one who both models effective thinking and encourages student emulation. Accordingly, the teacher's role is to develop the students' capability in inquiry rather than to present an organized body of knowledge. The cognitively oriented teacher undertakes to foster in students the ability to generalize the mode of inquiry and to extend it well beyond the course content to problems more typical of those that occur in life. In so doing, the teacher finds *individualization and adaptation* desirable, both as motivation and as providing real problems for which neither the means of solution nor the answers are readily available in the text. The teacher encourages *objectivity* while recognizing that complete separation of cognition and affect is neither possible nor desirable. *Standards* are high but harder to define than in a discipline-based course because the objectives and the tasks are broader and more inclusive. Furthermore, as students are encouraged to move toward defining their own standards, uniform appraisal procedures may become impossible. The cognitively oriented teacher is less concerned with covering a specified body of content than with fostering students' interest in learning as well as their understanding and ability to use what they have learned.

Student-Centered Affective Teaching

In student-centered affective teaching, the personal, social, and intellectual development of the individual is the primary goal of the teaching-learning process. Moreover, affective and social development, as a composite, is taken to be a prerequisite to significant intellectual development. Both course content and educative activities are selected and adjusted to accommodate this goal. Education is seen as therapeutic, and intensive interaction of individuals in groups is, therefore, regarded as an essential part of it.

In this orientation, *content* is secondary and is selected (or indistinguishably merged with activities) to help students mature and to confirm to them their emerging status as adults. The preferred *instructional methods* encourage student involvement, with emphasis on discussion sessions led by students or instructors (or perhaps simply convened with no leadership). Informality, frankness, and student *interaction* characterize the sessions. Since students are encouraged to work toward self-expression and self-determination, formal *assignments* are seldom evident. Students are evaluated or evaluate themselves on the basis of participation, self-expression, affective development, and personal satisfaction. Grades in the traditional sense are not used. The students' remarks tend to be highly objective and personal, although subject to group discussion and appraisal. In this mode, it is uncertain whether students become objectively subjective or entirely subjective by decrying objectivity. The affective orientation is found most commonly in the social sciences (sociology or psychology), occasionally in the humanities (literature or philosophy), and rarely in mathematics and the natural sciences. This distribution reflects distinctions among the disciplines and differences among the individuals attracted to them.

In Table 1, the major characteristics of the four teacher prototypes or teaching orientations just discussed are displayed in such a manner as to facilitate comparison and contrast.

Cognitive Versus Affective Orientation

Student-centered teaching may be focused on cognitive development, on affective development, or on the complex but natural commingling of affect and intellect that characterizes all human beings. Some people would regard this conception of teaching as based upon a humanistic point of view. Since we believe that cultivation of the intellect is the primary concern of higher education, we doubt the validity of teaching that is completely affective in orientation. This is not to say that affective outcomes are inappropriate, that they are not learned, or that they do not involve knowledge and reflection. Though self-insight, self-acceptance, and a start toward self-realization can be deeply educational experiences, such experiences, even when successful, are not necessarily accompanied by acquisition of skills and the ability to use them. The individual experiencing such affective development may be happier and better able to cope with life, but there seems to be no more reason for granting credits or degrees for this than for giving credits or a degree in medicine to someone who has recovered from infectious hepatitis.

At the other extreme, pure cognitively oriented teaching is impossible. Both teachers and students, whether or not they realize it, come to an educational experience with biases and value commitments. For example, most teachers attempt to communicate to students both the values and preconceptions of

Table 1
Characteristics of Four Teaching Orientations by Components

Components	Discipline-Centered Teaching	Instructor-Centered Teaching	Student-Centered Teaching *(Cognitive Approach)*	Student-Centered Teaching *(Affective Approach)*
Course content	Based on disciplinary concepts, principles, theories, and methods.	Based on teacher's preferences and perceptions.	Composed of materials interesting to students and productive of cognitive outcomes.	Secondary—used to help students in maturation.
Method of instruction	Lectures and standard text, with systematic coverage of the body of knowledge.	Lecture or teacher-dominated discussion highlighting teacher's personality.	Discussion, with special lectures to focus on important issues.	Emphasis on student involvement and interaction as a means of personal and social development.
Classroom setting	Emotion free, with emphasis on scholarly objectivity.	Teacher dominated and controlled.	Somewhat relaxed but intellectually stimulating.	Highly informal, encouraging free student expression of feelings and concerns.
Student-faculty interaction	Familiarity and intimacy with students discouraged.	Discussions with students focused on clarifying lecture points.	Interactions planned to be intellectually stimulating to students.	Interactions in groups, with instructors acting as moderators.
Assignments	All students in course given the same assignment.	Reflect the teacher's interests and views of the discipline.	Geared to cultivate the desire to move toward intellectual maturity.	No formal assignments—students encouraged to work toward self-expression.
Objectives and evaluation	Students judged and graded by comparison with mastery standards.	Students judged and graded on ability to imitate professorial approaches, perspectives, and formulations.	Students judged and graded on tasks that require new resources and strategies.	Students evaluated (perhaps by themselves and their peers) on participation and self-expression.
Professorial self-image	Identifies with the discipline rather than with teaching role.	Has strong ego and radiates self-confidence.	Developer of student's ability to analyze, reason, use language effectively, and solve problems.	Counselor and "resource person."
Students	Viewed as would-be majors and graduate school candidates.	Viewed as an audience or a source of acolytes.	Regarded as individuals who must become self-reliant in using their knowledge.	Viewed as individuals who must achieve self-insight and accept full responsibility for their own behavior and goals.
Adaptation to or in student groups	Course coverage standard for all sections.	Some adjustments made for different audiences.	Emphasis on the *how* and *why* of knowledge.	Group interaction used to motivate students to learn.
Originality or creativity	Students encouraged to use the standard way of solving prestructured problems.	Originality in student responses acceptable if it does not clash with teacher's views.	Originality in thinking encouraged.	Each student expected to achieve self-realization.
Individualization	Assignments designed to help students master materials presented.	Students expected to adapt to teacher's interests rather than develop their own.	Students encouraged to develop their own analytic abilities.	Allows individuals to develop and acquire new resources and new ways of organizing ideas.
Source of standards	Standards of mastery set for each unit of learning by experts in the field.	Teacher standards based upon acceptance of his or her views.	Students expected to develop and use high standards in their own work.	Standards individually derived and self-imposed.
Objectivity	Expression of opinion in the classroom minimized.	Teacher's seeming objectivity actually highly subjective.	Analytical, objective, and logical instructional methods.	Understanding and acceptance more prized than objectivity.

Note: This table was modified from one that appears in Paul L. Dressel, *Improving Degree Programs: A Guide to Curriculum Development, Administration, and Review* (San Francisco: Jossey-Bass, 1980), pp. 127–129.

the discipline and the satisfaction that accompanies knowing and using ideas, concepts, and methods that characterize it. Nevertheless, it is possible to approach teaching (especially in mathematics, logic, and the natural sciences) as though the disciplines taught are purely intellectual and theoretical enterprises. Some teachers appear not to have recognized any other view, whereas others have recognized affective potentials but have consciously striven to avoid them in their teaching. This conscious avoidance of affect is in itself an affective commitment, although not always so recognized. With some people, that avoidance results from profound convictions and deep-seated biases.

The distinction between cognitive orientation and affective orientation may be theoretically possible, but the complete separation of cognition and affect in actual teaching and learning is artificial, if not impossible. The difference between the two orientations is more one of intent and emphasis than it is a complete dichotomy. Similar arguments could be made for the interdependence of all four orientations. For example, an otherwise discipline-oriented teacher may be sensitive to individual differences and adapt assignments to them in reference to either ability or interest.

In fact, our observations and experiences to date with these four orientations suggest that most teachers fall athwart all four rather than into any one, and they may shift in emphasis from one to another as they deal with different content, course levels, and students. This is facilitated by the fact that the four orientations are related in pairs. The disciplinary orientation and the student-cognitive orientation can be regarded as extremes on an objective disciplinary continuum. At one extreme, the emphasis is on presenting the discipline as an organized body of knowledge, with some attention to modes of inquiry. At the other extreme, the emphasis is on developing student cognition by assimilation of the modes of inquiry. The instructor orientation and the student-affective orientation present a continuum along which the human element takes precedence over the discipline. Some teachers who find themselves preferring one continuum may have an eclectic disciplinary or human (personal or student) orientation rather than any extreme position. Other teachers may combine an instructor-centered orientation with either an orientation to a discipline or a student-cognitive and student-affective orientation. The one combination that seems unlikely (from observations of teachers and their responses to this structure) is that of discipline orientation and student-affective orientation. But even this composite may characterize some teachers in psychology or sociology.

We point out these possible combinations to emphasize, once again, that we do not claim that the four orientations are discrete types or that each teacher will perfectly fit one category. The four orientations are the result of observation and the logical analysis of tendencies rather than of statistical analysis, seeking independent types. The whole intent has been to develop a pattern of orientations that might be useful to teachers in self-analysis. We personally favor the student-cognitive orientation and question (at least at the undergraduate level) the extreme positions on the student-affective, instructor-centered, and discipline-centered orientations. But effective and stimulating teaching based upon any of these orientations or composites is surely possible for some teachers in selected courses and disciplines and with appropriate students. These teacher orientations have value as a way to improve teaching and learning by making teachers more conscious of their stances and the relevance of these stances to their objectives, courses, and students. Teaching practices and their underlying values are thereby brought to the teachers' attention, and the tendency unthinkingly to imitate others or to fall into rote patterns may be overcome.

Emphasis on Learning

If learning is embraced as the criterion of effective teaching, however, much of the emphasis on teaching may be misplaced. The verb *teach* may be either transitive or intransitive, but the intransitive usage implies nothing about the nature of teaching. The sentence "Jones teaches" states only that Jones engages in activities designated as teaching, whether by self-characterization or the judgment of others. The statement conveys no information about what Jones does or about the attendant circumstances. In its transitive form, *teach* indicates that someone learns something as a result of the activities of a teacher. A learner may be self-taught. The statement that Jones teaches history uses *teach* as a transitive verb, but it is no improvement over saying that Jones teaches. A disciplinary attachment is indicated, but the learner, the object of the teaching, is not. The sentence suggests that Jones does something to history, although history surely does not change significantly because of Jones's teaching. In fact, we should say that Jones teaches students *about* history rather than that he teaches history to students.

The success of teaching must then be determined by whether and what the students learn, not by what the teacher does or asks students to do, and most certainly not solely by the scholarly precision and verve with which Jones presents the historical materials. This is not to say that the materials, content, and forms of presentation are unimportant or irrelevant; rather, it emphasizes that these are subject to choice by the teacher guided by a concern for their effectiveness in promoting learning by students. Teaching and learning must always take place in some context and involve some content.

The term *content* evokes such words as discipline, knowledge, subject matter, values, abilities, and skills. But closer examination reveals that these are by no means equivalent terms. A discipline is both an organized body of knowledge and an organized mode of accumulating and ordering knowledge. As such, it includes disciplinary methods, skills, strategies, concepts, principles, structural elements, value commitments, and analytic and synthesizing modes of thought. Knowledge, understanding, and mastery of the methods, skills, and strategies are not taught so much as they are exemplified by the teacher and the materials used. Students emulate, assimilate, and learn in individual ways and often in ways not well understood by either the teachers or the students.

Content connotes what is in or what is covered by a course. As Table 1 indicates, content may be determined by a teacher or predetermined by the course description. The content of a course has much the same sense as the contents of a book. The term indicates the substantive material of the course without any implication of how, why, or where the material will be presented. Content and subject matter are often used interchangeably, but this ignores an important distinction. We prefer to regard subject matter as external to the discipline, referring rather to the problems or aspects of reality around which the discipline developed or to which its methods are being applied. This distinction is a significant factor in the teaching orientations. For example, the disciplines of physics and mathematics can be directed to the making of musical instruments, the building of bridges, or the analysis of human behavior. The application of a discipline to a distinctive subject matter involves values, abilities, and skills that are often ignored when a discipline is regarded solely as an organized body of knowledge. Subject matter is the problem or immediate focus of human concern, whereas course content involves the study of a subject matter by use of one or more disciplines. The problem approach to development of course content encourages, if it does not actually necessitate, interdisciplinary teaching.

To the extent that knowledge, values, abilities, and skills are acquired by students as intended consequences (objectives) of teaching, these outcomes justify the costs of education. These outcomes have personal, esthetic, social, economic, and political implications that are, by nature, interdisciplinary or supradisciplinary. The individual who acquires knowledge, values, abilities, and skills achieves some immediate personal satisfaction and develops the capacity for a more pleasurable and productive life. Society benefits both qualitatively and quantitatively from the presence and contributions of these educated individuals. The nation also benefits from their contributions to goal setting and political decision making. Teaching is supported because of these benefits, and these same benefits provide much of the satisfaction of those teachers whose vision of their roles extends beyond their interest in and commitment to their disciplines. For these reasons, we are convinced that the cognitive orientation, as earlier defined, is the most appropriate for undergraduate college teachers in a democratic society.

The concept of Jones teaching students about history resolves some of the previously noted ambiguities of the teaching task. However, teachers are generally well trained in their disciplines but are relatively uncertain about appraising and adjusting to differences in students or in program purposes. Hence teachers may confuse communication with teaching. The scholarly readers of a definitive research report become, at that moment, students of the writer, but at a very different level of specificity and understanding from that expected of college freshmen. Sensitive teaching, especially in a democratic society, must recognize and adjust to audience differences in sophistication and purpose. The concept *student* must be qualified by reference to the reason for and the nature of the learning sought. Is the student a graduate or undergraduate, a major or nonmajor? Each of these may have distinctive reasons for taking a course. The part-time adult student of age thirty to sixty and the full-time freshman of seventeen or eighteen bring sharply different backgrounds and purposes to the learning situation. If the teacher accepts responsibility for the students' learning, these differences among students must be taken into account. Learning objectives, instructional materials, and teaching methods should be adapted to individual differences in motivations and goals. Ever present should be the concern that the learner acquire increased independence in and motivation for pursuit of further learning.

One of our major assumptions is that class activities should motivate and direct learning inside and outside the classroom. Only if the teacher accepts and meets this responsibility is the role of the teacher as motivator and director of learning fully realized. But many professors think of teaching merely as appearing before a selective and relatively homogeneous student audience in a classroom for a specified period of time and at specified intervals to administer a carefully predetermined dose of information. This conception of teaching may produce learning for certain students, but such a teaching model is not the best for most undergraduate courses or for any other level of learning.

In only a very limited sense is teaching either an administratively imposed or a self-assumed role and responsibility. When one person learns from another, the latter has become a teacher, whether or not he or she realizes it. Being in the same room or living in the same age is not necessary for learning to be motivated by a teacher and achieved by a learner. Most of the difficulty with defining and evaluating good teaching lies in our lack of understanding of how individuals learn and in our inability or unwillingness to specify that which is most desirable to learn. In subsequent chapters, we shall focus upon student learning and ways of defining what is to be learned and the means of facilitating the learning process.

Suggestions for Further Reading

Anderson, J. "The Teacher as Model." *American Scholar,* 1961, *30,* 393–398, 400–401.

Axelrod, J. *The University Teacher as Artist: Toward an Aesthetics of Teaching with Emphasis on the Humanities.* San Francisco: Jossey-Bass, 1973.

Baird, L.L. "Teaching Styles." *Journal of Educational Psychology,* 1973, *64 (1),* 15–21.

Eble, K.E. *Professors as Teachers.* San Francisco: Jossey-Bass, 1972.

Eble, K.E. *The Craft of Teaching: A Guide to Mastering the Professor's Art.* San Francisco: Jossey-Bass, 1976.

Green, T.F. "The Concept of Teaching." In D. Vandenberg (Ed.), *Teaching and Learning.* Urbana: University of Illinois Press, 1969.

Hardy, N.T. "A Survey Designed to Refine an Inventory of Teaching Styles To Be Used by Individuals Preparing for College Teaching." Unpublished doctoral dissertation, Michigan State University, 1976.

Hyman, R.T. *Ways of Teaching.* Philadelphia: Lippincott, 1970.

Layton, D. (Ed.). *University Teaching in Transition.* Edinburgh, Scotland: Oliver and Boyd, 1968.

Pullias, E.V., Lockhard, A., and others. *Toward Excellence in College Teaching.* Dubuque, Iowa: Brown, 1964.

University of London Teaching Methods Unit. *Improving Teaching In Higher Education.* Leicester, England: Cavendish Press, 1976.

What Constitutes Masterful Teaching

JOSEPH LOWMAN

What all the great teachers appear to have in common is love of their subject, an obvious satisfaction in arousing this love in their students, and an ability to convince them that what they are being taught is deadly serious.

Epstein (1981, p. xii)

If I were to ask you to picture a masterful college teacher, any of a number of images could come to mind. One image might be that of an awe-inspiring scholar lecturing from the stage of an amphitheater to an audience of students who are leaning forward to catch every word. Another might be that of a warm, approachable person seated at a seminar table among a group of students, facilitating an animated discussion, firmly but gently guiding the students to insight, awareness, self-confidence, and a heightened ability to think critically. Still another image might be that of an instructor engaged with one or two students in freewheeling sessions in the professor's study, over a glass of beer in the students' haunt, or in the laboratory—sessions in which each student has the opportunity to see at close range the way the teacher thinks and perhaps to glimpse an older person attempting to live a life committed to ideas and knowledge.

Varied as these images are, they are alike in fundamental ways. In each of them the instructor is pictured not while studying alone or presenting a paper to learned colleagues but while interacting with students. The images all convey a sense of impact, of an instructor having a potentially profound effect on the students. In each, the students are emotionally as well as intellectually stimulated by the proceedings, whether as members of an audience or in one-to-one relationships.

If instruction is first rate, we can expect that several kinds of learning will occur. The learning of facts, theories, and methods will take place, to be sure. Beyond that, students will have the chance to gain an understanding of relationships among varied kinds of knowledge, sharpen their thinking and communication skills, and receive a perspective from which to evaluate information critically. This learning meets the broad goals of liberal education.

The three imaginary scenes illustrate and circumscribe the subject of this book: masterful college teaching. The view of outstanding college teaching presented here emphasizes the traditional skills of lecturing and leading discussions. In contrast to approaches that focus on detailed planning or rely on technological innovations, my perspective rests squarely on the assumption that college teaching is and should be interpersonal, that it is above all an enterprise involving human beings and their personalities, and that it is incapable of being reduced to mechanical cause-and-effect relationships. This book provides detailed, practical instruction that a graduate instructor or professor can use to fully master the art of college teaching.

The premise of this book is that superior college teaching involves two distinct sets of skills. The first is speaking ability. This includes skill not only in giving clear, intellectually exciting lectures but also in leading discussions. The second is interpersonal skills. Such skills allow one to create the sort of warm, close relationships with one's students that motivate them to work independently. To become an excellent instructor, one must be outstanding in one of these sets of skills and at least competent in the other. This first chapter considers the nature of the necessary and sufficient characteristics of masterful college teaching and presents the two-dimensional model of effective college instruction upon which the specific

"What Constitutes Masterful Teaching?" (Chapter 1), by Joseph Lowman, reprinted from *Mastering the Techniques of Teaching,* 1984, Jossey-Bass Publishers, Inc.

lent instructor, one must be outstanding in one of these sets of skills and at least competent in the other. This first chapter considers the nature of the necessary and sufficient characteristics of masterful college teaching and presents the two-dimensional model of effective college instruction upon which the specific suggestions offered in this book are based.

Is Knowledge Taught or Learned?

If the members of an academic community are polled on ways to improve the quality of education, the students are likely to suggest hiring and promoting faculty who are better teachers, while the faculty probably will suggest admitting brighter, better prepared, and more motivated students. Whose opinion is the more valid? How responsible, in fact, are the faculty for how much students learn and for how insightful they become? How responsible are faculty members for students' proficiencies in fundamental skills—reading, thinking, writing, and speaking—or for students' attitudes toward learning? Who is most to blame when students pursue college merely for vocational rewards or social distractions? Conversely, who deserves credit for those rare students who not only master basic content and skills but understand a discipline in fresh and original ways and are somehow able to integrate the knowledge they have gleaned in various areas into a single, personal vision?

In *College Professoring*, O. P. Kolstoe answers these questions by asserting that "nobody can't teach nobody nothing" (1975, p. 61). He is correct. No instructor can *make* students learn. Consequently, college teachers cannot claim full credit when a student learns something well, nor must they carry all the blame when students fail to learn. Given students' freedom to take or leave what we instructors have to offer, it is crucial that we take pains to see that they become involved in learning. The importance of this motivational function is immense.

What differences among students require different teaching methods? Individual differences in students' abilities to do academic work are foremost. Students learn a subject at different rates and with strikingly different levels of completeness. College teachers are often amazed at the brilliance of some students and the shallowness of others. Regardless of the amount of work some students put into their studies, the complexity of their thinking fails to match that of others. Our society's contemporary social ethic tends to deny the importance of differences in fundamental academic ability, but psychological research (Guilford, 1968; Scarr, 1981) and the experience of college teachers support the influence of intelligence on the quality of student learning. How fully students apply themselves also affects how much they learn, but motivation can go only so far in compensating for differences in ability.

We as instructors cannot be held responsible for the differences in ability students bring with them, but we *are* responsible for motivating all students, from the gifted to the barely adequate, to do their best work and to love the learning experience. College teachers have as much power to dampen students' enthusiasm for learning as to excite it.

Student Memories of Excellent Instructors

Everyone can remember a few college teachers who stood out from the rest. If we were lucky, we had several who were superb; however, each of us likely had more poor teachers than outstanding ones. We can all remember classes that were boring and frustrating, when we dreaded going to class or meeting the professor in the hallway, when we ritualistically counted off the number of classes remaining in the term. But we also had classes we attended eagerly and finished with regret. Remembering notable positive and negative examples from our past is useful in choosing ideals to emulate.

There are also written descriptions of highly esteemed instructors to consider. A particularly interesting collection is Joseph Epstein's *Masters: Portraits of Great Teachers* (1981), which contains essays that originally appeared in *The American Scholar*. Professors such as Christian Gauss of Princeton, Ruth Benedict of Columbia, Morris Cohen of City College, Alfred North Whitehead of Harvard, John William Miller of Williams, Frederick Teggart of Berkeley, F. O. Mathiessen of Harvard, and Hannah Arendt of the New School are included. Subjects taught by these masters included philosophy, political thought, literature, theoretical physics, history, and anthropology.

Epstein's contributors remember their instructors as particularly skilled in specific teaching settings. The specialty for some was lecturing to large introductory classes attended primarily by freshmen and sophomores. For others it was leading senior or graduate seminars. In all cases, however, the writers remark on the instructors' influence and skill in tutorials or informal one-to-one interactions.

The most striking thing about these portraits of twentieth-century college teachers is the importance of their lecture or seminar performance to the level of personal and intellectual impact they had on their students. Not only did these men and women have a great deal to offer their students; they were also highly skilled at getting it across. As Epstein relates in his introduction to the collection, they had individual styles, using "socratic teasing, sonorous lecturing, sympathetic discussion; passionate argument, witty exposition, dramatics and other sorts of derring-do; plain power of personal example, main force of intellect, and sometimes even bullying" (p. xii).

Finally, it is clear that all of these outstanding instructors took their teaching responsibilities very seriously. They put a great deal of themselves into their classes and expected a similar level of commitment from their students. The tremendous personal satisfaction they received from their teaching was evident to their students.

Outstanding Teaching as Portrayed by Contemporary Research

The large body of findings from empirical research on college teaching presents a consistent picture of the outstanding teacher. Studying questionnaires that assess students' satisfaction with professors' teaching skills has been very fruitful for educational research, although the routine use of such student ratings to give instructors personal feedback, to provide public information for course selection, and to aid in faculty personnel decisions has become an increasingly controversial topic (Chandler, 1978; Marg, 1979; Raskin and Plante, 1979; Ryan and others, 1980).

Faculty ambivalence about student ratings of instruction probably stems from a number of concerns, some noble (preserving academic freedom and faculty power, promoting excellent scholarship), some petty (jealousy of others, excuses for receiving low ratings). Beyond this ambivalence about student ratings may lie a deeper ambivalence about the importance of quality teaching. Colleges and academic departments differ in the amount of actual encouragement and reinforcement (as opposed to ritualistic lip service) they give to quality undergraduate teaching. It is a sad commentary on comtemporary higher education that among the varied arenas for achievement open to faculty (scholarship, grant-getting, consulting, or administration), classroom teaching ranks in importance near the bottom for many.

In contrast to this controversy among faculty, students very much favor evaluating their professors' teaching and consider it quite legitimate to do so (Gmelch and Glasman, 1978). Some teachers claim that student raters are not competent to evaluate instructors' command of subject or research expertise, and several studies indicate that students do not consider themselves able to evaluate professors in this way either (Kroman, 1978). Students do not generally believe they have sufficient knowledge to evaluate the depth of their instructors' contribution to a field. However, students *do* believe themselves capable of evaluating how well a college teacher taught them a subject and how much they were excited by the process of learning it. Regardless of individual attitudes toward the ways student evaluations are used, data from such instruments are highly relevant to the question of what constitutes outstanding teaching—especially in the eyes of instructional "consumers," the students themselves.

What does the research on student ratings of teaching effectiveness show about outstanding college instruction? Two types of research need to be discussed. One is studies relating overall teaching ratings to other kinds of information known about the classes, teachers, and students; this line of inquiry examines the external validity of the evaluation questionnaires. The other type of relevant research is studies focusing on relationships among the evaluation questions, with the aim of condensing the numerous items into the fundamental dimensions being measured.

In a number of studies the overall level of student ratings was found to have little if any relationship to the time of day courses were taught, the subject under consideration, the extent of the instructor's experience, or the size of the class. Though a number of studies have attempted to show that factors other than the instructor's teaching ability influence such ratings, on the whole it is clear that such variables have much less effect on ratings than the qualities students see in the individual college teachers (Braskamp, Ory, and Peiper, 1981; Freedman, Stumpf, and Aquano, 1979; Hoffman, 1978; Korth, 1979; Marsh, 1980; Marsh and Overall, 1981; Meredith, 1980).

A common notion among faculty is that ratings merely reflect instructor popularity, attractiveness, or grading stringency and have little to do with competence as a teacher. Arguing against this position are the results of studies showing that students consider the quality of teacher-student relationships to be second in importance to an instructor's ability to present material clearly (Abbot and Perkins, 1978; Reardon and Waters, 1979). The contention that students' ratings of teaching are functions of the amount of work an instructor assigns and the severity with which he or she evaluates it also is little supported by research (Abrami and others, 1980; Frey, 1978; Peterson and Cooper, 1980). Difficult, demanding professors are just as likely to be given outstanding student evaluations as are less demanding ones. Teachers of "slide" courses (available in quantity at most schools) frequently receive poor or mediocre student ratings, even though seats in their classes may be in demand. It is not accurate to say that most students are so concerned about grades that their satisfaction with a teacher is related mainly to the difficulty of the course. Grading practices and the attitude with which work is assigned can adversely affect class morale, but satisfaction with an instructor's teaching comes more from positive emotions (excitement, enthusiasm, respect) than from the absence of negative ones.

A variation of this misconception about difficulty is the belief that if students enjoy or are excited by an instructor, the quality of that teacher's material must be second rate. The source of this puritanical attitude toward learning and teaching is difficult to pin down, but there is nothing compelling about arguments for its validity. Great teachers demonstrate a pleasure in learning and create a love of learning in their students. The best protection against being seen as a modern-day sophist is to aim for substance as well as enjoyment. Stiff, businesslike, or aversive behavior in a teacher is no assurance of quality instruction.

Professors who believe that high student ratings must reflect sweetened or watered-down knowledge often have the covert hope that students who rate them poorly will one day value them more than the instructors they found satisfying at the time. In a growing number of studies, however, evaluations of faculty made several years after graduation (up to ten years in one case) have been found to be remarkably consistent with the students' original opinions (Firth, 1979; Marsh and Overall, 1979; Overall and Marsh, 1980). Student ratings thus cannot be dismissed as reflecting merely the poor judgment of youth.

Even if student ratings are consistent over time and classes (professors typically receive similar ratings across different semesters and courses), some will argue that they have no relationship to the way the teachers' peers would evaluate their effectiveness. Available evidence runs contrary to this notion as well (Aleamoni, 1978; Ballard, Rearden, and Nelson, 1976). One study compared student ratings, professors' evaluations of their own teaching, and expert judges' ratings of videotape recordings of the professors' classroom presentations. A similar pattern for each teacher was found with each of the three types of measures. Those college teachers seen as excellent by their students were also rated highly by the judges and by themselves; weaker instructors also were rated similarly by all three groups. The only notable difference among the ratings was that students tended to rate the faculty members lower than did the instructors or their peers (Marsh, Overall, and Kesler, 1979). If anything, students may be tougher judges of teaching than faculty.

But what, some may ask, do student ratings of teaching have to do with student learning, regardless of whether the ratings are valid? Is not student demonstration of what they have learned the only outcome of importance in education? The fact that some studies have found student achievement to have little correlation with student ratings (Braskamp, Caulley, and Costin, 1979; Costin, 1978; Hoffman, 1979; Moody, 1976; Palmer, Carliner, and Romer, 1978) is sometimes interpreted as support for this argument against the importance of student ratings. More research indicates that teacher ratings *are* positively associated with student learning, however (see Cohen's 1981 meta-analysis).

The overall level of student ratings, then, is mostly a function of the degree of students' satisfaction with the instruction they receive. Internal analysis of the various questions on student rating questionnaires tells us what students find satisfying and dissatisfying about teaching. In factor analytic studies of ratings, as many of six or seven mathematically distinct factors and as few as two or three have been reported (Feldman, 1976; Mannan and Traicoff, 1976; Marques, Lane, and Dorfman, 1979; Tennyson, Boutwell, and Frey, 1978). It is instructive to examine the different types of factors (or fundamental dimensions) that have been described in published studies.

The most prominent factors concern clarity of presentation. Specific items in this category usually deal with whether an instructor presents material clearly and in a logically organized way that is easy for students who know little about the subject to understand. Some studies suggest that frequent use of concrete examples is associated with the ability to present material understandably. Another strong factor is the instructor's ability to stimulate students' thinking about the material rather than simply encouraging them to absorb it. A factor found prominent in most studies is the instructor's ability to stimulate enthusiasm for the subject, a skill frequently related to the teacher's personal enthusiasm.

Secondarily, student ratings have been shown to reflect the quality of interpersonal relationships between instructor and students. Some studies refer to this factor as student-teacher rapport; others discuss the degree to which students perceive an instructor as being concerned about them as individuals. Questionnaire items contributing to this category ask how warm students perceive an instructor as being and how much the instructor seems to enjoy sharing knowledge with them. Students may learn something important from a class in which the instructor shows a lack of respect or a negative and cynical attitude toward them, but it will be in spite of the teacher's attitude rather than because of it.

Thus, studies of student ratings of instruction present a consistent picture of outstanding and, by contrast, undesirable teaching. Fundamentally, such ratings reflect how well the instructor presents material and fosters positive interpersonal relationships with students. These two categories closely resemble Bales's classic definition of "task" and "maintenance" functions of group leadership (Bales, 1950; Bales and Slater, 1955). The two-dimensional model of effective college teaching discussed in the next section has been built around them.

A Two-Dimensional Model of Effective College Teaching

The specific lessons in this book are based on a two-dimensional model of teaching effectiveness in which the quality of instruction results from a college teacher's skill at creating both intellectual excitement and positive rapport in students, the kinds of emotions and relationships that motivate them to do their best work. These two kinds of skills are relatively independent, and excellence at either can ensure effective teaching with some students and in certain kinds of classes. A teacher who is accomplished at both is most likely to be outstanding for all students and in any setting.

Dimension I: Intellectual Excitement

Skill at creating intellectual excitement has two components: the clarity of an instructor's communications and their positive emotional impact on students. Clarity is related to *what* one presents, and positive emotional impact results from the *way* in which material is presented.

Clarity can be no better than the accuracy of content, of course, but it is assumed that most instructors have mastered their content adequately. Knowing material well is quite different from being able to present it clearly, however.

Knowledge is far more than the accumulation of isolated facts and figures. It involves a deeper understanding, an ability to "walk around" facts and see them from different angles. As Bloom argues in his classic taxonomy of educational goals (Bloom, Madaus, and Hastings, 1981), knowledge includes the ability to analyze and integrate facts, to apply them to new situations, and to evaluate them critically within the broad context available to the educated person. For a teacher to do an excellent job, he or she must be able to do far more than simply present the details of a subject—and students seem to know this. They like to receive an overall perspective and love to compare and contrast different concepts in addition to learning individual facts.

To be able to present material clearly, instructors must approach and organize their subject matter as if they too know little about it. They must focus on the early observations, essential milestones, key assumptions, and critical insights in a subject and not be distracted by the qualifications and limitations that most concern them as scholars. Being able to do this leads to the ability to explain a complex subject simply.

Outstanding teachers share this facility for clear exposition. Ernest Rutherford, the nineteenth-century British physicist, believed that he had not completed a scientific discovery until he was able to translate it into readily understandable language (Highet, 1950). Similarly, the ancient Greek and Hebrew teachers were masters of metaphor, making complex points by using simple language and concrete images. It is false snobbery to claim that one's knowledge is too grand to be understandable by a reasonably intelligent outsider. Outstanding college teachers are able to explain ideas and the connections between them in ways that make eminently good sense to the uninitiated.

Most students who receive consistently clear presentations will be able to correctly define, illustrate, and compare and contrast concepts. However, understanding material is not the same thing as being intellectually excited about it—being, for example, so highly engaged in a presentation as to be free from distracting thoughts and fantasies, surprised when the class period is over, or compelled to talk about the class to others during the day. To have this kind of impact on students, an instructor must do far more than present material clearly. In other words, for maximum effectiveness on this first dimension, clarity is necessary but not sufficient. It must be accompanied by virtuosity at speaking in front of groups. Why is this believed to be the case?

College classrooms are fundamentally dramatic arenas in which the teacher is the focal point, just as the actor or orator is on a stage. The students are subject to the same influences—both satisfactions and distractions—as any audience. As Epstein's portraits demonstrate, teaching is undeniably a performing art. Excellent teachers use their voices, gestures, and movements to elicit and maintain attention and to stimulate students' emotions. Like other performers, teachers must convey a strong sense of presence, of highly focused energy. Some teachers do this by being overtly enthusiastic, animated, or witty, while others accomplish the same effect with a quieter, more serious and intense style. The ability to stimulate strong positive emotions in students separates the competent from the outstanding college teacher.

Table 1 describes instructors at the high, middle, and lower ranges of this dimension of intellectual excitement as seen by an outside observer and as experienced by students. A teacher at the upper end of this dimension is an unusually skilled individual. To master college teaching to this degree, an instructor must be able to do more than prepare an accurate, well-organized synopsis of a content area. He or she must also be able to organize and deliver the material with the skill of a seasoned speaker. Such teaching is not simply showmanship or gratuitous attention-getting, as is assumed by disparagers who refer to it as "hamming it up," "showing off," or "faking it." As followup research on the famous Dr. Fox experiment has demonstrated, exciting teaching is not merely acting or entertaining (Kaplan, 1974; Meier and Feldhusen, 1979; Naftulin, Ware, and Donnelly, 1973; Perry, Abrami, and Leventhal, 1979; Williams and Ware, 1977). Entertainment involves the stimulation of emotions and the creation of pleasure for their own sakes. Outstanding teaching is characterized by stimulation of emotions associated with intellectual activity: the excitement of considering ideas, understanding abstract concepts and seeing their relevance to one's life, and participating in the process of discovery.

Dimension II: Interpersonal Rapport

In theory, the college classroom is strictly an intellectual and rational arena. In reality, a classroom is a highly emotional interpersonal arena in which a wide range of psychological phenomena occur. For example, student's motivation to work will be reduced if they feel that they are disliked by their instructor or controlled in heavy-handed or autocratic ways. All students are vulnerable to such disrupting emotions, and some students are especially senstive to them. Also, like anyone else, students have a potential to react emotionally when they are being challenged and evaluated in group settings. Even students whose work is superior will become angry if testing and grading practices seem unfair.

Instructors are not immune to what happens in the classroom, either; many events can interfere with their enjoyment of teaching and lessen their motivation to teach well. Most professors have strong needs for achievement and success. The common desire to be at least average makes instructors' professional self-esteem vulnerable to their students' achievement and end-of-term ratings. This is especially true of those teaching for the first few times and for junior faculty facing tenure and promotion decisions. If students are not learning as much as expected, a teacher is only human in feeling threatened and being tempted to show anger by criticizing student efforts. Also, because they are human, instructors want to be liked and respected as individuals, and walking into a room of 50 to 100 strangers is guaranteed to raise interpersonal anxiety in anyone.

Psychologically, classes of students behave like other groups. The study of group phenomena has demonstrated convincingly that people in almost any kind of group situation, from digging a ditch to designing a research program, show predictable emotional reactions to their interactions with one another (Cartwright and Zander, 1960; Shaffer and Galinsky, 1974). Issues of *leadership* (or control) and *affection* (or the degree to which individuals feel respected and liked by others) will always be present.

College classrooms are no different. They are complex interpersonal arenas in which a variety of emotional reactions can influence how much is learned and how the participants feel about it. Richard Mann and his colleagues at the University of Michigan (1970) convincingly illustrated these college classroom phenomena by coding and analyzing individual comments of students and teachers in four introductory psychology classes. They offer a rich and insightful portrayal of this emotional substratum of

Table1
Dimension I: Intellectual Excitement

Level of Student Response	*Observer's Description of Teaching*	*Impact on Students*
High: Extremely clear and exciting	All content is extremely well organized and presented in clear language	Students know where the teacher is going and can distinguish important from unimportant material
	Relationships among specific concepts and applications to new situations are stressed	Students see connections among concepts and can apply them to new situations
	Content is presented in an engaging way, with high energy and strong sense of dramatic tension	Students have little confusion about material or about what the teacher has said
	Teacher appears to love presenting material	Students have a good sense of why concepts are defined as they are
		Ideas seem simple and reasonable, almost obvious, and are easily remembered
		It is very easy to pay attention to teacher (almost impossible to daydream)
		Class time seems to pass very quickly, and students may get so caught up in the ideas that they forget to take notes
		Students experience a sense of excitement about the ideas under study and generally hate to miss class
		Course and teacher are likely to be described as "great" or "fantastic"
Moderate: Reasonably clear and interesting	Facts and theories are presented clearly within an organized framework	Students' understanding of most concepts is accurate and complete; they find it easy to take good notes
	Material is presented in an interesting manner, with a moderate level of energy	Students can see connections between most concepts and understand examples offered in class or in the text
	Teacher seems moderately enthusiastic and involved in teaching the class	Class is moderately interesting and enjoyable for most students
		Course and teacher are likely to be described as "good" or "solid"
Low: Vague and dull	Some material is organized well and presented clearly, but much is vague and confusing	Students have little idea of where the teacher is going or why material is presented as it is or even at all
	Most material is presented with little energy or enthusiasm	Students experience confusion or uncertainty frequently

Table 1 *continued*

	Teacher may seem to hate teaching the class and to be as bored with it as the students	Most students find taking notes difficult
		Students see few relationships among concepts and little relevance of content to their own experience
		Students find it difficult to pay attention, and class time may seem to pass very slowly
		Students frequently experience a sense of frustration or anger and may dread coming to class and welcome excuses not to go
		Course and teacher are likely to be described as "boring" and "awful"

college classrooms, detailing teacher roles, students types, and predictable changes over a semester. . . .

Dimension II deals with an instructor's awareness of these interpersonal phenomena and with his or her skill at communicating with students in ways that increase motivation, enjoyment, and independent learning. This is done in essentially two ways. The first is to avoid stimulation of negative emotions, notably excessive anxiety and anger toward the teacher. The second is to promote positive emotions, such as the feeling that the instructor respects the students as individuals and sees them as capable of performing well. These sets of emotions strongly affect students' motivation to complete their assignments and learn material, whether their motivation is a desire for approval from the teacher or an attempt to meet their own personal standards.

Dimension II is especially critical to success in one-to-one teaching situations. For most settings, however, Dimension II is not as critical to outstanding teaching as Dimension I, although it does contribute significantly to class atmosphere and the conditions under which students are motivated to learn. It should also be noted that Dimension I refers almost totally to what an instructor does in the classroom, while Dimension II is significantly influenced by teacher-student interactions outside as well as inside class. Table 2 contains descriptions of teaching at three levels within this second dimension of teaching effectiveness.

Dimension II is admittedly more controversial than Dimension I. No one is likely to advocate that teachers be vague and dull, though some professors may believe that clarity is all that is required for good teaching and see attempts to be exciting or inspiring as demeaning. However, less consensus would be found among college faculties about the place on Dimension II where an outstanding instructor should fall—whether he or she should be autocratic and aloof or democratic and approachable. Some professors sincerely believe that recognizing students' personal reactions not only is irrelevant to teaching content but also impedes students' growth into mature and responsible adults because it indulges or coddles them. Other instructors are just as certain that a distant, autocratic style of teaching is a cruel vestige of the past and does not promote independent learning that is likely to continue when the class is over. Faculty holding this more humanistic position emphasize two-way interaction between teachers and students. Socrates is their ideal teacher, not the irascible "Herr Professor" of the nineteenth-century German lecture hall.

In contrast to faculty disagreement about Dimension II, the summary of research on student ratings shows that there is little question about which end of this continuum most students prefer. They prefer more democratic and approachable teachers (Uranowitz and Doyle, 1978)—provided first that the teachers are clear and interesting. Research indicates that students give relatively more weight to Dimension I than Dimension II (Keaveny and McGann, 1978; Marques, Lane, and Dorfman, 1979).

Table 2
Dimension II: Interpersonal Rapport

Level of Interpersonal Rapport	*Observer's Description of Teaching*	*Impact on Students*
High: Extremely warm and open; highly student-centered; predictable	Teacher appears to have strong interest in the students as individuals and high sensitivity to subtle messages from them about the way they feel about the material or its presentation	Students feel that the teacher knows who they are and cares about them and their learning a great deal
	Teacher acknowledges students' feelings about matters of class assignments or policy and encourages them to express such feelings; may poll their preferences on some matters	Students have positive, perhaps even affectionate, thoughts about the teacher; some may identify with him or her strongly
	Teacher encourages students to ask questions and seems eager for them to express personal viewpoints	Students believe teacher has confidence that they can learn and think independently about the subject
	Teacher communicates both openly and subtly that each student's understanding of the material is important to him or her	Students are highly motivated to do their best, in part so as not to disappoint the teacher's high expectation of them
	Teacher encourages students to be creative and independent in dealing with the material, to formulate their own views	Students are likely to describe teacher as a "fantastic person"
Moderate: Relatively warm, approachable, and democratic; predictable	Teacher is friendly and personable to students but makes no great effort to get to know most of them	Students have little fear or anxiety about the teacher or their ability to perform successfully in the class
	Teacher announces policies and discusses student reactions to them if the students complain	Students know what the teacher expects of them but feel little responsibility to go beyond that level of performance
	Teacher responds to student questions and personal comments politely and without apparent irritation	Students are reasonably well motivated to complete assigned work and to perform well
	Teacher is relatively consistent and predictable in behavior toward students; gives ample notice before announcing requirements or changes in schedule	Students are likely to describe teacher as a "nice person" or a "good guy" or "nice woman"
Low: Cold, distant, highly controlling; may also be unpredictable	Teacher shows little interest in students as persons; knows few of their names and may fail to recognize many of them out of class	Students feel teacher has no personal interest in them or their learning; some students may believe teacher actively dislikes them or is "out to get them"

Table 2 *continued*

	Teacher is occasionally sarcastic or openly disdainful about students, their level of performance in the course, or their nonacademic interests	Students believe teacher has a low opinion of their ability or motivation to learn course content
	Teacher seems irritated or rushed when students ask questions or drop by, even during office hours	Students generally are afraid to ask questions, and sometimes only the boldest will voice a personal opinion
	Teacher simply announces requirements and policies and seems defensive or angry if they are questioned	Students are motivated to work primarily by a fear of failure or ridicule by the teacher and see assignments as something the teacher imposes on them
	Teacher may be inconsistent and unpredictable, for example, by smiling when saying insulting things about students, by giving backhanded compliments, or by announcing assignments or requirements at the last minute	Even if students are interested in the content, they may dread studying it or may rethink their previous desire to major in the subject
		Students feel uneasy in class or around the teacher and may sometimes experience significant anxiety or anger
		Students are likely to describe teacher as a "bitch" or "bastard"

Combining Dimensions I and II

Table 3 presents the full model in which Dimensions I and II form nine combinations or cells, each representing a unique style of instruction associated with different probabilities that students will learn to their fullest potential from instructors following that style. The nine styles are numbered in ascending order of overall effectiveness, with cell 1 the least effective and cell 9 the most effective.

Keep in mind that the nine styles of teaching are generalizations and will not describe every college teacher exactly; individual instructors may show elements of more than one type. Instructors in cells 1, 2, and 3 are less than fully competent. The "Adequates" will be minimally successful in lecture classes and with relatively compliant students but need increased interpersonal skill to expand the range of students and situations in which they will be effective. Similarly, the "Marginals" need to improve their ability to present material. Teachers in cells 4 and 6 represent the most unusual combinations of skills. The "Socratics" excel at promoting independent work and will be ideal for students and subjects well suited to seminars. Their approach will be inadequate in larger classes requiring lecturing, however. Conversely, the "Intellectual Authorities" will be able to create intellectual excitement and promote achievement in students who are confident in their own abilities and comfortable with these instructors' distant manner, but younger or less able students are likely to experience anxiety under such instruction. An "Intellectual Authority" is more likely to be respected than loved by most students.

All instructors in cells 7, 8, and 9 are outstanding individual who have unquestionably attained excellence at college teaching. Students are likely to describe "Masterful Lecturers" as those who captivate them by sheer intellectual force and motivate them to learn material because it seems a terribly important and exciting thing to do. Students might also describe these cell 8 instructors as a bit mysterious—per-

Table 3
Two-Dimensional Model of Effective College Teaching

Dimension I:	*Dimension II: Interpersonal Rapport*		
Intellectual Excitement	*Low:* Cold, distant, highly controlling, unpredictable	*Moderate:* Relatively warm, approachable, and democratic; predictable	*High:* Warm, open, predictable, and highly student-centered
High: Extremely clear and exciting	*Cell 6: Intellectual Authorities* Outstanding for some students and classes but not for others	*Cell 8: Masterful Lecturers* Especially skilled at large introductory classes	*Cell 9: Complete Masters* Excellent for any student and situation
Moderate: Reasonably clear and interesting	*Cell 3: Adequates* Minimally adequate for many students in lecture classes	*Cell 5: Competents* Effective for most students and classes	*Cell 7: Masterful Facilitators* Especially skilled at smaller, more advanced classes
Low: Vague and dull	*Cell 1: Inadequates* Unable to present material or motivate students well	*Cell 2: Marginals* Unable to present material well but will be liked by some students	*Cell 4: Socratics* Outstanding for some students and situations but not for most

sons they would like to know better. Many students do their best work under such a teacher. However, younger students or those with limited academic skills and confidence are less likely to benefit maximally from what this instructor has to offer.

In contrast, students of "Masterful Facilitators" feel close to their instructors. Such instructors are likely to be able to stimulate independent work of high quality. They are sought out by students after class and are particularly effective in smaller, more advanced classes characterized by considerable discussion. "Masterful Facilitators" are also likely to become important in their students' personal lives; students may come to them for advice or attempt to model their lives or careers after them. Both "Masterful Lecturers" and "Masterful Facilitators" have their fortes, but each is capable of providing competent instruction in all situations.

The rare "Complete Masters" of cell 9 are able to perform superbly in both lecture hall and seminar room and to modify their approach so as to motivate all students, from the brilliant to the mediocre. Few if any of Epstein's portraits reach this degree of flexibility; of teachers I interviewed, I can classify in this cell only one or two.

Most students will do well under any cell 7, 8, or 9 instructor, and are likely to rate all these masterful types highly, but they may prefer one type or the other. Some will be more comfortable with the impersonality of "Masterful Lecturers," preferring to learn someone else's view of the content. On the other hand, students desiring to express their creativity, to tackle learning more independently, or to have more personal relationships and individualized instruction will prefer "Masterful Facilitators."

Outstanding instructors, then, are those who excel at one or both of these two dimensions of teaching effectiveness. Every competent teacher must have at least moderate skill in each dimension, but there is considerable room for variation. My model assumes that some students will learn more under one style of instruction than another but that all students will learn more and prefer college teachers in the masterful cells. It also assumes that instructor skill on Dimensions I and II is distributed normally; that is, that most teachers are competent, falling at the midrange of each dimension, and relatively few are above or below the norm. The lessons in the following chapters are designed to help those with less than adequate skills to improve and those already in the midrange to attain excellence.

Inside Feminist Classrooms: An Ethnographic Approach

FRANCES MAHER AND MARY KAY THOMPSON TETREAULT

The transformational impact of the last two decades of feminist scholarship on the academic disciplines and college curricula has been well documented. Feminist theorists and other postmodern scholars have shown us that all knowledge is a social construction and that the male-dominated disciplines have given us at best partial truths and at worst a discourse that silences or marginalizes other ways of knowing. Thus, feminist postmodernists have called attention to women's positions of oppression in society as sources of legitimate claims to truths, truths obscured heretofore by perceived universals based on the male experience. These theorists argue that only consciously partial perspectives such as those derived from women's various positions within society can guarantee the objectivity of knowledge, an objectivity based not on impartiality but on acknowledgement of particular contexts, experiences, and histories.

The pedagogical implications and classroom enactments of a developing feminist theory of knowledge are now being explored in an ethnographic research project done by the authors that systematically uses feminist theories to examine women as teachers, students, and knowers within the classroom context. Classroom pedagogies and the processes of knowledge construction that are emerging in the classrooms of feminist teachers are important topics to explore because they have wide-reaching implications for teaching and learning.

Feminist Pedagogies

Feminist teaching practices have emerged in the margins of and in sharp contrast to the practices of the traditional college classroom—a context marked by the rational critical discourse of positivism and the search for a single, universal, objective reality. There, students are expected to master materials and arguments and come to rational and objectively verifiable conclusions based on a falsely universal view of the world. At the heart of traditional pedagogy is the goal of mastery: an understanding of the truth of a work, what it really means, and thus an ability to dominate or control it the way that the authorities in the field have traditionally done. While the predominant mode of traditional teaching is lecturing, discussions also tend to aim, via the Socratic method or techniques of critical thinking, to overall generalizations that are meant to subsume or reconcile different points of view. One teacher captured the limitations of this form of teaching:

> I used to come into the classroom with a list of questions and I knew where they were leading. Very Socratic! I don't teach Socratically anymore. I think it's very manipulative. . . . I would get frustrated if the students didn't take the thing in the direction I thought they were supposed to . . . so I missed all these wonderful insights that they have to offer. They may not be able to develop such an insight in as sophisticated a way as you and I can, but they can sometimes come up with the absolute crucial starting point for a really interesting piece of interpretation, and the more they do it, the farther they can take it.

Another problem with traditional pedagogy is that it rewards learning that is associated with rational, objective approaches and as it happens, with male students. Frequently, the mark of success becomes the grade that a student achieves rather than the student's development of the ability to make meaning.

"Inside Feminist Classrooms: An Ethnographic Approach," by Frances Maher and Mary Kay Thompson Tetrault, reprinted from *Teaching For Diversity,* No. 49, edited by L. B. Border and N. Van Note Chism, 1992, Jossey-bass Publishers, Inc.

Belenky, Clinchy, Goldberger, and Tarule (1986) have identified this requirement of mastery as a hallmark of separate, rather than connected, knowing, whereby students learn disciplinary content and methods of analysis on the terms of the dominant culture but forgo—especially in the case of women and minority students—a personal emergence that comes from connecting their education to their own experiences, or from raising and answering their own questions and concerns. One of our female student informants describes how mastery works and her resistance to it: "I went through years of school without saying a word because the professor would ask something and I'd know what he wanted to hear, but I wouldn't tell him."

Feminist pedagogy was originally conceived as an alternative to these traditional pedagogical paradigms. Feminist pedagogy, culturally constituted and ascribed to women in general, has been defined as cooperative rather than competitive, attentive to student experiences, and concerned with the personal and relational aims and sources of knowledge. Its roots have been traced back to both the consciousness-raising groups that launched the women's movement (reframing *the personal is political* to *the personal is educational*) and the pedagogical practices associated with progressive, student-centered, and liberatory models of education.

Since the 1970s, there has been a growing literature on feminist pedagogy that has been useful to many teachers, but the work has been confined to self-reports and has come to seem overly prescriptive (Maher, 1985a, 1985b). The purpose of this chapter, therefore, is to summarize specific practices of two feminist teachers selected from a study of eighteen teachers in six different college environments. Their practices illustrate the wide variety of choices, conflicts, and creative possibilities faced in their classrooms. Here, we examine four issues: mastery of materials and what constitutes knowledge, student voice and identity, authority and the ways in which feminist teachers and students negotiate authority, and positionality, that is, the ways in which an individual's position in the classroom and in society affects learning.

Mastery, Voice, Authority, and Positionality

Our four major themes, *mastery, voice, authority,* and *positionality,* emerged from a complex combination of experience and reflection on data collected over several years of fieldwork. The themes evolved from transcripts of class discussions, conversations with informants, readings in feminist theory, and, finally, an examination of our own personal histories as students, feminist teachers, and feminist researchers over the past decade. (Our thinking about where learning, or mastery, is embedded has also benefited greatly from conversations with Jill Mattuck Tarule.)

Mastery has traditionally meant the goal of rational comprehension of material on the teachers' or experts' terms. In the feminist classrooms described in this chapter, students seek mastery on their own terms and in concert with others. Thus, individual mastery is embedded in the social construction of knowledge—it becomes collaborative, based on interaction among peers, rather than hierarchical. Rather than achieving rational comprehension of the material on the teachers' terms, students make increasingly more sophisticated connections with the topics. Universal notions of "the right answer" give way to notions of mastery as empowerment—an instrument for previously silenced students to "claim an education," to use Adrienne Rich's (1979) expression.

Voice has recently become a metaphor for the emergence of women's consciousness and experiences into the public sphere, symbolizing both personal awakenings and new visions of the world. For the classrooms that we studied, voice connotes the ways in which the students and teachers articulated their own sense of their experiences and their learning. It means speaking for oneself and bringing one's own questions and perspectives to the material. It connotes a connection of one's education to one's personal experience, a connection that women and other oppressed groups must often give up when they seek mastery on the terms of the dominant discourse of traditional pedagogy.

The third theme is that of authority. In traditional classrooms, teachers and students stand in a hierarchical relationship to knowledge and to scholarly expertise. The traditional teacher's authority comes from his or her role as interpreter of the knowledge of experts, who are believed to be closest to the ultimate truth of any event or idea. With new paradigms of knowledge construction that view truth as the product of multiple perspectives, feminist teachers must reevaluate the source and implications of their authority. The issue of authority then becomes problematic and challenges both teachers and students.

Teachers see themselves as facilitators and resources, viewing their expertise as derived from their own individual and collective experience rather than from a superior access to truth. They also see their authority as grounded in their own diverse commitments as feminists, with necessarily partial but still legitimate worldviews.

Positionality encompasses recent feminist thinking about how the validity of knowledge comes from an acknowledgment of the knower's specific position in any context, as defined by gender, race, class, and other variables. Linda Alcoff (1988) calls for an acknowledgment of women's various societal positions as the sources of feminist perspectives, with the concept of positionality replacing a biologically determined essential woman; Sandra Harding (1987) attempts to locate and describe a female standpoint; and Donna Haraway (1988) describes what she calls "situated knowledges," whereby objectivity comes not from a false impartiality but from the acknowledgment of all perspectives as partial and particular. The concept of positionality, first articulated for us by one of our teacher informants, points to contextual and relational factors as crucial for defining not only our identities but also our knowledge as women teachers or students in any given situation. Feminist teaching practices reposition the relationships among teachers, their students, and their materials, producing an epistemological shift away from the teacher as the sole authority and transforming the students' experiences of mastery and voice.

In this chapter we present sketches of two professors' teaching practices in terms of their goals, their classroom techniques, and their students' experiences of the class. To illustrate the ways in which each teacher challenges the traditional classroom by pursuing alternative pedagogies and forms of knowledge construction, we analyzed their teaching in relation to the four themes described above using both classroom transcripts and interviews with the teachers and their students.

Mastery, Authority, and the Construction of Knowledge

We first came to the theme of mastery after observing Laurie Finke, an English professor at Lewis and Clark College in Portland, Oregon. On the first day of class, while introducing her course on literary theory, Finke stressed that students should immerse themselves in the material, jot down in journals questions that arise as they do the reading, and come to class to pool the information that they have gathered, rather than trying to be "master of whatever materials we are reading." This charge to her students to give up mastery in favor of immersion was a way of making them coinvestigators and equals in the exploration of topics in the classroom. She wanted them to construct their own relationships with the materials, to be as active as the instructor in relation to the issues that would be raised.

As the class progressed, discussions usually began with students presenting questions and answers from their journal entries, rather than with Finke's own questions on the material. By instructing the students to ask and answer their own questions, she established an alternative way of constructing knowledge and transformed the role of mastery as a goal of teaching and learning. The practice of beginning with the students' questions rather than with the teachers' is an important innovation in feminist classrooms. The anthropologist Shirley Brice Heath (1983) has observed how heavily teachers have been socialized into thinking that they should teach by asking questions.

In the classroom that we studied, rather than head toward a rational comprehension of the material on the teacher's and experts' terms, Finke sought to enable students to seek learning on their own terms and in concert with others, thus initiating a collective rather than hierarchical learning process. She suggested this goal of collaboration when she said, "And as we come together to pool that information we may come up with more definitive answers." She also wanted her students to feel that "they have equal access to the agenda of the day."

How did students experience this shift toward construction of a collaborative relationship with the material that asked them to recognize their own questions and their own voices? Because the course focused on theory rather than fictional narrative, several of the students were silenced in this class, feeling they could not easily attain the equal access that Finke sought for them. Carole, a traditional student who was preparing to teach high school English, seldom spoke in class. She felt that before she could interact with the materials and participate as an equal in the classroom, she had to "assimilate and understand the material," in short, master it in the traditional sense of that concept. She said, "It's hard for me to do what Laurie wants us to do and criticize it, because I'm just assimilating it, understanding it . . . so I have a hard time contributing. [Yet] it's a great experience. It's the most challenging class I ever had." When, in accordance with our desire to get our teacher informants' views of what was happening in their classrooms, we showed her quotes to the teacher, Finke pointed out that students who have seldom achieved mastery in traditional ways might be especially loath to abandon that approach.

Another student, Jane, who was twenty-eight years old at the time of these observations and also preparing to be a teacher, felt that Finke helped her move through conventional concerns about mastery to a rewarding awakening as she wrote a paper for the college's annual Gender Studies Symposium. Jane described the process this way: "My rough draft was a synthesis of feminist theory in general, but I didn't come up with anything new." Stuck there, she went to Finke, who said, "This one sentence [at the end] is great. It could be the beginning sentence. Start with that sentence and write." Anxiety stricken because her presentation was the next day, Jane went home and went to bed, got up at four o'clock in the morning and wrote until nine o'clock that morning. She reported, "It was all organized. I got up there and read it and it went real well."

The experiences of these two students suggest that it may not be enough to instruct some students, particularly females, to bring their own questions to the materials. They may first need some confirmation that their own concerns and identities are legitimate. The insight of Belenky Clinchy, Goldberger, and Tarule (1986) that women are connected knowers suggests that many female students perceive themselves as having a subjective voice in relation to knowledge, not a separate, rational stance seeking objective truth. They need to make the material part of themselves, first, to assimilate it rather than master it.

Even though female students tended to be more silent than were the males in the class, the two male students that we interviewed talked more about *being* silenced in the class. The women-centered content of Finke's class put male and female students into a different relationship with the material. Male students may feel silenced in feminist classrooms because they are no longer the authorities and the dominant position of males in society is often in question. However, in Finke's class the males were also disturbed by the redefinition of mastery in her pedagogical approach.

The feminist practice of reconceptualizing the construction of knowledge as a collaborative effort did not lead male students to reflect on issues of mastery but rather on issues of authority. Two of the most talkative students, Ned and Robert, were more worried about their own positions vis-a-vis the other students and the teacher authority figure than their own development as learners. In courses with feminist teachers, they were taught to approach discussions in a more collaborative way, and they came to see their positions in these classes as problematic. Ned, the student who initiated the most topics for class discussion and who was a prominent debator on campus, appreciated Finke's democratic style but missed the old challenge of struggling with a dominant authority figure. He said, "I've been in classes where I've been encouraged to go after people. . . . If that class had consisted [of different students], we would have come closer to the level of Laurie's voice and I think we should have made her take back the power she relinquished. I think we would have made her take it back to defend it. . . . It wasn't a debate. There are plenty of people around here who would like to argue with an authoritative voice."

Comments such as these helped us to see authority as another of our major themes. Later in the interview, Ned acknowledged that he admired Finke for empowering students to approach the material with their own questions; yet he longed for combative discourse with an expert more powerful than he. Ned's desire for a debate also suggests, however, that he was still locked into the search for traditional mastery, for the ultimate truth of any event or idea, and into achievement through competitive struggle.

Robert, who was thirty-five years old and who referred to himself as a former member of Students for a Democratic Society, could be heard probing the relationship between gender and discourse when he said, "It's real easy to dominate, and I wouldn't want to do it [in Finke's class]. I mean I walk on eggshells." And Ned said, "If I were to try to be combative where I am one of six males in a class, in some ways I begin to replicate the problems of authority unintentionally. And you just don't want to set up that kind of situation." Both knew that class discussions often reproduce traditional gender relations with males as dominant, and yet they continued to be drawn to the traditional mode of discourse.

This examination of mastery and authority also entails an exploration of the various forms of authority contained in Finke's teaching role, as the expert, the resource, the evaluator, and the facilitator of discussion. How did she use her authority as the teacher to convey knowledge, to direct the course of discussion, and to encourage and to restrain the activities of different students? In the dialogue excerpts that follow, we present an example of an occasion where she engaged with the students' as an equal participant and yet also used her expertise to resolve a dispute by explaining a difficult concept, the concept of positionality.

This class on literary theory was an extended discussion of the ideas of three prominent French feminists—Hélène Cixous, Luce Irigaray, and Julia Kristeva (Moi, 1985). Comparison of their views led the class to question the relationship between gender and social class, and Robert had initiated an extended discussion of this issue by arguing with Jane and a few others that economic oppression was more important than gender oppression. Finke maintained a nonauthoritarian position by going along with their choice of topic and did not direct the discussion for a long time. When the students finally seemed stuck around the issue of gender versus class as primary oppositions, she tried to resolve it by introducing the concept of positionality.

> FINKE: What we need is a description that is not based on categories but, as Kristeva says, on positionality, on relations. In other words, in your example, although women generally are marginal in our culture, the example you give suggests a slightly different position in which the whole question of who is oppressed and who is central and who is marginal depends on its relation to what.
>
> MARGARET: Well, who created it as the center?
>
> FINKE: Well, no group is in and of itself oppressed or marginal. It's only in relation to something else. So that, for instance, women are marginal to men, but black women are marginal compared to white, middle-class women.
>
> NED: And there's no margin without center.
>
> FINKE: There's no center. We are falling into the whole androcentric trap of trying to find the center when what we need is to keep the whole model in motion.

(Later . . .)

> MARGARET: One of the things I thought about when Kristeva was talking about marginality is that positioning relates to man, the center, . . . is going in a straight line.... I think that if Kristeva sort of went one step further, . . . [and] created not only the wedge she talks about in language but a web that goes beyond language. Because in a web a binary opposition doesn't really have a chance to survive.
>
> FINKE: Right. Absolutely.

(Later . . .)

> FINKE: Yeah, you begin to create a margin which then reinscribes the same center margin dichotomy itself and what you need to do is keep deconstructing that, keep seeing it as relational. Keep seeing it as position.
>
> JANE: Do you think that there are ways in which this kind of approach or attitude can be dangerous for feminism in the sense that it sort of opens things up so that patriarchy can use that rationale to its advantage?
>
> FINKE: How?
>
> JANE: I don't know how. That's what I'm asking you guys. Do you think there is a possibility of that?
>
> FINKE: I mean, I tend to.
>
> SAM: [to Jane] It, isn't it sort of defusing the power of the movement sort of? Is that what you mean?
>
> JANE: I don t know what I mean.
>
> FINKE: That exactly comes from that mentality of seeing the women's struggle as being somehow divorced from the racial struggle or the class struggle. A relational kind of thing like this, I think, far from dividing and conquering, would encourage more cross-referencing across those different kinds of struggles. Instead of seeing them all as separate or all as the same struggle, you see a whole series of relationships. I mean, how does feminism keep from creating a white, middle-class feminist movement which is completely ignorant of what is happening in racial struggles or class struggles?

SAM: So, in other words, the division is going to be there and it's better to recognize them than to pretend they are not.

FINKE: Yeah.

JANE: [raises her point again] Your gender determines in some ways how much you can achieve, to some extent, I mean there is a tendency that way because of the binary opposition.

NED: I agree.

FINKE: But the fact is that all those things do. They all work together. You can't privilege one.

JANE: I'm using it as an example.

FINKE: Yeah, you can't privilege one over the other.

The discussion above focused on a collaborative exploration of the issues of gender, race, and class raised by the reading assignment, rather than a mastery of what the materials said. Even though Finke quoted Kristeva (or Moi, 1985), it was as if she were using the text to convey her own sense of the issues involved and her interpretation of them, rather than an authoritative final version. When she invoked the concept of positionality, she used it to resolve a dispute that several students had created. However, she was also using her authority as the teacher in a more subtle way. We thought that she was ignoring Jane's concern about the actual oppression of women in order to keep the theoretical relationships among different oppressions clear. Perhaps her teaching goal of "coming together to come up with more definitive answers" was brought into play here, as she pushed the students to a certain conclusion. And yet Jane hung in there, undaunted, so that the flavor was of an argument among equals rather than of the imposition of one view by the teacher.

Thus, in this excerpt, we see Finke both relinquishing and displaying her authority in several complex ways. She opened the discussion with students' questions rather than her own, and at many points she sat back in order to give the students full rein. When she did come in as the voice of expertise, she did so in order to resolve the dispute over whether women are a class. But even in this context, the students took her on and disputed her on the question of whether deconstruction (or positionality) is dangerous for feminism. Finke stated her position, and she did so at some length, but she expected and was challenged by student responses. In this excerpt, we see her definitions of mastery, namely, giving students equal access to the agenda of the day, being enacted. The students who were willing to take her on engaged with her as peers.

Issues of Voice and Positionality

Our second professor, Dorothy Berkson, also teaches English literature at Lewis and Clark College, where she is presently chair of the department and one of the prominent voices in the Gender Studies Program. One hallmark of her teaching was that she began class by having students read from their journals. Her purpose was to spark engagement, to get students to interact with the assigned texts and with one another, and to explore the positions that they had taken on the readings.

In her interview Berkson described her goals as "empowering students to think for themselves, to ask questions, to challenge virtually everything. . . . Of course I have the agenda of exposing them to feminist ideas. I think exposing them is probably the way I feel, not imposing it on them. It is a way of empowering them and I think it is a way for the male students to ask questions about power too."

The excerpts below are from a class on women writers taught in 1987, which included seventeen women and five men ranging from first-year students to seniors. At the previous class meeting, students had been struggling to interpret Emily Dickinson's poems. Berkson had ended that class by telling the students to go back and reread the poems and to do another journal entry based on what they had learned from the day's discussion. This current class began with her asking if anyone had taken her advice and tried to write about Emily Dickinson. Nancy, a very quiet Japanese American who often sat on the edge of the room, nodded and Berkson asked her to read what she had written. Nancy based her journal entry on the following Dickinson poem (all poetry citations from Johnson, 1967):

I'm Nobody! Who are you?
Are you—Nobody—Too?
Then there's a pair of us?
Don't tell! They'd advertise—
you know!
How dreary—to be—Somebody!
How public—like a frog—
To tell one's name—the live—
long June
to an admiring Bog!

Nancy's journal entry began as follows:

> I couldn't help thinking of the idea of a mute culture within a dominant culture. A "nobody" knowing she's different from the dominant culture keeps silent and is surprised to find out there are others who share this feeling. But they speak only to each other and hide otherwise. This is what it must have been like being a woman and thinking against the grain. But don't tell! At least if you are silent and no one knows, you can continue to live your inner life as you wish, your thoughts at least still belong to you. If "they," the somebodies find out, they'll advertise and you'll have to become one of them.
>
> But to be somebody! How dreary! How public! She says, "To tell one's name the livelong day to an admiring bog!" What is a name? I think she means an easily classifiable public identity. Names don't really tell you anything about what a person is like. So when you become a somebody and buy into the dominant culture, you have to live in their roles. You could call yourself a wife and the admiring bog says lovely, Yes. You could call yourself a spinster even and the bog would still admire you because you fit. But what if you don't want to be any of these things? Well then you stay a nobody. Nobodies, though silent and secretive at least have their peace, their solitude and are free from the judgment of the bog. (This could also be read about genius.)

Nancy was drawing here on what anthropologists Shirley and Edwin Ardener call "the wild zone." In Showalter's account of the Ardeners' conceptualization of culture, she states that women are a "muted group, the boundaries of whose culture and reality overlap but are not wholly contained by the dominant (male) group. Both muted and dominant groups generate beliefs or order ideas of social reality at the unconscious level but dominant groups control the forms or structures in which consciousness can be articulated" (Showalter, 1985, p. 29). Nancy also wrote some comments about the following Dickinson poem:

Before I got my eye put out
I liked as well to see—
As other Creatures, that have
Eyes
And know no other way—

But were it told to me—Today—
That I might have the sky
For mine—I tell you that my
heart
Would split, for size of me—

The Meadows—mine—
The Mountains—mine—
All Forests—Stintless Stars—

As much of Noon as I could
take
Between my finite eyes—

The Motions of the Dipping
Birds
The Morning's Amber Road—
for mine—to look at when I
liked—
The News would strike me dead—

So safer—guess—with must my
soul
Upon the Window pane—
Where other Creatures put their eyes—
Incautious—of the Sun

Nancy wrote the following comments about this poem:

> [Dickinson] said: But let me try to go back to the inner and outer circles of society or rather back to the ideas of the dominant and mute cultures and the dangers and opposition that exists.
>
> Those termed "mad" by the society, while more rewarded on a higher plane, still suffer here. You are either forced to conform and lose that sanity or you live under all sorts of social chains that keep you "still" and quiet, mute.
>
> But looking at [the poem] it's problematic, there is a price to pay, and it isn't always voluntary. Infinite vision seems to come from suffering through enforced pain. "Before I got my eye put out/I liked as well to see—/As other Creatures, that have/Eyes/and know no other way." You can run around in ignorant bliss until something breaks through this level of illusion, take out the "eye" that makes it through it, you can't go back, trying to face yourself backwards would "strike you dead." I'm not articulating this well but it's like growing awareness.
>
> A silly example: It's like watching a Walt Disney film as a child where Hayley Mills and these other girls dance and primp before a party singing "Femininity," how being a woman is all about looking pretty and smiling pretty and acting stupid to attract men. As a child I ate it up—at least it seemed benign, at the most I eagerly studied it. But once your eye gets put out and you realize how this vision has warped you, it would split your heart to try and believe that again, it would strike you dead. Much safer with your soul "upon the window pane."

Nancy's journal reading of the poem stopped the rest of the class dead. Berkson attempted to help the students engage with her ideas by asking Nancy to summarize, but the entry proved too complex for them. After a few of the students made unrelated comments, Berkson reviewed the concept of a mute culture within the dominant culture. She then tried again to draw students into a discussion of Nancy's ideas. When they did not respond, she turned to Nancy, as the authority, who then reiterated the meaning of what she had written. A discussion ensued between two students and Berkson, suggesting that Nancy's journal entry gave voice to all of them and revealed the ways that they thought about their relationship to the dominant culture.

> SUSAN [a white student described as one of the class leaders]: That's because it's like a gift that puts you in the dominant cultural role and then you kind of owe it something, you can't just have it both ways. You can't believe in the subculture because you've got this gift, and if you want to keep it, you've got to stay somebody and that's got a price to pay.
>
> BERKSON: This is really interesting. Anybody else?
>
> MARCY [another Asian-American student]: When I read it, it was more like when she's a nobody, you know she's proud of being a nobody, she's a person, she's someone other than the majority. She had identified with that and she's kind of shocked when she finds that there is actually another person who doesn't want to be part of the majority also. When she says, "Oh how dreary to be somebody," its like oh how dreary to be part of the major-

> ity. You don't stand out, you just kind of like go in and mix with the majority. Whereas when you are a nobody you are someone.
>
> BERKSON: Think about the person who doesn't want to be a member of the majority and who chooses to be a public flake, etcetera, but to be nobody is a different kind of choice, it is really to disappear from that public arena into the private sphere or the wild zone.
>
> MARCY: You don't have to answer to anyone and you just can be yourself.
>
> BERKSON: It's totally on your terms, it doesn't have to be on their terms at all.
>
> MARCY: You are your own individual.
>
> BERKSON: Yes.
>
> NANCY: To add to that of what I thought is just to maintain that, to be able to maintain that, you had to be silent, you couldn't let anyone know, kind of. You have to be really sneaky.
>
> BERKSON: To go back to Nancy's ideas about telling the truth "slant." It is like you don't want to give away too much of the truth in her terms. It can't be told straight out, there is a sense again that the usual structures somehow get slanted, get circumvented, get changed or altered or have to be gone around. The whole concept of the brightness that blinds is a power image for Dickinson.

Nancy's journal entries are a particularly powerful example of a previously silenced student coming to "voice." Nancy's imagery of "a nobody knowing she's different from the dominant culture," breaking through the illusion of "ignorant bliss," all combines to reveal this journal entry as a moment of awakening for her. She connected what she was learning—the Ardeners' concept of a mute culture within a dominant culture and Dickinson's poetry—with her experience as a woman, and perhaps as a minority woman. Nancy's identification with the positions of those who have been profoundly silenced was a perspective informed by and inseparable from her development as a knower and a learner. Her insights were subjective, not attempts at universal "truths."

In the conclusions of her journal entry, Nancy used powerful metaphors to depict her awakening. Her "silly example" implies that she was breaking through the illusion of a Japanese American patterning herself after Hayley Mills, a prototypical, blond teenager from the 1960s, and suggests that she was thinking of ethnicity as well as gender. However, while there are numerous references to gender in this journal entry, there is no explicit mention of race or ethnicity. When we first asked her if her journal entry related to her personal experience, she said that she did not "think about it in terms of an incident. Maybe an overlying personal experience. I really didn't think about that." But later in a follow-up interview she said the following:

> There's no way that it could not, because obviously it had to connect to something and even I think the fact that when I put in about the example—I don't think there's a way you could be able to think about that sort of a concept of culture if you have not felt like you've lived it. . . . You know just even thinking in terms of race, even thinking about different kinds of minority perspectives, I guess, things like that I think I've started to look more into experience instead of just thinking about these theories. . . . I think that is something that sort of came out of this class. . . . I really have grown up in this community where everybody is blond and tall. . . . We are the only Japanese people, and since we never had really any Japanese community, I was never aware of that aspect in myself. Which doesn't mean that that didn't have any influence on the interactions, it just meant that I was not aware of that as influencing.

Thus, while her ethnic position had not been mentioned in the class discussion, Nancy later began to think about "looking more into" her ethnic experience as a result of Berkson's class. This novelty suggests how little Nancy's previous education had attended to issues of race or ethnicity.

We see this class session as particularly evocative of the themes of positionality and voice. Not only did Nancy speak from the explicit position of someone on the margins, but Berkson here *repositioned* her own relationship to the students and the students' relationship to the materials, beginning when the students, not Berkson, raised questions and set the agenda. The first voice to be taken seriously was a student's. By acknowledging Nancy's responses to Dickinson, her powerful connection to her own experience, Berkson let in the disruptive voices, the voices from the wild zone. Nancy's journal entry opened up new truths for other students, truths coming from different perspectives, thus exposing the shortcomings of any purportedly universalized, single truth.

The influence of Berkson's repositioning was observed in several other ways as well. First, while some students contributed frequently and consistently to classroom discussions, quieter students such as Nancy spoke more after they had read from their journals. Second, while female students learned to see their positions as women (and minorities) as generating newly valid knowledge about the world, male students became more conscious of power relations in the classroom and learned to listen. Duke, one of the five males in the class, spoke in his interview about the importance of hearing female voices. He was interested in finding out how "women feel about these texts": "I could read Dickinson a thousand times and probably never try to relate to that because it just would never make an impression on me, but having the girls in that class interested in that particular topic—'How does that relate to me as a woman?'—then I sit back and I think that's a really good question, and although I'm male I can sit and learn something from this and learn how women react to women's texts as opposed to maybe the way I react to it or Dorothy reacts to it or something like that." As Duke's comment shows, this empowering of females occasioned a fundamental change in the males' positions as well.

Nancy's journal entry also turned out to be a revelatory moment for Berkson. Although issues of race and ethnicity were implicit in Nancy's striking metaphorical connection to Hayley Mills, and in Berkson's comments, issues of race and ethnicity were not explicitly discussed that day. Berkson, however, recognized immediately that the students who had the most profound response to Dickinson's representation of a mute culture were the Japanese-American women. This led her, a few days after the Dickinson discovery, to share her thinking about the limitations of the syllabus with her students: "I told the class today, the thing that is really wrong with this course is that it is too Wasp, too Wasp, too British-American mainstream women writers, and I really need to think about that and how to change that. You know, I just don't think that the issues of race and gender and the way that different groups are disempowered or lose their voices can be really separated and those issues have been touched on in the course, but not enough. White women writers are overrepresented. I really want to do something about that."

Thus, through her reliance on student journals to determine the direction of class discussions, Berkson gave Nancy a chance to create and display a new reading of Emily Dickinson's poems, a reading from the explicit standpoint of a woman and the implicit standpoint of a Japanese American. The awakening of this student's voice produced changes in others' positions as well—the males' views were no longer at the center of the discourse and the teacher herself was inspired to change her syllabus. Moreover, this class was able to construct knowledge out of the intersection of new and partial truths, truths coming from the explicit identification of perspectives not heard before as "gendered" and "cultured" voices.

Conclusion

How can we summarize the ways that these two teachers constructed their alternative pedagogies? In the traditional classroom, to oversimplify things a bit, teachers' pedagogical choices are the guiding theories and worldview of a particular discipline. However, feminist theorists (and postmodernists) say that all worldviews are necessarily limited, that truth is partial. Depending on one's position, truth is gendered, raced, and classed. It is also dependent on context, including the context of the classroom, so that, for example, a woman's text and a feminist teacher may bring new truths forward while marginalizing others that used to occupy center stage.

If truth is partial, dependent on context, and yet, paradoxically, available to us through attention to particular positions and the lenses that they employ, then feminist teachers must be newly conscious of some aspects of teaching hidden from us by the traditional paradigms. One aspect is that we are particular (and evolving) knowers—the sources of our authority lie in our experience and our history, not centrally in our greater mastery of the abstract universals of our disciplines. A second aspect is that along with the illusion of perfect mastery, there is the illusion of the perfect teacher. In the literature on feminist pedagogy, for example, we constructed her as the consummate feminist, a teacher who is cooperative, compassionate yet demanding, and open-minded yet clear and resolute.

In the real situations of real classrooms, in the face of the need to make specific choices based on their own positions and the backgrounds and needs of their students, our two teachers took particular stands, at odds with traditional forms but also different from each other. While these two professors used student journals to start discussions, their choice of readings in their courses set the terms for the very different directions that they took. Dorothy Berkson, out of her commitment to women's awakening voices, used women's literature to consciously empower her students and evoke voices from the margins of traditional discourse, but she also allowed herself to evolve from a white woman's standpoint as a result of learning from minority women's experiences. Laurie Finke's literary theory course sought to get the theory clear, to come to a kind of definitive closure more usually associated with traditional models of teaching. And yet, on the day cited here, the theory itself was about partial truths, about gender and race and class as relational, positional, and changing in dynamic contexts. In creating this clarity, however, Finke seemed to ignore at one point the material condition of women as articulated by a persistent Jane.

As each teacher made her choices, she repositioned the relationships among herself, the students, and the material, away from herself as authority and toward learning as a function of complex interactions among teacher and student voices. These choices had different effects on different students, that is, different students learned different things. Nancy, awakened by Berkson and by Emily Dickinson, taught Duke, who was not used to a woman's perspective (or, we would guess, of thinking of himself as having a particular perspective). Finke energized Ned, Sam, and Jane through their give and take, but Carole felt both challenged and silenced in the same class.

So what questions do such teaching practices raise for issues of pedagogy in general? Our own meanings as teachers are evolving these days, as we attempt to listen to our students' questions and to keep up with the shifting grounds of gendered knowledge construction in our disciplines. Our student bodies are already over 50 percent female and are becoming increasingly ethnically diverse; this multiplicity of student backgrounds gives us a constantly expanding set of perspectives to contend with and honor as valid. Feminist approaches are not a panacea, or even a ready-made set of techniques. Rather, they are ways of dealing with difficult and recurrent choices between confusion and complexity, on the one hand, and clarity at the expense of some people's voices, on the other. The solutions nowadays are to be sought at the level of process, and in terms of the demands and goals of a particular teacher and classroom. Therefore, we believe that the most useful and evocative texts about feminist pedagogy are probably ethnographic in nature, detailing the specifics of teaching in different contexts. Finally, if the goals of gender integration are really to empower all our students, then we have to seek this empowerment not only at the level of course content but also at the level of our pedagogy. As teachers, we need to acknowledge our own development as a process, our own truths as partial, and yet affirm our own commitments and experiences as the only valid bases for our authority. Then we can respond to the multiple and interacting perspectives given by our students' voices and create new processes of knowledge construction beyond the traditional paradigms.

References

Alcoff, L. "Cultural Feminism Versus Post-Structuralism: The Identity Crisis in Feminist Theory." *Signs*, 1988, *13* (3), 405–436.

Belenky, M.F, Clinchy, B.M., Goldberger, N.R., and Tarule, J.M. *Women's Ways of Knowing: The Development of Self, Body, and Mind.* New York: Basic Books, 1986.

Haraway, D. "Situated Knowledges: The Science Question in Feminism and Privilege of Partial Perspective." *Feminist Studies*, 1988, *14* (3), 575–599.

Harding, S. *The Science Question in Feminism.* Ithaca, N.Y.: Cornell University Press, 1987.

Heath, S.B. *Ways With Words: Language, Life, and Work in Communities and Classrooms.* New York: Cambridge University Press, 1983.

Johnson, T.H. (ed.). *Complete Poems of Emily Dickinson.* New York: Macmillan, 1967.

Maher, F. "Classroom Pedagogy and the New Scholarship on Women." In M. Culley and C. Portuges (eds.), *Gendered Subjects: The Dynamics of Feminist Teaching.* London, England: Routledge & Kegan Paul, 1985a.

Maher, F. "Pedagogies for the Gender Balanced Classroom." *Journal of Thought*, 1985b, *20* (3), 48–64.

Moi, T. *Sexual/Textual Politics: Feminist Literary Theory.* London, England: Methuen, 1985.

Rich, A. "Claiming an Education." In *On Lies, Secrets and Silences: Selected Prose, 1966–1978.* New York: Norton, 1979.

Showalter, E. (ed.). "Feminist Criticism in the Wilderness." In *The New Feminist Criticism: Essays on Women, Literature, and Theory.* New York: Pantheon, 1985.

What It Means to Be a Critically Reflective Teacher

STEPHEN D. BROOKFIELD

We teach to change the world. The hope that undergirds our efforts to help students learn is that doing this will help them act toward each other, and toward their environment, with compassion, understanding, and fairness. But our attempts to increase the amount of love and justice in the world are never simple, never unambiguous. What we think are democratic, respectful ways of treating people can be experienced by them as oppressive and constraining. One of the hardest things teachers have to learn is that the sincerity of their intentions does not guarantee the purity of their practice. The cultural, psychological, and political complexities of learning and the ways in which power complicates all human relationships (including those between students and teachers) mean that teaching can never be innocent.

Teaching innocently means thinking that we're always understanding exactly what it is that we're doing and what effect we're having. Teaching innocently means assuming that the meanings and significance we place on our actions are the ones that students take from them. At best, teaching this way is naive. At worst, it induces pessimism, guilt, and lethargy. Since we never have full awareness of our motives and intentions, and since we frequently misread how others perceive our actions, an uncritical stance toward our practice sets us up for a lifetime of frustration. Nothing seems to work out as it should. Our continuing inability to control what looks like chaos becomes, to our eyes, evidence of our incompetence.

The need to break this vicious circle of innocence and blame is one reason why the habit of critical reflection is crucial for teachers' survival. Without a critically reflective stance toward what we do, we tend to accept the blame for problems that are not of our own making. We think that all resistance to learning displayed by students is caused by our own insensitivity or unpreparedness. We read poor evaluations of our teaching (often written by only a small minority of our students) and immediately conclude that we're hopeless failures. We become depressed when ways of behaving toward students and colleagues that we think are democratic and respectful are interpreted as aloof or manipulative. A critically reflective stance toward our teaching helps us avoid these traps of demoralization and self-laceration. It might not win us easy promotion or bring us lots of friends, but it does enormously increase the chance that we will survive in the classroom with enough energy and sense of purpose to have some real effect on those we teach.

Reflection as Hunting Assumptions

Critical reflection is one particular aspect of the larger process of reflection. To understand critical reflection properly, we need first to know something about the reflective process in general. As Figure 2.1 in Chapter Two shows, the most distinctive feature of the reflective process is its focus on hunting assumptions.

Assumptions are the taken-for-granted beliefs about the world and our place within it that seem so obvious to us as not to need stating explicitly. In many ways, we *are* our assumptions. Assumptions give meaning and purpose to who we are and what we do. Becoming aware of the implicit assumptions that frame how we think and act is one of the most challenging intellectual puzzles we face in our lives. It is

"What It Means to Be a Critically Reflective Teacher," (Chapter 1), by Stephen D. Brookfield, reprinted from *Becoming a Critically Reflective Teacher,* 1995, Jossey-Bass Publishers, Inc.

also something we instinctively resist, for fear of what we might discover. Who wants to clarify and question assumptions she or he has lived by for a substantial period of time, only to find that they don't make sense? What makes the process of assumption hunting particularly complicated is that assumptions are not all of the same character. I find it useful to distinguish between three broad categories of assumptions—paradigmatic, prescriptive, and causal.

Paradigmatic assumptions are the hardest of the three kinds to uncover. They are the basic structuring axioms we use to order the world into fundamental categories. We may not recognize them as assumptions, even after they've been pointed out to us. Instead, we insist that they're objectively valid renderings of reality, the facts we know to be true. Some paradigmatic assumptions I have held at different stages of my life as a teacher are that adults are self-directed learners, that critical thinking is an intellectual function characteristic of adult life, that good adult educational processes are inherently democratic, and that education always has a political dimension. Paradigmatic assumptions are examined critically only after a great deal of resistance to doing so, and it takes a considerable amount of contrary evidence and disconfirming experiences to change them. But when they are challenged and changed, the consequences for our lives are explosive.

Prescriptive assumptions are assumptions about what we think ought to be happening in a particular situation. They are the assumptions that surface as we examine how we think teachers should behave, what good educational processes should look like, and what obligations students and teachers owe to each other. Inevitably, they are grounded in, and extensions of, our paradigmatic assumptions. For example, if you take it for granted that adults are self-directed learners, then you assume that the best teaching is that which encourages students to take control over designing, conducting, and evaluating their own learning.

Causal assumptions help us understand how different parts of the world work and the conditions under which processes can be changed. They are usually stated in predictive terms. An example of a causal assumption is that if we use learning contracts, this will increase students' self-directedness. Another is that if we make mistakes in front of students, this creates a trustful environment for learning, in which students feel free to make errors with no fear of censure or embarrassment. Of all the assumptions we hold, causal ones are the easiest to uncover. Most of the reflective exercises described in this book will, if they work well, clarify teachers' causal assumptions. But discovering and investigating these is only the start of the reflective process. We must then try to find a way to work back to the more deeply embedded prescriptive and paradigmatic assumptions we hold.

Hunting Assumptions: Some Examples

One way to demonstrate the benefits of the reflective habit is to point out what happens when it is absent. Without this habit, we run the continual risk of making poor decisions and bad judgments. We take action on the basis of assumptions that are unexamined and we believe unquestioningly that others are reading into our actions the meanings that we intend. We fall into the habits of justifying what we do by reference to unchecked "common sense" and of thinking that the unconfirmed evidence of our own eyes is always accurate and valid. "Of course we know what's going on in our classrooms," we say to ourselves. "After all, we've been doing this for years, haven't we?" Yet unexamined common sense is a notoriously unreliable guide to action.

Consider the following examples of how commonsense assumptions inform action. All these assumptions and actions are probably familiar to readers, particularly those who see themselves as progressive. After each example of a commonsense assumption, I give a plausible alternative interpretation that calls its validity into question.

> It's common sense to visit small groups after you've set them a task, since this demonstrates your commitment to helping them learn. Visiting groups is an example of respectful, attentive, student-centered teaching.

Visiting small groups after you've set them a task can seem like a form of assessment—a way of checking up to see whether they're doing what you told them to do. This can be insulting to students, since it implies that you don't trust them enough to do what you've asked. Students might change their behavior during your visit to their group as a way of impressing you with the kinds of behaviors they think you want to see. Their overwhelming concern is showing you what good, efficient, task-oriented learners they are rather than thoughtfully analyzing and critiquing the task at hand.

> It's common sense to cut lecturing down to a minimum, since lecturing induces passivity in students and kills critical thinking.

Before students can engage critically with ideas and actions, they may need a period of assimilation and grounding in a subject area or skill set. Lecturing may be a very effective way of ensuring this. Before students can be expected to think critically, they must see this process modeled in front of their eyes. A lecture in which a teacher questions her own assumptions, acknowledges ethical dilemmas hidden in her position, refers to inconvenient theories, facts, and philosophies that she has deliberately overlooked, and demonstrates an openness to alternative viewpoints encourages students to do likewise. Through lectures that stimulate critical analysis, a teacher sets a tone for learning. By first modeling the process herself, she earns the right to ask students to think critically.

> It's common sense to use learning contracts because they are democratic, cooperative forms of assessment that give students a sense of control and independence.

Unless the ground for learning contracts has been well prepared and a detailed case for them has been built, students may interpret their use as evidence of a teacher's laziness or of a laissez-faire intellectual relativism. Students can make informed decisions about what they need to know, how they can know it, and how they can know that they know it only on the basis of as full as possible an understanding of the learning terrain they are being asked to explore. Learning contracts should therefore be used only when students know the grammar of the activity. They should understand its internal rules of inquiry, the analytical processes it requires, and the criteria used to judge meritorious achievement in the area. Only if they know these can they make good choices about what and how to learn.

> It's common sense that students like group discussion because they feel involved and respected in such a setting. Discussion methods build on principles of participatory, active learning.

Democratic discourse—the ability to talk and listen respectfully to those who hold views different from our own—is a habit that is rarely learned or practiced in daily life. When discussion groups form, they reflect power dynamics and communicative inequities in the larger society. They also provide a showcase for egomaniacal grandstanding. Students will be highly skeptical of group discussion if the teacher has not earned the right to ask students to work this way by first modeling her own commitment to the process. One way to do this might be by holding several public discussions with colleagues early on in a course. In these discussions, teachers would model respectful disagreement and constructive criticism. Teachers would then work with students to create ground rules for democratic discourse that correct, as much as possible, for the inequities of race, class, and gender that are inevitably imported into the group from the wider society.

> It's common sense that respectful, empathic teachers will downplay their position of presumed superiority and acknowledge their students as coteachers .

To students who have made great sacrifices to attend an educational activity, a teacher's attempts to deconstruct her authority through avowals of how she'll learn more from the students than they will from her rings of false modesty. Students know teachers have particular expertise, experience, skill, and knowledge. To pretend otherwise is to insult students' intelligence and to create a tone of mistrust from the outset. Students will feel happy with their role as coteachers only after the teacher's credibility has been established to their satisfaction and after they have learned what she stands for.

> It's common sense that teaching is essentially mysterious, so if we try to dissect it or understand its essence, we will kill it.

Viewing teaching as a process of unfathomable mystery removes the necessity to think about what we do. Although a serious inquiry into practice may appear reductionistic and asinine, the teaching-as-mystery metaphor can be used as a convenient shield for incompetence. It excuses teachers from having to answer such basic questions as "How do you know when you are teaching well?" "How do you know your students are learning?" and "How could your practice be made more responsive?" To see teaching as mysterious works against the improvement of practice. If good and bad teaching are simply a matter of chance, then there is no point in trying to do better. The teaching-as-mystery idea also closes down the possibility of teachers sharing knowledge, insights, and informal theories of practice, since mystery is, by definition, incommunicable.

> It's common sense that teachers who have been working the longest have the best instincts about what students want and what approaches work best. If my own instincts as a novice conflict with what experienced teachers tell me is true, I should put these instincts aside and defer to the wisdom of their experience.

Length of experience does not automatically confer insight and wisdom. Ten years of practice can be one year's worth of distorted experience repeated ten times. The "experienced" teacher may be caught within self-fulfilling interpretive frameworks that remain closed to any alternative perspectives. Experience that is not subject to critical analysis is an unreliable and sometimes dangerous source of advice. "Experienced" teachers can collude in promoting a form of groupthink about teaching that serves to distance them from students and to bolster their own sense of superiority.

The assumptions just outlined are, in certain situations, entirely valid. Their apparent clarity and truth explain why they are so widely accepted. But as we can see, there are quite plausible arguments to be made against each of them. Central to the reflective process is this attempt to see things from a variety of viewpoints. Reflective teachers seek to probe beneath the veneer of a commonsense reading of experience. They investigate the hidden dimensions of their practice and become aware of the omnipresence of power.

What Makes Reflection Critical?

One of the consequences of a concept's popularity is an increased malleability in its meaning. As interest in reflective practice has widened, so have the interpretations given to it. Smyth (1992) and Zeichner (1994) have both pointed out that the concept becomes meaningless if people use it to describe any teaching they happen to like. In Zeichner's words: "It has come to the point now where the whole range of beliefs about teaching, learning, schooling, and the social order have become incorporated into the discourse about reflective practice. Everyone, no matter what his or her ideological orientation, has jumped on the bandwagon at this point, and has committed his or her energies to furthering some version of reflective teaching practice" (1994, p. 9).

Reflection is not, by definition, critical. It is quite possible to teach reflectively while focusing solely on the nuts and bolts of classroom process. For example, we can reflect about the timing of coffee breaks, whether to use blackboards or flip charts, the advantages of using a liquid crystal display (LCD) panel over previously prepared overheads, or how rigidly we stick to a deadline for the submission of students' assignments. All these decisions rest on assumptions that can be identified and questioned, and all of them can be looked at from different perspectives. But these are not, in and of themselves, examples of *critical* reflection.

Just because reflection is not critical does not mean it is unimportant or unnecessary. We cannot get through the day without making numerous technical decisions concerning timing and process. These decisions are made rapidly and instinctively. They are also usually made without an awareness of how the apparently isolated and idiosyncratic world of the classroom embodies forces, contradictions, and structures of the wider society. Reflection on the timing of breaks would become critical only if the right of teachers and administrators to divide learning up into organizationally manageable periods of time was questioned. Critical reflection on the merits of blackboards, flip charts, or LCD panels would name and investigate educators' and students' unequal access to technology. Reflection about the deadlines for students' submission of papers that led to an investigation and questioning of the sources of authority underlying the establishment of criteria of evaluation would be reflection that was critical.

What is it, then, that makes this kind of reflection critical? Is it a deeper, more intense, and more probing form of reflection? Not necessarily. Critical reflection on experience certainly does tend to lead to the uncovering of paradigmatic, structuring assumptions But the depth of a reflective effort does not, in and of itself, make it critical. To put it briefly, reflection becomes critical when it has two distinctive purposes. The first is to understand how considerations of power undergird, frame, and distort educational processes and interactions. The second is to question assumptions and practices that seem to make our teaching lives easier but actually work against our own best long-term interests.

Critical Reflection as the Illumination of Power

An awareness of how the dynamics of power permeate all educational processes helps us realize that forces present in the wider society always intrude into the classroom. Classrooms are not limpid, tranquil ponds, cut off from the river of social, cultural, and political life. They are contested spaces—whirlpools containing the contradictory crosscurrents of struggles for material superiority and ideological legitimacy that exist in the world outside. When we become aware of the pervasiveness of power, we start to notice the oppressive dimensions to practices that we had thought were neutral or even benevolent. We start to explore how power *over* learners can become power *with* learners (Kreisberg, 1992). Becoming alert to the oppressive dimensions of our practice (many of which reflect an unquestioned acceptance of values, norms, and practices defined for us by others) is often the first step in working more democratically and cooperatively with students and colleagues.

Let me give some examples of critical reflection focused on unearthing the ways in which the dynamics of power invade and distort educational processes.

The Circle

No practice is more beloved of progressive educators than that of having students sit in a circle rather than in rows. The circle is seen as a physical manifestation of democracy, a group of peers facing each other as respectful equals. Teachers like the circle because it draws students into conversation and gives everyone a chance to be seen and heard. Doing this respects and affirms the value of students' experiences. It places their voices front and center. In my own teaching, the circle has mostly been an unquestioned given.

However, as Gore (1993) points out, the experience of being in a circle is ambiguous. For students who are confident, loquacious, and used to academic culture, the circle holds relatively few terrors. It is an experience that is congenial, authentic, and liberating. But for students who are shy, self-conscious about their different skin color, physical appearance, or form of dress, unused to intellectual discourse, intimidated by disciplinary jargon and the culture of academe, or embarrassed by their lack of education, the circle can be a painful and humiliating experience. These students have been stripped of their right to privacy. They have also been denied the chance to check teachers out by watching them closely before deciding whether or not they can be trusted. Trusting teachers is often a necessary precondition for students' speaking out. This trust only comes with time, as teachers are seen to be consistent, honest, and fair. Yet the circle, with its implicit pressure to participate and perform, may deny the opportunity for this trust to develop.

So, beneath the circles democratic veneer, there may exist a much more troubling and uncertain reality. Students in a circle may feel implicit or explicit pressure from peers and teachers to say something, anything, just to be noticed, particularly if part of their grade is awarded for participation. Whether or not they feel ready to speak or whether or not they have anything particular they want to say becomes irrelevant. The circle can be experienced as a mechanism for mandated disclosure, just as much as it can be a chance for people to speak in an authentic voice. This is not to suggest that we throw the circle out and go back to the dark days of teachers talking uninterruptedly at rows of desks. I continue to use the circle in my own practice. But critical reflection makes me aware of the circle's oppressive potential and reminds me that I must continually research how it is experienced by students.

Teachers at One with Students

Teachers committed to working democratically often declare their "at-one-ness" with students. Believing themselves and their students to be moral equals, they like to say to them, "I'm no different from you, so treat me as your equal. Act as if I wasn't a teacher, but a friend. The fact that there's a temporary imbalance between us in terms of how much I know about this subject is really an accident. We're colearners and coteachers, you and I." However, culturally learned habits of reliance on, or hostility toward, authority figures (especially those from the dominant culture) cannot so easily be broken.

Like it or not, in the strongly hierarchical culture of higher education, with its power imbalances and its clear demarcation of roles and boundaries, teachers cannot simply wish away students' perception of their superior status. No matter how much they might want it to be otherwise, and no matter how informal, friendly, and sincere toward students they might be in their declarations of "at-one-ness," teachers *are* viewed as different, at least initially. Critically aware teachers will reject as naive the assumption that by saying you're the students' friend and equal, you thereby become so. Instead, they will research how their actions are perceived by their students and will try to understand the meaning and symbolic significance students ascribe to the things teachers say and do. They will come to realize that any authentic collaboration can happen only after they have spent considerable time earning students' trust by acting democratically and respectfully toward them.

The Teacher as Fly on the Wall

Teachers committed to a vision of themselves as nondirective facilitators of learning, or as resource people present only to serve needs defined by students, often adopt the "fly on the wall" approach to teaching. They will put students into groups, give only minimal instructions about what should happen, and then retreat from the scene to let students work as they wish. However, this retreat is only partial. Teachers rarely leave the room for long periods of time. Instead, they sit at their desk, or off in a corner, observing groups get started on their projects.

For students to pretend that a teacher is not in the room is almost impossible. Knowing that a teacher is nearby will cause some students to perform as good, task-oriented members of the group. Others will just clam up for fear of saying or doing something stupid while a teacher is watching. Students will wonder how the teacher thinks they're doing and will be observing him or her closely for any clues to approval or censure. Students' awareness of the power relationship that exists between themselves and their teachers is such that it pervades nearly all interactions between them.

A teacher cannot be a fly on the wall if that means being an unobtrusive observer. If you say nothing, this will be interpreted either as a withholding of approval or as tacit agreement. Students will always be wondering what your opinion is about what they're doing. Better to give some brief indication of what's on your mind than to have students obsessed with whether your silence means disappointment or satisfaction with their efforts. Critically reflective teachers will make sure that they find some way of regularly seeing what they do through students' eyes. As a result of learning about the different ways in which students view the teacher's silence, they will be in a much better position to make sure that their fly-on-the-wall presence has the helpful consequences they seek. They will learn when and how much to disclose, and they will know about the confidence-inducing effects of such disclosure. They will also know when keeping their own counsel leads to students' doing some productive reflection, and when it paralyzes them.

Discussion as Spontaneous Combustion

Teachers who, like myself, use discussion extensively often have particular image of an ideal discussion session. Usually, this is of a conversation in which the teacher says very little because students are talking so much. There is little silence in the room. What conversation there is focuses on relevant issues, and the level of discourse is suitably sophisticated. The Algonquin Roundtable, a Bloomsbury dinner party, a Woody Allen film script—these are the models for good conversation. Discussions in which teachers are mostly silent are often regarded as the best discussions of all. We walk away from animated conversations dominated by students' voices with a sense that our time has been well spent.

This sense may be justified. But other readings of these discussions are possible. It may well be that by standing back and not intervening in the conversation, we have allowed the reinforcement of differences of status existing in the wider society. As Doyle (1993) puts it, "The teacher closing a classroom door does not shut out the social, cultural, or historical realities of students" (p. 6). Students who see themselves as members of minority groups and whose past experiences have produced legitimate fears about how they will be treated in an academic culture may hold back. Out of a fear of being browbeaten by students of privilege, or from a desire not to look stupid, they may elect for silence (Fassinger, 1995). This silence will be broken only if a teacher intervenes to create a structured opportunity for all group members to say something. Also, students who are introverts, or those who need time for reflective analysis, may find the pace of conversation intimidating. In this instance, inequity caused by personality or learning style, rather than that caused by race, class, or gender, may be distorting what seems to be a conversation characterized by excitement and spontaneity.

A critically reflective teacher will be concerned to check whether or not her sense of pleasure in a discussion is matched by that of students. Such a teacher will find a way of conducting a regular emotional audit of how the conversation is experienced. On the basis of what she learns, she will be able to make a more informed decision about when her silence enhances students' sense of participating in a spontaneous experience. She will be better placed to know when to structure participation or when to call for silent reflective interludes.

The Mandated Confessional

Student journals, portfolios, and learning logs are all the rage among teachers who advocate experiential methods. Teachers believe that encouraging students to speak personally and directly about their experiences honors and encourages their authentic voices. That this often happens is undeniable. However, journals, portfolios, and logs also have the potential to become ritualistic and mandated confessionals (Usher and Edwards, 1995)—the educational equivalents of the tabloidlike, sensationalistic outpourings of talk show participants.

Students who sense that their teacher is a strong advocate of experiential methods may pick up the implicit message that good students reveal dramatic private episodes in their lives that lead to transformative insights. Students who don't have anything painful, traumatic, or exciting to confess may start to feel that their journal falls short. Not being able to produce revelations of sufficient intensity, they may decide to invent some, or they may start to paint quite ordinary experiences with a sheen of transformative significance. A lack of dramatic experiences or insights may be perceived by students as a sign of failure—an indication that their lives are somehow incomplete and lived at a level that is insufficiently self-aware or exciting.

A teacher committed to critical reflection will constantly inquire into how her students perceive her use of experiential methods such as journals, portfolios, and logs. She will get inside their heads to check whether her instructions are inadvertently encouraging them to produce certain kinds of revelations. If she discovers that this is the case, she will take steps to address the issue publicly. By adjusting the reward system, she will model a rejection of the belief that the more sensational the revelation, the better the grade.

Respect for Voice "I Want to Hear Your Opinion, Not Mine"

Teachers committed to democratic classrooms often believe that speaking too much or expressing their own opinions will create in students' minds a stock of "acceptable" beliefs that parrot those held by the teacher. They believe that declaring their own biases and perspectives encourages students to gain teacher approval by uncritically regurgitating these rather than thinking issues through for themselves. So, when faced with students who ask the question, "What do you think?", teachers will sometimes reply along the following lines: "Well, it's not important what *I* think, but it is important that *you* think this through by yourself. So I'm not going to tell you what I think until you've had the chance to air your own ideas." Done well, as in the "dialogic lecture" (Shor, 1992b), this withholding of opinions can encourage students' independence of thought. Done unreflectively, however, this apparently emancipatory prompt to critical analysis can induce mistrust and shut down learning.

From a student's viewpoint, teachers who withhold expression of their own opinions may be perceived as untrustworthy. Given the power relationship that pertains in a college classroom, teachers who refuse to say what they think can be seen as engaged in a manipulative game, the purpose of which is to trick students into saying the wrong thing. Students know that the teacher has the right answer, but for some reason it is not being given to them. Instead, the teacher is seen to be holding back the information that would enable them to perform well. He is asking students to risk declaring their own thinking without making public what he believes.

A critically reflective teacher would know the power—both positive and negative—of his withholding of speech. By examining his students' experiences, he would learn how to time his interventions more skillfully. By asking students about their best and worst experiences as learners, he would probably learn the importance of first modeling any risk-taking that he intends to request of students.

Critical Reflection as the Recognition of Hegemonic Assumptions

The second purpose of critical reflection is to uncover hegemonic assumptions. Hegemonic assumptions are those that we think are in our own best interests but that have actually been designed by more powerful others to work against us in the long term. As proposed by Antonio Gramsci (1978), the term *hegemony* describes the process whereby ideas, structures, and actions come to be seen by the majority of people as wholly natural, preordained, and working for their own good, when in fact they are constructed and transmitted by powerful minority interests to protect the status quo that serves those interests. The subtle tenacity of hegemony lies in the fact that, over time, it becomes deeply embedded, part of the cultural air we breathe. We cannot peel back the layers of oppression and identify any particular group or groups of people actively conspiring to keep others silent and disenfranchised. Instead, the ideas and practices of hegemony are part and parcel of everyday life—the stock opinions, conventional wisdom, and commonsense ways of seeing and ordering the world that many of us take for granted. If there is a conspiracy here, it is the conspiracy of the normal.

Hegemonic assumptions about teaching are eagerly embraced by teachers. They seem to represent what's good and true and therefore to be in their own best interests. Yet these assumptions actually have the effect of serving the interests of groups that have little concern for teachers' mental or physical health. The dark irony and cruelty of hegemony is that teachers take pride in acting on the very assumptions that work to enslave them. In working diligently to implement these assumptions, teachers become willing prisoners who lock their own cell doors behind them.

Critically reflective teachers are alert to hegemonic assumptions. Ideas about "good teaching" that may seem obvious, even desirable, are revealed as harmful and constraining. These teachers are able to see the insanity of aspiring to ways of teaching that, in the end, seriously threaten their own well-being. Let me give some examples of the kind of hegemonic assumptions I am talking about.

Teaching as a Vocation

Teachers sometimes speak of their work as a vocation. Thought of this way, teaching is a calling distinguished by selfless service to students and educational institutions. That teachers sometimes eagerly accept concepts of vocation and conscientiousness to justify their taking on backbreaking loads is evident from Campbell and Neill's studies (1994a, 1994b) of teachers' work. A sense of calling becomes distorted to mean that teachers should deal with larger and larger numbers of students, regularly teach overload courses, serve on search, alumni, and library committees, generate external funding by winning grant monies, and make occasional forays into scholarly publishing. And they should do all of this without complaining, which is the same as "whining."

Teachers who take the idea of vocation as the organizing concept for their professional lives may start to think of any day on which they don't come home exhausted as a day wasted—or at least a day when they have not been "all that they can be." (It's interesting that so many teachers have adopted a slogan to describe their work that first appeared in commercials for army recruitment.) Diligent devotion to the college's many ends—some of which are bound to be contradictory—may come to be seen as the mark of a good teacher.

Thus what seems on the surface to be a politically neutral idea on which all could agree—that teaching is a vocation calling for dedication and hard work—may be interpreted by teachers as meaning that they should squeeze the work of two or three jobs into the space where one can sit comfortably. "Vocation" thus becomes a hegemonic concept—an idea that seems neutral, consensual, and obvious, and that teachers gladly embrace, but that ultimately works against their own best interests. The concept of vocation serves the interests of those who want to run colleges efficiently and profitably while spending the least amount of money and employing the smallest number of staff that they can get away with.

Critically reflective teachers can stand outside their practice and see what they do in a wider perspective. They know that curriculum content and evaluative procedures are social products located in time and space that reproduce the inequities and contradictions of the wider culture. They are able to distinguish between a justifiable and necessary dedication to students' well-being and a self-destructive workaholism. They have a well-grounded rationale for their practice, which they can call on to help them make difficult decisions in unpredictable situations.

This rationale—a set of critically examined core assumptions about why one does what one does in the way that one does it—is a survival necessity. It grounds teachers in a moral, intellectual, and political project and gives them an organizing vision of what they are trying to accomplish. By prioritizing what is really important in their work, a critical rationale helps teachers keep in check their own tendency to translate a sense of vocation into a willingness to do everything asked of them.

The "Perfect Ten" Syndrome

Many teachers take an understandable pride in their craft wisdom and knowledge. They want to be good at what they do, and consequently, they set great store by students' evaluations of their teaching. When these are less than perfect—as is almost inevitable—teachers assume the worst. All those evaluations that are complimentary are forgotten, while those that are negative assume disproportionate significance. Indeed, the inference is often made that bad evaluations must, by definition, be written by students with heightened powers of pedagogic discrimination. Conversely, good evaluations are thought to be produced by students who are half-asleep.

The constant inability to obtain uniformly good evaluations leads to feelings of incompetence and guilt. When we keep these evaluations to ourselves (as is typical, given the privatized culture of many college campuses), the sense of failure becomes almost intolerable. We're convinced that we're the only ones who receive bad evaluations, and that everyone else is universally loved. In this way, an admirable desire to do good work turns into a source of demoralization.

Critically reflective teachers recognize the error of assuming that good teaching is always signaled by the receipt of uniformly good student evaluations. They know that the complexities of learning and the presence among students of diverse personalities, cultural backgrounds, genders, ability levels, learning styles, ideological orientations, and previous experiences make a perfect ten impossible to achieve. Given the diversity of college classrooms (particularly those in urban areas), no actions a teacher takes can ever be experienced as universally and uniformly positive. The critically reflective know, too, that teacher assessment and performance appraisal mechanisms that reward perfect scores don't always serve students' interests. For one thing, good evaluations are sometimes the result of teachers' pandering to students' prejudices. Teachers are almost bound to be liked if they never challenge students' automatic ways of thinking and behaving, or if they allow them to work only within their preferred learning styles. Since letting people stick with what comes easily to them is a form of cognitive imprisonment, one could almost say that anyone who consistently scores a perfect ten is just as likely to be doing something wrong as something right.

So, whose interests does the "perfect ten" assumption serve, if not those of students and teachers? Primarily, it serves individuals with a reductionist cast of mind who believe that the dynamics and contradictions of teaching can be reduced to a linear, quantifiable rating system. Such epistemologically challenged people sometimes work their way into positions of administrative and legislative power. Believing that learning and teaching are unidimensional, they carve curricula into discrete units and create standardized objectives that are meant to be context- and culture-proof. In their minds, teaching becomes the simple implementation of centrally produced curricula and objectives. Good or bad teaching is then numerically measured by how well these are put into effect.

Judging teaching by how many people say they like what you do supports a divisive professional ethic that rewards those who are the most popular. The "perfect ten" syndrome makes life easier for those who have the responsibility of deciding which faculty members are to be promoted. All they need do is consult student ratings, since according to this logic, the best teachers are obviously those with the highest scores. This turns professional advancement into a contest in which the winners are those who get the most students to say they like them. Administrators who use this rating system are not vindictive or oppressive. They are tired and burned out from making an unworkable system appear to be working. So if they come across a neat solution (giving promotion to those with the highest scores on student evaluations) to a difficult problem (deciding who of their staff advances), we can hardly blame them for embracing it.

Deep Space Nine: The Answer Must Be Out There Somewhere

For many teachers, the first response to encountering a problem of practice is to look for a manual, workshop, or person that can solve it. Students refusing to learn? Buy a book on dealing with resistance to learning. Classes full of students with different backgrounds, expectations, ability levels, and experiences? Enroll in that summer institute on dealing with diversity. Running discussions that are dominated by a handful of confident, articulate students? Go and see how that colleague across campus that everyone raves about runs her discussions.

All these resources for dealing with problems are useful and necessary. I have written chapters that dealt with resistance to learning, run workshops on responding to diversity, and invited colleagues to watch me teach, so I don't want to minimize the importance of doing such things. I do want to point out, however, that while reading books, attending workshops, or watching colleagues can give you some useful insights and techniques that will help you in dealing with your problem, it is wrong to assume that at some point in these activities, you will inevitably stumble on the exact answer to the problem you are experiencing.

To think this way is to fall victim to a fundamental epistemological distortion. This distortion holds that someone, or something, out there has the knowledge that constitutes the answer to our problems. We think that if we just look long and hard enough, we will find the manual, workshop, theory, or person that will tell us exactly what we need to do. Occasionally, this might happen. But more often than not, any ideas or suggestions we pick up will have to be sculpted to fit the local conditions in which we work. And that goes for all the suggestions I make in this book on how to become critically reflective.

Unless we challenge this epistemological distortion, we risk spending a great deal of energy castigating ourselves for our inability to make externally prescribed solutions fit the problems we're facing. It never occurs to us that what needs questioning is the assumption that neat answers to our problems are always waiting to be discovered outside our experience. It can take many demoralizing disappointments and misfirings—applications of standardized rules that vary wildly in their success—before we realize the fruitlessness of the quest for standardized certainty.

Critically reflective teachers have researched their teaching and their students enough to know that methods and practices imported from outside rarely fit snugly into the contours of their classrooms. They are aware that difficult problems never have standardized solutions. At best, such problems call forth a multiplicity of partial responses. The critically reflective also know that a significant but neglected starting point for dealing with these problems is the critical analysis of their own past experience. Taken at face value, autobiographical stories are suspect and subject to the dangers of distortion and overgeneralization. But when critically analyzed and combined with other sources of reflection such as colleagues' experiences, students' perceptions, and formal theory, autobiographies can be a powerful source of insight into the resolution of problems.

The idea that our complex questions of practice always have simple answers designed by others serves the interests of those who accrue power, prestige, and financial reward from designing and producing these answers. Consultants, authors, and production companies rarely say of their products, "These might be useful, but only if you research your local conditions and adapt what is here to your own circumstances." Neither do they advocate a mixing and matching of their products with elements from others marketed by their rivals. To say this would negate the chief appeal of these products, which is their promise that they will take care of our problems for us. We are thus relieved of the tiresome responsibility of having to analyze our own experiences critically or to research the contexts of our practice. However comfortable this may feel, it is ultimately damaging to our sense of ourselves as purposeful agents.

We Meet Everyone's Needs

The "meeting needs" rationale is alive and well in higher education. For example, when asked to explain why they've made a particular decision, administrators will often justify what they've done by saying that they're meeting the community's, the faculty's, or the students' needs. Likewise, teachers will say that the best classes are those in which every student feels that his or her needs have been met. The assumption that good teachers meet all students' needs all the time is guaranteed to leave us feeling incompetent and demoralized.

The trouble with the "meeting needs" rationale is not just that it sets up an unattainable standard, but that students sometimes take a dangerously narrow view of their needs. Students who define their need as never straying beyond comfortable ways of thinking, acting, and learning are not always in the best position to judge what is in their own best interests. I don't believe that teachers can force people to learn, but I do believe that they can lay out for students the consequences (especially the negative consequences) of their holding on to their own definitions of need. They can also suggest alternative, broadening definitions.

Critically reflective teachers know that while meeting everyone's needs sounds compassionate and student-centered, it is pedagogically unsound and psychologically demoralizing. They know that clinging to this assumption will only cause them to carry around a permanent burden of guilt at their inability to live up to this impossible task. They are aware that what seems to be an admirable guiding rule—and one that they are tempted to embrace—will end up destroying them.

The "meeting needs" assumption serves the interests of those who believe that education can be understood and practiced as a capitalist economic system. Higher education is viewed as a marketplace in which different businesses (colleges) compete for a limited number of consumers. Those who survive because they have enough consumers must, by definition, be doing a good job. State colleges need to attract and graduate large numbers of students if they are to continue to be funded. Private colleges depend on tuition revenue to survive. Under such circumstances, keeping the consumers (students) happy enough so that they don't buy the product (education) elsewhere is the bottom line for institutional success.

When education is viewed this way, we devote a lot of energy to keeping the customer satisfied. We definitely don't want him to feel confused or angry because we have asked him to do something he finds difficult and would rather avoid. The problem with this way of thinking about education is that it ignores pedagogic reality. Significant learning and critical thinking inevitably induce an ambivalent mix of feelings and emotions, in which anger and confusion are as prominent as pleasure and clarity. The most hallowed rule of business—that the customer is always right—is often pedagogically wrong. Equating good teaching with a widespread feeling among students that you have done what they wanted ignores the dynamics of teaching and prevents significant learning.

Why Is Critical Reflection Important?

Given that critical reflection entails all kinds of risks and complexities, there have to be some compelling reasons why anyone would choose to begin the critical journey. Few of us are likely to initiate a project that promises enlightenment only at the cost of torture. The choice to become critically reflective will be made only if we see clearly that it is in our own best interests. Otherwise, given the already overcrowded nature of our lives, why should we bother to take this activity seriously? I believe there are six reasons why learning critical reflection is important.

It Helps Us Take Informed Actions

Simple utilitarianism dictates that critical reflection is an important habit for teachers to develop. As is evident from the examples scattered throughout this chapter, becoming critically reflective increases the probability that we will take informed actions. Informed actions are those that can be explained and justified to ourselves and others. If a student or colleague asks us why we're doing something, we can show how our action springs from certain assumptions we hold about teaching and learning. We can then make a convincing case for their accuracy by laying out the evidence—experiential as well as theoretical—that undergirds them.

An informed action is one that has a good chance of achieving the consequences intended. It is an action that is taken against a backdrop of inquiry into how people perceive what we say and do. When we behave in certain ways, we expect our students and colleagues to see in our behaviors a certain set of meanings. Frequently, however, our words and actions are given meanings that are very different from, and sometimes directly antithetical to, those we intended. When we have seen our practice through others' eyes, we're in a much better position to speak and behave in ways that ensure a consistency of understanding between us, our students, and our colleagues. This consistency increases the likelihood that our actions have the effects we want.

It Helps Us Develop a Rationale for Practice

The critically reflective habit confers a deeper benefit than that of procedural utility. It embeds not only our actions but also our sense of who we are as teachers in an examined reality. We know why we believe what we believe. A critically reflective teacher is much better placed to communicate to colleagues and students—as well as to herself—the rationale behind her practice. She works from a position of informed commitment. She knows why she does what she does, why she thinks what she thinks. Knowing this, she communicates to students a confidence-inducing sense of being grounded. This sense of groundedness stabilizes her when she feels swept along by forces she cannot control.

A critical rationale grounds our most difficult decisions in core beliefs, values, and assumptions. As I found out when interviewing students for *The Skillful Teacher* (1990b), a teacher's ability to make clear what it is that she stands for, and why she believes this is important, is a crucial factor in establishing her credibility with students. Even students who disagree fundamentally with a teacher's rationale gain confidence from knowing what it is. In this instance, knowledge really is power. According to students, the worst position to be in is to sense that a teacher has an agenda and a preferred way of working, but not to know exactly what these are. Without this information, they complain, how can they trust the teacher or know what they're dealing with?

A critical rationale for practice is a psychological, professional, and political necessity. Without it, we are tossed about by whatever political or pedagogical winds are blowing at the time. A rationale serves as a methodological and ethical touchstone. It provides a foundational reference point—a set of continually tested beliefs that we can consult as a guide to how we should act in unpredictable situations. But a critical rationale for practice is not a static, immutable construct. It is shaped in a particular context and needs to keep adapting to circumstances. Although our foundational beliefs (such as a commitment to democratic process or a belief in critical thinking) can remain essentially unchanged, we keep learning different ways to realize them in our work.

It Helps Us Avoid Self-Laceration

If we are critically reflective, we are also less prone to self-laceration. A tendency of teachers who take their work seriously is to blame themselves if students are not learning. These teachers feel that at some level, they are the cause of the hostility, resentment, or indifference that even the best and most energetic of them are bound to encounter from time to time. Believing themselves to be the cause of these emotions and feelings, they automatically infer that they are also their solution. They take on themselves the responsibility for turning hostile, bored, or puzzled students into galvanized advocates for their subjects, brimming over with the joys of learning. When this doesn't happen (as is almost always the case), such teachers allow themselves to become consumed with guilt for what they believe is their pedagogic incompetence.

Critically reflective teachers who systematically investigate how their students are experiencing learning know that much student resistance is socially and politically sculpted. Realizing that resistance to learning often has nothing to do with what they've done as teachers helps them make a healthier, more realistic appraisal of their own role in, or responsibility for, creating resistance. They learn to stop blaming themselves and they develop a more accurate understanding of the cultural and political limits to their ability to convert resistance into enthusiasm.

It Grounds Us Emotionally

Critical reflection also grounds us emotionally. When we neglect to clarify and question our assumptions, and when we fail to investigate our students, we have the sense that the world is governed by chaos. Whether or not we do well seems to be largely a matter of luck. Lacking a reflective orientation, we place an unseemly amount of trust in the role of chance. We inhabit what Freire (1993) calls a condition of "magical consciousness." Fate or serendipity, rather than human agency, is seen as shaping educational process. The world is experienced as arbitrary, as governed by a whimsical God.

When we think this way, we are powerless to control the ebbs and flows of our emotions. One day, a small success inflates our self-confidence out of all proportion. The next, an equally small failure (such as one bad evaluative comment out of twenty good ones) is taken as a devastating indictment of our inadequacy. Teachers caught on this emotional roller coaster, where every action either confirms their brilliance or underscores their failure, cannot survive intact for long. Either they withdraw from the classroom or they are forced to suppress (at their eventual peril) the emotional content of their daily experiences. The critically reflective habit is therefore connected to teachers' morale in powerful ways.

It Enlivens Our Classrooms

It is important to realize the implications for our students of our own critical reflection. Students set great store by our actions, and they learn much from observing how we model intellectual inquiry and democratic process. A critically reflective teacher therefore activates her classroom by providing a model of passionate skepticism. As Osterman (1990) comments, "Critically reflective teachers—teachers who make their own thinking public, and therefore subject to discussion—are more likely to have classes that are challenging, interesting, and stimulating for students" (p. 139).

We know that students watch us closely and that they are quick to notice and condemn any inconsistency between what we say we believe and what we actually do. They tell us that seeing a teacher model critical thinking in front of them is enormously helpful to their own efforts to think critically. By openly questioning our own ideas and assumptions—even as we explain why we believe in them so passionately—we create an emotional climate in which accepting change and risking failure are valued. By inviting students to critique our efforts—and by showing them that we appreciate these critiques and treat them with the utmost seriousness—we deconstruct traditional power dynamics and relationships that stultify critical inquiry. A teacher who models critical inquiry in her own practice is one of the most powerful catalysts for critical thinking in her students. For this reason, if for no other, critical reflection should become perhaps the most important indicator we look for in any attempt to judge teachers' effectiveness.

It Increases Democratic Trust

What we do as teachers makes a difference in the world. In our classrooms, students learn democratic or manipulative behavior. They learn whether independence of thought is really valued or whether everything depends on pleasing the teacher. They learn that success depends either on beating someone to the prize using every available advantage or on working collectively. Standing above the fray and saying that our practice is apolitical is not an option for a teacher. Even if we profess to have no political stance, and to be concerned purely with furthering inquiry into a discrete body of objective ideas or practices, what we do counts. The ways we encourage or inhibit students' questions, the kinds of reward systems we create, and the degree of attention we pay to students' concerns all create a moral tone and a political culture.

Teachers who have learned the reflective habit know something about the effects they are having on students. They are alert to the presence of power in their classrooms and to its potential for misuse. Knowing that their actions can silence or activate students' voices, they listen seriously and attentively to what students say. They deliberately create public reflective moments when students' concerns—not the teacher's agenda—are the focus of classroom activity. Week in and week out, they make public disclosure of private realities, both to their students and to their colleagues. They make constant attempts to find out how students are experiencing their classes, and they make this information public. All their actions are explicitly grounded in relation to students' experiences, and students know and appreciate this.

Trust is the thread that ties these practices together. Through their actions, teachers build or diminish the amount of trust in the world. Coming to trust another person is the most fragile of human projects. It requires knowing someone over a period of time and seeing their honesty modeled in their actions. College classrooms provide the conditions in which people can learn to trust or mistrust each other. A teacher who takes students seriously and treats them as adults shows that she can be trusted. A teacher who emphasizes peer learning shows that it's important to trust other students. A teacher who encourages students to point out to her anything about her actions that is oppressive and who seeks to change what she does in response to their concerns is a model of critical reflection. Such a teacher is one who truly is trustworthy.

Conclusion

As this chapter has shown, critical reflection is inherently ideological. It is also morally grounded. It springs from a concern to create the conditions under which people can learn to love one another, and it alerts them to the forces that prevent this. Being anchored in values of justice, fairness, and compassion, critical reflection finds its political representation in the democratic process. Since it is difficult to show love to others when we are divided, suspicious, and scrambling for advantage, critical reflection urges us to create conditions under which each person is respected, valued, and heard. In pedagogic terms, this means the creation of democratic classrooms. In terms of professional development, it means an engagement in critical conversation. The rest of this book explores how both these projects can be realized.

B. Specific Strategies and Classroom Implementation

Seven Principles for Good Practice in Undergraduate Education

Arthur W. Chickering and Zelda F. Gamson*

Apathetic students, illiterate graduates, incompetent teaching, impersonal campuses—so rolls the drumfire of criticism of higher education. More than two years of reports have spelled out the problems. States have been quick to respond by holding out carrots and beating with sticks.

There are neither enough carrots nor enough sticks to improve undergraduate education without the commitment and action of students and faculty members. They are the precious resources on whom the improvement of undergraduate education depends.

But how can students and faculty members improve undergraduate education? Many campuses around the country are asking this question. To provide a focus for their work, we offer seven principles based on research on good teaching and learning in colleges and universities.

Good practice in undergraduate education:

1. Encourages contacts between students and faculty.
2. Develops reciprocity and cooperation among students.
3. Uses active learning techniques.
4. Gives prompt feedback.
5. Emphasizes time on task.
6. Communicates high expectations.
7. Respects diverse talents and ways of learning.

We can do it ourselves—with a little bit of help. . . .

A Focus for Improvement

These seven principles are not ten commandments shrunk to a twentieth century attention span. They are intended as guidelines for faculty members, students, and administrators—with support from state agencies and trustees—to improve teaching and learning. These principles seem like good common sense, and they *are*—because many teachers and students have experienced them and because research supports them. They rest on 50 years of research and on the way teachers teach and students learn, how students work and play with one another, and how students and faculty talk to each other.

While each practice can stand on its own, when all are present their effects multiply. Together, they employ six powerful forces in education:

- Activity
- Cooperation
- Diversity

"Seven Principles for Good Practice in Undergraduate Education," by Arthur W. Chickering and Zelda F. Gamson, reprinted by permission from *AAHE Bulletin*, March 1987, a publication of the American Association of Higher Education.

- Expectations
- Interaction
- Responsibility

Good practices hold as much meaning for professional programs as for the liberal arts. They work for many different kinds of students—white, black, Hispanic, Asian, rich, poor, older, younger, male, female, well-prepared, underprepared.

But the ways different institutions implement good practice depends very much on their students and their circumstances. In what follows, we describe several different approaches to good practice that have been used in different kinds of settings in the last few years. In addition, the powerful implications of these principles for the way states fund and govern higher education and for the way institutions are run are discussed briefly at the end.

As faculty members, academic administrators, and student personnel staff, we have spent most of our working lives trying to understand our students, our colleagues, our institutions, and ourselves. We have conducted research on higher education with dedicated colleagues in a wide range of schools in this country. We draw the implications of this research for practice, hoping to help us all do better.

We address the teacher's *how,* not the subject-matter *what,* of good practice in undergraduate education. We recognize that content and pedagogy interact in complex ways. We are also aware that there is much healthy ferment within and among the disciplines. What is taught, after all, is at least as important as how it is taught. In contrast to the long history of research in teaching and learning, there is little research on the college curriculum. We cannot, therefore, make responsible recommendations about the content of a good undergraduate education. That work is yet to be done.

This much we can say: An undergraduate education should prepare students to understand and deal intelligently with modern life. What better place to start but in the classroom and on our campuses? What better time than now?

Seven Principles of Good Practice

1. Encourages Contacts Between Students and Faculty

Frequent student-faculty contact in and out of classes is the most important factor in student motivation and involvement. Faculty concern helps students get through rough times and keep on working. Knowing a few faculty members well enhances students' intellectual commitment and encourages them to think about their own values and future plans.

Some examples: Freshman seminars on important topics, taught by senior faculty members, establish an early connection between students and faculty in many colleges and universities.

In the Saint Joseph's College core curriculum, faculty members who lead discussion groups in courses outside their fields of specialization model for students what it means to be a learner. In the Undergraduate Research Opportunities Program at the Massachusetts Institute of Technology, three out of four undergraduates have joined three-quarters of the faculty in recent years as junior research colleagues. At Sinclair Community College, students in the College Without Walls program have pursued studies through learning contracts. Each student has created a "resource group," which includes a faculty member, a student peer, and two "community resource" faculty members. This group then provides support and assures quality.

2. Develops Reciprocity and Cooperation Among Students

Learning is enhanced when it is more like a team effort than a solo race. Good learning, like good work, is collaborative and social, not competitive and isolated. Working with others often increases involvement in learning. Sharing one's own ideas and responding to others' reactions sharpens thinking and deepens understanding.

Some examples: Even in large lecture classes, students can learn from one another. Learning groups are a common practice. Students are assigned to a group of five to seven other students, who meet regularly during class throughout the term to solve problems set by the instructor. Many colleges use peer tutors for students who need special help.

Learning communities are another popular way of getting students to work together. Students involved in SUNY at Stony Brook's Federated Learning Communities can take several courses together. The courses, on topics related to a common theme like science, technology, and human values, are from different disciplines. Faculty teaching the courses coordinate their activities while another faculty member, called a "master learner," takes the courses with the students. Under the direction of the master learner, students run a seminar which helps them integrate ideas from the separate courses.

3. Uses Active Learning Techniques

Learning is not a spectator sport. Students do not learn much just by sitting in classes listening to teachers, memorizing pre-packaged assignments, and spitting out answers. They must talk about what they are learning, write about it, relate it to past experiences, apply it to their daily lives. They must make what they learn part of themselves.

Some examples: Active learning is encouraged in classes that use structured exercises, challenging discussions, team projects, and peer critiques. Active learning can also occur outside the classroom. There are thousands of internships, independent study, and cooperative job programs across the country in all kinds of colleges and universities, in all kinds of fields, for all kinds of students. Students also can help design and teach courses or parts of courses. At Brown University, faculty members and students have designed new courses on contemporary issues and universal themes; the students then help the professors as teaching assistants. At the State University of New York at Cortland, beginning students in a general chemistry lab have worked in small groups to design lab procedures rather than repeat prestructured exercises. At the University of Michigan's Residential College, teams of student periodically work with faculty members on a long-term original reserach project in the social sciences.

4. Gives Prompt Feedback

Knowing what you know and don't know focuses learning. Students need appropriate feedback on performance to benefit from courses. When getting started, students need help in assessing existing knowledge and competence. In classes, students need frequent opportunities to perform and receive suggestions for improvement. At various points during college, and at the end, students need chances to reflect on what they have learned, what they still need to know, and how to assess themselves.

Some examples: No feedback can occur without assessment. But assessment without timely feedback contributes little to learning.

Colleges assess students as they enter in order to guide them in planning their studies. In addition to the feedback they receive from course instructors, students in many colleges and universities receive counseling periodically on their progress and future plans. At Bronx Community College, students with poor academic preparation have been carefully tested and given special tutorials to prepare them to take introductory courses. They are then advised about the introductory courses to take, given the level of their academic skills.

Adults can receive assessment of their work and other life experiences at many colleges and universities through portfolios of their work or through standardized tests; these provide the basis for sessions with advisors.

Alverno College requires that students develop high levels of performance in eight general abilities such as analytic and communication skills. Performance is assessed and then discussed with students at each level for each ability in a variety of ways and by a variety of assessors.

In writing courses across the country, students are learning, through detailed feedback from instructors and fellow students, to revise and rewrite drafts. They learn, in the process, that feedback is central to learning and improving performance.

5. Emphasizes Time on Task

Time plus energy equals learning. There is no substitute for time on task. Learning to use one's time well is critical for students and professionals alike. Students need help in learning effective time management. Allocating realistic amounts of time means effective learning for students and effective teaching for faculty. How an institution defines time expectations for students, faculty, administrators, and other professional staff can establish the basis for high performance for all.

Some examples: Mastery learning, contract learning, and computer assisted instruction require that students spend adequate amounts of time on learning. Extended periods of preparation for college also give students more time on task. Maneo Ricci College is known for its efforts to guide high school students from the ninth grade to a B.A. in six years through a curriculum taught jointly by faculty at Seattle Preparatory School and Seattle University. Providing students with opportunities to integrate their studies into the rest of their lives helps them use time well.

Workshops, intensive residential programs, combinations of televised instruction, correspondence study, learning centers are all being used in a variety of institutions, especially those with many part-time students. Weekend colleges and summer residential programs, courses offered at work sites and community centers, clusters of courses on related topics taught in the same time block, and double-credit courses make more time for learning. At Empire State College, for example, students design degree programs organized in manageable time blocks; students may take courses at nearby institutions, pursue independent study, or work with faculty and other students at Empire State learning centers.

6. Communicates High Expectations

Expect more and you will get more. High expectations are important for everyone—for the poorly prepared, for those unwilling to exert themselves, and for the bright and well motivated. Expecting students to perform well becomes a self-fulfilling prophecy when teachers and institutions hold high expectations of themselves and make extra efforts.

Some examples: In many colleges and universities, students with poor past records or test scores do extraordinary work. Sometimes they outperform students with good preparation. The University of Wisconsin-Parkside has communicated high expectations for underprepared high school students by bringing them to the university for workshops in academic subjects, study skills, test taking, and time management. In order to reinforce high expectations, the program involves parents and high school counselors.

The University of California, Berkeley introduced an honors program in the sciences for underprepared minority students; a growing number of community colleges are establishing general honors programs for minorities. Special programs like these help. But most important are the day-to-day, week-in and week-out expectations students and faculty hold for themselves and for each other in all their classes.

7. Respects Diverse Talents and Ways of Learning

There are many roads to learning. People bring different talents and styles of learning to college. Brilliant students in the seminar room may be all thumbs in the lab or art studio. Students rich in hands-on experience may not do so well with theory. Students need the opportunity to show their talents and learn in ways that work for them. Then they can be pushed to learning in new ways that do not come so easily.

Some examples: Individualized degree programs recognize different interests. Personalized systems of instruction and mastery learning let students work at their own pace. Contract learning helps students define their own objectives, determine their learning activities, and define the criteria and methods of evaluation. At the College of Public and Community Service, a college for older working adults at the University of Massachusetts-Boston, incoming students have taken an orientation course that encourages them to reflect on their learning styles. Rockland Community College has offered a life-career-educational planned course. At the University of California, Irvine, introductory physics students may choose between a lecture-and-textbook course, a computer-based version of the lecture-and-textbook course, or a computer-based course based on notes developed by the faculty that allow students to program the computer. In both computer-based courses, students work on their own and must pass mastery exams.

Whose Responsibility Is It?

Teachers and students hold the main responsibility for improving undergraduate education. But they need a lot of help. College and university leaders, state and federal officials, and accrediting associations have the power to shape an environment that is favorable to good practice in higher education.

What qualities must this environment have?

- A strong sense of shared purposes.
- Concrete support from adminstrators and faculty leaders for those purposes.
- Adequate funding appropriate for the purposes.
- Policies and procedures consistent with the purposes.
- Continuing examination of how well the purposes are being achieved.

There is good evidence that such an environment can be created. When this happens, faculty members and administrators think of themselves as educators. Adequate resources are put into creating opportunities for faculty members, administrators, and students to celebrate and reflect on their shared purposes. Faculty members receive support and release time for appropriate professional development activities. Criteria for hiring and promoting faculty members, administrators, and staff support the institution's purposes. Advising is considered important. Departments, programs, and classes are small enough to allow faculty members and students to have a sense of community, to experience the value of their contributions, and to confront the consequences of their failures.

States, the federal government, and accrediting associations affect the kind of environment that can develop on campuses in a variety of ways. The most important is through the allocation of financial support. States also influence good practice by encouraging sound planning, setting priorities, mandating standards, and reviewing and approving programs. Regional and professional accrediting associations require self-study and peer review in making their judgments about programs and institutions.

These sources of support and influence can encourage environments for good practice in undergraduate education by:

- Setting policies that are consistent with good practice in undergraduate education.
- Holding high expectations for institutional performance.
- Keeping bureaucratic regulations to a minimum that is compatible with public accountability.
- Allocating adequate funds for new undergraduate programs and the professional development of faculty members, administrators, and staff.
- Encouraging employment of under-represented groups among administrators, faculty members, and student services professionals.
- Providing the support for programs, facilities, and financial aid necessary for good practice in undergraduate education.

Note

* Prepared with the assistance of Alexander W. Astin, Howard Bowen, Carol M. Boyer, K. Patricia Cross, Kenneth Ehle, Russell Edgerton, Jerry Gaff, Joseph Katz, C. Robert Pace, Marvin W. Peterson, and Richard C. Richardson, Jr.

This work was co-sponsored by the American Association for Higher Education and the Education Commission of the States. The Johnson Foundation supported the preparation of early drafts and a meeting for the authors at Wingspread in Racine, Wisconsin. William Boyd and Henry Halsted of the Johnson Foundation made useful contributions to the group's deliberations and to revisions.

References

Adelman, C. (1984). *Starting with students: Promising approaches in American higher education*. Washington, DC: National Institute of Education.

Astin, A.W. (1977). *Four critical years: Effects of college on beliefs, attitudes, and knowledge*. San Francisco: Jossey-Bass.

Astin, A.W. (1985). *Achieving educational excellence*. San Francisco: Jossey-Bass.

Bayer, A.E. (1975). Faculty composition, institutional structure, and students' college environment. *Journal of Higher Education*, 46(5), 549–555.

Beal, P.E., and Noel, L. (1980). *What works in student retention*. American College Testing Program.

Bouton, C., and Garth, R.Y. (1983). Learning in groups. *New Directions for Teaching and Learning*, 14. San Francisco: Jossey-Bass.

Bowen, H.R. (1977). *Investment in learning*. San Francisco: Jossey-Bass.

Boyer, C.M., and Ahlgren, A. (1987, July/August). Assessing undergraduates' patterns of credit distribution: Amount and specialization. *Journal of Higher Education*, 58(4), forthcoming.

Boyer, C.M., and Ewell, P.T., Finney, J.E., and Mingle, J.R. (1987). Assessment and outcomes measurement—A view from the states: Highlights of a new ECS survey. *AAHE Bulletin*, 39: 7, 8–12.

Chickering, A.W. (1969). *Education and identity*. San Francisco: Jossey-Bass.

Chickering, A.W., and McCormick, J. (1973). Personality development and the college experience. *Research in Higher Education*, 1, 43–70.

Chickering, A.W. (1974). *Commuting versus resident students: Overcoming the educational inequities of living off campus*. San Francisco: Jossey-Bass.

Chickering, A.W., and Associates (1981). *The modern American college: Responding to the new realities of diverse students and a changing society*. San Francisco: Jossey-Bass.

Claxton, C.S., and Ralston, Y. (1978). Learning styles: Their impacts on teaching and administration. *AAHE-ERIC/Higher Education, Research Report No. 10*. Washington, DC: American Association for Higher Education.

Cohen, E.G. (1986). *Designing groupwork: Strategies for the heterogeneous classroom*. New York: Teachers College Press.

Cross, K.P. (1986, March). Taking teaching seriously. Presentation at the Annual Meeting of the American Association for Higher Education.

Eble, K. (1976). *Craft of teaching*. San Francisco: Jossey-Bass.

Feldman, K.A., and Newcomb, T.M. (1969). *The impact of college on students*. San Francisco: Jossey-Bass.

Gamson, Z.F., and Associates. (1984). *Liberating education*. San Francisco: Jossey-Bass.

Gardner, H. (1983). *Frames of mind: A theory of multiple intelligence*. New York: Basic Books.

Heath, D. (1968). *Growing up in college*. San Francisco: Jossey-Bass.

Jacob, P.E. (1957). *Changing values in college*. New York: Harper.

Katz, J., and Associates. (1968). *No time for youth*. San Francisco: Jossey-Bass.

Keeton, M.T. (Ed.) (1976). *Experiential learning*. San Francisco: Jossey-Bass.

Kolb, D. (1984). *Experiential learning*. New Jersey: Prentice Hall.

Kulik, J.A. (1982). Individualized systems of instruction. In Harold E. Mitzel (Ed.), *Encyclopedia of educational research*, 2. New York: The Free Press.

Lowman, J. (1984). *Mastering the techniques of teaching*. San Francisco: Jossey-Bass.

McKeachie, W.J. (1985). *Improving undergraduate education through faculty development*. San Francisco: Jossey-Bass.

Messick, S., and Associates. (Ed.) (1976). *Individuality in learning*. San Francisco: Jossey-Bass.

Newcomb, T.M. (1943). *Personality and social change*. New York: Dryden Press.

Newcomb, T.M., and others. *Persistence and change: A college and its students after twenty-five years.* Huntington, NY: Krieger.

Pace, C.R. (1943). *Measuring outcomes of college: Fifty years of finding and recommending for future assessment.* San Francisco: Jossey-Bass.

Pascarella, E.T. (1980). Student-faculty informal contact and college outcomes. *Review of Educational Research,* 50, Winter, 545–595.

Pascarella, E.T., Terenzini, P.T., and Wolfe, L.M. (1986). Orientation to college and freshman year persistence/withdrawal decisions. *Journal of Higher Education,* 57, 155–175.

Perry, W.G., Jr. (1970). *Forms of intellectual and ethical development in the college years: A scheme.* New York: Holt, Rinehart and Winston.

Peterson, M.W., Jedamus, P., and Associates. (1981). *Improving academic management.* San Francisco: Jossey–Bass.

Richardson, R.C., Jr., Fisk, E.C., and Okun, M.A. (1983). *Literacy in the open access college.* San Francisco: Jossey-Bass.

Sanford, N. (Ed.) (1962). *The American college.* New York: John Wiley and Sons.

Wallace, W.L. (1966). *Student culture.* Chicago: Aldine.

Wilson, R.C., Gaff, J.G., Dienst, E.R., Wood, L., and Bavry, J.I. (1975). *College professors and their impact upon students.* New York: John Wiley and Sons.

Winter, D.G., McClelland, D.C., and Stewart, A.J. (1981). *A new case for the liberal arts.* San Francisco: Jossey-Bass.

Practical Proposals for Motivating Students

DONELSON R. FORSYTH AND JAMES H. MCMILLAN

Motivation is an irrelevancy to some college educators. Laborers may need to be properly motivated by their supervisors, football players may require pumping up before the big game, and listless high school students may need to be seduced into the excitement of learning—but college students? Aren't they supposed to be self-motivated?

Certainly some students come to the classroom ready to expend considerable time and effort in their quest to learn the course material and achieve personal goals of success. Yet, for many students, the motivational pump is unprimed. Students' degree programs often require certain courses, so students may not be interested in the material, since they did not choose the course themselves, or perhaps they consider its content irrelevant to their personal goals. The course may be so challenging or so easy that discouragement or disillusionment may set in. Students also have jobs and other life pursuits to contend with, and these extracurricular activities may be far more exciting or involving than the act of learning.

Given that self-motivated learners exist only rarely in the college classroom, what can teachers do to increase their students' motivation to learn? This chapter, by building on the theoretical analyses presented in the previous chapter, focuses on needs, expectations, and goals. We first consider how one particularly important need—achievement orientation—influences motivation, by examining ways of restructuring this orientation if it is not conducive to learning. Next, because even the most motivated students will not strive to achieve when they are certain that failure is inevitable, we examine ways to create the expectation of success. Last, we turn to ways to increase the value of academic outcomes, by helping students develop personal goals and identify the means of achieving these goals. Throughout, our focus is on methods that classroom instructors can use to modify these three determinants of motivation.

Need to Achieve

As noted in the preceding chapter, theorists have conceptualized learners' need to achieve in a variety of ways. To some, the key difference between high and low achievers is self-esteem: low achievers lack self-confidence and consider themselves failures (Purkey, 1970). Others, by contrast, emphasize individual variations in locus of control (Rotter, 1966), self-efficacy (Bandura, 1977), need for achievement (McClelland, 1985), competence motivation (White, 1959), self-control (Carver and Scheier, 1981), personal causation (deCharms, 1976, 1987), and intrinsic motivation (Deci and Ryan, 1985). These variations, however, need not be considered unalterable. Whereas early personality theorists felt that achievement orientation was a stable trait that remained constant across situations and was not easily altered, an interactional view assumes that one's general need to achieve interacts with features of the setting, to determine overall achievement motivation. A student who is unmotivated in one situation may become the epitome of the hard-striving, goal-oriented student in another. The key is to take care in structuring the classroom situation, so that motivation is gained rather than lost.

"Practical Proposals for Motivating Students," by Donelson R. Forsyth and James H. McMillan, reprinted from *New Directions for Teaching and Learning: College Teaching from Theory to Practice,* No. 45, edited by R. J. Menges and M. D. Svinicki, 1991, Jossey-Bass Publishers, Inc.

Capitalize on Intrinsic Motivation

The desire to learn—to discover, to comprehend, to synthesize, to develop—is an intrinsic part of human nature, and this intrinsic motivation to learn should be exploited. Although educators too frequently assume that students are reluctant learners, in many cases they become reluctant only after their initial intrinsic motivation is wiped away by hours of uninspired lectures in which instructors convey their own contempt for the subject matter. Instructors should do all they can to capitalize on intrinsic motivation, by taking certain simple steps (Ames, 1987; Brophy, 1987; Condry, 1987; Deci and Ryan, 1985; Lepper, 1983).

Introduce the course and each topic in an interesting, informative, and challenging way. You should not just review the syllabus during the first session or concentrate on how grades will be determined. Instead, you should highlight the stimulating intellectual tasks to be accomplished, pique students' curiosity, challenge traditional views, and hint at inconsistencies to be resolved.

Present material at a challenging level that communicates respect for your students and their abilities. Monitor the pace at which you present ideas, so that you maintain a balance between a slow pace that leads to boredom and a too-fast pace that leads to confusion.

Use varied and creative styles of teaching to avoid monotony and keep students' interest high. You should be unpredictable but not capricious. Introduce odd but provocative ideas, take the role of devil's advocate, and let students participate in the classroom process.

Focus on higher-order learning outcomes, such as application, analysis, synthesis, and evaluation, rather than on such lower-order outcomes as knowledge and comprehension. Make certain that evaluations favor students who achieve higher-order educational outcomes.

Model enthusiasm for the course content and for learning itself. Students assume that the instructor who habitually arrives late for class, seems preoccupied, reads directly from notes or from the book, and speaks in a monotone is bored with the class.

Give responsibility for learning back to the students. Allow them to design and select their learning experiences, topics, and methods of evaluation. Promote feelings of autonomy and personal involvement.

Avoid Extrinsic Motivators

Intrinsic motivation contrasts sharply with extrinsic motivation. Students, when intrinsically motivated, "experience interest and enjoyment, they feel competent and self-determining, they perceive the locus of causality for their behavior to be internal, and in some instances they experience flow" (Deci and Ryan, 1985, p. 34). When extrinsically motivated, by contrast, students are working for impersonal, external reasons. External motivators have a long history and possibly a permanent place in the classroom, but their negative impact on learning should be minimized, whenever possible, by basic precautions.

Use tests and other forms of evaluation to give students information about their accomplishments, but not to exert control or deny students' autonomy. Grades are the basic currency of the college classroom—the reward promised to students for good performance and the punishment threatened for failure. Instructors who stress tests, evaluations, and grades over all else, however, produce students who are striving to earn a particular grade rather than to learn the course material.

Exercise care when describing the need for grades, since even subtle nuances can influence motivation. Evaluations described as feedback to see how well students are doing have a less negative impact than evaluations designed to test whether they are performing as well as they should (Ryan, Mims, and Koestner, 1983). Similarly, students who are told that a grade of A means they are doing well in a subject perform better than students who are told that the A is a reward for working hard or for learning the material (Miller, Brickman, and Bolen, 1975).

Use the weakest extrinsic motivators possible. If you must use controlling methods—deadlines, pop quizzes, extra readings for poor performance, surveillance, penalties for nonattendance—then make certain that they are minimally sufficient to achieve compliance (Condry, 1987).

Minimize competition among students. Although introducing competition among students is a popular way to prompt them to expend greater effort, competition has many drawbacks. Competition focuses students' attention on winning, to the extent that they eventually conclude that "learning something new" is not nearly as important as "performing better than others" (Ames, 1987, p. 134). Failure in a competitive setting also undermines self-esteem and prompts students to blame their failures on lack of ability, rather than on lack of effort. Ames (1987), after thoroughly reviewing the literature, recommends excising all forms of competition from the college classroom by using criterion-based grading schemes (rather than norm-referenced schemes), by not posting grades and not grading on a curve, and by stressing the cooperative nature of learning.

Create a Mastery Orientation

Some of the most useful research into achievement motivation has been conducted by Dweck and her colleagues (Dweck, 1975; Dweck and Elliot, 1983; Dweck and Leggett, 1988). In her early research, Dweck found that students who think that their outcomes are within their control—mastery-oriented students—respond much differently from those who are helpless (Dweck and Licht, 1980; Dweck and Reppucci, 1973). After a failure, among mastery-oriented students, "effort is escalated, concentration is intensified, persistence is increased, strategy use becomes more sophisticated, and performance is enhanced"; by contrast, when helpless students fail, "efforts are curtailed, strategies deteriorate, and performance is often severely disrupted" (Dweck and Licht, 1980, p. 197). In one demonstration of these differences, Deiner and Dweck (1978) asked students who were failing on a cognitive task to "think out loud" about what they were doing. They discovered that 52 percent of the helpless questioned their ability, while none of the mastery-oriented students mentioned ability.

These findings suggest that instructors must remain sensitive to students' cognitive reactions to evaluations and test feedback. If students who do poorly in class conclude that there is nothing they personally can do to change their outcomes, then their failure may undermine their motivation and their satisfaction with themselves and academic work. If, however, the teacher encourages students to associate failure with factors that can be controlled, then the debilitating consequences of failure may be avoided. In addition, by emphasizing the importance of internal factors as causal agents after success, teachers may further ensure continued success. There are various methods for achieving this mastery orientation.

Encourage feelings of controllability in the classroom. Noel, Forsyth, and Kelley (1987) found that students who perform poorly often react very negatively and seek to blame their outcomes on lack of ability or on factors beyond their control: a poor teacher, a cold, a noisy roommate, and the like. Noel and his colleagues sought to undo these attributions by exposing some students to information that suggested that grades in college are caused by internal, controllable factors. The group was told, for example, that successful students generally believe they cause their own grades and have control over their performance. As predicted, on subsequent tests and on final examinations, these students earned higher grades than did control students who received no training.

Emphasize the extent to which grades and performance fluctuate over time. Wilson and Linville (1982, 1985), in studies of college students, succeeded in convincing first-year students that their grades were caused by unstable rather than stable factors. By comparison with "untreated" students, the students were told that, on the average, college students do improve their grades during their educational careers were less likely to drop out at the end of the second year, and they achieved greater increases in their grade point averages.

Identify ways for students to increase their control over their outcomes. Do not just tell students they have control; give them control over their studying, the course material, and the way it is taught. For example, you can hold workshops on study skills, time management, and effective reading; provide students with important and useful resources, such as supplementary readings, an outline of your notes, and question-and-answer sessions; and allow students to take a role in designing evaluation procedures. If students realize that they can take behavioral steps to improve their performance, their sense of autonomy and control in the classroom should prosper.

Expectations for Success

In a tradition extending back to Tolman (1955), virtually all theories of human motivation argue that individuals intuitively calculate the probability that they will succeed in a particular situation. Although these calculations initially reflect generalized expectancies based on past performances, these generalized expectations are translated into more specific expectancies as the individual gains more and more information in the particular setting. Given that even students who are high in achievement orientation may not strive for success in classes where they expect to fail, teachers should maximize positive expectations, avoid fear of failure, and help shape their students' attributions about the causes of future performances.

Maximize Optimism Regarding Outcomes

The power of positive expectations is startling. As Rosenthal and Jacobson (1968) illustrate in their study of teachers' self-fulfilling prophecies, teachers who expect a student to succeed act in ways that make the student's success more likely. Moreover, students who develop positive expectations about their performance, by comparison with students who have bleaker expectations, work harder on class assignments, take a more active role in their learning by asking questions, learn more material, and come to think of themselves as high achievers (Harris and Rosenthal, 1985; Rosenthal, 1973). Merely expecting success in no way ensures success, but a positive expectation about performance is a crucial link in the motivation-achievement chain. This link can be made stronger if instructors take the following steps.

Develop positive expectations about students' chances of success. Rosenthal's (1973) work suggests that even instructors who try to keep their expectations private communicate these expectations to their students through subtle forms of behavior. Because negative expectations can become self-fulfilling prophecies, instructors should expect the most from their classes in general, and from specific individual students within the class. High expectations are communicated as instructors learn students' names and call on them by name, ask difficult, challenging questions, allow a long time for students to respond, provide helpful cues and prompts, and give warm, positive, non-verbal messages (Good and Brophy, 1986).

Avoid norm-referenced grading systems. When instructors grade on a curve, they ensure that some students in the class will earn failing grades. This grading scheme reinforces negative expectations, promotes competition among students, and limits the number of students who receive positive reinforcement.

Monitor the level of difficulty of tests and assignments. Evidence indicates that the perceived difficulty of the task is one of the primary determinants of subjective probability of success (Heckhausen, Schmalt, and Schneider, 1985). Students' expectations for success erode rapidly when instructors repeatedly give tests that are very difficult.

Provide students with encouraging information about future outcomes. Rather than tell students that most students fail a course at least once or that it will be the hardest course they will take in college, tell students how many people passed the course the last time you taught it or how many people improved their performance over time.

Minimize Fear of Failure

McClelland (1985) maintains that for some people, in some situations, the desire for success is replaced by the fear of failure. Individuals who fear failure tend to express negative attitudes toward achievement. They fail to set performance goals, they experience polarized emotional reactions when they succeed or fail, and they avoid evaluations if possible. As a result, they tend to become enmeshed in a negative cycle of low motivation that only serves to guarantee poor performance. This negative cycle can be short-circuited, however.

Limit the scope of the tasks attempted. Give many tests, rather than a few major tests, and provide opportunities to redress poor performance with good performance. Students should realize that a single poor performance will not do irreversible damage to their course grades.

Monitor the difficulty of the goals and tasks that students choose for themselves. Evidence indicates that individuals who are high in fear of failure tend to select tasks that are either so easy that they feel no pride in their accomplishments or so difficult that they are bound to fail (Heckhausen, Schmalt, and Schneider, 1985). Students should be counseled to select moderately difficult goals that they can reasonably expect to achieve. Moreover, if they fail to establish suitable goals, you can help them identify the paths that they can take to achieve such goals. When you include help sessions, study sheets, review sessions, and workshops on study skills in your teaching, students are more likely to feel that even moderately difficult goals can be achieved.

Minimize competition and social comparison in the classroom. In competitive settings, students often take steps to minimize their embarrassment over a failure, including deliberately refusing to study, cutting classes, or expressing derisive attitudes about the class content. These self-protective mechanisms, however, interfere substantially with performance and opportunities for success.

Actively attack negative expectations based on cultural stereotypes. Instructors must be particularly sensitive to the motivational needs of minorities and women. Instructors in college courses in areas that are traditionally viewed as male- or Anglo-dominated must undo these negative stereotypes; otherwise, students may not feel that they have the ability to meet course requirements (Bartz, 1984; Farmer, 1987; Maruyama, 1984).

Encourage Attributions to Controllable Causes

Motivation prospers when students feel that their outcomes are under their personal control. Feelings of control do not just increase general feelings of personal ability; they also increase students' expectations concerning success. When success is produced by factors that students think they can control—effort, motivation, diligence—they can assume that good scores will occur again. If, however, good grades are attributed to uncontrollable, external factors—such as an easy test, an excellent teacher, or the simplicity of the topic—then successful students must wonder whether they can maintain their high level of achievement. Conversely, failing students who believe that they can control the cause of their poor performance can reasonably hope to improve on future tasks. If, however, they believe that their grades result from uncontrollable factors, such as low ability or a poor teacher, their expectations concerning future outcomes will remain negative (Forsyth and McMillan, 1981). These attributional processes can be made to work in the service of motivation, however.

Minimize references to the causal importance of uncontrollable factors, such as mood, inspired guessing, time of year, luck, the ease or difficulty of the particular unit, the presence of poor items on the test, and so on. Instead, emphasize the causal impact on performance of effort, note-taking skill, diligence, preparation, and other factors. Irrespective of performance, students who think they control the causes of their outcomes experience more positive emotions than students who think their performance is caused by uncontrollable factors (Forsyth, 1986).

Provide differentiated feedback, rather than global feedback. Even when a student tests poorly, some questions that he or she answered correctly can be found. The student's ability to answer these items should be highlighted and explained by his or her superior learning of the material tested, rather than by the ease of the items.

Minimize the emotional repercussions of failure. Attributional reactions following failure are closely linked to emotional reactions (Wiener, 1985). Even when steps are taken to make certain that failure does not threaten self-esteem, students who perform poorly react very emotionally to their outcomes. The negative impacts of these emotional processes on motivation and on the quality of the classroom setting can be limited by discussing them in advance, avoiding confrontation in the classroom setting, and letting the feelings abate gradually over time.

Identifying Valuable Goals

Researchers exploring productivity in industrial settings discovered long ago the motivating power of goals. People working at jobs ranging from hauling logs to generating creative ideas to proofreading were found to be unproductive if their goals were vague or absent but productive if they were laboring to attain clearly established goals (Locke and Latham, 1990; Locke, Shaw, Saari, and Latham, 1981). These findings, applied to the classroom, suggest that students will perform better if they know what goals they are seeking and if those goals are personally important to them (Kleinbeck, Quast, and Schwarz, 1989).

Help Students Set Realistic Goals

Why do students take a particular class? Asking students this question can be a sobering experience for the college teacher. Such answers as "I want an A," "It meets at a good time," "It's required," "I have a friend in the class," or "I heard good things about the instructor" abound, whereas answers like "I'm seeking knowledge about this fascinating area" or "I think this material will be useful to me in my career" are relatively few.

Because goals are important sources of motivation, it may be worthwhile to spend time helping your students identify the goals they are seeking. This goal clarification can be achieved by discussing the goals of the class during the initial class session and including the goals of the class on the course syllabus. Using a brainstorming format, you can also develop a long list of goals through class discussion and then have students review the goals and suggest ways to achieve them. You can also arrange, as one of the class assignments, to have students identify their goals, or you can develop a simple goal-setting project that can be completed outside class. Whichever method you use to set goals, however, you should try to help students develop goals that are positive, behaviorally specific, realistic, and personally important (Danish, Galambos, and Laquatra, 1983).

Emphasize positive goals (things desired) rather than negative goals (things to avoid). Students should be encouraged to study more, rather than procrastinate less; take clearer notes, rather than not daydream during lectures; come to class, rather than skip class.

Goals that describe a specific behavioral outcome are superior to "do your best" goals or no goals. Particularly for students who are not doing well in the class, such goals as "Take two pages of well-organized notes" and "Read five pages and make a list of the key ideas in each section" are more effective motivators than "Get an A on the next test" or "Work hard."

Goals should be ones that the student, through effort, can attain. They should be challenging but not so difficult that the student will fail. Many educators recommend a mastery approach to goal setting, whereby students begin to work toward a goal only after they have attained the previous one.

Avoid giving students goals. Instead, ask each student to identify his or her own personal goals. When students generate their own goals, their intrinsic motivation is less likely to suffer, their commitment to the goals is greater, and, in most cases, the goals themselves are viewed as much more valuable (Locke, Shaw, Saari, and Latham, 1981).

As necessary, remind students of their goals. When goals are salient, learners process information more efficiently than when goals are unspecified; "from the wealth of information available to an individual in his environment, only those aspects of the environment that serve the goal-oriented control of action are registered and processed" (Kleinbeck, Quast, and Schwarz, 1989, p. 25). The learner, awash in a sea of information, must pick and choose what to remember and what to forget.

Help students develop strategies for achieving their goals. In many cases, students will need to develop coherent plans for attaining broad, overall goals. For example, they may need to break major goals into smaller subgoals, or they may need to identify barriers that have prevented them from succeeding in the past.

Increase the Value of Academic Goals

Simply having a goal is not sufficient to produce increases in motivation. As expectancy-value theory argues, the motivational gains generated by goals depend to a large extent on the perceived value of the goals identified. A student, after identifying a series of positive, behaviorally specific, challenging goals, may still fail to work to achieve these goals if the goals are not viewed as personally meaningful or worthwhile.

Brophy (1987), drawing on analyses of classroom motivation, offers a number of recommendations aimed at increasing the attractiveness of educational outcomes. These recommendations, some of which are incorporated into the following paragraphs, work by changing students' perceptions of the course material and providing them with overarching goals related to the class and the educational experience.

Model enthusiasm and interest in the topic and in learning. Social learning theory recommends increasing the value of educational outcomes by providing an example for students (Bandura, 1977). Instructors who are interested in the material, who display a scholarly attitude while teaching, and who seem genuinely interested in achieving understanding are more likely to produce students who also display these values.

Expect interest, not boredom. Brophy notes that students will rise to the level of their instructors' expectations. If teachers think the students will find the material boring, then students typically react with indifference and boredom. If, however, teachers treat students as "active, motivated learners who care about their learning and are trying to understand" (Brophy, 1987, p. 195), then positive motivation is much more likely (Good and Brophy, 1986).

Directly address the importance of each new topic examined. When beginning a new subject, assigning a task, or asking students to read a chapter, highlight the value of the learning activity with a short overview. For example, explain the scholar's excitement over the particular topic ("When Darwin published *The Origin of Species,* the scientific community reeled"), your own interest in the material and how it relates to some personal incident in your life ("I first read *The Old Man and the Sea* when my family was vacationing at the shore"), the practical utility of the information about to be presented ("The principle of supply and demand explains why all the things you buy each day—from a cola to a fast-food burger—cost what they do"), or the long-term usefulness of a working knowledge of the topic ("Many of the ideas we have discussed so far will be of use to you in your career, but the principles of forecasting are perhaps the most essential"). Be careful, however, in phrasing your message (Brophy and Kher, 1986). Brophy found that even when teachers take the time to tell students that the upcoming material is stimulating and personally useful in the long run, they accidentally include threatening information as well. The teacher who says, "Once we finish this section, we will understand some of the puzzles that challenged even Plato and Socrates" is also likely to say, "It is so important that we will have a quiz next session to test your comprehension."

Make the material personally relevant to students. Novel, challenging, or unfamiliar ideas are more interesting to learners when they are tied to more familiar, personally relevant ideas. According to Brophy (1987, p. 197), "Teachers can promote personal identification with the content by relating experiences or telling anecdotes illustrating how the content applies to the lives of particular individuals."

Select topics and tasks that interest students. If you have the choice to teach one of two equally worthwhile topics, select the topic that students will find more enjoyable and exciting. When a number of methods can be used to accomplish a particular learning outcome, show a preference for methods that match students' existing interests. Allow students to choose among various options. Use novel introductions and activities that diverge from your usual method of teaching, and allow students to learn actively rather than passively. When you can, tie class activities and content to significant features of students' lives. Students' concerns about interpersonal relationships, for example, can be used to stimulate discussion about fundamental biological processes, research methods in psychology, changing views of love in art, sociological conceptions of the basis of political structures, and so on.

Take time to understand what students perceive as important and interesting. All too often, professors assume that they know what will be challenging or stimulating. Stress the importance of students' involvement in meaningful learning, and ask them to evaluate activities and content on this basis. If students do not agree with you, ask them to generate further options.

Summary

Motivation is, to a large extent, a basic dispositional quality of each learner, but savvy instructors can do much to raise motivation by structuring their classrooms carefully. The practical suggestions we have presented are based on theory, research, and our experiences as teachers. If we can keep students intrinsically motivated, provide meaningful feedback, and encourage the development of realistic, valuable, and achievable goals that students expect to achieve, their engagement in learning should be enhanced.

References

Ames, C. "The Enhancement of Student Motivation." In M.L. Maehr and D.A. Kleiber (eds.), *Advances in Motivation and Achievement*. Vol. 5. *Enhancing Motivation*. Greenwich, Conn.: JAI Press, 1987.

Bandura, A. *Social Learning Theory.* Englewood Cliffs, N.J.: Prentice-Hall, 1977.

Bartz, D.E. "Remediating Social and Psychological Harm Resulting from Segregative Acts." In D.E. Bartz and M.L. Maehr (eds.), *Advances in Motivation and Achievement*. Vol. 1. Greenwich, Conn.: JAI Press, 1984.

Brophy, J. "Socializing Students' Motivation to Learn." In M.L. Maehr and D.A. Kleiber (eds.), *Advances in Motivation and Achievement*. Vol. 5. *Enhancing Motivation*. Greenwich, Conn.: JAI Press, 1987.

Brophy, J., and Kher, N. "Teacher Socialization as a Mechanism for Developing Student Motivation to Learn." In R. Feldman (ed.), *Social Psychology Applied to Education*. New York: Cambridge University Press, 1986.

Carver, C.S., and Scheier, M.F. *Attention and Self-Regulation: A Control-Theory Approach to Human Behavior.* New York: Springer-Verlag, 1981.

Condry, J. "Enhancing Motivation: A Social Developmental Perspective." In M.L. Maehr and D.A. Kleiber (eds.), *Advances in Motivation and Achievement*. Vol. 5. *Enhancing Motivation*. Greenwich, Conn.: JAI Press, 1987.

Danish, S.J., Galambos, N.L., and Laquatra, I. "Life Development Interventions: Skill Training for Personal Competence." In R.D. Felner, L.A. Jason, J.N. Maritsugu, and S.S. Flarber (eds.), *Preventive Psychology: Theory, Research, and Practice*. New York: Pergamon Press, 1983.

deCharms, R. *Enhancing Motivation*. New York: Irvington, 1976.

deCharms, R. "The Burden of Motivation." In M.L. Maehr and D.A. Kleiber (eds.), *Advances in Motivation and Achievement*. Vol. 5. *Enhancing Motivation*. Greenwich, Conn.: JAI Press, 1987.

Deci, E.L., and Ryan, R.M. *Intrinsic Motivation and Self-Determination in Human Behavior*. New York: Plenum, 1985.

Diener, C.I., and Dweck, C.S. "An Analysis of Learned Helplessness: Continuous Changes in Performance, Strategy, and Achievement Cognitions Following Failure." *Journal of Personality and Social Psychology*, 1978, 36, 451–462.

Dweck, C.S. "The Role of Expectations and Attributions in the Alleviation of Learned Helplessness." *Journal of Personality and Social Psychology*, 1975, 31, 674–685.

Dweck, C.S., and Elliot, E.S. "Achievement Motivation." In E.M. Hetherington (ed.), *Handbook of Child Psychology*. Vol. 4. *Social and Personality Development*. (4th ed.) New York: Wiley, 1983.

Dweck, C., and Leggett, E.L. "A Social-Cognitive Approach to Motivation and Personality." *Psychological Bulletin*, 1988, 95, 256–273.

Dweck, C.S., and Licht, B.G. "Learned Helplessness and Intellectual Achievement." In M.E.P. Seligman and J. Garber (eds.), *Human Helplessness: Theory and Application*. Orlando, Fla.: Academic Press, 1980.

Dweck, C.S., and Reppucci, N.D. "Learned Helplessness and Reinforcement of Responsibility in Children." *Journal of Personality and Social Psychology*, 1973, 25, 109–116.

Farmer, H.S. "Female Motivation and Achievement: Implications for Interventions." In M.L. Maehr and D.A. Kleiber (eds.), *Advances in Motivation and Achievement*. Vol. 5. *Enhancing Motivation*. Greenwich, Conn.: JAI Press, 1987.

Forsyth, D.R. "An Attributional Analysis of Students' Reactions to Success and Failure." In R.S. Feldman (ed.), *The Social Psychology of Education*. New York: Cambridge University Press, 1986.

Forsyth, D.R., and McMillan, J.H. "Attributions, Affect, and Expectations: A Test of Weiner's Three-Dimensional Model." *Journal of Educational Psychology*, 1981, 73, 393–401.

Good, T.L., and Brophy, J.E. *Educational Psychology: A Realistic Approach*. (3rd ed.) New York: Longman, 1986.

Harris, M.J., and Rosenthal, R. "Mediation of Interpersonal Expectancy Effects." *Psychological Bulletin*, 1985, 97, 363–386.

Heckhausen, H., Schmalt, H-D., and Schneider, K. *Achievement Motivation in Perspective*. Orlando, Fla.: Academic Press, 1985.

Kleinbeck, U., Quast, H., and Schwarz, R. "Volitional Effects on Performance: Conceptual Considerations and Results from Dual-Task Studies." In R. Kanfer, P.L. Ackerman, and R. Cudeck (eds.), *Abilities, Motivation, and Methodology: The Minnesota Symposium on Learning and Individual Differences*. Hillsdale, N.J.: Erlbaum, 1989.

Lepper, M. "Extrinsic Reward and Intrinsic Motivation: Implications for the Classroom." In J. Levine and M. Wang (eds.), *Teacher and Student Perspectives: Implications for Learning*. Hillsdale, N.J.: Erlbaum, 1983.

Locke, E.A., and Latham, G.P. "Work Motivation and Satisfaction: Light at the End of the Tunnel." *Psychological Science*, 1990, *1*, 240–246.

Locke, E.A., Shaw, K.N., Saari, L.M., and Latham, G.P. "Goal Setting and Task Performance: 1969–1980." *Psychological Bulletin*, 1981, *90*, 125–152.

McClelland, D.C. *Human Motivation*. Glenview, Ill.: Scott, Foresman, 1985.

Maruyama, G. "What Causes Achievement? An Examination of Antecedents in Segregated and Desegregated Classrooms." In D.E. Bartz and M.L. Maehr (eds.), *Advances in Motivation and Achievement*. Vol. 1. Greenwich, Conn.: JAI Press, 1984.

Miller, R.L., Brickman, P., and Bolen, D. "Attribution Versus Persuasion as a Means for Modifying Behavior." *Journal of Personality and Social Psychology*, 1975, *31*, 430–441.

Noel, J., Forsyth, D.R., and Kelley, K.N. "Improving the Performance of Failing Students by Overcoming Their Self-Serving Attributional Biases." *Basic and Applied Social Psychology*, 1987, 8, 151–162.

Purkey, W.W. *Self-Concept and School Achievement*. Englewood Cliffs, N.J.: Prentice-Hall, 1970.

Rosenthal, R. "The Mediation of Pygmalion Effects: A Four-Factor 'Theory.'" *Papua New Guinea Journal of Education*, 1973, *9*, 1–12.

Rosenthal, R., and Jacobson, L. *Pygmalion in the Classroom: Teacher Expectation and Pupils' Intellectual Development*. New York: Holt, Rinehart & Winston, 1968.

Rotter, J.B. "Generalized Expectancies for Internal Versus External Control of Reinforcement." *Psychological Monographs*, 1966, *80* (entire issue 1).

Ryan, R.M., Mims, V., and Koestner, R. "Relation of Reward Contingency and Interpersonal Context to Intrinsic Motivation: A Review and Test Using Cognitive Evaluation Theory." *Journal of Personality and Social Psychology*, 1983, *45*, 736–750.

Tolman, E.C. "Principles of Performance." *Psychological Review*, 1955, *62*, 315–326.

Weiner, B. "An Attributional Theory of Achievement Motivation and Emotion." *Psychological Review*, 1985, *92*, 548–573.

White, R.M. "Motivation Reconsidered: The Concept of Competence." *Psychological Review*, 1959, *66*, 297–333.

Wilson, T.D., and Linville, P.W. "Improving the Academic Performance of College Freshmen: Attribution Therapy Revisited." *Journal of Personality and Social Psychology*, 1982, *42*, 367–376.

Wilson, T.D., and Linville, P.W. "Improving the Academic Performance of College Freshmen with Attributional Techniques." *Journal of Personality and Social Psychology*, 1985, *49*, 287–293.

Effective Social Arrangements for Teaching and Learning

JANET MANCINI BILLSON AND RICHARD G. TIBERIUS

What social arrangements are best suited to facilitate teaching and learning? In the previous chapter, we concluded that a new ideal for the social context of teaching and learning is emerging from contemporary theory and research. We described this ideal as an alliance between teachers and students. We identified five key features underlying the alliance: mutual respect; shared responsibility for learning and mutual commitment to goals; effective communication and feedback; cooperation and willingness to negotiate conflicts; and a sense of security in the classroom. In this chapter, we concentrate on how such social arrangements can be promoted, and we offer specific guidelines for promoting the alliance in the context of the classroom.

Promotion of the alliance requires us to shift our perception of the teacher as an agent of change in students to the teacher as a partner in the process of change. Shifting from the production/transmission metaphor to the dialogue metaphor—from controlling or managing students and classroom interaction to forming an alliance with students—is the critical change.

Guidelines for Strengthening the Alliance in the Classroom Group

Katz and Henry (1988) identify several basic learning principles that depend on the social context of the teaching-learning process. They conclude that teaching should be directed toward the transformation of students' passivity into active learning, through inquiry with others in a supportive atmosphere. We have argued that the alliance is central to the social context and have stressed the nature of the teacher-student relationship, but overcoming the sometimes impenetrable wall of students' passivity hinges on development of the student-student relationship and a commitment to collaborative inquiry. This leads us to a model for thinking of the class as a group and for using group activities in the classroom. In this section, we emphasize teaching as group facilitation and group leadership, rather than as one-way transmission of knowledge.

Keener awareness of group processes can enhance teaching effectiveness through improving participation levels, increasing individual and group motivation, stimulating enthusiasm, and facilitating communication in the classroom. Although the guidelines are presented here under the key features they are most readily associated with, all contribute to all features. The guidelines are applicable to our alliance with students as individuals and to our facilitative role in the classroom environment. They can be applied to any classroom, regardless of subject matter or, in some cases, size. They are explicated here in tandem with specific suggestions for course design and classroom management.

The principles of group interaction presented here are by no means exhaustive. Such issues as group emotion, transference (the tendency for students to relate to faculty in terms of feeling patterns developed toward their parents), social control, social status, or numerical propositions regarding group size are not directly addressed. An earlier version of several guidelines appears in Billson (1986); see also Billson (forthcoming).

"Effective Social Arrangements for Teaching and Learning," by Janet Mancini Billson and Richard G. Tiberius, reprinted from *New Directions for Teaching and Learning: Teaching from Theory to Practice,* No. 45, edited by R. J. Menges and M. D. Svinicki, 1991, Jossey-Bass Publishers, Inc.

Mutual Respect

In the previous chapter, we discussed the theory that communication has both content and relational components, with the latter providing the interpretive framework for the former. One implication of this theory is very encouraging. If learning about one another enhances the relational context, and if a better relational context facilitates understanding, then communication should become easier.

Guideline 1: Learn About Students. Teachers who wish to learn more about students should "listen for feelings as well as for thoughts, search for underlying messages, explore thoughts in depth by asking questions, and encourage expression of feelings by showing acceptance of students' feelings" (DeVito, 1986, p. 57). Since most of the contact between teachers and students takes place in classrooms, methods of gathering information during class should not be ignored. The old adage "Start where the student is" bears repeating. At the beginning of the term, three simple devices can help you gain more knowledge about your students:

1. Review results of institutional surveys of incoming freshmen.
2. Ask students to fill out 3 x 5 cards the first week of class, including name, major, age, career aspirations, current employment, residence, reasons for taking the course, other courses taken in the discipline, and other information of special interest.
3. Allow time for introductions at the term's beginning. Use name tags or desk cards to learn students' names. This is a minimum requirement for classes of thirty or fewer students.

Guideline 2: Help Students Learn About the Teacher. Scholl-Buchwald (1985, p. 17) recommends that teachers "share something about themselves that illuminates their values and styles and cuts through the stereotypes that students sometimes have of professors." He cites an example of a teacher who is bright, witty, and perhaps great fun at a party but who may intimidate students in the classroom. In order to dispel anxiety and improve attitudes toward learning, Scholl-Buchwald advises the teacher to disclose some of his or her own anxieties and shortcomings, or to playfully poke fun at offending characteristics in order to make light of them.

1. Begin the term by asking students to introduce each other in pairs. Participate in a pair yourself. Students can then introduce each other or themselves.
2. Open each class term with a brief introduction of yourself, your research and teaching interests, avocations, and approach to the course and to teaching.

Guideline 3: Develop Sensitivity to Nonverbal Cues. Another way teachers and students learn about each other is through nonverbal cues. Anderson (1986) reminds us of the importance of nonverbal communication, especially in learning about student preferences, values, beliefs, apprehensions, and interests. Nonverbal communication often provides the only data regarding attitudes of students in a large class.

Learning about students implies learning about their immediate reactions to the educational task at hand. Nonverbal cues can be misleading in this respect. Respectful silence can be mistaken for boredom or confusion. Attention to nonverbal cues is important for receiving and interpreting communication.

1. Attend to what students are doing—taking notes, looking at the handout, reading the newspaper. Frowning, fidgeting, sleeping, reading the college newspaper, slouching, and so on, may be as important feedback as that which students provide at the end of the term in a computerized questionnaire.
2. Have a class session videotaped and analyzed with a sympathetic colleague. An informal visit by a trusted colleague who attends to nonverbals may be equally instructive and less threatening.

Anderson supports the conclusion that nonverbal means of communication are well suited to disclosing teachers' attitudes toward their students. Eye contact, smiling, vocal expressiveness, physical proximity, gesturing, and body language can communicate feelings of warmth and support, or the opposite. Failure to attend to nonverbal cues hampers the teacher's ability to recognize incomprehension of or dissatisfaction with course materials and procedures. Students complain that the teacher is losing the class or over their heads. Often, they vote with their feet.

Guideline 4: Establish a Climate of Egalitarianism and Tolerance. Diverse backgrounds and interests can add to the richness of classroom interaction. They can also contribute to misunderstanding conflict, and uneven participation. Students, as people, bring to class their personalities, assumptions about the learning process, physical and emotional problems, and what happened on the way to class. (The same can be said of professors.) Although individuals may coalesce into a group as the term proceeds, this diversity underscores the need for informal preclass interaction, reiteration of clear norms and goals, and mechanisms that foster open participation.

Further, it is the responsibility of teachers and students to ensure that factors of race, gender, ethnicity, religion, sexual preference, lifestyle, and nationality are not allowed to exclude anyone directly or by implication. Inequality in classroom interaction has a poisonous effect on trust. Teachers should endeavor to establish egalitarian norms. The social context will be toxic if discriminatory comments are allowed to float unchallenged in the classroom. Students who feel excluded or slighted are likely to withdraw; both the victims and other students suffer from the loss of ideas. Invite each student to join the dialogue.

Egalitarian norms are as important in a chemistry or history class as they are in a sociology class on minority groups and race relations. Research on the classroom as a "chilly climate" for women indicates that teachers' behaviors that endanger security for women cover a wide range: recognizing and reinforcing comments from males more often than those from females, inviting males to solve math problems on the chalkboard more often than females, interrupting women's comments, making direct derogatory and sexist remarks, and offering more help outside the classroom to males (Constantinople, Cornelius, and Gray, 1988).

A safe climate for learning can be shattered by a remark such as "You girls won't understand this problem." We know of a math professor who taught calculation of the mean by asking females to give their bra sizes. Some withdrew in silent humiliation; others reported him to the affirmative action officer, in indignation. The problem with racist and sexist incidents is that all too many students withdraw rather than protest. Individualization and respect for differences in learning styles are also related to the development of tolerance for individual differences. As students are made more self-aware and respectful of their own strivings toward autonomy, they can also be helped to develop greater tolerance toward other differences that separate them.

1. Do not allow racist or sexist comments or actions to pass unnoticed. Draw students' attention to them, and help students explore the sources of prejudice and discrimination and how these inhibit full participation of all class members and hence the learning capacity of the class as the group.
2. Acknowledge feelings about differences, and create a safe climate for discussion. This fosters individual development as well as group solidarity.
3. Do not insist on a "politically correct" position. Help students explore all sides of a position and understand how they come to their various perspectives.

Guideline 5: Help Students Explore Differences and Find Commonalities on Key Issues. Students who discover, in the process of interacting with others, that their opinions, fears, or problems are not unique are less likely to feel timid in the future to express themselves. For example, a student who feels stupid in not solving an equation may experience a renewal of self-confidence and optimism when others admit the same difficulty. Ask simple questions in response to students' comments, especially unconventional or controversial ones: "Does anyone else ever feel that way?" "Have any of you ever had that problem or experience?" "Do you know anyone who has had that problem or experience?" This last question is particularly useful in stimulating discussion of social issues or psychological phenomena. Students who hesitate to discuss their own experiences or attitudes may be quick to discuss those of family members, neighbors, or friends. This paves the way to open discussion of their own prejudices, fears, biases, or questions.

Guideline 6: Remember That You Are a Role Model for Student Behavior. The leader of any group serves as a role model for its members. The way in which you play your role—including how you present expectations of students, carry out responsibilities, and handle privileges implicit in the professional role—has a profound effect on how students enact their role.

1. Early in the semester, model behavior you want your students to exhibit, particularly regarding punctuality, keeping agreements, tolerating dissent, respecting diversity, encour-

aging discussion, and being a good listener.

2. Model standards for academic productivity. If your syllabus is full of typographical and spelling errors, admonishments to students about turning in carefully prepared work will fall on deaf ears.
3. Keep ahead of the agreed-upon reading. If you are barely a page ahead of your students in reading assignments, encouraging them to read on schedule will hold little significance.
4. Try to teach courses that genuinely interest you. Students take the lead from you in terms of enthusiasm, energy, and excitement about subject matter. Chances are that if you are mildly bored with the course materials, your students will also be bored.
5. If you expect students to think critically, you should listen to divergent opinions, ask questions, and model critical thinking yourself.
6. If you want students to provide examples from their own experience, begin by sharing an experience of your own.
7. By saying "I don't know" when that is true, you help students to accept the limits of their own knowledge and to admit when they do not know or understand something.
8. By saying "But I know where we can find it," you help students believe that knowledge is worth pursuing.

Shared Responsibility and Mutual Commitment to Goals

As we argued in the previous chapter, an effective social context for teaching and learning is characterized by mutual commitment to the goals, methods, and evaluation of an educational experience. Every participant in a group is responsible for the outcome of the group interaction. A class consists of two roles, in complementary and reciprocal relationship—teacher and student. A teacher may suggest or assign readings; discussion will be vague and one-sided if students do not complete the reading on schedule. The class as a group will be held back from achieving its potential for meaningful and stimulating discussion.

Technically—because of contractual obligations, expertise, and power—the teacher has major responsibility for the outcome of a particular course. Yet college students, as adults (few are under eighteen), share a significant part of the responsibility for creating a successful learning experience. Making the shift from being a passive learner to an active one depends in large part on one's increasing willingness to accept shared responsibility for one's own educational experience.

This is a difficult concept for many students, who have been socialized into teacher-dependent learning relationships in elementary and secondary school. The task for young adults is in large part centered on establishing independence and autonomy from parents and other authority figures. For older adults, highly authoritarian classes can be an instant turnoff—they do not want to be treated "like children." The presumption of responsibility may make the difference between satisfaction with higher education and disgruntlement (see Kazmierski, 1989). Conducting the class as a cooperative learning group, which lessens the teacher's authority and strengthens peer relationships, can support that growth. Group interaction that stresses student responsibility, individuality, and diverse learning styles can reduce inhibition and foster growth.

Student discontent is often expressed outside the classroom and is never brought to the teacher's attention. Students may perceive themselves to be in a relatively powerless position as long as the teacher has the power of the final grade. A teacher who takes shared responsibility seriously and at the same time understands reluctance to ask questions or criticize a teacher's style or methods can try the following guidelines in order to promote student responsibility.

Guideline 7: Share Responsibility with the Learner. Flexibility in course organization and structure allows us to negotiate with each class as a particular constellation of individuals, with their special needs, interests, skills, and prior knowledge. This makes it more likely that students will be motivated to achieve those goals. They will be more willing to take responsibility not only for their own achievement but also for the success of the course. Frequent reference to the syllabus reinforces the relevance of commonly shared goals.

1. Explore at the beginning of each term the concept of joint responsibility, especially with regard to assignments and format.
2. Establish with students at the outset that their discontent, as well as yours, is "group business," and that you welcome their opinions and ideas. This sets the tone for openness and mutual responsibility toward course goals.
3. Prepare a few copies of a basic syllabus. Negotiate details of pacing, structure, and assignment weights during the first week of class. Distribute a revised syllabus the next week. Students feel more positive toward a course when they have had a meaningful role in planning it.
4. Give opportunities for students to plan certain segments of the course, to make class presentations under your guidance, or to suggest and arrange for discussion topics, debates, class speakers, and films.
5. Build in choices between papers and presentations, but invite those who write papers to share their work briefly with the class (or with a subgroup with similar interests).
6. Regardless of subject matter, students can contribute their ideas and information through formal and informal presentations. Simple techniques for facilitating such contributions include asking students to prepare definitions, find answers to directed questions, bring articles or research data for discussion in class, and work in small groups in class to generate questions (answers, policies, principles, theories, and so forth) for classwide deliberation.
7. Check out class sentiment early in the term, so that students' feedback can be incorporated, as appropriate, into the course format.
8. Encourage students to contribute course-structure ideas to a suggestion box, or set aside a few minutes for a periodic check on course progress.

Guideline 8: Strive Toward Balance Between the Socioemotional and Task Areas. As we pointed out in the previous chapter, the functions of any group fall into two fundamental areas: task and socioemotional. Morale, cohesion, solidarity, and effective problem solving rest on achieving a balance between them.

1. Help keep the class on schedule, or renegotiate meaningful deadlines.
2. Help keep the class on task by reiterating agreed-upon goals and initiating periodic assessments of progress toward them.
3. Attend to morale and cohesion by including them in periodic assessments.
4. Maintain good humor in working on tasks. Return to tasks after the use of humor and letting off steam.

Guideline 9: Encourage Emergent Student Leadership. Natural leaders may emerge among students and may function positively or negatively in the socioemotional and task areas. Roles such as joker, clown, negativist, organizer, or class spokesperson will materialize from time to time. As Benjamin (1978, p. 7) observes, "This leadership will encourage or discourage member involvement, form coalitions and factions, or attempt to rule unilaterally. It will operate with, oppose, or act independently of the formal group leader."

Student leadership can help create a strong alliance and contribute to productivity and morale. Nonconstructive, belligerent behavior can be redirected or discussed as part of class business. The teacher who is able to recognize informal leadership and other roles among students is likely to cope better with the class.

1. Notice student seating patterns, and observe informal conversations before and after class. Opinion leaders may be among the dominant participators in class, but some leadership will be expressed outside the classroom.

2. Encourage students who appear to be forming subgroups to bring their ideas and issues to the class as a whole.

3. Invite students who are comfortable with a leadership role to serve as facilitators or discussion leaders in subgroups.

Guideline 10: Build In Early Assessments. End-of-course evaluations may help assess teaching performance, but they do not afford students the opportunity to take real responsibility for the outcome of the course. Administer a simple instrument a few weeks into the course: "What do you like most about this course? What do you like least about it? Do you have any suggestions for improving it?" Responses are written and returned anonymously for discussion and possible fine-tuning or restructuring of the course format.

Guideline 11: Create Opportunities for Informal Interaction. The social climate of the classroom is elevated considerably by allowing a period at the beginning of each session for informal conversation. Coffee or stretch breaks and chatting before or after class are examples of informal interaction.

1. Each day, allow the class to warm up. Arrive a few minutes before class to afford a period of settling in. This is a time when students and teachers can learn more about each other.

2. Help students maintain contacts outside the classroom (this seems to be particularly important in commuter schools) by duplicating students' names and telephone numbers early in the term (with their permission, of course).

3. If logistically feasible, ask students to organize a refreshment pool for midclass breaks.

Students can hide more easily in larger classes, but because each individual is comparatively visible in classes of fewer than fifteen students, pressure to participate is greater on each individual and is also more likely to generate self-consciousness. The smaller the number of students, the more likely the student is to be called on or to be expected to participate. While this makes for a more personalized learning experience, it also may generate or tap into the self-consciousness that some students bring to the learning environment. For the most self-conscious students, building a safe climate is especially important.

Effective Communication and Feedback

Teaching strategies that afford multiple opportunities for individual and group feedback, both between teacher and student and among students, will contribute to a positive learning environment. Such strategies rely on open, multichannel communication, timely feedback, and the open flow of ideas.

Guideline 12: Break the Ice Early in the Group's Life. Some teachers use structured "ice breakers," especially early in the term, to help students get to know one another and to establish each particular classroom cohort as a group. Students will participate more readily when they have been given an opportunity to get to know each other and interact in subgroups before they interact in the group as a whole.

Breaking the ice with simple exercises will have long-term payoffs. Students can get a sense of the communication styles of other students and of the teacher. Ice breakers can be designed to serve simultaneously as catalysts for motivating students to master the course content.

1. Learn each student's name, where feasible, and use it.

2. Invite students to chat for a few minutes with the nearest person on either side. Encourage them to share information, such as why they are taking the course, their major, how they see the course fitting into their education, their concerns about the course, or other factors relevant to the course.

3. Serve as a model by sharing information about yourself, your interests, your educational and work background, why you teach the course.

4. Ask students to work in subgroups of three or four to define concepts central to the course: What is an atom? What is health? What is crime? What is literary criticism?

5. Ask students to pair off by numbers or by proximity. The topic they discuss is not particularly important. It may be biographical data on the first day of class, or an issue or problem relevant to course material. Give each pair ten minutes to talk. The dyadic form of in-

teraction is less threatening and establishes at least one bond for each student. Then ask each pair to join another pair and share information with other groups of four, then eights with eights, until one large group is created for a class discussion of what was learned in the smaller groups. This technique can also be used effectively with a class of thirty or more, but the progression must move in larger steps until the class is fully merged.

Although even one session of ice breaking will reduce barriers to communication and raise participation levels, shared responsibility and broad participation will be reinforced if students are asked to work in subgroups occasionally during the term.

Guideline 13: Emphasize Two-Way and Multichannel Communication. Boyer and Bolton (1971) distinguish between two types of communication and feedback patterns. In one-way communication, the flow of information is from one person to another (or to a group). This is typical of televised courses and lecture courses (regardless of size), in which the teacher leaves little time for questions or debate. In two-way communication, the flow of information is between and among two or more persons. The sender of a message has greater opportunity to receive immediate reactions from listeners. This is typical of seminars, small-group discussions, lecture/discussion courses, and study groups. (We prefer the term *multichannel* because it implies communication among students that is not directed to or through the teacher.) One-way communication is more efficient—a greater amount of material can be transmitted in a shorter amount of time. However, it is less accurate than two-way communication—the listener's understanding of the information is less complete. The teacher who is geared to straight lecturing may fail to take advantage of the opportunity for two-way communication.

A circle is the seating arrangement most conducive to effective feedback and communication, particularly if the teacher occupies a different place in the circle each session. Other suggestions for creating multichannel communication include the following:

1. Resist the temptation to answer all questions yourself. Redirect and rephrase questions for the class as a whole.
2. Encourage students to comment directly to each other, rather than through you.
3. Remind yourself of two-way communication: "The best general advice to the professor who would lecture well is still 'Don't lecture.' That is, for most of teaching, to think in terms of discourse—talk, conversation—rather than lecture" (Eble, 1976, p. 42).
4. Pause frequently to make sure students are still with you. "Lecturing creates the temptation to set one's voice on 'play' and forget everything else" (Eble, 1976, p. 48).
5. Avoid lecturing from a written script or text. If you do, provide students with a brief outline of your lectures. This allows them to listen more carefully to the flesh on the skeleton and helps them organize their listening.
6. During a lecture or discussion, frequently ask whether students have questions, comments, or reactions. This gatekeeping role also maintains student involvement and responsibility.
7. Allow silence after extending such an invitation. Students in general do not feel comfortable with silence, any more than teachers do. Someone will break the silence and pave the way to further discussion. Goldman-Eisler (1958) found that pauses in speech serve to introduce new and less predictable information. Thus the incidence of silence in group interaction may indicate flexibility in adapting to new situations and elasticity of group processes.
8. Make it a rule never to lecture all the way to the last minute of class, no matter how brilliant your lecture or how much you feel you must cover that day (see Highet, 1976).
9. Ensure that ample time is reserved during each class for student interaction and discussion of lectures, films, speakers, and so forth. This breaks the "transmission" metaphor of information and ideas flowing in one direction only. Even a class of five hundred students sitting in a lecture hall can be given a few minutes (in groups of three or four) to debate and discuss, apply concepts to examples, or clarify terms.

10. As a check on comprehension, ask students to analyze a situation or problem by employing the concepts or principles under discussion. This technique carries the message that you expect students to be active rather than passive learners.
11. Reward constructive participation with affirming comments and follow-up questions.

Guideline 14: Provide Multiple, Timely Opportunities for Feedback. The effectiveness of any group depends on the quality of the feedback contained in the interaction. Research shows that both teaching and learning are enhanced by timely, descriptive feedback and by interaction between teachers and students. This guideline reaches its logical conclusion in the recent trend toward mastery learning (Guskey, 1988), in which students are given scope to define issues, problems, and projects. Work and materials are broken into discrete blocks that can be targeted, attempted, and mastered, with many opportunities for immediate feedback, criticism, redirection, and consultation.

Other research (Egan, 1970, p. 247) shows that feeling-oriented, positive feedback results in the "greatest efficiency, least defensiveness, and greatest increase in participation." This is particularly important in discussing sensitive issues, stereotypical views, prejudices, and values.

1. Build in several points of evaluation, rather than one or two.
2. Return written work and exams in a timely fashion.
3. Remember that not all student work must be evaluated by the teacher. For example, written reactions to literary texts can receive feedback from other students working in small groups.
4. Ask students to give each other feedback on proposals for papers or projects before they are handed in to you. This gives them earlier feedback on their ideas, organization, and direction and helps students develop genuine interest in each other's work.
5. Build in a few minutes for students to work in pairs, giving each other feedback on draft papers or essays. Feedback can be structured in terms of what they found most interesting, what they would like to know more about, ideas for reorganization, further resources, and strengthening the introduction and conclusion.

Guideline 15: Foster Heterogeneity of Ideas. Teaching and learning profit from heterogeneity of ideas. Marton and Ramsden (1988) recommend several teaching strategies that will promote learning. One is to highlight inconsistencies in and consequences of learners' conceptions. Another is to offer new ways of seeing. By building on contradictions inherent in students' views of reality, you can lead them toward formulation of hypotheses, testing of myths, and reconceptualization. It is the tension created by competing or unusual views that makes the classroom intellectually fertile ground. Elbow (1986, p. 41) calls this "cooking." Ideas are channeled into the pool of information, opinions, concerns, and applications that is available for all in the classroom to work with. Elbow says that engaging the "competent, decent" student who is not particularly interested or involved requires this cross-fertilization of ideas and contrasting beliefs that can only come through group interaction.

Heterogeneity of ideas relies on and is a function of open communication. Even though students may be encouraged to feel more comfortable in the process of participating, they may still be reluctant regarding the content. Unconventional ideas and offbeat solutions to problems will emerge only if students feel safe in the classroom. If we want students to share responsibility for the outcome of a class, then it is critical to help them discover their interests, queries, concerns, confusions, and creative ideas. Tiberius (1986) finds evidence that effective teaching rests on meaningful material. Helping students become more self-reflexive in a secure environment helps unlock meaningful material. Creative and critical thinking can be amplified by even participation.

1. Use group techniques, such as brainstorming, to help students uncover beliefs, myths, values, and ideas. This is empowering rather than squelching, if organized effectively. The broader the pool of ideas, the better.
2. Organize a "fishbowl" discussion format, in which eight students sit in a circle to discuss an issue or solve a problem. Other students who wish to contribute raise their hands and

are admitted to the circle by those who are willing to give their seats up briefly. This seems to attract students who wish to make only one or two strong statements but are reluctant to participate.

3. Before discussing sensitive topics or solving complex problems, provide opportunities for students to express their ideas anonymously. For example, in teaching the concepts of prejudice, discrimination, and social distance, first ask students to fill out a brief questionnaire about their own ethnic identifications and attitudes.
4. For a science, mathematics, statistics, or research-design problem, ask students to write down their best attempts, even if they seem to be unorthodox solutions. Summarize the results, and present them anonymously at the next session. In this way, a wider range of ideas, values, and attitudes is available for discussion and problem solving.
5. For a history or literature question, ask students to write brief interpretations before the next class. These can be read in small groups, as a way of opening class discussion of a text or issue.
6. Reserve criticism or evaluation of contributions until they have become the property of the entire group and are less closely identified with any single contributor. Soliciting ideas individually or anonymously reduces the likelihood of receiving only conventional or conformist expressions and contributes to the heterogeneity of ideas available for discussion.

Guideline 16: Bring Each Class and Term to Appropriate Closure. All groups benefit from closure. Similarly, when a course ends, the termination process is important for continuity of the learning experience.

1. At the end of each class, summarize the main points of the day and suggest where they might lead in the next session.
2. At the end of each class, say goodbye and wish students a good day or weekend. These small closures serve to increase cohesion of the class as group and reinforce the alliance.

At the end of term, evaluation is a central part of closure. Teachers and students want to know how they fared in the course. There are scores of methods by which teachers can gather information about student opinions and attitudes regarding the teaching-learning situation (see Cross and Angelo, 1988; Weimer, 1987). Student ratings are the most popular form of course and teacher evaluation, but there is reason to believe that direct, face-to-face discussion between teachers and students may be more effective than written questionnaires, particularly in influencing teachers' and students' attitudes toward one another. This means that ratings must be administered prior to the end of the semester.

1. Ask students to engage in an informal feedback session, reflecting on the successes and failures of the course. This may be more instructive than the computerized evaluations typically conducted by departments.
2. Set aside at least one class to recapitulate major points of learning that occurred throughout the term, to reflect on how the class worked together as a group, and to link learning with future courses.

Unfortunately, evaluative information to students is often lacking at terms' end. Papers are graded and left in boxes for students to retrieve during the next semester. Final exams are taken, without discussion of results. Opportunities for self-evaluation are usually absent. Meaningful closure requires some major adjustments to standard course structures (and perhaps to institutional policies).

1. Term papers should be due well before the end of the course, so that information can be given to students in a meaningful way.
2. Give final exams one or two weeks prior to term's end, so that results can be discussed.
3. Invite students to write brief evaluations of what they have learned and what they have contributed to the class. These can be shared in small groups.

4. If time permits, hold a cooperative class party to say goodbye. This leaves a positive invitation with students to continue interacting with both you and each other after the course has ended.

Cooperation

This key feature of the alliance involves moving students from competition toward cooperation. Kohn (1986, pp. 123–124) summarizes a substantial body of literature that points to competition as one of the primary inhibitors of "the security that is so vital for healthy human development. We are anxious about losing, conflicted about winning, and fearful about the effects of competition on our relationships with others—effects that include hostility, resentment, and disapproval." Kohn reminds us about the well-documented negative effect of anxiety on performance. As an antidote, he recommends heavy doses of cooperation. His recommendation is supported by Johnson, Johnson, and Maruyama's (1983) review of ninety-eight studies, in which they conclude that cooperation promotes more positive relationships. Teachers can design classroom structures so that students gain by helping one another, rather than by beating one another (see Millis, 1990).

Guideline 17: Promote Cooperation and Teamwork. It is important to devote class time to discussing these issues and participating in activities that illustrate them.

1. Teach students how to become more aware of their own competitiveness. Inform them about the destructive potential of competition.

2. Shift to process competition, in which students engage in an activity for its own sake, rather than for some product or outcome.

Palmer (1987, p. 25) makes a distinction between healthy conflict and competition: conflict stimulates the active engagement of students in dialogue with one another, while "competitive individualism breeds silent, *sub rosa*, private combat for personal reward." Indeed, he argues that, to sustain healthy conflict, the destructive effects of competition must be reduced by group supportiveness, making learners feel emotionally safe in the group.

Billson (forthcoming) has devised a method of team exams in introductory-level criminology courses. Students work in pairs throughout the semester—reviewing materials, generating questions for class discussion and clarification, and testing each other on central concepts, trends, and theories. The pairs take three exams (without books or notes), working through a standard objective test of multiple-choice, true-false, and matching questions. The two students must negotiate the answers quietly, filling in the computer sheet only when they have reached a high level of agreement. This forces students to think through questions and answers and reduces "potshot" responses. Students also define several concepts and write an essay collaboratively. Under this model, which rests on team cooperation and some mild interteam competition, students' performance on exams is slightly higher than on individual exams. Class morale builds rapidly, teams tend to study harder than many individuals otherwise would, there is more commitment to asking questions about material, and the teacher has only half the exams to evaluate. Students who prefer to take individual exams are permitted to do so, but few choose that option.

Guideline 18: Foster Even Participation Levels. Students fall along a continuum of participation, from high (dominators) to low (quiet ones). Although most students want to participate, it is not unusual for a handful of students (and not always the brighter or best-prepared ones) to dominate discussion. This is true of most groups, unless specific efforts are made by the leader to elicit broader participation.

Although simultaneous talking and interrupting can be signs of a dynamic discussion and high involvement, they can also be used to close out less assertive members of a class. Very early in each course, students begin to be labeled as dominant or quiet. Labels tend to harden unless the teacher facilitates even participation. A variety of gatekeeping measures can be utilized for this purpose.

1. When a high-level participator makes a point, invite comments from others: "How do others feel about this?" "Any other ideas on this question?" "Let's hear from some who haven't had a chance to talk yet" "Are there other ways to look at this? Other solutions?"

2. Use nonverbal cues and body language to invite participation from other students.

3. Make eye contact with quieter students. Shift your stance toward them. Sit next to them.
4. If you use a circle for discussion, change your position each session. Never sit directly opposite a high participator who tends to monopolize the conversation.
5. Establish, with students' consent, a norm of noninterruption, to help quieter students who find it difficult to complete a sentence in an ongoing discussion and who succumb quickly to the efforts of dominants and interrupters.
6. Be cognizant of participation levels in forming work groups.
7. If the problem of a few dominants persists, consider engaging the class in a discussion of how they feel about the participation levels.

Many teachers are reluctant to call on students who do not voluntarily participate. However, good gatekeeping typically creates an atmosphere in which more students voluntarily participate, and in which being called on is not a traumatic experience.

Guideline 19: Work Toward Exploration and Resolution of Conflict. Being able to mediate conflicts and bring debates to some level of resolution is a central role for the facilitative teacher. In virtually any group, differences generate the formation of subgroups along certain lines (cleavages), such as gender, age, major, social class, race, residence, political views, and so forth. Students tend to form various subgroups in class. Efforts to explore and cut across cleavages heighten participation at the classwide level. Activities or discussions that cut across cleavages tend to reduce conflict and increase empathy among subgroups, thereby increasing participation.

1. Find ways to create heterogeneous work groups. You can ask students to count off, or ask students to work with others in their row, section of the classroom, or year in school. Better still, ask students to select others who they think may have different views.
2. When conflict emerges, invite students to break into brainstorming groups or focused-discussion groups, in order to explore the sources and nature of the conflict, as well as possible resolutions. Groups can reflect new combinations of students for each conflict.
3. When cleavages seem to cluster around two major positions (for example, opposing or supporting gun control, abortion, or intervention in world affairs), organize on-the-spot debates. Make sure that approximately half the class is on each side, by asking students to cross over to the minority position. It can be equally instructive for them to argue positions they do not hold. Give each side ten minutes to prepare arguments and select someone to make an opening statement. Ask students to raise their hands to be recognized, one person per side, one statement per person, until all students on both sides have had a chance to speak. Then ask the class as a whole to discuss the merits of each side's arguments.
4. Ask students to answer, on paper, the question "Who am I?" ten times. Then ask them to form groups of four or five and discuss their responses with each other. This is especially appropriate for stimulating class discussion of such concepts as identity, self-image, personality, and ethnic, racial, or gender identification. Empathy and tolerance may improve.
5. Stimulate debate and dissent while maintaining norms of respect and tolerance for differences of opinion.

Security and Trust

An effective social context requires students and teachers alike to work toward a safe, coercion-free environment. Student participation, performance, and evaluation of teachers are higher when the classroom is safe; when students feel threatened, they regress to surface learning strategies (Eizenberg, cited in Jones, 1989; Numell and Rosengren, 1986). Reciprocal feedback, cooperation, and mutual responsibility cannot occur in a climate of threat, anxiety, and fear of reprisal or putdowns. The alliance hinges on the student's sense of security and safety in the classroom.

In a safe climate, students will feel more comfortable about displaying either ignorance or knowledge. They will also be more willing to share experiences and expertise and to disagree with other points of view. Reduction of self-consciousness, apathy, and boredom will enhance dialogue; participation levels and class attendance will increase. The group climate affects students' sense of belonging and whether they look forward to class, participate, drop the class, or leave college altogether. Safety and security depend on many factors.

Although structural changes, such as separating the role of teacher as facilitator from the role of teacher as evaluator, are important, they require massive reordering of the university environment toward mastery learning or competency-based evaluation. Still, there is much that individual teachers can do to develop trust.

Guideline 20: Make It Safe to Take Risks and to Be Wrong. Svinicki (1989) reminds us that learning is a risky business, and teachers need to support learners to make learning safer. She describes four strategies for building a trusting relationship with the learner: modeling how to take risks, minimizing the pain of making an error, exuding organization and competence, and providing risk-taking opportunities. In practical terms, this may include the following strategies:

1. Work toward accepting criticism of your own ideas or methods.
2. Build in ungraded student minipresentations (risk taking, but minimizing pain of making errors).
3. Take offbeat ideas seriously.
4. Freely admit when you do not understand or know something. This helps students feel safe in doing the same.
5. Help students establish norms of not interrupting or ridiculing each other when they disagree.
6. Avoid personal comparison as a method of motivating students.

Guideline 21: Keep the Doors Open for All Students. A classroom that is dominated by a few students does not constitute an alliance. It is merely the interaction of a comfortable, vocal elite with the teacher. Others may feel left out and may find it too threatening to break into the dialogue. Work toward even participation, in which dominators are motivated to share classroom space with quieter students, and low participators feel safe to express themselves.

Guideline 22: Reduce the Status Differential Between Teacher and Student. According to Boyer and Bolton (1971), the professor who is perceived by students as having "psychological bigness" inhibits participation and the establishment of a positive climate. Psychological bigness stems from frequent reference to the teacher's high status and titles, a formal manner, displaying an overwhelming amount of detailed knowledge, and using sarcasm, ridicule, veiled or open threats, or terminal statements. These characteristics tend to be associated with domination, rather than with leadership. Here are some suggestions for not outranking students:

1. Resist cutting off questioning.
2. Include and invite multiple explanations of reality.
3. Do not insist that your position is the only correct one. Encourage students to do their own research and exploration.
4. Respond positively to a student's initial attempts to communicate, and invite further contributions. This will affect whether a student risks contributing again.
5. Respond to all comments. Avoid passing students over. Comments that are not quite on the mark can be responded to invitationally: "Good. Now let's take it a step farther." "Keep going." "That could become important later. Don't forget what you had in mind."
6. Avoid putdowns and close-off comments, such as "You're way off" or "You're the only one who doesn't understand" or "You've missed the whole point" or "You haven't heard of. . . ?"

7. Avoid sarcasm or ridicule.

8. Avoid making terminal statements, where no disagreement is possible.

9. Before dialogue has passed on to another focus, make healing comments to both sides of a conflict. This will ensure that students are not reluctant to participate again.

Guideline 23: Ask Questions in an Open and Constructive Manner. Another factor in creating a safe environment is the method of questioning to find out what students know or believe. Firing questions at students to determine their level of comprehension is likely to provoke protective silence. Questions should be constructed that encourage students to risk speaking out in class.

1. Begin by asking open-ended questions, or questions that require a group response rather than a single-person response.

2. Reserve a question period. Once you have decided to use this method, stick to it. Do not rush to fill the time by talking if questions are slow in coming.

3. Ask students to try out their questions first on someone who sits beside them in class.

4. Have students prepare questions between classes, which they submit in writing at the beginning of the next class. These set the tone for the lecture and other in-class activities.

Guideline 24: Handle Disturbing Behavior Constructively. Trust and security in the classroom also depend on how describing behavior is handled. Violation of classroom ground rules or of basic norms governing social conduct must be addressed if the classroom is to remain safe. Teachers who, for fear of making matters worse, allow one or two students to disrupt the classroom usually create growing resentment on the part of students who are oriented toward cooperative interaction. The majority must feel that their rights are being protected, too. At all times, however, the question of handling inappropriate behavior is a sensitive one.

1. Negotiate ground rules with students at the beginning of the course. Then, such classroom discourtesies as arriving late, leaving early, talking off subject, interrupting, horsing around, failing to hold up one's end in group projects, and so forth, can be addressed by referring the student back to those ground rules, which belong to the group, not to the teacher alone.

2. If disruptive behavior persists, suggest that the class reassess its ground rules.

Security becomes self-reinforcing. Participation broadens as trust increases. As students begin to open up, they discover they are not alone in their confusion or in their opinions. The resulting "all in the same boat" feeling increases trust and participation (Billson, 1986). There are many other devices for creating security, stimulating questions, and fostering interaction that helps teachers to learn about students. For large-group teaching, see Weimer (1987); for small-group teaching, see Tiberius (1990).

Guideline 25: Be Aware of the Development of Group Norms. A group will set its own norms of behavior and will expect conformity to them. These may extend to the teacher. Norms develop in every classroom group. Negative norms may emerge, such as entering late, leaving early, missing classes, relying on a handful of students to engage in pseudodiscussion, punishing "rate busters" who read and complete assignments on time, and manipulating extensions on due dates. Positive norms, such as being prepared to discuss readings, cooperating with others to solve problems, and showing tolerance of diversity, may also develop. In either case, it is more likely that emerging norms will be apparent to the teacher in a safe climate and when channels of communication are open.

1. As soon as you or students notice them, openly discuss norms that work against achieving the goals of the course.

2. Note the emergence of positive norms, and invite students to continue the good work. Chances are that they have also noticed that others are reading, contributing, or showing respect.

Conclusion

Schön (1987) points out the gap between our growing awareness of the importance of social arrangements in the classroom and the actual behavior of teachers. Translating theory into practice, or insight into a dynamic teaching-learning relationship, can be frustratingly elusive. Defining the classroom as a cooperative learning group that is subject to the same principles of interaction as other groups can contribute to our chances of making the shift from theory to practice. The guidelines delineated here can make us more aware of classroom interaction, process, and communication patterns. We can shape techniques of classroom management according to our understanding of group processes, through creating personalized strategies appropriate to subject areas and personal teaching styles.

Sensitivity to group-building and group-maintenance techniques can contribute to enhanced satisfaction, success, and retention by raising levels of both academic and social involvement in the learning process. Social arrangements between students and teachers can be strengthened in ways that foster intellectual and social growth for students and challenges for teachers. This in turn will nurture teachers' satisfaction with and enjoyment of teaching.

There are many roads to learning, and learning is enhanced in an atmosphere of cooperation (Tiberius, 1986). Viewing the teaching-learning process as an alliance, conceiving of the classroom as a group situation, and taking full account of the social context of educational experiences we share with students moves us toward the metaphor of dialogue and away from that of the transmission of banks of material. A secure classroom climate, in which students help set the agenda, improves chances that they will engage meaningfully in the learning process.

The effectiveness of a teacher's strategy depends on the nature of the alliance between teacher and students. In turn, the alliance rests on whether the methods a teacher chooses are helpful to students, are accepted by students, and are seen by students as the outcome of a caring teacher who is trying to facilitate learning.

How a teacher regards the alliance is partly a function of that teacher's stage of professional development. According to Pratt (1989), teachers at an early stage of development need the certainty of universal strategies. Teachers at this stage of readiness tend to view the alliance as a product of their own good performance. They may rigidly apply recommendations such as those described in this chapter in the hope of making an alliance happen. With luck, if circumstances are right, they may achieve more effective social arrangements with their students. However, their chances of success will be much greater as they begin to learn that recommended strategies, particularly those aimed at enhancing the social arrangements underlying teaching and learning, are not universal but apply only to certain well-defined situations. Knowing when to do what is a judgment that comes slowly, with experience and reflection.

During the second stage of teacher development, teachers shift "from fixing routines and flexible problem solving" (Pratt, 1989, p. 79). Teachers at this stage are more flexible in responding to the demands of the situation with constructions of their own that reflect a sensitivity to new situations. They regard all teaching strategies as conditional—that is, as dependent on the context and the situation. They begin to perceive their teaching situation "as a set of dynamic, interactive variables that require flexible and adaptive use of their existing knowledge" (Pratt, 1989, p. 80). Teachers at this stage of development tend to perceive the alliance between teachers and learners as more than a product of good teaching. They also view it as a vehicle or method for improving teaching and learning.

The third stage of professional development, according to Pratt (1989, p. 81), "is characterized by a consideration of the relationship between social and cultural values and teachers' professional knowledge. . . . Ways of thinking and acting are understood to be cultural as well as conditional." Teachers at this stage begin to realize that their perceptions of the alliance are formed by the metaphors of teaching and learning and by the implicit theories of teaching and learning that they and their students hold. They try to make their theories more explicit, and to incorporate those contextual factors into them, both within and beyond the classroom.

References

Anderson, J.F. "Instructor Nonverbal Communication: Listening to Our Silent Messages." In J.M. Civikly (ed.), *Communicating in College Classrooms.* New Directions for Teaching and Learning, no. 26. San Francisco: Jossey-Bass, 1986.

Benjamin, A. *Behavior in Small Groups.* Boston: Houghton Mifflin, 1978.

Billson, J.M. "The College Classroom as a Small Group: Some Implications for Teaching and Learning." *Teaching Sociology,* 1986, 14, 143–151.

Billson, J.M. "Group Process in the Classroom: Building Relationships for Learning." In C.B. Howery, N. Perrin, and J. Seem (eds.), *Teaching Applied Sociology: A Resource Book.* Washington, D.C.: American Sociological Association, forthcoming.

Boyer, R.K., and Bolton, C.K. *One-Way and Two-Way Communication Process in the Classroom.* Cincinnati, Ohio: Faculty Resource Center, University of Cincinnati, 1971.

Constantinople, A., Cornelius, R., and Gray, J. "The Chilly Climate: Fact or Artifact?" *Journal of Higher Education,* 1988, 59, 527–551.

Cross, K.P., and Angelo, T.A. *Classroom Assessment Techniques: A Handbook for Faculty.* Ann Arbor, Mich.: National Center for Research on Improving Postsecondary Teaching and Learning, 1988.

DeVito, J.A. "Teaching as Relational Development." In J.M. Civikly (ed.), *Communicating in College Classrooms.* New Directions for Teaching and Learning, no. 26. San Francisco: Jossey-Bass, 1986.

Eble, K.E. *The Craft of Teaching.* San Francisco: Jossey-Bass, 1976.

Egan, G. *Encounter: Group Processes for Interpersonal Growth.* Belmont, Calif.: Brooks/Cole, 1970.

Elbow, P. *Embracing Contraries: Explorations in Learning and Teaching.* New York: Oxford University Press, 1986.

Goldman-Eisler, F. "Speech Production and the Predictability of Words in Context." *Quarterly Journal of Experimental Psychology,* 1958, 10, 96–106.

Guskey, T.R. *Improving Student Learning in College Classrooms.* Springfield, Ill.: Thomas, 1988.

Highet, G. *The Immortal Profession.* New York: Weybright and Talley, 1976.

Johnson, D.W., Johnson, R.T. and Maruyama, G. "Interdependence and Interpersonal Attraction Among Heterogeneous Individuals: A Theoretical Formulation and a Meta-Analysis of the Research." *Review of Educational Research,* 1983, 53, 5–54.

Jones, J. "Students' Ratings of Teacher Personality and Teaching Competence." *Higher Education,* 1989, 18, 551–558.

Katz, J., and Henry, M. *Turning Professors into Teachers: A New Approach to Faculty Development and Student Learning.* New York: American Council on Education/Macmillan, 1988.

Kazmierski, P. "The Adult Learner." In D. Grieve (ed.), *Teaching in College: A Resource for College Teachers.* Cleveland, Ohio: INFO-TEC, 1989.

Kohn, A. *No Contest: The Case Against Competition.* Boston: Houghton Mifflin, 1986.

Marton, F., and Ramsden, P. "What Does It Take to Improve Teaching?" In P. Ramsden (ed.), *Improving Learning: New Perspectives.* London: Kogan Page, 1988.

Millis, B.J. "Helping Faculty Build Learning Communities Through Cooperative Groups." *To Improve the Academy,* 1990, 9, 43–58.

Numella, R.M., and Rosengren, T. M. "What's Happening in Students' Brains May Redefine Teaching." *Educational Leadership,* May 1986, pp. 49–53.

Palmer, P.J. "Community, Conflict, and Ways of Knowing." *Change,* 1987, 19 (5), 20–25.

Pratt, D.D. "Three Stages of Teacher Competence: A Developmental Perspective." In E. Hayes (ed.), *Effective Teaching Styles.* New Directions for Continuing Education, no. 43. San Francisco: Jossey-Bass, 1989.

Scholl-Buchwald, S. "The First Meeting of the Class." In J. Katz (ed.), *Teaching as Though Students Mattered.* New Directions for Teaching and Learning, no. 21. San Francisco: Jossey-Bass, 1985.

Schön, D.A. *Educating the Reflective Practitioner.* San Francisco: Jossey-Bass, 1987.

Svinicki, M. "If Learning Involves Risk-Taking, Teaching Involves Trust-Building." *Teaching Excellence: Toward the Best in the Academy,* Fall 1989, pp. 1–2.

Tiberius, R.G. "Metaphors Underlying the Improvement of Teaching and Learning." *British Journal of Educational Technology,* 1986, 17, 144–156.

Tiberius, R.G. *Small-Group Teaching: A Trouble-Shooting Guide.* Toronto, Canada: OISE Press, 1990.

Weimer, M.G. *Teaching Large Classes Well.* New Directions for Teaching and Learning, no. 32. San Francisco: Jossey-Bass, 1987.

The Kolb Model Modified for Classroom Activities

MARILLA D. SVINICKI AND NANCY M. DIXON

It's five minutes before the hour in a typical college classroom. As students wander in singly or in small groups, early comers read the student newspaper, chat about their evening's activities, glance over the reading assignment, compare notes on the homework, or set up their notebook for today's class. As the bell rings, the instructor makes his entrance, laden with books and notes which he piles on the desk at the front of the room. After a few brief announcements concerning upcoming assignments, he lays out his lecture notes on the podium and launches into today's material. The students dutifully begin to transcribe whatever seems relevant. Not much changes in that scene for the next fifty minutes, after which the bell rings and the class files out, only to be replaced by the same procedure for the next class period.

This scene is repeated innumerable times every day in classrooms across the country. While there is some variation, particularly in performance-based classes such as language or mathematics, the use of alternative activities in the college classroom is minimal at best. Instructors, being primarily subject matter experts, tend to focus their attention on the content of their courses, equating "teaching" with "covering the content" and giving much less thought to the instructional methodology they use. Thus they tend to rely on the standard instructional activities used by their own professors, such as lecture, discussion, and laboratories. A study conducted by Trani (1979) of 4,433 students in five midwestern institutions found the most frequently used teaching methods were the traditional ones of formal and informal lecture, discussion, laboratory, and audiovisual aids.

An interesting twist to this finding is that both students and faculty in Trani's study indicated that they would ideally like to experience less formal lecture and more of other teaching methods. If everyone in the classroom would like more variety, why don't instructors use more alternative methods? We believe there are many reasons for their reluctance, including time pressures, familiarity and comfort with the standard methods, and fear of failure. But an additional and perhaps more subtle source of a limited approach to instructional methodology could be the absence of a theoretical framework for selecting and organizing classroom activities to enhance learning.

Our purpose is to use an already well-established model that describes the process of learning as a basis for selecting and sequencing activities. An understanding of the model should help the instructor take maximum advantage of the tools with which he or she is already familiar and might even lead an instructor to create his or her own new learning activities appropriate to the particular course. Let's begin by examining the model and then see how it can be used in instructional design.

The Experiential Learning Model

The experiential learning model of Kolb (1984) provides a framework for examining the selection of a broader range of classroom activities than is in current use. Building on Dewey, Lewin and Piaget, Kolb has postulated that learning involves a cycle of four processes, each of which must be present for learning to occur most completely (see Figure 1). The cycle begins with the learner's personal involvement in a specific experience. The learner reflects on this experience from many viewpoints, seeking to find its meaning. Out of this reflection the learner draws logical conclusions (abstract conceptualization) and

"The Kolb Model Modified for Classroom Activities," by Marilla D. Svinicki and Nancy M. Dixon, reprinted from *College Teaching*, No. 35, 1987, Heldref Publications, 1319 Eighteenth St. N. W., Washington, D. C. 20036-1802. Reprinted by permission of the Helen Dwight Reid Foundation.

Figure 1
Experiential Learning Cycle

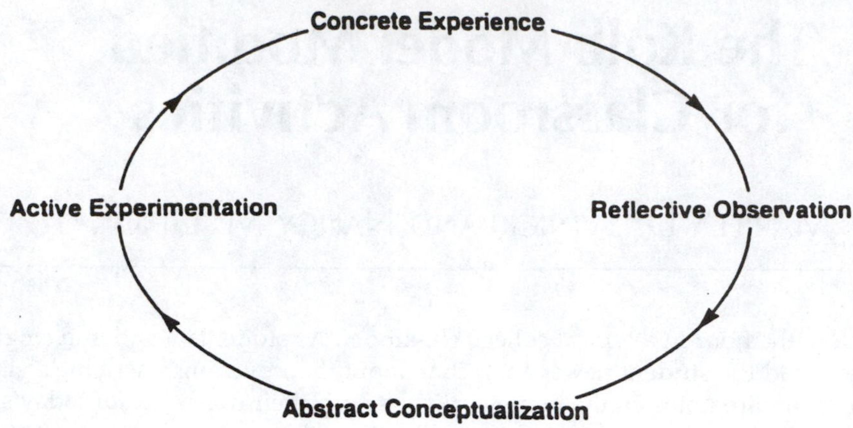

may add to his or her own conclusions the theoretical constructs of others. These conclusions and constructs guide decisions and actions (active experimentation) that lead to new concrete experiences.

The axes of the figure represent the two dimensions of the learning task. The vertical dimension (concrete experience to abstract conceptualization) represents the input of information either from experience or from abstractions. The horizontal dimension (reflective observation to active experimentation) refers to the processing of information by either internally reflecting on the experience or externally acting upon the conclusions which have been drawn.

Figure 2
Instructional activities that may support different aspects of the learning cycle

CONCRETE EXPERIENCE
laboratories
observations
primary text reading
simulations/games
field work
trigger films
readings
problem sets
examples

ACTIVE EXPERIMENTATION
simulations
case study
laboratory
field work
projects
homework

REFLECTIVE OBSERVATION
logs
journals
discussion
brainstorming
thought questions
rhetorical questions

ABSTRACT CONCEPTUALIZATION
lecture
papers
model building
projects
analogies

Experiential Learning as Instructional Design

We would add to this basic model the proposal that certain activities support different phases of this cycle. By constructing learning sequences that lead students through the full cycle, an instructor should be able to foster a more complete learning than can be gained from a single perspective. Figure 2 lists learning activities representative of each of the four poles of the learning cycle. For example, field experiences, inquiry laboratories, direct data collection, and the reading of primary sources such as poetry are all designed to give the learner firsthand, personal experiences with the content. Activities such as discussion and journal keeping force students to reflect on their experiences and the experiences of others. Model building exercises, research papers, or lectures that present a model foster abstract conceptualization. Simulations and projects force students to apply the models to problem situations.

Thus to produce a complete cycle, the instructor would select an activity from each pole and guide the students through them in order. For example, a unit designed for political science, which focuses on age variables related to political attitudes, might begin with field work. Students could conduct interviews with people of different age groups (concrete experience). Each student could categorize his or her own observations (reflective observation) and make initial speculations on differences between the ages represented. Next the class as a whole could pool their results and identify common age patterns to generate a model (abstract conceptualization) that describes how different age groups are likely to react to other political questions. Finally, the class could test their hypotheses by follow-up interviews with other members of the same age groups (active experimentation). Figure 3 illustrates a similar sequence of instructional activities in a number of different disciplines.

A specific activity, such as viewing a film, may fit into more than one category depending upon the instructional intent. In the political science unit discussed earlier, interviewing was used twice, first as a concrete experience and later as active experimentation. However, the purpose for which interviewing was employed at each point in the learning was different. In the first instance, the purpose was to "see what is," and in the second instance, the purpose was to verify a theory. Laboratory activities are another illustration of how an activity might fit into more than one step in the sequence. For example, when laboratory activities precede instruction, their intent may be exploratory, such as is used in inquiry teaching. When the laboratory activities occur later in the instructional sequence, they may serve as a way to apply what is being learned, i.e., they involve active experimentation.

A similar case could be drawn for the use of film, case study, simulations, projects, etc. Thus an instructor, in selecting learning activities to correspond with each of the four poles of the experiential learning model, must give greater consideration to the functional use of the activity than to the activity itself.

To assist the teacher in concentrating on the experience of the students when applying the model, we can modify the Kolb cycle slightly by designating the four activities with action verbs that describe the activity of the learner at each step. Thus, concrete experience becomes experiencing; reflective observation becomes examining; abstract conceptualization becomes explaining; and active experimentation becomes applying.

The second term of each of these pairs focuses our attention on what the student is doing at each phase of the cycle. We can specify that a film used during the concrete experience phase is intended to allow the student to "experience" some event or phenomenon, while a film used during the abstract conceptualization phase is intended to explain a concept. Discussion in the reflective observation phase is focused on examining an idea, while discussion in the abstract conceptualization phase would be conducted to allow students to develop an explanation of a concept.

Disciplinary Differences

While the proposed instructional framework has a great deal of intuitive appeal, there may be some other immediate considerations. For example, in selecting instructional activities to incorporate into the experiential learning cycle, it may be appropriate to take into account the fundamental differences in the nature of the discipline being taught. Kolb has suggested (Figure 4A) that the disciplines of humanities and social science are based in concrete experience and reflective observation, the natural sciences and mathematics in reflective observation and abstract conceptualization, the science-based professions in abstract conceptualization and active experimentation, and the social professions in active experimentation and concrete experience.

Figure 3
Sample Instructional Sequences

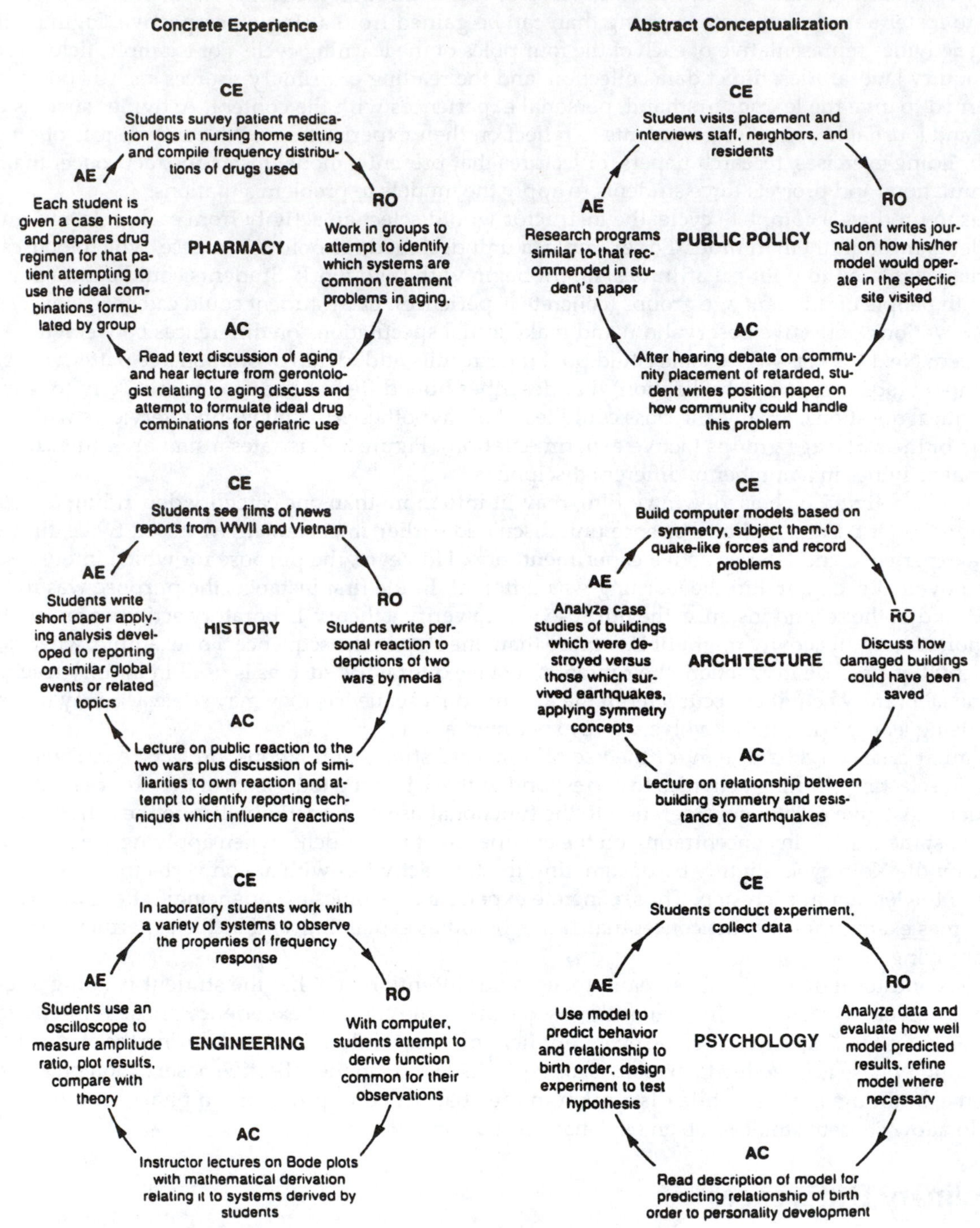

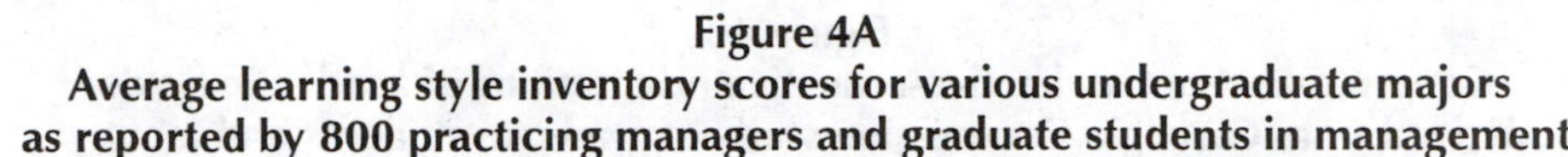

Figure 4A
Average learning style inventory scores for various undergraduate majors as reported by 800 practicing managers and graduate students in management

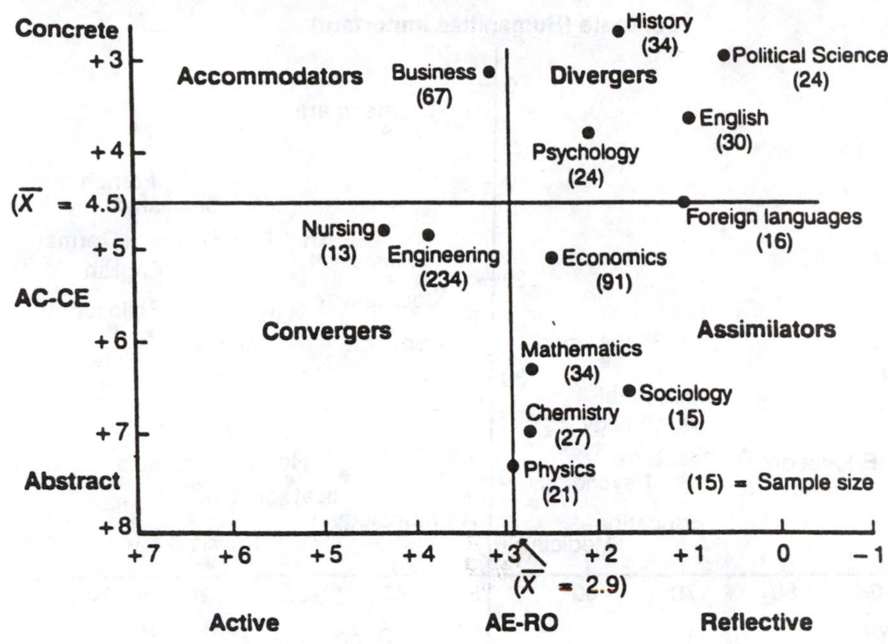

Source: Kolb, D.A. 1976. Management and learning processes. *California Management Review*, 18(3):21–31.

This construction was confirmed by Biglan (1973) when he asked faculty members to group different disciplines on the basis of similarity. Biglan found two dimensions, "soft-hard" and "pure-applied" which corresponded to Kolb's concrete-abstract and reflective-active dimensions. Biglan's results were supported with data collected in the Carnegie Commission on Higher Education 1969 study (Figure 4B).

If the general focus of a discipline is toward two specific poles of the experiential learning cycle, then the discipline itself may circumscribe an instructor's choice of learning activities. For example, in the abstract and reflective discipline of mathematics, it may be difficult to design activities which represent concrete experience and active experimentation. Likewise in history, which appears to be more concrete and reflective, activities which represent active experimentation may be more difficult to design. When such disciplinary constraints limit an instructor's choices, one possible solution, discussed in the next section, is to vary the instruction along another dimension, the student as actor versus student as receiver.

Student as Actor versus Student as Receiver

A second variable afffecting the application of this design model may be the nature of the student's role. This variable would be reflected in a continuum of action of activities placed at any one of the four poles of Kolb's model as seen earlier in Figure 2. The continuum would range from activities in which the student is the actor to those in which the student is a more passive receiver of the learning. Figure 5 illustrates this continuum for each of the poles of the experiential learning model. Activities at the outer edge of the circle most directly involve the student, while those closer to the center involve the student merely as an observer or listener.

The political science sequence cited earlier would fall near the outer circle of the graph. A political science sequence designed to be closer to the center, with students as receivers, might include activities such as: the instructor describes some examples of survey responses (concrete experience); the instructor shows graphed results of survey responses displayed in frequency and age distributions (reflective ob-

Figure 4B
Concrete-abstract and active-reflective orientations of academic fields derived from Carnegie Commission study of graduate students and faculty

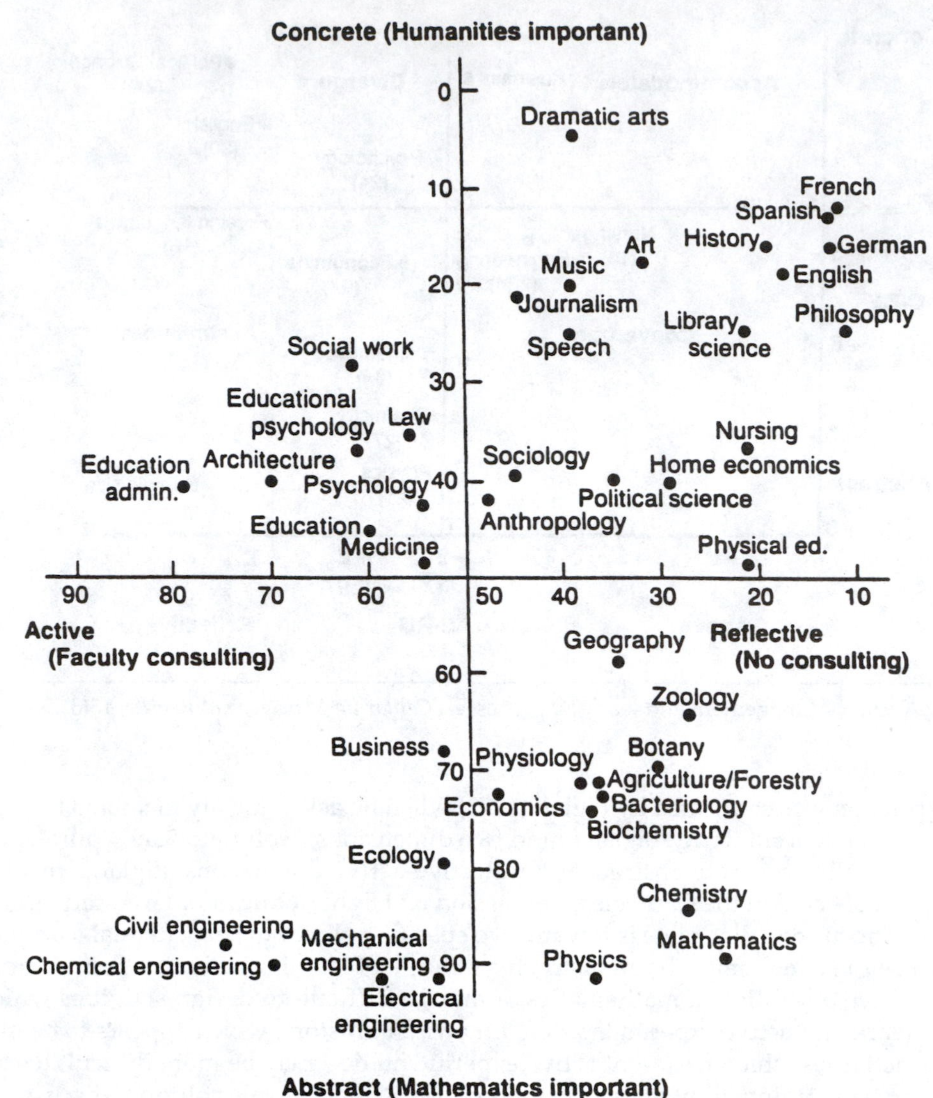

Source: Kolb, D.A. 1981. Learning styles and disciplinary differences. In *The modern American college*, edited by A.W. Chickering and Associates, San Francisco: Jossey-Bass.

servation); the instructor states the general principle being illustrated in the graph (abstract conceptualization); the instructor displays graphs from related studies to show how the principle applies more broadly (active experimentation). Such a sequence could conceivably take place using lectures as the only method.

One drawback of this actor/receiver dimension is that, in general, activities involving students as actors require a greater amount of time. For example, in the engineering unit illustrated in Figure 3, it would take longer for a student to work with a number of oscillating systems in order to observe the properties of frequency response than it would for the instructor to simply describe in class what the students would see if they had done the observation themselves. Likewise on the reflective observation pole, less time is consumed if the instructor provides the functions than if the students attempt to derive the functions themselves. And so on throughout the cycle. On the other hand, the active participation in learning has long been accepted as an important concept in learning. The value of active involvement must be weighed against the time limitations most instructors face.

Figure 5
Degree of direct student involvement in various teaching methods

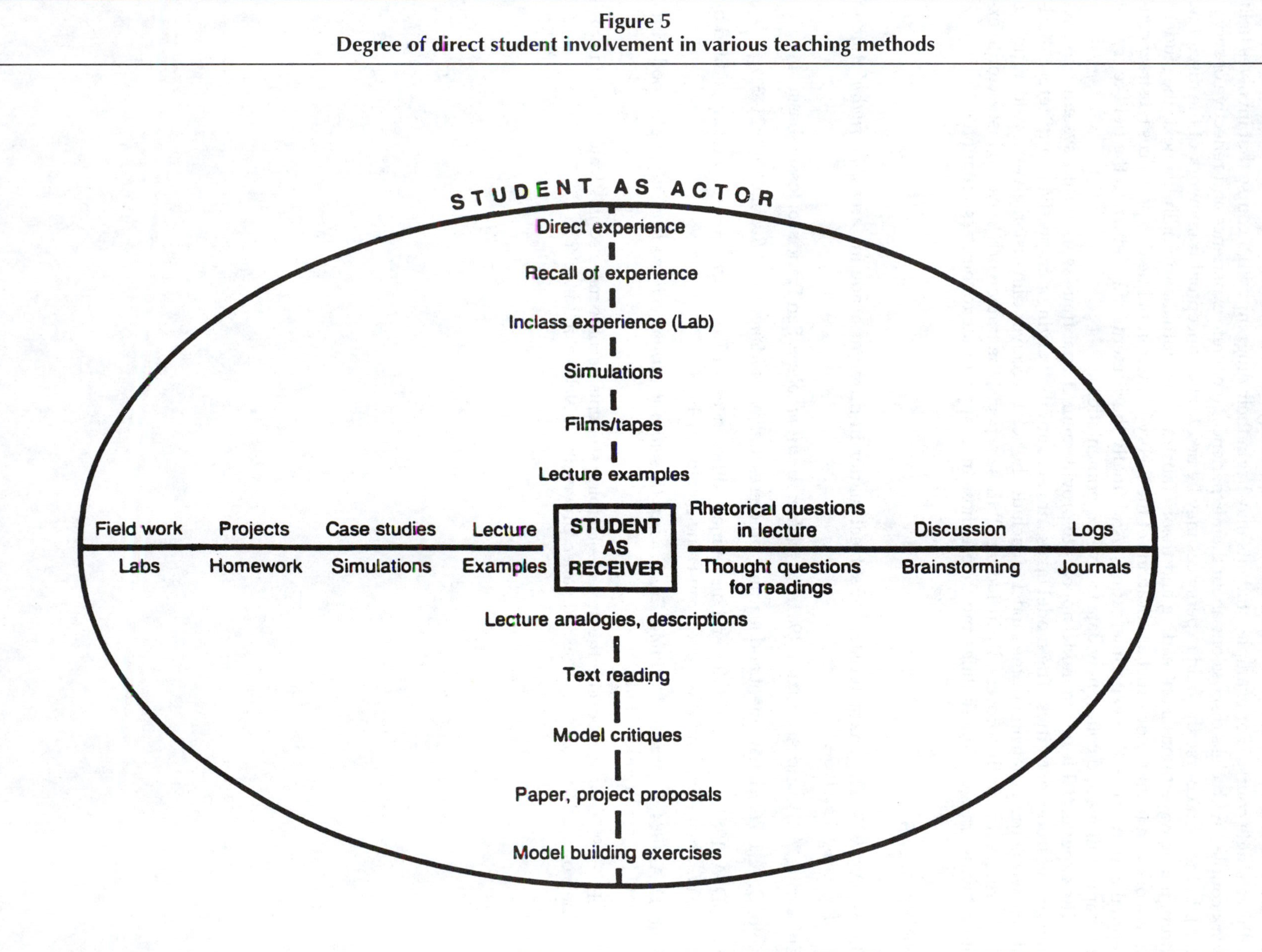

The Framework on a Larger Scale

It is also possible to think of the learning cycle as extending across a curriculum in addition to occurring within a single course. For example, students may begin their program with a course that involves field work coupled with class discussions about their experiences (concrete experience and reflective observation). In the next course the field experiences may be tied to the conceptual framework of the discipline through a heavy emphasis on reading and theory (abstract conceptualization). In the next, the student may work in a team to construct applications of the theory to their initial field experiences (abstract conceptualization and active experimentation). And finally the students may return to the field to try out their applications and collect new data (active experimentation).

The experiential learning model appears to provide a functional framework for the systematic selection of classroom activities. The model takes into account the varying perspectives of different disciplines, while the expansion of the model to include the actor/receiver dimension gives consideration to the learner's role in the process. By including all these aspects, the framework frees the instructor to explore a wider range of possibilities and choose those most appropriate to the class situation.

References

Biglan, A. 1973. The characteristics of subject matter in different academic areas. *Journal of Applied Psychology*, 57:195–203.

Chickering, A. W. and Associates. 1981. *The modern American college.* San Francisco: Jossey-Bass.

Kolb, D. A. 1976. Management and learning processes. *California Management Review*, 18(3):21–31.

Kolb, D. A. 1981. Learning styles and disciplinary differences. In *The modern American college*, edited by A. W. Chickering and Associates, San Francisco: Jossey-Bass.

Kolb, D. A. 1984. *Experiential learning: Experience as the source of learning and development.* Englewood Cliffs, New Jersey: Prentice-Hall.

Trani, E. P. 1979. Final report on the project—Helping students become more sophisticated consumers of their own education. Unpublished paper, University of Nebraska, Lincoln.

What Is Collaborative Learning?

BARBARA LEIGH SMITH AND JEAN T. MACGREGOR

As an "umbrella term" collaborative learning describes the many educational approaches involving "joint intellectual effort." Smith and MacGregor follow suit with cogent, carefully referenced descriptions of six major collaborative learning approaches along with their various sub-types. They tie each back to a series of assumptions about learning which crosses the varied approaches. The piece is remarkable in its expansiveness. It "maps" the collaborative learning territory and thereby makes orienting oneself to the rest of the sourcebook a much more manageable task.

Collaboration. Collaborative learning. Community. Communities of learners. Notions of collaboration and community have been informally linked to the learning process for many years, but they have become catch phrases in education in the 1980's and the 1990's. Collaborative learning is now finding prominence in college viewbooks, at conferences, and in journals on higher education. Although its various approaches are known by different names, collaborative learning is occurring in every discipline at every level of education. While these strategies are often called "innovative" and "new," they have engaged students and teachers throughout much of this century. We are simply developing new forms and adapting them to new contexts.

Collaborative learning is particularly timely now. In the 1980's an avalanche of reports underscored the problems of undergraduate education: the distance between faculty and students, the fragmentation of the curriculum, a prevailing pedagogy of lecture and routinized tests, an educational culture that reinforces student passivity, high rates of student attrition, and a reward system that gives low priority to teaching. In many ways, the academy mirrors larger social trends of fragmentation, lack of civil involvement, and undercurrents of alienation. Collaborative learning, with its emphasis on social and intellectual engagement and mutual responsibility, aims to counteract many of these educational and societal trends.

Collaborative learning holds enormous promise for improving student learning and revitalizing college teaching. It is a flexible and adaptable approach appropriate to any discipline. Nonetheless, teachers who adopt collaborative learning approaches find it challenging. They inevitably face fundamental questions about the purposes of their classes, teacher and student roles and responsibilities, the relationship between educational form and content, and the nature of knowledge itself. Collaborative learning represents a radical departure from contemporary practices in postsecondary education.

In this article, we describe collaborative learning and identify some of its underlying assumptions and goals. We describe some of the collaborative learning approaches most widely used in higher education, and we conclude with some observations on the challenges and opportunities that teachers encounter as they work to build collaboration and community into their classrooms.

Characterizing Collaborative Learning

"Collaborative learning" is an umbrella term for a variety of educational approaches involving joint intellectual effort by students, or students and teachers together. In most collaborative learning situations students are working in groups of two or more, mutually searching for understanding, solutions, or

"What Is Collaborative Learning?" by Barbara Leigh Smith and Jean T. MacGregor, reprinted from *Collaborative Learning: A Sourcebook for Higher Education,* by Anne S. Goodsell, Michelle R. Maher, Vincent Tinto, Barbara Leigh Smith, and Jean MacGregor, 1992, National Center on Postsecondary Teaching, Learning, and Assessment.

meanings, or creating a product. There is a wide variability in collaborative learning activities, but most center on the students' exploration or application of the course material, not simply the teacher's presentation or explication of it. Everyone in the class is participating, working as partners or in small groups. Questions, problems, or the challenge to create something drive the group activity. Learning unfolds in the most public of ways.

However practiced, collaborative learning represents a significant shift away from the typical teacher-centered or lecture-centered milieu in college. In collaborative classrooms, the lecturing/listening/note-taking process may not disappear entirely, but it lives alongside other processes that are based in students' discussion and active work with the course material. Teachers who use collaborative learning approaches tend to think of themselves less as expert transmitters of knowledge to students and more as expert designers of intellectual experiences for students—as coaches or mid-wives of a more emergent learning process (Belenky, Clinchy, Goldberger, & Tarule, 1985; Schön, 1983, 1987; Whipple, 1987).

Assumptions about Learning

Though collaborative learning takes on a variety of forms and is practiced by teachers of different disciplinary backgrounds and teaching traditions, the field is tied together by a number of important assumptions about learners and the learning process.

Learning is an active, constructive process. To learn new information, ideas, or skills, students have to work actively with them in purposeful ways. They need to attach this new material to, or integrate it with, what they already know—or use it to reorganize what they thought they knew. In collaborative learning situations, students are not simply taking in new information or ideas. They are creating something new with the information and ideas. These acts of intellectual processing—of constructing meaning or creating something new—are crucial to learning.

Learning depends on rich contexts. Recent research suggests that learning is fundamentally influenced by the context and activity in which it is embedded (Brown, Collins, & Duguid, 1989). Collaborative learning activities immerse students in challenging tasks or questions. Rather than beginning with facts and ideas and then moving to an application, collaborative learning activities frequently begin with problems, for which students must marshal pertinent facts and ideas. Instead of being distant observers of questions and answers, or problems and solutions, students become immediate practitioners. Rich contexts challenge students to practice and develop higher order reasoning and problem-solving skills. They invite students to join what Bruffee calls the conversation of the discipline with knowledgeable peers (Bruffee, 1984. See page 23 of this sourcebook.)

Learners are diverse. Students bring multiple perspectives to the classroom—diverse backgrounds, learning styles, experiences, and aspirations; teachers can no longer assume a one-size-fits-all approach. When students work together on their learning in class, teachers get a direct and immediate sense of how students are learning, and what experiences and ideas they bring to their learning. The diverse perspectives that emerge in collaborative activities are clarifying not just for teachers; they are illuminating for students as well.

Learning is inherently social. As Jeff Golub points out, "Collaborative learning has as its main feature a structure that allows for student talk: students are supposed to talk with each other . . . and it is in this talking that much of the learning occurs." (Golub, 1988).

In collaborative learning, there is the intellectual synergy of many minds coming to bear on a problem, and the social stimulation of mutual engagement in a common endeavor. This mutual exploration, meaning-making, and feedback often leads to better understanding on the part of students, and to the creation of new understandings as well.

Learning has affective and subjective dimensions. Collaborative tasks build connections between learners and ideas and between students and teachers. Listening to and acknowledging diverse perspectives, working in a cooperative spirit, becoming a peer teacher or a peer learner—all these activities are socially involving, as well as emotionally demanding. Such intense social interaction stimulates learners and learning. In collaborative learning situations, students generally experience a shift in their intellectual development as they learn to articulate their own point of view and listen to the views of others. They begin to see themselves not just as recipients of truths from textbooks or faculty members, or procedural knowers (going through the motions called for by the teacher), but as responsible creators of their own knowledge and meanings—a change that is essential to life-long learning and true intellectual development.

Goals for Education

While faculty members use collaborative learning because they believe it helps students to learn more effectively, many of them also place a high premium on teaching strategies that go beyond mere mastery of content and ideas; they believe that collaborative learning promotes a larger educational agenda. Still, there isn't just one rationale for collaborative learning, but rather several intertwined rationales.

Involvement. Today's college students are increasingly diverse in terms of background, prior experience, skills, and goals; they are commuter students with busy lives, full of distractions and multiple responsibilities. It should not surprise us that many of these students have little sense of connection to each other or the academic community as a whole. Calls to involve students more actively in their learning are coming from virtually every quarter of higher education (Astin, 1985; Bonwell & Eison, 1991; Kub et al., 1991; Study Group on the Conditions of Excellence in Higher Education, 1984). These exhortations are repeatedly borne out by studies both of students who leave college and those who stay, and by studies on what students find most important and meaningful to their learning (Light, 1990, 1991; Tinto, 1987). Involvement in learning, involvement with other students, and involvement with faculty are factors that make an overwhelming difference in student retention and success in college. By its very nature, collaborative learning is socially and intellectually involving. It invites students to build closer connections to other students, to their faculty, to their courses, and to their learning.

Cooperation and team-work. In collaborative endeavors, students inevitably encounter difference and must grapple with recognizing and working with it. Building the capacities for tolerating or resolving differences, for building agreement that honors all the voices in a group, for caring how others are doing—these abilities are crucial aspects of living in a community. Too often the development of these values and skills are relegated to what is called the "Student Life" side of the campus. Cultivation of team-work and leadership skills are legitimate and valuable classroom goals, not just extra-curricular ones.

As Alexander Astin points out in "Competition or Cooperation: Teaching Teamwork as a Basic Skill" (1987), there is both an implicit and an explicit curriculum embedded in the content and pedagogy of any course. Often, the implicit values are unexamined. Many educational reform efforts are unsuccessful because they fail to deal with the implicit values in the educational environment. Astin believes there is an underlying culture of individualism and competition that gets in the way of many current reform efforts. Collaborative learning represents a new and different value system, one that regards teamwork, cooperation, and community as just as important as academic achievement.

Civic responsibility. These collaborative skills and values are essential components in a larger civic landscape. If democracy is to sustain in any meaningful way, our educational system must foster habits of participation and a sense of responsibility to the larger community. Collaborative learning encourages students to acquire an active voice in shaping their ideas and values and a sensitive ear in hearing others. Dialogue, deliberation, and consensus-building out of differences are strong threads in the fabric of collaborative learning, and in civic life as well.

Collaborative Learning Approaches

Collaborative learning covers a broad territory of approaches, and there is wide variability in the amount of in-class or out-of-class time built around group work. Collaborative activities can range from classroom discussions interspersed with short lectures, through entire class periods, to study on research teams that last a whole term or a year. There is also enormous variability in the goals and processes of collaborative activities. Some faculty members design small group work around specific sequential steps, or tightly structured tasks. Others are comfortable with a more spontaneous agenda developing out of student interests or questions. In some collaborative learning settings, the task for students is to create a clearly delineated product; in others, the task is not to produce a product, but rather to participate in a process, an exercise of responding to each other's work or engaging in analysis and meaning making.

In the next section, we describe a number of widely used collaborative learning approaches. Some of these approaches, such as Guided Design and peer writing, evolved in a particular discipline and then spread to others. Others, such as seminars, peer teaching, and cooperative learning, have been used in many disciplines. Learning communities are a structural approach to curriculum reform that embraces multiple courses or disciplines.

While the approaches we describe are referred to by their distinctive names, there are myriad other small group teaching approaches that also constitute collaborative learning that we will not describe in detail. For example, many faculty punctuate their lectures with questions to student pairs or threesomes. (Johnson, Johnson, & Smith, 1991a). Others create "worksheet workshops" like those Finkel and Monk describe in a later article in this sourcebook (p. 50). In numerous lab and field courses, student pairs or student teams gather data together and produce reports. In every discipline, teachers are inventing more extended collaborative projects through presentations or debates, dramatizations and research papers. The possibilities are endless.

Cooperative Learning

Cooperative learning represents the most carefully structured end of the collaborative learning continuum. Defined as "the instructional use of small groups so that students work together to maximize their own and each other's learning,"(Johnson, Johnson, & Holubec, 1990) cooperative learning is based on the social interdependence theories of Kurt Lewin and Morton Deutsch (Deutsch, 1949; Lewin, 1935). These theories and associated research explore how the structure of social interdependence influences individual interaction within a given situation which, in turn, affects the outcomes of that interaction (Johnson & Johnson, 1989a). Pioneers in cooperative learning, David and Roger Johnson at the University of Minnesota, Robert Slavin at Johns Hopkins University, and Elizabeth Cohen at Stanford University, have devoted years of detailed research and analysis to clarify the conditions under which cooperative, competitive, or individualized goal structures affect or increase student achievement, psychological adjustment, self-esteem, and social skills.

Cooperative learning structures small group learning around precisely defined tasks or problems. Although numbers of cooperative strategies are workable in any discipline, there are several essential elements. Positive interdependence of effort is crucial. Cooperative learning activities are designed so that every learner contributes to the collaborative task. There is "promotive interaction"; students work constructively, talking face-to-face, helping each other complete the given task. At the same time, however, careful attention is given to individual accountability and personal responsibility to achieve the group's goals. Within the framework of group work, each student's performance is still individually assessed and each student is held responsible for contributing to the group's success.

In cooperative learning, the development of interpersonal skills is as important as the learning itself. The development of social skills in group work—learning to cooperate—is key to high quality group work, and many cooperative learning tasks are put to students with both academic objectives and social skills objectives. Many of the strategies involve the assigning of roles within each small group (such as recorder, participation encourager, summarizer) to ensure the positive interdependence of group participants and to enable students to practice different team-work skills. Built into cooperative learning work is regular group processing, a "debriefing" time where students reflect on how they are doing in order to learn how to become more effective in group learning settings (Johnson, Johnson, & Holubec, 1990).

For years, researchers in the cooperative learning field have focused their work on comparing cooperative learning contexts with competitive and individualized ones. As the Johnsons' summary and analysis of hundreds of studies concludes, cooperative learning situations foster more intrinsic motivation, more continuing interest and commitment to achievement, greater persistence, and the incentive for everyone to succeed together. On the other hand, the motivational environment associated with competitive or individualized learning situations fosters more extrinsic motivation, less continuing interest in achievement, and lower persistence on tasks. Moreover, competition seems to motivate only "winners," students with high ability to achieve in competitive situations (Johnson & Johnson, 1989a). Current cooperative learning research is now turning to the internal dynamics of cooperative learning groups, to understand more about the qualities of an effective learning group. Research findings in higher education, though less well explored, appear in more detail in Cooper and Mueck's (p. 68) and Slavin's (p. 97) articles which follow in this sourcebook.

Under the leadership of the Johnsons at the Cooperative Learning Center at the University of Minnesota, and David DeVries, Keith Edwards, and Robert Slavin at the Study for Social Organization of Schools at Johns Hopkins, cooperative learning has developed in the past 25 years into a forceful movement in K-12 education. Growing numbers of practitioners in higher education are adopting cooperative learning methods. The International Association for the Study of Cooperation in Education (IASCE) publishes the magazine *Cooperative Learning* and holds triennial conferences. More recently, with support from the Fund for the Improvement of Postsecondary Education, Jim Cooper and his colleagues at California State University Dominquez Hills established a Center for Cooperative Learning in Higher Education which disseminates and researches cooperative learning at the college level and publishes *Cooperative Learning in College Teaching*.

Problem-Centered Instruction

Problem-centered instruction, widely used in professional education, frequently is built around collaborative learning strategies. Many of these spring from common roots, especially the work of John Dewey in the early part of this century. Dewey endorsed discussion-based teaching and believed strongly in the importance of giving students direct experiential encounters with real-world problems. Guided Design, cases, and simulations are all forms of problem-centered instruction which immerse students in complex problems that they must analyze and work through together. These approaches develop problem solving abilities, understanding of complex relationships, and decision-making in the face of uncertainty. While problem-solving has long been a focus of professional education, it is increasingly regarded as an important aspect of the liberal arts as well. Our focus here is on problem-centered instruction that involves collaborative learning.

Guided Design. Guided Design is the most carefully structured approach to problem-centered instruction. The approach asks students working in small groups to practice decision making in sequenced tasks, with detailed feedback at every step. Developed in the late 1960's in the engineering program at West Virginia University, the Guided Design approach has since been adopted in many disciplines and professional programs, most notably in engineering, nursing, and pharmacy, but in many liberal arts and sciences courses as well (Borchardt, 1984; Day, Macy, & Jackson, 1984; deTornyay & Thompson, 1987; Miller, 1981; Roemer, 1981; Vogt, Cameron, & Dolan, in press). Each Guided Design activity presents a large and open-ended problem to students, but the problem is broken down into the following steps: (1) situation or problem definition, (2) statement of the goal, (3) generation of possible solutions, (4) evaluation of solutions, and (5) development of a plan of action. Each of these steps themselves involve open-ended questions. To answer them, students must marshal both information and the thinking skills of analysis, synthesis, and evaluation.

They also must build their social skills to work in a team, reconcile differences, and reach a common decision. After developing their response to each step of the "design," each student team receives written feedback from the faculty member, the "professional," about the strengths, weaknesses and implications of their decision. At each step of the process, there is an interplay between novice problem-solver and expert problem-solver. (Wales, Nardi, & Stager, 1987) Some designs take about a week to complete, while others run over several weeks of a course.

Careful guidance underpins this approach; it develops from the sequenced steps, from related homework assignments, from the thinking of other students, and from detailed feedback from the faculty member at each step in the process (Wales et al., 1978). Charles Wales at West Virginia University, Director of the Center for Guided Design, and Robert Stager at the University of Windsor co-developed this approach. Guided Design practitioners share their work under the auspices of the International Society for Exploring Teaching Alternatives (ISETA), an organization that promotes a variety of alternative teaching approaches.

Cases. Case studies have long been a staple for teaching and learning in the professions, particularly in the fields of business, law, and education, and they are now being used in many other disciplines as well. A case is a story or a narrative of a real life situation that sets up a problem or unresolved tension which the students analyze and resolve. The use of cases does not necessarily imply collaborative learning or small seminar discussion. However, case method teaching frequently asks small groups of students to tackle cases in class or in study group sessions.

Harvard University's Business School pioneered the development of the case method in the early part of this century. The dean of Harvard's first business program saw the case method as especially appropriate to educating managers and decision-makers. As one of Harvard's early professors put it, "[Business people must be able] to meet in action the problems arising out of new situations of an ever-changing environment. Education, accordingly, would consist of acquiring facility to act in the presence of new experience. It asks not how a man may be trained to know, but how a man be trained to act" (Dewing 1931, 23).

More recently, in *The Reflective Practitioner: How Professionals Think in Action*, Donald Schön examines how professionals solve problems and how they develop a highly valuable type of knowledge through reflection-in-action. He believes that education must be designed to promote this reflective practice by immersing students in the "complexity, uncertainty, instability, uniqueness, and value conflicts which are increasingly perceived as central to the world of professional practice" (Schön, 1983, 14). Cases provide a kind of classroom apprenticeship for professional decision-making.

Cases can describe an actual event or composites of several events. They can be developed from almost any materials—letters, business reports, legal documents, or descriptions of actual historical events. Effective cases are complex and realistic, with a strong sense of plot and character. Case narratives compress time and space but otherwise mirror real life in all its provocative complexity and ambiguity. Cases can be very brief, as short as several paragraphs, or quite lengthy. As Boehrer and Linsky point out, the definition of a case is quite elastic and the form of cases is changing: "today, video and computer technology come into increasing use, separately and together, both to present cases and to engage students in working through them" (Boehrer & Linsky, 1990, 56).

Harvard's professional schools have spent many years refining the case method and developing new ways of supporting it in the classroom through the development of new cases and faculty training seminars. Harvard remains the richest source of published cases on a wide variety of subjects in business, law, education, and public policy (Christensen & Hansen, 1987; McNair & Hersum, 1954). There is now a new renaissance of interest in teaching with cases, especially in schools of education and many professional graduate schools.

Problem-centered instruction in medical education. Problem-centered instruction has also emerged in recent decades in the field of medical education. This work began in England, then spread to Canada and ultimately to the United States. M. L. J. Abercrombie's research in England in the 1950's had a profound impact on collaborative learning in medical education both in England and North America (Abercrombie, 1970, 1961). She made a compelling case for discussion methods of teaching, contending that when people work in teams, they make more valid judgments than when working alone. McMaster University in Canada was one of the early pioneers in problem-centered medical education (Barrows & Tamblyn, 1980), followed by Western Reserve University, the University of New Mexico, and others.

In 1985, the Harvard Medical School adopted a problem-based curriculum entitled "New Pathways" that has garnered national attention. It was so successful in its pilot years that the program was quickly extended to all students. While several medical schools have ambitiously mounted whole curricula and extensive teaching support around problem-based instruction, many other campuses have embarked on more modest efforts, building individual courses around these approaches.

Simulations. Simulations are complex, structured role-playing situations that simulate real experiences. These complex scenarios provide one of the most open-ended forms of collaborative learning and often the most exciting way to get students involved. Most simulations ask students, working individually or in teams, to play the roles of opposing stakeholders in a problematic situation or an unfolding drama. Taking on the values and acting the part of a stakeholder usually gets students emotionally invested in the situation. The key aspect of simulations, though, is that of perspective-taking, both during the simulation exercise, and afterward. Following the simulation, there is usually a lengthy debriefing process, a discussion period where students reflect on the simulation and explore their own actions and those of others. This is where important concepts and lessons emerge.

When used in a carefully planned syllabus with a clear purpose, simulations enrich the learning process and provide a tangible underpinning to more theoretical material. A colleague of ours in a social science class asked students to read Machiavelli's *The Prince* and write an essay about their ideal society. Then, the class session played *Starpower*, a trading game about the distribution of power and authority in society. After a debriefing of the simulation, the students tackled a second writing assignment in which they were asked to juxtapose Machiavelli's analysis of power against their personal vision and their experience in the simulation.

There are now a large number of simulations or educational games, as they are sometimes called, relating to many disciplinary areas (Abt, 1987; Bratley, 1987). Some are quite extensive, taking from four hours to an entire quarter to complete. And a number of simulations utilize computers. Simulations can also be easily developed from everyday events, and many teachers find it useful to have groups of students develop their own simulations (Glazier, 1969). Some widely used commercially designed simulations are *CLUG: the Community Land Use Game* (Feldt, 1978); games designed to model prejudice and intergroup cultural communication and relationships such as *Bafa Bafa* and *Barnga: A Simulation on Cultural Clashes* (Intercultural Press, 1989); and simulations designed to study power and societal relationships such as *Starpower, SimSoc: Simulated Society*, and *What's News? A Game Simulation of TV News.* (Gamson, 1978, 1984). And for some time business schools have used a variety of simulation games called "operational games."

Writing Groups

Both in theory and practice, the most concentrated effort in undergraduate collaborative learning has focused on the teaching of writing. The writing group approach (known variously as peer response groups, class criticism, or helping circles) has transformed thousands of college writing classes. Through the spread of writing across the curriculum initiatives, writing groups increasingly are appearing in other courses as well. While many proponents of peer writing think of this approach as innovative, writing groups are actually as old as the nation. Anne Ruggles Gere's (1987) fascinating book on the subject describes how writing groups enjoy an extensive history in this country, both within and beyond the academy. Literary societies and writing clubs, developing in early American universities in the late 18th and early 19th centuries, met regularly to debate ideas, and to hear and respond to members' work. Benjamin Franklin and countless aspiring and established writers have met to share and critique their work. By the early part of this century, many educators were leading writing groups in high school and college classrooms and were convinced that these processes improved critical thinking as well as writing skills (Gere, 1987).

Using writing groups as a vehicle for reforming the teaching of college English visibly surfaced in the late 1960's, when American writing teachers learned about writing group approaches in Great Britain. Indeed, three seminal books advocating writing as a social process appeared in 1968 (Macrorie, 1968; Moffett, 1968; Murray, 1968). In the decades since, a large body of literature about the theory and practice has helped writing teachers move to more active, student-centered, sharing classrooms.

Writing teachers at both the secondary and undergraduate level have embraced peer writing because it helps students see writing as an emergent and social process. As Peter Elbow puts it, "Meaning is not what you start out with but what you end up with. Control, coherence, and knowing your mind are not what you start out with but what you end up with. Think of writing then not as a way to transmit a message but as a way to grow and cook a message" (Elbow, 1973, 14-15).

Peer writing involves students working in small groups at every stage of the writing process. Many writing groups begin as composing groups: they formulate ideas, clarify their positions, test an argument or focus a thesis statement before committing it to paper. This shared composing challenges students to think through their ideas out loud, to hear what they "sound like," so they will know "what to say" in writing.

Writing groups also serve as peer response groups. Students exchange their written drafts of papers and get feedback on them either orally or in writing. This is a challenging process, one that requires students to read and listen to fellow students' writing with insight, and to make useful suggestions for improvement. Word processors have helped peer writing enormously: In many writing labs, students share their drafts and revise them right on the screens.

Getting and giving feedback helps students understand that writing is a social process, not a solo performance. The mutual support of peer writing groups attempts to make the processes of composing and drafting less lonely and alienating (Spear, 1988). Sharing their writing with peers not only gives student writers an audience, it helps them understand the idea of audience (Maimon, 1979). John Bean puts it this way: "Good writing grows out of good talking." And, "Good talking means focused dialectical conversation where students can practice creating and testing their own arguments on an audience of peers" (Bean, 1991, 1990).

Peer writing also makes better writers. A major research study from the University of Chicago compared results of all the major approaches in teaching composition. It concluded that "having students work independently in small groups on purposefully designed and sequenced tasks produces significantly better results, as measured by the quality of thinking revealed in the writing, than does the lecture method, whole class discussion methods, or open-ended group work" (Hillocks, 1984, as summarized in Bean, 1991, 90).

Peer Teaching

With its roots in our one-room schoolhouse tradition, the process of students teaching their fellow students is probably the oldest form of collaborative learning in American education. In recent decades, however, peer thinking approaches have proliferated in higher education, under many names and structures. Many of these approaches have drawn on the peer teaching methods and studies developed by the Goldschmids at McGill University. Student pairs, called "learning cells," practice structured approaches for completing out-of-class assignments, as well as for teaching and quizzing each other on new material. In studies comparing the learning cells approach to seminars, discussion and independent study, the learning cell students at McGill not only outperformed others, but they preferred learning cells to the other approaches (Goldschmid & Goldschmid, 1976).

In his recent book surveying the literature on peer teaching, Neal Whitman offers a helpful typology of peer teaching approaches (Whitman, 1988). "Near -peers" are teachers who are slightly more advanced than the learners. They may be undergraduate teaching assistants who successfully complete a class and then return to assist the instructor in teaching it by leading discussion groups or help sessions. Another "near-peer" might be a tutor, also a previously successful student who works in one-to-one situations with fellow students in need of help in a specific course. Counselors is Whitman's term for near-peers who also work one-on-one with fellow students, but instead of being attached to a specific course, they offer broad help, perhaps on writing, study skills, or academic advising. A second type of peer tutor is the "co-peer," a student at the same level who helps another. Students may work in two-person partnerships or in larger work groups that share a common task.

Peer teaching designs and programs are prolific and naturally quite variable. The following examples represent three of the most successful and widely adapted peer teaching models.

Supplemental instruction. The supplemental instruction approach is an undergraduate teaching assistant model developed by Deanna Martin at the University of Missouri-Kansas City. It has been adopted at hundreds of colleges in the United States and abroad. This urban campus recognized the need to offer tutoring help to students, but budgetary constraints made one-to-one tutoring too expensive. Their search for an alternative approach led to "Supplemental Instruction." This approach focused not on "at risk students," but rather on "at-risk classes," entry level in health sciences, and later in general arts and sciences classes where more than 30% of the students were either withdrawing or failing. The university invited advanced undergraduates who had done well in those classes to become "SI leaders." These students are paid to attend the class and to convene Supplemental Instruction sessions at least three times a week at hours convenient to students in the class. All the students in the class are welcome to attend the SI sessions.

The course instructor works closely with the SI student leader to assess what students need to master the content of the class and to help the SI leader develop sessions to facilitate learning. Still, the SI leader is presented as a "student of the subject," not an expert of the subject—an approach meant to close the perceived gaps between teacher and student and subject matter. Evaluations of Supplemental Instruction at the University of Missouri-Kansas City and elsewhere have shown that if students attend the SI sessions consistently, their grades and their persistence in college are significantly higher, regardless of whether they are strong or weak academically (Blanc, DeBuhr, & Martin, 1983; "Supplemental Instruction," 1991).

Writing fellows. The writing fellows approach, pioneered by Tori Haring-Smith at Brown University, is a peer teaching approach somewhat parallel to supplemental instruction. The writing fellows are upper division students who are strong writers. After extensive training, these students are each deployed to an undergraduate class (generally in the discipline of their major) where they read and respond to the papers of all students. Haring-Smith calls this a "bottom-up approach" to sustaining writing across the curriculum initiatives, particularly in large classes where many faculty flag at assigning writing because there simply are too many papers to which they must respond. Over 50 colleges and universities have created writing fellows programs.

Mathematics workshops. A third peer teaching approach that spread rapidly in the late 1980's is the intensive mathematics workshops program developed by Uri Treisman while he was at the University of California at Berkeley. Treisman wanted to address the drawbacks of traditional tutoring models—particularly those geared to minority students in academic difficulty. Finding that study groups made a difference in student success, he created a co-peer teaching approach called the Professional Development

Program. The program assumes the culture of an honors program rather than a remedial program. Graduate instructors (usually doctoral candidates) lead math workshops built around small group problem-solving with an explicit emphasis on peer teaching. These workshops supplement the regular lecture and discussion sections of mathematics courses. This intensive small group workshop approach, which emphasizes developing strength rather than remediating weakness, and peer collaboration rather than solo competition, completely reversed the prevailing patterns of failure in calculus classes by Hispanic and African American students at Berkeley (Treisman, 1985). This intensive math workshop approach has since spread widely in the mathematics community in high schools, and in both two- and four-year colleges.

These peer teaching approaches and many others like them depart from many tutoring models that focus on the remediation or rescue of the drowning. Many of these newer models require all students to participate as teachers and learners in turn, or they invite all students to participate voluntarily. The tutors are available to all, and the learning context is one of collaboration and success. These programs lead to better learning and higher motivation both for the tutors and the learners. Also, peer teaching introduces countless undergraduates to the stimulation, challenge, and satisfaction of teaching—an important investment in developing the future professorate.

Discussion Groups and Seminars

The terms discussion group and seminar refer to a broad array of teaching approaches. In college settings we usually think of discussions as processes, both formal and informal, that encourage student dialogue with teachers and with each other. These are spaces within classes, where "instructors and groups of students consider a topic, issue, or problem and exchange information, experiences, ideas, opinions, reactions, and conclusions with each other" (Ewens, 1989). Seminar has several connotations; historically the seminar has been thought of as a course where advanced students take turns presenting research for discussion and critical feedback from student peers as well as the teacher. Seminar also refers to an extended discussion in which students and teacher examine a specific text or common experience.

While the terms group discussion and seminar are often used interchangeably, it is interesting to note that discussion derives from the Latin words meaning breaking apart, while the word seminar comes from words having to do with nurseries and seed plots. As the etymologies suggest, both these settings involve the interplay between the dissection of ideas and the cultivation of new ones, analysis and synthesis, the acknowledgment of diverse perspectives, and the creation of community. These are powerful arenas for collaborative learning, spaces in the curriculum where the conversation turns to mutual search for understanding.

All the approaches we have described above involve discussion. However most have distinct protocols, goals, or structures framing the activity. What we are describing here—more open-ended discussions or seminars—puts the onus on the teacher or the students to pose questions and build a conversation in the context of the topic at hand. There is enormous variability, then, in terms of who sets the agenda, who organizes and monitors the discussion, and who evaluates what. Some discussions or seminars may be heavily teacher-directed, others much more student-centered. There are a myriad possibilities for discussions, and many good resources on strategies (Christensen, Garvin, & Sweet, 1991; Eble, 1976; McKeachie, 1986; Neff & Weimer, 1989).

Learning Communities

Collaborative learning practitioners would say that all collaborative learning is about the building of learning communities. However, we are using the term learning community here in a broader and more specific sense, in terms of an intentional reconfiguration of the curriculum. In the past 15 years, a number of colleges have recognized that deep-seated structural factors weaken the quality of undergraduate learning and inhibit the development of community. These schools have attacked this problem directly by developing learning communities, a "purposeful restructuring of the curriculum to link together courses so that students find greater coherence in what they are learning and increased interaction with faculty and fellow students" (Gabelnick, MacGregor, Matthews, & Smith, 1990). As such, learning communities are a delivery system and a facilitating structure for the practice of collaborative learning.

Learning community curriculum structures vary from campus to campus, and can serve many different purposes, but they have two common intentions. They attempt to provide intellectual coherence for students by linking classes together and building relationships between subject matter, or by teaching a skill (e.g., writing or speaking) in the context of a discipline. Second, they aim to build both academic and social community for students by enrolling them together in a large block of course work. While the learning community approach goes back 60 years or more (Meiklejohn, 1932), we have seen a recent proliferation of learning community approaches on all sizes and types of campuses. Learning communities directly confront multiple problems plaguing undergraduate education: the fragmentation of general education classes, the isolation of students (especially on large campuses or commuter schools), the lack of meaningful connection-building between classes, the need for greater intellectual interaction between students and faculty, and the lack of sustained opportunities for faculty development.

Some learning community models are quite modest. In the Freshman Interest Group (FIG) model used at several large universities, cohorts of 25-30 freshman students enroll in three classes that are an appropriate introduction and platform for a major. In addition, the FI group meets in a discussion group once a week with a peer advisor. The faculty of the three classes teach them in the usual way, but they rapidly discover that the FIG students become the most active students in their class.

Other learning community models are more complex in terms of both pedagogy and curriculum redesign. In many linked classes, or three-course clusters, the faculty members co-plan their syllabi to address common themes or develop common assignments. Still other learning community models are completely team taught and involve a more ambitious reconfiguring of coursework around broad interdisciplinary themes. Not only are these closely integrated models exciting for students, they are revitalizing for faculty. Team teaching creates a unique opportunity for learning from each other's disciplinary perspectives and for creating and sharing teaching approaches.

By altering the curricular structure to provide larger units of study, learning communities frequently provide more time and space for collaborative learning and other more complicated educational approaches. Small group workshops and book seminars are staples of most learning communities. Peer writing groups and team projects associated with labs and field work are also fairly common. Study groups emerge in learning communities, both intentionally and spontaneously. These programs provide a unique social and intellectual glue for students that result in high rates of student retention, increased student achievement, and more complex intellectual development (MacGregor, 1991).

Collaborative Learning: Challenges and Opportunities

In the past decade, collaborative learning approaches quietly have begun to proliferate. Specific strategies are spreading across campuses and through disciplinary and professional networks. And as more faculty members use collaborative learning, the design and analysis of these approaches are becoming more diverse and more sophisticated. Research and evaluation on collaborative learning strategies are sharpening our definitions of student outcomes and giving us a clearer understanding of when collaborative activities do and do not work.

Creating a collaborative classroom is full of challenges and dilemmas. Few of us experienced collaborative work in our own undergraduate settings, and much of our graduate school training reinforced the teacher-centered, lecture-driven model of college teaching. For the individual teacher, stepping "out of the center" and engaging students in group activity is hard work, especially at first. For students and teachers alike, every collaborative activity is new and unpredictable in the way it unfolds. Everyone involved must takes some risks.

And designing collaborative learning situations requires a demanding yet important rethinking of one's syllabus, in terms of course content and time allocation. If some (or a great deal) of the classroom time is considered an important social space for developing understandings about course material, or if some of the out-of-class time is devoted to study groups or group projects, how then should the rest of the class time (lectures, assignments, examinations) be designed? How does the teacher ensure that students are learning and mastering key skills and ideas in the course, while at the same time addressing all the material of the course? Teaching in collaborative settings puts the tension between the process of student learning and content coverage front and center.

As teachers become more involved in using collaborative learning, they discover what radical questions it raises. Collaborative learning goes to the roots of long-held assumptions about teaching and learning. Classroom roles change: Both teachers and students take on more complex roles and responsibilities

(Finkel & Monk, 1983, available in this sourcebook p. 50; MacGregor, 1990). The classroom is no longer solo teacher and independent students—it becomes more an interdependent community. This degree of involvement often questions and reshapes assumed power relationships between teachers and students, a process that at first can be confusing and disorienting (Romer & Whipple, 1990). Not only is course content reshaped, so are definitions of student competence. The public nature of group work makes the demonstration of student learning continuous. Thus, for teachers and students, collaborative learning both complicates and enriches the evaluation process.

Challenges to collaborative learning at the classroom level are compounded by the traditional structures and culture of the academy, which continue to perpetuate the teacher-centered, transmission-of-information model of teaching and learning. The political economy of the academy is set up to front load the curriculum with large lower division classes in rooms immutably arranged for lectures, usually in classes limited to fifty-minute "hours." Student-student interaction; extended, careful examination of ideas; the hearing-out of multiple perspectives; the development of an intellectual community—all these are hard to accomplish under these physical and time constraints.

The lecture-centered model is reinforced (both subtly and blatantly) by institutional reward systems that favor limited engagement in teaching and give greater recognition to research. Achievement for teachers and students alike is assumed to be a scarce honor, which one works for alone, in competition with peers. This assumption of scarcity is the platform for norm-referenced grading, or "grading on the curve," a procedure that enforces distance between students and corrodes the trust on which collaborative learning is built. Moreover, our definitions of ourselves as teachers, as keepers and dispensers of disciplinary expertise, are still very much bound up in the lecture podium. As a young colleague of ours just beginning to use collaborative learning in her class acidly observed, "I know this works, but my colleagues don't respect it as real teaching. They associate group work with lazy, unprepared faculty members."

And there are compelling reasons to believe our colleagues. Lectures, the prevailing mode of classroom teaching in college, have only limited efficacy (Blackburn, Pellino, Boberg, & O'Connell, 1980; Costin, 1972, 1980; McKeachie, 1986; Penner, 1984; Thielens, 1987; Verner & Dickinson, 1967). The myths about interpersonal competition—that it is motivating, enjoyable, character-building, and necessary for success in a competitive workplace and world—have been debunked increasingly in the past twenty years, both in theoretical terms (Astin, 1987; Bricker, 1989; Nichols, 1989; Palmer, 1983) and through extensive research (Johnson & Johnson, 1989a; Kohn, 1986). Most troubling of all, more than 50% of the students who begin college leave, often never to return. Much of this student leaving has to do with feelings of isolation and a lack of involvement with the college environment (Tinto, 1987). Whether we measure these losses in wasted resources, in thwarted aspirations, or in workplace unpreparedness, the costs of this kind of attrition are too high.

While these reasons may motivate some teachers, what really propels teachers into collaborative classrooms is the desire to motivate students by getting them more actively engaged. Nonetheless, wanting to be a facilitator of collaborative learning and being good at it are very different things. As with all kinds of teaching, designing and guiding group work takes time to learn and practice. Most teachers start with modest efforts while others may work with colleagues, designing, trying, and observing each other's approaches.

Several years ago, two colleagues of ours embarked on collaborative learning because they were dissatisfied with their introductory biology course. Because it seemed students were having difficulty grasping the concepts in the textbook, these teachers found themselves devoting too much class time to re-explaining the text material. At the same time, they noticed how engaged students were with their occasional problem-solving exercises and small group seminars on journal articles.

Over a period of a year, these two biologists began to shift their lectured-centered course to one involving small group problem-solving workshops. They developed these workshops as applications and extensions of the textbook reading and required students to complete reading assignments in order to participate in class workshops. At the same time, these faculty members built support for their new approach with their biology department colleagues by asking for their help in defining the knowledge and understandings essential to completion of Introductory Biology. The rewards were immediate: The completion rate of the course soared, student achievement rose significantly, and the course became much more exciting to teach. These teachers have continued their collaboration, refining the workshops in the course and developing new ones.

The story of our biology colleagues is not anomalous. Faculty collaboration seems to be an important ingredient in the design of and experimentation with collaborative learning approaches. Learning new moves in the classroom need not be a lonely enterprise. Faculty development initiatives at the department or college-wide level need to acknowledge this as they work to create a supportive climate for dissemination of approaches as well as a forum for work on questions that arise. At several universities, collaborative and cooperative learning "users groups" have sprung up and become valuable structures for sharing approaches and problems. The team-teaching that is embedded in many learning community programs is a powerful strategy for enabling faculty to build their repertoires and confidence. Research and evaluation, from modest faculty-designed "classroom research" (Cross & Angelo, 1985) to more formal studies, can also help develop approaches and clarify their results. Sourcebooks like this one and growing networks, such as AAHE's Action Community on Collaborative Learning, will also continue to share resources and build momentum.

There is no getting around the challenging nature of collaborative learning. But when collaborative work becomes a regular feature of their class, faculty members usually find it enormously energizing and liberating. The specter of teaching becoming repetitive or routinized simply isn't an issue for these teachers. Every course and every class presents an intriguing opportunity. Teachers relish the intellectual challenges of creating (and re-creating) activities or problems that really engage students. They enjoy those moments when the class becomes a community. And they often speak of the new lens they gain on their students, which comes from watching them struggle with ideas and build meaningful connections to previous learning or personal experiences. They also remark on the fresh perspectives they gain on their subject matter, as it is enriched and challenged by continuous and diverse student examination and reshaping of it.

Ideally, collaborative learning leads students to become much more directly immersed in the ideas of the class. They will develop confidence and skills at entertaining ideas on their own while learning to raise questions, to listen carefully, and to respond to others' questions. They will develop the ability to stay focused, sustain an idea, build rapport with fellow students and learn the art of disagreeing with others with respect and courtesy. They may learn to recognize and acknowledge the limitations of their own points of view. These intellectual and interpersonal skills don't come easily to college students, not to mention college graduates! Their development requires extended and focused practice. As Finkel and Monk point out in one of the following articles, students' awkwardness and tentativeness can often discourage teachers, and drive them back into the comparative ease of lecturing (Finkel & Monk, 1983). Developing successful collaborative learning activities challenges teachers to become coaches and facilitators of complex social processes, but these are deeply important ones for true learning.

Ultimately, collaborative classrooms stimulate both students and teachers. In the most authentic of ways, the collaborative learning process models what it means to question, learn and understand in concert with others. Learning collaboratively demands responsibility, persistence, and sensitivity, but the result can be a community of learners in which everyone is welcome to join, participate, and grow.

Talking about Race, Learning about Racism: The Application of Racial Identity Development Theory in the Classroom

BEVERLY DANIEL TATUM

As many educational institutions struggle to become more multicultural in terms of their students, faculty, and staff, they also begin to examine issues of cultural representation within their curriculum. This examination has evoked a growing number of courses that give specific consideration to the effect of variables such as race, class, and gender on human experience—an important trend that is reflected and supported by the increasing availability of resource manuals for the modification of course content (Bronstein & Quina, 1988; Hull, Scott, & Smith, 1982; Schuster & Van Dyne, 1985).

Unfortunately, less attention has been given to the issues of process that inevitably emerge in the classroom when attention is focused on race, class, and/or gender. It is very difficult to talk about these concepts in a meaningful way without also talking and learning about racism, classism, and sexism.[1] The introduction of these issues of oppression often generates powerful emotional responses in students that range from guilt and shame to anger and despair. If not addressed, these emotional responses can result in student resistance to oppression-related content areas. Such resistance can ultimately interfere with the cognitive understanding and mastery of the material. This resistance and potential interference is particularly common when specifically addressing issues of race and racism. Yet, when students are given the opportunity to explore race-related material in a classroom where both their affective and intellectual responses are acknowledged and addressed, their level of understanding is greatly enhanced.

This article seeks to provide a framework for understanding students' psychological responses to race-related content and the student resistance that can result, as well as some strategies for overcoming this resistance. It is informed by more than a decade of experience as an African-American woman engaged in teaching an undergraduate course on the psychology of racism, by thematic analyses of student journals and essays written for the racism class, and by an understanding and application of racial identity development theory (Helms, 1990).

Setting the Context

As a clinical psychologist with a research interest in racial identity development among African-American youth raised in predominantly White communities, I began teaching about racism quite fortuitously. In 1980, while I was a part-time lecturer in the Black Studies department of a large public university, I was invited to teach a course called Group Exploration of Racism (Black Studies 2). A requirement for Black Studies majors, the course had to be offered, yet the instructor who regularly taught the course was no longer affiliated with the institution. Armed with a folder full of handouts, old syllabi that the previous instructor left behind, a copy of *White Awareness: Handbook for Anti-racism Training* (Katz, 1978), and my own clinical skills as a group facilitator, I constructed a course that seemed to meet the goals already outlined in the course catalogue. Designed "to provide students with an understanding of the psychological causes and emotional reality of racism as it appears in everyday life," the course incorporated the use of lectures, readings, simulation exercises, group research projects, and extensive class discussion to help students explore the psychological impact of racism on both the oppressor and the oppressed.

Though my first efforts were tentative, the results were powerful. The students in my class, most of whom were White, repeatedly described the course in their evaluations as one of the most valuable educational experiences of their college careers. I was convinced that helping students understand the ways in which racism operates in their own lives, and what they could do about it, was a social responsibility that I should accept. The freedom to institute the course in the curriculum of the psychology departments in which I would eventually teach became a personal condition of employment. I have successfully introduced the course in each new educational setting I have been in since leaving that university.

Since 1980, I have taught the course (now called the Psychology of Racism) eighteen times, at three different institutions. Although each of these schools is very different—a large public university, a small state college, and a private, elite women's college—the challenges of teaching about racism in each setting have been more similar than different.

In all of the settings, class size has been limited to thirty students (averaging twenty-four). Though typically predominantly White and female (even in coeducational settings), the class make-up has always been mixed in terms of both race and gender. The students of color who have taken the course include Asians and Latinos/as, but most frequently the students of color have been Black. Though most students have described themselves as middle class, all socioeconomic backgrounds (ranging from very poor to very wealthy) have been represented over the years.

The course has necessarily evolved in response to my own deepening awareness of the psychological legacy of racism and my expanding awareness of other forms of oppression, although the basic format has remained the same. Our weekly three-hour class meeting is held in a room with movable chairs, arranged in a circle. The physical structure communicates an important premise of the course—that I expect the students to speak with each other as well as with me.

My other expectations (timely completion of assignments, regular class attendance) are clearly communicated in our first class meeting, along with the assumptions and guidelines for discussion that I rely upon to guide our work together. Because the assumptions and guidelines are so central to the process of talking and learning about racism, it may be useful to outline them here.

Working Assumptions

1. Racism, defined as a "system of advantage based on race" (see Wellman, 1977), is a pervasive aspect of U.S. socialization. It is virtually impossible to live in U.S. contemporary society and not be exposed to some aspect of the personal, cultural, and/or institutional manifestations of racism in our society. It is also assumed that, as a result, all of us have received some misinformation about those groups disadvantaged by racism.

2. Prejudice, defined as a "preconceived judgment or opinion, often based on limited information," is clearly distinguished from racism (see Katz, 1978). I assume that all of us may have prejudices as a result of the various cultural stereotypes to which we have been exposed. Even when these preconceived ideas have positive associations (such as "Asian students are good in Math"), they have negative effects because they deny a person's individuality. These attitudes may influence the individual behaviors of people of color as well as of Whites, and may affect intergroup as well as intragroup interaction. However, a distinction must be made between negative racial attitudes held by individuals of color and White individuals, because it is only the attitudes of Whites that routinely carry with them the social power inherent in the systematic cultural reinforcement and institutionalization of those racial prejudices. To distinguish the prejudices of students of color from the racism of White students is *not* to say that the former is acceptable and the latter is not; both are clearly problematic. The distinction is important, however, to identify the power differential between members of dominant and subordinate groups.

3. In the context of U.S. society, the system of advantage clearly operates to benefit Whites as a group. However, it is assumed that racism, like other forms of oppression, hurts members of the privileged group as well as those targeted by racism. While the impact of racism on Whites is clearly different from its impact on people of color, racism has negative ramifications for everyone. For example, some White students might remember the pain of having lost important relationships because Black friends were not allowed to visit their homes. Others may express sadness at having been denied access to a broad range of experiences because of social segregation. These individuals often attribute the discomfort

or fear they now experience in racially mixed settings to the cultural limitations of their youth.

4. Because of the prejudice and racism inherent in our environments when we were children, I assume that we cannot be blamed for learning what we were taught (intentionally or unintentionally). Yet as adults, we have a responsibility to try and identify and interrupt the cycle of oppression. When we recognize that we have been misinformed, we have a responsibility to seek out more accurate information and to adjust our behavior accordingly.

5. It is assumed that change, both individual and institutional, is possible. Understanding and unlearning prejudice and racism is a lifelong process that may have begun prior to enrolling in this class, and which will surely continue after the course is over. Each of us may be at a different point in that process, and I assume that we will have mutual respect for each other, regardless of where we perceive one another to be.

To facilitate further our work together, I ask students to honor the following guidelines for our discussion. Specifically, I ask students to demonstrate their respect for one another by honoring the confidentiality of the group. So that students may feel free to ask potentially awkward or embarrassing questions, or share race-related experiences, I ask that students refrain from making personal attributions when discussing the course content with their friends. I also discourage the use of "zaps," overt or covert put-downs often used as comic relief when someone is feeling anxious about the content of the discussion. Finally, students are asked to speak from their own experience, to say, for example, "I think . . . " or "In my experience, I have found . . ." rather than generalizing their experience to others, as in "People say . . ."

Many students are reassured by the climate of safety that is created by these guidelines and find comfort in the nonblaming assumptions I outline for the class. Nevertheless, my experience has been that most students, regardless of their class and ethnic background, still find racism a difficult topic to discuss, as is revealed by these journal comments written after the first class meeting (all names are pseudonyms):

> The class is called Psychology of Racism, the atmosphere is friendly and open, yet I feel very closed in. I feel guilt and doubt well up inside of me. (Tiffany, a White woman)
>
> Class has started on a good note thus far. The class seems rather large and disturbs me. In a class of this nature, I expect there will be many painful and emotional moments. (Linda, an Asian woman)
>
> I am a little nervous that as one of the few students of color in the class people are going to be looking at me for answers, or whatever other reasons. The thought of this inhibits me a great deal. (Louise, an African-American woman)
>
> I had never thought about my social position as being totally dominant. There wasn't one area in which I wasn't in the dominant group. . . . I first felt embarrassed. . . . Through association alone I felt in many ways responsible for the unequal condition existing in the world. This made me feel like shrinking in a hole in a class where I was surrounded by 27 women and 2 men, one of whom was Black and the other was Jewish. I felt that all these people would be justified in venting their anger upon me. After a short period, I realized that no one in the room was attacking or even blaming me for the conditions that exist. (Carl, a White man)

Even though most of my students voluntarily enroll in the course as an elective, their anxiety and subsequent resistance to learning about racism quickly emerge.

Sources of Resistance

In predominantly White college classrooms, I have experienced at least three major sources of student resistance to talking and learning about race and racism. They can be readily identified as the following:

1. Race is considered a taboo topic for discussion, especially in racially mixed settings.
2. Many students, regardless of racial-group membership, have been socialized to think of the United States as a just society.
3. Many students, particularly White students, initially deny any personal prejudice, recognizing the impact of racism on other people's lives, but failing to acknowledge its impact

on their own.

Race as Taboo Topic

The first source of resistance, race as a taboo topic, is an essential obstacle to overcome if class discussion is to begin at all. Although many students are interested in the topic, they are often most interested in hearing other people talk about it, afraid to break the taboo themselves.

One source of this self-consciousness can be seen in the early childhood experiences of many students. It is known that children as young as three notice racial differences (see Phinney & Rotheram, 1987). Certainly preschoolers talk about what they see. Unfortunately, they often do so in ways that make adults uncomfortable. Imagine the following scenario: A White child in a public place points to a dark-skinned African-American child and says loudly, "Why is that boy Black?" The embarrassed parent quickly responds, "Sh! Don't say that." The child is only attempting to make sense of a new observation (Derman-Sparks, Higa, & Sparks, 1980), yet the parent's attempt to silence the perplexed child sends a message that this observation is not okay to talk about. White children quickly become aware that their questions about race raise adult anxiety, and as a result, they learn not to ask the questions.

When asked to reflect on their earliest race-related memories and the feelings associated with them, both White students and students of color often report feelings of confusion, anxiety, and/or fear. Students of color often have early memories of name-calling or other negative interactions with other children, and sometimes with adults. They also report having had questions that went both unasked and unanswered. In addition, many students have had uncomfortable interchanges around race-related topics as adults. When asked at the beginning of the semester, "How many of you have had difficult, perhaps heated conversations with someone on a race-related topic?", routinely almost everyone in the class raises his or her hand. It should come as no surprise then that students often approach the topic of race and/or racism with both curiosity and trepidation.

The Myth of the Meritocracy

The second source of student resistance to be discussed here is rooted in students' belief that the United States is a just society, a meritocracy where individual efforts are fairly rewarded. While some students (particularly students of color) may already have become disillusioned with that notion of the United States, the majority of my students who have experienced at least the personal success of college acceptance still have faith in this notion. To the extent that these students acknowledge that racism exists, they tend to view it as an individual phenomenon, rooted in the attitudes of the "Archie Bunkers" of the world or located only in particular parts of the country.

After several class meetings, Karen, a White woman, acknowledged this attitude in her journal:

> At one point in my life—the beginning of this class—I actually perceived America to be a relatively racist free society. I thought that the people who were racist or subjected to racist stereotypes were found only in small pockets of the U.S., such as the South. As I've come to realize, racism (or at least racially orientated stereotypes) is rampant.

An understanding of racism as a system of advantage presents a serious challenge to the notion of the United States as a just society where rewards are based solely on one's merit. Such a challenge often creates discomfort in students. The old adage "ignorance is bliss" seems to hold true in this case; students are not necessarily eager to recognize the painful reality of racism.

One common response to the discomfort is to engage in denial of what they are learning. White students in particular may question the accuracy or currency of statistical information regarding the prevalence of discrimination (housing, employment, access to health care, and so on). More qualitative data, such as autobiographical accounts of experiences with racism, may be challenged on the basis of their subjectivity.

It should be pointed out that the basic assumption that the United States is a just society for all is only one of many basic assumptions that might be challenged in the learning process. Another example can be seen in an interchange between two White students following a discussion about cultural racism, in which the omission or distortion of historical information about people of color was offered as an example of the cultural transmission of racism.

"Yeah, I just found out that Cleopatra was actually a Black woman."

"What?"

The first student went on to explain her newly learned information. Finally, the second student exclaimed in disbelief, "That can't be true. Cleopatra was beautiful!" This new information and her own deeply ingrained assumptions about who is beautiful and who is not were too incongruous to allow her to assimilate the information at that moment.

If outright denial of information is not possible, then withdrawal may be. Physical withdrawal in the form of absenteeism is one possible result; it is for precisely this reason that class attendance is mandatory. The reduction in the completion of reading and/or written assignments is another form of withdrawal. I have found this response to be so common that I now alert students to this possibility at the beginning of the semester. Knowing that this response is a common one seems to help students stay engaged, even when they experience the desire to withdraw.

Following an absence in the fifth week of the semester, one White student wrote, "I think I've hit the point you talked about, the point where you don't want to hear any more about racism. I sometimes begin to get the feeling we are all hypersensitive." (Two weeks later she wrote, "Class is getting better. I think I am beginning to get over my hump.")

Perhaps not surprisingly, this response can be found in both White students and students of color. Students of color often enter a discussion of racism with some awareness of the issue, based on personal experiences. However, even these students find that they did not have a full understanding of the widespread impact of racism in our society. For students who are targeted by racism, an increased awareness of the impact in and on their lives is painful, and often generates anger.

Four weeks into the semester, Louise, an African-American woman, wrote in her journal about her own heightened sensitivity:

> Many times in class I feel uncomfortable when White students use the term Black because even if they aren't aware of it they say it with all or at least a lot of the negative connotations they've been taught goes along with Black. Sometimes it just causes a stinging feeling inside of me. Sometimes I get real tired of hearing White people talk about the conditions of Black people. I think it's an important thing for them to talk about, but still I don't always like being around when they do it. I also get tired of hearing them talk about how hard it is for them, though I understand it, and most times I am very willing to listen and be open, but sometimes I can't. Right now I can't.

For White students, advantaged by racism, a heightened awareness of it often generates painful feelings of guilt. The following responses are typical:

> After reading the article about privilege, I felt very guilty. (Rachel, a White woman)

> Questions of racism are so full of anger and pain. When I think of all the pain White people have caused people of color, I get a feeling of guilt. How could someone like myself care so much about the color of someone's skin that they would do them harm? (Terri, a White woman)

White students also sometimes express a sense of betrayal when they realize the gaps in their own education about racism. After seeing the first episode of the documentary series *Eyes on the Prize*, Chris, a White man wrote:

> I never knew it was really that bad just 35 years ago. Why didn't I learn this in elementary or high school? Could it be that the White people of America want to forget this injustice? . . . I will never forget that movie for as long as I live. It was like a big slap in the face.

Barbara, a White woman, who also felt anger and embarrassment in response to her own previous lack of information about the internment of Japanese Americans during World War II. She wrote:

> I feel so stupid because I never even knew that these existed. I never knew that the Japanese were treated so poorly. I am becoming angry and upset about all of the things that I do not know. I have been so sheltered. My parents never wanted to let me know about the bad things that have happened in the world. After I saw the movie (*Mitsuye and Nellie*), I even called them up to ask them why they never told me this. . . . I am angry at them too for not teaching me and exposing me to the complete picture of my country.

Avoiding the subject matter is one way to avoid these uncomfortable feelings.

"I'm Not Racist, But . . ."

A third source of student resistance (particularly among White students) is the initial denial of any personal connection to racism. When asked why they have decided to enroll in a course on racism, White students typically explain their interest in the topic with such disclaimers as, "I'm not racist myself, but I know people who are, and I want to understand them better."

Because of their position as the targets of racism, students of color do not typically focus on their own prejudices or lack of them. Instead they usually express a desire to understand why racism exists, and how they have been affected by it.

However, as all students gain a better grasp of what racism is and its many manifestations in U.S. society, they inevitably start to recognize its legacy within themselves. Beliefs, attitudes, and actions based on racial stereotypes begin to be remembered and are newly observed by White students. Students of color as well often recognize attitudes they may have internalized about their own racial group or that they have believed about others. Those who previously thought themselves immune to the effects of growing up in a racist society often find themselves reliving uncomfortable feelings of guilt or anger.

After taping her own responses to a questionnaire on racial attitudes, Barbara, a White woman previously quoted, wrote:

> I always want to think of myself as open to all races. Yet when I did the interview to myself, I found that I did respond differently to the same questions about different races. No one could ever have told me that I would have. I would have denied it. But I found that I did respond differently even though I didn't want to. This really upset me. I was angry with myself because I thought I was not prejudiced and yet the stereotypes that I had created had an impact on the answers that I gave even though I didn't want it to happen.

The new self-awareness, represented here by Barbara's journal entry, changes the classroom dynamic. One common result is that some White students, once perhaps active participants in class discussion, now hesitate to continue their participation for fear that their newly recognized racism will be revealed to others.

> Today I did feel guilty, and like I had to watch what I was saying (make it good enough), I guess to prove I'm really *not* prejudiced. From the conversations the first day, I guess this is a normal enough reaction, but I certainly never expected it in me. (Joanne, a White woman)

This withdrawal on the part of White students is often paralleled by an increase in participation by students of color who are seeking an outlet for what are often feelings of anger. The withdrawal of some previously vocal White students from the classroom exchange, however, is sometimes interpreted by students of color as indifference. This perceived indifference often serves to fuel the anger and frustration that many students of color experience, as awareness of their own oppression is heightened. For example, Robert, an African-American man, wrote:

> I really wish the White students would talk more. When I read these articles, it makes me so mad and I really want to know what the White kids think. Don't they care?

Sonia, a Latina, described the classroom tension from another perspective:

> I would like to comment that at many points in the discussions I have felt uncomfortable and sometimes even angry with people. I guess I am at the stage where I am tired of listening to Whites feel guilty and watch their eyes fill up with tears. I do understand that everyone is at their own stage of development and I even tell myself every Tuesday that these people have come to this class by choice. Some days I am just more tolerant than others. . . . It takes courage to say things in that room with so many women of color present. It also makes courage for the women of color to say things about Whites.

What seems to be happening in the classroom at such moments is a collision of developmental processes that can be inherently useful for the racial identity development of the individuals involved. Nevertheless, the interaction may be perceived as problematic to instructors and students who are unfamiliar with the process. Although space does not allow for an exhaustive discussion of racial identity regarding the classroom dynamics when issues of race are discussed. It will also provide a theoretical framework for the strategies for dealing with student resistance that will be discussed at the conclusion of this article.

Stages of Racial Identity Development

Racial identity and racial identity development theory are defined by Janet Helms (1990) as

> a sense of group or collective identity based on one's *perception* that he or she shares a common racial heritage with a particular racial group . . . racial identity development theory concerns the psychological implications of racial-group membership, that is belief systems that evolve in reaction to perceived differential racial-group membership. (p. 3)

It is assumed that in a society where racial-group membership is emphasized, the development of a racial identity will occur in some form in everyone. Given the dominant/subordinate relationship of Whites and people of color in this society, however, it is not surprising that this developmental process will unfold in different ways. For purposes of discussion, William Cross's (1971, 1978) model of Black identity development will be described along with Helms's (1990) model of White racial identity development theory. While the identity development of other students (Asian, Latino/a, Native American) is not included in this particular theoretical formulation, there is evidence to suggest that the process for these oppressed groups is similar to that described for African Americans. (Highlen, et al., 1988; Phinney, 1990).[2] In each case, it is assumed that a positive sense of one's self as a member of one's group (which is not based on any assumed superiority) is important for psychological health.

Black Racial Identity Development

According to Cross's (1971, 1978, 1991) model of Black racial identity development, there are five stages in the process, identified as Preencounter, Encounter, Immersion/Emersion, Internalization, and Internalization-Commitment. In the first stage of Preencounter, the African American has absorbed many of the beliefs and values of the dominant White culture, including the notion that "White is right" and "Black is wrong." Though the internalization of negative Black stereotypes may be outside of his or her conscious awareness, the individual seeks to assimilate and be accepted by Whites, and actively or passively distances him/herself from other Blacks.[3]

Louise, an African-American woman previously quoted, captured the essence of this stage in the following description of herself at an earlier time:

> For a long time it seemed as if I didn't remember my background, and I guess in some ways I didn't. I was never taught to be proud of my African heritage. Like we talked about in class, I went through a very long stage of identifying with my oppressors. Wanting to be like, live like, and be accepted by them. Even to the point of hating my own race and myself for being a part of it. Now I am ashamed that I ever was ashamed. I lost so much of myself in my denial of and refusal to accept my people.

In order to maintain psychological comfort at this stage of development, Helms writes:

> The person must maintain the fiction that race and racial indoctrination have nothing to do with how he or she lives life. It is probably the case that the Preencounter person is bombarded on a regular basis with information that he or she cannot really be a member of the "in" racial group, but relies on denial to selectively screen such information from awareness. (1990, p. 23)

The de-emphasis on one's racial-group membership may allow the individual to think that race has not been or will not be a relevant factor in one's own achievement, and may contribute to the belief in a U.S. meritocracy that is often a part of a Preencounter worldview.

Movement into the Encounter phase is typically precipitated by an event or series of events that forces the individual to acknowledge the impact of racism in one's life. For example, instances of social rejection by White friends or colleagues (or reading new personally relevant information about racism) may lead the individual to the conclusion that many Whites will not view him or her as an equal. Faced with the reality that he or she cannot truly be White, the individual is forced to focus on his or her identity as a member of a group targeted by racism.

Brenda, a Korean-American student, described her own experience of this process as a result of her participation in the racism course:

> I feel that because of this class, I have become much more aware of racism that exists around. Because of my awareness of racism, I am now bothered by acts and behaviors that might not have bothered me in the past. Before when racial comments were said around me I would somehow ignore it and pretend that nothing was said. By ignoring comments such as these, I was protecting myself. It became sort of a defense mechanism. I never realized I did this, until I was confronted with stories that were found in our reading, by other people of color, who also ignored comments that bothered them. In realizing that there is racism out in the world and that there are comments concerning race that are directed towards me, I feel as if I have reached the first step. I also think I have reached the second step, because I am now bothered and irritated by such comments. I no longer ignore them, but now confront them.

The Immersion/Emersion stage is characterized by the simultaneous desire to surround oneself with visible symbols of one's racial identity and an active avoidance of symbols of Whiteness. As Thomas Parham describes, "At this stage, everything of value in life must be Black or relevant to Blackness. This stage is also characterized by a tendency to denigrate White people, simultaneously glorifying Black people. . . . (1989, p. 190). The previously described anger that emerges in class among African-American students and other students of color in the process of learning about racism may be seen as part of the transition through these stages.

As individuals enter the Immersion stage, they actively seek out opportunities to explore aspects of their own history and culture with the support of peers from their own racial background. Typically, White-focused anger dissipates during this phase because so much of the person's energy is directed toward his or her own group- and self-exploration. The result of this exploration is an emerging security in a newly defined and affirmed sense of self.

Sharon, another African-American woman, described herself at the beginning of the semester as angry, seemingly in the Encounter stage of development. She wrote after our class meeting:

> Another point that I must put down is that before I entered class today I was angry about the way Black people have been treated in this country. I don't think I will easily overcome that and I basically feel justified in my feelings.

At the end of the semester, Sharon had joined with two other Black students in the class to work on their final class project. She observed that the three of them had planned their project to focus on Black people specifically, suggesting movement into the Immersion stage of racial identity development. She wrote:

> We are concerned about the well-being of our own people. They cannot be well if they have this pinned-up hatred for their own people. This internalized racism is something that we all felt, at various times, needed to be talked about. This semester it has really been important to me, and I believe Gordon [a Black classmate], too.

The emergence from this stage marks the beginning of Internalization. Secure in one's own sense of racial identity, there is less need to assert the "Blacker than thou" attitude often characteristic of the Immersion stage (Parham, 1989). In general, "pro-Black attitudes become more expansive, open, and less defensive" (Cross, 1971, p. 24). While still maintaining his or her connections with Black peers, the internalized individual is willing to establish meaningful relationships with Whites who acknowledge and are respectful of his or her self-definition. The individual is also ready to build coalitions with members of other oppressed groups. At the end of the semester, Brenda, a Korean American, concluded that she had in fact internalized a positive sense of racial identity. The process she described parallels the stages described by Cross:

> I have been aware for a long time that I am Korean. But through this class I am beginning to really become aware of my race. I am beginning to find out that White people can be accepting of me and at the same time accept me as a Korean.
>
> I grew up wanting to be accepted and ended up almost denying my race and culture. I don't think I did this consciously but the denial did occur. As I grew older, I realized that I was different. I became for the first time, friends with other Koreans. I realized I had much in common them. This was when I went through my "Korean friend" stage. I began to enjoy being friends with Koreans more than I did with Caucasians.
>
> Well, ultimately, through many years of growing up, I am pretty much in focus about who I am and who my friends are. I knew before I took this class that there were people not of color that were understanding of my differences. In our class, I feel that everyone is trying to sincerely find the answer of abolishing racism. I knew people like this existed, but it's nice to meet with them weekly.

Cross suggests that there are few psychological differences between the fourth stage, Internalization, and the fifth stage, Internalization-Commitment. However, those at the fifth stage have found ways to translate their "personal sense of Blackness into a plan of action or a general sense of commitment" to the concerns of Blacks as a group, which is sustained over time (Cross, 1991, p. 220). Whether at the fourth or fifth stage, the process of Internalization allows the individual, anchored in a positive sense of racial identity, both to proactively perceive and transcend race. Blackness becomes "the point of departure for discovering the universe of ideas, cultures and experiences beyond blackness in place of mistaking blackness as the universe itself" (Cross, Parham, & Helms, 1991, p. 330).

Though the process of racial identity development has been presented here in linear form, in fact it is probably more accurate to think of it in a spiral form. Often a person may move from one stage to the next, only to revisit an earlier stage as the result of new encounter experiences (Parham, 1989), though the later experience of the stage may be different from the original experience. The image that students often find helpful in understanding this concept of recycling through the stages is that of a spiral staircase. As a person ascends a spiral staircase, she may stop and look down at a spot below. When she reaches the next level, she may look down and see the same spot, but the vantage point has changed.[4]

White Racial Identity Development

The transformations experienced by those targeted by racism are often paralleled by those of White students. Helms (1990) describes the evolution of a positive White racial identity as involving both the abandonment of racism and the development of a nonracist White identity. In order to do the latter,

> he or she must accept this or her own Whiteness, the cultural implications of being White, and define a view of Self as a racial being that does not depend on the perceived superiority of one racial group over another. (p. 49)

She identifies six stages in her model of White racial identity development: Contact, Disintegration, Reintegration, Pseudo-Independent, Immersion/Emersion, and Autonomy.

The contact stage is characterized by a lack of awareness of cultural and institutional racism, and of one's own White privilege. Peggy McIntosh (1989) writes eloquently about her own experience of this state of being:

> As a white person, I realized I had been taught about racism as something which puts others at a disadvantage, but had been taught not to see one of its corollary aspects, white privilege, which puts me at an advantage. . . . I was taught to see racism only in individual acts of meanness, not in invisible systems conferring dominance on my group. (p. 10)

In addition, the Contact stage often includes naive curiosity about or fear of people of color, based on stereotypes learned from friends, family, or the media. These stereotypes represent the framework in use when a person at this stage of development makes a comment such as, "You don't act like a Black person" (Helms, 1990, p, 57).

Those Whites whose lives are structured so as to limit their interaction with people of color, as well as their awareness of racial issues, may remain at this stage indefinitely. However, certain kinds of experiences (increased interaction with people of color or exposure to new information about racism) may lead to a new understanding that cultural and institutional racism exist. This new understanding marks the beginning of the Disintegration stage.

At this stage, the bliss of ignorance or lack of awareness is replaced by the discomfort of guilt, shame, and sometimes anger at the recognition of one's own advantage because of being White and the acknowledgment of the role of Whites in the maintenance of a racist system. Attempts to reduce discomfort may include the denial (convincing oneself that racism doesn't really exist, or if it does, it is the fault of its victims).

For example, Tom, a White male student, responded with some frustration in his journal to a classmate's observation that the fact that she had never read any books by Black authors in any of her high school or college English classes was an example of cultural racism. He wrote, "It's not my fault that Blacks don't write books."

After viewing a film in which a psychologist used examples of Black children's drawings to illustrate the potentially damaging effect of negative cultural messages on a Black child's developing self-esteem, David, another White male student, wrote:

> I found it interesting the way Black children drew themselves without arms. The psychologist said this is saying that the child feels unable to control his environment. It can't be because the child has notions and beliefs already about being Black. It must be built in or hereditary due to the past history of the Blacks. I don't believe it's cognitive but more biological due to a long past history of repression and being put down.

Though Tom's and David's explanations seem quite problematic, they can be understood in the context of racial identity development theory as a way of reducing their cognitive dissonance upon learning this new race-related information. As was discussed earlier, withdrawal (accomplished by avoiding contact with people of color and the topic of racism) is another strategy for dealing with the discomfort experienced at this stage. Many of the previously described responses of White students to race-related content are characteristic of the transition from the Contact to the Disintegration stage of development.

Helms (1990) describes another response to the discomfort of Disintegration, which involves attempts to change significant others' attitudes toward African Americans and other people of color. However, as she points out,

> due to the racial naiveté with which this approach may be undertaken and the person's ambivalent racial identification, this dissonance-reducing strategy is likely to be met with rejection by Whites as well as Blacks. (p. 59)

In fact, this response is also frequently observed among White students who have an opportunity to talk with friends and family during holiday visits. Suddenly they are noticing the racist content of jokes or comments of their friends and relatives and will try to confront them, often only to find that their efforts are, at best, ignored or dismissed as a "phase," or at worst, greeted with open hostility.

Carl, a White male previously quoted, wrote at length about this dilemma:

> I realized that it was possible to simply go through life totally oblivious to the entire situation or, even if one realizes it, one can totally repress it. It is easy to fade into the woodwork, run with the rest of society, and never have to deal with these problems. So many

> people I know from home are like this. They have simply accepted what society has taught them with little, if any, question. My father is a prime example of this. . . . It has caused much friction in our relationship, and he often tells me as a father he has failed in raising me correctly. Most of my high school friends will never deal with these issues and propagate them on to their own children. It's easy to see how the cycle continues. I don't think I could ever justify within myself simply turning my back on the problem. I finally realized that my position in all of these dominant groups gives me power to make change occur. . . . It is an unfortunate result often though that I feel alienated from friends and family. It's often played off as a mere stage that I'm going through. I obviously can't tell if it's merely a stage, but I know that they say this to take the attention off of the truth of what I'm saying. By belittling me, they take the power out of my argument. It's very depressing that being compassionate and considerate are seen as only phases that people go through. I don't want it to be a phase for me, but as obvious as this may sound, I look at my environment and often wonder how it will not be.

The societal pressure to accept the status quo may lead the individual from Disintegration to Reintegration. At this point the desire to be accepted by one's own racial group, in which the overt or covert belief in White superiority is so prevalent, may lead to a reshaping of the person's belief system to be more congruent with an acceptance of racism. The guilt and anxiety associated with Disintegration may be redirected in the form of fear and anger directed toward people of color (particularly Blacks), who are now blamed as the source of discomfort.

Connie, a White woman of Italian ancestry, in many ways exemplified the progression from the contact stage to Reintegration, a process she herself described seven weeks into the semester. After reading about the stages of White identity development, she wrote:

> I think mostly I can find myself in the disintegration stage of development. . . . There was a time when I never considered myself a color. I never described myself as a "White, Italian female" until I got to college and noticed that people of color always described themselves by their color/race. While taking this class, I have begun to understand that being White makes a difference. I never thought about it before but there are many privileges to being White. In my personal life, I cannot say that I have ever felt that I have had the advantage over a Black person, but I am aware that my race has the advantage.
>
> I am feeling really guilty lately about that. I find myself thinking: "I didn't mean to be White, I really didn't mean it." I am starting to feel angry towards my race for ever using this advantage towards personal gains. But at the same time I resent the minority groups. I mean, it's not our fault that society has deemed us "superior." I don't feel any better than a Black person. But it really doesn't matter because I am a member of a dominant race. . . . I can't help it . . . and I sometimes get angry and feel like I'm being attacked.
>
> I guess my anger toward a minority group would enter me into the next stage of Reintegration, where I am once again starting to blame the victim. This is all very trying for me and it has been on my mind a lot. I really would like to be able to reach the last stage, autonomy, where I can accept being White without hostility and anger. That is really hard to do.

Helms (1990) suggests that it is relatively easy for Whites to become stuck at the Reintegration stage of development, particularly if avoidance of people of color is possible. However, if there is a catalyst for continued self-examination, the person "begins to question her or his previous definition of Whiteness and the justifiability of racism in any of its forms . . ." (p. 61). In my experience, continued participation in a course on racism provides the catalyst for this deeper self-examination.

This process was again exemplified by Connie. At the end of the semester, she listened to her own taped interview of her racial attitudes that she had recorded at the beginning of the semester. She wrote:

> Oh wow! I could not believe some of the things that I said. I was obviously in different stages of the White identity development. As I listened and got more and more disgusted with myself when I was at the Reintegration stage, I tried to remind myself that these are stages that all (most) White people go through when dealing with notions of racism. I can remember clearly the resentment I had for people of color. I feel the one thing I enjoyed from listening to my interview was noticing how much I have changed. I think I am finally out of the Reintegration stage. I am beginning to make a conscious effort to seek out information about people of color and accept their criticism. . . . I still feel guilty about the feeling I had about people of color and I always feel bad about being privileged as a result of racism. But I am glad that I have reached what I feel is the Pseudo-Independent state of White identity development.

The information-seeking that Connie describes often marks the onset of the Pseudo-Independent stage. At this stage, the individual is abandoning beliefs in White superiority, but may still behave in ways that unintentionally perpetuate the system. Looking to those targeted by racism to help him or her understand racism, the White person often tries to disavow his or her own Whiteness through active affiliation with Blacks, for example. The individual experiences a sense of alienation from other Whites who have not yet begun to examine their own racism, yet may also experience rejection from Blacks or other people of color who are suspicious of his or her motives. Students of color moving from the Encounter to Immersion phase of their own racial identity development may be particularly unreceptive to the White person's attempts to connect with them.

Uncomfortable with his or her own Whiteness, yet unable to be truly anything else, the individual may begin searching for a new, more comfortable way to be White. This search is characteristic of the Immersion/Emersion stage of development. Just as the Black student seeks to redefine positively what it means to be of African ancestry in the United States through immersion in accurate information about one's culture and history, the White individual seeks to replace racially related myths and stereotypes with accurate information about what it means and has meant to be White in U.S. society (Helms. 1990). Learning about Whites who have been antiracist allies to people of color is a very important part of this process.

After reading articles written by antiracist activists describing their own process of unlearning racism, White students often comment on how helpful it is to know that others have experienced similar feelings and have found ways to resist the racism in their environments.[5] For example, Joanne, a White woman who initially experienced a lot of guilt, wrote:

> This article helped me out in many ways. I've been feeling helpless and frustrated. I know there are all these terrible things going on and I want to be able to do something. . . . anyway this article helped me realize, again, that others feel this way, and gave me some positive ideas to resolve my dominant class guilt and shame.

Finally, reading the biographies and autobiographies of White individuals who have embarked on a similar process of identity development (such as Barnard, 1987) provides White students with important models for change.

Learning about White antiracists can also provide students of color with a sense of hope that they can have White allies. After hearing a White antiracist activist address the class, Sonia, a Latina who had written about her impatience with expressions of White guilt, wrote:

> I don't know when I have been more impressed by anyone. She filled me with hope for the future. She made me believe that there are good people in the world and that Whites suffer too and want to change things.

For White students, the internalization of a newly defined sense of oneself as White is the primary task of the Autonomy stage. The positive feelings associated with this redefinition energize the person's efforts to confront racism and oppression in his or her daily life. Alliances with people of color can be more easily forged at this stage of development than previously because the person's antiracist behaviors and attitudes will be more consistently expressed. While Autonomy might be described as "racial self-actualization, . . . it is best to think of it as an ongoing process . . . wherein the person is continually open to new information and new ways of thinking about racial and cultural variables" (Helms, 1990, p. 66).

Annette, a White women, described herself in the Autonomy stage, but talked at length about the circular process she felt she had been engaged in during the semester:

If people as racist as C. P. Ellis (a former Klansman) can change, I think anyone can change. If that makes me idealistic, fine. I do not think my expecting society to change is naive anymore because I now *know* exactly what I want. To be naive means a lack of knowledge that allows me to accept myself both as a White person and as an idealist. This class showed me that these two are not mutually exclusive but are an integral part of me that I cannot deny. I realize now that through most of this class I was trying to deny both of them.

While I was not accepting society's racism, I was accepting society's telling me as a White person, there was nothing I could do to change racism. So, I told myself I was being naive and tried to suppress my desire to change society. This is what made me so frustrated—while I saw society's racism through examples in the readings and the media, I kept telling myself there was nothing I could do. Listening to my tape, I think I was already in the Autonomy stage when I started this class. I then seemed to decide that being White, I also had to be a racist which is when I became frustrated and went back to the Disintegration stage. I was frustrated because I was not only telling myself there was nothing I could do but I also was assuming society's racism was my own which made me feel like I did not want to be White. Actually, it was not being White that I was disavowing but being racist. I think I have now returned to the Autonomy stage and am much more secure in my position there. I accept my Whiteness now as just a part of me as is my idealism. I will no longer disavow these characteristics as I have realized I can be proud of both of them. In turn, I can now truly accept other people for their unique characteristics and not by the labels society has given them as I can accept myself that way.

While I thought the main ideas that I learned in this class were that White people need to be educated to end racism and everyone should be treated as human beings, I really had already incorporated these ideas into my thoughts. What I learned from this class is being White does not mean being racist and being idealistic does not mean being naive. I really did not have to form new ideas about people of color; I had to form them about myself—and I did.

Implications for Classroom Teaching

Although movement through all the stages of racial identity development will not necessarily occur for each student within the course of a semester (or even four years of college), it is certainly common to witness beginning transformations in classes with race-related content. An awareness of the existence of this process has helped me to implement strategies to facilitate positive student development, as well as to improve interracial dialogue within the classroom.

Four strategies for reducing student resistance and promoting student development that I have found useful are the following:

1. the creation of a safe classroom atmosphere by establishing clear guidelines for discussion;
2. the creation of opportunities for self-generated knowledge;
3. the provision of an appropriate developmental model that students can use as a framework for understanding their own process;
4. the exploration of strategies to empower students as change agents.

Creating a Safe Climate

As was discussed earlier, making the classroom a safe space for discussion is essential for overcoming students' fears about breaking the race taboo and will also reduce later anxieties about exposing one's own internalized racism. Establishing the guidelines of confidentiality, mutual respect, "no zaps," and speaking from one's own experience on the first day of class is a necessary step in the process.

Students respond very positively to these ground rules, and do try to honor them. While the rules do not totally eliminate anxiety, they clearly communicate to students that there is a safety net for the discussion. Students are also encouraged to direct their comments and questions to each other rather than always focusing their attention on me as the instructor, and to learn each other's names rather than referring to each other as "he," "she," or "the person in the red sweater" when responding to each other.[6]

The Power of Self-Generated Knowledge

The creation of opportunities for self-generated knowledge on the part of students is a powerful tool for reducing the initial stage of denial that many students experience. While it may seem easy for some students to challenge the validity of what they read or what the instructor says, it is harder to deny what they have seen with their own eyes. Students can be given hands-on assignments outside of class to facilitate this process.

For example, after reading *Portraits of White Racism* (Wellman, 1977), some students expressed the belief that the attitudes expressed by the White interviewees in the book were no longer commonly held attitudes. Students were then asked to use the same interview protocol used in the book (with some revision) to interview a White adult of their choice. When students reported on these interviews in class, their own observation of the similarity between those they had interviewed and those they had read about was more convincing than anything I might have said.

After doing her interview, Patty, a usually quiet White student, wrote:

> I think I learned a lot from it and that I'm finally getting a better grip on the idea of racism. I think that was why I participated so much in class. I really felt like I knew what I was talking about.

Other examples of creating opportunities for self-generated knowledge include assigning students the task of visiting grocery stores in neighborhoods of differing racial composition to compare the cost and quality of goods and services available at the two locations, and to observe the interactions between the shoppers and the store personnel. For White students, one of the most powerful assignments of this type has been to go apartment hunting with an African-American student and to experience housing discrimination firsthand. While one concern with such an assignment is the effect it will have on the student(s) of color involved, I have found that those Black students who choose this assignment rather than another are typically eager to have their White classmates experience the reality of racism, and thus participate quite willingly in the process.

Naming the Problem

The emotional responses that students have to talking and learning about racism are quite predictable and related to their own racial identity development. Unfortunately, students typically do not know this; thus they consider their own guilt, shame, embarrassment, or anger an uncomfortable experience that they alone are having. Informing students at the beginning of the semester that these feelings may be part of the learning process is ethically necessary (in the sense of informed consent), and helps to normalize the students' experience. Knowing in advance that a desire to withdraw from classroom discussion or not to complete assignments is a common response helps students to remain engaged when they reach that point. As Alice, a White woman, wrote at the end of the semester:

> You were so right in saying in the beginning how we would grow tired of racism (I did in October) but then it would get so good! I have *loved* the class once I passed that point.

In addition, sharing the model of racial identity development with students gives them a useful framework for understanding each other's processes as well as their own. This cognitive framework does not necessarily prevent the collision of developmental processes previously described, but it does allow students to be less frightened by it when it occurs. If, for example, White students understand the stages of racial identity development for students of color, they are less likely to personalize or feel threatened by an African-American student's anger.

Connie, a White student who initially expressed a lot of resentment at the way students of color tended to congregate in the college cafeteria, was much more understanding of this behavior after she learned about racial identity development theory. She wrote:

> I learned a lot from reading the article about the stages of development in the model of oppressed people. As a White person going through my stages of identity development, I do not take time to think about the struggle people of color go through to reach a stage of complete understanding. I am glad that I know about the stages because now I can understand people of color's behavior in certain situations. For example, when people of color stay to themselves and appear to be in a clique, it is not because they are being rude as I originally thought. Rather they are engaging perhaps in the Immersion stage.

Mary, another White student, wrote:

> I found the entire Cross model of racial identity development very enlightening. I knew that there were stages of racial identity development before I entered this class. I did not know what they were, or what they really entailed. After reading through this article I found myself saying, "Oh. That explains why she reacted this way to this incident instead of how she would have a year ago." Clearly this person has entered a different stage and is working through different problems from a new viewpoint. Thankfully, the model provides a degree of hope that people will not always be angry, and will not always be separatists, etc. Although I'm not really sure about that.

Conversely, when students of color understand the stages of White racial identity development, they can be more tolerant or appreciative of a White student's struggle with guilt, for example. After reading about the stages of white identity development, Sonia, a Latina previously quoted, wrote:

> This article was the one that made me feel that my own prejudices were showing. I never knew that Whites went through an identity development of their own.

She later told me outside of class that she found it much easier to listen to some of the things white students said because she could understand their potentially offensive comments as part of a developmental stage.

Sharon, an African-American woman, also found that an understanding of the respective stages of racial identity development helped her to understand some of the interactions she had had with White students since coming to college. She wrote:

> There is a lot of clash that occurs between Black and White people at college which is best explained by their respective stages of development. Unfortunately schools have not helped to alleviate these problems earlier in life.

In a course of the psychology of racism, it is easy to build in the provision of this information as part of the course content. For instructors teaching courses with race-related content in other fields, it may seem less natural to do so. However, the inclusion of articles on racial identity development and/or class discussion of these issues in conjunction with the other strategies that have been suggested can improve student receptivity to the course content in important ways, making it a very useful investment of class time. Because the stages describe kinds of behavior that many people have commonly observed in themselves, as well as in their own intraracial and interracial interactions, my experience has been that most students grasp the basic conceptual framework fairly easily, even if they do not have a background in psychology.

Empowering Students as Change Agents

Heightening students' awareness of racism without also developing an awareness of the possibility of change is a prescription for despair. I consider it unethical to do one without the other. Exploring strategies to empower students as change agents is thus a necessary part of the process of talking about race and learning about racism. As was previously mentioned, students find it very helpful to read about and hear from individuals who have been effective change agents. Newspaper and magazine articles, as well as biographical or autobiographical essays or book excerpts, are often important sources for this information.

I also ask students to work in small groups to develop an action plan of their own for interrupting racism. While I do not consider it appropriate to require students to engage in antiracist activity (since I believe this should be a personal choice the student makes for him/herself), students are required to think about the possibility. Guidelines are provided (see Katz, 1978), and the plans that they develop over several weeks are presented at the end of the semester. Students are generally impressed with each other's good ideas, and, in fact, they often do go on to implement their projects.

Joanne, a White student who initially struggled with feelings of guilt, wrote:

> I thought that hearing others' ideas for action plans was interesting and informative. It really helps me realize (reminds me) the many choices and avenues there are once I decided to be an ally. Not only did I develop my own concrete way to be an ally, I have found many other ways that I, as a college student, can be an active anti-racist. It was really empowering.

Another way all students can be empowered is by offering them the opportunity to consciously observe their own development. The taped exercise to which some of the previously quoted students have referred is an example of one way to provide this opportunity. At the beginning of the semester, students are given an interview guide with many open-ended questions concerning racial attitudes and opinions. They are asked to interview themselves on tape as a way of recording their own ideas for future reference. Though the tapes are collected, students are assured that no one (including me) will listen to them. The tapes are returned near the end of the semester, and students are asked to listen to their own tapes and use their understanding of racial identity development to discuss it in essay form.

The resulting essays are often remarkable and underscore the psychological importance of giving students the chance to examine racial issues in the classroom. The following was written by Elaine, a White woman:

> Another common theme that was apparent in the tape was that, for the most part, I was aware of my own ignorance and was embarrassed because of it. I wanted to know more about the oppression of people in the country so that I could do something about it. Since I have been here, I have begun to be actively resistant to racism. I have been able to confront my grandparents and some old friends from high school when they make racist comments. Taking this psychology of racism class is another step toward active resistance to racism. I am trying to educate myself so that I have a knowledge base to work from.
>
> When the tape was made, I was just beginning to be active and just beginning to be educated. I think I am now starting to move into the redefinition stage. I am starting to feel ok about being White. Some of my guilt is dissipating, and I do not feel as ignorant as I used to be. I think I have an understanding of racism; how it effects [*sic*] myself, and how it effects this country. Because of this I think I can be more active in doing something about it.

In the words of Louise, a Black female student:

> One of the greatest things I learned from this semester in general is that the world is not only Black and White, nor is the United States. I learned a lot about my own erasure of many American ethnic groups . . . I am in the (immersion) stage of my identity development. I think I am also dangling a little in the (encounter) stage. I say this because a lot of my energies are still directed toward White people. I began writing a poem two days ago and it was directed to White racism. However, I have also become more Black-identified. I am reaching to the strength in Afro-American heritage. I am learning more about the heritage and history of Afro-American culture. Knowledge = strength and strength = power.

While some students are clearly more self-reflective and articulate about their own process than others, most students experience the opportunity to talk and learn about these issues as a transforming process. In my experience, even those students who are frustrated by aspects of the course find themselves changed by it. One such student wrote in her final journal entry:

What I felt to be a major hindrance to me was the amount of people. Despite the philosophy, I really never felt at ease enough to speak openly about the feelings I have and kind of watched the class pull farther and farther apart as the semester went on . . . I think that it was your attitude that kept me intrigued by the topics we were studying despite my frustrations with the class time. I really feel as though I made some significant moves in my understanding of other people's positions in our world as well as of my feelings of racism, and I feel very good about them. I feel like this class has moved me in the right direction. I'm on a roll I think, because I've been introduced to so much.

Facilitating student development in this way is a challenging and complex task, but the results are clearly worth the effort.

Implications for the Institution

What are the institutional implications for an understanding of racial identity development theory beyond the classroom? How can this framework be used to address the pressing issues of increasing diversity and decreasing racial tensions on college campuses? How can providing opportunities in the curriculum to talk about race and learn about racism affect the recruitment and retention of students of color specifically, especially when the majority of the students enrolled are White?

The fact is, educating White students about race and racism changes attitudes in ways that go beyond the classroom boundaries. As White students move through their own stages of identity development, they take their friends with them by engaging them in dialogue. They share the articles they have read with roommates, and involve them in their projects. An example of this involvement can be seen in the following journal entry, written by Larry, a White man:

> Here it is our fifth week of class and more and more I am becoming aware of the racism around me. Our second project made things clearer, because while watching T.V. I picked up many kinds of discrimination and stereotyping. Since the project was over, I still find myself watching these shows and picking up bits and pieces every show I watch. Even my friends will be watching a show and they will say, "Hey, Larry, put that in your paper." Since they know I am taking this class, they are looking out for these things. They are also watching what they say around me for fear that I will use them as an example. For example, one of my friends has this fascination with making fun of Jewish people. Before I would listen to his comments and take them in stride, but now I confront him about his comments.

The heightened awareness of the White students enrolled in the class has a ripple effect in their peer group, which helps to create a climate in which students of color and other targeted groups (Jewish students, for example) might feel more comfortable. It is likely that White students who have had the opportunity to learn about racism in a supportive atmosphere will be better able to be allies to students of color in extracurricular settings, like student government meetings and other organizational settings, where students of color often feel isolated and unheard.

At the same time, students of color who have had the opportunity to examine the ways in which racism may have affected their own lives are able to give voice to their own experience, and to validate it rather than be demoralized by it. An understanding of internalized oppression can help students of color recognize the ways in which they may have unknowingly participated in their own victimization, or the victimization of others. They may be able to move beyond victimization to empowerment, and share their learning with others, as Sharon, a previously quoted Black woman, planned to do.

Campus communities with an understanding of racial identity development could become more supportive of special-interest groups, such as the Black Student Union or the Asian Student Alliance, because they would recognize them not as "separatist" but as important outlets for students of color who may be at the Encounter or Immersion stage of racial identity development. Not only could speakers of color be sought out to add diversity to campus programming, but Whites who had made a commitment to unlearning their own racism could be offered as models to those White students looking for new ways to understand their own Whiteness, and to students of color looking for allies.

It has become painfully clear on many college campuses across the United States that we cannot have successfully multiracial campuses without talking about race and learning about racism. Providing a forum where this discussion can take place safely over a semester, a time period that allows personal and group development to unfold in ways that day-long or weekend programs do not, may be among the most proactive learning opportunities an institution can provide.

Notes

1. A similar point could be made about other issues of oppression, such as anti-Semitism, homophobia and heterosexism, ageism, and so on.
2. While similar models of racial identity development exist, Cross and Helms are referenced here because they are among the most frequently cited writers on Black racial identity development and on White racial identity development, respectively. For a discussion of the commonalities between these and other identity development models, see Phinney (1989, 1990) and Helms (1990).
3. Both Parham (1989) and Phinney (1989) suggest that a preference for the dominant group is not always a characteristic of this stage. For example, children raised in households and communities with explicitly positive Afrocentric attitudes may absorb a pro-Black perspective, which then serves as the starting point for their own exploration of racial identity.
4. After being introduced to this model and Helms's model of White identity development, students are encouraged to think about how the models might apply to their own experience or the experiences of people they know. As is reflected in the cited journal entries, some students resonate to the theories quite readily, easily seeing their own process of growth reflected in them. Other students are sometimes puzzled because they feel as though their own process varies from these models, and may ask if it is possible to "skip" a particular stage, for example. Such questions provide a useful departure point for discussing the limitations of stage theories in general, and the potential variations in experience that make questions of racial identity development so complex.
5. Examples of useful articles include essays by McIntosh (1988), Lester (1987), and Braden (1987). Each of these combines autobiographical material, as well as a conceptual framework for understanding some aspect of racism that students find very helpful. Bowser and Hunt's (1981) edited book, *Impacts of Racism on Whites*, though less autobiographical in nature, is also a valuable resource.
6. Class size has a direct bearing on my ability to create safety in the classroom. Dividing the class into pairs or small groups of five or six students to discuss initial reactions to a particular article or film helps to increase participation, both in the small groups and later in the large group discussions.

References

Bernard, H. F. (Ed.). (1987). *Outside the magic circle: The autobiography of Virginia Foster Durr*. New York: Simon & Schuster. (originally published in 1985 by University of Alabama Press)

Bowser, B. P., & Hunt, R. G. (1981). *Impacts of racism on whites*. Beverly Hills: Sage.

Braden, A. (1987, April–May). Undoing racism: Lessons for the peace movement. *The Nonviolent Activist*, pp. 3–6.

Bronstein, P. A., & Quina, K. (Eds.). (1988). *Teaching a psychology of people: Resources for gender and sociocultural awareness*. Washington, DC: American Psychological Association.

Cross, W. E., Jr. (1971). The Negro to black conversion experience: Toward a psychology of black liberation. *Black World, 20*(9), 13–27.

Cross, W. E., Jr. (1978). The Cross and Thomas models of psychological nigrescence. *Journal of Black Psychology, 5*(1), 13–19.

Cross, W. E., Jr. (1991). *Shades of black: Diversity in African-American identity*. Philadelphia: Temple University Press.

Cross, W. E., Jr., Parham, T. A., & Helms, J. E. (1991). The stages of black identity development: Nigrescence models. In R. Jones (Ed.), *Black psychology* (3rd ed., pp. 319–338). San Francisco: Cobb and Henry.

Derman-Sparks, L., Higa, C. T., & Sparks, B. (1980). Children, race and racism: How race awareness develops. *Interracial Books for Children Bulletin, 11*(3/4), 3–15.

Helms, J. E. (Ed.). (1990). *Black and white racial identity: Theory, research and practice.* Westport, CT: Greenwood Press.

Highlen, P. S., Reynolds, A. L., Adams, E. M., Hanley, T. C., Myers, L. J., Cox, C., & Speight, S. (1988, August 13). *Self-identity development model of oppressed people: Inclusive model for all?* Paper presented at the American Psychological Association convention, Atlanta, GA.

Hull, G. T., Scott, P. B., & Smith, B. (Eds.). (1982). *All the women are white, all the blacks are men, but some of us are brave: Black women's studies.* Old Westbury, NY: Feminist Press.

Katz, J. H. (1978). *White awareness: Handbook for anti-racism training.* Norman: University of Oklahoma Press.

Lester, J. (1987). *What happens to the mythmakers when the myths are found to be untrue?* Unpublished paper, Equity Institute, Emeryville, CA.

McIntosh, P. (1988). *White privilege and male privilege: A personal account of coming to see correspondences through work in women's studies.* Working paper, Wellesley College Center for Research on Women, Wellesley, MA.

McIntosh, P. (1989, July/August). White privilege: Unpacking the invisible knapsack. *Peace and Freedom*, pp. 10–12.

Parham, T. A. (1989). Cycles of psychological nigrescence. *The Counseling Psychologist, 17*(2), 187–226.

Phinney, J. (1989). Stages of ethnic identity in minority group adolescents. *Journal of Early Adolescence, 9*, 34–39.

Phinney, J. (1990). Ethnic identity in adolescents and adults: Review of research. *Psychological Bulletin, 108*(3), 499–514.

Phinney, J. S., & Rotheram, M. J. (Eds.). (1987). *Children's ethnic socialization: Pluralism and development.* Newbury Park, CA: Sage.

Schuster, M. R., & Van Dyne, S. R. (Eds.). (1985). *Women's place in the academy: Transforming the liberal arts curriculum.* Totowa, NJ: Rowman & Allanheld.

Wellman, D. (1977). *Portraits of white racism.* New York: Cambridge University Press.

Implementing the Seven Principles: Technology as Lever

Arthur W. Chickering and Stephen C. Ehrmann

Since the Seven Principles of Good Practice were created in 1987, new communication and information technologies have become major resources for teaching and learning in higher education. If the power of the new technologies is to be fully realized, they should be employed in ways consistent with the Seven Principles. Such technologies are *tools* with multiple capabilities; it is misleading to make assertions like "Microcomputers will empower students" because that is only one way in which computers might be used.

Any given instructional strategy can be supported by a number of contrasting technologies (old and new), just as any given technology might support different instructional strategies. But for any given instructional strategy, some technologies are better than others: Better to turn a screw with a screwdriver than a hammer—a dime may also do the trick, but a screwdriver is usually better.

This essay, then, describes some of the most cost-effective and appropriate ways to use computers, video, and telecommunications technologies to advance the Seven Principles.

1. Good Practice Encourages Contacts Between Students and Faculty

> Frequent student-faculty contact in and out of class is a most important factor in student motivation and involvement. Faculty concern helps students get through rough times and keep on working. Knowing a few faculty members well enhances students' intellectual commitment and encourages them to think about their own values and plans.

Communication technologies that increase access to faculty members, help them share useful resources, and provide for joint problem solving and shared learning can usefully augment face-to-face contact in and outside of class meetings. By putting in place a more "distant" source of information and guidance for students, such technologies can strengthen faculty interactions with all students, but especially with shy students who are reluctant to ask questions or challenge the teacher directly. It is often easier to discuss values and personal concerns in writing than orally, since inadvertent or ambiguous nonverbal signals are not so dominant. As the number of commuting part-time students and adult learners increases, technologies provide opportunities for interaction not possible when students come to class and leave soon afterward to meet work or family responsibilities.

The biggest success story in this realm has been that of time-delayed (asynchronous) communication. Traditionally, time-delayed communication took place in education through the exchange of homework, either in class or by mail (for more distant learners). Such time-delayed exchange was often a rather impoverished form of conversation, typically limited to three conversational turns:

1. The instructor poses a question (a task).
2. The student responds (with homework).
3. The instructor responds some time later with comments and a grade.

"Implementing the Seven Principles: Technology as Lever," by Arthur W. Chickering and Stephen C. Ehrmann, reprinted from *AAHE Bulletin*, Vol. 49, No. 2, October 1996, American Association for Higher Education.

The conversation often ends there; by the time the grade or comment is received, the course and student are off on new topics.

Now, however, electronic mail, computer conferencing, and the World Wide Web increase opportunities for students and faculty to converse and exchange work much more speedily than before, and more thoughtfully and "safely" than when confronting each other in a classroom or faculty office. Total communication increases and, for many students, the result seems more intimate, protected, and convenient than the more intimidating demands of face-to-face communication with faculty.

Professor Norman Coombs reports that, after twelve years of teaching black history at the Rochester Institute of Technology, the first time he used email was the first time a student asked what he, a white man, was doing teaching black history. The literature is full of stories of students from different cultures opening up in and out of class when email became available. Communication also is eased when student or instructor (or both) is not a native speaker of English; each party can take a bit more time to interpret what has been said and compose a response. With the new media, participation and contribution from diverse students become more equitable and widespread.

2. Good Practice Develops Reciprocity and Cooperation Among Students

> Learning is enhanced when it is more like a team effort than a solo race. Good learning, like good work, is collaborative and social, not competitive and isolated. Working with others often increases involvement in learning. Sharing one's ideas and responding to others' improves thinking and deepens understanding.

The increased opportunities for interaction with faculty noted above apply equally to communication with fellow students. Study groups, collaborative learning, group problem solving, and discussion of assignments can all be dramatically strengthened through communication tools that facilitate such activity. The extent to which computer-based tools encourage spontaneous student collaboration was one of the earliest surprises about computers. A clear advantage of email for today's busy commuting students is that it opens up communication among classmates even when they are not physically together.

For example: One of us, attempting to learn to navigate the Web, took a course taught entirely by a combination of televised class sessions (seen live or taped) and by work on a course Web page. The hundred students in the course included persons in Germany and the Washington, DC, area.

Learning teams helped themselves "learn the plumbing" and solve problems. These team members never met face-to-face. but they completed and exchanged Myers-Briggs Type Inventories, surveys of their prior experience and level of computer expertise, and brief personal introductions. This material helped teammates size one another up initially; team interactions then built working relationships and encouraged acquaintanceship. This kind of "collaborative learning" would be all but impossible without the presence of the media we were learning about and with.

3. Good Practice Uses Active Learning Techniques

> Learning is not a spectator sport. Students do not learn much just sitting in classes listening to teachers, memorizing prepackaged assignments, and spitting out answers. They must talk about what they are learning, write reflectively about it, relate it to past experiences, and apply it to their daily lives. They must make what they learn part of themselves.

The range of technologies that encourage active learning is staggering. Many fall into one of three categories: tools and resources for learning by doing, time-delayed exchange, and real-time conversation. Today, all three usually can be supported with "worldware," i.e., software (such as word processors) originally developed for other purposes but now used for instruction, too.

We've already discussed communication tools, so here we will focus on learning by doing.

Apprentice-like learning has been supported by many traditional technologies: research libraries, laboratories, art and architectural studios, athletic fields. Newer technologies now can enrich and expand these opportunities. For example:

- Supporting apprentice-like activities in fields that themselves require the use of technology as a tool, such as statistical research and computer-based music, or use of the Internet to gather information not available in the local library.

- Simulating techniques that do not themselves require computers, such as helping chemistry students develop and practice research skills in "dry" simulated laboratories before they use the riskier, more expensive real equipment.
- Helping students develop insight. For example, students can be asked to design a radio antenna. Simulation software displays not only their design but the ordinarily invisible electromagnetic waves the antenna would emit. Students change their designs and instantly see resulting changes in the waves. The aim of this exercise is not to design antennae but to build deeper understanding of electromagnetism.

4. Good Practice Gives Prompt Feedback

> Knowing what you know and don't know focuses your learning. In getting started, students need help in assessing their existing knowledge and competence. Then, in classes, students need frequent opportunities to perform and receive feedback on their performance. At various points during college, and at its end, students need chances to reflect on what they have learned, what they still need to know, and how they might assess themselves.

The ways in which new technologies can provide feedback are many—sometimes obvious, sometimes more subtle. We already have talked about the use of email for supporting person-to-person feedback, for example, and the feedback inherent in simulations. Computers also have a growing role in recording and analyzing personal and professional performances. Teachers can use technology to provide critical observations for an apprentice; for example, video to help a novice teacher, actor, or athlete critique his or her own performance. Faculty (or other students) can react to a writer's draft using the "hidden text" option available in word processors: Turned on, the "hidden" comments spring up; turned off, the comments recede and the writer's prized work is again free of "red ink."

As we move toward portfolio evaluation strategies, computers can provide rich storage and easy access to student products and performances. Computers can keep track of early efforts, so instructors and students can see the extent to which later efforts demonstrate gains in knowledge, competence, or other valued outcomes. Performances that are time-consuming and expensive to record and evaluate—such as leadership skills, group process management, or multicultural interactions—can be elicited and stored, not only for ongoing critique but also as a record of growing capacity.

5. Good Practice Emphasizes Time on Task

> Time plus energy equals learning. Learning to use one's time well is critical for students and professionals alike. Allocating realistic amounts of time means effective learning for students and effective teaching for faculty.

New technologies can dramatically improve time on task for students and faculty members. Some years ago a faculty member told one of us that he used technology to "steal students' beer time," attracting them to work on course projects instead of goofing off. Technology also can increase time on task by making studying more efficient. Teaching strategies that help students learn at home or work can save hours otherwise spent commuting to and from campus, finding parking places, and so on. Time efficiency also increases when interactions between teacher and students, and among students, fit busy work and home schedules. And students and faculty alike make better use of time when they can get access to important resources for learning without trudging to the library, flipping through card files, scanning microfilm and microfiche, and scrounging the reference room.

For faculty members interested in classroom research, computers can record student participation and interaction and help document student time on task, especially as related to student performance.

6. Good Practice Communicates High Expectations

> Expect more and you will get it. High expectations are important for everyone—for the poorly prepared, for those unwilling to exert themselves, and for the bright and well motivated. Expecting students to perform well becomes a self-fulfilling prophecy.

New technologies can communicate high expectations explicitly and efficiently. Significant real-life problems, conflicting perspectives, or paradoxical data sets can set powerful learning challenges that drive students to not only acquire information but sharpen their cognitive skills of analysis, synthesis, application, and evaluation.

Many faculty report that students feel stimulated by knowing their finished work will be "published" on the World Wide Web.

With technology, criteria for evaluating products and performances can be more clearly articulated by the teacher, or generated collaboratively with students. General criteria can be illustrated with samples of excellent, average, mediocre, and faulty performance. These samples can be shared and modified easily. They provide a basis for peer evaluation, so learning teams can help everyone succeed.

7. Good Practice Respects Diverse Talents and Ways of Learning

> Many roads lead to learning. Different students bring different talents and styles to college. Brilliant students in a seminar might be all thumbs in a lab or studio; students rich in hands-on experience may not do so well with theory. Students need opportunities to show their talents and learn in ways that work for them. Then they can be pushed to learn in new ways that do not come so easily.

Technological resources can ask for different methods of learning through powerful visuals and well-organized print; through direct, vicarious, and virtual experiences; and through tasks requiring analysis, synthesis, and evaluation, with applications to real-life situations. They can encourage self-reflection and self-evaluation. They can drive collaboration and group problem solving. Technologies can help students learn in ways they find most effective and broaden their repertoires for learning. They can supply structure for students who need it and leave assignments more open-ended for students who don't. Fast, bright students can move quickly through materials they master easily and go on to more difficult tasks; slower students can take more time and get more feedback and direct help from teachers and fellow students. Aided by technologies, students with similar motives and talents can work in cohort study groups without constraints of time and place.

Evaluation and the Seven Principles

How are we to know whether given technologies are as useful in promoting the Seven Principles and learning as this article claims? One approach is to look and see, which is the aim of the "Flashlight Project," a three-year effort of the Annenberg/CPB Project to develop and share evaluation procedures. The Flashlight Project is developing a suite of evaluation tools that any campus can use to monitor the usefulness of technology in implementing the Seven Principles and the impacts of such changes on learning outcomes (e.g., the student's ability to apply what was learned in the academic program) and on access (e.g., whether hoped-for gains in time on task and retention are saving money for the institution and its funders).

[For more about the Flashlight Project, see Stephen Ehrmann's "Asking the Right Questions: What Does Research Tell Us About Technology and Higher Learning?" in the March/April 1995 *Change*. Or, check out the Flashlight Project's website at http://www.learner.org/content/ed/strat/eval.html.]

Technology Is Not Enough

The Seven Principles cannot be implemented by technophiles alone, or even by faculty alone. *Students* need to become familiar with the Principles and be more assertive with respect to their own learning. When confronted with teaching strategies and course requirements that use technologies in ways contrary to the Principles, students should, if possible, move to alternatives that serve them better. If teaching focuses simply on memorizing and regurgitating prepackaged information, whether delivered by a faculty lecture or computer, students should reach for a different course, search out additional resources or complementary experiences, establish their own study groups, or go to the professor for more substantial activities and feedback.

Faculty members who already work with students in ways consistent with the Principles need to be tough-minded about the software- and technology-assisted interactions they create and buy into. They need to eschew materials that are simply didactic, and search instead for those that are interactive, problem oriented, relevant to real-world issues, and that evoke student motivation.

Institutional policies concerning learning resources and technology support need to give high priority to user-friendly hardware, software, and communication vehicles that help faculty and students use technologies efficiently and effectively. Investments in professional development for faculty members, plus training and computer lab assistance for students, will be necessary if learning potentials are to be realized.

Finally, it is appropriate for legislators and other benefactors to ask whether institutions are striving to improve educational practice consistent with the Seven Principles. Much depends on the answer.

Note

This article draws on Arthur Chickering's participation in "The Future of Face-to-Face and Distance Learning in Post-Secondary Education," a workgroup chaired by W. L. Renwick as part of a larger effort examining *The Future of Post-Secondary Education and the Role of Information and Communication Technology: A Clarifying Report*, carried out by the Center for Educational Research and Innovation, Organization for Economic Cooperation and Development. Paris: 1993, 1994.

C. Instructional Improvement

from Taking Teaching Seriously: Meeting the Challenge of Instructional Improvement

MICHAEL B. PAULSEN AND KENNETH A. FELDMAN

Models of Change

Much of this section examines the nature of instructional improvement for individual teachers and the personal dynamics involved in the process. How is it that teachers become motivated to want to improve their teaching and to produce and maintain actual changes in behavior? Improving teaching is not solely the responsibility of individual faculty members and does not lie only in the realm of self-generating individual change. A variety of group, social-structural, and cultural forces are involved, yet ultimately it is the individual college teacher who must change something about his or her behavior if instruction is to be improved. This section explores the process of individual change that underlies instructional improvement.

Several useful models of instructional improvement have been developed. Each takes a different perspective and offers distinctive insights into the nature of the process. One approach has been to describe instructional improvement from a faculty perspective, explaining how college teachers interact with their environment in a familiar feedback loop (Menges 1991). Teachers receive input or feedback about their effectiveness from their environment, compare it with their internal standards for performance, and then restore equilibrium by changing their output (teaching behavior), feedback input, or internal performance standards.

> Feedback loops are easily discerned in instructional settings. Imagine that examination scores create dissonance because the teacher (comparator) finds them below her standard. She may deal with the discrepancy by gathering additional kinds of data, ultimately concluding that students are not deficient after all. Thus, equilibrium is restored. She may reflect on what she expects of students, decide that these expectations are too high, and adjust her expectations to restore equilibrium. Finally, she may schedule review sessions . . . to raise students' performance, thereby restoring equilibrium. . . . Many college teachers do this naturally. They solicit information as feedback; they reflect on their expectations, beliefs, and values; and they experiment with different ways of teaching (Menges 1991, p. 27).

Another model of instructional improvement postulates that formative evaluation (informative feedback) promotes optimum improvement in the effectiveness of teaching when four conditions are met (Centra 1993).

> Through formative evaluation the teachers must first learn something new about their teaching performance (new knowledge). Second, they must value the information; this generally means they must have confidence in the source and in the evaluation process (value). Third, teachers must understand how to make the changes called for (how to change). And finally, teachers must be motivated to make the changes (motivation). . . .

Excerpts from "Taking Teaching Seriously: Meeting the Challenge of Instructional Improvement," by Michael B. Paulsen and Kenneth A. Feldman, reprinted by permission from *ASHE-ERIC HIGHER EDUCATION REPORT,* No.2, 1995. Washington, D. C.: The George Washington University, School of Education and Human Development.

> This does not mean that improvement will not occur if only two or three conditions are fulfilled; however, in those instances, the changes are not likely to be so dramatic. The model can best be understood as a linear progression of the four conditions, with a final return loop. . . . The loop signifies that motivation not only affects the improvements but also may cause teachers to seek additional new knowledge about their instructional effectiveness (Centra 1993, pp. 9, 14–15).

A third model takes the straightforward approach of describing five steps that teachers must go through to improve their instructional effectiveness (Weimer 1990). While the previous two models were primarily explanatory or theoretical, this model is clearly more descriptive.

> First, faculty members develop instructional awareness, a clear understanding of the instructional strategies, techniques, and practices they use and the assumptions about teaching and learning implicit in them. Second, they gather information from students and peers to accomplish three objectives. The input from others (a) clarifies and elaborates further the instructor's own understanding of his or her teaching; (b) . . . offers feedback as to the impact of the policy, practice, behavior, or activity on the person offering the input; and (c) . . . generates a pool of alternative ideas—other (and perhaps more effective) ways to accomplish the instructor's objectives. Third, faculty members make choices about changes. This involves identifying the teaching strategies, techniques, or practices to be changed and the instructional alternatives that are appropriate solutions for the particular teacher to try. Fourth, the faculty member implements the changes systematically and incrementally. Fifth, the faculty member assesses the impact of the alterations (Weimer 1990, p. 34).

These models, providing us with meaningful ways of organizing our thoughts about instructional improvement, can be seen as implicitly grounded in the general theory of change in human systems pioneered by Lewin (1947) and elaborated and refined by Schein in studies of management development (1961), general personal change (1964), improvement in professional education (1972), organizational change (1992), and human relations training (Schein and Bennis 1965). This general theory of change comprises the three stages of unfreezing, changing, and refreezing.

Unfreezing: Motivating Change

During the unfreezing stage, the motivation to change is created when three criteria have been met. First, an individual experiences "disconfirmation" cues from his or her environment, that is, information indicating that the individual's present attitudes and behaviors are not achieving the goals or producing the results that would be consistent with his or her current self-image. The assumptions and beliefs a person holds about himself or herself (the self-image), however, are related to the assumptions and beliefs the person holds about the nature of a particular situation and others who are relevant to that situation. Therefore, the unfreezing process can be initiated through disconfirmation cues related to any of the aspects of a total situation (Schein 1964, p. 364). Second, the individual "compares" information on the outcomes of his or her actual behavior to outcomes that the individual desires and considers important or ideal. When this incongruence leads to a sense of guilt, anxiety, or inadequacy related to not achieving some aspect of one's ideal self-image, it suggests that the disconfirming cues have had an impact on some of the individual's primary sources of motivation. A desire to reduce or eliminate such disequilibrium could lead to a motivation to change. In order to be so motivated, a third condition must also be met: The individual must feel a sense of psychological "safety" associated with attempts to change. The person must be able to envision ways to change that will produce results that reestablish his or her positive self-image without feeling any loss of integrity or identity. "One essential component of this feeling of safety is that we finally see a way to work on the problem or see a direction of learning that we had not seen before" (Schein 1992, p. 301).

Unfreezing could motivate a professor to improve his or her teaching if disconfirming cues relate to important goals in a way that affects motivational patterns related to the professor's need to see himself or herself as an effective teacher. Evidence consistently indicates that college professors, like many other professionals, are motivated or satisfied in their jobs primarily as a result of the intrinsic rewards of academic work (Austin and Gamson 1983; B. Clark 1987a; McKeachie 1979, 1982; Olsen 1993). Intrinsic "motivation is based on the innate need to be competent and self-determining . . . this basic need leads people to situations and activities that interest them, that provide optimal challenges, that allow them to learn and achieve" (Deci and Ryan 1982, p. 28).

The intrinsically rewarding nature of faculty work, including teaching, can be clearly seen in terms of the "job characteristics model" of intrinsic motivation theory (Hackman and Oldham 1976). An individual, such as a college professor, who experiences a high need for personal growth and development will be more intrinsically motivated "to the extent that he *learns* (knowledge of results) that he *personally* (experienced responsibility) has performed well on a task that he *cares about* (experienced meaningfulness)" (pp. 255–56). Knowledge of results is enhanced by the availability of informative feedback on performance. A person's sense of personal responsibility for outcomes depends on the extent to which he or she experiences autonomy or self-determination in performing the various elements of the task. Finally, the perceived meaningfulness of work depends on the presence of three characteristics of the job: skill variety, task identity, and task significance. Skill variety is the "degree to which a job requires a variety of different activities . . . [that] involve the use of a number of different skills and talents." Task identity is "the degree to which the job requires completion of a 'whole' and identifiable piece of work; that is, doing a job from beginning to end with a visible outcome." And task significance is the "degree to which the job has a substantial impact on the lives or work of other people, whether in the immediate organization or in the external environment" (p. 257).

It is common, for example, for an instructor's first concern with disconfirming cues to arise from end-of-semester student ratings of their teaching. When the instructor compares these ratings with his or her own assumptions and beliefs about his or her teaching effectiveness, the instructor may find them to fall below his or her internal standards. Such disconfirming cues could easily affect the instructor's intrinsic motivational needs related to perceptions of competence, self-determination, and the meaningfulness or significance of his or her work. As a result, the instructor might feel discomfort or a sense of inadequacy and desire to explore change as a way of restoring equilibrium. The instructor must also see a way to experiment without impairing his or her self-image. Suppose a close colleague had shared with the instructor information about his own similar situation a year earlier; suppose further that the instructor had observed him change some factors and get higher ratings in the current year. Now the instructor can see a safe path to change that might well produce results that would reduce or eliminate his or her current discomfort.

A key factor in leading this instructor toward motivation to change is the presence of opportunities for interaction and discussion among colleagues about their teaching experiences. Opportunities for interaction with peers regarding teaching have been shown to be an important characteristic of a supportive teaching culture (LaCelle-Peterson and Finkelstein 1993; Massy, Wilger, and Colbeck 1994). Clearly, then, the content of a teaching culture can have an important impact, even on this first stage of the overall instructional improvement process.

Changing: Making It Happen

After the unfreezing stage has produced a "motivation to change, the person . . . will search out new ideas and new information . . . to develop new attitudes and responses [behaviors] that will be rewarded or confirmed" (Schein 1972, p. 79). During the changing stage, an individual learns new attitudes and behaviors through the acquisition and interpretation of this new information. The individual collects informative feedback from one or more sources to cognitively redefine the situation or revise the assumptions and beliefs held about oneself, others, and the relevant situation. As a result, some cognitive redefinition precedes each experiment with new behavior the person makes. Cognitive redefinition and resulting behavioral change result from two primary mechanisms: scanning and identification (Schein 1964, 1972, 1992; Schein and Bennis 1965). The mechanism of *scanning* involves collecting informative feedback from more than one (perhaps a variety) of the types of sources or persons in the environment. From each type of source, an individual collects the feedback that best fits the needs of the individual relevant to a particular situation he or she faces. In contrast, the mechanism of *identification* is based on the collection of informative feedback from only one source (or type of source) with whom the individual has come to identify. Information from this source alone—perhaps a role model—shapes cognitive redefinition. These mechanisms characterize the processes by which individuals attempt to locate solutions to the disequilibrium initiated during the unfreezing stage.

For example, to obtain additional informative feedback to guide his or her experiments at change, the instructor in our example could begin the next term by collecting informal feedback from his or her students early in the semester (Clark and Bekey 1979). Next, the instructor could reflect on this feedback (Chism and Sanders 1986) and then ask a trusted colleague to sit in on his or her class to obtain additional feedback from a peer (Katz and Henry 1988). Third, the instructor could visit with a teaching consultant at the campus teaching center to acquire additional guidance on how to change his or her teaching using the multiple sources of feedback the instructor has collected by scanning the environment (Lewis and Povlacs 1988). Finally, a supportive department chair could invite this instructor to sit in on one of the chair's own classes, share his or her own ideas about instructional improvement, and help the instructor develop additional plans for change (Vavrus, Grady, and Creswell 1988). In this example, the instructor assessed his or her instructional experiments by scanning the environment for informative feedback from five different sources: self, students, colleagues, consultants, and the department chair.

A central feature of this instructor's actual experimentation with change is the availability and use of multiple sources of informative feedback and guidance. When departmental and institutional teaching cultures are rich with opportunities to assess teaching, instructors can more easily experiment with their teaching and successfully scan the environment for various sources of informative feedback. Serious and rigorous evaluative information from different sources, such as students and peers, is an important characteristic of a supportive teaching culture (Massy, Wilger, and Colbeck 1994). Departments and campuses rich with information assessing teaching create an important aspect of a supportive teaching culture—sometimes referred to as the "culture of assessment" (Braskamp and Ory 1994). "In a culture of assessment, faculty members profit from discussion and reflection about how their individual achievements contribute to their personal gain and the common good" (p. 23).

Refreezing: Sustaining Change

After cognitive redefinition and experiments with new behavior have been carried out, further informative feedback is collected as part of the final stage of overall change. The refreezing stage refers to the ways in which additional informative feedback on new behaviors either encourages or discourages the maintenance of these changes. New behaviors can be sustained through two basic mechanisms: integration and reconfirmation. "Whatever new response [behavior] is attempted, it must fit into the total personality of the individual attempting it [integration], and it must fit sufficiently into the culture of which that person is a member to be confirmed and reinforced by others [reconfirmation]" (Schein 1972, p. 81).

For instance, suppose the instructor in our example does receive significantly higher ratings from students at the end of the next semester, particularly in the areas of teaching that he or she had specifically targeted for improvement. If the instructor once again perceives himself or herself to be competent and self-determining and feels that his or her teaching is meaningful and significant work, then the changes are likely to be integrated into the instructor's total personality, thereby helping to sustain the changed behavior. As the theory of change indicates, however, the teaching culture might have to supply reconfirming data for the instructor's instructional improvements to be sustained indefinitely. The instructor's efforts to improve, as well as his or her new teaching behaviors, might need to be supported by others in the environment.

The teaching culture provides informative feedback in various ways that reconfirm equilibrium and encourage the maintenance of change. For example, the dean or department chair might ask this instructor and several of the instructor's colleagues to lead a panel discussion of their experiences with instructional improvement at the next college or departmental faculty meeting. Opportunities to discuss teaching experiences with peers strengthens an instructor's intrinsic rewards from teaching, thereby contributing to a more supportive teaching culture (Froh, Menges, and Walker 1993). The panel discussion would also help communicate to these and other faculty that the administration is committed to improving instruction within the college or department. Administrative commitment has been found to be directly related to the success of efforts to improve instruction (Eble and McKeachie 1985). Further, the efforts to improve these instructors' teaching may be given serious consideration in evaluating the faculty. A strong connection between the evaluation of teaching effectiveness and promotion and tenure decisions is a characteristic of a supportive teaching culture (Jenrette and Napoli 1994; Wolverton and Richardson 1992).

A Model of Instructional Improvement that Includes Individual, Interpersonal, and Group Forces

Figure 1 illustrates a "general change model" that includes the recognition of a teaching culture within which sources of informative feedback—self, students, colleagues, consultants, and chairs—influence the various stages of the process of change. In several ways the model provides an underlying analytic framework for examining instructional improvement. First, for many years parts of this model have proven to be useful and popular for explaining human change across a wide variety of settings. Second, the model explicitly acknowledges the important influence of the content of organizational culture on the initiation, implementation, and persistence of behavioral change in human systems. This attribute makes the model especially useful as a heuristic device for exploring the influence of particular aspects of the teaching culture, such as the formal use of teaching portfolios in faculty evaluation, on the process of change (Hutchings 1993a; Seldin 1993). Third, because of its comprehensiveness and generalizability, the model encompasses many or all of the concepts and component parts of other models implicitly or explicitly derived from it. As a result, it is flexible enough to examine the importance of informative feedback at all stages of the process of change, which means that all of the primary sources of informative feedback (self, students, colleagues, consultants, and chairs) can be conceived of as having a potential bearing at every stage of the process. This feature is especially important, because most strategies for improving instruction can be discussed and even categorized according to their particular sources or means of acquiring informative feedback and guidance for change (Braskamp, Brandenburg, and Ory 1984; Centra 1993). Fourth, it explicitly considers the important influence of individual differences (for example, different

Figure 1
The Process of Instructional Improvement

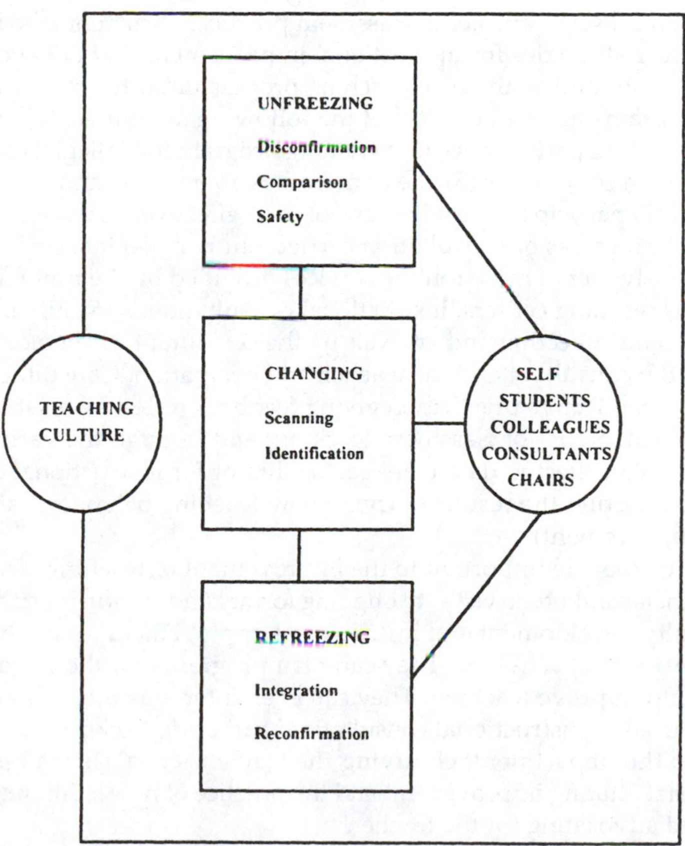

professional goals during different stages of development) on the process of change, allowing the model to be applied to the special needs of particular subgroups of faculty, such as new and junior faculty (Sorcinelli and Austin 1992).

. . .

This report has been particularly interested in the varieties of informative feedback—themselves facilitated by a supportive teaching culture—that drive the process of instructional improvement. Most strategies for improving instruction can be meaningfully arranged into categories according to the primary source of informative feedback that serves to initiate, direct, or sustain improvement in teaching. Prominent sources of such feedback are colleagues and consultants, chairs, students, and the teacher himself or herself.

With regard to, first, faculty colleagues as sources of informative feedback, faculty seminars, workshops, and colloquia are traditional (but still effective) practices for encouraging interaction and collaboration among faculty regarding teaching issues. Recent developments in a variety of areas—action science, reflective practice, adult learning theory, and the like—have encouraged an expanded range of strategies for improving instruction. One important set of activities, programs, and projects in this expansion is the renewed use of team teaching. Faculty collaboration through team teaching benefits professors by developing their teaching abilities, intellectually stimulating them, engaging them as self-directed learners, and more closely connecting them to the university or college as a community. The capacity of team teaching to improve instruction appears to derive from the opportunities for interaction provided by collaboration in teaching, through which colleagues come to trust one another, observe each other teach, and discuss their ideas and concerns about teaching. The various models of team teaching form a continuum from the least collaborative to the most collaborative. As far as can be told at this point, the most collaborative models seem to have the greatest success in improving teaching.

A second set of activities, programs, and projects that can be included in the expanded range of the use of faculty colleagues in improving instruction is collegial coaching. Two primary activities involved in collegial coaching are observation of classroom teaching and instructional consultation, including a review of course materials and discussions about classroom practices. Teachers who interact with their colleagues as coaches are using strategies for instructional improvement that engage them as self-directed learners. From the descriptions and analyses of coaching projects undertaken at a variety of colleges and universities, effective programs have all or most of the following attributes: (1) an underlying philosophy; (2) a procedure for selecting participants; (3) a training program for collegial coaches (observers/consultants); (4) a preobservation conference; (5) one or more classroom visits and observations; (6) a postobservation conference; and (7) participants' evaluations of their effectiveness.

Many of the informal processes of consultation carried out in collegial coaching projects have been formalized in a comprehensive set of more routine services provided by the trained consultants who constitute the staff of campus teaching centers. Instructional consultation is usually based on a comprehensive model that includes data collection and analysis by the consultant, strategies for improvement that are worked out between the consultant and the teacher, and evaluation. Consultation improves teaching primarily through the use of effective practices in giving feedback (often associated with student ratings and direct observation or videotapes of classroom teaching) and through the various interpersonal roles assumed by consultants (data collector, data manager, facilitator for instructional change, source of support to help analyze and interpret the results of trying new teaching behaviors, and information source about teaching and its improvement).

Chairs of departments, too, are important to the improvement of teaching. One way they help is by providing support—financial and otherwise—to ongoing formal and informal attempts to improve teaching. They can define faculty development and instructional improvement (as distinct from faculty evaluation) as important departmental activities. They can plan programs for the department, such as pedagogical colloquia, that help improve teaching. They can even intervene more directly by following a set of steps similar to those used in instructional consultation: gathering background information about the teaching of a member of the department; clarifying the teacher's goals and objectives; observing the teacher in the classroom; facilitating improvement and the practice of new skills; and monitoring progress toward improvement and advocating for the teacher.

Although it is sometimes forgotten, students are not "silent partners" in the enterprise of improving reaching. One way their voices can be heard is through filling out teacher and course evaluations. Research has shown persistently that feedback from students' ratings is of value in improving teaching, particularly if this feedback is accompanied by consultation with the teacher. Good evidence shows the utility of the teacher's sitting down with a colleague or teaching consultant to jointly interpret the feedback from students, select targets for improvement, and develop strategies for instructional change. And the more diagnostic the rating form used by students—for example, forms with items asking about specific or low-inference behaviors of teachers as contrasted with items about global or high inference behaviors—the more help they are likely to be.

The voice of students can be heard even more directly by talking with them. Student interviews can be successfully used in several different ways to give feedback to teachers: group discussions; small-group instructional diagnosis; the class interview; and quality-control circles. A particularly distinctive way of receiving feedback from students is for a professor to invite students into his or her classroom who are not "official" members of the class but who are trained in classroom observation. The primary purpose of this approach is to provide confidential observations to increase the instructor's effectiveness in helping students learn. Another strategy for "listening" to students, "classroom assessment," comprises a wide range of methods college teachers can use to obtain useful feedback on what, how much, and how well their students are learning. Classroom assessment helps instructors to monitor students' learning continuously so that they can identify (and respond with instructional changes to) gaps between what the teacher thinks he or she is teaching and what students are actually learning.

Teachers have an additional important source of feedback, another significant voice to listen to: their own. Because college teachers often have a strong need to seek self-determined competence by continuously scanning the instructional environment for informative feedback, their behavior can be examined—and the source of changes in their behavior understood—by viewing them as "reflective practitioners." Activities that constitute reflective practice or practice-centered inquiry—which have been shown to be useful strategies for instructional improvement—can be arranged along a continuum. At one end are the informal observations, questions, and realizations that arise in the act of teaching, coupled with the immediate reflections on them during and shortly after class. In the middle of the continuum are more persistent, yet still informal, efforts at observation and inquiry (for example, notes taken and records kept). At the other end of the continuum, reflective practice takes place within the framework of a more formal design for research.

The ultimate foundation of all reflective practice or self-reflection is the ability and opportunity to engage in self-evaluation or self-assessment. Two common methods of collecting feedback based on self-evaluation at universities involve the use of self-rating forms and self-reports. At some colleges and universities, for example, faculty are asked to complete the same (or slightly reworded) teaching evaluation questionnaires as their students. This procedure enables faculty to analyze their work and to reflect on their teaching along the same dimensions their students use to evaluate them. A second method, self-reports completed by college professors, has traditionally been limited to vitae and reports of activities; recently, however, the idea of self-reports has been conceptually and functionally expanded into the use of teaching portfolios. These portfolios essentially represent an elaborate and reflective form of self-evaluation. They usually contain the products of good teaching, material from the teachers themselves, and information from others. Unlike most other strategies for improving instruction, these portfolios provide opportunities for professors to reflect on their own teaching within the context of their own particular classes; thus, the concept of a teaching portfolio is based squarely on the notion of viewing a teacher as a reflective practitioner.

Although supportive teaching cultures and effective practices of informative feedback from a variety of sources are generally beneficial for the improvement of instruction, specific tailoring might be needed for certain categories of teachers. One such group consists of new and junior faculty. Because new faculty share common concerns about such things as workload and stress from multiple demands, uncertainty about what is expected of them, a desire for collegial support, and a need to develop teaching skills, a strong argument can be made for supplementing traditional, individual approaches of socialization that help them adjust to their new environment with a collective approach that addresses these common concerns. Workshops and what have been called "substantial" orientation programs for new faculty (which offer concrete assistance with the development of teaching skills and consider other matters of importance to new faculty) are being used successfully in a variety of colleges and universities. In addition, formal mentoring programs for new and junior faculty members are also being used at different schools to give concrete assistance with the development of teaching skills, to address various professional and personal concerns, and, in general, to counter the vagaries of the usually informal socialization of new college teachers.

Even the best informative feedback (within the context of the most supportive of teaching cultures) would come to naught if individual teachers ignored it or did not act upon it. What, then, motivates individual teachers to want to improve their teaching and to produce and maintain actual changes in attitudes and behavior? The general theory of change comprising the three stages of unfreezing, changing, and refreezing can be applied here. During unfreezing, the motivation to change is created. A teacher experiences "disconfirmation" cues from his or her environment. Such cues refer to information—including informative feedback from the various sources discussed in this report—indicating that the individual's present attitudes and behaviors are not achieving the goals or producing the kinds of results that would be consistent with his or her current self-image as a teacher. The teacher "compares" information on the outcomes of his or her actual behavior to outcomes that he or she would desire and consider important or ideal. Any incongruence could lead to a sense of anxiety or inadequacy related to not achieving some aspect of one's ideal self-image. A desire to eliminate such disequilibrium might well motivate change (provided that the individual can envision ways to change that will produce results that reestablish his or her positive self-image as a teacher without feeling any loss of integrity or identity).

After the unfreezing stage has produced a motivation to improve one's teaching, the individual searches out new ideas and new information (or considers ideas and information he or she has already received from various sources) to develop new attitudes and behaviors that will be rewarding and confirming (both by the self and others). Any cognitive redefinitions and changes in instructional behaviors and teaching practices are likely to be sustained (refreezing) when the new behaviors and practices are encouraged by others (reconfirmation) and fit into the total personality of the teacher (integration).

Instructional Interventions: A Review of the Literature on Efforts to Improve Instruction

MARYELLEN WEIMER AND LISA FIRING LENZE

Introduction

Efforts to improve college teaching continue. In some instances these are efforts of individual faculty members occurring independent of institutional involvement or support. In other instances institutions are engaged in activities designed to support and encourage faculty efforts in the classroom. Continuing concern about quality undergraduate education signals that interest in these efforts, particularly those at the institutional level, will remain high. Institutions need to know which resources and activities most positively affect instructional quality. Therefore, it is appropriate that the literature on efforts to improve instruction be reviewed frequently and regularly.

The bulk of these efforts at the institutional level occur via various "interventions," organized, systematic activities designed to impact, in a positive way, the instruction of an individual faculty member. A workshop on participation strategies or consultation with a faculty member over student evaluation data illustrate what is meant by intervention. It is important to note that the interventions, in and of themselves, do not improve instruction. They are the methods used to motivate and inform instructional change, but the faculty member alone implements the alterations. For example, the workshop on participation strategies may propose and describe a variety of techniques which effectively increase student involvement, but the faculty member is in charge of deciding whether or not to use any of the techniques in class tomorrow. Moreover, there is no guarantee that all change affects teaching performance positively. A consultant may offer bad advice, a faculty member may implement change at the wrong time, or it may be poorly suited for the student group to which it is directed.

This leads to the question: how then are the effects of the instructional interventions to be assessed? In the first review of this literature, Levinson-Rose and Menges (1981) used five categories which will be used in this review as well: 1) teacher attitude from self-report (participants offer opinions as to the effectiveness of the intervention); 2) teacher knowledge from tests or observer (pre- and post-tests or observations document any changes in teacher knowledge); 3) teacher skill from observer (instructional observation reports on changes in skill levels); 4) student attitude from self-report (student evaluation evidences change in teacher performance); and 5) student learning from tests or observer reports (tests or observation attest to changes in student learning). As Levinson-Rose and Menges (1981) note, "the strongest evidence for most interventions is impact on students (the last two categories), and the weakest is self-reported opinion of participants (the first category)" (p. 403).

Continuing interest in instructional improvement mandates an update of the 1981 review focusing on literature published during the intervening years. Moreover, while many of the instructional interventions originally considered are still widely used, various emphases have changed necessitating a different categorization than that used by Levinson-Rose and Menges (1981). Five interventions will be considered in this review; workshops, consultation, instructional grants, distribution of resource material, and efforts of colleagues on behalf of each other's instruction. Each of these interventions will be introduced

"Instructional Interventions: A Review of the Literature on Efforts to Improve Instruction," by Maryellen Weimer and Lisa Firing Lenze, reprinted by permission from *Higher Education: Handbook of Theory and Research,* Vol. 7, edited by J. C. Smart, 1991, Agathon Press.

briefly at this point and their inclusion justified as a means of illustrating how efforts to improve instruction have changed during the '80s.

As was the case in 1981, workshops, seminars, and programs continue to be the most widely used of all instructional interventions. They range from hour-long sessions, to week-long retreats, to year-long programs. They offer advice and information on virtually every aspect of instruction. They employ a wide range of instructional methods including lecture, discussion, and collaborative learning. More so during this decade than previous ones, workshop programs are complex. They use a variety of interventions in the context of a single program; like a three-day orientation activity for new faculty with lectures on instructional techniques, individual consultation, and the possibility of a microteaching experience.

During the decade, the use of consultation has grown. Here an instructional expert, most often a faculty or instructional developer, offers individual advice and information to faculty members, usually in the context of a face-to-face interview. It typically occurs in three arenas: over student ratings, over a videotaped teaching sample or microteaching experience, or over a more general instructional issue or concern. The Levinson-Rose and Menges (1981) review does not consider consultation as an independent intervention. However, research on consultation over student ratings is considered as part of a larger intervention labeled "feedback from ratings by students." Analysis and critique of microteaching experiences is considered separately. The consideration of consultation as an independent intervention reflects a change in practice that has occurred during the decade.

As was true in 1981, instructional grants continue to be used as a faculty development intervention. Most often now the grants are of small amounts and are awarded competitively to individual faculty members. Monies are targeted to some instructional, often course-related project. New materials may be designed, a new set of assignments conceived, course content significantly revised, or a computer component developed for the course.

It is difficult to document the extent to which resource materials aimed at improving instruction were being distributed to faculty prior to 1981, However, their widespread use today justifies their consideration as an improvement intervention. To illustrate, many instructional and faculty development centers publish newsletters; others distribute published articles to faculty; several new interdisciplinary and disciplinary pedagogical journals are being published; and marketed resource manuals, workbooks, and sourcebooks offer advice on everything from test construction to discussion techniques.

Although not reviewed previously, the effect of resource materials like these on instructional quality merits review.

Finally, although not used as widely as the previous interventions and not considered in the Levinson-Rose and Menges (1981) review, increasingly colleagues are being used to intervene in the instruction of each other. Their use in part reflects the chronic lack of staff in many instructional and faculty development units. Faculty volunteers were commandeered to help, but what was quickly discovered was their effectiveness as instructional improvers. Most often they are being used to observe other faculty teach, not as evaluators, but as colleagues interested in exploring the impact of a set of instructional policies and practices on student learning.

To summarize, this review considers two interventions considered by Levinson-Rose and Menges (1981), it recategorizes activities associated with the consultation intervention, and it adds two new interventions. It does not consider feedback from ratings independent of consultation since it has been shown that summative rating feedback alone has much less impact on instructional improvement (Murray, 1984), and it does not consider concept-based training since data do not document the prevalent use of this intervention.

One other change in efforts to improve instruction has occurred since 1981. Current efforts are being targeted at particular faculty groups more than they were previously. Specifically, if instructional and faculty development units exist at institutions where teaching assistants are employed, chances are those units sponsor, coordinate, or work closely with other academic departments in activities designed to prepare teaching assistants for instructional responsibilities. TA training existed before 1981. The difference here is one of degree. Instructional interventions with TAs are far more widespread than they used to be.

The interest in the instructional preparation of TAs has spawned efforts directed at a target group not previously focused on by those interested in instructional improvement—new faculty. Many of the programs and activities first offered teaching assistants are now being extended to new faculty.

Why are TAs and new faculty being targeted for instructional interventions more than other faculty groups? Is their instruction less effective? Certainly they are less experienced, and experience is seen as one of the conditions contributing to the development of pedagogical prowess. They are also the faculty groups an institution has most control over and are therefore the easiest to "require" to participate in efforts to improve instruction. Does that have an impact on the effectiveness of these interventions?

The attention focused on TAs and new faculty may also stem from larger issues confronting higher education. Many are concerned with the impending change in faculty populations. Most institutions anticipate significant percentages of retirements in the decade. This is seen not so much as a problem as an opportunity—the chance to intervene in instruction of faculty and potential faculty at the beginning of their careers. Germane to this review is the implicit assumption that somehow it is easier and more effective to "intervene" at this point in a teaching career. Does research evidence substantiate that assumption?

As the activities, programs, and resources offered TAs and new faculty are reviewed, it is readily apparent that the interventions most often used are those being considered in this review. In other words, no special, unique, or different interventions are being used despite the distinctions between TAs and new faculty, and other faculty groups. Are these interventions the most effective ones for TAs and new faculty?

Questions like these make it clear why efforts to target interventions at specific subgroups within the larger faculty population merit review and assessment. Research and other relevant literature on the effects of these interventions with new faculty will be considered in this review. A recent review of research on training TAs has been published, so literature in that area will be summarized and relevant references included.

This review is modeled on the original work of Levinson-Rose and Menges (1981), but with several important distinctions. It is a more comprehensive look at the literature. Levinson-Rose and Menges (1981) elected not to include description or discussion of studies where evaluation occurred only at the level of teacher attitude from self-report and teacher knowledge. A number of these are considered in this review and for several reasons. First, the extent of evaluation at this level warrants documentation. Second and considerably more important, efforts to improve instruction are occurring within the realm of practice. That is, practice is preceding research. Unlike the arena of student evaluation, where sizable research effort occurred first and stimulated to a large degree the adoption and adaptation of the evaluative practices, instructional interventions are being used prior to rigorous empirical exploration. Of concern is the considerable delay between implementation and exploration. It is hoped that by including some of what qualifies more as a literature of practice than a literature of research, the much needed research effort will be stimulated. These are cases and ongoing operations that could be studied. It is further hoped that by recognizing what is occurring in the arenas of both practice and research, those interested in one will see the merit of the other and be encouraged to collaborate.

A second distinction between this review and the Levinson-Rose and Menges (1981) effort is the more detailed description of inquiries that aim to assess the impact of the interventions at the more significant levels of observable change in classroom behaviors and student outcomes. First, the limited number of studies at this level permits it, and it is hoped the more detailed descriptions will serve as models, again to stimulate more rigorous investigation.

Finally, the conclusions as to the effectiveness of any single intervention are more qualitative than quantitative. No statistical methods of comparison were employed, primarily because the number of available studies precludes them. Rather the intent is to offer more general conclusions with specific and elaborate calls for more research.

The individual interventions are considered separately. For each a brief history is included. Current data documenting the prevalence of the practice precede a general but detailed description of the intervention, including specific, published examples of programs. An assessment of studies and results follows. Consideration of the intervention concludes with a discussion section. New faculty and TAs are considered following review of all the interventions. The review concludes with a recommendation and discussion section.

Workshops, Seminars, and Programs

History

In early efforts to improve college teaching, the workshop was the main staple in the instructional improver's cupboard. Centra's (1978) first survey of those responsible for improvement efforts yielded

45 different instructional development practices. Oblique (promax) rotation of the data suggested four major categories of practices, and one of those, labeled "high faculty involvement," included a variety of workshop, seminar, and program activities.

Levinson-Rose and Menges (1981) assert, "workshops and seminars are probably the most frequent but least evaluated instructional improvement activities" (p. 406). Their review assessed research done primarily with graduate teaching assistants. The impact of workshops and seminars on teaching was assessed in three different areas: student ratings, observer ratings, and student learning. As to the overall effectiveness of this intervention they conclude: "Workshops and seminars are useful to motivate and to raise consciousness under certain conditions. But most workshops and seminars, even those with specific training goals, are unlikely to produce lasting changes in teacher behavior or lasting impact on students unless participants continue skill practice and receive critical feedback on their efforts" (p. 419).

Prevalence

Early reliance on workshops, seminars, and programs has continued in the years since the Levinson-Rose and Menges (1981) review. Konrad's (1983) replication of the Centra survey in 25 Canadian universities documented "fairly common" (p. 24) use of workshops with programs exploring "various methods or techniques of instruction, . . . testing and evaluating student performance, . . . [and] new or different approaches to develop curricula" (p. 18). Of the 687 community colleges responding to Smith's (1981) survey of 1,315 of these institutions, 236 report using workshops to promote effective instruction. Of the 36 Illinois community colleges responding to Hansen's (1983) survey, 89 percent reported doing single session workshops, making them the most common faculty development activity listed. Seventy-five percent reported doing multisession workshops/seminars. Richardson and Moore (1987) surveyed 62 community colleges in Texas; of the 52 which responded, 69 percent reported using single-session workshops and 62 percent used all-day programs for full-time faculty, making this intervention the most common after orientation activities (many of which also used the workshop programming). Erickson (1986) reports that of the 630 four-year institutions responding to his survey, 63 percent offered workshops on various methods of instruction, 55 percent gave sessions on academic advising and counseling, and 36 percent sponsored programs on understanding college students and how they learn.

Most recently Bland and Schmitz (1988) reviewed literature which offered "either strategies or recommendations for developing full-time faculty members, departments or institutions" (p. 191). In their collection of 288 references they identified 49 different strategies and found that workshops were the most frequent strategy, mentioned in 73 sources.

Description

As might be expected with continued use of an intervention across better than 20 years now, a considerable amount of diversification has occurred. Workshop programs now vary across several important dimensions. First, they vary as to the topics presented. Sessions share information on subjects as diverse as cooperative learning, time management, learning disabilities, and cultural diversity. Recent literature does not document which of these and many other topics are used most commonly.

Second, these programs vary as to the instructional methods used to deliver the content. The large orientation sessions for TAs rely on traditional lecture methods, sessions for seasoned faculty tend more toward interactive modes, and some workshop sponsors try the collaborative/cooperative techniques they recommend to faculty. In recent years more elaborate programs that combine a variety of methods, content, and even interventions themselves have been used. Herr (1988) describes a semester-long workshop used at Colorado State University. Seventeen faculty enrolled in the program that focused on weekly observation in the courses of award-winning faculty. Participants observed in pairs and met privately to discuss the observation. During meetings (held every other week) the group explored the characteristics of the effective teaching they were observing. They also discussed, received information about, and participated in activities related to a number of other instructional issues such as mid-term evaluation and teaching assumptions.

Third, in recent years workshops have been directed to target populations within the larger faculty group. Since 1981, as already mentioned, both the number and scope of programs for TAs, many relying heavily on the workshop intervention (Weimer, Svinicki, and Bauer, 1990), have increased dramatically, witnessed by two national conferences on the training and employment of TAs, both with published proceedings (Chism, 1987, and Nyquist, Abbott, Wulff and Sprague, in press). In addition to workshops, seminars, and minicourses designed for TAs, in recent years programs for new faculty have also proliferated. Again, most commonly these are orientation workshops and seminars, although increasingly these are evolving into the more involved programs mentioned earlier. A number of specific examples appear in the section on new faculty as a target group. Reliance on part-time, adjunct, and fixed-term faculty has also grown during the past decade, necessitating workshop programs for this faculty population. Less common but not unusual are workshops designed for faculty populations who share instructional settings; for example, those who teach large courses, those who teach required introductory courses to non-majors, and those who teach lab courses.

Finally, workshop programs vary in length—all the way from two-hour, one-shot sessions to semester-, and in a few cases, year-long programs. Between are half-day, full-day, two-day, week-long, biweekly, monthly, and weekly meetings of faculty groups which explore single or multiple instructional issues.

Assessment

Given the diversity of current workshop programming, assessment is difficult in any sort of general way. What is the impact of workshops on instructional effectiveness? The question is too broad. Programs for new faculty may work, but sessions less than four hours may not have measurable effects across the life of a course, for example. In other words, the research on workshops needs to be analyzed across different dimensions. This review begins that more detailed assessment by looking at workshops (in this section) of varying length and (in a subsequent section) targeted to different faculty populations. Unfortunately, the actual research on workshop effectiveness is so meager that it makes assessment across any dimension a moot point. However, the diversity of the phenomenon in question demands this more detailed analysis. Perhaps the categorization will stimulate subsequent investigation.

Short-term Programs: those less than four hours in length. Despite the prevalence of these programs, no published research assesses the effectiveness of these programs in any of the categories being used: 1) teacher attitude from self-report, 2) teacher knowledge from tests or observer, 3) teacher skill from observer, 4) student attitude from self-report (evaluations), and 5) student learning from tests or observer reports.

Long Programs: those between four hours and six days in duration. Brown and Daines (1983) report on a the effectiveness of a two-day program on lecturing and explaining which incorporated microteaching experiences. Sixty-six videotapes of new lecturers' explanations given during the workshop were rated by two trained independent observers. "The results indicate that, for this group of lecturers, the course yielded perceptible and significant improvements in the opening moves of an explanation, its structure and interest, and in the use of audiovisual aids" (p. 67). In addition, Brown and Daines studied transcripts of 65 explanations, also recorded during the program. Analysis of six variables via regression techniques documented "significant changes in structuring tactics such as the use of explaining links, signposts, and frames but not in the use of foci. The frequency of hesitations, stumbles, and incomplete sentences were reduced but not significantly" (p. 68).

Long, Sadker, and Sadker (1986) report on the effectiveness of a two-and-a-half-day training session that focused on the elimination of sex-biased teacher-student interactions in the classroom and the distribution, precision, and quality of teacher responses to students' verbal behavior. The 46 faculty participants were divided into experimental and control groups. Training included review of videotapes demonstrating both the desired and undesirable behaviors and a microteaching experience. Participants were observed teaching three times by five trained observers. The researchers summarized the results. "Training increased interaction by 38 percent, reduced the percentage of salient students who monopolize interaction, and also reduced the percentage of silent or nonparticipating students" (p. 3). As for gender issues, "this study revealed significant bias in favor of male students in the control group while the experimental group approached equity" (p. 3).

Mini Courses: longer than six days and incorporating more than one instructional intervention. Friedman and Stomper (1983) studied the effectiveness of a semester-long training program for selected mathematics faculty aimed at improving student achievement in a basic mathematics course. Five faculty members were selected for the training sessions; eight others constituted a control group. The training program encouraged the use of several instructional strategies, advocated responding to designated student needs, and provided feedback on videotaped teaching samples. Investigators controlled for the entry status of students in the classes used. In the experimental group, 59.1 percent of the students passed compared with 49.4 percent in the control group. The group average for test score means was 59.4 for the experimental group and 51.5 for the control group. These differences were corroborated by two additional videotaped recordings made at the beginning and end of the course for those in the experimental group. Analysis documented behavior changes in the direction of the strategies proposed. Investigators conclude that this program resulted in "large differences in student achievement in favor of the experimental group" (p. 60).

Menges and others (1988) report on a program of interdisciplinary faculty renewal workshops. Faculty from different institutions took part in two-week summer sessions conducted by Stanford faculty on a common humanistic and interdisciplinary theme. Participants were invited to return for a weekend "reunion" one or two years (or both) after the original session. Surveys were sent to all 189 participants with 123 returning them. Generally high levels of satisfaction appear in the responses. Most highly impacted were "knowledge of my discipline," "knowledge of related disciplines," and "scholarly enthusiasm" (p. 295), although when assessing results of participation, 57 percent indicated their teaching had been impacted.

As already described, Herr (1988) reports on a workshop-observation program used with 15 faculty at Colorado State University to identify the characteristics of effective teaching. Eleven of those participants returned evaluations. Of those, 91 percent indicated the workshop had met their expectation and 100 percent recommended it be repeated.

Gibbs, Browne, and Keeley (1989) report on a program designed to teach faculty critical thinking skills. Program participants (who received $200 for their involvement) had to: 1) attend six four-hour programs, 2) create a three- to four-page plan for integrating critical thinking into a course to be taught during the semester immediately following the program, 3) share plans with other participants, and 4) cooperate in evaluating the program. Seventy-two participants were randomly assigned to either an experimental and control group. In addition to qualitative data, investigators collected quantitative data via The Watson Glaser Critical Thinking Appraisal Test administered to faculty prior to participation to determine whether the two groups differed on initial critical thinking ability. They did not. Following the fifth session, faculty completed the Ennis-Weir Critical Thinking Test as a post-test. Those in the control group had statistically significant higher post-test scores than those in the experimental group. During the term in which the plan for teaching critical thinking was being integrated into the course, a randomly selected student sample completed the Watson-Glaser Test and the Class Activities Questionnaire. Students selected from the classes of the experimental group did not differ significantly from those in the control group on either measure. The investigators maintain the findings have limited implications for a number of reasons, among them their sense that even a workshop of this length was too short to significantly change critical thinking abilities for faculty, and that the intervention period may have been too brief for changes in student outcomes to manifest themselves.

Some of those surveying institutions about faculty and instructional development activities have collected general assessments of the effectiveness of the intervention. In Hansen's (1983) survey of 36 Illinois community colleges a rating of good or excellent was given by 75 percent of those holding one-day workshops, by 78 percent conducting day-long programs and by 80 percent of those offering multisession workshops. In Richardson and Moore's survey of 56 Texas community colleges, a rating of good or excellent was given by 76 percent of those holding one day workshops, by 100 percent of those conducting day-long programs, and by 93 percent of those offering multisession workshops. Moses (1985) surveyed 17 directors of academic development units in Australia asking, "What three approaches to improvement of teaching have worked best in your institution?" (p. 77) Workshops and seminars were mentioned by 15; making them, in the judgment of these unit heads, the best way to improve instruction.

Discussion

In addition to the assessment of specific programs and general conclusions, other relevant information about the evaluation of workshops exists. Hansen (1983) summarizes evaluation methods used to assess the effectiveness of workshop programs: "There was heavy dependence on verbal feedback and questionnaire evaluative techniques. Only three respondents indicated the use of classroom observation to see if improved instruction was occurring as a result of faculty development activities. Testing of students as a measure of improvement of instruction was never used as an evaluative device" (p. 223). Richardson and Moore (1987) asked the Texas Community College respondents to their survey how many of them were evaluating programs and what assessment methods they were employing. For workshop activities of varying sorts, 62 to 71 percent reported they were using evaluation. As for specifics, 57 to 71 percent reported using verbal feedback, 29 to 50 percent said they had participants respond to questionnaires, 4 to 6 percent used pre- and post-tests, 4 percent tested student outcomes, and zero percent reported using classroom observation.

Returning to the five levels of intervention assessment proposed by Levinson-Rose and Menges (1981), as was the case at the time of that review, the bulk of program assessment, if it occurs at all, occurs at the level of faculty attitude as reported by them. That's the bad news. As Levinson-Rose and Menges (1981), Richardson and Moore (1987), and others have consistently pointed out, this is the least significant way to measure the effectiveness of these programs. These data mean that in the opinion of the faculty participants the programs were useful, relevant, or informative. It does not prove that the programs caused them to change any of their instructional behaviors, nor does it establish any relationship between program participation and significantly improved learning outcomes.

There is some good news. At least faculty surveyed in these studies do respond favorably to workshop programming. They see the programs as contributing to their instructional effectiveness. And although the accuracy of that perception remains unproven, faculty attitudes toward teaching do affect their instructional policies and practices. What remains unclear is how long or to what degree new or recharged attitudes influence what happens in the classroom.

And added to the small number of studies in the Levinson-Rose and Menges (1981) that assess impact across the other four levels are a few additional studies completed during this decade. Brown and Daines (1983) and Gibbs, Browne, and Keeley (1989) did test participant knowledge. Brown and Daines (1983), Friedman and Stomper (1983), and Long, Sadker, and Sadker (1986) assessed changes in skill levels through independent observation. And Friedman and Stomper (1983) and Gibbs, Browne, and Keeley (1989) did test student achievement affected by program participation. Although the data pool is too small to warrant any conclusions, all studies except Gibbs, Browne, and Keeley (1989) report positive results, meaning the workshop, seminar, or program effectively improved instruction.

These studies have been categorized by the length of the program even though the amount of research makes it impossible to tell whether that dimension has an effect on the intervention. It is interesting to note that the programs reviewed here with positive effects, excepting Gibbs, Browne, and Keeley (1989), do tend to be longer and to involve more than one intervention. This provides further corroboration of the earlier Levinson-Rose and Menges (1981) conclusion that programs with more lasting impacts are those in which participants continue to practice and receive feedback on their efforts. However, short programs remain unstudied, so this trend in the research may be noted but its significance remains to be determined.

Despite this modest "good news," discussion of this intervention cannot be concluded without considerable concern again expressed about the extensive use of a method to improve instruction with so little corroboration of its effectiveness. Those who have reviewed these interventions previously, among them Richardson and Moore (1983), have warned that in times of tight budgets instructional and faculty development efforts will have to justify the methods used. Perhaps budgets are not tight enough yet, but to date that call for solid proof has not come from those who supply the funds. If seems the interest in documenting the effectiveness of an intervention ought to be more intrinsic. Why are those using the intervention not more interested in finding out whether or not what they are doing impacts instruction? Most of them do work hard at designing and presenting these programs. Assessing their effectiveness seems the next logical step. However, it is not just those who rely on the intervention who are ignoring its study. The same could be said of those who study teaching, learning, and its improvement in post-secondary education. If ever there was a case in point illustrating the need for greater collaboration between those who research and those who practice, the study and use of workshops to improve instruction demonstrates it.

Consultation

History

Like workshops and seminars, consulting has been a common faculty development intervention. Centra (1978) found instructional consultation among the practices under a factor labeled, "high faculty involvement." He concluded that consultations "involve a high proportion of the faculty at the colleges that use them" (p. 154).

Much of what is known about consulting has been learned via experience and not research. Several different authors articulate the theoretical foundations and models that underlie current practice. Boud and McDonald (1981) describe consultants' original purpose as providing "solutions to educational problems," "carrying out a survey or a study for an individual or for a whole institution," or, simply, functioning as "experts" (p. 2). They outline three traditional models consultants initially adopted: the Professional Service Model, in which the consultant brings "organizational or technical expertise" (p. 3) to the consultation; the Counseling Model, in which the consultant aims to help the teacher-client realize his or her teaching problems and devise a plan to deal with the problem; and the Collegial Model, in which two peers serve as consultants for one another, "each taking equal responsibility and each having the same stake in the outcomes" (p. 5). However, Boud and McDonald (1981) point out that faculty often see consultants who ascribe to these models as "technicians," "shrinks," or "blind leading the blind." Consequently, they propose an Eclectic Model, which is to say that "the educational consultant needs to draw from each of these [previous] models . . . to work flexibly and eclectically in order to respond to the unique demands of *each situation*" (p. 5).

Lewis (1988) suggests that consultants must wear the "many hats" (p. 76) of data collector, data manager, facilitator, support system, counselor, and information source in order to meet the particular needs of each teacher-client. In a slightly more prescriptive sense, Nyquist and Wulff (1988) also depart from the traditional models of consultancy, proposing that the consulting process be viewed through a research perspective. Like Boud and McDonald's Eclectic Model, Nyquist and Wulff's (1988) Research Perspective draws on many of the *skills* used in preceding models (e.g., collecting and interpreting data, working collaboratively, etc.), but then recommends four specific steps (paralleling the steps in the research process) which will focus attention on the individual teacher-client and her or his unique teaching style and situation.

Taylor-Way (1988) also acknowledges the importance of "analyzing, reflecting on, and evaluating" specific teaching "events" (p. 161) when consulting with faculty. Murray (1985) provides empirical support for addressing individual teaching behaviors when consulting with faculty for the purpose of improving teaching. Thus, the current focus for instructional consultation has evolved out of practice. It involves looking at, interpreting, and analyzing the individual teacher-client's unique teaching behaviors in a collaborative, investigative fashion.

Prevalence

Widespread use of consultation continues, documented by all the survey data collected in the 1980s except Konrad (1983) whose survey of 25 Canadian universities showed that only eight percent of the institutions surveyed indicated use, by over 20 percent of their faculty, of consultations "by faculty with expertise." Contrastingly, in Hansen's (1983) survey of 36 Illinois community colleges, 64 percent offered "individual informal consultations." In Richardson and Moore's (1987) survey of 56 Texas community colleges, 44 percent offered "individual teaching consultations." Interestingly, in his survey of 630 four-year United States institutions, Erickson (1986) notes, separately, the percentage that use consultations over student evaluations, the percentage that use consultations over observations, and the percentage of institutions that use consultations over teaching issues, in general. Erikson found that only 38 percent of the 95 percent who used student evaluations offered consultations in conjunction with the evaluation data. More encouragingly, 51.5 percent of the respondents in his survey reported using consultations with videotaping of classroom instruction; and 49.5 percent reported using consultations for discussing teaching issues, in general.

Description

Although the discussion of faculty consultation has focused only on instructional improvement, a subset of a larger consulting arena, even this single area of instructional consulting (henceforth to be referred to simply as "consultation") must be subdivided. Face-to-face interactions between teacher-client and consultants occur over three main issues: student evaluation data, a videotaped teaching sample or microteaching experience, and instructional concerns in general.

Other models of instructional consultation occur: when the consultant visits an actual classroom and offers feedback (more often colleagues fulfill this role and that contributions is described in a subsequent section), when students are trained to observe and offer feedback (Helling and Kuhlmann, 1988), when the consultation is part of a larger inquiry into the classroom teaching (Provlacs, 1988), and when small student groups offer input (Tiberius, 1988). Although these models propose innovative ways of using instructional consultation, they are not the norm and are therefore not considered in this review.

Although Erikson's (1986) survey indicates that receiving student evaluation feedback in conjunction with consultation is not as *prevalent* as receiving student evaluation feedback alone, consultation over student evaluations has been shown to be significantly more *effective* in improving teaching than receiving student evaluation feedback without consultation. Levinson-Rose and Menges (1981) report five of seven studies reviewed, with regard to "ratings with consultation," support the conclusion that consultation over student evaluation data improves teaching. The case is further supported by more recent research reviewed by Murray (1984).

But what does consultation over student evaluation entail? It may involve either a visit to the consultant's office or to the teacher-client's office to discuss the results of a mid-semester or end-of-semester student evaluation. The most productive discussions often focus on the instructor's behaviors; for when talking about specific, individual, observable behaviors, instructors acquire concrete suggestions to put into action when trying to implement change (Murray, 1984; Wilson, 1986). The consultant may request that the teacher-client bring with him or her past student evaluations, so as to compare performance across semesters. In all cases where improvement of teaching is the goal, the object of the consultation should be to work collaboratively to translate student data into teacher practices, or principles (Taylor-Way, 1988), that the client can use to maintain, modify, or eliminate certain elements of his or her teaching style.

Probably the most inhibiting of the three types of consultation involves recording a sample of teaching on videotape which the teacher-client and consultant then critique, or teaching a mini-lesson before a small audience of peers and/or consultants who then critique the instruction. This second method is usually called microteaching. Much more has been written about consultation over a videotaped teaching sample than microteaching experiences. Most often microteaching experiences are embedded in a longer seminar or program.

Consultation over videotape requires instructors to confront themselves as others actually see them (rather than as they think others see them). Taylor-Way (1988) suggests that videotaping allows the teacher-client to focus on the actual classroom behaviors observed (which allows the client to "own" the experience), rather than only on the particular behaviors noted in the observer-consultant's or colleague's notes (as is most often the case with personal observations). However, as he notes, instructors wishing to improve the teaching should not be forced into being videotaped; thus, in class observation (although not as descriptive as videotaping) is sometimes used to provide an unbiased account of the instructor's teaching behaviors. Often this feedback takes the form of a checklist with the observer-consultant's or colleague's notes attached.

The last, and the least well described, form of consultation is consultation over instructional issues in general. This type of consultation usually takes place in the consultant's office, and the teacher-client determines the content of the conversation. Issues raised may range from eliciting student participation, to dealing with classroom management issues, to improving presentational skills. This type of consultation also varies in the amount of time the instructor and consultant spend working together. The time period may consist of one meeting or may extend across the course of a semester.

Assessment

As was the case with workshops and seminars, much of the assessment as to whether consultations improve teacher effectiveness is at the attitudinal level. With regard to consultations generally, Centra (1978) found that 56 percent of college coordinators surveyed perceived "classroom visitations by an instructional resource person, simulation procedures to help faculty practice new skills, and the use of in-class videotapes" as effective. Centra also noted that in terms of perceived effectiveness, consultations and the other intervention strategies within the category "instructional assistance practices" ranked second out of six total categories of interventions (second only to the category "grants and travel funds").

Also regarding consultations in general, Moses (1985) surveyed 17 directors of academic development units in Australia and asked them what three approaches to improving teaching worked best in their institution. "Individual consultation" ranked third (behind workshops and student evaluations). Moses explained that "individual consultations were judged to be effective because they are based on the needs of individual teachers, they are initiated by them, and follow-up is feasible and usually occurs. . . . Thus, it is often possible to observe a change in teaching or in student reaction to teaching" (p. 79). Similarly, in Konrad's (1983) survey of Canadian universities, he found that, although not the most widely utilized, "assessment practices followed by some types of consultation appeared to be among the most effective for development purposes."

These attitudinal studies all focused on consultation in general. There are, however, a few studies that report on the individual types of consultation and their ability to increase instructional effectiveness.

Consultation Over Student Evaluation Data

Since the Levinson-Rose and Menges (1981) review, research on the impact of consultation over ratings has continued to be explored. In Murray's (1984) review of the impact of student evaluation on improvement, he states that although "the weight of evidence suggests that feedback from student ratings produces a small but significant improvement in teaching effectiveness. . .student feedback supplemented by expert consultation produces a much larger improvement in teaching" (p. 124). Two more recent studies add still more support.

Wilson (1986) studied the effects of a consultation process that focused on teaching behaviors. Before consulting with client-teachers about their student evaluations, he asked award-winning teachers to identify their teaching behaviors. From the interviews, Wilson compiled a list of behaviors that conveyed certain characteristics of effective teaching. Wilson next conducted student evaluations with a group of teacher-clients. He then consulted with each client about his or her teaching behaviors, careful to incorporate suggestions (from the list of behaviors generated by the master teachers) of other possible behaviors to try. After an intervening semester a second evaluation was administered. He found no difference in evaluation ratings for a comparison group who administered two evaluations but received no consultation. However, the teacher-client consultations were "associated with statistically important change in overall teaching effectiveness ratings for 52 percent of the faculty clients" (p. 209). In addition, the data showed that the "items on which the greatest number of faculty showed statistically important change were those for which the suggestions were most concrete, specific and behavioral" (p. 209).

In another study, Stevens and Aleamoni (1985) conducted a retrospective analysis to assess the effectiveness of consultations promoting instructional improvement over a 14-year intervening period. The original study (Aleamoni, 1978) compared the instructional improvement of teachers who received student evaluation feedback with consultation and teachers who received student evaluation feedback without consultation. The second study looked at the student evaluation ratings of 17 of the original study's participants at two time intervals; seven years after the initial study, and 14 years after the initial study. The results showed that "provision of consultation in addition to student ratings feedback resulted in an increase in student ratings that was maintained over time" (p. 303). On the other hand, the evaluations of instructors who had not originally received consultation with their student evaluation data did not result in consistent increases.

Stevens and Aleamoni (1985) call further longitudinal research in the area of consultations over student evaluation data to further substantiate these findings and suggest that student evaluation feedback "must be integrated with a system of instructor training and available instructional support services" (p. 303).

Consultation Over Videotaping and Microteaching

There is little direct evidence establishing the effectiveness of consultation over a videotaped teaching sample or microteaching experience. However the support Levinson-Rose and Menges (1981) summoned for microteaching and the indirect evidence of the intervening decade establish a strong potential for this improvement intervention.

Perlberg (1983) draws on research and theory related to effective use of video feedback and consultation in other contexts to propose potential uses in higher education as an improvement strategy. Perlberg concludes: "To exploit the full potential of video as an adjunct to a consultant's interventions, and in some cases as the focus of training and consultation, we need more research on its effectiveness and optimal uses" (p. 659).

The most significant evidence of the impact of video as an intervention has been collected in efforts to train teaching assistants. Sharp (1981) showed that TAs who viewed a tape modeling effective lecturing techniques did teach differently than those who did not see the tape. The differences were documented by trained observers who reviewed a videotape of a microteaching experience scheduled after the tape had been viewed. The Long, Sadker, and Sadker (1986) study described in the workshop section also supports Sharp's findings. Dalgaard (1982) videotaped 22 inexperienced TAs prior to a training program that included feedback over the initial tape and workshop presentations designed to help TAs plan and organize course content and involve students. TAs were taped again after the training, and teaching experts who rated the tapes documented significantly higher ratings for those who participated in the training as compared with a control group who did not.

Personal testimony to the Taylor-Way Videotape Recall method (1988) suggests that consultation over videotaping is very effective. Taylor-Way (1988) reports that "in most cases I can see specific improvement even from the first to the second videotaping and this perception is equally shared by the teacher involved" (p. 187). He elaborates, "The primary sources of data I have to support this statement are the completed recall forms of my clients (cognitive and affective indices) and their teaching behaviors comparing first and second videotapes (behavioral indiced)" (p. 187).

Finally, as general evidence of the effectiveness of this intervention in Konrad's (1983) small sample of universities, he found that 33 percent of the institutions that used analysis of in-class video tapes rated the practice effective.

Consultation Over Teaching Issues, in General

Studies assessing consultation over teaching issues, in general, are by far the scarcest. Again, in Konrad's (1983) survey of 25 Canadian universities, he noted that of institutions which do practice consultation over general teaching issues, 31 percent rated this practice effective. Hansen's (1983) survey of 36 Illinois community colleges provides more support for the perceived usefulness, of general consultations. In Hansen's study, 73 percent of the 64 percent that use individual informal consultations rated this practice as good or excellent in terms of its usefulness. In Richardson and Moore's (1987) survey of 56 Texas community colleges, 86 percent of the 44 percent that use individual teaching consultations rated them as good or excellent in terms of usefulness. Once again empirical research is needed to verify the perceptions of those who use this intervention.

Discussion

Evidence continues to support the effectiveness of consultation over ratings in positively affecting subsequent evaluations. Certainly enough evidence exists to strongly commend the practice to those who use student evaluation and are interested in increasing its impact on instruction. Despite the solid evidence supporting the effectiveness of this intervention some important questions remain unanswered. What exactly is it about the addition of a consultation session to student evaluation feedback that makes instructors improve? Murray (1985), Wilson (1986), and others who suggest translating evaluation data into behaviors' seem to suggest that talking about behaviors is the key. In addition Wilson (1986) states, "it may be . . . that interpersonal expectations established in the consultation sessions create for some faculty a desire to fulfill an implied contract with their consultant" (p. 211). Gil (1987) suggests that it is simply "the human element" (p. 59)—the fact that someone takes an interest—that provides the impetus for change.

Obviously, further research is needed to clarify which of these elements, or combination of elements, it may be that helps faculty use student evaluation data to make instructional changes.

In addition, research to date has not yet addressed how long consultative sessions ought to be, how soon after the evaluative event they should be scheduled, if continuing consultation across several semesters adds to the impact, or if consultation works more effectively with certain groups of faculty, i.e. those with low or high ratings, those with limited or extensive teaching experience, and so on. The Stevens and Aleamoni (1985) call for further research as to effects of rating consultation over time needs response as well. At this point, consultation over ratings has been shown to make a difference; the scope, nature, and variables contributing to that impact remain to be discovered.

Evidence documenting the effectiveness of videotaping and microteaching as instructional improvement interventions continues to offer tantalizing possibilities. Unfortunately, most of the evidence is peripheral to the larger and more direct question: Does a videotape or microteaching experience with consultation improve instruction? The peripheral evidence provided by research done in this decade coupled with research on microteaching reported earlier seems to indicate a positive impact, but once again the extent of that impact, its continued effect over time, what the consultative component adds to the intervention, all remain unclear. As with consultation over student evaluation results, the effects of videotaping and microteaching on learning outcomes remains untested. Research in both these areas does tend to go beyond the level of faculty attitudes and knowledge, but to date it does not show that these interventions cause students to learn more.

In terms of consultations over general teaching issues, much remains unknown. For example, to name a few unresolved questions: What are the most common issues brought to the consultant? What are the implications in terms of effects of the models proposed in the historical section? Does experience and/or training of the consultant make a difference? Are the effects of consultation sustainable across time?

The use of instructional consultation as it occurs over ratings, over videotaped teaching samples and microteaching experiences, and over general instructional issues has grown during the '80s. In terms of the criteria being used to assess research on the interventions, more of the research in this area has occurred at the level of observable behavior changes and changes in student evaluation. Unfortunately, the body of research remains small, in some cases only peripherally related to the intervention and to date not at all assessing the effects of consultation on student learning outcomes. Much needed work in this area remains to be done.

Grants for Instructional Improvement Projects

History

Generally small grants, in most cases available from the institution, have been used as an instructional intervention from the beginning of the instructional and faculty development efforts that started in the '60s. In the first survey of instructional improvement activities, Centra (1978) reports that of the 756 two- and four-year institutions responding to his survey, 58 percent indicated they had a grants program. Levinson-Rose and Menges (1981) reviewed instructional grants programs in terms of interinstitutional projects, campus-wide programs and individual faculty projects at the national (some offered by the professional associations of particular disciplines) and state level, as well as those offered by local institutions. They reference some survey studies completed in the '70s where those associated with grant programs were queried as to methods of evaluation. Only a small percentage went beyond soliciting faculty reactions. Centra's (1978) data indicate that fewer than one-fifth of those with grants programs had attempted evaluation and most of those used unsophisticated designs. Levinson-Rose and Menges summarize the status of research on the grant intervention in 1981. "Few generalizations about effective granting programs can be made on the basis of this research. Such programs possess face validity, since persons completing a grant-supported project are likely to have gained new knowledge and skills. Nevertheless, impact on students remains to be studied in relation to specific features of particular programs" (p. 406).

Prevalence

Throughout the '80s, institutions continued to use small grants programs to intervene in the quality of instruction at the institution. Smith (1981), using a survey design modeled on Centra's (1978), asked 1,315 community colleges about staff development goals and activities. Of the 413 institutions having organized staff development programs, 324 used grants to faculty "for developing new or different approaches to courses or teaching" (p. 214). Hansen (1983) reports that 50 percent of the community colleges in Illinois who responded to a survey of faculty development activities and their impact used "institutional grants for instructional projects" (p. 218). Richardson and Moore (1987) found similarly in their survey of Texas community colleges. Forty-nine percent of the 56 institutions reported making grants available to support instructional programs. Of the 25 Canadian institutions responding to Konrad's (1983) survey, 40 percent indicated that "summer grants for projects to improve instruction or courses" existed. In Erickson's (1986) survey of four-year institutions, including responses from 630 colleges and universities, 60 percent had "summer grants for projects to improve instruction or courses" and 64.5 percent had "grants for faculty members developing new or different approaches to courses or teaching" (p. 188). The sum of this evidence warrants this conclusion: the use of grants as an intervention to improve instruction continues in all types of post-secondary institutions.

Description

Although no data were located which document the extent to which these programs share design details, there is a general sense among faculty and instructional developers that during this decade there are fewer interinstitutional projects, fewer campus-wide programs, and more institutional grants to individual faculty. In general, these grants tend to be small, ranging between $500 and $5,000. They are awarded competitively, with faculty writing grant proposals and faculty-administrative committees awarding the funds. Funds are used to purchase instructional materials, pay personnel, support travel, provide access to consultants, or buy release time.

Jacobsen's (1989) study of the impact of faculty incentive grants on teaching effectiveness at a college in Pennsylvania was the only published study of a particular grant program located during this review of up to $5,000 each annually to four instructors. Faculty members must submit "student evaluations of teaching performance during the preceding calendar year, . . . evidence of effective advising, . . . a course evaluation that has been completed by a fellow faculty member, . . . a letter from the department chair indicating quality performance in both teaching and advising, . . . and a proposal for how the award money will be used" (p. 4). Summarized in the assessment section are Jacobsen's findings with regard to the effect of this program on faculty members' student evaluations.

Assessment

Most of the assessment of the effectiveness of grants as an instructional intervention is general data collected in the survey's mentioned throughout this review. In other words, those who oversee or have knowledge of an institution's instructional grants program (not faculty who received the grants) offer opinions as to their effectiveness. Of Smith's (1981) community college respondents, 70 percent saw the use of grants by faculty as effective or very effective. Of Hansen's (1983) Illinois community college respondents, 89 percent gave grants excellent or good ratings, making them the highest evaluated improvement activity. Furthermore, 84 percent gave release time to develop instructional projects excellent or good ratings, making them the second most highly evaluated activity. Of Richardson and Moore's (1987) Texas community college respondents, 88 percent gave institutional grants for instructional projects excellent or good ratings; 90 percent gave the same ratings to release time to develop instructional projects. In Konrad's (1983) survey of Canadian institutions, 50 percent felt summer grants programs were effective. Erickson (1986) did not ask the faculty and instructional developers he surveyed to assess the effectiveness of the interventions they reported using.

Only two other assessments of grants as instructional intervention were located. The first appears in a book by Eble and McKeachie (1985) which describes and evaluates the Bush Foundation Faculty Development Project in Minnesota and the Dakotas. The foundation aimed to improve undergraduate education by supporting a variety of different programs (24 for the first three years) at a variety of different institutions in the region. Using interview and survey techniques, Eble and McKeachie (1985) compare and contrast individual programs and the interventions they employed. They write: "Projects involving *course development* and *curricular change* were also rated as highly productive by our faculty respondents" (p. 198). Later they qualify: "Grant programs are unlikely to affect norms unless a purposeful effort is made to use the grants as catalysts for institutional change through faculty forums, newsletters, and follow-up activities drawing upon the experience of the grantees and relating their learning to the interests and needs of other faculty members. . . . Our impression is that the degree to which faculty grants eventually affected teaching and learning was related to the degree to which a faculty development committee or officer consulted with grantees about teaching and the relevance of the grant to teaching" (p. 199).

The second assessment of grants as an instructional intervention appeared in the already mentioned Jacobsen (1989) study. Jacobsen defines the "Excellence in Teaching" grant as a reward (rather than incentive) grant since faculty members applying for the grant must supply proof of effective teaching and advising, in addition to a grant proposal. Jacobsen compared, over two time periods (pre-grant program and post-grant program), student evaluations for those instructors who received grants, those who applied for but did not receive grants, and those who did not apply for grants. She found that, overall, pre- and post-grant program evaluations for the whole college remained constant; instructors who were awarded grants were better teachers than their colleagues; instructors with grants did not see improved evaluations as a result of the grant received; and those who did see improved evaluations were the instructors who applied for a grant and did not receive one.

Additionally, she interviewed ten faculty members (some who received grants, some who applied but did not receive grants, and some who did not apply) and asked them, among other questions, "What effect has the Excellence in Teaching Award program had on teaching effectiveness at this college?" (p. 16). She found that no one indicated a positive effect, six reported no effect, and four indicated a negative effect.

Discussion

The evidence found to support the effectiveness of grants as an instructional improvement intervention justifies no conclusion. Most of it fails to meet even the first category of assessment proposed by Levinson-Rose and Menges (1981). Here even faculty participants have only rarely been asked to offer self-reports of instructional experiences related to receipt of a grant. More often those who administer the grant, perhaps have even had a hand in designing the program, have been asked for general opinions as to the effectiveness of the intervention. The only study that did assess faculty improvement (Jacobsen, 1989) reported that grants did not increase recipients' student evaluations. For this review no evidence was discovered which substantiates that grants change faculty instructional knowledge, in-class instructional behaviors, that they change student evaluations of instruction, or that they in any way change learning outcomes. It seems almost unbelievable that an intervention so widely used and that involves measurable amounts of money (to say nothing of time and effort) remains so unstudied. The decade has produced gains in experience, although even those have not been shared in a published form, but it has produced no gains in research-based knowledge. Whether or not grants have any measurable effects on instructional quality is still not known.

Resource Materials

History

Neither Centra (1978) nor Levinson-Rose and Menges (1981) considered those efforts to intervene in instructional quality by distributing to faculty various materials about teaching and learning. Therefore, no evidence as to the prevalence or effectiveness of this intervention has been reviewed previously. However, materials on teaching have been available and circulated to faculty prior to this decade. A number of discipline-specific pedagogical journals, *The Journal of Chemical Education* and *Teaching Psychology,* to name just two of many, have been published for decades. The interdisciplinary journal *College Teaching* began publication in the '50s. Early instructional and faculty development units did prepare and circulate local newsletters and other resources on teaching and learning.

Prevalence

Some of the survey data collected during the '80s does document the extent to which this intervention is used. In Konrad's (1983) survey of Canadian universities, 80 percent of those responding indicated that newsletters and articles pertinent to teaching were circulated. Of the 630 four-year institutions responding to Erickson's (1986) survey, 48 percent indicated they did circulate newsletters and articles on instructional issues.

Description

Materials on teaching and learning circulated to faculty take a variety of different forms. Newsletters are probably the most frequently discussed in faculty and instructional development circles. In a newsletter on writing newsletters Border and Fisch (1988) propose that these publications can achieve a number of important goals: present information about effective teaching, stimulate discussion and promote the sharing of good ideas, provide instructional support, and showcase examples of instructional excellence, among others. Besides infusing the instruction of faculty with new and pertinent information, newsletters also call attention to those units offering instructional resources and services.

Some instructional and faculty development units circulate articles to faculty or make them available upon faculty request. These articles may address teaching effectiveness generally or may relate to a specific instructional issue like constructing multiple-choice exams, or getting students participating in discussion, or using clear examples.

Some programs develop their own materials, perhaps a resource book for new faculty, or a monograph on test construction, or a bibliography of sources on how students learn. These may be distributed to faculty at large, to those who request them, or they may be part of a larger collection of instructional resources generally housed in the instructional or faculty development unit

Assessment

This review uncovered no inquiry into the effectiveness of instructional materials distributed to faculty. Of those who use them in Canadian universities, according to Konrad (1983), only 30 percent list them as effective.

Weimer (1988), in an article written for faculty, offers a number of reasons why reading ought to improve instruction, among them that it infuses teaching with a stream of concrete, practical, new ideas; that it forces faculty to become aware of how they teach and how they might teach differently; and that it can help to alleviate some of the psychological burnout associated with teaching by providing motivational descriptions of teaching and learning. She does point out, however, that none of these claims have been subjected to empirical inquiry.

Discussion

No conclusions can be drawn as to the effectiveness of resource materials on instructional quality. In the case of this intervention as with others in this review, a fairly extensive use of an intervention can be documented, and yet for all intents and purposes absolutely no evidence exists supporting its effectiveness in the improvement of instruction. Perhaps a larger body of research can be summoned to make the case. Students of all sorts can and do learn by reading materials. There is nothing to indicate that faculty reading materials on teaching and learning are different than any other students who learn by reading, but that qualifies as general support, not the specific evidence needed to establish the efficacy of the case in point.

Colleagues Helping Colleagues

History

Neither the Centra (1978) or Levinson-Rose and Menges (1981) review considered the effects of colleague interventions on teaching quality. The practice was not widespread in early instructional and faculty development efforts. The use of colleague intervention increased when understaffed and underfunded instructional and faculty development units began using faculty volunteers and discovered the benefits of their involvement, and when reviews of literature like Cohen and McKeachie's (1980) concluded that colleagues would do best by intervening formatively in the instructional efforts of one another.

Prevalence

The prevalence of this activity is currently difficult to document. Those collecting data on instructional and faculty development practices do not clearly differentiate between the presence of colleagues in each other's classrooms for the purposes of preparing an evaluation to be used in a promotion and tenure decision, and the presence of colleagues in each other's classrooms for the purpose of instructional improvement. This may account for the low effectiveness rating given by community college personnel responding to Smith's (1981) survey. Only 38 percent of the 255 of them who reported using "formal assessments by colleagues for teaching or course improvement" (p. 216) labeled it an effective practice. In Erickson's (1986) survey, 64.5 percent of the four-year institutions who responded reported using classroom observation by peers as an instructional improvement intervention.

Description

Instructional and faculty developers are using colleagues to intervene with each other in a variety of ways. Most often they observe each other teach; sometimes one (possibly trained and experienced) observes the other, and sometimes the visitation is reciprocal. After the visitation there is a discussion of what was observed with suggestions offered for improvement. Faculty are sometimes used to offer input on course materials, or to respond to an instructional concern they have faced (for example, teaching a large, lower division, required course), or a practice they use (for example, student managed tutoring groups).

Millis (1989) describes a program typical in many respects of the kind of activities being used in this instructional intervention. At the University of Maryland a group of peer visitors are selected from a group of faculty who have distinguished themselves in the classroom as indicated by student evaluations and administrative recommendations. They are trained both in the observation of instruction and the communication of feedback. These peer visitors attend one class session of several target faculty groups: those new to the university, those nominated for teaching awards, randomly selected experienced faculty, and faculty perceived as needing assistance. Although some resistance occurs from faculty in the last two categories, most respond favorably to the opportunity.

Probably the most elaborate colleague instructional intervention is one described by Katz and Henry (1988). Their model was developed in two separate projects: one funded by FIPSE and the other by the Ford Foundation. It involves colleagues in an elaborate and comprehensive inquiry into the learning experiences of students in their courses. Colleagues attend class and then individually interview selected students from the class as to how they are attempting to learn course content. Those learning experiences are then related to the professor teaching the class and the two colleagues explore what instructional policies and practices might more effectively impact student learning experiences. Versions of this program have been used at a variety of different institutions throughout the country, most recently in the institutions in New Jersey's Department of Higher Education. Participants are asked to prepare a paper describing what knowledge they have gained through their interviews, observation, and discussions. A published assessment of those outcomes was not located for this review.

Assessment

Evaluation of the effects of colleagues interventions is spotty. Annis (1989) reports on a project at Ball State University where nine colleague pairs observed and interacted with each other for two quarters. Students completed a Teaching Analysis By Students (TABS) evaluation instrument prior to the program's start and once again at its conclusion. Comparisons between average student responses on the pre- and post-evaluations revealed improvement on six of seven primary teaching components. In a case study, two English professors (Rorschach and Whitney, 1986) describe the positive effects of a course-long observation experience in each other's composition courses.

Discussion

Despite the growing number of colleague interventions, the effectiveness of this means to improve instruction remains for all intents and purposes unstudied. Theoretical grounding for the intervention exists, as does experience in a number of different programs and activities. What remains unproven is the effect of colleague interventions on the instructional practices of each other, on student evaluations, and on learning outcomes.

Target Group: New Faculty

Background and Current Status

A focus on the instructional efforts of new faculty stems from two assumptions. First, since the graduate school experiences continues to ignore instructional preparation (except perhaps for those with teaching assistantships), new faculty come to college teaching with little or no prior experience or training, and it is assumed that instructional quality suffers as a consequence. That assumption rests on some evidence, described subsequently, but mostly on the prior experience of faculty who teach in college today. Few wish to repeat (or even recall) their early teaching experiences. Second, since new faculty generally do not come to an institution with tenure, it is assumed the institution is in a better position to "encourage" these faculty to do "something" about teaching effectiveness during these years.

Neither of these two assumptions, however, can explain the current surge of interest in new faculty. It may be an extension of the concern about teaching assistants. *All* new college teachers face many of the same challenges: preparing course materials, constructing a syllabus, establishing credibility and control, devising equitable grading systems, to name a few. Instructional faculty developers, and their institutions have discovered what concerns TAs is equally needed and of interest to new faculty. Or, current interest may be in anticipation of the large numbers of new faculty who will join colleges and universities in the '90s to replace retirees. Institutions have an opportunity to intervene with faculty over instruction to an extent unknown in recent decades. Whatever the reason, interest in instructional interventions with new faculty is on the rise, as witnessed by several studies focusing on the instructional experiences of new faculty, published pieces describing and assessing the use of various interventions with them, and new materials being developed for them.

To date, the prevalence of activities targeted for new faculty has been partially documented. Hansen (1983) surveyed chief academic officers of Illinois community colleges and found that of the 36 institutions responding, 94 percent conducted orientation activities (mostly workshops) for new faculty. Richardson and Moore (1987) found that in the 56 Texas community colleges responding to their survey 89 percent reported having orientation activities (most often workshops) for full-time, new faculty. In Konrad's (1983) survey of 25 Canadian universities, 20 percent of the institutions indicated they gave new faculty lighter than normal teaching loads for the first year. Only 40 percent assessed it an "effective" practice. Likewise in the Smith (1981) survey of 413 community colleges nationwide, this technique fell in the "least favorable" category with only 32 percent listing it as "effective."

However, recent research on new faculty reflects current interest in this target group. Fink (1984) studied nearly 100 beginning college teachers in geography collecting information on their "origin, distribution, preparation, situation and performance . . . from the new teachers themselves, their colleagues, from students, and from site visits by the research director" (p. 95). Interestingly, in light of previous assessments of lighter loads for new faculty, Fink found that student evaluations revealed that "an increase in the number of separate preparations during a single term had a strong, straight-line negative effect on teaching performance" (p. 99). Participants were also asked to indicate whether they had found "intellectual companionship" (p. 100) with colleagues. One third said yes, one half said only to a limited degree, and one sixth said no. "The less companionship they found, the lower was their average teaching evaluation score" (p. 100). Also of interest to the topic of instructional improvement were Fink's attempts to assess the instructional performance of these first-year faculty. He summarizes, "The student ratings and the self-rating both indicated that one sixth of the new teachers performed well above average compared with other, experienced teachers. One half did about average, and one third had problems. In other words, there was a range in their performance, but the distribution was overrepresented in the lower half of the scale" (p. 102).

Sorcinelli (1988) interviewed 54 new tenure-track appointments at a large mid-western university. About half her sample reported stresses in teaching. "The major culprit was the time it took to develop courses (several designed four new courses their first year), teach, evaluate, and advise students" (p. 126). New faculty in this survey also reported a "lack of collegial relations as the most surprising and disappointing aspect of their first year" (p. 126).

Turner and Boice (1989) report on a large interview/observation project undertaken across the first four semesters 100 new faculty were at a large regional university. "The study's goals included collection of information about how new faculty reacted to recruiting and orienting practices, how they coped with pressures to master teaching while initiating research and scholarly writing, how they were socialized to departmental and campus mores, how they perceived the stresses and satisfactions of new faculty status, and their perceptions of senior faculty as sources of collegiality and intellectual stimulation" (p. 52).

Specifically, in regard to teaching most new professors in this survey reported spending from 16 to 20 hours a week preparing their lectures and other course materials. The majority received "good" or "excellent" student evaluations. Those not teaching well seemed to share a common pattern. "They reported feeling highly motivated but notably insecure in their own knowledge and skills. They reported spending 35 hours a week preparing lectures. And, they came across as stiff, formal, and generally uncomfortable in the classroom" (p. 54) With regard to colleagues, "nearly 50% of all new tenure track faculty rated the overall quality of collegial relations in their department as only 'fair' or 'poor' " (p. 55).

Interventions

Three of the instructional interventions under consideration in this review are being used in efforts designed for new faculty: workshop programming, consultation (almost exclusively via some form of mentoring model), and resource materials. Each of these interventions will be considered separately in terms of the prevalence of its use (provided an indication of this exists), a general description and specific illustrations of the intervention, and the assessment measures being used to determine its effectiveness.

Workshop, Seminars, and Programs

Many of these occur under the rubric of orientation activities, and the prevalence of those has been mentioned previously. Additionally, Eison (1989) reports data from a survey of faculty developers at 70 different institutions where 85 percent of the respondents report providing a special workshop or program for new faculty. Approximately one third of those programs are less than a day in length, one third last one full day, and the final third are longer than one day.

Typically orientation activities for new faculty occur just prior to or shortly after the first teaching experience at the institution. The shorter orientations include introductions to various aspects of the institution and a review of relevant policies and practices, with some instructional "survival skills" thrown in for good measure. The longer programs tend to include more information on teaching and rely on a greater variety of instructional methods and interventions.

A particularly complete description of the development, implementation, and evolution of a week-long, mandatory workshop for new faculty is provided by Bonwell and Eison (1987) and Eison (1989). This workshop seeks to accomplish four goals: 1) to convey the university's view that teaching excellence should be the number one goal of the faculty, 2) to create a positive first impression of the university, faculty, staff, and community, 3) to provide new faculty with an opportunity to develop the attitudes, knowledge base, and pedagogical skills associated with instructional excellence, and 4) to provide new faculty with an opportunity to meet and work with each other, and with faculty members recognized as excellent teachers. Based on their discovery that not all new hired faculty are new to teaching, that mandatory attendance sometimes engenders defensiveness, and that participants wanted information about all sorts of issues in addition to instructional ones, program organizers have continued to revise what they offer new faculty and how they offer it. Participants each year in the program evaluate it via open and closed-ended instruments. Those assessments reported in 1989 are favorable.

Foster and Moore (1987) describe an orientation workshop for new faculty first offered at their institution in the 1960s. Forty percent of the content of the current workshop focuses on teaching methods. Participants also prepare and are videotaped delivering a 10- to 15-minute lesson. The group evaluates each presentation. Assessments of the activity delivered in group discussion sessions and in written comments indicate the "large majority of participants are enthusiastic about the workshop" (p. 749).

Certainly one of the most comprehensive and oldest programmatic interventions with new faculty is a fellowship program supported by the Lilly Endowment. Begun in 1974, the Teaching Fellows Programs offer research institutions a way to assist junior, untenured faculty members to learn about, reflect on, and develop teaching expertise, while they simultaneously pursue research activities at their institution of appointment. Yearly grants are awarded to institutions with the possibility of renewal for three years. Although the programs at the individual institutions vary, typically they involve regular group meetings to discuss teaching-related topics, individual projects focused on teaching, some release time from usual course responsibilities, and often, senior faculty mentors. At least five Fellows must be appointed annually. A recent evaluation of the program completed by Austin (1990) assessed the impact of the program on individual Fellows, on their institutions, and on higher education policy issues. The 568 former Fellows were surveyed, all with a written instrument, some with phone interviews. All program directors were surveyed and interviewed as well as archival material studied. As for impact on the individual participants, Austin concludes: "In sum, evidence from the Fellows, the Program Directors, Deans, and Department Chairs leads to the unmistakable conclusion that, with only a few exceptions, the Teaching Fellows Program typically affects faculty participants in important, positive, identifiable ways" (p. 3). At the 30 universities where programs have been located, nine have continued the program with internal funding. Eighteen (some included in the nine) have established other faculty development programs that are the result, partially or fully, of the Lilly program.

Some general assessment of the effectiveness of the workshop activity with new faculty has occurred. Hansen (1983) asked those surveyed in Illinois community colleges if they considered orientation activities for new faculty to be useful for the improvement of instruction. Seventy-eight percent considered them to be an excellent or good way to improve instruction. Richardson and Moore (1987) report that 63 percent of the community colleges in Texas report they do evaluate their orientation activities for new faculty. Seventy-two percent evaluate via verbal feedback from participants; 57 percent use written feedback. Virtually no other form of assessment is reported by those surveyed.

Consultation via Mentoring Models

This review located very little material documenting the prevalence of this intervention with new faculty. Konrad's (1983) survey of Canadian institutions reported that 44 percent of those interviewed did not use this intervention, but of those who did (percentage not reported), 43 percent considered it an effective practice.

The interest in mentoring models for new faculty probably stems from a variety of different sources. Mentoring activities for newcomers in an organization are popular in various contexts right now. It appeals particularly to faculty who harbor traditions of collegiality and rely on experience for much of what they have learned about effective instruction. Perhaps those who propose it are attempting to respond to the earlier evidence documenting dissatisfaction on the part of new faculty with collegial experiences. Whatever its cause, a variety of different programs and approaches are being taken which share two common objectives: help new faculty better understand an institution's goals and objectives, and get them started on activities designed to meet those goals.

Several published descriptions of programs exist. Boice and Turner (1989) report on an elaborate FIPSE supported mentoring project undertaken with faculty at California State University, Long Beach. Fourteen new faculty were given faculty mentors, picked "on the basis of our observations of their prowess and balance as teachers, researchers, and colleagues" (p. 119). New faculty were selected for the project based on "our judgments about their need for mentoring and their willingness, eventually, to become mentors themselves" (p. 119). During this year-long program mentors and mentees agreed to: 1) meet in mentor-mentee meetings at least weekly for an academic year, 2) attend monthly meetings of all project pairs, 3) keep regular records of their pair meetings, and 4) submit to weekly or biweekly observations and surveys conducted by project directors. Mentoring pairs reported they discussed research/scholarship/publication most often during the year, and teaching second most often. They reported the following as most helpful aspects of the experience (in rank order): help with academic policies, emotional support, help with faculty, help with scholarship, and time management/goal setting.

Freudenthal and DiGiorgio (1989) report on a new faculty program at Trenton State College where the institution assumes the mentor role. An advisory committee of selected faculty, department chairs, deans, and an administrative representative designed a formal mentoring program aimed at impacting the teaching, research, and service activities of new faculty members, including both those new to college teaching and new to the institution, and supporting faculty efforts throughout their entire first year. The program has five components: mentoring meetings (biweekly), departmental mentoring, development of a scholarly plan, "paper" mentoring that includes providing in an organized and coherent collection all published information about the college, and a one course reduction in teaching load. Participants have responded favorably to surveys asking for their feedback about the program.

Holmes (1988) reports on a mentoring component of a larger new faculty orientation program at the University of Wisconsin, Stevens Point. Here new faculty are assigned mentors from within their departments. In her survey of 44 mentors, Holmes found that most mentors reported spending six to fifteen hours with the mentee during the first semester and zero to five the second semester. The most frequently discussed topics by the pairs included talking about teaching, about the department, about testing and grading, about the administration, about the local community, and about research and scholarly activity. Surprisingly, since mentoring programs are generally constructed to benefit the mentee, Holmes' mentors reported several significant benefits had occurred to them as well. Thirty-eight percent reported an increased enthusiasm for teaching. Twenty-three percent indicated that they had in fact modified their own teaching style as a result of the program.

Resource Materials

No evidence was located that establishes the prevalence or use of materials written especially for new faculty. However, materials do exist, not the least of which is a text, *Tips for Teachers: A Guidebook for Beginning College Teachers* by Wilbert McKeachie (1986). This particular book, currently available in its eighth edition, holds the distinction of being the only book on college teaching. More recently an anthology of readings for new faculty has been published, *Teaching College: Collected Readings for the New Instructor,* edited by Weimer and Neff (1990). Two recent articles have also appeared, "Confidence in the Classroom: Ten Maxims for New Teachers" by Eison (1990) and "Achieving Excellence: Advice to New Teachers" by Browne and Keeley (1985). This review of instructional interventions uncovered no study of the effectiveness of these published materials on the improvement of the instruction of new faculty.

Discussion

In assessing the effectiveness of these three interventions with new faculty against the five levels proposed by Levinson-Rose and Menges (1981), it becomes clear quickly that no general statement as to the effectiveness of any or all the new faculty interventions can be offered. Empirical evidence establishing the effect of these interventions on faculty classroom behaviors and learning outcomes simply does not exist. In this case, the only evidence exists at the level of faculty attitude as reported by them. For orientation workshop programming there is some evidence that faculty "like" these programs and see them as useful and relevant to their initial experiences at the institution. In the case of consultation via mentoring, there is some of the same evidence as reported by both mentors and mentees depending on the published report.

As the summary of the literature described in this section shows, this is not the literature of research, but the literature of practice. To date no one has attempted to design and test a new faculty intervention using experimental controls, nor has anyone tried to assess an existing intervention in terms of its effects at these more objective, measurable levels. This, despite the fact that research cited in this section documents the need for such interventions, and the survey results reported document a widespread use of activities designed to improve the instruction of new faculty.

Target Group: Teaching Assistants

Two reviews of research describe the status of current research on efforts to prepare teaching assistants for their instructional responsibilities. Carroll (1980) reviewed the research in terms of the effects of training on TA and student variables. For TA variables, he reports on eight studies which assessed TA feedback about the program (the Levinson-Rose and Menges category of attitude by self-report). Programs were evaluated favorably. Inconclusive evidence existed to determine whether or not training programs effectively changed TA knowledge, or TA attitudes toward specific methods and techniques. More evidence documented the success of TA training programs at changing observed teaching behavior. With student variables, Carroll concludes: "Quasi-experimental research has indicated that training programs covering a wide range of teaching skills generally improved student attitudes, achievement, and ratings of instruction. However, studies with true experimental designs have tended to isolate a narrow set of teaching skills, and the results have been inconsistent" (p. 177).

Recently, Abbott, Wulff, and Szego (1989) attempted to update the Carroll (1980) review. They focused on training programs studied via a research design that manipulated variables with training and no training groups, or employed pre- and post-testing. They found studies which met this criteria in the area of student ratings with consultation or interpretation, and conclude that the evidence there suggests that "consultation based on student rating can be useful in helping TAs improve their teaching" (p. 113). With general training combined with videotaping, the evidence reviewed also suggests that these interventions can be effective in producing change in TAs. Two studies were assessed which attempted training in specific disciplines. Both were successful. Two additional studies focused on training TAs in specific instructional approaches and both were successful.

Authors of this recent review summarize the current status of research on TA training efforts:

> *Empirical research on TA training is still lacking.* Carroll (1980) suggested that there was a paucity of research that dealt specifically with training TAs. That deficiency still exists. We originally planned to report the results of our review in a meta-analysis and to make recommendations based on effect sizes, but we identified too few relevant studies to undertake such a procedure. Our review also discovered few case studies that employed modern qualitative approaches to examine TA training, and little research examining the generalizability of results across disciplines. (p 120)

Nonetheless, by comparison more research has studied the effects of TA training on instructional improvement than has studied efforts with new faculty. To date, though, none of the assumptions underlying efforts to reach particular parts of the larger faculty population are being tested. Is the beginning of the teaching career the best time to intervene? Are the interventions considered in this review the best means to intervene? Until those questions are addressed efforts directed at these target teacher groups remain on questionable ground.

Discussion and Recommendations

Based on this description and assessment of the literature in the 1980s on the effectiveness of five interventions to improve instruction (workshops, consultation, grants, resource materials, and colleagues helping colleagues), and the effectiveness of efforts to use these interventions with two target groups (new faculty and teaching assistants), concluding remarks and recommendations for future research can be offered.

First and most fundamentally, *more research must be undertaken.* That is probably the most obvious, but nonetheless most important conclusion of this review. In colleges and universities across this country and others, instructional interventions are being used with virtually no empirical justification as to their effectiveness. They have become the "traditional" and "customary" means of intervening to improve instruction. This is not to denigrate unnecessarily the wisdom of practice and the voice of experience present in the literature. Instructional and faculty developers are trained and experienced professionals. Their assessment of the effectiveness of these interventions should not be discounted, nor should the opinions of faculty participants be ignored. The problem is simply that they are not enough. The involvement and vested interest of these professionals in the success of the interventions place them in a biased position. The same may be said of faculty participants themselves who attend a workshop or experience visitation from a colleague. There is an inherent bias in favor of those experiences. All who support efforts to improve instruction will benefit from further evidence documenting how, why, and the extent to which these interventions succeed or fail.

Why has so little research on instructional interventions been conducted during this decade and the years preceding it? Those who use the interventions should not be excused from their lack of research, but to some degree it can be explained. Faculty and instructional developers for the most part are practitioners, not researchers. Many are faculty from other academic disciplines, assuming positions as heads and directors of faculty and instructional development units out of deep love for and concern about teaching. They are not familiar with educational research, either in terms of what is known about teaching or learning or in terms of methodology. Most also run offices chronically underfunded and understaffed. There is simply no time to do research beyond the most pragmatic levels—Did faculty like the program? Will they come if we sponsor one like it next year?

Despite these realities, during this decade the calls for more research and more comprehensive program evaluations are being made in the professional associations of these groups. Published materials are appearing which point out the need and value and then propose models and methods. Menges and Svinicki (1989) illustrate.

As much as more research is needed, *greater sophistication in empirical design is needed* even more. Granted, on some of the interventions reviewed (distribution of resource material, for example) any evidence would be an improvement, but for most of the interventions, evidence which does more than collect and summarize self-reported attitudes is essential. Favorable attitudes do not guarantee what is in fact needed if instruction is to be improved. Faculty must change what they do in class. Those changes must be obvious to independent observers, students, and must result in measurable differences in student learning. In other words, the effects of instructional interventions in these substantive realms must be established before any definitive claim can be made about current efforts to improve instruction.

Design sophistication also relates to the complexity that has come to characterize the use of a number of these interventions. Workshops and consultation provide the most compelling examples. Each of these interventions needs to be studied across different dimensions. Does the length of a workshop program correlate with its ability to change faculty behaviors? Do certain topics accomplish better results than other topics? What about consultation? Is it more effective over student evaluation results or a videotaped teaching sample? Individual interventions need to be studied across the different dimensions that have come to characterize their use.

In addition to deeper study of the interventions themselves, their relative strengths and weaknesses in the improvement process need to be assessed. It remains unclear, for example, whether participation in workshop programs more efficiently and permanently changes teaching behaviors than, say, consultation over a videotaped teaching sample. To date the association of more than one intervention in a packaged program—a week-long orientation to college teaching that combines, e. g., seminars, a microteaching experience, and consultation—remains unstudied. Does their power as impetuses to improve instruction grow or diminish by virtue of their association with each other? More sophisticated designs are needed if important questions like these are to be explored.

Finally, the targeting of instructional interventions to certain faculty groups needs study. Are efforts to intervene in the instruction of TAs and new faculty only occurring because those are the most "captive" of faculty groups? Stronger justification would include evidence that interventions like the ones reviewed in this study are effective in changing the behaviors, student assessments, and learning outcomes in the classes of faculty in these groups. More specific evidence would identify which of the interventions are most successful for each target group.

The call of this review for more rigorous empirical inquiry is not new. It has been made previously. Why are these interventions not being studied? First, as previously noted, those who use them are not qualified to complete the needed research agenda. Those with the qualifications may be avoiding the research because these are not easy phenomena to study. Researchers seldom have access to faculty subjects and even those who do quickly learn how difficult it is to "require" faculty to do anything. Moreover, the interventions themselves are difficult to study. Many intervening and confounding variables cloud results. It is easy to understand, by comparison, why the plethora of research on student evaluation continues. There vast quantities of data can be collected in much more tightly controlled environments. The study of instructional interventions requires field research with all its confounding logistical liabilities.

Do these realities preclude all possibilities of completing this research agenda? No. A closer collaboration between those who use the interventions, and those interested in studying them could help to overcome a number of obstacles. Those associated with faculty and instructional development programs do have access to faculty subjects. Most would be amenable to using interventions in the more structured and systematic way research treatments require. Most also are part of a network of fellow professionals who might add to the potential number of subjects and the data pool. This interinstitutional collaboration would help to alleviate still another weakness of this research, identified by Levinson-Rose and Menges (1981). "Cross-campus collaboration is absent. Most studies are isolated efforts of investigators on individual campuses. Intercampus research networks are potentially powerful tools for dealing with several of these problems, particularly random assignment and small numbers" (p. 419).

For years calls have been made for greater cooperation between those who research and those who practice. Here is yet another illustration of how that association could profitably benefit both groups. But will it occur? It will if those who research and those who practice, who do in fact share common goals and objectives, determine to make it so.

In addition to the need for more research and more rigorous empirical design of the research, there is also a need for *different kinds of inquiry.* Quantitative inquiries are not enough. They are by their nature ill-suited to answer all that needs to be known. Here little can be done but to re-echo the call made in the previous review. Levinson-Rose and Menges (1981) observe that quantitative methods "tend to distance researcher from participants in the name of objectivity and to oversimplify teaching and learning in the name of control. . . . To advance the field we need careful classroom ethnographies, disciplined case studies, and sensitive clinical interview as well as rigorous experimentation" (p. 419).

Finally, *the study of instructional interventions needs to derive from theoretical or conceptual bases.* In the research to date the underlying assumptions and grounding principles are rarely made explicit. Virtually no attempt is made to connect these interventions to related fields of knowledge. Several examples will illustrate. Faculty learning to teach more effectively are adult learners confronted with a new learning task. Much is known about how adults learn, what instructional strategies work best with them, and what learning activities they respond to favorably, but seldom is that knowledge applied to the use of instructional interventions with faculty. After an initial exploration of the applicability of adult learning theory to faculty development efforts, Geis and Smith (1989) conclude: ". . . we come away from this exploration of Adult Education and its application to the concerns and problems of faculty development with optimism and vitality. We suggest that much can be learned from the Adult Education literature, especially that part produced by those involved with continuing education in the professions" (p. 162).

Even closer to the sphere in which instructional interventions function is the work applying diffusion of innovation theories to faculty who adopt instructional innovations. Kozma's pioneering efforts (1978 and 1985) of faculty who adopted instructional technology innovations has large implications for the design and use of instructional interventions. Building on his work, Stevens' (1989) small but significant interview project with faculty innovators proposes a theoretical framework ripe for testing with more structured inquiries involving the interventions reviewed here.

Finally, work on motivation, specifically as it applies to the motivation faculty, do or do not have for teaching has large implications for the improvement of instruction. Bess' (1977) initial work in this area remains unapplied to improvement efforts, although the issues he identified have been repeated and reinforced by other literature; Bennan and Skeff (1988), for example.

Interest in instructional improvement has continued unabated during the '80s. That interest shows no signs of impending decline. As more time, effort, and money are devoted to better college teaching, the contribution of various instructional interventions remains an issue. Do these efforts to stimulate faculty attention to teaching make a difference in the realms, like student learning, that matter most? Research reviewed here offers some support for them, but it is feeble, inconclusive support at best. Regrettably, this is the conclusion arrived at by virtually everyone who has assessed the literature. Hopefully those who review the literature at the end of this decade will tell a different story.

References

Abbott, R. D., Wulff, D. A. and Szego, C. K. (1989). Review of research on TA training. In J. D. Nyquist, R. D. Abbott and D. H. Wulff (eds.), *New Directions for Teaching and Learning: Teaching Assistant Training in the 1990s.* San Francisco: Jossey-Bass.

Aleamoni, L. M. (1978). The usefulness of student evaluations in improving college teaching. *Instructional Science* 7: 95–105.

Annis, L. F. (1989). Partners in teaching improvement. *Journal of Staff, Program, and Organizational Development* 7(1): 7–12.

Austin, A. E. (1990). To leave an indelible mark: encouraging good teaching in universities through faculty development. A report for the Lilly Foundation presented at the Annual Meeting of the American Association of Higher Education, San Francisco, March.

Berman, J., and Skeff, K. M. (1988). Developing the motivation for improving university teaching. *Innovative Higher Education* 12: 114–125.

Bess, J. L. (1977). The motivation to teach. *Journal of Higher Education* 48(3): 243–258.

Bland, C., and Schmitz, C. C. (1988). Faculty vitality on review: retrospect and prospect. *Journal of Higher Education* 59(2): 190–224.

Boice, R., and Turner, J. L. (1989). The FIPSE-CSULB mentoring project for new faculty. *To Improve the Academy* 8: 117–139.

Bonwell, C., and Eison, J. (1987). Mandatory teaching effectiveness workshops for new faculty: lessons learned the hard way. *The Journal of Staff, Program, and Organizational Development* 5(3): 114–118.

Border, L., and Fisch, L. (1988). A newsletter on newsletters. In E. Wadsworth (ed.), *A Handbook for New Practitioners.* Stillwater, OK: New Forums Press.

Boud, D., and McDonald, R. (1981). *Educational Development Through Consultancy.* Surrey, England: Society for Research into Higher Education.

Brown, G., and Daines, J. (1983). Creating a course on lecturing and explaining. *Programmed Learning and Educational Technology* 20: 64–69.

Browne, M. N., and Keely, S. M. (1985). Achieving excellence: advice to new teachers. *College Teaching* 33(2): 78–83.

Carroll, J. G. (1980). Effects of training programs for university teaching assistants. *Journal of Higher Education* 51(2): 167–183.

Centra, J. A. (1978). Types of faculty development programs. *Journal of Higher Education* 49: 151–162.

Chism, N. (ed.) (1987). *Employment and Education of Teaching Assistants: Readings from a National Conference.* Columbus, Ohio: The Ohio State University.

Cohen, P. A., and McKeachie, W. (1980). The role of colleagues in the evaluation of college teaching. *Improving College and University Teaching* 28(4): 147–154.

Dalgaard, K. A. (1982). Some effects of training on teaching effectiveness of untrained university teaching assistants. *Research in Higher Education* 17(1): 39–50.

Eble, K., and McKeachie, W. (1985). *Improving Undergraduate Education Through Faculty Development.* San Francisco: Jossey-Bass.

Eison, J. A. (1990). Confidence in the classroom: ten maxims for new teachers. *College Teaching* 38(1): 21–25.

Eison, J. A. (1989). Mandatory teaching effectiveness workshops for new faculty: what a difference three years make. *The Journal of Staff, Program, and Organizational Development* 7(2): 59–66.

Erickson, G . (1986). A survey of faculty development practices. *To Improve the Academy* 5:182–194.

Fink, L. D . (1984). *New Directions for Teaching and Learning: The First Year of College Teaching.* San Francisco: Jossey-Bass.

Foster, J. M., and Moore, R. M. (1987). A workshop for new faculty. *Engineering Education* 77(7/8): 748–749.

Freudenthal, N. R., and DiGiorgio, A. J. (1989). New faculty mentoring: the institution as mentor. *The Journal of Staff, Program, and Organizational Development* 7(2): 67–72.

Friedman, M., and Stomper, C. (1983). The effectiveness of a faculty development program: a process-product experimental study. *The Review of Higher Education* 7(1): 49–65.

Geis, G. L., and Smith, R. A. (1989). If professors are adults. *The Journal of Staff, Program, and Organizational Development* 7(4): 155–163.

Gibbs, L. E., Browne, M. N., and Keeley, S. M. (1989). Critical thinking: a study's outcome. *The Journal of Professional Studies* 13(1): 44–59.

Gil, D. H. (1987). Instructional evaluation as a feedback process. In L. M. Aleamoni (ed.), *New Directions for Teaching and Learning: Techniques for Evaluating and Improving Instruction.* San Francisco: Jossey-Bass.

Hansen, D. W. (1983). Faculty development activities in the Illinois Community College System. *Community/Junior College Quarterly* 7: 207–230.

Helling, B., and Kuhlmann, D. (1988). The faculty visitor program: helping teachers to see themselves. In K. G. Lewis (ed.), *Face to Face.* Stillwater, OK: New Forums Press.

Herr, K. U. (1988). Exploring excellence in teaching: it can be done! *The Journal of Staff, Program, and Organization Development* 6(1): 11–16.

Holmes, S. K. (1988). New faculty mentoring: benefits to the mentor. *The Journal of Staff, Program, and Organization Development* 6(1): 17–20.

Jacobsen, R. H. (1989). The impact of faculty incentive grants on teaching. A paper given at the Annual Meeting of the American Educational Research Association, San Francisco, March.

Katz, J., and Henry, M. (1988). *Turning Professors into Teachers.* New York: Macmillan.

Konrad, A. C. (1983). Faculty development practices in Canadian universities. *The Canadian Journal of Higher Education* 13(2): 13–25.

Kozma, R. B. (1985). A grounded theory of instructional innovation in higher education. *Journal of Higher Education* 56(3): 300–319.

Kozma, R. B. (1978). Faculty development and the adoption and diffusion of classroom innovations. *Journal of Higher Education* 49(5): 438–449.

Levinson-Rose, J., and Menges, R. F. (1981). Improving college teaching: a critical review of research. *Review of Educational Research* 51(3): 403–434.

Lewis, K. G. (1988). Individual consultation: its importance to faculty development programs. In E. Wadsworth (ed.), *A Handbook for New Practitioners.* Stillwater, Oklahoma: New Forums Press.

Long, J. E., Sadker, D., and Sadker, M. (1986). The effects of teacher sex equity and effectiveness training on classroom interaction at the university level. Paper given at the Annual Meeting of the American Educational Research Association, San Francisco, April.

McKeachie, W. J. (1986). *Tips for Teachers: A Guidebook for Beginning College Teachers.* Lexington, Mass.: Heath.

Menges, R. J., and Svinicki, M. (1989). Designing program evaluations: a circular model. *To Improve the Academy* 8: 81–97.

Menges, R. J., and others. (1988). Strengthening professional development. *Journal of Higher Education* 59(3): 291–304.

Millis, B. J. (1989). Colleagues helping colleagues: a peer observation program model. *The Journal of Staff, Program, and Organizational Development* 7(1): 15–21.

Moses, I. (1985). Academic development units and the improvement of teaching. *Higher Education* 14: 75–100.

Murray, H. G. (1985). Classroom behaviors related to college teaching effectiveness. In J. G. Donald and A. M. Sullivan (eds.), *New Directions for Teaching and Learning: Using Research to Improve Teaching.* San Francisco: Jossey-Bass.

Murray, H. G. (1984). The impact of formative and summative evaluation of teaching in North American universities. *Assessment and Evaluation in Higher Education* 9(2): 117–132.

Nyquist, J., Abbott, B., Wulff, D., and Sprague, J. (in press). *Preparing the Professoriate of Tomorrow to Teach: Selected Readings on TA Training.* Dubuque, Iowa: Kendall Hunt.

Nyquist, J. D., and Wulff, D. H. (1988). Consultation using a research perspective. In K.G. Lewis (ed.), *Face to Face.* Stillwater, Oklahoma: New Forum Press.

Perlberg, A. (1983). When professors confront themselves: towards a theoretical conceptualization of video self-confrontation in higher education. *Higher Education* 12: 633–63.

Provlacs, J. (1988). The teaching analysis program and the role of the consultant. In K. G. Lewis (ed.), *Face to Face.* Stillwater, Oklahoma: New Forums Press.

Richardson, R., and Moore, W. (1987). Faculty development and evaluation in Texas community colleges. *Community/Junior College Quarterly of Research and Practice* 11(1): 19–32.

Rorschach, E., and Whitney, R. (1986). Relearning to teach: peer observation as a means of professional development. *English Education* 18: 159–172.

Sharp, G. (1981). Acquisition of lecturing skills by university teaching assistants: some effects of interest, topic relevance, and viewing a model videotape. *American Educational Research Journal* 18(4): 491–502.

Sorcinelli, M. D. (1988). Satisfactions and concerns of new university teachers. *To Improve the Academy* 7: 121–133.

Smith, A. (1981). Staff development goals and practices in U.S. community colleges. *Community/Junior College Research Quarterly* 2: 209–225.

Stevens, E. (1989). Explorations in faculty innovation. *The Journal of Staff, Program, and Organization Development* 7(4): 191–200.

Stevens, J. J., and Aleamoni, L. M. (1985). The use of evaluative feedback for instructional improvement: a longitudinal perspective. *Instructional Science* 13: 285–304.

Taylor-Way, D. (1988). Consultation with video: memory management through stimulated recall. In K. G. Lewis (ed.), *Face to Face.* Stillwater: New Forums Press. (159–191).

Tiberius, R. (1988). The use of the discussion group for the fine-tuning of teaching. In K. G. Lewis (ed.) *Face to Face.* Stillwater, Oklahoma: New Forums Press.

Turner, J. L., and Boice, R. (1989). Experiences of new faculty. *The Journal of Staff, Program, and Organizational Development* 7(2): 51–57.

Weimer, M. (1988). Reading your way to better teaching. *College Teaching* 36(2): 48–51.

Weimer, M., and Neff, R. A. (1990). *Teaching College: Collected Readings for the New Instructor.* Madison: Magna Publications.

Weimer, M., Svinicki, M., and Bauer, G. (1990). Designing programs to prepare TAs to teach. In J. D. Nyquist, R. D. Abbott, and D. H. Wulff (eds.), *New Directions for Teaching and Learning: Teaching Assistant Training in the 1990s.* San Francisco: Jossey-Bass.

Wilson, R. (1986). Improving faculty teaching: effective use of student evaluations and consultants. *Journal of Higher Education* 57: 196–211.

Introduction to Classroom Research

K. PATRICIA CROSS AND MIMI HARRIS STEADMAN

> *The richness of faculty talent should be celebrated, not restricted. Only as the distinctiveness of each professor is affirmed will the potential of scholarship be fully realized. Surely, American higher education is imaginative and creative enough to support and reward not only those scholars uniquely gifted in research but also those who excel in the integration and application of knowledge, as well as those especially adept in the scholarship of teaching. Such a mosaic of talent, if acknowledged, would bring renewed vitality to higher learning and to the nation.*
>
> Boyer, *Scholarship Reconsidered*, 1990, p. 27

The Carnegie report titled *Scholarship Reconsidered* (Boyer, 1990) has received widespread interest, and many colleges and universities are especially interested in implementing its recommendation to give greater attention to the "scholarship of teaching." But what exactly is the scholarship of teaching? The Carnegie report gives scant attention to an operational definition, but it does say what good teachers do. They "stimulate active, not passive learning and encourage students to be critical, creative thinkers, with the capacity to go on learning after their college days are over." Further, "good teaching means that faculty, as scholars, are also learners. . . . Through reading, through classroom discussion, and surely through comments and questions posed by students, professors themselves will be pushed in creative new directions" (p. 24). Well, maybe.

We believe that the learning required for the scholarship of teaching goes considerably beyond the traditional classroom activities of reading, class discussion, and being "pushed in creative new directions" by the comments and questions of students. Just as students must be actively engaged in formulating their own learning questions and thinking critically about them, so teachers must be actively engaged in formulating their own questions about learning and the impact of their teaching upon it. Teachers have an exceptional opportunity to engage actively in the scholarship of teaching by using their classrooms as laboratories for the study of teaching and learning. Observing students in the act of learning, reflecting and discussing observations and data with teaching colleagues, and reading the literature on what is already known about learning is one way teachers can implement the scholarship of teaching. It is what we call *Classroom Research*.

Classroom Research may be simply defined as ongoing and cumulative intellectual inquiry by classroom teachers into the nature of teaching and learning in their own classrooms. At its best, Classroom Research should benefit both teachers and students by actively engaging them in the collaborative study of learning as it takes place day by day in the particular context of their own classrooms. Teachers are learning how to become more effective teachers, and students are learning how to become more effective learners. In the next section, we describe the specific characteristics of Classroom Research.

Characteristics of Classroom Research

Many of the characteristics of Classroom Research (specifically learner-centered, teacher-directed, context-specific, and continual, or ongoing) are shared by Classroom Assessment (see Angelo and Cross, 1993, pp. 4–6).

"Introduction to Classroom Research," by K. Patricia Cross and Mimi Harris Steadman, reprinted from *Classroom Research: Implementing the Scholarship of Teaching*, 1996, Jossey-Bass Publishers, Inc.

Learner-Centered

Classroom Research focuses the primary attention of teachers and students on observing and improving *learning*, rather than on observing and improving teaching. In Classroom Research, it is learner responses to teaching rather than teacher performance that is the subject for study. Through systematic and careful study of learning as it takes place day by day in the classroom, teachers are gaining insight and understanding into how to make their teaching more effective, and students are gaining the lifelong skills of assessing and improving their learning.

Teacher-Directed

Classroom Research is dedicated to the proposition that college teachers are quite capable of conducting useful and valid research on classroom learning. Although Classroom Research does not obviate the need for technically trained educational researchers, it does change the focus from teachers as consumers of research to teachers as active investigators, engaged in studies of learning in their discipline.

Collaborative

Classroom Research requires the active engagement of students and teachers. In most circumstances, students become partners in the research and share in the analysis and interpretation of the results. Classroom Research is also enriched by discussion and collaboration with teaching colleagues. Because the purpose of Classroom Research is to deepen understandings about how people learn, it benefits from full discussion and participation by all who have something to learn and something to contribute.

Context-Specific

Classroom Research is conducted to shed light on the specific questions of an identified classroom. It involves the teaching of a particular discipline to a known group of students. Although the results may be generalizable to other populations and other disciplines, Classroom Research does not require technical research skills such as sampling and making statistical inferences.

Scholarly

Classroom Research is intellectually demanding and professionally responsible. It builds upon the knowledge base of research on teaching and learning. It requires the identification of a researchable question, the careful planning of an appropriate Research design, and consideration of the implications of the research for practice.

Practical and Relevant

The questions selected for investigation in Classroom Research are practical questions that the teacher faces in teaching the class. The primary purpose of Classroom Research is not to advance knowledge in general or to publish findings but rather to deepen personal understandings. Although Classroom Research projects may be related to theory and topics in the literature and may be published or otherwise shared with colleagues, the measure of the quality of the project is its contribution to the knowledge and practice of the teacher.

Continual

Classroom Research is ongoing. Frequently, a Classroom Research project will raise new questions, leading to cascading investigations, with new projects emerging from past investigations. Classroom Research is also continual in the sense that changes suggested by the research are treated as experiments requiring continual evaluation and modification. Classroom Research is more a process than a product.

Roots of Classroom Research

Because Classroom Research is just one of many efforts to improve the quality of undergraduate education, it may be best understood in the context of its relationship to four additional major efforts to improve teaching and learning in higher education: (1) the application of educational research to practice, (2) faculty development, (3) the assessment of student learning, and (4) the Carnegie proposals to broaden the definition of scholarship. All of these approaches to the improvement of teaching and learning exist in some strength today, but they were established in different times in recent history. In fact, each decade since the 1960s has featured a distinctive effort to improve teaching and learning.

In the 1960s, a huge and expensive effort was launched to create large federally sponsored R&D (research and development) centers to conduct research and engage in the development and dissemination that would make the research useful to educational practitioners. The 1970s were a decade of growth nationwide for *faculty development*, which usually meant the creation of an office of special consultants on campus to work with faculty toward the improvement of teaching (Centra, 1976). The 1980s, especially in the years following the publication of *A Nation at Risk* (National Commission on Excellence in Education, 1983), generated intense and widespread involvement in the assessment of student learning outcomes. The 1990s opened with the publication of *Scholarship Reconsidered* (Boyer, 1990). Its recommendation for recognition of the scholarship of teaching has met with widespread interest, and it promises to make the 1990s a decade (or perhaps more) of emphasis on the recognition and reward of good teaching.

All of these approaches have made, and continue to make, important contributions to the improvement of teaching and learning. A major problem for each of the first three approaches, however, is that they cast people other than teachers as the "experts" in teaching and learning. This means that major efforts must go into making the knowledge from the various experts available and useful to those who can use the knowledge to improve practice, namely teachers and students. One can picture a chasm with teachers on one side and various campus resources for the improvement of teaching on the other. Bridge building across this chasm has been difficult.

In the 1960s, major efforts went into building bridges between research and its application by practitioners through R&D. Every large educational research center had on its staff specialists in development and dissemination whose task it was to convert the findings of research into practice. The envied solution was the extremely successful agriculture extension model, in which discoveries in the laboratories of the universities were taken to the farmers in the field by agriculture extension agents. Unfortunately, in education we have never come close to matching the success of agriculture in demonstrating the usefulness of research and delivering it for implementation to teachers (Cross, 1988b). "Practitioners seldom read the research literature," writes Elliot Eisner of Stanford. "Even when they do, this literature contains little that is not so qualified or so compromised by competing findings, rival hypotheses, or faulty design that the framework could scarcely be said to be supported in some reasonable way by research" (1984, p. 258). Research on learning makes some advances with each passing decade of investigation, but despite the best efforts of R&D, discipline-oriented faculty remain largely unaware of—and sometimes resistant to—applying pedagogical research to their teaching practices.

Faculty development offices, often directed and staffed by experts knowledgeable about teaching practices, continue their efforts to get faculty involved, to educate faculty to the latest findings of research, and to coordinate efforts for the improvement of instruction on campus, but many such offices exist precariously on the edge of budget cuts, and in the most prestigious universities, they are sometimes advised to "keep a low profile" and "not make waves," lest they alienate faculty. The credibility gap between the pedagogical knowledge of the faculty development specialists and the disciplinary knowledge of the faculty has proved hard to bridge. Yet faculty development specialists have access to a rich network of professional colleagues and resources that are valuable in joining the "wisdom of practice" (Shulman, 1987) to the knowledge of research.

There are, in all institutions of higher education, clusters of faculty intensely interested in teaching. Peer review of teaching and the analysis of case studies are examples of currently popular activities for faculty who are sincerely interested in making constructive contributions to the improvement of teaching, but these activities often proceed without any knowledge input from the specialists in educational research, faculty development, and assessment. Under these circumstances, the interested faculty retain credibility with their colleagues but paradoxically, for educators, reject academic knowledge about teaching in favor of employing experience as their base of knowledge about teaching and learning. Their assumption is that experience alone will improve teaching, if that experience is widely shared. Without a doubt, college teachers can learn a great deal about teaching through experience—their own as well as that of their colleagues. But it is our contention that these well-motivated faculty groups have much to gain from—and much to contribute to—building bridges to reach academic knowledge bases of teaching and learning.

Finally, the recent emphasis on assessment has made a major contribution by focusing on the quality of *learning* as the ultimate criterion of good teaching. Assessment, however, is frequently left to the "measurement experts," who duly collect reams of data and then file them in institutional offices to fulfill the requirements of governmental and accrediting agencies. It has been a major problem to get faculty involved in the assessment process and to complete the feedback loop that would enable teachers to use these data to improve student learning.

These lessons from the past have powerful implications for Classroom Research. Classroom Research *starts* with the faculty and students. Its purpose is to assist teachers to assess the quality of learning in the classroom and to provide feedback (assessment) to both their students and themselves, to conduct investigations into the nature of learning and to apply the results to teaching and learning (research and development), and to join with faculty colleagues in recognizing and improving teaching and learning throughout the campus (faculty development).

The premise of Classroom Research is that if faculty are encouraged to become active participants in the search for knowledge about teaching and learning, they will become interested in building bridges across the chasm that separates the practice of teaching from knowledge about assessment, research, and faculty development.

The remainder of this chapter defines Classroom Research further by describing its relationship to these other ongoing efforts to improve teaching and learning, concluding with a discussion of the relationship of Classroom Research to the present high interest in the scholarship of teaching.

Further Defining Classroom Research

It is, perhaps, important to state explicitly that Classroom Research is proposed as a supplement to and not as a replacement for any of the established approaches to the improvement of teaching and learning. It is derived from and indebted to work in assessment, research on teaching and learning, and faculty development, but it is critic as well as friend of these major efforts. As the character of Classroom Research continues to emerge and take shape, it is defined as much by its departure from established approaches to the improvement of instruction as it is by its heritage in them.

We shall begin with an analysis of the relationship of Classroom Research to assessment, because our development of Classroom Research really began with Classroom Assessment. Although our early work used the term Classroom Research as a generic term that included Classroom Assessment (Cross, 1986), we started with Classroom Assessment for pragmatic as well as logical reasons. The assessment movement was in full swing in the late 1980s, and people were eager to involve faculty more directly in the assessment efforts. Thus, it seemed practical to capitalize on the high interest in assessment by defining a form of assessment that was especially relevant to teaching faculty and for which we could devise some operational methods and instructions (Angelo and Cross, 1993; Cross and Angelo, 1988). Logically, it made sense to start with Classroom Assessment because it was more concrete and easier to define and illustrate than Classroom Research and because the methodology for Classroom Assessment could benefit from larger efforts to develop sophisticated assessment methods.

Although today the terms *Classroom Assessment* and *Classroom Research* are frequently used interchangeably, Classroom Assessment is the more limited concept. It is frequently a part of Classroom Research. Classroom Assessment usually addresses the "what" questions about classroom behaviors—*What* did students learn from the class discussion?—whereas Classroom Research is concerned with the "why" questions—*Why* did students respond as they did? Classroom Assessment describes what *is* happening; Classroom Research tries to find out *why*.

Relationship to the Assessment Movement

Classroom Assessment is intimately related to institutional assessment. It has its heritage in the fundamental notion that learning can and should be monitored and that feedback from assessment should lead to more effective instruction, with the ultimate goal of improved learning. But much of the distinctive character of Classroom Assessment lies in its departure from mainstream assessment.

Most people think of assessment as a *large-scale* testing program, conducted *periodically* at the *institutional or state level,* usually by measurement experts, to determine what students *have learned in college.* Classroom Assessment questions almost every working word in that image. Its contrasting definition is this: Classroom Assessment consists of *small-scale* assessments conducted *continually* in college *classrooms* by discipline-based *teachers* to determine what students *are learning in that class.*

The advantage of thinking small in assessment is that if the ultimate purpose of assessment is to improve teaching and learning, then the results of successful assessment must eventually bear directly on the actions of teachers in their classrooms. This means that the feedback from assessment must reach classroom teachers and be perceived by them as relevant to the way they do their jobs. Because classroom assessment was born partly in support of and partly in protest against what assessment was becoming, it is helpful to look at the characteristics and promise of its parent assessment movement, which swept the nation with remarkable speed and breadth considering the number of people affected and the decision-making mechanisms involved.

In the beginning of the assessment movement, much attention was given to the demonstration of the accountability of educational institutions to the society that supported them. Assessment-for-accountability is illustrated in this remark of Missouri governor John Ashcroft in his role as chair of the Governors' Task Force on College Quality: "The public has the right to know what it is getting for its expenditure of tax resources; the public has a right to know and understand the quality of undergraduate education that young people receive from publicly funded colleges and universities" (National Governors' Association, 1986, p. 154).

As the assessment movement matured, attention turned more heavily to the uses of assessment to improve the quality of education. The assessment-for-improvement perspective was expressed by William Turnbull, late president of Educational Testing Service, when he wrote, "The overriding purpose of gathering [assessment] data is to provide a basis for improving instruction, rather than keeping score or allocating blame" (Turnbull, 1985, p. 25).

Although ultimately the purpose of both kinds of assessment is to improve education, the most important distinction between assessment-for-accountability and assessment-for-improvement lies in what is done with the results of the assessment. Those who, by virtue of their positions, are interested in accountability usually have indirect responsibilities for teaching and learning. They are usually not on the campus or in the classroom and must use assessment results in whatever ways they can to influence the behavior of those who are in a position to affect teaching and learning directly. The further removed one is from the scene of the action in teaching and learning, the more one is dependent on manipulating reward and punishment to bring about desired ends. Thus, motivation for improved teaching in accountability models usually takes the form of extrinsic rewards: increased funding for institutions; larger budgets or more positions for departments demonstrating accountability; promotion, tenure, or a "teacher of the year" award for good teachers; and usually, lack of reward (rather than punishment) for poor teachers.

Conversely, in assessment-for-improvement models, the results of the assessment go directly to those who can, through their own efforts, make the improvements indicated. For example, departments may collect data to show how their graduates perform on tests for graduate and professional schools, and they may directly change the curriculum when indicated. Classroom teachers are directly involved in instruction; through their *own* actions, they can change the quality of teaching and learning in the classroom. Reward systems in this model are usually intrinsic: teacher satisfaction in seeing students learn, stimulation of intellectual curiosity about the learning process, and increased professional knowledge and self-esteem.

The importance of the *feedback loop,* of getting the results of the assessment to those who can do something about it, can be illustrated through an analogy to learning archery. Imagine a group of people learning archery in a darkened room, where both the target and the feedback on hitting it are invisible. The learners might be provided with the best and most sophisticated equipment that money can buy; have one-on-one coaching from an expert who demonstrates effectively how to hold the bow, get the right tension in the string, and place the arrow; and have access to study materials on the dynamics of flight and the arc of the trajectory. Despite all this input, it is pretty clear that they are not going to improve their performance until they get some feedback on whether they are hitting the target. Herein lies the enormous contribution of the assessment movement. Targets are identified and the results of hitting them fed back continually to the archers.

Those of us in education do not pay a lot of attention right now to giving students feedback on their progress as learners. Almost all students get grades that tell them how they have done relative to their classmates, but that sort of information is not useful feedback on their progress as learners, nor does it help them develop the skills they need for self-assessment as lifelong learners. The assessment-for-accountability models do not address these learning issues either. The situation now in many institutional assessment programs is akin to turning on the lights in the target practice room after the students have left and reporting on the total number of hits to whoever is paying for the archery lessons. Turning on the lights after practice—as is beginning to be done with some to the educational outcomes assessments—is probably better than being left permanently in the dark. When the lights go on, the institution, at least, gets feedback on how well students did. The problem is that there is no useful information about what caused good or poor performance because the lights were off during practice. We might carry this analogy further to point out that if research showed that even a dim light in the room improved scores dramatically, then the message would be clear: it would tell institutions that they should turn on the lights during practice so students and teachers, not just institutions, can see what they are doing.

Although some faculty members are currently involved in designing or approving institutional assessment programs, they are acting as representatives of the collective faculty, which is a different role from assessing their own effectiveness as teachers. It is assumed in most forms of institutional assessment that if college teachers as a group are made aware that students lack knowledge or skills in areas considered important, the collective faculty will then take steps to correct the deficiency—usually through changing the curriculum or increasing requirements. The changes made are frequently *additions* of courses or requirements, leaving the impression that education is additive, that is that more requirements equal more learning. Virtually ignored is the fact that much of what is taught is not learned.

If teachers could reduce the gap between teaching and learning, they could not only increase the productivity of the present workforce but could also begin to visualize learning as transformational rather than merely additive. Learning, correctly understood, consists of new learning transforming what already exists in the minds of learners, leading them to deeper understandings and appreciations. In this view, learning is more than the accumulation and storage of knowledge; it is dynamic and interactive, constantly changing and evolving. Classroom Assessment operates on the premise that learning is constantly in process and that assessments must be conducted frequently and the results made available immediately to both students and teachers so that any necessary changes can be made while there is time to benefit from them.

In summary, Classroom Assessment has its roots in the assessment movement. Its assessment parentage is clearly visible in its search for valid measures of students' learning and in its systematic monitoring of progress. To its credit, assessment has come a long way from a decade ago when accountability models launched the movement. The departure of Classroom Assessment from that assessment heritage is most apparent in the changed locale of the power to directly influence the quality of teaching and learning. Whereas in accountability models the power usually resides in the experts who design the assessment and in the legislators and administrators who reward the performance, Classroom Assessment empowers teachers to design assessments that are meaningful to them and that can be used to improve their own teaching. Once again, the rewards of Classroom Assessment are more intrinsic than extrinsic.

Relationship to Traditional Educational Research

In much the same way that Classroom Assessment both parallels and diverges from the direction of the assessment movement, so Classroom Research is both allied with and critical of traditional educational research. It shares with educational research the broad goal of improving education through the systematic study of teaching and learning. But it questions the heavy dependence on the current "scientific method" as the only or most valid approach to knowledge. We believe that the experience and insights of teachers, their knowledge of the subject matter they are trying to teach, their continuing association with students in the process of learning, and their opportunities to observe both the struggles and triumphs of learning are just as important as the "scientific objectivity" of external researchers seeking generalizable knowledge about learning.

Research in the social sciences is undergoing slow but obvious change, generally away from the rigidities of scientism. (*Scientism* is defined in *Webster's New World Dictionary*, Third College Edition, as "the principle that scientific methods can and should be applied in all fields of investigation.") Educational research has many faces, and at this time, the research community is vigorously debating future directions for educational research and evaluation and their potential for improving education (Eisner, 1984; Guba, 1979; Keller, 1985; Lincoln, 1989; Mishler, 1979; Reichardt and Rallis, 1994). The meaning of Classroom Research can be further defined by tracing briefly the issues under discussion in traditional research and the position of Classroom Research with respect to each. Let us look first at the criticisms of educational research within the social science research community.

The "scientific method" is under attack primarily on the grounds that it has become a "virtual orthodoxy—*the* way of getting at the truth" (Guba, 1979, p. 268). Even though the assumptions of scientism have worked remarkably well in the natural and physical sciences, their application to inquiry in the social sciences remains problematic. The points of contention fall into two major categories: (1) The nature of the *questions* to be investigated and (2) the research *methods* to be used. Both these seemingly concrete issues, however, are embedded in larger philosophical or epistemological debates over positivism versus any number of emerging isms, including feminism, constructivism, and functionalism. Because today's literature consists largely of attacks on positivism, we shall attempt to present briefly the essence of the arguments for change launched by the critics of traditional research.

Yvonna Lincoln (1989), one of the outspoken critics of traditional research, has analyzed some of the criticisms of logical positivism as a basis for research in the social sciences, categorizing the criticisms into issues of "debate." Because it is important for Classroom Researchers to understand these criticisms in order to gain maximum benefits from their research, we shall review briefly those aspects of Lincoln's critique that have specific implications for Classroom Research.

- *The Exception Debate.* This is the term Lincoln uses to describe a cluster of criticisms directed at specific axioms of scientific inquiry. Positivism in science, for example, assumes that "truth" is "out there" and will be discovered as scientific investigation converges on that single reality. But generalizations about "truth" in human behavior are so problematic that a widely respected research scholar has suggested that in this field, it would be preferable to abandon the search for general truths in favor of "working hypotheses," to be tested in each new context (Cronbach, 1975).

  Classroom Research is based on the premise that generalizations across classrooms are, at best, tentative hypotheses, to be tested within the specific context of a given classroom. Experienced teachers know that even when the same teacher teaches the same subject in the same classroom at the same hour of the day, the learning environment, or context, can differ greatly from one semester to the next. Classroom Researchers will ultimately build a base of knowledge about what works for them in their discipline with their students. A Classroom Research project is not a one-shot effort that is completed, published, and assumed to contribute one more brick to building the wall of truth. Rather, Classroom Research projects can be described as continual and cascading, the conclusion from one project suggesting the beginning of another.

- *The Exclusion Debate.* The conventional paradigm for science research is considered by many to represent a majority, male, and elitist view. Indeed, many of the descriptive terms most often applied to science and "scientific" research are also considered descriptive of males—objective, analytical, cool, and impersonal—as opposed to characteristics more often considered descriptive of females—sensitive, warm, caring, and personal. It is thus not surprising that the most vigorous criticisms with respect to the exclusion debate have come from feminist scholars—although people of color and other excluded populations have joined in the criticism that science is mobilized to defend the status quo by excluding researchers without the accepted training.

  Until a few years ago, research on college students was conducted largely by middle-class white male researchers studying middle-class white male students, and according to critics, resulted in conclusions that are sexist, biased, misleading, and unreliable (Lincoln, 1989; Namenwirth, 1986; Stage 1990). Women researchers, such as Gilligan (1982) and Belenky, Clinchy, Goldberger, and Tarule (1986) have demonstrated through their own research, that the male norm is not necessarily the human norm. Similarly, ethnic researchers and gerontologists have shown wide cultural departures from the norms of young white middle-class males. Because the student population today is diverse in almost every respect, and students who are not young, white, male, or middle-class are not only frequently found in college classrooms but often make up the majority in those classrooms—it is clear that Classroom Research cannot accept a science that excludes any aspect of student diversity.

Even more important to the concept of Classroom Research, however, is the axiom that research on teaching and learning in the classroom cannot exclude those who are most involved and most affected, namely teachers and students. Ironically, traditional educational researchers often reject teachers and students as investigators (on the grounds that they lack technical research skills and "objectivity") while these same researchers are struggling to gain teachers' and students' cooperation as subjects for research. Moreover, the subordination implied in the expert-subject relationship is not completely alleviated by placing teachers and students on "advisory" committees to inform the experts about investigations that would improve practice. Thus, Classroom Researchers support the argument that exclusion exists. Indeed, a science predicated on bringing into the classroom an outside expert to study what teachers and students know best is both exclusionary and inadequate. We do not intend to imply that educational research should not be done in and on classrooms. We do believe, however, that reliance on "scientific" research as the "best" or "most legitimate" source of knowledge about teaching and learning has failed to demonstrate its usefulness.

The major tenet of Classroom Research is that college teachers are capable of doing their own research on the questions that interest them. Classroom Research capitalizes on the talents and competencies that teachers bring to the systematic study of teaching and learning: knowledge of the subject matter, experience in teaching it to others, and an interest in gaining a greater understanding of how students in their classrooms learn what teachers are trying to teach.

- *The Whole Paradigm Debate.* One of the most basic axioms of traditional research is that science can get at an understanding of the whole through studying the parts individually. The common practice of "controlling" some variables while studying others or, in statistical studies, of "holding constant" some variables while abstracting others out for intense study is coming under increasing criticism in a variety of disciplines. The penchant for "context stripping," which is a "key feature of our standard methods of experimental design, measurement, and statistical analysis," says Mishler (1979, p. 2), "treats context as though it were the enemy of understanding rather than the resource for understanding."

  Classroom Research welcomes the context of the classroom in all its complexity as a resource for understanding. Certain types of learning can be isolated for study in the laboratory, but teaching never can be. Teaching is necessarily interactive; it requires a teacher, a learner, and a context.

  Because interaction is *the* important characteristic in the learning environment of the classroom, a science that in the interest of rigor and neatness, attempts to separate this variable from its environment, is at best inadequate and most likely misleading. Classroom Research is interested in the interaction between teachers and learners in the context of their natural environment.

- *The Impoverished Debate.* A major criticism of traditional research based in a logical positivist framework is that its emphasis on quantitative methods is impoverished. The inclusion of qualitative methods, it is argued, would add richness, texture, and greater depth of understanding to investigations. Because it is hard to refute the reasonableness of this argument, we would like to think that the impoverishment debate is now moot. However, as the continuing debates over methods suggest (and is shown later in this chapter), the issue remains alive—at least among career researchers, who tend to develop high levels of expertise in either quantitative or qualitative methods, and who therefore have a vested interest in their use.

The indications that the debate between the "quants" and the "quals" (Rossi, 1994) is still alive and vigorous are revealed in Reichardt and Rallis's *The Qualitative-Quantitative Debate: New Perspectives* (1994). Their introduction comments that "the origins" of their book "can be found in the long-standing antagonism between qualitative and quantitative researchers in evaluation. This antagonism was part of the reason that the field of evaluation gave birth in the 1970s to two separate professional organizations: the Evaluation Network (ENet) and the Evaluation Research Society (ERS). When ENet and ERS decided to merge to form the American Evaluation Association (AEA) in the mid-1980s, the antagonism did not disappear, it was merely suppressed" (p. 1).

These suppressed hostilities surfaced in three successive conventions of the American Evaluation Association in the early 1990s (Fetterman, 1992; Lincoln, 1991; Sechrest, 1992), adding fuel to the charge that academic social scientists have devoted too much attention to methods and not enough to the formulation of meaningful questions for investigation. But that is not a new charge. "Historically," writes House, "methodology has been greatly overemphasized at the expense of content" (1994, p. 14). This was especially true in the heyday of behaviorist psychology, leading Chomsky to call behaviorism "a methodology without a subject matter" (1977, p. 46).

The problem of maintaining a constructive balance between methods and questions for study is captured by Donald Schön in his description of the dilemma of "rigor versus relevance."

> In the varied topography of professional practice, there is a high, hard ground where practitioners can make effective use of research-based theory and technique, and there is a swampy lowland where situations are confusing "messes" incapable of technical solution. The difficulty is that the problems of the high ground, however great their technical interest, are often relatively unimportant to clients or to the larger society, while in the swamp are the problems of greatest human concern. Shall the practitioner stay on the high, hard ground where he can practice rigorously, as he understands rigor, but where he is constrained to deal with problems of relatively little social importance? Or shall he descend to the swamp where he can engage the most important and challenging problems if he is willing to forsake technical rigor?
>
> There are those who choose the swampy lowlands. They deliberately involve themselves in messy but crucially important problems and, when asked to describe their methods of inquiry, they speak of experience, trial and error, intuition, and muddling through [1983, p. 42].

Classroom Research is not completely comfortable with either the "high, hard ground" of rigorous methods or the "swampy lowlands" of practical relevance. Classroom Researchers are most interested in building a bridge across the swamp, not necessarily to the high ground of rigorous methodology but at least to more solid ground, where teaching is subject to systematic investigation. Forced to choose, however, Classroom Research would opt for relevance over rigor, for two reasons.

First, if the question for study is not highly relevant to the real-life needs of the Classroom Researcher, then there is no point at all in doing the study. The purpose of Classroom Research is more to enhance the understanding of the researcher than to report findings to the research community.

Second, Classroom Researchers are, by definition, not methodologists with technical research competence in the social sciences. Their great strength as researchers lies in their understanding of the classroom context, their closeness to the learning problems, their experience in the practical realities of teaching, and their knowledge of the subject matter being taught. More often than not, Classroom Researchers will opt for careful observation, interviews with students, and understanding in the swamps of the natural environment over working on the high hard ground of experimental and statistical methods.

However much we might wish for a resolution to the "paradigm wars" (Lincoln, 1989), the conflict has a long history and, to many, a competitive present. Rossi, a self-identified quant, says, "In my home base discipline, sociology, the struggle between the quants and the quals is alive and well today, but it has been alive and well since sociology first turned away from being an armchair discipline and started to undertake empirical investigations" (1994, p. 24). Rossi argues that the quals and the quants have usefully different functions in today's evaluation programs. Large-scale well-funded projects using quantitative methods are generally feasible only for large research firms (dominated today by economists, significantly) and are most useful to policy makers, whereas small local projects dominated by people with "extensive practical and theoretical knowledge, further illuminated by a rich and intimate knowledge of the program in question and its ecology" (p. 32) are more appropriate for stakeholders. Although it is conceivable that Classroom Research might have some implications for policy makers somewhere in the future, it is specifically designed for stakeholders. Faculty and students are stakeholders in the academic enterprise.

One practical objection to the standard statistical methods employed by the quants is that they are most useful with large samples—fine for lecture classes numbering in the hundreds but of dubious value in the typical classroom of twenty to forty students. More serious, however, is that statistical analysis is based in probability theory. The question in statistical analysis is, What is the *probability* that the findings differ from chance? Although that is a useful question for policy makers, it is not an appropriate question for classroom teachers who are interested not only in how the majority confirm a hypotheses but also in why individual learners may depart from it. Indeed, understanding the exceptions in the classroom may tell teachers far more about the learning process than understanding the majority; teachers must be just as concerned with the 30 precent who do not change "significantly" as with the 70 percent who do. Classroom Researchers are not looking for a law of human behavior, an if-then formula to tell them that *if* they teach in a certain way, *then* a certain kind of learning will occur—or even that such learning will occur predictably in 62 percent of the students. Classroom Researchers are primarily interested in gaining the insights and understandings that will strengthen their base of professional knowledge about teaching. They want to know *what* works, of course, but they are even more interested in knowing *why* it works. They want to understand learning as a process, and they consider insights as important as findings.

It is extremely important that Classroom Researchers use the methods that will address their questions. They need make no apology for their lack of advanced study in methodology—either quantitative or qualitative. The tide is turning now to greater concern about the relevance of the research, and it would be hard to find researchers who are more relevant to the issues of teaching and learning than teachers and students. The strengths they bring to classroom investigations are different from, but at least as important as, academic methodological sophistication.

Classroom Research makes a point of encouraging a wide variety of research measures—quantitative, qualitative, or performance—whatever measure serves up information about what the teacher wants to know. Indeed, Classroom Researchers are encouraged to place no arbitrary restrictions on data collection and even to invent their own methods. Classroom Assessment Techniques (CATs) for example, are common sources of data for Classroom Researchers, and they come in a wide variety of forms: quantitative, qualitative, and performance measures and what might be called modest pedagogical experiments. Because the results of Classroom Research are frequently tentative and suggestive of further experimentation and development, data may consist of almost any sort of information that adds to a teacher's understanding of teaching and learning.

Again, although we have been critical of the current heavy emphasis on traditional research to ferret out the complexities of teaching and learning, our argument is not for the abolition or even diminution of traditional educational research. Rather, it is for the legitimate addition of Classroom Research. In the present academic climate, because Classroom Researchers are not well grounded in current methods of research, their efforts are still not considered quite legitimate. Classroom Research faces the same uphill battle that qualitative researchers faced ten years ago—and in many places still face.

Our argument is that Classroom Researchers bring to the study of teaching and learning in the classroom some particularly valuable talents and opportunities that educational researchers do not have—just as traditional researchers bring to their investigations background, experience, and training that classroom teachers do not have. We need both, and each should enrich the other. The more Classroom Researchers learn about the practical questions that interest them, the more appreciative and interested they will be in the knowledge of educational researchers. Likewise, the more educational researchers can learn about Classroom Research, the more specifics from that research will enrich their own investigations.

Relationship to Faculty Development

Classroom Research is an important form of faculty development. Its purpose, consistent with the broad purposes of faculty development, is to engage faculty in a program of continual learning about how to improve their own teaching. The assumption behind Classroom Research is that as teachers become involved in systematically inquiring into the impact of their teaching on students' learning, they will raise questions about their own teaching and seek further knowledge about it. Thus, Classroom Research serves as a motivator for faculty to take advantage of faculty development programs and to contribute to them.

As is the case with traditional assessment and research, Classroom Research is consistent with but different from traditional emphases in faculty development. Differences are most likely to take place over the actual program of activities and, most importantly, in the focus of attention. The direct goal of faculty development is to improve the performance of *teachers* by inculcating teaching skills and techniques, increasing the self-confidence and performance of teachers, and creating a supportive institutional climate that recognizes good teaching and is conducive to its growth. Classroom Research is also interested in effective teaching, but the attention of Classroom Research is on *students* rather than on teachers. The premise is that it makes no difference how perfectly a teacher is teaching if students are not responding in their learning.

Thus, the two stances are quite different. Faculty development starts with the fundamental assumption that through orientation, workshops, and the like, faculty can learn how to lecture, lead discussions, construct tests, assign grades, and use such varied techniques of teaching as collaborative learning, case studies, role-playing, and most recently, techniques employing technology and computers. (See the chapter headings in such popular books as McKeachie's ninth revision of *Teaching Tips*, 1994, and Davis's new *Tools for Teaching*, 1993, for example). There is no denying that these are important teaching functions or that most faculty have had little or no exposure to them in graduate school. Thus, traditional faculty development programs are, without doubt, making an important contribution to the improvement of teaching. How much they contribute to the improvement of learning is an open question, but one that can be addressed by educational researchers as well as Classroom Researchers.

There are two major arguments for including Classroom Research in faculty development. One addresses the psychological advantage of focusing on student rather than faculty performance. A major hurdle for any faculty development program to overcome is the faculty perception that there is something wrong with the teaching of those who participate in faculty development—or worse yet in some cases, that an interest in improving teaching may mean that the faculty member is on the slow track in research. It is far easier in most faculty cultures to admit an interest in scholarly inquiry about student learning than is to profess an interest in or a need for improving one's own teaching.

The second reason for suggesting that faculty development programs might be enhanced by the addition of Classroom Research is based in motivational and learning theory. Teachers, like students, need to be active learners in order to remain motivated. Just as one-shot lectures to students may have little impact on their behavior, so a one-shot program on how to lead a discussion may have little impact on teaching practices. A profession, by definition, requires lifelong learning. If teachers are to remain motivated to learn how to teach, they need to be actively involved in formulating questions about how to teach and seeking the answers; they need continual feedback on how well they are doing; they need the support and encouragement of their colleagues. In short, learning for teachers has the same requirements that it has for students. Teachers are—or should be—lifelong students of the teaching-learning connection.

It is instructive to look at the concept of teaching as lifelong learning through the lens of the well-known seven principles for good practice in undergraduate education (Chickering and Gamson, 1991). The seven principles were devised by a task force of scholars and researchers brought together in July 1986 by Zelda Gamson and Arthur Chickering to identify the key principles of learning derived from decades of research on undergraduate learning. Those key principles have been widely distributed (150,000 copies ordered in the first eighteen months!) and are perhaps the most succinct, comprehensive, and respected research-based conclusions about learning to be widely distributed to discipline-oriented college teachers. Although the principles were derived from research on undergraduate learning, they are far broader than that, incorporating information about cognition and motivation that is useful with any age group. With only occasional paraphrasing, the seven principles can be applied to teachers as lifelong learners and can serve as a rationale for Classroom Research as a productive learning experience for both teachers and students.

1. **Good Practice Encourages Student-Faculty Contact**. A substantial body of research has concluded that students showing the greatest gains in intellectual commitment, personal development, and motivation report high contact with faculty in and out of class

(Sorcinelli, 1991). The same appears to be true for faculty in their contacts with students. Wilson and his colleagues (Wilson and others, 1975), in a four-year research project involving eight institutions, found that teachers nominated by students and colleagues as especially effective teachers reported more interaction with students than those less frequently nominated.

Students, over some twelve years of schooling, have developed some well-honed practices for hiding their confusion or lack of knowledge from teachers. Teachers who rely on body language or eye contact are often greatly surprised when they ask students for their reactions. The more a teacher can gain understanding of and show interest in students' learning, the more both teacher and students are likely to gain from contact.

Significantly, one of Classroom Assessment's best-known and most frequently used CATs, the Minute Paper, came from a study of effective teachers on the Berkeley campus of the University of California (Wilson, 1986). When researchers interviewed teachers to find out what teachers *did* that resulted in an exceptional number of student nominations for effective teaching, one physics teacher described the way he asked students to take a few minutes at the end of the class session to write anonymously what they had learned from that day's lesson. (See Angelo and Cross, 1993, pp. 148-153 for a more complete description of the Minute Paper.) Students had rated him especially high on "knowing how well students are understanding," and he suspected that at least part of the reason was his use of the Minute Paper. It is reasonable to suspect that he probably *did* know better than most teachers how well students were understanding but also that students were aware of his concern about their learning.

Interpersonal rapport shows up on virtually every list of the characteristics of effective teachers (Cross, 1988a; Feldman, 1994), and Lowman (1984) has reduced the characteristics of good teaching to two essential dimensions—"intellectual excitement" and "interpersonal rapport," the latter of which includes sensitivity to how students feel about the material and its presentation. He claims that outstanding teachers excel in one of these two dimensions and are at least competent in the other.

Aside from the evidence that appears with some consistency in research on effective teaching, it does not take much stretch of the imagination to conclude that student-faculty contact increases the understanding about learning and its progress on the part of both teachers and students. Thus, the first of the seven principles of good practice applies to the learning of teachers as well as students. One way for a teacher to learn how to teach effectively—and to continue to do so throughout the years of teaching and changing student populations—is to learn to know students, and especially to monitor their progress in learning.

2. **Good Practice Encourages Cooperation Among Students—and Colleagues.** There is a great deal of emphasis today on the importance of encouraging faculty to work with faculty on the improvement of instruction. Hutchings notes that "there's a growing recognition that what's really needed to improve teaching is a campus culture in which good practice can thrive, one where faculty talk together about teaching, inquire into its effects, and take collective responsibility for its quality" (1993, p. v). For college faculty, much of the credibility of teaching improvement programs lies in faculty members' faith in the knowledge and experience of their peers. Faculty development offices today are encouraging faculty initiative, "ownership," and responsibility for cooperative endeavors. Maryellen Weimer advises that college faculty members must be put in charge of their own improvement because "better teaching cannot be done by one party to another. . . . It is the teacher alone who changes the teaching" (1990, p. 25).

Empirical research on student-centered methods supports the contention that working together on learning (and learning how to teach) has clear advantages. In their extensive review of research on instructional methods, McKeachie, Pintrich, Lin, and Smith concluded that, "the best answer to the question, 'What is the most effective method of teaching?,' is that it depends on the goal, the student, the content, and the teacher. But the next best answer is, 'Students teaching other students' " (1986, p. 63). And so it would seem with faculty. Increasingly, there is good information about human learning being supplied by researchers and scholars in education and psychology, but the research suggests that when it comes to motivation, concept development, and application, peer learning has most of the advantages (McKeachie, Pintrich, Lin, and Smith, 1986, p. 68).

One of the most important—and surprising—conclusions of our experiences in working with faculty members on Classroom Assessments and Classroom Research is that these activities are highly social. Initially, we had thought that one of the advantages of Classroom Research was that it could be done independently, without participating in endless committee meetings or seeking anyone's blessing or approval. And it can be. As it turns out, however, once teachers begin to observe and study the effectiveness of their own teaching, they have a strong desire to share their findings and questions with others (Angelo and Cross, 1993). Thus, the colleges where Classroom Research has made the strongest inroads as part of the faculty culture are places where faculty regularly come together to share experiences and learn from one another.

3. **Good Practice Encourages Active Learning.** Perhaps no principle of learning has received more attention in recent years than this one. The Study Group on the Conditions of Excellence in American Higher Education selected active involvement in learning as one of their three "critical conditions for excellence" in the quality of undergraduate education. The study group contends that "there is now a good deal of research evidence to suggest that the more time and effort students invest in the learning process and the more intensely they engage in their own education, the greater will be their growth and achievement, their satisfaction with their educational experiences, and their persistence in college, and the more likely they are to continue their learning" (1984, p. 17).

   Clearly, if teachers are to experience satisfaction and achievement in their teaching, they must be actively engaged in learning all they can about the impact of their teaching on students' learning. Classroom Research requires active involvement in learning about teaching. Teachers must not only raise their own questions about their teaching but then they must devise appropriate ways of investigating those questions. Researchers on cognition today recognize this model of self-initiated inquiry as one of the most effective for learning.

4. **Good Practice Gives Prompt Feedback.** The importance of prompt feedback ranks right up there with active involvement as a basic and fundamental requirement for learning. Like active involvement, it has been given major attention in recent years and is the very foundation of the assessment movement in education. The authors of the influential reform report *Involvement in Learning* (Study Group on the Conditions of Excellence in American Higher Education, 1984) write that "the use of assessment information to redirect effort is an essential ingredient in effective learning and serves as a powerful lever for involvement. This is true whether the learner is a student, a faculty member monitoring the progress of students, or an administrator seeking to identify the educational strengths and weaknesses of a college and its academic programs" (p. 21).

   Providing prompt and regular feedback is certainly an important if not the most important function of Classroom Assessment. Teachers need feedback on their teaching as much as students need feedback on their learning. Good teachers spend a lot of time grading papers, making comments, redirecting efforts, and in general providing feedback on student progress. But teachers themselves, often working behind closed doors, rarely get any feedback on their teaching other than student ratings of teaching, which usually appear only after the semester has ended, when both students and teachers have forgotten the specifics and teachers have little motivation to incorporate suggestions for improvement into their lesson plans.

   Research on the usefulness of student ratings to improve teaching has so far been disappointing—although in a study at the nine campuses of the University of California, 78 percent of the faculty reported making changes in their teaching based on student evaluations (Outcalt, 1980). Centra, in reviewing the research on actual change as a result of student evaluations, terms the impact "modest" (1993, p. 10). But most student ratings of instruction are designed and used more for summative evaluation (making judgments) than for formative evaluation (making improvements). Faculty have little control over these rating instruments, and Centra (1993) and Weimer (1990) are in staunch agreement that unless the faculty member values the feedback and it has high credibility for him or her, it will most likely have little effect.

Classroom Research preserves the feedback so important to learning, but it leaves the design and control of the method of getting that feedback in the hands of faculty, thereby preserving value and credibility. Critics see this as a problem for Classroom Research, saying that poor teachers can fool themselves by asking only for feedback that they believe will be positive. Our experience, however, suggests that teachers are somewhat more likely to ask for feedback on their weaknesses than on their strengths. As Centra reminds us, "Whatever the source, the evaluation must be a balance between challenge and support or it will be perceived as a threat and provoke the same anxious and self-defeating reaction" (1993, p. 10). And even if a defensive teacher designs Classroom Assessment and Classroom Research projects that give an overly positive view of his or her teaching, that may not be all bad for teachers with few bright spots in their teaching day. With a boost to the teachers' self-confidence, they may be encouraged to investigate other aspects of their teaching. Nevertheless, as suggested in principle 2, colleagues can be extremely helpful in preventing isolation and helping one another develop a realistic and constructive approach to getting and using feedback.

The major function of Classroom Assessment and Classroom Research is to give feedback about students' learning. The purpose of Classroom Assessment, in particular, is to monitor student learning throughout the semester and to provide information to both teacher and students while there is still time to take corrective action.

5. **Good Practice Emphasizes Time on Task.** Although much of the writing on this principle is laden with the educational jargon of "time on task" and "academic learning time" (ALT) (Berliner, 1984), it should come as no surprise that research concludes that the more time students spend actively engaged in the learning task, the more they learn. Students recognize this; there are "consistently significant correlations between the effective use of class time and overall ratings of course, instructor, and amount learned" (Sorcinelli, 1991, p. 20). We do not know of any research that has attempted to relate time spent on teaching with amount or quality of student learning. But it takes no great leap of faith to conclude that time spent productively on the task of teaching results in better use of class time.

   Research by Steadman (1994) found that one of the major problems for teachers using Classroom Assessment was the amount of time required. This sets up a conflict for teachers. Is it better to spend time on learning content or to assess how effectively learning time is spent? To the extent that time is taken from learning content to collect information from students on their learning progress, one could argue that doing Classroom Assessment and Classroom Research is not consistent with the good practice of emphasizing time on task. However, that argument assumes that class time is maximally effective and that if the teacher and students were not taking time to monitor learning students would be using that time to actively engage in the task of learning itself. Research shows, however, that teachers are not very good judges of their own effectiveness, and they are quite likely to overestimate how much students learn. In one study, teachers thought students would know 75 percent of the items on a final exam, when in fact they knew only 58 percent (Fox and LeCount, 1991). Thus, the counterargument is that time spent in Classroom Assessment checks the assumption of maximal effectiveness of the teaching and the learning. Research on cognition shows that monitoring learning makes an important contribution to learning; therefore, Classroom Assessment also contributes to the lifelong learning skills of students in monitoring their own learning.

6. **Good Practice Communicates High Expectations.** Research documents the wisdom that teachers get from students about what they expect. Teachers who expect high performance will usually get it and, in the process, win the respect of their students. "The literature consistently shows, contrary to faculty belief, that students give higher ratings to difficult

courses in which they have to work hard" (Sorcinelli, 1991, p. 21). Research on cognition and motivation, however, suggests that there is an optimal level of expectation; if expectations are set too low, students will do less than they are capable of; if expectations are too high, students will engage in any number of counterproductive ego-protective devices (Corno and Mandinach, 1983; Covington and Berry, 1976).

Classroom Research and Classroom Assessment communicate high expectations in the sense that they assume that both teachers and students take the business of education seriously and are mature enough to want performance feedback with implications for improvement. The trend today in teacher evaluation is to expect teachers to collect information about their teaching, preferably along with reflections about their teaching (Edgerton, Hutchings, and Quinlan, 1991). We have questioned the use of Classroom Assessment and Classroom Research data in portfolios that are to be used for making decisions about promotion and tenure, on the grounds that Classroom Research might be distorted, in both design and interpretation, to show only favorable results. However, the fact that a teacher is designing and using Classroom Assessment and Classroom Research for his or her own improvement might be quite relevant to high self-expectations and self-improvement. Thus, a teaching portfolio might well include information about how a teacher was engaging in the lifelong development of his or her teaching effectiveness.

7. **Good Practice Respects Diverse Talents and Ways of Learning—and Teaching.** Just as students have different talents and learning styles, so teachers have diverse talents and styles of teaching. Although research on learning has been rather negative about lecturing as a style of teaching, this does not mean that a brilliant and inspiring lecturer cannot engage the minds of students in active learning or that the talented lecturer should revert to discussion groups. Just as a teacher should respect diverse talents and ways of learning, so institutions should respect and reward diverse talents and ways of teaching.

   The contributing of Classroom Assessment and Classroom Research to respecting diverse teaching talents is that the assessment and research methods are highly diverse and flexible. Teachers across a wide array of disciplines may select from a large number of designs already available (for example, the fifty Classroom Assessment Techniques in Angelo and Cross, 1993) or may invent personal assessments and research studies to provide the kind of information most useful to their own style and talents. The rationale for Classroom Research is that it must be personally designed by the teacher in order to address the questions relevant to that teacher.

Relationship to the Scholarship of Teaching

As mentioned at the beginning of this chapter, The Carnegie Foundation for the Advancement of Teaching has launched what appears to be a very promising nationwide movement to combat the overemphasis on disciplinary research as the singular form of scholarship in academe. Ernest Boyer (1990) calls for the recognition of four separate but overlapping functions of scholarship—the scholarship of discovery, the scholarship of integration, the scholarship of application, and the scholarship of teaching.

The Carnegie proposals are widely interpreted to mean that teaching should be recognized as one of the four forms of scholarship. We heartily endorse the Carnegie proposals to recognize more varied forms of scholarship, but we also believe that teaching itself, if it is to be a real profession, should involve *all four* forms of scholarship.

"The scholarship of *discovery*, at its best," says the Carnegie report, "contributes not only to the stock of human knowledge but also to the intellectual climate of a college or university. . . . The advancement of knowledge can generate an almost palpable excitement in the life of an educational institution" (p. 17). There should also be a palpable excitement in the life of a teaching institution. Should not all teachers and students be engaged daily in the excitement of discovery about how people learn? We are not talking here about casual discovery or the occasional but welcome "aha" experience, Classroom Research involves systematic and scholarly inquiry into the nature of learning—specifically into the nature of learning English, or math, or psychology, or any other subject in which faculty have become lifelong learners. Dedicated college teachers have much to gain—and much to contribute—to the advancement of teaching as a profession through the scholarship of discovery in teaching and learning. Teachers employ the scholarship of discovery when they use Classroom Research to inquire about the learning taking place in their own classrooms and their own disciplines.

The scholarship of *integration*, according to the Carnegie definitions, involves making connections across disciplines and making interpretations that fit research into larger intellectual patterns. The very purpose of a liberal education, say Pascarella and Terenzini, is "to foster the integration and synthesis of knowledge rather than learning discrete bits of information" (1991, p. 136). Richard Light, director of the Harvard Assessment Seminars, writes in his first report that early on in the seminars, he asked faculty members that what single change would most improve their current teaching. "Two ideas swamped all others," says Light. "One is the importance of enhancing students' awareness of 'the big picture,' the 'big point of it all,' and not just the details of a particular topic. The second is the importance of helpful and regular feedback from students so a professor can make mid-course corrections" (1990, p. 35). Classroom Research can respond to both of these expressed needs of college teachers. Regular feedback from students to teachers is, of course, the linchpin of Classroom Assessment, and Classroom Research, at its best, is integrative scholarship in the sense that it studies learning as it occurs in students—assessing not individual bits and pieces of the lesson but how students integrate them into a meaningful whole.

The scholarship of *application*, according to the Carnegie report, addresses the question, "How can knowledge be responsibly applied to consequential problems?" Law, business, medicine, engineering, and all the professional and preprofessional programs are committed to the application of knowledge. But teaching, for the most part, has not applied what is known about teaching and learning to improve the profession. Most teachers teach as they were taught. If teaching is to become a true profession, then teachers must *apply* what is known about learning to the teaching-learning process. Classroom Research concerns the application of knowledge from each teacher's own research as well as that of others.

Finally, there is the scholarship of *teaching*. Teaching, says the Carnegie report, is "a dynamic endeavor involving all the analogies, metaphors, and images that build bridges between a teacher's understanding and the students' learning. Pedagogical procedures must be carefully planned, continually examined, and relate directly to the subject taught. . . . Great teachers create a common ground of intellectual commitment. They stimulate active, not passive, learning and encourage students to be critical creative thinkers with the capacity to go on learning after their college days are over. . . . Teaching, at its best, means not only transmitting knowledge, but *transforming* and *extending* it as well" (pp. 23–24).

It is encouraging that the Carnegie report has been so well received. Many colleges and universities are beginning to build into their promotion and tenure procedures a broader definition of scholarship. That is both desirable and necessary, but there are broader and deeper implications of the report that have not been addressed.

The Carnegie recommendations are important not only as a *correction* for the existing problem of too much emphasis on research and not enough on teaching but also as an *opportunity* for institutions to take leadership in the advancement of teaching as a profession by encouraging faculties to involve themselves in the *multiple* scholarships of teaching.

Conclusion

This introduction has examined the place of Classroom Research in the context of modern approaches to the improvement of teaching and learning. Classroom Research has its roots in all four of today's institutional efforts to improve teaching and learning. It borrows from all, but it has its own distinctive character. It is none of them and all of them.

from The Teaching Portfolio

RUSSELL EDGERTON, PATRICIA HUTCHINGS, AND KATHLEEN QUINLAN

Teaching as a Scholarly Act

A movement that K. Patricia Cross labeled "Taking Teaching Seriously" is spreading throughout the country. Campus after campus is reexamining its commitment to teaching and beginning to explore ways that teaching might be rewarded and improved.

This movement is in part a response to important changes in public attitudes toward higher education. Students and parents, faced with the escalating costs of college attendance, are asking new and demanding questions about the value of undergraduate education. State policy makers are not only facing unrelenting budgetary demands; they are learning, through their involvement in the reform of schools, about "active learning" and other effective practices and wondering why colleges don't practice these too. In short, the heat is on.

But the new seriousness about teaching is also propelled from within academe. It is driven not only by residents and trustees who want to reposition their campuses as teaching institutions but by faculty who care deeply about teaching and sense a new legitimacy for their concerns in the emerging interest in undergraduate reform.

For both external and internal reasons, then, we see this as an opportune moment to consider the role of teaching in higher education. But how will that opportunity unfold? How deep will this reexamination go? Will campuses simply make cosmetic changes and issue empty proclamations? Or will they reexamine such basic academic practices as the grounds for hiring and promoting faculty?

We believe that many campuses are indeed grappling with fundamental issues of practice, especially that lurking academic octopus, "the reward system." Moreover, there have now emerged some fresh perspectives from which these slippery old issues can be tackled. Two of these new perspectives are especially pertinent to the teaching portfolio.

The first new perspective is contained in *Scholarship Reconsidered*, a report issued in 1990 by the Carnegie Foundation for the Advancement of Teaching. In this report, Ernest Boyer argues that it is time to reformulate the tired debate about teaching *versus* research. Boyer argues that the categories of teaching, research, and service have become too segregated. Instead, we should begin with the premise that all faculty, whatever type of institution they might be working in, are *scholars*. Then we should consider the various ways in which their scholarship is expressed. Drawing on a formulation of scholarly roles developed by Eugene Rice (now provost at Antioch College), Boyer makes a case for thinking of faculty work in terms of four, overlapping functions; the scholarship of *discovery* (as in specialized research); the scholarship of *integration* (as in writing a textbook); the scholarship of *application* (as in consulting); and the scholarship of *teaching*.

This last category is, we think, particularly hard to grasp. What does it mean to talk about "the scholarship of teaching"? At bottom, the concept entails a view that teaching, like other scholarly activities (whether by Boyer's labels or by the more traditional ones of research, service, and teaching) relies on a base of expertise, a "scholarly knowing" that needs to and *can* be identified, made public, and evaluated; a scholarship that faculty themselves must be responsible for monitoring. That's a task, we'll argue in the pages that follow, that the teaching portfolio is distinctly suited to.

"The Teaching Portfolio: Capturing the Scholarship in Teaching," by Russell Edgerton, Patricia Hutchings, and Kathleen Quinlan, reprinted from *American Assocaition for Higher Education*, 1991.

The second new perspective that bears on the teaching portfolio can be found in the stream of research authored and sponsored by Lee Shulman, professor of education and psychology at Stanford University. As we described in the Foreword, whereas the Carnegie report *asserts* that teaching is an expression of scholarship, Shulman's research explicates what the knowledge base of teaching actually is.

Shulman's research approach is itself novel. By and large, educators and psychologists who study teaching have concerned themselves with developing scientific principles about teaching—principles that would stand up to the tests of social science. But in doing so, Shulman believes, they have abstracted teaching from the particular situations—the fluid, untidy, unstructured realities of classroom life—in which teaching takes place. They have neglected the "knowing" in teaching that is hard to codify into scientific principles but is nonetheless a crucial part of teaching expertise.

Shulman illustrates this point through the analogy of chess playing. We recognize, he says, that a master chess player knows things that an ordinary chess player does not. But this knowledge is not a knowledge of principles; it is a knowledge of situations and ways of responding to them—the knowledge that comes of *having been there before,* and of *which precedents might best apply* in a new situation (in press).

Through intensive observation of practicing teachers, Shulman concluded that "master" teachers know many things that ordinary teachers do not. Most importantly, they have a command of the "pedagogy of substance"—a repertoire of ways to *transform* the particular concepts of their field into terms that can be understood by the particular students they teach. The exemplary economics teacher doesn't simply define "the demand curve" and gallop on to the next concept; rather, she knows a range of ways to help students understand the concept, apply it, and internalize it as their own.

Taken together, Boyer's call for broadening our view of scholarship and Shulman's vision of the knowing that informs good teaching form a conception of teaching as an act of scholarship. No longer can we think of teaching in the terms of the old formula; subject-matter expertise plus generic methods (how to plan a lecture, lead a discussion group...) equals good teaching. Effective teaching is also a matter of transforming one's knowledge of a subject in ways that lead to student understanding.

This view of teaching will not, we're aware, surprise faculty who are experienced teachers; they know at a deep level the kinds of things that Shulman's research confirms. However, these insights are *not*, typically, the topic of conversation in conferences and workshops about teaching; nor is a faculty member's ability to transform knowledge in ways that particular students can grasp at a deep level the basis for the evaluation of collegiate teaching. The teaching portfolio can, we believe, help document and display a conception of teaching that is indeed a "pedagogy of substance"—recognized and valued as a form of scholarly work.

The Promise of Portfolios

What is a teaching portfolio? Why should anyone bother with it? What purposes can portfolios serve, and what distinctive advantages do they offer?

In an essay on the possibilities inherent in the concept of portfolios, Tom Bird observes that they would be much less appealing if they were called "the teacher's personnel file" (p. 242). Indeed, the suggestiveness of the notion lies in the analogy to portfolios kept by architects, designers, painters, and photographers to display their best work. What would happen, Bird asks, if teachers borrowed that practice? What would a "teaching portfolio" look like? How would it work?

The Power of Analogy

Beginning, as Bird does, with a view of the teaching portfolio as a suggestive analogy is precisely right, we think. It makes clear a point with which this monograph also begins: that there is no single thing called "a teaching portfolio"; neither the concept nor its practice is all figured out. What we have now are ideas (and also lots of questions) about what a teaching portfolio *might* be.

Within higher education, one such idea appears in a line of work begun in Canada some years ago under the aegis of the Canadian Association of University Teachers (CAUT). With an aim to improve the body of evidence about teaching that administrators could take into account in personnel actions, CAUT published a guide called *The Teaching Dossier* (Shore 1986). According to this guide, a teaching dossier is "a summary of a professor's major teaching accomplishments and strengths. It is to a professor's teaching what lists of publications, grants, and academic honors are to research" (p. 1). Peter Seldin's recent monograph, *The Teaching Portfolio*, employs an almost identical definition, adding "It is a factual description of a professor's major strengths and teaching achievements" (p. 3).

Here, then, is a first image of the teaching portfolio—the portfolio as a kind of "extended teaching resume." Indeed, Seldin recommends that faculty think of their portfolio as a "special insert" in their curriculum vitae under the heading of "Teaching" (p. 8). These portfolios aim for a brief but comprehensive account of teaching activity over a defined period of time.

Still other images of what portfolios might be appear in versions of them now being used on campuses across the country. Evergreen State College has long used portfolios as the primary tool for decisions about promotion and tenure; they consist primarily of self-reflective essays by faculty. At Roberts Wessleyan College, the emphasis is on faculty development; portfolios there are being incorporated into a "faculty growth contract" and are kept separate from personnel decision making. At the University of Pittsburgh, portfolios have recently been used in the selection of teaching-award winners; a wide range of materials are included, from annotated student work samples to self-reflective statements of teaching philosophy.

Yet another image of what a portfolio might be appears in the work of Stanford's Teacher Assessment Project. Kenneth Wolf, a member of the project team, drawing on earlier work by Tom Bird, describes possibilities that the group considered:

> Should the school teacher's portfolio be more like a photographer's presentation of his very best work, or the pilot's log in which every flight is recorded? Should the portfolio display all of a person's work—the good, the bad, and the ugly—or only the work that the person is most proud of? Or, is teaching so dissimilar from any of these occupations that the model for the school teacher's portfolio should not be borrowed from any of these existing images? (p. 134)

Wolf and his colleagues came down on the side of the portfolio as a *display of best work*. In their view, the portfolio need not be a *comprehensive* record of performance over time, but a *selective* account—one that highlights what is unique about an individual's approach to teaching. Thus, the organizing image emerging from the Stanford project is of portfolios more like those used by professional artists, who provide samples of their best work to illustrate their distinctive style.

So what is a teaching portfolio? In the broadest sense, the teaching portfolio is a container into which many different ideas can be poured. Rather than settle on any fixed view of what the "it" is, we hope that campuses will explore many images of what portfolios might be.

At the same time, it seems to us that some versions of the portfolio are likely to be much more powerful in advancing good teaching—and therefore more learning—than others. Thus, this monograph describes and argues for a rather particular image of the portfolio.

At the heart of the portfolio as we envision it are *samples of teaching performance*: not just what teachers say about their practice but artifacts and examples of what they actually do. We argue, too, that portfolios should be *reflective*: work samples would be accompanied by faculty commentary and explanation that reveal not only what was done but why, the thinking behind the teaching. Finally, we argue for portfolios that are structured and selective: not (as one practitioner of portfolios for student assessment put it) "pack-ratting run rampant," but a careful selection of evidence organized around agreed upon categories, which themselves represent key dimensions of the scholarship of teaching.

What excites us about this image, and informs our view of what the portfolio might contain, is its potential for fostering the creation of a culture in which thoughtful disclosure about teaching becomes the norm.

Why Bother? The Case for Portfolios

Since portfolios can take different shapes and serve various purposes, the case for developing them will vary as well. The strongest case, however—one that applies to a variety of types of portfolios but particularly to the one type described in our next chapter—can be captured in four interrelated propositions.

First, portfolios can capture the intellectual substance and "situated-ness" of teaching in ways that other methods of evaluation cannot. Second, because of this capacity, portfolios encourage faculty to take important, new roles in the documentation, observation, and review of teaching. Third, because they prompt faculty to take these new roles, portfolios are a particularly powerful tool for improvement. Fourth, as more faculty come to use them, portfolios can help forge a new campus culture of professionalism about teaching.

1. Portfolios capture the complexities of teaching.

A fillet knife can be used to chop up many things in the kitchen. But until we use it to fillet fish, we aren't exploiting the potential inherent in its particular design. So it is, we believe, with portfolios. Portfolios, as Shulman notes,

> . . . are messy to construct, cumbersome to store, difficult to score, and vulnerable to misrepresentation. But in ways that no other assessment method can, portfolios provide a connection to the contexts and personal histories that characterize real teaching and make it possible to document the unfolding of both teaching and learning over time (Shulman 1988).

Through portfolios, faculty can present evidence and reflection about their teaching in ways that keep this evidence and reflection *connected* to the particulars of what is being taught to whom under what conditions. As later sections of this monograph will make clear, in preparing entries for their portfolios, faculty can present concrete "pictures" of their practice successively syllabi of a course that has evolved over time, "before and after" samples of student work, videotapes of lessons on key concepts, and so forth.

Moreover, in a portfolio, faculty can arrange and "annotate" these pictures in ways that document an overall approach to teaching. Entries constitute a considerable advance over the practice of classroom visits by an outside observer, a method of evaluation that at best provides only an isolated snapshot. With portfolios, discrete pictures of teaching can be presented in their context as part of an ongoing "documentary movie," a larger story. When maintained over several semesters, the portfolio can even allow a look at the gradual unfolding of expertise in a way that no other method makes possible.

2. Portfolios place responsibility for evaluating teaching in the hands of faculty.

Portfolios not only have properties that enable us to illuminate deeper dimensions of teaching; they enable faculty—indeed, *require* them—to become more important actors in monitoring and evaluating the quality of their own work.

First and most obviously, portfolios entail a shift of initiative. When it comes to research, faculty take it for granted that it is their responsibility to present evidence of accomplishment. In the case of teaching, however, evaluation often appears to be something that happens *to* faculty—be it through student course ratings or obligatory classroom visits by chairs or deans. Portfolios place the initiative for documenting and displaying teaching back in the hands of the person who is *doing* it; they put the teacher back in charge . . . selecting, assembling, and explaining portfolio entries that accurately represent actual performance.

Second, portfolios invite faculty to participate in the examination of *one another's* teaching. Faculty can work collaboratively in constructing their portfolios; they can also use portfolios as windows to view and share perspectives on one another's teaching. Such collaboration is almost certain to be powerful where the aim is to improve teaching. When teaching is being evaluated for purposes of personnel decisions, faculty collaboration around portfolios might constitute a real sea change.

The contrast with prevailing practice is striking. On most campuses, student ratings are the "method of choice" for evaluating teaching, supplemented by a classroom visit or two and perhaps testimonial letters. By and large, faculty colleagues are not involved, or only secondarily as judges of evidence and perspectives submitted by others. What is "peer reviewed" is not the process of teaching and its products (the learning that the teaching enabled) but the observations and ratings submitted by students and assorted others.

This situation is in part a function of faculty uneasiness about the intrusion of colleagues in their classrooms. But underneath this unease lies a more troubling circumstance: the lack of clarity about why faculty *should* be observers of one another's teaching.

This lack of clarity is no surprise. One need only note that the aspects of teaching most often evaluated are classroom management and interpersonal skills. We ask how clear the assignments are, whether grades are fair, how promptly student work is returned, whether student ideas are respected...questions students are indeed qualified to answer.

But there's more to teaching than what's critiqued on student evaluation forms. What's missing in such evaluation are precisely those aspects of teaching that *faculty* are uniquely qualified to observe and judge: issues about how appropriately courses are organized, whether crucial content is covered (and more incidental material left out), and how well key concepts are represented. In short, there are aspects of the teaching/learning transaction—those things Lee Shulman has in mind when he refers to "the pedagogy of substance"—that *require* peer perspectives and review.

Here is where portfolios can help. Classroom visitation is a desirable practice; it's a form of peer review that can indeed address the most substantive, scholarly aspects of teaching. But classroom visitation is far from universal. Many campuses practice it not at all; some do so in only perfunctory ways. The good news is that portfolios offer an attractive, nonthreatening *step toward* classroom visitation. A professor can work up samples of her teaching, including videotapes, and present them to her colleagues for comment; her colleagues can observe her teaching without setting foot in her classroom. In time, we hope, as faculty come to appreciate through work on portfolios the value of peer perspectives, classroom visitation will seem a natural next step.

Finally, portfolios involve faculty in setting *standards* for effective teaching. An entry in "Professor Smith's" portfolio includes a creative assignment in a biology lab. Do his colleagues in the department agree with Smith that this is a creative and appropriate way to teach the principles of genetics involved in this assignment? Do they believe that the teaching in question will lead to *learning*? What kinds of learning—what levels of understanding—do they believe most matter in the teaching of genetics? These are some of the questions that the review of the portfolio might naturally raise; the "answers" (obviously such questions won't have any single answer) constitute an important step toward the articulation of standards for effective teaching. And with a *set* of portfolios on the table for review and discussion, larger, collective discussion of campus expectations for teaching can occur.

3. Portfolios can prompt more reflective practice and improvement.

There are many routes to the improvement of teaching, but teaching portfolios can have a special power to involve faculty in reflection on their own practice and how to improve it. This potential for improvement is the single most-cited benefit of portfolio use to date.

The reasons are not hard to understand. In the very process of assembling portfolios, faculty reflect on their teaching selecting best work, organizing evidence so that it creates a larger, authentic picture of their practice. Because faculty are the makers of their own portfolios, the level of "investment" is also high—a necessary condition for change, and one that is sometimes missing in evaluation by student rating.

Moreover, because portfolios display not only the final products of teaching but its processes—the thoughts behind the actions—they also reveal much about teaching to colleagues involved in the development and review of portfolios. Whether at the department level or across departments, occasions where faculty examine one another's portfolios could be occasions for cultivating new and richer ways of thinking about and inquiring into the scholarship of teaching, which bring us to the portfolio's fourth advantage.

4. Portfolios can foster a culture of teaching and a new discourse about it.

Teaching is examined at many points and occasions in a faculty member's life. On the one hand, there are all the occasions at which personnel decisions are made: hiring, assigning course workloads, annual evaluations for salary and promotion, the granting or withholding of tenure. And on the other hand, there are occasions and processes where the agenda is not to judge or select but to diagnose and improve: consultation with instructional-development professionals, mentoring programs, and team teaching, for example.

Teaching portfolios can introduce more compelling, authentic evidence about teaching into all of these occasions. Annual-review and tenure committees might require candidates to submit portfolios as evidence of their teaching performance. But institutions or departments might also turn to portfolios purely to cultivate a more thoughtful discussion about the elements of good teaching.

Are some uses for portfolios better—or more appropriate—than others? The underlying theme of this monograph is that there is a scholarship in teaching that has yet to be fully acknowledged and discussed; bringing that scholarship out in the open would enrich faculty discourse about teaching and cultivate a new respect for the profession of teaching. In truth, the teaching portfolio is a technology yet to be invented for a culture that on many campuses doesn't yet exist—a culture of professional inquiry about good teaching. We believe that the kind of portfolio described in the next chapter can help foster such a culture by uncovering the scholarship in teaching.

The Format and Content of a Portfolio

What should go into a portfolio? What would a "typical" portfolio look like? Obviously, the different understandings about what portfolios are, and the different ways they can be used, all have bearing on the determination of what a portfolio should contain. The first step in sorting through the possibilities, in our view, is to be clear about the *reasons* why a campus might wish to prescribe the format or content of a portfolio in the first place.

Determining Needs and Purposes

Portfolios, as we've said, can be used for purposes ranging from evaluating a candidate for promotion and tenure to facilitating good conversation about teaching; *which* use one intends will drive decisions about format and content. The more the portfolio becomes a basis for important personnel decisions, for example, the more likely it is that people will feel the need for *requiring* that it contain specified (even uniform) kinds of information.

Consider the "possible items for inclusion" listed in the 1986 Canadian Association of University Teachers publication *The Teaching Dossier* (Shore), shown on [the next two pages]. The forty-nine items are grouped under the headings "The Products of Good Teaching," "Material from Oneself," and "Information From Others." For purposes or occasions of professional development, it's possible to imagine a portfolio that includes *no* "information from others"—such as student rating and colleague evaluations. But in making decisions about promotion and tenure, most committees charged with this task would want to see *many* kinds of evidence—including ratings from students and evaluations from colleagues.

Another circumstance that might affect portfolio contents is that in which portfolios are being compared with one another. For example, portfolios might be used (and are on several campuses) for selecting candidates to receive a teaching award. The need here is for some degree of standardization, some common structure that enables reviewers to compare portfolios.

The experience of campuses with *student* portfolios offers an instructive lesson on this point. The College of William and Mary, looking for an alternative to standardized tests, turned to portfolios to examine student learning in general education. They started with open-ended portfolios and quickly discovered that without common categories of evidence, the portfolios were impossible to evaluate. The College is now working to design more structured portfolios for assessing student learning and program effects.

Both CAUT's *Teaching Dossier* and Seldin's *The Teaching Portfolio*—the only two general guidelines now available—recognize these considerations of purpose and how they affect the issue of portfolio contents. But it is noteworthy that neither takes a position on the relative value of the options. CAUT offers the forty-nine "possible items for inclusion" to stimulate faculty thinking on what choices they might consider, but there is no framework provided for choosing among them.

The Portrayal of Teaching

There is, however, *another* perspective from which one might derive ideas about portfolio format and content: that is, a perspective about *how teaching can best be documented and displayed*, which, in turn, presumes a view of *teaching itself*. That is, the more we understand about what is important in teaching, the more we understand about how acts of teaching can best be captured and revealed for others to review. It

Possible Items for Inclusion

(These items are explained in detail in Part 4.)

Faculty members should recognize which of the items which might be included in a teaching dossier would most effectively give a favorable impression of teaching competence and which might better be used for self-evaluation and improvement. The dossier should be compiled to make the best possible case for teaching effectiveness.

The Products of Good Teaching

1. Students' scores on teacher-made or standardized tests, possibly before and after a course has been taken as evidence of learning.
2. Student laboratory workbooks and other kinds of workbooks or logs.
3. Student essays, creative work, and project or field-work reports.
4. Publications by students on course-related work.
5. A record of students who select and succeed in advanced courses of study in the field.
6. A record of students who elect another course with the same professor.
7. Evidence of effective supervision of Honors, Master's or Ph.D. theses.
8. Setting up or running a successful internship program.
9. Documentary evidence of the effect of courses on student career choice.
10. Documentary evidence of help given by the professor to students in securing employment.
11. Evidence of help given to colleagues on teaching improvement.

Material from Oneself

Descriptive material on current and recent teaching responsibilities and practices.

12. List of course titles and numbers, unit values or credits, enrollments with brief elaboration.
13. List of course materials prepared for students.
14. Information on professor's availability to students.
15. Report on identification of student difficulties and encouragement of student participation in courses or programs.
16. Description of how films, computers or other nonprint materials were used in teaching.
17. Steps taken to emphasize the interrelatedness and relevance of different kinds of learning.

Description of steps taken to evaluate and improve one's teaching.

18. Maintaining a record of the changes resulting from self-evaluation.
19. Reading journals on improving teaching and attempting to implement acquired ideas.
20. Reviewing new teaching materials for possible application.
21. Exchanging course materials with a colleague from another institution.
22. Conducting research on one's own teaching or course.
23. Becoming involved in an association or society concerned with the improvement of teaching and learning.
24. Attempting instructional innovations and evaluating their effectiveness.
25. Using general support services such as the Education Resources Information Centre (ERIC) in improving one's teaching.
26. Participating in seminars, workships and professional meetings intended to improve teaching.

27. Participating in course or curriculum development.
28. Pursuing a line of research that contributes directly to teaching.
29. Preparing a textbook or other instructional materials.
30. Editing or contributing to a professional journal on teaching one's subject.

Information from Others

Students:

31. Student course and teaching evaluation data which suggest improvements or produce an overall rating of effectiveness or satisfaction.
32. Written comments from a student committee to evaluate courses and provide feedback.
33. Unstructured (and possibly unsolicited) written evaluation by students, including written comments on exams and letters received after a course has been completed.
34. Documented reports of satisfaction with out-of-class contacts.
35. Interview data collected from students after completion of a course.
36. Honors received from students, such as being elected "teacher of the year."

Colleagues:

37. Statements from colleagues who have observed teaching either as members of a teaching team or as independent observers of a particular course, or who teach other sections of the same course.
38. Written comments from those who teach courses for which a particular course is a prerequisite.
39. Evaluation of contributions to course development and improvement.
40. Statements from colleagues from other institutions on such matters as how well students have been prepared for graduate studies.
41. Honors or recognition such as a distinguished teacher award or election to a committee on teaching.
42. Requests for advice or acknowledgments of advice received by a committee on teaching or similar body.

Other sources:

43. Statements about teaching achievements from administrators at one's own institution or from other institutions.
44. Alumni ratings or other graduate feedback.
45. Comments from parents of students.
46. Reports from employers of students (e.g., in a work-study or "cooperative" program).
47. Invitations to teach for outside agencies.
48. Invitations to contribute to the teaching literature.
49. Other kinds of invitations based on one's reputation as a teacher (for example, a media interview on a successful teaching innovation).

"Possible Items for Inclusion," by Shore, reprinted from *The Teaching Dossier,* 1986, Canadian Association of University Teachers.

is from those understandings that one comes to a recognition of the importance of a framework for determining what goes into a teaching portfolio.

Here, we believe, is where the Stanford Teacher Assessment Project has a major contribution to make to a portfolio design. In the course of the project, the team came up with a number of provocative ideas about what kind of portfolio "entries" would be most revealing about a teacher's approach to teaching. And they also developed some ideas about how these entries could be arrayed so as to present a reasonably complete picture of that teacher's performance.

Reflecting on Samples of Actual Performance

The Stanford team began with the premise that portfolios should be based in actual performance. The team was unwilling to allow teachers (as some campus versions of portfolios now do) simply to report what they did in their classroom. Reflective essays *alone* would not do. "The aim," as Kenneth Wolf put it, is to look at "what teachers actually do, not what they *say* they do" (p. 132).

In addition to believing that portfolios should be connected to actual performance, the project team worked on the premise that good teaching was highly situational. Teachers were not simply good "in general." Whether they were good or not depended on the *particulars* of the situation—exactly what was being taught to whom and under what conditions. So to capture good teaching, the team decided that it was important to zero in on *particular episodes* of actual teaching. They assumed, in short, that the more complex aspects of good teaching would best be revealed by looking at *discrete samples of actual work.*

What, then, might a work sample be? Well, the team decided, there were all the materials that are generated in the giving of a course: syllabi, daily assignments, special reading lists, laboratory exercises, student papers, student examinations . . . all the *artifacts* of teaching. And second, there were *reproductions* and representations of what happened: videotapes of classroom situations, photographs, diaries, journals. Both categories would provide evidence of what actually happened.

But, the team realized, these samples of actual work don't speak for themselves. To fill a portfolio with artifacts such as syllabus, lesson plans, and student examinations would be like handing your secretary your "in-box" and saying, "Please act on these items right away." What's missing—what's *needed*—is an explanation.

And so we come to the punch line, the major insight we find in the work of the Stanford project. General reflection, divorced from evidence of actual performance, fails to capture the situated nature of teaching. Work samples alone aren't intelligible. But work samples *plus* reflection make a powerful formula. The reflection is "grounded" by being connected to a particular instance of teaching; the work sample is made meaningful and placed in context through reflection. Thus, out of the Stanford project comes a sense of what the character of a portfolio entry might be: a professor's reflections about a sample of actual work.

Covering the Critical Tasks of Teaching

We came away from our immersion in the Stanford project with the notion that reflections on samples of actual teaching can be the basic building blocks of a portfolio. But there remained another problem to be solved. Faculty preparing a portfolio of such entries, left to their own devices, might simply select samples from one small corner of their classroom work. Suppose a biologist prepared a portfolio that included only entries from the laboratory sections of the courses. Anyone reviewing the portfolio would immediately ask, what of the rest of the experience? What, for instance, of this professor's ability to lecture or to help students make sense of textbook readings?

So, in addition to specifying the nature of portfolio entries, we need to confront the question: What should the sample entries be samples *of*? What guidance might any instructions for portfolio development provide about the domains of teaching performance that entries should reflect?

In our view, this is still an unsettled question. The answers might well vary according to the type of institution and discipline that the professor preparing the portfolio is in. Some campuses consider advising and out-of-classroom contact with students to be an important aspect of teaching performance. Others might feel that those activities have no place in the professional role and therefore in a teaching portfolio. Similarly, to require an entry that focuses on teaching aimed at "experiential learning" might make sense in some disciplines but would need to be understood quite differently in English and nursing. There is much to be learned from experimenting with portfolios in diverse settings.

But there is an appealing place to start. In considering the issue of domain, the task force on the Stanford project that developed portfolios in the field of biology decided that every teacher confronted *four core tasks:*

- course planning and preparation;
- actual teaching;
- evaluating student learning and providing feedback; and
- keeping up with the professional field in areas related to teaching performance.

While not necessarily the final answer, we are taken with the simplicity of this scheme.

Examples of Entries for Each Task

Imagine, for example, that you are preparing a portfolio. You are required to prepare an entry that illustrates your approach to each of these four tasks. What might you include?

In the category of *course planning*, you might begin with the syllabus—or several syllabi—for a course revised over successive years. The syllabi would be your "work sample." The "reflective" portion of the entry might then be a commentary on why the current syllabus contains what it does, how it had changed from one year to the next and why. Had new literature appeared? Had your students changed? Had your experience of teaching the course given you new ideas about what did and did not work?

The syllabus, to be sure, is only one way to document course planning. Alternatively, the work sample might be a series of assignments that you gave your students throughout the semester. The reflective portion of the entry would be your rationale for each of the assignments as well as for the set as a whole. Or suppose you wished to focus on the way you approached the teaching of a key concept in your field. Here, you might use your assignments and your lecture notes as your work sample. Your reflection might deal with how and why your approach to the concept has changed over time, with attention to the returns in student understanding.

For the second task—your actual *teaching of the course*—there are numerous possibilities. You might have a colleague visit your class and then base your reflections on the notes and observations your colleague produced. (There is much to be said for classroom visitation, but also—and particularly on campuses where faculty have little experience observing one another—some things to overcome: your colleague might not be a skilled observer, your students might behave differently in your colleague's presence, and so on.) Alternatively, you could develop an entry by having your teaching videotaped, then selecting segments that best reveal your distinctive style of teaching, accompanied by your reflection on those segments. Still another alternative would be to enlist several students in an effort to keep detailed journals, using these as the basis for your reflections.

The third task—*evaluating and giving feedback to students* about their work—also lends itself to many possibilities. You might take a student paper that illustrated a high standard of performance and comment on why the standard was appropriate, and what you had done as a teacher to enable the student to achieve that standard. Alternatively, you might use a paper or an exam that reflects misconceptions students often bring to the course, and then comment on how you handle those misconceptions. Such an entry would capture for public discussion a dimension of learning that educators have come to see as particularly key in the last decade.

An entire repertoire of ways to assess student learning and give feedback are available in the publications by K. Patricia Cross and Tom Angelo on "Classroom Research." The "one-minute paper"—a simple strategy designed to reveal what students did *and* didn't understand from a given class session—would be excellent grist for an entry that reflects on the gaps between what you as a teacher say on the one hand, and what students hear and learn on the other.

Wrap-up: Format of a Teaching Portfolio

Having now looked at the character of individual entries, one comes to questions about the whole. What might a complete portfolio look like? What format might it take? Again, there's no single answer; each campus needs to think through and design its own version of the portfolio. But here's a rough sketch of one possible version:

Section one might be called *Background Information*. Everyone reviewing a portfolio, no matter what kind of portfolio it is or how it will be used, will need a context for understanding the entries. Two categories of contextual information seem important.

The first is the professional biography of the person who is preparing the portfolio. At a minimum, this could be a traditional resume. But it might also be useful to have the person write about key stages in his or her development as a teacher.

The second is information about the specific environment in which the individual works...what the campus and department expect in terms of teaching, research, and service; what specific classes the individual faculty member teaches; and the important details about these classes that affect teaching—such as course size and the characteristics, abilities, and motivations of the students.

Section two might be called *Selected Entries*. If the teaching terrain were divided into the four critical tasks described above, then each of these tasks would become a subsection. Alternatively, portfolio guidelines might simply require the individual preparing the portfolio to document and display entries that illustrated *diverse* aspects of his or her performance. Each entry would have a caption, and the various documents—be they artifacts, reproductions, or reflective commentary—would be clearly labeled.

How many entries is enough? The Stanford project—as we discuss further in Chapter Four—found that raters of portfolios made up their minds after reviewing just a few entries per category. More was not necessarily better. This is, to us, good news indeed; it reinforces our view that a selected, limited number of sample entries can be highly revealing.

For some purposes and occasions, portfolios with these two sections would suffice. For other purposes a campus might wish to add *other sections of required information*.

Many campuses, when a critical personnel decision has to be made, for example, will want faculty to provide evaluations and ratings done by students, faculty peers, and/or administrators. Since such data can easily become unwieldy, careful thought should be given (as ever) to what data are really needed. Requiring all student rating sheets, for example, without any summary or perspective from which to view them, doesn't strike us as very sensible. On the other hand, a summary of the data, and—better yet—a reflective essay on how the professor responded to them, might be quite revealing.

Some campuses might ask faculty members to write reflective essays about their teaching that are not necessarily tied to particular acts of performance. A number of institutions, such as the University of Maryland's University College and Evergreen State College, do this now.

The list could go on. And of course the portfolio need not (and probably should not) be the only source of evidence for decisions about faculty; one might, for instance, decide that student evaluations provide important information but that they do not belong in the portfolio itself. The important point here—the image we most want to stress—is the portfolio as a set of entries that combine real work samples with reflection. That image leaves lots of maneuvering room, but within it we'd vote to keep portfolios as lean and lively as they can possibly be.

The Teaching Culture

MICHAEL B. PAULSEN AND KENNETH A. FELDMAN

In spring . . . 1990, the American Association for Higher Education (AAHE) established a new program aimed at improving college teaching and learning. Though now encompassing a variety of projects and lines of work, the Teaching Initiative (as we call it) continues to pursue a single, unifying vision: what is needed for improvement of instruction is a culture in which teaching and learning are the subject of serious, sustained discussion and debate; where people talk about teaching, inquire into its effects, and work together for improvement (Hutchings 1993b, p. 63).

I like the way the chair of the English Department at Stanford put it: "What we're trying to do," he said, "is to create a culture of teaching, one in which the conversations, the priorities [and, I would add, the rituals and kinship systems] of the department have teaching at their center." . . . To change academic culture in this way will not be easy. But colleges and universities have always taken justifiable pride in their commitment to inquiry and criticism in all fields, even those where dogma and habit make real scrutiny uncomfortable. Now we must turn this tough scrutiny on our own practices, traditions, and culture. Only by doing so will we make teaching truly central to higher education (Shulman 1993, p. 7).

Concepts of Organizational Culture

College instructors do not teach in a vacuum. They are part of an organization whose culture could both positively and negatively affect their teaching. The intellectual origins of modern cultural analysis of organizations are predominantly in anthropology and sociology (Allaire and Firsirotu 1984; Ouchi and Wilkins 1985). Anthropologists and other ethnographic scholars have long studied cultures, but it was not until the early 1980s that a growing number of organizational researchers began to view organizations as "culture-bearing milieux" (Louis 1992, p. 509). The cultural perspective in the study of organizations challenges and contradicts the assumptions and approaches to research associated with the traditional, rational-structural perspectives on organizational behavior (Sergiovanni 1992; Shafritz and Ott 1992). One important and distinctive contribution of the cultural perspective is that it draws our attention to the "expressive, nonrational . . . subjective, interpretive aspects of organizational life" (Smircich 1983, p. 355).

Although "the essence of a group's culture is its pattern of shared, taken-for-granted basic assumptions, the culture will manifest itself at the levels of observable artifacts and shared espoused values, norms, and rules of behavior" (Schein 1992, p. 26). Thus, the content of organizational culture can be analyzed at various levels along a continuum extending from the most implicit essence of culture to the most explicit expressions of that culture. The deepest level of cultural content is the essence or "substance" of organization culture—the webs of shared meanings that constitute deeply embedded assumptions and beliefs common to members of a group. While the substance of an organization's culture is largely implicit, intangible, and unconscious, it is expressed to group members on a more tangible surface level in terms of more explicit cultural "forms"—artifacts, such as rites and ceremonials, and other symbols that are more readily observable (Trice and Beyer 1984, p. 654). The substance of culture comprises the tacit underlying assumptions, beliefs, values, philosophies, and ideologies that essentially shape organizational behavior. The forms of culture include a variety of observable artifacts, such as rites, rituals, ceremonials, myths, sagas, stories, language, gestures, architecture, informal and formal rules, practices,

Excerpt from "Taking Teaching Seriously: Meeting the Challenge of Instructional Improvement," by Michael B. Paulsen and Kenneth A. Feldman, reprinted from *ASHE-ERIC Higher Education Report,* No. 2, 1995.

norms, patterns of behavior and interaction, and other symbolic processes (Kuh and Whitt 1988; Peterson, Cameron, Jones, Mets, and Ettington 1986; Peterson and Spencer 1990; Shafritz and Ott 1992; Tierney and Rhoads 1993; Trice and Beyer 1984). Cultural forms provide most of the available evidence about the core or substance of culture.

Although culture can and should be thought of as a source of stability in organizations in many ways (Hatch 1993; Parsons and Platt 1973; Schein 1992), it is important to remember that organizational cultures are constantly evolving, being constructed and reconstructed, both shaping human interaction as well as being shaped by it (Jelinek, Smircich, and Hirsch 1983, p. 331). And many approaches have been recommended and applied in the promotion of change in organizational cultures (Chaffee and Tierney 1988; Deal and Kennedy 1982; Hatch 1993; Kilmann, Saxton, Serpa, and Associates 1985; Peterson et al. 1986; Rhoads and Tierney 1992; Sathe 1983; Schein 1992; Trice and Beyer 1984).

As revealed in a "cultural audit," the shared basic assumptions constituting the essence, core, or substance of culture are very difficult to discern. Group members are not fully and consciously aware of basic cultural assumptions and therefore take them for granted, rarely challenging them or even thinking or talking about them. When asked about such assumptions, individuals have difficulty discussing them directly. Instead, they speak of their organization's distinctiveness by describing concrete examples of surface-level artifacts or expressions of deeper cultural content. Describing a familiar ritual or telling a story is their way of communicating what the culture means to them (Wilkins 1983).

Challenges in studying organizational culture thus arise "because culture is implicit, and we are all embedded in our own cultures. In order to observe organizational culture, the researcher must find its visible and explicit manifestations" (Masland 1985, p. 160). Such overt, tangible, and accessible cultural forms provide "windows on organizational culture" (p. 160). As a result, most researchers of organizational culture work hard to discern the meanings of the elusive, essential substance of culture through analysis of the cultural content that is expressed in more accessible, surface-level cultural forms. When studying the work culture of an organization, inquiries regarding the nature of work that is expected and the type of work that is rewarded can be particularly revealing (Wilkins 1983, p. 30).

The recent rediscovery of the cultural perspective for organizational analysis began in the late 1980s with some well-known applications to the study of business organization (Deal and Kennedy 1982; Ouchi 1981; Peters and Waterman 1982). The findings of these studies supported the contention that strong, congruent cultures promote effective organizational performance. Following some early and well-known studies of the organizational cultures of academic institutions (B. Clark 1970, 1972; Riesman and Jencks 1962), a growing number of such studies began to appear in the late 1980s (Bergquist 1992; Cameron and Ettington 1988; Chaffee and Tierney 1988; Peterson and Spencer 1993; Rice and Austin 1988; Tierney 1988a). The study of subcultures within academic institutions began with the exploration of student cultures (Bushnell 1962; Clark and Trow 1966; Feldman 1972; Feldman and Newcomb 1969; Hughes, Becker, and Geer 1962) and has expanded to include insights into various dimensions of faculty cultures (Austin 1990a; Boice 1992b; B. Clark 1985, 1987a, 1987b; Schuster and Bowen 1985; Tierney and Rhoads 1993; Wergin 1994; Whitt 1991) and finally, cultural perspectives on the college presidency (Bensimon 1989; Tierney 1988b).

The Teaching Culture and Its Place in Colleges and Universities

> Many . . . well-researched and persuasive critiques of higher education focus on the inadequacy of our commitment to the quality of instruction and the limited prestige of teaching in the values and reward system of academic culture. . . . There are historic reasons for the gradual shift toward a research model on American campuses, particularly at institutions with graduate programs. But there is also compelling evidence that concern for teaching has never been absent or silent, even on these campuses. Instead, teaching has perhaps been submerged—and deserves to take its rightful place once again in our institutional culture (Shelton and DeZure 1993, p. 27).

From 1636 through the late 19th century, American colleges were predominantly teaching institutions, based largely on an adapted English model of higher education devoted to the development of the student as a whole person (Brubacher and Rudy 1968; Carnegie Commission 1973; Rudolph 1990). Essentially, a culture of student development (primitive by modern standards and concepts of college student development) was the dominant culture of American higher education for over two centuries.

During this time, the teaching culture represented an important subculture of the overall collegiate culture, in some ways contributing to students' development and in other ways constraining it (Cowley 1958; Fuhrmann and Grasha 1983).

Two important developments in the late 19th and early 20th centuries promoted a reconstruction of the faculty work cultures in American institutions of higher education. First, thousands of new professors, who had been educated in Germany, joined our faculty ranks. These professors were greatly influenced by some powerful assumptions embedded in the cultures of German universities, and when these cultural influences were selectively combined, taken out of context, and adapted to the American university, research and the advancement of knowledge for its own sake became impressive and valued undertakings. The "practice of research became elevated into an all-encompassing ideal" (Veysey 1965, p. 127). Second, during the same period, faculty and administrators were shaping a distinctively American service ideal as an important mission of academic work. Reaching its zenith in the Progressive Era, this ideal placed research in the highly valued role of helping to solve society's problems. In effect, "the American university united two divergent conceptions of research" (Metzger 1961, p. 107).

From the perspective of cultural dynamics, the research ideal initially entered American institutions at the level of artifacts—faculty practices or behaviors—that met with success, as viewed by some members of the academy. When the appreciation of the value of such work spread among a wider audience, both inside and outside the university, a critical mass of group members began to espouse the value of research work. And when the ongoing success of these valued research activities began to be taken for granted, the high status of research became part of an underlying assumption about the kind of faculty work expected and rewarded (Hatch 1993; Schein 1992).

Based on his study of faculty culture in American higher education, the author of *The Academic Life: Small Worlds, Different Worlds* observes that the research ideal has resulted in "hierarchies of status" stretching from the highest-status research universities to other doctoral universities to comprehensive universities to liberal arts colleges to the lowest-status community colleges (B. Clark 1987a, p. xxvii). He further concludes that the "greatest paradox of academic work in modern America is that most professors teach most of the time, and large proportions of them teach all the time, but teaching is not the activity most rewarded by the academic profession nor most valued by the system at large" (pp. 98–99).

Institutions at all levels in the hierarchy express a desire for more of the prestige associated with the research ideal. This "research surge" has intensified in the past decade or two (Schuster and Bowen 1985, p. 16). Because of the large supply of new Ph.D.'s from top research universities who are already socialized into the research ideal, the desire on campus for research-related status is growing. But "the goal of becoming 'a leading research university' [has been] espoused explicitly at many doctoral-granting universities that are still some distance from achieving distinction" (Schuster and Bowen 1985, p. 16).

To some extent, pursuit of the prestige of the research ideal is even felt at institutions where the primary criterion for tenure and promotion has long been effective teaching. Faculty dedicated to the teaching imperatives of community colleges seek ways to keep up with advances in their disciplines, to be viewed as scholars, and to conduct some research (Palmer and Vaughan 1992; Vaughan and Palmer 1991). At the same time, research and other doctoral universities often refuse tenure to outstanding teachers because their research record is considered inadequate.

> Such repetitive professional behavior on the part of the evaluating academics results not from personal willfulness but from the underlying structure of commitments and related rewards. . . . This underlying problem has not and will not go away. In the inability to reward undergraduate teaching, we find the Achilles heel of the American research university. . . . Serious reform that seeks . . . changes are somewhere on the drawing board in virtually every major university, challenging administrators and faculty to creatively alter rewards for the professoriate, even at the risk of creating a division between a teaching faculty and a research faculty. Some small gains are made in stiffening the teaching criterion in promotion decisions. But with competition for scholarly status powerfully concentrating the institutional mind, the tides run strong in the opposite direction (B. Clark 1987a, pp. 265–66).

To the extent that the research-based hierarchies of status clearly affect the dominant culture of a higher education institution, the teaching culture of that college or university can be meaningfully viewed as a *sub*culture. Nearly every type of organization, including colleges and universities, is characterized by a dominant culture as well as one or more subcultures (Bergquist 1992; Gregory 1983; Sackmann 1992).

The embedded values of an organization's dominant culture are manifested in observable artifacts that express the basic beliefs shared by most members. The subcultures that normally develop either support, contradict, or are largely independent of the shared values of the dominant culture of the organization.

Three types of subcultures have been identified: enhancing, countercultural, and orthogonal (Martin and Siehl 1983). An enhancing subculture can be found among organizational subgroups where members' commitment to the basic beliefs of the dominant culture is stronger than the commitment of other members of the organization (pp. 53–54). A supportive teaching culture is most likely to be an enhancing subculture in a community college or a small private college where the research ideal is weak and the teaching ideal is strong. In these highly teaching-oriented institutions, subgroups of faculty often actively support or serve on faculty or staff development committees and participate regularly and enthusiastically in a wide range of instructional improvement activities promoted by the committee and its administrative supporters.

A counterculture exists when some of the basic beliefs of a subgroup in the organization "present a direct challenge to the core values of a dominant culture. Thus a dominant culture and a counterculture exist in an uneasy symbiosis, taking opposite positions on value issues that are critically important to each of them" (Martin and Siehl 1983, p. 54). In larger doctoral and research universities, where the research-based, status-seeking ideal is prominent, a subculture highly supportive of teaching is more likely to match the characteristics of a counterculture. Faculty's perceptions of the conflicting work demands placed on them by the dominant research cultures and the teaching subcultures at such universities have been well documented (Bowen and Schuster 1986; Boyer 1990; Carnegie Foundation 1989; Dey et al. 1993; Gray, Froh, and Diamond 1992; Ratcliff and Associates 1995; Schuster and Bowen 1985).

Finally, "in an orthogonal subculture, the members would simultaneously accept the core values of the dominant culture and a separate, unconflicting set of values particular to themselves" (Martin and Siehl 1983, p. 54).

> A president at a doctorate university, in commenting on the mission of his institutions, put it this way: "This campus should be a place where both great teachers and great researchers function side by side. We should have the confidence to say, 'Look, you're a great researcher and we are eager to have you here doing what you do best.'" He then added, "We should also be able to say to a colleague, 'You are terrific with students, but you are not publishing. Still, we want you to help us perform an important mission on the campus.'" This is precisely the kind of division of labor that should be clarified and strengthened at doctorate-granting institutions (Boyer 1990, pp. 58–59).

In such a doctorate-granting university, which has traditionally adhered strongly to the research mode, a supportive teaching culture would fit well the characteristics of an orthogonal substructure. In an orthogonal teaching subculture, for example, members of the relevant subgroup would be committed to both the basic beliefs of the dominant culture of research and to a set of shared beliefs regarding the importance of the contribution of teaching and instructional improvement to that culture.

The Teaching Culture: A Subculture or a Dominant Culture?

Research cultures are not the dominant culture at all colleges and universities, despite certain trends in that direction. In fact, the degree to which one or another culture is dominant in a school still varies across institutions of higher education. At some schools, a teaching culture could be as dominant as—or even more dominant than—the research culture. In addition, some recently published reports (see, in particular, Boyer 1990 and Pister 1991) have prompted many universities to begin the process of formulating new institutional policies that seek to restructure faculty roles and rewards so that quality of teaching and instructional improvement are promoted, evaluated, and rewarded on a level comparable to research (Roberts, Wergin, and Adam 1993). Regardless of which culture dominates at a particular school, it can still support (enhance), contradict (counter), or be neutral to (orthogonal) the other.

Some analysts maintain that teaching and research are mutually supportive (see, e.g., Leary 1959), whereas others take the opposite view that the two are mutually antagonistic (see, e.g., Cutten 1958). Perhaps neither is the case. A meta-analysis of a number of studies found that, when results were averaged across an number of different colleges and universities, the research productivity of individual faculty members was positively associated with their teaching effectiveness (as measured by the perceptions and evaluations of their students) but only to a very small degree ($r = +.12$) (Feldman 1987). On the basis of this small positive correlation between research productivity and teaching effectiveness, it could be maintained that the two are at best slightly beneficial to one another. But it could just as well be argued that the correlation is so small that for all practical purposes the variables in question are generally independent of each other.

Faculty obviously could separate themselves into more than just two cultures. Just as those interested in academia have come to realize that there are different types of scholarship—for example, research, teaching, application, and integration (see Boyer 1990; Rice 1991; Richlin 1993; Schon 1995)—so the possibility of a type of subculture or culture associated with each arises. One reconceptualization of scholarship uses the Parsonian four-function paradigm as an analytic framework from which to deduce a somewhat different set of categories of scholarship: research and graduate training; teaching; service; and academic citizenship (Paulsen and Feldman 1995). Again, each could well be associated with a separate culture on campus.

In recent years, institutions have been increasingly encouraged to capitalize on the diverse dimensions of scholarship. Some institutions might wish to focus their mission and their faculty's scholarship relatively more on one of these several dimensions than on others. Liberal arts colleges, comprehensive colleges, and research universities—as three different types of institutions—might wish to emphasize more the scholarly activities of teaching, service and research, respectively. In contrast, some institutions might wish to encourage their individual faculty members to specialize in their most preferred scholarly activities—those that capitalize on their distinctive talents. This latter approach is appropriate for many doctoral universities to consider.

> These institutions typically see themselves as being "in transition," embracing to a very large degree the research model. . . . [But] doctorate-granting institutions need also to recognize professors who make exceptional contributions to other scholarly areas: integration, application, and teaching. At these institutions, perhaps more than any others, the mosaic of talent should be carefully considered (Boyer 1990, p. 58).

Regardless of whether the teaching culture is the dominant culture or a subordinate subculture at a particular school, and regardless of whether it enhances, contradicts, or is orthogonal to other cultures or subcultures at the particular school, the characteristics of a supportive teaching culture are of great importance. The effectiveness of all strategies to improve instruction clearly benefits from the presence of a culture that supports teaching. The next subsection draws upon the wisdom, experience, and research generated by instructional developers, administrators, faculty leaders, and other higher education scholars to synthesize what has been learned about the characteristics of a supportive teaching culture.

In Search of a Supportive Teaching Culture

Most research on the characteristics of cultures that support teaching in today's colleges and universities has focused on identifying forms or artifacts common to institutional or departmental cultures that place a high value on teaching and its improvement. In particular, the focus is primarily on organizational structures, behaviors, interactions, documents, policies, and practices that appear to be outward manifestations of the values, beliefs, and assumptions constituting those academic cultures that promote, support, and reward efforts to improve the quality of teaching. The research literature consists primarily of qualitative studies, case studies, and surveys. In combination, these studies have consistently identified a number of prominent characteristics of cultures that support teaching and its improvement. Eight of them are especially salient.

Commitment and Support from High-Level Administrators

To promote the improvement of instruction, the unambiguous commitment and support of senior administrators is necessary. It is important that "teaching improvement activities [be] given high visibility by the senior administration in order to illustrate their importance" (Wright and O'Neil 1994, p. 26). High-level administrators perform the critical role of communicating the institution's mission in terms of the value placed on teaching. In general, faculty need to be convinced that the administration's positive rhetoric about excellent teaching "is not merely polite language to satisfy various external constituents and that it will indeed drive the reward system" (Armour 1995, p. 20). An evaluative study of the Lilly Endowment Teaching Fellows Program at 30 research universities illustrates the important impact that supportive senior administrators can have on the way teaching is valued.

> One example is provided by the University of Massachusetts, where, even in the midst of serious financial constraints, the teaching fellows program has continued without external funding and, additionally, a center for teaching has been established, This success owes much to the considerable involvement of the associate vice chancellor for academic affairs in the program, especially during its earliest years, and his strong public advocacy of the importance of teaching at the institution and the contribution made by the teaching fellows program (Austin 1992, p. 83).

A recent case study of the efforts of the University of Massachusetts at Amherst to "encourage a culture on campus that values teaching" has also emphasized how important it is for the campus community—especially faculty—to feel that the administration clearly values teaching highly (Aitken and Sorcinelli 1994, p. 64). The findings also indicate, however, that at research universities such as this one, administrators might be hesitant to speak out in favor of the value of teaching because they are concerned that faculty and administrative support for teaching and its improvement are interdependent. In other words, faculty and administrators must come together to establish shared values about teaching.

Faculty Involvement, Shared Values, and a Sense of Ownership

While the strong support of senior administrators is an essential component of a culture that encourages the improvement of instruction, the widespread involvement of faculty in every aspect of planning and implementing improved teaching is necessary to increase the chances for shared values between administrators and faculty. In-depth case studies of 10 liberal arts colleges where faculty were highly committed to teaching revealed that "participatory leadership" and "organizational structures" that encourage "active involvement of faculty in making important institutional decisions" were common characteristics of the teaching cultures of these exemplary colleges (Rice and Austin 1990, pp. 28–29).

Miami-Dade Community College's Teaching and Learning Project was the first recipient of TIAA-CREF's Theodore M. Hesburgh Award for the most outstanding faculty development program dedicated to the enhancement of the quality of teaching. The "blueprint for change" underlying this project serves as a model for all colleges and universities seeking to create a culture supportive of teaching. The project director and a member of the steering committee describe how they worked to promote shared values about the importance of teaching among members of the campus community:

> The first area to be addressed was that of institutional values related to teaching and learning. . . . The Teaching/Learning Values Subcommittee . . . began with an intensive research review of college-produced documents, self-studies, and material written about Miami-Dade. From this review they identified implicit values [that] were then placed into a survey and sent to all college personnel as well as a sampling of students and community members. Several cycles of activity followed . . . [and] a set of seven institutional values related to teaching/learning . . . articulated. . . . This values document then became the cornerstone of the entire project (Jenrette and Napoli 1994, p. 6).

The results of case studies at 12 other community colleges indicate that institutional cultures characterized by shared values between administrators and faculty "centered on the importance of promoting [students'] achievement" are the most likely to manifest faculty behaviors that promote students' learning (Richardson 1993, p. 106). Further, among colleges and universities participating in the Bush Foundation Faculty Development Project, researchers found that institutional cultures characterized by shared faculty-administrative leadership that promoted a sense of "faculty ownership" had more successful faculty development programs (Eble and McKeachie 1985, p. 216).

A Broader Definition of Scholarship

After nearly a full century since the construct of scholarship was given its contemporary meaning, the 1990s have witnessed growing efforts to reconceptualize and expand the meaning of scholarship (Boyer 1990; Lynton and Elman 1987; Paulsen and Feldman, 1995; Rice 1991; Schon 1995). The results of four recent case studies of institutions ranging from a large research university to a small liberal arts college indicate that one of the factors that influences the relationship between the culture of the campus and the value it places on teaching is "an appropriate balance between teaching and scholarship" (Armour 1995, p. 20). For example, at Syracuse University in 1992, Chancellor Kenneth A. Shaw promoted a broader conception of scholarship that was to include discovery, integration, application, and teaching. In response, academic departments have been reformulating the evaluation of faculty to take into account a broader range of scholarly activities. In particular, research on effective teaching in one's own discipline is now given more attention during evaluation. A study of 10 exemplary liberal arts colleges found that each college in its own way challenged the restrictive view that scholarship equals research. These schools value as scholarship various forms of faculty work, including teaching, research, and service. This expanded view "allows faculty to build on their own scholarly strengths and be rewarded for them" (Rice and Austin 1990, p. 33).

A Teaching Demonstration or Pedagogical Colloquium as Part of the Hiring Process

Campus cultures that highly value teaching regularly include some demonstration of effective teaching as part of interviewing and hiring new faculty (Jenrette and Napoli 1994; Rice and Austin 1988). A recent survey of faculty development professionals found that the policy of "hiring practices [that] require demonstration of teaching ability" was ranked among the top 10 institutional practices in terms of its capacity to contribute to the improvement of teaching (Wright and O'Neil 1994, p. 10).

A "disciplinary teaching colloquium" or a "pedagogical colloquium" would provide an opportunity during the interview process for a candidate "to do something that begins to demonstrate [his or her] understanding of the teaching of [the] discipline" (Schulman 1995, p. 7). Three models have been proposed for this colloquium. The first is a "course narrative or course argument" approach, in which the candidate uses a syllabus to explain how he or she would teach the course, what would be studied, and what the teacher and students would experience—thereby unveiling the candidate's philosophies of teaching and learning in the discipline. The second approach is a "colloquium centered on an essential idea or concept," in which the candidate selects one disciplinary concept that is well known to be very difficult for students to learn and explains various approaches he or she would use to promote learning of that concept. In the third approach, a "dilemma-centered colloquium," the candidate is asked to think out loud about an inherent problem in teaching the discipline, such as "the right balance between breath and depth in an introductory course" (pp. 7–8).

The pedagogical colloquium model has been used at Georgetown University. In the German Department, for example, the course narrative and dilemma-centered approaches are introduced during the interview to encourage candidates to talk about how they would teach an introductory course. The associate vice chancellor for academic affairs at the university justifies the university's use of the pedagogical colloquium approach: "[We especially] needed to know more about what these candidates could contribute to a campus that prides itself, I think quite correctly, on quality teaching" (Byrnes 1995, p. 7).

> In the end, we found ourselves thinking how much more certain we could be about having chosen the right candidate to be our future colleague by our close attention to teaching in that pivotal moment that hiring is in any department (Byrnes 1995, p. 10).

Frequent Interaction, Collaboration, and Community Among Faculty

Institutional and departmental cultures that support teaching are characterized by opportunities for frequent interaction among faculty regarding teaching-related issues (Ferren 1989; Massy, Wilger, and Colbeck 1994; Wright and O'Neil 1994). Interviews of 88 faculty at six research universities indicate that one of the important institutional characteristics that can help increase the intrinsic rewards of teaching is the availability of "opportunities to talk about teaching"; in discussions with peers as well as students, faculty are able to remind themselves of the intrinsic rewards of teaching (Froh, Menges, and Walker 1993, p. 93). Results of an 11-campus study of "institutional efforts to create and/or maintain positive teaching climates" demonstrate that one of the most important characteristics of a positive teaching culture is the opportunity for collegial interaction and collaboration about teaching (LaCelle-Peterson and Finkelstein 1993, p. 22):

> Frequently, faculty report these interactions in the context of team teaching. . . . Faculty who had taught in such course clusters . . . report that the experience was the occasion for their most meaningful teaching interactions (LaCelle-Peterson and Finkelstein 1993, p. 28).

A relatively recent review of the literature on faculty collaboration in teaching identifies three major benefits to teachers: improvement of teaching ability, increased intellectual stimulation, and reduction in the degree of isolation associated with traditional teaching (Austin and Baldwin 1991, pp. 41–43).

After the original three-year funding period for universities participating in the Lilly Endowment's Teaching Fellows Program ended, many of the universities continued to fund the program without external support. A comprehensive evaluative study of these programs reveals that one of the characteristics of the campus cultures that fostered the continuation of such programs was the substantial sense of community that had been established among faculty associated with the program in previous years. It was customary to make clear to new teaching fellows that they were "joining a group of faculty committed to teaching and spanning university departments and years of involvement in the program" (Austin 1990b, p. 72). The creation of a community of teachers such as this has demonstrated the potential to defend "the program if budget constraints threaten its existence" (p. 72).

> Whether through peer visits, informal study groups, conferences, or social events, the input of others offers new and original ideas, provides intellectual stimulation around teaching issues, and creates a sense of community that helps to break down the isolation felt by many college teachers (Aitken and Sorcinelli 1994).

A Faculty Development Program or Campus Teaching Center

Campus cultures that value teaching are characterized by extensive faculty development programs (LaCelle-Peterson and Finkelstein 1993; Rice and Austin 1990; Richardson 1993), often coordinated by the staff of a campus teaching center (Aitken and Sorcinelli 1994; Ambrose 1995; Austin 1990b; Fenton 1991; Jenrette and Napoli 1994; Wright and O'Neil 1994). A typical campus teaching center is a university-funded branch of the office of academic affairs. It is commonly operated by a director and trained teaching consultants. The tasks performed by the Center for Teaching at the University of Massachusetts at Amherst, for example, are representative of those performed by most centers.

> Since its inception, the center has offered an ever-increasing range of resources and programs for enhancing teaching and learning. They include individual consultations, departmental consultations, workshops, seminars, conferences, teaching assistant training programs, annual award programs [like] the Teaching Fellows Program and Faculty Grants for Teaching, materials on teaching development and institutional participation in grants and research on teaching and faculty development (Aitken and Sorcinelli 1994, p. 66).

In a recent survey, faculty development professionals ranked a "[campus teaching] center to promote effective instruction" as one of the top 10 institutional practices in terms of its capacity to improve teaching (Wright and O'Neil 1994, p. 10). A recent case study of the development of the University Teaching Center at Carnegie-Mellon University reveals a number of ways in which it "has had a marked effect on the culture of the university" (Ambrose 1995, p. 88). Support for the center persisted through a major change in the central administration; moreover, the most recent president created a new senior academic administrative position in charge of "innovation in undergraduate education," and the university "created the Center for Innovation in Learning" as a focus for research connected to the work of the teaching center (p. 88). Because of the center's success as the campus forum for discussion of issues related to teaching, this function has been expanded and included in the regular activities of other campus institutions. Recently, the center was moved to a new and prominent campus location, symbolizing "to the campus community the ever-increasing importance of teaching" at the university (p. 88). Every semester the rate of faculty participation in the center's activities has continued to increase.

Supportive and Effective Department Chairs

Recent empirical work offers strong support for the earlier conviction of higher education scholars (particularly Lucas 1989, 1990, 1994) that one of the most critical characteristics of institutional and departmental cultures that value teaching is the presence and activities of supportive and effective department chairs. A recent qualitative investigation of the characteristics of departmental cultures that either support or inhibit faculty's efforts to work toward effective teaching included interviews with nearly 300 faculty at eight research universities, four doctoral universities, and three liberal arts colleges (Massy, Wilger, and Colbeck 1994). This ongoing study of faculty across humanities, social sciences, and science departments reveals that a supportive department chair is of pivotal importance in creating a culture that really values teaching.

> The chair may well represent the single most important factor in determining whether or not a department actively supports teaching. Interviewees cited in the crucial role the chair plays in creating an environment conducive to effective teaching. In two departments, the current chair is credited with revolutionary changes in the department—with resolving long-standing issues related to undergraduate education. . . . As one faculty member said, "Faculty never moved away from their commitment to teaching—it just wasn't rewarded as seriously as research. [The chair] wants the quality of both [teaching and research] to improve and has tried to revitalize and reemphasize teaching" (Massy, Wilger, and Colbeck 1994, pp. 17–18).

A national sample of faculty development professionals recently ranked "[deans'] and chairpersons' recognition of teaching as an important aspect of academic responsibility" in the top institutional practices in terms of its potential to improve teaching; they ranked this role of the supportive chair second out of a possible 36 institutional practices (Wright and O'Neil 1994, p. 15). Studies of both liberal arts colleges and research universities show that the department chair is essential in a campus culture that supports teaching;

> Department chairs can convey to faculty members information about how teaching efforts are valued, how time is most profitably allocated, and on what basis rewards are determined. . . . Without the support of department chairs, many incentives to encourage good teaching may be fruitless (Rice and Austin 1990, p. 39).

A Connection Between Rigorous Evaluation of Teaching and Decisions about Tenure and Promotion

A number of recent case studies of institutions with campus cultures that value teaching have consistently demonstrated that a common and outstanding characteristic of such cultures is the rigorous (peer and student) evaluation of teaching and the connection of this evaluation with decisions about tenure and promotion (Armour 1995; Jenrette and Napoli 1994; Richardson 1993). In a recent international survey of faculty development professionals in the United States (N = 165), Canada (N = 51), the United Kingdom (N = 82), and Australasia (N = 33), respondents in each sample country and region ranked "recognition of teaching in tenure and promotion decisions" as the number one institutional practice in terms of its "potential to improve the quality of teaching" (Wright and O'Neil 1995, pp. 12–13). Clearly, those who probably know the most about teaching cultures at colleges and universities around the world have in common the perception that the quality of teaching is particularly likely to be enhanced in campus cultures where the evaluation of teaching is connected to decisions about tenure and promotion (p. 18).

Further, interviews with 300 faculty on 15 campuses reveal that departmental cultures that support quality teaching are more likely to value rigorous peer and student evaluation of teaching and to connect such evaluation to decisions about tenure and promotion. According to one faculty member:

> We are scrupulous in promotion and tenure decisions about the evaluation of teaching. We insist that teaching be very good. We review faculty members on a set schedule. Assistant professors are reviewed every two years, associates every five years, and full professors every seven years. The review includes both teaching and research, as well as service and other contributions to the field (Massy, Wilger, and Colbeck 1994, pp. 16–17).

Even at research universities, departments with cultures that support teaching differ from others in important ways.

> These departments scrutinize their junior members' teaching skills and offer guidance and assistance before crucial decision points. They are changing the standard line, "Good teaching can't help you, but only terrible teaching can hurt you," to "Good (not necessarily excellent) teaching is a necessary but not sufficient condition for tenure" (Massy, Wilger, and Colbeck 1994, p. 17).

In sum, strategies to improve instruction are both nurtured by and help to create more supportive teaching cultures on college and university campuses. Supportive teaching cultures facilitate the informative feedback to teachers so important to improving teaching—feedback that comes from the teachers themselves as reflective practitioners, from students, and from colleagues, consultants, and department chairs. The next three sections consider these various sources of informative feedback and the strategies of instructional improvement associated with them.

From Teaching to Learning: A New Paradigm for Undergraduate Education

ROBERT B. BARR AND JOHN TAGG

The significant problems we face cannot be solved at the same level of thinking we were at when we created them

—Albert Einstein

A paradigm shift is taking hold in American higher education. In its briefest form, the paradigm that has governed our colleges is this: A college is an institution that exists *to provide instruction.* Subtly but profoundly we are shifting to a new paradigm: A college is an institution that exists *to produce learning.* This shift changes everything. It is both needed and wanted.

We call the traditional, dominant paradigm the "Instruction Paradigm." Under it, colleges have created complex structures to provide for the activity of teaching conceived primarily as delivering 50-minute lectures—the mission of a college is to deliver instruction.

Now, however, we are beginning to recognize that our dominant paradigm mistakes a means for an end. It takes the means or method—called "instruction" or "teaching"—and makes it the college's end or purpose. To say that the purpose of colleges is to provide instruction is like saying that General Motors' business is to operate assembly lines or that the purpose of medical care is to fill hospital beds. We now see that our mission is not instruction but rather that of producing *learning* with every student by *whatever* means work best.

The shift to a "Learning Paradigm" liberates institutions from a set of difficult constraints. Today it is virtually impossible for them to respond effectively to the challenge of stable or declining budgets while meeting the increasing demand for postsecondary education from increasingly diverse students. Under the logic of the Instruction Paradigm, colleges suffer from a serious design flaw: it is not possible to increase outputs without a corresponding increase in costs, because any attempt to increase outputs without increasing resources is a threat to quality. If a college attempts to increase its productivity by increasing either class sizes or faculty workloads, for example, academics will be quick to assume inexorable negative consequences for educational quality.

Just as importantly, the Instruction Paradigm rests on conceptions of teaching that are increasingly recognized as ineffective. As Alan Guskin pointed out in a September/October 1994 *Change* article premised on the shift from teaching to learning, "the primary learning environment for undergraduate students, the fairly passive lecture-discussion format where faculty talk and most students listen, is contrary to almost every principle of optimal settings for student learning." The Learning Paradigm ends the lecture's privileged position, honoring in its place whatever approaches serve best to prompt learning of particular knowledge by particular students.

The Learning Paradigm also opens up the truly inspiring goal that each graduating class learns more than the previous graduating class. In other words, the Learning Paradigm envisions the institution itself as a learner—over time, it continuously learns how to produce more learning with each graduating class, each entering student.

"From Teaching to Learning: A New Paradigm for Undergraduate Education," Robert B. Barr and John Tagg, reprinted from *Change,* Vol. 27, No. 6, November/December 1995, Hildref Publications, 1319 Eighteenth St. N. W., Washington, D. C. 20036-1802.

For many of us, the Learning Paradigm has always lived in our hearts. As teachers, we want above all else for our students to learn and succeed. But the heart's feeling has not lived clearly and powerfully in our heads. Now, as the elements of the Learning Paradigm permeate the air, our heads are beginning to understand what our hearts have known. However, none of us has yet put all the elements of the Learning Paradigm together in a conscious, integrated whole.

Lacking such a vision, we've witnessed reformers advocate many of the new paradigm's elements over the years, only to see few of them widely adopted. The reason is that they have been applied piecemeal within the structures of a dominant paradigm that rejects or distorts them. Indeed, for two decades the response to calls for reform from national commissions and task forces generally has been an attempt to address the issues *within the framework of the Instruction Paradigm*. The movements thus generated have most often failed, undone by the contradictions within the traditional paradigm. For example, if students are not learning to solve problems or think critically, the old logic says we must teach a class in thinking and make it a general education requirement. The logic is all too circular: What students are learning in the classroom doesn't address their needs or ours; therefore, we must bring them back into another classroom and instruct them some more. The result is never what we hope for because, as Richard Paul, director of the Center for Critical Thinking observes glumly, "critical thinking is taught in the same way that other courses have traditionally been taught, with an excess of lecture and insufficient time for practice."

To see what the Instruction Paradigm is we need only look at the structures and behaviors of our colleges and infer the governing principles and beliefs they reflect. But it is much more difficult to see the Learning Paradigm, which has yet to find complete expression in the structures and processes of any college. So we must imagine it. This is what we propose to do here. As we outline its principles and elements, we'll suggest some of their implications for colleges—but only some, because the expression of principles in concrete structures depends on circumstances. It will take decades to work out many of the Learning Paradigm's implications. But we hope here that by making it more explicit we will help colleagues to more fully recognize it and restructure our institutions in its image.

That such a restructuring is needed is beyond question: the gap between what we *say* we want of higher education and what its structures *provide* has never been wider. To use a distinction made by Chris Argyris and Donald Schön, the difference between our espoused theory and our theory-in-use is becoming distressingly noticeable. An "espoused theory," readers will recall, is the set of principles people offer to explain their behavior; the principles we can infer from how people or their organization actually behave is their "theory-in-use." Right now, the Instruction Paradigm is our theory-in-use, yet the *espoused* theories of most educators more closely resemble components of the Learning Paradigm. The more we discover about how the mind works and how students learn, the greater the disparity between what we say and what we do. Thus so many of us feel increasingly constrained by a system increasingly at variance with what we believe. To build the colleges we need for the 21st century—to put our minds where our hearts are, and rejoin acts with beliefs—we must consciously reject the Instruction Paradigm and restructure what we do on the basis of the Learning Paradigm.

The Paradigms

When comparing alternative paradigms, we must take care: the two will seldom be as neatly parallel as our summary chart suggests (see pages 16 and 17). A paradigm is like the rules of a game: one of the functions of the rules is to define the playing field and domain of possibilities on that field. But a new paradigm may specify a game played on a larger or smaller field with a larger or smaller domain of legitimate possibilities. Indeed, the Learning Paradigm expands the playing field and domain of possibilities and it radically changes various aspects of the game. In the Instruction Paradigm, a specific methodology determines the boundary of what colleges can do; in the Learning Paradigm, student learning and success set the boundary. By the same token, not all elements of the new paradigm are contrary to corresponding elements of the old; the new includes many elements of the old within its larger domain of possibilities. The Learning Paradigm does not prohibit lecturing, for example. Lecturing becomes one of many possible methods, all evaluated on the basis of their ability to promote appropriate learning.

In describing the shift from an Instruction to a Learning Paradigm, we limit our address in this article to undergraduate education. Research and public service are important functions of colleges and universities but lie outside the scope of the present discussion. Here, as in our summary chart, we'll compare the two paradigms along six dimensions: mission and purposes, criteria for success, teaching/learning structures, learning theory, productivity and funding, and nature of roles.

Mission and Purposes

In the Instruction Paradigm, the mission of the college is to provide instruction, to teach. The method and the product are one and the same. The means is the end. In the Learning Paradigm, the mission of the college is to produce learning. The method and the product are separate. The end governs the means.

Some educators may be uncomfortable with the verb "produce." We use it because it so strongly connotes that the college takes *responsibility* for learning. The point of saying that colleges are to *produce* learning—not provide, not support, not encourage—is to say, unmistakably, that they are responsible for the degree to which students learn. The Learning Paradigm shifts what the institution takes responsibility for: from quality instruction (lecturing, talking) to student learning. Students, the co-producers of learning, can and must, of course, take responsibility for their own learning. Hence, responsibility is a win-win game wherein two agents take responsibility for the same outcome even though neither is in complete control of all the variables. When two agents take such responsibility, the resulting synergy produces powerful results.

The idea that colleges cannot be responsible for learning flows from a disempowering notion of responsibility. If we conceive of responsibility as a fixed quantity in a zero-sum game, then students must take responsibility for their own learning, and no one else can. This model generates a concept of responsibility capable of assigning blame but not of empowering the most productive action. The concept of responsibility as a framework for action is quite different: when one takes responsibility, one sets goals and then acts to achieve them, continuously modifying one's behavior to better achieve the goals. To take responsibility for achieving an outcome is not to guarantee the outcome, nor does it entail the complete control of all relevant variables; it is to make the achievement of the outcome the criterion by which one measures one's own efforts. In this sense, it is no contradiction to say that students, faculty, and the college as an institution can all take responsibility for student learning.

In the Learning Paradigm, colleges take responsibility for learning at two distinct levels. At the organizational level, a college takes responsibility for the aggregate of student learning and success. Did, for example, the graduating class's mastery of certain skills or knowledge meet our high, public standards for the award of the degree? The college also takes responsibility at the individual level, that is, for each individual student's learning. Did Mary Smith learn the chemistry we deem appropriate for a degree in that field? Thus, the institution takes responsibility for both its institutional outcomes and individual student outcomes.

Turning now to more specific purposes, in the Instruction Paradigm, a college aims to transfer or deliver knowledge from faculty to students; it offers courses and degree programs and seeks to maintain a high quality of instruction within them mostly by assuring that faculty stay current in their fields. If new knowledge or clients appear, so will new course work. The very purpose of the Instruction Paradigm is to offer courses.

In the Learning Paradigm, on the other hand, a college's purpose is not to transfer knowledge but to create environments and experiences that bring students to discover and construct knowledge for themselves, to make students members of communities of learners that make discoveries and solve problems. The college aims, in fact, to create a series of ever more powerful learning environments. The Learning Paradigm does not limit institutions to a single means for empowering students to learn; within its framework, effective learning technologies are continually identified, developed, tested, implemented, and assessed against one another. The aim in the Learning Paradigm is not so much to improve the quality of instruction—although that is not irrelevant—as it is to improve continuously the quality of learning for students individually and in the aggregate.

Under the older paradigm, colleges aimed to provide access to higher education, especially for historically underrepresented groups such as African-Americans and Hispanics. Too often, mere access hasn't served students well. Under the Learning Paradigm, the goal for under-represented students (and *all* students) becomes not simply access but success. By "success" we mean the achievement of overall student educational objectives such as earning a degree, persisting in school, and learning the "right" things—the skills and knowledge that will help students to achieve their goals in work and life. A Learning Paradigm college, therefore, aims for ever-higher graduation rates while maintaining or even increasing learning standards.

Chart I
Comparing Educational Paradigms

The Instruction Paradigm	The Learning Paradigm
Mission and Purposes	
• Provide/deliver instruction	• Produce learning
• Transfer knowledge from faculty to students	• Elicit student discovery and construction of knowledge
• Offer courses and programs	• Create powerful learning environments
• Improve the quality of instruction	• Improve the quality of learning
• Achieve access for diverse students	• Achieve success for diverse students
Criteria for Success	
• Inputs, resources	• Learning and student-success outcomes
• Quality of entering students	• Quality of exiting students
• Curriculum development, expansion	• Learning technologies development, expansion
• Quantity and quality of resources	• Quality and quality of outcomes
• Enrollment, revenue growth	• Aggregate learning growth, efficiency
• Quality of faculty, instruction	• Quality of students, learning
Teaching/Learning Structures	
• Atomistic; parts prior to whole	• Holistic; whole prior to parts
• Time held constant, learning varies	• Learning held constant, time varies
• 50-minute lecture, 3-unit course	• Learning environments
• Classes start/end at same time	• Environment ready when student is
• One teacher, one classroom	• Whatever learning experience works
• Independent disciplines, departments	• Cross discipline/department collaboration
• Covering material	• Specified learning results
• End-of-course assessment	• Pre/during/post assessments
• Grading within classes by instructors	• External evaluations of learning
• Private assessment	• Public assessment
• Degree equals accumulated credit hours	• Degree equals demonstrated knowledge and skills
Learning Theory	
• Knowledge exists "out there"	• Knowledge exists in each person's mind and is shaped by individual experience
• Knowledge comes in "chunks" and "bits" delivered by instructors	• Knowledge is constructed, created, and "gotten"
• Learning is cumulative and linear	• Learning is a nesting and interacting of frameworks
• Fits the storehouse of knowledge metaphor	• Fits learning how to ride a bicycle metaphor
• Learning is teacher centered and controlled	• Learning is student centered and controlled
• "Live" teacher, "live" students required	• "Active" learner required, but not "live" teacher
• The classroom and learning are competitive and individualistic	• Learning environments and learning are cooperative, collaborative, and supportive
• Talent and ability are rare	• Talent and ability are abundant
Productivity/Funding	
• Definition of productivity: cost per hour of instruction per student	• Definition of productivity: cost per unit of learning per student
• Funding for hours of instruction	• Funding for learning outcomes

Chart 1 *continued*

Nature of Roles	
• Faculty are primarily lecturers	• Faculty are primarily designers of learning methods and environments
• Faculty and students act independently and in isolation	• Faculty and student work in teams with each other and other staff
• Teachers classify and sort students	• Teachers develop every student's competencies and talents
• Staff serve/support faculty and the process of instruction	• All staff are educators who produce student learning and success
• Any expert can teach	• Empowering learning is challenging and complex
• Line governance; independent actors	• Shared governance; teamwork

By shifting the intended institutional outcome from teaching to learning, the Learning Paradigm makes possible a continuous improvement in productivity. Whereas under the Instruction Paradigm a primary institutional purpose was to optimize faculty well-being and success—including recognition for research and scholarship—in the Learning Paradigm a primary drive is to produce learning outcomes more efficiently. The philosophy of an Instruction Paradigm college reflects the belief that it cannot increase learning outputs without more resources, but a Learning Paradigm college expects to do so continuously. A Learning Paradigm college is concerned with learning productivity, not teaching productivity.

Criteria for Success

Under the Instruction Paradigm, we judge our colleges by comparing them to one another. The criteria for quality are defined in terms of inputs and process measures. Factors such as selectivity in student admissions, number of PhDs on the faculty, and research reputation are used to rate colleges and universities. Administrators and boards may look to enrollment and revenue growth and the expansion of courses and programs. As Guskin put it, "We are so wedded to a definition of quality based on resources that we find it extremely difficult to deal with the *results* of our work, namely student learning."

The Learning Paradigm necessarily incorporates the perspectives of the assessment movement. While this movement has been under way for at least a decade, under the dominant Instruction Paradigm it has not penetrated very far into normal organizational practice. Only a few colleges across the country systematically assess student learning outcomes. Educators in California community colleges always seem to be surprised when they hear that 45 percent of first-time fall students do not return in the spring and that it takes an average of six years for a student to earn an associate's (AA) degree. The reason for this lack of outcomes knowledge is profoundly simple: under the Instruction Paradigm, student outcomes are simply irrelevant to the successful functioning and funding of a college.

Our faculty evaluation systems, for example, evaluate the performance of faculty in teaching terms, not learning terms. An instructor is typically evaluated by her peers or dean on the basis of whether her lectures are organized, whether she covers the appropriate material, whether she shows interest in and understanding of her subject matter, whether she is prepared for class, and whether she respects her students' questions and comments. All these factors evaluate the instructor's performance in teaching terms. They do not raise the issue of whether students are learning, let alone demand evidence of learning or provide for its reward.

Many institutions construe teaching almost entirely in terms of lecturing. A true story makes the point. A biology instructor was experimenting with collaborative methods of instruction in his beginning biology classes. One day his dean came for a site visit, slipping into the back of the room. The room was a hubbub of activity. Students were discussing material enthusiastically in small groups spread out across the room; the instructor would observe each group for a few minutes, sometimes making a comment, sometimes just nodding approval. After 15 minutes or so the dean approached the instructor and said, "I came today to do your evaluation. I'll come back another time when you're teaching."

In the Instruction Paradigm, teaching is judged on its own terms; in the Learning Paradigm, the power of an environment or approach is judged in terms of its impact on learning. If learning occurs, then the environment has power. If students learn more in environment A than in environment B, then A is more powerful than B. To know this in the Learning Paradigm we would assess student learning routinely and constantly.

Institutional outcomes assessment is analogous to classroom assessment, as described by K. Patricia Cross and Thomas Angelo. In our own experience of classroom-assessment training workshops, teachers share moving stories about how even limited use of these techniques has prompted them to make big changes in their teaching, sometimes despite years of investment in a previous practice. Mimi Steadmen, in a recent study of community college teachers using classroom assessment, found that "eighty-eight percent of faculty surveyed reported that they had made changes in their teaching behaviors as a result." This at first was startling to us. How could such small amounts of information produce such large changes in teaching behavior?

Upon reflection, it became clear. The information was feedback about learning, about results—something teachers rarely collect. Given information that their students were not learning, it was obvious to these teachers that something had to be done about the methods they had been using. Likewise, we think, feedback on learning results at the institutional level should have a correspondingly large impact on an institution's behavior and on the means it uses to produce learning.

Of course, some will argue, true education simply cannot be measured. You cannot measure, for example, true appreciation of the beauty of a work of art. Certainly some learning is difficult, even impossible to measure. But it does not follow that useful and meaningful assessment is impossible.

If we compare outcomes assessment with the input measures controlling policy in the Instruction Paradigm, we find that measures of outcome provide far more genuine information about learning than do measures of input. Learning outcomes include whatever students do as a result of a learning experience. Any measurement of students' products from an educational experience is a measure of a learning outcome. We could count the number of pages students write, the number of books they read, their number of hours at the computer, or the number of math problems they solve.

Of course, these would be silly methods to determine institutional incentives, and we do not recommend them. Any one of them, however, would produce more useful information on learning than the present method of measuring inputs and ignoring outcomes. It would make more sense to fund a college on the number of math problems students solve, for example, than to fund it on the number of students who sit in math classes. We suspect that *any* system of institutional incentives based on outcomes would lead to greater learning than any system of incentives based on inputs. But we need not settle for a system biased toward the trivial. Right now, today, we can construct a good assessment regime with the tools we have at hand.

The Learning Paradigm requires us to heed the advice of the Wingspread Group: "New forms of assessment should focus on establishing what college and university graduates have learned—the knowledge and skill levels they have achieved and their potential for further independent learning."

Teaching/Learning Structures

By structures we mean those features of an organization that are stable over time and that form the framework within which activities and processes occur and through which the purposes of the organization are achieved. Structure includes the organization cart, role and reward systems, technologies and methods, facilities and equipment, decision-making customs, communication channels, feed-back loops, financial arrangements, and funding streams.

Peter Senge, in *The Fifth Discipline*, a book about applying systems theory to organizational learning, observes that institutions and their leaders rarely focus their attention on systemic structures. They seldom think, he says, to alter basic structures in order to improve organizational performance, even though those structures generate the patterns of organizational action and determine which activities and results are possible. Perhaps the recent talk about restructuring, re-engineering, and reinvention in higher education reflects a change in focus and a heightened awareness of both the constraining and liberating power of organizational structures.

There is good reason to attend to structure. First, restructuring offers the greatest hope for increasing organizational efficiency and effectiveness. Structure is leverage. If you change the structure in which people work, you increase or decrease the leverage applied to their efforts. A change in structure can either increase productivity or change the nature of organizational outcomes. Second, structure is the concrete manifestation of the abstract principles of the organization's governing paradigm. Structures reflecting an old paradigm can frustrate the best ideas and innovations of new-paradigm thinkers. As the governing paradigm changes, so likewise must the organization's structures.

In this section, we focus on the main structures related to the teaching and learning process; funding and faculty role structures are discussed later under separate headings. The teaching and learning structure of the Instruction Paradigm college is atomistic. In its universe, the "atom" is the 50-minute lecture, and the "molecule" is the one-teacher, one-classroom, three-credit-hour course. From these basic units the physical architecture, the administrative structure, and the daily schedules of faculty and students are built. Dennis McGrath and Martin Spear, professors at the Community College of Philadelphia, note that "education proceeds everywhere through the vehicle of the three-credit course. Faculty members [and everyone else, we might add] have so internalized that constraint that they are long past noticing that it is a constraint, thinking it part of the natural order of things."

The resulting structure is powerful and rigid. It is, of course, perfectly suited to the Instruction Paradigm task of offering one-teacher, one-classroom courses. It is antithetical to creating almost any other kind of learning experience. A sense of this can be obtained by observing the effort, struggle, and rule-bending required to schedule even a slightly different kind of learning activity such as a team-taught course.

In the "educational atomism" of the Instruction Paradigm, the parts of the teaching and learning process are seen as discrete entities. The parts exist prior to and independent of any whole; the whole is no more than the sum of the parts, or even less. The college interacts with students only in discrete, isolated environments, cut off from one another because the parts—the classes—are prior to the whole. A "college education" is the sum the student's experience of a series of discrete, largely unrelated, three-credit classes.

In the Instruction Paradigm, the teaching and learning process is governed by the further rule that time will be held constant while learning varies. Although addressing public elementary and secondary education, the analysis of the National Commission of Time and Learning nonetheless applies to colleges:

> Time is learning's warden. Our time-bound mentality has fooled us all into believing that schools can educate all of the people all of the time in a school year of 180 six-hour days. . . . If experience, research, and common sense teach nothing else, they confirm the truism that people learn at different rates, and in different ways with different subjects. But we have put the cart before the horse: our schools . . . are captives of clock and calendar. The boundaries of student growth are defined by schedules . . . instead of standards for students and learning.

Under the rule of time, all classes start and stop at the same time and take the same number of calendar weeks. The rule of time and the priority of parts affect every instructional act of the college.

Thus it is, for example, that if students come into college classes "unprepared," it is not the job of the faculty who teach those classes to "prepare" them. Indeed, the structure of the one-semester, three-credit class makes it all but impossible to do so. The only solution, then, is to create new courses to prepare students for the existing courses; within the Instruction Paradigm, the response to educational problems is always to generate more atomized, discrete instructional units. If business students are lacking a sense of ethics, then offer and require a course in business ethics. If students have poor study skills, then offer a "master student" course to teach such skills.

Instruction Paradigm colleges atomistically organize courses and teachers into departments and programs that rarely communicate with one another. Academic departments, originally associated with coherent disciplines, are the structural home bases for accomplishing the essential work of the college: offering courses. "Departments have a life of their own," notes William D. Schaefer, professor of English and former executive vice chancellor at UCLA. They are "insular, defensive, self-governing, [and] compelled to protect their interests because the faculty positions as well as the courses that justify funding those positions are located therein."

Those globally applicable skills that are the foundation of meaningful engagement with the world—reading, writing, calculating, reasoning—find a true place in this structure only if they have their own independent bases: the English or math or reading departments. If students cannot reason or think well, the college creates a course on reasoning and thinking. This in turn produces pressure to create a corresponding department. "If we are not careful," warns Adam Sweeting, director of the Writing Program at the Massachusetts School of Law at Andover, "the teaching of critical thinking skills will become the responsibility of one university department, a prospect that is at odds with the very idea of a university."

Efforts to extend college-level reading, writing, and reasoning "across the curriculum" have largely failed. The good intentions produced few results because, under the Instruction Paradigm, the teacher's job is to "cover the material" as outlined in the disciplinary syllabus. The instructor charged with implementing writing or reading or critical thinking "across the curriculum" often must choose between doing her job or doing what will help students learn—between doing well, as it were, or doing good.

From the point of view of the Learning Paradigm, these Instruction Paradigm teaching and learning structures present immense barriers to improving student learning and success. They provide no space and support for redesigned learning environments or for experimenting with alternative learning technologies. They don't provide for, warrant, or reward assessing whether student learning has occurred or is improving.

In a Learning Paradigm college, the structure of courses and lectures becomes dispensable and negotiable. Semesters and quarters, lectures, labs, syllabi—indeed, classes themselves—become options rather than received structures or mandatory activities. The Learning Paradigm prescribes no one "answer" to the question of how to organize learning environments and experiences. It supports any learning method and structure that works, where "works" in defined in terms of learning outcomes, not as the degree of conformity to an ideal classroom archetype. In fact, the Learning Paradigm requires a constant search for new structures and methods that work better for student learning and success, and expects even these to be redesigned continually and to evolve over time.

The transition from Instruction Paradigm to Learning Paradigm will not be instantaneous. It will be a process of gradual modification and experimentation through which we alter many organizational parts in light of a new vision for the whole. Under the Instruction Paradigm, structures are assumed to be fixed and immutable; there is no ready means for achieving the leverage needed to alter them. The first structural task of the Learning Paradigm, then, is to establish such leverage.

The key structure for changing the rest of the system is an institutionwide assessment and information system—an essential structure in the Learning Paradigm, and a key means for getting there. It would provide constant, useful feedback on institutional performance. It would track transfer, graduation, and other completion rates. It would track the flow of students through learning stages (such as the achievement of basic skills) and the development of in-depth knowledge in a discipline. It would measure the knowledge and skills of program completers and graduates. It would assess learning along many dimensions and in many places and stages in each student's college experience.

To be most effective, this assessment system would provide public institutional-level information. We are not talking about making public the status of individual students by name, but about making the year-to-year graduation rate—or the mean score of graduating seniors on a critical thinking assessment, for example—"public" in the sense that they are available to everyone in the college community. Moreover, in the Learning Paradigm college, such data are routinely talked about and acted upon by a community ever dedicated to improving its own performance.

The effectiveness of the assessment system for developing alternative learning environments depends in part upon its being *external* to learning programs and structures. While in the Instruction Paradigm students are assessed and graded within a class by the same instructor responsible for teaching them, in the Learning Paradigm much of the assessment would be independent of the learning experience and its designer, somewhat as football games are independent measures of what is learned in football practice. Course grades alone fail to tell us what students know and can do; average grades assigned by instructors are not reliable measures of whether the institution is improving learning.

Ideally an institution's assessment program would measure the "value-added" over the course of students' experience at the college. Student knowledge and skills would be measured upon entrance and again upon graduation, and at intermediate stages such as at the beginning and completion of major programs. Students could then be acknowledged and certified for what they have learned; the same data aggregated, could help shift judgments of institutional quality from inputs and resources to the value-added brought to student learning by the college.

The college devoted to learning first identifies the knowledge and skills it expects its graduates to possess, without regard to any particular curriculum or educational experiences. It then determines how to assess them reliably. It assesses graduating students, and the resulting information is then used to redesign and improve the processes and environments leading to such outcomes. In this manner, enhancing intellectual skills such as writing and problem solving and social skills such as effective team participation become the project of *all* learning programs and structured experience. The whole would govern the parts.

Information from a sophisticated assessment system will gradually lead to the transformation of the college's learning environments and supporting structures. Such a system seeks out "best practice" benchmarks against which improvements in institutional performance can be measured in learning terms. It is the foundation for creating an institutional capacity to develop ever more effective and efficient ways of empowering learning. It becomes the basis for generating revenue or funding according to learning results rather than hours of instruction. Most importantly, it is the key to the college's and its staff's taking responsibility for and enjoying the progress of each student's education.

Instead of fixing the means—such as lectures and courses—the Learning Paradigm fixes the ends, the learning results, allowing the means to vary in its constant search for the most effective and efficient paths to student learning. Learning outcomes and standards thus would be identified and held to for all students—or *raised* as learning environments became more powerful—while the time students took to achieve those standards would vary. This would reward skilled and advanced students with speedy progress while enabling less prepared students the time they needed to actually master the material. By "testing out," students could also avoid wasting their time being "taught" what they already know. Students would be given "credit" for degree-relevant knowledge and skills regardless of how or where or when they learned them.

In the Learning Paradigm, then, a college degree would represent not time spent and credit hours dutifully accumulated, but would certify that the student had demonstrably attained specified knowledge skills. Learning Paradigm institutions would develop and publish explicit exit standards for graduates and grant degrees and certificates only to students who met them. Thus colleges would move away from educational atomism and move toward treating holistically the knowledge and skills required for a degree.

Learning Theory

The Instruction Paradigm frames learning atomistically. In it, knowledge, by definition, consists of matter dispensed or delivered by an instructor. The chief agent in the process is the teacher who delivers knowledge; students are viewed as passive vessels, ingesting knowledge for recall on tests. Hence any expert can teach. Partly because the teacher knows which chunks of knowledge are most important, the teacher controls the learning activities. Learning is presumed to be cumulative because it amounts to ingesting more and more chunks. A degree is awarded when a student has received a specified amount of instruction.

The Learning Paradigm frames learning holistically, recognizing that the chief agent in the process is the learner. Thus, students must be active discoverers and constructors of their own knowledge. In the Learning Paradigm, knowledge consists of frameworks or wholes that are created or constructed by the learner. Knowledge is not seen as cumulative and linear, like a wall of bricks, but as a nesting and interacting of frameworks. Learning is revealed when those frameworks are used to understand and act. Seeing the whole of something—the forest rather than the trees, the image of the newspaper photo rather than its dots—gives meaning to its elements, and that whole becomes more than a sum of component parts. Wholes and frameworks can come in a moment—a flash of insight—often after much hard work with the pieces, as when one suddenly knows how to ride a bicycle.

In the Learning Paradigm, learning environments and activities are learner-centered and learner-controlled. They may even be "teacherless." While teachers will have designed the learning experiences and environments students use—often through teamwork with each other and other staff—they need not be present for or participate in every structured learning activity.

Many students come away from college with a false notion of what learning is and come to believe falsely that learning—at least for some subjects—is too difficult for them. Many students cruise through schools substituting an ersatz role-playing exercise for learning.

The first time I (Barr) studied calculus as a college freshman, I did well by conventional standards. However, while I could solve enough problems to get A's on exams, I really didn't feel that I understood the Limit Theorem, the derivative, or much else. But 15 years later, after having completed college and graduate school and having taught algebra and geometry in high school, I needed to relearn calculus so that I could tutor a friend., In only two, albeit intense, days, I relearned—or really learned for the first time, so it seemed—two semesters of calculus. During those days, I wondered how I ever thought that calculus was difficult and why I didn't see the Limit Theorem and derivative for the simple, obvious things they are.

What was the difference between my first learning of calculus and the second? It certainly wasn't a higher IQ. And I don't think it was because I learned or remembered much from the first time. I think it was that I brought some very powerful intellectual frameworks to the learning the second time that I didn't have the first time. Having taught algebra and geometry, I had learned their basic structure, that is, the nature of a mathematical system. I had learned the lay of the land, the whole. Through many years of schooling and study, I had also learned a number of other frameworks that were useful for learning calculus. Thus learning calculus the second time within these "advanced" frameworks was easy compared to learning, or trying to learn, calculus without them as I did as a freshman.

So much of this is because the "learning" that goes on in Instruction Paradigm colleges frequently involves only rudimentary, stimulus-response relationships whose cues may be coded into the context of a particular course but are not rooted in the student's everyday, functioning understanding.

The National Council on Vocational Educational summarizes the consequences in its 1991 report, *Solutions*: "The result is fractionation, or splitting into pieces: having to learn disconnected sub-routines, items, and sub-skills without an understanding of the larger context into which they fit and which gives them meaning." While such approaches are entirely consistent with educational atomism, they are at odds with the way we think and learn. The same report quotes Sylvia Farnham-Diggory's summary of contemporary research: "Fractionated instruction maximizes forgetting, inattention, and passivity. Both children and adults acquire knowledge from active participation in holistic, complex, meaningful environments organized around long-term goals. Today's school programs could hardly have been better designed to prevent a child's natural learning system from operating."

The result is that when the contextual cues provided by the class disappear at the end of the semester, so does the learning. Howard Gardner points out that "researchers at Johns Hopkins, MIT, and other well-regarded universities have documented that students who receive honor grades in college-level physics courses are frequently unable to solve basic problems and questions encountered in a form slightly different from that on which they have been formally instructed and tested."

The Learning Paradigm embraces the goal of promoting what Gardner calls "education for understanding"—"a sufficient grasp of concepts, principles, or skills so that one can bring them to bear on new problems and situations, deciding in which way one's present competencies can suffice and in which ways one may require new skills or knowledge." This involves the mastery of functional, knowledge-based intellectual frameworks rather than the short-term retention of fractionated, contextual cues.

The learning theory of the Instruction Paradigm reflects deeply rooted societal assumptions about talent, relationships, and accomplishment: that which is valuable is scarce; life is a win-lose proposition; and success is an individual achievement. The Learning Paradigm theory of learning reverses these assumptions.

Under the Instruction Paradigm, faculty classify and sort students, in the worst cases into those who are "college material" and those who cannot "cut it," since intelligence and ability are scarce. Under the Learning Paradigm, faculty—and everybody else in the institution—are unambiguously committed to each student's success. The faculty and the institution take an R. Buckminster Fuller view of students: human beings are born geniuses and designed for success. If they fail to display their genius or fail to succeed, it is because their design function is being thwarted. This perspective is founded not in wishful thinking but in the best evidence about the real capabilities of virtually all humans for learning. As the Wingspread Group points out, "There is growing research evidence that all students can learn to much higher standards than we now require." In the Learning Paradigm, faculty find ways to develop every student's vast talents and clear the way for every student's success.

Under the Instruction Paradigm, the classroom is competitive and individualistic, reflecting a view that life is a win-lose proposition. The requirement that the students must achieve individually and solely through their own efforts reflects the belief that success is an individual accomplishment. In the Learning

Paradigm, learning environments—while challenging—are win-win environments that are cooperative, collaborative, and supportive. They are designed on the principle that accomplishment and success are the result of teamwork and group efforts, even when it appears one is working alone.

Productivity and Funding

Under the Instruction Paradigm, colleges suffer from a serious design flaw—they are structured in such a way that they cannot increase their productivity without diminishing the quality of their product. In the Instruction Paradigm, productivity is defined as cost per hour of instruction per student. In this view, the very quality of teaching and learning is threatened by any increase in the student-to-faculty ratio.

Under the Learning Paradigm, productivity is redefined as the cost per unit of learning per student. Not surprisingly, there is as yet no standard statistic that corresponds to this notion of productivity. Under this new definition, however, it *is* possible to increase outcomes without increasing costs. An abundance of research shows that alternatives to the traditional semester-length, classroom-based lecture method produce more learning. Some of these alternatives are less expensive; many produce more learning for the same cost. Under the Learning Paradigm, producing more with less becomes possible because the more that is being produced is learning and not hours of instruction. Productivity, in this sense, cannot even be measured in the Instruction Paradigm college. All that exists is a measure of exposure to instruction.

Given the Learning Paradigm's definition, increases in productivity pose no threat to the quality of education. Unlike the current definition, this new definition requires that colleges actually produce learning. Otherwise, there is no "product" to count in the productivity ratio.

But what should be the definition of "unit of learning" and how can it be measured? A single, permanent answer to that question does not and need not exist. We have argued above that learning, or at least the effects of learning, can be measured, certainly well enough to determine what students are learning and whether the institution is getting more effective and efficient at producing it.

The Instruction Paradigm wastes not only institutional resources but the time and energy of students. We waste our students' time with registration lines, bookstore lines, lock-step class scheduling, and redundant courses and requirements. We do not teach them to learn efficiently and effectively. We can do a lot, as D. Bruce Johnstone, former chancellor of SUNY, suggests, to reduce the false starts and aimless "drift" of students that slow their progress toward a degree. Now let's consider how colleges are funded. One of the absurdities of current funding formulas is that an institution could utterly fail its educational mission and yet its revenue would remain unaffected. For example, attendance at public colleges on the semester system is measured twice, once in the fall and again in the spring. Normally, at California community colleges, for example, about two-thirds of fall students return for the spring term. New students and returning stop-outs make up for the one-third of fall students who leave. Even if only half—or none at all—returned, as long as spring enrollments equal those of the fall, these institutions would suffer no loss of revenue.

There is no more powerful feedback than revenue. Nothing could facilitate a shift to the Learning Paradigm more swiftly than funding learning and learning-related institutional outcomes rather than hours of instruction. The initial response to the idea of outcomes-based funding is likely to be "That's not possible." But, of course, it is. As the new paradigm takes hold, forces and possibilities shift and the impossible becomes the rule.

Nature of Roles

With the shift to the Learning Paradigm comes a change in roles for virtually all college employees.

In the Instruction Paradigm, faculty are conceived primarily as disciplinary experts who impart knowledge by lecturing. They are the essential feature of the "instructional delivery system." The Learning Paradigm, on the other hand, conceives of faculty as primarily the designers of learning environments; they study and apply best methods for producing learning and student success.

If the Instruction Paradigm faculty member is an actor—a sage on a stage—then the Learning Paradigm faculty member is an inter-actor—a coach interacting with a team. If the model in the Instruction Paradigm is that of delivering a lecture, then the model in the Learning Paradigm is that of designing and then playing a team game. A coach not only instructs football players, for example, but also designs football practices and the game plan; he participates in the game itself by sending in plays and making other decisions. The new faculty role goes a step further, however, in that faculty not only design game plans but also create new and better "games," ones that generate more and better learning.

Roles under the Learning Paradigm, then, begin to blur. Architects of campus buildings and payroll clerks alike will contribute to and shape the environments that empower student learning. As the role structures of colleges begin to loosen up and as accountability for results (learning) tightens up, organizational control and command structures will change. Teamwork and shared governance over time replace the line governance and independent work of the Instruction Paradigm's hierarchical and competitive organization.

In the Learning Paradigm, as colleges specify learning goals and focus on learning technologies, interdisciplinary (or nondisciplinary) task groups and design teams become a major operating mode. For example, faculty may form a design team to develop a learning experience in which students networked via computers learn to write about selected texts or on a particular theme.

After developing and testing its new learning module, the design team may even be able to let students proceed through it without direct faculty contact except at designated points. Design teams might include a variety of staff: disciplinary experts, information technology experts, a graphic designer, and an assessment professional. Likewise, faculty and staff might form functional teams responsible for a body of learning outcomes for a stated number of students. Such teams could have the freedom that no faculty member has in today's atomized framework, that to organize the learning environment in ways that maximize student learning.

Meeting the Challenge

Changing paradigms is hard. A paradigm gives a system integrity and allows it to function by identifying what counts as information within the infinite ocean of data in its environment. Data that solve problems that the paradigm identifies as important are information; data that are irrelevant to those problems are simply noise, static. Any system will provide both channels for transmitting information relevant to the system and filters to reduce noise.

Those who want to change the paradigm governing an institution are—from the institution's point of view—people who are listening to the noise and ignoring the information. They appear crazy or out of touch. The quartz watch was invented by the Swiss. But the great Swiss watchmakers responded to the idea of gearless timepieces in essentially the same way that the premiere audience responded to Stravinsky's *The Rite of Spring*. They threw tomatoes. They hooted it off the stage.

The principle also operates in the other direction. From the point of view of those who have adopted a new paradigm, the institution comes to sound like a cacophony-generating machine, a complex and refined device for producing more and louder noise. From the perspective of the governing paradigm, the advocates of the insurgent paradigm seem willing to sacrifice the institution itself for pie-in-the-sky nonsense. But from the perspective of the insurgents, the defenders of the present system are perpetuating a system that no longer works.

But paradigms do change. The Church admits Galileo was right. *The Rite of Spring* has become an old warhorse. Paradigms can even change quickly. Look at your watch.

Paradigms change when the ruling paradigm loses its capacity to solve problems and generate a positive vision of the future. This we very much see today. One early sign of a paradigm shift is an attempt to use the tools and ideas of a new paradigm within the framework provided by the old, or to convey information intelligible in the new paradigm through the channels of the old. This, too, is now happening.

In our experience, people will suffer the turbulence and uncertainty of change if it promises a better way to accomplish work they value. The shift to the Learning Paradigm represents such an opportunity.

The Learning Paradigm doesn't answer all the important questions, of course. What it does do is lead us to a set of new questions and a domain of possible responses. What knowledge, talents, and skills do college graduates need in order to live and work fully? What must they do to master such knowledge, talents, and skills? Are they doing those things? Do students find in our colleges a coherent body of experiences that help them to become competent, capable, and interesting people? Do they understand what they've memorized? Can they act on it? Has the experience of college made our students flexible and adaptable learners, able to thrive in a knowledge society?

How do you begin to move to the new paradigm? Ultimately, changing paradigms means doing everything differently. But we can suggest three areas where changes—even small ones—can create leverage for larger change in the future.

First, you begin by speaking. You begin to speak *within* the new paradigm. As we come to understand the Learning Paradigm, we must make our understanding public. Stop talking about the "quality of instruction" or the "instructional program." Instead, talk about what it takes to produce "quality learning" and refer to the college's "learning programs." Instead of speaking of "instructional delivery," speak about "learning outcomes."

The primary reason the Instruction Paradigm is so powerful is that it is invisible. Its incoherencies and deficiencies appear as inherent qualities of the world. If we come to see the Instruction Paradigm as a product of our own assumptions and not a force of nature, then we can change it. Only as you begin to experiment with the new language will you realize just how entrenched and invisible the old paradigm is. But as you and your colleagues begin to speak the new language, you will then also begin to think and act out of the new paradigm.

Second, if we begin to talk about the "learning outcomes" of existing programs, we'll experience frustration at our nearly complete ignorance of what those outcomes are—the Learning Paradigm's most important category of information is one about which we know very little now. The place to start the assessment of learning outcomes is in the conventional classroom; from there, let the practice grow to the program and institutional levels. In the Learning Paradigm, the key structure that provides the leverage to change the rest is a system for requiring the specification of learning outcomes and their assessment through processes external to instruction. The more we learn about the outcomes of existing programs, the more rapidly they will change.

Third, we should address the legally entrenched state funding mechanisms that fund institutions on the basis of hours of instruction. This powerful external force severely constrains the kinds of changes that an institution can make. It virtually limits them to changes within classrooms, leaving intact the atomistic one-teacher, one-classroom structure. We need to work to have state legislatures change the funding formulas of public colleges and universities to give institutions the latitude and incentives to develop new structures for learning. Persuading legislators and governors should not be hard; indeed, the idea of funding colleges for results rather than seat time has an inherent political attractiveness. It is hard to see why legislators would resist the concept that taxpayers should pay for what they get out of higher education, and get what they pay for.

Try this thought experiment. Take a team of faculty at any college—at your college—and select a group of students on some coherent principle, any group of students as long as they have something in common. Keep the ratio of faculty to students the same as it already is. Tell the faculty team. "We want you to create a program for these students so that they will improve significantly in the following knowledge and cognitive skills by the end of one year. We will assess them at the beginning and assess them at the end, and we will tell you how we are going to do so. Your task is to produce learning with these students. In doing so, you are not constrained by any of the rules or regulations you have grown accustomed to. You are free to organize the environment in any way you like. The only thing you are required to do is to produce the desired result—student learning."

We have suggested this thought experiment to many college faculty and asked them whether, if given this freedom, they could design a learning environment that would get better results than what they are doing now. So far, no one has answered that question in the negative. Why not do it?

The change that is required to address today's challenges is not vast or difficult or expensive. It is a small thing. But it is a small change that changes everything. Simply ask, how would we do things differently if we put learning first? Then do it.

Those who say it can't be done frequently assert that environments that actually produce learning are too expensive. But this is clearly not true. What we are doing now is too expensive by far. Today, learning is prohibitively expensive in higher education; we simply can't afford it for more and more of our students. The high cost of learning is an artifact of the Instruction Paradigm. It is simply false to say that we cannot afford to give our students the education they deserve. We can, but we will not as long as we allow the Instruction Paradigm to dominate our thinking. The problem is not insoluble. However, to paraphrase Albert Einstein, we cannot solve our problem with the same level of thinking that created it.

Buckminster Fuller used to say that you should never try to change the course of a great ship by applying force to the bow. You shouldn't even try it by applying force to the rudder. Rather you should apply force to the trim-tab. A trim-tab is a little rudder attached to the end of the rudder. A very small force will turn it left, thus moving the big rudder to the right, and the huge ship to the left. The shift to the Learning Paradigm is the trim-tab of the great ship of higher education. It is a shift that changes everything.

Additional Readings

I. The Evolution of College Teaching and Learning in America

Boyer, E. L. (1990). *Scholarship reconsidered: Priorities of the professoriate.* Princeton, NJ: Carnegie Foundation for the Advancement of Teaching.

Brubacher, J. S., and Rudy, S. W. (1958). Early methods of instruction. In J. S. Brubacher and S. W. Rudy, *Higher education in transition: A history of American colleges and universities, 1636-1976* (pp. 84-99). New York: Harper and Row.

Cowley, W. H. (1953). A century of college teaching. *Improving College and University Teaching, 1* (3), 3–10.

Cowley, W. H. (1958). College and university teaching, 1858–1958. In R. M. Cooper (Ed.), *The two ends of the log: Learning and teaching in today's college* (pp. 101–124). Minneapolis, MN: University of Minnesota Press.

Highet, G. (1950). *The art of teaching*. New York: Vintage Books.

McKeachie, W. J. (1970). *Research on college teaching: A review.* (Report No. 6). Washington, D. C.: ERIC Clearinghouse on Higher Education, George Washington University.

McKeachie, W. J. (1963). Research on teaching at the college and university level. In N. L. Gage (Ed.), *Handbook of research on teaching* (pp. 1118–1172). Skokie, IL: Rand-McNally.

McKeachie, W. J., and Kulik, J. A. (1975). Effective college teaching. *Review of Research in Education*, 3, 165–209.

Paulsen, M. B., and Feldman, K. A. (1995). Toward a reconceptualization of scholarship: A human action system with functional imperatives. *Journal of Higher Education, 66*, 615–640.

Richlin, L. (Ed.). (1993). *Preparing faculty for the new conceptions of scholarship* (New Direction for Teaching and Learning, No. 54). San Francisco: Jossey–Bass.

Schon, D. A. (1995). The new scholarship requires a new epistemology: Knowing in action. *Change, 27* (6), 26–34.

Weimer, M. (1966). Why scholarship is the bedrock of good teaching. In R. J. Menges and M. Weimer (Eds.), *Teaching on solid ground: Using scholarship to improve practice* (pp. 1–12). San Francisco: Jossey-Bass.

II. Understanding Students as Learners

Adams, M. (1992). Cultural inclusion in the American college classroom. In L. L. B. Border and N. Van Note Chism (Eds.), *Teaching for diversity* (New Directions for Teaching and Learning, No. 49, pp. 5–17). San Francisco: Jossey-Bass.

Anderson, J. A. (1988). Cognitive styles and multicultural populations. *Journal of Teacher Education, 39*, 2–9.

Anderson, J. A. and Adams, M. (1992). Acknowledging the learning styles of diverse student populations: Implications for instructional design. In L. L. B. Border and N. Van Note Chism (Eds.), *Teaching for diversity* (New Directions for Teaching and Learning, No. 49, pp. 19–33). San Francisco: Jossey-Bass.

Baxter Magolda, M. B. (1990). Gender differences in epistemological development. *Journal of College Student Development, 31*, 555–561.

Baxter Magolda, M. B. (1992). *Knowing and reasoning in college: Gender-related patterns in students' intellectual development*. San Francisco: Jossey-Bass.

Belenky, M. F., Clinchy, B. M., Goldberger, N. R., and Tarule, J. M. (1986). *Women's ways of knowing: The development of self, body, and mind*. New York: Basic Books.

Bower, G. H., and Hilgard, E. R. (1981). *Theories of learning* (5th ed.). Englewood Cliffs, NJ: Prentice-Hall.

Brookfield, S. D. (1986). *Understanding and facilitating adult learning*. San Francisco: Jossey-Bass.

Bruning, R. H., Schraw, G. J., and Ronning, R. R. (1995). *Cognitive psychology and instruction*. Englewood Cliffs, NJ: Prentice-Hall.

Claxton, C. S., and Murrell, P. H. (1987). *Learning styles: Implications for improving educational practices*. (ASHE-ERIC Higher Education Report No. 4). Washington, D. C.: Association for the Study of Higher Education.

Cross, K. P. (1981). *Adults as learners: Increasing participation and facilitating learning*. San Francisco: Jossey-Bass.

Entwistle, N. J., and Ramsden, P. (1983). *Understanding student learning*. London: Croom Helm.

Entwistle, N., and Tate, H. (1995). Approaches to studying and perceptions of the learning environment across disciplines. In N. Hativa and M. Marincovich (Eds.), *Disciplinary differences in teaching and learning: Implications for practice* (New Directions for Teaching and Learning, No. 64, pp. 93–103). San Francisco: Jossey-Bass.

Feldman, K. A., and Newcomb, T. M. (1969). *The impact of college on students*. San Francisco: Jossey-Bass.

Gagne, R. M., and Driscoll, M. P. (1988). *Essentials of learning for instruction* (2nd ed.). Englewood Cliffs, NJ: Prentice-Hall.

Gardner, H. (1993). *Multiple intelligences: The theory in practice*. San Francisco: Harper and Row.

Gilligan, C. (1982). *In a different voice: Psychological theory and women's development*. Cambridge, MA: Harvard University Press.

Goldberger, N. R., Tarule, J. M., Clinchy, B. M., and Belenky, M. F. (1996). *Knowledge, difference, and power: Essays inspired by Women's Ways of Knowing*. New York: Basic Books.

Griggs, S. A., and Dunn, R. (1989). The learning styles of multicultural groups. *Journal of Multicultural Counseling and Development, 17*, 146–155.

Hofer, B. K., and Pintrich, P. R. (1997). The development of epistemological theories: Beliefs about knowledge and knowing and their relation to learning. *Review of Educational Research 67*, 88–140.

Jenkins, C. A., and Bainer, D. L. (1991). Common instructional problems in the multicultural classroom. *Journal on Excellence in College Teaching, 2*, 77–88.

Joyce, B., and Weil, M. (1986). The thinking, feeling student: Alternative models of learning. In B. Joyce and M. Weil, *Models of teaching* (3rd ed., pp. 1–22). Englewood Cliffs, NJ: Prentice-Hall.

Knapper, C. K. (1988). Technology and college teaching. In R. E. Young and K. E. Eble (Eds.), *College teaching and learning: Preparing for new commitments* (New Directions for Teaching and Learning, No. 33, pp. 31–46). San Francisco: Jossey-Bass.

Kolb, D. A. (1984). *Experiential learning: Experience as the source of learning and development*. New York: Prentice-Hall.

Kozma, R. B. (1991). Learning with media. *Review of Educational Research, 61*, 179–211.

Kuh, G. D., Douglas, K. B., Lund, J. P., and Ramin-Gyurnek, J. (1994). *Student learning outside the classroom* (ASHE-ERIC Higher Education Report No. 8). Washington, D.C.: The George Washington University, School of Education and Human Development.

Larose, S., and Roy, R. (1995). Test of reactions and adaptation in college (TRAC): A new measure of learning propensity for college students. *Journal of Educational Psychology*, *87*, 293–306.

Lefrancois, G. R. (1991). *Psychology for teaching* (7th ed.). Belmont, CA: Wadsworth.

Love, P. G., and Love, A. G. (1995). *Enhancing student learning: Intellectual, social and emotional integration* (ASHE-ERIC Higher Education Report No. 4). Washington, D.C.: The George Washington University, School of Education and Human Development.

Marton, F., Hounsell, D., and Entwistle, N. (1984). *The experience of learning*. Edinburgh: Scottish Academic Press.

McEwen, M. K., Roper, L. C., Byrant, D. B., and Langa, M. J. (1990). Incorporating the development of African-American students into psychosocial theories of student development. *Journal of College Student Development*, *31*, 429–436.

McKeachie, W. J. (1993). Learning and cognition in the college classroom. In W. J. McKeachie, *Teaching tips: Strategies, research, and theory for college and university teachers* (pp. 279–295). Lexington, MA: D.C. Heath.

McMillan, J. H., and Forsyth, D. R. (1991). What theories of motivation say about why learners learn. In R. J. Menges and M. D. Svinicki (Eds.), *College teaching: From theory to practice* (New Directions for Teaching and Learning, No. 45, pp. 39–52). San Francisco: Jossey-Bass.

Merriam, S. B. (1993). *An update on adult learning theory* (New Directions for Adult and Continuing Education, No. 57). San Francisco: Jossey-Bass.

Merriam, S. B., and Caffarella, R. S. (1991). *Learning in adulthood: A comprehensive guide*. San Francisco: Jossey-Bass.

Milton, O., Pollio, H. R., and Eison, J. (1986). Learning for grades versus learning for its own sake. In O. Milton, H. R. Pollio, and J. Eison, *Making sense of college grades* (pp. 124–149). San Francisco: Jossey-Bass.

Novak, J. D., and Gowin, D. B. (1984). *Learning how to learn*. New York: Cambridge University Press.

Pascarella, E. T. and Terenzini, P. T. (1991). *How college affects students: Findings and insights from twenty years of research*. San Francisco: Jossey-Bass.

Pascarella, E. T., Whitt, E. J., Nora, A., Edison, M., Hagedorn, L. S., and Terenzini, P. T. (1996). What have we learned from the first year of the national study of student learning? *Journal of College Student Development*, *37*, 182–192.

Paulsen, M. B., and Wells, C. T. (in press). Domain differences in the epistemological beliefs of college students. *Research in Higher Education 39* .

Pintrich, P. R. (1988). A process-oriented view of student motivation and cognition. In J. S. Stark and L. A. Mets (Eds.), *Improving teaching and learning through research* (New Directions for Institutional Research, No. 57, pp. 65–79). San Francisco: Jossey-Bass.

Pintrich, P. R. (1988). Student learning and college teaching. In R. E. Young and K. E. Eble (Eds.), *College teaching and learning: Preparing for new commitments* (New Directions for Teaching and Learning, No. 33, pp. 71–86). San Francisco: Jossey-Bass.

Pintrich, P.R. (Ed.). (1995). *Understanding self-regulated learning* (New Directions for Teaching and Learning No. 63). San Francisco: Jossey-Bass.

Pintrich, P. R., and Schunk, D. H. (1996). *Motivation in education: Theory, research, and applications.* Englewood Cliffs, NJ: Prentice-Hall.

Ramsden, P. (1985). Student learning research: Retrospect and prospect. *Higher Education Research and Development*, *4*, 51–69.

Rodgers, R. F. (1989). Student development. In U. Delworth, G. Hanson, and Associates (Eds.), *Student services: A handbook for the profession* (2nd ed.). San Francisco: Jossey-Bass.

Rodgers, R. F. (1990). Recent theories and research underlying student development. In D. G. Creamer and Associates (Eds.), *College student development theory and practice for the 1990s* (pp. 27–29). Alexandria, VA: American College Personnel Association.

Schommer, M. (1993). Comparisons of beliefs about the nature of knowledge and learning among post-secondary students. *Research in Higher Education, 34*, 355–370.

Schommer, M. (1994). Synthesizing epistemological belief research: Tentative understandings and provocative confusions. *Educational Psychology Review, 6*, 293–319.

Schunk, D. H. (1996). *Learning theories* (2nd ed.). Englewood Cliffs, NJ: Prentice-Hall.

Schunk, D.H., and Zimmerman, B. J. (Eds.). (1994). *Self-regulation of learning and performance: Issues and educational applications*. Hillsdale, NJ: Lawrence Erlbaum.

Shulman, L. (1987). Knowledge and teaching: Foundation of the new reform. *Harvard Educational Review, 57*, 1–22.

West, C. K., Farmer, J. A., and Wolff, P. M. (1991). *Instructional design: Implications from cognitive science.* Englewood Cliffs, NJ: Prentice-Hall.

III. Understanding Students and Teachers in the Classroom

Abrami, P. C., d'Apollonia, S., and Cohen, P. (1990). The validity of student ratings of instruction: What we know and what we do not. *Journal of Educational Psychology, 82*, 219–231.

Abrami, P. C., d'Apollonia, S., and Rosenfield, S. (1996). The dimensionality of student ratings of instruction: What we know and what we do not. In J. C. Smart (Ed.), *Higher Education: Handbook of theory and research* Vol. 11 (pp. 213–264). New York: Agathon Press.

Auster, C. J., and MacRone, M. (1994). The classroom as a negotiated social setting: An empirical study of the effects of faculty members' behavior on students' participation. *Teaching Sociology, 22*, 289–300.

Becker, H. S., Geer, B., and Huges, E. (1968). *Making the grade: The academic side of college life.* New York: John Wiley & Sons, Inc.

Billson, J. M. (1986). The college classroom as a small group: Some implications for teaching and learning. *Teaching Sociology, 14*, 143–151.

Boersma, P. D., Gay, D., Jones, R. A. Morrison, L. and Remick, H. (1981). Sex differences in college student interaction: Factor fantasy? *Sex Roles, 7*, 775–784.

Boice, R. (1992). *The new faculty member: Supporting and fostering professional development*. San Francisco: Jossey-Bass.

Bryant, J., Comisky, P., and Zillmann, D. (1979). Teachers' humor in the college classroom. *Communication Education, 28*, 110–118.

Calista, D. J. (1975). Reassessing college students' instructional expectations and evaluations. *Sociology of Education, 48*, 186–201.

Cashin, W. E. (1995). *Student ratings of teaching: The research revisited* (IDEA paper No. 32). Manhattan, KS: Center for Faculty Evaluation and Development, Kansas State University.

Cashin, W. E., and Downey, R. G. (1995). Disciplinary differences in what is taught and in students' perceptions of what they learn and of how they are taught. In N. Hativa and M. Marincovich (Eds.), *Disciplinary differences in teaching and learning: Implications for practice* (New Directions for Teaching and Learning, No. 64, pp. 81–92). San Francisco, CA: Jossey-Bass.

Centra, J. A. (1993). *Reflective faculty evaluation: Enhancing teaching and determining faculty effectiveness.* San Francisco: Jossey-Bass.

Chickering, A. (1972). Undergraduate academic experience. *Journal of Educational Psychology, 63*, 134–143.

Cohen, P. A. (1981). Student ratings of instruction and student achievement. *Review of Educational Research, 51*, 281–309.

Condon, J. D. (1986). The ethnographic classroom. In J. M. Civikly (Ed.), *Communication in college classrooms* (New Directions in Teaching and Learning, No. 26, pp. 11–20). San Francisco: Jossey-Bass.

Constantinople, A. Cornelius, R., and Gray, J. (1988). The chilly climate: Fact or artifact? *Journal of Higher Education, 59*, 527–550.

Cooper, C., Lorban, D., Henry, R., and Townsend, J. (1983). Teaching and storytelling: An ethnographic study of the instructional process in the college classroom. *Instructional Science, 12*, 171–190.

Duell, O. K., Lynch, D. J., Ellsworth, R., and Moore, C. A. (1991). Wait-time in college classes taken by education majors. *Research in Higher Education, 33*, 483–495.

Dunkin, M. J., and Barnes, J. (1986). Research on teaching in higher education. In M. C. Wittrock (Ed.), *Handbook of research on teaching* (pp. 754–777). New York: Macmillan.

Ellner, C. L., and Barnes, C. P. (1983). *Studies of college teaching: Experimental results, theoretical interpretations, and new perspectives.* Lexington, MA: D. C. Heath.

Ellsworth, E. (1989). Why doesn't it feel empowering? Working through the repressive myths of critical pedagogy. *Harvard Educational Review, 59*, 297–324.

Erekson, O. H. (1992). Joint determination of college student achievement and effort: Implications for college teaching. *Research in Higher Education, 33*, 433–446.

Fassinger, P. A. (1995). Understanding classroom interaction: Students' and professors' contributions to students' silence. *Journal of Higher Education, 66*, 87–96.

Feldman, K. A. (1976). The superior college teacher from the students' view. *Research in Higher Education, 5*, 243–288.

Feldman, K. A. (1989). Instructional effectiveness of college teachers as judged by teachers themselves, current and former students, colleagues, administrators, and external (neutral) observers. *Research in Higher Education, 30*, 137–194.

Feldman, K. A. (1989). The association between student ratings of specific instructional dimensions and student achievement: Refining and extending the synthesis of data from multisection validity studies. *Research in Higher Education, 30*, 583–645.

Feldman, K. A. (1990). An afterword for "The association between student ratings of specific instructional dimensions and student achievement: Refining and extending the synthesis of data from multisection validity studies." *Research in Higher Education, 31*, 315–318.

Feldman, K. A. (1992). College students' views of male and female college teachers: Part I—evidence from the social laboratory and experiments. *Research in Higher Education, 33*, 317–375.

Feldman, K. A. (1993). College students' views of male and female college teachers: Part II—evidence from students' evaluations of their classroom teachers. *Research in Higher Education, 34*, 151–211.

Feldman, K. A. (1998). Reflections on the study of effective college teaching and student ratings: One continuing quest and two unresolved issues. In J. C. Smart (Ed.), *Higher education: Handbook of theory and research* (Vol. 13, pp35-74). New York: Agathon Press.

Fink, L. D. (1984). *The first year of college teaching.* (New Directions for Teaching and Learning, No. 17). San Francisco: Jossey-Bass.

Franklin, J. F., and Theall, M. (1995). The relationship of disciplinary differences and the value of class preparation time to student ratings of teaching. In N. Hativa and M. Marincovich (Eds.), *Disciplinary differences in teaching and learning: Implications for practice* (New Directions for Teaching and Learning, No. 64, pp. 41–48). San Francisco: Jossey-Bass.

Gamson, Z. (1967). Performance and personalism in student-faculty relations. *Sociology of Education, 40,* 279–301.

Gardner, S., Dean, C., and McKaig, D. (1989). Responding to differences in the classroom: The politics of knowledge, class, and sexuality. *Sociology of Education, 62,* 64–74.

Gaggled, R. J., and Bechtel, F. S. (1990). Attributional bias and course evaluations. *Journal of Educational Psychology, 82,* 341–351.

Hall, R. M., and Sandler, B. R. (1982). *The classroom climate: A chilly one for women?* (Project on the Status and Education of Women). Washington, D. C.: Association of American Colleges. (ED 215 628)

Howard, J. R., Short, L. B., and Clark, S. (1996). Students' participation in the mixed-age college classroom. *Teaching Sociology, 24,* 8–24.

Karabenick, S. A., and Sharma, R. (1994). Perceived teacher support of student questioning in the college classroom: Its relation to student characteristics and role in the classroom questioning process. *Journal of Educational Psychology, 86,* 90–113.

Keller, J. W., Mattie, N., Vodanovich, S. J., and Piotrowski, C. (1991). Teaching effectiveness: Comparisons between traditional and nontraditional college students. *Innovative Higher Education, 15,* 177–184.

Kozma, R. B. (1991). Learning with media. *Review of Educational Research, 61,* 179–211.

Krupnick, C. C. (1988). Women and men in the classroom: Inequality and its remedies. *On Teaching and Learning, 1,* 18–25.

Kulik, C-L., Kulik, J. A., and Cohen, P. A. (1980). Instructional technology and college teaching. *Teaching of Psychology, 7,* 199–205.

Mann, R. D., Arnold, S. M., Bender, J., Cytrynbaum, S., Newman, B. M., Ringwald, B., Ringwald, J., and Rosenwein, R. (1970). *The college classroom: Conflict, change and learning.* New York: Wiley.

Marsh, H. W. (1987). Students' evaluations of university teaching: Research findings, methodological issues, and directions for future research. *International Journal of Educational Research, 11,* 253–388.

Marsh, H. W., and Dunkin, M. J. (1992). Students' evaluations of university teaching: A multidimensional perspective. In J. C. Smart (Ed.), *Higher education: Handbook of theory and research* (Vol. 8, pp. 143–233). New York: Agathon Press.

McCord, M. T. (1985). Methods and theories of instruction. In J. C. Smart (Ed.), *Higher education: Handbook of theory and research* (Vol. 1, pp. 97–132). New York: Agathon Press.

McKeachie, W. J. (1980). Class size, large classes, and multiple sections. *Academe, 66,* 24–27.

McKeachie, W. J. (1987). Instructional evaluation: Current issues and possible improvements. *Journal of Higher Education, 58,* 344–350.

Mills, T. M. (1964). *Group transformation: An analysis of a learning group.* Englewood Cliffs, NJ: Prentice-Hall.

Moriber, G. (1971). Wait-time in college science classes. *Science Education, 55,* 321–328.

Murray, H. G. (1991). Effective teaching behaviors in the college classroom. In J. C. Smart (Ed.), *Higher education: Handbook of theory and research* (Vol. 7, pp. 135–172). New York: Agathon Press.

Nunn, C. E. (1996). Discussion in the college classroom: Triangulating observational and survey results. *Journal of Higher Education, 67,* 243–266.

Perry, R. P. (1991). Perceived control in college students: Implications for instruction in higher education. In J. C. Smart (Ed.), *Higher education: Handbook of theory and research* (Vol. 7, pp. 1–56).

Perry, R. P., and Smart, J. E. (Eds.). *Effective teaching in higher education: Research and practice*. New York: Agathon Press.

Richardson, R., Fisk, E., and Okum, M. (1983). *Literacy in the open-access college*. San Francisco: Jossey-Bass.

Runkel, P., Harrison, R., and Runkel, M. (Eds.). (1969). *The changing college classroom*.

Smart, J. C., and Ethington, C. A. (1995). Disciplinary and institutional differences in undergraduate education goals. In N. Hativa and M. Marincovich (Eds.), *Disciplinary differences in teaching and learning: Implications for practice* (New Directions for Teaching and Learning, No. 64, pp. 49–57). San Francisco, CA: Jossey-Bass.

Stark, J., Lowther, M. A., Ryan, M. P., Bomotti, S. S., Genthon, M., Haven, C. L., and Martens, G. (1988). *Reflections on course planning: Faculty and students consider influences and goals*. Ann Arbor, MI: National Center for Research to Improve Postsecondary Teaching and Learning, University of Michigan.

Sternglanz, S. H., and Lyberger-Ficek, S. (1977). Sex differences in student-teacher interactions in the college classroom. *Sex Roles, 3*, 345–352.

Theall, M. and Franklin, J. (Eds.). (1990). *Student ratings of instruction: Issues for improving practice* (New Directions for Teaching and Learning, No. 43). San Francisco: Jossey-Bass.

Thielens, W., Jr. (1971). Teacher-student interaction, higher education: Student viewpoint. In L. C. Deighton (Ed.), *The encyclopedia of education* (Vol. 9, pp. 54–63). New York: Macmillan.

Thielens, W., Jr. (1977). Undergraduate definitions of learning from teachers. *Sociology of Education, 50*, 159–181.

Wilson, R. C., Gaff, J. G., Dienst, E. R., Wood, L., and Bavry, J. L. (1975). *College professors and their impact on students*. New York: Wiley.

Wilson, R. C., Woods, L., and Gaff, J. G. (1974). Social-psychological accessibility and faculty-student interaction beyond the classroom. *Sociology of Education, 47*, 74–92.

Winston, R. B., Jr., Vahala, M. E., Nichols, E. C., Gillis, M. E., Wintrow, M., and Rome, K. D. (1994). A measure of college classroom climate: The College Classroom Environment Scales. *Journal of College Student Development, 35*, 11–18.

Wyatt, G. (1992). Skipping class: An analysis of absenteeism among first-year college students. *Teaching Sociology, 20*, 201–207.

Yourglich, A. (1955). Study on correlations between college teachers' and students' concepts of "ideal-student" and "ideal-teacher." *Journal of Educational Research, 49*, 59–64.

IV. Understanding and Implementing Effective Teaching and Learning

Adams, J. Q., Niss, J. F., and Suarez, C. (Eds.). (1991). *Multicultural education: Strategies for implementation in colleges and universities*. Macomb, IL: Western Illinois University Foundation.

Adams, J. Q., and Welsch, J. R. (Eds.). (1992). *Multicultural education: Strategies for implementation in colleges and universities* (Volume 2). Macomb, IL: Illinois Staff and Curriculum Developers Association.

Anderson, E. (Ed.). (1993). *Campus use of the teaching portfolio: Twenty-five profiles*. Washington, D. C.: American Association for Higher Education.

Angelo, T. D., and Cross, K. P. (1993). *Classroom assessment techniques: A handbook for college teachers* (2nd ed.). San Francisco: Jossey-Bass.

Angelo, T. A. (Ed.). (1991). *Classroom research: Early lessons from success* (New Directions for Teaching and Learning, No. 46). San Francisco: Jossey-Bass.

Angelo, T. A. (1993). A "teacher's dozen": Fourteen general, research-based principles for improving higher learning in our classrooms. *AAHE Bulletin, 46*, 3–13.

Argyris, C., Putnam, R., and Smith, D.M. (1985). *Action science.* San Francisco: Jossey-Bass.

Association of American Colleges. (1985). *Integrity in the college curriculum: A report to the academic community.* Washington, D. C.: Association of American Colleges.

Axelrod, J. (1973). *The university teacher as artist.* San Francisco: Jossey-Bass.

Bess, J. L. (1997). *Teaching well and liking it: Motivating faculty to teach effectively.* Baltimore, MD: Johns Hopkins University Press.

Boice, R. (1991). Quick starters: New faculty who succeed. In M. Theall, and J. Franklin (Eds.), *Effective practices for improving teaching* (New Directions for Teaching and Learning, No. 48, pp. 111–121). San Francisco: Jossey-Bass.

Boice, R. (1996). *First-order principles for college teachers: Ten basic ways to improve the teaching process.* Bolton, MA: Anker Publishing..

Bonwell, C. C., and Eison, J. A. (1991). *Active learning: Creating excitement in the classroom* (ASHE-ERIC Higher Education Report No. 1). Washington, D. C.: The George Washington University, School of Education and Human Development.

Border, L. L. B., and Chism, N. V. N. (Eds.). (1992). *Teaching for diversity* (New Directions for Teaching and Learning, No. 49, pp. 19–33). San Francisco: Jossey-Bass.

Bosworth, K., and Hamilton, S. J. (Eds.). (1994). *Collaborative learning: Underlying processes and effective techniques* (New Directions for Teaching and Learning, No. 59). San Francisco: Jossey-Bass.

Boyer, E. (1987). *College.* New York: Harper and Row.

Braskamp, L. A., and Ory, J. C. (1994). *Assessing faculty work: Enhancing individual and institutional performance.* San Francisco: Jossey-Bass.

Braxton, J. M. (1995). Disciplines with an affinity for the improvement of undergraduate education. In N. Hativa and M. Marincovich (Eds.), *Disciplinary differences in teaching and learning: Implications for practice* (New Directions for Teaching and Learning, No. 64, pp. 59–64). San Francisco: Jossey-Bass.

Braxton, J. M., Eimers, M. T., and Bayer, A. E. (1996). The implications of teaching norms for the improvement of undergraduate education. *Journal of Higher Education, 67*, 603–625.

Brinko, K. T. (1993). The practice of giving feedback to improve teaching: What is effective? *Journal of Higher Education, 64*, 574–593.

Brookfield, S. D. (1990). *The skillful teacher: On technique, trust, and responsiveness in the classroom.* San Francisco: Jossey-Bass.

Butler, K. A. (1987). *Learning and teaching style: In theory and practice.* Columbia, CT: The Learner's Dimension.

Cannon, L. W. (1990). Fostering positive race, class, and gender dynamics in the classroom. *Women's Studies Quarterly, 18*, 126–134.

Cashin, W. E. (1979). *Motivating students* (IDEA paper No. 1). Manhattan, KS: Center for Faculty Evaluation and Development, Kansas State University.

Cashin, W. E., and Clegg, V. L. (1993). *Periodicals related to college teaching* (IDEA paper No. 28). Manhattan, KS: Center for Faculty Evaluation and Development, Kansas State University.

Chickering, A. W., and Gamson, Z. F. (Eds.). (1991). *Applying the seven principles for good practice in undergraduate education* (New Directions for Teaching and Learning, No. 47). San Francisco: Jossey-Bass.

Cohen, P. A. (1980). Effectiveness of student-rating feedback for improving college instruction: A meta-analysis of findings. *Research in Higher Education, 13*, 321–341.

Cones III, J. H., Noonan, J. F., and Janha, D. (Eds.). (1983). *Teaching minority students* (New Directions for Teaching and Learning, No. 16). San Francisco: Jossey-Bass.

Cooper, J., and Mueck, R. (1990). Student involvement in learning: Cooperative learning and college instruction. *Journal on Excellence in College Teaching, 1*, 68–76.

Cooper, J. L., Prescott, S., Cook, L., Smith, L., Mueck, R., and Cuseo, J. (1990). *Cooperative learning and college instruction: Effective use of student learning teams*. Long Beach, CA: Institute of Teaching and Learning.

Cross, K. P. (1990). Teaching to improve learning. *Journal on Excellence in College Teaching, 1*, 9–22.

Cross, K. P., and Angelo, T. A. (1988). *Classroom assessment techniques: A handbook for faculty*. Ann Arbor: National Center for Research to Improve Postsecondary Teaching and Learning, University of Michigan.

Davis, B. G. (1993). *Tools for teaching*. San Francisco: Jossey-Bass.

DeVito, J. A. (1986). Teaching as relational development. In J. M. Civikly (Ed.), *Communicating in college classrooms* (New Directions for Teaching and Learning, No. 26, pp. 51–59). San Francisco: Jossey-Bass.

Donald, J. (1997). *Improving the environment for learning*. San Francisco: Jossey-Bass.

Eble, K. A. (1988). *The craft of teaching: A guide to mastering the professor's art*. San Francisco: Jossey-Bass.

Eble, K. E., and McKeachie, W. J. (1985). *Improving undergraduate education through faculty development*. San Francisco: Jossey-Bass.

Ericksen, S. C. (1984). *The essence of good teaching: Helping students learn and remember what they learn*. San Francisco: Jossey-Bass.

Erickson, B. L., and Strommer, D. W. (1991). *Teaching college freshmen*. San Francisco: Jossey-Bass.

Freire, P. (1970). *Pedagogy of the oppressed*. New York: The Seabury Press.

Fuhrmann, B. S., and Grasha, A. F. (1983). Behaviorist and humanistic perspectives on learning: Classroom applications. In B. S. Fuhrmann and A. F. Grasha, *A practical handbook for college teachers* (pp. 67–100). Boston: Little, Brown and Company.

Fuhrmann, B. S., and Grasha, A. F. (1983). Cognitive perspective on learning: Classroom applications. In B. S. Fuhrmann and A. F. Grasha, *A practical handbook for college teachers* (pp. 42–66). Boston: Little, Brown and Company.

Gabelnick, F., MacGregor, J., Matthews, R. S., and Smith, B. L. (Eds.). (1990). *Learning communities: Creating connections among students, faculty, and disciplines* (New Directions for Teaching and Learning, No. 41). San Francisco: Jossey-Bass.

Gamson, Z. (1991). A brief history of the seven principles for good practice in undergraduate education. In A. W. Chickering, and Z. F. Gamson (Eds.), *Applying the seven principles for good practice in undergraduate education* (New Directions for Teaching and Learning, No. 47, pp. 5–12). San Francisco: Jossey-Bass.

Goodsell, A., Maher, M., Tinto, V., Smith, B. L., and MacGregor, J. (Eds.). (1992). *Collaborative learning: A sourcebook for higher education*. University Park, PA: National Center on Postsecondary Teaching, Learning, and Assessment, The Pennsylvania State University.

Grasha, A. F. (1996). *Teaching with style*. Pittsburgh, PA: Alliance Publishers.

Green, M. F. (Ed.). (1988). *Minorities on campus: A handbook for enhancing diversity*. Washington, D. C.: American Council on Education.

Gullette, M. M. (ed.). (1984). *The art and craft of teaching*. Cambridge, MA: Harvard University Press.

Hatfield, S. R. (1995). *The seven principles in action*. Bolton, MA: Anker Publishing.

Johnson, G. R., Eison, J. A., Abbott, R., Meiss, G. T., Moran, K., Morgan, J. A., Pasternack, T. L., and Zaremba, E. (1991). *Teaching tips for users of the motivated strategies for learning questionnaire*. Ann Arbor, MI: National Center for Research to Improve Postsecondary Learning and Teaching, University of Michigan.

Johnson, D. W., Johnson, R. T., and Smith, K. A. (1991). *Active learning: Cooperation in the college classroom*. Edina, MN: Interaction Book Company.

Joyce, B., and Weil, M. (1986). *Models of teaching* (3rd ed.). Englewood Cliffs, NJ: Prentice-Hall.

Katz, J., and Henry, M. (1988). *Turning professors into teachers: A new approach to faculty development and student learning*. New York: MacMillan Publishing.

Keller, J. M. (1983). Motivational design of instruction. In C. M. Reigeluth (Ed.), *Instructional-design theories and models: An overview of their current status* (pp. 383–434). Hillsdale, NJ: Lawrence Erlbaum Associates.

Kurfiss, J. G. (1988). *Critical thinking: Theory, research, practice, and possibilities*. (ASHE-ERIC Higher Education Report No. 2). Washington, D. C.: Association for the Study of Higher Education.

Leistyna, P., Woodrum, A., and Sherblom, S.A. (1996). *Breaking free: The transformative power of critical pedagogy*. Cambridge, MA: The President and Fellows of Harvard College.

Levinson-Rose, J., and Menges, R. J. (1981). Improving college teaching: A critical review of research. *Review of Educational Research, 51*, 403–434.

Lewis, M., and Simon, R. (1986). A discourse not intended for her: Learning and teaching within patriarchy. *Harvard Educational Review, 56*, 297–324.

Lowman, J. (1984). *Mastering the techniques of teaching*. San Francisco: Jossey-Bass.

Lucas, A. F. (1990). Using psychological models to understand student motivation. In M. D. Svinicki (Ed)., *The changing face of college teaching* (New Directions for Teaching and Learning, No. 42, pp. 103–114). San Francisco: Jossey-Bass.

Lucas, A. F. (Ed.). (1989). *The department chairperson's role in enhancing college teaching* (New Directions for Teaching and Learning, No. 37). San Francisco: Jossey-Bass.

Luke, C., and Gore, J. (Eds.). (1992). *Feminisms and critical pedagogy*. New York: Routledge.

Maher, F. (1985). Classroom pedagogy and the new scholarship on women. In M. Culley and C. Portuges (Eds.), *Gendered subjects: The dynamics of feminist teaching*. London: Routledge and Kegan Paul.

Maher, F. A. (1987). Toward a richer theory of feminist pedagogy: A comparison of "liberation" and " gender" models for teaching and learning. *Journal of Education, 169*, 91–100.

Maher, F. A., and Tetreault, M. K. T. (1994). *The feminist classroom*. New York: Basic Books.

McKeachie, W. J. (1994). *Teaching tips: Strategies, research, and theory for college and university teachers* (9th ed.). Lexington, MA: D. C. Heath.

Menges, R. J. (1990). Using evaluative information to improve instruction. In P. Seldin and Associates (Eds.), *How administrators can improve teaching: Moving from talk to action in higher education*. San Francisco: Jossey-Bass.

Menges, R. J. (1993). Improving your teaching. In W. J. McKeachie, *Teaching tips: Strategies, research, and theory for college and university teachers* (9th edition, pp. 297–312). Lexington, MA: D. C. Heath.

Menges, R. J., and Brinko, K. T. (1986). *Effects of student evaluation feedback: A meta-analysis of higher education research*. Paper presented at the annual meeting of the American Educational Research Association, San Francisco.

Menges, R. J., and Mathis, B. C. (1988). *Key resources on teaching, learning, curriculum, and faculty development*. San Francisco: Jossey-Bass.

Menges, R. J., and Weimer, M. (1996). *Teaching on solid ground: Using scholarship to improve practice.* San Francisco: Jossey-Bass.

Meyers, C., and Jones, T. B. (1993). *Promoting active learning: Strategies for the college classroom.* San Francisco: Jossey-Bass.

Mezirow, J. (1990). *Fostering critical reflection in adulthood: A guide to transformative and emancipatory learning* San Francisco: Jossey-Bass.

Mezirow, J. (1991). *Transformative dimensions of adult learning*. San Francisco: Jossey-Bass.

Millis, B. J. (1991). Fulfilling the promise of the "seven principles" through cooperative learning: An action agenda for the university classroom. *Journal on Excellence in College Teaching, 2*, 139–144.

Millis, B. J. (1990). Helping faculty build learning communities through cooperative groups. *To Improve the Academy: Resources for Student, Faculty, and Institutional Development, 10*, 43–58.

Murray, J. P. (1995). *Successful faculty development and evaluation: The complete teaching portfolio* (ASHE-ERIC Higher Education Report No. 8). Washington, D. C.: The George Washington University, Graduate School of Education and Human Development.

National Institute of Education. (1984). *Involvement in learning: Realizing the potential of American higher education*. Washington, D. C.: U. S. Government Printing Office.

Osajima, K. (1991). Challenges to teaching about racism: Breaking the silence. *Teaching Education, 4*, 145–152.

Palmer, P. J. (1993). *To know as we are known: Education as a spiritual journey*. San Francisco: Harper and Row.

Pemberton, G. (1988). *On teaching the minority student: Problems and strategies*. Brunswick, ME: Bowdoin College.

Pintrich, P. R., and Johnson, G. R. (1990). Assessing and improving students' learning strategies. In M. D. Svinicki (Ed)., *The changing face of college teaching*. (New Directions for Teaching and Learning, No. 42, pp. 83–92). San Francisco: Jossey-Bass.

Polson, C. J. (1993). *Teaching adult students* (IDEA paper No. 29). Manhattan, KS: Center for Faculty Evaluation and Development, Kansas State University.

Rando, W. C., and Lenze, L. F. (1994). *Learning from students: Early term student feedback in higher education.* The Pennsylvania State University: National Center on Postsecondary Teaching, Learning, and Assessment.

Rando, W. C., and Menges, R. J. (1991). How practice is shaped by personal theories. In R. J. Menges and M. D. Svinicki (Eds.), *College teaching: From theory to practice* (New Directions for Teaching and Learning, No. 45, pp. 7–14). San Francisco: Jossey-Bass.

Richlin, L., and Cox, M. D. (Eds.). (1995). *Journal on Excellence in College Teaching, Special Focus: Evaluation of Teaching, 6*.

Sadker, M., and Sadker, D. (1990). Confronting sexism in the college classroom. In S. Gabriel and I. Smithson (Eds.), *Gender in the classroom* (pp. 176–187). Champaign: University of Illinois Press.

Sadker, M., and Sadker, D. (1992). Ensuring equitable participation in college classes. In L. L. B. Border and N. Van Note Chism. (1992). (Eds.), *Teaching for diversity* (New Directions for Teaching and Learning, No. 49, pp. 49–56). San Francisco: Jossey-Bass.

Schniedewind, N. (1987). Teaching feminist process. *Women's Studies Quarterly, 15* (3 and 4), 15–31.

Schon, D.A. (1983). *The reflective practitioner*. New York: Harper Collins.

Seldin, P. (1991). *The teaching portfolio*. Bolton, MA: Anker Publishing.

Seldin, P. (1993). *Successful use of teaching portfolios*. Bolton, MA: Anker Publishing.

Seldin, P. (Ed.). (1995). *Improving college teaching*. Bolton, MA: Anker Publishing.

Seldin, P. and Associates. (Eds.). (1990). *How administrators can improve teaching: Moving from talk to action in higher education*. San Francisco: Jossey-Bass.

Shrewsbury, C. M. (1987). What is feminist pedagogy? *Women's Studies Quarterly, 15* (3 and 4), 6–13.

Sorcinelli, M. D. (1991). Research findings on the seven principles. In A. W. Chickering, and Z. F. Gamson (Eds.), *Applying the seven principles for good practice in undergraduate education*. (New Directions for Teaching and Learning, No. 47, pp. 13–25). San Francisco: Jossey-Bass.

Stice, J. E. (Ed.). (1987). *Developing critical thinking and problem-solving abilities*. (New Directions for Teaching and Learning, No. 30). San Francisco: Jossey-Bass.

Sutherland, T. E., and Bonwell, C. C. (Eds.). (1996). *Using active learning in college classes: A range of options for faculty* (New Directions for Teaching and Learning, No. 67). San Francisco: Jossey-Bass.

Svinicki, M. D. (Ed.). (1990). *The changing face of college teaching*(New Directions for Teaching and Learning, No. 42). San Francisco: Jossey-Bass.

Svinicki, M. D. (1991). Practical implications of cognitive theories. In R. J. Menges and M. D. Svinicki (Eds)., *College teaching: From theory to practice* (New Directions for Teaching and Learning, No. 45, pp. 27–38). San Francisco: Jossey-Bass.

Theall, M., and Franklin, J. (Eds.). (1991). *Effective practices for improving teaching*. (New Directions for Teaching and Learning, No. 48). San Francisco: Jossey-Bass.

Tiberius, R. G., and Billson, J. M. (1991). The social context of teaching and learning. In R. J. Menges and M. D. Svinicki (Eds.), *College teaching: From theory to practice* (New Directions for Teaching and Learning, No. 45, pp. 67–86). San Francisco: Jossey-Bass.

Travis, J. E. (1995). *Models for improving college teaching: A faculty resource* (ASHE-ERIC Higher Education Report No. 6). Washington, D. C.: The George Washington University, Graduate School of Education and Human Development.

Weimer, M. G. (1990). *Improving college teaching: Strategies for developing instructional effectiveness*. San Francisco: Jossey-Bass.

Weimer, M. G. (1990). Study your way to better teaching. In M. D. Svinicki (Ed)., *The changing face of college teaching*. (New Directions for Teaching and Learning, No. 42, pp. 117–130). San Francisco: Jossey-Bass.

Weimer, M. (Ed.). (1993). *Faculty as teachers: Taking stock of what we know*. The Pennsylvania State University: National Center on Postsecondary Teaching, Learning, and Assessment.

Weinstein, C. E., and Meyer, D. K. (1991). Cognitive learning strategies and college teaching. In R. J. Menges and M. D. Svinicki (Eds.), *College teaching: From theory to practice* (New Directions for Teaching and Learning, No. 45, pp. 7–14). San Francisco: Jossey-Bass.

Weinstein, C. E., Meyer, D. K., and Stone, G. V. M. (1993). Teaching students how to learn. In W. J. McKeachie, *Teaching tips: Strategies, research, and theory for college and university teachers* (pp. 359–367). Lexington, MA: D. C. Heath.

West, C. K., Farmer, J. A., and Wolff, P. M. (1991). *Instructional design: Implications from cognitive science*. Englewood Cliffs, NJ: Prentice-Hall.

Wilkerson, L., and Gijselaers, W. H. (Eds.). (1996). *Bringing problem-based learning to higher education: Theory and practice* (New Directions for Teaching and Learning, No. 68). San Francisco: Jossey-Bass.

Wolverton, M. (1994). *A new alliance: Continuous quality and classroom effectiveness* (ASHE ERIC Higher Education Report No. 6). Washington, D.C.: The George Washington University, School of Education and Human Development.

Wright, W. A. (Ed.). (1995). *Teaching improvement practices*. Bolton, MA: Anker Publishing.